# DATA-BOOK OF HAPPINESS

# DATA-BOOK OF HAPPINESS

*A Complementary Reference Work to 'Conditions of Happiness' by the same author*

RUUT VEENHOVEN

*with the assistance of*

TON JONKERS

*Erasmus University Rotterdam*
*Department of Sociology*

D. REIDEL PUBLISHING COMPANY

A MEMBER OF THE KLUWER ACADEMIC PUBLISHERS GROUP

DORDRECHT / BOSTON / LANCASTER

**Library of Congress Cataloging in Publication Data**

CIP

Veenhoven, R.
Data-Book of Happiness

Bibliography: p.
Includes indexes.
1. Happiness-Case Studies. I. Jonkers, Ton.
II. Veenhoven, R. Conditions of Happiness. III. Title.
BJ1481.v443 1984 152.4 84-9196
ISBN 90-277-1793-1
ISBN 90-277-1794-X (set) (in combination with Conditions of Happiness, ISBN 90-277-1792-3)

---

Published by D. Reidel Publishing Company
P.O. Box 17, 3300 AA Dordrecht, Holland

Sold and distributed in the U.S.A. and Canada by Kluwer Academic Publishers
190 Old Derby Street, Hingham, MA 02043, U.S.A.

In all other countries, sold and distributed by Kluwer Academic Publishers Group,
P.O. Box 322, 3300 AH Dordrecht, Holland



Printed in The Netherlands

A second edition of this book will be published in 1988. It will cover investigations up to and including 1985. Investigators are therefore invited to send a copy of their reports to the author. Suggestions about relevant publications are also welcome; in particular suggestions about reports published before 1975 but not covered in this volume. Please send to: Dr. Ruut Veenhoven; Erasmus University Rotterdam; Department of Sociology; P.O.B. 1738, 3000 DR Rotterdam, The Netherlands.

# TABLE OF CONTENTS

## ACKNOWLEDGMENT

This book is one of the products of a research program on happiness on the Erasmus University Rotterdam. Funds were provided by the Department of Sociology of that University and also by the Dutch Ministry of Social Affairs by means of allotment of assistence.

Several people assisted in excerpting reports and ordering the findings, among others: Peter Bakker, Rob Feuth, Hans Hordijk, Ton Jonkers, Gerrit van Kooten and Lies Kokee. Ton Jonkers, in particular, did a great deal. Technical advice was given by Lies Nuyten. The typework was done by Janet de Raad, Jeanne Hidskes and for the major part by Elly Graven. Sasqia Chin-Hon-Foei drew up the index.

R.V.

Erasmus University Rotterdam, The Netherlands
January, 1984.

# PART I

# DESIGN

## 1. PURPOSE OF THE STUDY.

Since Classical times philosophers have been fascinated by the question of how happiness can effectively and lastingly be promoted. In that context many have wondered why all people are not equally happy, even not when living in identical conditions. There is now a vast amount of literature on the matter. However, we are little wiser.

There are several reasons why differences in happiness are so little understood as yet. One is that most students of the subject have tended to confuse moralizing and reality, the bulk of the literature dealing in fact with moral rules for living. Another reason is that speculation often predominated systematic observation. There was therefore little accumulation of knowledge.

It had been expected that the emerging social sciences would take up the empirical study of happiness and that conclusions would eventually be arrived at. Several founders of psychology and sociology saw grounds for hope: with the naïve optimism of their time they professed the discovery of universal laws of happiness and announced the possibility of a scientifically guided reconstruction of society on that basis.

Yet the matter stopped with such declarations. With the exception of a few isolated attempts the subject was abandoned. Only since the 1960's has any appreciable amount of empirical investigations been performed. To some extent this was a by-product of the so-called 'social indicators movement'. Policymakers in affluent western nations instigated large scale surveys to assess the well-being of citizens and to sound out the demand for state sponsored services. Several of these marketing-like studies involved attempts to assess the appreciation of life - in Britain for example carried out by Hall (1976); in the Netherlands by Pommer & van Praag (1978) and in the US by Bradburn (1969), Campbell (1976) and Andrews & Whithey (1976). Independently of them some stray psychologists picked up the subjects as well, as did some clinical psychologists while studying the healthy personality (among others Wessman & Ricks, 1966). A few social psychologists became interested in the issue in the course of their work on social comparison (among others Brickman & Campbell, 1971). Several gerontologists 'discovered' happiness when studying the adjustment to retirement and old age (among others Thompson et al., 1960).

This book is part of that revival. It is in fact an account of the results yielded so far. Though the promised systematic study of happiness was never produced, stray investigations on the matter provide a quite sizable body of data. If ever it comes to the redemption of this old mission, a chart of these data will be valuable.

Earlier surveys. This is not the first attempt to take stock of the results of empirical investigations on happiness. In fact there are already nine literature surveys. Two of these deal exclusively with happiness in elderly persons Adams, 1971 ; Larson, 1978). The other seven are not restricted to special categories (Fellows, 1966; Wilson, 1967; Veenhoven, 1970; Fordyce, 1972; Robinson & Shaver, 1973; Arkoff, 1975; Nettler, 1976). All suffer from imperfections, the one by Veenhoven (first author of this book) not excluded. These imperfections are the rationale for the present study, so they deserve a short enumeration.

Most surveys did not start from any clear conception of happiness. They tend to gather research reports on phenomena the investigator labeled as 'happiness' or the like. There being various connotations in usage, a babel of tongues is characteristically the result. Fordyce's survey contains for instance studies on 'mood', 'life satisfaction' and 'peak experiences' (p. 19). Curiously most reviewers noted that the term 'happiness' carried different meanings, but failed to make motivated choice. Veenhoven's review did start with a formal definition of happiness, but did not use it sufficiently consistently in selecting the studies. Though all reviewers noted that some of the measures of happiness used were somewhat dubious, no one got around to sorting out the valid from the less valid. All merely reported the results whether sound or not. Only Fordyce pointed out some doubtful indicators afterwards.

The earlier surveys cover only part of the investigations that were actually available at the time they were drawn up. The most complete review is the one by Fordyce in 1972. He claims his collection to be 'exhaustive'. Yet he covers only 18 of the 69 publications we found published prior to 1970. The flow of investigations after 1970 has not yet been reviewed at all. All surveys focus heavily on research in the US and overlook the considerable number of European studies.

The earlier reviewers did not enumerate all the findings actually presented in the publications covered. Only Fordyce tried to present the findings completely. All the others simply selected the most interesting ones from their point of view. Thus they tended to omit non-correlates and factors that did not fit in their theoretical scheme. Though inevitable in the context of short review articles, this practice involves a considerable loss of information.

Parallelbook 'Conditions of Happiness'. This volume is an inventory of facts. It does not go into their interpretation. The consequences of the various findings are considered in a simultaneously published book, titled 'Conditions of Happiness', for which the present volume served in fact as a source (Veenhoven, 1984). The introductory chapters of that book provide more detail about this study, in particular about the conceptual delineation of happiness and the problems of measurement. Hence these subjects will be mentioned only shortly in the next two sections of this chapter.

## 2. THE CONCEPT OF HAPPINESS.

The term 'happiness' has various subtly different meanings. Its many connotations have often proved confusing, thereby hindering the scientific study of happiness to a great extent. Thus a first step is to decide on a clear definition.

### a. Overall happiness.

The term 'happiness' is used to refer to an experiental phenomenon. Overall happiness is defined as the degree to which an individual judges the overall quality of his life favorably. In other words: how well he likes the life he leads. The key terms in this definition may be elucidated as follows:

Degree. The word 'happiness' does not denote an optimal appreciation of life. In this language it depicts a degree, like the concepts of 'length' or 'weight'; it denotes more or less of something. When saying a person is happy, it is meant he/she judges his or her life favorably rather than unfavorably.

Individual. The term happiness is used to describe the state of an individual person only. The term does not apply to collectivities, objects or events. So a nation cannot be said to be happy. At best, a majority of its citizens considers itself happy. Happiness denotes a subjective appreciation of life by an individual. So there is no given standard for happiness. While a person who thinks he has a heart condition may or may not have one, a person who thinks he is (un)happy really is (un)happy.

Judges. The word 'happiness' is used where somebody made an overall judgment about the quality of his life. This implies an intellectual activity. Making an overall judgment implies assessing past experiences and estimating future experiences. Both require marshalling facts into a convenient number of cognitive categories. It also requires awarding relative values and setting priorities. Thus happiness is not a simple sum of pleasures, but rather a congnitive construction which the individual puts together from his various experiences.

One consequence of this conceptualization is that the word 'happiness' can not be used for those who did not make up their mind. One cannot say whether a person is happy or not if he is intellectually unable to construct an overall judgment. Thus the concept cannot be used for animals, little children and retarded people. Similarly it does not apply to people who simply never thought about the matter.

Overall. The evaluation of life aimed at is an overall judgment. It embodies all criteria for appreciation which figure in the mind. Ancient hedonists used to equate happiness with sensory pleasures only. But other modes of appreciation are far from negligible. Apart from the senses, affect and cognition enable men to appreciate life as well; in so far as judgments are made intellectually, they may be based on various values or preferences.

The word 'happiness' refers to a judgment which integrates all the appreciation criteria used explicitly or implicitly by the person himself. Thus the contention that one has all one ever desired does not necessarily make a person happy. Despite all earthly endowments he may suffer pain or feel depressed. Similarly the awareness that life is exciting does not necessarily make it as happy either.

Life as a whole. We do not use the word 'happiness' to characterize specific aspects of life. 'Happiness' refers to life as a whole. Thus it covers past, present and anticipated experiences. This does not mean that all things ever experienced are given equal weight in the evaluation process. As stated above, evaluation involves sifting and ordering. In this process some experiences may be emphasized and others ignored. Past life-experiences for example seldom enter into the evaluation process in their original phenomenological Gestalt. What is taken into consideration is mostly a shallow representation of what one tasted previously.

His/her. The term 'happiness' concerns the evaluation of one's own life; not of life in general. A pessimistic 'Weltanschauung' does not necessarily characterize someone as 'unhappy'.

Favourably. Evaluations always embody appreciation; a conclusion as to whether one likes something or not. The term 'happiness' refers to judgments concerning this aspect only. Happiness judgments concern the dimension extending from appreciation to depreciation; from like to dislike. All humans are capable of appraisals of this kind. People of all cultures are acquainted with evaluations in terms of good versus bad (Osgood, 1971: 37/38) and all persons seem able to communicate appreciation by means of facial expressions (see

Schlossberg, 1954).

This criterion of 'favourableness' is very close to what is called 'pleasantness'. However, it is not quite the same. The term 'favourableness' concerns the appreciation involved in a cognitive evaluation. On the other hand the term 'pleasantness' refers exclusively to direct affective experience. As such it is more characteristic of the affective component of happiness (to be discussed below) than of overall happiness itself.

When evaluating the favourableness of their lives, people tend to use two more or less distinct sources of information: their affects and their thoughts. These two approaches may result in different judgments of life as a whole. An individual can decide that he feels fine most of the time and he can also judge that life seems to meet his conscious demands. These judgments do not necessarily coincide. A person may feel fine generally, but nevertheless be aware that he failed to realize his aspirations. Or he may have surpassed his aspirations but nevertheless feel miserable. Using the word 'happiness' in these cases would result in two different kinds of happiness. Therefore we opted to restrict the word 'happiness' to those cases where these evaluations were integrated into one final judgment. The two aspect-judgments can best be conceived as separate issues. They are labeled 'hedonic level of affect' and 'contentment' respectively. This inventory study will cover data on these 'components' of happiness as well.

b. <u>Hedonic level of affect</u>.

Hedonic level of affect is the degree to which the various affects a person experiences are pleasant in character. Hedonic level of affect is not the same as 'mood'. People experience different kinds of moods: elated moods, calm moods, restless moods, moody moods, etc. Each of these moods is characterized by a special mixture of affectional experiences, one of which is 'hedonic tone' or 'pleasantness'. The concept of hedonic level concerns only the pleasantness experienced in affects; the pleasantness in feelings, in emotions, as well as in moods. So a high hedonic level may be based on strong but passing emotions of love as well as on moods of steady calmness.

Hedonic tone is an experiental quality that exists in all human affects. Several investigators have shown this to be so (Arnold, 1960: 38; Davitz, 1970: 256; Schlossberg, 1954; Plutchnik, 1980: 75/77 and Sjöberg et al., 1979). It exists even in brain-injured patients who have lost their abstract capacity and can therefore not enjoy happiness in the meaning employed here (Goldstein, 1952: 370). Probably animals do experience hedonic tone as well. As we cannot ask them, we will never know for sure, however.

A person's average hedonic level of affect can be assessed over different periods of time: an hour, a week, a year as well as over a lifetime. The concept does not presume subjective awareness of this level. A baby that is laughing all day probably feels fine. However, it is not likely to be aware of that. Contrary to the concepts of 'happiness' and of 'contentment' the concept of 'hedonic level' does not cover anticipated experience.

Hedonic level is probably a constituting factor in the overall evaluation of life called 'happiness'. However, it is not what is usually referred to as 'the affective aspect' of the attitude towards life. The affective aspect of an attitude is the whole of emotional associations which go together with the appraisal of the object at hand. In the case of happiness they denote the affective reaction on the awareness of being either happy or unhappy. The concept of hedonic level is broader. It covers all affective experience, among which all the 'raw' experiences that exist more or less independently of deliberate appraisals of life.

c. Contentment.

Contentment is the degree to which an individual perceives his aspirations to be met. The concept presupposes that the individual developed some conscious wants and that he formed an idea about their realization. Whether this idea is factually correct or not is unimportant. The concept concerns the individual's subjective perception.

When an individual assesses the degree to which his wants are being met, he may look both backwards and forwards. He may assess what life brought up to now and he may estimate what it is likely to yield in the future. Usually people combine both the past and the future in their assessments.

Like hedonic level, contentment serves probably as a formative element in the overall evaluation of life. Yet it is not precisely what is commonly understood as 'the cognitive aspect' of that attitude. The 'cognitive aspect' of an attitude is all one knows about its object. The perception of success in aspirations is part of the knowledge about one's life, but not all there is.

d. Related terms.

Happiness, as defined here, is mostly not the same as what is commonly referred to by terms like 'well-being', 'quality of life', 'morale', 'mental health', and 'adjustment'. These terms being used in varying ways, they sometimes correspond with the present definition and sometimes not.

Likewise the phenomenon termed happiness here is currently given other names as well. Terms like 'life-satisfaction', 'contentment' and 'positive attitudes towards life' sometimes cover the same notion.

## 3. INDICATORS OF HAPPINESS.

Happiness can be assessed only by asking people about it. That is at least true for 'overall happiness' and 'contentment'. 'Hedonic level' can to some extent be inferred from non-verbal cues.

Several doubts are being raised about the quality of responses to questions about happiness; especially about the validity of direct questions about overall happiness. It is suggested that people do not know, that they are reluctant to discuss the matter, that they fool themselves, that they try to appear happier than they know they are, etc. In the parallel book 'Conditions of happiness' the reality value of these doubts is considered in detail (Chapter 3). It appears that most can be discarded on the basis of empirical evidence. It was for example shown that people have typically quite definite ideas on whether they are happy or not and that it is hence unlikely that questions on the matter tap hot air only. Not all objections could be discarded, however; especially not the objection that people sometimes fool themselves or their interviewers by pretending to be happier than they in fact are. Yet these objections have not been proven true either.

Next to doubts about validity there are questions about the technical reliability of self-reports of happiness. It is objected that responses tend to be heavily biassed by among other things interviewer characteristics, answer formats and contextual cues. Sofar checked empirically, these distortions do not appear too dramatic, however.

Though not convincingly demonstrated, the various objections are still serious enough to be taken into account. They suggest at least four working rules: Firstly, selfratings are to be preferred to ratings by others. Secondly, anonymous questionnaires work better than personal interviews. Thirdly, the context of the questionnaire as well as the key-questions must be focused clearly on the issue aimed at: in the case of overall happiness on an 'overall' appreciation of 'life-as-a-whole'. Fourthly, questions must leave room for 'no answer' or 'don't know' responses.

Fewer solutions seem available for the problem of comparison. We are not sure whether two people, both claiming to be happy, are in fact talking about identical levels of appreciation. This implies that respondents can be ranked for happiness only rather crudely. In practice this means that statistical correlations of measured happiness will be somewhat less pronounced than correlations of true happiness. Possibly one or more of the various objections to happiness testing will in due course be convincingly substantiated. For the time being attempts to measure happiness deserve the benefit of doubt.

Happiness has been measured in many different ways. There is a particularly great variety of questions and interrogation techniques. Most of these methods were proposed by investigators who failed to define happiness formally or who had in mind another concept than the one used here.

We therefore inspected all current formats for 'face validity'. This involved close reading of questions, instructions and eventual further devices, in order to assess whether or not they referred exclusively to one of the phenomena defined above. This procedure is reported in full detail in chapter 4 of 'Conditions of happiness'.

The main selection rules are specified below. For most indicators it was rather clear whether or not they meet these demands. Yet there were also cases of doubt, several indicators having both strong and weak sides. Choices on that matter were complicated by the fact that validity demands are not identical for all three happiness variants and that not all observational methods can be judged by the same criteria.

Many indicators appeared unacceptable, several dealing in fact with essentially different matters, such as 'social adjustment', zestful living', 'optimism', etc. In many cases it appeared entirely unclear what was actually tapped. Many investigators used for example long lists of questions referring to various items that have at one time or another been associated with 'well-being'. In spite of their statistical validity these investories are theoretically meaningless.

Overall happiness can be assessed by direct questioning only: indirect questions tap essentially different matters. Direct questions referring to 'satisfaction with life' are preferrable to questions using the word 'happiness' as a key-term. Though not ideal, the latter were nevertheless deemed acceptable. Questions can be framed in different formats: in one or more closed questions, in open-ended questions and in focused interviews. In the latter two cases clear instructions for content analysis of responses are required.

Hedonic level can be assessed in three ways: by direct questioning, by indirect questioning and by ratings on the basis of non-verbal behaviour. Again the method of direct questioning is to be preferred: especially when the individual is asked several times during a certain period how pleasant he feels there and then.

Though generally less dependable, indirect methods can sometimes do as well. Some projective tests seem for example to be reasonably valid. Ratings by others will also suffice, provided that rating instructions are sufficiently specific.

Contentment can be measured by means of direct questions only. Like overall happiness it cannot validly be assessed by indirect questions or by peer ratings. Direct questions must again be specific. They probably work best when preceded by an enumeration of one's major aspirations. Questions can again be framed in various formats.

Composites. Finally there are several acceptable indicators that cover two or more of these happiness variants. The majority of these consists of single direct questions which by wording or answer formats refer to both overall happiness and hedonic level. In sofar they did not labour specific deficits these questions were accepted. Next some indicators work with multiple questions. Characteristically these questions cover both overall happiness and one or both of the discerned components. When all items met the demands outlined above, such composite indicators were accepted. A last format to be mentioned in this context is the focused interview of which the 'depth interview' is a variant. Such interrogations tend to broach all three happiness variants. By lack of clear reports about themes of enquiry and ratings procedures it is mostly difficult to assess their face validity.

The inspection resulted in a rejection of more than half of the currently used indicators of happiness. A typology of the accepted ones is presented in exhibit 1.

## 4. SEARCHING EMPIRICAL HAPPINESS STUDIES.

Having established which indicators of happiness can be deemed acceptable, the next problem was to take stock of investigations that had used such indicators. This was a labourious job. There is no international reference system that covers all of the research reports that have been ever produced by social scientists throughout the world. Neither is there any bibliographical system that uses a classification that fits with the present conceptualization of happiness. Trying to trace reports of all the empirical happiness studies ever performed is rather like searching for a needle in a haystack.

### a Search problems.

More specifically we met with the following problems:

Exhibit 1: Indicators of happiness in empirical investigations between 1911 - 1975.[1)]

**OVERALL HAPPINESS**

| Code | Type of indicator | Number of studies |
|---|---|---|
| HAPP 1 | Questions using the term 'happiness' | |
| 1.1 | - Single closed question | 130 |
| 1.2 | - Index of closed questions | 1 |
| 1.3 | - Open-ended question | |
| 1.4 | - Focused interview | |
| HAPP 2 | Questions using terms like 'satisfaction with life' | |
| 2.1 | - Single closed question | 67 |
| 2.2 | - Index of closed questions | |
| 2.3 | - Open-ended question | |
| 2.4 | - Focused interview | |
| HAPP 3 | Other questions focusing exclusively on overall happiness | |
| 3.1 | - Single closed question | 45 |
| 3.2 | - Index of closed questions | |
| 3.3 | - Open- ended question | |
| 3.4 | - Focused interview | |
| HAPP 4 | Composites, combining two or more of the above mentioned indicators | |
| | | 243 |

**HEDONIC LEVEL OF AFFECT**

| Code | Type of indicator | Number of studies |
|---|---|---|
| AFF 1 | Questions on perceived hedonic level in general (indefinite period) | |
| 1.1 | - Single closed questions | 10 |
| 1.2 | - Index of closed questions | |
| 1.3 | - Index of closed questions (on occurrence of specific affects) | 7 |
| 1.4 | - Open-ended question | |
| 1.5 | - Focused interview | |
| AFF 2 | Questions on perceived hedonic level over last period (one week to about a year) | |
| 2.1 | - Single closed question | 3 |
| 2.2 | - Index of closed questions | |
| 2.3 | - Index of closed questions (on occurrence of specific affects) | 35 |
| 2.4 | - Open-ended questions | |
| 2.5 | - Focused interview | |
| AFF 3 | Repeated questions on momentaneous hedonic level (periods of one day at most) | |
| 3.1 | - Repeated single closed question | 13 |
| 3.2 | - Repeated index of closed questions | |
| 3.3 | - Repeated index of closed questions (on occurrence of specific affects) | 6 |
| 3.4 | - Repeated open-ended question | 1 |
| 3.5 | - Repeated focused interview | |
| AFF 4 | Projective measures | |
| AFF 5 | Ratings by others | |
| 5.1 | - Clinical ratings | 4 |
| 5.2 | - Peer ratings | 2 |
| 5.3 | - Ratings by teachers, nurses, parents, etc. | 2 |
| AFF 6 | Composites, combining two or more of the above-mentioned indicators | 3 |
| | | 86 |

**CONTENTMENT**

| Code | Type of indicator | Number of studies |
|---|---|---|
| CON 1 | Questions on contentment | |
| 1.1 | - Single closed question | 5 |
| 1.2 | - Index of closed questions | |
| 1.3 | - Open-ended question | |
| 1.4 | - Focused interview | 1 |
| CON 2 | Expert ratings of contentment on the basis of longer clinical contact | |
| CON 3 | Composites, combining two or more of the above mentioned indicators | |
| | | 6 |

**COMPOSITES**

| Code | Type of indicator | Number of studies |
|---|---|---|
| COMP 1 | Questions covering both overall happiness and perceived hedonic level of affect | |
| 1.1 | - Single closed question | 16 |
| 1.2 | - Index of closed questions | 5 |
| 1.3 | - Open-ended question | |
| 1.4 | - Focused interview | 1 |
| COMP 2 | Questions covering both overall happiness and contentment | |
| 2.1 | - Single closed question | |
| 2.2 | - Index of closed questions | 1 |
| 2.3 | - Open-ended question | |
| 2.4 | - Focused interview | |
| COMP 3 | Questions covering both perceived hedonic level and contentment | |
| 3.1 | - Single closed question | |
| 3.2 | - Index of closed questions | |
| 3.3 | - Open-ended question | |
| 3.4 | - Focused interview | |
| COMP 4 | Questions covering both overall happiness, perceived hedonic level and contentment | |
| 4.1 | - Single closed question | 2 |
| 4.2 | - Index of closed questions | 1 |
| 4.3 | - Open-ended question | 1 |
| 4.4 | - Focused interview | 1 |
| COMP 5 | Expert ratings on happiness on the basis of clinical contact | 2 |
| | | 30 |

(1) Some investigations used more than one indicator

Happiness variously labeled. The meaning attached to the word 'happiness' here is obviously not shared by everybody. As we have seen, titles using the term 'happiness' often refer to other matters, while reports that use other labels sometimes deal with it. Hence it was not enough to amass publications that use 'happiness' as a keyword, but we had to cover various other search entries as well. Titles often being misleading, we had to inspect all promising publications in order to assess whether they actually dealt with 'happiness' or not. More than a thousand were considered. Several of these research reports did not specify precisely what they measured. In these cases the investigator was asked for more details. Unfortunately we could not get in touch with all the authors concerned.

Too broad entries. Happiness and related terms were not used in most indexes at the time of this investigation. Hence we were forced to inspect rather broader categories, such as 'emotion', 'mental health' and 'attitudes'. This required a lot of work. Fortunately several bibliographical systems were computerized when we were halfway. This enabled not only to select titles that used promising keywords, but also to identify publications which used these words in their abstract.

Book publications difficult to trace. Current bibliographical systems cover journal articles better than book publications. Nevertheless, the few books that deal exclusively with happiness could be easily spotted. However, many empirical data on happiness are reported in books that deal with quite different matters, such as 'health', 'ageing' and 'alcoholism'. As yet there is no reference system that adequately covers such sidelines in book publications. In order to detect such publications we had to rely on references in other publications, on hints and on good luck. Another problem was that many of these book-like reports have a very limited circulation. We struck several that had not left the research institute: among others reports from opinion poll agencies and unpublished theses.

Non-English publications underrepresentated. Most international reference systems cover publications in the English language more thoroughly than publications in other languages. As a result we found only a few reports in German and French and not a single one in Spanish, Japanese or Russian. Combing out libraries in the countries concerned would probably yield more of them. It is planned to do so when preparing a sequel to this book, which will cover the empirical literature up to and including 1985.

When to stop? As we will see in the next section, the number of empirical investigations on happiness has grown considerably in the last decade. Hence we were confronted with an ever growing list of promising titles. It was decided to take January 1, 1976 as a cut-off date. About a hundred more investigations were reported since.

b Search procedure.

We started with an examination of the 'Psychological Abstracts' from 1928 to 1972. All abstracts that were listed under the following keyword were scanned: 'adaptation', 'affect', 'adjustment', 'aspiration', 'awareness', 'conflict', 'depression', 'deprivation', 'emotion', 'expectancy', 'frustration', 'happiness', 'life satisfaction', 'mental health', 'motivation', 'morale', 'mood', 'satisfaction', 'self evaluation', 'stress' and 'suicide'. Whenever an abstract seemed to refer to empirical data about happiness, the original report was ordered and inspected. This procedure yielded some thirty usable reports. In the references contained in these reports we found several more.

In 1976 four abstract systems had been computerized to some extent, namely the 'Psychological Abstracts' (1967-1975), the 'Sociological Abstracts' (1963-1974), the 'Educational Resources Information Center' (1966-1975) and the Social Sciences Citation Index ' (1972-1975). These files were mechanically scanned for the following keywords: 'happiness', 'morale', 'life satisfaction', 'evaluation of life', 'general satisfaction', 'hedonic level', 'elation', 'general mood', 'attitude towards life', 'contentment with life', 'emotional satisfaction', 'psychological well-being', 'inner well-being', 'mood level' and 'daily mood'. This resulted in 2159 abstracts, a hundred of which turned out to refer to an investigation that had used an acceptable indicator of happiness. In some of these reports we again found references to other publications.

Furthermore we searched several libraries in the Netherlands and inspected the indexes of many books on related subjects, thus coming across several more reports.

Finally we consulted the authors of acceptable reports; we sent them a copy of the excerpt we made from their publication and enclosed a list of the titles found sofar. The authors were asked whether they knew any more. Thus we received a few dozen tips.

This procedure was very time consuming, in particular because the search criteria were adjusted several times. The criteria for the valid measurement of happiness have in fact sharpened a great deal as we got a better view of the variety of methods that had been used. All in all the search took almost a year work.

c  The studies found.

We managed to find 150 publications reporting altogether 156 acceptable research projects, which covered 245 samples. Each set of observation in a sample will be referred to as an 'investigation'. Probably this is not all that is in fact available. Though incomplete, this crop is nevertheless richer than any of the earlier literature reviews made surmise. Remember that the best documented article mentioned only fifty titles, while it set out to cover a broader field (Fordyce, 1972). In fact that review signalized only 18 reports from the present collection and missed 69 ones in the period meant to cover.

The investigations found concern different populations at different moments and used a great variety of happiness indicators. Let's take a closer look at their characteristics.

Periods. The first empirical investigation on happiness was one in 1912 among English students and schoolboys. It focused on hedonic level. In the decades that followed several small studies in the US dealt with hedonic level of students as well. After World War II the number of investigations increased and emphasis shifted to overall happiness and general population surveys. See exhibit 2. Since 1970 the number increased even more and the stream still swells in the early 1980's. At first sight this gradual rise in the number of investigations might suggest that social scientists are becoming more aware of their calling to study happiness and that the subject is gaining a more prominent place in the order of research priorities. Yet we should realize that the entire volume of social research has expanded almost as much during that period; in fact the subject is still the Cinderella it always was.

Populations. More than half of the investigations concern North-America; with two exceptions the US. About seventy come from European countries, of which fourteen from Britain, eight from France, twelve from the Netherlands and eight from Western Germany. In each of the other parts of the world only a few happiness investigations have been performed. See exhibit 3.

The relatively large number of investigations from the Netherlands is not only due to the flourishing social sciences in that country, but also to the fact that we happen to live there and thus had a better chance of finding reports that have not reached any international reference system. In fact only five of the Dutch reports could have been traced that way.

Most of the investigations at hand were based on probability samples in national populations. Next some twenty investigations focused on regional populations, most of them based on probability samples as well. The remaining inves-

<u>Exhibit 2:</u> Number[1)] of empirical investigations on happiness between 1911 and 1975[2)], by continent, type of population covered and happiness variant[3)] involved.

| | 1911–1920 | 1921–1930 | 1931–1940 | 1941–1950 | 1951–1960 | 1961–1965 | 1966–1970 | 1971–1975 | Total |
|---|---|---|---|---|---|---|---|---|---|
| Africa | – | – | – | – | 1 | 1 | – | 1 | 3 |
| Asia | – | – | – | – | 1 | 8 | 1 | 7 | 17 |
| Australia | – | – | – | 2 | – | – | 1 | 1 | 4 |
| Europe | 2 | 1 | – | 14 | 2 | 8 | 6 | 33 | 66 |
| Anglo America | 2 | 4 | 5 | 10 | 15 | 19 | 33 | 58 | 146 |
| Latin America | – | – | – | 1 | 2 | 3 | – | 3 | 9 |
| | | | | | | | | | |
| National population | – | – | – | 23 | 13 | 23 | 10 | 62 | 131 |
| Regional/local population | – | – | – | – | – | 7 | 3 | 11 | 21 |
| Students/pupils | 4 | 3 | 5 | 3 | 2 | 3 | 10 | 8 | 38 |
| Aged people | – | – | – | – | 5 | 2 | 2 | 7 | 16 |
| Other categories | – | 2 | – | 1 | 1 | 4 | 16 | 15 | 39 |
| | | | | | | | | | |
| Overall happiness | – | 1 | 2 | 25 | 20 | 37 | 29 | 89 | 203 |
| Hedonic level of affect | 4 | 5 | 3 | 1 | 2 | 11 | 18 | 36 | 80 |
| Contentment | – | – | – | – | 2 | 2 | 1 | 1 | 6 |
| | | | | | | | | | |
| Total | 4 | 5 | 5 | 27 | 21 | 39 | 41 | 103 | 245 |

(1) The number of separate samples was counted, not the number of publications.
(2) If no date of data gathering was reported, the data are presumed to have been gathered one year before publication.
(3) Some investigations covered more than one happinessvariant.

Exhibit 3: Number[1] of empirical investigations on happiness between 1911 and 1975, by population[2] covered and type of sample[3].

| | National population | | Regional population | | Students / pupils | | Aged people | | Other special groups | | Total | |
|---|---|---|---|---|---|---|---|---|---|---|---|---|
| | prob. | non-prob. | prob. | non-prob. | prob. | non-prob. | prob. | non-prob. | prob. | non-prob. | prob. | non-prob. |
| Africa | 2 | 1 | - | - | - | - | - | - | - | - | 2 | 1 |
| Asia | 12 | - | 3 | - | - | - | - | - | 1 | 1 | 16 | 1 |
| India | 3 | - | - | - | - | - | - | - | - | - | 3 | - |
| Israel | 1 | - | 2 | - | - | - | - | - | 1 | 1 | 4 | 1 |
| Japan | 3 | - | - | - | - | - | - | - | - | - | 3 | - |
| other | 5 | - | 1 | - | - | - | - | - | - | - | 6 | - |
| Australia | 4 | - | - | - | - | - | - | - | - | - | 4 | - |
| Europe | 48 | 3 | 2 | 1 | - | 6 | - | - | 1 | 5 | 51 | 15 |
| Britain/England | 8 | 1 | - | 1 | - | 2 | - | - | - | 2 | 8 | 6 |
| France | 8 | - | - | - | - | - | - | - | - | - | 8 | - |
| W. Germany | 6 | - | - | - | - | - | - | - | - | 2 | 6 | 2 |
| Italy | 5 | - | - | - | - | - | - | - | - | - | 5 | - |
| The Netherlands | 6 | - | 2 | - | - | 2 | - | - | 1 | 1 | 9 | 3 |
| Scandinavia | 5 | 1 | - | - | - | 1 | - | - | - | - | 5 | 2 |
| other | 10 | 1 | - | - | - | 1 | - | - | - | - | 10 | 2 |
| Anglo America | 46 | 6 | 14 | 1 | 6 | 26 | 7 | 9 | 13 | 18 | 86 | 60 |
| USA | 44 | 6 | 13 | 1 | 6 | 26 | 7 | 9 | 13 | 17 | 83 | 59 |
| Canada | 2 | - | 1 | - | - | - | - | - | - | 1 | 3 | 1 |
| Latin America | 9 | - | - | - | - | - | - | - | - | - | 9 | - |
| Brazil | 2 | - | - | - | - | - | - | - | - | - | 2 | - |
| Mexico | 2 | - | - | - | - | - | - | - | - | - | 2 | |
| other | 5 | - | - | - | - | - | - | - | - | - | 5 | - |
| Total | 121 | 10 | 19 | 2 | 6 | 32 | 7 | 9 | 15 | 24 | 168 | 77 |

(1) The number of separate samples was counted, not the number of publications.

(2) Major countries are listed under the continents. The 'other' categories contain investigations in countries not presented, or in different combinations of countries. The number behind the major regions are sumscores.

(3) In some cases type of sample construction was not reported. In these cases 'representative' samples were considered as probability samples, and other samples as non-probability samples.

tigations covered various more specific populations, the most frequently studied ones being 'elderly people' and 'students'. There are furthermore some stray investigations among e.g. 'workers', 'university professors', 'military personel', 'housewives' and 'farmers'.

Indicators. Most investigations focused on overall happiness. Some eighty dealt with hedonic level and only a few assessed contentment. Let us now examine in more detail what indicators were involved. Exhibit 1 lists all types of indicators deemed acceptable. Next it shows how often each of these was used.

Overall happiness was most frequently tapped by means of single closed questions using the word 'happiness'. Direct closed questions on 'life satisfaction' were second in popularity among investigators. Surprisingly few investigators worked with open-ended questions or focused interviews.

Hedonic level was often assessed by means of sum scores of questions on specific affects: mostly by variants of the so-called 'Affect Balance Scale' (ABS), developed by Bradburn & Caplovitz (1965:177). In several instances it was also measured by repeated questions on the momentaneous level of cheerfulness, mostly by means of the 'Elation-Depression Scale' of Wessman & Ricks (1960: 273). A few investigations used ratings by others. Open-ended questions and focused interviews hardly appear.

The few investigations that assessed contentment all used single direct closed questions , except one that worked with focused interviews.

Finally some thirty investigations involved composite indicators, covering more than one of the happiness variants at the same time. More than half of these combined questions on overall happiness and hedonic level. The two 'clinical ratings' probably covered matters of contentment as well.

d Some further characteristics.

Part of the harvest consists of public opinion polls which provide no more information than frequency distributions of answers to happiness questions by certain populations at a certain time. We found 66 of them. Taken individually, these investigations are not very interesting, but together they allow comparison across time and culture.

Most investigations do more than counting happy and unhappy people; generally they also investigate whether certain characteristics are more frequent among the former than among the latter. We found 179 such correlational studies. Most of these used zero-order correlations, but quite a few specified at least some of the correlations found: correlations between happiness and income have for example been specified by variables such as 'gender', 'age' and 'social rank'. Most investigations are rather superficial and haphazard in this respect, only about thirty of them involving broad and systematic elaborations.

Almost all investigations at hand are synchronic ones and only eight involved longitudinal observations of happiness, mostly over the periods no longer than a year. Six other ones related synchronic observations on happiness to longitudinal data on other variables.

## 5 PRESENTING THE FINDINGS.

Filling a bookcase with acceptable studies is just the first step. The next was to order the abundant findings conveniently. To that end the reports were first excerpted in a uniform way. In a shortened version these excerpts are presented in Part II of this volume. Next the correlational findings were arranged according to subject. Over 2500 correlations were involved, their presentation taking the bulk of this book. These data are enumerated in Part III. Part IV presents the results of the 66 non-correlational studies that assessed the level of happiness in particular countries and of some correlational studies that assessed national averages as well.

This procedure may look simpler than it actually was. It is worthwhile having a look at the problems involved and the way dealt with them.

### a Hinderances in getting an overview.

Excerpting the reports was necessary for several reasons: to mention one: several were rather chaotic and their findings therefore hard to trace. Some had relevant information hidden in footnotes and appendices, while others presented information in separate (and not easily accessible) statistical supplements.

Another problem was that not all reports used the same language. Not only were not all the reports in English, they moreover used subtly differing technical vocabularies. Together with the great number of investigations these problems render it impossible to get a general view, even for the interested scholar who is willing to spend several months reading. Uniform excerpts were thus necessary in order to prevent the information gathered from getting lost.

In excerpting the reports we struck on the following technical problems.

Different labeling of variables. As noted before, not all investigators used the same word to depict 'happiness'. The same problem appears in labeling variables that were related to it; essentially similar co-varying factors being adorned with quite different names. Answers to questions about 'self esteem' for instance were labeled with terms as 'mental health', 'role adjustment' and 'identity'. On the other hand, one and the same term sometimes covers distinct concepts. The term 'health' for example refers sometimes to 'absence of apparent disease', sometimes to 'frequency of complaints' and in an other instance to 'longevity'. As in the case of happiness the problem was solved by forgetting the theoretical lables used and by focusing on what had been actually observed and how. When ordering the findings later on, we classified them on the basis of this information and devised labels for the categories thus constructed.

Differents technical vocabulary. Another problem was that the studies do not use the same technical terms to describe the design of the investigation. The term 'reliability' for example was used sometimes to refer to similarity in response to the same question asked twice and sometimes to the association between answers on different questions believed to represent the same variable. Likewise terms such as 'scale', 'non-response' and 'sample' carry different meanings. This confusion of tongues is nicely illustrated by van de Merwe's 'Thesaurus of Social Research Terminology', a volumnious book, the purpose of which is to list current technical jargon (van der Merwe, 1974). Obviously this situation can easily lead to misunderstanding. I felt therefore obliged to define all the technical terms I used in the excerpts and to translate all the reports into that terminology. The resulting list can be found in Appendix A.

Incomparable statistics. Several investigators report their results in frequency distributions of happiness, split up for other variables. Such tables do not allow comparison with other studies very easily. Moreover, they are too voluminous to be inserted into the excerpts. Therefore we reduced the data reported in such tables by computing association values. As most of the tables contained data on the ordinal level of measurement, we computed Gammas. In the excerpts these values are marked with an accent (G'). In cases where no Gammas could be computed due to lack of information, it sufficed to indicate the direction of the relation as shown in the tables (+ or -)-

Most investigators computed association values themselves, generally product moment correlations ($r_{pm}$). Unfortunately there are various measures of association. These measures are based on slightly different assumptions about the mathematical qualities of the data and for that reason they are not quite comparable. This is a serious problem in comparative research, a problem to which there is no adequate answer. The best we could do was to record the statistical measures used in each case and to sketch their characteristics in an appendix. See Appendix B.

Though varying somewhat in their methods and assumptions, most measures of association are nevertheless expressed in values ranging from zero to one. For all measures the value of 'zero' implies absence of any common variance, whereas the value of 'one' implies absolute association. The meaning of the interjacent values may differ, however. Gamma of +.30 does not always reflect the same correspondence between two variables as an $r_{pm}$ of +.30. Yet standardized measures of association permit at least a rough comparison. Unfortunately not all measures of association are expressed in standardized values ranging from zero to one. The much used '$Chi^2$' for example has a theoretical range from zero to infinite. In these cases comparison is even more hazardous. We therefore decided not to mention such values in the excerpts, but simply to note the direction of the statistical relationship. For the same reason we did not mention most differences in means. A difference in mean happiness scores range from 1 to 10. The noting down of a '+' or '-' had to suffice.

Several investigators further tried to establish whether the correlations they found were significant or not (mostly significantly deviating from a zero correlation in the population the sample was drawn from). To that end they used again a great variety of methods. These test statistics are summarized in Appendix C. In the cases we computed Gammas ourselves we also assessed the significance of these. The resulting values are once more marked with an accent (Gt' for 'Gammatest').

b Excerpting the reports.

The excerpts were not exactly 'summaries'. They were not meant to cover all the issues the author had raised, but focused exclusively on his empirical observations on happiness. The excerpts were made by means of a notation sheet. A completed version is printed on the next page. The report dealt with there is an article by Thompson et al. (1960). As noted above, the technical terms used in this excerpt are explained in Appendix A. We saw to it that the excerpts reflected all the findings of the reports, not only the findings that were stressed by the author or that seemed most relevant to us. We did not restrict to significant correlations either; non-correlations were noted as well. This required a careful inspection of both the text and the tables in the reports.

Excerpting involves the possibility of making mistakes, in particular of selective attention and theoretically guided misperception. Therefore each report was excerpted twice by two different excerpters. The excerpts were then compared and differences settled on the basis of a careful re-examination of the report. In cases where the author(s) could be traced, the excerpt was also sent

Exhibit 4 : A typical excerpt

AUTHOR: Thompson, W.E., Streib, G.F. & Kosa, J.

TITLE: The effect of retirement on personal adjustment: a panel analysis.

SOURCE: Journal of Gerontology, 1960; vol. 15, nr. 2, p. 165-169.

THOMP 60

GOAL OF THE STUDY: Test and specification of assumed negative relation between retirement and personal adjustment.

REFERS TO: Theory of adjustment among retirees; Havighurst & Albrecht (1953); Kutner et al. (1956).

TYPE OF STUDY: explanatory, explorative, special group, longitudinal, non-experimental

DATA GATHERING: Structured interview administered at the respondent's place of work, followed by 2 mailed questionnaires at one or two years interval.

DATE OF DATA: 1952 - 1956

POPULATION: Aged males, USA

SAMPLE CONSTRUCTION: Non-probability accidental sample using volunteers. All males were born in 1887, 1888 or 1889; relatively more prosperous and better educated individuals from relatively larger, more affluent and more progressive organizations from all parts of the country;1082 Ss gainfully employed throughout and 477 Ss retired between 1952-1954

NON-RESPONSE:

N: 1559

LABEL: Satisfaction with life

INSTRUMENT: COMP 1.2: Index of closed questions (devised through the use of the Guttman (1944) scaling technique):

1. All in all, how much happiness would you say you find in life today? (negative response:'almost none' or 'some , but not very much')
2. In general, how would you say you feel most of the time, in good spirits or in low spirits? (negative response:'I'm usually in low spirits' or 'sometimes in good spirits, sometimes in low spirits')
3. On the whole, how satisfied would you say you are with your way of life today? (negative response: 'fairly satisfied' , 'not very satisfied' or 'not satisfied at all')

RELIABILITY: Reproducibility: +.96
Error Ratio : +.55

VALIDITY:

DISTRIBUTION: Almost symmetric: in 1952: 51% satisfied, 49% dissatisfied
in 1954: 43% satisfied, 57% dissatisfied

REMARKS: The publication focuses on longitudinal changes in satisfaction with life rather than on correlates of present satisfaction with life. Compared were persons satisfied in 1952 who became dissatisfied in 1954 (N=788) and persons dissatisfied in 1952 who became satisfied in 1954 (N=771). For our purpose we computed correlates of satisfaction with life in 1954, when possible we made elaborations for satisfaction with life in 1952.

| page | association | | significance | | correlates of happiness found | | |
|---|---|---|---|---|---|---|---|
| | measure | value | test | p < | conceptualization | operationalization | elaboration/remarks |
| 167 | G' | -.07 | Gt' | ns | Retirement | Gainfully employed vs retired between 1952 and 1954 | Among those who were satisfied in 1952 : G' = -.21<br>Among those who were dissatisfied in 1952 : G' = +.11<br>When the gainfully employed were compared with retirees who had a positive orientation towards retirement before they were retired : G' = +.13<br>When the gainfully employed were compared with retirees who had a negative pre-retirement attitude towards retirement : G' = -.27<br>Unaffected by voluntary vs compulsory retirement. |
| 168 | G' | -.08 | | 01 | Compulsory retirement | Voluntary vs administrative retirement | Computed for those who retired between 1952 and 1954 only.<br>Unaffected by pre-retirement attitude towards retirement. |
| 168 | G' | +.40 | Gt' | 01 | Positive pre-retirement attitude towards retirement | 3-item index of closed questions indicating a negative vs a positive orientation towards retirement | Computed for those who had retired between 1952 and 1954 only. |
| 168 | G' | -.55 | Gt' | 01 | Economic deprivation | not deprived vs economically deprived | Computed for those who were satisfied in 1952 only.<br>Among the gainfully employed : G' = -.54(01)<br>Among retirees who had a positive pre-retirement attitude towards retirement : G' = -.53(01)<br>Among retirees who had a negative pre-retirement attitude towards retirement : G' = -.40(ns) |
| 168 | G' | +.58 | Gt' | 01 | Subjective health | poor vs good | Computed for those who were satisfied in 1952 only.<br>Among the gainfully employed : G' = +.65(01)<br>Among retirees who had a positive pre-retirement attitude towards retirement : G' = +.46(01)<br>Among retirees who had a negative pre-retirement attitude towards retirement : G' = +.23(ns) |
| 168 | G' | -.49 | Gt' | 01 | Having difficulties in keeping occupied | Closed question: no vs yes | Computed for those who were satisfied in 1952 only.<br>Among the gainfully employed : G' = -.43(01)<br>Among retirees who had a positive pre-retirement attitude towards retirement : G' = -.38(05)<br>Among retirees who had a negative pre-retirement attitude towards retirement : G' = -.64(01) |

CONCLUSIONS: In general, retirement appears to have a negative effect on personal adjustment only when retirement is involuntary and economic deprivation is felt. The findings do suggest that the work-role is not as central to the personality as many writers would contend.

to him (them) for inspection. Altogether 120 were sent out (to 93 authors), 73 of which were returned (by 55 authors). Several of the latter enclosed additional information that had not been published in their excerpted report. Where relevant, that information was added.

Close reading of the reports revealed many defects. Relevant information was often found to be missing and several reports appeared to contain mistakes. If possible the author was consulted. The correct information was then included in the excerpt.

Altogether these excerpts ran to some 400 pages. That was too much to print. The excerpts in Part II are therefore short ones. The actual findings are omitted because these appear in Part III (See contents of part III on page 191-194). The shortened excerpts thus reflect only the design of the investigation and its conclusions. See page 170 for the shortened version of the excerpt of the article by Thompson et al.

Not all reports were excerpted, only the ones that present 'correlates' of happiness. As noted there are also 66 investigations that assessed the 'distribution' of happiness in certain populations, mostly highly standardized opinion polls. Their results are presented separately in Part IV of this volume.

The excerpting of the reports turned out to be a laborious job. Not the excerpting as such, but rather the development of a manageable vocabulary and rules. All in all it took two full man-years.

c <u>Classifying the findings</u>.

Together the reports appeared to contain some 4000 correlates of happiness- too much to survey. The next problem was hence to categorize these abundant findings conveniently. When sorting out the findings we took care not to squeeze them into conceptual categories of some a priori theory of happiness. Rather we tried to figure out which categorization would show the wealth of data to its fullest advantage. Thus we arrived at forty-two main categories which we ordered alphabetically. These main categories were subdivided into some two hundred further ones. The resulting classification is presented on page 191-194. In classifying the correlates by subject-matter, we ignored the theoretical labels the investigators had attached to them, but focused on what they had actually observed. Several findings appeared to fit in more than one category of the classification and were hence presented more than once.

When classifying the findings of different investigations in subject categories, we could obviously not obliterate their contextural differences. Hence we did not merely list statistics, but presented each finding with shortened information about the methods of measurement used and the population concerned. See for instance the pages 291 to 295 which summarize the findings on the relationship between happiness and physical health. On page 292 we meet again with one of the findings of Thompson et al. summarized in exhibit 4. The codenumbers in the headline on p.291 refer to the classification shown on p. 191-194. The horizontal columns summarize information drawn from the various investigations. The first vertical column records how the variable concerned was labeled by the investigator. The second one notes how that variable has actually been measured. The third column presents eventual elaborations that were made by the investigator. If left blank the investigator made do with zero-order correlations. The fourth column contains codes referring to the kind of happiness measures used: 'HAPP' meaning 'overall happiness', 'AFF' 'hedonic level of affect', etc. These codes are the ones contained in exhibit 1. The fifth column notes the measures of association used; the symbols are explained in Appendix C. The eigth column mentions the resulting 'p' value. If these latter two colums are left blank no test for significance has been carried out. Almost at the right side of the page column nine describes shortly which population was studied, what kind of sample had been involved and when the data were gathered. Finally the last column mentions the source. The reader who wants more information can revert to the excerpt in Part II or even the original report. To that end column ten also mentions the page in the original report.

This job also required a lot of work, especially the setting up of a reliable classification. It took another full year to organize the data conveniently. Finally a 350 page inventory resulted which served as Part III of this volume. Thus a bookcase full of different reports was reduced to a one inch thick systematic volume. This reduction did not involve a loss of essential information, as least not as far as empirical data about happiness were concerned.

# PART II

# EXCERPTS

**Excerpts of 150 Reports on Empirical Investigations on Happiness between 1911 and 1975. Presented in Alphabetical Order of Author's Names.**

ABRAM 72

AUTHOR: Abrams, M. & Hall, J.

TITLE: The condition of the British people: report on a pilot survey using self-rating scales.

SOURCE: Unpublished paper, Social Science Research Council, London. Partly reported in 'Measuring the quality of life using sample surveys', in Stöber et al. 'Technology assessment and the quality of life', Amsterdam, 1973, Elsevier.

---

GOAL OF THE STUDY: To produce a questionnaire which could be used in large scale sample surveys to measure 'the aspirations, attitudes, satisfactions, disappointments, grievances, expectations and values of the British people.

REFERS TO: Happiness research; Campbell & Converse (1970), Bradburn (1969)

TYPE OF STUDY: explanatory, explorative, national population, snapshot, non-experimental

DATA GATHERING: Halfstructured questionnaire, using both open-ended and closed questions.

DATE OF DATA: March, 1971

POPULATION: National population, Britain

SAMPLE CONSTRUCTION: Non-probability quota sample.
age 15+; overrepresentation of middle class people (48% vs 35%)

NON-RESPONSE:

N: 213

AUTHOR'S HAPPINESS LABEL: Satisfaction in general

OUR CONCEPTUALIZATION: Happiness

INSTRUMENT: HAPP 2.1: Single closed question rated on an 11-point self-anchoring scale (based on the Cantril Satisfaction with Life Rating; see CANTR 65/2):

How dissatisfied would you say you are with things in general today? This is a scale with complete satisfaction at the top and complete dissatisfaction at the bottom.
Whereabouts on the ladder would you put yourself?

RELIABILITY:

VALIDITY:

DISTRIBUTION: almost symmetric
possible range: 0 (low) to 10 (high); actual range: 20% low (0-3), 56% medium (4-7), 24% high (8-10); mean: 5.53

REMARKS:

CORRELATES: Age (A 3); Anomy (D 1); Gender (G 1.1); Changes in happiness (H 1.6); Wish to change life (H 3.1.1); Income (I 1.1); various indicators of Life quality (L 2.1.1, L 2.3); Marital status (M 1.6); Being an old age pensioner (R 2.1); various Domainsatisfactions (S 1); Social grade (S 5.1); Occupation (W 2.2)

CONCLUSION:

AUTHOR: Alexander, W.E.

ALEXA 68

TITLE: Some sociological aspects of psychological well-being in a schizophrenic population: social class, participation and work.

SOURCE: Unpublished doctoral dissertation, 1968, Syracuse University, U.S.A.

---

GOAL OF THE STUDY: Assessment of relations between psychological well-being and mental illness, social class, social participation and work.

REFERS TO: Theory of mental health; Smith (1959), Scott (1958)

TYPE OF STUDY: explanatory, explorative, special group, snapshot, non-experimental

DATA GATHERING: Analysis of psychiatric case register, psychiatric ratings by clinical interview, interview with family member, and highly structured questionnaire.

DATE OF DATA: 1964 - 1965

POPULATION: Non-hospitalized schizophrenic males, Monroe County, New York, U.S.A.

SAMPLE CONSTRUCTION: Probability sample, drawn from the Monroe County psychiatric case register including all persons who had ever contacted the diagnostic source.
The sample was limited to those patients who had first psychiatric contact between January, 1960 and June, 1963; who had no history of psychiatric hospitalization prior to initial contact, and had received at least one diagnosis of schizophrenia.
Later the sample was limited to non-hospitalized patients. The number of separate schizophrenic diagnoses received ranged from 1 to 19, and the proportion of schizophrenic diagnoses received varied from 10% to 100%.
24% possible schizophrenic, 76% definitely schizophrenic; 37% never hospitalized, 25% less than one month hospitalized, 38% hospitalized for more than one month in mental hospital; 18% unemployed, 82% employed (only 34% of unskilled workers are employed, whereas 84% of the highest occupational prestige grouping are employed); age 20 - 50.

NON-RESPONSE: 28%, most of them patients' or family member refusal

N: 178

AUTHOR'S HAPPINESS LABEL: Psychological well-being

OUR CONCEPTUALIZATION: Happiness (first instrument) and Hedonic level of affect (second instrument)

FIRST INSTRUMENT: HAPP 1.1: Single closed question using the term 'happiness', rated on a 3-point scale (see GURIN 60).

RELIABILITY:

VALIDITY:

DISTRIBUTION: symmetric distribution: 22% very happy, 59% pretty happy, 19% not too happy

SECOND INSTRUMENT: AFF 2.3: Index of closed questions on perceived occurrence of specific affects during the last week (Bradburn & Caplovitz Affect Balance Score; see BRADB 65 and BRADB 69):

As in the BRADB 65 instrument Ss were told:

'The following list describes some of the ways people feel at different times. Please indicate how often you felt each way during the last week. . .'
not at all / once / several times / often

The 10 items from the BRADB 69 instrument were used.

The dichotomized variables (not at all = 0, other = 1) were correlated with the multivalued variables (not at all = 0, once = 1, several times = 2, often = 3) and yielded a correlation coefficient of .88 for the positive items and .94 for the negative items.
The two-valued variable on each feeling is used.
The Affect Balance Score was calculated by substracting the negative affect score from the positive affect score.

RELIABILITY: equivalence: positive items : $r_{pm}$ ranging from +.13 to +.43
negative items : $r_{pm}$ ranging from +.09 to +.45
positive x negative items: $r_{pm}$ ranging from -.25 to +.14
positive affect score x negative affect score: R = .07 (ns)

VALIDITY:

DISTRIBUTION: possible range: positive affect: 1 (low positive) to 5 (high positive); negative affect: 1 (low negative) to 5 (high negative); affect balance: -4 (low positive, high negative) to +4 (high positive, low negative)
means : positive affect: 2.9; negative affect: 2.7

REMARKS:

CORRELATES: Educational level (E 1.1.1); Hedonic level x happiness (H 1.2.1); Mental health (H 2.3.2); Income (I 1.1); Job satisfaction (S 1.9.1); various indicators of Social participation (S 4); S.E.S. (S 5.1); Employment history (W 2.1); Occupation (W 2.2); Interaction in the job setting (W 2.6)

CONCLUSION: The Bradburn-Caplovitz measures of well-being are also appropriate for schizophrenics. It was found that both positive and negative affect were correlated with happiness, that negative and positive affect were independent of one another, and that affect balance bore a stronger relation to happiness than either negative or positive affect alone.

AUTHOR: Alston, J.P., Lowe, G.D. & Wrigley, A

ALSTO 74

TITLE: Socioeconomic correlates for four dimensions of self-perceived satisfaction.

SOURCE: Human Organization, 1974, vol. 33, nr 1, p. 99-102.

---

**GOAL OF THE STUDY:** To explore the relationship between socioeconomic status and four dimensions of satisfaction (work, financial situation, health and happiness ).

**REFERS TO:** Happiness research; Wessman (1956), Gurin et al. (1960), Bradburn & Caplovitz (1965)

**TYPE OF STUDY:** explanatory, explorative, national population, shapshot, non-experimental

**DATA GATHERING:**

**DATE OF DATA:** March, 1972

POPULATION: Non-institutionalized adults, U.S.A.

**SAMPLE CONSTRUCTION:** Probability sample, conducted by NORC.
1342 whites, 260 blacks

**NON-RESPONSE:**

N: 1602

**AUTHOR'S HAPPINESS LABEL:** Happiness

**OUR CONCEPTUALIZATION:** Happiness

INSTRUMENT: HAPP 1.1: Single closed question using the term 'happiness', rated on a 3-point scale (see GURIN 60).

RELIABILITY:

VALIDITY:

DISTRIBUTION: 31% very happy

REMARKS: Our computation of Gammas (G') is based on the proportions 'very happy' answers .

CORRELATES: Age (A 3); Educational level (E 1.1.1); Race (E 2.1); Gender (G 1.1); Income (I 1.1); Satisfaction with health (S 1.6); Satisfaction with work (S 1.9.1); Occupational level (W 2.2)

CONCLUSION:

| | |
|---|---|
| AUTHOR: | Andrews, F.M. & Withey, S.B. — ANDRE 74 |
| TITLE: | Developing measures of perceived life quality: Results from several national surveys. |
| SOURCE: | Social Indicators Research; 1974, vol. 1, p. 1-26. |

---

GOAL OF THE STUDY: Development of an instrument for the assessment of perceived life quality in the diverse domains most important for predicting people's general satisfaction with their lives.

REFERS TO: Theory of social indicators

TYPE OF STUDY: explanatory, explorative, national population, snapshot, non-experimental

DATA GATHERING: Structured interview using highly structured questionnaires

DATE OF DATA: first sample: May, 1972; second sample: November, 1972; third sample: November, 1972

POPULATION: National adult population, U.S.A.

SAMPLE CONSTRUCTION: Probability area samples of adults (age 18+) living in non-institutional dwelling units of the 48 coterminous states.
The first sample appeared to be representative for the total population with respect to age, sex and race. Both other samples were not tested for representativeness, but no gross biases are expected.
The second and the third sample were limited to American citizens.
first sample: 547 males, 750 females.

NON-RESPONSE: first sample: 76%, second sample: 62%; third sample: 62%

N: first sample: 1297; second sample: 1118; third sample: 1072

AUTHOR'S HAPPINESS LABEL: Perceived life quality

OUR CONCEPTUALIZATION: Happiness (first to fifth instrument) and Hedonic level of affect (sixth instrument)

FIRST INSTRUMENT: HAPP 3.1: Single closed question rated on a 7-point scale:

How do you feel about your life as a whole ?

| 1 | 2 | 3 | 4 | 5 | 6 | 7 |
|---|---|---|---|---|---|---|
| delighted | pleased | mostly satisfied | mixed (about equally satisfied and dissatisfied) | mostly dissatisfied | unhappy | terrible |

REMARKS: In the first and third sample the question has been asked twice during the interview. The interval was about 8 to 12 minutes. During this interval the respondent was questioned on quality-of-life issues. Here the arithmetic mean of the coded responses was used as a happiness measure. If the associations with either the first or the second question show remarkable differences we reported them in the 'elaboration/remarks' column (Part III).
In the second sample the question has been asked only once.

RELIABILITY: repeat-reliability:
- correlation between first and second questioning: $r_{pm}$ = +.71 (third sample); $r_{pm}$ = +.61 (first sample)
- correlation between mean and first questioning : $r_{pm}$ = +.92 (third sample); $r_{pm}$ = +.90 (first sample)
- correlation between mean and second questioning : $r_{pm}$ = +.93 (third sample); $r_{pm}$ = +.90 (first sample)

VALIDITY:

DISTRIBUTION:

SECOND INSTRUMENT: HAPP 2.1: Single closed question rated on a 7-point scale:

How satisfied are you with your life as a whole these days?
completely satisfied . . . . . . . completely dissatisfied.

RELIABILITY:

VALIDITY:

DISTRIBUTION:

THIRD INSTRUMENT: COMP 1.1: Single closed question rated on a graphic scale:

Where would you put your life as a whole on a feeling thermometer?
very cold (negative) . . . . . . . . . . . . . very warm (positive)

RELIABILITY:

VALIDITY:

DISTRIBUTION:

FOURTH INSTRUMENT: HAPP 1.1: Single closed question using the term 'happiness' rated on a 3-point scale (see GURIN 60)

RELIABILITY:

VALIDITY:

DISTRIBUTION:

FIFTH INSTRUMENT: HAPP 3.1: Single closed question rated on a 7-point scale:

How do you feel about how happy you are?
delighted / pleased / mostly satisfied / mixed / mostly dissatisfied / unhappy / terrible (see first instrument)

RELIABILITY:

VALIDITY:

DISTRIBUTION:

SIXTH INSTRUMENT: AFF 2.3: Index of closed questions on perceived occurrence of specific affects during the past few weeks (Bradburn Affect Balance Score; see BRADB 69).

The affect balance score was obtained by substracting the Negative affect score from the Positive affect score.

RELIABILITY: equivalence : positive affect x negative affect: $r_{pm}$ = +.01 (third sample)
positive affect x affect balance : $r_{pm}$ = +.71 (third sample)
negative affect x affect balance : $r_{pm}$ = -.70 (third sample)

VALIDITY:

DISTRIBUTION:

REMARKS: This study is more fully reported in Andrews & Withey (1976). Because the present inventorization only covers reports dated 1975 or earlier, that later report is not included.
For the first sample only correlates of the first instrument are offered; for the second sample correlates of the first, second and third instrument; and for the third sample correlates of all instruments.
Most data concern the first instrument only.

CORRELATES: Age (A 3); Educational level (E 1.1.1); Race (E 2.1); Gender (G 1.1); Family life cycle (F 1.4); Happiness x happiness (H 1.1.1); Hedonic level x happiness (H 1.2.1); Wish to change life (H 3.1.1); Income (I 1.1); Feelings about the good/poor parts of life (L 2.1.1); Amount of worrying (P 5.2.1); various Domainsatisfactions (S 1); Satisfaction with oneself (S 2.1.5)

CONCLUSION: Additive combinations of affective responses to domains of life provide moderately good explanations of people's overall sense of life quality. Good predictions of life quality can be made with an unweighted additive combination of relatively few domain satisfactions.

AUTHOR: Antonovsky, A., Maoz, B., Dowty, N. & Wijsenbeek, H.

ANTON 71

TITLE: Twenty-five years later: A limited study of the sequelae of the concentration camp experience.

SOURCE: Social Psychiatry, 1971, vol. 6, nr 4, p. 186-193.

---

**GOAL** OF THE STUDY: To investigate maladaptive and malfunctional long-range effects of concentration camp experience.

REFERS TO: Theory of the consequences of concentration camp experience; Krystal (1968)

**TYPE** OF STUDY: explanatory, explorative, special group, snapshot, non-experimental

**DATA** GATHERING: Structured interview administered at home and medical examination; semi-structured psychiatric interview with 43 females (24 of the best and 19 of the poorest adapted, judged on basis of interview and medical examination)

**DATE** OF DATA: 1968

POPULATION: Females in the age of 45-54, Israel.

**SAMPLE** CONSTRUCTION: Probability sample of females, born between 1914 and 1923 in Central Europe, stratified by ethnicity.
All respondents are inhabitants of a fair sized Israeli city; 77 with and 210 without concentration camp experience.

**NON**-RESPONSE: 52%: 24% unattainable, 29% incomplete; unaffected by age

N: 287

**AUTHOR'S HAPPINESS** LABEL: Overall life situation

**OUR CONCEPTUAL**IZATION: Happiness

INSTRUMENT: HAPP 3.1: Single closed question on personal situation as compared with best and worst possible life, rated on an 11-point self-anchoring scale (Cantril Present Personal rating; see CANTR 65).

RELIABILITY:

VALIDITY:

DISTRIBUTION: slightly negatively skewed
possible range: 0 (low) to 10 (high); means: camp survivors 5.6, and Ss without camp experience 6.5

REMARKS:

CORRELATES: Having concentration camp experience (W 1.1)

CONCLUSION: People with concentration camp experience are more poorly adapted than people with no such experience. However, many concentration camp survivors are well adapted. This might be due to an initial underlying strength, a subsequent environment which provided opportunities to re-establish a satisfying and meaningful existence, and a 'hardening' process which allows the survivor to view current stress with some equanimity. The literature, especially psychiatric case studies, pointing to inevitable breakdown, is questioned.

AUTHOR: Bachman, J.G., Kahn, R.L., Mednick, M., Davidson, T.N. & Johnson, L.D. (Volume I).
Bachman, J.G. (Volume II).

BACHM 67/70

TITLE: Youth in transition. Vol. I : Blueprint for a longitudinal study of adolescent boys.
Vol. II: The impact of family background on intelligence in tenth-grade boys.

SOURCE: Ann Arbour, Michigan, 1967 (vol. I) and 1970 (Vol. II), Institute for Social Research.

---

**GOAL OF THE STUDY:** Exploration of the effects of different social environments on individual growth and change in adolescence.

REFERS TO: Research in education; Flanagan et al. (1962), Coleman et al. (1966)

**TYPE OF STUDY:** explanatory, explorative, special group, longitudinal, non-experimental

**DATA GATHERING:** (half-) structured interviews, tests, and highly structured questionnaires; also questionnaires to principals, counselors, and sample of teachers

**DATE OF DATA:** fall, 1966; spring, 1968; and spring, 1969

POPULATION: Public highschool boys, U.S.A.

**SAMPLE CONSTRUCTION:** Probability multi-stage sample selecting resp. geographic areas, one public high school in each area, and ± 30 tenth grade boys within each school by random sampling (in fall, 1966).
A supplementary probability sample of tenth-grade boys in 10 outstanding high schools was also included.

**NON-RESPONSE:** 2,8 % incomplete information in 1966

N: 2213 in 1966, 1886 in 1968 and 1799 in 1969

**AUTHOR'S HAPPINESS LABEL:** Happiness

**OUR CONCEPTUALIZATION:** Happiness

**INSTRUMENT:** COMP 1.2: Index of closed questions:

Ss were asked to 'describe the kind of person you are. Please read each sentence, then mark how often it is true for you'
almost always true / often true / sometimes true / seldom true / never true

1. I feel like smiling
2. I generally feel in good spirits
3. I feel happy
4. I am satisfied with life
5. I find a good deal of happiness in life
6. I feel sad

RELIABILITY: repeat reliability: $T_1 - T_3$ (30 mos.): $r_{pm} = +.47$
$T_1 - T_2$ (18 mos.): $r_{pm} = +.54$
$T_2 - T_3$ (12 mos.): $r_{pm} = +.63$

VALIDITY:

DISTRIBUTION: positively skewed
mean: 3.77; S.D.: .61

REMARKS: If not mentioned otherwise the data presented come from the first stage of the project (fall, 1966; N = 2213). All the correlations are presented in Volume II of the Youth in Transiti on study.

More data including interview waves in 1970 and 1974 are presented in Volume VI of the Youth in Transition study and in a correlation matrix (available at the authors on request). These data are not presented here because they were published after 1975. They will be reported in our follow-up publication.

CORRELATES: Aggression (A 2.2.1); Negative affect states (A 2.2.21, L 2.1.2); various Cognitive characteristics (C 1.3); various indicators of Deviance (D 1); various factors concerning School (E 1.2, E 1.3); Positive evaluation of family relations (F 1.1.3.2); Psychosomatic symptoms (H 2.2); Trust in government (N 1.1.2); various Personality characteristics (P 1); Political knowledge (P 3.1); Self-esteem (S 2.1.3); various factors concerning S.E.S. (S 5); Job-preferences (W 2.5); Acceptance of social values (V 1.1)

CONCLUSION:

| | |
|---|---|
| AUTHOR: | Bakker, P. & Berg, N. van de |

BAKKE 74

| | |
|---|---|
| TITLE: | Determinants and correlates of happiness.<br>(in Dutch: Determinanten en correlaten van geluk). |
| SOURCE: | Unpublished thesis, 1974, Erasmus University Rotterdam, The Netherlands. |

---

| | |
|---|---|
| GOAL OF THE STUDY: | Exploration of differences in factors contributing to happiness for several socio-cultural groups. |
| REFERS TO: | Theory of adaptive behavior; Aakster (1972) |
| TYPE OF STUDY: | explanatory, testing, national population, snapshot, non-experimental |
| DATA GATHERING: | Structured interview |
| DATE OF DATA: | June, 1968 |
| POPULATION: | National adult population, The Netherlands |
| SAMPLE CONSTRUCTION: | Probability area sample.<br>Aakster (1972) sample; age 20-65.<br>In comparison with the total population underrepresentation of single persons; women from the northern, eastern and southern parts of the Netherlands, and people living in the smaller cities. |
| NON-RESPONSE: | 34% refusal and unattainable |
| N: | 1552 |
| AUTHOR'S HAPPINESS LABEL: | Happiness |
| OUR CONCEPTUALIZATION: | Happiness |
| INSTRUMENT: | HAPP 1.1: Single closed question rated on an open graphic scale (later translated in a 7-point scale): |

Generally speaking, are you a happy person?

| very happy | very unhappy |
|---|---|

In Dutch: Bent U in het algemeen gesproken een gelukkig mens?

| zeer gelukkig | zeer ongelukkig |
|---|---|

Each S could indicate his position with an X.

| | |
|---|---|
| RELIABILITY: | |
| VALIDITY: | |
| DISTRIBUTION: | possible range: 1 (high) to 7 (low); actual range: 62% score 1, 18% score 2, 10% score 3, 8% score 4, 2% score 5, 6 or 7. |
| REMARKS: | |
| CORRELATES: | Depression (A 2.2.4); Educational level (E 1.1.1); Number of children (F 1.2.2); Worries concerning family members (F 1.4, P 5.2.2.1); various indicators of Physical health (H 2.1); Psychosomatic complaints (H 2.2); Worries about health (H 2.5); Life change (L 1.2); Doubt about meaningfulness of one's existence (L 2.1.2); various Life style characteristics (L 3.1, L 3.2, L 3.4); Community size (L 4.1); Subjective adaptation to change (P 1.2); various Personality traits concerning interpersonal functioning (P 1.8); Pregnancy (P 2.3); various Domainsatisfactions (S 1); Like to have other people around (S 4.5); S.E.S. (S 5.1); Social mobility (S 5.3); Variables associated with neurosis/depression (X 1) |
| CONCLUSION: | |

BARSC 51

AUTHOR: Barschak, E.

TITLE: A study of happiness and unhappiness in the childhood and adolescence of girls in different cultures.

SOURCE: Journal of Psychology, 1951, vol. 32, p. 173-215, separatedly published by the Journal Press, Province Town (Mass.).

---

**GOAL OF THE STUDY:** To make a comparison of attitudes of adolescent girls of four different societies.

REFERS TO:

**TYPE OF STUDY:** explanatory, explorative, special group, retrospective snapshot, non-experimental

**DATA GATHERING:** Half-structured questionnaire containing closed and open-ended questions administered in classroom situation

**DATE OF DATA:** 1949 - 1951

POPULATION: Female college students, western world

**SAMPLE CONSTRUCTION:** Wall (1948) non-probability chunk sample using female freshmen students of education in the U.S.A. (N = 128), Switzerland (N = 65), W.Germany (N = 164): 47 Ss from Berlin, 117 Ss from Goettingen) and England (N = 128)
age 17 - 24; predominantly middle class

**NON-RESPONSE:**

N: 493

**AUTHOR'S HAPPINESS LABEL:** Happiness

**OUR CONCEPTUALIZATION:** Happiness

INSTRUMENT: HAPP 1.2: Index of closed happiness questions:

- Have you on the whole been happy since age of 12 - 13? Yes / no
- Were you on the whole happy during childhood? Yes / no

On the basis of these questions Ss were classified as:
- happy in both childhood and adolenscense
- happy in childhood or adolescence
- unhappy during both periods

RELIABILITY:

VALIDITY:

DISTRIBUTION: highly positively skewed (both ir memory of childhood and adolescence)

REMARKS:

CORRELATES: Confrontation with war (W 1.1)

CONCLUSION:

AUTHOR: Baxter M.F., Yamada, K. & Washburn, M.F. | BAXTE 17

TITLE: Directed recall of pleasant and unpleasant experiences.

SOURCE: American Journal of Psychology, 1917, vol. 28, p. 155-157.

---

GOAL OF THE STUDY: To see whether there is some kind of a test of the optimistic or pessimistic tendencies of individuals.

REFERS TO:

TYPE OF STUDY: explanatory, explorative, special group, snapshot, non-experimental

DATA GATHERING: Verbal projective techniques and questions in laboratory situation

DATE OF DATA:

POPULATION: Female college students, U.S.A.

SAMPLE CONSTRUCTION: Non-probability chunk sample.

NON-RESPONSE:

N: 69

AUTHOR'S HAPPINESS LABEL: Cheerfulness

OUR CONCEPTUALIZATION: Hedonic level of affect

INSTRUMENT: AFF 5.2: Peer-rating of hedonic level of affect:
Each S was judged by 3 acquaintances. Each acquaintance was asked:
'Do you think that A. (the S in question) tends in general to be optimistic and cheerful of pessimistic and uncheerful?'

RELIABILITY:

VALIDITY:

DISTRIBUTION: positively skewed

REMARKS:

CORRELATES: Promptness of pleasant associations in connection with verbal stimuli (P 1.6)

CONCLUSION:

AUTHOR: Beiser, M. | BEISE 74

TITLE: Components and correlates of mental well-being.

SOURCE: Journal of Health and Social Behavior, 1974, vol. 15, nr 4, p. 320-327.

---

GOAL OF THE STUDY: Delineation of components of emotional well-being.

REFERS TO: Theory of mental well-being; Bradburn & Caplovitz (1965)

TYPE OF STUDY: explanatory, explorative, local population, snapshot, non-experimental

DATA GATHERING: Unstructured and structured interview and ratings by psychiatrists

DATE OF DATA: 1963 - 1968

POPULATION: Residents of Stirling County, Maritime Canada

SAMPLE CONSTRUCTION: Probability sample stratified by sex, age, socio-environmental circumstances and mental health (as rated by 2 psychiatrists).

NON-RESPONSE: 10%

N: 112

AUTHOR'S HAPPINESS LABEL: Pleasure involvement and Negative affect (first instrument) and General well-being (second instrument)

OUR CONCEPTUALIZATION: Hedonic level of affect (first instrument) and Happiness (second instrument)

FIRST INSTRUMENT: AFF 2.3: Index of closed questions on perceived occurrence of specific affects during the past few months (adapted Bradburn indices of positive and negative affects; see BRADB 69):

Ss were asked: 'During the past few months have you felt . . . . often, sometimes, or never'

On the basis of factor analysis the item 'On top of the world' was excluded from the index of positive affects. The index of negative affects was unchanged.
No overall affect balance scores were computed.

RELIABILITY: equivalence: common variance: 18.5% for index of positive affects and 19.9% for index of negative affects
positive affect score x negative affect score: $r_{pm} = -.13$ (ns)

VALIDITY:

DISTRIBUTION:

SECOND INSTRUMENT: HAPP 1.1: Single closed question using the term 'happiness' rated on a 3-point scale (see GURIN 60).

RELIABILITY:

VALIDITY:

DISTRIBUTION:

REMARKS:

CORRELATES: Age (A 3); Educational level (E 1.1.1); Hedonic level x happiness (H 1.2.1); Psycho-physiological condition (H 2.2); Psychiatric 'caseness' (H 2.3.1); Material style of life (I 1.6); Long-term satisfaction (L 2.1.2); Having hobbies (L 3.3.1); Role-related planning abilities (P 1.2); Interpersonal reactivity (P 1.8.1); Socially participant behavior (S 4.2)

CONCLUSION: At least three affects - negative affect, pleasure involvement, and long-term satisfaction - make separate contributions to feelings of general well-being. Well-being is the resultant effect of a complex intrapsychic process in which a person's general level of satisfaction with life interacts with more short-lived and fluctuating affective states.

BENDO 74

AUTHOR: Bendo, A.A. & Feldman, H.

TITLE: A comparison of the self-concept of low-income women with and without husbands present.

SOURCE: Cornell Journal of Social Relations, 1974, vol. 9, nr 1, p. 53-85.

---

GOAL OF THE STUDY: Assessment of the relationship between a positive self-concept and marital status of low-income women.

REFERS TO: Research on women in poverty; Kreisberg (1970), Marsden (1969)

TYPE OF STUDY: explanatory, testing, special group, snapshot, no-experimental

DATA GATHERING: Structured interview at home

DATE OF DATA:

POPULATION: Low-income women with children, New York State, U.S.A.

SAMPLE CONSTRUCTION: Probability systematic random sample, stratified by employed status and marital status, drawn from twelve welfare jurisdictions.
Stage of family life cycle was held constant by selecting women with a teenage child only. The study was carried out in cities with less than 100,000 inhabitants and the small towns and rural areas dependent on these cities.
693 husband-absent women and 632 husband-prsent women

NON-RESPONSE:

N: 1325

AUTHOR'S HAPPINESS LABEL: Happiness (first instrument) and Satisfaction with life in general (second instrument)

OUR CONCEPTUALIZATION: Happiness

FIRST INSTRUMENT: HAPP 1.1: Single closed question rated on a 5-point scale:
How do you feel personally, how happy do you feel?

RELIABILITY:

VALIDITY:

DISTRIBUTION: positively skewed
possible range: 0 (low) to 4 (high); mean: 2.63

SECOND INSTRUMENT: HAPP 2.1: Single closed question on satisfaction with overall life situation, rated on a 10-point ladder scale.

RELIABILITY:

VALIDITY:

DISTRIBUTION: positively skewed
mean: 5.55

REMARKS:

CORRELATES: Welfare status (I 1.6); Husband absent vs present (M 1.1.5); Employed status (W 2.1)

CONCLUSION: Husband-absent women tend to find satisfaction outside the home as workers, whereas for married women it is easier to derive satisfaction from their children, husband and housework.

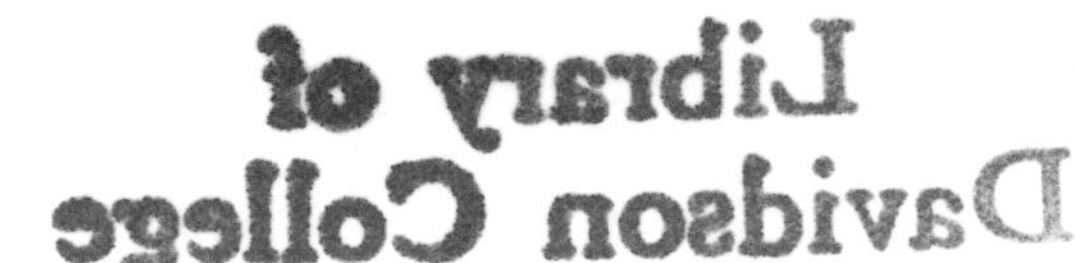

AUTHOR: Berkman, P.L.

BERKM 71

TITLE: Life stress and psychological well-being: a replication of Langner's analysis in the Midtown Manhattan Study.

SOURCE: Journal of Health and Social Behavior, 1971, vol. 12, nr 3, p. 35-45.

---

GOAL OF THE STUDY: To determine the mental health validity of a psychological measure based on items included in a mail questionnaire study of generic health and ways of living.

REFERS TO: Theory of mental health; Langner & Michael (1963)

TYPE OF STUDY: explanatory, explorative, local population, snapshot, non-experimental

DATA GATHERING: Mailed highly structure questionraire

DATE OF DATA: 1965

POPULATION: Adults, Alameda County, U.S.A.

SAMPLE CONSTRUCTION: Probability sample of households (see also RENNE 70).

NON-RESPONSE:

N: 6928

AUTHOR'S HAPPINESS LABEL: Psychological well-being

OUR CONCEPTUALIZATION: Hedonic level of affect

INSTRUMENT: AFF 1.3: Index of closed questions on perceived occurrence of specific affects in general (adapted Bradburn & Caplovitz Affect Balance Score; see BRADB 65).

The component items were asked in mixed order, introduced by the statement:
'Here is a list that describes some of the ways people feel at different times. How often do you feel each of these ways?'
never / sometimes / often

The 5-item index of negative affects was unchanged. From the 4-item index of positive affects the item 'proud because someone complimented you on something you had done' was excluded.

RELIABILITY:

VALIDITY: Test for external validity shows corresponding correlates with stressfactors as psychiatric diagnosis did in the Langner & Michael (1963) study.

DISTRIBUTION: slightly positively skewed
possible range: positive affect: 0 (low) to 9 (high); negative affect: 0 (low) to 15 (high); affect balance: 1 (high positive, low negative) to 7 (low positive, high negative)
actual range : affect balance: 1 (6.9%) to 7 (3.5%)

REMARKS:

CORRELATES: various characteristics of Family of origin (F 1.1, L 1.1); Physical health (H 2.1.3); Self-evaluated financial situation (I 1.6); Stress (L 2.2.2); Parental worries (F 1.2.4, P 5.2.2.1); Marital satisfaction (S 1.7.2); Poor interpersonal relations (S 4.3); S.E.S. (S 5.1)

CONCLUSION: The number of stressfactors mentioned offers a better prediction of life-satisfaction than the quality or patterns of the different stressfactors do. Stress is more frequent in the lower S.E.S. - classes and though stress exerts a significant influence on psychological well-being in all classes, this influence is stronger in the lower classes.

AUTHOR: Blood, M.R.

BLOOD 69

TITLE: Work values and job satisfaction.

SOURCE: Journal of Applied Psychology, 1969, vol. 53, nr 6, p. 456-459.

---

GOAL OF THE STUDY: Development of an instrument for the measurement of work values.

REFERS TO: Work values related to the ideals of the Protestant Ethic; Weber (1958), Lenski (1961)

TYPE OF STUDY: explanatory, explorative, special group, snapshot, non-experimental

DATA GATHERING: Highly structured questionnaire

DATE OF DATA:

POPULATION: Airmen, U.S.A.F., U.S.A.

SAMPLE CONSTRUCTION: Non-probability chunk sample, using 114 fulltime students in courses in aircraft maintenance and 306 Ss permanently assigned on a variety of low skill level tasks.

NON-RESPONSE: 6%

N: 420

AUTHOR'S HAPPINESS LABEL: Satisfaction with life in general

OUR CONCEPTUALIZATION: Happiness

INSTRUMENT: HAPP 2.1: Single closed question on satisfaction with life in general, scored on the Kunin (1955) pictorial rating scale

RELIABILITY:

VALIDITY:

DISTRIBUTION:

REMARKS:

CORRELATES: Disagreement with protestant ethic (V 1.1)

CONCLUSION: The more a worker agrees with the ideals of the Protestant Ethic, the more he will be satisfied in his work and with his life in general.

AUTHOR: Bohn, C.J. | BOHN 72

TITLE: The effect of children upon life satisfaction. A thesis in child development and family relationships.

SOURCE: Unpublished master thesis, 1972, Pennsylvania State University.

---

GOAL OF THE STUDY: To determine the effect of presence or absence of children upon one's overall feelings of status and well-being.

REFERS TO: Theory of marital satisfaction; Rollins & Feldman (1970), Renne (1970)

TYPE OF STUDY: explanatory, testing, (inter-) national population, snapshot, non-experimental

DATA GATHERING: Half-structured interview by native interviewers in each country

DATE OF DATA: ± 1960

POPULATION: Adults in the Dominican Republic, Panama and Yugoslavia

SAMPLE CONSTRUCTION: Pooling of the Cantril (1965) samples of the Dominican Republic, Panama and Yugoslavia (see CANTR 65).

NON-RESPONSE:

N: 5228

AUTHOR'S HAPPINESS LABEL: Life satisfaction

OUR CONCEPTUALIZATION: Happiness

INSTRUMENT: HAPP 3.1: Single closed question on personal situation as compared with the best and the worst possible life, rated on an 11-point self-anchoring scale (Cantril Present Personal rating; see CANTR 65).

RELIABILITY:

VALIDITY:

DISTRIBUTION: possible range: 0 (low) to 10 (high); mean: 3.38; S.D.: 2.59

REMARKS: See also BORTN 74B

CORRELATES: Age (A 3); Gender (G 1.1); Having children (F 1.2.1); Child-centered attitude (F 1.2.4); Socio-economic level (I 1.1); Urban residence (L 4.2); various Marital status comparisons (M 1)

CONCLUSION: In countries, where children are an economic asset, they raise the satisfaction with life of their parents. In other countries children either lessen or raise the status of the parents, depending on social class, residence and the presence or absence of a child-centered attitude on the part of the parents.

AUTHOR: Bortner, R.W. & Hultsch, D.F. BORTN 70

TITLE: A multivariate analysis of correlates of life satisfaction in adulthood.

SOURCE: Journal of Gerontology, 1970, vol. 25, nr 1, p. 41-47.

---

GOAL OF THE STUDY: Examination of demographic and social psychological variables related to life satisfaction and their impact.

REFERS TO: Happiness research; Cantril (1965), Neugarten et al. (1961)

TYPE OF STUDY: explanatory, explorative, national population, snapshot, non-experimental

DATA GATHERING: Cantril (1965) U.S.A.-data, gathered by structured interview (see CANTR 65).

DATE OF DATA: 1959

POPULATION: National adult population, U.S.A.

SAMPLE CONSTRUCTION: Modified probability sample (Cantril U.S.A. sample; see CANTR 65).
Test for sample representativiness showed non-significant differences for age, race, economic level and education; overrepresentation of divorced females; underrepresentation of widowed females (as assessed by the 1960 census of the continental United States). Ss lacking identifying demographic data were eliminated.
age 20-88; 681 males, 728 females; 117 blacks, 1292 whites

NON-RESPONSE: 9% incomplete information

N: 1406

AUTHOR'S HAPPINESS LABEL: Life satisfaction (first and second instrument) and Success in goals (third instrument)

OUR CONCEPTUALIZATION: Happiness (first and second instrument) and Contentment (third instrument)

FIRST INSTRUMENT: HAPP 2.1: Single closed question on satisfaction with life rated on an 11-point self-anchoring scale (Cantril Satisfaction with Life rating; see CANTR 65/2).

RELIABILITY:

VALIDITY:

DISTRIBUTION: positively skewed
posssible range: 0 (low) to 10 (high); mean: 7.6; S.D.: 2.0

SECOND INSTRUMENT: HAPP 3.1: Single closed question on personal situation as compared with best and worst possible life, rated on an 11-point self-anchoring scale (Cantril Present Personal rating; see CANTR 65/1).

RELIABILITY:

VALIDITY:

DISTRIBUTION: positively skewed
possible range: 0 (low) to 10 (high); mean: 6.6; S.D.: 2.3

THIRD INSTRUMENT: CON 1.1: Single closed question on contentment, rated on an 11-point self-anchoring scale (Cantril Success in achieving Goals rating; see CANTR 65/2).

RELIABILITY:

VALIDITY:

DISTRIBUTION: positively skewed
possible range: 0 (low) to 10 (high); mean: 6.7; S.D. 2.2

REMARKS:

CORRELATES: Age (A 3); Educational level (E 1.1.1); Race (E 2.1); Opportunity to do things one likes (F 2.2); Gender (G 1.1); various factors concerning Happiness (H 1); Economic level (I 1.1); Enjoyment of previous day (L 2.1.1); Marital status (M 1.6); Positive evaluation of national situation (N 1.1.1); Efficacy (P 1.1); Extent of perceived troubles and obstacles in life (P 5.1.1); Extent of worrries and fears that things might get worse (P 5.2.1); Religiousness (R 1.1); Satisfaction with the way things are going in the U.S.A. (S 1.3.1); Self-respect (S 2.1.3); Self-confidence (S 2.1.4); Occupational level (W 2.2)

CONCLUSION: The social psychological variables are more predictive of life satisfaction than the demographic variables.

| | | |
|---|---|---|
| AUTHOR: | Bortner, R.W. & Hultsch, D.F. | BORTN 72 |
| TITLE: | Personal time perspective in adulthood. | |
| SOURCE: | Developmental psychology, 1972, vol. 7, nr 2, p. 98-103. | |

---

GOAL OF THE STUDY: Examination of age differences in time perspective and assessment of factors affecting time perspective.

REFERS TO: Theory of time perspective; Wohlford (1966)

TYPE OF STUDY: explanatory, explorative, national population, snapshot, non-experimental

DATA GATHERING: Cantril (1965) U.S.A.-data, gathered by structured interview (see CANTR 65)

DATE OF DATA: 1959

POPULATION: National adult population, U.S.A.

SAMPLE CONSTRUCTION: Modified probability sample (Cantril U.S.A. sample; see CANTR 65 and BORTN 70).

NON-RESPONSE: 9% incomplete information

N: 1409

AUTHOR'S HAPPINESS LABEL: Life satisfaction (first and second instrument) and Success in goals (third instrument)

OUR CONCEPTUALIZATION: Happiness (first and second instrument) and Contentment (third instrument)

INSTRUMENTS: See BORTN 70

REMARKS: In this article the authors refer to correlates of the second and the third instrument, which are also presented in Bortner & Hultsch (1970) (see BORTN 70).

AUTHOR: Bortner, R.W. & Hultsch, D.F.

BORTN 74A

TITLE: Patterns of subjective deprivation in adulthood.

SOURCE: Development Psychology, 1974, vol. 10, nr 4, p. 534-545.

---

GOAL OF THE STUDY: Investigation into age related subjective deprivation and assessment of which of them represent an ontogenetic developmental sequence.

REFERS TO: Theory of deprivation; Stouffer et al. (1949), Cantril (1965)

TYPE OF STUDY: explanatory, explorative, national population, snapshot, non-experimental

DATA GATHERING: Cantril (1965) U.S.A.-data, gathered by structured interview (see CANTR 65)

DATE OF DATA: 1959

POPULATION: National adult population , U.S.A.

SAMPLE CONSTRUCTION: Modified probability sample (Cantril U.S.A. sample; see CANTR 65 and BORTN 70).

Ss were classified according to type of age-related subjective deprivation as assessed by Cantril (1965) present-self, past-self and future-self ratings on 'best possible life' question (Cantril personal rating; see CANTR 65):

- stereotyped non-deprivation (SND, N = 140): present rating higher than past rating, and future rating 1 or 2 points higher than present rating.
- great expectations deprivation (GED, N = 194): present rating higher than past rating, and future rating 3 or more points higher than present rating.
- temporary deprivation (TD, N = 170): present rating lower than past rating, and future rating higher than present rating.
- anticipatory deprivation (AD, N = 75): present rating higher than past rating, and future rating lower than present rating.
- continuous deprivation (CD, N = 69): present rating lower than past rating, and future rating lower than present rating.

unclassified Ss (N = 665) were excluded from analysis

NON-RESPONSE: 17% incomplete information

N: 1294

AUTHOR'S LABEL: Success in goals (first instrument) and Life satisfaction (second instrument)

OUR CONCEPTUALIZATION: Contentment (first instrument) and Happiness (second instrument)

FIRST INSTRUMENT: CON 1.1: Single closed question on contentment, rated on an 11-point self-anchoring scale (Cantril Success in achieving Goals rating; see CANTR 65).

RELIABILITY:

VALIDITY:

DISTRIBUTION: see BORTN 70

SECOND INSTRUMENT: HAPP 2.1: Single closed question on satisfaction with life, rated on an 11-point self-anchoring scale (Cantril Satisfaction with Life rating; see CANTR 65).

RELIABILITY:

VALIDITY:

DISTRIBUTION: see BORTN 70

REMARKS:

CORRELATES: Type of subjective age-related deprivation (L 2.3)

CONCLUSION:

AUTHOR: Bortner, R.W., Bohn, C.J. & Hultsch, D.F. | BORTN 74B

TITLE: A cross-cultural study of the effects of children on parental assessment of past, present and future.

SOURCE: Journal of Marriage and the Family, May 1974, P. 370-378.

---

GOAL OF THE STUDY: Assessment and elaboration of the relation between having children and happiness in past, present and future.

REFERS TO: Parent-child interaction ; Rollings & Feldman (1970)

TYPE OF STUDY: explanatory, explorative, national populations, snapshot, non-experimental

DATA GATHERING: Cantril (1965) data, gathered by structured interview, using native interviewers in each country (see CANTR 65)

DATE OF DATA: 1960

POPULATION: married people in the Dominican Republic, Panama and Yugoslavia.

SAMPLE CONSTRUCTION: Married people from the Cantril (1965) samples of the Dominican Republic (N = 1977), Yugoslavia (N = 1177) and Panama (N = 959) (see CANTR 65 and BOHN 72)
2409 males, 1704 females; 2232 age 21-39, 1878 age 40+; 3650 with children, 483 without children; 2721 rurals, 1392 urbans; 857 upper S.E.S., 3140 lower S.E.S.

NON-RESPONSE:

N: 4113

AUTHOR'S HAPPINESS LABEL: Satisfaction with life in general

OUR CONCEPTUALIZATION: Happiness

INSTRUMENT: HAPP 3.1: Single closed question on personal situation as compared with best and worst possible life, rated on an 11-point self-anchoring scale (Cantril Present Personal rating; see CANTR 65).

RELIABILITY:

VALIDITY:

DISTRIBUTION:

REMARKS: This article is a summary of an unpublished master thesis by Bohn (1972) and provides information already reported there (see BOHN 72).

AUTHOR: Bradburn, N.M. & Caplovitz, D. — BRADB 65/1

TITLE: Reports on happiness.

SOURCE: Chicago, 1965, Aldine Publishing Company.

---

GOAL OF THE STUDY: To develop an inventory for the periodical assessment of the social-psychological state of the nation's population.

REFERS TO: Theory of mental health; Jahoda (1958)

TYPE OF STUDY: explanatory, explorative, local populations, snapshot, non-experimental

DATA GATHERING: 2 methods: - long form : personal structured interviews (males of age 25-49 only, N = 393)
- short form: self-adminstered highly structured questionnaire delivered at home (517 males and 1097 females)

DATE OF DATA: March, 1962

POPULATION: Inhabitants of 4 small communities, Illinois, U.S.A.

SAMPLE CONSTRUCTION: Probability multi-stage samples in 4 communities of comparable size, selected in view of their economic situations: 2 communities in chronic economic depression, 1 improving from chroniceconomic depression and 1 economically well-off.
909 males, 1097 females; non-clinical population

NON-RESPONSE:

N: 2006

AUTHOR'S HAPPINESS LABEL: Psychological well-being

OUR CONCEPTUALIZATION: Happiness (first instrument) and Hedonic level of affect (second instrument)

FIRST INSTRUMENT: HAPP 1.1: Single closed question using the term 'happiness', rated on a 3-point scale (see GURIN 60).

RELIABILITY: retest reliability (after 8 months): r = +.62

VALIDITY:

DISTRIBUTION: slightly positively skewed: 24% very happy, 59% pretty happy, 17% not too happy

SECOND INSTRUMENT: AFF 2.3: Index of closed questions on perceived occurrence of specific affects during the last week (Bradburn & Caplovitz Affect Balance Score):

We are interested in the way people are feeling these days. The following list describes some of the ways people feel at different times. Please indicate how often you felt each way during the last week.

How often last week did you feel . . . .    not at all / once / several times / often

1. On top of the world?
2. Very lonely or remote from other people?
3. Angry at something that usually wouldn't bother you?
4. That you couldn't do something because you just couldn't get going?
5. Particularly excited or interested in something?
6. Depressed or very unhappy?
7. Pleased about having accomplished something?
8. Bored?
9. Proud because someone complimented you on something you had done?
10. So restless you couldn't sit long in a chair?
11. That you had more things to do than you could get done?
12. Vaguely uneasy about something without knowing why?

The items 3, 4 and 11 did not correlate with the others and were excluded.
Positive feelings (1, 5, 7 and 9) and negative feelings (2, 6, 8, 10, 12) are used in a balance score: the Affect Balance Score. High A.B.S. means high scores on the 4-item index of positive affects and relative low scores on the 5-item index of negative affects.

The males in the age of 25-49 who were personally interviewed (see data gathering) were asked:
'During the past week did you ever feel . . .' yes / no
If yes: 'How often did you feel that way?' once / several times / often

RELIABILITY: equivalence (on the basis of the responses of the males who were personally interviewed; N = 393):

- positive items : $r_{pm}$ ranging from +.26 to +.47
- negative items : $r_{pm}$ ranging from +.31 to +.54
- positive x negative items : $r_{pm}$ ranging from -.19 to +.11
- positive affect score x negative affect score: $R_{pm}$= .07 (ns)

VALIDITY:

DISTRIBUTION: - Affect balance : 13% more positive than negative affects, 32% as many positive and negative affects, 37% more negative than positive affects
- Positive affect: 36% high, 34% medium, 30% low
- Negative affect: 53% high, 9% medium, 38% low

REMARKS: In Part III $G'^{(x)}$ indicates that the gamma is computed on the basis of the proportion 'not too happy' answers.

CORRELATES: Age (A3); various Concerns (C 2); Educational level (E 1.1.1); Gender (G 1.1); Contact with relatives (F 1.4); Hedonic level x happiness (H 1.2.1); Anxiety (H 2.2); Income (I 1.1); Overall role adjustment (L 2.2.2); various Specific leisure activities (L 3.3.2); Economic climate of local environment (L 4.4); various Marital status comparisons (M 1); Marital tension (M 2.4, P 5.1.2); Worrying (P 5.2.1); Participation in religious events (R 1.3); Job satisfaction (S 1.9.1); various indicators of Social participation (S 4); S.E.S. (S 5.1); Participating in sports (S 6.1); Attending sports (S 6.2); Employment status (W 2.1)

CONCLUSION: Happiness can be conceived as a balance of positive and negative feelings, which turn out to vary independently and show different correlates. It is strongly affected by activity, social participation, and social position. Environmental factors turn out to be less influential.

BRADB 65/2

GOAL OF THE STUDY: Assessment of psychological effects of a period of national stress.

REFERS TO:

TYPE OF STUDY: explanatory, explorative, local populations, longitudinal, non-experimental

DATA GATHERING: Structured interview

DATE OF DATA: October, 1962. At that time the 'Cuban crisis' took place; a political confrontation between the Sovjet Union and the U.S.A., which might have resulted in a (nuclear) war.

POPULATION: Inhabitants of 2 small communities, Illinois, U.S.A.

SAMPLE CONSTRUCTION: Probability multi-stage samples in 2 communities.
Reinterview of those Ss used in the first study (see BRADB 65/1) who are living in the most prosperous and the most depressed community of the 4 communities used.

NON-RESPONSE:

N: 547

AUTHOR'S HAPPINESS LABEL: Psychological well-being

OUR CONCEPTUALIZATION: Happiness (first instrument) and Hedonic level of affect (second instrument)

INSTRUMENTS: see BRADB 65/1

CORRELATES: Living in a period of national crisis (N 1.2)

CONCLUSION: A national crisis has little bearing on the state of people's feelings. The impact of the crisis may have been conditioned by personal characteristics of the respondents.

AUTHOR: Bradburn, N.M. BRADB 69

TITLE: The structure of psychological well-being.

SOURCE: Chicago, 1969, Aldine Publishing Company.

---

GOAL OF THE STUDY: Assessment of the influences of every day life events on well-being and investigation of effects of social change on well-being.

REFERS TO: Happiness reasearch; Bradburn & Caplovitz (1965)

TYPE OF STUDY: explanatory, explorative, local populations, longitudinal, non-experimental

DATA GATHERING: Repeated interviews at home using highly structured questionnaires

DATE OF DATA: January, 1963 (wave 1); June, 1963 (wave 2); October, 1963 (wave 3); January, 1964 (wave 4) (see also 'sample construction')

POPULATION: Adults, urban areas, U.S.A.

SAMPLE CONSTRUCTION: Probability area samples in:

- Suburban county near Washington D.C.
  The population was chosen because of expected changes by an experimental community mental health program.
  predominantly middle class; 17% semi- or unskilled laborers (N: 1277; non-response: 26%, 20% dropouts; date of data: population interviewed in January, 1963 and in October, 1963)
- Working class neighborhood, Chicago
  The population was chosen because of expected race tensions.
  40% semi- or unskilled laborers (N: 252; non-response: 15%, 30% dropouts; date of data: population interviewed in January, 1963 and in October, 1963)
- All-white suburb, Detroit
  The city of Detroit was chosen because of expected changes in the automobile industry.
  many skilled workers in automobile industry; both white-collar and skilled blue-collar; 25% semi- or unskilled laborers (N: 542; non-response: 15 - 20%, 21% dropouts; date of data: January, 1963; June, 1963; October, 1963; January, 1964)
- Negro inner city population, Detroit
  The city of Detroit was chosen because of expected changes in the automobile industry.
  many workers in automobile industry; predominantly lower economic status; 75% semi- or unskilled laborers; 62% females (N: 446, non-response: 15 - 26%, 21% dropouts; date of data: January, 1963 and October, 1963)
- Ten metropolitan areas
  The population was chosen as comparison group.
  the sample resembles the U.S.A. population rather well; 25% semi- or unskilled laborers (N: 270; non-response: 15-26%, 23% dropouts; date of data: January, 1963 and October, 1963)

NON-RESPONSE: ± 20%

N: 2787

AUTHOR'S HAPPINESS LABEL: Psychological well-being

OUR CONCEPTUALIZATION: Hedonic level of affect (first instrument), Happiness (second instrument) and Contentment (third instrument)

FIRST INSTRUMENT: AFF 2.3 Index of closed questions on perceived occurrence of specific affects during the past few weeks (adapted Bradburn & Caplovitz Affect Balance Score; see BRADB 65):

During the past few weeks, did you ever feel . . . yes / no

1. Particularly exited or interested in something?
2. So restless that you couldn't sit long in a chair?
3. Proud because someone complimented you on something you had done?
4. Very lonely or remote from other people?
5. Pleased about having accomplished something?
6. Bored?
7. On top of the world?
8. Depressed or very unhappy?
9. That things were going your way?
10. Upset because someone criticized you?

Index of Positive Affects: items 1, 3, 5, 7 and 9
Index of Negative Affects: items 2, 4, 6, 8 and 10

RELIABILITY: equivalence:
- positive items : Q ranging from +.23 to +.72
- negative items : Q ranging from +.41 to +.71
- positive x negative items: Q ranging from -.28 to +.25
- positive affect score x negative affect score: wave 1: G = +.08, wave 3: G = +.02

| | | |
|---|---|---|
| Washington suburban country | : wave 1: G = +.13, | wave 3: G = +.07 |
| Working class neighborhood, Chicago | : wave 1: G = +.04, | wave 3: G = -.06 |
| All-white suburb, Detroit | : wave 1: G = +.08, | wave 3: G = +.14 |
| Negro inner city, Detroit | : wave 1: G = +.04, | wave 3: G = -.20 |
| Ten metropolitan areas | : wave 1: G = +.11, | wave 3: G = +.02 |

white suburb Detroit only:
- retest reliability (retest after 3 days, N = 174): Affect Balance Scale : G = +.76
Index of Positive Affects: G = +.83
Index of Negative Affects: G = +.81
- positive items: Q ranging from +.86 to +.96
- negative items: Q ranging from +.90 to +.97
- repeat reliability: Non-significant differences in average Ridit values in the four interviews for affect balance, positive affect and negative affect.

VALIDITY:

DISTRIBUTION: positively skewed
possible range: -5 (low) to +5 (high); actual range: 2% score - 4 or -5, 5% -3, 10% -2, 14% -1, 21% 0, 20% +1, 15% +2, 10% +3, 3% +4 or +5

SECOND INSTRUMENT: HAPP 1.1: Single closed question rated on a 3-point scale (adapted Gurin et al. question; see GURIN 60):

Taken all together, how would you say things are these days? - would you say that you are very happy, pretty happy, or not too happy?

RELIABILITY: repeat reliability: wave 1 - wave 3: G = +.74 for males, G = +.71 for females

All-white suburb, Detroit only: wave 1 - wave 2: G = +.65 for males, G = +.79 for females
wave 2 - wave 3: G = +.68 for males, G = +.79 for females
wave 3 - wave 4: G = +.80 for males, G = +.84 for females

VALIDITY:

DISTRIBUTION: positively skewed (wave 1):
- Washington suburban county : 35% very happy, 57% pretty happt, 8% not too happy
- Working class neighborhood, Chicago : 31% very happy, 50% pretty happy, 19% not too happy
- All-white suburb, Detroit : 36% very happy, 57% pretty happy, 7% not too happy
- Negro inner city, Detroit : 17% very happy, 56% pretty happy, 27% not too happy
- Ten metropolitan areas : 33% very happy, 59% pretty happy, 8% not too happy

THIRD INSTRUMENT: CON 1.1: Single closed question rated on a 3-point scale:

In getting the things you want out of life, would you say that you are doing pretty well, or not too well right now?

In wave 3 three response categories were offered: very well, pretty well, not too well.

RELIABILITY:

VALIDITY:

DISTRIBUTION: positively skewed:
- Washington suburban county : wave 1: 86% pretty well, 13% not too well
wave 3: 30% very well, 62% pretty well, 8% not too well
- Working class neighborhood, Chicago : wave 1: 68% pretty well, 32% not too well
wave 3: 26% very well, 57% pretty well, 16% not too well
- All-white suburb, Detroit : wave 1: 84% pretty well, 16% not too well
wave 3: 29% very well, 61% pretty well, 9% not too well
- Negro inner city, Detroit : wave 1: 50% pretty well, 50% not too well
wave 3: 21% very well, 47% pretty well, 31% not too well
- Ten metropolitan areas : wave 3: 27% very well, 65% pretty well, 8% not too well

REMARKS: This excerpt presents the results of the first interview wave in January, 1963. Results of the other waves are presented only if they differ from the first.

CORRELATES: Age (A 3); Educational level (E 1.1.1); Race (E 2.1); Number of children under 21 (F 1.2.2); Contacts with relatives (F 1.4); Gender (G 1.1); Hedonic level x happiness (H 1.2.1); Contentment x happiness (H 1.3.1); Contentment x hedonic level (H 1.3.2); Illness (H 2.1.3); various indicators of Psychosomatic complaints (H 2.2); Ever expected a nervous breakdown (H 2.3.2); Wish to change life (H 3.1.1); various factors concerning Income, financial situation (I 1); various factors concerning Use of leisure time (L 3.3); various Marital status comparisons (M 1); various factors concerning Marriage (M 2.3, M 2.4); Esteem for others (P 1.8.2); various factors concerning Problems, worries and fears (P 5); Marital happiness (S 1.7.2); Satisfaction with social life (S 1.7.3); Job satisfaction (S 1.9.1); various indicators of Social participation (S 4); S.E.S. (S 5.1); Job advancement (S 5.3); various factors concerning Work (W 2)

CONCLUSION: Positive and negative feelings vary almost independently from each other.
Income, social involvement, and new experiences are related to positive affect only, while indicators of mental and physical dysfunctioning are related to negative affect only. Aspects of work and marriage are related to both positive and negative affects.

AUTHOR: Bradbury, B.R. | BRADB 67

TITLE: A study of guilt and anxiety as related to certain psychological and sociological variables.

SOURCE: Unpublished doctoral dissertation, 1967, Denton, Texas, U.S.A.

---

GOAL OF THE STUDY: Providing a conceptual linkage between feelings of guilt and anxiety and certain psychological and sociological variables.

REFERS TO: Theory of guilt and anxiety; Symonds (1946), Mosher (1961)

TYPE OF STUDY: explanatory, testing, special group, snapshot, non-experimental

DATA GATHERING: Psychological tests and highly structured questionnaire, administered in class-room situation

DATE OF DATA: 1966 - 1967

POPULATION: University students, North Texas State University, U.S.A.

SAMPLE CONSTRUCTION: Non-probability chunk sample of students enrolled in freshman (sociology and psychology) and graduate (cross section of majors) classes during the 1966 - 1967 academic year.
162 males, 151 females; 124 freshmen, 103 graduates, 86 other

NON-RESPONSE:

N: 313

AUTHOR'S HAPPINESS LABEL: Happiness

OUR CONCEPTUALIZATION: Happiness

INSTRUMENT: HAPP 1.1: Single closed question rated on a 3-point scale:
Do you consider yourself to be: generally happy, moderately happy, generally unhappy?

RELIABILITY:

VALIDITY:

DISTRIBUTION: positively skewed: 72% generally happy, 18% moderately happy or generally unhappy

REMARKS:

CORRELATES: various indicators of Guilt (A 2.2.8); Anxiety (H 2.2)

CONCLUSION: Unhappiness plays a part in the genesis of guilt and anxiety.

AUTHOR: Brenner, B. | BRENN 67

TITLE: Patterns of alcohol use, happiness and the satisfaction of wants.

SOURCE: Quarterly Journal of Studies on Alcohol, 1967, vol. 28, p. 667-675.

---

GOAL OF THE STUDY: Examination of the impact of various patterns of alcohol use on happiness.

REFERS TO: Theory of social patterns (alcohol use); Fallding (1964)

TYPE OF STUDY: descriptive, explorative, national population, snapshot, non-experimental

DATA GATHERING: Structured interview

DATE OF DATA: Summer, 1963

POPULATION: Non-institutionalized adult population, U.S.A.

SAMPLE CONSTRUCTION: Probability multi-stage sample.
At block level non-probability quota sample, with quotas based on sex, age, race and employment.
age 21+

NON-RESPONSE: 4% incomplete

N: 1453

AUTHOR'S HAPPINESS LABEL: Happiness (first instrument) and Satisfaction of wants (second instrument)

OUR CONCEPTUALIZATION: Happiness (first instrument) and Contentment (second instrument)

FIRST INSTRUMENT: HAPP 1.1: Single closed question using the term 'happiness', rated on a 3-point scale (see GURIN 60).

RELIABILITY:

VALIDITY:

DISTRIBUTION: positively skewed: 33% very happy, 51% pretty happy, 16% not too happy

SECOND INSTRUMENT: CON 1.1: Single closed question rated on a 2-point scale:

When you think of the things you want from life, would you say that you're doing pretty well or you're not doing too well now in getting the things you want?

RELIABILITY:

VALIDITY:

DISTRIBUTION: highly positively skewed: 82% doing pretty well, 18% doing not too well

REMARKS:

CORRELATES: Contentment x happiness (H 1.3.1); various factors concerning Alcohol consumption (L 3.1.2)

CONCLUSION: Having never been an alcohol user and drinking usually small amounts of alcohol at one setting appears to be the drinking patterns most consistent with happiness. However, among persons (especially drinkers) who are not doing well, drinking medium or large amounts appears to be the pattern most consistent with happiness, provided that there are no problems due to drinking. Those who drink medium or large amounts and have encountered problems due to drinking, and those who are ex-drinker are appreciably less happy.

AUTHOR: Brenner, B. BRENN 70

TITLE: Social factors in mental well-being at adolescence.

SOURCE: Unpublished doctoral dissertation, 1970, The American University, Washington D.C., U.S.A.

---

GOAL OF THE STUDY: To explore the influence of social factors (esp. participation in extracurricular activities and family social class) on mental well-being among adolenscents.

REFERS TO: Theory of happiness and mental well-being; Gurin et al. (1960), Bradburn (1969)

TYPE OF STUDY: explanatory, explorative, special group, snapshot, non-experimental

DATA GATHERING: Highly structured questionnaire

DATE OF DATA: 1960

POPULATION: Juniors and seniors attending public high schools in New York State, U.S.A.

SAMPLE CONSTRUCTION: Probability cluster sample of 10 public high schools in New York State.
Six schools were randomly selected from those in communities with a population of over 100,000, three from communities of 10,000 to 100,000, one from communities of 2,500 - 10,000, and one from communities of 2,500 or less. One high school in a medium-sized community refused cooperation. In each of the appropriate classrooms (juniors/seniors) three questionnaires were alternately distributed to the students, thereby selecting a subsample A (N = 1682), a subsample B (N = 1664), and a subsample C (N = 1678)

NON-RESPONSE: 1%

N: 5204

AUTHOR'S HAPPINESS LABEL: Happiness (first instrument) and Usual mood (second instrument)

OUR CONCEPTUALIZATION: Happiness (first instrument) and Hedonic level of affect (second instrument)

FIRST INSTRUMENT: HAPP 1.1: Single closed question rated on a 4-point scale:

On the whole, how happy would you say you are?
very happy / fairly happy / not very happy / very unhappy

RELIABILITY:

VALIDITY:

DISTRIBUTION: positively skewed: 35% very happy, 59% fairly happy, 6% not happy

SECOND INSTRUMENT: AFF 1.1: Single closed question rated on a 5-point scale:

In general, how would you say you feel most of the time - in good spirits or in low spirits?
very good spirits / fairly good spirits / neither good spirits nor low spirits / fairly low spirits / very low spirits

RELIABILITY:

VALIDITY:

DISTRIBUTION: positively skewed: 23% in very good spirits, 62% in fairly good spirits, 15% not in good spirits

REMARKS: In the analysis 'not very happy' and 'very unhappy' are combined into 'not happy' and 'neither good spirits nor low spirits', 'fairly low spirits' and 'very low spirits' into 'not in good spirits'.
The happiness question (first instrument) was only put in the subsamples A and B (N = 3031), the question on spirits (second instrument) in all the samples (N = 4942).

CORRELATES: Frequency of low mood (A 2.2.4); School social class (E 1.3); Gender (G 1.1); various characteristics of Family of origin (F 1.1); Hedonic level x happiness (H 1.2.1); Anxiety (H 2.2); Having fun in life (L 2.1.2); Tending to be a lonely person (L 2.1.2, S 4.1.5); Tending to be a discouraged person (L 2.1.2, P 1.2); Extracurricular activities (L 3.3.1); various Personality characteristics concerning interpersonal functioning (P 1.8); Sensitivity to criticism (P 1.5.2); Sensitivity to failure (P 1.9); various Formal aspects of self-image (S 2.1); Extent of dating (S 4.1.2); various factors concerning S.E.S. (S 5); Hours spent on work for pay (W 2.1)

CONCLUSION: Happiness appears to be largely determined by usual mood, frequency of high mood and frequency of low mood. The influence of anxiety upon happiness is smaller. Insofar as anxiety does reduce happiness, it appears to do so mainly by increasing the frequency of low mood.
Particularly among students who might otherwise be under-involved, participation in extracurricular activities tends to foster each aspect of mental well-being, partly by increasing fun in life and decreasing loneliness. However, this tendency is reduced and even reversed among students for whom participation is likely to mean over-involvement, and given such unfavourable circumstances as unstable self-image and factors associated with lower class, home and school environment.
With increasing social class, students tend to be happier, usually in better spirits, more likely to find much fun in life, less discouraged, less lonely and less anxious. In fact, the greater fun in life and less loneliness associated with social class seem largely responsible for the other associations. However, a greater likelihood of frequent low moods is also associated with social class, reducing the relation with mental well-being.

BRENN 75A

AUTHOR: Brenner, B.

TITLE: Quality of affect and self-evaluated happiness.

SOURCE: Social Indicators Research, 1975, vol. 2, nr 3, p. 315-331.

---

GOAL OF THE STUDY: Assessment of the relation between quality of affect and self-evaluated happiness.

REFERS TO: Happiness research; Bradburn (1969), Wessman & Ricks (1966)

TYPE OF STUDY: descriptive, explorative, local population, snapshot, non-experimental

DATA GATHERING: Structured interview

DATE OF DATA: Summer, 1973 to summer, 1974.

POPULATION: Local population, Washington County, Maryland, U.S.A.

SAMPLE CONSTRUCTION: Probability cluster sample of households.
Out of each household 1 S was chosen at random.
age 18+

NON-RESPONSE: 25%

N: 916

AUTHOR'S HAPPINESS LABEL: Self-evaluated happiness (first instrument) and Quality of affect (second to sixth instrument)

OUR CONCEPTUALIZATION: Happiness (first to third instrument) and Hedonic level of affect (fourth to sixth instrument)

FIRST INSTRUMENT: HAPP 1.1: Single closed question using the term 'happiness', rated on a 3-point scale (see GURIN 60).

RELIABILITY:

VALIDITY:

DISTRIBUTION: positively skewed: 35% very happy, 59% pretty happy, 6% not too happy

SECOND INSTRUMENT: COMP 1.2: Index of closed questions (Two component Quality of Affect Scale):

1. How often do you feel that you are really enjoying life?
   Would you say very often, fairly often, occasionally, rarely or never.
2. How often do you feel downcast or dejected?
   Would you say very often, fairly often, occasionally, rarely or never.

RELIABILITY:

VALIDITY:

DISTRIBUTION: positively skewed
possible range: 0 (low) to 6 (high); actual range: 0 (0.2%) to 6 (11.9%)

THIRD INSTRUMENT: COMP 1.2: Index of closed questions (Three Component Quality of Affect Scale):

1. How often do you feel that you are really enjoying life?
   Would you say very often, fairly often, occasionally, rarely or never.
2. How often do you feel downcast or dejected?
   Would you say very often, fairly often, occasionally, rarely or never
3. In general how would you say you feel most of the time?
   Would you say very good spirits, fairly good spirits, neither good spirits nor low spirits, fairly low spirits, or very low spirits.

RELIABILITY: equivalence: item 1 & 2: G = -.52 (.001)
item 2 & 3: G = -.56 (.001)
item 1 & 3: G = +.76 (.001)

VALIDITY:

DISTRIBUTION: positively skewed
possible range: 0 (low) to 6 (high); actual range: 0 (0.1%) to 6 (8.6%)

FOURTH INSTRUMENT: AFF 2.3: Index of closed questions on perceived occurrence of specific affects during the past week (Going-Your-Way / Depressed-or-Unhappy Scale; from the Bradburn & Caplovitz Affect Balance Scale; see BRADB 65):

1. How often did you feel that things were going your way during the past week?
 not at all / once / several times / often
2. How often did you feel depressed or very unhappy during the past week?
 not at all / once / several times / often

RELIABILITY: equivalence: G = -.52 (.001)

VALIDITY:

DISTRIBUTION: very positively skewed
possible range: 0 (low) to 4 (high); actual range: 0 (2.8%) to 4 (40.9%)

FIFTH INSTRUMENT: AFF 2.3: Index of closed questions on perceived occurrence of specific affects during the past week (Enjoyed / Depressed Scale):

Please tell me how often you have felt this way during the past week . . . rarely or none of the time / some or a little of the time / occasionally or a moderate amount of time / most or all of the time
- I enjoyed life
- I felt depressed
(selected items from interview schedule)

RELIABILITY: equivalence: G = -.72 (.001)

VALIDITY:

DISTRIBUTION: very positively skewed
possible range: 0 (low) to 4 (high); actual range: 0 (2.0%) to 4 (64.1%)

SIXTH INSTRUMENT: AFF 2.3: Index of closed questions on perceived occurrence of specific affects during the past week (Happy / Sad Scale):

Please tell me how often you have felt this way during the past week . . . rarely or none of the time / some or a little of the time / occasionally or a moderate amount of time / most or all of the time
- I felt happy
- I felt sad
(selected items from interview schedule)

RELIABILITY: equivalence: G = -.71 (.001)

VALIDITY:

DISTRIBUTION: very positively skewed
possible range: 0 (low) to 4 (high); actual range: 0 (1.4%) to 4 (63.5%)

REMARKS: All measures of association are based on frequencies which have been weighted according to the number of adults living in the household of the person selected for interview.

CORRELATES: Depressive affect (A 2.2.4); Happiness x happiness (H 1.1.1); Hedonic level x happiness (H 1.2.1)

CONCLUSION: Assessment of the extent of marked positive affect, negative affect, and the modal quality of affect provides a useful description of the quality of a person's current pattern of affect.
The association between quality of affect and self-evaluated happiness is substantial. The latter appears to be influenced by each of the quality of affect components with the influence of positive affect predominating.

BRENN 75B

AUTHOR: Brenner, B.

TITLE: Enjoyment as a preventive of depressive affect.

SOURCE: Journal of Community Psychology, 1975, vol. 3, nr 4, p. 346-357.

---

GOAL OF THE STUDY: Assessment of relations between satisfaction, enjoyment, depressive affect, and psychophysiologic problems to determine whether enjoyment decreases the likelihood of depressive affect.

REFERS TO: Theory of enjoyment and depressive affect; Heath (1964), Ferster (1965)

TYPE OF STUDY: explanatory, testing, regional population, snapshot, non-experimental

DATA GATHERING: Structured interview

DATE OF DATA: 1972

POPULATION: Adults, U.S.A.

SAMPLE CONSTRUCTION: Probability cluster sample using households in Washington County, Maryland (N = 1268), and probability multi-stage sample in Kansas City, Missouri (N = 900).
In each household the individual to be interviewed was chosen at random.
age 18+

NON-RESPONSE: 19% in Washington County, and 25% in Kansas City

N: 2168

AUTHOR'S HAPPINESS LABEL: Enjoyment of life

OUR CONCEPTUALIZATION: Happiness

INSTRUMENT: COMP 1.1: Single closed question rated on a 5-point scale:

How often do you feel that you are really enjoying life?
Would you say very often, fairly often, occasionally, rarely or never?

RELIABILITY:

VALIDITY:

DISTRIBUTION: positively skewed: 80% often, 16% occasionally, 4% rarely enjoys life

REMARKS:

CORRELATES: Feeling downcast or dejected (A 2.2.4 ); Psycho-physiologic problems (H 2.2); Satisfaction with major life areas (S 1.11)

CONCLUSION: The findings are consistent with the proposition that satisfaction with major life areas is a factor in finding enjoyment in life, thereby a factor in avoiding depressive affect and thereby a factor in avoiding psychophysiologic problems.

AUTHOR: Brim, J.A.

BRIM 74

TITLE: Social network correlates of avowed happiness.

SOURCE: Journal of Nervous and Mental Disease, 1974, vol. 158, nr 6, p. 432-439.

---

GOAL OF THE STUDY: Assessment of correlates between avowed happiness and social network characteristics and description of a technique for obtaining quantified data on these social network characteristics.

REFERS TO: Theory of social networks; Bott (1955, 1957)

TYPE OF STUDY: explanatory, explorative, special group, snapshot, non-experimental

DATA GATHERING: Highly structured questionnaire

DATE OF DATA:

POPULATION: Females from the Seatlle - Washington area, U.S.A.

SAMPLE CONSTRUCTION: Non-probability chunk sample using all members of a woman's rights organization and random selection of one other woman from each block where a woman's rights organization member lived.
92 members, 61 non-members; 113 married, 40 not married

NON-RESPONSE:

N: 153

AUTHOR'S HAPPINESS LABEL: Avowed happiness

OUR CONCEPTUALIZATION: Happiness

INSTRUMENT: HAPP 1.1: Single closed question rated on a 9-point scale (adapted Gurin et al. question; see GURIN 60):

Taken all things together, how would you say things are these days - would you say you're very happy, pretty happy, or not too happy?
Please put a circle around the appropriate number to indicate how happy you are these days.

| very happy | | | | pretty happy | | | | not too happy |
|---|---|---|---|---|---|---|---|---|
| 9 | 8 | 7 | 6 | 5 | 4 | 3 | 2 | 1 |

RELIABILITY:

VALIDITY:

DISTRIBUTION:

REMARKS:

CORRELATES: various indicators of the Marital relationship (M 2.4); various indicators of Social participation (S 4); Value similarity (V 1.2)

CONCLUSION: Several dimensions of social network relationship content have been shown to be significantly related to avowed happiness. One plausible explanation for this is that characteristics of a person's social network directly affect his psychological state, but several rival explanations cannot be ruled out.

BUCHA 53

AUTHOR: Buchanan, W. & Cantril, H.

TITLE: How nations see each other. A study in public opinion.

SOURCE: Urbans, U.S.A., 1953, University of Illinois Press.

---

GOAL OF THE STUDY: Exploration of the relationships between public opinions about foreign people, human nature, peace, etc., and factors as nationality, culture, class and income.

REFERS TO:

TYPE OF STUDY: descriptive, explorative, international population, snapshot, non-experimental

DATA GATHERING: Structured interview

DATE OF DATA: 1948 - 1949

POPULATION: Adult population of 9 countries

SAMPLE CONSTRUCTION: Probability samples proportionally stratified by sex, age, occupation, S.E.S. and education.
Adults of: Australia (N = 945), Britain (N = 1195), France (N = 1000), W.Germany (N = 3371), Italy (N = 1078), Mexico (N = 1752), The Netherlands (N = 942), Norway (N = 1030), U.S.A. (N = 1015).

NON-RESPONSE:

N: 13402

AUTHOR'S HAPPINESS LABEL: Satisfaction

OUR CONCEPTUALIZATION: Happiness

INSTRUMENT: HAPP 2.1: Single closed question rated on a 4-point scale:

How satisfied are you with the way you are getting on now?
very satisfied / all right / dissatisfied / don't know

RELIABILITY:

VALIDITY:

DISTRIBUTION:

| | | | | |
|---|---|---|---|---|
| Australia | : symmetric : | 22% very satisfied, | 57% all right, | 20% dissatisfied |
| Britain: | : negatively skewed: | 12% very satisfied, | 52% all right, | 33% distatisfied |
| France | : negatively skewed: | 2% very satisfied, | 27% all right, | 56% dissatisfied |
| W.Germany | : negatively skewed: | 2% very satisfied, | 51% all right, | 44% dissatisfied |
| Italy | : negatively skewed: | 5% very satisfied, | 45% all right, | 46% dissatisfied |
| The Netherlands | : negatively skewed: | 8% very satisfied, | 54% all right, | 34% dissatisfied |
| Mexico | : negatively skewed: | 20% very satisfied, | 18% all right, | 61% dissatisfied |
| Norway | : positively skewed: | 21% very satisfied, | 67% all right, | 10% dissatisfied |
| U.S.A. | : negatively skewed: | 15% very satisfied, | 57% all right, | 26% dissatisfied |

REMARKS:

CORRELATES: Age (A 3); Educational level (E 1.1.1); Gender (G 1.1); Retirement (R 2.1); S.E.S. (S 5.1); Occupation (W 2.1, W 2.2)

CONCLUSION:

AUTHOR: Bulatao, R.A.

BULAT 73

TITLE: Measures of happiness among Manila residents.

SOURCE: Philippine Sociological Review, 1973, vol. 2, nr 3-4, p. 229-238.

---

GOAL OF THE STUDY: Assessment of personal happiness in Greater Manila and evaluation of the usefulness of 3 measures of happiness.

REFERS TO: Happiness research; Bradburn & Caplovitz (1965), Davitz (1969), Cantril (1965)

TYPE OF STUDY: explanatory, explorative, local population, snapshot, non-experimental

DATA GATHERING: Structured interview

DATE OF DATA: January - April, 1972

POPULATION: Adults, Metro Manila, Philippines

SAMPLE CONSTRUCTION: Probability area sample
age 21+

NON-RESPONSE:

N: 941

AUTHOR'S HAPPINESS LABEL: Happiness (first and second instrument), Enhancement and Discomfort (third instrument)

OUR CONCEPTUALIZATION: Happiness (first and second instrument) and Hedonic level of affect (third instrument)

FIRST INSTRUMENT: HAPP 1.1: Single closed question rated on a 3-point scale (adapted Gurin et al. question; see GURIN 60):

Considering everything that has happened to you recently, how would you say things are with you - would you say you're very happy, pretty happy or not too happy?

RELIABILITY:

VALIDITY:

DISTRIBUTION: negatively skewed: 15% very happy, 56% pretty happy, and 30% not so happy

SECOND INSTRUMENT: HAPP 3.1: Single closed qusestion on personal situation as compared with worst and best possible life, rated on an 11-point self-anchoring scale (Cantril Present Personal rating; see CANTR 65).

RELIABILITY:

VALIDITY:

DISTRIBUTION: slightly positively skewed: steps 0-3 18%, steps 4-6 57%, and steps 7-10 25%
possible range: 0 (low) to 10 (high); actual range: 0 (2%) to 10 (2%); mean: 5.2

THIRD INSTRUMENT: AFF 2.3: index of closed questions on perceived occurrence of specific affects during the past week (most items were selected from the Bradburn & Caplovitz indices of positive and negative affects; see BRADB 65):

The total measure consisted of a set of 12 feelings that respondents could admit having experienced 'never / once / several times / often' during the week before the interview. On the basis of a principal axis factor analysis four factors were extracted, of which 2 in combination appeared to be a valid indicator of hedonic level of affect:

Index of positive affects (Enhancement):
1. Particularly interested in or excited about something
2. Pleased about having accomplished something
3. On top of the world
4. Pity for some people you know

Index of negative affects (Discomfort):
1. Helpless, with no control over situations
2. Bored
3. Vaguely uneasy about something without knowing why
4. Angry about something that usually wouldn't bother you

RELIABILITY:

VALIDITY:

DISTRIBUTION: positively skewed

REMARKS:

CORRELATES: Loneliness (A 2.2.21); Age (A 3); Educational level (E 1.1.1); Happiness x happiness (H 1.1.1); Hedonic level x happiness (H 1.2.1); Change orientation (H 3.4); Household income (I 1.1); various factors concerning Use of leisure time (L 3.3, L 3.4); Living conditions in neighborhood (L 4.4, L 4.5); Marital status (M 1.6); Going to church (R 1.3); Marital happiness (S 1.7.2); Attending parties (S 4.1.2); Participating in sports (S 6.1); Employed status (W 2.1)

CONCLUSION:

AUTHOR: Cameron, P., v. Hoeck, D., Weiss, N. & Kostin, M.

CAMER 71

TITLE: Happiness or life satisfaction of the malformed.

SOURCE: Proceedings, 79th Annual Convention, A.P.A., 1971, vol. 6, p. 641-642.

---

GOAL OF THE STUDY: Comparing life-satisfaction of handicapped children and adults with normal controls.

REFERS TO:

TYPE OF STUDY: explanatory, explorative, special group, snapshot, non-experimental

DATA GATHERING: Highly structured questionnaire

DATE OF DATA:

POPULATION: Physically defective and normal persons, Detroit, U.S.A.

SAMPLE CONSTRUCTION: Non-probability purposive samples of physically defectives and normals (control group).
The handicapped were matched with normals as to sex, age and situation (outpatient, inpatient or student). Where possible inpatient controls were matched as to length of hospitalization.
144 handicapped: age 12-81 (mean 37.6); 1/3 outpatient, 1/3 inpatient, 1/3 student
151 normals : age 14-76 (average 30.1)
The normals had a higher income level than the handicapped.

N: 295

AUTHOR'S HAPPINESS LABEL: Life satisfaction

OUR CONCEPTUALIZATION: Happiness (first instrument) and Hedonic level of affect (second instrument)

FIRST INSTRUMENT: HAPP 2.1: Single closed question rated on a 5-point scale:
These days my life is . . . .
just great / more than satisfactory / less than satisfactory / miserable

RELIABILITY:

VALIDITY:

DISTRIBUTION: positively skewed

SECOND INSTRUMENT: AFF 1.1: Single closed question rated on a 3-point scale:
How would you describe your general mood?
happy / neutral / sad

RELIABILITY:

VALIDITY:

DISTRIBUTION: positively skewed

REMARKS:

CORRELATES: Bodily defect (H 2.1.4); Income (I 1.1)

CONCLUSION: Both normals and malformed claim to value life to about the same degree. As long as permanently socially disadvantaged persons do not believe that their potential is being unjustly and unreasonably crimped, the 'objective' social situation could be expected to have no effect on their appraisals of happiness.

AUTHOR: Cameron, P., Titus, D.G., Kostin, J. & Kostin, M.

TITLE: The life-satisfaction of non-normal persons.

CAMER 73/1-3

SOURCE: Journal of Consulting and Clinical Psychology, 1973, vol. 41, nr 2, p. 207-214.

---

GOAL OF THE STUDY: Test of the proposition that membership in a fixed social status category is unrelated to life satisfaction.

REFERS TO: happiness research; Cameron et al. (1971), Gruhn & Krause (1968)

TYPE OF STUDY: explanatory, testing, special groups, snapshot, non-experimental

CAMER 73/1

DATA GATHERING: Highly structured questionnaire

DATE OF DATA:

POPULATION: Physically defective and normal persons, Detroit, U.S.A.

SAMPLE CONSTRUCTION: Cameron et al. (1971) non-probability purposive samples of physically defectives and normals (control group) (see CAMER 71).

NON-RESPONSE:

N: 295

AUTHOR'S HAPPINESS LABEL: Life satisfaction

OUR CONCEPTUALIZATION: Happiness

INSTRUMENT: HAPP 2.1: Single closed question on satisfaction with life, rated on a 5-point scale (see CAMER 71, first instrument).

RELIABILITY:

VALIDITY:

DISTRIBUTION:

CORRELATES: Happy mood (A 2.2.5); Age (A 3); Bodily defect (H 2.1.4); Income (I 1.1); various indicators of Life quality (L 2.1.2, L 2.2.1); Liking others (P 1.8.4); Appraised liking by others (P 4.2); Religiousness (R 1.1); Futurity (T 1.2)

CAMER 73/2

DATA GATHERING: Highly structured questionnaire

DATE OF DATA:

POPULATION: Physically handicapped and normal persons, Detroit, U.S.A.

SAMPLE CONSTRUCTION: Non-probability purposive samples of 46 physically handicapped and 44 normals (control group). The handicapped were matched with the normals as to sex, race and age.

NON-RESPONSE: 2% of the handicapped excluded because matching was impossible (lack of data)

N: 90

AUTHOR'S HAPPINESS LABEL: Life satisfaction

OUR CONCEPTUALIZATION: Happiness

INSTRUMENT: HAPP 2.1: Single closed question on satisfaction with life, rated on a 5-point scale (see CAMER 71, first instrument).

RELIABILITY:

VALIDITY:

DISTRIBUTION:

CORRELATES: Physical handicap (H 2.1.4); Income (I 1.1)

CAMER 73/3

DATA GATHERING: Disguised structured field observation and questioning teachers and parents of the children.

DATE OF DATA:

POPULATION: Mentally retarded and normal children, U.S.A.

SAMPLE CONSTRUCTION: Probability sample of 40 mentally retarded and non-probability purposive sample of 40 normal children (control group) out of 6 classrooms provided by the Louisville Parochial School System, (4 classrooms with retarded children and 2 with normal children).
retarded: mean IQ 70.8; age 6-19, mean age 13; 20 boys and 20 girls
normals : mean IQ 97.5; age 12-15, mean age 13; 20 boys and 20 girls
Non-Caucasian children were excluded.

N: 80

AUTHOR'S HAPPINESS LABEL: Life satisfaction

OUR CONCEPTUALIZATION: Hedonic level of affect

FISRT INSTRUMENT: AFF 5.1: Clinical rating of hedonic level of affect on the basis of observation of expressive behavior:
Rating by two independent observers
One of the observers was familiar with the general aims of the study whereas the other one was not familiar with these.
Each child was observed twice in both a class situation and at reces. It was observed for one minute and then later for another minute in the same situation by both observers independently and then rated as happy, neutral or unhappy over that minute in that situation.

RELIABILITY: interjudge agreement: average agreement of 97.7%

VALIDITY:

DISTRIBUTION:

SECOND INSTRUMENT: AFF 5.3: Rating of hedonic level of affect by the teachter and by the parents of the children; each on the basis of a single closed question, rated on a 5-point scale:

How would you rate this child's general level of happiness?
always or almost always unhappy / more often unhappy than happy / equal periods or amounts of happiness and unhappiness / more often happy than unhappy / always or almost always happy

RELIABILITY:

VALIDITY:

DISTRIBUTION:

CORRELATES: Being retarded (C 1.5)

CONCLUSION: As long as a class of persons does not believe that its potential is being unjustly or unreasonably crimped, the 'objective' social situation could be expected to have no effect on the class's appraisals of happiness.

AUTHOR: Cantril, H.

CANTR 65/1

TITLE: The pattern of human concerns.

SOURCE: New Brunswick, New Jersey, 1965, Rutgers University Press.

---

GOAL OF THE STUDY: To discover the spectrum of values a person is preoccupied with and by means of which he evaluates his own life.

REFERS TO:

TYPE OF STUDY: explanatory, explorative, snapshot, international population, non-experimental

DATA GATHERING: Structured interview using native interviewers in each country

DATE OF DATA: ± 1960 (see also below at 'sample construction')

POPULATION: Adult population of 14 countries: 5 Westernized nations (U.S.A., W. Germany, Yugoslavia, Poland, Japan), 3 underdeveloped giants (Brazil, Nigeria, India), 2 countries in the Middle East (Israel, Egypt), 3 Caribbean nations (Cuba, Dominican Republic, Panama) and the Philippines.

SAMPLE CONSTRUCTION: Representative samples, partly using random procedures:

- Brazil : Probability samples of both urban and rural population; date: 1960-1961; N: 2168 (after weighting 2739); 1713 rural, 1026 urban; 1242 males, 1479 females; age 18+
- Cuba Probability area sample; date: April-May, 1960; N: 992 (1490); urban population only: 487 Ss from Havana and 1003 Ss other; 833 males, 633 females; age 20+
- Dominican Republic : Probability samples of both the urban and rural publics; date: April, 1962; N: 814 (2442); 1884 rural, 558 urban; 1588 males, 854 females; age 21+
- Egypt : Non-probability accidental sample, proportionally poststratified by dwelling; overrepresentation of better educated and urban segments of the population; date: fall, 1960; N: 499 (1237); 820 rural, 417 urban; 848 males, 363 females; age 15+
- India : Probability sample, proportionally poststratified by dwelling; date: late summer, 1962; N: 2366 (5720); 4472 rural, 1248 urban; 5188 males, 532 females
- Israel : Probability sample; date: November, 1961 - June, 1962; N: 1170; 578 males, 592 females. A separate sample of members of 10 Kibbutzim was drawn: N: 300; 167 males, 133 females
- Japan : Probability sample; date: fall, 1962; N: 972; 437 males, 533 females; age 21+
- Nigeria : Probability sample, proportionally stratified by dwelling and region; date: September, 1962 - spring, 1963; N: 1200 (2876); 1054 rural, 822 urban; 580 west, 700 east, 1596 north; 2328 males, 552 females; age 21+
- Panama : Probability sample , proportionally poststratified by dwelling and mortality; date: January - March, 1962; N: 642 (1351); 786 rural, 565 urban; 622 males, 698 females; age 21+
- Philippines : Probability sample, proportionally poststratified by dwelling; date: spring, 1959; N: 500 (1388); 1036 rural, 164 semi-urban, 188 urban; 780 males, 608 females; age 21+
- Poland : Probability samples of urban and rural populations; date: spring, 1962; N: 1464 (1950); 972 rural, 978 urban; 929 males, 1021 females; age 18+
- U.S.A. : Probability sample; date: August, 1959; N: 1549 (2696); 2432 white, 264 non-white; 128 males, 1413 females; age 21+
- W. Germany : Probability area sample; date: September, 1957; N: 480; 219 males, 261 females
- Yugoslavia : Probability sample; date: spring, 1962; N: 1523; 727 rural, 83 semi-urban, 706 urban; 761 males, 762 females; age 21+

N: 18.653 After weighting procedures , mostly for dwelling, the total number of card-units was 33.327 (see also 'sample construction')

AUTHOR'S HAPPINESS LABEL:

OUR CONCEPTUALIZATION: Happiness

INSTRUMENT: HAPP 3.1: Single closed question, rated on an 11-point self-anchoring scale (Cantril Present Personal rating):

Here is a picture of a ladder. Suppose we say that the top of the ladder represents the best possible life for you and the bottom represents the worst possible life for you.
Where on the ladder do you feel you personally stand at the present time?

Ss were also asked where on the ladder they stood five years ago and where on the ladder they thought to stand five years from now.

| 10 |
|---|
| 9 |
| 8 |
| 7 |
| 6 |
| 5 |
| 4 |
| 3 |
| 2 |
| 1 |
| 0 |

RELIABILITY: reliability between coders of around 95%

VALIDITY:

DISTRIBUTION:

(to be continued on next page)

DISTRIBUTION: possible range: 0 (low) to 10 (high); actual range: 31% low (step 0-3), 42% medium (step 4-6), 20% high (step 7-10); average mean rating: 5.0

| | | | | | | |
|---|---|---|---|---|---|---|
| - Brazil | : negatively skewed: | 28% low, | 35% medium, | 18% high; | mean: 4.6 |
| - Cuba | : positively skewed: | 9% low, | 43% medium, | 45% high; | mean: 6.4 |
| - Dominican Republic: | negatively skewed: | 84% low, | 13% medium, | 1% high; | mean: 1.6 |
| - Egypt | : positively skewed: | 17% low, | 51% medium, | 30% high; | mean: 5.5 |
| - India | : negatively skewed: | 39% low, | 42% medium, | 4% high; | mean: 3.7 |
| - Israel | : positively skewed: | 19% low, | 50% medium, | 29% high; | mean: 5.3 |
| Kibbutzim | : positively skewed: | | | | mean: 7.0 |
| - Japan | : symmetric : | | | | mean: 5.2 |
| - Nigeria | : negatively skewed: | 28% low, | 46% medium, | 21% high: | mean: 4.8 |
| - Panama | : negatively skewed: | 26% low, | 54% medium, | 18% high; | mean: 4.8 |
| - Philippines | : symmetric : | 24% low, | 54% medium, | 21% high; | mean: 4.9 |
| - Poland | : negatively skewed: | | | | mean: 4.4 |
| - U.S.A. | : positively skewed: | 7% low, | 41% medium, | 51% high; | mean: 6.6 |
| - W. Germany | : positively skewed: | 14% low, | 59% medium, | 24% high; | mean: 5.3 |
| - Yugoslavia | : symmetric : | 21% low, | 57% medium, | 21% high; | mean: 5.0 |

REMARKS: Most correlates concern the total world sample. However, a number of variables concern one or more of the national samples only.

CORRELATES: Age (A 3); Educational level (E 1.1.1); Ethnicity / Race (E 2); Gender (G 1.1); Personal hopes and aspirations (H 3.2.1); Hopes and aspirations for one's country (H 3.2.2); Socio-economic level / Income (I 1.1); Community size (L 4.1); Rural vs urban dwelling (L 4.2); Region (L 4.3, L 4.4); Positive evaluation of national situation (N 1.1.1); Socio-economic development of one's country (N 1.2); Political concern (P 3.1); Personal worries and fears (P 5.2.2.1); Worries and fears for one's country (P 5.2.2.3); Religious denomination (R 1.2); S.E.S. (S 5.1); Fear of war (W 1.2); Occupation (W 2.1, W 2.2)

## CANTR 65/2

GOAL OF THE STUDY: To learn something about variables that might be involved in producing the psychological matrix experienced as 'satisfaction'.

REFERS TO:

TYPE OF STUDY: explanatory, explorative, national population, snapshot, non-experimental

DATA GATHERING: Structured interview

DATE OF DATA: August, 1959

POPULATION: National adult population, U.S.A.

SAMPLE CONSTRUCTION: Probability sample (see U.S.A. sample of CANTR 65/1)

NON-RESPONSE:

N: 1549 (after weighting procedures to get the 'not-at-home' the total number of card-units was 2696)

AUTHOR'S HAPPINESS LABEL: Satisfaction with life (second instrument) and Success in achieving goals (third instrument)

OUR CONCEPTUALIZATION: Happiness (first and second instrument) and Contentment (third instrument)

FIRST INSTRUMENT: HAPP 3.1: Single closed question on personal situation as compared with best and worst possible life, rated on an 11-point self-anchoring scale (Cantril Present Personal rating; see CANTR 65/1).

RELIABILITY:

VALIDITY :

DISTRIBUTION: positively skewed: 7% low, 41% middle, 51% high
possible range: 0 (low) to 10 (high); mean: 6.6

SECOND INSTRUMENT: HAPP 2.1: Single closed question rated on an 11-point self-anchoring scale (Cantril Satisfaction with Life rating):

Suppose that a person who is entirely satisfied with his life would be at the top of the ladder and a person who is extremely dissatisfied with his life would be at the bottom of the ladder. Where would you put yourself on the ladder at the present stage of your life in terms of how satisfied or dissatisfied you are with your personal life?

RELIABILITY:

VALIDITY:

DISTRIBUTION: positively skewed
possible range: 0 (low) to 10 (high); mean: 7.6

THIRD INSTRUMENT: CON 1.1: Single closed question rated on an 11-point self-anchoring scale (Cantril Success in achieving Goals rating):

How would you rate yourself as to how successful or unsuccessful you have been in terms of achieving your own goals and aims in life? Think of the top of the ladder as being completely successful, the bottom being entirely unsuccessful.

RELIABILITY:

VALIDITY:

DISTRIBUTION: positively skewed
possible range: 0 (low) to 10 (high); mean: 6.7

REMARKS:

CORRELATES: Opportunity to do thinks one likes (F 2.2); Happiness x happiness (H 1.1.1); Contentment x happiness (H 1.3.1); Enjoyment of previous day (L 2.1.1); Ability to do things (P 1.1); Feeling that life is full of troubles and obstacles (P 5.1.1); Extent of worries or fears that things night get worse (P 5.2.1); Religiousness (R 1.1); Respect for oneself (S 2.1.3); Confidence in oneself (S 2.1.4)

CONCLUSION: The data confirm the truth of Aristotle's observation that 'happiness comes from the exercise powers along lines of excellence in a life affording them scope'.
People denied a scope for their lives because they live in poorer countries, are less satisfied and are not resigned to their situation. An apparent characteristic of man is never to be satisfied, always to want to experience some new value satisfactions, as well as to protect those he already enjoys. In a world where more and more people are becoming aware of what other people have and hence what is potentially available to them, they perceive and assess their own situations in terms of the relative differences between what is and what might be for them in terms of their own purposes.

CANTR 71

AUTHOR: Cantril, A.H. & Roll, C.W. Jr

TITLE: Hopes and fears of the American people.

SOURCE: New York, 1971, Universe Books.

---

GOAL OF THE STUDY: To attain a sense of the basic hopes and fears of the American people.

REFERS TO:

TYPE OF STUDY: descriptive, explorative, national population, snapshot, non-experimental

DATA GATHERING: Structured interview

DATE OF DATA: January, 1971

POPULATION: Non-institutionalized national adult population, U.S.A.

SAMPLE CONSTRUCTION: Multi-stage probability sample stratified by size of locality.
age 21+

NON-RESPONSE:

N: 1588

AUTHOR'S HAPPINESS LABEL:

OUR CONCEPTUALIZATION: Happiness

INSTRUMENT: HAPP 3.1: Single closed question on personal situation compared with best and worst possible life, rated on an 11-point self-anchoring scale (Cantril Present Personal rating; see CANTR 65/1).

RELIABILITY:

VALIDITY:

DISTRIBUTION: positively skewed
possible range: 0 (low) to 10 (high); mean: 6.6

REMARKS: Data from a study in the U.S.A. in 1964, conducted by the Institute for Social Research, were also presented in this publication. The same happiness question was used.
In Part III we presented these 1964 data in the 'elaboration / remarks' column in brackets behind the original data from 1971.

CORRELATES: Age (A 3); Educational level (E 1.1.1); Race (E 2.2); Gender (G 1.1); Income (I 1.1); Community size (L 4.1); Region (L 4.3); Political affiliation (P 3.3); Occupation (W 2.1, W 2.2)

CONCLUSION:

AUTHOR: Cherlin, A. & Reeder, L.G. | CHERL 75

TITLE: The dimensions of psychological well-being. A critical review.

SOURCE: Sociological Methods & Research, 1975, vol. 4, nr 2, p. 189-214.

---

GOAL OF THE STUDY: Replication and critical examination of the Bradburn (1969) study, and refinement of his theoretical model.

REFERS TO: Happiness research; Bradburn (1969), and Phillips (1967)

TYPE OF STUDY: explanatory, explorative, local population, snapshot, non-experimental

DATA GATHERING: Highly structured questionnaire

DATE OF DATA: Spring, 1972 and spring, 1973

POPULATION: Adults, Los Angeles County, U.S.A.

SAMPLE CONSTRUCTION: Probability multi-stage samples of households.
Los Angeles Metropolitan Area Survey V (in 1972) and VI (in 1973).

NON-RESPONSE: 20% in 1972 and 23% in 1973

N: 1078 in 1972 and 1008 in 1973

AUTHOR'S HAPPINESS LABEL: Psychological well-being

OUR CONCEPTUALIZATION: Hedonic level of affect

INSTRUMENT: AFF 2.3: Index of closed questions on perceived occurrence of specific affects during the past few weeks (Bradburn Affect Balance Score; see BRADB 69).

RELIABILITY: Equivalence: positive affect score x negative affect score: r = -.07 (01) in 1972
r = -.09 (01) in 1973

VALIDITY:

DISTRIBUTION:

REMARKS:

CORRELATES: Educational level (E 1.1.1); Need for help (H 2.3.2); Internal control (P 1.1); Employed status (W 2.1)

CONCLUSION:

AUTHOR: Chiriboga, D. & Lowenthal, M.F. | CHIRI 71

TITLE: Psychological correlates of perceived well-being.

SOURCE: Proceedings of the 79th Annual Convention, A.P.A., 1971.

---

GOAL OF THE STUDY: Investigation of the comparative relationship between psychological deficits and resources to the subjective sense of well-being.

REFERS TO: Happiness research; Bradburn (1969)

TYPE OF STUDY: explanatory, explorative, special group, snapshot, non-experimental

DATA GATHERING: Depth interviews and tests, averaging 9 hours in administration

DATE OF DATA:

POPULATION: People in transition, U.S.A.

SAMPLE CONSTRUCTION: Stratified random sample out of a community based population of people undergoing a process of normative transition:
- high school seniors (mean age 17)
- newlyweds ( mean age 24)
- empty-nesters (parents, whose youngest child leaves home, mean age 50)
- pre-retired (mean age 60)

NON-RESPONSE:

N: 216

JTHOR'S HAPPINESS LABEL: Perceived well-being

OUR CONCEPTUALIZATION: Happiness (first instrument) and Hedonic level of affect (second instrument)

FIRST INSTRUMENT: HAPP 1.1: Single closed question rated on a 3-point scale:

In general how happy are you these days?
very happy / pretty happy / not too happy

RELIABILITY:

VALIDITY:

DISTRIBUTION:

SECOND INSTRUMENT: AFF 2.3: Index of closed questions on perceived occurrence of specific affects during the past week (adapted Bradburn & Caplovitz Affect Balance Score; see BRADB 65).

The questions were dealing with 8 positive and negative affective experiences during the past 7 days.

RELIABILITY: Equivalence: positive affect score x negative affect score: $r_{pm} = +.18$

VALIDITY:

DISTRIBUTION:

REMARKS:

CORRELATES: Hedonic level x happiness (H 1.2.1); Mental health (H 2.3.1)

CONCLUSION: Indicators of positive and negative mental health vary relatively independently as do positive and negative feelings. They both predict well-being, but a consideration of both dimensions adds considerably to predictive efficiency (as does the combination of positive and negative feelings in ABS - scores).
So happy people are not necessarily free from psychopathologic symptoms and neither are healthy people necessarily happy.

AUTHOR: Clum, G.A. & Clum, J.

CLUM 73

TITLE: Choice of defense mechanisms and their relationship to mood level.

SOURCE: Psychological Reports, 1973, vol. 32, nr 2, p. 507-510.

---

GOAL OF THE STUDY: Assessment of the relation between preferences for defense mechanisms and average mood level.

REFERS TO: Theory of depression; Gleser & Ihilivich (1969), Wessman & Ricks (1966)

TYPE OF STUDY: explanatory, testing, special group, snapshot, non-experimental

DATA GATHERING: Highly structured questionnaire

DATE OF DATA:

POPULATION: Undergrates at San Diego State College, U.S.A.

SAMPLE CONSTRUCTION: Non-probability chunk sample.
23 males : mean age 22
32 females: mean age 24

NON-RESPONSE:

N: 55

AUTHOR'S HAPPINESS LABEL: Mood

OUR CONCEPTUALIZATION: Hedonic level of affect

INSTRUMENT: AFF 3.1: Repeated single closed question on overall hedonic level for the past day rated on a 10-point scale (Wessman & Ricks Elation - Depression Scale; see WESSM 60).

The scale was scored at the end of each day for average mood level during 30 consecutive days.

RELIABILITY:

VALIDITY:

DISTRIBUTION:

REMARKS: Correlations were presented for males only.

CORRELATES: various Defense mechanisms (P 1.3)

CONCLUSION: It may be more accurate to conceptualize depression as involving an increase in aggressive thoughts directed against others, without a proportionate increase in the probability of responding on a motor level to those thoughts.

AUTHOR: Commission of the European Communities. COMMI 75

TITLE: European men and women.
A comparison of their attitudes to some of the problems facing society.

SOURCE: Commission of the European Communities, 1975, Brussels, Belgium.
(data available at the Belgian Archives for the Social Sciences (BASS), Louvain-la-Neuve, Belgium)

---

GOAL OF THE STUDY: To contribute to a better understanding of European men and women's attitudes to certain problems of our society, especially problems regarding the changing role of women.

REFERS TO:

TYPE OF STUDY: explanatory, explorative, international population, snapshot, non-experimental

DATA GATHERING: Structured interview

DATE OF DATA: May, 1975

POPULATION: National populations of nine European countries

SAMPLE CONSTRUCTION: Type of sample construction not reported.
Representative national samples; age 15+; 1699 age 15-24, 4959 age 25-54, 2947 age 55+; 4622 (4592) males, 4983 (4951) females; 6410 married, 120 living as married, 2028 single, 845 widowed, 142 divorced, 64 separated (see 'REMARKS')

- Belgium : N: 1555 (1507); 746 (728) males, 809 (779) females
- Denmark : N: 1039 (1073); 491 (505) males; 548 (568) females
- France : N 1196 (1156); 582 (563) males; 614 (593) females
- W.Germany : N: 1039 (1039); 483 (483) males; 556 (556) females
- Italy : N: 1043 (1043); 526 (526) males; 517 (517) females
- Ireland : N: 999 (996); 477 (475) males; 522 (521) females
- Luxembourg : N: 324 (311); 156 (151) males; 168 (160) females
- The Netherlands : N: 1093 (1093); 539 (539) males; 554 (554) females
- United Kingdom (including N.Ireland) : N: 1317 (1325); 622 (622) males; 695 (703) females; 300 Ss from N.Ireland

NON-RESPONSE:

N: 9605 (or 9543; see 'REMARKS')

AUTHOR'S HAPPINESS LABEL: Life satisfaction (first instrument) and Happiness (second instrument)

OUR CONCEPTUALIZATION: Happiness

FIRST INSTRUMENT: HAPP 2.1: Single closed question, rated on a 5-point scale:

All things considered, how satisfied or dissatisfied are you with your life as a whole these days?
very satisfied / fairly satisfied / not very satisfied / not satisfied / don't know

RELIABILITY: Retest after nearly two years (September, 1973 - May, 1975) indicates perfect stability.

VALIDITY:

DISTRIBUTION:

| | | | | | |
|---|---|---|---|---|---|
| Belgium | : positively skewed: | 39% very satisfied, | 52% fairly satisfied, | 5% not very satisfied, | 2% not satisfied at all |
| Denmark | : positively skewed: | 51% very satisfied, | 41% fairly satisfied, | 4% not very satisfied, | 0% not satisfied at all |
| France | : almost symmetric : | 16% very satisfied, | 59% fairly satisfied, | 16% not very satisfied, | 7% not satisfied at all |
| W.Germany | : almost symmetric : | 13% very satisfied, | 66% fairly satisfied, | 16% not very satisfied, | 2% not satisfied at all |
| Italy | : negatively skewed: | 7% very satisfied, | 52% fairly satisfied, | 28% not very satisfied, | 10% not satisfied at all |
| Ireland | : positively skewed: | 36% very satisfied, | 52% fairly satisfied, | 9% not very satisfied, | 3% not satisfied at all |
| Luxembourg | : positively skewed: | 26% very satisfied, | 45% fairly satisfied, | 15% not very satisfied, | 7% not satisfied at all |
| The Netherlands | : positively skewed: | 33% very satisfied, | 52% fairly satisfied, | 7% not very satisfied, | 2% not satisfied at all |
| United Kingdom | : positively skewed: | 33% very satisfied, | 53% fairly satisfied, | 9% not very satisfied, | 3% not satisfied at all |
| Total | : almost symmetric : | 20% very satisfied, | 57% fairly satisfied, | 16% not very satisfied, | 5% not satisfied at all |

SECOND INSTRUMENT: HAPP 1.1: Single closed question using the term 'happiness', rated on a 3-point scale (see GURIN 60).

RELIABILITY:

VALIDITY:

DISTRIBUTION:

| | | | | |
|---|---|---|---|---|
| Belgium | : positively skewed: | 36% very happy, | 52% pretty happy, | 10% not too happy |
| Denmark | : positively skewed, | 38% very happy, | 49% pretty happy, | 6% not too happy |
| France | : negatively skewed: | 16% very happy, | 55% pretty happy, | 27% not too happy |
| W.Germany | : negatively skewed: | 11% very happy, | 63% pretty happy, | 21% not too happy |
| Italy | : negatively skewed: | 6% very happy, | 48% pretty happy, | 44% not too happy |
| Ireland | : negatively skewed: | 17% very happy, | 53% pretty happy, | 30% not too happy |
| Luxembourg | : positively skewed: | 24% very happy, | 50% pretty happy, | 21% not too happy |
| The Netherlands | : positively skewed: | 31% very happy, | 54% pretty happy, | 10% not too happy |
| United Kingdom | : almost symmetric : | 22% very happy, | 50% pretty happy, | 27% not too happy |
| Total | : negatively skewed: | 16% very happy, | 54% pretty happy, | 27% not too happy |

REMARKS: The publication presents no measures of association, but tables of frequencies presenting percentages only. By using tables of frequencies presenting exact numbers of responcents, offered by the Belgian Archives for the Social Sciences (BASS), we were able to compute our measure of association (G').

Probably due to weighting problems small differences exist in most cases between the number of respondents as presented in the tables offered by BASS and the numbers presented in the publication. In these cases we give the numbers as presented in the publication in brackets behind the number of respondents as offered by BASS. Otherwise the data are from BASS.

Except for the data concerning marital status of which crosstabulations were sent to us by BASS, the Gammas concerning associations in separate countries are based on the percentages 'very satisfied' or 'very happy' answers.

CORRELATES: Age (A 3); Educational level (E 1.1.1); Gender (G 1.1); Family income (I 1.1); Size of locality (L 4.1); various Marital status comparisons (M 1)

CONCLUSION: Satisfaction with the way of life in men tends to reflect the individual's career as well as the general evolution of living conditions in society, whereas in women, increasing age, often accompanied by widowhood and a large drop in material well-being brings about more frequent dissatisfaction.

AUTHOR: Constantinople, A.P. CONST 65

TITLE: Some correlates of happiness and unhappiness in college students.

SOURCE: Unpublished doctoral dissertation, 1965, University of Rochester, U.S.A.

---

GOAL OF THE STUDY: Assessment of interrelationships between personality development, happiness, academic achievement, and attitude toward college, for college students.

REFERS TO: Theory of personality development and happiness; Erikson (1959), Wessman & Ricks (1966)

TYPE OF STUDY: explanatory, explorative, special group, snapshot, non-experimental

DATA GATHERING: Highly structured questionnaire in classroom situation and additional highly structured questionnaire for freshmen and juniors administered at home (± 70% return)

DATE OF DATA: March, 1965

POPULATION: Undergraduate full-time college students, University of Rochester, U.S.A.

SAMPLE CONSTRUCTION: Non-probability chunk sample of undergraduate students recruited from classes of students from 10 departments of the University of Rochester.
513 males : 150 freshmen, 126 sophomores, 133 juniors, 104 seniors.
439 females: 124 freshmen, 120 sophomores, 98 juniors, 115 seniors.

NON-RESPONSE:

N: 952

AUTHOR'S HAPPINESS LABEL: Happiness

OUR CONCEPTUALIZATION: Hedonic level of affect

INSTRUMENT: AFF 2.1: Single closed question on perceived overall hedonic level during the current academic year, rated on a 10-point scale (Wessman & Ricks Elation - Depression Scale; see WESSM 60).

Ss were asked to indicate which statement best describes their typical mood for the current academic year.

RELIABILITY: retest - reliability: In pilot study (N = 152): r = +.85 between two administrations of the scale occurring two weeks apart.

VALIDITY: congruent validity: In pilot study (N = 152) correlations of the instrument with the Nowlis (1965) MACL surgency plus Elation factors administered 4 times were +.30 for males and +.48 for females.
In the same pilot study correlations with the Marlowe-Crowne Social Desirability scale were +.02 (ns) for males and +.20 (ns) for females.

DISTRIBUTION: possible range: 1 (low) to 10 (high); mean: 5.9

REMARKS: see also CONST 67 and PORTE 67

CORRELATES: various Wessman & Ricks Personal feeling scales (A 2.2); Academic status (C 1.3, E 1.2.2); Attitudes towards college (E 1.2.1); Stage of study (E 1.2.3); Gender (G 1.1); Psycho-social development (P 1.4.1); Satisfaction with university (S 1.10)

CONCLUSION: The happiness level for the several sex/class groups can be used as an indication of differences in the process of adaption to the college environment. It can be interpreted as reflections both of the general nature of psycho-social development in men and women and the operation of specific factors in the University environment.

AUTHOR: Constantinople, A.

CONST 67

TITLE: Perceived instrumentality of the college as a measure of attitudes toward college.

SOURCE: Journal of Personality and Social Psychology, 1967, vol. 5, p. 196-201.

---

GOAL OF THE STUDY: Test of the hypothesis that happier students will perceive the university as more helpful in their progress toward important goals than less happy students.

REFERS TO: Theory of attitudes; Peak (1955)

TYPE OF STUDY: explanatory, testing, special group, snapshot, non-experimental

DATA GATHERING: Highly structured questionnaire in classroom situation and additional highly structured questionnaire administered at home

DATE OF DATA: March, 1965

POPULATION: Undergraduate college students, University of Rochester, U.S.A.

SAMPLE CONSTRUCTION: Non-probability chunk sample of undergraduate students recruited from classes of students from 10 departments of the University of Rochester. (see also CONST 65).
Freshmen and juniors who returned the second questionnaire were used in this study.
99 male freshmen, 89 female freshmen, 90 male juniors, 75 female juniors.

NON-RESPONSE:

N: 353

AUTHOR'S HAPPINESS LABEL: Happiness

OUR CONCEPTUALIZATION: Hedonic level of affect

INSTRUMENT: AFF 2.1: Single closed question on perceived overall hedonic level during the current academic year, rated on a 10-point scale (Wessman & Ricks Elation - Depression Scale; see WESSM 60 and CONST 65)

RELIABILITY: see CONST 65

VALIDITY: see CONST 65

DISTRIBUTION:

REMARKS: The data presented in this publication were already presented in the Constantinople (1965) publication: see CONST 65.

CONCLUSION: Happy students see college as more instrumental for their goals than unhappy students do. However, it is unclear whether this is a result of a causal relation or an effect of general optimism of happy students.

AUTHOR: Constantinople, A. | CONST 70

TITLE: Some correlates of average level of happiness among college students.

SOURCE: Developmental Psychology, 1970, vol. 2, nr 3, p. 447 (brief report).
Unpublished paper (extended report).

---

GOAL OF THE STUDY: Test of relationships among happiness, personality development and attitudes towards college.

REFERS TO: Happiness research; Wessman & Ricks (1966), Constantinople (1967)

TYPE OF STUDY: explanatory, testing, special group, longitudinal, non-experimental

DATA GATHERING: Highly structured questionnaires administered in classroom situation or at home and mailed highly structured questionnaire three years later for freshmen (± 50% return)

DATE OF DATA: March, 1965 and March, 1968 (N = 88)

POPULATION: Undergraduate college students, University of Rochester, U.S.A.

SAMPLE CONSTRUCTION: Non-probability chunk sample of undergraduate students recruited from classes of students from 10 departments of the University of Rochester (students from the Constantinople (1965) sample; see CONST 65).
157 male freshmen and sophomores, 125 male juniors and seniors, 189 female freshmen and sophomores, 110 female juniors and seniors. A follow-up study of 88 freshmen (48 males, 40 females) in their senior years was made too.

NON-RESPONSE:

N: 581

AUTHOR'S HAPPINESS LABEL: Happiness

OUR CONCEPTUALIZATION: Hedonic level of affect

INSTRUMENT: AFF 2.1: Single closed question on perceived overall hedonic level during the current academic year, rated on a 10-point scale (Wessman & Ricks Elation - Depression Scale; see WESSM 60 and CONST 65).

RELIABILITY: see CONST 65

VALIDITY: see CONST 65

DISTRIBUTION:

REMARKS:

CORRELATES: Perceived instrumentality of college (E 1.2.1); Gender (G 1.1); Psycho-social development (P 1.4.1)

CONCLUSION: Males begin their college careers in a relatively less happy state than females, but become happier during the course of the four college years, whereas females do not. This might be due to the fact that for the females the joys of academic work for its own sake become increasingly less relevant as their life-goals of marriage and motherhood become more important.

DYSIN 37

AUTHOR: Dysinger, D.W.

TITLE: A study of mood.

SOURCE: Psychological Records, 1937, vol. 1, p. 147-156.

---

GOAL OF THE STUDY: To investigate whether or not a graphic method is suitable to be used in studying the variability of mood, and determination of factors which are operative in bringing about these variations.

REFERS TO: Happiness research; Cason (1931), Sullivan (1922)

TYPE OF STUDY: explanatory, explorative, special group, snapshot, non-experimental

DATA GATHERING: Lowly structured questionnaire

DATE OF DATA:

POPULATION: University students and staff members, U.S.A.

SAMPLE CONSTRUCTION: Non-probability chunk sample of undergraduate psychology students (N = 9) and graduate students or staff members (N = 7).

NON-RESPONSE: 38% incomplete information

N: 16

AUTHOR'S HAPPINESS LABEL: Mood

OUR CONCEPTUALIZATION: Hedonic level of affect

INSTRUMENT: AFF 3.1: Repeated single question on present overall hedonic level, rated on a open graphic scale, marked two times a day for periods ranging from 18 to 64 days:

Consider the extreme of depression to be the most depressed state that you have ever experienced, and the extreme of cheerfulness to be the most cheerful state that you have ever experienced. Draw a line across the base line of the scale at a point which indicates your present mood in relation to these extremes

depressed ------------------------+------------------------ cheerful (total: 80 mm)

The recorded judgements were read in centimeters, using the midpoint of each line as the point of reference.
Judgments of cheerfulness were considered plus, those of depression minus.

RELIABILITY: Retest reliability after a few months

VALIDITY:

DISTRIBUTION: positively skewed
possible range: -40 (low) to +40 (high); actual range on the basis of individual mean scores: -14.2 to +23.6

REMARKS:

CORRELATES: Physical condition (H 2.1.2)

CONCLUSION: Physical condition is a factor of secondary importance in producing moods. The routine affairs and interests of the day are of more importance.

| | | |
|---|---|---|
| AUTHOR: | Dysinger, D.W. | DYSIN 38 |
| TITLE: | The fluctuations of mood. | |
| SOURCE: | Psychological Records, 1938, vol. 2, p. 115-123. | |

---

GOAL OF THE STUDY: To check previous findings in respect to the relationship between mood and physical condition, and to determine whether or not more frequent daily reports would give indications of periodic mood fluctuations.

REFERS TO: Happiness research; Dysinger (1937)

TYPE OF STUDY: explanatory, explorative, special group, snapshot, non-experimental

DATA GATHERING: Lowly structured questionnaire

DATE OF DATA: March - April, ?

POPULATION: University students, U.S.A.

SAMPLE CONSTRUCTION: Non-probability chunk sample of undergraduate psychology students.
15 males, 9 females

NON-RESPONSE:

N: 24

AUTHOR'S HAPPINESS LABEL: Mood

OUR CONCEPTUALIZATION: Hedonic level of affect

INSTRUMENT: AFF 3.1: Repeated single question on present overall hedonic level, rated on an open graphic scale, marked 3 times a day during 5 weeks (adapted Dysinger instrument; see DYSIN 37).

All subjects recorded their judgments within the same periods of each day. An 86 mm. scale was used here.

RELIABILITY:

VALIDITY:

DISTRIBUTION: positively skewed
possible range: -43 (low) to +43 (high); actual range on the basis of individual mean scores: -4.0 to +35.5

REMARKS:

CORRELATES: Physical condition (H 2.1.2)

CONCLUSION: It appears that generally the physical condition is a contributing factor rather than a direct cause of mood, except in cases of actual illness.

ESTES 73

AUTHOR: Estes, R.

TITLE: Determinants of differential stress levels among university students.

SOURCE: Journal of the American College Health Association, 1973, vol. 21, nr 5, p. 470-476.

---

GOAL OF THE STUDY: Identification of major subgroups within the student population which experience high levels of emotional sress.

REFERS TO: Theory of emotional stress among students; Davis et al. (1971), Nicholi (1967)

TYPE OF STUDY: explanatory, explorative, special group, snapshot, non-experimental

DATA GATHERING: Structured interview for patients and highly structured questionnaire for patients and controls

DATE OF DATA: 1971 / 1972

POPULATION: Full-time university students, Berkeley Campus, California, U.S.A.

SAMPLE CONSTRUCTION: Probability samples of patients and controls.
Patients having consulted the Psychiatric Clinic of the Student Health Service during the 1971 - 1972 academic year.
140 patients, 140 controls; both patients and controls are representative of students at all levels of educational experience

NON-RESPONSE:

N: 280

AUTHOR'S HAPPINESS LABEL: Feeling in good spirits

OUR CONCEPTUALIZATION: Hedonic level of affect

INSTRUMENT: AFF 1.1: Single closed yes/no question on feeling in good spirits usually.

RELIABILITY:

VALIDITY:

DISTRIBUTION: negatively skewed: 38% usually and 62% not usually in good spirits

REMARKS:

CORRELATES: Having received psychiatric treatment (H 2.3.3)

CONCLUSION:

AUTHOR: Fischer, C.S.

FISCH 73/1-5

TITLE: Urban malaise.

SOURCE: Social Forces, 1973, vol. 52, nr 2, p. 221-235.

---

GOAL OF THE STUDY: Determine whether malaise increases along with urbanism and whether urban residence is independently related to urban malaise.

REFERS TO: Theory of urbanism; Wirth (1938), Fischer (1972)

TYPE OF STUDY: explanatory, testing, snapshot, non-experimental, national population (special group in study 4)

DATA GATHERING: Highly structured questionnaire.

DATE OF DATA: 1952 (study 1), 1957 (study 2), 1963 (study 3), 1968 (study 4), 1967 (study 5).

POPULATION: National population, U.S.A. (study 1-4) and national population, France (study 5)

SAMPLE CONSTRUCTION:
- Gallup national probability samples (study 1-3)
- University of Michigan Survey Research election poll; double sampling of black respondents (study 4)
- survey from the COFREMCA Institute, Paris, France (study 5)

NON-RESPONSE:

N: 2970 (study 1), 1605 (study 2), 1555 (study 3), 1440 (study 4), 2175 (study 5)

AUTHOR'S HAPPINESS LABEL: Malaise

OUR CONCEPTUALIZATION: Happiness

INSTRUMENTS: study 1-3: HAPP 1.1: Single closed question rated on a 3-point scale:

In general, how happy would you say you are?
very happy / pretty happy / not very happy

study 4 : HAPP 2.1: Single closed question rated on a 3-point scale:

In general, how satisfying do you find the way you're spending your life these days?
Would you call it: completely satisfying / pretty satisfying / not very satisfying

study 5: COMP 1.1: Single closed question rated on a 21-point self-anchoring scale (based on Cantril; see CANTR 65):

There are moments you feel your work and your personal affairs are going well. Sometimes without any specific reason you feel good and confident towards the future. There are also moments that things seem to go bad; that you feel anxious and worried about the future. Now here is a picture of a ladder running from 0 to 20. Suppose 0 represents the time in your life you felt most miserable and 20 represents the best time you ever had. Where on the ladder are you now?

In French:
Il y a des moments dans la vie personelle et professionelle où on a le sentiment que les choses vont bien, même sans savoir pourquoi; on se sent bien et confiant dans l'avenir. Il y a des moments où on a le sentiment que les choses vont mal; on est inquiet et peu confiant dans l'avenir. Voici une échelle de 0 à 20. Vous allez vous situer sur cette échelle: 0 correspond à la période de votre vie où vous vous êtes senti le plus inquiet et malheureux. 20 correspond à la période où vous vous êtes senti le plus heureux et confident. Où vous situerez-vous en ce moment?

RELIABILITY:

VALIDITY:

DISTRIBUTION:
study 1: positively skewed: 47% very happy, 43% pretty happy, 10% not very happy
study 2: positively skewed: 54% very happy, 43% pretty happy, 3% not very happy
study 3: positively skewed: 47% very happy, 48% pretty happy, 4% not very happy
study 4: positively skewed: 23% completely satisfying, 66% pretty satisfying, 11% not very satisfying
study 5: positively skewed: mean: 12.6 (possible range: 0 (low) to 20 (high))

REMARKS:

CORRELATES: Community size (L 4.1)

CONCLUSION: Only in the largest cities people are unhappier.

AUTHOR: Flügel, J.C.

FLUGE 25

TITLE: A quantative study of feeling and emotion in very day life.

SOURCE: British Journal of Psychology, 1925, vol. 15, p. 318-355.

---

GOAL OF THE STUDY: Assessment of nature and proportion of pleasure and pain.

REFERS TO: Theory of pleasure and pain

TYPE OF STUDY: explorative, explanatory, special group, snapshot, non-experimental

DATA GATHERING: Lowly structured diary of emotions, used each hour during 30 days

DATE OF DATA:

POPULATION: Intellectuals, England

SAMPLE CONSTRUCTION: Non-probability accidental sample using friends of the investigators and other volunteers.
Each respondent had received some psychological training; 5 females, 4 males; age 19-42

NON-RESPONSE:

N: 9

AUTHOR'S HAPPINESS LABEL: Pleasure (hedonic feeling)

OUR CONCEPTUALIZATION: Hedonic level of affect

INSTRUMENT: AFF 3.4: repeated open-ended qeestions on momentaneous hedonic level of affect:

Several times per hour the respondents noted in a diary:
1. the emotion(s) they had experienced the last few minutes
2. the number of minutes they experienced these feelings
3. the hedonic dimension they experienced in these feelings, rated from +3 to -3

The total percentage of unpleasure was divided by the total percentage of pleasure to obtain the measure used here.

RELIABILITY: Odd / even test for equivalence: r ranging from +.45 to +.96
lowest for most extreme feelings

VALIDITY: Respondents declared that this proportion of pleasure and unpleasure was fairly characteristic for their life as a whole

DISTRIBUTION: positively skewed
possible range: 1 (high) to 100 (low); actual range: +.12 to +.78

REMARKS: In the publication several variations of the reported instrument were presented. We did not include these measures because they did not provide more useful information.

CORRELATES: Intensity of feelings (A 2.1.3); Variability of feelings (A 2.1.4)

CONCLUSION: Those who tend to experience the most extreme degrees of feelings are on the whole less happy than those whose feelings are usually less intense.

AUTHOR: Fordyce, M.W. FORDY 72

TITLE: Happiness, its daily variation and its relation to values.

SOURCE: Unpublished doctoral dissertation, 1972, United States International University.

---

GOAL OF THE STUDY: Experimental investigation of the relationship between happiness and values and between happiness and other aspects of daily mood.

REFERS TO: Happiness research; Wessman & Ricks (1966), Cantril (1965)

TYPE OF STUDY: explanatory, explorative, special group, snapshot, non-experimental

DATA GATHERING: Highly structured questionnaires and content analysis

DATE OF DATA: November - December, 1971

POPULATION: Undergraduate university students, California, U.S.A.

SAMPLE CONSTRUCTION: Non-probability chunk sample of undergraduate students enrolled in three introductory Sociology courses at the United States International University. 38 males and 48 females, representing all four years: freshman through senior; predominantly upper-middle or lower-upper class background

NON-RESPONSE:

N: 86

AUTHOR'S HAPPINESS LABEL: Happiness (daily mood)

OUR CONCEPTUALIZATION: Hedonic level of affect

FIRST INSTRUMENT: AFF 3.1: Repeated single closed question on overall hedonic level for the past day, rated on a 10-point scale (adapted Wessman & Ricks Elation-Depression Scale; see WESSM 60):

On the average, how happy or unhappy did you feel today?

1. Extremely unhappy. Utterly depressed. Completely down.
2. Very unhappy. Depressed. Spirits very low.
3. Pretty unhappy. Somewhat 'blue'. Spirits down.
4. Mildly unhappy. Just a little low.
5. Barely unhappy. Just this side of neutral.
6. Barely happy. Just this side of neutral.
7. Mildly happy. Feeling fairly good and somewhat cheerful.
8. Pretty happy. Spirits high. Feeling good.
9. Very happy. Feeling really good. Elated.
10. Extremely happy. Feeling ecstatic, joyous, fantastic.

The scale was scored every evening before retiring during 3 weeks. The three weeks mean was used as happiness measure.

RELIABILITY:

VALIDITY: External congruent validity: in pilot study the happiness scale produced a much greater range of responding than did the original Wessman & Ricks scale. The scales intercorrelated +.93 (001)

DISTRIBUTION: positively skewed: 84% of mean happiness scores were above the midpoint
possible range: 1 (low) to 10 (high); actual range of means: 3.6 - 8.7; mean: 6.8; S.D. 1.15

SECOND INSTRUMENT: AFF 3.1: Repeated closed questions on overall hedonic level for the past day, scored every evening before retiring during 3 weeks:

- What percentage of the time you were awake today did you feel happy?
- What percentage of the time did you feel unhappy?
- What percentage of the time did you feel neutral (neither happy nor unhappy) ?

Ss were told that the three percentages should add up to equal 100%. The three week averages were used in the analysis.

RELIABILITY: Equivalence: % happy mood x % unhappy mood : $r_{pm}$ = -.67 (.01)
% happy mood x % neutral mood : $r_{pm}$ = -.72 (.01)
% unhappy mood x % neutral mood: $r_{pm}$ = -.02 (ns)

VALIDITY:

DISTRIBUTION: percentage of day in happy moods : mean: 52.9%, S.D.: 17.69%
percentage of day in unhappy moods: mean: 20.4%, S.D.: 10.51%
percentage of day in neutral moods: mean: 26.6%, S.D.: 14.92%

REMARKS: Regarding the correlations for the whole sample the separate correlations for males and females are sometimes a bit strange. We were not able to contact the author in order to obtain more information.

CORRELATES: Mood variability (A 2.1.4); Number of (un)happy moods per day / Affect balance (A 2.2.5); Gender (G 1.1); Hedonic level x hedonic level (H 1.2.2); various Value dimensions (V 1.1); Day of week (X 1); Special day (X 1)

CONCLUSION: Only a few values are related to happiness. The relationship between values and happiness may be higly culturally relative. The sex distinctions may be explained by differences in sex-role expectations. So happy females are concerned about others and social values, while happy males show a definite lack of concern for others.

AUTHOR: Fowler, F.J. & McCalla, M.E.

FOWLE 69

TITLE: Correlates of morale among aged in greater Boston.

SOURCE: Proceedings of the 77th Annual Convention, A.P.A., 1969, p. 733-734.

---

GOAL OF THE STUDY: Assessment of conditions that imfluence the morale of the aged.

REFERS TO: Theory of morale

TYPE OF STUDY: explanatory, explorative, special group, snapshot, non-experimantal

DATA GATHERING: Highly structured questionnaire administered at home

DATE OF DATA: 1965

POPULATION: Aged persons, Metropolitan Boston, U.S.A.

SAMPLE CONSTRUCTION: Probability area sample.
age 65+

NON-RESPONSE:

N: 1335

AUTHOR'S HAPPINESS LABEL: Morale

OUR CONCEPTUALIZATION: Hedonic level of affect

INSTRUMENT: AFF 1.1: Single closed question rated on a 4-point scale:
In general, how good would you say your spirits are these days - excellent, very good, fair or poor?

RELIABILITY:

VALIDITY:

DISTRIBUTION:

REMARKS:

CORRELATES: Age (A 3); Educational level (E 1.1.1); Foreign born (E 2.2); Reported health (H 2.1.2); Living arrangement (H 4.1); Family income (I 1.1); Number of social contacts (S 4.1.1)

CONCLUSION: It seems possible that people car tolerate some amount of basic problems but require a compensating number of fulfilled needs.

| | | |
|---|---|---|
| AUTHOR: | Gaitz, C.M. & Scott, J. | GAITZ 72 |
| TITLE: | Age and the measurement of mental health. | |
| SOURCE: | Journal of Health and Social Behavior, 1972, vol. 13, p. 55-67. | |

---

GOAL OF THE STUDY: Assessment of the influence of age on mental health

REFERS TO: Theory of mental health; Offer & Sabshin (1966)

TYPE OF STUDY: explanatory, explorative, special group, snapshot, non-experimental

DATA GATHERING: Structured interview

DATA OF DATA: Autumn, 1969

POPULATION: Adults, Houston, Texas, U.S.A.

SAMPLE CONSTRUCTION: Non-probability purposive quota sample stratified by age, sex, occupational skill level and ethnicity.
ethnicity: Anglo, Black and Mexican-American; as many males as females; as many low as high occupational skill levels; age 20+

NON-RESPONSE: 2%; aged Mexican-Americans of high socio-economic status only.

N: 1441

AUTHOR'S HAPPINESS LABEL: Psychological well-being

OUR CONCEPTUALIZATION: Hedonic level of affect (first instrument) and Happiness (second instrument)

FIRST INSTRUMENT: AFF 2.3: Index of closed questions on perceived occurrence of specific affects during the past few weeks (Bradburn Affect Balance Score; see BRADB 69).

Affect Balance Score = positive affect score - negative affect score + 5

RELIABILITY: equivalence:
- affect balance score x negative affect score : $r_{pm}$ = -.07 (.01)
- affect balance score x positive affect score : $r_{pm}$ = +.72 (.01)
- positive affect score x negative affect score: $r_{pm}$ = -.01 (ns)

VALIDITY:

DISTRIBUTION: positively skewed
possible range: 0 (low) to 10 (high); actual range: 0 (0.5%) to 10 (3.3%)

SECOND INSTRUMENT: COMP 1.1: Single closed question rated on a 3-point scale:

All things considered, how happy would you say you are right now - very happy, pretty happy, or not too happy?

RELIABILITY:

VALIDITY:

DISTRIBUTION: positively skewed: 43% very happy, 45% pretty happy, 12% not too happy

REMARKS:

CORRELATES: Age (A 3); Ethnicity (E 2.2); Gender (G 1.1); Hedonic level x happiness (H 1.2.1); Self-perceived health (H 2.1.2); Mental illness (H 2.3.1); Satisfaction with oneself (S 2.1.5); Occupational skill level (W 2.2)

CONCLUSION: Older people are inclined to report fewer feelings.
Bradburn's findings on the structure of happiness are confirmed.

AUTHOR: Garber, D.L. | GARBE 71

TITLE: Retired soldiers in second careers: self-assessed change, reference group salience, and psychological well-being.

SOURCE: Unpublished doctoral dissertation, 1971, University of Southern California.

---

GOAL OF THE STUDY: To investigate the relationship between the individual's experience of change in social environment in middle age and his level of psychological well-being among Army retirees.

REFERS TO: Theory of military retirement; Biderman & Sharp (1967a, 1967b, 1968)

TYPE OF STUDY: explanatory, testing, special group, snapshot, non-experimental

DATA GATHERING: Highly structured mailed questionnaire

DATE OF DATA: August, 1970

POPULATION: Middle-aged, presently employed army retirees, California, U.S.A.

SAMPLE CONSTRUCTION: Probability simple random sample of retired Army personnel residing in Los Angeles and Orange Counties.
Afterwards those Ss were selected who have had a military career of at least 10 years and are currently engaged in a civilian career.

NON-RESPONSE: 63%; 21% no return of questionnaire, 13% incomplete information, and 29% discarded

N: 362

AUTHOR'S HAPPINESS LABEL: Psychological well-being

OUR CONCEPTUALIZATION: Hedonic level of affect

INSTRUMENT: AFF 2.3: Index of closed questions on perceived occurrence of specific affects during the past few weeks (Bradburn Affect Balance Score; see BRADB 69).

Affect Balance Score = positive affect score - negative affect score + 5

RELIABILITY:

VALIDITY:

DISTRIBUTION: positively skewed
possible range: 1 (low) to 9 (high); actual range: 1 ($\pm$ 3.5%) to 9 ($\pm$ 10%); mean: 5.97; medium: 6.55

REMARKS:

CORRELATES: various factors concerning Retirement / Change of work (R 2.3 / W 2.3)

CONCLUSION: The nature of change an individual assesses upon retirement from the Army is related to his level of psychological well-being. Prestige continuity is a major factor related to a high level of well-being.
Also related to well-being is identification with the civilian community, while there is no evidence of such relationship between identification with the military and well-being.

AUTHOR: Garrity, T.F.

GARRI 73

TITLE: Social involvement and activeness as predictors of morale six months after first myocardinal infarction.

SOURCE: Social Science and Medicine, 1973, vol. 7, nr 3, p. 199-207.

---

GOAL OF THE STUDY: Testing the proposition that predictors of morale are the same for the experience of a heart attack as they are for the experience of aging.

REFERS TO: Theory of social involvement and morale; Rosen & Bibring (1966), Maddox (1963)

TYPE OF STUDY: explanatory, testing, special group, snapshot, non-experimental

DATA GATHERING: Structured interview in hospital, highly structured mailed questionnaire and content analysis of hospital records

DATE OF DATA: 1970

POPULATION: White males who had experienced a first heart attack, Durham, North Carolina, U.S.A.

SAMPLE CONSTRUCTION: Non-probability quota sample of patients from 3 hospitals.
respondents survived at least six months after their hospital discharge; age 37-74, mean age 54; 93% married

NON-RESPONSE: 20%

N: 56

AUTHOR'S HAPPINESS LABEL: Morale

OUR CONCEPTUALIZATION: Happiness

INSTRUMENT: COMP 1.1: Single closed question rated on an 11-point self-anchoring scale (based on Cantril; see CANTR 65).
Ladder rating, ranging from 'the happiest I could be' at the top, down to 'the saddest I could be' at the bottom.

RELIABILITY:

VALIDITY:

DISTRIBUTION:

REMARKS:

CORRELATES: Age (A 3); various indicators of Physical health (H 2.1); Leisure activity (L 3.3.1); Participation in informal sociability (S 4.1.2); Participation in community organizations (S 4.2); S.E.S. (S 5.1); Having gainful employment (W 2.1)

CONCLUSION: Not a high level of activity and social involvement, but the health perception of the heart patients is the strongest predictor of morale.

AUTHOR: Gillo, M.W. GILLO 73

TITLE: Studies on the nature of the relationships between job and life satisfactions: towards a comprehensive model.

SOURCE: Unpublished doctoral dissertation, 1973, University of Kansas, U.S.A.

---

GOAL OF THE STUDY: Review of the literature on job satisfaction, and identification of variables that predict overall work and leisure happiness as a multivariate criterion.

REFERS TO: Theory of job satisfaction; Quinm & Kahn (1967), Schwab & Cummings (1970)

TYPE OF STUDY: explanatory, explorative, special group, snapshot, non-experimental

DATA GATHERING: Highly structured mailed questionnaire administered at home

DATE OF DATA:

POPULATION: Workers of a utility union, Greater Kansas City area, U.S.A.

SAMPLE CONSTRUCTION: Probability cluster sample of workers, drawn from the ranks of a large utility union.
Union members in three rather different plants: a manufacturing plant with assembly line operations, a public service plant, and an electronic equipment maintenance and installation plant.
both males and females

NON-RESPONSE: 73%, no return of mailed questionnaire
unaffected by age, sex, Local's membership, and length of employment

N: 213

AUTHOR'S HAPPINESS LABEL: Overall happiness

OUR CONCEPTUALIZATION: Happiness

INSTRUMENT: HAPP 1.1: Single closed question rated on an 11-point self-anchoring scale (based on Cantril; see CANTR 65):

Consider the ladder. It has 11 steps, from 0 to 10. Think of this ladder as representing different levels of happiness. Step 0 would stand for the least happy you could ever be. Step 10 would stand for the most happy you could ever be. Taking everything together, where on this ladder do you stand regarding your happiness?

RELIABILITY:

VALIDITY:

DISTRIBUTION: possible range = 0 (low) to 10 (high); S.D. = 1.99

REMARKS:

CORRELATES: Happiness with leisure time activities (S 1.1.1); Happiness with job (S 1.9.1)

CONCLUSION: Job related variables are more important to satisfaction with life than leisure variables, so satisfaction and/or dissatisfaction of a person with respect to his working conditions are most central to his overall happiness.

| | |
|---|---|
| AUTHOR: | Glenn, N.D. — GLENN 75A/1-3 |
| TITLE: | Psychological well-being in the postparental stage: Some evidence from national surveys. |
| SOURCE: | Journal of Marriage and the Family, 1975, vol. 37, nr 1, P 105-110. |

| | |
|---|---|
| GOAL OF THE STUDY: | A cross-sectional comparison of persons in the parental and postparental stage on reported psychological well-being. |
| REFERS TO: | Theory of the post-parental stage ; Deutscher (1964) |
| TYPE OF STUDY: | explanatory, testing, special group, snapshot, non-experimental |
| DATA GATHERING: | Highly structured questionnaires |
| DATE OF DATA: | 1963/1966 (study 1), 1972/1973 ( study 2), 1971 (study 3) |
| POPULATION: | Non-institutionalized middle-aged females, U.S.A. |
| SAMPLE CONSTRUCTION: | Pooling of 3 Gallup surveys (study 1), Pooling of 2 NORC surveys (study 2), Rooper survey (study 3)<br>age 40-59 (study 1 and 2), age 35 - 64 (study 3) |
| NON-RESPONSE: | |
| N: | 902 (study 1), 425 (study 2), 319 (study 3) |
| AUTHOR'S HAPPINESS LABEL: | Psychological well-being |
| OUR CONCEPTUALIZATION: | Happiness |
| INSTRUMENTS: | study 1: HAPP 1.1: Single closed question rated on a 3-point scale:<br>In general, how happy would you say you are - very happy, fairly happy or not too happy?<br><br>study 2: HAPP 1.1: Single closed question using the term 'happiness', rated on a 3-point scale (see BRADB 69).<br><br>study 3: COMP 1.1: Single closed question rated on a 3-point scale:<br>Thinking of your life as you live it day by day, which of these statements best expresses the way you feel?<br>1. Mostly I enjoy life, although at times I just go through the days.<br>2. Half of the time I enjoy life, and half of the time I just go through the days.<br>3. Sometimes I enjoy life, but most of the time I just go through the days. |
| RELIABILITY: | |
| VALIDITY: | |
| DISTRIBUTION: | study 1: 52% very happy; study 2: 40% very happy; study 3: 82% mostly enjoys life |
| REMARKS: | Gammas (G') were computed by us on the basis of the proportions 'very happy' and 'mostly enjoys life' answers. |
| CORRELATES: | Post-parental stage (F 1.2.3, H 4.1) |
| CONCLUSION: | Children leaving home seems to have a moderate positive effect on the psychological well-being of females. |

AUTHOR: Glenn, N.D. | GLENN 75B

TITLE: The contribution of marriage to the psychological well-being of males and females.

SOURCE: Journal of Marriage and the Family, 1975, vol. 37, nr 3, p. 594-601.

---

GOAL OF THE STUDY: To investigate the relationship of marital happiness and psychological well-being for males and females.

REFERS TO: Theory of marriage and psychological well-being; Bernard (1972), Bradburn (1969)

TYPE OF STUDY: explanatory, testing, national population, snapshot, non-experimental.

DATA GATHERING: Highly structured questionnaire

DATE OF DATA: 1972-1974

POPULATION: National adult population, U.S.A.

SAMPLE CONSTRUCTION: Combined data from 3 U.S. General Surveys conducted by the National Opinion Research Center in 1972, 1973 and 1974
1841 males, 2012 females; age 18+; blacks excluded

NON-RESPONSE:

N: 3853

AUTHOR'S HAPPINESS LABEL: Happiness

OUR CONCEPTUALIZATION: Happiness

INSTRUMENT: HAPP 1.1: Single closed question using the term 'happiness', rated on a 3-point scale (see BRADB 69).

RELIABILITY:

VALIDITY:

DISTRIBUTION: 37% very happy, 63% pretty happy or not too happy

REMARKS: Gammas (G') were computed by us on the basis of the proportions 'very happy' answers.
The number of widowed males of age 18-39 and 40-59, and the number of widowed females of age 18-39 were too small to make computations reliable.

CORRELATES: Age (A 3); Gender (G 1.1); various Marital status comparisons (M 1); Marital happiness (S 1.7.2)

CONCLUSION: Contemporary American marriage, in spite of its limitations, is typically beneficial to both husbands and wives. It is likely that women, as a whole, exceed men in both the stress and the satisfaction derived from marriage.

AUTHOR: González, J.R. GONZA 67

TITLE: Study of student teachers' life adjustment.

SOURCE: Unpublished doctoral dissertation, 1967, University of North Carolina, Chapel Hill, U.S.A.

---

GOAL OF THE STUDY: To explore feelings of adjustment and methods of handling emotional problems among students teachers.

REFERS TO: Theory of mental health; Gurin et al. (1960)

TYPE OF STUDY: explanatory, explorative, special group, snapshot, non-experimental

DATA GATHERING: Structured interview using open-ended questions and highly structured questionnaire

DATE OF DATA: Spring, 1967

POPULATION: Students teachers, Chapel Hill, U.S.A.

SAMPLE CONSTRUCTION: Probability sample of student teachers enrolled in the student teaching program in the School of Education at the University of California, proportionally stratified by teaching level.

NON-RESPONSE:

N: 75

AUTHOR'S HAPPINESS LABEL: Happiness

OUR CONCEPTUALIZATION: Happiness

INSTRUMENT: HAPP 1.1: Single closed question using the term 'happiness', rated on a 3-point scale (see GURIN 60).

RELIABILITY:

VALIDITY:

DISTRIBUTION: positively skewed: 47% very happy, 49% pretty happy, 4% not too happy

REMARKS:

CORRELATES: Teaching level (E 1.2.3); Subject matter majors (E 1.3); Gender (G 1.1); Expected future happiness (H 1.6.2); Mental health (H 2.3.1); Readiness for self-referral (H 2.6); Extent of worries (P 5.2.1)

CONCLUSION: Unhappiness and worrying are similar in reflecting a high number of frustrating and unhappy experiences and particular kinds of stresses, but they differ in that unhappiness also reflects an absence of positive areas of satisfaction in life, whereas worrying does not seem to imply such a lack.

AUTHOR: Gordon, F.E. & Hall, D.T.

GORDO 74

TITLE: Self image and stereotypes of feminity; their relationship to women's role conflicts and coping.

SOURCE: Journal of Applied Psychology, 1974, vol. 59, nr 2, p. 241-243.

---

GOAL OF THE STUDY: To explore the relationships of types of role conflicts and methods of coping behavior to (a) the woman's self image, (b) her image of a feminine woman, and (c) her perception of the male image of a feminine woman.

REFERS TO: Theory of role conflict; Hall & Lawler (1971)

TYPE OF STUDY: explanatory, explorative, special group, snapshot, non-experimental

DATA GATHERING: Highly structured mailed questionnaire

DATE OF DATA: 1971

POPULATION: Married female graduates of the liberal arts college, University of Connecticut, U.S.A.

SAMPLE CONSTRUCTION: Probability cluster sample selected from five graduating classes.

NON-RESPONSE: 49%

N: 229

AUTHOR'S HAPPINESS LABEL: Happiness

OUR CONCEPTUALIZATION: Happiness

INSTRUMENT: HAPP 1.1: Single closed question rated on a 5-point scale ranging from 'very unhappy' to 'very happy':

In general, how happy would you say you are?

RELIABILITY:

VALIDITY:

DISTRIBUTION:

REMARKS:

CORRELATES: Emotionality (A 2.1.3); Sex-role attitudes (G 1.2); Content of real self-image (S 2.2.1)

CONCLUSION:

| | |
|---|---|
| AUTHOR: | Gorman, B.S. — GORMA 71 |
| TITLE: | A multivariate study of the relationship of cognitive control and cognitive style principles to reported daily mood experiences. |
| SOURCE: | Unpublished doctoral dissertation, 1971, the City University of New York, U.S.A. |

---

| | |
|---|---|
| GOAL OF THE STUDY: | Exploration of the relationship of cognitive control and cognitive style variables to subjective mood reports. |
| REFERS TO: | Theories of cognition and affect; Gardner et al. (1959), Witkin et al. (1954, 1962), Wessman & Ricks (1966) |
| TYPE OF STUDY: | explanatory, explorative, special group, snapshot, non-experimental |
| DATA GATHERING: | Administration of highly structured questionnaire in classroom situation and daily records administered at home during 28 days |
| DATE OF DATA: | Summer, 1970 |
| POPULATION: | Undergraduate students, Nassau Community College, U.S.A. |
| SAMPLE CONSTRUCTION: | Non-probability chunk sample using volunteering undergraduate students enrolled in an abnormal psychology course.<br>20 males, 47 females; age 18-40, median age 20; subjects from solidly middle-class backgrounds. |
| NON-RESPONSE: | 4%; 3% refusal, 1% incomplete information |
| N: | 67 |
| AUTHOR'S HAPPINESS LABEL: | Mood (first instrument) and Happiness (second instrument) |
| OUR CONCEPTUALIZATION: | Hedonic level of affect (first instrument) and Happiness (second instrument) |
| FIRST INSTRUMENT: | AFF 3.1: Repeated single closed question on overall hedonic level for the past day, rated on a 10-point scale (Wessman & Ricks Elation - Depression Scale; see WESSM 60).<br>The scale was scored every night for highest, lowest and average mood level ('your overall summary of the day') during 28 consecutive days. The mean daily average was used as happiness measure here. |
| RELIABILITY: | |
| VALIDITY: | |
| DISTRIBUTION: | possible range: 0-9; mean: 5.41; S.D.: .71 |
| SECOND INSTRUMENT: | HAPP 3.1: Single closed question on personal situation as compared with best and worst possible life, rated on an 11-point self-anchoring scale (Cantril Present Personal rating; see CANTR 65). |
| RELIABILITY: | |
| VALIDITY: | |
| DISTRIBUTION: | possible range: 0-10; mean: 6.37; S.D.: 1.67 |
| REMARKS: | see also GORMA 74 |
| CORRELATES: | various indicators concerning Affect (A 2.2); various Cognitive characteristics (C 1); Pressure of academic work (E 1.3); Gender (G 1.1); Hedonic level x happiness (H 1.2.1); various factors concerning Past / Future happiness (H 1.4.1, H 1.5, H 1.6); Self-perceived health (H 2.1.2); various Life style characteristics (L 3.1.2, L 3.2); various Personality characteristics (P 1); Temporal orientation (T 1.3) |
| CONCLUSION: | Happier subjects are more extrovert, more optimistic and have a more developed sense of self-confidence and efficacy. |

AUTHOR: Gorman, B.S. & Wessman, A.E.

GORMA 74

TITLE: The relationship of cognitive styles and moods.

SOURCE: Journal of Clinical Psychology, 1974, vol. 30, p. 18-25.

---

GOAL OF THE STUDY: Exploration of the relationship of cognitive control and cognitive style variables to subjective mood reports.

REFERS TO: Theories of cognition and affect; Cantril (1965), Wessman & Ricks (1966)

TYPE OF STUDY: explanatory, explorative, special group, snapshot, non-experimental

DATA GATHERING: Administration of highly structured questionnaire in classroom situation and daily records administered at home during 28 days

DATE OF DATA: Summer, 1970

POPULATION: Undergraduate students, Nassau Community College, U.S.A.

SAMPLE CONSTRUCTION: Non-probability chunk sample, using paid volunteering undergraduate students enrolled in an abnormal psychology course (see GORMA 71).
age 18 - 40

NON-RESPONSE: 4%; 3% refusal, 1% incomplete information

N: 67

AUTHOR'S HAPPINESS LABEL: Mood (first instrument) and happiness (second instrument)

OUR CONCEPTUALIZATION: Hedonic level of affect (first instrument) and happiness (second instrument)

INSTRUMENTS: See GORMA 71

REMARKS: This publication provides information already reported in an other publication of Gorman: see GORMA 71

| | |
|---|---|
| AUTHOR: | Graney, M.J. — GRANE 73A |
| TITLE: | The Affect Balance Scale and old age. |
| SOURCE: | Paper presented at the Annual Meeting of the Midwest Sociological Society, April 26, 1973, Milwaukee, Wisconsin. |

---

GOAL OF THE STUDY: To extend the use of the Affect Balance Scale to the study of old age and aging.

REFERS TO: Happiness research; Bradburn & Caplovitz (1965), Phillips (1967)

TYPE OF STUDY: explanatory, explorative, special group, longitudinal, non-experimental

DATA GATHERING: Structured interview at home

DATE OF DATA: 1967 - 1971

POPULATION: Aged female public housing residents, U.S.A.

SAMPLE CONSTRUCTION: Probability systematic random sample of residents of public housing for the elderly from the rosters of a metropolitan housing and redevelopment authority.
All women were initially in good health, able to keep house, and lived alone.
age 62 - 89

NON-RESPONSE: 27%; 24% unattainable, 3% incomplete

N: 44

AUTHOR'S HAPPINESS LABEL: Happiness

OUR CONCEPTUALIZATION: Hedonic level of affect

INSTRUMENT: AFF 2.3: Index of closed questions on perceived occurrence of specific affects during the past few weeks (Bradburn Affect Balance Score; see BRADB 69).

RELIABILITY:

VALIDITY:

DISTRIBUTION: slightly positively skewed: 30% happy, 45% neutral, 25% unhappy (in 1971)

REMARKS:

CORRELATES: Age (A 3); Physical ability (H 2.1.4 ); Gains in social status (L 1.2); Orientation towards social participation (S 4.5)

CONCLUSION:

| | |
|---|---|
| AUTHOR: | Graney, M.J. & Graney, E.E. |
| TITLE: | Scaling adjustment in older people. |
| SOURCE: | International Journal of Aging and Human Development, 1973, vol. 4, nr 4, p. 351-359. |

GRANE 73B

---

| | |
|---|---|
| GOAL OF THE STUDY: | To provide an empirical example of the usefulness of distinct evaluation of happiness and personal adjustment. |
| REFERS TO: | Theory of attitudes and adjustment of aged people; Landis (1940) |
| TYPE OF STUDY: | explanatory, testing, special group, longitudinal, non-experimental |
| DATA GATHERING: | Structured interview |
| DATE OF DATA: | 1967 - 1971 |
| POPULATION: | Aged female public housing residents, U.S.A. |
| SAMPLE CONSTRUCTION: | Probability systematic random sample.<br>Graney (1973) sample (see GRANE 73A) |
| NON-RESPONSE: | 27%; 24% unattainable, 3% incomplete |
| N: | 44 |
| AUTHOR'S HAPPINESS LABEL: | Happiness |
| OUR CONCEPTUALIZATION: | Hedonic level of affect |
| INSTRUMENT: | AFF 2.3: Index of closed questions on perceived occurrence of specific affects during the past few weeks (Bradburn Affect Balance Score; see BRADB 69). |
| RELIABILITY: | |
| VALIDITY: | |
| DISTRIBUTION: | slightly positively skewed: 30% happy, 45% neutral, 25% unhappy (in 1971) |
| REMARKS: | |
| CORRELATES: | Personal adjustment (S 4.7) |
| CONCLUSION: | There is empirical evidence for the distinction between personal adjustment and happiness. |

GRANE 75

AUTHOR: Graney, M.J.

TITLE: Happiness and social participation in aging.

SOURCE: Journal of Gerontology, 1975, vol. 30, nr 6, p. 701-706.

---

GOAL OF THE STUDY: To examine happiness as a criterion of well-being in analysis of longitudinal data on social activities of elderly women.

REFERS TO: Happiness research; Morgan (1937), Cavan et al. (1949)

TYPE OF STUDY: explanatory, explorative, special group, longitudinal, non-experimental

DATA GATHERING: Structured interview at home

DATE OF DATA: 1967 - 1971

POPULATION: Aged female public housing residents, U.S.A.

SAMPLE CONSTRUCTION: Probability systematic random sample.
Graney (1973) sample (see GRANE 73A).

NON-RESPONSE: 27%; 24% unattainable, 3% incomplete

N: 44

AUTHOR'S HAPPINESS LABEL: Happiness

OUR CONCEPTUALIZATION: Hedonic level of affect

INSTRUMENT: AFF 2.3: Index of closed questions on perceived occurrence of specific affects during the past few weeks (Bradburn Affect Balance Score; see BRADB 69).

RELIABILITY:

VALIDITY:

DISTRIBUTION: slightly positively skewed: 30% happy, 45% neutral, 25% unhappy (in 1971)

REMARKS:

CORRELATES: various factors concerning Use of leisure time (L 3.3); Attending religious services (R 1.3)

CONCLUSION: Happiness and social participation activities are positively related in old age and in aging. Increases in activity over time were often related to happiness, and declines in activity were related to unhappiness. The association between changes in levels of activity over time and happiness was stronger among the oldest elderly.

AUTHOR: Greenhaus, J.H.

GREEN 74

TITLE: Career salience as a moderator of the relationship between satisfaction with occupational preference and satisfaction with life in general.

SOURCE: Journal of Psychology, 1974, vol. 86, p. 53-55.

---

GOAL OF THE STUDY: Test of the hypothesis that the correlation between the satisfaction with an occupational preference and the satisfaction with life in general is moderated by career salience.

REFERS TO: Theory of career salience; George (1965), Greenhaus (1973)

TYPE OF STUDY: explanatory, testing, special group, snapshot, non-experimental

DATA GATHERING: Highly structured questionnaire administered in classroom setting

DATE OF DATA:

POPULATION: Undergraduates, U.S.A.

SAMPLE CONSTRUCTION: Non-probability chunk sample of undergraduates at two eastern colleges.

NON-RESPONSE:

N: 203

AUTHOR'S HAPPINESS LABEL: Satisfaction with life in general

OUR CONCEPTUALIZATION: Happiness

INSTRUMENT: COMP 1.2: Index of closed questions:

1. Taking all aspects of yourself and your life into account, which of the following best describes your own feelings of satisfaction with your life?
   - I am extremely satisfied with my life
   - I am satisfied with my life
   - I am somewhat satisfied with my life
   - I am only slightly satisfied with my life
   - I am not at all satisfied with my life
2. In very general terms, about what proportion of the time do you feel satisfied with your life?
   all of the time / most of the time / some of the time / rarely / never

RELIABILITY:

VALIDITY:

DISTRIBUTION:

REMARKS: Career salience was measured by 3 factorially derived dimensions: 1. relative priority of work and a career compared to other sources of life satisfaction, 2. general attitudes towards work, 3. concern for career advancement and planning.

CORRELATES: Satisfaction with occupational preference (S 1.10)

CONCLUSION: One dimension of career salience - career advancement and planning - stands out as the most effective moderator of the relationship between satisfaction with occupational preference and satisfaction with life in general for both males and females.

AUTHOR: Gubrium, J.F.

GUBRI 74

TITLE: Marital desolation and the evaluation of everyday life in old age.

SOURCE: Journal of Marriage and the Family, February, 1974, p. 107-113.

---

GOAL OF THE STUDY: To consider the impact of continuity versus discontinuity in marital status on the evaluation of everyday life in old age.

REFERS TO: Theory of widowhood; Townsend (1957), Tunstall (1966)

TYPE OF STUDY: explanatory, testing, special group, snapshot, non-experimental

DATA GATHERING: Structured interview

DATE OF DATA:

POPULATION: Aged persons, Detroit, U.S.A.

SAMPLE CONSTRUCTION: Probability systematic random sample stratified by 3 types of housing:
- large multiple-unit dwellings exclusively housing aged persons, none of which were considering nursing or convalescent homes
- appartment and high-rise building with mixed age groups
- housing consisting of single homes

59 married, 22 single, 15 divorced, 114 widowed; age 60 - 90; Ss' demographic characteristics were similar to that of the U.S.A. population of aged persons.

N: 210

AUTHOR'S HAPPINESS LABEL: Life satisfaction (first instrument) and Happiness (second instrument)

OUR CONCEPTUALIZATION: Happiness

FIRST INSTRUMENT: HAPP 2.1: Single closed questions rated on a 3-point scale:

On the whole, how satisfied would you say you are with your way of life today?
Would you say: very satisfied, fairly satisfied, or not satisfied?

RELIABILITY:

VALIDITY:

DISTRIBUTION: positively skewed: 38% very satisfied, 51% fairly satisfied, 11% not satisfied

SECOND INSTRUMENT: HAPP 1.1: Single closed question rated on a 3-point scale:

All in all, how much unhappiness would you say you find in life today?
Would you say: almost none, some unhappiness, or great unhappiness

RELIABITLIY:

VALIDITY:

DISTRIBUTION: positively skewed: 9% great unhappiness, 38% some unhappiness, 53% almost none

REMARKS: In Part III the + and - values of the associations between unhappiness (second instrument) and the variables mentioned are turned to indicate the direction of the associations with happiness.

CORRELATES: various Marital status comparisons (M 1)

CONCLUSION: Single and married persons, the former being isolates but not desolates, both tend to be less negative in their evaluations of everyday life than widowed and divorced persons. Only the latter two would be categorized as desolate. So it may be useful to make a distinction between isolation and desolation.

AUTHOR: Gurin, G., Veroff, J. & Feld, S.

GURIN 60

TITLE: Americans view their mental health. A nation wide interview survey.

SOURCE: New York, 1960, Basic Books Inc.

---

GOAL OF THE STUDY: Assessment of how people feel they have adjusted to life and how they cope with their problems.

REFERS TO: Theory of mental health; Jahoda (1958)

TYPE OF STUDY: explanatory, explorative, national population, snapshot, non-experimental

DATA GATHERING: Lengthy structured interviews administered at home

DATE OF DATA: Spring, 1957

POPULATION: Non-institutionalized adults, U.S.A.

SAMPLE CONSTRUCTION: Probability multi-stage area sample.
1077 males, 1383 females; age 21+; people living in private households only; transients and all individuals in hospitals, prisons or other institutions were excluded.

NON-RESPONSE: 13%; 5% not at home, 8% refusals

N: 2460

AUTHOR'S HAPPINESS LABEL: Happiness

OUR CONCEPTUALIZATION: Happiness

INSTRUMENT: HAPP 1.1: Single closed question rated on a 3-point scale:

Taking all things together, how would you say things are these days - would you say you're very happy, pretty happy or not too happy these days?

RELIABILITY:

VALIDITY:

DISTRIBUTION: positively skewed: 35% very happy, 54% pretty happy, 11% not too happy

REMARKS: Gammas concerning a number of variables are computed by us on the basis of data not presented in the book but in a 'Tabular Supplement' (available at the authors on request).

CORRELATES: Age (A 3); Educational level (E 1.1.1); Ethnicity (E 2.2); Gender (G 1.1); Broken home background (F 1.1.2); Family size (F 1.2.2); Expected future happiness (H 1.6.2); Perceived sources of happiness (H 1.8); Readiness for self-referral (H 2.6); Income (I 1.1); Community size (L 4.1); Region (L 4.3); various Marital status comparisons (M 1); Being a wife of a skilled worker (M 2.3); Extent of worries (P 5.2.1); Religious denomination (R 1.2); Church attendance (R 1.3); Marital happiness (S 1.7.2); Occupation (W 2.2)

CONCLUSION: In explaining varying patterns of adjustment, it is important to make a distinction between the meaning of a demographic variable in terms of gratification-potential and its meaning in terms of involvement and aspirations.
First of all, demographic variables seem to be important when they differentiate population subgroups in terms of the potential rewards and gratifications derived from life. Secondly, they are important when they represent differences in the expectations and demands the subgroup members make of themselves and life, or differences in introspectiveness and tendencies towards a psychological view of life and the problems it presents.

AUTHOR: Gurman, A.S. | GURMA 72

TITLE: Therapists' mood patterns and therapeutic facilitativeness.

SOURCE: Journal of Counseling Psychology, 1972, vol. 19, nr 2, p. 169-170.

---

**GOAL OF THE STUDY:** To examine the relationships between therapeutic facilitativeness and therapists' mood patterns.

REFERS TO: Theory of quality of therapeutic relationships; Truax & Carkhuff (1967), Bergin & Solomon (1970)

**TYPE OF STUDY:** explanatory, testing, special group, snapshot, non-experimental

**DATA GATHERING:** Content analysis of audiotape recordings of individual psychotherapy sessions, and structured questionnaire

**DATE OF DATA:** 1970

POPULATION: Therapists, Columbia University, U.S.A.

**SAMPLE CONSTRUCTION:** Non-probability chunk sample of postinternship doctoral students in clinical and counseling psychology.
7 males, 5 females; mean age 29.3

**NON-RESPONSE:** none

N: 12

**AUTHOR'S HAPPINESS LABEL:** Elation

**OUR CONCEPTUALIZATION:** Hedonic level of affect

**INSTRUMENT:** AFF 3.1: Repeated closed question on overall hedonic level for the past day, rated on a 10-point scale (Wessman & Ricks Elation - Depression Scale; see WESSM 60).

The therapists completed the scale for 14 consecutive nights, reporting the average mood level experienced during the past day.

RELIABILITY:

VALIDITY:

DISTRIBUTION:

REMARKS:

CORRELATES: Therapist's functioning (P 1.8.1)

CONCLUSION: The more facilitative therapists are happier.

AUTHOR: Haavio-Mannila, E. | HAAVI 71

TITLE: Satisfaction with family, work, leisure and life among men and women.

SOURCE: Human Relations, 1971, vol. 24, nr 6, p. 585-601.

---

GOAL OF THE STUDY: Examination of the satisfaction-value of three major institutions (work, family and leisure) for men and women.

REFERS TO: Happiness research; Bradburn & Caplovitz (1965)

TYPE OF STUDY: explanatory, explorative, national population, snapshot, non-experimental

DATA GATHERING: Structured interview

DATE OF DATA: Spring - summer, 1966

POPULATION: Persons of age 15 - 64, Finland

SAMPLE CONSTRUCTION: Probability samples in Helsinki and in 5 Finnish rural communes.
Helsinki : 229 males, 215 females
rural communes: 251 males, 253 females

NON-RESPONSE:

N: 948

AUTHOR'S HAPPINESS LABEL: Overall life satisfaction

OUR CONCEPTUALIZATION: Happiness

INSTRUMENT: HAPP 2.1: Single closed question rated on a 4-point scale ranging from 'very satisfied' to 'very unsatisfied'.

RELIABILITY:

VALIDITY:

DISTRIBUTION: positively skewed: 72% very satisfied, 22% fairly satisfied, 5% not satisfied

REMARKS:

CORRELATES: Gender (G 1.1); Anxiety (H 2.2); Urban setting (L 4.2); Not married vs married (M 1.5); various Domainsatisfactions (S 1); Employed status (W 2.1); Social stratum (W 2.4); Reasons for employment (W 2.9)

CONCLUSION: The most important social institution for central life satisfaction is the family; particularly for low S.E.S. groups. Upper status people rely on a wider range of institutions.

AUTHOR: Hacker, S.L. & Gaitz, C.M.

HACKE 69

TITLE: The moral career of the elderly mental patient.

SOURCE: The Gerontologist, 1969, vol. 9, p. 120-127.

---

**GOAL OF THE STUDY:** Assessment of the key elements of the moral career of the elderly mental patient.

REFERS TO: Theory of hospitalization of the mental patient; Goffman (1959)

TYPE OF STUDY: explanatory, explorative, special group, snapshot, non-experimental

**DATA GATHERING:** Interview using direct open-ended questions, spaced one year apart.

**DATE OF DATA:** 1966

POPULATION: Aged mental patients, U.S.A.

**SAMPLE CONSTRUCTION:** Non-probability accidental sample, using patients in a psychiatric screeningward, 1 year after entrance.
18 Ss in state hospital, 18 Ss released (13 had been in state hospital)

**NON-RESPONSE:** 66% drop-outs: 33% dead, 17% could not be located, 16% incoherent or refusal

N: 36

**AUTHOR'S HAPPINESS LABEL:** Psychological well-being

**OUR CONCEPTUALIZATION:** Hedonic level of affect

INSTRUMENT: AFF 2.3: Index of closed questions on perceived occurrence of specific affects over the last period (adapted Bradburn & Caplovitz Affect Balance Score; see BRADB 65):

Ss were asked if they had recently felt lonely, pleased at some accomplishment, upset at some criticism, proud, depressed, restless, and so on. No further information was offered.

RELIABILITY:

VALIDITY:

DISTRIBUTION:

REMARKS:

CORRELATES: Mental illness (H 2.3.3)

CONCLUSION: Ex-patients feel better than in-patients. This difference is probably due to the environment the subject lives in rather than to psychiatric disorders.

AUTHOR: Hall, J.

HALL 73

TITLE: Measuring the quality of life using sample surveys.

SOURCE: Stöber, J. et al.: 'Technology assessment and the quality of life', Amsterdam, Elsevier, 1973.

---

GOAL OF THE STUDY: Finding social indicators for measuring the quality of life.

REFERS TO: Happiness research; Bradburn (1969), Campbell & Converse (1970)

TYPE OF STUDY: explanatory, explorative, local population, snapshot, non-experimental

DATA GATHERING: Questionning by means of a highly structured questionnaire containing direct closed questions

DATE OF DATA: October - November, 1971

POPULATION: Adult population of 8 major British conurbations

SAMPLE CONSTRUCTION: Non-probability quota sample.

NON-RESPONSE:

N: 593

AUTHOR'S HAPPINESS LABEL: Satisfaction with life as a whole

OUR CONCEPTUALIZATION: Happiness

INSTRUMENT: HAPP 2.1: Single closed question rated on a 7-point self-anchoring scale ranging from 'completely dissatisfied' to 'completely satisfied' (adapted Cantril Satisfaction with Life rating; see CANTR 65).

RELIABILITY:

VALIDITY:

DISTRIBUTION:

REMARKS:

CORRELATES: various Domainsatisfactions (S 1)

CONCLUSION:

AUTHOR: Harder, J.M. | HARDE 69

TITLE: Self-actualization, mood, and personality adjustment in married women.

SOURCE: Unpublished doctoral dissertation, 1969, Teachers College, Columbia University, U.S.A.

---

GOAL OF THE STUDY: Attempt to improve the measurement of self-actualization, and assessment of relationships between self-actualization measures and mood.

REFERS TO: Theory of self-actualization; Cofer & Appley (1964), Maslow (1954), Fromm (1955)

TYPE OF STUDY: explanatory, explorative, special group, snapshot, non-experimental

DATA GATHERING: Judge ratings, structured interview in test situation, and highly structured questionnaire administered at home during 3 weeks.

DATE OF DATA:

POPULATION: Married females, U.S.A.

SAMPLE CONSTRUCTION: Non-probability purposive sample by expert choice of married females, manifesting varying degrees of self-actualization.
Of the 239 females who were rated, the 62 females rated by the most reliable judges were used in the analysis.
age 29 - 69, mean age 45; 16% had never attended college, 32% some college, 52% at least one college degree; 71% one or two children

NON-RESPONSE:

N: 62

AUTHOR'S HAPPINESS LABEL: Happiness (first instrument) and mood (second instrument)

OUR CONCEPTUALIZATION: Hedonic level of affect

FIRST INSTRUMENT: AFF 2.1: Single closed question on perceived overall hedonic level during the past year, rated on a 10-point scale (Wessman & Ricks Elation - Depression Scale; see WESSM 60):

Ss were asked: 'In thinking over the past year, indicate how elated or depressed, happy or unhappy you have felt'.

RELIABILITY:

VALIDITY:

DISTRIBUTION: positively skewed; possible range: 0-9; mean: 5.6; median: 6.3; S.D.: 1.1

SECOND INSTRUMENT: AFF 3.1: Repeated single closed question on overall hedonic level for the past day, rated on a 10-point scale (Wessman & Ricks Elation - Depression Scale; see WESSM 60).

The scale was scored at the end of each day during three weeks for the 'highest', the 'lowest' and the 'average mood' (how you felt most of the time during the day).

The three weeks mean of daily averages was used as happiness measure here.

RELIABILITY:

VALIDITY:

DISTRIBUTION: possible range: 0 - 9
average mood: actual range: 4.4 - 7.4; mean: 5.6; S.D.: .65
peak mood : actual range: 4.9 - 8.1; mean: 6.4; S.D.: .88
through mood: actual range: 2.3 - 7.2; mean: 4.7; S.D.: .88

REMARKS:

CORRELATES: various Wessman & Ricks Personal feeling scales (A 2.2); Fullness of life (A 2.2.7); Hedonic level x hedonic level (H 1.2.2); Anxiety (H 2.2); Neuroticism (H 2.3.2); various Personality characteristics (P 1); Satisfaction with role (S 1.9.1); Time competence (T 1.1)

CONCLUSION: There is some evidence that self-actualization in women is positively related to mood level.

AUTHOR: Heeren, S.D.

HEERE 69

TITLE: Entrepreneurial vs bureaucratic fathers as related to family structure, happiness and two measures of independence.

SOURCE: Unpublished doctoral dissertation, 1969, University of Kansas, U.S.A.

---

GOAL OF THE STUDY: To test the effects of the father's work setting (entrepreneurial or bureaucratic) and childrearing practices on the independence of the children.

REFERS TO: Theory of socialization; Marcuse (1963), Bronfenbrenner (1967)

TYPE OF STUDY: explanatory, testing, special group, snapshot, non-experimental

DATA GATHERING: Highly structured questionnaire, filled out within a week

DATE OF DATA: ± 1967

POPULATION: Male undergraduates, University of Kansas, U.S.A.

SAMPLE CONSTRUCTION: Non-probability chunk sample of students enrolled in the introductory psychology class.

NON-RESPONSE: 5% incomplete information

N: 103

AUTHOR'S HAPPINESS LABEL: Happiness

OUR CONCEPTUALIZATION: Happiness

INSTRUMENT: HAPP 1.1: Single closed question, rated on a 9-point scale:

How happy would you say your life is in general?

| 1 | 2 | 3 | 4 | 5 | 6 | 7 | 8 | 9 |
|---|---|---|---|---|---|---|---|---|
| very unhappy | | | | neither happy nor unhappy | | | | very happy |

RELIABILITY:

VALIDITY:

DISTRIBUTION:

REMARKS:

CORRELATES: Age (A 3); Stage of study (E 1.2.3); various indicators of Freedom in youth (F 2.1); various characteristics of Family of origin (F 1.1); Size of home town (L 4.1); Living in an urban area (L 4.2); Other-directedness (P 1.1); Independence of judgment (P 1.1); Need for social approval (P 1.5.2)

CONCLUSION: Happiness is being allowed to develop relatively unrestricted by confident parents who provide loving support and enjoy each other and their marriage.
Other-directedness is related to the expression of less happiness with life in general.

AUTHOR: Henley, B. & Davis, M.S.

HENLE 67

TITLE: Satisfaction and dissatisfaction: A study of the chronically-ill aged patient.

SOURCE: Journal of Health and Social Behavior, 1967, vol. 8, p. 65-75.

---

GOAL OF THE STUDY: Exploration of the relationships between one's global perception of satisfaction and a variety of subjective and objective aspects of the life situation.

REFERS TO: Theory of adaptation to old age; Cavan et al .(1949), Cumming & Henry (1961)

TYPE OF STUDY: explanatory, testing, special group, longitudinal, non-experimental

DATA GATHERING: Structured interview at clinic or at home

DATE OF DATA: 1959

POPULATION: Aged chronically-ill patients, U.S.A.

SAMPLE CONSTRUCTION: Probability sample out of aged chronically-ill attendants of a medical clinic.
predominantly females; European-born or first generation American; white population; low income; average of three chronic illnesses; age 60+

NON-RESPONSE: 24% not available because of death, mental deterioration, unknown address or refusal; unaffected by age, marital status, religion and place of birth; overrepresentation of males

N: 167

AUTHOR'S HAPPINESS LABEL: General satisfaction

OUR CONCEPTUALIZATION: Happiness

INSTRUMENT: HAPP 2.1: Single closed question, rated on a 4-point scale:

In general, how satisfied are you with your way of life?
quite satisfied / fairly satisfied / sometimes dissatisfied / usually dissatisfied

RELIABILITY: Stability as assessed by repeating the same question after three years showed 73% unchanged.

VALIDITY: External concurrent validity as assessed by comparison with the impression of clinic nurses of patient's satisfaction: 71% agreement.

DISTRIBUTION: positively skewed: 29% quite satisfied, 42% fairly satisfied, 10% sometimes dissatisfied, 19% usually dissatisfied

REMARKS:

CORRELATES: Age (A 3); Educational level (E 1.1.1); Race (E 2.1); Gender (G 1.1); Family contact outside the home (F 1.4, S 4.1.2); Self-perceived health (H 2.1.2); Availability of help (H 2.6); Household composition (H 4.1); Income (I 1.1); Perceived financial adequacy (I 1.2); various Marital status comparisons (M 1); Religiousness (R 1.1); Quality of contact with household members (H 4.1, S 4.1.3); Employed status (W 2.1)

CONCLUSION: The specific meaning attached by the respondents to their financial situation, health and interpersonal relationships is more relevant than objective circumstances to understand the morale of the elderly chronically ill.

AUTHOR: Hermans, H.J.M. & Tak-van de Ven, J.C.M.

HERMA 73

TITLE: Are there arguments in favour of an original dimension 'positive psychological well-being'?
(In Dutch: Bestaat er een oorspronkelijke dimensie 'positief innerlijk welbevinden'?)

SOURCE: Nederlands Tijdschrift voor de Psychologie en haar Grensgebieden, 1973, vol. 27, nr 11, p. 731-754.

---

GOAL OF THE STUDY: To investigate whether it is justified to treat 'positive psychological well-being' as a factor separate from negative mental characteristics such as neuroticism, anxiety, etc.

REFERS TO: Happiness research, Bradburn & Caplovitz (1965)

TYPE OF STUDY: explanatory, explorative, special group, snapshot, non-experimental

DATA GATHERING: Highly structured questionnaire administered in classroom situation

DATE OF DATA:

POPULATION: Secondary school pupils, The Netherlands

SAMPLE CONSTRUCTION: Non-probability chunk sample using 3 highest classes of 3 secondary schools of different level.
144 boys, 152 girls

NON-RESPONSE: 2%

N: 291

AUTHOR'S HAPPINESS LABEL: Happiness

OUR CONCEPTUALIZATION: Happiness

FIRST INSTRUMENT: COMP 1.1: Single closed question rated on a 4-point scale:

Moments that I feel happy I have
often / not often / seldom / never

In Dutch:
Momenten dat ik me gelukkig voel heb ik
vaak / niet zo vaak / zelden / nooit

RELIABILITY:

VALIDITY:

DISTRIBUTION:

SECOND INSTRUMENT: COMP 1.1: Single closed question rated on a 3-point scale:

I feel
rarely unhappy / rather often unhappy / very often unhappy

In Dutch:
Ik voel me
zelden ongelukkig / tamelijk vaak ongelukkig / zeer vaak ongelukkig

RELIABILITY:

VALIDITY:

DISTRIBUTION:

REMARKS: In Part III the + and - values of the associations between unhappiness (second instrument) and the variables mentioned are turned to indicate the direction of the associations with happiness.

CORRELATES: Positive / negative inner well-being (L 2.1.2)

CONCLUSION:

AUTHOR: Hulin, C.L.

HULIN 69

TITLE: Sources of variation in job and life satisfaction: The role of community and job-related variables.

SOURCE: Journal of Applied Psychology, 1969, vol. 53, nr 4, p. 279-291.

---

GOAL OF THE STUDY: Test of hypothesis that economic circumstances of a community have no direct effect on pay-satisfaction of workers, but that the effects are mediated through intervening psychological variables.

REFERS TO: Theory of job satisfaction; Blood & Hulin (1967), Katzell et al. (1961)

TYPE OF STUDY: explanatory, testing, special group, snapshot, non-experimental

DATA GATHERING: Highly structured questionnaire using direct closed questions administered in the workshop

DATE OF DATA:

POPULATION: Workers, Columbia, Canada

SAMPLE CONSTRUCTION: Non-probability purposive sample by expert choice.
salaried white-collar workers living in 2 'company' towns in British Coloumbia; 388 males, 82 females

NON-RESPONSE: 24%

N: 470

AUTHOR'S HAPPINESS LABEL: Satisfaction with life in general

OUR CONCEPTUALIZATION: Happiness

INSTRUMENT: HAPP 3.1: Single closed question rated on a 7-point scale (based on the Kunin (1955) 11-point General Motors Faces Scale).

The scale consisted of three smiling faces, one neutral face, and three scowling faces. The workers were asked to indicate how they felt about their life in general, considering everything about their present situation, by checking the appropriate face.

RELIABILITY:

VALIDITY:

DISTRIBUTION:

REMARKS:

CORRELATES: Satisfaction with various aspects of Living environment (S 1.2.3, S 1.2.4); Satisfaction with various aspects of one's job (S 1.9.2)

CONCLUSION:

AUTHOR: Hynson Jr, L.M. HYNSO 75

TITLE: Rural-urban differences in satisfaction among the elderly.

SOURCE: Rural Sociology, 1975, vol. 40, nr 1, p. 64-66.

---

GOAL OF THE STUDY: To examine rural-urban differences in satisfaction.

REFERS TO: Theory of urbanism; Wirth (1938), Fischer (1972)

TYPE OF STUDY: explanatory, explorative, special group, snapshot, non-experimental

DATA GATHERING: Highly structured questionnaire

DATE OF DATA: 1973

POPULATION: Aged persons, U.S.A.

SAMPLE CONSTRUCTION: NORC (1973) national probability sample.
age 60+

NON-RESPONSE:

N: 319

AUTHOR'S HAPPINESS LABEL: Happiness

OUR CONCEPTUALIZATION: Happiness

INSTRUMENT: HAPP 1.1: Single closed question using the term 'happiness', rated on a 3-point scale (see BRADB 69).

RELIABILITY:

VALIDITY:

DISTRIBUTION:

REMARKS:

CORRELATES: Community size (L 4.1)

CONCLUSION: The city relates negatively to the aged population's sense of community satisfaction, general sense of happiness, and fear.

AUTHOR: Iris, B. & Barrett, G.V.

IRIS 72

TITLE: Some relations between job and life satisfaction and job importance.

SOURCE: Journal of Applied Psychology, 1972, vol. 56, nr 4, p. 301-304.

---

GOAL OF THE STUDY: Examination of relations among dimensions of employee job satisfaction, life satisfaction, and the importance of job factors.

REFERS TO: Theory of job attitudes and life satisfaction; Hulin (1969), Kornhauser (1965)

TYPE OF STUDY: explanatory, explorative, special group, snapshot, non-experimental

DATA GATHERING: Highly structured questionnaire

DATE OF DATA:

POPULATION: Male supervisors of a chemical plant, U.S.A.

SAMPLE CONSTRUCTION: Probability samples of first level male supervisors from two departments, A or B, of a large southern chemical plant.
Each sample contained approximately 20% of the foremen of that department.
Sample A (N = 34) contained Ss of lower age, less education, lower income, shorter length of tenure in comparison with sample B (N = 35).
Sample A had been identified as a 'problem' group with low morale.
Sample B foremen were significantly more satisfied with life ($t = 3.91$, $p < .01$), leisure ($t = 2.24$, $p < .05$) and job ($t = 2.63$, $p < .05$) than were those of sample A.

N: 69

AUTHOR'S HAPPINESS LABEL: Overall satisfaction with life in general

OUR CONCEPTUALIZATION: Happiness

INSTRUMENT: HAPP 2.1: Single closed question rated on a 5-point scale (from Kornhauser, 1965):

Which of these statements here comes nearest to saying how you feel about your life in general?
Would you say you are . . . competely satisfied / well satisfied / neither satisfied nor dissatisfied / a little dissatisfied / very dissatisfied

RELIABILITY:

VALIDITY:

DISTRIBUTION:

REMARKS:

CORRELATES: Satisfaction with specific aspects of one's job (S 1.9.2); Perceived importance of specific aspects of one's job (W 2.8)

CONCLUSION: When men are in a job situation that provides little job satisfaction, disavowing the importance of the job may be a healthy response and leading to greater satisfaction with life in general.

AUTHOR: Iisager, H.

IISAG 48

TITLE: Factors contributing to happiness among Danish college students.

SOURCE: Journal of Social Psychology, 1948, vol. 28, p. 237-246 .

---

GOAL OF THE STUDY: To find out which factors were rated as most essential to happiness in general and to what extent differences in definitions make for differences in composition of the contributing factors.

REFERS TO: Happiness reasearch; Watson (1930)

TYPE OF STUDY: descriptive, explorative, special group, snapshot, non-experimental

DATA GATHERING: Structured questionnaire, using closed and half-open questions, administered in a classroom

DATE OF DATA: 1946 - 1947

POPULATION: Adult college students, Denmark

SAMPLE CONSTRUCTION: Non-probability chunk sample out of adult students of a peoples college.

NON-RESPONSE: 5%

N: 113

AUTHOR'S HAPPINESS LABEL: Happiness in general

OUR CONCEPTUALIZATION: Happiness

INSTRUMENT: COMP 1.1: Single closed question rated on a 5-point scale:

Underline the sentence which comes nearest to the truth:
I am: almost always unhappy / more often unhappy than happy / about as often happy as unhappy / more often happy than unhappy / almost always happy.

RELIABILITY:

VALIDITY:

DISTRIBUTION: positively skewed

REMARKS:

CORRELATES: Gender (G 1.1); Perceived sources of one's happiness (H 1.8)

CONCLUSION: The essentials of happiness for most people are among the stable elements of life (friends, work, nature), not among the stimulants (alcohol, clubs, churches, dancing, cards, automobiles or arts).

AUTHOR: Jong-Gierveld, J. de

JONG 69

TITLE: The unmarried.
(In Dutch: De ongehuwden).

SOURCE: Alphen a/d Rijn, The Netherlands, 1969, Samson N.V.

---

GOAL OF THE STUDY: To investigate living conditions and psychological disposition of never married persons.

REFERS TO: Theory of social participation; Kwant (1962), Dean (1961)

TYPE OF STUDY: explanatory, testing, special group, snapshot, non-experimental

DATA GATHERING: Structured interview and low structured questionnaire administered at home

DATE OF DATA: September - December, 1965

POPULATION: Adults, Amsterdam, The Netherlands

SAMPLE CONSTRUCTION: Probability systematic random sample stratified by sex and marital status.
150 never married males, 150 married males, 150 never married females and 150 married females; age 30 - 55

NON-RESPONSE: 31%; 4% changed marital status: overrepresentation of singles; 14% unattainable: overrepresentation of singles; 13% refusal, unaffected by sex and marital status; total non-response: unaffected by age and living area, overrepresentation of singles.

N: 600

AUTHOR'S HAPPINESS LABEL: General satisfaction

OUR CONCEPTUALIZATION: Happiness

INSTRUMENT: HAPP 2.1: Single closed question rated on a 5-point scale:

Would you tell me: which of the following statements is best applicable to your own life these days?
- I am very satisfied with the way things are going in my life.
- There are problems, but I am satisfied.
- I don't know whether I should be satisfied or not. In fact I am.
- I don't know whether I should be satisfied or not. In fact I am not.
- I am disappointed in life.
- Own choice:. . . . . . . .

In Dutch:
Wilt U mij zeggen: welke van deze uitspraken vindt U het beste op uw eigen leven, zoals het thans verloopt, van toepassing?
- Ik ben zeer tevreden met de gang van zaken in mijn leven.
- Er zijn problemen, maar ik ben tevreden.
- Ik weet niet of ik nu tevreden moet zijn of niet. Eigenlijk wel.
- Ik weet niet of ik nu tevreden moet zijn of niet. Eigenlijk niet.
- Ik ben door het leven teleurgesteld.
- Eigen keuze, nl. . . . . . .

RELIABILITY:

VALIDITY:

DISTRIBUTION: Highly positively skewed: 23% very satisfied, 56% satisfied, 11% don't know / satisfied, 6% don't know / not satisfied, 4% disappointed in life.

REMARKS: Most correlates were presented in a tabular supplement. In a number of cases the page numbers presented in Part III refer to this supplement.

CORRELATES: Age (A 3); Educational level (E 1.1.1); Freedom on one's job (F 2.2, W 2.6); Gender (G 1.1); Social contacts of one's family (F 1.4); Living alone (H 4.1); Loneliness (L 2.1.2); Never married vs married (M 1.1.1); Self-image (M 1.7); Perceived image (M 1.7); Expected satisfaction if married (M 2.2); various factors concerning Religion (R 1); various Domainsatisfactions (S 1); Being homosexual (S 3.3); various indicators of Social participation (S 4); Occupational prestige (W 2.4); Perceived appreciation on job (W 2.7); Prefer to change job (W 2.10)

CONCLUSION: Feelings of loneliness and discontentedness are much more associated with the attitudes of life of individuals than with their social and material situation, although the association with the social situation is stronger among unmarried than among married individuals.

KAHAN 75

AUTHOR: Kahana, B. & Kahana, E.

TITLE: The relationship of impulse control to cognition and adjustment among institutionalized aged women.

SOURCE: Journal of Gerontology, 1975, vol. 30, nr 6, p. 679-687.

---

GOAL OF THE STUDY: Evaluation of the relationships between several dimensions of impulse control and intelligence, mental status and adjustment.

REFERS TO: Theory of aging; Kahana & Kahana (1966)

TYPE OF STUDY: explanatory, explorative, special group, snapshot, non-experimental

DATA GATHERING: Structured interview

DATE OF DATA:

POPULATION: Institutionalized white females of age 55+, U.S.A.

SAMPLE CONSTRUCTION: Non-probability purposive sample of 'well' residents (i.e. those without incapacitating physical impairment and judged by staff to be interviewable).
age 55 - 97, mean age 79

NON-RESPONSE:

N: 91

AUTHOR'S HAPPINESS LABEL: Life satisfaction

OUR CONCEPTUALIZATION: Happiness

INSTRUMENT: HAPP 2.1: Single closed question rated on a 10-point self-anchoring scale (based on the Cantril Satisfaction with Life rating; see CANTR 65).

Ss were asked to rate themselves on an 1 - 10 rating ladder in terms of their self-perceived life satisfaction.

RELIABILITY:

VALIDITY:

DISTRIBUTION: positively skewed
possible range: 1 (low) to 10 (high); mean: 7.88; S.D.: 1.98

REMARKS:

CORRELATES: Impulse control (P 1.9)

CONCLUSION:

AUTHOR: Knupfer, G., Clark, W. & Room, R.

KNUPF 66

TITLE: The mental health of the unmarried.

SOURCE: The American Journal of Psychiatry, 1966, vol. 122, nr 2, p. 841-851.

---

GOAL OF THE STUDY: To report and assess some constituent dimensions of maladjustment of single persons.

REFERS TO: Theory of mental health; Gurin et al. (1960)

TYPE OF STUDY: explanatory, testing, special group, snapshot, non-experimental

DATA GATHERING: Structured interview during 3½ hours using closed as well as open-ended questions and highly structured mailed questionnaire.

DATE OF DATA: 1964

POPULATION: Adults, San Francisco, U.S.A.

SAMPLE CONSTRUCTION: Probability area sample, poststratified by drinking habits.
Knupfer & Room (1964) sample; overrepresentation by heavy drinkers; unaffected by major demographic variables; age 23+

NON-RESPONSE: 29% incomplete

N: 979

AUTHOR'S HAPPINESS LABEL: Overall happiness

OUR CONCEPTUALIZATION: Happiness

INSTRUMENT: COMP 1.1: Single closed question rated on a 2-point scale:

Most of the time I feel happy . . . true /false

RELIABILITY:

VALIDITY:

DISTRIBUTION:

REMARKS:

CORRELATES: Gender (G 1.1); Never married vs married (M 1.1.1)

CONCLUSION: Mental health is highest for married males and lowest for unmarried males. Females score in-between; single females being somewhat healthier than married females.
These differences may be due to selective factors as well as reactive factors. Single males have more childhood problems and are more isolated and antisocial.

AUTHOR: Levy, S. & Guttman, L.

LEVY 75/1-2

TITLE: On the multivariate structure of well-being.

SOURCE: Social Indicators Research, 1975, vol. 2, p. 361-388.

---

GOAL OF THE STUDY: Presentation of a theory for the structure of well-being and its test with empirical data.

REFERS TO: Theory of well-being; Bradburn & Caplovitz (1965), Andrews (1974)

TYPE OF STUDY: explanatory, testing, special group, snapshot, non-experimental

DATA GATHERING: Structured interview at home

DATE OF DATA: Spring, 1973 (Study 1) and summer, 1973 (Study 2)

POPULATION: Urban adult Jewish population, Israel

SAMPLE CONSTRUCTION: Probability area samples using dwelling units, from a continuing survey conducted jointly by the Israel Institute of Applied Social Research and the Communications Institute of the Hebrew University.

Ss residing in the larger cities of Israel: Jerusalem, Tel Aviv, Haifa, and Beersheva

NON-RESPONSE:

N: 1940 (Study 1) and 1830 (Study 2)

AUTHOR'S HAPPINESS LABEL: Happiness (first instrument) and Mood (second instrument)

OUR CONCEPTUALIZATION: Happiness (first instrument) and Hedonic level of affect (second instrument)

FIRST INSTRUMENT: HAPP 1.1: Single closed question rated on a 6-point scale, ranging from 'very happy' to 'very unhappy':

Generally speaking, are you happy these days?

RELIABILITY:

VALIDITY:

DISTRIBUTION:

SECOND INSTRUMENT: AFF 1.1: Single closed question rated on a 5-point scale, ranging from 'very good all the time' to 'not good almost all the time':

How is your mood these days?

RELIABILITY:

VALIDITY:

DISTRIBUTION:

REMARKS: Some correlates come from one of the two studies, others from both studies

CORRELATES: Positive evaluation of one's family life (F 1.4, S 4.1.3); Hedonic level x happiness (H 1.2.1); Health (H 2.1.2); Sufficient family income (I 1.2) Being able to save (I 1.6); Perceived safety of living environment (L 4.4); Attitude towards neighborhood (L 4.5); Positive evaluation of national situation (N 1.1); Success in acquiring friends (P 1.8.1); various Domainsatisfactions (S 1); Positive evaluation of work relations (W 2.6); Success in performing job (W 2.7)

CONCLUSION:

LEWIN 72

AUTHOR: Lewinsohn, P.M. & Libet, L.

TITLE: Pleasant events, activity schedules, and depressions.

SOURCE: Journal of Abnormal Psychology, 1972, vol. 79, nr 3, p. 291-295.

---

GOAL OF THE STUDY: To test the general hypothesis that intensity of depression is a function of amount of positive reinforcement.

REFERS TO: Theory of depression; Lubin (1965), Lewinsohn et al. (1969)

TYPE OF STUDY: explanatory, testing, special group, snapshot, non-experimental

DATA GATHERING: Mailed highly structured questionnaire administered each day during one month.

DATE OF DATA: February - March, 1971

POPULATION: College undergraduates, Oregon, U.S.A.

SAMPLE CONSTRUCTION: Non-probability purposive sample by expert choice of paid college undergraduates at the University of Oregon, stratified by psychic status and sex.
15 males, 15 females
Ss were classified into three groups: depressed, psychiatric controls, and normal controls, each consisting of 5 males and 5 females.

NON-RESPONSE:

N: 30

AUTHOR'S HAPPINESS LABEL: Depression (mood)

OUR CONCEPTUALIZATION: Hedonic level of affect

INSTRUMENT: AFF 3.3: Repeated index of closed questions on the occurrence of specific affects during the past day (Lubin (1965) Depression Adjective Check Lists).

The checklist was administered at the end of each day for 30 consecutive days.

It contains words which describe different kinds of moods and feelings.
Each S is asked 'to check the words which describe How You Feel Now - Today. Some of the words may sound alike, but we want you to check all the words that describe your feelings. Work rapidly and check all of the words which describe how you feel today'.
Typical adjectives are: hopeless, sad, low-spirited, fine, enthusiastic, sorrowful, clean, melancholy, bright, alert, great, lonely, free, grieved, suffering, healthy, elated, etc.

Three scores were computed:
- Depression score 1: number of 'good' (positive affect) adjectives not checked;
- Depression Score 2: number of 'bad' (negative affect) adjectives checked and
- Depression Score 3: score 1 + 2

In Part III associations with each Depression score are presented in the 'elaboration / remarks' column.

RELIABILITY:

VALIDITY:

DISTRIBUTION:

REMARK: In Part III the + and - values of the associations between Depression and the variables mentioned are turned to indicate the direction of the association with hedonic level of affect

CORRELATES: Doing things one likes (L 2.1.2)

CONCLUSION: The major finding in the study of a significant association between pleasant activities and mood state is consistent with the major tenet of the behavioral theory of depression that there is an association between rate of positive reinforcement and intensity of depression.

AUTHOR: Lewinsohn, P.M. & Graf, M.

LEWIN 73

TITLE: Pleasant activities and depression.

SOURCE: Journal of Consulting and Clinical Psychology, 1973, vol. 41, nr 2, p. 261-268.

---

GOAL OF THE STUDY: Examination of the relation between pleasure in activities and mood, using age as a control variable, and examination of the nature of the activities that are associated with mood.

REFERS TO: Theory of depression; Lewinsohn (1973), Lewinsohn & Libet (1972)

TYPE OF STUDY: explanatory, explorative, local population, snapshot, non-experimental

DATA GATHERING: Mailed highly structured questionnaire administered each day during one month

DATE OF DATA:

POPULATION: Adults, Oregon, U.S.A.

SAMPLE CONSTRUCTION: Non-probability purposive sample by expert choice of paid individuals recruited from a wide variety of sources, including an inpatient psychiatric facility, several clinics, voluntary organizations, churches, newspapers, etc.
The sample was stratified by:
- psychic status: 30 depressed, 30 psychiatric controls (those experiencing psychological disorders other than depression), and 30 normal controls
- age : 30 of age 18 - 29, 30 of age 30 - 49, and 30 of age 50+
- sex : 45 males, 45 females
The males and females and the different age groups were evenly divided over the 3 diagnostic groups.

N: 90

AUTHOR'S HAPPINESS LABEL: Depression (mood)

OUR CONCEPTUALIZATION: Hedonic level of affact

INSTRUMENT: AFF 3.3: Repeated index of closed questions on the occurrence of specific affects during the past day (Lubin (1965) Depression Adjective Check List; see LEWIN 72).

The checklist was administered at the end of each day for 30 consecutive days.

RELIABILITY:

VALIDITY:

DISTRIBUTION:

REMARKS: In Part III the ; and - values of the associations between Depression and the variables mentioned are turned to indicate the direction of the association with hedonic level of affect.

CORRELATES: Doing things one likes (L 2.1.2)

CONCLUSION: The findings provide support for the behavioral theory of depression.

AUTHOR: Lewis, M.A.

LEWIS 72

TITLE: Actual and perceived age differences in self-concept and psychological well-being for Catholic sisters.

SOURCE: Unpublished doctoral dissertation, 1972, Syracuse University, New York.

---

GOAL OF THE STUDY: Investigation of conceptions of self and other sisters and of the relationship between self-concept and psychological well-being among Catholic sisters of different age cohorts.

REFERS TO: Happiness research; Cavan et al. (1949), Kuhlen (1959), and other theories

TYPE OF STUDY: explanatory, testing, special group, snapshot, non-experimental

DATA GATHERING: Highly structured mailed questionnaire

DATE OF DATA:

POPULATION: Catholic sisters, U.S.A.

SAMPLE CONSTRUCTION: Non-probability chunk sample of Catholic sisters who are members of the Eastern American Province, which is a geographical subdivision including New York, Virginia, Florida, Illinois, Missouri and Colorado.
age 24 - 75; 74 of age 23 - 34, 69 of age 35 - 49, 49 of age 50+

NON-RESPONSE: 34%

N: 183

AUTHOR'S HAPPINESS LABEL: Psychological well-being

OUR CONCEPTUALIZATION: Hedonic level of affect (first instrument) and Happiness (second instrument)

FIRST INSTRUMENT: AFF 2.3: Index of closed questions on perceived occurrence of specific affects during the past few weeks (Bradburn Affect Balance Score; see BRADB 69).
The Affect Balance Score is positive affect score - negative affect score

RELIABILITY:

VALIDITY:

DISTRIBUTION: positively skewed: 42% +3 or more, 33% +1 or +2, 14% 0, 11% -1 or less
possible range : -5 (low) to +5 (high)

SECOND INSTRUMENT: HAPP 1.1: Single closed question rated on a 3-point scale (see BRADB 69).

RELIABILITY:

VALIDITY:

DISTRIBUTION: positively skewed: 30% very happy, 64% pretty happy, 6% not too happy

REMARKS:

CORRELATES: Age (A 3); Hedonic level x happiness (H 1.2.1); Positive self-concept (S 2.1.3); Self-concept components (S 2.2.1)

CONCLUSION: The concept the sisters have of their own self-worth, especially of their ability to adjust to the recent changes in the life style, may be the force which influences their basic motivations, and in turn their psychological well-being.

AUTHOR: Lowenthal, M.F. & Boler, D.

LOWEN 65

TITLE: Voluntary vs involuntary social withdrawal.

SOURCE: Journal of Gerontology, 1965, vol. 20, p. 363-371.

---

GOAL OF THE STUDY: Qualification of disengagement theory of morale in old age for voluntarity of withdrawal.

REFERS TO: Theory of adaptation to old age; Cumming & Henry (1961)

TYPE OF STUDY: explanatory, testing, special group, longitudinal, non-experimental

DATA GATHERING: Interviews using open questions during 3 days

DATE OF DATA: 1960 - 1964

POPULATION: Non-institutionalized aged persons, San Francisco, U.S.A.

SAMPLE CONSTRUCTION: Probability sample stratified by sex, age and social living arrangement.
survivors from the Lowenthal (1964) sample
age 60+

NON-RESPONSE: 55%: 22% refusals, 9% deaths, 22% unattainable

N: 269

AUTHOR'S HAPPINESS LABEL: Morale

OUR CONCEPTUALIZATION: Happiness (first and second instrument) and Hedonic level of affect (third instrument)

FIRST INSTRUMENT: HAPP 1.1: Single closed question (from Thompson et al.; see THOMP 60):
All in all, how much happiness would you say you find in life today?

RELIABILITY:

VALIDITY:

DISTRIBUTION: 10% none

REMARKS: In Part III the Gammas (G') are based on the proportions 'none' answers.

SECOND INSTRUMENT: HAPP 2.1: Single closed question (from Thompson et al.; see THOMP 60):
On the whole, how satisfied would you say you are with your way of life today?

RELIABILITY:

VALIDITY:

DISTRIBUTION: 12% not very satisfied

REMARKS: In Part III the Gammas (G') are based on the proportions 'not very' answers

THIRD INSTRUMENT: AFF 1.1: Single closed question (from Thompson et al.; see THOMP 60):
In general, how would you say you feel most of the time, in good spirits or in low spirits?

RELIABILITY:

VALIDITY:

DISTRIBUTION: 13% sometimes or usually low

REMARKS: In Part III the Gammas (G') are based on the proportions 'sometimes of usually low' answers.

CORRELATES: Deprivation (L 2.2.2); Social withdrawal (S 4.4)

CONCLUSION: Presence or absence of deprivation has a greater bearing on morale than recent social withdrawal. The voluntary withdrawn (withdrawn but not deprived) have only slightly lower morale than those neither withdrawn nor deprived, and the involuntary withdrawn (withdrawn and deprived) have the lowest morale but not much lower than the deprived not-withdrawn.

AUTHOR: Ludwig, L.D. | LUDWI 70

TITLE: Intra- and interindividual relationships between elation-depression and desire for excitement.

SOURCE: Journal of Personality, 1970, vol. 38, nr 2, p. 167-176.

---

GOAL OF THE STUDY: To examine the relationships between elation-depression and desire for excitement.

REFERS TO: Happiness research; Nowlis & Nowlis (1956), Wessman & Ricks (1966)

TYPE OF STUDY: explanatory, testing, special group, snapshot, non-experimental

DATA GATHERING: Highly structured questionnaire completed every night for 20 consecutive days

DATE OF DATA:

POPULATION: University students, University of Wisconsin, U.S.A.

SAMPLE CONSTRUCTION: Probability sample of 45 out of a sample of 84 undergraduate and graduate students, stratified by desire for excitement.
18 males, 27 females

NON-RESPONSE:

N: 45

AUTHOR'S HAPPINESS LABEL: Elation

OUR CONCEPTUALIZATION: Hedonic level of affect

INSTRUMENT: AFF 3.1: Repeated closed question on overall hedonic level for the past day, rated on a 10-point scale (Wessman & Ricks Elation - Depression Scale; see WESSM 60).

The scale was scored each night for at least 20 days.

RELIABILITY:

VALIDITY:

DISTRIBUTION:

REMARKS:

CORRELATES: Tranquility (A 2.2.20); Excitement (A 2.2.21); various indicators of Desire for excitement (P 1.5.3)

CONCLUSION: The data fail to confirm that elation-depression and desire for excitement are related.

LUDWI 71/75

AUTHOR: Ludwig, L.D.

TITLE: Elation - Depression and skill as determinants of desire for excitement.

SOURCE: Unpublished doctoral dissertation, 1971, University of Wisconsin, U.S.A.
Partly published in the Journal of Personality, 1975, vol. 43, p. 1-22.

---

GOAL OF THE STUDY: To examine the influence of trait elation-depression, manipulated elation-depression, stable skill, and manipulated skill upon desire for excitement.

REFERS TO: Theory of elation-depression ard desire for excitement; Ludwig (1970), Wessman & Ricks (1966)

TYPE OF STUDY: explanatory, testing, special group, snapshot, experimental

DATA GATHERING: Hihgly structured questionnaires, including direct closed questions, a Rorschach inkblot and a 'doodle'; and interview

DATE OF DATA:

POPULATION: Female undergraduates, University of Wisconsin, U.S.A.

SAMPLE CONSTRUCTION: Random sample of paid female undergraduates, poststratified by acting ability and depression.
The large majority were freshmen and sophomores.

NON-RESPONSE: 81%; 61% refusal, 5% eliminated on basis of screening data, 15% miscellaneous reasons

N: 72

AUTHOR'S HAPPINESS LABEL: Trait elation-depression

OUR CONCEPTUALIZATION: Hedonic level of affect

INSTRUMENT: AFF 6: Composite, including closed questions on both perceived hedonic level in general and actual hedonic level, rated on 10-point scales (Wessman & Ricks Elation - Depression Scale; see WESSM 60):

1. Which of these phrases best describes the way you feel now?
2. Which of the phrases best describes the worst you felt today?
3. Which of the phrases most accurately describes the best you felt today?
4. Which of the phrases most accurately describes the best you feel in a typical day?
5. Which of the phrases best describes the worst you feel in a typical day?
6. Which of the phrases best describes your average feelings in a typical day?

RELIABILITY:

VALIDITY:

DISTRIBUTION: positively skewed
possible range: 1 (low) to 10 (high); mean: 6.17

REMARKS:

CORRELATES: Depression (A 2.2.4); Elated mood during experiment (A 2.2.5); Numbering speed (C 1.5); Number of leading roles played in a play (L 3.3.2); Self-perceived creativity and maturity (P 1.4.2); various indicators of Desire for excitement (P 1.5.3); Self-esteem (S 2.1.3); various Preferences with respect to social participation (S 4.5); Perceived acting ability (X 1); Writing firmness (X 1)

CONCLUSION: Compared to trait-depressed subjects, those who were trait-elated behaviorally and attitudinally expressed greater desire for social, not for non-social, excitement. In avoiding social excitement, the depressed person misses out on many potentially enjoyable experiences.

AUTHOR: Makarczyk, W.

MAKAR 62

TITLE: Factors affecting life satisfaction among people in Poland.

SOURCE: Polish Sociological Bulletin, 1962, vol. 1, p. 105-116.

---

GOAL OF THE STUDY: Assessment of adjustment of people in Poland to their circumstances.

REFERS TO:

TYPE OF STUDY: explanatory, explorative, national population, snapshot, non-experimental

DATA GATHERING: Administration of a structured questionnaire using direct closed questions

DATE OF DATA: June - July, 1960

POPULATION: National adult population, Poland

SAMPLE CONSTRUCTION: Non-probability purposive quota sample stratified by sex, age, type of local community, employment and S.E.S. Excluded were individual farmers owning farms of less than 2 ha., and pupils and students not gainfully employed.

NON-RESPONSE: 5%

N: 2387

AUTHOR'S HAPPINESS LABEL: Satisfaction with life in general

OUR CONCEPTUALIZATION: Happiness

INSTRUMENT: HAPP 2.1: Single closed question rated on a 5-point scale:

On the whole, are you satisfied with life?
definitely yes / rather yes / don't know / rather no / definitely no / no reply

RELIABILITY:

VALIDITY:

DISTRIBUTION: positively skewed: 16% definitely yes, 53% rather yes, 10% don't know, 16% rather no, 5% definitely no, 1% no reply

REMARKS: A number of correlates concern subsamples of the total population: farm owners, housewives, etc.

CORRELATES: Nervousness (A 2.2.21, H 2.2); Age (A 3); Educational level (E 1.1.1); Gender (G 1.1); Getting on well with one's family (F 1.4); Self-perceived health (H 2.1.2); Income (I 1.6); Expected increase in income (I 1.7); Attitudes towards time spent on entertainment (L 3.3.4); Getting on well with local authorities (L 4.4); Anxiety about future of farm (P 5.2.2.1); Marital happiness (S 1.7.2); Job satisfaction (S 1.9.1); various indicators of Social participation (S 4.1); various factors concerning Work (W 2)

CONCLUSION: The rural group derives less life satisfaction from work and interpersonal relations than the non-rural group.

MANNI 72

AUTHOR: Manning Gibbs, B.A.

TITLE: Relative deprivation and self-reported happiness of blacks: 1946 - 1966.

SOURCE: Unpublished doctoral dissertation, 1972, University of Texas at Austin, U.S.A.

---

GOAL OF THE STUDY: Attempt to test the relative deprivation theory for blacks.

REFERS TO: Theory of reference groups and relative deprivation; Merton & Rossi (1968)

TYPE OF STUDY: explanatory, testing, national population, snapshots, non-experimental

DATA GATHERING: Secondary analysis of 10 A.I.P.C. polls (American Institute of Public Opinion Surveys)

DATE OF DATA: April, 1946; June, 1947; December, 1947; May, 1948; August, 1948; August, 1956; September, 1956; September, 1966; October, 1966

POPULATION: National adult population, U.S.A.

SAMPLE CONSTRUCTION: Non-probability quota samples in 1946 and 1947, and probability area samples in the later 1950's and 1960's.

three groups of data were compared:

1) 5 surveys between 1946 and 1948 (referred to as 1946): N = 12185: 447 blacks, 11738 whites
2) 3 surveys in 1956 : N = 6445: 566 blacks, 5879 whites
3) 2 surveys in 1966 : N = 6987: 603 blacks, 6384 whites

N: 25617

AUTHOR'S HAPPINESS LABEL: Happiness (Psychological well-being)

OUR CONCEPTUALIZATION: Happiness

INSTRUMENT: HAPP 1.1: Single closed question rated on a 3 or 4-point scale:

In general, how happy would you say you are?

RELIABILITY:

VALIDITY:

DISTRIBUTION: positively skewed: in 1946: 40% very happy, in 1956: 52% very happy, in 1966: 46% very happy

REMARKS: Throughout the surveys under consideration the response categories of the happiness question varied. Only the 'very happy' response alternative is consistently offered. It is for this reason that the analysis (and our computation of Gammas) was based on proportions 'very happy' answers.

CORRELATES: Age (A 3); Educational level (E 1.1.1); Race (E 2.1); Income (I 1.1); Community size (L 4.1); Region (L 4.3); Occupational level (W 2.2)

CONCLUSION: Between 1946 and 1966 negroes became less happy, especially negroes with higher educational, occupational and income levels. This might be due to the fact that especially these negroes are increasingly using whites as a comparative reference group, leading to the development of a feeling of relative deprivation.

AUTHOR: Matlin, N.

MATLI 66

TITLE: The demography of happiness.

SOURCE: University of Puerto Rico, School of Medicine, Department of Public Health, 1966, San Juan.

---

GOAL OF THE STUDY: To explore the internal relationships of the dimensions of happiness and to assess the relationships of demographic variables and health with happiness.

REFERS TO: Happiness research; Bradburn (1964), Bradburn & Caplovitz (1965)

TYPE OF STUDY: explanatory, explorative, national population, snapshot, non-experimental

DATA GATHERING: Structured interview

DATE OF DATA: November, 1963 - January, 1964 and August - October, 1964

POPULATION: National adult population, Puerto Rico

SAMPLE CONSTRUCTION: Probability simple random sample of Puerto Ricans of age 20+.
validation sample: 114 out-patients of psychiatric hospital, who had been diagnosed by psychiatrists as anxious (N = 56) or depressed (N = 58)

NON-RESPONSE:

N: 1417 (excluding validation sample)

AUTHOR'S HAPPINESS LABEL: Happiness

OUR CONCEPTUALIZATION: Happiness (first instrument) and Hedonic level of affect (second instrument)

FIRST INSTRUMENT: HAPP 1.1: Single closed question rated on a 3-point scale:

All things considered, how would you describe yourself these days? Would you say you are very happy, fairly happy, or not too happy?

RELIABILITY:

VALIDITY: external congruent validity: Validation sample was significantly less happy than the Puerto Ricans (see variable 'mental disturbances' in Part III, H 2.3.3)

DISTRIBUTION: negatively skewed: 17% very happy, 50% fairly happy, 33% not too happy

SECOND INSTRUMENT: AFF 2.3: Index of closed questions on perceived occurrence of specific affects during the past week (adapted Bradburn & Caplovitz Affect Balance Score; see BRADB 65):

Ss were asked: 'During the past week did you ever feel . . .' yes / no.

To the index of negative affects the item 'Could not do anything simply because you could not start it' was added.

From the Index of Positive Affects the item 'particularly excited or interested in something' was excluded.

RELIABILITY: equivalence:

| | | |
|---|---|---|
| positive items | : Q ranging from +.36 to +.58 | For correlations with the separate items of this instrument, see A 2.2 (Part III) |
| negative items | : Q ranging from +.66 to +.84 | |
| positive x negative items | : Q ranging from -.05 to +.30 | |
| positive affect score x negative affect score: | G' = -.14 (01) | |

VALIDITY: external congruent validity: Validation sample had a significantly lower Affect Balance Score than the Puerto Ricans (see variable 'mental disturbances' in Part III, H 2.3.3)

DISTRIBUTION: possible range: -6 (low) to +3 (high); actual range: 15% score -3 or less; 19% score -1 or -2; 29% score 0; 23% score 1, 14% score 2 or 3

REMARKS:

CORRELATES: Age (A 3); Educational level (E 1.1.1); Gender (G 1.1); Hedonic level x happiness (H 1.2.1); Hedonic level x hedonic level (H 1.2.2); Self-perceived health (H 2.1.2); Mental disturbances (H 2.3.3); Income (I 1.1); Enjoying life (L 2.1.1); various Marital status comparisons (M 1); Economic prosperity of one's country (N 1.2)

CONCLUSION: In Puerto Rico happiness is more closely related to absence of negative feelings than in the USA, where almost exclusively a relation with the amount of positive feelings exists.

AUTHOR: McGrade, B.J.

MCGRA 68

TITLE: Newborn activity and emotional response at eight months.

SOURCE: Child Development, 1968, vol. 39, nr 4, p. 1247-1252.

---

GOAL OF THE STUDY: To relate newborn activity measures to ratings of emotional response.

REFERS TO: Theory of newborn activity; McGrade et al. (1965)

TYPE OF STUDY: explanatory, explorative, special group, longitudinal, non-experimental

DATA GATHERING: Observation of motion pictures (newborn measures) and developmental testing by a (project) psychologist, using 4 rating scales (8 months measures).

DATE OF DATA:

POPULATION: 8 months old infants, U.S.A.

SAMPLE CONSTRUCTION: Non-probability quota sample of infants whose mothers were patients in the obstetic clinic of Yale-New Haven Hospital.
13 boys, 11 girls

NON-RESPONSE: 46% unattainable

N: 24

AUTHOR'S HAPPINESS LABEL: Happiness

OUR CONCEPTUALIZATION: Hedonic level of affect

INSTRUMENT: AFF 5.1: Clinical ratings on the basis of repeated observations of expressive behavior (Bayley Infant Behavior Profile, Research Form 1959; see also SCHAE 63):

General emotional tone: unhappy - happy

1. Child seems unhappy throughout the period.
2. Mostly unhappy, but not consistently so.
3. At times rather unhappy, but may respond happily to interesting procedures.
4. Seems calm and contented.
5. Happy: may become upset by some procedures, but recovers fairly easily.
6. Appears generally in a happy state of well-being.
7. Consistently happy, radiating a gay mood, only rarely disturbed by an annoying situation.
8. Radiantly happy; nothing is upsetting; animated.

RELIABILITY:

VALIDITY:

DISTRIBUTION:

REMARKS:

CORRELATES: Newborn activity (A 1.5, P 1.9); Tension (P 1.9); Fearfulness (P 1.9); Length of labor (X 1)

CONCLUSION:

AUTHOR: Miller, H. & Wilson, W. MILLE 68

TITLE: Relation of sexual behavoirs, values and conflict to avowed happiness and personal adjustment.

SOURCE: Psychological Reports, 1968, vol. 23, p. 1075-1086.

GOAL OF THE STUDY: Providing empirical information about the relation of sexual liberality and adjustment.

REFERS TO: Theory of sexual liberality and adjustment; Swensen (1963), Mowrer (1961)

TYPE OF STUDY: explanatory, testing, special group, snapshot, non-experimental

DATA GATHERING: Highly structured questionnaire administered in classroom situation

DATE OF DATA: 1966/1967

POPULATION: Undergraduate students, Kent State University at Ashtabula, Ohio, U.S.A.

SAMPLE CONSTRUCTION: Non-probability accidental sample using attendants of a psychology course.
68 males (mean age 22), and 64 females (mean age 21)

NON-RESPONSE:

N: 132

AUTHOR'S HAPPINESS LABEL: Avowed happiness

OUR CONCEPTUALIZATION: Happiness

INSTRUMENT: COMP 1.1: Single closed question rated on a 9-point scale:

Please estimate your happiness on the scale below by marking a number 1 to 9.

| 1 | 2 | 3 | 4 | 5 | 6 | 7 | 8 | 9 |
|---|---|---|---|---|---|---|---|---|
| not very happy most of the time | | | | happy most of the time | | | | very happy most of the time |

RELIABILITY:

VALIDITY:

DISTRIBUTION:

REMARKS:

CORRELATES: Age (A 3); Maladjustment (H 2.3.1); Religiousness (R 1.1); various indicators of Sexual attitudes (S 3.1)

CONCLUSION: A small overall correlation exists between liberal vs conflictual attitude towards sexuality and both adjustment and happiness. This may be because American society places persons in a conflict between sexual frustration, loneliness and abstention from rewarding emotional relations on the one hand and guilt, social disapproval and concern about pregnancy on the other hand.
People reveal very little of their sexual behavior, probably because these behaviors, though often rewarding, are socially taboo.

AUTHOR: Morgan, E., Mull, H.K. & Washburn, M.F.

MORGA 19

TITLE: An attempt to test moods or temperaments of cheerfulness and depression by directed recall of emotionally toned experiences.

SOURCE: American Journal of Psychology, 1919, vol. 30, p. 302-304.

---

GOAL OF THE STUDY: Trying to measure moods or temperaments of cheerfulness and depression by directed recall of emotionally toned experiences.

REFERS TO:

TYPE OF STUDY: descriptive, testing, special group, snapshot, non-experimental

DATA GATHERING: Open interview during five successive days, using a verbal projective technique

DATE OF DATA:

POPULATION: Female college students, U.S.A.

SAMPLE CONSTRUCTION: Non-probability chunk sample using attendants of a psychology course.

NON-RESPONSE:

N: 97

AUTHOR'S HAPPINESS LABEL: Optimism

OUR CONCEPTUALIZATION: Hedonic level of affect

INSTRUMENT: AFF 5.2: Peer-rating of hedonic level of affect on the basis of two questions:

Is A.B. inclined to be optimistic and cheerful, or pessimistic and depressed most of the time?
Is she steady or fluctuating in mood?

Ss were classified as: steadily optimistic / variable tending to optimism / indifferent or fluctuating / variable tending to pessimism / steadily pessimistic.

RELIABILITY:

VALIDITY:

DISTRIBUTION: positively skewed

REMARKS:

CORRELATES: Recalling pleasant associations in connection with verbal stimuli (P 1.6)

CONCLUSION: There is a real positive correlation between exceeding or falling below the average number of pleasant associations in five successive days, and the judgments of a person s intimate associates regarding his temperament.

AUTHOR: Moriwaki, S.Y.

MORIW 73

TITLE: Self-disclosure, significant others and psychological well-being.

SOURCE: Journal of Health and Social Behavior, 1973, vol. 14, p. 266-232.

---

GOAL OF THE STUDY: Examination of the relation between psychological well-being and number of significant others in old age,using self-disclosure as an intervening variable.

REFERS TO: Happiness research; Lowentnai & Haven (1968), Rosow (1967), Jourard (1959)

TYPE OF STUDY: explanatory, testing, special group, snapshot, non-experimental

DATA GATHERING: Structured interview

DATE OF DATA: 1971

POPULATION: Aged retired persons, Los Angeles County, USA.

SAMPLE CONSTRUCTION: Non-probability purposive quota sample of aged persons from two metropolitan health plans, proportionally stratified by marital status. Overrepresentation of healthy and financially secure Ss; 49% males, 51% females; age 60-84, median age 70.4; median income $ 7200.-

NON-RESPONSE:

N: 71

AUTHOR'S HAPPINESS LABEL: Psychological well-being

OUR CONCEPTUALIZATION: Hedonic level of affect

INSTRUMENT: AFF 2.3: Index of closed questions on perceived occurrence of specific affects during the past few weeks (Bradburn Affect Balance Score; see BRADB 69).

RELIABILITY:

VALIDITY:

DISTRIBUTION:

REMARKS:

CORRELATES: Age (A 3); Role loss (L 1.2, R 2.3); Number of significant others (S 4.1.1); Supported self-disclosure (S 4.1.3)

CONCLUSION: The number of significant others is directly related to psychological well-being, regardless of the level of supported self-disclosure to these others, role loss, or age.

AUTHOR: Moriwaki, S.Y. MORIW 74

TITLE: The Affect Balance Scale: A validity study with aged samples.

SOURCE: Journal of Gerontology, 1974, vol. 29, nr 1, 73-78.

---

GOAL OF THE STUDY: To examine the validity of the Affect Balance Scale using older peoply.

REFERS TO: Theory of psychological well-being; Cavan et al. (1949), Bradburn & Caplovitz (1965)

TYPE OF STUDY: explanatory, explorative, special group, snapshot, non-experimental

DATA GATHERING: Structured interview

DATE OF DATA: 1971

POPULATION: Aged persons, Los Angeles County, U.S.A.

SAMPLE CONSTRUCTION: 2 samples: - Psychiatric outpatients group: Non-probability purposive sample by expert choice of psychiatric outpatients from 2 mental health clinics during a 4-months period.
- Normal community subjects : Non-probability purposive sample by expert choice of Lutheran Church members judged to be physically and mentally healthy and without prior psychiatric hospital experience.
age 60+; sample 1 predominantly males (63%), sample 2 predominantly females (63%)

NON-RESPONSE:

N: 27; sample 1: N = 8, sample 2: N = 19

AUTHOR'S HAPPINESS LABEL: Psychological well-being

OUR CONCEPTUALIZATION: Hedonic level of affect (first instrument) and Happiness (second instrument)

FIRST INSTRUMENT: AFF 1.3: Index of closed questions on perceived occurrence of specific affects in general (adapted Bradburn Affect Balance Score; see BRADB 69).
The items were unchanged.
Ss were asked: 'Looking at your present life situation, have you ever felt. . .' yes / no.

RELIABILITY: equivalence (on the basis of data from sample 2): positive affects score x negative affect score: r = -.32 (ns)

VALIDITY:

DISTRIBUTION:

SECOND INSTRUMENT: HAPP 1.1: Single closed question using the term 'happiness', rated on a 3-point scale (see GURIN 60).

RELIABILITY:

VALIDITY:

DISTRIBUTION:

REMARKS:

CORRELATES: Hedonic level x happiness (H 1.2.1); Mental health (H 2.3.3)

CONCLUSION: The Affect Balance Scale is a better predictor for overall psychological well-being than either positive or negative affect alone. The scale is applicable to aged populations.

MOSER 69

AUTHOR: Moser - Peters, C.M.J.

TITLE: Backgrounds of happiness feelings.
(In Dutch: Achtergronden van geluksgevoel).

SOURCE: Nederlands Instituut voor Preventieve Geneeskunde (T.N.O.), 1969, Leiden, The Netherlands.

---

GOAL OF THE STUDY: Exploration of the relations between happiness and various situational and personal characteristics.

REFERS TO: Happiness research; Jahoda (1958), Gurin et al. (1960), Bradburn & Caplovitz (1965)

TYPE OF STUDY: descriptive, explorative, local population, snapshot, non-experimental

DATA GATHERING: Structured interview

DATE OF DATA: Autumn, 1967

POPULATION: Adults, Utrecht, The Netherlands

SAMPLE CONSTRUCTION: Probability sample stratified by age.
183 males, 117 females; 88 of age 21 - 35, 93 of age 35 - 50, 119 of age 50 - 65; overrepresentation of males and older people

NON-RESPONSE: 14% unattainable etc.

N: 300

AUTHOR'S HAPPINESS LABEL: Happiness

OUR CONCEPTUALIZATION: Happiness

INSTRUMENT: HAPP 1.1: Single closed question rated on a 5-point scale:

Taken all things together, how would you say you are these days?
extremely happy / very happy / happy / pretty happy / not too happy

In Dutch:
Hoe gelukkig voelt U zich alles bij elkaar genomen op het ogenblik?
buitengewoon gelukkig / zeer gelukkig / gelukkig / tamelijk gelukkig / niet zo gelukkig

RELIABILITY:

VALIDITY:

DISTRIBUTION: positively skewed: 15% extremely happy, 27% very happy, 43% happy, 13% pretty happy, 2% not too happy
possible range: 1 (low) to 5 (high); mean 3.41; modus: 3.30

REMARKS:

CORRELATES: Nervousness (A 2.2.21); Age (A 3); Law and order attitude (D 1, V 1.1); Dissatisfaction with socio-political order (D 1, V 1.1); Educational level (E 1.1.1); Gender (G 1.1); various indicators of Physical health (H 2.1.3); Psychosomatic complaints (H 2.2); Income (I 1.6); various Marital status comparisons (M 1); Social isolation (P 1.8.2); various factors concerning Religion (R 1); various Domainsatisfactions (S 1); Social uncertainty (S 2.1.4); various indicators of Social participation (S 4); Achievement (S 5.3); Occupational level (W 2.4)

CONCLUSION: The majority of Ss feels happy, and this feeling seems relatively independent of the socio-situational conditions in which they live. This is indicative of man's adaptive capacities.

AUTHOR: Neugarten, B.L., Havighurst, R.J. & Tobin, S.S.

NEUGA 61

TITLE: The measurement of life satisfaction.

SOURCE: Journal of Gerontology, 1961, vol. 16, p. 134-143.

---

**GOAL OF THE STUDY:** Development of a measure of successful aging that uses the individual's own evaluation as the point of reference and is relatively independent of level of activity or social participation.

REFERS TO: Theory of adaptation to old age; Havighurst & Albrecht (1953), Cavan et al. (1949), Kutner et al. (1956)

TYPE OF STUDY: explanatory, explorative, special group, snapshot, non-experimental

DATA GATHERING: 4 repeated and lengthy interviews in a period of two and a half years

DATE OF DATA:

POPULATION: White adult population of age 50+, Kansas City, U.S.A.

**SAMPLE CONSTRUCTION:** Panel group: Stratified probability sample of middle and working class persons, age 50 - 70 (N = 103)
Quasi panel: Non-probability quota sample of middle and working class persons, age 70 - 90 (N = 74)
Tobin & Neugarten (1961) sample

NON-RESPONSE: Panel group: 16% refusal; 74% remained after 4 interviews
Quasi panel: 83% remained after 4 interviews

N: 177 (after 4 interviews)

**AUTHOR'S HAPPINESS LABEL:** Congruence between desired and achieved goals ( first instrument) and Mood tone (second instrument)

**OUR CONCEPTUALIZATION:** Perceived realization of aspirations (first instrument) and Happiness (second instrument)

FIRST INSTRUMENT: CON 1.4: Expert rating on the basis of a focussed interview:

Content analysis of interview records by independent judges:
The extent to which R feels he has achieved his goals in life, whatever those goals might be; feels he has succeeded in accomplishing what he regards as important. High ratings go, for instance, to R who says: 'I've managed to keep out of jail', just as to R who says: 'I managed to send all my kids through college'. Low ratings go to R who feels he's missed most of his opportunities, or who says: 'I've never been suited to my work', or 'I always wanted to be a doctor, but never could get there'. Also to R who wants most to be 'loved', but instead feels merely 'approved'. (Expressions of regret for lack of education are not counted because they are stereotyped responses among all but the group of highest social status).

The variable was rated on a 5-point scale:

5. Feels he has accomplished what he wanted to do. He has achieved or is achieving his own personal goals.
4. Regrets somewhat the chances missed during life. 'Maybe I could have made more of certain opportunities'. Nevertheless feels that he has been fairly successful in accomplishing what he wanted to do in life.
3. Has a fifty-fifty record of opportunities taken and opportunities missed. Would have done some things differently, if he had his life to live over. Might have gotten more education.
2. Has regrets about major opportunities missed but feels good about accomplishment in one area (may be his avocation).
1. Feels he has missed most opportunities in life.

Ratings were made on each case by two judges working independently. In all, 14 judges rated the 177 cases.

RELIABILITY: Inter-judge agreement: 92% of the paired judgements showed exact agreement or 1-step disagreement
Retest reliability : 73% exact agreement of 1-step disagreement between paired judgements and psychologist rating on the basis of interview $1\frac{1}{2}$ - 2 years later (N = 80)

VALIDITY: purpose of investigation

DISTRIBUTION:

SECOND INSTRUMENT: COMP 1.4: Expert rating on the basis of a focussed interview:

Content analysis of interview records by independent judges:
High ratings for R who expresses happy, optimistic attitudes and mood; who uses spontaneous positively-toned affective terms for people and things; who takes pleasure from life and expresses it. Low ratings for depression, 'feel blue and lonely'; for feelings of bitterness; for frequent irritability and anger. (Here not only R's verbalized attitudes in the interview were considered, but interferences were made from all the knowledge of his interpersonal relationships, how others react towards him).

The variable was rated on a 5-point scale:

5. 'This is the best time of my life'. Is nearly always cheerful, optimistic. Cheerfulness may seem unrealistic to an observer, but R shows no sign of 'putting up a bold front'.
4. Gets pleasure out of life, knows it and shows it. There is enough restraint to seem appropriate to a younger person. Usually feels positive affect. Optimistic.
3. Seems to move along on an even temperamental keel. Any depressions are neutralized by positive mood swings. Generally neutral-to-positive affect. May show some irritability.
2. Wants things quiet and peaceful. General neutral-to-negative affect. Some depression.
1. Pessimistic, complaining, bitter. Complaints of being lonely. Feels 'blue' a good deal of the time. May get angry when in contact with people.

Ratings were made on each case by two judges working independently. In all, 14 judges rated the 177 cases.

RELIABILITY: Inter-judge agreement: 92% of the paired judgements showed exact agreement or 1-step disagreement
Retest reliability : 69% exact agreement or 1-step disagreement between paired judgements and psychologist rating on the basis of interview 1½ - 2 years later (N = 80)

VALIDITY: purpose of investigation

DISTRIBUTION:

REMARKS: Both instruments are components of the Life Satisfaction Rating (LSR) developed by the authors. The other three components of the LSR and thus the overall LSR cannot be considered as valid indicators of happiness (see also under CORRELATES).
The other two indicators of 'life satisfaction' presented in the publication (Life Satisfaction Index A and B) must be considered invalid too.

CORRELATES: Zest vs apathy (A 1.8); Contentment x happiness (H 1.3.1); Resolution and fortitude (P 1.2); Positive self-concept (S 2.1.3)

CONCLUSION:

AUTHOR: N.I.P.O.

NIPO 49

TITLE: The things that make people happy.
(In Dutch: Wat de mensen gelukkig maakt.)

SOURCE: De publieke opinie, 1949, vol. 3, nr 1, p. 3-4.

---

**GOAL OF THE STUDY:** Investigation of factors that make people happy and comparison of the degree of happiness in The Netherlands and some other countries.

REFERS TO:

TYPE OF STUDY: descriptive, explorative, national population, snapshot, non-experimental

DATA GATHERING: Interview

DATE OF DATA: 1948

POPULATION: National adult population, The Netherlands

**SAMPLE CONSTRUCTION:**

NON-RESPONSE: 7%

N: Unknown

**AUTHOR'S HAPPINESS LABEL:** Happiness

**OUR CONCEPTUALIZATION:** Happiness

INSTRUMENT: HAPP 1.1: Single closed question, rated on a 3-point scale:

Are you happy, pretty happy, or unhappy?

In Dutch:
Vindt U zichzelf gelukkig, tamelijk gelukkig, of ongelukkig?

RELIABILITY:

VALIDITY:

DISTRIBUTION: positively skewed: 43% happy, 44% pretty happy, 6% unhappy, 7% non-response

REMARKS:

CORRELATES: Age (A 3); Educational level (E 1.1.1); Gender (G 1.1); Self-perceived health (H 2.1.2); Income (I 1.1); Having a good life (L 2.1.1); Unmarried vs married (M 1.1.5); Political affiliation (P 3.3); Religious denomination (R 1.1, R 1.2); Marital happiness (S 1.7.2); Job satisfaction (S 1.9.1)

CONCLUSION:

| | | |
|---|---|---|
| AUTHOR: | Palmore, E.B. | PALMO 69 |

TITLE: 2 publications: - Physical, mental, and social factors in predicting longevity.
- Predicting longevity: a follow up controlling for age.

SOURCE: Gerontologist, 1969, vol. 9, p. 103-108 / 247-250.

---

**GOAL OF THE STUDY:** Examination of the relative importance by physical, mental and social factors in predicting longevity for various age, sex, and race categories by using a longevity quotient.

REFERS TO: Theory of longevity; Jarvik & Falek (1963), Riegel et al. (1967)

**TYPE OF STUDY:** explanatory, explorative, special group, longitudinal, non-experimental

**DATA GATHERING:** Personal interview, medical examination in a hospital setting and administration of questionnaire

**DATE OF DATA:** 1955 - 1959

**POPULATION:** Aged non-institutionalized persons, North Carolina, U.S.A.

**SAMPLE CONSTRUCTION:** Non-probability accidental sample, using volunteers.
age 60 - 94, median age 70; ambulatory, non-institutionalized Ss; sex, racial and occupational distribution approximated that of the area (Central North Carolina)

**NON-RESPONSE:**

N: 268

**AUTHOR'S HAPPINESS LABEL:** Happiness

**OUR CONCEPTUALIZATION:** Happiness

**INSTRUMENT:** COMP 4.4: Rating of happiness by the interviewer, using flexible standards relative to the age of the subject.

RELIABILITY:

VALIDITY:

DISTRIBUTION:

REMARKS:

CORRELATES: Longevity (H 2.4)

CONCLUSION: Happiness is one of the strongest predictors of longevity, even stronger than health. Other important factors are work satisfaction, health and tobacco use.

AUTHOR: Palmore, E.B. & Luikart, C.

PALMO 72

TITLE: Health and social factors related to life satisfaction.

SOURCE: Journal of Health & Social Behavior, 1972, vol. 13, p. 68-80.

---

GOAL OF THE STUDY: Analysis of the relative influence of health, activity, social-psychological and socio-economic variables upon life satisfaction in early and late middle age and analysis of the interrelations between these variables by using multiple regression analysis.

REFERS TO: Happiness research; Cantril (1965), Berkman (1971), Bradburn & Caplovitz (1965)

TYPE OF STUDY: explanatory, testing, special group, snapshot, non-experimental

DATA GATHERING: Personal interview, administration of questionnaire and medical examination at a hospital

DATE OF DATA: 1968

POPULATION: People of 46 and older, Duke, U.S.A.

SAMPLE CONSTRUCTION: Probability systematic random sample, using a membership list of a local major health insurance association, stratified by age and sex.
268 age 46 - 59, 234 age 60 - 71 ; 261 males, 241 females; white race only; underrepresentation of lower S.E.S. groups

NON-RESPONSE: 52%; reasons: too busy or not interested in free medical examination. Probably psychological differences; no substantial differences in terms of age, sex, health or S.E.S.

N: 502

AUTHOR'S HAPPINESS LABEL: Life satisfaction

OUR CONCEPTUALIZATION: Happiness

INSTRUMENT: HAPP 3.1: Single closed question on personal situation as compared with best and worst possible life, rated on a 10-point self-anchoring scale (adapted Cantril Present Personal rating; see CANTR 65).

A 10-point scale was used here instead of the 11-point scale, used by Cantril.
The same question as used by Cantril was offered.

RELIABILITY:

VALIDITY:

DISTRIBUTION: positively skewed
possible and actual range: 0 (low) to 9 (high); mean 7.0; S.D.: 1.5

REMARKS:

CORRELATES: Productivity (A 1.1); Age (A 3); Intelligence (C 1.3); Educational level (E 1.1.1); Gender (G 1.1); Physical health (H 2.1); Income (I 1.1); Geographic mobility (L 1.2, L 4.5); Social activity (L 3.3.1); Being married (M 1.1.5); Internal control (P 1.1); Sexual enjoyment (S 3.2); various indicators of Social participation (S 4); Upward career anchorage (S 5.4, W 2.5); Employed status (W 2.1)

CONCLUSION: Self-perceived health is most important for life satisfaction for both males and females and for all age groups. Second important is involvement in social organizations. Third important is belief in internal control (two-way effect). Life satisfaction of the males is more dependent on a variety of active roles than among the females.
Age, sex, number of social contacts, career anchorage, marital status and intelligence are not or slightly related to life satisfaction.

PALMO 75

AUTHOR: Palmore, E.

TITLE: The honorable elders. A cross-cultural analysis of aging in Japan.

SOURCE: Durham, North Carolina, 1975, Duke University Press.

---

GOAL OF THE STUDY: An attempt both to broaden the base for the emerging science of gerontology and to enlarge our vision of possible ways to improve the quality of our later years.

REFERS TO: Theory of aging; Palmore (1969), Cumming & Henry (1961)

TYPE OF STUDY: explanatory, explorative, national population, snapshot, non-experimental

DATA GATHERING: Structured interview

DATE OF DATA: September, 1973

POPULATION: Adults, Japan

SAMPLE CONSTRUCTION: Probability sample out of the Japanese adult population.

NON-RESPONSE:

N: 2000 or more

AUTHOR'S HAPPINESS LABEL: Life satisfaction

OUR CONCEPTUALIZATION: Happiness

INSTRUMENT: HAPP 3.1: Single closed question on present situation as compared with best and worst possible life, rated on an 11-point self-anchoring scale (Cantril Present Personal rating; see CANTR 65).

RELIABILITY:

VALIDITY:

DISTRIBUTION:

REMARKS:

CORRELATES: Like doing voluntary activities (A 1.8); Age (A 3); Retirement (R 2.1)

CONCLUSION: Activity in old age is associated with better health and more life satisfaction. Activity, health and satisfaction are three mutually reinforcing factors.

AUTHOR: Pandey, C. PANDE 71

TITLE: Popularity, rebelliousness, and happiness among institutionalized retarded males.

SOURCE: American Journal of Mental Deficiency, 1971, vol. 76, nr 3, p. 325-331.

---

GOAL OF THE STUDY: To investigate the interrelationships among popularity, rebelliousness, happiness and restrictiveness of setting among retardates.

REFERS TO: Theory of popularity of retardates; Dentler & Mackler (1961)

TYPE OF STUDY: explanatory, testing, special group, snapshot, non-experimental

DATA GATHERING: Structured interview, content analysis of hospital records, and rating by staff members familiar with the patients.

DATE OF DATA:

POPULATION: Institutionalized mentally retarded males, U.S.A.

SAMPLE CONSTRUCTION: Non-probability chunk sample of retarded males occupying two wards in a state hospital. The two wards differed greatly in populations being roughly comparable.
Ward A (N = 82): mean age 15.5; average person lived in hospital for 6 years; more open
Ward B (N = 67): mean age 21 ; average person lived in hospital for 7.5 years; more restrictive

NON-RESPONSE:

N: 149

AUTHOR'S HAPPINESS LABEL: Happiness

OUR CONCEPTUALIZATION: Hedonic level of affect

INSTRUMENT: AFF 5.1: Expert rating on the basis of longer clinical contact:

The patients were rated independently by two experienced staff-members who were familiar with all the patients on a 7-point 'Happy - Depressed' scale. The average of the two ratings was used as happiness score.

RELIABILITY:

VALIDITY:

DISTRIBUTION: positively skewed

REMARKS:

CORRELATES: Aggressiveness (A 2.2.1); Age (A 3); Intelligence (C 1.3); Speech (C 1.5); Cooperativeness (D 1); Race (E 2.2); various indicators of Physical health (H 2.1); various factors concerning Institutional living (I 2); various Physical characteristics (P 2.1); Popularity (P 4.1); various indicators of Social participation (S 4.1.1)

CONCLUSION: In both settings, happiness seems more related to social interaction variables than to any personal or physical characteristics.

AUTHOR: Payne, R.L. | PAYNE 74

TITLE: N.M. Bradburn's measures of psychological well-being: an attempt at replication.

SOURCE: Memo Mo: 61, MRC Social and Applied Psychology Unit, Department of Psychology, University of Sheffield, Sheffield S10 2TN, England, 1974.

---

GOAL OF THE STUDY: Replication of Bradburn's results on a British sample and an attempt to improve Bradburn's two independent measures of positive and negative affect.

REFERS TO: Happiness research; Bradburn & Caplovitz (1965), Bradburn (1969)

TYPE OF STUDY: explanatory, explorative, special group, snapshot, non-experimental

DATA GATHERING: Structured interview and highly structured questionnaire administered at home

DATE OF DATA:

POPULATION: Employed males, England

SAMPLE CONSTRUCTION: Non-probability purposive quota sample.
Interviewers were instructed to obtain a sample which contained 80% persons who supervised other people
Compared with the general population underrepresentation of very low skilled workers.
Age 30 - 60; almost 100% whites

NON-RESPONSE: 4% incomplete

N: 192

AUTHOR'S HAPPINESS LABEL: Psychological well-being

OUR CONCEPTUALIZATION: Hedonic level of affect (first instrument); Happiness (second instrument) and Contentment (third instrument)

FIRST INSTRUMENT: AFF 2.3: Index of closed questions on perceived occurrence of specific affects during the past four weeks (adapted Bradburn & Caplovitz indices of positive and negative affects; see BRADB 69):

Each Ss was asked: 'During the past four weeks have you ever felt. . .' yes/no. If yes: 'How often during the past four weeks have you ever felt. . .' every day / several times a week / once a week / 2 or 3 times a month / once a month

Index of positive affects:
1. Pleased about having accomplished something.
2. Things going my way.
3. Proud because someone complimented me on something I had done.
4. Particularly excited or interested in something.
5. On top of the world.
6. A deep sense of joy.
7. Pleased because my life feels orderly and secure.

Index of negative affects:
1. Bored
2. Very lonely and remote from other people.
3. Jealous of somebody.
4. Angry with someone.
5. Disappointed in myself.
6. Unhappy about the small number of times I have pleasant feelings and experiences.

An overall Affect Balance Score was not computed.

RELIABILITY: Equivalence: positive items : Q ranging from -.17 to +.70
negative items : Q ranging from +.03 to +.56
positive x negative items: Q ranging from -.15 to +.74
positive affect score x negative affect score: G = +.39

VALIDITY:

DISTRIBUTION:

SECOND INSTRUMENT: HAPP 1.1: Single closed question on 'how happy these days', rated on a 3-point scale.
very happy / pretty happy / not too happy

RELIABILITY:

VALIDITY:

DISTRIBUTION:

THIRD INSTRUMENT: CON 1.1: Single closed question on 'getting things wanted from life', rated on a 2-point scale.

doing pretty well now / not doing too well now

RELIABILITY:

VALIDITY:

DISTRIBUTION:

REMARKS: It is likely that the second and third instrument are the same questions as those used in the Bradburn study (see BRADB 69). The complete questions are not presented.

CORRELATES: Encountered new stimulating ideas (A 1.6, C 1.5); Having sufficient energy (A 2.2.6); Hedonic level x happiness (H 1.2.1); Contentment x hedonic level (H 1.3.2); Illness (H 2.1.3); Psychosomatic symptoms (H 2.2); Expected nervous breakdown (H 2.3.2); Wish to change life (H 3.1.1); New activities or hobbies engaged in (L 3.3.3); Satisfaction with specific aspects of one's job (S 1.9.2); Self-esteem (S 2.1.3); Contacts with friends (S 4.1.2); New people met (S 4.4)

CONCLUSION: In contrast to Bradburn's findings positive and negative affect were not found always unrelated. It is possible that the relation holds only in different categories of people; also there may be cultural differences. It is also likely that some people are more sensitive to affects of both kinds.

AUTHOR: Payne, R.L.

PAYNE 75

TITLE: Recent life changes and the reporting of psychological states.

SOURCE: Journal of Psychosomatic Research, 1975, vol. 19, p. 99-103.

---

GOAL OF THE STUDY: Exploration of relationships between recent life changes and psychological states.

REFERS TO: Theory of recent life changes; Rahe (1972)

TYPE OF STUDY: explanatory, explorative, special group, snapshot, non-experimental

DATA GATHERING: Structured interview and highly structured questionnaire administered at home

DATE OF DATA:

POPULATION: Employed males, England

SAMPLE CONSTRUCTION: Non-probability purposive quota sample (see PAYNE 74)

NON-RESPONSE: 4% incomplete

N: 192

AUTHOR'S HAPPINESS LABEL: Psychological well-being

OUR CONCEPTUALIZATION: Hedonic level of affect

INSTRUMENT: AFF 2.3: Index of closed questions on perceived occurrence of specific affects during the past few weeks (adapted Bradburn & Caplovitz indices of positive and negative affects; see PAYNE 74, first instrument).

RELIABILITY:

VALIDITY:

DISTRIBUTION:

REMARKS:

CORRELATES: Recent life changes (L 1.2)

CONCLUSION:

AUTHOR: Peretti, P.O. & Wilson, C.

PERET 75

TITLE: Voluntary and involuntary retirement of aged males and their effect on emotional satisfaction, usefulness, self-image, emotional stability and interpersonal relationships.

SOURCE: International Journal of Aging and Human Development, 1975, vol. 6, nr. 2, p. 131-138.

---

GOAL OF THE STUDY: To determine to what extent voluntary and involuntary retirement affect the emotional stability, usefulness, self-image, emotional satisfaction and interpersonal relationships of aged males.

REFERS TO: Theory of retirement; Reichard (1962), Tobin & Neugarten (1961)

TYPE OF STUDY: explanatory, explorative, special group, snapshot, non-experimental

DATA GATHERING: Highly structured questionnaire, followed by a structured interview with open-ended questions

DATE OF DATA:

POPULATION: Retired institutionalized aged males, Chicago, Illinois, U.S.A.

SAMPLE CONSTRUCTION: Non-probability purposive quota sample of retired males from a retirement hotel for the aged.
70 Ss were involved in voluntary and 70 in involuntary retirement.
Ss were matched on years of retirement, age, nature of retirement, occupational classification and length of stay at the establishment.
age 60 - 70; retired 2 to 3 years ago from (semi-) skilled occupations; physically and mentally healthy.

NON-RESPONSE:

N: 140

AUTHOR'S HAPPINESS LABEL: Emotional satisfaction

OUR CONCEPTUALIZATION: Happiness

INSTRUMENT: COMP 4.2: 7-item index containing yes/no questions, indicative for contentment, good spirits, happiness and satisfaction with present status or condition.

On basis of these questions Ss were dichotomized in emotionally satisfied vs not emotionally satisfied.

RELIABILITY:

VALIDITY:

DISTRIBUTION: Positively skewed (negative among involuntary retirees)

REMARKS:

CORRELATES: (In)Voluntary retirement (R 2.2)

CONCLUSION: Voluntary retirement tends to have a more positive effect on aged males than does involuntary retirement.

AUTHOR: Pesznecker, B.L. & McNell, J.

PESZN 75

TITLE: Relationship among health habits, social assets, psychological well-being, life change, and alterations in health status.

SOURCE: Nursing Research, 1975, vol. 4, nr 6, p. 442-447.

---

GOAL OF THE STUDY: Examination of the relationship between life change and alterations in health and the relationship of 3 variables (health habits, social assets and psychological well-being) to alterations in health status and life change.

REFERS TO: Theory of physical health; Mechanic (1968), Crawford (1971)

TYPE OF STUDY: explanatory, explorative, local population, snapshot, non-experimental

DATA GATHERING: Highly structured mailed questionnaire

DATE OF DATA:

POPULATION: Adults, Renton, Washington, U.S.A.

SAMPLE CONSTRUCTION: Probability systematic random sample of households listed in a commercial 'householders' directory, taking one adult per household.
age 18+, mean age 39; 236 males, 300 females; 525 white, 6 black, 5 oriental; 453 married, 54 divorced, 29 single.

NON-RESPONSE: 55%; 185 unattainable, 12 incomplete, 412 refusals

N: 536

AUTHOR'S HAPPINESS LABEL: Psychological well-being

OUR CONCEPTUALIZATION: Hedonic level of affect

INSTRUMENT: AFF 1.3: Index of closed questions on perceived occurrence of specific affects in general (adapted Bradburn & Caplovitz Affect Balance Score; see BERKM 71).

RELIABILITY:

VALIDITY:

DISTRIBUTION: possible and actual range: 0 (high) to 7 (low); mean: 3.98

REMARKS:

CORRELATES: Alterations in health status (H 2.5); Life change (L 1.2)

CONCLUSION: The notion that psychological well-being fosters health by tempering life change did not receive strong support in the data.

PHILI 66

AUTHOR: Philips Nederland, N.V.

TITLE: The Dutch housewife.
(In Dutch: De Nederlandse huisvrouw.)

SOURCE: Eindhoven, 1966, Philips Nederland.

---

GOAL OF THE STUDY: Description of time use, domestic appliances, house and attitudes of the Dutch housewife.

REFERS TO:

TYPE OF STUDY: descriptive, explorative, special group, snapshot, non-experimental

DATA GATHERING: Structured interview administered at home

DATE OF DATA: Autumn, 1964

POPULATION: Housewives, The Netherlands

SAMPLE CONSTRUCTION: Probability area sample.

NON-RESPONSE:

N: 1800. The data concerning happiness are based on the answers of 450 housewives.

AUTHOR'S HAPPINESS LABEL: Happiness

OUR CONCEPTUALIZATION: Happiness

INSTRUMENT: HAPP 1.1: Single closed question rated on a 5-point scale:

How happy or unhappy do you think you are?
very happy / happy / moderately happy / fairly unhappy / very unhappy?

In Dutch:
Hoe gelukkig of ongelukkig vindt U zichzelf?
heel gelukkig / gelukkig / matig gelukkig / tamelijk ongelukkig / erg ongelukkig?

RELIABILITY:

VALIDITY:

DISTRIBUTION: positively skewed: 29% very happy, 51% happy, 16% moderately happy, 3% fairly unhappy, 0% very unhappy

REMARKS:

CORRELATES: Age (A 3); Having children (F 1.2.1); Self-perceived health (H 2.1.2); Enjoying domestic work (H 4.2); Income (I 1.1); Having a good life (L 2.1.1); Community size (L 4.1); Satisfaction with marriage (S 1.7.2); Satisfaction with marriage, job and health (S 1.11)

CONCLUSION:

AUTHOR: Phillips, D.L. PHILL 67A

TITLE: Social participation and happiness.

SOURCE: The American Journal of Sociology, 1967, vol. 72, nr 5, p. 479-488.

---

**GOAL OF THE STUDY:** Examination of the effects of voluntary social participation on self-reports of happiness.

REFERS TO: Happiness research; Bradburn & Caplovitz (1965), Homans (1961)

TYPE OF STUDY: explanatory, testing, local population, snapshot, non-experimental

DATA GATHERING: Structured interview at home

DATE OF DATA:

POPULATION: Adults, New Hampshire, U.S.A.

**SAMPLE CONSTRUCTION:** Probability sample.
Study 750, National Opinion Research Center (NORC).

NON-RESPONSE:

N: 600

**AUTHOR'S HAPPINESS LABEL:** Happiness (first instrument) and Affect (second instrument)

**OUR CONCEPTUALIZATION:** Happiness (first instrument) and Hedonic level of affect (second instrument)

FIRST INSTRUMENT: HAPP 1.1: Single closed question using the term 'happiness', rated on a 3-point scale (see GURIN 60).

RELIABILITY:

VALIDITY:

DISTRIBUTION: positively skewed: 41% very happy, 52% pretty happy, 7% not too happy

SECOND INSTRUMENT: AFF 2.3: Index of closed questions on perceived occurrence of specific affects during the past few weeks (Bradburn Affect Balance Score; see BRADB 69).

RELIABILITY:

VALIDITY:

DISTRIBUTION: positively skewed
possible range: -5 (low) to +5 (high); actual range: 19% +3 or more, 40% +1 or2, 19% 0, 22% -1 or less

REMARKS: No correlations with the overall Affect Balance Score were presented. On the basis of data available we were able to compute a Gamma (G') for the association between Affect Balance and Happiness (first instrument).

The data reported in this publication are from the same investigation as reported in two other articles by the same author (see PHILL 67B and PHILL 69). These latter two publications present elaborations of the zero-order correlations reported in this publication. In Part III we combined these results for reasons of convenience.

Correlations presented in the 'elaboration / remarks' column (in Part III) are based on the proportions 'very happy' answers (first instrument), or on the proportions 'high positive' or 'high negative' feelings (second instrument).

CORRELATES: Age (A 3); Educational level (E 1.1.1); Gender (G 1.1); Hedonic level x happiness (H 1.2.1); Religious denomination (R 1.2); various indicators of Social participation (S 4)

CONCLUSION: Social participation is related to happiness and positive feelings, but not to negative feelings.

AUTHOR: Phillips, D.L.

PHILL 67B

TITLE: Mental health status, social participation and happiness.

SOURCE: Journal of Health and Social Behavior, 1967, vol. 18, p. 285-291.

---

GOAL OF THE STUDY: To determine the extent to which mental health status and social participation contribute to the level of happiness which people experience.

REFERS TO: Happiness research; Bradburn & Caplovitz (1965)

TYPE OF STUDY: explanatory, testing, local population, snapshot, non-experimental

DATA GATHERING: Structured interview at home

DATE OF DATA:

POPULATION: Adults, New Hampshire, U.S.A.

SAMPLE CONSTRUCTION: Probability sample.
NORC study 750 (see PHILL 67A).
430 mentally well, 163 mentally ill

NON-RESPONSE: 1%

N: 593

AUTHOR'S HAPPINESS LABEL: Happiness

OUR CONCEPTUALIZATION: Happiness

INSTRUMENT: HAPP 1.1: Single closed question using the term 'happiness', rated on a 3-point scale (see GURIN 60).

RELIABILITY:

VALIDITY:

DISTRIBUTION: positively skewed: 41% very happy, 52% pretty happy, 7% not too happy

REMARKS: This publications contains some correlates of Happiness also mentioned in an earlier publication by the same author (see PHILL 67A). It also reports elaborations of relationships mentioned in the PHILL 67A publication. In Part III these data are presented together at PHILL 67A.

CORRELATES: Mental health (H 2.3.1)

CONCLUSION: Happiness is contingent both on people's state of mental health and the extent to which they participate in social interaction with others. Each of these factors exerts an independent influence on happiness.

AUTHOR: Phillips, D.L. | PHILL 69

TITLE: Social class, social participation, and happiness: A consideration of 'interaction opportunities' and 'investment'.

SOURCE: The Sociological Quarterly, 1969, vol. 10, nr 1, p. 3-21.

---

GOAL OF THE STUDY: Examination of the effects of S.E.S. upon the relationship between social participation and happiness.

REFERS TO: Happiness research; Bradburn (1964), Homans (1961)

TYPE OF STUDY: explanatory, explorative, local population, snapshot, non-experimental

DATA GATHERING: Structured interview at home

DATE OF DATA:

POPULATION: Adults, New Hampshire, U.S.A.

SAMPLE CONSTRUCTION: Probability sample.
NORC study 750 (see PHILL 67A).

NON-RESPONSE:

N: 600

AUTHOR'S HAPPINESS LABEL: Happiness (first instrument) and Affect (second instrument)

OUR CONCEPTUALIZATION: Happiness (first instrument) and Hedonic level of affect (second instrument)

FIRST INSTRUMENT: HAPP 1.1: Single closed question using the term 'happiness', rated on a 3-point scale (see GURIN 60).

RELIABILITY:

VALIDITY:

DISTRIBUTION: positively skewed: 41% very happy, 52% pretty happy, 7% not too happy

SECOND INSTRUMENT: AFF 2.3: Index of closed questions on perceived occurrence of specific affects during the past few weeks (Bradburn Affect Balance Score; see BRADB 69).

RELIABILITY:

VALIDITY:

DISTRIBUTION: —

REMARKS: This publication contains some correlates of Happiness also mentioned in an earlier publication by the same author (see PHILL 67A). It also reports elaborations of relationships mentioned in the PHILL 67A publication. In Part III these data are presented together at PHILL 67A.

CORRELATES: S.E.S. (S 5.1)

CONCLUSION: Social participation is related to happiness and positive feelings.
This relationship is stronger in lower S.E.S. groups because they have fewer voluntary social participation opportunities, leading to a greater investment in available participation opportunities.

| | | |
|---|---|---|
| AUTHOR: | Phillips, D.L. & Clancy, K.J. | PHILL 73 |
| TITLE: | Some effects of 'social desirability' in survey studies. | |
| SOURCE: | American Journal of Sociology, 1972, vol. 77, nr 5, p. 921-940. | |

---

GOAL OF THE STUDY: To test the effects of people's judgement of trait desirability and their need for social approval on responses to questions on happiness, religiosity, friends, marital happiness, prejudice and visiting a doctor.

REFERS TO: Theory of social desirability; Cook & Selltiz (1964)

TYPE OF STUDY: explanatory, testing, special group, snapshot, non-experimental

DATA GATHERING: Structured interview by telephone

DATE OF DATA:

POPULATION: Adults in the New England and Mid-Atlantic States, U.S.A.

SAMPLE CONSTRUCTION: Probability cluster sample of adults from households with a listed telephone.

NON-RESPONSE:

N: 404

AUTHOR'S HAPPINESS LABEL: General happiness

OUR CONCEPTUALIZATION: Happiness

INSTRUMENT: HAPP 1.1: Single closed question using the term 'happiness', rated on a 3-point scale (see GURIN 60).

RELIABILITY:

VALIDITY:

DISTRIBUTION: 32% very happy

REMARKS: Our computation of Gammas (G') is based on the proportions 'very happy' answers.

CORRELATES: Gender (G 1.1); Perceived desirability of happiness (H 1.10); Need for social approval (P 1.5.2)

CONCLUSION:

PIERC 73

AUTHOR: Pierce. R.C. & Clark, M.M.

TITLE: Measurement of morale in the elderly.

SOURCE: International Journal of Aging and Human Development, 1973, vol. 4, nr 2, p. 83-101.

---

GOAL OF THE STUDY: Exploration of the relationship between dimensions of morale and mental health.

REFERS TO: Theory of morale in old age; Cumming et al. (1958), Neugarten et al. (1961)

TYPE OF STUDY: explanatory, explorative, special group, snapshot, non-experimental

DATA GATHERING: Structured interview taking 2 to 4 hours

DATE OF DATA:

POPULATION: Aged persons, San Fransisco, U.S.A.

SAMPLE CONSTRUCTION: Community subjects: probability sample stratified by age, sex, and social living arrangement (N = 264).
Hospital subjects : non-probability chunk sample of persons admitted to a psychiatric hospital during 1959 (N = 171); 90 discharged, 81 inpatients.
Both samples were survivors from the Löwenthal (1964) sample of elderly San Fransisco residents.
206 males, 229 females; age 60+

NON-RESPONSE: 62% dropouts after 2 interviews (2 years)

N: 435

AUTHOR'S HAPPINESS LABEL: Happiness

OUR CONCEPTUALIZATION: Happiness (first & third instrument) and Hedonic level of affect (second instrument)

FIRST INSTRUMENT: HAPP 1.1: Single closed question rated on a 3-point scale (from Thompson et al.; see THOMP 60)

All in all, how much happiness would you say you find in life today?
lots / some / almost none

RELIABILITY:

VALIDITY:

DISTRIBUTION:

SECOND INSTRUMENT: AFF 1.1: Single closed question rated on a 3-point scale (from Thompson et al.; see THOMP 60):

In general, how would you say you feel most of the time, in good spirits or in low spirits?
good / both / low

RELIABILITY:

VALIDITY:

DISTRIBUTION:

THIRD INSTRUMENT: HAPP 2.1: Single closed question rated on a 3-point scale (from Thompson et al.; see THOMP 60):

On the whole, how satisfied would you say you are with your way of life today?
very / fairly / not very

RELIABILITY:

VALIDITY:

DISTRIBUTION:

REMARKS:

CORRELATES: Mental illness (H 2.3.3)

CONCLUSION: Among the elderly good morale seems to be related to three essential factors: being able to look on one's life with a sense of satisfaction and perhaps accomplishment; an equable and unruffled approach to present day-to-day living; and a sense of anticipation for the future.

AUTHOR: Porter J.

PORTE 67

TITLE: Sex-role concepts, their relationships to psychological well-being and to future plans in female seniors.

SOURCE: Unpublished doctoral dissertation, 1967, University of Rochester, New York, U.S.A.

---

GOAL OF THE STUDY: To determine sex-role attitudes of female college seniors and its relationships with psychological well-being and other attitudes and behaviors.

REFERS TO: Theory of sex-role attitudes and happiness research; Wessman et al. (1960), Douvan (1960), Vaught (1965)

TYPE OF STUDY: explanatory, explorative, special group, longitudinal, non-experimental

DATA GATHERING: Highly structured questionnaire, administered in classroom situation

DATE OF DATA: May - June, 1966

POPULATION: Female college seniors, University of Rochester, U.S.A.

SAMPLE CONSTRUCTION: Non-probability chunk sample of women in the class of 1966.
The sample represented 92% of the female senior class.
age 19 - 28, mean age 21

NON-RESPONSE: 8%; unaffected by place of residence

N: 162

AUTHOR'S HAPPINESS LABEL: Psychological well-being (average typical mood)

OUR CONCEPTUALIZATION: Hedonic level of affect

INSTRUMENT: AFF 2.1: Single closed question on perceived overall hedonic level during the current semester, rated on a 10-point scale (Wessman & Ricks Elation - Depression Scale; see WESSM 60).

The scale was introduced by the following statement:
'Mood is usually applied to states lasting for minutes or hours, but most people can estimate their average or typical mood over a long period of time. Using the following scale, please indicate which statement best describes your typical mood for the current spring semester.
Draw a circle around the number of the statement which best describes your average level of happiness or unhappiness during this semester'.

RELIABILITY:

VALIDITY:

DISTRIBUTION:

REMARKS: Constantinople (see CONST 65) administered the Elation - Depression Scale and the personal importance of specific goals measure to a number of the subjects in the present study during the preceding academic year. Junior Elation - Depression scores were therefore available for 75 of the 162 Ss, and indicators of personal goals for 60 of the 75 Ss.

CORRELATES: Age (A 3); various Sex-role attitudes (G 1.2); Ego-strength (H 2.1.3); Personal goals (H 3.2.1); Level of attachment to male partner (M 1.6); Satisfaction with next year's plans (S 1.10)

CONCLUSION: A causal relationship between happiness and attachment is not made clear by these data, but the data do suggest that the two variables are not independent. Perhaps more mature women are happier, and also more likely to establish enduring relationships.

PORTE 72

AUTHOR: Porter Gump, J.

TITLE: Sex-role attitudes and psychological well-being.

SOURCE: Journal of Social Issues, 1972, vol. 28, nr 2, p. 79-92.

---

GOAL OF THE STUDY: Exploration of the relation of sex-role concepts of senior college women to ego strength, happiness and achievement plans.

REFERS TO: Theory of sex-role attitudes and happiness; Wessman et al. (1960), Wessman & Ricks (1966), Constantinople (1965)

TYPE OF STUDY: descriptive, explorative, special group, longitudinal, non-experimental

DATA GATHERING: Highly constructed questionnaire, administered in classroom situation

DATE OF DATA: May - June, 1966

POPULATION: Female college seniors, University of Rochester, U.S.A.

SAMPLE CONSTRUCTION: Non-probability chunk sample (see PORTE 67).
Most females were accepting rather a progressive than a traditional sex-role definition.

NON-RESPONSE:

N: 162

AUTHOR'S HAPPINESS LABEL: Happiness

OUR CONCEPTUALIZATION: Hedonic level of affect

INSTRUMENT: AFF 2.1: Single closed question on perceived overall hedonic level during the current semester, rated on a 10-point scale (Wessman & Ricks Elation - Depression Scale; see WESSM 60 and PORTE 67).

RELIABILITY:

VALIDITY:

DISTRIBUTION:

REMARKS: see remarks at PORTE 67

CORRELATES: various Sex-role attitudes (G 1.2)

CONCLUSION: Self and other orientated women differ with respect to the goals towards they consciously strive, but they do not differ with respect to establishing serious relationships with men, nor with respect to their level of happiness.

RAHE 71

AUTHOR: Rahe, R.H., Rubin, R.T., Gunderson, K.E. & Arthur, R.J.

TITLE: Psychological correlates of serum cholesterol in man. A longitudinal study.

SOURCE: Psychosomatic Medicine, 1971, vol. 33, nr 5, p. 399-410.

---

**GOAL OF THE STUDY:** To investigate the magnitude and variability over time of the correlations between psychological moods and feelings and serum cholesterol level.

REFERS TO: Theory of serum cholesterol level and mood and feelings; Groover et al. (1960), Cathey et al (1957)

TYPE OF STUDY: descriptive, explorative, special group, snapshot, non-experimental

DATA GATHERING: Highly structured questionnaire and cholesterol determinations in laboratory during the first months of an extensive training program.

DATE OF DATA:

POPULATION: Trainees on the U.S. underwater demolition team, U.S.A.

**SAMPLE** CONSTRUCTION: Rahe & Arthur (1967) probability sample of a class of U.D.T. trainees.

**NON**-RESPONSE: The non-response during the 16 measurements varied from 4 to 0 Ss.

N: 16 - 20

**AUTHOR'S HAPPINESS** LABEL: Happiness

**OUR CONCEPTUALIZATION:** Hedonic level of affect

**INSTRUMENT:** AFF 3.3: Repeated index of closed questions on momentaneous occurrence of specific affects, scored 15 times during 2 months:

The adjective ckecklist contained 7 factorally derived items: contented, calm, happy, pleased, satisfied, cheerful, and good.
Response values were: not at all / somewhat or slightly / mostly or generally

RELIABILITY: equivalence: intercorrelations ranged between +.86 and +.94

VALIDITY:

DISTRIBUTION:

REMARKS:

CORRELATES: Serum Cholesterol level (P 2.3)

CONCLUSION: Serum cholesterol level is strongly positively associated with moods and feelings of depression, anger, fear and lethargy, and strongly negatively associated with moods and feelings of motivation, arousal and happiness.

AUTHOR: Ramzy-Saleh Guirguis, N. & Hermans, H.J.M.

RAMZY 73

TITLE: Correlates of psychological well-being and emotionality.

SOURCE: Gedrag, 1973, vol. 1, p. 64-91 (Dutch periodical).

---

**GOAL** OF THE STUDY: Exploration of the positive and negative dimensions of well-being.

REFERS TO: Happiness research; Bradburn & Caplovitz (1965), Wessman & Ricks (1966)

TYPE OF STUDY: descriptive, explorative, special group, snapshot, non-experimental

DATA GATHERING: Administration of a highly structured questionnaire in a classroom situation and precoded daily record of personal feelings and behavior during 28 days.

DATE OF DATA: After 1970

POPULATION: Secondary school pupils, The Netherlands

**SAMPLE** CONSTRUCTION: Non-probability accidental sample of volunteer pupils from the top class of their secondary education from 4 schools.
36 boys, 53 girls

NON-RESPONSE: 47%

N: 89

AUTHOR'S HAPPINESS LABEL: Elation

OUR CONCEPTUALIZATION: Hedonic level of affect

INSTRUMENT: AFF 3.1: Repeated single closed question on overall hedonic level for the past day, rated on a 10-point scale (Wessman & Ricks Elation - Depression Scale; see WESSM 60).

The scale was scored every night during 20 - 28 days

RELIABILITY:

VALIDITY:

DISTRIBUTION:

REMARKS:

CORRELATES: Emotionality (A 2.1.3); Happiness (L 2.1.2)

CONCLUSION:

RENNE 70

**AUTHOR:** Renne, K.S.

**TITLE:** Correlates of dissatisfaction in marriage.

**SOURCE:** Journal of Marriage and the Family, 1970, vol. 32, p. 54-67.

---

**GOAL OF THE STUDY:** Examination of factors related to marital happiness

**REFERS TO:** Theory of marital happiness; Blood & Wolfe (1960)

**TYPE OF STUDY:** explanatory, explorative, special group, snapshot, non-experimental

**DATA GATHERING:** Highly structured mailed questionnaire and structured interview

**DATE OF DATA:** 1965

**POPULATION:** Married adults, Alameda County, California, U.S.A.

**SAMPLE CONSTRUCTION:** Probability area sample of households (see also BERKM 71 and RENNE 74).
The sample was limited to married Ss living with their spouse only. Most of them were couples.

**NON-RESPONSE:** 26%

**N:** 5163

**AUTHOR'S HAPPINESS LABEL:** Happiness

**OUR CONCEPTUALIZATION:** Happiness

**INSTRUMENT:** HAPP 1.1: Single closed question rated on a 3-point scale:

All in all, how happy are you these days?
very happy / pretty happy / not too happy

**RELIABILITY:**

**VALIDITY:**

**DISTRIBUTION:**

**REMARKS:**

**CORRELATES:** Marital satisfaction (S 1.7.2)

**CONCLUSION:** Marital satisfaction is an integral part of emotional or physical well-being. So marital happiness was found to be closely associated with general morale or happiness.

AUTHOR: Renne, K.S.

RENNE 74

TITLE: Measurement of social health in a general population survey.

SOURCE: Social Science Research, 1974, vol. 3, nr 1, p. 25-44.

---

GOAL OF THE STUDY: To define and measure the social health of individuals in terms of the degree in which they are functioning members of their community.

REFERS TO: Theory of health (physical, psychological and social); Belloc et al. (1971), Berkman (1971)

TYPE OF STUDY: explanatory, explorative, local population, snapshot, non-experimental

DATA GATHERING: Highly structured questionnaire adminstered at home

DATE OF DATA: 1965

POPULATION: Adults, Alameda County, California, U.S.A.

SAMPLE CONSTRUCTION: Probability multi-stage sample of households (see also BERKM 71).
Subjects were 20 years or older, or 16 - 19 and ever married.

NON-RESPONSE: 14%

N: 6928

AUTHOR'S HAPPINESS LABEL: Psychological well-being

OUR CONCEPTUALIZATION: Hedonic level of affect

INSTRUMENT: AFF 1.3: Index of closed questions on perceived occurrence of specific affects in general (adapted Bradburn & Caplovitz Affect Balance Score; see BRADB 65).

The instrument is almost identical with the one, used by Berkman (see BERKM 71). The only difference is that four, instead of five, negative affect items were used here.

RELIABILITY:

VALIDITY:

DISTRIBUTION:

REMARKS:

CORRELATES: Social health (L 2.2.2)

CONCLUSION: Psychological health and social health reinforce each other.

AUTHOR: Rose, A.M.

ROSE 55

TITLE: Factors associated with the life satisfaction of middle-class, middle aged persons.

SOURCE: Marriage and Family Living, 1955, p. 15-19.

---

GOAL OF THE STUDY: To test the hypothesis that differences in factors associated with life satisfaction between the sexes will reflect the need for women to find a new central role as their role as homemaker necessarily declines..

REFERS TO: Theory of central roles in life; Rose (1951)

TYPE OF STUDY: explanatory, testing, special group, snapshot, non-experimental

DATA GATHERING: Highly structured questionnaire administered at home and rating by college student offspring

DATE OF DATA: 1952 - 1953

POPULATION: Middle aged, middle-class married couples, U.S.A.

SAMPLE CONSTRUCTION: Non-probability accidental sample of married couples, using parents of sociology students.

NON-RESPONSE: 50%

N: 416

AUTHOR'S HAPPINESS LABEL: Satisfaction with life

OUR CONCEPTUALIZATION: Happiness

INSTRUMENT: HAPP 2.1: Single closed question rated on a 5-point scale:

In general, how satisfied are you with your life?
very satisfied / satisfied / average / somewhat dissatisfied / very satisfied

RELIABILITY:

VALIDITY:

DISTRIBUTION: positively skewed

REMARKS:

CORRELATES: various factors concerning one's Children (F 1.2); Closeness of the total family life (F 1.4, S 4.1.3); various Wishes (H 3.2.3); Household work (H 4.2); various factors concerning Use of leisure time (L 3.3); various factors concerning Marriage (M 2); Job satisfaction (S 1.9.1); Formal social participation (S 4.2); Desire for participation in organizations and activities (S 4.5); Employed status (W 2.1)

CONCLUSION: The life satisfaction of middle-class women as they enter middle age is a function of the degree to which they are able to assume another central role to substitute for their necessarily declining role as homemakers. Earning an income and engaging in organizational activities are among the additional roles that make for life satisfaction.

AUTHOR: Schaefer, E.S. & Bayley, N.

SCHAE 63

TITLE: Maternal behavior, child behavior, and their intercorrelations from infancy through adolenscence.

SOURCE: Monographs of the Society for Research in Child Development, Serial no. 87, vol. 28, nr 3.

---

GOAL OF THE STUDY: Investigation into the relationship of maternal behavior to the social and emotional development of the child.

REFERS TO: Theory of maternal behavior and personality development; Schaefer (1959), Hall & Lindzey (1957)

TYPE OF STUDY: explanatory, explorative, special group, longitudinal, non-experimental

DATA GATHERING: Structured and unstructured observations of overt behavior of mothers and their children during the children's first three years, and of the children's behavior until the age of 18, and interviews with the mothers between the children's age of 9 to 14 years.

DATE OF DATA: 1928 - 1943

POPULATION: Children and their mothers, Berkeley, California, U.S.A.

SAMPLE CONSTRUCTION: Non-probability chunk sample of children, born in two Berkeley hospitals in 1928 and 1929, and their mothers (Berkeley Growth Study; see Bayley 1933). full-term infants of white, English speaking parents; 27 boys, 27 girls

NON-RESPONSE: 13% drop-outs (7 children and their mothers)

N: 108 (54 children and their mothers) during the first years of the children's life. The sample is smaller at higher ages but never less than 13 boys and 13 girls. For the interview with mothers in the period of the children's age from 9 to 14 years, data of 34 mothers were available.

AUTHOR'S HAPPINESS LABEL: Emotional tone (for children in the ages of 10 - 36 months only).

OUR CONCEPTUALIZATION: Hedonic level of affect

INSTRUMENT: AFF 5.1: Clinical ratings on the basis of repeated observations of expressive behavior (see also MCGRA 68).

Only the children were rated during the first 3 years of their lives. They were rated 12 times (after 10, 11, 12, 13, 14, 15, 18, 21, 24, 27, 30 and 36 months of living) for 'Emotional tone: unhappy - happy' on a 7-point scale.
Later the ratings of 10 - 12, 13 - 15, 18 - 24, and 27 - 36 months were combined.

RELIABILITY: retest reliability within combined months:

10 - 12 months: for boys r = +.83, for girls r = +.56
13 - 15 months: for boys r = +.80, for girls r = +.85
18 - 24 months: for boys r = +.78, for girls r = +.47
27 - 36 months: for boys r = +.66, for girls r = +.63

retest reliability between combined months:

10 - 12 x 13 - 15 months: for boys r = +.64 (05), for girls r = +.72 (05)
10 - 12 x 18 - 24 months: for boys r = +.61 (05), for girls r = +.51 (05)
10 - 12 x 27 - 36 months: for boys r = +.50 (05), for girls r = +.48 (05)
13 - 15 x 18 - 24 months: for boys r = +.65 (05), for girls r = +.69 (05) ($r = r_{pm}$)
13 - 15 x 27 - 36 months: for boys r = +.68 (05), for girls r = +.48 (05)
18 - 24 x 27 - 36 months: for boys r = +.64 (05), for girls r = +.72 (05)

VALIDITY:

DISTRIBUTION:

REMARKS: This study has yielded a wealth of data. It has assessed many variables at many different points in time. Hedonic level has been assessed at several ages. These measures have been related to variables which have also been assessed at different ages. For practical reasons in Part III all correlates thus produced are brought together in schemes like the following one:

| | | happiness measured at the age of (months): | | | |
|---|---|---|---|---|---|
| | | 10 - 12 | 13 - 15 | 18 - 24 | 27 - 36 |
| other variable | 10 - 12 | ... | ...[x] | ... | ...[x] |
| measured at the | 13 - 15 | ... | ... (correlations) | ... | ... |
| age of (months): | 18 - 14 | ... | ... | ... | ... |
| | 27 - 36 | ... | ... | ... | ... |

([x] indicates $p < .05$)

The investigators have also assessed the mothers' happiness. This measure must be considered invalid, however, because one of its items concerns 'a sense of humor'.

Information concerning measurements of maternal behavior data were more fully reported in Schaefer et al. (1959).

CORRELATES: various Characteristics of the mother (F 1.1.3, F 2.1); various Personality traits (P 1.9)

CONCLUSION:

AUTHOR: Schneider, F.W. & Coppinger, N.W.

SCHNE 71

TITLE: Staff-resident perception of the needs and adjustment of nursing home residents.

SOURCE: Aging and Human Development, 1971, vol. 2, p. 59-65.

---

GOAL OF THE STUDY: Assessment of the relation between self- and staff perceived needs of nursing home residents and determination whether this relation is reflected in both the staff's judgement of the resident's adjustment and the resident's feelings of personal satisfaction.

REFERS TO:

TYPE OF STUDY: explanatory, testing, special group, snapshot, non-experimental

DATA GATHERING: Structured interview

DATE OF DATA:

POPULATION: Male residents of a chronic care Veterans Administration nursing home, U.S.A.

SAMPLE CONSTRUCTION: All the residents of a 41-bed chronic care Veterans Administration nursing home.
age 46 - 89, mean age 69.7

NON-RESPONSE: 51% unobtainables, because of physical incapacity or inability to understand the instructions

N: 20

AUTHOR'S HAPPINESS LABEL: Life satisfaction

OUR CONCEPTUALIZATION: Happiness

INSTRUMENT: COMP 5: Expert ratings on happiness on the basis of longer clinical contact:

Ratings by 16 members of the staff of the happiness and satisfaction with present and past life each resident displays, on the basis of lasting face-to-face interaction.

RELIABILITY: interjudge agreement: $t_k = +.24$ (001)

VALIDITY:

DISTRIBUTION:

REMARKS:

CORRELATES: various factors concerning Institutional living (I 2, D 1); Satisfaction with life (L 2.1.2)

CONCLUSION: The degree of misperception of the resident's needs by the staff are only related to external adjustment criteria, such as adjustment and cooperation ratings by the staff, but not to internal adjustment criteria: the resident's feelings of satisfaction.

AUTHOR: Schwarz, D. & Strian, F.

SCHWA 72/1-2

TITLE: Psychometric investigations on well-being in psychiatric and medical patients.
(In German: Psychometrische Untersuchungen zur Befindlichkeit psychiatrischer und inter-medizinischer Patienten).

SOURCE: Archiv für Psychiatrie und Nervenkrankheiten, 1972, vol. 216, nr 1, p. 70-81 (German periodical).

---

GOAL OF THE STUDY: To validate the v. Zerssen well-being scale using depressive patients.

REFERS TO: Happiness research; v. Zerssen et al. (1970)

TYPE OF STUDY: explanatory, explorative, special group, snapshot, experimental

DATA GATHERING: Highly structured questionnaire and ratings by doctors

DATE OF DATA:

POPULATION: Psychiatric patients (study 1) and medical patients (study 2), W. Germany

SAMPLE CONSTRUCTION: study 1: Non-probability chunk sample of psychiatric patients in therapy.
10 neurotic depressed patients, 30 internal depressed patients, 16 depressed schizophrenic patients
study 2: Unknown.
90 males, 90 females

NON-RESPONSE:

N: 56 (study 1), 180 (study 2)

AUTHOR'S HAPPINESS LABEL: Well-being

OUR CONCEPTUALIZATION: Hedonic level of affect

INSTRUMENT: AFF 3.3: Repeated index of closed questions on momentaneous occurrence of specific affects (v. Zerssen et al. (1970) Befindlichkeitsskala).

The well-being score is the mean of the ratings of every other day during the treatment (study 1), the mean of the rating before treatment and the rating 4 weeks later (study 2).

RELIABILITY:

VALIDITY:

DISTRIBUTION:

REMARKS:

CORRELATES: Depression (A 2.2.4)

CONCLUSION:

SKRAB 69

AUTHOR: Skrabanek, R.L.

TITLE: Adjustment of former university faculty members to retirement.

SOURCE: Proceedings of the Southwestern Sociological Association, April 1969, vol. 19, p. 65-69.

---

GOAL OF THE STUDY: To investigate the adjustment to retirement.

REFERS TO:

TYPE OF STUDY: explanatory, explorative, special group, snapshot, non-experimental

DATA GATHERING: Highly structured mailed questionnaire

DATE OF DATA: 1968

POPULATION: Retired university faculty members, U.S.A.

SAMPLE CONSTRUCTION: Probability systematic random sample.
161 males, 386 females

NON-RESPONSE: 52%

N: 547

AUTHOR'S HAPPINESS LABEL: Happiness

OUR CONCEPTUALIZATION: Happiness

INSTRUMENT: HAPP 1.1: Single closed question using the term 'happiness', rated on a 5-point scale:
very happy / happy / neutral / unhappy / very unhappy.

RELIABILITY:

VALIDITY:

DISTRIBUTION: positively skewed: 39% very happy, 47% happy, 5% neutral, 2% unhappy, 4% very unhappy, 7% no answer

REMARKS:

CORRELATES: Gender (G 1.1); various factors concerning Retirement (R 2)

CONCLUSION: Former university faculty members may be generally more favorably adjusted to retirement than persons in most other occupations.

AUTHOR: Snyder, E.E. & Spreitzer, E.A. | SNYDE 74

TITLE: Involvement in sports and psychological well-being.

SOURCE: International Journal of Sport Psychology, 1974, vol. 5, p. 28-40.

---

GOAL OF THE STUDY: Assessment of psychological consequences of sport involvement among adults.

REFERS TO: Theory of involvement in sports, Kenyon (1969)

TYPE OF STUDY: explanatory, explorative, local population, snapshot, non-experimental

DATA GATHERING: Highly structured mailed questionnaire

DATE OF DATA: 1973

POPULATION: Adults, Toledo, Ohio, U.S.A.

SAMPLE CONSTRUCTION: Systematic random sample, using the City Directory of Toledo.
25% suburbans, 75% urbans; 49% females, 51% males; mean age 42; mean number of years of completed education 13

NON-RESPONSE: 46%

N: 510

AUTHOR'S HAPPINESS LABEL: Psychological well-being

OUR CONCEPTUALIZATION: Happiness

FIRST INSTRUMENT: HAPP 1.1: Single closed question using the term 'happiness', rated on a 3-point scale (see GURIN 60).

RELIABILITY:

VALIDITY:

DISTRIBUTION: positively skewed: 25% very happy, 62% pretty happy, 13% not too happy

SECOND INSTRUMENT: HAPP 2.1: Single closed question rated on a 3-point scale (from Robinson & Shaver, 1969):
In general how satisfying do you find the way you are spending your life these days?
completely satisfying / pretty satisfying / not very satisfying

RELIABILITY:

VALIDITY:

DISTRIBUTION: positively skewed: 22% completely satisfying, 66% pretty satisfying, 12% not very satisfying

REMARKS:

CORRELATES: Age (A 3); Educational level (E 1.1.1); Satisfaction received from sports (S 1.1.1); Participation in voluntary associations (S 4.2); various factors concerning Sports (S 6); Occupational prestige (W 2.4).

CONCLUSION: Involvement in sports is associated with greater psychological well-being. The relation with behavioral involvement in sports is stronger among females whereas affective involvement in sports is a stronger predictor of positive affect among males.
These results may be due to the positive effects of social interaction in general on the individual's well-being and to the specific fun of sports.

AUTHOR: Snyder, E.E. & Kivlin, J.E.

SNYDE 75

TITLE: Women athletes and aspects of psychological well-being and body image.

SOURCE: Research Quarterly, 1975, vol. 46, nr 2, p. 191-199.

---

GOAL OF THE STUDY: To examine the relationship between being a woman athlete and psychological well-being, suggesting type of sport as an explaining variable.

REFERS TO: Theory of women in sports; Landers (1970), Metheny (1965)

TYPE OF STUDY: explanatory, testing, special group, snapshot, non-experimental

DATA GATHERING: sample I : highly structured questionnaire
sample II: highly structured mailed questionnaire

DATE OF DATA:

POPULATION: College women and women athletes, U.S.A.

SAMPLE CONSTRUCTION: College women (I) : Non-probability chunk sample of women enrolled in sociology classes at Blowing Green State University. N = 275.
Women athletes (II): Non-probability chunk sample of women athletes who participated in the 1972 Woman's National Intercollegiate Championships or who participated in the 1972 Olympic tryouts (only women doing basketball, gymnastics, swimming and diving, and track and field). N = 328.

NON-RESPONSE: Sample II: 35%

N: 603

AUTHOR'S HAPPINESS LABEL: Psychological well-being

OUR CONCEPTUALIZATION: Hedonic level of affect (first instrument) and Happiness (second and third instrument)

FIRST INSTRUMENT: AFF 1.1: Single closed question, rated on a 3-point scale:
Generally feel in good spirits:
most of the time / much of the time / some / seldom

RELIABILITY:

VALIDITY:

DISTRIBUTION: positively skewed

SECOND INSTRUMENT: COMP 1.1: Singel closed question, rated on a 3-point scale:
very satisfied with life:
most of the time / much of the time / some / seldom

RELIABILITY:

VALIDITY:

DISTRIBUTION: positively skewed

THIRD INSTRUMENT: COMP 1.1: Single closed question, rated on a 3-point scale:
Find much happiness in life:
most of the time / much of the time / some / seldom

RELIABILITY:

VALIDITY:

DISTRIBUTION: positively skewed

REMARKS:

CORRELATES: Being an athlete (S 6.1); Being a basketball player vs gymnast (S 6.1)

CONCLUSION: Even though women athletes have frequently received negative sanctions, their participation in sports has apparently been psychologically satisfying and rewarding.

AUTHOR: Sondermeijer, B. SONDE 75

TITLE: Health correlates of happiness.

SOURCE: Unpublished report, 1975, Rotterdam.

---

GOAL OF THE STUDY: Analysis of the influence of biophysical, biomedical and social factors on the development of heart diseases.

REFERS TO:

TYPE OF STUDY: explanatory, explorative, special group, snapshot, non-experimental

DATA GATHERING: Highly structured questionnaire administered by medical assistent

DATE OF DATA:

POPULATION: Male employees of age 40 – 65, The Netherlands

SAMPLE CONSTRUCTION: Non-probability chunk sample of employees of all levels of various organizations: banks, university, shipping, glass industry, local government.

NON-RESPONSE: 5%

N: 13,000

AUTHOR'S HAPPINESS LABEL: Life satisfaction

OUR CONCEPTUALIZATION: Happiness

INSTRUMENT: HAPP 2.1: Single closed question rated on a 2-point scale:

All in all, are you satisfied? yes / no

In Dutch:
Hebt U het over het algemeen naar Uw zin? ja / nee

RELIABILITY:

VALIDITY:

DISTRIBUTION: Highly positively skewed

REMARKS:

CORRELATES: Self-perceived overactivity (A 1.8); Feeling cheerful (A 2.2.5); Feeling irritable (A 2.2.21); Age (A 3); Illness of parents (F 1.1.4); Number of children at home (F 1.2.3, H 4.1); Family problems (F 1.4, P. 5.1.2); Psychosomatic complaints (H 2.2); Cigarette smoking (L 3.1.2); Active leisure time (L 3.3.1); Relative weight (P 2.1); Blood pressure (P 2.3); various Domainsatisfactions (S 1); Feeling uncertain (S 2.1.4); Achieving higher job (S 5.3); Actual sporting (S 6.1); various Characteristics of one's job (W 2.6); Laughing and singing often (X 1)

CONCLUSION:

AUTHOR: Spreitzer, E. & Snyder, E.E.

SPREI 74

TITLE: Correlates of life satisfaction among the aged.

SOURCE: Journal of Gerontology, 1974, vol. 29, nr 4, p. 454-458.

---

GOAL OF THE STUDY: To replicate and extend earlier studies of the correlates of life satisfaction among older persons.

REFERS TO: Theory of aging and retirement; Streib & Schneider (1971), Maddox (1968)

TYPE OF STUDY: explanatory, explorative, national population, snapshot, non-experimental

DATA GATHERING: Structured interview

DATE OF DATA: 1972 - 1973

POPULATION: Non-institutionalized married or widowed adults, U.S.A.

SAMPLE CONSTRUCTION: Pooling of 2 NORC (1972 and 1973) national probability samples.
The sample was limited to married and widowed persons only; age 18+

NON-RESPONSE:

N: 1547

AUTHOR'S HAPPINESS LABEL: Life satisfaction

OUR CONCEPTUALIZATION: Happiness

INSTRUMENT: HAPP 1.1: Single closed question using the term 'happiness', rated on a 3-point scale (see GURIN 60).

RELIABILITY:

VALIDITY:

DISTRIBUTION: positively skewed: 33% very happy, 52% pretty happy, 15% not too happy

REMARKS:

CORRELATES: Age (A 3); Educational level (E 1.1.1); Race (E 2.1); Gender (G 1.1); Self-perceived health (H 2.1.2); Family income (I 1.1); Widowed vs married (M 1.1.2); Church attendance (R 1.3); Retirement (R 2.1); S.E.S. (S 5.1); Occupational prestige (W 2.4)

CONCLUSION: Men tend to reach their high point in terms of life satisfaction during the very same period (age 65-70) when women reach their low point. Subjective indicators of socio-economic position are stronger predictors of life satisfaction than more objective indicators.

AUTHOR: Spreitzer, E., Snyder, E.E. & Larson, D.

SPREI 75

TITLE: Age, marital status, and labor force participation as related to life satisfaction.

SOURCE: Sex Roles, 1975, vol. 1, nr 3, p. 235-247.

---

GOAL OF THE STUDY: To replicate and extend the research tradition of survey studies on life satisfaction.

REFERS TO: Happiness research; Andrews & Withey (1973)

TYPE OF STUDY: explanatory, explorative, national population, snapshot, non-experimental

DATA GATHERING: Structured interview

DATE OF DATA: Spring, 1973

POPULATION: Non-institutionalized adults, U.S.A.

SAMPLE CONSTRUCTION: NORC (1973, nr 1) national probability sample
698 males, 802 females; age 18+

NON-RESPONSE:

N: 1500

AUTHOR'S HAPPINESS LABEL: Life satisfaction

OUR CONCEPTUALIZATION: Happiness

INSTRUMENT: HAPP 1.1: Single closed question using the term 'happiness', rated on a 3-point scale (see GURIN 60).

RELIABILITY:

VALIDITY:

DISTRIBUTION: positively skewed: 36% very happy, 51% pretty happy, and 13% not too happy

REMARKS:

CORRELATES: Age (A 3); Educational level (E 1.1.1); Gender (G 1.1); various Marital status comparisons (M 1); Employed status (W 2.1)

CONCLUSION: Age, marital status, and employment status explain very little of the variation in reported life satisfaction.

AUTHOR: Stanfiel, J.D., Tompkins, W.G. & Brown, H.L.

STANF 71

TITLE: A daily activities list and its relation to measures of adjustment and early environment.

SOURCE: Psychological Reports, 1971, vol. 28, p. 691-699.

---

GOAL OF THE STUDY: Assessment of congruent validity of a Daily Activities List (D.A.L.) as an index of psychological adjustment.

REFERS TO: Theory of activity and psychological adjustment; Katz & Lyerly (1963)

TYPE OF STUDY: descriptive, testing, special group, snapshot, non-experimental

DATA GATHERING: Highly structured questionnnaire and open, personal history and clinical interview during four weeks of radiotherapy

DATE OF DATA:

POPULATION: Adult cancer patients, U.S.A.

SAMPLE CONSTRUCTION: Non-probability accidental sample using volunteering cancer patients receiving radiotherapy each weekday.
9 males, 12 females; age 22 - 65, median age 48; 18 outpatients, all ambulatory, and 3 Ss varying in ambulatory status

NON-RESPONSE:

N: 21

AUTHOR'S HAPPINESS LABEL: Euphoric mood state

OUR CONCEPTUALIZATION: Hedonic level of affect

INSTRUMENT: AFF 3.3: Repeated index of closed questions on momentaneous occurrence of specific affects, administered twice a week (Raskin et al. (1969) mood scale):

This scale is an objectively scored, self report 52-item adjective check-list designed to measure the immediate subjective feeling state of mood, such as feelings of anxiety, depression, fatigue, etc. The factor scores were combined in this study into an over-all score for each mood scale completed. High scores indicate a strong dysphoric mood state.

Ss completed a mean of 7.5 mood scales during the first four weeks of treatment. A mean score was computed for each patient including all mood scales completed during this period. These mean scores were employed for the analysis.

RELIABILITY:

VALIDITY:

DISTRIBUTION:

REMARKS:

CORRELATES: Activity level (A 1.1)

CONCLUSION: Activity level is significantly associated with psychological well-being. Activity level, as defined by the Daily Activities List, does not in itself define clinical syndromes or psychological health, but comprises an associated behavioral pattern which tends to reflect the psychological state of the individual.

AUTHOR: Storandt, M., Wittels, J. & Botwinick, J.

STORA 75

TITLE: Predictors of a dimension of well-being in the relocated healthy aged.

SOURCE: Journal of Gerontology, 1975, vol. 30, nr 1, p. 97-102.

---

GOAL OF THE STUDY: To determine the relationships between test performances of elderly people around the time of their moving into an appratment complex and assessment to their well-being 11 to 19 months afterwards.

REFERS TO: Theory of well-being in old age; Lawton & Cohen (1974), Aldrich (1964)

TYPE OF STUDY: explanatory, explorative, special group, snapshot, non-experimental

DATA GATHERING: Structured interview at home and independent ratings by 2 psychologists at home

DATE OF DATA:

POPULATION: Aged residents of an appartment building for the elderly, U.S.A.

SAMPLE CONSTRUCTION: Non-probability accidental sample
age 61 - 88

NON-RESPONSE: 50%; 47% unattainable, 3% incomplete

N: 122

AUTHOR'S HAPPINESS LABEL: Life satisfaction

OUR CONCEPTUALIZATION: Happiness

INSTRUMENT: HAPP 2.1: Single closed question rated on an 11-point self-anchoring scale (Cantril Satisfaction with Life rating; see CANTR 65).

RELIABILITY:

VALIDITY:

DISTRIBUTION:

REMARKS:

CORRELATES: Well-being (L 2.2.1)

CONCLUSION:

AUTHOR: Suchman, E.A., Phillips, B.S. & Streib, G.F.

SUCHM 58

TITLE: An analysis of the validity of health questionnaires.

SOURCE: Social Forces, 1958, vol. 36, p. 223-232.

---

GOAL OF THE STUDY: Validation of self-administered questionnaire items dealing with health.

REFERS TO: Theory of physical health, attitudes and behavior; Streib (1956), Kutner et al. (1956)

TYPE OF STUDY: descriptive, testing, special group, snapshot, non-experimental

DATA GATHERING: Self-administered questionnaires and medical examination by physicians

DATE OF DATA: 1952 - 1954

POPULATION: Aged persons, U.S.A.

SAMPLE CONSTRUCTION: Non-probability quota sample of residents of all parts of the U.S.A. from widely divergent backgrounds.
age 65+

NON-RESPONSE:

N: 2993

AUTHOR'S HAPPINESS LABEL: Happiness

OUR CONCEPTUALIZATION: Happiness

INSTRUMENT: HAPP 1.1: Single closed question rated on a 3-point scale:

All in all how much happiness would you say you find in life today?
almost none / some, but not very much / a good deal

RELIABILITY:

VALIDITY:

DISTRIBUTION: positively skewed: 89% reporting 'a good deal of happiness'

REMARKS:

CORRELATES: Various indicators of Physical health (H 2.1)

CONCLUSION:

| | | |
|---|---|---|
| AUTHOR: | Symonds, P.M. | SYMON 37 |
| TITLE: | Happiness as related to problems and interests. | |
| SOURCE: | Journal of Educational Psychology, 1937, vol. 28, p. 290-294. | |

---

GOAL OF THE STUDY: Exploration of some of the relations between happiness and interests of people.

REFERS TO:

TYPE OF STUDY: explanatory, explorative, special group, snapshot, non-experimental

DATA GATHERING: Administration of questionnaire

DATE OF DATA:

POPULATION: Students, U.S.A.

SAMPLE CONSTRUCTION: Non-probability chunk sample of 887 high school students, 584 college students and 180 graduate students.

NON-RESPONSE:

N: 1651

AUTHOR'S HAPPINESS LABEL: Happiness

OUR CONCEPTUALIZATION: Happiness

INSTRUMENT: Comp 4.1: Single closed question rated on a 7-point scale:

Check one of the following groups of adjectives which best describes you

7. full of deep joy, excitedly happy, enthousiastic, thrilled
6. cheerful, successful, optimistic, lighthearted
5. satisfied, comfortable, life goes smoothly, peaceful
4. contented at times and at other times discontented, life has both favorable and unfavorable features
3. restless, impatient, uncertain, dull, cross, confined
2. anxious, irritated, discouraged, disappointed, discontented
1. gloomy, miserable, a failure, no pleasure in anything

RELIABILITY:

VALIDITY:

DISTRIBUTION: positively skewed: 23% score 6 or 7, 19% score 5, 56% score 4 (neutral), 2% score 1, 2 and 3

REMARKS: Differences in average rankings which are more than twice the standard error of that difference are considered as significant.

CORRELATES: various Interests (C 2); various Problems (P 5.1.2)

CONCLUSION: Happy and unhappy people are remarkably alike in their problems and interests. The unhappy do not have peculiar problems but make less satisfactory adjustments to their problems. The happy are more concerned with affairs outside themselves while the unhappy are more concerned with themselves and with their relations to others.

AUTHOR: Tessler, R. & Mechanic, D.

TESSL 75

TITLE: Consumer satisfaction with prepaid group practice: A comparative study.

SOURCE: Journal of Health and Social Behavior, 1975, vol. 16, nr 4 pt 1, p. 95-113.

---

GOAL OF THE STUDY: To compare consumers satisfaction with participation in prepaid group practice and alternative health insurance plans.

REFERS TO: Theory of satisfaction with medical health care; Mechanic (1972), Weinerman (1964)

TYPE OF STUDY: explanatory, explorative, special group, snapshot, non-experimental

DATA GATHERING: Stuctured interview

DATE OF DATA: Summer, 1973

POPULATION: Families of hourly workers and salaried employees, U.S.A.

SAMPLE CONSTRUCTION: Sample from two large industrial firms that offer their employees a choice between prepaid group practice and a fee-for-service insurance plan.
Firm 1: Primarily (semi-) skilled hourly employees:
- all subscribers who joined the prepaid practice in July, 1972 and who were still eligible to receive care at the time of the interview
- random sample of employees choosing the fee-for-service plan

Firm 2: Salaried white collar group of higher S.E.S.:
- all subscribers who used the prepaid group practice from June 1972 until the time of the interview
- random sample of comparable employees choosing the fee-for-service plan

The prepaid practice group and the fee-for-service group were of the same size. When possible, women (usually wives of employees) were interviewed.

NON-RESPONSE:

N: 712

AUTHOR'S HAPPINESS LABEL: Mood

OUR CONCEPTUALIZATION: Hedonic level of affect

INSTRUMENT: AFF 1.1: Single closed question rated on a 3-point scale:
Would you say that your spirits most of the time are very good, fair, or low?

RELIABILITY:

VALIDITY:

DISTRIBUTION:

REMARKS:

CORRELATES: Subjective health status (H 2.1.2); various factors concerning Health care (H 2.6, S 1.2.3); Major life changes (L 1.2); Not currently married vs married (M 1.1.5); Being a housewife (W 2.1)

CONCLUSION:

AUTHOR: Thompson, W.E., Streib, G.F. & Kosa, J. | THOMP 60

TITLE: The effect of retirement on personal adjustment: a panel analysis.

SOURCE: Journal of Gerontology, 1960, vol. 15, nr 2, p. 165-169.

---

GOAL OF THE STUDY: Test and specification of the assumed negative relation between retirement and personal adjustment.

REFERS TO: Theory of adjustment among retirees; Havighurst & Albrecht (1953), Kutner et al. (1956)

TYPE OF STUDY: explanatory, explorative, special group, longitudinal, non-experimental

DATA GATHERING: Structured interview administered at the respondent's place of work, followed by 2 mailed questionnaires at 1 or 2 years interval

DATE OF DATA: 1952 - 1956

POPULATION: Aged males, U.S.A.

SAMPLE CONSTRUCTION: Non-probability accidental sample using volunteers.
All males were born in 1887, 1888 or 1889; relatively more prosporous and better educated individuals from relatively larger, more affluent and more progressive organizations from all parts of the country; 1082 Ss gainfully employed throughout, and 477 Ss retired between 1952 and 1954.

NON-RESPONSE:

N: 1559

AUTHOR'S HAPPINESS LABEL: Satisfaction with life

OUR CONCEPTUALIZATION: Happiness

INSTRUMENT: COMP 1.2: Index of closed questions (devised through the use of the Guttman (1944) scaling technique):

1. All in all, how much happiness would you say you find in life today?
   (negative response: 'almost none' or 'some, but not very much')
2. In general, how would you say you feel most of the time, in good spirits or in low spirits?
   (negative response: 'I am usually in low spirits' or ' sometimes in good spirits, sometimes in low spirits')
3. On the whole, how satisfied would you say you are with your way of life today?
   (negative response: 'fairly satisfied', 'not very satisfied' or 'not satisfied at all')

RELIABILITY: Reproducibility: +.96
Error ratio : +.55

VALIDITY:

DISTRIBUTION: almost symmetric: in 1952: 51% satisfied, 49% dissatisfied
in 1954: 43% satisfied, 57% dissatisfied

REMARKS: The publication focusses on longitudinal changes in satisfaction with life rather than on correlates of present satisfaction with life. Compared were persons satisfied in 1952 who became dissatisfied in 1954 (N = 788), and persons dissatisfied in 1952 who became satisfied in 1954 (N = 771).
For our purposes we computed correlates of satisfaction with life in 1954, when possible we made elaborations for satisfaction with life in 1952.

CORRELATES: Having difficulties in keeping occupied (A 1.8, P 5.1.2); Subjective health (H 2.1.2); Economic deprivation (I 1.6); various factors concerning Retirement (R 2)

CONCLUSION: In general retirement appears to have a negative effect on personal adjustment only when retirement is involuntary and economic deprivation is felt. The findings do suggest the work-role is not as central to the personality as many writers would contend.

AUTHOR: Tissue, T. | TISSU 72

TITLE: Another look at self-rated health among the elderly.

SOURCE: Journal of Gerontology, 1972, vol. 27, nr 1, p. 91-94.

---

GOAL OF THE STUDY: To examine the nature of health measured by self-ratings.

REFERS TO: Theory of self-rated health; Friedsam & Martin (1963), Sullivan (1966)

TYPE OF STUDY: explanatory, explorative, special group, snapshot, non-experimental

DATA GATHERING: Structured interview

DATE OF DATA: 1969

POPULATION: Non-institutionalized aged welfare recipients, U.S.A.

SAMPLE CONSTRUCTION: Non-probability purposive quota sample of aged welfare recipients.
111 males, 145 females; mean age 68

NON-RESPONSE:

N: 256

AUTHOR'S HAPPINESS LABEL: Morale

OUR CONCEPTUALIZATION: Hedonic level of affect (first instrument), Contentment (second instrument) and Happiness (third instrument)

FIRST INSTRUMENT: AFF 2.3: Index of closed questions on perceived occurrence of specific affects during the past few weeks (Bradburn Affect Balance Score; see BRADB 69).

RELIABILITY:

VALIDITY:

DISTRIBUTION:

SECOND INSTRUMENT: CON 1.1: Single closed question on belief regarding achievement of own life goals, rated on a 3-point scale (most, some / few).

RELIABILITY:

VALIDITY:

DISTRIBUTION:

THIRD INSTRUMENT: HAPP 1.1: Single closed question using the term 'happiness', rated on a 3-point scale (very happy / pretty happy , not too happy).

RELIABILITY:

VALIDITY:

DISTRIBUTION:

REMARKS:

CORRELATES: Self-perceived health (H 2.1.2)

CONCLUSION: Self-rated health is not merely another measure of morale, self-image, or happiness.

AUTHOR: Veenhoven, R. | VEENH 74

TITLE: Is there an innate need for children?

SOURCE: European Journal of Social Psychology, 1974, vol. 14, p. 495-501.

---

GOAL OF THE STUDY: Analysis of the belief that all human beings have an inner urge to have children and examination of its tenability.

REFERS TO: Theory of parenthood; Kephart (1966), Deutsch (1945)

TYPE OF STUDY: explanatory, testing, special group, snapshot, non-experimental

DATA GATHERING: Structured interview

DATE OF DATA: June, 1968

POPULATION: Married adults, The Netherlands

SAMPLE CONSTRUCTION: Married persons of age 25 - 65, from the Aakster (1972) probability area sample (see also BAKKE 74 and VEENH 75).

NON-RESPONSE: 34%; 23% unattainable, 10% non-response

N: 1376

AUTHOR'S HAPPINESS LABEL: Happiness

OUR CONCEPTUALIZATION: Happiness

INSTRUMENT: HAPP 1.1: Single closed question using the term 'happiness', rated on a open graphic scale (see BAKKE 74).

RELIABILITY:

VALIDITY:

DISTRIBUTION:

REMARKS:

CORRELATES: Childlessness (F 1.2.1); Pregnancy (P 2.3)

CONCLUSION: The procreation-instinct theory fails to find empirical support.

AUTHOR: Veenhoven, R. & Bakker, P. | VEENH 75

TITLE: Schooleducation and psychological wel—being.

SOURCE: Unpublished paper, 1975, Department of Sociology, Erasmus University Rotterdam, The Netherlands.

---

GOAL OF THE STUDY: Investigation of the effects of schooleducation on the sense of personal well-being in adulthood.

REFERS TO: theory on effects of education; Jencks et al. (1972)

TYPE OF STUDY: explanatory, explorative, national population, snapshot, non-experimental

DATA GATHERING: Structured interview

DATE OF DATA: June, 1968

POPULATION: National adult population, The Netherlands

SAMPLE CONSTRUCTION: Probability area sample (see also BAKKE 74).

NON-RESPONSE: 34%

N: 1534

AUTHOR'S HAPPINESS LABEL: Psychological well-being

OUR CONCEPTUALIZATION: Happiness

INSTRUMENT: HAPP 1.1: Single closed question using the term 'happiness', rated on an open graphic scale (see BAKKE 74).

RELIABILITY:

VALIDITY:

DISTRIBUTION:

REMARKS:

CORRELATES: Educational level (E 1.1.1); Social mobility (S 5.3)

CONCLUSION: Unlike common thought, there is no universal, direct and clear-cut relation between level of education and psychological well-being.

AUTHOR: Veroff, J., Feld, S. & Gurin, G.

VEROF 62

TITLE: Dimensions of subjective adjustment.

SOURCE: Journal of Abnormal and Social Psychology, 1962, vol. 64, nr 3, p. 192-205.

---

GOAL OF THE STUDY: Assessment of relations between different indices of subjective adjustment by using factor-analysis.

REFERS TO: Theory of mental health; Jahoda (1958)

TYPE OF STUDY: explanatory, explorative, special group, snapshot, non-experimental

DATA GATHERING: Structured interview

DATE OF DATA: Spring, 1957

POPULATION: Adult married population with children, U.S.A.

SAMPLE CONSTRUCTION: Probability area sample of adults, living in private households in the U.S.A. (N = 2460; see also GURIN 60), poststratified by married status, employed status and having children:
- working, currently married males with children (N = 255)
- currently married females with children (N = 542)

NON-RESPONSE:

N: 797

AUTHOR'S HAPPINESS LABEL: Happiness

OUR CONCEPTUALIZATION: Happiness

INSTRUMENT: HAPP 1.1: Single closed question using the term 'happiness', rated on a 3-point scale (see GURIN 60).

RELIABILITY:

VALIDITY:

DISTRIBUTION:

REMARKS:

CORRELATES: various factors concerning one's Children (F 1.2.4); Expected future happiness (H 1.6.2); Self-perceived physical health (H 2.1.3); various Psychosomatic symptoms (H 2.2); Ever expected a nervous breakdown (H 2.3.2); various Problems (P 5.1.2); Worrying (P 5.2.1); Job satisfaction (S 1.9.1); various factors concerning Self-image (S 2.1.6, S 2.3); Job performance (W 2.7)

CONCLUSION: In the factor analysis of various indices of mental functioning five distinctive factors emerged for men and four for women. There was considerable apparent overlap between the two factor structures. For both men and women the factors were identified as: felt psychological disturbance; unhappiness; social inadequacy; lack of identity. For men the fifth factor was labeled physical distress.

AUTHOR: Washburn, M.F., Harding, L., Simons, H. & Tomlinson, D.

WASHB 25

TITLE: Further experiments on directed recall as a test of cheerful and depressed temperaments.

SOURCE: American Journal of Psychology, 1925, vol. 36, p. 454-456.

---

GOAL OF THE STUDY: Assessment of the assumed relationship between temperamental tendencies to cheerfulness or depression and tendencies to recall pleasant or unpleasant ideas in connection with verbal stimuli.

REFERS TO: Happiness research; Morgan et al. (1919)

TYPE OF STUDY: explanatory, explorative, special group, snapshot, non-experimental

DATA GATHERING: Projective verbal techniques in test-room situation during three successive days

DATE OF DATA:

POPULATION: Female psychology students, U.S.A.

SAMPLE CONSTRUCTION: Non-probability chunk sample using attendants of a psychology course, poststratified by temperament.
Cheerful group: N = 33; depressed group: N = 34 (see 'REMARKS')

NON-RESPONSE:

N: 67

AUTHOR'S HAPPINESS LABEL: Cheerfulness

OUR CONCEPTUALIZATION: Hedonic level of affect

FIRST INSTRUMENT: AFF 1.1: Single closed question rated on a 4-point scale:

Each Ss was asked to judge herself using one of the four terms:
steadily cheerful / variable tendency to cheerfulness / variable tending to depression / steadily depressed

RELIABILITY:

VALIDITY:

DISTRIBUTION: positively skewed

SECOND INSTRUMENT: AFF 6: Composite of hedonic level of affect containing self-perceived cheerfulness and peer ratings of cheerfulness:

Each S was asked to judge herself on a 4-point scale (see first instrument)
Also the judgements of three friends were obtained, using the same terms.
For all judgements 'steadily cheerful' was rated as 4 points; 'variable tending to cheerfulness' as 3 points, 'variable tending to depression' as 2 points; and 'steadily depressed' as 1 point. For each S the self-judgement and the judgements of her friends were added to obtain a total score.

RELIABILITY: -

VALIDITY:

DISTRIBUTION: positively skewed
possible range: 4 - 16; median score: 12.5

REMARKS: The analysis was performed by comparing the cheerful group (those who had rated themselves as 'steadily cheerful') with the depressed group (those who had rated themselves as 'variable tending to depression' or 'steadily depressed'). Those who had rated themselves as 'variable tending to cheerfulness' were excluded.

CORRELATES: Recalling pleasant associations in connection with verbal stimuli (P 1.6); Galvanic skin response (P 2.3)

CONCLUSION: Directed recall seems to be a rather good measure of cheerful and depressed temperaments.

| | | |
|---|---|---|
| AUTHOR: | Washburn, M.F., Booth, M.E., Stocker, S. & Glicksmann, E. | WASHB 26 |
| TITLE: | A comparison of directed and free recalls of pleasant and unpleasant experiences, as tests of cheerful and depressed temperaments. | |
| SOURCE: | American Journal of Psychology, 1926, vol. 37, p. 278-280. | |

---

| | |
|---|---|
| GOAL OF THE STUDY: | Testing the validity of two projective, verbal techniques as measures of cheerful or depressed temperaments. |
| REFERS TO: | Happiness research; Morgan et al. (1919), Washburn et al. (1925) |
| TYPE OF STUDY: | explanatory, explorative, special group, snapshot, non-experimental |
| DATA GATHERING: | Projective verbal techniques in test-room situation during three successive days |
| DATE OF DATA: | |
| POPULATION: | Female psychology students, U.S.A. |
| SAMPLE CONSTRUCTION: | Non-probability chunk sample using attendants of a psychology course, poststratified by temperament.<br>Cheerful group: N = 64; depressed group: N = 59 (see 'REMARKS') |
| NON-RESPONSE: | |
| N: | 123 |
| AUTHOR'S HAPPINESS LABEL: | Cheerfulness |
| OUR CONCEPTUALIZATION: | Hedonic level of affect |
| INSTRUMENT: | AFF 6: Composite of hedonic level of affect containing self-perceived cheerfulness and peer ratings of cheerfulness (see WASHB 25, second instrument).<br>As in the WASHB 25 study the self judgement and the judgements of the 3 friends were added to obtain the total score. |
| RELIABILITY: | |
| VALIDITY: | |
| DISTRIBUTION: | positively skewed<br>possible range: 4 - 16 |
| REMARKS: | The analysis was performed by comparing the cheerful group (with hedonic level scores from 14 to 16) and the depressed group (with scores up to and including 10). The other Ss were excluded. |
| CORRELATES: | Recalling pleasant associations in connection with verbal stimuli (P 1.6); Promptness of pleasant associations (P 1.6) |
| CONCLUSION: | Both techniques have value for the determination of cheerful or depressed temperaments. The technique using the average association time appears to have a slight superiority. |

WASHB 41

AUTHOR: Washburne, J.N.

TITLE: Factors related to the social adjustment of college girls.

SOURCE: Journal of social Psychology, 1941, vol. 13, p. 281-189.

---

GOAL OF THE STUDY: To find out to what extent the social and emotional adjustment of college girls is related to certain factors in their home background, school activities and college status.

REFERS TO:

TYPE OF STUDY: explanatory, explorative, special group, snapshot, non-experimental

DATA GATHERING: Questionnaire and intelligence-test administered in classroom situation

DATE OF DATA:

POPULATION: Female college students, New York, U.S.A.

SAMPLE CONSTRUCTION: Type of construction unclear.
119 freshmen and 119 junior girls of the Syracuse University

NON-RESPONSE:

N: 238

AUTHOR'S HAPPINESS LABEL: Happiness

OUR CONCEPTUALIZATION: Happiness

INSTRUMENT: COMP 2.2: Index of closed questions indicating both happiness and a sense of contentment and well-being (Happiness subtest of the Washburne Social Adjustment Inventory).

RELIABILITY: Equivalence: reliability coefficient for the happiness subtest of at least .80

VALIDITY: Each item shows a difference of at least 2½ times the probable error of the difference between the answers of well-adjusted and maladjusted groups. These groups were selected by 3 competent judges and the individuals in them were paired for age, grade, sex and intelligence.

DISTRIBUTION:

REMARKS:

CORRELATES: Intelligence (C 1.3); Stage of study (E 1.2.3); Educational status of father (F 1.1.1, S 5.1); Broken home background (F 1.1.2); Campus activity level (L 3.3.1); Living in a city/town (L 4.2); Participation in church activities (R 1.3, S 4.2); Sorority membership (S 4.2); Playing sports (S 6.1); Having outside work (W 2.1)

CONCLUSION: Superior scores in happiness are most clearly and consistently associated with coming from unbroken homes, participation in sports, and high intelligence among juniors. These relations are rather strong in the lower happiness groups and disappear almost among very happy girls.

AUTHOR: Watson, G.

WATSO 30

TITLE: Happiness among adult students of education.

SOURCE: Journal of Educational Psychology, 1930, vol. 21, nr 2, p. 79-109.

---

GOAL OF THE STUDY: Applying the techniques of psychological study to the understanding of happiness.

REFERS TO:

TYPE OF STUDY: explanatory, explorative, special group, snapshot, non-experimental

DATA GATHERING: Lowly structured questionnaire

DATE OF DATA:

POPULATION: Graduate students of education (teachers), Columbia University, U.S.A.

SAMPLE CONSTRUCTION: Non-probability chunk sample using attendants of a psychology course.
average age 30

NON-RESPONSE:

N: 388. Most of the analysis is based on the answers of 50 males and 124 females (N = 174).

AUTHOR'S HAPPINESS LABEL: Happiness

OUR CONCEPTUALIZATION: Happiness (first and second instrument) and Hedonic level of affect (third instrument)

FIRST INSTRUMENT: COMP 4.1: Single closed question rated on a 10-point scale:

Among the following descriptions arranged in miscellaneous order, choose the one which comes nearest to fitting you. None will be likely to fit exactly. (The assigned values for each discription are presented in brackets behind the desctiptions)

a. Finding life rather disappointing and disillusioning, comfortable in many ways, moderately successful, but far from realizing the hopes of youth. (3)
b. Cheerful, gay spirits most of the time. Occasionally bothered by something but can usually laugh it off. (9)
c. Calm, quiet sort of satisfaction. Life has been pretty good. Not everything one desires comes, of course, but on the whole there is much for which to be serenely thankful. (8)
d. Ups and downs, now happy about things, now depressed. About balanced in the long run. (5)
e. Life often seems so worthless that there is little to keep one going. Nothing matters very much, there has been so much of hurt that laughter would be empty mockery. (1)
f. Keeping a brave front, others think everything is all right. Inside life seems rather black. (2)
g. Usually sad, weep readily, smile seldom. (1)
h. Radiant, find every day full of interest, amusing things, and worthwhile things. (10)
i. Seriously hurt by certain things, for which the good aspects of life cannot quite make up. (3)
j. Quite objective. Like some experiences, dislike others. Not aware of any prevalent happiness or unhappiness. (5)

RELIABILITY:

VALIDITY:

DISTRIBUTION:

SECOND INSTRUMENT: COMP 4.3: Single open-ended question:

Now write in your own words a sentence of two, something like those above (statements of the first instrument) which you believe willl most truly describe your own general happiness in life.

The answers were rated by three judges on an 11-point scale ranging from 0 to 10

RELIABILITY:

VALIDITY:

DISTRIBUTION:

THIRD INSTRUMENT: AFF 1.3: Index of closed questions on perceived occurrence of specific affects in general:

Below is a list of words and phrases. Check every term which you believe could fairly be applied to yourself in prevalent attitudes.

| | | |
|---|---|---|
| - Enthousiastic | - Morbid | - Disappointed |
| - Distressed | - Cheerful | - Prosperous |
| - Frivolous | - Troubled | - Annoyed |
| - Calm | - Miserable | - Thrilled |
| - Irritable | - Buoyant | - Joyful |

The total list contained fifty adjectives, half positive and half negative.
The score was obtained by substracting the number of 'unhappy' traits mentioned from the number of 'happy' ones.

RELIABILITY:

VALIDITY:

DISTRIBUTION:

REMARKS:

CORRELATES: Intelligence (C 1.3); Perceived happy image (L 2.3); Perceived popularity (P 4.2)

CONCLUSION:

WEBB 15

AUTHOR: Webb, E.

TITLE: Character and intelligence.
An attempt at an exact study of character.

SOURCE: London, 1915, Cambridge University Press.

---

GOAL OF THE STUDY: To provide a scientific framework for the study of character and intelligence.

REFERS TO: Theory of character; Heymans & Wiersma (1906), Ach (1910)

TYPE OF STUDY: explanatory, explorative, special group, snapshot, non-experimental

DATA GATHERING: Structured participant observation (by peers, teachers, doctors, captains of sports) and projective verbal techniques.

DATE OF DATA: 1912 - 1913

POPULATION: Male students and schoolboys, England

SAMPLE CONSTRUCTION: Non-probability chunk sample of male students at a training college (N = 194, average age 21) and schoolboys in four different schools in London (N = 140, average age 12).

NON-RESPONSE:

N: 334

AUTHOR'S HAPPINESS LABEL: General tendency to be cheerful (as opposed to being depressed and low spirited)

OUR CONCEPTUALIZATION: Hedonic level of affect

INSTRUMENT: Students : AFF 5.2: Peer rating of hedonic level of affect
Schoolboys: AFF 5.3: Class-master rating of hedonic level of affect

Both the students and the schoolboys were rated on a 7-point scale on the basis of observation during 6 months.

RELIABILITY:

VALIDITY:

DISTRIBUTION:

REMARKS: In one of the correlation tables it appeared that the number of the variables did not correspond with the list of variables presented elsewhere. In most cases we were able to recover the correct numbering.

CORRELATES: Bodily activity (A 1.5); Mental activity (A 1.6); various indicators concerning Affect (A 2.2); various Cognitive characteristics (C 1); Physical health (H 2.1.1); Activity in pursuit of pleasures (L 3.3.1); various Personality characteristics (P 1); Religiousness (R 1.1); Self-esteem (S 2.1.3); Belief in one's powers (S 2.1.4); various Preferences with respect to Social participation (S 4.5); Athletic skill (S 6.1); Working with distant objects in view (T 1.2)

CONCLUSION:

AUTHOR: Wessman, A.E. WESSM 56

TITLE: A psychological inquiry into satisfaction and happiness.

SOURCE: Unpublished doctoral dissertation, 1956, Princeton University, U.S.A.

---

GOAL OF THE STUDY: Assessment and interpretation of relationships between avowed happiness - unhappiness and various social-psychological background characteristics, experience in important life areas and general attitudes.

REFERS TO: Happiness research; Jones (1953)

TYPE OF STUDY: explanatory, explorative, national population, snapshot, non-experimental

DATA GATHERING: Structured interview

DATE OF DATA: February, 1946

POPULATION: National adult population, U.S.A.

SAMPLE CONSTRUCTION: Non-probability quota sample.
Comparison with the appropriate census figures shows that for all intents and purposes the sample may be considered as a representative national sample of the adult population of the United States.
age 21+

NON-RESPONSE:

N: 2377

AUTHOR'S HAPPINESS LABEL: Avowed happiness

OUR CONCEPTUALIZATION: Happiness

INSTRUMENT: HAPP 1.1: Single closed question rated on a 3-point scale:

In general, how happy would you say that you are - very happy, fairly happy, or not very happy?

RELIABILITY:

VALIDITY:

DISTRIBUTION: positively skewed: 46% very happy, 45% fairly happy, 8% not very happy, 1% don't know and no answer

REMARKS:

CORRELATES: Age (A 3); Educational level (E 1.1.1); Race (E 2.1); Gender (G 1.1); Childlessness (F 1.2.1); State of family relationships (F 1.4, S 4.1.3); Contentment x happiness (H 1.3.1); various other indicators concerning Happiness (H 1.7 - H 1.10); Self-percieved health (H 2.1.2); Desired personal changes (H 3.1); Unfulfilled aspirations (H 3.3.2); Economic status (I 1.1); Time spent in disliked activities (L 2.1.2); various Marital status comparisons (M 1); Positive attitude towards marriage (M 2.2); Caring about what others think about you (P 1.5.2); Ease of making friends (P 1.8.1); various Physical characteristics (P 2.1); Amount of worrying (P 5.1.2); Most important worry (P 5.2.2.2); various factors concerning Religion (R 1); various Domainsatisfactions (S 1)

CONCLUSION: The majority of contemporary Americans avow themselves as being happy. This might be due to the high material standard of living, but it could also be that the majority of Americans are incapable of the damaging admission that they might possibly be unhappy, which would be admission of failure in life. A third interpretation is that people do not set their demands and expectances to levels that will expose them to persistent thwarting. When situations are incapable of fully gratifying one's aspirations, one abandons or alters those aspirations.

AUTHOR: Wessman, A.E., Ricks, D.F. & McIlvaine Tyl, M.

WESSM 60

TITLE: Characteristics and concomitants of mood fluctuation in college women.

SOURCE: Journal of Abnormal and Social Psychology, 1960, vol. 60, nr 1, p. 117-126.

---

GOAL OF THE STUDY: Assessment of relations between self-concept and mood fluctuations.

REFERS TO: Happiness research; Flügel (1925), Johnson (1937)

TYPE OF STUDY: explanatory, testing, special group, snapshot, non-experimental

DATA GATHERING: Daily administration of mood-scale and psychological tests during 6 weeks

DATE OF DATA: October - December, 1957

POPULATION: Female college students, U.S.A.

SAMPLE CONSTRUCTION: Non-probability chunk sample of volunteering Radcliffe college students (see also WESSM 66/1).

NON-RESPONSE: 44% dropouts

N: 14

AUTHOR'S HAPPINESS LABEL: Elation - depression

OUR CONCEPTUALIZATION: Hedonic level of affect

INSTRUMENT: AFF 3.1: Repeated single closed question on overall hedonic level for the past day, rated on a 10-point scale (Wessman & Ricks Elation - Depression Scale).

The scale was marked each night just before retiring during 6 weeks for: (a) the best S had felt during the day, (b) the worst S had felt during the day, and (c) S's average for the day.
The mean value of the average mood for the day was used as happiness measure here.

The mood scale contained 10 phrases, ranging from expressions of extreme depression through more neutral feelings to those expressive of extreme elation. The phrases were choosen so that (a) there would be apporximately equal subjective gradations between units, and (b) the ends of the scale would be so extreme that few Ss would experience them, and these few would do so on rare accasions.

Elation vs Depression (how elated or depressed, happy or unhappy you felt today)

10. Complete elation, rapturous joy and soaring ecstacy.
9. Very elated and in very high spirits. Tremendous delight and buoyancy.
8. Elated and in high spirits.
7. Feeling very good and cheerful.
6. Feeling pretty good, 'OK'.
5. Feeling a little bit low. Just so-so.
4. Spirits low and somewhat 'blue'.
3. Depressed and feeling very low. Definitely 'blue'.
2. Tremendously depressed. Feeling terrible, really miserable, 'just awful'.
1. Utter depression and gloom. Completely down. All is black and leaden. Wish it were all over.

RELIABILITY: Repeat reliability: between-subject variance in scores of daily mood shown to be greater than variances within individual daily records (significant at 01 level).

VALIDITY:

DISTRIBUTION: positively skewed
individual means of the daily average ratings varied from 5.43 to 7.37; mean of their means: 6.14; median: 6.14

REMARKS:

CORRELATES: Mood fluctuation (A 2.1.4); various factors concerning Self-image (S 2)

CONCLUSION: Happiness is inversely related to correspondence of real and ideal self image. The less happy girls meet their standards, primarily concerned with intellectual achievement, in elation while the happier have more interests, are more sociable and even in elation experience discrepancy between real and ideal self.

AUTHOR: Wessman, A.E. & Ricks, D.F. — WESSM 66/1,2

TITLE: Mood and personality.

SOURCE: Holt, 1966, New York

---

GOAL OF THE STUDY: To contribute to the understanding of moods and affective experience in every day life.

REFERS TO: Happiness research; Flügel (1925), Johnson (1937)

TYPE OF STUDY: explanatory, explorative, special group, longitudinal, non-experimental

DATA GATHERING: Daily adminstration of personal feelings questionnaire during at least 30 days (study 1 + 2), and repeated interviews and psychological tests during three years (study 2 only).

DATE OF DATA: ± 1960

POPULATION: Female college students (study 1) and male college students (study 2), U.S.A.

SAMPLE CONSTRUCTION: Non-probability chunk samples of volunteering Radcliffe college students (study 1; see also WESSM 60) and of Harvard undergraduates, volunteering as paid participants in a three year research project (study 2).

All students superior in intelligence and academic performance; most of them of favored S.E.S., broad cultural backgrounds and interests; above average in the qualities of being introspective, self-aware and articulate.

NON-RESPONSE: 16% (study 1); 37%: 9 dropouts, incomplete; about the same happiness distribution (study 2)

N: 21 (study 1); 17 (study 2)

AUTHOR'S HAPPINESS LABEL: Hedonic level (relative happiness - unhappiness)

OUR CONCEPTUALIZATION: Hedonic level of affect

INSTRUMENT: AFF 3.1: Repeated single closed question on overall hedonic level for the past day, rated on a 10-point scale (Wessman & Ricks Elation - Depression Scale; see WESSM 60).

The scale was marked each night just before retiring during 6 weeks (at least 30 days) for daily peak, average and trough.
The six week mean of daily averages was used as happiness measure here.

RELIABILITY:

VALIDITY: external congruent validity (study 2 only):

- correlations ($r_{pm}$) with composite clinical rank order of happiness from 6 months earlier by 6 staff psychologists (inter-judge agreement: r = +.80) : r = +.71 with mean daily average, r = +.44 with mean daily peak, r= +.63 with mean daily trough
- correlations with questionnaire items indicative of avowed happiness from 2 years earlier: r = +.67 with mean daily average, r = +.66 with peak, r = +.32 with trough
- correlations with a system of scoring TAT themes supposedly indicative of happiness; r = +.27 with mean daily average, r = +.19 with peak, r = +.13 with trough
- correlations with clinical rank on present happiness, stressing possible aware subjective feelings, from a half year after: r = +.76 with mean daily average, r = +.57 with peak, r= +.56 with trough
- correlations with overall composite clinical rank on happiness from half a year after, using all clinical data and knowledge over 3 years: r = +.69 with mean daily average, r = +.48 with peak, r = +.42 with trough

external concurrent validity (study 2 only):

- correlations with MMPI Depression Scale, taken 2 years previously: r= -.83 with mean daily average, r= -.63 with peak, r= -.51 with trough
- correlations with clinical rank on happy life history, stressing autobiographic reports and information concerning past life experiences up to the time of entering college: r= +.48 with mean daily average, r= +.42 with peak, r= +.34 with trough

DISTRIBUTION: positively skewed

| possible range: 1 (low) to 10 (high); | actual range | median | mean | S.D. | |
|---|---|---|---|---|---|
| | 5.4 - 7.4; | 6.14; | 6.14; | .98 | (study 1) |
| | 5.1 - 6.7; | 6.0 | 5.96; | .94 | (study 2) |

REMARKS:

CORRELATES: Affective complexity (A 2.1.1); Variability in hedonic level (A 2.1.4); Hedonic level of most eleated/depressed moments (A 2.2.5); Wessman & Ricks Personal Feelings Scales (A 2.2); Physical condition (H 2.1.2); Pressure of academic work (E 1.3)

- study 1 only: Menstruation (P 2.3)
- study 2 only: Past depression and insecurity (A 2.2.4); projective Guilt (A 2.2.8); various other Emotional characteristics (A 2.3); Intellectual ability (C 1.3); Hedonic level x happiness (H 1.2.1); Contentment x hedonic level (H 1.3.2); Past happiness (H 1.4.2); Future happiness (H 1.5); Valuation of happiness (H 1.10); various indicators of Life history (L 1.1); Projective happiness (L 2.1.1); Optimism (L 2.1.2); Amount of sleep (L 3.2); various factors concerning Personality (P 1), Self-image (S 2), Time perspective (T 1)

CONCLUSION: The hedonic level is broadly indicative for all one's daily affective experiences. This hedonic level is relatively stable through time. High hedonic level persons tend to be more optimistic, possessed of self-esteem and confidence. They show ego-strength and a gratifying sense of identity. There is a good organization and purpose in their life, together with the necessary mastery of themselves and interpersonal situations to attain their goals.

| | |
|---|---|
| AUTHOR: | Wessman, A.E. — WESSM 73 |
| TITLE: | Personality and the subjective experience of time. |
| SOURCE: | Journal of Personality Assessment, 1973, vol. 37, nr 2, p. 103-114. |

| | |
|---|---|
| GOAL OF THE STUDY: | Assessment of some important dimensions of individual differences in reported experience and use of time, and personality characteristics associated with these dimensions. |
| REFERS TO: | Theory of personality and experience of time; Brayley & Freed (1971), Cottle (1971). |
| TYPE OF STUDY: | explanatory, explorative, special group, longitudinal, non-experimental |
| DATA GATHERING: | Queationnaires, repeated interviews, and psychological tests during 3 years |
| DATE OF DATA: | ± 1960 |
| POPULATION: | Male college students, U.S.A. |
| SAMPLE CONSTRUCTION: | Non-probability chunk sample of Harvard undergraduates, participating in a three-year personality assessment and research project (Wessman & Ricks sample; see WESSM 66/2). |
| NON-RESPONSE: | |
| N: | 17 |
| AUTHOR'S HAPPINESS LABEL: | Mood (first instrument) and Happiness (second instrument) |
| OUR CONCEPTUALIZATION: | Hedonic level of affect (first instrument) and Happiness (second instrument) |
| FIRST INSTRUMENT: | AFF 3.1: Repeated single closed question on overall hedonic level for the past day, rated on a 10-point scale (Wessman & Ricks Elation - Depression Scale; see WESSM 60 and WESSM 66/2).<br>The scale was scored each night during 6 weeks. |
| RELIABILITY: | |
| VALIDITY: | |
| DISTRIBUTION: | |
| SECOND INSTRUMENT: | COMP 5: Composite clinical rank order of happiness by 6 staff psychologists, based on a lasting, intensive study (see also WESSM 66 under VALIDITY). |
| RELIABILITY: | |
| VALIDITY: | |
| DISTRIBUTION: | |
| REMARKS: | |
| CORRELATES: | Experience and Use of time (T 1.1) |
| CONCLUSION: | |

WILSO 65

AUTHOR: Wilson, W.R.

TITLE: Relation of sexual behaviors, values, and conflicts to avowed happiness.

SOURCE: Psychological Reports, 1965, vol. 17, p. 371-378.

---

GOAL OF THE STUDY: Exploration of the relation between sexual conflicts and neurosis.

REFERS TO: Theory of neurosis; Mowrer (1961)

TYPE OF STUDY: explanatory, explorative, special group, snapshot, non-experimental

DATA GATHERING: Administration of highly structured questionnaire in a classroom situation

DATE OF DATA:

POPULATION: Undergraduate colleges students, Hawaii

SAMPLE CONSTRUCTION: Non-probability accidental sample using volunteering attendants of several psychology and anthropology courses.
32 males, 69 females

NON-RESPONSE:

N: 101

AUTHOR'S HAPPINESS LABEL: Happiness

OUR CONCEPTUALIZATION: Happiness

INSTRUMENT: COMP 1.1: Single closed question rated on an 11-point scale:

| 0 | 1 | 2 | 3 | 4 | 5 | 6 | 7 | 8 | 9 | 10 |
|---|---|---|---|---|---|---|---|---|---|---|
| Completely and utterly unhappy. Terrible depression and gloom all of the time. | | | Not very happy most of the time. | | Happy most of the time. | | Very happy almost all of the time. | | Completely and supremely happy. Tremendous joy and elation all of the time. | |

RELIABILITY:

VALIDITY:

DISTRIBUTION: slightly positively skewed
actual range: 1 - 9

REMARKS:

CORRELATES: Age (A 3); Gender (G 1.1); Perceived liberality of sexual attitudes of parents (F 1.1.3.2); Religiousness (R 1.1); various indicators of Sexual attitudes (S 3.1)

CONLCUSION: Religiousness, conservatism in sexual attitudes, and moderate sexual conflicts are associated with happiness.

YOUNG 37A

AUTHOR: Young, P.T.

TITLE: Laughing and weeping, cheerfulness and depression: A study of moods among college students.

SOURCE: Journal of Social Psychology, 1937, vol. 8, p. 311-334.

---

GOAL OF THE STUDY: Yielding information upon laughing and weeping, cheerfulness and depression.

REFERS TO: Theory of moods; Cason (1931)

TYPE OF STUDY: explanatory, explorative, special group, snapshot, experimental

DATA GATHERING: Highly structured questionnaire, filled out twice by the test-retest group with an interval of 16 days and daily for a period of 3½ weeks by the permanent group

DATE OF DATA: 1934/1935

POPULATION: College students, U.S.A.

SAMPLE CONSTRUCTION: Non-probability chunk sample using attendants of a psychology course.
- test-retest group: N = 180; 96 males, 84 females
- permanent group : N = 56; 48 males, 8 females
age 17 - 24, average age 19

NON-RESPONSE:

N: 236

AUTHOR'S HAPPINESS LABEL: Cheerfulness

OUR CONCEPTUALIZATION: Hedonic level of affect.

INSTRUMENT: AFF 3.1: Repeated single closed question on hedonic level for the past day, rated on a 7-point scale.

The scale was scored twice with an interval of 16 days (test-retest group); or daily, except on Saturdays and Sundays, for a period of three and a half weeks (permanent group).

Consider your experience during the past 24 hours, being as objective and matter-of-fact as possible. Estimate honestly the prevailing or dominant level of your mood, and put a cross through the term which most accurately describes your prevailing feeling.

highly elated / moderately cheerful / mildly cheerful / indifferent / mildly depressed / moderately depressed / extremely gloomy

RELIABILITY:

VALIDITY:

DISTRIBUTION: positively skewed

REMARKS:

CORRELATES: Mood variablity (A 2.1.4); Gender (G 1.1); Frequency of laughing (X 1); Weather conditions during experiment (X 1)

CONCLUSION: Moods of cheerfulness and depression are dependent primarily upon meaningful events within the social environment.

YOUNG 37B

AUTHOR: Young, P.T.

TITLE: Is cheerfulness-depression a general temperamental trait?

SOURCE: Psychological Review, 1937, vol. 44, p. 313-319.

---

GOAL OF THE STUDY: Test of the hypothesis that a cheerful average daily mood is related to a positive response to various other stimuli.

REFERS TO: Theory of affective processes: Young (1937)

TYPE OF STUDY: explanatory, testing, special group, snapshot, experimental

DATA GATHERING: Administration of mood scale, odors-test and word-test in laboratory situation during at least 4 days with a maximum of 13 days

DATE OF DATA: 1934 - 1935

POPULATION: College students, U.S.A.

SAMPLE CONSTRUCTION: Non-probability chunk sample using attendants of a psychology course.
'Permanent group' of Young sample (see YOUNG 37A).

NON-RESPONSE: 39% dropouts

N: 34

AUTHOR'S HAPPINESS LABEL: Cheerfulness

OUR CONCEPTUALIZATION: Hedonic level of affect

INSTRUMENT: AFF 3.1: Repeated single closed question on hedonic level for the past day, rated on a 7-point scale (see YOUNG 37A).
The scale was scored on at least 4 days, with a maximum of 13 days

RELIABILITY: Reasonable repeat reliability as assessed by little variation in individual average deviations over 13 days (from 0.00 to 1.50 with most frequent average deviations between 0.61 and 0.90 scale points).

VALIDITY:

DISTRIBUTION:

REMARKS:

CORRELATES: Inclination to recall pleasant words (P 1.6); Being readily pleased by odors (P 1.6)

CONCLUSION: The temperamental trait of cheerfulness is not wholly general.
The neural mechanisms which regulate affective reactions to odors are automatically distinct from those which regulate moods.

# PART III

# CORRELATES

**More than 3500 Correlational Findings Ordered in 42 Main Subject Categories. Presented in Alphabetical Order.**

# CONTENTS PART III



(to be continued on next page)

(to be continued on next page)

P 1 - PERSONALITY (p. 368) . . . . . . . . . . . . see also S 2, H 2.3, A 2

P 1.1 Locus of control

P 1.2 Coping capacity (Effectiveness) . . . . . . see also P 1.8.1, H 2.3, S 2, T 1.1, C 1, P 5

P 1.3 Defensiveness

P 1.4 Stages of personality development
1.4.1 - Erikson's stages of psycho-social development
1.4.2 - Other indicators of personality development

P 1.5 Needs . . . . . . . . . . . . . . . . . . . see also C 2, H 3, V 1
1.5.1 - Achievement motivation . . . . . . . . . see also S 1.8, S 2.2, G 1.2, W 2.9
1.5.2 - Need for social approval
1.5.3 - Desire for excitement
1.5.4 - Desire for social participation . . . . . see S 4 (esp. S 4.5)
1.5.5 - Various needs

P 1.6 Tendency to react positively

P 1.7 Morality . . . . . . . . . . . . . . . . . see also A 2.2.8, A 2.2.13, V 1

P 1.8 Personality traits concerning interpersonal functioning . . . . . . . . . . . . . . . . see also S 4, P 4, S 2.2, I 2
1.8.1 - Interpersonal capability
1.8.2 - Trust in people
1.8.3 - Influence
1.8.4 - Various traits concerning interpersonal functioning

P 1.9 Various personality traits

P 2 - PHYSICAL CHARACTERISTICS (p. 395)

P 2.1 Physical appearance . . . . . . . . . . . . see also E 2

P 2.2 Physical health . . . . . . . . . . . . . . see H 2.1

P 2.3 Various physiological characteristics

P 3 - POLITICS (p. 397)

P 3.1 Political concern

P 3.2 Attitudes towards political situation . . . see also N 1.1, S 1.3

P 3.3 Political preference

P 4 - POPULARITY (p. 401)

P 4.1 Actual popularity

P 4.2 Perceived popularity . . . . . . . . . . . see also A 2.2.18

P 4.3 Various factors concerning popularity

P 5 - PROBLEMS, WORRIES AND FEARS (p. 403) . . . . see also C 2, L 2

P 5.1 Problems
5.1.1 - Amount of problems
5.1.2 - Specific problems

P 5.2 Worries and fear
5.2.1 - Amount of worries and fears
5.2.2 - Specific worries and fears
5.2.2.1 - Personal worries and fears
5.2.2.2 - Most important worry
5.2.2.3 - Worries and fears concerning one's country

R 1 - RELIGION (p. 410) . . . . . . . . . . . . . . see also V 1

R 1.1 Religiousness

R 1.2 Religious denomination

R 1.3 Religious participation

R 1.4 Various factors concerning religion

R 2 - RETIREMENT (p. 414)

R 2.1 Being retired

R 2.2 Compulsory vs voluntary retirement

R 2.3 Various factors concerning retirement

S 1 - SATISFACTION WITH . . . (p. 418)

S 1.1 Satisfaction with leisure
1.1.1 - Leisure activities
1.1.2 - Leisure time

S 1.2 Satisfaction with living environment
1.2.1 - Housing
1.2.2 - Neighborhood
1.2.3 - Specific facilities
1.2.4 - Various aspects of the living environment

S 1.3 Satisfaction with nation
1.3.1 - Nation in general
1.3.2 - Government
1.3.3 - Various aspects of the nation

S 1.4 Satisfaction with oneself . . . . . . . . . see S 2.1

S 1.5 Satisfaction with one's own life . . . . . see H 1, L 2

S 1.6 Satisfaction with physical health

S 1.7 Satisfaction with social life
1.7.1 - Family, relatives
1.7.2 - Marriage
1.7.3 - Friends, social contacts
1.7.4 - Various aspects of social life

S 1.8 Satisfaction with socio-economic level
1.8.1 - S.E.S. in general
1.8.2 - Level of education
1.8.3 - Income, standard of living . . . . . . . see also S 1.9.2

S 1.9 Satisfaction with work, job . . . . . . . . see also A 2.2.14
1.9.1 - Work in general
1.9.2 - Specific aspects of the job

S 1.10 Various domainsatisfactions

S 1.11 Satisfaction sumscores

S 2 - SELF-IMAGE (p. 437 ) . . . . . . . . . . . . see also P 1

S 2.1 Formal aspects of self-image
2.1.1 - Congruency between real and ideal self-image
2.1.2 - Stability of self-image
2.1.3 - Self-esteem
2.1.4 - Self-confidence . . . . . . . . . . . . . see also A 2.2.16
2.1.5 - Satisfaction with oneself
2.1.6 - Various indicators of a positive self-image . . . . . . . . . . . . . . . . . . see also A 2.2.18

S 2.2 Content of self-image
2.2.1 - Content of real self-image
2.2.2 - Content of ideal self-image . . . . . . . see also V 1.1

S 2.3 Various factors concerning self-image

S 3 - SEXUALITY (p. 446)

S 3.1 Attitudes towards sex
3.1.1 - One's own attitudes
3.1.2 - Perceived attitudes of others
3.1.3 - Attitudinal conflicts

S 3.2 Quality of sex life . . . . . . . . . . . . see also A 2.2.11

S 3.3 Various factors concerning sex

S 4 - SOCIAL PARTICIPATION (p. 450)

S 4.1 Social participation in interpersonal networks
4.1.1 - Number of interpersonal relationships
4.1.2 - Frequency of interpersonal contacts
4.1.3 - Quality of interpersonal relationships . see also F 1, M 2, P 1.8
4.1.4 - Other characteristics of interpersonal relationships
4.1.5 - Various indicators of participation in interpersonal networks . . . . . . . . . see also A 2.2.3, A 2.2.11, A 2.2.17, P 1.8, S 2.2

(to be continued on next page)

# A1 ACTIVITY



## A 1.1 - GENERAL ACTIVITY

| | | | | | | | | | |
|---|---|---|---|---|---|---|---|---|---|
| PRODUCTIVITY | Number of hours spent during the last typical week working or doing housework, doing volunteer work for church, relatives, yard care, repairing, and other such activities | | HAPP 3.1 | r | +.12 | | | People of 46 and older, Duke, U.S.A.<br>Probability systematic random sample stratified by age and sex<br>N: 502, date: 1968 | PÅLMO 72<br>p. 70 |
| ACTIVITY LEVEL | 32-item inventory of daily activities (Daily Activities List).<br>The DAL was scored for the number of activities engaged in on the preceding day. Whenever possible it was administered each weekday during the first 4 weeks of treatment. | Analysis on the basis of a comparison between the 10 Ss with the lowest DAL scores and the 10 Ss with the highest scores | AFF 3.3 | $r_{pm}$ | +.53 | t | 05 | Adult cancer patients, U.S.A.<br>Non-probability accidental sample<br>N: 21, date: — | STANF 71<br>p. 696 |

## A 1.2 - WORK ACTIVITY

see 'Work' (W 2), 'Household Work' (H 4.2)

## A 1.3 - LEISURE ACTIVITY

see 'Use of Leisure Time' (L 3.3)

## A 1.4 - SOCIAL ACTIVITY

see 'Social Participation' (S 4)

## A 1.5 - PHYSICAL ACTIVITY

see also 'Sports' (S 6)

| | | | | | | | | | |
|---|---|---|---|---|---|---|---|---|---|
| NEWBORN ACTIVITY: | Observation of movements of hands and feet (by method of Kessen et al., 1961), using motion pictures of four observations on two consecutive days | Newborn activity was correlated with hedonic level at eight months. | | | | | | 8 months old infants, U.S.A.<br>Non-probability quota sample<br>N: 24, date: — | MCGRA 68<br>p. 1249 |
| - NEWBORN ACTIVITY | Observation of movements of hands and feet | | AFF 5.1 | $r_{pm}$ | +.06 | | ns | | |
| - NEWBORN REACTIVITY | Difference between unstimulated activity and activity after S's forehead was rubbed | | AFF 5.1 | $r_{pm}$ | -.09 | | ns | | |

| | | | | | | | | | |
|---|---|---|---|---|---|---|---|---|---|
| - NEWBORN REACTIVITY | Difference between unstimulated activity and activity after removal of nipple | | AFF 5.1 | $r_{pm}$ | -.51 | | 01 | | |
| ACTIVITY | Examination by a psychologist using a 9-point scale<br>(Activity: inactive-vigorous rating scale; from Bayley Infant Behavior Profile; see also below) | Both activity and hedonic level were assessed at 8 months | AFF 5.1 | $r_{pm}$ | +.59 | | 01 | 8 months old infants, U.S.A.<br>(see last page) | MCGRA 68<br>p. 1249 |
| ACTIVITY | Repeated expert rating on the basis of observation of expressive behavior on a bipolar 7-point 'inactive - vigorous' scale | Each child was rated 12 times between the ages of 10 and 36 months on both hedonic level and the variable mentioned.<br>Ratings at the ages of 10, 11 and 12; 13, 14 and 15; 18, 21 and 24; 27, 30 and 36 months were combined.<br>See also instrument and remarks in excerpt (Part II) and 'Various Personality Traits during Childhood' (Part III, P 1.9). | | | | | | Children, Berkeley, California, U.S.A.<br>Non-probability chunk sample<br>N: 54, date: 1928 - 1943 | SCHAE 63<br>p. 29 |
| | | boys: 10-12 / 13-15 / 18-24 / 27-36<br>10-12: -.08 / -.18 / -.06 / -.27<br>13-15: -.02 / +.03 / -.01 / -.17<br>18-24: +.19 / +.24 / +.65[x] / +.29<br>27-36: +.25 / +.07 / +.21 / +.14<br><br>girls: 10-12 / 13-15 / 18-24 / 27-36<br>10-12: +.03 / +.11 / +.07 / -.07<br>13-15: +.01 / +.09 / +.29 / +.10<br>18-24: +.07 / +.12 / +.34 / +.01<br>27-36: +.06 / +.02 / +.20 / +.23 | AFF 5.1 | $r_{pm}$ | | | | | |
| SPEED OF MOVEMENTS | Repeated expert rating on the basis of observation of expressive behavior on a 7-point 'slow - rapid' scale | See above<br><br>boys: 10-12 / 13-15 / 18-24 / 27-36<br>10-12: -.18 / -.31 / -.26 / -.39[x]<br>13-15: -.05 / -.13 / -.07 / -.29<br>18-24: +.06 / -.06 / +.35 / -.02<br>27-36: +.10 / +.05 / +.13 / +.02<br><br>girls: 10-12 / 13-15 / 18-24 / 27-36<br>10-12: -.02 / +.10 / +.11 / -.07<br>13-15: -.05 / +.10 / +.28 / -.01<br>18-24: +.01 / -.04 / +.06 / -.27<br>27-36: +.02 / -.03 / -.04 / -.27 | AFF 5.1 | $r_{pm}$ | | | | See above | SCHAE 63<br>p. 29 |
| BODILY ACTIVITY IN PURSUIT OF PLEASURES (games, etc.) | Class-master rating on a 7-point scale on the basis of observation | | AFF 5.3 | $r_{pm}$ | +.47 | | | Schoolboys, England<br>Non-probability chunk sample<br>N: 140, date: 1912 - 1913 | WEBB 15<br>p. 27 |
| BODILY ACTIVITY IN PURSUIT OF PLEASURES (games etc.) | Trained peer rating on a 7-point scale on the basis of observation | | AFF 5.2 | $r_{pm}$ | +.36 | | | Male students, England<br>Non-probability chunk sample<br>N: 194, date: 1912 - 1913 | WEBB 15<br>p. 26 |
| BODILY ACTIVITY DURING SCHOOL HOURS | Class-master rating on a 7-point scale on the basis of observation | | AFF 5.3 | $r_{pm}$ | +.59 | | | Schoolboys, England<br>Non-probability chunk sample<br>N: 140, date: 1912-1913 | WEBB 15<br>p. 27 |
| BODILY ACTIVITY DURING BUSINESS HOURS | Trained peer rating on a 7-point scale on the basis of observation | | AFF 5.2 | $r_{pm}$ | +.44 | | | Male students, England<br>Non-probability chunk sample<br>N: 194, date: 1912 - 1913 | WEBB 15<br>p. 26 |

| | | | | | | | | | |
|---|---|---|---|---|---|---|---|---|---|
| PHYSICAL ACTIVITY | Closed question: none or very little / little / neither much nor little / rather much / very much | | HAPP 1.1 | G | +.18 | | | National adult population, The Netherlands<br>Probability area sample<br>N: 1552, date: June, 1968 | BAKKE 74<br>p. 28 |

## A 1.6 - MENTAL ACTIVITY

see also 'Cognition' (C 1)

| | | | | | | | | | |
|---|---|---|---|---|---|---|---|---|---|
| MENTAL WORK BESTOWED UPON PLEASURES (games etc.) | Class-master rating on a 7-point scale on the basis of observation | | AFF 5.3 | $r_{pm}$ | +.43 | | | Schoolboys, England<br>Non-probability chunk sample<br>N: 140, date: 1912 - 1913 | WEBB 15<br>p. 27 |
| MENTAL WORK BESTOWED UPON PLEASURES (games etc.) | Trained peer rating on a 7-point scale on the basis of observation | | AFF 5.2 | $r_{pm}$ | +.27 | | | Male students, England<br>Non-probability chunk sample<br>N: 194, date: 1912 - 1913 | WEBB 15<br>p. 26 |
| MENTAL WORK BESTOWED UPON USUAL STUDIES | Class-master rating on a 7-point scale on the basis of observation | | AFF 5.3 | $r_{pm}$ | +.41 | | | Schoolboys, England<br>Non-probability chunk sample<br>N: 140, date: 1912 - 1913 | WEBB 15<br>p. 27 |
| MENTAL WORK BESTOWED UPON USUAL STUDIES | Trained peer rating on a 7-point scale on the basis of observation | | AFF 5.2 | $r_{pm}$ | -.02 | | | Male students, England<br>Non-probability chunk sample<br>N: 194, date: 1912 - 1913 | WEBB 15<br>p. 26 |
| NECOUNTERED NEW STIMULATING IDEAS | Closed question; during last few weeks | Index of Positive Affects: G = +.22<br>Index of Negative Affects: G = +.08 | AFF 2.3 | G | | | | Employed males, England<br>Non-probability purposive quota sample<br>N: 192, date: — | PAYNE 74<br>p. 17 |

## A 1.7 - ENERGY LEVEL

see 'Types of Affect: Energy' (A 2.2.6)

## A 1.8 - VARIOUS FACTORS CONCERNING ACTIVITY

| | | | | | | | | | |
|---|---|---|---|---|---|---|---|---|---|
| SELF-PERCEIVED OVERACTIVITY | Closed question: no vs yes | | HAPP 2.1 | G | -.48 | $Chi^2$ | 000 | Male employees of age 40+, The Netherlands<br>Non-probability chunk sample<br>N: 13000, date: — | SONDE 75 |
| LIKE DOING VOLUNTARY ACTIVITIES | Don't like voluntary activities vs like voluntary activities | Computed for those of age 60+ only<br>Among those who like voluntary activities, 84% have life satisfaction, while among those who do not like voluntary activities, 66% have life satisfaction. | HAPP 3.1 | D% | + | | | Adults, Japan<br>Probability sample<br>N: 2000 or more, date: September, 1973 | PALMO 75<br>p. 124 |
| HAVING DIFFICULTIES IN KEEPING OCCUPIES | Closed question: no vs yes | See remarks in excerpt (Part II).<br>Among the gainfully employed G' = -.43 (01)<br>Among retirees who had a positive orientation to retirement before they were retired: G' = -.38 (05)<br>Among retirees who had a negative orientation to retirement: G' = =.64 (01) | COMP 1.2 | G' | -.49 | Gt' | 01 | Aged males, U.S.A., (those satisfied in 1952)<br>Non-probability accidental sample<br>N: 787, date: 1952-1954 | THOMP 60<br>p. 168 |

| | | | | | | | | | |
|---|---|---|---|---|---|---|---|---|---|
| ZEST vs apathy | Content analysis of interview records by 2 independent judges (Component of Life Satisfaction Rating) | See remarks in excerpt (Part II) | CON 1.4<br>COMP 1.4 | r<br>r | +.56<br>+.84 | | | White population of age 50+, Kansas City, U.S.A.<br>Stratified probability sample and non-probability quota sample<br>N: 177, date: — | NEUGA 61<br>p. 139 |

# A 2 AFFECT



## A 2.1 – QUALITIES OF AFFECT

### A 2.1.1 – COMPLEXITY

| | | | | | | | | |
|---|---|---|---|---|---|---|---|---|
| AFFECTIVE COMPLEXITY | Number of factors that independently explain a considerable proportion of the variation in mood change | Eight factors were used, that were extracted from the highest, average and lowest moods reported each day during 6 weeks on 11 Personal Feeling Scales and 3 closed questions on physical health, menstruation and pressure of academic work.<br>See also under 'Correlates' in excerpt (Part II).<br>More detailed information concerning the Personal Feeling Scales is given under 'Types of Affect' (Part III, A 2.2). | AFF 3.1 | $r_{pm}$ | +.23 | t | ns | Female college students, U.S.A.<br>Non-probability chunk sample<br>N: 21, date: $\pm$ 1960 | WESSM 66/1<br>p. 73 |
| AFFECTIVE COMPLEXITY | Number of factors that independently explain a considerable proportion of the variation in mood change | Six factors were used, that were extracted from the highest, average and lowest moods reported each day during 6 weeks on the 16 Personal Feeling Scales and 3 closed questions on physical health, hours of sleep and pressure of academic work.<br>See also under 'Correlates' in excerpt (Part II) and under 'Types of Affect' (Part III, A 2.2). | AFF 3.1 | $r_{pm}$ | -.30 | t | ns | Male college students, U.S.A.<br>Non-probability chunk sample<br>N: 17, date: $\pm$ 1960 | WESSM 66/2<br>p. 73 |
| MOOD DIFFERENTIATION AND COMPLEXITY | P-technique factor analysis, usi the highest, average and lowest mood report ach day during 28 days on 14 Wessman & Ricks Personal Feeling Scales.<br>Four measures were deducted: | See also above. | | | | | | Undergraduate students, U.S.A.<br>Non-probability chunk sample<br>N: 67, date: summer, 1970 | GORMA 71<br>p. 216 |
| | – Percentage of variance explained by the first factor (indicative of low differentiation and complexity). | | HAPP 3.1 | $r_{pm}$ | +.08 | | ns | | |
| | | | AFF 3.1 | $r_{pm}$ | +.12 | | ns | | |
| | – Average correlation among mood ratings (indicative of a lack of differentiation) | | HAPP 3.1 | $r_{pm}$ | +.08 | | ns | | |
| | | | AFF 3.1 | $r_{pm}$ | +.12 | | ns | | |

| | | | | | | | | | |
|---|---|---|---|---|---|---|---|---|---|
| | - Number of factors needed to explain 90% of the variance (indicative of high complexity and differentiation) | | HAPP 3.1<br>AFF 3.1 | $r_{pm}$<br>$r_{pm}$ | +.10<br>-.01 | | ns<br>ns | | |
| | - Number of factors explaining more than 10% of the variance each (indicative of high complexity and differentiation) | | HAPP 3.1<br>AFF 3.1 | $r_{pm}$<br>$r_{pm}$ | -.24<br>-.10 | | 05<br>ns | | |

## A 2.1.2 - HEDONIC LEVEL

See 'Hedonic Level of Affect' (H 1.2)

## A 2.1.3 - INTENSITY

| | | | | | | | | | |
|---|---|---|---|---|---|---|---|---|---|
| EMOTIONALITY: level of emotion | Factor derived from a semantic differential of 28 bipolar 7-point self-rating adjective scales | | HAPP 1.1 | r | -.25 | | 01 | Married female graduates of the Liberal Arts College, U.S.A.<br>Probability cluster sample<br>N: 229, date: 1971 | GORDO 74<br>p. 243 |
| EMOTIONALITY | Ss with few negative and few positive feelings (n = 15) vs Ss with many negative and many positive feelings (n = 16) as assessed by the I.W. questionnaire (see Hermans & Tak-v.d.Ven, 1973) | | AFF 3.1 | | - | | | Secondary school pupils, The Netherlands<br>Non-probability accidental sample<br>N: 89, date: after 1970 | RAMZY 73<br>p. 77 |
| INTENSITY OF FEELINGS | Proportion of intense pleasure or unpleasure reported during 30 days | See also instrument in excerpt (Part II).<br>For tendency to experience intense pleasure:<br>r = -.37<br>For tendency to experience intense displeasure:<br>r = -.75 | AFF 3.4 | r | - | | | Intellectuals, England<br>Non-probability accidental sample using friends<br>N: 9, date: — | FLÜGE 25<br>p. 335/336 |
| SHALLOW AFFECT | 20-item index, referring to a general lack of feeling of involvement in activities and to avowed emotional insensitivity (DPI Shallow Affect Scale; see Jackson & Messick, 1964) | | AFF 3.1<br>HAPP 3.1 | $r_{pm}$<br>$r_{pm}$ | -.04<br>-.10 | | ns<br>ns | Undergraduate students, U.S.A.<br>Non-probability chunk sample<br>N: 67, date: summer, 1970 | GORMA 71<br>p. 215/219 |

## INTENSITY OF SPECIFIC AFFECTS

| | | | | | | | | | |
|---|---|---|---|---|---|---|---|---|---|
| EXTREME ANGER, occasional liability to - | Trained peer-rating on a 7-point scale on the basis of observation | | AFF 5.2 | $r_{pm}$ | -.16 | | | Male students, England<br>Non-probability chunk sample<br>N: 194, date: 1912 - 1913 | WEBB 15<br>p. 26 |
| EXTREME DEPRESSION, occasional liability to - | Trained peer-rating on a 7-point scale on the basis of observation | | AFF 5.2 | $r_{pm}$ | -.53 | | | See above | WEBB 15<br>p. 26 |

## A 2.1.4 - VARIABILITY

| Variable | Operationalization | Remarks | Instrument | Statistic | Value | | Sig. | Population | Source |
|---|---|---|---|---|---|---|---|---|---|
| MOOD FLUCTUATION | 20-item index referring to day-to-day and within-day mood fluctuation (Mood Fluctuation Scale; see Jackson & Messick, 1964) | | AFF 3.1<br>HAPP 3.1 | $r_{pm}$<br>$r_{pm}$ | -.32<br>-.11 | | 01<br>ns | Undergraduate students, U.S.A.<br>Non-probability chunk sample<br>N: 67, date: summer, 1970 | GORMA 71<br>p. 215/219 |
| VARIABILITY OF FEELINGS | Standard deviation of the average proportion of different degrees of feeling intensity during 30 days | See also instrument in excerpt (Part II). | AFF 3.4 | r | -.73 | | | Intellectuals, England<br>Non-probability accidental sample using friends<br>N: 9, date: — | FLÜGE 25<br>p. 334 |
| VARIABILITY OF FEELINGS | Mean variation of the average proportion of different degrees of feeling intensity during 30 days | See also instrument in excerpt (Part II). | AFF 3.4 | r | -.18 | | | See above | FLÜGE 25<br>p. 334 |

## VARIABILITY IN HEDONIC LEVEL

| Variable | Operationalization | Remarks | Instrument | Statistic | Value | | Sig. | Population | Source |
|---|---|---|---|---|---|---|---|---|---|
| MOOD VARIABILITY, day to day - | Comparison of averages and average deviations on a 7-point mood scale, scored daily over a period of 3½ weeks | See instrument in excerpt (Part II). | AFF 3.1 | | - | | ns | College students, U.S.A.<br>Non-probability chunk sample (permanent group)<br>N: 56, date: 1934/1935 | YOUNG 37A<br>p. 329 |
| MOOD FLUCTUATION, within day - | Mean difference between the lowest and highest mood reported each day during 6 weeks on the Elation-Depression Scale | The Elation-Depression Scale was scored each night for lowest, average and highest mood experienced that day over a period of 6 weeks. See also instrument in excerpt (Part II). | AFF 3.1 | $r_{pm}$ | +.36 | | ns | Female college students, U.S.A.<br>Non-probability chunk sample<br>N: 21, date: October - December, 1957 | WESSM 60<br>p. 121<br>WESSM 66/1<br>p. 61 |
| MOOD FLUCTUATION, day to day - | Standard deviation of the average mood reported each day during 6 weeks on the Elation-Depression Scale | See above | AFF 3.1 | $r_{pm}$ | -.17 | | ns | See above | WESSM 60<br>p. 121<br>WESSM 66/1<br>p. 61 |
| VARIATION IN HEDONIC LEVEL, within day - | Mean difference between the lowest and highest mood reported each day during 6 weeks on the Elation-Depression Scale | See above | AFF 3.1 | $r_{pm}$ | +.29 | t | ns | Male college students, U.S.A.<br>Non-probability chunk sample<br>N: 17, date: ± 1960 | WESSM 66/2<br>p. 61 |
| VARIATION IN HEDONIC LEVEL, day to day - | Standard deviation of the average mood reported each day during 6 weeks on the Elation-Depression Scale | See above | AFF 3.1 | $r_{pm}$ | +.03 | t | ns | See above | WESSM 66/2<br>p. 61 |
| VARIABILITY IN ELATION vs depression, day to day - | Standard deviation of lowest, average and highest mood reported each day during one month on the Wessman & Ricks Elation-Depression Scale | The Elation-Depression Scale was scored each night for lowest, average and highest mood experienced that day over a period of 6 weeks. See also instrument in excerpt (Part II).<br>daily highest: r = -.03 (ns)<br>daily average: r = +.08 (ns)<br>daily lowest : r = +.24 (05) | HAPP 3.1 | $r_{pm}$ | | | | Undergraduate students, U.S.A.<br>Non-probability chunk sample<br>N: 67, date: summer, 1970 | GORMA 71<br>p. 231 |
| MOOD VARIABILITY, day to day - | Standard deviation of the daily happiness score reported each day during 6 weeks on an adapted Wessman & Ricks Elation-Depression Scale | See also first instrument in excerpt (Part II). | AFF 3.1<br>(1st instr.) | $r_{pm}$ | -.43 | | 01 | Undergraduate University students, California, U.S.A.<br>Non-probability chunk sample<br>N: 86, date: November - December, 1971 | FORDY 72<br>p. 151 |
| QUICK OSCILLATION BETWEEN CHEERFULNESS AND DEPRESSION | Trained peer rating on a 7-point scale on the basis of observation | | AFF 5.2 | $r_{pm}$ | -.27 | | | Male students, England<br>Non-probability chunk sample<br>N: 194, date: 1912 - 1913 | WEBB 15<br>p. 26 |

## VARIABILITY IN OTHER AFFECTS

| | | | | | | | | | |
|---|---|---|---|---|---|---|---|---|---|
| DAY TO DAY VARIABILITY in specific moods: | Standard deviation of the lowest, average and highest scores reported each day during one month on the Wessman & Ricks Personal Feeling Scales (see Wessman & Ricks, 1966) | Each of the Personal Feeling Scales was scored each night for the lowest, average and highest mood experienced that day.<br>For Personal Feeling Scales see also under 'Types of Affect' (Part III, A 2.2). | | | | | | Undergraduate students, U.S.A.<br>Non-probability chunk sample<br>N: 67, date: summer, 1970 | GORMA 71<br>p. 230/231 |
| - COMPANIONSHIP vs being isolated | | daily highest: r = -.06 (ns)<br>daily average: r = +.05 (ns)<br>daily lowest : r = +.09 (ns) | HAPP 3.1 | $r_{pm}$ | + | | ns | | |
| - ENERGY vs fatigue | | daily highest: r = -.00 (ns)<br>daily average: r = +.04 (ns)<br>daily lowest : r = +.09 (ns) | HAPP 3.1 | $r_{pm}$ | + | | ns | | |
| - HARMONY vs anger | | daily highest: r = +.15 (ns)<br>daily average: r = +.23 (ns)<br>daily lowest : r = +.13 (ns) | HAPP 3.1 | $r_{pm}$ | + | | ns | | |
| - IMPULSE EXPRESSION vs self-restraint | | daily highest: r = -.05 (ns)<br>daily average: r = +.08 (ns)<br>daily lowest : r = +.04 (ns) | HAPP 3.1 | $r_{pm}$ | + | | ns | | |
| - LOVE and SEX | | daily highest: r = +.00 (ns)<br>daily average: r = +.01 (ns)<br>daily lowest : r = +.13 (ns) | HAPP 3.1 | $r_{pm}$ | + | | ns | | |
| - OWN SOCIABILITY vs withdrawal | | daily highest: r = -.04 (ns)<br>daily average: r = +.04 (ns)<br>daily lowest : r = +.10 (ns) | HAPP 3.1 | $r_{pm}$ | + | | ns | | |
| - PERSONAL FREEDOM vs external constraint | | daily highest: r = +.01 (ns)<br>daily average: r = +.07 (ns)<br>daily lowest : r = +.05 (ns) | HAPP 3.1 | $r_{pm}$ | + | | ns | | |
| - PERSONAL MORAL JUDGEMENT | | daily highest: r = -.03 (ns)<br>daily average: r = +.02 (ns)<br>daily lowest : r = +.02 (ns) | HAPP 3.1 | $r_{pm}$ | + | | ns | | |
| - PRESENT WORK | | daily highest: r = +.16 (ns)<br>daily average: r = +.15 (ns)<br>daily lowest : r = +.19 (ns) | HAPP 3.1 | $r_{pm}$ | + | | ns | | |
| - RECEPTIVITY towards the world | | daily highest: r = -.02 (ns)<br>daily average: r = +.03 (ns)<br>daily lowest : r = -.05 (ns) | HAPP 3.1 | $r_{pm}$ | + | | ns | | |
| - SELF-CONFIDENCE vs feeling of inadequacy | | daily highest: r = -.04 (ns)<br>daily average: r = +.06 (ns)<br>daily lowest : r = +.12 (ns) | HAPP 3.1 | $r_{pm}$ | + | | ns | | |
| - THOUGHT PROCESSES | | daily highest: r = -.03 (ns)<br>daily average: r = -.03 (ns)<br>daily lowest : r = +.05 (ns) | HAPP 3.1 | $r_{pm}$ | - | | ns | | |
| - TRANQUILLITY vs anxiety | | daily highest: r = +.08 (ns)<br>daily average: r = +.15 (ns)<br>daily lowest : r = +.28 (ns) | HAPP 3.1 | $r_{pm}$ | + | | ns | | |

## A 2.2 - TYPES OF AFFECT

### A 2.2.1 - ANGER / AGGRESSION

See also 'Harmony' (A 2.2.9)

| Variable | Operationalization | Remarks | Code | Statistic | Value | Test | Signif. | Population / Sample | Source |
|---|---|---|---|---|---|---|---|---|---|
| AGGRESSION, impulse to - | 4-item index of closed questions on feelings of swearing, losing temper at teachers, being rude to teachers, picking a fight with parents | | COMP 1.2 | $r_{pm}$ | -.33 | | 001 | Public highschool boys, U.S.A.<br>Probability multi stage sample<br>N: 2213 in 1966, 1886 in 1968 and 1799 in 1969<br>date: fall 1966, spring 1968 and spring 1969 | BACHM 67/70<br>p. 122 |
| AGGRESSIVENESS | Rating by staffmembers on a 7-point aggressive-passive scale | Open ward : r = -.24 (05)<br>Closed ward: r = -.34 (01)<br>(see excerpt, Part II) | AFF 5.1 | $r_{pm}$ | - | | 05 | Institutionalized mentally retarded males, U.S.A.<br>Non-probability chunk sample<br>N: 149, date: - | PANDE 71<br>p. 329 |
| READINESS TO BECOME ANGRY | Class-master rating on a 7-point scale on the basis of observation | | AFF 5.3 | $r_{pm}$ | -.21 | | | Schoolboys, England<br>Non-probability chunk sample<br>N: 140, date: 1912 - 1913 | WEBB 15<br>p. 27 |
| READINESS TO RECOVER FROM ANGER | Class-master rating on a 7-point scale on the basis of observation | | AFF 5.3 | $r_{pm}$ | +.22 | | | See above | WEBB 15<br>p. 27 |
| READINESS TO BECOME ANGRY | Trained peer-rating on a 7-point scale on the basis of observation | | AFF 5.2 | $r_{pm}$ | -.10 | | | Male students, England<br>Non-probability chunk sample<br>N: 194, date: 1912 - 1913 | WEBB 15<br>p. 26 |
| READINESS TO RECOVER FROM ANGER | Trained peer-rating on a 7-point scale on the basis of observation | | AFF 5.2 | $r_{pm}$ | +.43 | | | See above | WEBB 15<br>p. 26 |
| EXTREME ANGER, occasional liability to - | Trained peer rating on a 7-point scale on the basis of observation | | AFF 5.2 | $r_{pm}$ | -.16 | | | See above | WEBB 15<br>p. 26 |

### A 2.2.2 - ANXIETY

See 'Tranquility' (A 2.2.20)
See also 'Psycho-somatic Symptoms' (H 2.2)

### A 2.2.3 - COMPANIONSHIP

| Variable | Operationalization | Remarks | Code | Statistic | Value | Test | Signif. | Population / Sample | Source |
|---|---|---|---|---|---|---|---|---|---|
| COMPANIONSHIP vs being isolated | Repeated closed question on 'the extent to which you felt emotionally accepted by, or isolated from other people', rated on a 10-point scale:<br>10. Complete participation in warm, intimate friendship.<br>9. Enjoy the warmth of close companionship.<br>8. Thoroughly and genuinely liked.<br>7. Feel accepted and liked.<br>6. More or less accepted.<br>5. Feel a little bit left out.<br>4. Feel somewhat neglected and lonely.<br>3. Very lonely. No one seems to care about me. | The scale was scored each night for lowest, average and highest mood experienced that day, over a period of 6 weeks.<br>The means of the lowest, average and highest daily scores were correlated with the mean average score on the Elation-Depression Scale (see instrument in excerpt, Part II).<br>daily highest: r= +.38 (ns)<br>daily average: r= +.43 (ns)<br>daily lowest: r= +.08 (ns) | AFF 3.1 | $r_{pm}$ | +.43 | t | ns | Male college students, U.S.A.<br>Non-probability chunk sample<br>N: 17, date: ± 1960 | WESSM 66/2<br>p. 66/282 |

| | | | | | | | | | |
|---|---|---|---|---|---|---|---|---|---|
| | 2. Tremendously lonely. Friendless and forlorn.<br>1. Completely isolated and forsaken. Abandoned. Ache with loneliness.<br>(Wessman & Ricks Companionship vs Being Isolated Scale) | | | | | | | | |
| COMPANIONSHIP vs being isolated | Wessman & Ricks Companionship vs Being Isolated Scale, scored once for the current academic year (see above under WESSM 66/2) | Analysis on the basis of data from freshmen and juniors who returned the second questionnaire. N= 353: 188 freshmen (99 males, 89 females) and 165 juniors (90 males and 75 females)<br>Unaffected by sex<br>males: r= +.31 (05)<br>females: r= +.30 (05) | AFF 2.1 | $r_{pm}$ | + | | 05 | Undergraduate full time college students, U.S.A.<br>Non-probability chunk sample<br>N: 952, date: March, 1965 | CONST 65<br>p. 59 |
| COMPANIONSHIP vs being isolated | Wessman & Ricks Companionship vs Being Isolated Scale, scored at the end of each day for lowest, average and highest mood experienced that day during three weeks (see above under WESSM 66/2) | The means of the lowest, average and highest daily scores were correlated with the mean average score on the Elation-Depression Scale. (see second instrument in excerpt, Part II)<br>daily highest: r= +.42 (01)<br>daily average: r= +.66 (01)<br>daily lowest: r= +.60 (01) | AFF 3.1 | $r_{pm}$ | + | | 01 | Married females, U.S.A.<br>Non-probability purposive sample by expert choice<br>N: 62, date: — | HARDE 69<br>p. 118 |
| COMPANIONSHIP vs being isolated | Wessman & Ricks Companionship vs Being Isolated Scale, scored each night for lowest, average and highest mood experienced that day during one month (see above under WESSM 66/2) | The means of the lowest, average and highest daily scores were correlated with the mean average score on the Elation-Depression Scale. (see first instrument in excerpt, Part II)<br>daily highest: r= +.74 (01)<br>daily average: r= +.80 (01)<br>daily lowest: r= +.70 (01) | AFF 3.1 | $r_{pm}$ | + | | 01 | Undergraduate students, U.S.A.<br>Non-probability chunk sample<br>N: 67, date: summer, 1970 | GORMA 71<br>p. 215/221 |
| | | Analysis on the basis of the mean lowest, average and highest daily scores<br>daily highest: r= +.38 (01)<br>daily average: r= +.36 (01)<br>daily lowest: r= +.31 (05) | AFF 3.1 | $r_{pm}$ | + | | 01 | | |

## A 2.2.4 - DEPRESSION

see also 'Elation' (A 2.2.5) and 'Hedonic Level of Affect' (H 1.2)

| | | | | | | | | | |
|---|---|---|---|---|---|---|---|---|---|
| DEPRESSIVE AFFECT | Closed question on frequency of depression during past week<br>rarely / occasionally / most days | G= -.48 (001) when controlled for satisfaction with major life areas<br>G= -.48 (001) when controlled for usual quality of affect (closed question on spirits)<br>G= -.44 (001) when controlled for both satisfaction with major life areas and usual quality of affect | COMP 1.1 | G | -.57 | | 001 | Adults, U.S.A.<br>Probability cluster sample using households and probability multi-stage sample<br>N: 2168, date: 1972 | BRENN 75B<br>p. 351 |
| FEELING DOWNCAST OR DEJECTED | Closed question:<br>never / rarely / occasionally / fairly often / very often | See second and third instrument in excerpt (Part II).<br>Unaffected by sex, age and educational level<br>When enjoying life and usual affect (question on spirits) are held constant: $G_{pt}$ = -.31 (001) | HAPP 1.1 | G | -.46 | | 001 | Local population, Washington County, U.S.A.<br>Probability cluster sample of households<br>N: 916, date: summer, 1973 - summer, 1974 | BRENN 75A<br>p. 324 |

| Variable | Operationalization | Specification | Code | Statistic | Value | Test | Significance | Population / sample | Source |
|---|---|---|---|---|---|---|---|---|---|
| **FREQUENCY OF LOW MOOD** | Closed question on feeling downcast and dejected never / rarely / occasionally / fairly often / very often | When standardized on:<br>- having fun in life and usual mood: $G_s = -.40$<br>- having fun in life: $G_s = -.44$<br>- usual moods: $G_s = -.44$<br>- tending to be a discouraged person: $G_s = -.47$<br>- tending to be a lonely person: $G_s = -.44$<br>- anxiety symptoms: $G_s = -.54$<br>- social class: $G_s = -.56$<br>Stronger among females: $G = -.61$<br>Lower among males: $G = -.54$ | HAPP 1.1 | G<br>V | -.56<br>.31 | $Chi^2$ | 01 | Juniors and seniors attending public high schools in New York State, U.S.A.<br>Probability cluster sample of 10 public high schools<br>sample A: N= 1682, sample B: N= 1664<br>date: 1960 | BRENN 70<br>p. 64/71/75/87/88<br>262/263 |
| | | Unaffected by sex | AFF 1.1 | G<br>V | -.49<br>.27 | $Chi^2$ | 01 | | |
| DEPRESSION | 21-item index containing closed questions on pessimism, failure, dissatisfaction, sadness, guilt, punishment, disappointment, inferiority, suicide, crying, irritation, losing interest, indecisiveness, ugliness, inability to work, sleeplessness, tiredness, lack of appetite, loss of weight, concern about health, sexual listlessness<br>(Depression Inventory; see Beck et al., 1961) | | AFF 6 | $r_{pm}$ | -.47 | | 01 | Female undergraduate college students, U.S.A.<br>Random sample<br>N: 72, date: — | LUDWI 71/75<br>p. 64 |
| PAST DEPRESSION | MMPI Depression Scale, taken 2 years previously (see Gough, 1953) | | AFF 3.1 | $r_{pm}$ | -.83 | t | 05 | Male college students, U.S.A.<br>Non-probability chunk sample<br>N: 17, date: ± 1960 | WESSM 66/2<br>p. 103-115 |
| PAST DEPRESSION AND INSECURITY | Score derived from a 212-item inventory of past life experiences | | AFF 3.1 | $r_{pm}$ | -.46 | t | 10 | See above | WESSM 66/2<br>p. 122 |
| DEPRESSED OR UNHAPPY | Closed question:'During the past week, did you ever feel depressed or unhappy?'<br>no vs yes | See second instrument in excerpt (Part II). | HAPP 1.1 | Q | -.73 | | | National adult population, Puerto Rico<br>Probability simple random sample<br>N: 1417, date: November, 1963 - January, 1964 + August - October, 1964 | MATLI 66<br>p. 8 |
| EXTREME DEPRESSION, occasional liability to - | Trained peer rating on a 7-point scale on the basis of observation | | AFF 5.2 | $r_{pm}$ | -.53 | | | Male students, England<br>Non-probability chunk sample<br>N: 194, date: 1912 - 1913 | WEBB 15<br>p. 26 |
| DEPRESSION | Expert rating on a 9-point scale | Stronger among internal depressed patients<br>Lower among depressed schizophrenic patients and among neurotic depressed patients | AFF 3.3 | r | - | | 01 | Psychiatric patients, W.Germany<br>Non-probability chunk sample<br>N: 56, date: — | SCHWA 72/1<br>p. 74 |
| DEPRESSION | Expert rating (see Hamilton, 1960) | | AFF 3.3 | $r_{pm}$ | -.86 | | | Medical patients, W.Germany<br>N: 180, date: — | SCHWA 72/2<br>p. 75 |
| DEPRESSION | Self-rating scale (Zimmerman & v.Zerssen 'Depressions-Skala') | | AFF 3.3 | $r_{pm}$ | -.98 | | | See above | SCHWA 72/2<br>p. 75 |
| DEPRESSION | Two questions on amount and severity of sad whims, rated on graphic scales | | HAPP 1.1 | G | -.34 | | | National adult population, The Netherlands<br>Probability area sample<br>N: 1552, date: June, 1968 | BAKKE 74<br>p. 28 |

## A 2.2.5 - ELATION

The variables in this category are conceptually close to Hedonic Level of Affect. However, they cannot be accepted as valid indicators of that phenomenon. For valid indicators see 'Hedonic Level of Affect' (H 1.2).

| Variable | Measure | Procedure | Indicator | Statistic | Value | | Significance | Sample | Source |
|---|---|---|---|---|---|---|---|---|---|
| HEDONIC LEVEL OF MOST ELATED MOMENTS | Repeated closed question on highest mood experienced during the past day, rated on a 10-point scale during 6 weeks (Wessman & Ricks Elation-Depression Scale) | See instrument in excerpt (Part II). The 6 weeks mean of the 'daily highest mood' score was correlated with the 6 weeks mean of the 'daily average mood' scores. | AFF 3.1 | $r_{pm}$ | +.82 | | 05 | Female college students, U.S.A. Non-probability chunk sample N: 21, date: ± 1960 | WESSM 66/1 p. 277 |
| HEDONIC LEVEL OF MOST DEPRESSED MOMENTS | Repeated closed question on lowest mood experienced during the past day, rated on a 10-point scale during 6 weeks (Wessman & Ricks Elation-Depression Scale) | See above. The mean 'daily lowest mood 'score was correlated with the mean 'daily average mood' score. | AFF 3.1 | $r_{pm}$ | +.41 | | ns | See above | WESSM 66/1 p. 277 |
| HEDONIC LEVEL OF MOST ELATED MOMENTS | Repeated closed question on highest mood experienced during the past day, rated on a 10-point scale during 6 weeks (Wessman & Ricks Elation-Depression Scale) | See instrument in excerpt (Part II). The mean 'daily highest mood' score was correlated with the mean 'daily average mood' score. | AFF 3.1 | $r_{pm}$ | +.75 | | 05 | Male college students Non-probability chunk sample N: 17, date: ± 1960 | WESSM 66/2 p. 283 |
| HEDONIC LEVEL OF MOST DEPRESSED MOMENTS | Repeated closed question on lowest mood experienced during the past day, rated on a 10-point scale during 6 weeks (Wessman & Ricks Elation-Depression Scale) | See above. The mean 'daily lowest mood' score was correlated with the mean 'daily average mood' score. | AFF 3.1 | $r_{pm}$ | +.43 | | ns | See above | WESSM 66/2 p. 283 |
| HEDONIC LEVEL OF MOST ELATED MOMENTS | Repeated closed question on highest mood experienced during the past day, rated on a 10-point Scale during one month (Wessman & Ricks Elation-Depression Scale) | See first and second instrument in excerpt (Part II). The mean 'daily highest mood' score was correlated with the mean 'daily average mood ' score (first instrument) and with the happiness measure (second instrument). | AFF 3.1<br>HAPP 3.1 | $r_{pm}$<br>$r_{pm}$ | +.81<br>+.29 | | 01<br>05 | Junior College students, U.S.A. Non-probability chunk sample N: 67, date: summer, 1970 | GORMA 71 p. 216/222 |
| HEDONIC LEVEL OF MOST DEPRESSED MOMENTS | Repeated closed question on lowest mood experienced during the past day, rated on a 10-point scale during one month (Wessman & Ricks Elation-Depression Scale) | See above. The mean 'daily lowest mood' score was correlated with the mean 'daily average mood' score and with the happiness measure. | AFF 3.1<br>HAPP 3.1 | $r_{pm}$<br>$r_{pm}$ | +.73<br>+.16 | | 01<br>ns | See above | GORMA 71 p. 216/222 |
| NUMBER OF HAPPY MOODS PER DAY | Repeated direct question of number of happy moods experienced during the past day, scored every evening during three weeks | Correlations with % happy mood : r = +.44 (01)<br>% unhappy mood: r = -.29 (01)<br>% neutral mood: r = -.32 (01) | AFF 3.1 (1st instr.)<br>AFF 3.1 (2nd instr.) | $r_{pm}$<br>$r_{pm}$ | +.44<br>+ | | 01<br>01 | Undergraduate university students, California, U.S.A. Non-probability chunk sample N: 86, date: November - December, 1971 | FORDY 72 p. 146 |
| NUMBER OF UNHAPPY MOODS PER DAY | Repeated direct question on number of unhappy moods experienced during the past day, scored every evening during three weeks | Correlations with % happy mood : r = -.33 (01)<br>% unhappy mood: r = +.49 (01)<br>% neutral mood: r = +.07 (ns) | AFF 3.1 (1st instr.)<br>AFF 3.1 (2nd instr.) | $r_{pm}$<br>$r_{pm}$ | -.49<br>- | | 01<br>01 | See above | FORDY 72 p. 146 |
| RELATIVE AFFECT BALANCE | Ratio of number of happy moods over number of unhappy moods per day, as assessed for a period of three weeks (see above) | | AFF 3.1 (1st instr.) | $r_{pm}$ | +.54 | | 01 | See above | FORDY 72 p. 149 |
| ABSOLUTE AFFECT BALANCE | Difference score between number of happy moods and number of unhappy moods per day, as assessed for a period of three weeks (see above) | | AFF 3.1 (1st instr.) | $r_{pm}$ | +.22 | | 05 | See above | FORDY 72 p. 149 |

| Variable | Measure | Comments | Code | Stat | Value | Test | Sign. | Population / Sample | Source |
|---|---|---|---|---|---|---|---|---|---|
| ON TOP OF THE WORLD | Closed question: 'During the past week, did you ever feel on top of the world?' no vs yes | See second instrument in excerpt (Part II). | HAPP 1.1 | Q | +.44 | | | National adult population, Puerto Rico<br>Probability simple random sample<br>N: 1417, date: November, 1963 - January, 1964 + August - October, 1964 | MATLI 66<br>p. 8 |
| HAPPY MOOD | Closed question on mood during past half-hour<br>sad / neutral / happy | Among normals : r = +.50 (01)<br>Among the handicapped: r = +.41 (01) | HAPP 2.1 | r | + | | 01 | Physically defective and normal persons, Detroit, U.S.A.<br>Non-probability purposive samples<br>N: 295, date: — | CAMER 73/1<br>p. 209 |
| FEELING CHEERFUL | Closed question: no vs yes | | HAPP 2.1 | G | +.72 | Chi | 000 | Male employees of age 40+, The Netherlands<br>Non-probability chunk sample<br>N: 13000, date: — | SONDE 75 |
| ELATION MOOD DURING EXPERIMENT | 5-item elation cluster from the Nowlis-Green Mood Adjective Checklist, containing adjectives scored for 'how do you feel at the moment' (see Nowlis, 1965) | Unaffected by manipulated self-esteem<br>Among happy Ss elation is unaffected by bolstered self-esteem and slightly decreased by reduced self-esteem. Among unhappy Ss elation is unaffected by reduced self-esteem and increased by bolstered self-esteem. | AFF 6 | $r_{pm}$ | +.31 | | 05 | Female undergraduates, U.S.A.<br>Random sample<br>N: 72, date: — | LUDWI 71/75<br>p. 64 |
| ELATED MOOD DURING EXPERIMENT | 4-item index of closed questions on mood right now, the best you felt today, the worst you felt today, and the way you usually feel; scored on the Wessman & Ricks Elation vs Depression Scale (see excerpt WESSM 60, Part II) | Affected by manipulated self-esteem (.10)<br>Among happy Ss elation is increased by reduced self-esteem and slightly decreased by bolstered self-esteem.<br>Among unhappy Ss elation is higher by bolstered self-esteem than by reduced self-esteem. | AFF 6 | $r_{pm}$ | +.33 | | 01 | See above | LUDWI 71/75<br>p. 64 |

## A 2.2.6 - ENERGY

| Variable | Measure | Comments | Code | Stat | Value | Test | Sign. | Population / Sample | Source |
|---|---|---|---|---|---|---|---|---|---|
| ENERGY vs fatigue | Repeated closed question on 'how energetic, or tired and weary, you felt' rated on a 10-point scale:<br>10. Limitless zeal. Surging with energy. Vitality spilling over.<br>9. Exuberant vitality, tremendous energy, great zest for activity.<br>8. Great energy and drive.<br>7. Very fresh, considerable energy.<br>6. Fairly fresh. Adequate energy.<br>5. Slightly tired, indolent. Somewhat lacking in energy.<br>4. Rather tired. Lethargic. Not much energy.<br>3. Great fatigue. Sluggish. Can hardly keep going. Meager resources.<br>2. Tremendously weary. Nearly worn out and practically at a standstill. Almost no resources.<br>1. Utterly exhausted. Entirely worn out. Completely incapable of even the slightest effort.<br>(Wessman & Ricks Energy vs Fatigue Scale) | The scale was scored each night for lowest, average and highest mood experienced that day over a period of 6 weeks. The means of the lowest, average and highest daily scores were correlated with the mean average score on the Elation-Depression Scale (see instrument in excerpt, Part II)<br>daily highest: r= +.37 (ns)<br>daily average: r= +.76 (05)<br>daily lowest: r= +.48 (05) | AFF 3.1 | $r_{pm}$ | + | t | 05 | Female college students, U.S.A.<br>Non-probability chunk sample<br>N: 21, date: ± 1960 | WESSM 66/1<br>p. 64/276 |
| ENERGY vs fatigue | See above | See above<br>daily highest: r= +.76 (05)<br>daily average: r= +.75 (05)<br>daily lowest: r= +.02 (ns) | AFF 3.1 | $r_{pm}$ | + | t | 05 | Male college students, U.S.A.<br>Non-probability chunk sample<br>N: 17, date: ± 1960 | WESSM 66/2<br>p. 66/282 |

| | | | | | | | | | |
|---|---|---|---|---|---|---|---|---|---|
| ENERGY vs fatigue | Wessman & Ricks Energy vs Fatigue Scale, scored once for the current academic year (see last page under WESSM 66/1) | Analysis on the basis of data from freshmen and juniors who returned the second questionnaire. N= 353: 188 freshmen (99 males, 89 females) and 165 juniors (90 males and 75 females)<br>Unaffected by sex<br>males: r= +.41 (05)<br>females: r= +.44 (05) | AFF 2.1 | $r_{pm}$ | + | | 05 | Undergraduate full time college students, U.S.A.<br>Non-probability chunk sample<br>N: 952, date: March, 1965 | CONST 65<br>p. 59 |
| ENERGY vs fatigue | Wessman & Ricks Energy vs Fatigue Scale, scored at the end of each day for lowest, average and highest mood experienced that day during three weeks (see last page under WESSM 66/1) | The means of the lowest, average and highest daily scores were correlated with the mean average score on the Elation-Depression Scale (see second instrument in excerpt, Part II).<br>daily highest: r= +.71 (01)<br>daily average: r= +.81 (01)<br>daily lowest: r= +.73 (01) | AFF 3.1 | $r_{pm}$ | + | | 01 | Married females, U.S.A.<br>Non-probability purposive sample by expert choice<br>N: 62, date: — | HARDE 69<br>p. 118 |
| ENERGY vs fatigue | Wessman & Ricks Energy vs Fatigue Scale, scored each night for lowest, average and highest mood experienced that day during one month (see last page under WESSM 66/1) | The means of the lowest, average and highest daily scores were correlated with the mean average score on the Elation-Depression Scale (see first instrument in excerpt, Part II).<br>daily highest: r= +.65 (01)<br>daily average: r= +.85 (01)<br>daily lowest: r= +.61 (01) | AFF 3.1 | $r_{pm}$ | + | | 01 | Undergraduate students, U.S.A.<br>Non-probability chunk sample<br>N: 67, date: summer, 1970 | GORMA 71<br>p. 216/222 |
| | | Analysis on the basis of the mean lowest, average and highest daily scores<br>daily highest: r= +.34 (01)<br>daily average: r= +.28 (05)<br>daily lowest: r= +.06 (ns) | HAPP 3.1 | $r_{pm}$ | + | | 05 | | |
| INERTIA | Closed question: 'During the past week, did you ever feel that you could not do anything simply because you could not start it?' no vs yes | See second instrument in excerpt (Part II). | HAPP 1.1 | Q | -.53 | | | National adult population, Puerto Rico<br>Probability simple random sample<br>N: 1417, date: November, 1963 - January, 1964 + August - October, 1964 | MATLI 66<br>p. 8 |
| HAVING SUFFICIENT ENERGY to do things one wants | Closed question: no vs yes | Index of Positive Affects: G = -.45<br>Index of Negative Affects: G = -.27<br>In Bradburn's sample of adults, urban areas, U.S.A. (see excerpt BRADB 69, Part II) the relationship was as follows:<br>Index of Positive Affects: G = -.39<br>Index of Negative Affects: G = +.13<br>Bradburn did not report these findings. | AFF 2.3 | | | | | Employed males, England<br>Non-probability purposive quota sample<br>N: 192, date: — | PAYNE 74<br>p. 17 |

## A 2.2.7 - FULLNESS OF LIFE

| | | | | | | | | | |
|---|---|---|---|---|---|---|---|---|---|
| FULLNESS vs emptiness of life | Repeated closed question on 'how emotionally satisfying, abundant or empty, your life felt today', rated on a 10-point scale:<br>10. Consummate fulfillment and abundance.<br>9. Replete with life's abundant goodness.<br>8. Filled with warm feelings of contentment and satisfaction.<br>7. My life is ample and satisfying.<br>6. Life seems fairly adequate and relatively satisfying. | The scale was scored each night for lowest, average and highest mood experienced that day over a period of 6 weeks.<br>The means of the lowest, average and highest daily scores were correlated with the mean average score on the Elation-Depression Scale (see instrument in excerpt, Part II).<br>daily highest: r= +.60 (05)<br>daily average: r= +.88 (05)<br>daily lowest: r= +.69 (05) | AFF 3.1 | $r_{pm}$ | + | t | 05 | Female college students, U.S.A.<br>Non-probability chunk sample<br>N: 21, date: ± 1960 | WESSM 66/1<br>p. 64/276 |

| | | | | | | | | | |
|---|---|---|---|---|---|---|---|---|---|
| | 5. Some slight sense of lack, vague and mildly troubling.<br>4. My life seems deficient, dissatisfying.<br>3. Life is pretty empty and barren.<br>2. Desolate, drained dry, impoverished.<br>1. Gnawing sense of emptiness, hollowness, void.<br>(Wessman & Ricks Fullness vs Emptiness of Life Scale) | | | | | | | | |
| FULLNESS vs emptiness of life | See above | See above<br>daily highest: r= +.76 (05)<br>daily average: r= +.90 (05)<br>daily lowest: r= +.58 (05) | AFF 3.1 | $r_{pm}$ | + | t | 05 | Male college students, U.S.A.<br>Non-probability chunk sample<br>N: 17, date: ± 1960 | WESSM 66/2<br>p. 66/282 |
| FULLNESS vs emptiness of life | Wessman & Ricks Fullness vs Emptiness of Life Scale, scored once for the current academic year (see above under WESSM 66/1) | Analysis on the basis of data from freshmen and juniors who returned the second questionnaire. N= 353: 188 freshmen (99 males, 89 females) and 165 juniors (90 males and 75 females)<br>Unaffected by sex<br>males: r= +.67 (05)<br>females: r= +.69 (05) | AFF 2.1 | $r_{pm}$ | + | | 05 | Undergraduate full time college students, U.S.A.<br>Non-probability chunk sample<br>N: 952, date: March 1965 | CONST 65<br>p. 59 |
| FULLNESS vs emptiness of life | Wessman & Ricks Fullness vs Emptiness of Life Scale, scored once for the past year (see above under WESSM 66/1) | | AFF 2.1 | $r_{pm}$ | +.67 | | 01 | Married females, U.S.A.<br>Non-probability purposive sample by expert choice<br>N: 62, date: — | HARDE 69<br>p. 50 |
| FULLNESS vs emptiness of life | Wessman & Ricks Fullness vs Emptiness of Life Scale, scored at the end of each day for lowest, average and highest mood experienced that day during three weeks (see above under WESSM 66/1) | The means of the lowest, average and highest daily scores were correlated with the mean average score on the Elation-Depression Scale (see second instrument in excerpt, Part II).<br>daily highest: r= +.65 (01)<br>daily average: r= +.86 (01)<br>daily lowest: r= +.76 (01) | AFF 3.1 | $r_{pm}$ | + | | 01 | See above | HARDE 69<br>p. 118 |
| FULLNESS OF LIFE | Factor which has strong positive correlations with fullness of life in past year (+.87), elation in past year (+.80), and self-actualization (+.64) | | AFF 2.1<br>AFF 3.1 | $r_{pm}$<br>$r_{pm}$ | +.80<br>+.16 | | 01<br>ns | See above | HARDE 69<br>p. 52/65 |

## A 2.2.8 - GUILT

See also 'Personal Moral Judgment' (A 2.2.13)

| | | | | | | | | | |
|---|---|---|---|---|---|---|---|---|---|
| GUILT FEELINGS | 50-item sentence completion blank (Mosher Incomplete Sentences Test (MIST); see Mosher, 1961) | | HAPP 1.1 | DM | - | $r_1$ | 01 | University students, U.S.A.<br>Non-probability chunk sample<br>N: 313, date: 1966 - 1967 | BRADB 67<br>p. 64 |
| HOSTILE GUILT | MIST subscale (see above) | | HAPP 1.1 | DM | - | $r_1$ | 01 | See above | BRADB 67<br>p. 64 |
| SEX GUILT | MIST subscale (see above) | | HAPP 1.1 | DM | - | $r_1$ | 05 | See above | BRADB 67<br>p. 64 |
| MORALITY-CONSCIENCE GUILT | MIST subscale (see above) | | HAPP 1.1 | DM | - | $r_1$ | ns | See above | BRADB 67<br>p. 64 |

| | | | | | | | | | |
|---|---|---|---|---|---|---|---|---|---|
| PROJECTIVE GUILT | Score from stories told to the standard Thematic Apperception Test cards (see Murray, 1943) | | AFF 3.1 | $r_{pm}$ | -.44 | t | 10 | Male college students, U.S.A.<br>Non-probability chunk sample<br>N: 17, date: ± 1960 | WESSM 66/2<br>p. 120 |
| PROJECTIVE GUILT-RELIEF | Score from stories told to the standard Thematic Apperception Test cards (see Murray, 1943) | | AFF 3.1 | $r_{pm}$ | +.44 | t | 10 | See above | WESSM 66/2<br>p. 120 |

## A 2.2.9 - HARMONY

| | | | | | | | | | |
|---|---|---|---|---|---|---|---|---|---|
| HARMONY vs anger | Repeated closed question on 'how well you got along with, or how angry you felt toward, other people' rated on a 10-point scale:<br>10. Boundless good will and complete harmony.<br>9. Enormous good will and great harmony.<br>8. Considerable good will.<br>7. Get along well and rather smoothly.<br>6. Get along pretty well, more or less good feeling.<br>5. A little bit annoyed, somewhat 'put out'. Minor irritations.<br>4. Annoyed, irritated, provoked.<br>3. Very angry. Ill will.<br>2. Enraged. Seething with anger and hostility.<br>1. Violent hate and fury. Desire to attack, destroy.<br>(Wessman & Ricks Harmony vs Anger Scale) | The scale was scored each night for lowest, average and highest mood experienced that day over a period of 6 weeks. The means of the lowest, average and highest daily scores were correlated with the mean average score on the Elation-Depression Scale (see instrument in excerpt, Part II).<br>daily highest: r= +.58 (05)<br>daily average: r= +.81 (05)<br>daily lowest: r= +.58 (05) | AFF 3.1 | $r_{pm}$ | + | t | 05 | Female college students, U.S.A.<br>Non-probability chunk sample<br>N: 21, date: ± 1960 | WESSM 66/1<br>p. 64/276 |
| HARMONY vs anger | See above | See above<br>daily highest: r= +.68 (05)<br>daily average: r= +.41 (ns)<br>daily lowest: r= +.07 (ns) | AFF 3.1 | $r_{pm}$ | + | t | ns | Male college students, U.S.A.<br>Non-probability chunk sample<br>N: 17, date: ± 1960 | WESSM 66/2<br>p. 66/282 |
| HARMONY vs anger | Wessman & Ricks Harmony vs Anger Scale, scored once for the current academic year (see above under WESSM 66/1) | Analysis on the basis of data from freshmen and juniors who returned the second questionnaire. N= 353, 188 freshmen (99 males, 89 females) and 165 juniors (90 males and 75 females)<br>Stronger among females: r= +.24 (05)<br>Lower among males: r= +.17 (05) | AFF 2.1 | $r_{pm}$ | + | | 05 | Undergraduate full time college students, U.S.A.<br>Non-probability chunk sample<br>N: 952, date: March, 1965 | CONST 65<br>p. 59 |
| HARMONY vs anger | Wessman & Ricks Harmony vs Anger Scale, scored each night for lowest, average and highest mood experienced that day during one month (see above under WESSM 66/1) | The means of the lowest, average and highest daily scores were correlated with the mean average score on the Elation-Depression Scale (see first instrument in excerpt, Part II).<br>daily highest: r= +.68 (01)<br>daily average: r= +.74 (01)<br>daily lowest: r= +.56 (01) | AFF 3.1 | $r_{pm}$ | + | | 01 | Undergraduate students, U.S.A.<br>Non-probability chunk sample<br>N: 67, date: summer, 1970 | GORMA 71<br>p. 215/219 |
| | | Analysis on the basis of the mean lowest, average and highest daily scores<br>daily highest: r= +.30 (05)<br>daily average: r= +.27 (05)<br>daily lowest: r= +.16 (ns) | HAPP 3.1 | $r_{pm}$ | + | | 05 | | |

## A 2.2.10 - IMPULSE EXPRESSION

| | | | | | | | | | |
|---|---|---|---|---|---|---|---|---|---|
| IMPULSE EXPRESSION vs self-restraint | Repeated closed question on 'how expressive and impulsive or internally restrained and controlled you felt', rated on a 10-point scale:<br>10. Wild and complete abandon. No impulse denied.<br>9. Exhilarating sense of release. Say whatever I feel, and do just as I want.<br>8. Quick to act on every immediate desire.<br>7. Allowing my impulses and desires a pretty free rein.<br>6. Moderate acceptance and expression of my own needs and desires.<br>5. Keep a check on most whims and impulses.<br>4. On the straight and narrow path. Keeping myself within strong bounds.<br>3. Obeying rigorous standards. Strict with myself.<br>2. Refuse to permit the slightest self-indulgence or impulsive action.<br>1. Complete renunciation of all desires. Needs and impulses totally conquered.<br>(Wessman & Ricks Impulse Expression vs Self-Restraint Scale) | The scale was scored each night for lowest, average and highest mood experienced that day over a period of 6 weeks. The means of the lowest, average and highest daily scores were correlated with the mean average score on the Elation-Depression Scale (see instrument in excerpt, Part II).<br>daily highest: r= +.69 (05)<br>daily average: r= +.62 (05)<br>daily lowest: r= +.05 (ns) | AFF 3.1 | $r_{pm}$ | + | t | 05 | Male college students, U.S.A.<br>Non-probability chunk sample<br>N: 17, date: ± 1960 | WESSM 66/2<br>p. 66/282 |
| IMPULSE EXPRESSION vs self-restraint | Wessman & Ricks Impulse Expression vs Self-Restraint Scale, scored once for the current academic year (see above under WESSM 66/2) | Analysis on the basis of data from freshmen and juniors who returned the second questionnaire. N= 353: 188 freshmen (99 males, 89 females) and 165 juniors (90 males and 75 females)<br>Stronger among females: r= +.18 (05)<br>Lower among males: r= +.07 (ns) | AFF 2.1 | $r_{pm}$ | + | | | Undergraduate full time college students, U.S.A.<br>Non-probability chunk sample<br>N: 952, date: March, 1965 | CONST 65<br>p. 59 |
| IMPULSE EXPRESSION vs self-restraint | Wessman & Ricks Impulse Expression vs Self-Restraint Scale, scored each night for lowest, average and highest mood experienced that day during one month (see above under WESSM 66/2) | The means of the lowest, average and highest daily scores were correlated with the mean average score on the Elation-Depression Scale (see first instrument in excerpt, Part II).<br>daily highest: r= +.53 (01)<br>daily average: r= +.69 (01)<br>daily lowest: r= +.65 (01) | AFF 3.1 | $r_{pm}$ | + | | 01 | Undergraduate students, U.S.A.<br>Non-probability chunk sample<br>N: 67, date: summer, 1970 | GORMA 71<br>p. 216/222 |
| | | Analysis on the basis of the mean lowest, average and highest daily scores.<br>daily highest: r= +.39 (01)<br>daily average: r= +.38 (01)<br>daily lowest: r= +.35 (01) | HAPP 3.1 | $r_{pm}$ | + | | 01 | | |

## A 2.2.11 - LOVE AND SEX

| | | | | | | | | | |
|---|---|---|---|---|---|---|---|---|---|
| LOVE AND SEX | Repeated closed question on 'the extent to which you felt loving and tender, or sexually frustrated and unloving', rated on a 10-point scale: | The scale was scored each night for lowest, average and highest mood experienced that day over a period of 6 weeks. The means of the lowest, average and highest daily scores were | AFF 3.1 | $r_{pm}$ | + | t | ns | Female college students, U.S.A.<br>Non-probability chunk sample<br>N: 21, date: ± 1960 | WESSM 66/1<br>p. 64/276 |

| | | | | | | | | | |
|---|---|---|---|---|---|---|---|---|---|
| | 10. Feel the rapture of full, joyous and complete love.<br>9. Tremendous gratification, delight, love, and trust.<br>8. Warm sharing of intimacy and affection.<br>7. Pleasant companionship and some affection. Sharing interests and good times.<br>6. Fairly satisfying experiences or expectations. Some mutual interest and understanding.<br>5. Not much feeling of mutual understanding. Some lack of interest. Slightly frustrated.<br>4. Little feeling of relationship. Considerable indifference. Moderately frustrated.<br>3. Feel unable to maintain good relationships. Unloved. Much frustration.<br>2. Hurt, bewildered, incapable of loving or being loved. Vast amount of frustration.<br>1. Hopeless, cold, unloved and unloving.<br>(Wessman & Ricks Love and Sex Scale) | correlated with the mean average score on the Elation-Depression Scale (see instrument in excerpt, Part II).<br>daily highest: r= +.23 (ns)<br>daily average: r= +.22 (ns)<br>daily lowest: r= +.15 (ns) | | | | | | | |
| LOVE AND SEX | See above | See above<br>daily highest: r= +.40 (ns)<br>daily average: r= +.56 (05)<br>daily lowest: r= +.44 (ns) | AFF 3.1 | $r_{pm}$ | + | t | 05 | Male college students, U.S.A.<br>Non-probability chunk sample<br>N: 17, date: ± 1960 | WESSM 66/2<br>p. 66/282 |
| LOVE AND SEX | Wessman & Ricks Love and Sex Scale, scored once for the current academic year (see above under WESSM 66/1) | Analysis on the basis of data from freshmen and juniors who returned the second questionnaire. N= 353: 188 freshmen (99 males, 89 females) and 165 juniors (90 males and 75 females)<br>Unaffected by sex<br>males: r= +.31 (05)<br>females: r= +.37 (05) | AFF 2.1 | $r_{pm}$ | + | | 05 | Undergraduate full time college students, U.S.A.<br>Non-probability chunk sample<br>N: 952, date: March, 1965 | CONST 65<br>p. 59 |
| LOVE AND SEX | Wessman & Ricks Love and Sex Scale, scored each night for lowest, average and highest mood experienced that day during one month (see above under WESSM 66/1) | The means of the lowest, average and highest daily scores were correlated with the mean average score on the Elation-Depression Scale (see first instrument in excerpt, Part II).<br>daily highest: r= +.46 (01)<br>daily average: r= +.58 (01)<br>daily lowest: r= +.61 (01) | AFF 3.1 | $r_{pm}$ | + | | 01 | Undergraduate students, U.S.A.<br>Non-probability chunk sample<br>N: 67, date: summer, 1970 | GORMA 71<br>p. 216/221 |
| | | Analysis on the basis of the mean lowest, average and highest daily scores<br>daily highest: r= +.22 (ns)<br>daily average: r= +.30 (05)<br>daily lowest: r= +.31 (05) | HAPP 3.1 | $r_{pm}$ | + | | 05 | | |

## A 2.2.12 - PERSONAL FREEDOM

| | | | | | | | | | |
|---|---|---|---|---|---|---|---|---|---|
| PERSONAL FREEDOM vs external constraint | Repeated closed question on 'how much you felt you were free or not free to do as you wanted', rated on a 10-point scale: | The scale was scored each night for lowest, average and highest mood experienced that day over a period of 6 weeks. The means of the lowest, | AFF 3.1 | $r_{pm}$ | + | t | ns | Male college students, U.S.A.<br>Non-probability chunk sample<br>N: 17, date: ± 1960 | WESSM 66/2<br>p. 66/282 |

| | | | | | | | | | |
|---|---|---|---|---|---|---|---|---|---|
| | 10. Absolutely free to consider and try any new and adventuresome prospect.<br>9. Independent and free to do as I like.<br>8. Ample scope to go my own way.<br>7. Free, within broad limits, to act much as I want to.<br>6. Can do a good deal on my own initiative and in my own fashion. No particularly restrictive limitations.<br>5. Somewhat constrained and hampered. Not free to do things my own way.<br>4. Checked and hindered by too many demands and constraints.<br>3. Hemmed in. Cooped up. Forced to do things I don't want to do.<br>2. Trapped, oppressed.<br>1. Overwhelmed, smothered. Can't draw a free breath.<br>(Wessman & Ricks Personal Freedom vs External Constraint Scale) | average and highest daily scores were correlated with the mean average score on the Elation-Depression Scale (see instrument in excerpt, Part II).<br>daily highest: r= +.36 (ns)<br>daily average: r= +.15 (ns)<br>daily lowest: r= -.18 (ns) | | | | | | | |
| PERSONAL FREEDOM vs external constraint | Wessman & Ricks Personal Freedom vs External Constraint Scale, scored once for the current academic year (see above under WESSM 66/2) | Analysis on the basis of data from freshmen and juniors who returned the second questionnaire. N= 353: 188 freshmen (99 males, 89 females) and 165 juniors (90 males and 75 females)<br>stronger among males: r= +.24 (05)<br>lower among females: r= +.11 (ns) | AFF 2.1 | $r_{pm}$ | + | | | Undergraduate full time college students, U.S.A.<br>Non-probability chunk sample<br>N: 952, date: March, 1965 | CONST 65<br>p. 59 |
| PERSONAL FREEDOM vs external constraint | Wessman & Ricks Personal Freedom vs External Constraint Scale, scored each night for lowest, average and highest mood experienced that day during one month (see above under WESSM 66/2) | The means of the lowest, average and highest daily scored were correlated with the mean average score on the Elation-Depression Scale (see first instrument in excerpt, Part II).<br>daily highest: r= +.56 (01)<br>daily average: r= +.62 (01)<br>daily lowest: r= +.55 (01) | AFF 3.1 | $r_{pm}$ | + | | 01 | Undegraduate students, U.S.A.<br>Non-probability chunk sample<br>N: 67, date: summer, 1970 | GORMA 71<br>p. 215/219 |
| | | Analysis on the basis of the mean lowest, average and highest daily scores<br>daily highest: r= +.28 (05)<br>daily average: r= +.28 (05)<br>daily lowest: r= +.30 (05) | HAPP 3.1 | $r_{pm}$ | + | | 05 | | |

## A 2.2.13 – PERSONAL MORAL JUDGEMENT

| | | | | | | | | | |
|---|---|---|---|---|---|---|---|---|---|
| PERSONAL MORAL JUDGEMENT | Repeated closed question on 'how self-approving, or how guilty, you felt', rated on a 10-point scale:<br>10. Have a transcendent feeling of moral perfection and virtue.<br>9. I have a sense of extraordinary worth and goodness.<br>8. In high favor with myself. Well up to my own best standards.<br>7. Consider myself pretty close to my own best self. | The scale was scored each night for lowest, average and highest mood experienced that day over a period of 6 weeks. The means of the lowest, average and highest daily scores were correlated with the mean average score on the Elation-Depression Scale (see instrument in excerpt, Part II).<br>daily highest: r= +.37 (ns)<br>daily average: r= +.50 (05)<br>daily lowest: r= +.57 (05) | AFF 3.1 | $r_{pm}$ | + | t | 05 | Female college students, U.S.A.<br>Non-probability chunk sample<br>N: 21, date: ± 1960 | WESSM 66/1<br>p. 64/276 |

| | | | | | | | | |
|---|---|---|---|---|---|---|---|---|
| | 6. By and large, measuring up to most of my moral standards.<br>5. Somewhat short of what I ought to be.<br>4. I have a sense of having done wrong.<br>3. Feel that I have failed morally.<br>2. Heavy laden with my own moral worthlessness.<br>1. In anguish. Tormented by guilt and self-loathing.<br>(Wessman & Ricks Personal Moral Judgment Scale) | | | | | | | | |
| PERSONAL MORAL JUDGMENT | See above | See above<br>daily highest: r= +.62 (05)<br>daily average: r= +.44 (ns)<br>daily lowest: r= -.07 (ns) | AFF 3.1 | $r_{pm}$ | + | t | ns | Male college students, U.S.A.<br>Non-probability chunk sample<br>N: 17, date: ± 1960 | WESSM 66/2<br>p. 66/282 |
| PERSONAL MORAL JUDGMENT | Wessman & Ricks Personal Moral Judgment Scale, scored once for the current academic year (see above under WESSM 66/1) | Analysis on the basis of data from freshmen and juniors who returned the second questionnaire. N= 353: 188 freshmen (99 males, 89 females) and 165 juniors (90 males and 75 females)<br>stronger among males: r= +.46 (05)<br>lower among females: r= +.10 (ns)<br>The difference is significant (01) | AFF 2.1 | $r_{pm}$ | + | | | Undergraduate full time college students, U.S.A.<br>Non-probability chunk sample<br>N: 952, date: March, 1965 | CONST 65<br>p. 59 |
| PERSONAL MORAL JUDGMENT | Wessman & Ricks Personal Moral Judgment Scale, scored each night for lowest, average and highest mood experienced that day during one month (see above under WESSM 66/1) | The means of the lowest, average and highest daily scores were correlated with the mean average score on the Elation-Depression Scale (see first instrument in excerpt, Part II).<br>daily highest: r= +.57 (01)<br>daily average: r= +.61 (01)<br>daily lowest: r= +.52 (01) | AFF 3.1 | $r_{pm}$ | + | | 01 | Undergraduate students, U.S.A.<br>Non-probability chunk sample<br>N: 67, date: summer, 1970 | GORMA 71<br>p. 216/222 |
| | | Analysis on the basis of the mean lowest, average and highest daily scores<br>daily highest: r= +.46 (01)<br>daily average: r= +.39 (01)<br>daily lowest: r= +.32 (01) | HAPP 3.1 | $r_{pm}$ | + | | 01 | | |

## A 2.2.14 - PRESENT WORK

| | | | | | | | | | |
|---|---|---|---|---|---|---|---|---|---|
| PRESENT WORK | Repeated closed question on 'how satisfied or dissatisfied you were with your work', rated on a 10-point scale:<br>10. Tremendous, intense delight in my work. Proud of my purpose, skill, and accomplishment.<br>9. Great pleasure and enjoyment in my work. Much fulfillment through work.<br>8. Considerable satisfaction with my work. Eager to continue.<br>7. Satisfied with my work. Encouraged to go on with it.<br>6. More or less satisfied with my work. Keep plugging along. | The scale was scored each night for lowest, average and highest mood experienced that day over a period of 6 weeks. The means of the lowest, average and highest daily scores were correlated with the mean average score on the Elation-Depression Scale (see instrument in excerpt, Part II).<br>daily highest: r= +.40 (ns)<br>daily average: r= +.53 (05)<br>daily lowest: r= +.54 (05) | AFF 3.1 | $r_{pm}$ | + | t | 05 | Female college students, U.S.A.<br>Non-probability chunk sample<br>N: 21, date: ± 1960 | WESSM 66/1<br>p. 64/276 |

| | | | | | | | | |
|---|---|---|---|---|---|---|---|---|
| | 5. Somewhat dissatisfied with my work. Not much enjoyment doing it.<br>4. Dissatisfied with my work. Can't see much good in it. Moderately frustrated.<br>3. Greatly dissatisfied with my work. Not doing a good job. Markedly frustrated.<br>2. Tremendously dissatisfied and frustrated in my work. Befuddled. Disorganized.<br>1. Completely dissatisfied and frustrated in my work. Hopeless, useless chaos.<br>(Wessman & Ricks Present Work Scale) | | | | | | | |
| PRESENT WORK | See above | See last page<br>daily highest: r= +.85 (05)<br>daily average: r= +.85 (05)<br>daily lowest: r= +.57 (05) | AFF 3.1 | $r_{pm}$ | + | t | 05 | Male college students, U.S.A.<br>Non-probability chunk sample<br>N: 17, date: ± 1960 | WESSM 66/2<br>p. 66/282 |
| PRESENT WORK | Wessman & Ricks Present Work Scale, scored once for the current academic year (see last page under WESSM 66/1) | Analysis on the basis of data from freshmen and juniors who returned the second questionnaire.<br>N- 353: 188 freshmen (99 males, 89 females) and 165 juniors (90 males and 75 females)<br>Unaffected by sex<br>males: r= +.42 (05)<br>females: r= +.43 (05) | AFF 2.1 | $r_{pm}$ | + | | 05 | Undergraduate full time college students, U.S.A.<br>Non-probability chunk sample<br>N: 952, date: March, 1965 | CONST 65<br>p. 59 |
| PRESENT WORK | Wessman & Ricks Present Work Scale, scored each night for lowest, average and highest mood experienced that day during one month (see last page under WESSM 66/1) | The means of the lowest, average and highest daily scores were correlated with the mean average score on the Elation-Depression Scale (see first instrument in excerpt, Part II).<br>daily highest: r= +.41 (01)<br>daily average: r= +.47 (01)<br>daily lowest: r= +.48 (01) | AFF 3.1 | $r_{pm}$ | + | | 01 | Undergraduate students, U.S.A.<br>Non-probability chunk sample<br>N: 67, date: summer, 1970 | GORMA 71<br>p. 216/222 |
| | | Analysis on the basis of the mean lowest, average and highest daily scores<br>daily highest: r= +.36 (01)<br>daily average: r= +.32 (01)<br>daily lowest: r= +.24 (05) | HAPP 3.1 | $r_{pm}$ | + | | 01 | | |

## A 2.2.15 - RECEPTIVITY TOWARDS WORLD

| | | | | | | | | |
|---|---|---|---|---|---|---|---|---|
| RECEPTIVITY TOWARDS THE WORLD | Repeated closed question on 'how interested and responsive you felt to what was going on around you', rated on a 10-point scale:<br>10. Passionately absorbed in the world's excitement. My sensations and feelings incredibly intensified.<br>9. Tremendously stimulated. Enormously receptive.<br>8. Senses lively. Great interest and delight in everything around me.<br>7. Open and responsive to my world and its happenings. | The scale was scored each night for lowest, average and highest mood experienced that day over a period of 6 weeks. The means of the lowest, average and highest daily scores were correlated with the mean average score on the Elation-Depression Scale (see instrument in excerpt, part II).<br>daily highest: r= +.66 (05)<br>daily average: r= +.78 (05)<br>daily lowest: r= +.63 (05) | AFF 3.1 | $r_{pm}$ | + | t | 05 | Female college students, U.S.A.<br>Non-probability chunk sample<br>N: 21, date: ± 1960 | WESSM 66/1<br>p. 64/276 |

| | | | | | | | | |
|---|---|---|---|---|---|---|---|---|
| | 6. Moderately interested and fairly responsive.<br>5. Slightly disinterested and unresponsive.<br>4. Bored. Life pretty monotonous and uninteresting.<br>3. Dull and apathetic. Almost no interest or desire for anything.<br>2. Mired down in apathy. My only desire is to shut out the world.<br>1. Life is too much trouble. Sick of everything, want only oblivion.<br>(Wessman & Ricks Receptivity towards and Stimulation by the World Scale) | | | | | | | | |
| RECEPTIVITY TOWARDS THE WORLD | See above | See last page<br>daily highest: r= +.77 (05)<br>daily average: r= +.89 (05)<br>daily lowest: r= +.37 (ns) | AFF 3.1 | $r_{pm}$ | + | t | 05 | Male college students, U.S.A.<br>Non-probability chunk sample<br>N: 17, date: ± 1960 | WESSM 66/2<br>p. 66/282 |
| RECEPTIVITY TO THE WORLD | Wessman & Ricks Receptivity towards and Stimulation by the World Scale, scored once for the current academic year (see above under WESSM 66/1) | Analysis on the basis of data from freshmen and juniors who returned the second questionnaire.<br>N= 353: 188 freshmen (99 males, 89 females) and 165 juniors (90 males and 75 females)<br>Unaffected by sex<br>males: r= +.41 (05)<br>females: r= +.44 (05) | AFF 2.1 | $r_{pm}$ | + | | 05 | Undergraduate full time college students, U.S.A.<br>Non-probability chunk sample<br>N: 952, date: March, 1965 | CONST 65<br>p. 59 |
| RECEPTIVITY TOWARDS THE WORLD | Wessman & Ricks Receptivity towards and Stimulation by the World Scale, scored each night for lowest, average and highest mood experienced that day during one month (see above under WESSM 66/1) | The means of the lowest, average and highest daily scores were correlated with the mean average score on the Elation-Depression Scale (see first instrument in excerpt, Part II).<br>daily highest: r= +.60 (01)<br>daily average: r= +.79 (01)<br>daily lowest: r= +.64 (01) | AFF 3.1 | $r_{pm}$ | + | | 01 | Undergraduate students, U.S.A.<br>Non-probability chunk sample<br>N: 67, date: summer, 1970 | GORMA 71<br>p. 215/219 |
| | | Analysis on the basis of the mean lowest, average and highest daily scores<br>daily highest: r= +.35 (01)<br>daily average: r= +.33 (01)<br>daily lowest: r= +.22 (ns) | HAPP 3.1 | $r_{pm}$ | + | | 01 | | |

## A 2.2.16 - SELF-CONFIDENCE

| | | | | | | | | | |
|---|---|---|---|---|---|---|---|---|---|
| SELF-CONFIDENCE vs feeling of inadequacy | Repeated closed question on 'how self-assured and adequate, or helpless and inadequate, you felt', rated on a 10-point scale:<br>10. Nothing is impossible to me. Can do anything I want.<br>9. Feel remarkable self-assurance. Sure of my superior powers.<br>8. Highly confident of my capabilities.<br>7. Feel my abilities sufficient and my prospects good.<br>6. Feel fairly adequate. | The scale was scored each night for lowest, average and highest mood experienced that day over a period of 6 weeks. The means of the lowest, average and highest daily scores were correlated with the mean average score on the Elation-Depression Scale (see instrument in excerpt, Part II).<br>daily highest: r= +.73 (05)<br>daily average: r= +.77 (05)<br>daily lowest: r= +.37 (ns) | AFF 3.1 | $r_{pm}$ | + | t | 05 | Male college students, U.S.A.<br>Non-probability chunk sample<br>N: 17, date: ± 1960 | WESSM 66/2<br>p. 66/282 |

| | | | | | | | | |
|---|---|---|---|---|---|---|---|---|
| | 5. Feel my performance and capabilities somewhat limited.<br>4. Feel rather inadequate.<br>3. Distressed by my weakness and lack of ability.<br>2. Wretched and miserable. Sick of my own incompetence.<br>1. Crushing sense of weakness and futility. I can do nothing.<br>(Wessman & Ricks Self-confidence vs Feeling of Inadequacy Scale) | | | | | | | |
| SELF-CONFIDENCE | Wessman & Ricks Self-confidence vs Feeling of Inadequacy Scale, scored once for the current academic year (see above under WESSM 66/2) | Analysis on the basis of data from freshmen and juniors who returned the second questionnaire. N= 353: 188 freshmen (99 males, 89 females) and 165 juniors (90 males and 75 females)<br>slightly stronger among males: r= +.49 (05)<br>lower among females: r= +.43 (05) | AFF 2.1 | $r_{pm}$ | + | | 05 | Undergraduate full time college students, U.S.A.<br>Non-probability chunk sample<br>N: 952, date: March, 1965 | CONST 65<br>p. 59 |
| CONFIDENCE vs feeling of inadequacy | Wessman & Ricks Self-confidence vs Feeling of Inadequacy Scale, scored each night for lowest, average and highest mood experienced that day during one month (see above under WESSM 66/2) | The means of the lowest, average and highest daily scores were correlated with the mean average score on the Elation-Depression Scale (see first instrument in excerpt, Part II).<br>daily highest: r= +.72 (01)<br>daily average: r= +.82 (01)<br>daily lowest: r= +.71 (01) | AFF 3.1 | $r_{pm}$ | + | | 01 | Undergraduate students, U.S.A.<br>Non-probability chunk sample<br>N: 67, date: summer, 1970 | GORMA 71<br>p. 216/222 |
| | | Analysis on the basis of the mean lowest, average and highest daily scores<br>daily highest: r= +.34 (01)<br>daily average: r= +.31 (05)<br>daily lowest: r= +.29 (05) | HAPP 3.1 | $r_{pm}$ | + | | 05 | | |

## A 2.2.17 - SOCIABILITY

| | | | | | | | | |
|---|---|---|---|---|---|---|---|---|
| OWN SOCIABILITY vs withdrawal | Repeated closed question on 'how socially outgoing or withdrawn you felt today', rated on a 10-point scale:<br>10. Immensely sociable and outgoing.<br>9. Highly outgoing, congenial and friendly.<br>8. Very sociable and involved in things.<br>7. Companionable. Ready to mix with others.<br>6. Fairly sociable. More or less accessible.<br>5. Not particularly outgoing. Feel a little bit unsociable.<br>4. Retiring, would like to avoid people.<br>3. Feel detached and withdrawn. A great distance between myself and others.<br>2. Self-contained and solitary.<br>1. Completely withdrawn. Want no human contact.<br>(Wessman & Ricks Own Sociability vs Withdrawal Scale) | The scale was scored each night for lowest, average and highest mood experienced that day over a period of 6 weeks. The means of the lowest, average and highest scores were correlated with the mean average score on the Elation-Depression Scale (see instrument in excerpt, Part II).<br>daily highest: r= +.56 (05)<br>daily average: r= +.78 (05)<br>daily lowest: r= +.51 (05) | AFF 3.1 | $r_{pm}$ | + | t | 05 | Female college students, U.S.A.<br>Non-probability chunk sample<br>N: 21, date: ± 1960 | WESSM 66/1<br>p. 64/276 |

| | | | | | | | | | |
|---|---|---|---|---|---|---|---|---|---|
| OWN SOCIABILITY vs withdrawal | See last page | See last page<br>daily highest: r= +.66 (05)<br>daily average: r= +.61 (05)<br>daily lowest: r= +.06 (ns) | AFF 3.1 | $r_{pm}$ | + | t | 05 | Male college students, U.S.A.<br>Non-probability chunk sample<br>N: 17, date: ± 1960 | WESSM 66/2<br>p. 66/282 |
| SOCIABILITY vs withdrawal | Wessman & Ricks Own Sociability vs Withdrawal Scale, scored once for the current academic year (see last page under WESSM 66/1) | Analysis on the basis of data from freshmen and juniors who returned the second questionnaire. N= 353: 188 freshmen, 99 males, 89 females) and 165 juniors (90 males and 75 females)<br>stronger among females: r= +.30 (05)<br>lower among males: r= +.15 (05) | AFF 2.1 | $r_{pm}$ | + | | 05 | Undergraduate full time college students, U.S.A.<br>Non-probability chunk sample<br>N: 952, date: March, 1965 | CONST 65<br>p. 59 |
| OWN SOCIABILITY vs withdrawal | Wessman & Ricks Own Sociability vs Withdrawal Scale, scored each night for lowest, average and highest mood experienced that day during one month (see last page under WESSM 66/1) | The means of the lowest, average and highest daily scores were correlated with the mean average score on the Elation-Depression Scale (see first instrument in excerpt, Part II).<br>daily highest: r= +.72 (01)<br>daily average: r= +.80 (01)<br>daily lowest: r= +.67 (01) | AFF 3.1 | $r_{pm}$ | + | | 01 | Undergaduate students, U.S.A.<br>Non-probability chunk sample<br>N: 67, date: summer, 1970 | GORMA 71<br>p. 215/219 |
| | | Analysis on the basis of the mean lowest, average and highest daily scores<br>daily highest: r= +.35 (01)<br>daily average: r= +.29 (05)<br>daily lowest: r= +.15 (ns) | HAPP 3.1 | $r_{pm}$ | + | | 01 | | |

## A 2.2.18 - SOCIAL RESPECT

| | | | | | | | | | |
|---|---|---|---|---|---|---|---|---|---|
| SOCIAL RESPECT vs social contempt | Repeated closed question on 'how you felt other people regarded you, or felt about you, today', rated on a 10-point scale:<br>10. Excite the admiration and awe of everyone who matters.<br>9. Stand extremely high in the estimation of people whose opinions count with me.<br>8. People I admire recognize and respect my good points.<br>7. Confident that some people think well of me.<br>6. Feel I am appreciated and respected to some degree.<br>5. Some people don't seem to see much value in me.<br>4. I am looked upon as being of small or of no account.<br>3. People have no respect for me at all.<br>2. I am scorned, slighted, pushed aside.<br>1. Everyone despises me and holds me in contempt.<br>(Wessman & Ricks Social Respect vs Social Contempt Scale) | The scale was scored each night for lowest, average and highest mood experienced that day over a period of 6 weeks. The means of the lowest, average and highest daily scores were correlated with the mean average score on the Elation-Depression Scale (see instrument in excerpt, Part II).<br>daily highest: r= +.42 (ns)<br>daily average: r= +.45 (ns)<br>daily lowest: r= +.03 (ns) | AFF 3.1 | $r_{pm}$ | + | t | ns | Male college students, U.S.A.<br>Non-probability chunk sample<br>N: 17, date: ± 1960 | WESSM 66/2<br>p. 66/282 |

| | | | | | | | | | |
|---|---|---|---|---|---|---|---|---|---|
| SOCIAL RESPECT vs social contempt | Wessman & Ricks Social Respect vs Social Contempt Scale, scored once for the current academic year (see last page under WESSM 66/1) | Analysis on the basis of data from freshmen and juniors who returned the second questionnaire. N= 353: 188 freshmen (99 males, 89 females) and 165 juniors (90 males and 75 females)<br>Stronger among males: r= +.42 (05)<br>Lower among females: r= +.25 (05) | AFF 2.1 | $r_{pm}$ | + | | 05 | Undergraduate full time college students, U.S.A.<br>Non-probability chunk sample<br>N: 952, date: March, 1965 | CONST 65<br>p. 59 |

## A 2.2.19 - THOUGHT PROCESSES

| | | | | | | | | | |
|---|---|---|---|---|---|---|---|---|---|
| THOUGHT PROCESSES | Repeated closed question on 'how readily your ideas came and how valuable they seemed', rated on a 10-point scale:<br>10. I am a surging torrent of spectacular insights.<br>9. Brilliant penetrating ideas emerging spontaneously and with great rapidity.<br>8. Ideas coming quickly and effortlessly.<br>7. Clever and keen.<br>6. Quite alert. Thoughts fairly quick and clear.<br>5. Not particularly alert. My ideas trivial and commonplace.<br>4. My mind feels ponderous and dull. My thoughts are slow and monotonous.<br>3. My thoughts all seem weary, stale, flat and unprofitable.<br>2. My mind is stagnant. Almost nothing freshens it.<br>1. My mind is cold, dead. Nothing moves.<br>(Wessman & Ricks Thought Processes Scale) | The scale was scored each night for lowest, average and highest mood experienced that day over a period of 6 weeks. The means of the lowest, average and highest daily scores were correlated with the mean average score on the Elation-Depression Scale (see instrument in excerpt, Part II).<br>daily highest: r= +.57 (05)<br>daily average: r= +.82 (05)<br>daily lowest: r= +.74 (05) | AFF 3.1 | $r_{pm}$ | + | t | 05 | Female college students, U.S.A.<br>Non-probability chunk sample<br>N: 21, date: ± 1960 | WESSM 66/1<br>p. 64/276 |
| THOUGHT PROCESSES | See above | See above<br>daily highest: r= +.72 (05)<br>daily average: r= +.74 (05)<br>daily lowest: r= +.36 (ns) | AFF 3.1 | $r_{pm}$ | + | t | 05 | Male college students, U.S.A.<br>Non-probability chunk sample<br>N: 17, date: ± 1960 | WESSM 66/2<br>p. 66/282 |
| THOUGHT PROCESSES | Wessman & Ricks Thought Processes Scale, scored once for the current academic year (see above under WESSM 66/1) | Analysis on the basis of data from freshmen and juniors who returned the second questionnaire. N= 353: 188 freshmen (99 males, 89 females) and 165 juniors (90 males and 75 females)<br>Unaffected by sex<br>males: r= +.22 (05)<br>females: r= +.19 (05) | AFF 2.1 | $r_{pm}$ | + | | 05 | Undergraduate full time college students, U.S.A.<br>Non-probability chunk sample<br>N: 952, date: March, 1965 | CONST 65<br>p. 59 |
| THOUGHT PROCESSES | Wessman & Ricks Thought Processes Scale, scored each night for lowest, average and highest mood experienced that day during one month (see above under WESSM 66/1) | The means of the lowest, average and highest daily scores were correlated with the mean average score on the Elation-Depression Scale (see first instrument in excerpt, Part II).<br>daily highest: r= +.65 (01)<br>daily average: r= +.79 (01)<br>daily lowest: r= +.71 (01) | AFF 3.1 | $r_{pm}$ | + | | 01 | Undergraduate students, U.S.A.<br>Non-probability chunk sample<br>N: 67, date: summer, 1970 | GORMA 71<br>p. 216/221 |
| | | Analysis on the basis of the mean lowest, average and highest daily scores: | HAPP 3.1 | $r_{pm}$ | + | | ns | | |

| | | | | | | | | |
|---|---|---|---|---|---|---|---|---|
| | | daily highest: r= +.27 (05)<br>daily average: r= +.19 (ns)<br>daily lowest: r= +.10 (ns) | | | | | | |

## A 2.2.20 - TRANQUILITY

| | | | | | | | | |
|---|---|---|---|---|---|---|---|---|
| TRANQUILITY vs anxiety | Repeated closed question on 'how calm or troubled you felt', rated on a 10-point scale:<br>10. Perfect and complete tranquility. Unshakably secure.<br>9. Exceptional calm, wonderfully secure and carefree.<br>8. Great sense of well-being. Essentially secure, and very much at ease.<br>7. Pretty generally secure and free from care.<br>6. Nothing particularly troubling me. More or less at ease.<br>5. Somewhat concerned with minor worries or problems. Slightly ill at ease, a bit troubled.<br>4. Experiencing some worry, fear, trouble or uncertainty. Nervous, jittery, on edge.<br>3. Considerable insecurity. Very troubled by significant worries, fears, uncertainties.<br>2. Tremendous anxiety and concern. Harassed by major worries and fears.<br>1. Completely beside myself with dread, worry, fear. Overwhelmingly distraught and apprehensive. Obsessed or terrified by insoluble problems and fears.<br>(Wessman & Ricks Tranquility vs Anxiety Scale) | The scale was scored each night for lowest, average and highest mood experienced that day over a period of 6 weeks. The means of the lowest, average and highest daily scores were correlated with the mean average score on the Elation-Depression Scale (see instrument in excerpt, Part II).<br>daily highest: r= +.66 (05)<br>daily average: r= +.89 (05)<br>daily lowest: r= +.76 (05) | AFF 3.1 | $r_{pm}$ | + | t | 05 | Female college students, U.S.A.<br>Non-probability chunk sample<br>N: 21, date: ± 1960 | WESSM 66/1<br>p. 64/276 |
| TRANQUILITY vs anxiety | See above | See above<br>daily highest: r= +.80 (05)<br>daily average: r= +.67 (05)<br>daily lowest: r= +.12 (ns) | AFF 3.1 | $r_{pm}$ | + | t | 05 | Male college students, U.S.A.<br>Non-probability chunk sample<br>N: 17, date: ± 1960 | WESSM 66/2<br>p. 66/282 |
| TRANQUILITY vs anxiety | Wessman & Ricks Tranquility vs Anxietv Scale) scored once for the current academic year (see above under WESSM 66/1) | Analysis on the basis of data from freshmen and juniors who returned the second questionnaire. N= 353: 188 freshmen (99 males, 89 females) and 165 juniors (90 males and 75 females)<br>Stronger among females: r= +.56 (05)<br>Lower among males: r= +.44 (05)<br>The difference is non-significant | AFF 2.1 | $r_{pm}$ | + | | 05 | Undergraduate full time college students, U.S.A.<br>Non-probability chunk sample<br>N: 952, date: March, 1965 | CONST 65<br>p. 59 |
| TRANQUILITY vs anxiety | Wessman & Ricks Tranquility vs Anxiety Scale) scored at the end of each day for lowest, average and highest mood experienced that day during 3 weeks (see above under WESSM 66/1) | The means of the lowest, average and highest daily scores were correlated with the mean average score on the Elation-Depression Scale (see second instrument in excerpt, Part II).<br>daily highest: r= +.77 (01)<br>daily average: r= +.92 (01)<br>daily lowest: r= +.79 (01) | AFF 3.1 | $r_{pm}$ | + | | 01 | Married females, U.S.A.<br>Non-probability purposive sample by expert choice<br>N: 62, date: — | HARDE 69<br>p. 118 |

| | | | | | | | | | |
|---|---|---|---|---|---|---|---|---|---|
| TRANQUILITY vs Anxiety | Wessman & Ricks Tranquility vs Anxiety Scale, scored each night for lowest, average and highest mood experienced that day during one month (see last page under WESSM 66/1) | The means of the lowest, average and highest daily scores were correlated with the mean average score on the Elation-Depression Scale (see first instrument in excerpt, Part II).<br>daily highest: r= +.75 (01)<br>daily average: r= +.86 (01)<br>daily lowest: r= +.69 (01) | AFF 3.1 | $r_{pm}$ | + | | 01 | Undergraduate students, U.S.A.<br>Non-probability chunk sample<br>N: 67, date: summer, 1970 | GORMA 71<br>p. 216/221 |
| | | Analysis on the basis of the mean lowest, average and highest daily scores<br>daily highest: r= +.30 (05)<br>daily average: r= +.30 (05)<br>daily lowest: r= +.25 (05) | HAPP 3.1 | $r_{pm}$ | + | | 05 | | |
| TRANQUILITY | Repeated closed question on to what extent Ss felt like doing calm and tranquil things during the day, rated each night on a 4-point scale for at least 20 days | Analysis on the basis of the mean rating | AFF 3.1 | r | +.16 | | ns | University students, U.S.A.<br>Probability sample<br>N: 45, date: — | LUDWI 70<br>p. 173 |

## A 2.2.21 - VARIOUS TYPES OF AFFECT

| | | | | | | | | | |
|---|---|---|---|---|---|---|---|---|---|
| EXCITEMENT | Repeated closed question on to what extent Ss felt like doing exciting things during the day, rated each night on a 4-point scale for at least 20 days | Analysis on the basis of the mean rating | AFF 3.1 | r | -.16 | | ns | University students, U.S.A.<br>Probability sample<br>N: 45, date: — | LUDWI 70<br>p. 173 |
| READINESS TO SHOW FEAR in the face of bodily danger | Class-master rating on a 7-point scale on the basis of observation | | AFF 5.3 | $r_{pm}$ | -.33 | | | Schoolboys, England<br>Non-probability chunk sample<br>N: 140, date: 1912 - 1913 | WEBB 15<br>p. 27 |
| FEELING IRRITABLE | Closed question: no vs yes | | HAPP 2.1 | G | -.76 | Chi | 000 | Male employees of age 40+, the Netherlands<br>Non-probability chunk sample<br>N: 140, date: 1912 - 1913 | SONDE 75 |
| NERVOUSNESS | Closed question on being a nervous person: definitely no / rather no / rather yes / decidedly yes | | HAPP 2.1 | $T^2$ | -.11 | $Chi^2$ | 001 | National adult population, Poland<br>Non-probability purposive quota sample, stratified by sexe, age, type of local community, employment and S.E.S.<br>N: 2387, date: June - July, 1960 | MAKAR 62<br>p. 115 |
| NERVOUSNESS | Have taken 'something against the nerves' during the last 14 days | | HAPP 1.1 | G' | -.41 | Gt' | 01 | Adults, Utrecht, The Netherlands<br>Probability sample stratified by age<br>N: 300, date: autumn, 1967 | MOSER 69<br>p. 37 |
| PLEASED AT ACCOMPLISHMENT | Closed question: During the past week, did you ever feel pleased about having accomplished something? no vs yes | See second instrument in excerpt (Part II). | HAPP 1.1 | Q | +.10 | | | National adult population, Puerto Rico<br>Probability simple random sample<br>N: 1417, date: November, 1963 - January, 1964 + August - October, 1964 | MATLI 66<br>p. 8 |
| PROUD OF COMPLIMENT | Closed question: During the past week, did you ever feel proud because someone complimented you on something you had done? no vs yes | See above | HAPP 1.1 | Q | +.14 | | | See above | MATLI 66<br>p. 8 |
| LONELY OR REMOTE | Closed question: During the past week, did you ever feel very lonely or remote from other people? no vs yes | See above | HAPP 1.1 | Q | -.70 | | | See above | MATLI 66<br>p. 8 |

| | | | | | | | | | |
|---|---|---|---|---|---|---|---|---|---|
| BORED | Closed question: 'During the past week, did you ever feel bored?' no vs yes | See second instrument in excerpt (Part II). | HAPP 1.1 | Q | -.73 | | | National adult population, Puerto Rico (See last page) | MATLI 66 p. 8 |
| RESTLESS | Closed question: 'During the past week, did you ever feel so restless that you couldn't sit long in a chair?' no vs yes | See above | HAPP 1.1 | Q | -.56 | | | See above | MATLI 66 p. 8 |
| UNEASY | Closed question: 'During the past week, did you ever feel vaguely uneasy about something?' no vs yes | See above | HAPP 1.1 | Q | -.60 | | | See above | MATLI 66 p. 8 |
| LONELINESS | 2-item index of closed questions on feeling very lonely or remote from other people, and depressed or very unhappy during the past week | | HAPP 1.1<br>HAPP 3.1 | r<br>r | ± 0<br>± 0 | | | Adults, Metro Manila, Philippines<br>Probability area sample<br>N: 941, date: January - April, 1972 | BULAT 73 p. 233 |
| NEGATIVE AFFECT STATES | 40-item index of closed questions on irritability (7 items), general anxiety (7 items), anxiety and tension (5 items), depression (6 items), anomie (8 items) and resentment (7 items) | | COMP 1.2 | $r_{pm}$ | -.51 | | 001 | Public highschool boys, U.S.A.<br>Probability multi-stage sample<br>N: 2213 in 1966, 1886 in 1968 and 1799 in 1969, date: fall, 1966, spring, 1968 and spring, 1969 | BACHM 67/70 p. 122 |

## A 2.3 - VARIOUS EMOTIONAL CHARACTERISTICS

| | | | | | | | | | |
|---|---|---|---|---|---|---|---|---|---|
| BEING MORE INFLUENCED BY PEAKS OF FEELING than by troughs | Comparison of associations between daily lowest and daily average moods on the one side and daily highest and daily average moods on the other side for both unhappy and happy men | A positive relation (05) was found when daily lowest, average and highest scores during 6 weeks on the Elation-Depression Scale (see instrument in excerpt, Part II) were correlated and compared. For most of the other Personal Feeling Scales (see excerpt, Part II) the same pattern was found. | AFF 3.1 | | + | t | s | Male college students, U.S.A.<br>Non-probability chunk sample<br>N: 17, date: ± 1960 | WESSM 66/2 p. 81 |
| GENERAL REPRESSION AND DENIAL of unpleasant and disturbing affects | Clinical rank order on the basis of general clinical experience with the subjects and observation in experimental situations | | AFF 3.1 | $r_{pm}$ | -.01 | t | ns | See above | WESSM 66/2 p. 104 |
| SUPPRESSIVITY AND CONCEALMENT of emotions | Clinical rank order on the basis of general clinical experience with the subjects and observation in experimental situations | | AFF 3.1 | $r_{pm}$ | +.42 | t | ns | See above | WESSM 66/2 p. 105 |

## A3 AGE

| | | | | | | | | | |
|---|---|---|---|---|---|---|---|---|---|
| AGE | -29 / 30-49 / 50+ | | HAPP 3.1 | G' | +.05 | Gt' | 01 | Adult population of 5 Westernized nations, 3 under-developed giants, 2 countries in the Middle East, 3 Caribbean nations and the Philippines<br>N: 18.653, date: ± 1960 | CANTR 65/1<br>p. 259 |
| AGE | 20-29 / 30-39 / 40-49 / 50-59 / 60-69 / 70 | See remarks in excerpt (Part II)<br>in 1946: negroes: G' = -.00 (ns)<br>whites: G' = -.10 (01)<br>in 1956: negroes: G' = +.14 (05)<br>whites: G' = -.11 (01)<br>in 1966: negroes: G' = +.05 (ns)<br>whites : G' = -.08 (01) | HAPP 1.1 | G' | | Gt' | | National adult population, U.S.A.<br>Non-probability quota samples and probability area samples<br>N: 25.617, date: 1946 - 1948, 1956, 1966 | MANNI 72<br>p. 59 |
| AGE | 20-39 / 40-59 / 60+ | Unaffected by sex<br>U-shaped curves: males of age 30-39 and females of age 20-29 being most happy | HAPP 1.1 | G' | -.13 | Gt' | 01 | National adult population, U.S.A.<br>Non-probability quota sample<br>N: 2377, date: February, 1946 | WESSM 56<br>p. 176 |
| AGE | 21-29 / 30-49 / 50-65 / over 65 | | HAPP 2.1 | G' | +.01 | Gt' | ns | National adult population, U.S.A.<br>Probability sample proportionally stratified by sex, age, occupation, S.E.S., and education<br>N: 1015, date: 1948 - 1949 | BUCHA 53<br>p. 213 |
| AGE | 21-34 / 35-44 / 45-54 / 55+ | | HAPP 1.1 | G' | -.20 | Gt' | 01 | Non-institutionalized adults, U.S.A.<br>Probability multi-stage area sample<br>N: 2460, date: spring, 1957 | GURIN 60<br>p. 43 |
| AGE | 20-29 / 30-39 / 40-49 / 50-59 / 60-69 / 70+ | | HAPP 2.1<br>HAPP 3.1<br>CON 1.1 | r<br>r<br>r | +.09<br>+.05<br>+.11 | | | National adult population, U.S.A.<br>Cantril (1965) modified probability sample<br>N: 1406, date: 1959 | BORTN 70<br>p. 44 |
| AGE | -29 / 30-49 / 50+ | | HAPP 3.1 | G' | +.04 | | ns | National adult population, U.S.A.<br>Probability sample<br>N: 1549, date: ± 1960 | CANTR 65/1<br>p. 378 |
| AGE | 21-29 / 30-49 / 50+ | See remarks in excerpt (Part II)<br>age 21-29: Mean = 6.3 (6.4)<br>age 30-49: Mean = 6.6 (6.8)<br>age 50+ : Mean = 6.7 (7.0) | HAPP 3.1 | DM | + | | | Non-institutionalized national adult population, U.S.A.<br>Multi-stage probability sample, stratified by size of locality<br>N: 1588, date: January, 1971 (and 1964) | CANTR 71<br>p. 66 |

| | | | | | | | | | |
|---|---|---|---|---|---|---|---|---|---|
| AGE | -35 / 35–44 / 45+ | See remarks in excerpt (Part II).<br>Slightly negative among whites: G' = –.03 (ns)<br>Positive among blacks : G' = +.36 (01) | HAPP 1.1 | G' | .00 | Gt' | ns | Non-institutionalized adults, U.S.A.<br>Type of sample construction unclear<br>N: 1602, date: March, 1972 | ALSTO 74<br>p. 100 |
| AGE | | | AFF 2.3 | $h^2$ | .09 | | | National adult population, U.S.A.<br>Probability area sample (first sample)<br>N: 1297, date: May, 1972 | ANDRE 74<br>p. 20 |
| AGE | 18–24 / 25–34 / 35–44 / 45–54 / 55–64 / 65–70 / 71+ | Positive among males : G = +.11 (01)<br>males of age 65–70 are most happy<br>Negative among females: G = –.07 (01)<br>females of age 65–70 are most unhappy.<br>Unaffected by S.E.S. | HAPP 1.1 | $r_{pm}$ | –.06 | | 05 | Non-institutionalized adults, U.S.A.<br>Probability samples<br>N: 1547, date: 1972, 1973 | SPREI 74<br>p. 456 |
| AGE | 18–39 / 40–59 / 60+ | Males:<br>total group : G' = +.19 (01)<br>married : G' = +.14 (01)<br>divorced /<br>separated : G' = +.39 (05)<br>never married: G' = +.23 (ns)<br><br>Females:<br>total group : G' = +.01 (ns)<br>married : G' = +.00 (ns)<br>divorced /<br>separated : G' = +.17 (ns)<br>never married: G' = +.45 (01) | HAPP 1.1 | G' | +.09 | Gt' | 01 | National adult population, U.S.A.<br>Combined data from 3 U.S. general surveys<br>N: 3853, date: 1972, 1973, 1974 | GLENN 75B<br>p. 596 |
| AGE | 18–24 / 25–34 / 35–44 / 45–54 / 55–64 / 65–70 / 71+ | Slightly positive among males<br>Slightly negative among females<br>For both males and females U-shaped curve:<br>males of age 65–70 being most happy and<br>females of age 65–70 being most unhappy. | HAPP 1.1 | D% | $\pm 0$ | | | Non-institutionalized adults, U.S.A.<br>National probability sample<br>N: 1500, date: spring, 1973 | SPREI 75<br>p. 239 |
| AGE | -30 / 30–39 / 40–49 / 50–59 / 60–69 / 70+ | | HAPP 1.1 | G' | –.18 | Gt' | 01 | Inhabitants of 4 small communities, Illinois, U.S.A.<br>Probability multi-stage samples<br>N: 2006, date: March, 1962 | BRADB 65/1<br>p. 9/23 |
| | | U-shaped curve: Ss of age 50–59 being most happy.<br>After age 60 stronger positive relation between age and the Index of Negative Affects. | AFF 2.3 | G' | –.05 | Gt' | ns | | |
| AGE | 21–29 / 30–39 / 40–49 / 50–59 | For people with income of less than $ 5000.– only<br>Reversed among low educated people: $D\bar{R}$ = +.04<br><br>Index of Positive Affects: $D\bar{R}$ = –.15 (05)<br>Index of Negative Affects: $D\bar{R}$ = –.08 (05) | AFF 2.3 | $D\bar{R}$ | –.04 | BCI | 05 | Adults, urban areas, U.S.A.<br>Probability area samples<br>N: 2787, date: January, 1963 – January, 1964 | BRADB 69<br>p. 45/91 |
| | | | HAPP 1.1 | G' | –.10 | | ns | | |
| AGE | 21–49 vs 50+ | Index of Positive Affects: D% = –<br>Index of Negative Affects: D% = $\pm 0$ | AFF 2.3 | D% | – | | | Adults, New Hampshire, U.S.A.<br>Probability sample<br>N: 600, date: – | PHILL 67A<br>p. 485 |
| | | | HAPP 1.1 | D% | – | | | | |
| AGE | 45–49 / 50–54 / 55–59 / 60–64 / 65–69 | | HAPP 3.1 | r | –.04 | | ns | People of 46 and older, Duke, U.S.A.<br>Probability systematic random sample, stratified by age and sex<br>N: 502, date: 1968 | PALMO 72<br>p. 70 |

| | | | | | | | | | |
|---|---|---|---|---|---|---|---|---|---|
| AGE | 20-39 / 40-64 / 65+ | Lower scores on both the Index of Positive Affects (01) and the Index of Negative Affects (05) in old age<br>When controlled for sex and occupational level significant (05) for Anglo high skill group only (F-test). | AFF 2.3 | | - | $Chi^2$ | ns | Adults, Houston, Texas, U.S.A.<br>Non-probability purposive quota sample, stratified by age, sex, occupational skill level and ethnicity<br>N: 1441, date: autumn, 1969 | GAITZ 72<br>p. 62/64 |
| | | | COMP 1.1 | | - | $Chi^2$ | ns | | |
| AGE | | | HAPP 1.1<br>HAPP 2.1 | G<br>G | +.04<br>+.02 | | | Adults, Toledo, Ohio, U.S.A.<br>Systematic random sample<br>N: 510, date: 1973 | SNYDE 74<br>p. 32 |
| AGE | | | AFF 2.1 | | | | ns | Female college seniors, U.S.A.<br>Non-probability chunk sample<br>N: 162, date: May - June, 1966 | PORTE 67<br>p. 96 |
| AGE | 18-19 / 20-21 / 22-23 / 24+ | | HAPP 1.1 | $r_{pm}$ | | t | ns | Male college undergraduates, U.S.A.<br>Non-probability chunk sample<br>N: 103, date: ± 1967 | HEERE 69<br>p. 28 |
| AGE | | Stonger among females: r = -.20 (ns)<br>Lower among males : r = -.05 (ns) | COMP 1.1 | $r_{pm}$ | - | | ns | Undergraduate students, Ohio, U.S.A.<br>Non-probability accidental sample<br>N: 132, date: 1966/1967 | MILLE 68<br>p. 1082 |
| AGE | | | COMP 1.1 | $r_{pm}$ | -.02 | | ns | Undergraduate college students, Hawaii<br>Non-probability accidental sample<br>N: 101, date: — | WILSO 65<br>p. 375 |
| AGE | 24-34 / 35-49 / 50+ | At age 50+ significantly lower scores on both the Index of Positive Affects and the Index of Negative Affects | AFF 2.3 | DM | ± 0 | NK | ns | Catholic Sisters, U.S.A.<br>Non-probability chunk sample<br>N: 183, date: — | LEWIS 72<br>p. 62 |
| AGE | | | COMP 1.1 | $r_{pm}$ | -.09 | | ns | White males who had experienced a first heart attack, Durham, North Carolina, U.S.A.<br>Non-probalitity quota sample<br>N: 56, date 1970 | GARRI 73<br>p. 201 |
| AGE | | Stronger among handicapped: r = -.21 (05)<br>Lower among normals : r = -.07 (ns) | HAPP 2.1 | r | - | | | Physically defective and normal persons, Detroit, U.S.A.<br>Non-probability purposive samples<br>N: 295, date: — | CAMER 73/1<br>p. 209 |
| AGE | 60-74 vs 75+ | | HAPP 2.1 | G' | -.20 | Gt' | ns | Aged chronically ill patients, U.S.A.<br>Probability sample<br>N: 167, date: 1959 | HENLE 67<br>p. 69 |
| AGE | 65-70 vs 75+ | Negative relation disappears when controlled for health status | AFF 1.1 | | ± 0 | $Chi^2$ | ns | Aged persons, Metropolitan Boston, U.S.A.<br>Probability area sample<br>N: 1335, date: 1965 | FOWLE 69<br>p. 733 |
| AGE | 66-76 / 77-81 / 82-92 | | AFF 2.3 | tau | .00 | | ns | Aged female public housing residents, U.S.A.<br>Probability systematic random sample<br>N: 44, date: 1967-1971 | GRANE 73A<br>p. 6 |
| AGE | | | AFF 2.3 | r | -.16 | | ns | Aged retired persons, Los Angeles County, U.S.A.<br>Non-probability purposive quota sample, proportionally stratified by marital status<br>N: 71, date: 1971 | MORIW 73<br>p. 229 |
| AGE | Data obtained from hospital records | Open ward : r = -.14 (ns)<br>Closed ward: r = -.19 (ns) | AFF 5.1 | $r_{pm}$ | - | | ns | Institutionalized mentally retarded males, U.S.A.<br>Non-probability chunk sample<br>N: 149, date: — | PANDE 71<br>p. 329 |

| | | | | | | | | | |
|---|---|---|---|---|---|---|---|---|---|
| AGE | 18–35 / 36–64 / 65+ | Non-significant for both the Index of Positive Affects and the Index of Negative Effects | AFF 2.3 | $r_{pm}$ | | | ns | Residents of Stirling County, Maritime, Canada<br>Probability sample stratified by sex, age, socio-environmental circumstances and mental health<br>N: 112, date: 1963 – 1968 | BEISE 74<br>p. 325 |
| AGE | –29 / 30–49 / 50+ | | HAPP 3.1 | G' | +.02 | Gt' | ns | National adult population, Dominican Republic<br>Probability samples<br>N: 814, date: ± 1960 | CANTR 65/1<br>p. 378 |
| AGE | 21–29 / 30–49 / 50–65 / over 65 | | HAPP 2.1 | G' | –.05 | Gt' | ns | National adult population, Mexico<br>Probability sample proportionally stratified by sex, age occupation, S.E.S., and education<br>N: 1752, date: 1948 – 1949 | BUCHA 53<br>p. 188 |
| AGE | –29 / 30–49 / 50+ | | HAPP 3.1 | G' | +.05 | Gt' | ns | National adult population, Panama<br>Probability sample proportionally poststratified by dwelling and mortality<br>N: 642, date: ± 1960 | CANTR 65/1<br>p. 378 |
| AGE | –29 / 30–49 / 50+ | | HAPP 3.1 | G' | –.07 | Gt' | ns | National adult population, Cuba<br>Probability area sample<br>N: 992, date: ± 1960 | CANTR 65/1<br>p. 378 |
| AGE | 20–29 / 30–39 / 40–49 / 50–59 / 60+ | Reversed among those with incomes of more than $ 3000<br>Unaffected by education<br>Reversed among those with fair or poor health | HAPP 1.1 | G' | –.06 | Gt' | ns | National adult population, Puerto Rico<br>Probability simple random sample<br>N: 1417, date: November, 1963 – January, 1964 and August – October, 1964 | MATLI 66<br>p. 18 |
| | | | AFF 2.3 | G' | –.01 | Gt' | ns | | |
| AGE | –29 / 30–49 / 50+ | | HAPP 3.1 | G' | 0 | Gt' | ns | National adult population, Brazil<br>Probability samples<br>N: 2168, date: ± 1960 | CANTR 65/1<br>p. 378 |
| AGE | 21–39 vs 40+ | Lower among those who have children: DM = + (ns)<br>Stronger among those who have no children: DM = + (01) | HAPP 3.1 | DM | + | DMRT | 05 | Adults in the Dominican Republic, Panama and Yugoslavia (Married people only)<br>Pooling of the three Cantril (1965) samples<br>N: 4113, date: — | BOHN 72<br>p. 31 |
| AGE | 15–24 / 24–54 / 55+ | Positive among males : G' = +.05 (05)<br>Negative among females : G' = –.07 (01) | HAPP 2.1 | G' | –.01 | Gt' | ns | National populations of nine European countries<br>Type of sample construction not reported<br>N: 9605 (or 9543, see Remarks in excerpt, Part II)<br>date: May, 1975 | COMMI 75<br>p. 139/153 |
| | | Stronger among females : G' = –.19 (01)<br>No relation among males: G' = –.00 (ns) | HAPP 1.1 | G' | –.10 | Gt' | 01 | | |
| AGE | 15–24 / 25–54 / 55+ | Positive among males : G' = +.13 (05)<br>Negative among females : G' = –.18 (01) | HAPP 2.1 | G' | –.04 | Gt' | | National population, Belgium<br>N: 1555 (1507), date: May, 1975 | COMMI 75<br>p. 143/155 |
| | | Stronger among females : G' = –.20 (01)<br>Lower among males : G' = –.09 (ns) | HAPP 1.1 | G' | –.14 | Gt' | | | |
| AGE | 15–24 / 25–54 / 55+ | Stronger among females : G' = –.17 (05)<br>Lower among males : G' = –.10 (ns) | HAPP 2.1 | G' | –.13 | Gt' | | National population, Denmark<br>N: 1039 (1073), date: May, 1975 | COMMI 75<br>p. 143/155 |
| | | Unaffected by sex<br>males : G' = –.17 (05)<br>females: G' = –.19 (ns) | HAPP 1.1 | G' | –.18 | Gt' | | | |
| AGE | 21–29 / 30–49 / 50–65 / over 65 | | HAPP 2.1 | G' | –.04 | Gt' | ns | National adult population, France<br>Probability sample, proportionally stratified by sex, age, occupation, S.E.S. and education<br>N: 1000, date: 1948 – 1949 | BUCHA 53<br>p. 147 |

| | | | | | | | | | |
|---|---|---|---|---|---|---|---|---|---|
| AGE | 51-24 / 25-54 / 55+ | Positive among males : G' = +.27 (01)<br>No relation among females: G' = +.02 (ns) | HAPP 2.1 | G' | +.11 | Gt' | | National population, France<br>N: 1196 (1156), date: May, 1975 | COMMI 75<br>p. 143/155 |
| | | Negative among females : G' = -.23 (05)<br>No relation among males : G' = +.01 (ns) | HAPP 1.1 | G' | -.12 | Gt' | | | |
| AGE | 21-29 / 30-49 / 50-65 / over 65 | | HAPP 2.1 | G' | -.11 | Gt' | 01 | National adult population, W. Germany<br>Probability sample, proportionally stratified by sex, age occupation, S.E.S. and education<br>N: 3371, date: 1948 - 1949 | BUCHA 53<br>p. 156 |
| AGE | -29 / 30-49 / 50+ | | HAPP 3.1 | G' | +.06 | Gt' | ns | National population, W.Germany<br>Probability area sample<br>N: 480, date: ± 1960 | CANTR 65/1<br>p. 378 |
| AGE | 15-25 / 25-54 / 55+ | Positive among males : G' = +.31 (01)<br>Negative among females: G' = -.47 (01) | HAPP 2.1 | G' | -.02 | Gt' | | National population, W.Germany<br>N: 1039 (1039), date: May, 1975 | COMMI 75<br>p. 143/155 |
| | | Positive among males : G' = +.27 (05)<br>Negative among females: G' = -.31 (01) | HAPP 1.1 | G' | -.03 | Gt' | | | |
| AGE | 21-29 / 30-49 / 50-65 / over 65 | | HAPP 2.1 | G' | -.01 | Gt' | ns | National adult population, Italy<br>Probability sample, proportionally stratified by sex, age, occupation, S.E.S. and education<br>N: 1078, date: 1948 - 1949 | BUCHA 53<br>p. 176 |
| AGE | 15-24 / 25-54 / 55+ | Positive among males : G' = +.25 (05)<br>Negative among females: G' = -.12 (ns) | HAPP 2.1 | G' | +.14 | Gt' | | National population, Italy<br>N: 1043 (1043), date: May, 1975 | COMMI 75<br>p. 143/155 |
| | | Negative among females : G' = -.26 (ns)<br>No relation among males: G' = +.04 (ns) | HAPP 1.1 | G' | -.11 | Gt' | ns | | |
| AGE | 15-24 / 25-54 / 55+ | Negative among males : G' = -.06 (ns)<br>Positive among females: G' = +.15 (ns) | HAPP 2.1 | G' | +.06 | Gt' | ns | National population, Luxembourg<br>N: 324 (311), date: May, 1975 | COMMI 75<br>p. 143/155 |
| | | Stronger among females: G' = +.23 (ns)<br>Lower among males : G' = +.06 (ns) | HAPP 1.1 | G' | +.13 | Gt' | ns | | |
| AGE | | | HAPP 1.1 | | ± 0 | | ns | National adult population, The Netherlands<br>N: at least 1000, date: 1948 | NIPO 49<br>p. 4 |
| AGE | 21-29 / 30-49 / 50-65 / over 65 | U-shaped curve: Ss of age 50-65 being most unhappy | HAPP 2.1 | G' | -.09 | Gt' | ns | National adult population, The Netherlands<br>Probability sample, proportionally stratified by age, sex, occupation, S.E.S. and education<br>N: 942, date: 1948 - 1949 | BUCHA 53<br>p. 197 |
| AGE | 15-24 / 25-54 / 55+ | Positive among males : G' = +.13 (ns)<br>Negative among females: G' = -.12 (ns) | HAPP 2.1 | G' | +.00 | Gt' | ns | National population, The Netherlands<br>N: 1093 (1093), date: May, 1975 | COMMI 75<br>p. 143/155 |
| | | Negative among females : G' = -.23 (01)<br>No relation among males: G' = +.03 (ns) | HAPP 1.1 | G' | -.08 | Gt' | | | |
| AGE | 5-point scale | | HAPP 2.1 | G | +.10 | $Chi^2$ | 000 | Male employees of age 40+, The Netherlands<br>Non-probability chunk sample<br>N: 13.000, date: — | SONDE 75 |
| AGE | -35 / 35-49 / 50+ | | HAPP 1.1 | $r_{pm}$ | -.18 | | | Housewives, The Netherlands<br>Probability area sample<br>N: 450, date: autumn, 1964 | PHILI 66<br>p. 66 |

| | | | | | | | | | |
|---|---|---|---|---|---|---|---|---|---|
| AGE | 30-34 / 35-39 / 40-44 / 45-49 / 50-54 | Unmarried males : r = +.00 (ns)<br>Married males : r = -.06 (ns)<br>Unmarried females: r = -.03 (ns)<br>Married females : r = +.24 (ns) | HAPP 2.1 | $r_{pm}$ | | $Chi^2$ | ns | Adults, Amsterdam, The Netherlands<br>Probability systematic random sample, stratified by sex and marital status<br>N: 600, date: September - December, 1965 | JONG 69<br>p. 190 |
| AGE | 21-35 / 35-50 / 50-65 | Males: G' = -.16 (ns)<br>Stronger among those of lower educational level, in jobs that often ask hard physical labour(.10)<br>Females: G' = -.04 (ns)<br>U-shaped curve: females of age 35-49 being least happy | HAPP 1.1 | G' | - | Gt' | ns | Adults, Utrecht, The Netherlands<br>Probability sample, stratified by age<br>N: 300, date: autumn, 1967 | MOSER 69<br>p. 13 |
| AGE | 21-29 / 30-49 / 50-65 / over 65 | U-shaped curve: Ss of age 50-65 being most happy | HAPP 2.1 | G' | +.13 | Gt' | 05 | National adult population, Norway<br>Probability sample, proportionally stratified by sex, age, occupation, S.E.S. and education<br>N: 1030, date: 1948-1949 | BUCHA 53<br>p. 205 |
| AGE | | | HAPP 2.1 | $T^2$ | | $Chi^2$ | ns | National adult population, Poland<br>Non-probability purposive quota sample, stratified by sex, age, type of local community, employment and S.E.S.<br>N: 2387, date: June/July, 1960 | MAKAR 62<br>p. 106 |
| AGE | 18-29 / 30-39 / 40-49 / 50+ | age 18-29: Mean = 4.5<br>age 30-39: Mean = 4.3<br>age 40-49: Mean = 4.3<br>age 50+ : Mean = 4.6 | HAPP 3.1 | DM | + | | | National adult population, Poland<br>Probability samples<br>N: 1464, date: ± 1960 | CANTR 65/1<br>p. 374 |
| AGE | 15-24 / 25-54 / 55+ | Unaffected by sex<br>females: G' = +.03 (ns)<br>males : G' = +.00 (ns) | HAPP 2.1 | G' | +.04 | Gt' | ns | National population, United Kingdom (including Northern Ireland)<br>N: 1317 (1325), date: May, 1975 | COMMI 75<br>p. 143/155 |
| | | Negative among males : G' = -.11 (ns)<br>No relation among females: G' = -.00 (ns) | HAPP 1.1 | G' | -.05 | Gt' | ns | | |
| AGE | 21-29 / 30-49 / 50-65 / over 65 | U-shaped curve: Ss of age 30-65 being most happy | HAPP 2.1 | G' | +.01 | Gt' | ns | National adult population, Britain<br>Probability sample, proportionally stratified by sex, age, occupation, S.E.S. and education<br>N: 1195, date: 1948 -1949 | BUCHA 53<br>p. 137 |
| AGE | 15-34 / 35-54 / 55+ | age 15-34: Mean = 5.5<br>age 35-54: Mean = 5.8<br>age 55+ : Mean = 5.3 | HAPP 2.1 | DM | - | | | National population, Britain<br>Non-probability quota sample<br>N: 213, date: March, 1971 | ABRAM 73<br>p. 4 |
| AGE | 15-24 / 25-54 / 55+ | Positive among males : G' = +.15 (ns)<br>Negative among females: G' = -.10 (ns) | HAPP 2.1 | G' | +.02 | Gt' | ns | National population, Ireland<br>N: 999 (996), date: May, 1975 | COMMI 75<br>p. 143/155 |
| | | Stronger among females: G' = -.21 (05)<br>Lower among males : G' = -.09 (ns) | HAPP 1.1 | G' | -.17 | Gt' | | | |
| AGE | -29 / 30-49 / 50+ | | HAPP 3.1 | G' | -.05 | Gt' | ns | National adult population, Yugoslavia<br>Probability sample<br>N: 1523, date: ± 1960 | CANTR 65/1<br>p. 378 |
| AGE | -29 / 30-49 / 50+ | Gamma based on estimated number of respondents in each category | HAPP 3.1 | G' | -.03 | Gt' | ns | National population, Egypt<br>Non-probability accidental sample, proportionally poststratified by dwelling<br>N: 499, date: ± 1960 | CANTR 65/1<br>p. 378 |
| AGE | -29 / 30-49 / 50+ | | HAPP 3.1 | G' | -.05 | Gt' | ns | National population, Israel<br>Probability sample<br>N: 1170, date: ± 1960 | CANTR 65/1<br>p. 378 |

| | | | | | | | | | |
|---|---|---|---|---|---|---|---|---|---|
| AGE | -30 vs 30+ | age -30: Mean = 6.8<br>age 30+: Mean = 7.1 | HAPP 3.1 | DM | + | | | Members of kibbutzim, Israel<br>Non-probability purposive quota sample<br>N: 300, date: ± 1960 | CANTR 65/1<br>p. 370 |
| AGE | -29 / 30-49 / 50+ | | HAPP 3.1 | G' | +.17 | Gt' | 01 | National adult population, Nigeria<br>Probability sample, proportionally stratified by dwelling and region<br>N: 1200, date: ± 1960 | CANTR 65/1<br>p. 378 |
| AGE | -29 / 30-49 / 50+ | Gamma based on estimated numbers of respondents in each category | HAPP 3.1 | G' | +.09 | Gt' | 01 | National population, India<br>Probability sample, proportionally poststratified by dwelling<br>N: 2366, date: 1958 | CANTR 65/1<br>p. 378 |
| AGE | 21-29 / 30-44 / 45-64 / 65+ | age 21-29: Mean = 5.4<br>age 30-44: Mean = 5.1<br>age 45-64: Mean = 5.2<br>age 65+ : Mean = 5.2 | HAPP 3.1 | DM | - | | | National adult population, Japan<br>Probability sample<br>N: 972: date: ± 1960 | CANTR 65/1<br>p. 370 |
| AGE | 21-64 vs 65+ | age 21-64: Mean = 5.2<br>age 65+ : Mean = 5.2 | HAPP 3.1 | DM | 0 | | | Adults, Japan<br>Probability sample<br>N: 2000 or more, date: September, 1973 | PALMO 75<br>p. 117 |
| AGE | -29 / 30-49 / 50+ | | HAPP 3.1 | G' | +.14 | Gt' | 01 | National adult population, The Philippines<br>Probability sample, proportionally poststratified by dwelling<br>N: 500, date: ± 1960 | CANTR 65/1<br>p. 378 |
| AGE | | Unaffected by sex<br>females: G = -.01<br>males : G = -.00 | HAPP 1.1 | G | ± 0 | | | Adults, Metro Manila, The Philippines<br>Probability area sample<br>N: 941, date: January - April, 1972 | BULAT 73<br>p. 234 |
| | | Positive among males : G = +.04<br>Negative among females: G = -.08 | HAPP 3.1 | G | | | | | |
| | | Index of Positive Affects:<br>Positive among males : G = +.03<br>Negative among females: G = -.06<br>Index of Negative Affects:<br>males : G = -.14<br>females: G = -.12 | AFF 2.3 | G | - | | | | |
| AGE | 21-29 / 30-49 / 50-65 / over 65 | U-shaped curve: Ss of age 50-65 being most unhappy | HAPP 2.1 | G' | -.08 | Gt' | ns | National adult population, Australia<br>Probability sample, proportionally stratified by sex, age, occupation, S.E.S. and education<br>N: 945, date: 1948 - 1949 | BUCHA 53<br>p. 130 |

# C 1 COGNITION



## C 1.1 - CONCEPTUAL DIFFERENTIATION AND CATEGORIZATION STYLES

| | | | | | | | |
|---|---|---|---|---|---|---|---|
| OBJECT SORTING ABILITY (broad equivalence range) | Clayton & Jackson Object Sorting Test, asking subjects to sort 50 objects in logical order, scored for number of groups formed (see Clayton & Jackson, 1961) | AFF 3.1<br>HAPP 3.1 | $r_{pm}$<br>$r_{pm}$ | +.16<br>+.00 | ns<br>ns | Undergraduate students, U.S.A. Non-probability chunk sample N: 67, date: summer, 1970 | GORMA 71 p. 215/218 |
| OBJECT SORTING ABILITY (compartmentalization style) | Clayton & Jackson Object Sorting Test, scored for number of objects left ungrouped (see Clayton & Jackson, 1961) | AFF 3.1<br>HAPP 3.1 | $r_{pm}$<br>$r_{pm}$ | +.07<br>+.02 | ns<br>ns | See above | GORMA 71 p. 215/218 |
| NATION SORTING ABILITY | Scott Nation Sorting Test, asking subjects to sort 28 countries in logical order, scored for number of groups formed (see Scott, 1962) | AFF 3.1<br>HAPP 3.1 | $r_{pm}$<br>$r_{pm}$ | +.06<br>-.09 | ns<br>ns | See above | GORMA 71 p. 215/218 |
| NATION SORTING ABILITY | Scott Nation Sorting Test, scored for number of countries left ungrouped (see Scott, 1962) | AFF 3.1<br>HAPP 3.1 | $r_{pm}$<br>$r_{pm}$ | -.01<br>-.08 | ns<br>ns | See above | GORMA 71 p. 215/218 |
| CATEGORY WIDTH | Pettigrew Category Width Test, asking subjects to choose estimates of the largest and smallest values of a given object of known average value (see Pettigrew, 1958) | AFF 3.1<br>HAPP 3.1 | $r_{pm}$<br>$r_{pm}$ | +.11<br>+.00 | ns<br>ns | See above | GORMA 71 p. 215/218 |
| LANGUAGE FACILITY | Advanced Vocabulary Test V-4; a multiple choice questionnaire scored for the number of words correctly matched (see French et al., 1963) | AFF 3.1<br>HAPP 3.1 | $r_{pm}$<br>$r_{pm}$ | +.16<br>+.07 | ns<br>ns | See above | GORMA 71 p. 215/218 |
| MOOD WORD FLUENCY | Assessment of mood repertoire using the number of words mentioned in three minutes | AFF 3.1<br>HAPP 3.1 | $r_{pm}$<br>$r_{pm}$ | +.12<br>+.01 | ns<br>ns | See above | GORMA 71 p. 215/218 |

## C 1.2 - FIELD DEPENDENCE

| | | | | | | | |
|---|---|---|---|---|---|---|---|
| FIELD INDEPENDENCE | Hidden Figures Test - Cf-1; a 16-item multiple choice test asking which one of five simple figures was embedded in a given complex figure, scored for number of simple figures correctly identified | AFF 3.1<br>HAPP 3.1 | $r_{pm}$<br>$r_{pm}$ | +.14<br>+.09 | ns<br>ns | Undergraduate students, U.S.A. Non-probability chunk sample N: 67, date: summer, 1970 | GORMA 71 p. 215/216 |

| | | | | | | | | | |
|---|---|---|---|---|---|---|---|---|---|
| | (part of Kit of Reference Test for Cognitive Factors; see French et al., 1963) | | | | | | | Undergraduate students, U.S.A. (see last page) | GORMA 71 p. 215/216 |
| FIELD DEPENDENCE | Number of items on the Hidden Figures Test - Cf - 1 which were attempted incorrectly (see above) | | AFF 3.1 | $r_{pm}$ | -.17 | | ns | See above | GORMA 71 p. 215/216 |
| | | | HAPP 3.1 | $r_{pm}$ | -.19 | | ns | | |
| FIELD INDEPENDENCE | Hidden Patters Test - Cf - 2, asking to check the instances in which 200 complex figures contained a given simple figure (part of Kit of Reference Test for Cognitive Factors; see French et al., 1963) | | AFF 3.1 | $r_{pm}$ | +.23 | | ns | See above | GORMA 71 p. 215/216 |
| | | | HAPP 3.1 | $r_{pm}$ | +.24 | | 05 | | |

## C 1.3 - INTELLIGENCE

see also 'Level of Education' (E 1.1.1), and 'School Ability' (E 1.2.2)

| | | | | | | | | | |
|---|---|---|---|---|---|---|---|---|---|
| INTELLIGCENCE | Experimental test containing paired words of opposite meaning, and reconstructing disarranged sentences | | AFF 5.3 | $r_{pm}$ | +.20 | | | Schoolboys, England<br>Non-probability chunk sample<br>N: 140, date: 1912 - 1913 | WEBB 15 p. 27 |
| INTELLIGENCE | Otis S-A test of mental ability | Unaffected by sex | COMP 4.1 | $r_{pm}$ | -.04 | | ns | Graduate students of education, U.S.A.<br>Non-probability chunk sample<br>N: 388, date: — | WATSO 30 p. 88/89 |
| | | Males only | COMP 4.3 | $r_{pm}$ | -.04 | | ns | | |
| | | Unaffected by sex<br>males: r = -.03<br>females: r = -.09 | AFF 1.3 | $r_{pm}$ | - | | ns | | |
| INTELLIGENCE | Those below vs those above the 75th percentile of college students in the Ohio State University Psychological Examination - Form 17 | Stronger among freshmen<br>Lower among juniors<br>L-shaped curve: significant among unhappy students only | COMP 2.2 | | + | | s | Female college students, New York, U.S.A.<br>Type of construction unclear<br>N: 238, date: — | WASHB 41 p. 283 |
| INTELLIGENCE | Quick Test of Intelligence (see Amons & Amons, 1962) | Happiness was measured in each of the 3 interview waves.<br>The following associations are reported:<br>intell. ($t_1$) x hap. ($t_1$): r = -.00<br>intell. ($t_1$) x hap. ($t_2$): r = -.00<br>intell. ($t_1$) x hap. ($t_3$): r = -.02 | COMP 1.2 | $r_{pm}$ | $\pm$ 0 | | ns | Public highschool boys, U.S.A.<br>Probability multi stage sample<br>N: 2213 in 1966, 1886 in 1968 and 1799 in 1969, date: fall, 1966; spring, 1968 and spring, 1969 | BACHM 67/70 p. 209 |
| SELF-PERCEIVED SCHOOL ABILITY | 3-item index of closed questions on self-perceived ability, intelligence, and reading ability compared with other boys of the same age | | COMP 1.2 | $r_{pm}$ | +.12 | | 01 | See above | BACHM 67/70 p. 242 |
| INTELLECTUAL ABILITY AT COLLEGE ENTRANCE | Scholastic aptitude score (S.A.T.) | | AFF 3.1 | $r_{pm}$ | +.12 | t | ns | Male college students, U.S.A.<br>Non-probability chunk sample<br>N: 17, date: $\pm$ 1960 | WESSM 66/2 p. 123 |
| INTELLECTUAL ABILITY AT COLLEGE ENTRANCE | Mathematical aptitude score (M.A.T.) | | AFF 3.1 | $r_{pm}$ | +.17 | t | ns | See above | WESSM 66/2 p. 123 |
| ACADEMIC STATUS | S.A.T.-verbal score in the form of local percentile rank | Analysis on the basis of a comparison of happy and unhappy students (resp. 120 males, 157 females and 154 males, 94 females: N = 525)<br>Unaffected by sex and stage of study | AFF 2.1 | DM | $\pm$ 0 | t | ns | Undergraduate full-time college students, U.S.A.<br>Non-probability chunk sample<br>N: 952, date: March, 1965 | CONST 65 p. 68 |

| | | | | | | | | | |
|---|---|---|---|---|---|---|---|---|---|
| INTELLIGENCE | Four subtests of the Wechsler Adult Intelligence scale (see Wechsler, 1955) | | HAPP 3.1 | r | +.05 | | | People of 46 and over, Duke, U.S.A.<br>Probability, systematic random sample, stratified by age and sex<br>N: 502, date: 1968 | PALMO 72<br>p. 70 |
| IQ | Data obtained from hospital records | Open ward: r = +.04 (ns)<br>Closed ward: r = –.16 (ns) | AFF 5.1 | $r_{pm}$ | | | ns | Institutionalized mentally retarded males, U.S.A.<br>Non-probability chunk sample<br>N: 149, date: — | PANDE 71<br>p. 329 |

## C I.4 – RIGIDITY

| | | | | | | | | | |
|---|---|---|---|---|---|---|---|---|---|
| RIGIDITY | Breskin 15-item Rigidity Test, scored for the number of pairs out of 15 pairs in which the 'good fit' figure was chosen (see Breskin, 1968) | | AFF 3.1<br>HAPP 3.1 | $r_{pm}$<br>$r_{pm}$ | –.45<br>–.15 | | 01<br>ns | Undergraduate students, U.S.A.<br>Non-probability chunk sample<br>N: 67, date: summer, 1970 | GORMA 71<br>p. 215/216 |
| RIGIDITY | Barron-Welsh Art Scale, scored for the number of unusual figures selected out of a set of figures differing in complexity, shading and symmetry (see Barron & Welsh, 1952) | | AFF 3.1<br>HAPP 3.1 | $r_{pm}$<br>$r_{pm}$ | +.08<br>–.22 | | ns<br>ns | See above | GORMA 71<br>p. 215/216 |
| RIGIDITY | Barron-Welsh Art Scale, Forced Choice Form, scored for the number of pairs out of 20 pairs in which the more elaborate figure was chosen (Figure Choices Test, see Messick & Kogan, 1965) | | AFF 3.1<br>HAPP 3.1 | $r_{pm}$<br>$r_{pm}$ | +.16<br>–.15 | | ns<br>ns | See above | GORMA 71<br>p. 215/218 |

## C I.5 – VARIOUS COGNITIVE CHARACTERISTICS

see also 'Types of Affect: Thought Processes' (A 2.2.19) and 'Various Personality Traits during Childhood' (P 1.9)

| | | | | | | | | | |
|---|---|---|---|---|---|---|---|---|---|
| QUICKNESS OF APPREHENSION | Class-master rating on a 7-point scale on the basis of observation | | AFF 5.3 | $r_{pm}$ | +.52 | | | Schoolboys, England<br>Non-probability chunk sample<br>N: 140, date: 1912 – 1913 | WEBB 15<br>p. 27 |
| QUICKNESS OF APPREHENSION | Trained peer rating on a 7-point scale on the basis of observation | | AFF 5.2 | $r_{pm}$ | +.42 | | | Male students, England<br>Non-probability chunk sample<br>N: 194, date: 1912 – 1913 | WEBB 15<br>p. 26 |
| PROFOUNDNESS OF APPREHENSION | Class-master rating on a 7-point scale on the basis of observation | | AFF 5.3 | $r_{pm}$ | +.48 | | | Schoolboys, England<br>Non-probability chunk sample<br>N: 140, date: 1912 – 1913 | WEBB 15<br>p. 27 |
| PROFOUNDNESS OF APPREHENSION | Trained peer rating on a 7-point scale on the basis of observation | | AFF 5.2 | $r_{pm}$ | +.20 | | | Male students, England<br>Non-probability chunk sample<br>N: 194, date: 1912 – 1913 | WEBB 15<br>p. 26 |
| SOUNDNESS OF COMMON SENSE | Class-master rating on a 7-point scale on the basis of observation | | AFF 5.3 | $r_{pm}$ | +.47 | | | Schoolboys, England<br>Non-probability chunk sample<br>N: 140, date: 1912 – 1913 | WEBB 15<br>p. 27 |
| SOUNDNESS OF COMMON SENSE | Trained peer rating on a 7-point scale on the basis of observation | | AFF 5.2 | $r_{pm}$ | +.24 | | | Male students, England<br>Non-probability chunk sample<br>N: 194, date: 1912 – 1913 | WEBB 15<br>p. 26 |

| | | | | | | | | | |
|---|---|---|---|---|---|---|---|---|---|
| ORIGINALITY OF IDEAS | Class-master rating on a 7-point scale on the basis of observation | | AFF 5.3 | $r_{pm}$ | +.57 | | | Schoolboys, England<br>Non-probability chunk sample<br>N: 140, date: 1912 - 1913 | WEBB 15<br>p. 27 |
| ORIGINALITY OF IDEAS | Trained peer rating on a 7-point scale on the basis of observation | | AFF 5.2 | $r_{pm}$ | +.43 | | | Male students, England<br>Non-probability chunk sample<br>N: 194, date: 1912 - 1913 | WEBB 15<br>p. 26 |
| POWER OF GETTING THROUGH MENTAL WORK RAPIDLY | Trained peer rating on a 7-point scale on the basis of observation | | AFF 5.2 | $r_{pm}$ | +.37 | | | See above | WEBB 15<br>p. 26 |
| VOCABULARY LEVEL | General Aptitude Test Battery - Part J: Vocabulary<br>(GATB-J; see Super, 1957) | | COMP 1.2 | $r_{pm}$ | +.02 | | ns | Public high school boys, U.S.A.<br>Probability multi-stage sample<br>N: 2213 in 1966, 1886 in 1968 and 1799 in 1969<br>date: fall, 1966, spring, 1968 and spring 1969 | BACHM 67/70<br>p. 242 |
| READING COMPREHENSION ABILITY | Test of Reading Comprehension<br>(see Gates, 1958) | | COMP 1.2 | $r_{pm}$ | +.02 | | ns | See above | BACHM 67/70<br>p. 242 |
| NUMBERING SPEED | Time necessary to number backwards from 100 to 1 | | AFF 6 | $r_{pm}$ | +.02 | | ns | Female undergraduates, U.S.A.<br>Random sample<br>N: 72, date: — | LUDWI 71/75<br>p. 64 |
| ENCOUNTERED NEW STIMULATING IDEAS | Closed question; during last few weeks | Index of Positive Affects: G = +.22<br>Index of Negative Affects: G = +.08 | AFF 2.3 | G | | | | Employed males, England<br>Non-probability purposive quota sample<br>N: 192, date: — | PAYNE 74<br>p. 17 |
| SPEECH | Ratings by 2 experienced staff members on a 7-point scale, ranging from 'talks unintelligible' to 'talks well' | Open ward : r = -.00 (ns)<br>Closed ward: r = -.08 (ns) | AFF 5.1 | $r_{pm}$ | - | | ns | Institutionalized mentally retarded males, U.S.A.<br>Non-probability chunk sample<br>N: 149, date: — | PANDE 71<br>p. 329 |
| BEING RETARDED | Normal vs retarded children<br>(see sample construction in excerpt, Part II) | males only:<br>- in class situation:<br>- first judge : sign. at .02<br>- second judge: sign. at .001<br>- at recess:<br>- first judge : sign. at .10<br>- second judge: sign. at .01 | AFF 5.1 | | + | $Chi^2$ | s | Mentally retarded and normal children, U.S.A.<br>Probability sample and non-probability purposive sample<br>N: 80, date: — | CAMER 73/3<br>p. 211 |
| | | almost all of the variance contributed by the males | AFF 5.3 | F | +4.38 | | 04 | | |

# C2 CONCERNS, INTERESTS

see also 'Hopes, aspirations and goals' (H 3)
'Problems, worries and fears' (P 5)
'Needs' (P 1.5)

| | | | | | | | | | |
|---|---|---|---|---|---|---|---|---|---|
| INTERESTS: | 15-item inventory of closed questions | | | | | | | Students, U.S.A.<br>Non-probability chunk sample<br>N: 1651, date: — | SŸMON 37<br>p. 292 |
| - HEALTH | | College students only<br>L-shaped curve: significant among unhappier students only | COMP 4.1 | | – | | | | |
| - SEX | | | COMP 4.1 | | | | ns | | |
| - SAFETY | | | COMP 4.1 | | | | ns | | |
| - MONEY | | | COMP 4.1 | | | | ns | | |
| - MENTAL HYGIENE | | | COMP 4.1 | | | | ns | | |
| - STUDY HABITS | | | COMP 4.1 | | | | ns | | |
| - RECREATION | | | COMP 4.1 | | | | ns | | |
| - PERSONAL AND MORAL QUALITIES | | | COMP 4.1 | | | | ns | | |
| - FAMILY RELATIONSHIPS | | | COMP 4.1 | | | | ns | | |
| - MANNERS | | | COMP 4.1 | | | | ns | | |
| - PERSONAL ATTRACTIVENESS | | High school students only<br>U-shaped curve: students of 'average' happiness being most interested in personal attractiveness | COMP 4.1 | | + | | | | |
| - DAILY SCHEDULE | | High school students only | COMP 4.1 | | – | | s | | |
| - CIVIC INTERESTS | | College students only<br>L-shaped curve: stronger among unhappier students | COMP 4.1 | | + | | s | | |
| - GETTING ALONG WITH OTHERS | | | COMP 4.1 | | | | ns | | |
| - PHILOSOPHY OF LIFE | | College students only<br>L-shaped curve: stronger positive among unhappier students | COMP 4.1 | | + | | s | | |

| | | | | | | | | | |
|---|---|---|---|---|---|---|---|---|---|
| UNCONTROLLABLE CONCERNS: | Closed questions: 'Last week how often did you think about . . .'<br>not at all / sometimes / often | The authors label these questions as referring to 'worries'. However a more appropriate label seems to be 'concerns'.<br>Gammas are computed on the basis of the proportions 'often' answers | | | | | | Inhabitants of 4 small communities, Illinois, U.S.A.<br>Probability multi-stage samples<br>N: 2006, date: March, 1962 | BRADB 65/1<br>p. 54 |
| - GROWING OLD | | Unaffected by S.E.S.<br>high S.E.S.: G' = -.55 (01)<br>low S.E.S. : G' = -.52 (01) | HAPP 1.1 | G' | - | Gt' | | | |
| - DEATH | | low S.E.S.-group only | HAPP 1.1 | G' | -.34 | Gt' | 01 | | |
| - HEALTH | | Lower among those of high S.E.S. : G' = -.31 (01)<br>Stronger among those of low S.E.S.: G' = -.37 (01) | HAPP 1.1 | G' | - | Gt' | | | |
| - ATOM BOMB OR FALLOUT | | Lower among those of high S.E.S. : G' = -.04 (ns)<br>Stronger among those of low S.E.S.: G' = -.26 (05) | HAPP 1.1 | G' | - | Gt' | | | |
| CONTROLLABLE CONCERNS: | See above | See above | | | | | | See above | BRADB 65/1<br>p. 54 |
| - GETTING AHEAD | | high S.E.S.-group only | HAPP 1.1 | G' | -.06 | Gt' | ns | | |
| - MONEY | | Unaffected by S.E.S. | HAPP 1.1 | G' | -.22 | Gt' | 01 | | |
| - PERSONAL ENEMIES | | Stronger among those of high S.E.S.:G' = -.32 (01)<br>Lower among those of low S.E.S. :G' = -.27 (05) | HAPP 1.1 | G' | - | Gt' | | | |
| - WORK | | Unaffected by S.E.S.<br>high S.E.S.: G' = -.08 (ns)<br>low S.E.S. : G' = -.11 (05) | HAPP 1.1 | G' | - | Gt' | | | |
| - MARRIAGE | | Unaffected by S.E.S.<br>high S.E.S.: G' = -.07 (ns)<br>low S.E.S. : G' = -.03 (ns) | HAPP 1.1 | G' | - | Gt' | | | |
| - BRINGING UP CHILDREN | | Unaffected by S.E.S.<br>high S.E.S.: G' = +.06 (ns)<br>low S.E.S. : G' = +.02 (ns) | HAPP 1.1 | G' | + | Gt' | | | |

# D 1 DEVIANCE

## ATTITUDINAL INDICATORS:

| | | | | | | | | |
|---|---|---|---|---|---|---|---|---|
| ANOMY | 13-item index of statements rated on 5-point agree - disagree scales, measuring anomy and alienation (modified Srole - Christie scale; see Srole et al., 1962). Typical items are: 'the average man probably is better off to-day than he ever was', 'most people don't really care what happens to the next person', and 'if you try hard enough you can ususally get what you want'. | HAPP 2.1 | $r_{pm}$ | -.32 | | | National population, Britain<br>Non-probability quota sample<br>N: 213, date: March, 1971 | ABRAM 73<br>p. 21 |
| LAW AND ORDER ATTITUDE | 4-item index containing children need law and order; one should feel love and respect for one's parents; there are merely strong and weak people (item from a shortened F-scale; see Weima, 1963) | HAPP 1.1 | G' | +.21 | Gt' | 05 | Adults, Utrecht, The Netherlands<br>Probability sample stratified by age<br>N: 300, date: autumn, 1967 | MOSER 69<br>p. 39 |
| DISSATISFACTION WITH PRESENT SOCIO-POLITICAL ORDER | 5-item index indicating anomy and powerlessness; we need less laws and institutions and more courageous leaders; most politicians are incapable; people should talk less and lead a more natural and active way of life (items from a shortened F-scale; see Weima, 1963) | HAPP 1.1 | G' | +.13 | Gt' | ns | See above | MOSER 69<br>p. 40 |
| SATISFACTION WITH STANDARDS AND VALUES OF TODAY'S SOCIETY | Closed question: 'How do you feel about . . . .' terrible / unhappy / mostly dissatisfied / mixed / mostly satisfied / pleased / delighted | HAPP 3.1 | $r^2$ | .26 | | | National adult population, U.S.A.<br>Probability area sample (third sample)<br>N: 1072, date: November, 1972 | ANDRE 74<br>p. 19 |

## BEHAVIORAL INDICATORS:

| | | | | | | | | |
|---|---|---|---|---|---|---|---|---|
| DELINQUENT BEHAVIORS | 26-item index of closed questions on running away from home, hitting parents, stealing, fighting, drinking alcohol without permission, etc. (adapted from Gold, 1966) | COMP 1.2 | $r_{pm}$ | -.21 | | 001 | Public high school boys, U.S.A.<br>Probability multi-stage sample<br>N: 2213 in 1966, 1886 in 1968 and 1799 in 1969<br>date: fall 1966, spring 1968 and spring 1969 | BACHM 67/70<br>p. 247 |
| REBELLIOUS BEHAVIORS IN SCHOOL | 13-item index of closed questions on fighting with other students, not working hard, skipping classes, copying someone else's assignments, etc. | COMP 1.2 | $r_{pm}$ | -.26 | | 001 | See above | BACHM 67/70<br>p. 243 |

| | | | | | | | | | |
|---|---|---|---|---|---|---|---|---|---|
| IMPULSE TO AGGRESSION | 4-item index of closed questions on feelings of swearing, losing temper at teachers, being rude to teachers, picking a fight with parents | | COMP 1.2 | $r_{pm}$ | -.33 | | 001 | Public high school boys, U.S.A.<br>(see last page) | BACHM 67/70<br>p. 122 |
| COOPERATION WITH STAFF | Overall staff-ratings on cooperation with the staff, conformity to rules, and conduct | For 12 out of the 16 staff members a significant (05) relationship between their ranking on cooperation and satisfaction (= happiness measure) was found (range of r = +.32 to +.63) | COMP 5 | $t_k$ | +.46 | | 01 | Male residents of a chronic care Veterans Administration nursing home, age 46-89, U.S.A.<br>N: 20, date: — | SCHNE 71<br>p. 63 |
| ADJUSTMENT | Overall staff-ratings based on the staff's own conceptualization of adjustment | Analysis of results suggests that in evaluating the residents the staff equated adjustment with external criteria, such as cooperation and conduct, more than with internal criteria, such as the feelings of the residents.<br>For 8 out of the 12 staff members a significant (05) relationship between their rankings on adjustment and satisfaction (= happiness measure) was found (range of r = +.27 to +.51) | COMP 5 | $t_k$ | +.35 | | 02 | See above | SCHNE 71<br>p. 63 |
| COOPERATIVENESS | Ratings by two experienced staff members who are familiar with all the patients on a 7-point 'rebellious - cooperative' scale | open ward : r = +.56 (001)<br>closed ward: r = +.60 (001) | AFF 5.1 | $r_{pm}$ | + | | 001 | Institutionalized mentally retarded males, U.S.A.<br>Non-probability chunk sample<br>N: 149, date: — | PANDF 71<br>p. 329 |

# E 1 EDUCATION AND SCHOOL



## E 1.1 - EDUCATION

### E 1.1.1 - LEVEL OF EDUCATION

| | | | | | | | | |
|---|---|---|---|---|---|---|---|---|
| EDUCATIONAL LEVEL | Level of school education: low / middle / high | | HAPP 3.1 | G' | +.35 | Gt' | 01 | Adult populations of 5 Westernized nations, 3 underdeveloped giants, 2 countries in the Middle East, 3 Caribbean nations and the Philippines<br>Representative samples<br>N: 18653, date: ± 1960 | CANTR 65/1 p. 259 |
| EDUCATIONAL LEVEL | 8th grade or less / high school incomplete / high school graduate / college incomplete / college graduate | See remarks in excerpt (Part II).<br>in 1946: negroes: G' = +.08 (ns)<br>whites : G' = +.18 (01)<br>in 1956: negroes: G' = -.07 (ns)<br>whites : G' = +.19 (01)<br>in 1966: negroes: G' = -.18 (05)<br>whites : G' = +.19 (01) | HAPP 1.1 | G' | | Gt' | | National adult population, U.S.A.<br>Non-probability quota samples and probability area samples<br>N: 25617, date: 1946, 1947, 1948, 1956, 1966 | MANNI 72 p. 39 |
| EDUCATIONAL LEVEL | No school or grammar school / high school / college | | HAPP 1.1 | G' | +.20 | Gt' | 01 | National adult population, U.S.A.<br>Non-probability quota sample<br>N: 2377, date: February, 1946 | WESSM 56 p. 188 |
| EDUCATIONAL LEVEL | Primary / secondary / university | | HAPP 2.1 | G' | +.16 | Gt' | 01 | National adult population, U.S.A.<br>Probability sample, proportionally stratified by sex, age occupation, S.E.S. and education<br>N: 1015, date: 1948 - 1949 | BUCHA 53 p. 213 |
| EDUCATIONAL LEVEL | Grade school / high school / college | Unaffected by age, sex and income | HAPP 1.1 | G' | +.32 | Gt' | 01 | Non-institutionalized adults, U.S.A.<br>Probability multi-stage area sample<br>N: 2460, date: spring, 1957 | GURIN 60 p. 47 |
| EDUCATIONAL LEVEL | None to 4 years / 5-7 years / 8 years / high school incomplete / technical trade or business school / college incomplete / college complete | | HAPP 2.1<br>HAPP 3.1<br>CON 1.1 | r<br>r<br>r | +.03<br>+.16<br>+.06 | | | National adult population, U.S.A.<br>Cantril (1965) modified probability sample<br>N: 1406, date: 1959 | BORTN 70 p. 44 |
| EDUCATIONAL LEVEL | Grammar school / high school / college | | HAPP 3.1 | G' | +.23 | | 01 | National adult population, U.S.A.<br>Probability sample<br>N: 1549, date: ± 1960 | CANTR 65/1 p. 378 |

| | | | | | | | | | |
|---|---|---|---|---|---|---|---|---|---|
| EDUCATIONAL LEVEL | Grade school / high school / college | See remarks in excerpt (Part II).<br>College : Mean = 7.0 (7.3)<br>high school : Mean = 6.5 (6.8)<br>grade school: Mean = 6.3 (6.7) | HAPP 3.1 | DM | + | | | Non-institutionalized national adult population U.S.A.<br>Multi-stage probability sample, stratified by size of locality<br>N: 1588, date: January, 1971 (+1964) | CANTR 71<br>p. 66 |
| EDUCATIONAL LEVEL | 0-8 yrs / 1-4 yrs high school / college | See remarks in excerpt (Part II).<br>Stronger among whites: G' = +.12 (05)<br>Reversed among blacks: G' = -.37 (01) | HAPP 1.1 | G' | +.09 | Gt' | 05 | Non-institutionalized adults, U.S.A.<br>N: 1602, date: March, 1972 | ALSTO 74<br>p. 100 |
| EDUCATIONAL LEVEL | | | HAPP 3.1 | $h^2$ | .07 | | | National adult population, U.S.A.<br>Probability area sample (first sample)<br>N: 1297, date: May, 1972 | ANDRE 74<br>p. 20 |
| EDUCATIONAL LEVEL | | Unaffected by S.E.S.<br>Lower among those under age 65 : r = +.08<br>Stronger among those over age 65: r = +.15<br>The difference between the correlations is not significant | HAPP 1.1 | $r_{pm}$ | +.10 | | 01 | Non-institutionalized adults, U.S.A.<br>Probability sample<br>N: 1547, date: 1972, 1973 | SPREI 74<br>p. 457 |
| EDUCATIONAL LEVEL | | Unaffected by sex | HAPP 1.1 | | ± 0 | | | Non-institutionalized adults, U.S.A.<br>National probability sample<br>N: 1500, date: spring, 1973 | SPREI 75<br>p. 243-246 |
| EDUCATIONAL LEVEL | 8th grade or less / less than high school graduate / high school graduate / part college / college graduate or more | Lower income categories:<br>Stronger positive relationship<br>Unaffected by age<br>Higher income categories:<br>Negative relationship<br>When elaborated for age U-shaped curve:<br>under age 40: slightly positive<br>age 40-59 : no relationship<br>age 60+ : negative | HAPP 1.1<br>AFF 2.3 | G'<br>G' | +.18<br>+.31 | Gt'<br>Gt' | 01<br>01 | Inhabitants of 4 small communities, Illinois, U.S.A.<br>Probability multi-stage samples<br>N: 2006, date: March, 1962 | BRADB 65/1<br>p. 9-23 |
| EDUCATIONAL LEVEL | 8th grade or less / part high school / high school graduate / part college / college graduate or more | Lower among high income levels: $\bar{DR}$ = +.04<br>Lower among the aged : $\bar{DR}$ = +.05<br>Index of Positive Affects: $\bar{DR}$ = +.21 (05)<br>Index of Negative Affects: $\bar{DR}$ = -.05 (ns) | AFF 2.3 | $\bar{DR}$ | +.18 | BCI | 05 | Adults, urban areas, U.S.A.<br>Probability area samples<br>N: 2787, date: January, 1963 - January, 1964 | BRADB 69<br>p. 45/91 |
| | | | HAPP 1.1 | G' | +.15 | | | | |
| EDUCATIONAL LEVEL | Less than high school / high school graduate / college training | Index of Positive Affects: D% = +<br>Index of Negative Affects: D% = ± 0 | HAPP 1.1<br>AFF 2.3 | D%<br>D% | +<br>+ | | | Adults, New Hampshire, U.S.A.<br>Probability sample<br>N: 600, date: — | PHILL 67A<br>p. 485 |
| EDUCATION | Years of schooling completed | In 1972: Affect Balance Score : r = +.22 (001)<br>Index of Positive Affects: r = +.26 (001)<br>Index of Negative Affects: r = -.07 (05)<br>In 1973: Affect Balance Score : r = +.20 (001)<br>Index of Positive Affects: r = +.28 (001)<br>Index of Negative Affects: r = -.01 (ns) | AFF 2.3 | r | + | | 001 | Adults, Los Angeles County, U.S.A.<br>Multi-staged probability samples of households<br>N: 1078 in 1972 and 1008 in 1973, date: 1972/1973 | CHERL 75<br>p. 197 |
| EDUCATION | | | HAPP 1.1<br>HAPP 2.1 | G<br>G | -.08<br>-.04 | | | Adults, Toledo, Ohio, U.S.A.<br>Systematic random sample<br>N: 510, date: 1973 | SNYDE 74<br>p. 32 |
| EDUCATION | Highest grade of regular school or college ever attended by the respondent | Unaffected by age<br>Slightly stronger in low income category:<br>below $ 7.000 : r = +.06<br>$ 7.000 or more: r = -.04 | HAPP 3.1 | r | +.03 | | ns | People of 46 and older, Duke, U.S.A.<br>Probability systematic random sample, stratified by age and sex<br>N: 502, date: 1968 | PALMO 72<br>p. 70 |

| | | | | | | | | | |
|---|---|---|---|---|---|---|---|---|---|
| EDUCATIONAL LEVEL | | Positive relation disappears when controlled for income. | AFF 1.1 | | + | $Chi^2$ | | Aged persons, Metropolitan Boston, U.S.A.<br>Probability area sample<br>N: 1335, date: 1965 | FOWLE 69<br>p. 733 |
| EDUCATIONAL PRESTIGE | 8th grade or less / part high school / high school / trade school / some college / collage graduate or more | Ss with some college are less happy than high school graduates. | HAPP 1.1 | $t_{k_c}$ | +.10 | | 05 | Non-hospitalized schizophrenic males, Monroe County, New York, U.S.A.<br>Probability sample drawn from the Monroe County Psychiatric Case Register<br>N: 178, date: 1964 - 1965 | ALEXA 68<br>p. 97 |
| EDUCATIONAL LEVEL | None / 1-4 years / 5 - high school / post high school | | HAPP 2.1 | G' | +.19 | Gt' | ns | Aged chronically ill patients, U.S.A.<br>Probability sample<br>N: 167, date: 1959 | HENLE 67<br>p. 69 |
| EDUCATIONAL LEVEL | | Index of Negative Affects: ns | AFF 2.3 | $r_{pm}$ | | | ns | Residents of Stirling County, Maritime, Canada<br>Probability sample , stratified by sex, age, socio-environmental circumstances and mental health<br>N: 112, date: 1963 - 1968 | BEISE 74<br>p. 325 |
| EDUCATIONAL LEVEL | No schooling / some primary / some secondary | | HAPP 3.1 | G' | +.69 | Gt' | 01 | National adult population, Dominican Republic<br>Probability samples<br>N: 1314, date: ± 1960 | CANTR 65/1<br>p. 378 |
| EDUCATIONAL LEVEL | Stage of education reached<br>primary / secondary / university | | HAPP 2.1 | G' | +.20 | Gt' | 01 | National adult population, Mexico<br>Probability sample, proportionally stratified by sex, age, occupation, S.E.S. and education<br>N: 1752, date: 1948 - 1949 | BUCHA 53<br>p. 189 |
| EDUCATIONAL LEVEL | No schooling / some primary / some secondary | | HAPP 3.1 | G' | +.72 | Gt' | 01 | National adult population, Panama<br>Probability sample, proportionally poststratified by dwelling and mortality<br>N: 642, date: ± 1960 | CANTR 65/1<br>p. 378 |
| EDUCATIONAL LEVEL | Elementary; none / secondary / higher | | HAPP 3.1 | G' | +.09 | Gt' | ns | National adult population, Cuba<br>Probability area sample<br>N: 992, date: ± 1960 | CANTR 65/1<br>p. 378 |
| EDUCATIONAL LEVEL | 3rd grade or less / 4th - 7th grade / 8th - 11th grade / H.S. graduate / part college / college graduate | Unaffected by income<br>Unaffected by age | HAPP 1.1<br>AFF 2.3 | G'<br>G' | +.19<br>+.16 | Gt'<br>Gt' | 01<br>01 | National adult population, Puerto Rico<br>Probability, simple random sample<br>N: 1417, date: November, 1963 - January, 1964 + August - October, 1964 | MATLI 66<br>p. 19 |
| EDUCATIONAL LEVEL | Illiterate / low / middle / high | | HAPP 3.1 | G' | +.50 | Gt' | 01 | National adult population, Brazil<br>Probability samples<br>N: 2168, date: ± 1960 | CANTR 65/1<br>p. 378 |
| EDUCATIONAL LEVEL | Low / average / high | U-shaped curve: Ss of average education being most happy. | HAPP 2.1<br>HAPP 1.1 | G'<br>G' | +.14<br>+.20 | Gt'<br>Gt' | 01<br>01 | National populations of nine European countries<br>Type of sample-construction not reported<br>N: 9605 (or 9543, see remarks in excerpt, Part II), date: May, 1975 | COMMI 75<br>p. 139 |
| EDUCATIONAL LEVEL | Stage of education reached<br>primary / secondary / university | | HAPP 2.1 | G' | +.09 | Gt' | ns | National adult population, Britain<br>Probability sample, proportionally stratified by sex, age, occupation, S.E.S. and education<br>N: 1195, date: 1948 - 1949 | BUCHA 53<br>p. 138 |
| EDUCATIONAL LEVEL | Stage of education reached<br>primary / secondary / university | | HAPP 2.1 | G' | +.20 | Gt' | 01 | National adult population, France<br>Probability sample, proportionally stratified by sex, age, occupation, S.E.S. and education<br>N: 1000, date: 1948 - 1949 | BUCHA 53<br>p. 148 |

| | | | | | | | | | |
|---|---|---|---|---|---|---|---|---|---|
| EDUCATIONAL LEVEL | Stage of education reached<br>primary / secondary / university | | HAPP 2.1 | G' | -.03 | Gt' | ns | National adult population, W. Germany<br>Probability sample, proportionally stratified by sex, age, occupation, S.E.S. and education<br>N: 3371, date: 1948 - 1949 | BUCHA 53<br>p. 157 |
| EDUCATIONAL LEVEL | low / middle / high | | HAPP 3.1 | G' | +.07 | Gt' | ns | National population, W. Germany<br>Probability area sample<br>N: 480, date: ± 1960 | CANTR 65/1<br>p. 378 |
| EDUCATIONAL LEVEL | Stage of education reached<br>primary / secondary / university | | HAPP 2.1 | G' | +.13 | Gt' | 05 | National adult population, Italy<br>Probability sample, proportionally stratified by sex, age, occupation, S.E.S. and education<br>N: 1078, date: 1948 - 1949 | BUCHA 53<br>p. 176 |
| EDUCATIONAL LEVEL | | | HAPP 1.1 | | ± 0 | | ns | National adult population, The Netherlands<br>N: at least 1000, date: 1948 | NIPO 49<br>p. 4 |
| EDUCATIONAL LEVEL | Stage of education reached<br>primary / secondary / university | | HAPP 2.1 | G' | +.37 | Gt' | 01 | National adult population, The Netherlands<br>Probability sample, proportionally stratified by sex, age, occupation, S.E.S. and education<br>N: 942, date: 1948 - 1949 | BUCHA 53<br>p. 197 |
| EDUCATIONAL LEVEL | Number of years of schooling and level of school education | Unaffected by sex. Significant among young persons (G = -.16), among those of high S.E.S. (G = -.17) and among those who experienced a downward inter-generational mobility (G = -.24) only. | HAPP 1.1 | G | -.12 | | 05 | National adult population, The Netherlands<br>Probability area sample<br>N = 1552, date: June, 1968 | BAKKE 74<br>p. 27<br>VEENH 75<br>p. 11 |
| EDUCATION | Direct question | Married females only. | HAPP 2.1 | $r_{pm}$ | -.12 | $Chi^2$ | | Adults, Amsterdam, The Netherlands<br>Probability systematic random sample, stratified by sex and marital status<br>N: 600, date: September - December, 1965 | JONG 69<br>p. 203 |
| EDUCATIONAL LEVEL | 3-point scale | Unaffected by sex and age | HAPP 1.1 | G' | -.05 | Gt' | ns | Adults, Utrecht, The Netherlands<br>Probability sample, stratified by age<br>N: 300, date: autumn, 1967 | MOSER 69<br>p. 20 |
| EDUCATIONAL LEVEL | Stage of education reached<br>primary / secondary / university | | HAPP 2.1 | G' | +.24 | Gt' | 01 | National adult population, Norway<br>Probability sample, proportionally stratified by sex, age, occupation, S.E.S. and education<br>N: 1030, date: 1948 - 1949 | BUCHA 53<br>p. 205 |
| EDUCATIONAL LEVEL | Some primary / some secondary / some higher | some higher : Mean = 5.1<br>some secondary: Mean = 4.7<br>some primary : Mean = 4.1 | HAPP 3.1 | DM | + | | | National adult population, Poland<br>Probability samples<br>N: 1464, date: ± 1960 | CANTR 65/1<br>p. 374 |
| EDUCATIONAL LEVEL | | | HAPP 2.1 | | | | ns | National adult population, Poland<br>Non-probability, purposive quota sample, stratified by sex, age, type of local community, employment and S.E.S.<br>N: 2387, date: June/July, 1960 | MAKAR 62<br>p. 106 |
| EDUCATIONAL LEVEL | No schooling / some primary / some high school or primary complete / high school or higher | | HAPP 3.1 | G' | +.48 | Gt' | 01 | National adult population, Yugoslavia<br>Probability sample<br>N: 1523, date: ± 1960 | CANTR 65/1<br>p. 378 |
| EDUCATIONAL LEVEL | Elementary incomplete / secondary or elementary complete / university | | HAPP 3.1 | G' | +.49 | Gt' | 01 | National population, Israel<br>Probability sample<br>N: 1170, date: ± 1960 | CANTR 65/1<br>p. 378 |
| EDUCATIONAL LEVEL | Illiterate / no school but literate / some primary / some secondary or university | Ss with no school education, but literate are most happy, followed by resp. Ss with some sedondary, the illiterates and Ss with some primary school education. | HAPP 3.1 | G' | +.23 | Gt' | 01 | National adult population, Nigeria<br>Probability sample, proportionally stratified by dwelling and region<br>N: 1200, date: ± 1960 | CANTR 65/1<br>p. 378 |

| | | | | | | | | | |
|---|---|---|---|---|---|---|---|---|---|
| EDUCATIONAL LEVEL | Illiterate / under matriculate / matriculate / higher | | HAPP 3.1 | G' | +.31 | Gt' | 01 | National population, India<br>Probability sample, proportionally poststratified by dwelling<br>N: 2366, date: 1958 | CANTR 65/1<br>p. 378 |
| EDUCATIONAL LEVEL | 0 – 9 years schooling / high school incomplete / high | high: : Mean = 5.7<br>high school incomplete: Mean = 5.4<br>-9 years school : Mean = 5.0 | HAPP 3.1 | DM | + | | | National adult population, Japan<br>Probability sample<br>N: 972, date: ± 1960 | CANTR 65/1<br>p. 370 |
| EDUCATIONAL LEVEL | Elementary incomplete / elementary complete / high school incomplete / high school complete / college incomplete / college complete | | HAPP 3.1 | G' | +.23 | Gt' | 01 | National adult population, The Philippines<br>Probability sample, proportionally poststratified by dwelling<br>N: 500, date: ± 1960 | CANTR 65/1<br>p. 378 |
| EDUCATIONAL LEVEL | | Lower among males : G = +.17<br>Stronger among females: G = +.41 | HAPP 1.1 | G | + | | | Adults, Metro Manila, Philippines<br>Probability area sample<br>N: 941, date: January – April, 1972 | BULAT 73<br>p. 232 |
| | | Unaffected by sex | HAPP 3.1 | G | +.52 | | | | |
| | | Index of Positive Affects:<br>males : G = +.22<br>females: G = +.22<br>Index of Negative Affects:<br>positive among males: G = +.14<br>not among females : G = –.00 | AFF 2.3 | G | + | | | | |
| EDUCATIONAL LEVEL | Stage of education reached<br>primary / secondary / university | | HAPP 2.1 | G' | –.01 | Gt' | ns | National adult population, Australia<br>Probability sample, proportionally stratified by sex, age, occupation, S.E.S. and education<br>N: 945, date: 1948 – 1949 | BUCHA 53<br>p. 130 |

## E 1.1.2 - ATTITUDES TOWARDS LEVEL OF EDUCATION

| | | | | | | | | | |
|---|---|---|---|---|---|---|---|---|---|
| SATISFACTION WITH EDUCATION | Closed question rated on a 7-point self-anchoring scale, based on Cantril (1965) | | HAPP 2.1 | r | +.27 | | | Adult population of 8 major British conurbations<br>Non-probability quota sample<br>N: 593, date: October – November, 1971 | HALL 73<br>p. 100 |
| SATISFACTION WITH EDUCATIONAL LEVEL | Closed question ranging from 'very unsatisfied' to 'very satisfied' | | HAPP 1.1<br>AFF 1.1 | mc<br>mc | +.26<br>+.31 | | | Urban adult Jewish population, Israel<br>Probability area sample using dwelling units<br>N: 1940, date: spring, 1973 | LEVY 75/1<br>p. 232 |
| DESIRE FOR LONGER SCHOOLING | | 75% of the relatively dissatisfied and 58% of the very satisfied desire longer schooling.<br>Unaffected by sex | HAPP 2.1 | D% | – | | s | Middle-aged, middle class married couples, U.S.A.<br>Non-probability accidental sample of couples<br>N: 416, date: 1952 – 1953 | ROSE 55<br>p. 17 |
| UNFULFILLED ASPIRATIONS: EDUCATION, FOLLOW A TALENT | Open-ended question on unfulfilled aspirations.<br>other aspirations vs aspirations mentioned | Computed for those having unfulfilled aspirations only (N = 1646) | HAPP 1.1 | G' | +.06 | Gt' | ns | National adult population, U.S.A.<br>Non-probability quota sample<br>N: 2377, date: February, 1946 | WESSM 56<br>p. 210 |
| DESIRED PERSONAL CHANGES: MORE EDUCATION | Open-ended question on desired personal changes.<br>other changes vs change mentioned | Computed for those who desire to change only (N = 1591) | HAPP 1.1 | G' | –.14 | Gt' | ns | See above | WESSM 56<br>p. 211 |

## E 1.2 - SCHOOL

## E I.2.1 - ATTITUDES TOWARDS SCHOOL

| Concept | Operationalization | Results | Code | | Stat | Dir | Test | Sig | Population | Source |
|---|---|---|---|---|---|---|---|---|---|---|
| SATISFACTION WITH UNIVERSITY | Closed question on satisfaction with one's experience as a student at the University of Rochester, rated on a 7-point graphic scale extremely dissatisfied / neither satisfied nor dissatisfied / extremely satisfied | The 16 most happy and the 16 most unhappy students in each of 8 sex/class groups (N=256) were compared. The happy students had a mean score of 5.5 and the unhappy a score of 3.7. | AFF | 2.1 | DM | + | t | 01 | Undergraduate full-time college students, University of Rochester, U.S.A.<br>Non-probability chunk sample<br>N: 952, date: March, 1965 | CONST 65 p. 71 |
| SATISFACTION WITH UNIVERSITY | Direct yes/no question:<br>'Given the same alternatives, would you again choose to come to the University of Rochester?' | N = 256 (see above).<br>71% of the happy students and 37.5% of the unhappy students responded affirmatively. | AFF | 2.1 | D% | + | | | See above | CONST 65 p. 74 |
| <u>ATTITUDE TOWARD SPECIFIC ASPECTS OF COLLEGE:</u> | Product score of the subjective relevance of the goal mentioned and perceived instrumentality of the University of Rochester for the attainment of that goal; as assessed by a 14-item inventory of important goals (Perceived Instrumentality of College Test) | Analysis on the basis of data from freshmen and juniors who returned the second questionnaire. N= 353: 188 freshmen (99 males and 89 females), 165 juniors (90 males and 75 females)<br>Correlations of the Elation-Depression Scale with both the individual subjective relevance scores and the Rochester instrumentality scores for each goal indicate that happiness is more closely associated with perceived Rochester instrumentality than with subjective relevance of each goal. In most cases the correlations of happiness with the subjective relevance scores are less than .10 (ns). | | | | | | | See above. | CONST 65 p. 65 |
| - LEARNING HOW TO LEARN FROM BOOKS AND TEACHERS | | fresman males : r = +.29 (05)<br>freshman females: r = +.07 (ns)<br>junior males : r = +.16 (ns)<br>junior females : r = +.00 (ns) | AFF | 2.1 | $r_{pm}$ | + | | | | |
| - ACQUIRING AN APPRECIATION OF IDEAS | | freshman males : r = +.25 (05)<br>freshman females: r = +.25 (05)<br>junior males : r = +.05 (ns)<br>junior females : r = +.02 (ns) | AFF | 2.1 | $r_{pm}$ | + | | | | |
| - ESTABLISHING OWN PERSONAL, SOCIAL AND ACADEMIC VALUES | | freshman males : r = +.15 (ns)<br>freshman females: r = +.44 (05)<br>junior males : r = +.31 (05)<br>junior females : r = +.17 (ns) | AFF | 2.1 | $r_{pm}$ | + | | | | |
| - DEVELOPING RELATIONSHIPS WITH THE OPPOSITE SEX | | freshman males : r = +.29 (05)<br>freshman females: r = +.29 (05)<br>junior males : r = +.18 (ns)<br>junior females : r = +.14 (ns) | AFF | 2.1 | $r_{pm}$ | + | | | | |
| - CONTRIBUTING IN A DISTINGUISHED, MEANINGFUL MANNER TO SOME CAMPUS GROUP | | freshman males : r = +.11 (ns)<br>freshman females: r = +.29 (05)<br>junior males : r = -.02 (ns)<br>junior females : r = +.21 (05) | AFF | 2.1 | $r_{pm}$ | + | | | | |
| - DEVELOPING THE ABILITY TO GET ALONG WITH DIFFERENT KINDS OF PEOPLE | | freshman males : r = +.19 (ns)<br>freshman females: r = +.14 (ns)<br>junior males : r = +.15 (ns)<br>junior females : r = +.14 (ns) | AFF | 2.1 | $r_{pm}$ | + | | | | |
| - BECOMING SELF-CONFIDENT | | freshman males : r = +.39 (05)<br>freshman females: r = +.02 (ns)<br>junior males : r = +.38 (05) | AFF | 2.1 | $r_{pm}$ | + | | | | |

| | | | | | | | | | |
|---|---|---|---|---|---|---|---|---|---|
| | | junior females : r = +.32 (05) | | | | | | | |
| - PERSONAL INDEPENDENCE | | freshman males : r = +.24 (05)<br>freshman females: r = +.17 (ns)<br>junior males : r = +.28 (05)<br>junior females : r = +.05 (ns) | AFF 2.1 | $r_{pm}$ | + | | | | |
| - FINDING A SPOUSE | | freshman males : r = +.21 (05)<br>freshman females: r = +.20 (05)<br>junior males : r = +.18 (ns)<br>junior females : r = +.11 (ns) | AFF 2.1 | $r_{pm}$ | + | | | | |
| - ACHIEVING ACADEMIC DISTINCTION | | freshman males : r = +.27 (05)<br>freshman females: r = +.08 (ns)<br>junior males : r = +.24 (05)<br>junior females : r = +.03 (ns) | AFF 2.1 | $r_{pm}$ | + | | | | |
| - HAVING MANY GOOD FRIENDS | | freshman males : r = +.36 (05)<br>freshman females: r = +.28 (05)<br>junior males : r = +.17 (ns)<br>junior females : r = +.19 (ns) | AFF 2.1 | $r_{pm}$ | + | | | | |
| - DISCOVERING OWN STRONG POINTS AND LIMITATIONS | | freshman males : r = +.12 (ns)<br>freshman females: r = +.10 (ns)<br>junior males : r = +.20 (05)<br>junior females : r = +.07 (ns) | AFF 2.1 | $r_{pm}$ | + | | | | |
| - PREPARING FOR A CAREER WHICH BEGINS RIGHT AFTER GRADUATION | | freshman males : r = +.11 (ns)<br>freshman females: r = +.13 (ns)<br>junior males : r = +.05 (ns)<br>junior females : r = +.15 (ns) | AFF 2.1 | $r_{pm}$ | + | | | | |
| - PREPARING FOR A CAREER WHICH REQUIRES FURTHER STUDY BEYOND THE B.A. OR B.S. | | freshman males : r = +.36 (05)<br>freshman females: r = +.04 (ns)<br>junior males : r = +.28 (05)<br>junior females : r = +.07 (ns) | AFF 2.1 | $r_{pm}$ | + | | | | |
| ATTITUDE TOWARD COLLEGE | Product score of subjective importance of a goal and perceived instrumentality of the University of Rochester for the attainment of that goal, using a list of 14 goals (see above). Scores were summed to obtain a total score | Analysis on the basis of data from the 16 most happy and 16 least happy freshman and junior males and females (N= 4 x 32 = 128) who returned the second questionnaire.<br>Strongest among freshman males (01)<br>Lowest among junior females (ns)<br>Significant among junior males and freshman females (05) | AFF 2.1 | DM | + | t | | Undergraduate full-time college students, University of Rochester, U.S.A.<br>(see last page) | CONST 65<br>p. 63 |
| ATTITUDE TOWARD COLLEGE | Product score of subjective importance of a goal and what the ideal university could contribute to the attainment of that goal, minus product score of subjective importance and Rochester instrumentality for that goal, using a list of 14 goals (see above). | Analysis on the basis of data from the 16 most happy and 16 least happy freshman and junior males and females (N= 4 x 32 = 128) who returned the second questionnaire.<br>Strongest among freshman females (01)<br>Lowest among junor females (ns)<br>Significant among males only (05) | AFF 2.1 | DM | + | t | 05 | See above | CONST 65<br>p. 61 |
| <u>PERCEIVED INSTRUMENTALITY OF COLLEGE FOR SPECIFIC GOALS:</u> | Closed questions on the degree to which the the university is perceived as helping or hindering progress toward each of the goals mentioned.<br>(Perceived Instrumentality of College Test; see Constantinople 1965, 1967) | See also above under CONST 65<br>The goals were each scored for their importance as a goal in the S's own college experience too. These rating generally correlate less than .10 with happiness. | | | | | | Undergraduate college students, University of Rochester, U.S.A.<br>Non-probability chunk sample<br>N: 581, date: — | CONST 70<br>p. 11 |

| | | | | | | | |
|---|---|---|---|---|---|---|---|
| - LEARNING HOW TO LEARN FROM BOOKS AND TEACHERS | | freshman males : r = -.09 (ns)<br>senior males : r = +.23 (01)<br>freshman females: r = +.06 (ns)<br>senior females : r = +.03 (ns) | AFF 2.1 | r | + | | |
| - ACQUIRING AN APPRECIATION OF IDEAS | | freshman males : r = +.14 (ns)<br>senior males : r = +.29 (01)<br>freshman females: r = +.07 (ns)<br>senior females : r = +.17 (05) | AFF 2.1 | r | + | | |
| - ESTABLISHING OWN PERSONAL, SOCIAL AND ACADEMIC VALUES | | freshman males : r = +.11 (ns)<br>senior males : r = +.34 (01)<br>freshman females: r = +.20 (05)<br>senior females : r = -.01 (ns) | AFF 2.1 | r | + | | |
| - DEVELOPING RELATIONSHIPS WITH OPPOSITE SEX | | freshman males : r = +.17 (05)<br>senior males : r = +.30 (01)<br>freshman females: r = +.30 (01)<br>senior females : r = +.06 (ns) | AFF 2.1 | r | + | | |
| - CONTRIBUTING IN A DISTINGUISHED, MEANINGFUL MANNER TO SOME CAMPUS GROUP | | freshman males : r = +.08 (ns)<br>senior males : r = +.10 (ns)<br>freshman females: r = +.11 (ns)<br>senior females : r = +.22 (05) | AFF 2.1 | r | + | | |
| - DEVELOPING ABILITY TO GET ALONG WITH DIFFERENT KINDS OF PEOPLE | | freshman males : r = +.27 (01)<br>senior males : r = +.26 (01)<br>freshman females: r = +.18 (05)<br>senior females : r = +.30 (01) | AFF 2.1 | r | + | | |
| - BECOMING SELF-CONFIDENT | | freshman males : r = +.32 (01)<br>senior males : r = +.32 (01)<br>freshman females: r = +.28 (01)<br>senior females : r = +.23 (01) | AFF 2.1 | r | + | | |
| - PERSONAL INDEPENDENCE | | freshman males : r = +.07 (ns)<br>senior males : r = +.22 (05)<br>freshman females: r = +.05 (ns)<br>senior females : r = +.09 (ns) | AFF 2.1 | r | + | | |
| - FINDING A SPOUSE | | freshman males : r = +.01 (ns)<br>senior males : r = +.30 (01)<br>freshman females: r = +.25 (01)<br>senior females : r = +.01 (ns) | AFF 2.1 | r | + | | |
| - ACHIEVING ACADEMIC DINSTINCTION | | freshman males : r = +.16 (05)<br>senior males : r = +.23 (01)<br>freshman females: r = +.19 (05)<br>senior females : r = -.01 (ns) | AFF 2.1 | r | + | | |
| - HAVING MANY GOOD FRIENDS | | freshman males : r = +.24 (01)<br>senior males : r = +.22 (05)<br>freshman females: r = +.15 (ns)<br>senior females : r = +.11 (ns) | AFF 2.1 | r | + | | |
| - DISCOVERING OWN STRONG POINTS AND LIMITATIONS | | freshman males : r = +.10 (ns)<br>senior males : r = +.28 (01)<br>freshman females: r = +.22 (01)<br>senior females : r = +.24 (01) | AFF 2.1 | r | + | | |
| - PREPARING FOR CAREER WHICH BEGINS RIGHT AFTER GRADUATION | | freshman males : r = +.05 (ns)<br>senior males : r = -.03 (ns)<br>freshman females: r = +.05 (ns)<br>senior females : r = +.27 (01) | AFF 2.1 | r | + | | |

| | | | | | | | | | |
|---|---|---|---|---|---|---|---|---|---|
| - PREPARING FOR A CAREER WHICH REQUIRES FURTHER STUDY BEYOND THE B.A. OR B.S. | | freshman males : r = +.16 (05)<br>senior males : r = +.27 (01)<br>freshman females: r = +.10 (ns)<br>senior females : r = -.08 (ns) | AFF 2.1 | r | + | | | Undergraduate college students, University of Rochesterm U.S.A.<br>Non-probability chunk sample<br>N: 581, date: — | CONST 70<br>p. 11 |
| POSITIVE ATTITUDE TOWARD SCHOOL | 15-item index containing items that stress the intrinsic value of education | | COMP 1.2 | $r_{pm}$ | +.38 | | 001 | Public highschool boys, U.S.A.<br>Probability multi-stage sample<br>N: 2213 in 1966, 1886 in 1968 and 1799 in 1969, date: fall, 1966, spring, 1968 and spring, 1969 | BACHM 67/70<br>p. 242 |
| NEGATIVE ATTITUDE TOWARD SCHOOL | 8-item index containing questions ranging from general dissatisfaction with school to a devaluation of school in comparison to other sources of experience | | COMP 1.2 | $r_{pm}$ | -.24 | | 001 | See above | BACHM 67/70<br>p. 242 |
| HAVING PLANS TO GO TO COLLEGE | Open question on future plans; other plans vs plan to enter post- high school education | | COMP 1.2 | $r_{pm}$ | +.07 | | 05 | See above | BACHM 67/70<br>p. 243 |

## E I.2.2 - SCHOOL ABILITY

| | | | | | | | | | |
|---|---|---|---|---|---|---|---|---|---|
| EXAMINATIONAL ABILITY | Rating on a 7-point scale on the basis of 3 terminal examinations<br>The result of the first and the third were pooled to give one set of values, and the second furnished the other. | | AFF 5.2 | $r_{pm}$ | +.09 | | | Male students, England<br>Non-probability chunk sample<br>N: 194, date: 1912 - 1913 | WEBB 15<br>p. 26 |
| INTELLECTUAL PERFORMANCE IN COLLEGE | Student's yearly grade average | freshman year : r = +.50 (05)<br>sophomore year: r = +.53 (05)<br>junior year : r = +.15 (ns)<br>senior year : r = +.31 (ns) | AFF 3.1 | $r_{pm}$ | +.43 | t | 10 | Male college students, U.S.A.<br>Non-probability chunk sample<br>N: 17, date: ± 1960 | WESSM 66/2<br>p. 123 |
| ACADEMIC PERFORMANCE RELATIVE TO POTENTIAL ABILITIES | Discrepancy between predicted rank list (PRL) before college entrance and actual grade average for the four years | The PRL = expected college grade average on the basis of the student's previous secondary school record, level of preparation, and aptitude tests | AFF 3.1 | $r_{pm}$ | -.34 | t | ns | See above | WESSM 66/2<br>p. 123 |
| ACADEMIC STATUS | SAT - Verbal score in the form of local percentile rank | Analysis on the basis of a comparison of happy and unhappy students (resp. 120 males, 157 females and 154 males, 94 females: N= 525)<br>Unaffected by sex and stage of study | AFF 2.1 | DM | ± 0 | t | ns | Undergraduate full-time college students, U.S.A.<br>Non-probability chunk sample<br>N: 952, date: March, 1965 | CONST 65<br>p. 68 |
| ACADEMIC STATUS | Cumulative grade point average (GPA) | Analysis is based on a comparison of happy and unhappy students (N= 525, see above)<br>Positive among males only<br>Significant (05) among sophomore males only<br>Unaffected by stage of study among females | AFF 2.1 | DM | + | t | 01 | See above | CONST 65<br>p. 67 |
| ACADEMIC STATUS (DISCREPANCY BETWEEN APTITUDE AND ACHIEVEMENT) | Achievement index computed by subtracting the SAT - Verbal score from that associated with the cumulative grade point average (see above) | Computed for freshmen and juniors only (N = 274) | AFF 2.1 | D% | + | t | ns | See above | CONST 65<br>p. 69 |
| ACADEMIC STATUS | Cumulative grade point average | | AFF 2.1 | | | | ns | Female college seniors, U.S.A.<br>Non-probability chunk sample<br>N: 162, date: May - June, 1966 | PORTE 67<br>p. 96 |

| | | | | | | | | | |
|---|---|---|---|---|---|---|---|---|---|
| ACADEMIC ACHIEVEMENT (GRADES) | Question on average grade in past year | | COMP 1.2 | $r_{pm}$ | +.10 | | 01 | Public highschool boys, U.S.A.<br>Probability multi-stage sample<br>N: 2213 in 1966, 1886 in 1968 and 1799 in 1969, date: fall, 1966, spring, 1968 and spring, 1969 | BACHM 67/70<br>p. 247 |
| SELF-PERCEIVED SCHOOL ABILITY | 3-item index of closed questions on self-perceived school ability, intelligence, and reading ability compared with other boys of the same age | | COMP 1.2 | $r_{pm}$ | +.12 | | 01 | See above | BACHM 67/70<br>p. 242 |

## E I.2.3 - STAGE OF STUDY

| | | | | | | | | | |
|---|---|---|---|---|---|---|---|---|---|
| BEING A FRESHMAN | Junior vs freshman | L-shaped curve: positive relationship among unhappy students only | COMP 2.2 | | + | | ns | Female college students, New York, U.S.A.<br>Type of construction unclear<br>N: 238, date: — | WASHB 41<br>p. 283 |
| STAGE OF STUDY | Freshmen / sophomores / juniors / seniors | Stronger among males<br>L-shaped curve among males: Stronger relationship from freshman to junior years<br>U-shaped curve among females: sophomores being most unhappy | AFF 2.1 | DM | + | t | 01 | Undergraduate full-time college students, U.S.A.<br>Non-probability chunk sample<br>N: 952, date: March, 1965 | CONST 65<br>p. 50 |
| EDUCATIONAL LEVEL | freshman / sophomore / junior / senior / graduate student / other | | HAPP 1.1 | $r_{pm}$ | | t | ns | Male undergraduates, U.S.A.<br>Non-probability chunk sample<br>N: 103, date: ± 1967 | HEERE 69<br>p. 28 |
| TEACHING LEVEL | Elementary / secondary / fifth year | | HAPP 1.1 | G' | +.09 | Gt' | ns | Student teachers, Chapel Hill, U.S.A.<br>Probability sample, proportionally stratified by teaching level<br>N: 75, date: spring, 1967 | GONZA 67<br>p. 82 |

## E I.2.4 - EXTRACURRICULAR ACTIVITIES

see 'Use of Leisure Time' (L 3.3)

## E I.3 - VARIOUS FACTORS CONCERNING EDUCATION AND SCHOOL

| | | | | | | | | | |
|---|---|---|---|---|---|---|---|---|---|
| SUBJECT-MATTER MAJORS (IN THE PROGRAM OFFERED BY THE SCHOOL OF EDUCATION) | Foreign Languages / Humanities / English / Elementary Education / Physical or Special Education / Natural Sciences / Social Sciences / Mathematics | The firstmentioned subject-matter is reported mostly by unhappy students; the last most by happy students | HAPP 1.1 | D% | + | | | Student teachers, Chapel Hill, U.S.A.<br>Probability sample, proportionally stratified by teaching level<br>N: 75, date: spring, 1967 | GONZA 67<br>p. 84 |
| PRESSURE OF ACADEMIC WORK | Repeated closed question on immediate pressure during past day, scored every day during six weeks<br>none / rather light / moderate / fairly heavy / very heavy / extremely heavy | | AFF 3.1 | $r_{pm}$ | -.33 | t | ns | Female college students, U.S.A.<br>Non-probability chunk sample<br>N: 21, date: ± 1960 | WESSM 66/1<br>p. 277 |
| PRESSURE OF ACADEMIC WORK | See above | | AFF 3.1 | $r_{pm}$ | -.34 | t | ns | Male college students, U.S.A.<br>Non-probability chunk sample<br>N: 17, date: ± 1960 | WESSM 66/2<br>p. 66 |

| | | | | | | | | | |
|---|---|---|---|---|---|---|---|---|---|
| PRESSURE OF ACADEMIC WORK | Repeated closed question on immediate pressure during past day, scored every day during one month<br>none / rather light / moderate / fairly heavy / very heavy / extremely heavy | | AFF 3.1<br>HAPP 3.1 | $r_{pm}$<br>$r_{pm}$ | +.21<br>-.07 | | ns<br>ns | Undergraduate students, U.S.A.<br>Non-probability chunk sample<br>N: 67, date: summer, 1970 | GORMA 71<br>p. 216/222 |
| BEING INTERESTED IN STUDY HABITS | Closed question | | COMP 4.1 | | | | ns | Students, U.S.A.<br>Non-probability chunk sample<br>N: 1651, date: — | SYMON 37<br>p. 292 |
| HAVING PROBLEMS WITH STUDY HABITS | Closed question | High school students only<br>L-shaped curve: significantly positive among happier students only | COMP 4.1 | | + | | | See above | SYMON 37<br>p. 292 |
| MENTAL WORK BESTOWED UPON USUAL STUDIES, extent of - | Class-master rating on a 7-point scale on the basis of observation | | AFF 5.3 | $r_{pm}$ | +.41 | | | Schoolboys, England<br>Non-probability chunk sample<br>N: 140, date: 1912 - 1913 | WEBB 15<br>p. 27 |
| BODILY ACTIVITY DURING SCHOOL HOURS, degree of - | See above | | AFF 5.3 | $r_{pm}$ | +.59 | | | See above | WEBB 15<br>p. 27 |
| MENTAL WORK BESTOWED UPON USUAL STUDIES, extent of - | Trained peer-rating on a 7-point scale on the basis of observation | | AFF 5.2 | $r_{pm}$ | -.02 | | | Male students, England<br>Non-probability chunk sample<br>N: 194, date: 1912 - 1913 | WEBB 15<br>p. 26 |
| BODILY ACTIVITY DURING BUSINESS HOURS, degree of - | See above | | AFF 5.2 | $r_{pm}$ | +.44 | | | See above | WEBB 15<br>p. 26 |
| REBELLIOUS BEHAVIORS IN SCHOOL | 13-item index of closed question on fighting with other students, not working hard, skipping classes, copying someone else's assignments | | COMP 1.2 | $r_{pm}$ | -.26 | | 001 | Public highschool boys, U.S.A.<br>Probability multi-stage sample<br>N: 2213 in 1966, 1886 in 1968 and 1799 in 1969, date: fall, 1966, spring, 1968 and spring, 1969 | BACHM 67/70<br>p. 243 |
| SCHOOL SOCIAL CLASS | Score on the basis of the percentage of juniors and seniors of 'upper class' status | When standardized on participation in extra-curricular activities: $G_s = +.12$<br>Stronger in middle and upper class: G = +.11<br>Lower in the lower class: G = +.05 | HAPP 1.1 | G<br>V | +.14<br>.08 | $Chi^2$ | 01 | Juniors and seniors attending public high schools in New York State, U.S.A.<br>Probability cluster sample of 10 public high schools<br>N: sample A: 1682, sample B: 1664, sample C: 1678, date: 1960 | BRENN 70<br>p. 113/346 |
| | | When standardized on participation in extra-curricolair activities: $G_s = +.04$.<br>Unaffected by social class. | AFF 1.1 | G<br>V | +.07<br>.04 | $Chi^2$ | 01 | | |

# E2 ETHNICITY



## E 2.1 - BLACK - WHITE DIFFERENCES IN THE U.S.A.

| BLACK RACE | White vs black | See remarks in excerpt (Part II) | HAPP 1.1 | G' | - | Gt' | | National adult populations, U.S.A. Non-probability quota samples and probability area samples N: 25617, date: 1946 - 1948 (5 surveys referred to as 1946), 1956 (3 surveys), 1965 (2 surveys) | MANNI 72 p. 37-59 |
|---|---|---|---|---|---|---|---|---|---|

| | 1946 | 1956 | 1966 |
|---|---|---|---|
| total population : | -.04 | $-.26^{xx}$ | $-.37^{xx}$ |
| college graduate : | +.11 | $-.50^{xx}$ | $-.64^{xx}$ |
| college incomplete: | -.15 | $-.50^{xx}$ | -.29 |
| high school grad. : | -.00 | $-.38^{xx}$ | $-.60^{xx}$ |
| high sch. incompl.: | -.08 | $-.21^{x}$ | $-.40^{xx}$ |
| 8th grade & less : | +.11 | -.04 | -.09 |
| (semi-) prof'ls : | +.03 | $-.38^{x}$ | $-.72^{xx}$ |
| business ex. : | -.26 | $-.52^{xx}$ | $-.82^{xx}$ |
| white collar : | -.22 | $-.32^{x}$ | $-.54^{xx}$ |
| skilled workers : | -.11 | $-.34^{xx}$ | $-.30^{x}$ |
| semi- & unsk.work.: | $+.22^{xx}$ | $-.16^{x}$ | $-.19^{x}$ |
| service workers : | -.03 | $-.26^{x}$ | $-.36^{xx}$ |
| farmers : | -.14 | +.08 | -.00 |
| non-manual : | $+.17^{x}$ | $+.41^{xx}$ | $+.68^{xx}$ |
| manual : | -.04 | $+.22^{x}$ | $+.29^{xx}$ |
| high income : | -.04 | | $-.80^{xx}$ |
| average income : | -.08 | | $-.43^{xx}$ |
| low income : | +.02 | | $-.13^{x}$ |
| city size: | | | |
| 500,000 + : | -.03 | $-.35^{xx}$ | -.03 |
| 100,000 - 499,999 : | -.08 | $-.24^{xx}$ | -.08 |
| 10,000 - 99,999 : | -.02 | $-.39^{xx}$ | $-.50^{xx}$ |
| 2500 - 9999 : | -.03 | $-.84^{xx}$ | (X) |
| rural non-farm : | +.32 | -.10 | -.01 |
| farm : | -.11 | +.04 | -.34 |
| non-south : | +.06 | $+.29^{xx}$ | $+.30^{xx}$ |
| south : | +.07 | $+.14^{x}$ | $+.12^{x}$ |
| age 70+ : | +.11 | -.23 | +.08 |
| age 60 - 69 : | $+.29^{x}$ | +.03 | $-.49^{x}$ |
| age 50 - 59 : | -.03 | -.05 | -.30 |
| age 40 - 49 : | -.17 | -.08 | $-.60^{xx}$ |
| age 30 - 39 : | $-.19^{x}$ | $-.48^{xx}$ | $-.44^{xx}$ |
| age 20 - 29 : | -.03 | $-.46^{xx}$ | $-.35^{x}$ |

$G' = ^{x}$ means: $p < .05$
$G' = ^{xx}$ means: $p < .01$
(X) means N is too small

| | | | | | | | | | |
|---|---|---|---|---|---|---|---|---|---|
| WHITE RACE | negro vs white | | HAPP 1.1 | G' | +.01 | Gt' | ns | National adult population, U.S.A.<br>Non-probability quota sample<br>N: 2377, date: February, 1946 | WESSM 56<br>p. 183 |
| WHITE RACE | black vs white | | HAPP 2.1<br>HAPP 3.1<br>CON 1.1 | r<br>r<br>r | +.08<br>+.12<br>+.11 | | | National adult population, U.S.A.<br>Cantril (1965) modified probability sample<br>N: 1406, date: 1959 | BORTN 70<br>p. 44 |
| WHITE RACE | black vs white | Gammas based on proportions 'very happy' answers.<br>age 45+ : G' = +.22 (05)<br>age 35 - 44 : G' = +.21 (ns)<br>age -35 : G' = +.67 (01)<br>Unaffected by sex<br>high education : G' = +.60 (01)<br>medium education: G' = +.51 (01)<br>low education : G' = -.01 (ns)<br>high income : G' = +.48 (01)<br>medium income : G' = +.38 (01)<br>low income : G' = +.16 (ns)<br>white collar : G' = +.65 (01)<br>blue collar : G' = +.19 (ns) | HAPP 1.1 | G' | +.36 | Gt' | 01 | Non-institutionalized adults, U.S.A.<br>Type of sample construction unclear<br>N: 1602, date: March, 1972 | ALSTO 74<br>p. 100 |
| WHITE RACE | black vs white | Unaffected by age | HAPP 1.1 | $r_{pm}$ | +.12 | | 01 | Non-institutionalized adults, U.S.A.<br>Probability samples<br>N: 1547, date: 1972, 1973 | SPREI 74<br>p. 457 |
| RACE | | | HAPP 3.1<br>(1st instr.) | $h^2$ | .03 | | | National adult population, U.S.A.<br>Probability area sample (first sample)<br>N: 1297, date: May, 1972 | ANDRE 74<br>p. 20 |
| WHITE RACE | negro vs white | Gamma based on proportion 'not too happy' answers.<br>Unaffected by educational level<br>Stronger at lower income levels, especially among those of high education | HAPP 1.1 | G' | +.54 | Gt' | 01 | Adults, urban areas, U.S.A.<br>Probability area samples<br>N: 2787, date: January, 1963 - January, 1964 | BRADB 69<br>p. 47-49 |
| WHITE RACE | negro vs white | | HAPP 2.1 | G' | -.17 | Gt' | ns | Aged chronically-ill patients, U.S.A.<br>Probability samples<br>N: 167, date: 1959 | HENLE 67<br>p. 69 |

## E 2.2 - FURTHER ETHNIC DIFFERENCES IN THE U.S.A.

| | | | | | | | | | |
|---|---|---|---|---|---|---|---|---|---|
| ETHNICITY | | | HAPP 1.1 | | | | ns | Non-institutionalized adults, U.S.A.<br>Probability multi-stage area sample<br>N: 2460, date: spring, 1957 | GURIN 60<br>p. 207 |
| WHITE RACE | non-white ve white | non-white: Mean = 5.3<br>white : Mean = 6.7 | HAPP 3.1 | DM | + | | | National adult population, U.S.A.<br>Probability sample<br>N: 1549, date: ± 1960 | CANTR 65/1<br>p. 375 |
| RACE | non-white vs white | See remarks in excerpt (Part II).<br>non-white: Mean = 5.77 (5.84)<br>white : Mean = 6.63 (6.96) | HAPP 3.1 | DM | + | | | Non-institutionalized adult population, U.S.A.<br>Multi-stage probability sample stratified by size of locality<br>N: 1588, date: January, 1971 (+ 1964) | CANTR 71<br>p. 66 |

| | | | | | | | | | |
|---|---|---|---|---|---|---|---|---|---|
| ETHNICITY | Anglo / Black / Mexican-American | Mexican-American: males : Mean = 6.5<br>females: Mean = 5.9<br>Black : males : Mean = 6.2<br>females: Mean = 6.0<br>Anglo : males : Mean = 6.1<br>females: Mean = 5.9 | AFF 2.3 | DM | + | | ns | Adults, Houston, Texas, U.S.A.<br>Non-probability purposive quota sample stratified by age, sex, occupational skill level and ethnicity<br>N: 1441, date: autumn, 1969 | GAITZ 72<br>p. 63 |
| RACE | | Open ward : r = +.05 (ns)<br>closed ward: r = +.20 (ns) | AFF 5.1 | $r_{pm}$ | + | | ns | Institutionalized mentally retarded males, U.S.A.<br>Non-probability chunk sample<br>N: 149, date: — | PANDE 71<br>p. 329 |
| FOREIGN BORN | Native born vs foreign born | Negative relationship disappears when controlled for income | AFF 1.1 | | - | $Chi^2$ | | Persons over 65, Metropolitan Boston, U.S.A.<br>Probability area sample<br>N: 1335, date: 1965 | FOWLE 69<br>p. 733 |

## E 2.3 - ETHNIC DIFFERENCES IN OTHER COUNTRIES

| | | | | | | | | | |
|---|---|---|---|---|---|---|---|---|---|
| RACE | negro / mixed / white | mixed: Mean = 5.9<br>negro: Mean = 6.0<br>white : Mean = 6.5 | HAPP 3.1 | DM | + | | | National adult population, Cuba<br>Probability area sample<br>N: 992, date: ± 1960 | CANTR 65/1<br>p. 366 |
| NATIONALITY | Slovenian / Serbian / Croatian / other | Slovenian: Mean = 5.3<br>Serbian : Mean = 5.2<br>Croatian : Mean = 4.8<br>other : Mean = 4.8 | HAPP 3.1 | DM | - | | | National adult population, Yugoslavia<br>Probability sample<br>N: 1523, date: ± 1960 | CANTR 65/1<br>p. 377 |

# F 1 FAMILY

see also 'Marital status' (M 1)
'Marriage' (M 2)



## F 1.1 - FAMILY OF ORIGIN

### F 1.1.1 - SOCIO-ECONOMIC BACKGROUND

| | | | | | | | | | |
|---|---|---|---|---|---|---|---|---|---|
| HIGH EDUCATIONAL STATUS OF FATHER | Non-graduate vs college graduate | U-shaped curve: girls with a non-graduate father reporting significantly more 'average happiness' | COMP 2.2 | . | ± 0 | | ns | Female college students, New York, U.S.A.<br>Type of construction unclear<br>N: 238, date: — | WASHB 41<br>p. 283 |
| EDUCATIONAL LEVEL OF FATHER | Some grade school or grade school graduate / some high school or high school graduate / some college or college graduate / post graduate college work | | HAPP 1.1 | G<br>V | +.04<br>.03 | $Chi^2$ | ns | Juniors and seniors attending public high schools in New York State, U.S.A.<br>Probability cluster sample of 10 public high schools<br>Sample A: N= 1682, sample B: N= 1664, sample C: N= 1678<br>date: 1960 | BRENN 70<br>p. 113/338 |
| | | | AFF 1.1 | G<br>V | +.03<br>.02 | $Chi^2$ | ns | | |
| EDUCATIONAL LEVEL OF MOTHER | Some grade school or grade school graduate / some high school or high school graduate / some college or college graduate / post graduate college work | When standardized on:<br>- participation in extracurricular activities: $G_s$ = +.09<br>- social class: $G_s$ = +.06 | HAPP 1.1 | G<br>V | +.09<br>.04 | $Chi^2$ | 05 | See above | BRENN 70<br>p. 113/334 |
| | | | AFF 1.1 | G<br>V | +.04<br>.03 | $Chi^2$ | ns | | |
| INCOME LEVEL OF FATHER'S OCCUPATION | Under $ 3400 / $ 3400 - $ 5000 / over $ 5000 | | HAPP 1.1 | G<br>V | +.07<br>.04 | $Chi^2$ | ns | See above | BRENN 70<br>p. 113/334 |
| | | | AFF 1.1 | G<br>V | +.01<br>.02 | $Chi^2$ | ns | | |
| SOCIAL CLASS | Weighted score based on the medium score of father's occupation, father's education and father's primary source of income<br>lower / middle / upper | When standardized on:<br>- having fun in life: $G_s$ = +.07<br>- frequency of low mood: $G_s$ = +.15<br>- tending to be a lonely person: $G_s$ = +.08<br>- self-esteem: $G_s$ = +.08<br>- having faith in people: $G_s$ = +.09<br>- sensivity to criticism: $G_s$ = +.09<br>- presenting a false self: $G_s$ = +.13<br>- participation in extracurricular activities: $G_s$ = +.14<br>- extent of dating: $G_s$ = +.14<br>- hours spent on work for pay: $G_s$ = +.12<br>- disruption of family relationships: $G_s$ = +.12<br>- number of children in the family: $G_s$ = +.10<br>- school social class: $G_s$ = +.12<br>having fun in life and tending to be a lonely person: $G_s$ = +.07<br>(to be continued on next page) | HAPP 1.1 | G<br>V | +.12<br>.05 | $Chi^2$ | ns | See above | BRENN 70<br>p. 113/330 |

| | | | | | | | | | |
|---|---|---|---|---|---|---|---|---|---|
| | | - having fun in life, and self-esteem: $G_s = +.06$<br>- tending to be a lonely person, and self-esteem : $G_s = +.06$<br>- having faith in people, and self-esteem $G_s = +.07$<br>- sensitivity to criticism, and self-esteem : $G_s = +.05$<br>When Ss are regrouped, so that the upper third of middle class = upper class, and lower third of middle class = lower class : $G = +.06$<br>When standardized on educational level of mother : $G_s = +.04$<br><br>When standardized on:<br>- having fun in life: $G_s = +.03$<br>- frequency of low mood: $G_s = +.08$<br>- tending to be a lonely person: $G_s = +.04$<br>- self-esteem: $G_s = +.03$<br>- having faith in people: $G_s = +.02$<br>- sensitivity to criticism: $G_s = +.04$<br>presenting a false self: $G_s = +.06$<br>- participation in extracurricular activities: $G_s = +.06$<br>- extent of dating: $G_s = +.07$<br>- hours spent on work for pay: $G_s = +.03$<br>- disruption of family relationships: $G_s = +.05$<br>- number of children in the family: $G_s = +.05$<br>- school social class: $G_s = +.05$<br>- tending to be a lonely person, and having fun in life: $G_s = +.04$<br>- self-esteem, and having fun in life: $G_s = +.01$<br>- self-esteem, and tending to be a lonely person: $G_s = +.02$<br>- self-esteem, and having faith in people: $G_s = +.01$<br>- self-esteem, and sensitivity to criticism: $G_s = +.02$<br>When Ss are regrouped, so that the upper third of middle class = upper class, and the lower third of middle class = lower class: $G = +.01$<br>When standardized on educational level of mother: $G_s = .00$ | AFF 1.1 | G<br>V | +.05<br>.03 | $Chi^2$ | ns | | |
| WORK SETTING OF FATHER | Closed question: father works for himself and / or income from profits or fees vs works in organization and / or income from wages or a salary | | HAPP 1.1 | $r_{pm}$ | | t | ns | Male undergraduates, U.S.A.<br>Non-probability chunk sample<br>N: 103, date: ± 1967 | HEERE 69<br>p. 28 |

## F 1.1.2 - BROKEN HOME BACKGROUND

| | | | | | | | | | |
|---|---|---|---|---|---|---|---|---|---|
| PARENTS ARE LIVING TOGETHER | Broken vs unbroken homes | L-shaped curve: significant for the 'unhappy' only | COMP 2.2 | | + | | s | Female college students, New York, U.S.A.<br>Type of construction unclear<br>N: 238, date: — | WASHB 41<br>p. 283 |
| BROKEN HOME BACKGROUND | S lived with both of his real parents until he was 16 years of age vs separated from at least one of his parents through divorce. | Analysis on the basis of proportion 'not too happy' answers. | HAPP 1.1 | G' | -.30 | Gt' | 01 | Non-institutionalized adults, U.S.A.<br>Probability multi-stage sample<br>N: 2460, date: spring, 1957 | GURIN 60<br>p. 246 |

| | | | | | | | | | |
|---|---|---|---|---|---|---|---|---|---|
| BROKEN HOME BACKGROUND | S lived with both of his real parents until he was 16 years of age vs separation through the death of one or both parents. | Analysis on the basis of proportion 'not too happy' answers. | HAPP 1.1 | G' | -.11 | Gt' | ns | Non-institutionalized adults, U.S.A.<br>(See last page) | GURIN 60<br>p. 246 |
| DISRUPTION OF FAMILY RELATIONSHIPS | 2-item index of closed questions on parents living together / divorced / separated / separated by death, and ever had stepparents, foster parents or guardians | When standardized on social class: G = -.21 | HAPP 1.1<br><br>AFF 1.1 | G<br>V<br>G<br>V | -.21<br>.07<br>-.05<br>.04 | $Chi^2$<br><br>$Chi^2$ | 01<br><br>01 | Juniors and seniors attending public highschools in New York State, U.S.A.<br>Probability cluster sample of 10 public highschools<br>N: sample A: 1682, sample B: 1664, sample C: 1678<br>date: 1960 | BRENN 70<br>p. 113/350 |
| PARENTS ARE LIVING TOGETHER | Closed question: divorced / separated / living together | | HAPP 1.1 | $r_{pm}$ | + | t | s | Male undergraduates, U.S.A.<br>Non-probability chunk sample<br>N: 103, date: ± 1967 | HEERE 69<br>p. 28 |
| BROKEN HOMES IN CHILDHOOD | S lived with real father/mother during the first 15 years of his life yes vs no | | AFF 1.3 | $\bar{DR}$ | - | | 05 | Adults, Alameda County, U.S.A.<br>Probability sample<br>N: 6928, date: 1965 | BERKM 71<br>p. 42 |

## F 1.1.3 - SOCIO-PSYCHOLOGICAL CLIMATE IN FAMILY OF ORIGIN

### F 1.1.3.1 - RELATIONSHIP BETWEEN ONE'S PARENTS

| | | | | | | | | | |
|---|---|---|---|---|---|---|---|---|---|
| WARM RELATIONSHIP BETWEEN PARENTS | Closed question rated on a 9-point scale cool and distant / neither cool nor warm / very warm and close | | HAPP 1.1 | $r_{pm}$ | +.46 | t | s | Male undergraduates, U.S.A.<br>Non-probability chunk sample<br>N: 103, date: ± 1967 | HEERE 69<br>p. 28 |
| PARENTS ENJOY EACH OTHER'S COMPANY | Closed question rated on a 5-point scale not really / very much so | | HAPP 1.1 | $r_{pm}$ | + | t | s | See above | HEERE 69<br>p. 28 |
| PARENTS ENJOY DOING THINGS TOGETHER | Closed question rated on a 5-point scale very few / average / a great many | | HAPP 1.1 | $r_{pm}$ | +.39 | t | s | See above | HEERE 69<br>p. 28 |
| MARITAL HAPPINESS DURING THE CHILD'S AGE FROM 9 TO 14 YEARS | Rating of expressive behavior, made by three judges on the basis of interview-protocols (one to three interviews) for:<br>'Does this mother have a good marital relationship?'<br>8-item index: each item scored on a 7-point scale ranging from 'not at all true' to 'extremely true' | This variable was correlated with the child's hedonic level at the ages of 10-36 months. See also instrument and remarks in excerpt (Part II). For boys N= 15, for girls N=16.<br>10-12 / 13-15 / 18-24 / 27-36<br>boys: -.04 / -.08 / +.08 / +.08<br>girls: +.13 / -.04 / -.25 / +.00 | AFF 5.1 | $r_{pm}$ | | | | Children and their mothers, Berkeley, California, U.S.A.<br>Non-probability chunk sample<br>N: 108, date: 1928 - 1943 | SCHAE 63<br>p. 117/118 |
| HAPPINESS OF PARENTS' MARRIAGE IN CHILDHOOD | Closed question: very unhappy / unhappy / somewhat unhappy / somewhat happy / happy / very happy | | AFF 1.3 | $\bar{DR}$ | +.08 | | 05 | Adults, Alameda County, U.S.A.<br>Probability sample<br>N: 6928, date: 1965 | BERKM 71<br>p. 42 |

# F 1.1.3.2 - PARENTAL CHARACTERISTICS AND BEHAVIOR

## PARENTAL CHARACTERISTICS AS PERCEIVED BY THE SUBJECT

| | | | | | | | | |
|---|---|---|---|---|---|---|---|---|
| HAVING A DOMINANT FATHER | Closed question rated on a 9-point scale very submissive / moderate / very dominant | HAPP 1.1 | $r_{pm}$ | - | t | s | Male undergaduates, U.S.A. Non-probability chunk sample N: 103, date: ± 1967 | HEERE 69 p. 28 |
| HAVING A DOMINANT MOTHER | Closed question rated on a 9-point scale very submissive / moderate / very dominant | HAPP 1.1 | $r_{pm}$ | - | t | s | See above | HEERE 69 p. 28 |
| FATHER IS DEMANDING VERY LITTLE | Closed question rated on a 9-point scale demands a lot / moderate / very little | HAPP 1.1 | $r_{pm}$ | | t | ns | See above | HEERE 69 p. 28 |
| MOTHER IS DEMANDING VERY LITTLE | Closed question rated on a 9-point scale demands a lot / moderate / very little | HAPP 1.1 | $r_{pm}$ | +.21 | t | s | See above | HEERE 69 p. 28 |
| HAVING AN AFFECTIONATE FATHER | Closed question rated on a 5-point scale detached and aloof / quite openly affectionate | HAPP 1.1 | $r_{pm}$ | +.24 | t | s | See above | HEERE 69 p. 28 |
| HAVING AN AFFECTIONATE MOTHER | Closed question rated on a 5-point scale detached and aloof / quite openly affectionate | HAPP 1.1 | $r_{pm}$ | +.21 | t | s | See above | HEERE 69 p. 28 |
| FATHER HAS HIGH EXPECTATIONS | Closed question: no / to some extent / yes | HAPP 1.1 | $r_{pm}$ | | t | ns | See above | HEERE 69 p. 28 |
| FATHER IS 'WEARING THE PANTS' IN THE FAMILY | Closed question: mother / neither (equal in influence) / father | HAPP 1.1 | $r_{pm}$ | -.18 | t | s | See above | HEERE 69 p. 28 |
| FATHER IS SEEN AS A STRONG PERSON | Closed question rated on a 9-point scale weak and passive / neither weak nor strong / very strong | HAPP 1.1 | $r_{pm}$ | +.47 | t | s | See above | HEERE 69 p. 28 |
| MOTHER IS SEEN AS A STRONG PERSON | Closed question rated on a 9-point scale weak and passive / neither weak nor strong / very strong | HAPP 1.1 | $r_{pm}$ | | t | ns | See above | HEERE 69 p. 28 |
| FATHER HAS CLEAR AND STRONG BELIEFS | Closed question rated on a 9-point scale beliefs very uncertain / some uncertainty / very strong and clear beliefs | HAPP 1.1 | $r_{pm}$ | +.26 | t | s | See above | HEERE 69 p. 28 |
| CLOSE RELATIONSHIP WITH FATHER | Closed question rated on a 5-point scale not close at all / very close | HAPP 1.1 | $r_{pm}$ | + | t | s | See above | HEERE 69 p. 28 |
| WARMTH AND SPONTANEOUSNESS OF MOTHER | Closed question rated on a 9-point scale very cool and restrained / moderately so / very warm and spontaneous | HAPP 1.1 | $r_{pm}$ | + | t | s | See above | HEERE 69 p. 28 |
| PROTECTION AND SUPPORT FROM PARENTS IN MOMENTS OF STRESS | Closed question: no / to some extent / yes | HAPP 1.1 | $r_{pm}$ | + | t | s | See above | HEERE 69 p. 28 |
| PARENTS WERE PERMISSIVE AND LENIENT | Closed question rated on a 9-point scale very strict / about average / very permissive and lenient | HAPP 1.1 | $r_{pm}$ | | t | ns | See above | HEERE 69 p. 28 |
| BEING SHELTERED BY PARENTS | Closed question rated on a 5-point scale not at all / very much | HAPP 1.1 | $r_{pm}$ | | t | ns | See above | HEERE 69 p. 28 |
| ENCOURAGEMENT AND GUIDANCE BY PARENTS | Closed question rated on a 9-point scale pretty much on my own / some guidance / parents gave lots of guidance | HAPP 1.1 | $r_{pm}$ | | t | ns | See above | HEERE 69 p. 28 |

| | | | | | | | | | |
|---|---|---|---|---|---|---|---|---|---|
| PARENTS ARE SURE IN THEIR DECISIONS HAVING TO DO WITH ONE'S DISCIPLINE | Closed question rated on a 9-point scale always very doubtful / sometimes / always certain and sure | | HAPP 1.1 | $r_{pm}$ | +.20 | t | s | Male undergraduates, U.S.A.<br>(See last page) | HEERE 69<br>p. 28 |
| BEING OFTEN ALLOWED BY PARENTS TO MAKE OWN DECISIONS | Closed question rated on a 9-point scale almost never / sometimes / nearly all the time | | HAPP 1.1 | $r_{pm}$ | +.33 | t | s | | HEERE 69<br>p. 28 |
| FREEDOM TO DECIDE HOW LATE TO STAY OUT | Closed question rated on a 5-point scale not at all (parents decide) / completely free | | HAPP 1.1 | $r_{pm}$ | | t | ns | See above | HEERE 69<br>p. 28 |
| FREEDOM TO DRINK ALCOHOL | Closed question rated on a 5-point scale not at all (parents decide) / completely free | | HAPP 1.1 | $r_{pm}$ | | t | ns | See above | HEERE 69<br>p. 28 |
| FREEDOM TO STAY OVERNIGHT AT SOMEONE'S HOUSE | Closed question rated on a 5-point scale not at all (parents decide) / completely free | | HAPP 1.1 | $r_{pm}$ | | t | ns | See above | HEERE 69<br>p. 28 |
| FREEDOM TO TAKE OWN TRIPS OR GO TRAVELLING | Closed question rated on a 5-point scale not at all (parents decide) / completely free | | HAPP 1.1 | $r_{pm}$ | | t | ns | See above | HEERE 69<br>p. 28 |
| FREEDOM IN DATING | Closed question rated on a 5-point scale not at all (parents decide) / completely free | | HAPP 1.1 | $r_{pm}$ | | t | ns | See above | HEERE 69<br>p. 28 |
| FREEDOM TO FOLLOW OWN INTERESTS | Closed question rated on a 9-point scale not much / some / considerable freedom | | HAPP 1.1 | $r_{pm}$ | +.30 | t | s | See above | HEERE 69<br>p. 28 |
| DECISIONS THOROUGHLY DISCUSSED IN THE FAMILY | Closed question rated on a 9-point scale usually no discussion / some discussion / very thorough discussion | | HAPP 1.1 | $r_{pm}$ | +.33 | t | s | See above | HEERE 69<br>p. 28 |
| PAST PARENTAL TREATMENT AND RELATIONSHIPS | Scores derived from a 212-item inventory of past life experiences | A number of scores on parental treatments or relationships were derived. None of them appeared to show much relationship to mood level. | AFF 3.1 | | | t | ns | Male college students, U.S.A.<br>Non-probability chunk sample<br>N: 17, date: $\pm$ 1960 | WESSM 66/2<br>p. 122 |
| PERCEIVED LIBERALITY OF SEXUAL ATTITUDES OF PARENTS | 6-item questionnaire containing sexual behaviors varying in intimacy, scored for sexual behaviors, which one's parents would not seriously disapprove | Happiness was also correlated with discrepancy scores between the attitude of his parents and his own pragmatic and ideal sexual attitudes (indicative of external sexual conflicts).<br>In both cases these correlations were non-significant (see under 'Sexuality', Part III, S 3) | COMP 1.1 | $r_{pm}$ | -.04 | | ns | Undergraduate college students, Hawaii<br>Non-probability accidental sample<br>N: 101, date: — | WILSO 65<br>p. 375 |
| POSITIVE EVALUATION OF FAMILY RELATIONS | 21-item index containing closeness to father (4 items), closeness to mother (3 items), amount of reasoning with son (4 items), and parental punitiveness (10 items) | Both variables were measured in each of the three interview waves (See excerpt, Part II).<br>The following associations were reported:<br>fam. rel. $(t_1)$ x happ. $(t_1)$ : $r_{pm}$ = +.38<br>fam. rel. $(t_1)$ x happ. $(t_2)$ : $r_{pm}$ = +.32<br>fam. rel. $(t_1)$ x happ. $(t_3)$ : r = +.23<br>fam. rel. $(t_2)$ x happ. $(t_1)$ : r = +.30<br>fam. rel. $(t_2)$ x happ. $(t_2)$ : r = +.41<br>fam. rel. $(t_2)$ x happ. $(t_3)$ : r = +.30 | COMP 1.2 | $h^2$ | +.37 | | 001 | Public highschool boys, U.S.A.<br>Probability multi-stage sample<br>N: 2213 in 1966, 1886 in 1968 and 1799 in 1969<br>date: fall 1966, spring 1968 and spring 1969 | BACHM 67/70<br>p. 211 |
| POSITIVE EVALUATION OF MOTHER AND FATHER AS A PARENT | Closed question for mother and father separately worse / about the same / better than most mothers/fathers | | AFF 1.3 | $\bar{DR}$ | +.08 | | 05 | Adults, Alameda County, U.S.A.<br>Probability sample<br>N: 6928, date: 1965 | BERKM 71<br>p. 42 |

# PARENTAL CHARACTERISTICS AND BEHAVIOR AS RATED BY OUTSIDERS

| MATERNAL CHARACTERISTICS DURING THE FIRST THREE YEARS OF THE CHILD'S LIFE: | Ratings of expressive behavior on 7-point scales ranging from 'not at all true' to 'extremely true' by three judges on the basis of notes on observations of about 20 testing sessions | Each variable was correlated with the child's hedonic level at the ages of 10 - 36 months. See also instrument and remarks in excerpt (Part II). For boys N=15, for girls N = 16. | | | | | | | Children and their mothers, Berkeley, California, U.S.A. Non-probability chunk sample N: 108 (54 children and their mothers), date: 1928 - 1943 | SCHAE 63 p. 109/110 |
|---|---|---|---|---|---|---|---|---|---|---|
| | | age: | 10-12 | 13-15 | 18-24 | 27-36 | | | | |
| - PERMITS AND STIMULATES AUTONOMY | 'Does the mother think the child should be free to act independently and be allowed to work or play apart from the parents?' 5-item index | boys:<br>girls: | +.18<br>-.09 | +.15<br>-.08 | +.26<br>-.12 | +.29<br>-.14 | AFF 5.1 | $r_{pm}$ | | |
| - IGNORING | 'Does the mother ignore or reject her child?' 7-item index | boys:<br>girls: | -.03<br>+.04 | -.23<br>-.11 | -.26<br>-.40x | -.35<br>-.38x | AFF 5.1 | $r_{pm}$ | | |
| - PERCEIVES CHILD AS BURDEN | 'Does the mother perceive the child as more a burden and inconvenience than a source of happiness?' 7-item index | boys:<br>girls: | -.18<br>-.16 | -.32<br>-.32 | -.54x<br>-.42x | -.53x<br>-.39x | AFF 5.1 | $r_{pm}$ | | |
| - USE OF FEAR TO CONTROL | 'Does the mother attempt to use fear as a way of controlling and teaching the child?' 5-item index | boys:<br>girls: | -.13<br>-.29 | -.20<br>-.26 | -.39x<br>-.49x | -.38x<br>-.52x | AFF 5.1 | $r_{pm}$ | | |
| - PUNISHMENT | 'Does the mother believe in punishment as an effective method of influencing the child's behavior?' 7-item index | boys:<br>girls: | -.06<br>-.20 | -.19<br>-.26 | -.36<br>-.40x | -.41x<br>-.44x | AFF 5.1 | $r_{pm}$ | | |
| - INTRUSIVENESS | 'Does the mother seem to be unaware of the fact that a child has a mind of his own and that he should be able to do his own thinking without forceful intrusion by the mother?' 4-item index | boys:<br>girls: | -.36<br>+.12 | -.34<br>+.07 | -.35<br>+.02 | -.40x<br>-.07 | AFF 5.1 | $r_{pm}$ | | |
| - CONCERN ABOUT CHILD'S HEALTH | 'Does this mother seem to be preoccupied with her child's health?' 5-item index | boys:<br>girls: | -.25<br>+.12 | -.11<br>+.12 | -.13<br>+.30 | +.10<br>+.26 | AFF 5.1 | $r_{pm}$ | | |
| - ACHIEVEMENT DEMAND | 'Does she concern herself about the child's achievement?' 4-item index | boys:<br>girls: | -.22<br>+.27 | -.04<br>+.18 | -.11<br>+.30 | -.18<br>+.35 | AFF 5.1 | $r_{pm}$ | | |
| - EXCESSIVE CONTACT WITH CHILD | 'Does the mother wish to keep the child closely attached to herself?' 4-item index | boys:<br>girls: | -.12<br>+.00 | -.08<br>+.07 | -.16<br>+.29 | -.14<br>+.30 | AFF 5.1 | $r_{pm}$ | | |
| - FOSTERING DEPENDENCY ON CHILD | 'Does this mother tend to baby her child or foster dependency on him?' 6-item index | boys:<br>girls: | -.39x<br>+.12 | -.32<br>+.08 | -.27<br>+.20 | -.17<br>+.35 | AFF 5.1 | $r_{pm}$ | | |
| - EMOTIONAL INVOLVEMENT WITH CHILD | 'Extent and intensity of emotional and behavioral involvement with the child' 5-item index | boys:<br>girls: | -.08<br>+.17 | +.02<br>+.27 | +.00<br>+.46x | -.07<br>+.49x | AFF 5.1 | $r_{pm}$ | | |

| | | age: | 10–12 | 13–15 | 18–24 | 27–36 | | |
|---|---|---|---|---|---|---|---|---|
| - EXPRESSION OF AFFECTION FOR CHILD | 'Does the mother openly express her love and affection for her child?' 6-item index | boys:<br>girls: | +.03<br>+.16 | +.15<br>+.22 | +.23<br>+.42x | +.21<br>+.48x | AFF 5.1 | $r_{pm}$ |
| - EQUALITARIANISM | 'Does the mother tend to relate to the child as an equal?' 5-item index | boys:<br>girls: | +.22<br>+.37 | +.26<br>+.39x | +.49x<br>+.53x | +.44x<br>+.55x | AFF 5.1 | $r_{pm}$ |
| - POSITIVE EVALUATION OF CHILD | 'Does the mother tend to have a positive evaluation of the child as a person?' 6-item index | boys:<br>girls: | +.17<br>+.15 | +.26<br>+.22 | +.42x<br>+.42x | +.28<br>+.48x | AFF 5.1 | $r_{pm}$ |
| - SUPPRESSION OF AGGRESSION | 'Does the mother's ideal seem to be a quiet, passive child rather than an active, aggressive one?' 4-item index | boys:<br>girls: | -.39x<br>-.08 | -.21<br>-.36 | -.30<br>-.40x | -.31<br>-.22 | AFF 5.1 | $r_{pm}$ |
| - PUNITIVENESS | 'Does the mother seem punitive and unkind?' 4-item index | boys:<br>girls: | -.06<br>-.28 | -.25<br>-.31 | -.48x<br>-.44x | -.46x<br>-.38x | AFF 5.1 | $r_{pm}$ |
| - STRICTNESS (rigidity) | 'Does the mother believe in rigid rules and strict enforcement of those rules?' 5-item index | boys:<br>girls: | -.15<br>-.33 | -.06<br>-.37 | -.29<br>-.56x | -.11<br>-.57x | AFF 5.1 | $r_{pm}$ |
| - IRRITABILITY | 'Does the mother tend to be irritable?' 6-item index | boys:<br>girls: | -.29<br>-.24 | -.42x<br>-.30 | -.57x<br>-.32 | -.69x<br>-.34 | AFF 5.1 | $r_{pm}$ |
| - ANXIETY | 'Does this mother appear overtly anxious during the session?' 5-item index | boys:<br>girls: | -.39x<br>-.20 | -.36<br>-.19 | -.58x<br>-.04 | -.62x<br>+.15 | AFF 5.1 | $r_{pm}$ |
| - NEGATIVE EMOTIONAL STATES | 'Does she tend towards negative emotional states?' 5-item index | boys:<br>girls: | -.07<br>-.43x | -.34<br>-.41x | -.44x<br>-.44x | -.30<br>-.37 | AFF 5.1 | $r_{pm}$ |
| - MOOD SWINGS | 'Does she show mood swings?' 5-item index | boys:<br>girls: | -.29<br>-.17 | -.31<br>-.25 | -.50x<br>-.32 | -.56x<br>-.16 | AFF 5.1 | $r_{pm}$ |
| - DOMINANCE | 'Does the mother show competitive, domineering behavior in the family and examining situation?' 6-item index | boys:<br>girls: | -.21<br>+.23 | -.15<br>+.14 | -.34<br>+.16 | -.40x<br>+.28 | AFF 5.1 | $r_{pm}$ |
| - SELF-ABASEMENT | 'Does this mother seem self-abasing?' 6-item index | boys:<br>girls: | -.23<br>-.08 | -.02<br>-.24 | -.27<br>-.01 | -.11<br>+.02 | AFF 5.1 | $r_{pm}$ |
| - DEPENDENCY | 'Is she a dependent mother?' 7-item index | boys:<br>girls: | -.39x<br>+.33 | -.24<br>+.09 | -.16<br>+.13 | -.34<br>+.30 | AFF 5.1 | $r_{pm}$ |
| - OVER-CONSCIENTIOUSNESS | 'Is she an over-conscientious mother?' 3-item index | boys:<br>girls: | -.17<br>+.10 | +.06<br>-.07 | -.11<br>+.26 | +.10<br>+.27 | AFF 5.1 | $r_{pm}$ |
| - SOCIABILITY | 'Does this mother tend to be a social person?' 6-item index | boys:<br>girls: | -.02<br>+.48x | +.08<br>+.35 | +.10<br>+.37 | -.22<br>+.24 | AFF 5.1 | $r_{pm}$ |

| Variable | Item | age | 10–12 | 13–15 | 18–24 | 27–36 | | | Sample | Source |
|---|---|---|---|---|---|---|---|---|---|---|
| - COOPERATIVENESS | 'Does this mother seem cooperative overtly?' (excluding officiousness, interventions, self-abasing cooperation)<br>7-item index | boys:<br>girls: | +.34<br>-.09 | +.35<br>+.07 | +.45$^x$<br>+.33 | +.68$^x$<br>+.29 | AFF 5.1 | $r_{pm}$ | | |
| - NARCISSISM | 'Does she try to draw attention to herself?'<br>3-item index | boys:<br>girls: | -.30<br>+.55$^x$ | -.23<br>+.35 | -.15<br>+.33 | -.40$^x$<br>+.23 | AFF 5.1 | $r_{pm}$ | | |
| - REJECTION OF HOMEMAKING ROLE | 'Does she seem to reject the role of homemaker?'<br>5-item index | boys:<br>girls: | +.03<br>+.19 | -.10<br>+.01 | -.21<br>-.15 | -.37<br>-.06 | AFF 5.1 | $r_{pm}$ | | |
| - ESTIMATED INTELLIGENCE | 'Does this mother have a high intelligence?'<br>4-item index | boys:<br>girls: | +.43$^x$<br>+.16 | +.51$^x$<br>+.07 | +.52$^x$<br>+.30 | +.56$^x$<br>+.34 | AFF 5.1 | $r_{pm}$ | | |
| - POOR PHYSICAL HEALTH | 'Is this mother physically healthy?'<br>3-item index | boys:<br>girls: | -.07<br>-.03 | -.27<br>-.05 | -.28<br>+.09 | -.48$^x$<br>-.10 | AFF 5.1 | $r_{pm}$ | | |
| - FINANCIAL STRESS | 'Does this mother seem to be subject to financial strain?'<br>5-item index | boys:<br>girls: | -.32<br>-.35 | -.38$^x$<br>-.16 | -.52$^x$<br>-.06 | -.44$^x$<br>-.23 | AFF 5.1 | $r_{pm}$ | | |
| MATERNAL CHARACTERISTICS DURING THE CHILD'S AGE FROM 9–14 YEARS: | Ratings of expressive behavior on 7-point scales ranging from 'not at all true' to 'extremely true' by three judges on the basis of interview protocols (one to three interviews). | Each variable correlated with the child's hedonic level at the ages of 10–36 months. See also instrument and remarks in excerpt (Part II). For boys: N = 15; for girls: N = 16 | | | | | | | Children and their mothers, Berkeley, California, U.S.A.<br>Non-probability chunk sample<br>N: 108 (54 children and their mothers), date: 1928 – 1943 | SCHAE 63<br>p. 117/118 |
| | | age | 10–12 | 13–15 | 18–24 | 27–36 | | | | |
| - IGNORING | 'Does the mother ignore or reject her child?'<br>5-item index | boys:<br>girls: | -.31<br>-.27 | -.41<br>-.37 | -.39<br>-.30 | -.39<br>-.44 | AFF 5.1 | $r_{pm}$ | | |
| - PERCEIVES CHILD AS A BURDEN | 'Does this mother perceive the child as more a burden and inconvenience than a source of happiness?'<br>5-item index | boys:<br>girls: | -.40<br>+.27 | -.33<br>-.28 | -.28<br>-.14 | -.03<br>-.02 | AFF 5.1 | $r_{pm}$ | | |
| - USE OF FEAR TO CONTROL | 'Does this mother attempt to use fear as a way of controlling and teaching the child?'<br>5-item index | boys:<br>girls: | -.26<br>+.10 | -.35<br>-.03 | -.28<br>-.07 | -.28<br>-.19 | AFF 5.1 | $r_{pm}$ | | |
| - WISH TO CONTROL THE CHILD | 'Does this mother seem to wish to control the child?'<br>5-item index | boys:<br>girls: | -.24<br>-.02 | -.19<br>+.03 | -.09<br>-.03 | -.09<br>-.23 | AFF 5.1 | $r_{pm}$ | | |
| - KEEPS CHILD SOCIALLY ISOLATED | 'Does this mother tend to keep her child socially isolated?'<br>5-item index | boys:<br>girls: | +.21<br>-.01 | +.21<br>-.12 | +.21<br>-.22 | +.21<br>-.49 | AFF 5.1 | $r_{pm}$ | | |
| - INTRUSIVENESS | 'Does this mother seem to be unaware of the fact that a child has a mind of his own and that he should be able to do his own thinking without forceful intrusion by the mother?'<br>4-item index | boys:<br>girls: | -.03<br>-.06 | +.28<br>-.18 | +.16<br>-.30 | +.16<br>-.45 | AFF 5.1 | $r_{pm}$ | | |

| | | age | 10–12 | 13–15 | 18–24 | 27–36 | | |
|---|---|---|---|---|---|---|---|---|
| – EXCESSIVE CONTACT WITH CHILD | 'Does the mother wish to keep the child closely attached to herself?' 5-item index | boys: | +.20 | +.29 | +.12 | +.12 | AFF 5.1 | $r_{pm}$ |
| | | girls: | -.34 | -.17 | -.13 | -.33 | | |
| – FOSTERING DEPENDENCY IN CHILD | 'Does this mother tend to baby her child or foster dependency in him?' 5-item index | boys: | +.33 | +.57$^{x}$ | +.41 | +.41 | AFF 5.1 | $r_{pm}$ |
| | | girls: | -.16 | -.27 | -.06 | +.12 | | |
| – ACHIEVEMENT DEMAND | 'Does the mother set high standards of achievement for the child?' 6-item index | boys: | +.48 | +.65$^{x}$ | +.60$^{x}$ | +.68$^{x}$ | AFF 5.1 | $r_{pm}$ |
| | | girls: | +.32 | +.21 | +.00 | +.23 | | |
| – EMOTIONAL INVOLVEMENT WITH CHILD | 'Extent and intensity of emotional and behavioral involvement with the child' 6-item index | boys: | +.46 | +.79$^{x}$ | +.72$^{x}$ | +.72$^{x}$ | AFF 5.1 | $r_{pm}$ |
| | | girls: | -.03 | +.06 | +.19 | +.39 | | |
| – POSITIVE EVALUATION OF CHILD | 'Does this mother have a positive evaluation of the child?' 6-item index | boys: | +.06 | +.30 | +.36 | +.36 | AFF 5.1 | $r_{pm}$ |
| | | girls: | +.31 | +.38 | +.12 | +.48 | | |
| – EXPRESSION OF AFFECTION FOR CHILD | 'Does this mother openly express her love and affection for the child?' 5-item index | boys: | +.14 | +.34 | +.22 | +.22 | AFF 5.1 | $r_{pm}$ |
| | | girls: | -.12 | -.02 | -.02 | +.34 | | |
| – EQUALITARIANISM | 'Does this mother relate to the child as an equal?' 4-item index | boys: | +.36 | +.57$^{x}$ | +.51 | +.51 | AFF 5.1 | $r_{pm}$ |
| | | girls: | +.03 | +.08 | +.04 | +.40 | | |
| – POSITIVE MOTHER-CHILD RELATIONSHIP | 'Positiveness of mother-child relationship?' (differentiated from over-possessiveness) 7-item index | boys: | +.29 | +.32 | +.28 | +.28 | AFF 5.1 | $r_{pm}$ |
| | | girls: | +.12 | +.13 | +.05 | +.35 | | |
| – PERMITS AND STIMULATES AUTONOMY | 'Does the mother think the child should be free to act independently and should be allowed to work or play apart from his parents?' 5-item index | boys: | -.20 | -.45 | -.34 | -.34 | AFF 5.1 | $r_{pm}$ |
| | | girls: | +.19 | +.01 | -.05 | +.26 | | |
| – PUNITIVENESS | 'Does the mother seem positive and unkind?' 6-item index | boys: | -.34 | -.33 | -.32 | -.32 | AFF 5.1 | $r_{pm}$ |
| | | girls: | -.05 | -.08 | +.03 | -.31 | | |
| – IRRITABILITY | 'Does this mother tend to be irritable?' 5-item index | boys: | -.15 | -.24 | -.23 | -.23 | AFF 5.1 | $r_{pm}$ |
| | | girls: | -.03 | -.21 | -.03 | -.19 | | |
| – STRICTNESS (rigidity) | 'Does this mother believe in rigid rules and strict enforcement of those rules?' 4-item index | boys: | -.06 | -.28 | -.12 | +.07 | AFF 5.1 | $r_{pm}$ |
| | | girls: | +.28 | +.16 | -.06 | -.07 | | |
| – ANXIETY | 'Does the mother appear overtly anxious?' 5-item index | boys: | -.24 | -.15 | +.05 | +.05 | AFF 5.1 | $r_{pm}$ |
| | | girls: | -.21 | -.06 | +.21 | +.06 | | |
| – EMOTIONAL WITHDRAWAL | 'Does this mother withdraw from external involvements?' 6-item index | boys: | +.06 | -.08 | +.31 | +.31 | AFF 5.1 | $r_{pm}$ |
| | | girls: | -.28 | +.01 | +.21 | -.08 | | |

| | | age: | 10–12 | 13–15 | 18–24 | 27–36 | | | | | | | |
|---|---|---|---|---|---|---|---|---|---|---|---|---|---|
| - DEPENDENCY | 'Is she a dependent mother?'<br>8-item index | boys:<br>girls: | -.06<br>+.19 | +.07<br>+.03 | +.18<br>+.09 | +.36<br>+.19 | AFF 5.1 | $r_{pm}$ | | | | | |
| - SOCIABILITY | 'Is this mother a sociable person?'<br>6-item index | boys:<br>girls: | +.28<br>+.25 | +.31<br>+.03 | +.40<br>+.02 | +.40<br>+.34 | AFF 5.1 | $r_{pm}$ | | | | | |
| - COOPERATIVENESS | 'Does this moter seem cooperative overtly?' (excluding officiousness, interventions, self-abasing cooperation)<br>7-item index | boys:<br>girls: | +.32<br>+.18 | +.20<br>+.18 | +.26<br>+.14 | +.26<br>+.29 | AFF 5.1 | $r_{pm}$ | | | | | |
| - POSITIVE EMOTIONAL STATE | 'Does this mother tend towards positive emotional states?'<br>7-item index | boys:<br>girls: | +.62[x]<br>-.16 | +.57[x]<br>-.21 | +.58[x]<br>-.17 | +.46<br>+.08 | AFF 5.1 | $r_{pm}$ | | | | | |
| - COMMUNICATIVENESS | 'Does this mother communicate freely in the interview?'<br>5-item index | boys:<br>girls: | +.34<br>+.14 | +.08<br>-.02 | -.04<br>+.06 | -.04<br>+.19 | AFF 5.1 | $r_{pm}$ | | | | | |
| - REJECTION OF HOMEMAKING ROLE | 'Does this mother seem to reject the role of homemaker?'<br>5-item index | boys:<br>girls: | -.21<br>-.28 | -.15<br>-.23 | -.28<br>+.14 | -.28<br>+.00 | AFF 5.1 | $r_{pm}$ | | | | | |
| - ESTIMATED INTELLIGENCE | 'Does this mother have a high intelligence?'<br>6-item index | boys:<br>girls: | +.33<br>+.34 | +.26<br>+.02 | +.41<br>-.10 | +.41<br>+.12 | AFF 5.1 | $r_{pm}$ | | | | | |

## F 1.1.4 - VARIOUS FACTORS CONCERNING FAMILY OF ORIGIN

| | | | | | | | | | |
|---|---|---|---|---|---|---|---|---|---|
| NUMBER OF CHILDREN IN THE FAMILY | | Stronger in lower class : G = -.27<br>Not in the middle and upper class: G = +.01 | HAPP 1.1 | G<br>V | -.04<br>.06 | $Chi^2$ | 02 | Juniors and seniors attending public high schools in New York State, U.S.A.<br>Probability cluster sample of 10 public highschools<br>N: sample A: 1682, sample B: 1664, sample C: 1678; date: 1960 | BRENN 70<br>p. 113/354 |
| | | Stronger in lower class : G = -.11<br>Not in the middle and upper class: G = .00 | AFF 1.1 | G<br>V | -.01<br>.02 | $Chi^2$ | ns | | |
| BEING OLDEST OR ONLY CHILD | | | HAPP 1.1 | $r_{pm}$ | - | t | s | Male undergraduates, U.S.A.<br>Non-probability chunk sample<br>N: 103, date: ± 1967 | HEERE 69<br>p. 28 |
| PAST SIBLING CONFLICT | Score derived from a 212-item inventory of past life experiences | | AFF 3.1 | $r_{pm}$ | -.39 | t | ns | Male college students, U.S.A.<br>Non-probability chunk sample<br>N: 17, date: ± 1960 | WESSM 66/2<br>p. 122 |
| ILLNESS OF PARENTS | 2-item index of diseases of parents including infarction, stroke, hypertension and diabetes | | HAPP 2.1 | G | -.03 | $Chi^2$ | ns | Male employees of age 40-65, The Netherlands<br>Non-probability chunk sample<br>N: 13000, date: — | SONDE 75 |
| LONG OR SERIOUS ILLNESS IN FAMILY DURING CHILDHOOD | Closed question: no vs yes | | AFF 1.3 | $\bar{DR}$ | -.02 | | 05 | Adults, Alameda County, U.S.A.<br>Probability sample<br>N: 6928, date: 1965 | BERKM 71<br>p. 42 |

| | | | | | | | | | |
|---|---|---|---|---|---|---|---|---|---|
| CHILDHOOD STRESS | 4-factor score containing childhood broken homes, evaluation of mother and father as parents, happiness of parents's marriage during childhood, illness of family members during childhood | | AFF 1.3 | $\bar{DR}$ | -.09 | | s | Adults, Alameda County, U.S.A.<br>(See last page) | BERKM 71<br>p. 43 |
| FATHER WAS ABLE TO BE AROUND THE HOME A LOT | Closed question rated on a 9-point scale gone a lot / average / home a good deal of the time | | HAPP 1.1 | $r_{pm}$ | | t | ns | Male undergraduates, U.S.A.<br>Non-probability chunk sample<br>N: 103, date: ± 1967 | HEERE 69<br>p. 28 |

## F 1.2 - CHILDREN

### F 1.2.1 - HAVING CHILDREN

| | | | | | | | | | |
|---|---|---|---|---|---|---|---|---|---|
| CHILDLESSNESS | Having children vs not | Computed for married Ss only | HAPP 1.1 | G' | +.02 | Gt' | ns | National adult population, U.S.A.<br>Non-probability quota sample<br>N: 2377, date: February, 1946 | WESSM 56<br>p. 193 |
| HAVING CHILDREN | Having no children vs having children | | HAPP 1.1 | $r_{pm}$ | +.09 | | | Housewives, The Netherlands<br>Probability area sample<br>N: 450, date: autumn, 1964 | PHILI 66<br>p. 66 |
| HAVING CHILDREN | Absence vs presence of living children | Negative among married persons (05).<br>Married persons with children are less happy (05) than married Ss without children, singles without children and singles with children.<br><br>Among married persons:<br>- positive in Dominican Republic (05), esp. in rural areas<br>- negative in Panama (01) in both urban and rural areas<br>- negative in Yugoslavia (01), esp. in rural areas<br><br>- negative among females (01)<br>- positive among males (05)<br><br>- negative among those of age 40+ (01)<br>- not among those of age 21-39 (ns)<br><br>- negative among those of high S.E.S. (01)<br>- not among those of lower S.E.S. (ns) | HAPP 3.1 | DM | - | DMRT | ns | Adults in the Dominican Republic, Panama and Yugoslavia<br>Pooling of the Cantril (1965) samples of Dominican Republic, Panama and Yugoslavia<br>N: 5228, date: — | BOHN 72<br>p. 26-38 |
| CHILDLESSNESS | Having children vs not | Age 25 - 29: G = +.09 (ns)<br>30 - 34: G = +.26 (ns<br>35 - 39: G = +.60 (05)<br>40 - 44: G = +.23 (ns)<br>45 - 49: G = +.01 (ns)<br>50 - 54: G = +.08 (ns)<br>55 - 59: G = +.48 (ns)<br>60 - 65: G = +.20 (ns)<br><br>Unaffected by sex | HAPP 1.1 | G | +.12 | | ns | Married adults, The Netherlands<br>Probability area sample<br>N: 1376, date: June, 1968 | VEENH 74<br>p. 499 |

## F 1.2.2 - NUMBER OF CHILDREN

| | | | | | | | | | |
|---|---|---|---|---|---|---|---|---|---|
| NUMBER OF CHILDREN | | Reported for females only | HAPP 2.1 | D% | ± 0 | | ns | Middle-aged, middle class married couples, U.S.A.<br>Non-probability accidental sample of couples<br>N: 416, date: 1952 - 1953 | ROSE 55<br>p. 16 |
| FAMILY SIZE | | | HAPP 1.1 | | | | ns | Non-institutionalized adults, U.S.A.<br>Probability multi-stage area sample<br>N: 2460, date: spring, 1957 | GURIN 60<br>p. 207 |
| NUMBER OF CHILDREN | Open-ended question | | HAPP 1.1 | G | +.09 | | ns | National adult population, The Netherlands<br>Probability area sample<br>N: 1552, date: June, 1968 | BAKKE 74<br>p. 27 |
| NUMBER OF CHILDREN UNDER 21 | 0-1 / 2 / 3 / 4 or more | Computed for married Ss only<br>Significant in lowest income group only (less than $ 5,000 per year) | AFF 2.3 | D̄R | -.06 | BCI | | Adults, urban areas, U.S.A.<br>Probability area samples<br>N: 2787, date: January, 1963 - January, 1964 | BRADB 69<br>p. 99 |

## F 1.2.3 - NUMBER OF CHILDREN AT HOME

| | | | | | | | | | |
|---|---|---|---|---|---|---|---|---|---|
| NUMBER/PERCENTAGE OF CHILDREN LIVING AT HOME | | Reported for females only | HAPP 2.1 | D% | ± 0 | | ns | Middle-aged middle class married couples, U.S.A.<br>Non-probability accidental sample of couples<br>N: 416, date: 1952 - 1953 | ROSE 55<br>p. 16 |
| POSTPARENTAL STAGE | Children still living with parents vs 'empty nest' | Stronger among those of age 40-49: G' = +.29 (01)<br>Reversed among those of age 50-59: G' = -.11 (ns | HAPP 1.1 | G' | +.16 | Gt' | 05 | Non-institutionalized middle-aged females, U.S.A.<br>Pooling of three Gallup Surveys<br>N: 902, date: 1963, 1966 | GLENN 75A/1<br>p. 106 |
| POSTPARENTAL STAGE | Children still living with parents vs 'empty nest' | Lower among those of age 40-49 : G' = +.10 (ns)<br>Stronger among those of age 50-59: G' = +.27 (ns) | HAPP 1.1 | G' | +.12 | Gt' | ns | Non-institutionalized middle-aged females, U.S.A.<br>Pooling of NORC Surveys<br>N: 425, date: 1972, 1973 | GLENN 75A/2<br>p. 106 |
| POSTPARENTAL STAGE | Children still living with parents vs 'empty nest' | Lower among those of age 35-49 : G' = +.19 (ns)<br>Stronger among those of age 50-64: G' = +.32 (ns) | COMP 1.1 | G' | +.12 | Gt' | ns | Non-institutionalized middle-aged females, U.S.A.<br>Roper Survey<br>N: 319, date: 1971 | GLENN 75A/3<br>p. 107 |
| CHILDREN AT HOME | Number of children | | HAPP 2.1 | G | +.06 | $Chi^2$ | 002 | Male employees of age 40-65, The Netherlands<br>Non-probability chunk sample<br>N: 13000, date: — | SONDE 75 |

## F 1.2.4 - VARIOUS FACTORS CONCERNING ONE'S CHILDREN

| | | | | | | | | | |
|---|---|---|---|---|---|---|---|---|---|
| CHILD-CENTERED ATTITUDE | Children were mentioned in response to open-ended questions on wishes and hopes and/or fears and worries for the future | Computed for married persons only<br>negative among those of lower S.E.S. without children (05)<br>positive among those of lower S.E.S. with children (01)<br>slightly negative among those of high S.E.S. without children (ns)<br>(to be continued on next page) | HAPP 3.1 | DM | + | DMRT | 05 | Adults in the Dominican Republic, Panama and Yugoslavia (married people only)<br>Pooling of the Cantril (1965) samples of Dominican Republic, Panama and Yugoslavia<br>N: 4113, date: — | BOHN 72<br>p. 31 |

| | | | | | | | | | |
|---|---|---|---|---|---|---|---|---|---|
| | | slightly negative among those of high S.E.S. with children (ns) | | | | | | | |
| WISH ONE HAD LARGER OR SMALLER NUMBER OF CHILDREN | | Reported for females only | HAPP 2.1 | D% | $\pm 0$ | | ns | Middle-aged, middle class married couples, U.S.A.<br>Non-probability accidental sample of couples<br>N: 416, date: 1952 - 1953 | ROSE 55<br>p. 16 |
| THINKING OFTEN ABOUT BRINGING UP CHILDREN | Closed question: not at all / sometimes / often during the week | Gammas computed on the basis of the 'often' answers<br>Unaffected by S.E.S.<br>high S.E.S.: G' = +.06 (ns)<br>low S.E.S. : G' = +.02 (ns) | HAPP 1.1 | G' | + | Gt' | | Inhabitants of 4 small communities, Illinois, U.S.A.<br>Probability multi-stage samples<br>N: 2006, date: March, 1962 | BRADB 65/1<br>p. 54 |
| PARENTAL WORRIES | Score derived from an agree/disagree statement on children giving their parents more trouble than pleasure, and 13-item inventory of parental problems | | AFF 1.3 | $D\bar{R}$ | - | | 05 | Adults, Alameda County, U.S.A.<br>Probability sample<br>N: 6928, date: 1965 | BERKM 71<br>p. 42 |
| NEGATIVE ORIENTATION TO CHILDREN | Coder rating of answers on open-ended question on changes in a person's life as a result of having children<br>positive / neutral / negative | Unaffected by sex<br>males : $t_k$ = -.04 (ns)<br>females: $t_k$ = -.06 (05) | HAPP 1.1 | $t_k$ | - | | | Adult married population with children, U.S.A.<br>Probability area sample<br>N: 797, date: spring, 1957 | VEROF 62<br>p. 196 |
| PERCEIVED SHORTCOMINGS IN THE SELF | Question on how one would like his children to be different from oneself<br>does not want child to be different vs wants child to be different | Stronger among males : $t_k$ = -.10 (05)<br>Not among females : $t_k$ = -.00 (ns) | HAPP 1.1 | $t_k$ | - | | | See above | VEROF 62<br>p. 196 |
| HAVING PROBLEMS IN RAISING CHILDREN | Open-ended question on main problems:<br>never had problems vs mentions problems | Stronger among males: $t_k$ = -.20 (01)<br>Lower among females: $t_k$ = -.05 (ns) | HAPP 1.1 | $t_k$ | - | | | See above | VEROF 62<br>p. 196 |
| FEELING INADEQUATE AS A PARENT | Closed question on frequency of these feelings:<br>never / once in a while / a lot of times | Unaffected by sex<br>males : $t_k$ = -.08 (05)<br>females: $t_k$ = -.03 (ns) | HAPP 1.1 | $t_k$ | - | | | See above | VEROF 62<br>p. 196 |
| SATISFACTION WITH CHILDREN'S EDUCATION | Closed question rated on an 11-point self-anchoring scale, based on Cantril (1965) | | HAPP 2.1 | $r_{pm}$ | +.14 | | | National population, Britain<br>Non-probability quota sample<br>N: 213, date: March, 1971 | ABRAM 73<br>p. 21 |
| FONDNESS OF CHILD FOR PARENTS | College student offspring rating | Positive among females only<br>The mother's life-satisfaction was just as closely related to her child's fondness for his father as it was to the child's fondness for her. The child's fondness for both of his parents was not related to the father's life-satisfaction | HAPP 2.1 | D% | + | | s | Middle-aged, middle class married couples, U.S.A<br>Non-probability accidental sample of couples<br>N: 416, date: 1952 - 1953 | ROSE 55<br>p. 16 |

## F 1.3 - SATISFACTION WITH ONE'S FAMILY

see 'Satisfaction with Family, Relatives' (S 1.7.1)

## F 1.4 - VARIOUS FAMILY FACTORS

| | | | | | | | | | |
|---|---|---|---|---|---|---|---|---|---|
| POSITIVE EVALUATION OF ONE'S FAMILY LIFE | Closed question ranging from very bad to very good | | HAPP 1.1<br>AFF 1.1 | mc<br>mc | +.65<br>+.51 | | | Urban adult Jewish population, Israel<br>Probability area sample using dwelling units<br>N: 1940, date: spring, 1973 | LEVY 75/1<br>p. 372 |

| | | | | | | | | | |
|---|---|---|---|---|---|---|---|---|---|
| STATE OF FAMILY RELATIONSHIPS | Closed question: 'How do you and your family get along?'<br>only so-so / fairly well / very well | Stronger among those who are dissatisfied with job and/or friends | HAPP 1.1 | G' | +.64 | Gt' | 01 | National adult population, U.S.A.<br>Non-probability quota sample<br>N: 2377, date: February, 1946 | WESSM 56<br>p. 194 |
| GETTING ON WELL WITH ONE'S FAMILY | Closed question: very badly / rather badly / average / fairly well / very well | | HAPP 2.1 | $T^2$ | +.22 | $Chi^2$ | 001 | Non-agricultural population, Poland<br>Non-probability, purposive quota sample<br>N: 1385, date: June - July, 1960 | MAKAR 62<br>p. 108 |
| GETTING ON WELL WITH ONE'S FAMILY | See above | | HAPP 2.1 | $T^2$ | +.14 | $Chi^2$ | 001 | Individual farm-owners and their families, Poland<br>Non-probability, purposive quota sample<br>N: 1002, date: June - July, 1960 | MAKAR 62<br>p. 109 |
| CLOSENESS OF TOTAL FAMILY LIFE | College student offspring rating | Positive among females only.<br>Among very satisfied women in 48% of the cases the college student offspring described total family life as being very close; among satisfied women this percentage was 28%, and among the relatively dissatisfied mothers it was only 20%. | HAPP 2.1 | D% | + | | s | Middle-aged, middle class married couples, U.S.A.<br>Non-probability accidental sample of couples<br>N: 416, date: 1952 - 1953 | ROSE 55<br>p. 16 |
| SOCIAL CONTACTS OF OWN FAMILY | 2-item index of closed questions on frequency of contact and appreciation of contact | Computed for married persons only.<br>Males: r = +.00<br>Females: r = +.36 | HAPP 2.1 | $r_{pm}$ | + | $Chi^2$ | | Adults, Amsterdam, The Netherlands<br>Probability systematic random sample stratified by sex and marital status<br>N: 600, date: September - December, 1965 | JONG 69<br>p. 26 |
| CONTACTS WITH RELATIVES | Open-ended question on number of families:<br>no / 1 / 2 / 3 or more families during last week | Computed for Index of Positive Affects only:<br>G' = +.22 (01)<br>Unrelated to Index of Negative Affects<br>Unaffected by S.E.S. | AFF 2.3 | G' | + | Gt' | | Males of age 25-49, 4 small communities, Illinois, U.S.A.<br>Probability multi-stage samples<br>N: 393, date: March, 1962 | BRADB 65/1<br>p. 43 |
| FREQUENCY OF CONTACTS WITH RELATIVES | Open-ended question; during past few weeks | Index of Positive Affects: G = +.10<br>Index of Negative Affects: G = +.03 | AFF 2.3 | G | + | | | Adults, urban areas, U.S.A.<br>Probability area samples<br>N: 2787, date: January, 1963 - January, 1964 | BRADB 69<br>p. 127 |
| EXTENT OF FAMILY CONTACT OUTSIDE THE HOME | Respondents were classified according to the number of their living relatives, multiplied by the frequency of contacts.<br>sparse / occasional / many | | HAPP 2.1 | G' | +.28 | Gt' | 05 | Aged chronically ill patients, U.S.A.<br>Probability sample<br>N: 167, date: 1959 | HENLE 67<br>p. 71 |
| BEING INTERESTED IN FAMILY RELATIONSHIPS | Closed question | | COMP 4.1 | | | | ns | Students, U.S.A.<br>Non-probability chunk sample<br>N: 1651, date: — | SYMON 37<br>p. 292 |
| HAVING PROBLEMS WITH FAMILY RELATIONSHIPS | Closed question | Highschool students only<br>L-shaped curve: significant negative among happier students only | COMP 4.1 | | - | | | See above | SYMON 37<br>p. 292 |
| REPORT OF HOPES CONCERNING THE FAMILY | Open-ended question on personal wishes and hopes for the future<br>Responses rated as concerning happy family life; concern and hopes for relatives, children; etc. | | HAPP 3.1 | G' | +.11 | Gt' | 01 | Adult population of 14 countries<br>Representative samples<br>N: 18653, date: ± 1960 | CANTR 65/1<br>p. 263 |
| REPORT OF FEARS CONCERNING THE FAMILY | Open-ended question on personal worries and fears for the future<br>Responses rated as concerning no or unhappy family life; worries and fears regarding relatives, children; etc. | | HAPP 3.1 | G' | +.08 | Gt' | 01 | See above | CANTR 65/1<br>p. 263 |
| UNFULFILLED ASPIRATIONS: MARRIAGE, CHILDREN, HUSBAND | Open-ended question on unfulfilled aspirations. other aspirations vs aspirations mentioned | Computed for those having unfulfilled aspirations only (N = 1646) | HAPP 1.1 | G' | -.27 | Gt' | 05 | National adult population, U.S.A.<br>Non-probability quota sample<br>N: 2377, date: February, 1946 | WESSM 56<br>p. 210 |

| | | | | | | | | | |
|---|---|---|---|---|---|---|---|---|---|
| MOST IMPORTANT WORRY: FAMILY AND CHILDREN | Open-ended question on most important worry. other worries vs worry mentioned | Computed for those having worries only (N = 2040) | HAPP 1.1 | G' | +.10 | Gt' | 05 | National adult population, U.S.A.<br>(See last page) | WESSM 56<br>p. 213 |
| WORRIES ABOUT FUTURE OF FAMILY MEMBERS | Direct question rated on an open graphic scale ranging from 'not worried' to 'very worried' | | HAPP 1.1 | G | +.30 | | ns | National adult population, The Netherlands<br>Probability area sample<br>N: 1552, date: June, 1968 | BAKKE 74<br>p. 28 |
| WORRIES ABOUT RELATIONSHIP TO FAMILY MEMBERS | See above | Lower among those of age 40-50<br>Stronger among those of low S.E.S.<br>Not among those of higher education<br>Unaffected by sex | HAPP 1.1 | G | +.45 | | 05 | See above | BAKKE 74<br>p. 28 |
| FAMILY PROBLEMS | Closed question: no vs yes | | HAPP 2.1 | G | -.55 | $Chi^2$ | 000 | Male employees of age 40-65, The Netherlands<br>Non-probability chunk sample<br>N: 13000, date: — | SONDE 75 |
| FAMILY LIFE CYCLE | | | HAPP 3.1<br>(1st instr.) | $h^2$ | .20 | | | National adult population, U.S.A.<br>Probability area sample (first sample)<br>N: 1297, date: May, 1972 | ANDRE 74<br>p. 20 |

# F 2 FREEDOM

F 2.1 Freedom in youth

F 2.2 Freedom in adulthood

see also 'Personal freedom' (A 2.2.12)



## F 2.1 - FREEDOM IN YOUTH

| Variable | Measure | Results | | | Sample | Source |
|---|---|---|---|---|---|---|
| FREEDOM ALLOWED BY THE MOTHER DURING THE FIRST THREE YEARS OF THE CHILD'S LIFE: | Ratings of expressive behavior on 7-point scales ranging from 'not at all true' to 'extremely true' by three judges on the basis of notes on observations of about 20 testing sessions | Each variable was correlated with the child's hedonic level at the ages of 10-36 months. See also instrument and remarks in excerpt (Part II).<br>For boys N = 15, for girls N = 16 | | | Children and their mothers, Berkeley, California, U.S.A.<br>Non-probability chunk sample<br>N: 108 (54 children and their mothers), date: 1928-1943 | SCHAE 63<br>p. 109-110 |
| - PERMITS AND STIMULATES AUTONOMY | 'Does the mother think the child should be free to act independently and be allowed to work or play apart from the parents?'<br>5-item index |   10-12 13-15 18-24 27-36<br>boys: +.18 +.15 +.26 +.29<br>girls: -.09 -.08 -.12 -.14 | AFF 5.1 | $r_{pm}$ | | |
| - INTRUSIVENESS | 'Does the mother seem to be unaware of the fact that a child has a mind of his own and that he should be able to do his own thinking without forceful intrusion by the mother?'<br>4-item index |   10-12 13-15 18-24 27-36<br>boys: -.36 -.34 -.35 -.40[x]<br>girls: +.12 +.07 +.02 -.07 | AFF 5.1 | $r_{pm}$ | | |
| - STRICTNESS (rigidity) | 'Does the mother believe in rigid rules and strict enforcement of those rules?'<br>5-item index |   10-12 13-15 18-24 27-36<br>boys: -.15 -.06 -.29 -.11<br>girls: -.33 -.37 -.56[x] -.57[x] | AFF 5.1 | $r_{pm}$ | | |
| - FOSTERING DEPENDENCY ON CHILD | 'Does this mother tend to baby her child or foster dependency on him?'<br>6-item index |   10-12 13-15 18-24 27-36<br>boys: -.39[x] -.32 -.27 -.17<br>girls: +.12 +.08 +.20 +.35 | AFF 5.1 | $r_{pm}$ | | |
| - EXCESSIVE CONTACT WITH CHILD | 'Does the mother wish to keep the child closely attached to herself?'<br>4-item index |   10-12 13-15 18-24 27-36<br>boys: -.12 -.08 -.16 -.14<br>girls: +.00 +.07 +.29 +.30 | AFF 5.1 | $r_{pm}$ | | |
| FREEDOM ALLOWED BY THE MOTHER DURING THE CHILD'S AGE FROM 9-14 YEARS: | Ratings of expressive behavior on 7-point scales ranging from 'not at all true' to 'extremely true' by three judges on the basis of interview-protocols (one to three interviews) | Each variable was correlated with the child's hedonic level at the ages of 10-36 months. See also instrument and remarks in excerpt (Part II). | | | See above | SCHAE 63<br>p. 117-118 |
| - PERMITS AND STIMULATES AUTONOMY | 'Does the mother think the child should be free to act independently and should be allowed to work and play apart from his parents?'<br>5-item index |   10-12 13-15 18-24 27-36<br>boys: -.20 -.45 -.34 -.34<br>girls: +.19 +.01 -.06 +.26 | AFF 5.1 | $r_{pm}$ | | |

| Variable | Measure | Results | Code | Stat. | Value | Test | Sig. | Sample | Source |
|---|---|---|---|---|---|---|---|---|---|
| - INTRUSIVENESS | 'Does the mother seem to be unaware of the fact that a child has a mind of his own and that he should be able to do his own thinking without forceful intrusion by the mother?'<br>4-item index | 10-12 13-15 18-24 27-36<br>boys: -.03 +.28 +.16 +.16<br>girls: -.06 -.18 -.30 -.45 | AFF 5.1 | $r_{pm}$ | | | | | |
| - STRICTNESS (rigidity) | 'Does the mother believe in rigid rules and strict enforcement of those rules?'<br>4-item index | 10-12 13-15 18-24 27-36<br>boys: -.06 -.28 -.12 +.07<br>girls: +.28 +.16 -.06 -.07 | AFF 5.1 | $r_{pm}$ | | | | | |
| - WISH TO CONTROL THE CHILD | 'Does the mother seem to wish to control the child?'<br>5-item index | 10-12 13-15 18-24 27-36<br>boys: -.24 -.19 -.09 -.09<br>girls: -.02 +.03 -.03 -.23 | AFF 5.1 | $r_{pm}$ | | | | | |
| - FOSTERING DEPENDENCY IN CHILD | 'Does his mother tend to baby her child or foster dependency in him?'<br>5-item index | 10-12 13-15 18-24 27-36<br>boys: +.33 +.57[x] +.41 +.41<br>girls: -.16 -.27 -.06 +.12 | AFF 5.1 | $r_{pm}$ | | | | | |
| - EXCESSIVE CONTACT WITH CHILD | 'Does the mother wish to keep the child closely attached to herself?'<br>5-item index | 10-12 13-15 18-24 27-36<br>boys: +.20 +.29 +.12 +.12<br>girls: -.34 -.17 -.13 -.33 | AFF 5.1 | $r_{pm}$ | | | | | |
| - KEEPS CHILD SOCIALLY ISOLATED | 'Does this mother tend to keep her child socially isolated?' | 10-12 13-15 18-24 27-36<br>boys: +.21 +.21 +.21 +.21<br>girls: -.01 -.12 -.22 -.49 | AFF 5.1 | $r_{pm}$ | | | | | |
| HAVING A DOMINANT FATHER | Closed question rated on a 9-point scale very submissive / moderate / very dominant | | HAPP 1.1 | $r_{pm}$ | - | t | s | Male undergraduates, U.S.A.<br>Non-probability chunk sample<br>N: 103, date: ± 1967 | HEERE 69 p. 28 |
| HAVING A DOMINANT MOTHER | See above | | HAPP 1.1 | $r_{pm}$ | - | t | s | See above | HEERE 69 p. 28 |
| FATHER IS DEMANDING VERY LITTLE | Closed question rated on a 9-point scale demands a lot / moderate / very little | | HAPP 1.1 | $r_{pm}$ | | t | ns | See above | HEERE 69 p. 28 |
| MOTHER IS DEMANDING VERY LITTLE | See above | | HAPP 1.1 | $r_{pm}$ | +.21 | t | s | See above | HEERE 69 p. 28 |
| BEING OFTEN ALLOWED BY PARENTS TO MAKE OWN DECISIONS | Closed question rated on a 9-point scale almost never / sometimes / nearly all the time | | HAPP 1.1 | $r_{pm}$ | +.33 | t | s | See above | HEERE 69 p. 28 |
| PARENTS WERE PERMISSIVE AND LENIENT | Closed question rated on a 9-point scale very strict / about average / very permissive and lenient | | HAPP 1.1 | $r_{pm}$ | | t | ns | See above | HEERE 69 p. 28 |
| FREEDOM IN DATING | Closed question rated on a 5-point scale not at all / parents decided / completely free | | HAPP 1.1 | $r_{pm}$ | | t | ns | See above | HEERE 69 p. 28 |
| FREEDOM TO DECIDE HOW LATE TO STAY OUT | See above | | HAPP 1.1 | $r_{pm}$ | | t | ns | See above | HEERE 69 p. 28 |
| FREEDOM TO STAY OVERNIGHT AT SOMEONE'S HOUSE | See above | | HAPP 1.1 | $r_{pm}$ | | t | ns | See above | HEERE 69 p. 28 |
| FREEDOM TO DRINK ALCOHOL | See above | | HAPP 1.1 | $r_{pm}$ | | t | ns | See above | HEERE 69 p. 28 |

| | | | | | | | | |
|---|---|---|---|---|---|---|---|---|
| FREEDOM TO TAKE OWN TRIPS OR GO TRAVELLING | Closed question rated on a 5-point scale<br>not at all / parents decided / completely free | | HAPP 1.1 | $r_{pm}$ | | t | ns | Male undergraduates, U.S.A.<br>(See last page) | HEERE 69<br>p. 28 |
| FREEDOM TO FOLLOW OWN INTERESTS | Closed question rated on a 9-point scale<br>not much / some / considerable freedom | | HAPP 1.1 | $r_{pm}$ | +.30 | t | s | See above | HEERE 69<br>p. 28 |

## F 2.2 - FREEDOM IN ADULTHOOD

| | | | | | | | | |
|---|---|---|---|---|---|---|---|---|
| EXTENT OF OPPORTUNITY TO DO WHAT ONE LIKES | Closed question rated on an 11-point self-anchoring scale | | HAPP 3.1<br>HAPP 2.1<br>CON 1.1 | $r_{pm}$<br>$r_{pm}$<br>$r_{pm}$ | +.32<br>+.46<br>+.36 | | | National adult population, U.S.A.<br>Probability sample<br>N: 1549, date: 1959 | CANTR 65/2<br>p. 268-415 |
| OPPORTUNITIES TO DO WHAT YOU WOULD LIKE TO DO | Closed question rated on an 11-point self-anchoring scale | | HAPP 3.1<br>HAPP 2.1<br>CON 1.1 | r<br>r<br>r | +.33<br>+.43<br>+.39 | | | National adult population, U.S.A.<br>Cantril (1965) modified probability sample<br>N: 1406, date: 1959 | BORTN 70<br>p. 44 |
| SATISFACTION WITH OPPORTUNITY TO CHANGE THINGS | Closed question: 'How do you feel about . . .?'<br>terrible / unhappy / mostly dissatisfied / mixed / mostly satisfied / pleased / delighted | | HAPP 3.1 | $h^2$ | .37 | | | National adult population, U.S.A.<br>Probability area sample (third sample)<br>N: 1072, date: November, 1972 | ANDRE 74<br>p. 19 |
| FREEDOM ON THE JOB | Closed question: none / some / much freedom | | HAPP 2.1 | $r_{pm}$ | + | $Chi^2$ | ns | Adults, Amsterdam, The Netherlands<br>Probability systematic random sample stratified by sex and marital status<br>N: 600, date: September - December, 1965 | JONG 69<br>p. 191 |
| RESTRICTIVENESS OF SETTING | Ward A (open ward) vs ward B (closed ward)<br>(see 'Sample construction' in excerpt, Part II) | The mean happiness score in ward A was 4.7 and in ward B 5.4 | AFF 5.1 | DM | + | | 001 | Institutionalized mentally retarded males, U.S.A.<br>Non-probability chunk sample<br>N: 149, date: — | PANDE 71<br>p. 328 |

# G 1 GENDER

G 1.1 Male vs female sex

G 1.2 Gender-role attitudes

## G 1.1. - MALE VS FEMALE SEX

| | | | | | | | | | |
|---|---|---|---|---|---|---|---|---|---|
| MALE SEX | Female vs male | | HAPP 3.1 | G' | -.04 | Gt' | 05 | Adult population of 5 Westernized nations, 3 underdeveloped giants, 2 countries in the Middle East, 3 Caribbean nations and the Philippines<br>Representative samples<br>N: 18.653, date: ± 1960 | CANTR 65/1 p. 259 |
| MALE SEX | | | HAPP 1.1 | G' | -.07 | Gt' | ns | National adult population, U.S.A.<br>Non-probability quota sample<br>N: 2377, date: February, 1946 | WESSM 56 p. 177 |
| MALE SEX | | | HAPP 2.1 | G' | +.14 | Gt' | 05 | National adult population, U.S.A.<br>Probability sample, proportionally stratified by sex, age, occupation, S.E.S. and education<br>N: 1015, date: 1948 - 1949 | BUCHA 53 p. 213 |
| MALE SEX | | Strong negative relation among the never married<br>Positive relation among the divorced or separated<br>Negative relation among the widowed | HAPP 1.1 | G' | -.02 | Gt' | ns | Non-institutionalized adults, U.S.A.<br>Probability multi-stage area sample<br>N: 2460, date: spring, 1957 | GURIN 60 p. 42 |
| MALE SEX | | | HAPP 2.1<br>HAPP 3.1<br>CON 1.1 | r<br>r<br>r | -.01<br>-.03<br>-.07 | | | National adult population, U.S.A.<br>Cantril (1965) modified probability sample<br>N: 1406, date: 1959 | BORTN 70 p. 44 |
| MALE SEX | | | HAPP 3.1 | G' | +.02 | | ns | National adult population, U.S.A.<br>Probability sample<br>N: 1549, date: ± 1960 | CANTR 65/1 p. 378 |
| MALE SEX | | See remarks in excerpt (Part II)<br>males : Mean = 6.4 (6.8)<br>females: Mean = 6.6 (6.9) | HAPP 3.1 | DM | - | | | Non-institutionalized national adult population, U.S.A.<br>Multi-stage probability sample, stratified by size of locality<br>N: 1588, date: January, 1971 (+1964) | CANTR 71 p. 66 |
| MALE SEX | | See remarks in excerpt (Part II).<br>Unaffected by race | HAPP 1.1 | G' | -.06 | Gt' | ns | Non-institutionalized adults, U.S.A.<br>Type of sample construction unclear<br>N: 1602, date: March, 1972 | ALSTO 74 p. 100 |
| SEX | | | HAPP 3.1 (1st instr.) | $h^2$ | .04 | | | National adult population, U.S.A.<br>Probability area sample (first sample)<br>N: 1297, date: May, 1972 | ANDRE 74 p. 20 |

| | | | | | | | | | |
|---|---|---|---|---|---|---|---|---|---|
| MALE SEX | | Stronger among those of age 18 - 65: r = -.09<br>Reversed among those of age 65+ : r = +.18<br>This difference is significant (05)<br>Unaffected by S.E.S. | HAPP 1.1 | $r_{pm}$ | -.05 | | 05 | Non-institutionalized adults, U.S.A.<br>Probability samples<br>N: 1547, date: 1972, 1973 | SPREI 74<br>p. 457 |
| MALE SEX | | See remarks in excerpt (Part II)<br>age 18-39 : G' = -.25 (01)<br>age 40-59 : G' = -.06 (ns)<br>age 60+ : G' = -.00 (ns)<br>Married : G' = -.20 (01)<br>Widowed : G' = -.18 (ns)<br>Divorced/separated: G' = +.05 (ns)<br>Never married : G' = -.14 (ns) | HAPP 1.1 | G' | -.13 | Gt' | 01 | National adult population, U.S.A.<br>Combined data from 3 U.S. General Surveys<br>N: 3853, date: 1972, 1973, 1974 | GLENN 75B<br>p. 596 |
| MALE SEX | | Negative among those of age 18-64<br>Positive among those of age 65+ | HAPP 1.1 | D% | | | | Non-institutionalized adults, U.S.A.<br>National probability sample<br>N: 1500, date: spring, 1973 | SPREI 75<br>p. 239 |
| MALE SEX | | Strong negative relation among the never married<br>Also negative among the divorced/separated and the widowed | HAPP 1.1<br>AFF 2.3 | G'<br>G' | +.04<br>-.04 | Gt'<br>Gt' | ns<br>ns | Inhabitants of 4 small communities, Illinois, U.S.A.<br>Probability multi stage samples<br>N: 2006, date: March, 1962 | BRADB 65/1<br>p. 9 |
| MALE SEX | | Index of Positive Affects: $\bar{DR}$ = -.02 (ns)<br>Index of Negative Affects: $\bar{DR}$ = -.07 (05)<br>Unaffected by having a job | AFF 2.3 | $\bar{DR}$ | +.04 | BCI | 05 | Adults, urban areas, U.S.A.<br>Probability area samples<br>N: 2787, date: January, 1963 - January, 1964 | BRADB 69<br>p. 45/91 |
| | | Positive among job performers | HAPP 1.1 | G' | -.03 | Gt' | ns | | |
| MALE SEX | | Negative among those reporting low social participation only<br>Index of Positive Affects: D% = -<br>Index of Negative Affects: D% = - | HAPP 1.1<br>AFF 2.3 | D%<br>D% | - | | | Adults, New Hampshire, U.S.A.<br>Probability sample<br>N: 600, date: — | PHILL 67A<br>p. 485 |
| MALE SEX | | Positive among the married: G' = +.23 (ns)<br>Negative among singles : G' = -.52 (ns) | COMP 1.1 | G' | | Gt' | ns | Adults, San Francisco, U.S.A.<br>Probability area sample, poststratified by drinking habits<br>N: 979, date: 1964 | KNUPF 66<br>p. 844 |
| MALE SEX | | | HAPP 3.1 | r | +.02 | | ns | People of 46 and older, Duke, U.S.A.<br>Probability, systematic random sample, stratified by age and sex<br>N: 502, date: 1968 | PALMO 72<br>p. 70 |
| MALE SEX | | Stronger among Mexican-Americans<br>Only small differences between the different age-groups among Blacks and Anglo's | AFF 2.3 | DM | + | | | Adults, Houston, Texas, U.S.A.<br>Non-probability purposive quota sample, stratified by age, sex, occupational skill level and ethnicity<br>N: 1441, date: autumn, 1969 | GAITZ 72<br>p. 63 |
| MALE SEX | | Stronger among those scoring high on perceived desirability of happiness: Q = -.32<br>Not among those scoring low on perceived desirability of happiness : Q = +.03 | HAPP 1.1 | G' | -.16 | Gt' | ns | Adults in the New England and Mid-Atlantic States, U.S.A.<br>Probability cluster sample<br>N: 404, date: — | PHILL 72<br>p. 932 |
| MALE SEX | | | AFF 3.1 | | - | | ns | College students, U.S.A.<br>Non-probability chunk sample (test-retest group)<br>N: 180, date: autumn, 1934/1935 | YOUNG 37A<br>p. 325 |
| MALE SEX | | | HAPP 1.1<br>AFF 1.1 | G'<br>G' | -.14<br>-.10 | | | Juniors and seniors attentding public high schools in New York State, U.S.A.<br>Probability cluster sample of 10 public high schools<br>sample A: N=1682, sample B: N=1664, sample C: N=1678<br>date: 1960 | BRENN 70<br>p. 85 |

| | | | | | | | | | |
|---|---|---|---|---|---|---|---|---|---|
| MALE SEX | | Strongest among freshmen (01)<br>No relation among sophomores and juniors<br>Negative among seniors | AFF 2.1 | DM | - | t | 01 | Undergarduate full-time college students, U.S.A.<br>Non-probability chunk sample<br>N: 952, date: March, 1965 | CONST 65<br>p. 50 |
| MALE SEX | | Computed for the 88 freshmen who were examined twice only (see excerpt, Part II).<br>Reversed in senior years (ns) | AFF 2.1 | DM | - | t | 01 | Undergraduate college students, U.S.A.<br>Non-probability chunk sample<br>N: 581, date: — | CONST 70<br>p. 7 |
| MALE SEX | | males : Mean = 6.7<br>females: Mean = 6.4 | AFF 3.1<br>HAPP 3.1 | $r_{pm}$<br>$r_{pm}$ | +.17<br>-.15 | | ns<br>ns | Undergraduate students, U.S.A.<br>Non-probability chunk sample<br>N: 67, date: summer, 1970 | GORMA 71<br>p. 215/219 |
| MALE SEX | | males : Mean = 6.7<br>females: Mean = 6.4 | AFF 3.1<br>(1st instr.) | DM | - | t | ns | Undergraduate university students, California, U.S.A.<br>Non-probability chunk sample<br>N: 86, date: November - December, 1971 | FORDY 72<br>p. 144 |
| | | non-significant differences between males and females for % of day in happy moods, neutral moods and unhappy moods | AFF 3.1<br>(2nd instr.) | DM | - | t | ns | | |
| MALE SEX | | | COMP 1.1 | $r_{pm}$ | -.16 | | ns | Undergraduate college students, Hawaii<br>Non-probability accidental sample<br>N: 101, date: — | WILSO 65<br>p. 375 |
| MALE SEX | | | HAPP 1.1 | G' | +.38 | Gt' | ns | Student teachers, Chapel Hill, U.S.A.<br>Probability sample, proportionally stratified by teaching level<br>N: 75, date: spring, 1967 | GONZA 67<br>p. 80 |
| MALE SEX | | 91% of the retired women indicated that they were happy as contrasted with only 85% of the men. | HAPP 1.1 | D% | - | | | Retired university faculty members, U.S.A.<br>Probability systematic random sample<br>N: 547, date: 1968 | SKRAB 69<br>p. 67 |
| MALE SEX | | | HAPP 2.1 | G' | +.02 | Gt' | ns | Aged, chronically ill patients, U.S.A.<br>Probability sample<br>N: 167, date: 1959 | HENLE 67<br>p. 69 |
| MALE SEX | | | HAPP 3.1 | G' | -.12 | Gt' | ns | National adult population, Dominican Republic<br>Probability sample<br>N: 814, date: ± 1960 | CANTR 65/1<br>p. 378 |
| MALE SEX | | | HAPP 2.1 | G' | -.04 | Gt' | ns | National adult population, Mexico<br>Probability sample, proportionally stratified by sex, age, occupation, S.E.S. and education<br>N: 1752, date: 1948 - 1949 | BUCHA 53<br>p. 188 |
| MALE SEX | | | HAPP 3.1 | G' | -.08 | Gt' | ns | National adult population, Panama<br>Probability sample, proportionally poststratified by dwelling and mortality<br>N: 642, date: ± 1960 | CANTR 65/1<br>p. 378 |
| MALE SEX | | | HAPP 3.1 | G' | -.07 | Gt' | ns | National adult population, Cuba<br>Probability area sample<br>N: 992, date: ± 1960 | CANTR 65/1<br>p. 378 |
| MALE SEX | | | HAPP 1.1<br>AFF 2.3 | G'<br>G' | +.17<br>+.04 | Gt'<br>Gt' | 01<br>ns | National adult population, Puerto Rico<br>Probability, simple random sample<br>N: 1417, date: November, 1963 - January, 1964 and August - October, 1964 | MATLI 66<br>p. 16 |

| | | | | | | | | | |
|---|---|---|---|---|---|---|---|---|---|
| MALE SEX | | | HAPP 3.1 | G' | -.26 | Gt' | 01 | National adult population, Brazil<br>Probability samples<br>N: 2168, date: ± 1960 | CANTR 65/1<br>p. 378 |
| MALE SEX | | Stronger among those who have no children: DM= - (01)<br>Lower among those who have children: DM= - (01) | HAPP 3.1 | DM | - | DMRT | 01 | Adults in the Dominican Republic, Panama and Yugoslavia (married people only)<br>Pooling of the three Cantril (1965) samples<br>N: 4113, date: ± 1960 | BOHN 72<br>p. 31 |
| MALE SEX | | age 15-24: G'= -.05 (ns)<br>age 25-54: G'= +.05 (ns)<br>age 55+: G'= +.15 (01) | HAPP 2.1 | G' | +.07 | Gt' | 01 | National populations of nine European countries<br>Type of sample construction not reported<br>N: 9605 (or 9543, see remarks in excerpt, Part II).<br>date: May, 1975 | COMMI 75<br>p. 139/153 |
| | | age 15-24: G'= -.23 (01)<br>age 25-54: G'= -.04 (ns)<br>age 55+: G'= +.09 (01) | HAPP 1.1 | G' | -.04 | Gt' | 05 | | |
| MALE SEX | | | HAPP 2.1 | G' | -.04 | Gt' | ns | National population, Belgium<br>N: 1555 (1507), date: May, 1975 | COMMI 75<br>p. 143/155 |
| | | | HAPP 1.1 | G' | -.08 | Gt' | ns | | |
| MALE SEX | | | HAPP 2.1 | G' | +.02 | Gt' | ns | National adult population, Britain<br>Probability sample, proportionally stratified by sex, age, occupation, S.E.S. and education<br>N: 1195, date: 1948 - 1949 | BUCHA 53<br>p. 137 |
| SEX | | Both males and females had a mean happiness score of 5.5 | HAPP 2.1 | DM | 0 | | | National population, Britain<br>Non-probability quota sample<br>N: 213, date: March, 1971 | ABRAM 73<br>p. 4 |
| MALE SEX | | | HAPP 2.1 | G' | -.02 | Gt' | ns | National population, United Kingdom (including Northern Ireland)<br>N: 1317 (1325), date: May, 1975 | COMMI 75<br>p. 143/155 |
| | | | HAPP 1.1 | G' | -.18 | Gt' | 01 | | |
| MALE SEX | | | HAPP 2.1 | G' | -.08 | Gt' | ns | National population, Denmark<br>N: 1039 (1073), date: May, 1975 | COMMI 75<br>p. 143/155 |
| | | | HAPP 1.1 | G' | -.13 | Gt' | 05 | | |
| MALE SEX | | | COMP 1.1 | | - | | ns | Adult students, Denmark<br>Non-probability chunk sample<br>N: 113, date: 1946 - 1947 | IISAG 48<br>p. 241 |
| MALE SEX | | Unaffected by marital status<br><br>Helsinki: G'= -.21 (05)<br>Stronger among those of low S.E.S.<br>Rural communes: G'= -.12 (ns) | HAPP 2.1 | G' | -.17 | Gt' | 05 | Persons of age 15-64, Finland<br>Probability sample<br>N: 948, date: spring - summer, 1966 | HAAVI 71<br>p. 587 |
| MALE SEX | | | HAPP 2.1 | G' | +.00 | Gt' | ns | National adult population, France<br>Probability sample, proportionally stratified by sex, age, occupation, S.E.S. and education<br>N: 1000, date: 1948 - 1949 | BUCHA 53<br>p. 147 |
| MALE SEX | | | HAPP 2.1 | G' | -.22 | Gt' | 01 | National population, France<br>N: 1196 (1156), date: May, 1975 | COMMI 75<br>p. 143/155 |
| | | | HAPP 1.1 | G' | -.14 | Gt' | ns | | |
| MALE SEX | | | HAPP 2.1 | G' | -.05 | Gt' | ns | National adult population, W. Germany<br>Probability sample, proportionally stratified by sex, age, occupation, S.E.S. and education<br>N: 3371, date: 1948 - 1949 | BUCHA 53<br>p.156 |
| MALE SEX | | | HAPP 3.1 | G' | +.17 | Gt' | ns | National population, W. Germany<br>Probability area sample<br>N: 480, date: ± 1960 | CANTR 65/1<br>p. 378 |

| | | | | | | | | | |
|---|---|---|---|---|---|---|---|---|---|
| MALE SEX | | | HAPP 2.1<br>HAPP 1.1 | G'<br>G' | +.35<br>+.10 | Gt'<br>Gt' | 01<br>ns | National population, W.Germany<br>N: 1039 (1039), date: May, 1975 | COMMI 75<br>p. 143/155 |
| MALE SEX | | | HAPP 2.1<br>HAPP 1.1 | G'<br>G' | -.07<br>-.18 | Gt'<br>Gt' | ns<br>05 | National population, Ireland<br>N: 999 (996), date: May, 1975 | COMMI 75<br>p. 143/155 |
| MALE SEX | | | HAPP 2.1 | G' | -.10 | Gt' | ns | National adult population, Italy<br>Probability sample, proportionally stratified by sex, age, occupation, S.E.S. and education<br>N: 1078, date: 1948 - 1949 | BUCHA 53<br>p. 175 |
| MALE SEX | | | HAPP 2.1<br>HAPP 1.1 | G'<br>G' | +.45<br>-.10 | Gt'<br>Gt' | 01<br>ns | National population, Italy<br>N: 1043 (1043), date: May, 1975 | COMMI 75<br>p. 143/155 |
| MALE SEX | | | HAPP 2.1<br>HAPP 1.1 | G'<br>G' | -.05<br>-.12 | Gt'<br>Gt' | ns<br>ns | National population, Luxembourg<br>N: 324 (311), date: May, 1975 | COMMI 75<br>p. 143/155 |
| MALE SEX | | | HAPP 1.1 | G' | +.05 | Gt' | 05 | National adult population, The Netherlands<br>N: at least 1000, date: 1948 | NIPO 49<br>p. 4 |
| MALE SEX | | | HAPP 2.1 | G' | -.05 | Gt' | ns | National adult population, The Netherlands<br>Probability sample, proportionally stratified by sex, age, occupation, S.E.S. and education<br>N: 942, date: 1948 - 1949 | BUCHA 53<br>p. 197 |
| MALE SEX | | | HAPP 2.1<br>HAPP 1.1 | G'<br>G' | -.02<br>+.05 | Gt'<br>Gt' | ns<br>ns | National population, The Netherlands<br>N: 1093 (1093), date: May, 1975 | COMMI 75<br>p. 143/155 |
| MALE SEX | | Lower among married Ss: G'= -.03 (ns)<br>Stronger among singles: G'= -.13 (ns) | HAPP 2.1 | G' | -.07 | Gt' | ns | Adults, Amsterdam, The Netherlands<br>Probability systematic random sample, stratified by sex and marital status<br>N: 600, date: September - December, 1965 | JONG 69<br>p. 188 |
| MALE SEX | | Stronger among married Ss (10) | HAPP 1.1 | G' | -.02 | Gt' | ns | Adults, Utrecht, The Netherlands<br>Probability sample, stratified by age<br>N: 300, date: autumn, 1967 | MOSER 69<br>p. 12 |
| MALE SEX | | | HAPP 2.1 | G' | -.16 | Gt' | 01 | National adult population, Norway<br>Probability sample, proportionally stratified by sex, age, occupation, S.E.S. and education<br>N: 1030, date: 1948 - 1949 | BUCHA 53<br>p. 205 |
| SEX | | | HAPP 2.1 | | | | ns | National adult population, Poland<br>Non-probability purposive quota sample, stratified by sex, age, type of local community, employment and S.E.S.<br>N: 2387, date: June - July, 1960 | MAKAR 62<br>p. 106 |
| MALE SEX | | males : Mean = 4.3<br>females: Mean = 4.4 | HAPP 3.1 | DM | - | | | National adult population, Poland<br>Probability samples<br>N: 1464, date: ± 1960 | CANTR 65/1<br>p. 374 |
| MALE SEX | | | HAPP 3.1 | G' | +.05 | Gt' | ns | National adult population, Yugoslavia<br>Probability sample<br>N: 1523, date: ± 1960 | CANTR 65/1<br>p. 378 |
| MALE SEX | | | HAPP 3.1 | G' | -.07 | Gt' | ns | National population, Egypt<br>Non-probability accidental sample, proportionally poststratified by dwelling<br>N: 499, date: ± 1960 | CANTR 65/1<br>p. 378 |

| | | | | | | | | |
|---|---|---|---|---|---|---|---|---|
| MALE SEX | | | HAPP 3.1 | G' | -.15 | Gt' | 01 | National population, Israel<br>Probability sample<br>N: 1170, date: ± 1960 | CANTR 65/1<br>p. 378 |
| MALE SEX | | | HAPP 3.1 | G' | +.23 | Gt' | 01 | National adult population, Nigeria<br>Probability sample, proportionally stratified by dwelling and region<br>N: 1200, date: ± 1960 | CANTR 65/1<br>p. 378 |
| MALE SEX | | | HAPP 3.1 | G' | -.14 | Gt' | 01 | National population, India<br>Probability sample, proportionally poststratified by dwelling<br>N: 2366, date: 1958 | CANTR 65/1<br>p. 378 |
| MALE SEX | | males : Mean = 5.1<br>females: Mean = 5.3 | HAPP 3.1 | DM | - | | | National adult population, Japan<br>Probability sample<br>N: 972, date: ± 1960 | CANTR 65/1<br>p. 370 |
| MALE SEX | | | HAPP 3.1 | G' | -.08 | Gt' | ns | National adult population, The Philippines<br>Probability sample, proportionally poststratified by dwelling<br>N: 500, date: ± 1960 | CANTR 65/1<br>p. 378 |
| MALE SEX | | | HAPP 2.1 | G' | +.08 | Gt' | ns | National adult population, Australia<br>Probability sample, proportionally stratified by sex, age, occupation, S.E.S. and education<br>N: 945, date: 1948 - 1949 | BUCHA 53<br>p. 130 |

## G 1.2 - GENDER-ROLE ATTITUDES

| | | | | | | | | | |
|---|---|---|---|---|---|---|---|---|---|
| PROGRESSIVE SEX-ROLE ATTITUDE (SELF-ORIENTEDNESS) | 12-item index of agree / disagree statements on various views of the woman's role, indicative of a more progressive outlook: one is more concerned with achievement and maximalization of one's own potential.<br>(items from the revised Fand Inventory; see Fand, 1955) | Self-oriented women were less happy during the preceding academic year: $r_{pm} = -.22$ (01).<br>(N = 75; see remarks in excerpt of PORTE 67, Part II). | AFF 2.1 | | | | ns | Female college seniors, Rochester, U.S.A.<br>Non-probability chunk sample<br>N: 162, date: May - June, 1966 | PORTE 67<br>p. 78<br>PORTE 72<br>p. 87 |
| TRADITIONAL SEX-ROLE ATTITUDE (OTHER-ORIENTEDNESS) | 12-item index of agree / disagree statements on various views of the woman's role, indicative of a traditional outlook: one finds personal fulfillment through fostering the fulfillment of others, usually husband and children.<br>(items from the revised Fand Inventory; see Fand, 1955) | Other-orientedness was not related to happiness during the preceding academic year either.<br>N = 75; see above) | AFF 2.1 | | | | ns | See above | PORTE 67<br>p. 79<br>PORTE 72<br>p. 87 |
| <u>SEX-ROLE ATTITUDE:</u> | 24-item inventory indicative of a self- or other orientation<br>(revised Fand Inventory; see above) | Seven factors and two composite scores were derived<br>(See above for composite scores) | | | | | | See above | PORT 72<br>p. 87 |
| - IDENTITY DERIVED THROUGH TRADITIONAL ROLES | Factor indicative of identity derived through the status conferred by marriage and children, rather than through own efforts (other-orientation) | | AFF 2.1 | | | | ns | | |
| - WOMAN'S ROLE IS SUBMISSIVE | Factor indicative of a traditional, submissive sex-role attitude (other-orientation) | | AFF 2.1 | | | | ns | | |
| - NEED FOR INDIVIDUALISTIC ACHIEVEMENT AND SATISFACTION | Factor indicative of a need for personal fulfillment and development (self-orientation) | | AFF 2.1 | | | | ns | | |

| | | | | | | | | | |
|---|---|---|---|---|---|---|---|---|---|
| - HOME ORIENTATED, DUTY TO CHILDREN STRESSED | Factor indicative of the belief that the 'good mother' remains at home to care for her children (other orientation) | | AFF 2.1 | | | | ns | | |
| - TRADITIONAL ROLE IMPLIES SOME RELINQUISHING OF NEEDS FOR PERSONAL FULFILLMENT | Factor indicative of a feeling of some inherent contradiction in fulfilling oneself as an individual and fulfilling oneself as a wife and mother (other-orientation) | This factor was negatively correlated with hedonic level during the preceding academic year: $r_{pm}$ = -.24 (05). N = 75; see remarks in excerpt of PORTE 67, Part II) | AFF 2.1 | | | | ns | | |
| - SENSE OF AUTONOMY AND HEIGHTENED INDEPENDENCE | Factor indicative of a concern with personal development and not with the approval of other people (self-orientation) | | AFF 2.1 | | | | ns | | |
| - FAMILY INADEQUATE TO COMPLETELY FULFULL NEEDS | Factor indicative of a need of something over and beyond a family to fulfull oneself (self-orientation) | | AFF 2.1 | | | | ns | | |
| IMAGE OF A FEMININE WOMAN | Each subject was asked to rate her image of a feminine woman on a semantic differential of 27 bi-polar 7-point adjective scales. | Four factors were derived. None of them was related to happiness. For factors used see under 'Content of real self-image' (Part III, S 2.2.1). | HAPP 1.1 | r | $\pm$ 0 | | ns | Married female graduates of the Liberal Arts College, U.S.A. Probability cluster sample N: 229, date: 1971 | GORDO 74 p. 243 |
| PERCEIVED MALE IMAGE OF A FEMININE WOMAN | Each subject was asked to rate what she perceived to be the average man's image of a feminine woman on a semantic differential (see above) | See above | HAPP 1.1 | r | $\pm$ 0 | | ns | See above | GORDO 74 p. 243 |

# H 1 HAPPINESS

see also 'Life quality' (L 2)
'Satisfaction with ...' (S 1)
'Affect' (A 2)



## H 1.1 - OVERALL HAPPINESS OR LIFE SATISFACTION

### H 1.1.1 - HAPPINESS AND HAPPINESS

| | | | | | | | | | |
|---|---|---|---|---|---|---|---|---|---|
| SATISFACTION WITH LIFE | Closed question rated on an 11-point self-anchoring scale (Cantril satisfaction with life rating) (HAPP 2.1) | See second instrument (happiness measure presented in the second column) resp. first instrument (happiness measure mentioned in next column) in excerpt (Part II). | HAPP 3.1 | $r_{pm}$ | +.36 | | | National adult population, U.S.A. Probability sample N: 1549, date: 1960 | CANTR 65/2 p. 415 |
| LIFE SATISFACTION | Closed question rated on an 11-point self-anchoring scale (Cantril satisfaction with life rating; see above) (HAPP 2.1) | See first, resp. second instrument in excerpt (Part II). | HAPP 3.1 | $r$ | +.43 | | | National adult population, U.S.A. Cantril (1965) modified probability sample N: 1406, date: 1959 | BORTN 70 p. 44 |
| HAPPINESS | Closed question: not too happy / pretty happy / very happy (HAPP 1.1) (see Gurin et al., 1960) | See fourth, resp first instrument in excerpt (Part II). | HAPP 3.1 | $r_{pm}$ | +.53 | | | National adult population, U.S.A. Probability area sample (first sample) N: 1297, date: May, 1972 | ANDRE 74 p. 15 |
| SATISFACTION WITH LIFE AS A WHOLE | Closed question rated on a 7-point scale raging from 'completely dissatisfied' to 'completely satisfied' (HAPP 2.1) | See second resp. first instrument | HAPP 3.1 | $r_{pm}$ | +.56 | | | National adult population, U.S.A. Probability area sample (second sample) N: 1118, date: November, 1972 | ANDRE 74 p. 15 |
| FEELING WARM ABOUT LIFE | Closed question rated on a graphic scale ranging from 'very cold' to 'very warm' (COMP 1.1) | See third resp. first instrument | HAPP 3.1 | $r_{pm}$ | +.49 | | | See above | ANDRE 74 p. 15 |
| | | See third resp. second instrument | HAPP 2.1 | $r_{pm}$ | +.46 | | | | |
| SATISFACTION WITH LIFE AS A WHOLE | Closed question rated on a 7-point scale ranging from 'completely dissatisfied' to 'completely satisfied' (HAPP 2.1) | See second resp. first instrument | HAPP 3.1 | $r_{pm}$ | +.70 | | | National adult population, U.S.A. Probability area sample (third sample) N: 1072, date: November, 1972 | ANDRE 74 p. 15 |
| FEELING WARM ABOUT LIFE | Closed question rated on a graphic scale ranging from 'very cold' to 'very warm' (COMP 1.1) | See third resp. first instrument | HAPP 3.1 | $r_{pm}$ | +.53 | | | See above | ANDRE 74 p. 15 |
| | | See third resp. second instrument | HAPP 2.1 | $r_{pm}$ | +.47 | | | | |
| HAPPINESS | Closed question: not too happy / pretty happy / very happy (HAPP 1.1) (see Gurin et al., 1960) | See fourth resp. first instrument | HAPP 3.1 | $r_{pm}$ | +.59 | | | See above | ANDRE 74 p. 15 |
| | | See fourth resp. second instrument | HAPP 2.1 | $r_{pm}$ | +.49 | | | | |
| | | See fourth resp. third instrument | COMP 1.1 | $r_{pm}$ | +.39 | | | | |

| | | | | | | | | | |
|---|---|---|---|---|---|---|---|---|---|
| HAPPINESS | Closed question on feelings about own happiness: terrible / unhappy / mostly dissatisfied / mixed/ mostly satisfied / pleased / delighted (HAPP 3.1) | See fifth resp. first instrument in excerpt (Part II). | HAPP 3.1 | $r_{pm}$ | +.77 | | | National adult population, U.S.A. (see last page) | ANDRE 74 p. 15 |
| | | See fifth resp. second instrument | HAPP 2.1 | $r_{pm}$ | +.63 | | | | |
| | | See fifth resp. third instrument | COMP 1.1 | $r_{pm}$ | +.50 | | | | |
| | | See fifth resp. fourth instrument | HAPP 1.1 | $r_{pm}$ | +.57 | | | | |
| QUALITY OF AFFECT | 2-item index of closed questions on enjoying life and feeling downcast or dejected (COMP 1.2) (Two Component Quality of Affect Scale) | See second resp. first instrument in excerpt (Part II).<br>Unaffected by sex, age and educational level | HAPP 1.1 | G | +.59 | | 001 | Local population, Washington County, U.S.A.<br>Probability cluster sample of households<br>N: 916, date: summer, 1973 - summer, 1974 | BRENN 75A p. 324 |
| QUALITY OF AFFECT | 3-item index of closed questions on enjoying life, feeling downcast or dejected, and usual affect (question on spirits) (COMP 1.2) (Three Component Quality of Affect Scale) | See third resp. first instrument<br>Unaffected by sex, age and educational level | HAPP 1.1 | G | +.62 | | 001 | See above | BRENN 75A p. 324 |
| ENJOYING LIFE | Closed question: never / rarely / occasionally / fairly often / very often | Item of second and third instrument (see above)<br>Unaffected by sex, age and educational level<br>When feeling downcast or dejected and usual affect are kept constant: $G_{pt}$ = +.79 (001) | HAPP 1.1 | G | +.84 | | 001 | See above | BRENN 75A p. 324 |
| HAPPINESS | Closed question rated on an 11-point self-anchoring scale (Cantril present personal rating; see Cantril, 1965) (HAPP 3.1) | See second resp. first instrument in excerpt (Part II).<br>Lower among males : G = +.31<br>Stronger among females: G = +.43 | HAPP 1.1 | G | + | | | Adults, Metro Manila, Philippines<br>Probability area sample<br>N: 941, date: January - April, 1972 | BULAT 73 p. 231 |

## H 1.1.2 - HAPPINESS AND HEDONIC LEVEL OF AFFECT

see below (H 1.2.1)

## H 1.1.3 - HAPPINESS AND CONTENTMENT

see below (H 1.3.1)

## H 1.2 - HEDONIC LEVEL OF AFFECT

see also 'Elation' (A 2.2.5)

### H 1.2.1 - HEDONIC LEVEL AND HAPPINESS

| | | | | | | | | | |
|---|---|---|---|---|---|---|---|---|---|
| RELATIVE BALANCE OF POSITIVE AND NEGATIVE FEELINGS (AFFECT BALANCE) | 9-item index of closed questions on specific affects (Bradburn & Caplovitz Affects Balance Score) (AFF 2.3). | See second instrument (measure of hedonic level presented in second column) resp. first instrument (happiness measure mentioned in next column) in excerpt (Part II).<br>Association with Index of Positive Affects: G' = +.38 (01)<br>Stronger among males<br>Association with Index of Negative Affects: G' = -.49 (01) | HAPP 1.1 | G' | +.50 | Gt' | 01 | Inhabitants of four small communities, Illinois, U.S.A.<br>Probability multi stage samples<br>N: 2006, date: March, 1962 | BRADB 65/1 p. 18-20 |

| | | | | | | | | | |
|---|---|---|---|---|---|---|---|---|---|
| PSYCHOLOGICAL WELL-BEING | 10-item index of closed questions on specific affects (Bradburn Affect Balance Score) (AFF 2.3) | See first resp. second instrument in excerpt (Part II).<br>Association with Index of Positive Affects: G = +.34 (05)<br>Association with Index of Negative Affects: G = -.33 (05) | HAPP 1.1 | G | +.45 | | 05 | Adults, urban areas, U.S.A.<br>Probability area samples<br>N: 2787, date: January, 1963 - January, 1964 | BRADB 69<br>p. 63-68 |
| AFFECT BALANCE | 10-item index of closed questions on specific affects (Bradburn Affect Balance Score) (AFF 2.3) | See sixth resp. first instrument in excerpt (Part II).<br>Correlation with Index of Positive Affects: r = +.36<br>Correlation with Index of Negative Affects: r = -.32 | HAPP 3.1 | $r_{pm}$ | +.48 | | | National adult population, U.S.A.<br>Probability area sample (third sample)<br>N: 1072, date: November, 1972 | ANDRE 74<br>p. 15 |
| | | See sixth resp. second instrument<br>Index of positive Affects: r = +.30<br>Index of Negative Affects: r = -.31 | HAPP 2.1 | $r_{pm}$ | +.43 | | | | |
| | | See sixth resp. third instrument<br>Index of Positive Affects: r = +.25<br>Index of Negative Affects: r = -.20 | COMP 1.1 | $r_{pm}$ | +.32 | | | | |
| | | See sixth resp. fourth instrument<br>Index of Positive Affects: r = +.34<br>Index of Negative Affects: r = -.31 | HAPP 1.1 | $r_{pm}$ | +.50 | | | | |
| | | See sixth resp. fifth instrument<br>Index of Positive Affects: r = +.36<br>Index of Negative Affects: r = -.30 | HAPP 3.1 | $r_{pm}$ | +.47 | | | | |
| AFFECT BALANCE | 10-item index of closed questions on specific affects (Bradburn Affect Balance Score) (AFF 2.3) | See second resp. first instrument in excerpt (Part II). | HAPP 1.1 | G' | +.55 | Gt' | 01 | Adults, New Hampshire, U.S.A.<br>Probability sample<br>N: 600, date: — | PHILL 67A<br>p. 483 |
| PSYCHOLOGICAL WELL-BEING | 10-item index of closed questions on specific affects (Bradburn Affect Balance Score) (AFF 2.3) | See first resp. second instrument in excerpt (Part II).<br>Index of Positive Affects: r = +.19 (01)<br>Index of Negative Affects: r = -.32 (01) | COMP 1.1 | $r_{pm}$ | +.36 | $Chi^2$ | 01 | Adults, Houston, Texas, U.S.A.<br>Non-probability purposive quota sample, stratified by age, sex, occupational skill level and ethnicity<br>N: 1441, date: autumn, 1969 | GAITZ 72<br>p. 65 |
| AFFECT BALANCE | 10-item index of closed questions on specific affects (adapted Bradburn Affect Balance Score) (AFF 1.3) | See first resp. second instrument in excerpt (Part II).<br>Computed for normals only (N=19)<br>Index of Positive Affects: G = +.49 (05)<br>Index of Negative Affects: G = -.20 (ns) | HAPP 1.1 | G | +.40 | | ns | Aged persons, Los Angeles County, U.S.A.<br>Non-probability purposive samples by expert choice of psychiatric out-patients and normal community subjects<br>N: 27, date: 1971 | MORIW 74<br>p. 76 |
| PSYCHOLOGICAL WELL-BEING | 10-item index of closed questions on specific affects (Bradburn Affect Balance Score) (AFF 2.3) | See first resp. second instrument in excerpt (Part II). | HAPP 1.1 | G' | +.76 | Gt' | 01 | Catholic sisters, U.S.A.<br>Non-probability chunk sample<br>N: 183, date: — | LEWIS 72<br>p. 66 |
| AFFECT BALANCE | 8-item index of closed questions on specific affects (adapted Bradburn & Caplovitz Affect Balance Score) (AFF 2.3) | See second resp. first instrument in excerpt (Part II).<br>Index of Positive Affects: r > +.18 (05)<br>Index of Negetive Affects: r > -.18 (05) | HAPP 1.1 | $r_{pm}$ | > +.18 | | 05 | People in transition, U.S.A.<br>Stratified random sample<br>N: 216, date: — | CHIRI 71<br>p. 603 |

| | | | | | | | | | |
|---|---|---|---|---|---|---|---|---|---|
| AFFECT BALANCE | 10-itm index of closed questions on specific affects (adapted Bradburn & Caplovitz Affect Balance Score) (AFF 2.3) | See second resp. first instrument in excerpt (Part II).<br>When all 'pretty happy' Ss were deleted: G = +.89<br>Index of Possitive Affects: tau = +.30 : G = +.42<br>Index of Negative Affects: tau = -.29 ; G = -.42<br>When happiness is used as a dependent variable<br>affect balance : d = +.34<br>positive affect: d = +.24<br>negative affect: d = -.25 | HAPP 1.1 | tau<br>G | +.39<br>+.56 | | 001 | Non-hospitalized schizophrenic males, Monroe County, New York, U.S.A.<br>Probability sample, drawn form the Monroe County Psychiatric Case Register<br>N: 178, date: 1964 - 1965 | ALEXA 68<br>p. 49-53/84 |
| PLEASURE INVOLVEMENT | 4-item index of closed questions on specific positive affects (adapted Bradburn Index of Positive Affects) (AFF 2.3) | See first resp. second instrument in excerpt (Part II).<br>When controlled for 'negative affect' and 'long-term satisfaction': $r_{pc}$ = +.31 (001) | HAPP 1.1 | $r_{pm}$ | +.38 | | 001 | Residents of Stirling County, Maritime, Canada<br>Probability sample, stratified by sex, age, socio-environmental circumstances and mental health<br>N: 112, date: 1963 - 1968 | BEISE 74<br>p. 325 |
| NEGATIVE AFFECT | 5-item index of closed questions on specifec negative affects (adapted Bradburn Index of Negative Affects) (AFF 2.3) | See first resp. second instrument in excerpt (Part II).<br>When controlled for 'pleasure involvement' and 'long-term satisfaction': $r_{pc}$ = -.30 (001) | HAPP 1.1 | $r_{pm}$ | -.44 | | 001 | See above | BEISE 74<br>p. 325 |
| AFFECT BALANCE | 9-item index of closed questions on specific affects (adapted Bradburn & Caplovitz Affect Balance Score) (AFF 2.3) | See second resp. first instrument in excerpt (Part II).<br>Index of Positive Affects: G' = +.19 (01)<br>Index of Negative Affects: G' = -.54 (01) | HAPP 1.1 | G' | +.52 | Gt' | 01 | National adult population, Puerto Rico<br>Probability simple random sample<br>N: 1417, date: November, 1963 - January, 1964 ; August - October, 1964 | MATLI 66<br>p. 10-13 |
| PSYCHOLOGICAL WELL-BEING | 13-item index of closed questions on specific affects (based on Bradburn & Caplovitz Affect Balance Score) (AFF 2.3) | See first resp. second instrument in excerpt (Part II).<br>Index of Positive Affects: G = +.06<br>Index of Negative Affects: G = -.22 | HAPP 1.1. | G | + | | | Employed males, England<br>Non-probability purposive quota sample<br>N: 192, date: — | PAYNE 74<br>p. 17 |
| ENHANCEMENT | 4-item index of closed questions on specific positive affects (based on Bradburn & Caplovitz Index of Positive Affects) (AFF 2.3) | See third resp. first instrument in excerpt (Part II). | HAPP 1.1 | r | +.24 | | | Adults, Metro Manila, Philippines<br>Probability sample<br>N: 941, date: January - April, 1972 | BULAT 73<br>p. 233 |
| | | See third resp. second instrument in excerpt (Part II). | HAPP 3.1 | r | +.24 | | | | |
| DISCOMFORT | 4-item index of closed questions on specific negative affects (based on Bradburn & Caplovitz Index of Negative Affects) (AFF 2.3) | See third resp. first instrument in excerpt (Part II). | HAPP 1.1 | r | -.20 | | | See above | BULAT 73<br>p. 233 |
| | | See third resp. second instrument in excerpt (Part II). | HAPP 3.1 | r | ± 0 | | | | |
| HAPPINESS | Overall composite clinical rank on 'happiness - unhappiness'; using all clinical data and knowledge over a period of three years, including evidence of possible repressed or latent problems at deeper levels of the personality. (COMP 5) | This clinical rank on happiness was made a half year after the Elation-Depression Scale (see instrument in excerpt, Part II) was employed.<br>Correlations between this clinical rank on happiness and hedonic level, as assessed by the Elation-Depression Scale, were as follows:<br>-with mean daily average mood: r = +.69<br>-with mean daily highest mood: r = +.48<br>-with mean daily lowest mood : r = +.42 | AFF 3.1 | $r_{pm}$ | +.69 | | | Male college students, U.S.A.<br>Non-probability chunk sample<br>N: 17, date: ± 1960 | WESSM 66/2<br>p. 104 |
| ELATION vs depression | Repeated closed question rated on a 10-point scale, scored every night for 28 consecutive days (Wessman & Ricks Elation - Depression Scale; see above) (AFF 3.1) | See first resp. second instrument in excerpt (Part II).<br>Correlations were as follows:<br>-with mean daily average mood: r = +.26 (05)<br>-with mean daily highest mood: r = +.29 (05)<br>-with mean daily lowest mood : r = +.16 (ns) | HAPP 3.1 | $r_{pm}$ | +.26 | | | Undergraduate students, U.S.A.<br>Non-probability chunk sample<br>N: 67, date: summer, 1970 | GORMA 71<br>p. 216 |

| | | | | | | | | |
|---|---|---|---|---|---|---|---|---|
| USUAL MOOD | Closed question on spirits: very low spirits / fairly low spirits / neither good spirits nor low spirits / fairly good spirits / very good spirits (AFF 1.1) | See second resp. first instrument in excerpt (Part II).<br>When standardized on:<br>- having fun in life, and frequency of low mood : $G_s$ = +.62<br>- having fun in life : $G_s$ = +.68<br>- frequency of low mood : $G_s$ = +.74<br>- tending to be a discouraged person: $G_s$ = +.73<br>- tending to be a lonely person : $G_s$ = +.72<br>- anxiety symptoms : $G_s$ = +.77<br>Unaffected by sex | HAPP 1.1 | G<br>V | +.78<br>.39 | <br>$Chi^2$ | <br>01 | Juniors and seniors attending public high schools in New York State, U.S.A.<br>Probability cluster sample of 10 public high schools<br>N: sample A: 1682, sample B: 1664, sample C: 1878<br>date: 1960 | BRENN 70<br>p. 64/71/75/87-88/262 |
| USUAL AFFECT | Closed question on spirits: very low spirits / fairly low spirits / neither good nor low spirits / fairly good spirits / very good spirits (AFF 1.1) | Third item of third instrument (see excerpt, Part II).<br>When enjoying life and feeling downcast or dejected are kept constant: $G_{pt}$ = +.64 (001)<br>Unaffected by sex, age and educational level | HAPP 1.1 | G | +.75 | | 001 | Local population, Washington County, U.S.A.<br>Probability cluster sample of households<br>N: 916, date: summer, 1973 - summer, 1974 | BRENN 75A<br>p. 324 |
| QUALITY OF AFFECT | 2-item index of closed questions on feeling that things were going your way, and feeling depressed or unhappy (Going-Your-Way / Depressed-or-Unhappy Scale) (AFF 2.3) | See fourth resp. first instrument in excerpt (Part II).<br>See fourth resp. third instrument | HAPP 1.1<br>COMP 1.2 | G<br>G | +.60<br>+.60 | | 001<br>001 | See above | BRENN 75A<br>p. 327 |
| QUALITY OF AFFECT | 2-item index of closed questions on enjoying life and feeling depressed (Enjoyed / Depressed Scale) (AFF 2.3) | See fifth resp. first instrument<br>See fifth resp. third instrument | HAPP 1.1<br>COMP 1.2 | G<br>G | +.61<br>+.68 | | 001<br>001 | See above | BRENN 75A<br>p. 328 |
| QUALITY OF AFFECT | 2-item index of closed questions on feeling happy and feeling sad (Happy/Sad Scale) (AFF 2.3) | See sixth resp. first instrument<br>See sixth resp. third instrument | HAPP 1.1<br>COMP 1.2 | G<br>G | +.61<br>+.59 | | 001<br>001 | See above | BRENN 75A<br>p. 328 |
| MOOD | Closed question on mood-level, rated on a 5-point scale ranging from 'not good almost all the time' to 'very good all the time' (AFF 1.1) | See second resp. first instrument in excerpt (Part II). | HAPP 1.1 | mc | +.77 | | | Urban adult Jewish population, Israel<br>Probability area sample, using dwelling units<br>N: 1940, date: spring, 1973 | LEVY 75/1<br>p. 372 |
| MOOD | Closed question on mood-level (see above) | See above | HAPP 1.1 | mc | +.71 | | | Urban adult Jewish population, Israel<br>Probability area sample, using dwelling units<br>N: 1830, date: summer, 1973 | LEVY 75/2<br>p. 373 |

## H 1.2.2 - HEDONIC LEVEL AND HEDONIC LEVEL

| | | | | | | | | |
|---|---|---|---|---|---|---|---|---|
| RELATIVE AFFECT BALANCE | Ratio of percent of day in happy moods over percent of day in unhappy moods (AFF 3.1) | This ratio was based on repeated open-ended questions on percentage of day in happy, neutral and unhappy moods (see second instrument in excerpt, Part II)<br>The ratio and the separate questions were correlated with the Elation-Depression Scale (see first instrument in excerpt, Part II).<br>Correlations with the separate questions were as follows: % happy moods : r = +.83 (01)<br>% neutral moods: r = -.40 (01)<br>% unhappy moods: r = -.77 (01) | AFF 3.1 | $r_{pm}$ | +.57 | | 01 | Undergraduate university students, California, U.S.A.<br>Non-probability chunk sample<br>N: 86, date: November - December, 1971 | FORDY 72<br>p. 149 |
| ABSOLUTE AFFECT BALANCE | Difference score between percent of day in happy moods and percent of day in unhappy moods (AFF 3.1) | This difference-score was based on the same questions as the above-mentioned ratio (relative affect balance) | AFF 3.1 | $r_{pm}$ | +.87 | | 01 | See above | FORDY 72<br>p. 149 |
| BEING IN GOOD SPIRITS | Closed question: very low spirits / low spirits / good spirits / very good spirits most of the time (AFF 1.1) | Index of Positive Affects: G' = +.09 (ns)<br>Index of Negative Affects: G' = -.59 (01) | AFF 2.3 | G' | +.56 | Gt' | 01 | National adult population, Puerto Rico<br>Probability simple random sample<br>N: 1417, date: winter, 1963/64 + autumn, 1964 | MATLI 66<br>p. 13 |

| | | | | | | | | | |
|---|---|---|---|---|---|---|---|---|---|
| ELATION vs depression | Repeated closed question rated on a 10-point scale, scored every night during three weeks (Wessman & Ricks Elation-Depression Scale) (AFF 3.1) | See second resp. first instrument in excerpt (Part II).<br>Correlations were as follows:<br>- with mean daily average mood: r = +.21 (ns)<br>- with mean daily highest mood: r = +.29 (05)<br>- with mean daily lowest mood : r = +.22 (ns) | AFF 2.1 | $r_{pm}$ | +.21 | | ns | Married females, U.S.A.<br>Non-probability purposive sample by expert choice<br>N: 62, date: — | HARDE 69<br>p. 83 |

## H 1.2.3 - HEDONIC LEVEL AND CONTENTMENT

s e e b e l o w (H 1.3.2)

## H 1.3 - CONTENTMENT

## H 1.3.1 - CONTENTMENT AND HAPPINESS

| | | | | | | | | | |
|---|---|---|---|---|---|---|---|---|---|
| HAVING NO UNFULFILLED ASPIRATIONS | Open-ended direct question on unfulfilled aspirations (CON 1.3)<br>mentions unfulfilled aspirations vs says to have no unfulfilled aspirations | See also under 'Perceived unfulfilled aspirations' (Part III, H 3.3.2) | HAPP 1.1 | G' | +.23 | Gt' | 01 | National adult population, U.S.A.<br>Non-probability quota sample<br>N: 2377, date: February, 1946 | WESSM 56<br>p. 210 |
| SUCCESS IN ACHIEVING GOALS | Closed question rated on an 11-point self-anchoring scale (CON 1.1) | See third instrument (measure of contentment presented in the second column) resp. first instrument (happiness measure mentioned in the next column) in excerpt (Part II). | HAPP 3.1 | $r_{pm}$ | +.39 | | | National adult population, U.S.A.<br>Probability sample<br>N: 1549, date: 1960 | CANTR 65/2<br>p. 268/415 |
| | | See third resp. second instrument | HAPP 2.1 | $r_{pm}$ | +.45 | | | | |
| SUCCESS IN ACHIEVING GOALS | Closed question rated on an 11-point self-anchoring scale, based on Cantril (see above) (CON 1.1) | See third resp. first instrument in excerpt (Part II). | HAPP 2.1 | r | +.45 | | | National adult population, U.S.A.<br>Cantril (1965) modified probability sample<br>N: 1406, date: 1959 | BORTN 70<br>p. 44 |
| | | See third resp. second instrument | HAPP 3.1 | r | +.41 | | | | |
| SATISFACTION OF WANTS (doing well) | Closed question: not doing too well vs doing pretty well (CON 1.1) | See second resp. first instrument in excerpt (Part II). | HAPP 1.1 | G' | +.66 | Gt! | 01 | Non-institutional adult population, U.S.A.<br>Probability multi stage sample<br>N: 1453, date: summer, 1963 | BRENN 67<br>p. 671 |
| GETTING WHAT ONE WANTS FROM LIFE | Closed question: doing not too well / pretty well / very well (CON 1.1) | See third resp. second instrument in excerpt (Part II).<br>Unaffected by sex: males : G = +.69<br>females: G = +.70 | HAPP 1.1 | G | + | | | Adults, urban areas, U.S.A.<br>Probability area sample<br>N: 2787, date: January, 1963 - January, 1964 | BRADB 69<br>p. 51 |
| CONGRUENCE BETWEEN DESIRED AND ACHIEVED GOALS | Content analysis of interview records by two independent judges (component of Life Satisfaction Rating) (CON 1.4) | See first resp. second instrument in excerpt (Part II).<br>See also remarks in excerpt (Part II). | COMP 1.4 | r | +.57 | | | White adult population, Kansas City, U.S.A.<br>Stratified probability sample and non-probability quota sample<br>N: 177, date: — | NEUGA 61<br>p. 139 |

## H 1.3.2 - CONTENTMENT AND HEDONIC LEVEL

| | | | | | | | | | |
|---|---|---|---|---|---|---|---|---|---|
| GETTING WHAT ONE WANTS FROM LIFE | Closed question: not doing too well / pretty well / very well (CON 1.1) | See third resp. first instrument in excerpt (Part II).<br>Index of Positive Affects: G = +.37 (05)<br>Index of Negative Affects: G = -.35 (05) | AFF 2.3 | G | +.47 | | 05 | Adults, urban areas, U.S.A.<br>Probability area samples<br>N: 2787, date: January, 1963 - January, 1964 | BRADB 69<br>p. 63/68 |

| | | | | | | | | |
|---|---|---|---|---|---|---|---|---|
| FEELINGS OF FAILURE TO FULFILL AMBITIONS | Content analysis of a 60-item Q sort, filled out both in very elated and in very depressed moods for self-concept ('an accurate picture of yourself as you honestly feel and believe you are'). (CON 1.3). See also 'Content of real self-image' (Part III, S 2.2.1) | Analysis on the basis of comparison between 9 relatively happy and 8 relatively unhappy males, both in elation and in depression. The unhappy men appeared to be more ambitious, but are also less able to fulfill their ambitions. Especially in depression they feel ineffective, unable to get what they want, pessimistic, and unable to absorb frustration. | AFF 3.1 | $r_{pm}$ | - | t | 05 | Male college students, U.S.A.<br>Non-probability chunk sample<br>N: 17, date: ± 1960 | WESSM 66/2<br>p. 110 |
| GETTING WHAT ONE WANTS FROM LIFE | Closed question: not doing too well now / doing pretty well now (CON 1.1) (based on Bradburn; see last page under BRADB 69) | See third resp. first instrument in excerpt (Part II).<br>Index of Positive Affects: G = -.19<br>Index of Negative Affects: G = -.15 | AFF 2.3 | G | | | | Employed males, England<br>Non-probability purposive quota sample<br>N: 192, date: — | PAYNE 74<br>p. 17 |

## H 1.3.3 - CONTENTMENT AND CONTENTMENT

no research on this matter as yet

## H 1.4 - PAST HAPPINESS

### H 1.4.1 - PERCEIVED PAST HAPPINESS

| | | | | | | | | |
|---|---|---|---|---|---|---|---|---|
| PERCEIVED LIFE SATISFACTION | Closed question rated on an 11-point self-anchoring scale (Cantril past personal rating; see Cantril, 1965) | The question on 'best possible life' (see instrument in excerpt of CANTR 65/1, Part II) was scored here for 5 years ago. | HAPP 2.1<br>HAPP 3.1<br>CON 1.1 | r<br>r<br>r | +.11<br>+.36<br>+.18 | | | National adult population, U.S.A.<br>Cantril (1965) modified probability sample<br>N: 1406, date: 1959 | BORTN 70<br>p. 44 |
| PERCEIVED HAPPINESS 5 YEARS AGO | Closed question rated on an 11-point self-anchoring scale (Cantril past personal rating; see above). | | AFF 3.1<br>HAPP 3.1 | $r_{pm}$<br>$r_{pm}$ | +.00<br>+.27 | | ns<br>05 | Undergraduate students, U.S.A.<br>Non-probability chunk sample<br>N: 67, date: summer, 1970 | GORMA 71<br>p. 215-216 |

### H 1.4.2 - ACTUAL PAST HAPPINESS

| | | | | | | | | |
|---|---|---|---|---|---|---|---|---|
| AVOWED HAPPINESS | Questionnaire items indicative of avowed happiness - unhappiness | This happiness measure was employed two years before hedonic level was assessed by means of the Elation - Depression Scale (see instrument in excerpt, Part II).<br>Correlations were as follows:<br>- with mean daily highest mood: r = +.66<br>- with mean daily average mood: r = +.67<br>- with mean daily lowest mood : r = +.32 | AFF 3.1 | $r_{pm}$ | +.67 | | | Male college students, U.S.A.<br>Non-probability chunk sample<br>N: 17, date: ± 1960 | WESSM 66/2<br>p. 103 |
| HAPPINESS | Composite clinical rank order of happiness by 6 staff psychologists, based on two years of experience with the subjects | This clinical rank was made 6 months before hedonic level was assessed (see above).<br>Correlations were as follows:<br>- with mean daily highest mood: r = +.44<br>- with mean daily average mood: r = +.71<br>- with mean daily lowest mood : r = +.63 | AFF 3.1 | $r_{pm}$ | +.71 | | | See above | WESSM 66/2<br>p. 103 |

| Concept | Measure | Remarks | Corr. with | Stat. | Value | Test | Sign. | Population | Source |
|---|---|---|---|---|---|---|---|---|---|
| HAPPY LIFE HISTORY | Clinical rank on 'happy - unhappy life story', stressing auto-biographic reports and information for three years, concerning past life experiences up to the time of entering college | This clinical rank was made half a year after hedonic level was assessed ( see above).<br>Correlations were as follows:<br>- with mean daily highest mood: r = +.42<br>- with mean daily average mood: r = +.48<br>- with mean daily lowest mood : r = +.34 | AFF 3.1 | $r_{pm}$ | +.48 | t | 05 | Male college students, U.S.A.<br>(see last page) | WESSM 66/2<br>p. 104 |

## H 1.5 - FUTURE HAPPINESS

| Concept | Measure | Remarks | Corr. with | Stat. | Value | Test | Sign. | Population | Source |
|---|---|---|---|---|---|---|---|---|---|
| EXPECTED LIFE SATISFACTION 5 YEARS FROM NOW | Closed question rated on an 11-point self-anchoring scale (Cantril future personal rating; see Cantril, 1965) | The question on 'best possible life' (see instrument in excerpt of CANTR 65/1, Part II) was scored here for 5 years from now | HAPP 2.1 | r | +.28 | | | National adult population, U.S.A.<br>Cantril (1965) modified probability sample<br>N: 1406, date: 1959 | BORTN 70<br>p. 44 |
| | | | HAPP 3.1 | r | +.58 | | | | |
| | | | CON 1.1 | r | +.27 | | | | |
| EXPECTED HAPPINESS 5 YEARS FROM NOW | Closed question rated on an 11-point self-anchoring scale (Cantril future personal rating; see above) | | AFF 3.1 | $r_{pm}$ | +.23 | | ns | Undergraduate students, U.S.A.<br>Non-probability chunk sample<br>N: 67, date: summer, 1970 | GORMA 71<br>p. 215-216 |
| | | | HAPP 3.1 | $r_{pm}$ | +.44 | | 01 | | |
| HAPPINESS | Clinical rank on present happiness - unhappiness, stressing possible aware subjective feelings | This clinical rank was made half a year after hedonic level was assessed by means of the Elation - Depression Scale (see instrument in excerpt, Part II).<br>Correlations were as follows:<br>- with mean daily highest mood: r = +.57<br>- with mean daily average mood: r = +.76<br>- with mean daily lowest mood: r = +.56 | AFF 3.1 | $r_{pm}$ | +.76 | | | Male college students, U.S.A.<br>Non-probability chunk sample<br>N: 17, date: ± 1960 | WESSM 66/2<br>p. 104 |

## H 1.6 - CHANGES IN HAPPINESS

### H 1.6.1 - PAST CHANGES IN HAPPINESS

| Concept | Measure | Remarks | Corr. with | Stat. | Value | Test | Sign. | Population | Source |
|---|---|---|---|---|---|---|---|---|---|
| BEING MORE SATISFIED WITH LIFE THAN 5 YEARS AGO (retrotension) | Actual difference in scores on questions on satisfaction with life now, and 5 years ago (Cantril present and past personal ratings; see Cantril, 1965) | For present and past personal ratings, see resp. second instrument in excerpt (Part II), and under 'Perceived past happiness' (Part III, H 1.4.1). | HAPP 3.1 | r | +.24 | | | National adult population, U.S.A.<br>Cantril (1965) modified probability sample<br>N: 1406, date: 1959 | BORTN 70<br>p. 44 |
| | | | HAPP 2.1 | r | +.45 | | | | |
| | | | CON 1.1 | r | +.16 | | | | |
| PERCEIVED IMPROVEMENT OF LIFE | Actual difference in scores on questions on satisfaction with life now, and 5 years ago (Cantril present and past personal ratings; see Cantril, 1965) | See resp. second instrument in excerpt (Part II). and under 'Perceived past happiness' (Part III, H 1.4.1) | AFF 3.1 | $r_{pm}$ | +.03 | | ns | Undergraduate students, U.S.A.<br>Non-probability chunk sample<br>N: 67, date: summer, 1970 | GORMA 71<br>p. 215-216 |
| | | | HAPP 3.1 | $r_{pm}$ | +.09 | | ns | | |

| | | | | | | | | | |
|---|---|---|---|---|---|---|---|---|---|
| INCREASE IN SATISFACTION DURING 4 – 5 YEARS | Actual difference in scores on questions on satisfaction with life now, and 5 years ago (based on Cantril, 1965) | See first instrument in excerpt (Part II). The same scale was also scored for 'yourself as you were about 4 or 5 years ago' | HAPP 2.1 | $r_{pm}$ | +.62 | | | National population, Britain<br>Non-probability quota sample<br>N: 213, date: March, 1971 | ABRAM 73<br>p. 21 |
| PERCEIVED INCREASE IN SATISFACTION DURING 4 – 5 YEARS | Closed question on satisfaction now compared with 4 or 5 years ago<br>lot less / little less / same / little more / lot more | | HAPP 2.1 | $r_{pm}$ | +.40 | | | See above | ABRAM 73<br>p. 21 |

## H 1.6.2 – EXPECTED CHANGES IN HAPPINESS

| | | | | | | | | | |
|---|---|---|---|---|---|---|---|---|---|
| EXPECTED IMPROVEMENT IN LIFE SATISFACTION DURING NEXT 5 YEARS (protension) | Actual difference in scores on questions on satisfaction with life now, and expected satisfaction 5 years from now (Cantril present and future personal ratings; see Cantril, 1965) | For present and future personal ratings see resp. second instrument in excerpt (Part II), and under 'Future Happiness' (Part III, H 1.5) | HAPP 2.1<br>HAPP 3.1<br>CON 1.1 | r<br>r<br>r | +.10<br>+.08<br>+.04 | | | National adult population, U.S.A.<br>Cantril (1965) modified probability sample<br>N: 1406, date: 1959 | BORTN 70<br>p. 44 |
| EXPECTED IMPROVEMENT OF LIFE | Actual difference in scores on questions on satisfaction with life now, and expected satisfaction 5 years from now (Cantril present and future personal ratings; see Cantril 1965) | See resp. second instrument in excerpt (Part II), and under 'Future Happiness' (Part III, H 1.5). | AFF 3.1<br>HAPP 3.1 | $r_{pm}$<br>$r_{pm}$ | -.11<br>-.74 | | ns<br>01 | Undergraduate students, U.S.A.<br>Non-probability chunk sample<br>N: 67, date: summer, 1970 | GORMA 71<br>p. 215-216 |
| SUBJECTIVE CONFIDENCE AND HOPE | Actual difference in scores on questions on satisfaction with life 5 years ago, and expected satisfaction 5 years from now (Cantril past and future personal ratings; see Cantril, 1965) | For past and future personal ratings see resp. under 'Perceived Past Happiness' (Part III, H 1.4.1) and under 'Future Happiness' (Part III, H 1.5). | AFF 3.1<br>HAPP 3.1 | $r_{pm}$<br>$r_{pm}$ | +.11<br>-.06 | | ns<br>ns | See above | GORMA 71<br>p. 215-216 |
| EXPECTED INCREASE IN SATISFACTION DURING NEXT 4 – 5 YEARS | Actual difference in scores on questions on satisfaction with life now, and 4 or 5 years from now (based on Cantril, 1965) | See first instrument in excerpt (Part II). The same scale also was scored for 'yourself as you expect to be about 4 or 5 years from now'. | HAPP 2.1 | $r_{pm}$ | -.25 | | | National population, Britain<br>Non-probability quota sample<br>N: 213, date: March, 1971 | ABRAM 73<br>p. 21 |
| EXPECTED FUTURE HAPPINESS | Closed question on anticipation of happiness 5 or 10 years from now, compared with present life<br>less happy / about the same / happier | Unaffected by age | HAPP 1.1 | G' | +.16 | Gt' | 01 | Non-institutionalized adults, U.S.A.<br>Probability multi-stage area sample<br>N: 2460, date: spring, 1957 | GURIN 60<br>p. 34 |
| EXPECTED FUTURE HAPPINESS | Closed question on anticipation of happiness 5 or 10 years from now, compared with present life<br>not as happy / about the same / happier | Positieve among males : $t_k$ = +.04 (ns)<br>Negative among females: $t_k$ = -.04 (ns) | HAPP 1.1 | $t_k$ | | | ns | Adult married population with children, U.S.A.<br>Probability area sample<br>N: 797, date: spring, 1957 | VEROF 62<br>p. 196 |
| EXPECTED FUTURE HAPPINESS | Closed question on anticipation of happiness 5 or 10 years from now, compared with present life<br>less happy / about the same / happier | | HAPP 1.1 | G' | -.43 | Gt' | 05 | Student teachers, Chapel Hill, U.S.A.<br>Probability sample, proportionally stratified by teaching level<br>N: 75, date: spring, 1967 | GONZA 67<br>p. 75 |

## H 1.7 – HAPPIEST PERIOD

| | | | | | | | | | |
|---|---|---|---|---|---|---|---|---|---|
| PERCEIVED HAPPIEST PERIOD: | Open-ended direct question<br>Other periods vs period mentioned | | | | | | | National adult population, U.S.A.<br>Non-probability quota sample<br>N: 2377 date: February, 1946 | WESSM 56<br>p. 220 |
| - CHILDHOOD, SCHOOL DAYS, COLLEGE, WHEN I WAS SINGLE | | | HAPP 1.1 | G' | -.32 | Gt' | 01 | | |
| - NOW, RECENTLY, UNTIL NOW | | | HAPP 1.1 | G' | +.23 | Gt' | 01 | | |
| - MARRIED LIFE | | | HAPP 1.1 | G' | +.36 | Gt' | 01 | | |
| - HAVING BABIES, RAISING CHILDREN, WHEN CHILDREN WERE SMALL | | | HAPP 1.1 | G' | +.10 | Gt' | ns | | |
| - FALLING IN LOVE, GETTING MARRIED, EARLY MARRIED LIFE | | | HAPP 1.1 | G' | -.07 | Gt' | ns | | |
| - WHEN FAMILY WAS TOGETHER, BEFORE HUSBAND OR WIFE DIED | | | HAPP 1.1 | G' | -.16 | Gt' | ns | | |
| - EARLY WORKING DAYS | | | HAPP 1.1 | G' | -.48 | Gt' | 01 | | |
| - ALWAYS HAPPY | | | HAPP 1.1 | G' | +.47 | Gt' | 01 | | |
| - NEVER HAPPY | | | HAPP 1.1 | G' | -1.00 | Gt' | 01 | | |
| - NO OPINION | | | HAPP 1.1 | G' | -.37 | Gt' | 01 | | |
| PERCEIVED HAPPIEST PERIOD: | Open-ended direct question (see above)<br>Other periods vs period mentioned | Closely related code categories were combined here. | | | | | | See above | WESSM 56<br>p. 221 |
| - MARRIAGE AND FAMILY LIFE | | | HAPP 1.1 | G' | +.17 | Gt' | 01 | | |
| - CHILDHOOD, YOUTH, AND EARLY ADULTHOOD | | | HAPP 1.1 | G' | -.35 | Gt' | 01 | | |
| - PRESENT, NOW | | | HAPP 1.1 | G' | +.23 | Gt' | 01 | | |
| - ALWAYS HAPPY | | | HAPP 1.1 | G' | +.49 | Gt' | 01 | | |
| - NEVER HAPPY | | | HAPP 1.1 | G' | -1.00 | Gt' | 01 | | |
| - OTHER AND NO OPINION | | | HAPP 1.1 | G' | -.05 | Gt' | ns | | |

## H I.8 - PERCEIVED SOURCES OF HAPPINESS

| | | | | | | | | | |
|---|---|---|---|---|---|---|---|---|---|
| PERCEIVED SOURCES OF HAPPINESS: | Open-ended question: 'What are some of the things you feel pretty happy about these days?' | If a specific source of satisfaction is mentioned more often by the 'very happy' than by the 'not too happy' a positive relationship is assumed, if reversed a negative one. | | | | | | Non-institutionalized adults, U.S.A.<br>Probability multi-stage area sample<br>N: 2460, date: spring, 1957 | GURIN 60<br>p. 31-32 |
| - FAMILY | | | HAPP 1.1 | | + | | | | |
| - MARRIAGE | | | HAPP 1.1 | | + | | | | |
| - ECONOMIC AND MATERIAL FACTORS | | | HAPP 1.1 | | ± 0 | | | | |
| - HEALTH | | | HAPP 1.1 | | - | | | | |

| | | | | | | | | | |
|---|---|---|---|---|---|---|---|---|---|
| **PERCEIVED SOURCES OF UNHAPPINESS:** | Open-ended question: 'What are some of the things you're not too happy about these days?' | If a specific source of dissatisfaction is mentioned more often by the 'very happy' than by the 'not too happy' a positive relationship is assumed, if reversed a negative one. | | | | | | Non-institutionalized adults, U.S.A. (see last page) | GURIN 60 p. 31-32 |
| - CHILDREN | | | HAPP 1.1 | | - | | | | |
| - MARRIAGE | | | HAPP 1.1 | | - | | | | |
| - ECONOMIC AND MATERIAL FACTORS | | | HAPP 1.1 | | ± 0 | | | | |
| - HEALTH | | | HAPP 1.1 | | - | | | | |
| NUMBER OF SOURCES OF HAPPINESS MENTIONED | Less than 2 vs 2 or more sources mentioned on open-ended direct question (see above) | | HAPP 1.1 | G' | +.38 | Gt' | 01 | See above | GURIN 60 p. 33 |
| NUMBER OF SOURCES OF UNHAPPINESS MENTIONED | Less than 2 vs 2 or more sources mentioned on open-ended direct question (see above) | | HAPP 1.1 | G' | -.33 | Gt' | 01 | See above | GURIN 60 p. 33 |
| **PERCEIVED MAJOR FACTOR IN PEOPLE'S HAPPINESS:** | Open-ended question: 'What one thing would you say makes people happy more than anything else?' Other factors vs factor mentioned | | | | | | | National adult population, U.S.A. Non-probability quota sample N: 2377, date: February, 1946 | WESSM 56 p. 215-216 |
| - MARRIAGE, FAMILY, CHILDREN, HAVING HAPPY HOME LIFE | | | HAPP 1.1 | G' | +.10 | Gt' | ns | | |
| - UNDERSTANDING PEOPLE, MAKING OTHER PEOPLE HAPPY, BEING UNSELFISH | | | HAPP 1.1 | G' | +.20 | Gt' | 01 | | |
| - CONTENTED, BEING ADJUSTED TO ONE'S SURROUNDINGS, FREEDOM FROM WORRY | | | HAPP 1.1 | G' | -.00 | Gt' | ns | | |
| - HEALTH | | | HAPP 1.1 | G' | -.11 | Gt' | 05 | | |
| - MONEY, HAVING ENOUGH TO GET ALONG ON | | | HAPP 1.1 | G' | -.41 | Gt' | 01 | | |
| - GETTING ALONG WITH PEOPLE, CONGENIALITY GOOD FRIENDS | | | HAPP 1.1 | G' | +.11 | Gt' | ns | | |
| - SUCCESS IN CHOSEN WORK, ACHIEVEMENT, SECURITY | | | HAPP 1.1 | G' | -.03 | Gt' | ns | | |
| - RELIGION, OBEYING GOD'S WILL | | | HAPP 1.1 | G' | +.25 | Gt' | 01 | | |
| - LOVE, AFFECTION | | | HAPP 1.1 | G' | +.10 | Gt' | ns | | |
| - HAVING FUN, ENJOYMENT | | | HAPP 1.1 | G' | -.24 | Gt' | ns | | |
| - NO OPINION | | | HAPP 1.1 | G' | -.21 | Gt' | 05 | | |
| **PERCEIVED MAJOR FACTOR IN PEOPLE'S UNHAPPINESS:** | Open-ended question: 'What one thing would you say makes people unhappy more than anything else?' Other factors vs factor mentioned | | | | | | | See above | WESSM 56 p. 217 |
| - LACK OF MONEY, DESIRE FOR MONEY | | | HAPP 1.1 | G' | -.13 | Gt' | 01 | | |
| - UNHAPPY HOMELIFE, ARGUMENTS, INLAWS | | | HAPP 1.1 | G' | -.05 | Gt' | ns | | |

| | | | | | | | | | |
|---|---|---|---|---|---|---|---|---|---|
| - JEALOUSY, SUSPICION, LACK OF UNDER-STANDING | | | HAPP 1.1 | G' | +.28 | Gt' | 01 | | |
| - FEAR, WORRY, DISCONTENT | | | HAPP 1.1 | G' | +.02 | Gt' | ns | | |
| - SELFISHNESS, GREED, BAD CHARACTER, OR DISPOSITION | | | HAPP 1.1 | G' | +.15 | Gt' | 05 | | |
| - SICKNESS, POOR HEALTH | | | HAPP 1.1 | G' | -.32 | Gt' | 01 | | |
| - DRINKING, RUNNING AROUND | | | HAPP 1.1 | G' | -.03 | Gt' | ns | | |
| - NOT GETTING ALONG WITH NEIGHBORS AND FRIENDS | | | HAPP 1.1 | G' | +.15 | Gt' | ns | | |
| - FAILURE, LACK OF SUCCESS, LACK OF SECURITY, IDLENESS | | | HAPP 1.1 | G' | -.15 | Gt' | ns | | |
| - LACK OF RELIGION, LEAVING OUT GOD, SIN | | | HAPP 1.1 | G' | +.31 | Gt' | 01 | | |
| - NO OPINION | | | HAPP 1.1 | G' | -.01 | Gt' | ns | | |
| POSITIVE ATTITUDE TOWARDS MARRIAGE | Closed question: 'In general, which do you think is happier - married people or single people?' single / no difference / married | | HAPP 1.1 | G' | +.32 | Gt' | 01 | National adult population, U.S.A. (see last page) | WESSM 56 p. 191 |
| PERCEIVED IMPORTANCE FOR OWN HAPPINESS OF: | 31-item inventory. Each item was scored for its importance for the attainment of happiness by each subject | Analysis on the basis of a comparison of the 'happy' subjects and those reporting 'about as often happy and unhappy' or 'unhappy most of the time'. | | | | | | Adult students, Denmark Non-probability chunk sample N: 113, date: 1946 - 1947 | IISAG 48 p. 241 |
| - ART | | | COMP 1.1 | | | CR | ns | | |
| - BEAUTY | | | COMP 1.1 | | | CR | ns | | |
| - CLEAR CONSCIENCE | | | COMP 1.1 | | + | CR | s | | |
| - ECONOMIC INDEPENDENCE | | | COMP 1.1 | | - | CR | s | | |
| - ENTERTAINMENTS (dance, cinema, restaurants) | | | COMP 1.1 | | | CR | ns | | |
| - EXCITEMENT AND THRILLS | | | COMP 1.1 | | | CR | ns | | |
| - FREEDOM (of speech and behaviour) | | | COMP 1.1 | | | CR | ns | | |
| - FRIENDS | | | COMP 1.1 | | | CR | ns | | |
| - GOOD FELLOWSHIP | | | COMP 1.1 | | | CR | ns | | |
| - GOOD FOOD | | | COMP 1.1 | | | CR | ns | | |
| - GOOD HEALTH | | | COMP 1.1 | | | CR | ns | | |
| - HELPING OTHERS | | | COMP 1.1 | | | CR | ns | | |
| - HUMOUR | | | COMP 1.1 | | | CR | ns | | |
| - JOY OF COLLECTING | | | COMP 1.1 | | | CR | ns | | |

| | | | | | | | | |
|---|---|---|---|---|---|---|---|---|
| - JOY OF WORK | | COMP 1.1 | | | CR | ns | | |
| - KNOWLEDGE | | COMP 1.1 | | | CR | ns | | |
| - LIQUOR | | COMP 1.1 | | | CR | ns | | |
| - LITERATURE | | COMP 1.1 | | | CR | ns | | |
| - LOVE | | COMP 1.1 | | | CR | ns | | |
| - MONEY | | COMP 1.1 | | | CR | ns | | |
| - MUSIC | | COMP 1.1 | | | CR | ns | | |
| - NATURE | | COMP 1.1 | | | CR | ns | | |
| - POLITICS | | COMP 1.1 | | | CR | ns | | |
| - POPULARITY | | COMP 1.1 | | | CR | ns | | |
| - POWER | | COMP 1.1 | | | CR | ns | | |
| - PRESTIGE | | COMP 1.1 | | | CR | ns | | |
| - RELIGION | | COMP 1.1 | | | CR | ns | | |
| - SECURITY | | COMP 1.1 | | | CR | ns | | |
| - SPORTS | | COMP 1.1 | | | CR | ns | | |
| - THINKING | | COMP 1.1 | | | CR | ns | | |
| - TRAVELS | | COMP 1.1 | | - | CR | s | | |

## H 1.9 - MEANING ATTACHED TO THE WORD 'HAPPINESS'

| | | | | | | | | |
|---|---|---|---|---|---|---|---|---|
| MEANING ATTACHED TO THE WORD 'HAPPINESS' | Open-ended question: 'Will you tell me in your own words what the word 'happiness' means to you?<br>Other meanings vs meaning mentioned | | | | | | National adult population, U.S.A.<br>Non-probability quota sample<br>N: 2377, date: February, 1946 | WESSM 56<br>p. 214 |
| - CONTENTED, BEING ADJUSTED TO ONE'S SURROUNDING, FREEDOM FROM WORRY | | HAPP 1.1 | G' | -.01 | Gt' | ns | | |
| - MARRIAGE, FAMILY, CHILDREN, HAVING A HAPPY HOME LIFE | | HAPP 1.1 | G' | +.19 | Gt' | 01 | | |
| - HEALTH | | HAPP 1.1 | G' | -.01 | Gt' | ns | | |
| - MONEY, HAVING ENOUGH TO GET ALONG ON | | HAPP 1.1 | G' | -.26 | Gt' | 01 | | |
| - SUCCESS IN CHOSEN WORK, ACHIEVEMENT, SECURITY | | HAPP 1.1 | G' | -.07 | Gt' | ns | | |
| - UNDERSTANDING PEOPLE, MAKING OTHER PEOPLE HAPPY, BEING UNSELFISH | | HAPP 1.1 | G' | +.08 | Gt' | ns | | |
| - GETTING ALONG WITH PEOPLE, CONGENIALITY, GOOD FRIENDS | | HAPP 1.1 | G' | -.04 | Gt' | ns | | |

| | | | | | | | | |
|---|---|---|---|---|---|---|---|---|
| - HAVING FUN, ENJOYMENT | | | HAPP 1.1 | G' | -.11 | Gt' | ns | National adult population, U.S.A.<br>(see last page) | WESSM 56<br>p. 214 |
| - RELIGION, OBEYING GOD'S WILL | | | HAPP 1.1 | G' | +.41 | Gt' | 01 | | |
| - LOVE, AFFECTION | | | HAPP 1.1 | G' | +.18 | Gt' | ns | | |
| - NO OPINION | | | HAPP 1.1 | G' | -.26 | Gt' | 01 | | |

## H 1.10 - ATTITUDES TOWARDS HAPPINESS

| | | | | | | | | | |
|---|---|---|---|---|---|---|---|---|---|
| HOLDING IDEA OF NATURAL HAPPINESS | Closed question: 'Would you say that by nature you are a happy person?'<br>no vs yes | 90% affirmative answers | HAPP 1.1 | G' | +.76 | Gt' | 01 | National adult population, U.S.A.<br>Non-probability quota sample<br>N: 2377, date: February, 1946 | WESSM 56<br>p. 219 |
| VALUATION OF HAPPINESS | Scale, containing agree / disagree statements | The happier men were more likely to agree with such statements as:'Happiness is one of the primary goals of life' and 'Find me a truly happy man and I'll show you a man who is mature and creative'.<br>The less happy tended to agree with statements to the effect:'Only cows are contented', 'Most people who say they are happy close their eyes to the sufferings of the world', and 'I don't want to be happy: I want to be utterly alive'. | AFF 3.1 | $r_{pm}$ | +.48 | t | 05 | Male college students, U.S.A.<br>Non-probability chunk sample<br>N: 17, date: ± 1960 | WESSM 66/2<br>p. 116-117 |
| PERCEIVED DESIRABILITY OF HAPPINESS AS A TRAIT | Rating of 'happiness' on a 9-point scale of desirability:<br>low / medium / high desirability | Gamma's computed on the basis of proportions 'very happy' answers<br>Stronger among females: Q = +.40<br>Lower among males : Q = +.10<br>Stronger among those reporting a high need for social approval : G' = +.33 (ns)<br>Also stronger among those with a medium need for social approval : G' = +.30 (05)<br>Lower among those with a low need for social approval : G' = +.22 (ns) | HAPP 1.1 | G' | +.28 | Gt' | 01 | Adults in the New England and Mid-Atlantic States, U.S.A.<br>Probability cluster sample<br>N: 404, date: — | PHILL 7?<br>p. 927 |

# H2 HEALTH AND HEALTHCARE



## H 2.1 - PHYSICAL HEALTH

### H 2.1.1 - EXPERT RATINGS OF GENERAL HEALTH

| | | | | | | | | | |
|---|---|---|---|---|---|---|---|---|---|
| PERFORMANCE STATUS (PHYSICAL HEALTH) | Rating given by a physician based on his examination, the medical history, and the results of laboratory tests. The ratings had a theoretical range of 1 for 'moribund; fatal processes progressing rapidly' to 10 for 'normal; no complaints; no evidence of disease'. | Unaffected by sex and age | HAPP 3.1 | r | +.11 | | | People of 46 and older, Duke, U.S.A.<br>Probability systematic random sample stratified by age and sex<br>N: 502, date: 1968 | PALMO 72<br>p. 70 |
| PHYSICAL HEALTH | Physician's rating: very poor / poor / fair / good / excellent | The relationship disappears when controlled for self-rated general health and self-rated health problems. | HAPP 1.1 | G' | +.14 | Gt' | ns | Aged persons, U.S.A.<br>Non-probability quota sample<br>N: 2993, date: 1952 - 1954 | SUCHM 58<br>p. 227 |
| PHYSIQUE (SOUNDNESS OF BODILY CONSTITUTION) | Ratings by a visiting doctor and by the lecturer in physical excercises and hygiene | | AFF 5.2 | $r_{pm}$ | +.30 | | | Male students, England<br>Non-probability chunk sample<br>N: 194, date: 1912 - 1913 | WEBB 15<br>p. 26 |
| PHYSIQUE (SOUNDNESS OF BODILY CONSTITUTION) | Class-master rating on a 7-point scale on the basis of observation | | AFF 5.3 | $r_{pm}$ | +.31 | | | Schoolboys, England<br>Non-probability chunk sample<br>N: 140, date: 1912 - 1913 | WEBB 15<br>p. 27 |
| PHYSICAL STRENGTH | Rating by staff members on a 7-point scale ranging from 'physically weak' to 'physically strong' | Open ward : r = -.07 (ns)<br>Closed ward: r = -.04 (ns) | AFF 5.1 | $r_{pm}$ | - | | ns | Institutionalized mentally retarded males, U.S.A.<br>Non-probability chunk sample<br>N: 149, date: — | PANDE 71<br>p. 329 |

### H 2.1.2 - SELF-PERCEIVED GENERAL HEALTH

| | | | | | | | | | |
|---|---|---|---|---|---|---|---|---|---|
| SELF-PERCEIVED HEALTH | Closed question: poor / fair / good | | HAPP 1.1 | G' | +.37 | Gt' | 01 | National adult population, U.S.A.<br>Non-probability quota sample<br>N: 2377, date: February, 1946 | WESSM 56<br>p. 179 |
| SELF-PERCEIVED HEALTH | Closed question: poor / fair / good / excellent | Lower among those under the age of 65: r = +.21<br>Stronger among those of age 65+ : r = +.40<br>The difference between the correlations is significant (05).<br>Unaffected by S.E.S. | HAPP 1.1 | $r_{pm}$ | +.25 | | 01 | Non-institutionalized adults, U.S.A.<br>Probability samples<br>N: 1547, date: 1972, 1973 | SPREI 74<br>p. 457 |

| Variable | Measurement | Remarks | Happiness measure | Statistic | Value | Test | Sig. | Population / sample | Source |
|---|---|---|---|---|---|---|---|---|---|
| PHYSICAL AILMENTS | Number of medical conditions reported 0 / 1 / 2 / 3 / 4 / 5+ | Positive relationship with the Index of Negative Affects | HAPP 1.1 | G' | -.26 | Gt' | 01 | National adult population, Puerto Rico<br>Probability simple random sample<br>N: 1417, date: November, 1963 - January, 1964 and August - October, 1964 | MATLI 66<br>p. 25/30 |
| | | Unrelated to the Index of Positive Affects | AFF 2.3 | DM | - | | | | |
| SELF-PERCEIVED HEALTH | Closed question: poor / fair / good / excellent | Stronger among those of age 20-39: G' = +.59<br>Lower among those of age 40+ : G' = +.31 | HAPP 1.1 | G' | +.47 | Gt' | 01 | See above | MATLI 66<br>p. 28-31 |
| | | Index of Negative Affects only | AFF 2.3 | G' | +.40 | Gt' | 01 | | |
| SELF-PERCEIVED PHYSICAL HEALTH | Closed question: poor / not so good / pretty good / very good | Index of Positive Affects: r = +.18 (01)<br>Index of Negative Affects: r = -.23 (01) | AFF 2.3 | $r_{pm}$ | +.28 | $Chi^2$ | 01 | Adults, Houston, Texas, U.S.A.<br>Non-probability purposive quota sample stratified by age, sex, occupational skill level and ethnicity<br>N: 1441, date: autumn, 1969 | GAITZ 72<br>p. 65 |
| | | | COMP 1.1 | $r_{pm}$ | +.34 | $Chi^2$ | 01 | | |
| SUBJECTIVE HEALTH STATUS | Closed question: poor / fair / good / excellent | | AFF 1.1 | $r_{pm}$ | +.28 | | 001 | Families of hourly workers and salaried employees, U.S.A.<br>N: 712, date: summer, 1973 | TESSL 75<br>p. 103 |
| SELF-RATED HEALTH | Direct question rated on a 10-point self-anchoring scale (based on Cantril, 1965), with the bottom of the ladder representing the most serious illness and the top of the ladder representing perfect health. | Unaffected by sex and age | HAPP 3.1 | r | +.43 | | 05 | People of 46 and older, Duke, U.S.A.<br>Probability systematic random sample stratified by age and sex<br>N: 502, date: 1968 | PALMO 72<br>p. 70 |
| SELF-RATED HEALTH | Closed question: poor / fair / good / excellent | | HAPP 3.1 | r | +.26 | | 05 | See above | PALMO 72<br>p. 73 |
| SELF-RATED GENERAL HEALTH | Closed question: very poor / poor / fair / good/ excellent | Unaffected by physician's health rating, and self-rated health problems | HAPP 1.1 | G' | +.48 | Gt' | 01 | Aged persons, U.S.A.<br>Non-probability quota sample<br>N: 2993, date: 1952 - 1954 | SUCHM 58<br>p. 227 |
| REPORTED HEALTH | Direct question | Unaffected by income and social participation | AFF 1.1 | | + | $Chi^2$ | s | Aged persons, Metropolitan Boston, U.S.A.<br>Probability area sample<br>N: 1335, date: 1965 | FOWLE 69<br>p. 734 |
| SELF-PERCEIVED HEALTH | Closed question: poor / fair / good | | AFF 2.3 | G | +.45 | $Chi^2$ | 001 | Non-institutionalized aged welfare recipients, U.S.A.<br>Non-probability purposive quota sample<br>N: 256, date: 1969 | TISSU 72<br>p. 92 |
| | | | CON 1.1 | G | +.20 | $Chi^2$ | ns | | |
| | | | HAPP 1.1 | G | +.17 | $Chi^2$ | ns | | |
| SUBJECTIVE HEALTH | poor vs good | See remarks in excerpt (Part II)<br>Among the gainfully employed : G' = +.65 (01)<br>Among retirees who had a positive orientation to retirement at the moment of retirement : G' = +.46 (01)<br>Among retirees who had a negative orientation to retirement : G' = +.23 (ns) | COMP 1.2 | G' | +.58 | Gt' | 01 | Aged males, U.S.A. (those satisfied in 1952)<br>Non-probability accidental sample<br>N: 787, date: 1952 - 1956 | THOMP 60<br>p. 168 |
| SELF-PERCEIVED HEALTH | Direct question rated on a 10-point self-anchoring scale (based on Cantril, 1965), ranging from 'worst possible health' to 'best possible health' | | COMP 1.1 | $r_{pm}$ | +.62 | | 01 | White males who had experienced a first heart attack, Durham, North Carolina, U.S.A.<br>Non-probability quota sample<br>N: 56, date: 1970 | GARRI 73<br>p. 201 |
| SELF-PERCEIVED HEALTH | Closed question: poor, fair vs good, very good | | HAPP 2.1 | G' | +.42 | Gt' | 01 | Aged chronically-ill patients, U.S.A.<br>Probability sample<br>N: 167, date: 1959 | HENLE 67<br>p. 70 |

| | | | | | | | | | |
|---|---|---|---|---|---|---|---|---|---|
| PHYSICAL CONDITION | Repeated direct question rated on an open graphic scale ranging from 'poor' to 'excellent' | Both the scale for physical condition and the one measuring hedonic level were marked 2 times a day for periods ranging from 18 - 64 days.<br>Individual correlations vary from -.36 to +.74. Of the 16 correlations only 1 is negative and 10 of the remaining 15 are significant. | AFF 3.1 | $r_{pm}$ | + | | | University students and staff members, U.S.A.<br>Non-probability chunk sample<br>N: 16, date: — | DYSIN 37<br>p. 152 |
| PHYSICAL CONDITION | See above | Both the scale for physical condition and the one measuring hedonic level were marked 3 times a day during 5 weeks<br>Individual correlations vary from -.39 to +.71. Of the 24 correlations only 2 are negative and 19 of the remaining 22 are significant, with 11 of these over +.50. | AFF 3.1 | $r_{pm}$ | + | | | University students, U.S.A.<br>Non-probability chunk sample<br>N: 24, date: — | DYSIN 38<br>p. 118 |
| PHYSICAL HEALTH | Repeated closed question on physical health during the past day, scored every evening during 6 weeks<br>very sick / sick / rather poor / fair / good / excellent | | AFF 3.1 | $r_{pm}$ | +.12 | t | ns | Female college students, U.S.A.<br>Non-probability chunk sample<br>N: 21, date: ± 1960 | WESSM 66/1<br>p. 277 |
| PHYSICAL HEALTH | See above | | AFF 3.1 | $r_{pm}$ | -.31 | t | ns | Male college students, U.S.A.<br>Non-probability chunk sample<br>N: 17, date: ± 1960 | WESSM 66/2<br>p. 283 |
| SELF-PERCEIVED PHYSICAL HEALTH | Repeated closed question on health during the past day, scored every evening during one month<br>very sick / sick / rather poor / fair / good / excellent | | AFF 3.1<br>HAPP 3.1 | $r_{pm}$<br>$r_{pm}$ | +.39<br>+.13 | | 01<br>ns | Undergraduate students, U.S.A.<br>Non-probability chunk sample<br>N: 67, date: summer, 1970 | GORMA 71<br>p. 216/222 |
| POSITIVE EVALUATION OF HEALTH | Closed question ranging from 'not at all good' to 'very good' | | HAPP 1.1<br>AFF 1.1 | mc<br>mc | +.56<br>+.60 | | | Urban adult Jewish population, Israel<br>Probability area sample, using dwelling units<br>N: 1940, date: spring, 1973 | LEVY 75/1<br>p. 372 |
| HEALTH CONDITION | Closed question | | HAPP 1.1<br>AFF 1.1 | mc<br>mc | +.54<br>+.60 | | | Urban adult Jewish population, Israel<br>Probability area sample using dwelling units<br>N: 1830, date: summer, 1973 | LEVY 75/2<br>p. 373 |
| SELF-PERCEIVED HEALTH | Closed question: poor / fair / good | | HAPP 1.1 | G' | +.50 | Gt' | 01 | National adult population, The Netherlands<br>N: at least 1000, date: 1948 | NIPO 49<br>p. 3 |
| SUBJECTIVE HEALTH FEELING | Direct question rated on an open graphic scale ranging from 'very sick' to 'very healthy' | Unaffected by age<br>Stronger among those of lower S.E.S.<br>Stronger among those with lower educational level<br>Stronger among males than among females | HAPP 1.1 | G | +.50 | | 05 | National adult population, The Netherlands<br>Aakster (1972) sample<br>N: 1552, date: June, 1968 | BAKKE 74<br>p. 28 |
| SELF-PERCEIVED HEALTH | Direct question: less than good / good / excellent | | HAPP 1.1 | $r_{pm}$ | +.29 | | | Housewives, The Netherlands<br>Probability area sample<br>N: 450, date: autumn, 1964 | PHILI 66<br>p. 66 |
| SELF-PERCEIVED HEALTH | Closed question: very poor / poor / average / fairly good / very good | | HAPP 2.1 | $T^2$ | +.18 | $Chi^2$ | 001 | National adult population, Poland<br>Non-probability purposive quota sample stratified by sex, age, type of local community, employment and S.E.S.<br>N: 2387, date: June - July, 1960 | MAKAR 62<br>p. 115 |

## H 2.1.3 - VARIOUS INDICATORS OF PHYSICAL HEALTH

see also 'Types of Affect: Energy' (A 2.2.6), 'Satisfaction with Physical Health' (S 1.6)

| | | | | | | | | | |
|---|---|---|---|---|---|---|---|---|---|
| POOR PHYSICAL HEALTH | 2-item index of closed questions on general health (poor / fair / good / excellent), and number of times one stayed at a hospital, sanitarium, or nursing home during the past 5 years | | AFF 1.3 | $\bar{DR}$ | -.15 | | 05 | Adults, Alameda county, U.S.A.<br>Probability sample<br>N: 6928, date: 1965 | BERKM 71<br>p. 42 |
| SELF-PERCEIVED PHYSICAL HEALTH | Factor containing yes / no questions on feeling bothered by pains and ailments, and feeling healthy enough to carry out the things one would like to do<br>(3 ranks). | males : $t_k$ = +.14 (01)<br>females: $t_k$ = +.10 (01) | HAPP 1.1 | $t_k$ | + | | 01 | Adult married population with children, U.S.A.<br>Probability area sample<br>N: 797, date: spring, 1957 | VEROF 62<br>p. 196 |
| HAVING PROBLEMS WITH HEALTH | Closed question | | COMP 4.1 | | | | ns | Students, U.S.A.<br>Non-probability chunk sample<br>N: 1651, date: — | SYMON 37<br>p. 292 |
| SELF-RATED HEALTH PROBLEMS | Closed question: no vs yes | Unaffected by physician's health ratings and self-rated general health | HAPP 1.1 | G' | -.32 | Gt' | 01 | Aged persons, U.S.A.<br>Non-probability quota sample<br>N: 2993, date: 1952 - 1954 | SUCHM 58<br>p. 227 |
| HAVING CHRONIC HEALTH PROBLEMS | Absence vs presence of chronic health problems (other than heart disease); obtained from hospital records | | COMP 1.1 | $r_{pm}$ | -.14 | | ns | White males who had experienced a first heart attack, Durham, North Carolina, U.S.A.<br>Non-probability quota sample<br>N: 56, date: 1970 | GARRI 73<br>p. 201 |
| LONG-TERM ILLNESS | Direct yes / no questions on long-standing physical or health trouble and whether this kept one from doing the things one might like to do | Index of Positive Affects: G = -.05<br>Index of Negative Affects: G = +.19 | AFF 2.3 | G | - | | | Adults, urban areas, U.S.A.<br>Probability area samples<br>N: 2787, date: January, 1963 - January, 1964 | BRADB 69<br>p. 118 |
| RECENT ILLNESS | Direct yes / no questions on sickness during the past few weeks and whether it caused a cut down in one's usual activities | Index of Positive Affects: G = -.04<br>Index of Negative Affects: G = +.13 | AFF 2.3 | G | - | | | See above | BRADB 69<br>p. 118 |
| ILLNESS | 2-item index of closed questions on both recent and long-term illnesses (see above)<br>low / medium / high | Computed for Index of Negative Affects only:<br>$\bar{DR}$ = +.14 (05)<br>Stronger among those with low anxiety and not among those with high anxiety<br>Stronger among those, esp. females, reporting low physical symptoms, and not among those having a lot of physical symptoms | AFF 2.3 | $\bar{DR}$ | - | BCI | | See above | BRADB 69<br>p. 119 |
| LONG-STANDING ILLNESS | Direct question on long-standing physical or health trouble | Index of Positive Affects: G = +.04<br>Index of Negative Affects: G = -.03 | AFF 2.3 | G | + | | | Employed males, England<br>Non-probability purposive quota sample<br>N: 192, date: — | PAYNE 74<br>p. 17 |
| RECENT ILLNESS | Direct question on sickness during the last few weeks | Index of Positive Affects: G = +.20<br>Index of Negative Affects: G = -.04 | AFF 2.3 | G | + | | | See above | PAYNE 74<br>p. 17 |
| RECENT ILLNESS | Closed question on number of days one stayed in bed due to illness during the past three months: not a single day / a few days / about 1 week / 2 weeks - 1 month / 1-3 months / 3 months | | HAPP 1.1 | G | -.29 | | | National adult population, The Netherlands<br>Probability area sample<br>N: 1552, date: June, 1968 | BAKKE 74<br>p. 28 |
| RECENT ILLNESS | Direct question on number of times one stayed in bed due to illness during the last three months<br>not in bed vs in bed | When eleborated for age, significant among those of age 50-65 only | HAPP 1.1 | G' | -.31 | Gt' | 05 | Adults, Utrecht, The Netherlands<br>Probability sample stratified by age<br>N: 300, date: autumn, 1967 | MOSER 69<br>p. 31 |

| | | | | | | | | | |
|---|---|---|---|---|---|---|---|---|---|
| NUMBER OF DOCTOR'S CONSULTS | Direct question on number of consults during the past three months:<br>0 / 1 / 2 / 3-4 / 5-10 / more than 10 | | HAPP 1.1 | G | -.18 | | | National adult population, The Netherlands<br>Probability area sample<br>N: 1552, date: June, 1968 | BAKKE 74<br>p. 28 |
| NUMBER OF DOCTOR'S CONSULTS | Direct question on number of doctor's consults during last year:<br>0 / 1-3 / 4 or more | When elaborated for age significant among those of age 50 - 65 only | HAPP 1.1 | G' | -.10 | Gt' | ns | Adults, Utrecht, The Netherlands<br>Probability sample stratified by age<br>N: 300, date: autumn, 1967 | MOSER 69<br>p. 31 |
| HOSPITALIZATION | Direct questions on number of admissions into hospital during last year | | HAPP 1.1 | | | $Chi^2$ | ns | See above | MOSER 69<br>p. 31 |
| MEDICINE USE | Direct question on medicine use during last two weeks | | HAPP 1.1 | | | $Chi^2$ | ns | See above | MOSER 69<br>p. 31 |

## H 2.1.4 - SPECIFIC PHYSICAL HEALTH CHARACTERISTICS

see also 'Psychosomatic Symptoms' (H 2.2)

| | | | | | | | | | |
|---|---|---|---|---|---|---|---|---|---|
| PRESENCE OF BODILY DEFECT | 'normal' vs handicapped Ss | Reversed among those with incomes above $ 15,000.- | HAPP 2.1<br>AFF 1.1 | G'<br>G' | -.13<br>-.17 | Gt'<br>Gt' | ns<br>ns | Physically defective and normal persons, Detroit, U.S.A.<br>Non-probability purposive samples<br>N: 295, date: — | CAMER 71<br>p. 641-642<br>CAMER 73/1<br>p. 210 |
| PRESENCE OF PHYSICAL HANDICAP | 'normal' vs handicapped Ss | | HAPP 2.1 | | | $Chi^2$ | ns | Physically handicapped and normal persons, U.S.A.<br>Non-probability purposive samples<br>N: 90, date: — | CAMER 73/2<br>p. 210 |
| BORN WITH PHYSICAL HANDICAP | Ss who acquired their defect vs Ss who had had their defect since birth | Computed for handicapped Ss only | HAPP 2.1 | | | $Chi^2$ | ns | See above | CAMER 73/2<br>p. 210 |
| MOVING ONE'S LIMBS EASILY | Direct question rated on an open graphic scale ranging from 'very easily' to 'with much difficulty' | | HAPP 1.1 | G | +.31 | | | National adult population, The Netherlands<br>Probability area sample<br>N: 1552, date: June, 1968 | BAKKE 74<br>p. 28 |
| MOTOR ABILITY; GENERAL COORDINATION | Rating by the hospital's research staff | Open ward : r = +.10 (ns)<br>Closed ward: r = +.11 (ns) | AFF 5.1 | $r_{pm}$ | + | | ns | Institutionalized mentally retarded males, U.S.A.<br>Non-probability chunk sample<br>N: 149, date: — | PANDE 71<br>p. 329 |
| HEARING ABILITY | See above | Open ward : r = -.09 (ns)<br>Closed ward: r = -.09 (ns) | AFF 5.1 | $r_{pm}$ | - | | ns | See above | PANDE 71<br>p. 329 |
| VISUAL ABILITY | See above | Open ward : r = +.22 (05)<br>Closed ward: r = -.09 (ns) | AFF 5.1 | $r_{pm}$ | | | | See above | PANDE 71<br>p. 329 |
| PHYSICAL ABILITY | 3-item index of direct questions on ease of reading, bending, and use of tub or shower without help | | AFF 2.3 | $t_k$ | +.22 | | 02 | Aged female public housing residents, U.S.A.<br>Probability systematic random sample<br>N: 44, date: 1967 / 1971 | GRANE 73A<br>p. 7 |
| SEVERITY OF INITIAL HEART ATTACK | number of cardiogenic complications of the acute heart attack; obtained from hospital reports | | COMP 1.1 | $r_{pm}$ | +.21 | | ns | White males who had experienced a first heart attack, Durham, North Carolina, U.S.A.<br>Non-probability quota sample<br>N: 56, date: 1970 | GARRI 73<br>p. 201 |

## H 2.2 - PSYCHOSOMATIC SYMPTOMS

see also Types of Affect: 'Anxiety' (A 2.2.2) and 'Tranquility' (A 2.2.20)

### SYMPTOM INVENTORIES

| | | | | | | | | | |
|---|---|---|---|---|---|---|---|---|---|
| ANXIETY | 6-item index of closed questions on dizziness, general aches and pains, headaches, muscle twitches, nervousness, and rapid heart beat; during last week<br>(items from Stouffer et al., 1949) | Index of Positive Affects: G' = +.02 (ns)<br>Index of Negative Affects: G' = +.53 (01) | AFF 2.3<br><br>HAPP 1.1 | G'<br><br>G' | -<br><br>-.33 | Gt'<br><br>Gt' | <br><br>01 | Inhabitants of 4 small communities, Illinois, U.S.A.<br>Probability multi-stage samples<br>N: 2006, date: March, 1962 | BRADB 65/1<br>p. 29 |
| PHYSICAL SYMPTOMS | 5-item index of closed questions on general aches and pains, headaches, dizziness, rapid heart beat, and hands sweating and feeling damp and clammy; during the past few weeks<br>(items from Stouffer et al., 1950) | Index of Positive Affects:<br>males : G = +.00<br>females: G = -.02<br>Index of Negative Affects:<br>males : G = +.30<br>females: G = +.36<br>Stronger among those who are healthy<br>Not among those who are sick | AFF 2.3 | G | - | | | Adults, urban areas, U.S.A.<br>Probability area samples<br>N: 2787, date: January, 1963 - January, 1964 | BRADB 69<br>p. 110/119 |
| PSYCHOLOGICAL ANXIETY | 3-item index of closed questions on nervousness or tenseness during the last few weeks, having trouble getting to sleep at night, and having enough energy to do the things one would like to do | Index of Positive Affects:<br>males : G = +.04<br>females: G = +.02<br>Index of Negative Affects:<br>males : G = +.47<br>females: G = +.45<br>Stronger among those who are healthy than among those who are sick<br>Unaffected by expecting a nervous breakdown | AFF 2.3 | G | - | | | See above | BRADB 69<br>p. 110/117/119 |
| DECREASING ANXIETY | 3-item index (see above)<br>The index was employed twice with an interval of ± 10 months (in wave 1 and 3)<br>stable vs decreasing anxiety | See remarks in excerpt (Part II)<br>Computed for Index of Negative Affects only:<br>$\bar{DR}$ = -.11 | AFF 2.3 | $\bar{DR}$ | + | BCI | 05 | See above | BRADB 69<br>p. 111 |
| INCREASING ANXIETY | See above<br>stable vs increasing anxiety | Computed for Index of Negative Affects only:<br>$\bar{DR}$ = +.08 | AFF 2.3 | $\bar{DR}$ | - | BCI | 05 | See above | BRADB 69<br>p. 111 |
| PHYSICAL ANXIETY | Factor containing direct questions on having ever been bothered by shortness of breath, and by one's heart beating hard<br>never / hardly ever / sometimes / many times<br>(6 ranks) | males : $t_k$ = -.12 (01)<br>females: $t_k$ = -.15 (01) | HAPP 1.1 | $t_k$ | - | | 01 | Adult married population with children, U.S.A.<br>Probability area sample<br>N: 797, date: spring, 1957 | VEROF 62<br>p. 196 |
| PSYCHOLOGICAL ANXIETY | Factor of closed questions on having trouble falling asleep or staying asleep and being bothered by nervousness, feeling fidgety and tense | males : $t_k$ = -.16 (01)<br>females: $t_k$ = -.19 (01) | HAPP 1.1 | $t_k$ | - | | 01 | See above | VEROF 62<br>p. 196 |
| IMMOBILIZATION | Factor containing direct questions on difficulties with getting up in the morning, and sweating hands<br>(6 ranks) | Stronger among males: $t_k$ = -.12 (01)<br>Not among females : $t_k$ = -.02 (ns) | HAPP 1.1 | $t_k$ | - | | | See above | VEROF 62<br>p. 196 |
| PSYCHO-SOMATIC SYMPTOMS | Summary score of 16 symptoms indicative of psychological and psychosomatic symptom complaints<br>(10 ranks)<br>(adapted from McMillan, 1957) | males : $t_k$ = -.24 (01)<br>females: $t_k$ = -.18 (01) | HAPP 1.1 | $t_k$ | - | | 01 | See above | VEROF 62<br>p. 196 |

| | | | | | | | | | |
|---|---|---|---|---|---|---|---|---|---|
| PSYCHO-PSYCHOLOGIC PROBLEMS | 3-item index of closed questions on problems with energy, appetite, and/or sleep during past week<br>rarely / occasionally / most days | When controlled for depressive affect: G = -.31 | COMP 1.1 | G | -.43 | | 001 | Adults, U.S.A.<br>Probability cluster sample using households, and probability multi-stage sample<br>N: 2168, date: 1972 | BRENN 75B<br>p. 352 |
| ANXIETY | Index containing statements about feelings of nervousness, strain, distraction, embarrassment and fear<br>(Taylor Manifest Anxiety Scale; see Taylor,1953) | | AFF 2.1 | $r_{pm}$ | -.24 | | ns | Married females, U.S.A.<br>Non-probability purposive sample by expert choice<br>N: 62, date: — | HARDE 69<br>p. 50 |
| ANXIETY SYMPTOMS | 10-item index of closed questions on sleeping problems, trembling hands, nervousness, heart beating hard, pressures or pains in head, biting fingernails, shortness of breath, sweating hands, sick headaches, nightmares<br>(see Rosenberg, 1965) | When standardized on:<br>- usual mood : $G_s$ = -.21<br>- having fun in life : $G_s$ = -.20<br>- frequency of low mood : $G_s$ = -.18<br>- tending to be a discouraged person: $G_s$ = -.20<br>- tending to be a lonely person : $G_s$ = -.19<br>Stronger among females: G = -.35<br>Lower among males : G = -.28 | HAPP 1.1 | G | -.28 | | | Juniors and seniors attending public high schools in New York State, U.S.A.<br>Probability cluster sample of 10 public high schools<br>N: sample A: 1682, sample B: 1664, date: 1960 | BRENN 70<br>p. 71/272 |
| | | Stronger among females: G = -.32<br>Lower among males : G = -.23 | AFF 1.1 | G<br>V | -.24<br>.11 | $Chi^2$ | 01 | | |
| SOMATIC SYMPTOMS | 18-item checklist of physical complaints containing nervousness, headaches, loss of appetite, upset stomach, trouble getting out of bed, work affected by ill health, shortness of breath, hard heart beating, dizziness, nightmares, losing weight, trembling hands, sweating hands, troubles to get going, bad health, having a cold, trouble falling asleep, absent from school because of illness<br>(adapted from Gurin et al., 1960) | | COMP 1.2 | $r_{pm}$ | -.28 | | 001 | Public high school boys, U.S.A.<br>Probability multi-stage sample<br>N: 2213 in 1966, 1886 in 1968 and 1799 in 1969<br>date: fall, 1966; spring, 1968 and spring 1969 | BACHM 67/70<br>p. 122 |
| NEGATIVE AFFECT STATES | 40-item index of closed questions on irritability (7 items), general anxiety (7 items), anxiety and tension (5 items), depression (6 items), anomie (8 items) and resentment (7 items) | | COMP 1.2 | $r_{pm}$ | -.51 | | 001 | See above | BACHM 67/70<br>p. 122 |
| ANXIETY | 40-item questionnaire scored as 'true' or 'false'<br>(IPAT Anxiety Scale Questionnaire; Self Analysis Form; see Cattell & Scheier, 1963) | | HAPP 1.1 | DM | - | $r_1$ | 001 | University students, U.S.A.<br>Non-probability chunk sample<br>N: 313, date: 1966 - 1967 | BRADB 67<br>p. 64 |
| PSYCHO-PHYSIOLOGICAL CONDITION | Number of psycho-psychological disorders reported, e.g. psychophysiologic gastrointestinal reaction, asthma, hypertension, etc. | Index of Negative Affects: r = +.37 (01)<br>Unrelated to Index of Positive Affects | AFF 2.3 | $r_{pm}$ | - | | | Residents of Stirling County, Maritime, Canada<br>Proability sample stratified by sex, age, socio-environmental circumstances and mental health<br>N: 112, date: 1963 - 1968 | BEISE 74<br>p. 325 |
| HEALTH STATUS | 13-item index of physical and psychological symptoms; e.g. dizziness, headaches, upset stomach, nervousness | Index of Positive Affects: G = +.02<br>Index of Negative Affects: G = +.13 | AFF 2.3 | G | - | | | Employed males, England<br>Non-probability purposive quota sample<br>N: 192, date: — | PAYNE 74<br>p. 17 |
| ANXIETY | Question on anxiousness about things, using a symptoms list, including nervousness, headache, insomnia, excessive appetite, nightmares, loneliness, chest pains, bad appetite, or trembling hands | unmarried employed males : r = -.22 (ns)<br>unmarried employed females : r = -.29 (05)<br>married employed males : r = -.18 (05)<br>married employed females : r = -.10 (ns)<br>married non-employed females: r = +.07 (ns) | HAPP 2.1 | $r_{pm}$ | - | | | Inhabitants of Helsinki, Finland<br>Probability sample<br>N: 442, date: spring - summer, 1966 | HAAVI 71<br>p. 590 |
| PSYCHO-SOMATIC COMPLAINTS | 88-item inventory containing symptoms indicative of both physical bad health, and psycho-somatic and social problems | Unaffected by age and sex<br>Lowest among those of medium S.E.S. and strongest among those of lower S.E.S.<br>Stronger among those with lower education. | HAPP 1.1 | G | -.41 | | 05 | National adult population, The Netherlands<br>Probability area sample<br>N: 1552, date: June, 1968 | BAKKE 74<br>p. 28 |

| | | | | | | | | |
|---|---|---|---|---|---|---|---|---|
| PSYCHO-SOMATIC COMPLAINTS | 21-item index of psycho-somatic complaints (from the VOEG; see Dirken, 1967)<br>no complaints / some complaints / a lot of complaints | U-shaped curve: Ss with some complaints being most happy | HAPP 1.1 | G' | -.10 | Gt'<br>$Chi^2$ | ns<br>05 | Adults, Utrecht, The Netherlands<br>Probability sample stratified by age<br>N: 300, date: autumn, 1967 | MOSER 69<br>p. 36 |
| **SPECIFIC SYMPTOMS** | | | | | | | | | |
| STOMACH COMPLAINTS | 3-item index of direct questions on stomach complaints and gall-stones | | HAPP 2.1 | G | -.18 | $Chi^2$ | 000 | Male employees of age 40 - 65, The Netherlands<br>Non-probability chunk sample<br>N: 13000, date: — | SONDE 75 |
| CHEST PAINS | 10-item index of direct questions on various pains in one's chest | | HAPP 2.1 | G | -.29 | $Chi^2$ | 000 | See above | SONDE 75 |
| CARDIAC PRESSURE | 3-item index of direct questions on swollen ankles and feet , sleeping on high pillow, and often need to urinate at night | | HAPP 2.1 | G | -.27 | $Chi^2$ | 000 | See above | SONDE 75 |
| SHORT OF BREATH | 4-item index of direct questions on complaints when walking up a hill, walking normally, being exhausted when walking, when awaking | | HAPP 2.1 | G | -.24 | $Chi^2$ | 000 | See above | SONDE 75 |
| RESPIRATORY COMPLAINTS | 5-item index of direct questions on complaints when awaking, during the day, and on periods during the year | | HAPP 2.1 | G | -.17 | $Chi^2$ | 000 | See above | SONDE 75 |
| DIZZINESS | Closed question: no vs yes | | HAPP 2.1 | G | -.33 | $Chi^2$ | 000 | See above | SONDE 75 |
| SLEEPLESSNESS | Closed question: no vs yes | | HAPP 2.1 | G | -.54 | $Chi^2$ | 000 | See above | SONDE 75 |
| FEELING TIRED | Closed question: no vs yes | | HAPP 2.1 | G | -.75 | $Chi^2$ | 000 | See above | SONDE 75 |
| FEELING IRRITABLE | Closed question: no vs yes | | HAPP 2.1 | G | -.76 | $Chi^2$ | 000 | See above | SONDE 75 |
| FEELING RESTLESS | Closed question: 'During the past week did you ever feel so restless that you couldn't sit long in a chair?'<br>no vs yes | See second instrument in excerpt (Part II). | HAPP 1.1 | Q | -.56 | | | National adult population, Puerto Rico<br>Probability simple random sample<br>N: 1417, date: November, 1963 - January, 1964 and August - October, 1964 | MATLI 66<br>p. 8 |
| FEELING UNEASY | Closed question: 'During the past week, did you ever feel vaguely uneasy about something?'<br>no vs yes | See above | HAPP 1.1 | Q | -.60 | | | See above | MATLI 66<br>p. 8 |
| NERVOUSNESS (psychological tension) | Direct question: 'Have you taken something against the nerves, during the last 14 days?'<br>nothing vs swallowed something | | HAPP 1.1 | G' | -.41 | Gt' | 01 | Adults, Utrecht, The Netherlands<br>Probability sample stratified by age<br>N: 300, date: autumn, 1967 | MOSER 69<br>p. 37 |
| NERVOUSNESS | Closed question on being a nervous person<br>definitely no / rather no / rather yes / decidedly yes | | HAPP 2.1 | $T^2$ | -.11 | $Chi^2$ | 001 | National adult population, Poland<br>Non-probability purposive quota sample stratified by sex, age, type of local community, employment and S.E.S.<br>N: 2387, date: June - July, 1960 | MAKAR 62<br>p. 115 |

## H 2.3 - MENTAL HEALTH

see also 'Types of Affect' (A 2.2), 'Life Quality' (L 2), 'Personality' (P 1), 'Problems, Worries and Fears' (P 5), 'Self-Image' (S 2)

### H 2.3.1 - GENERAL MENTAL HEALTH RATINGS

| | | | | | | | | | |
|---|---|---|---|---|---|---|---|---|---|
| MENTAL HEALTH | Twenty-two Item Screening Score of psychiatric symptoms indicating impairment (see Langner, 1962) | Unaffected by age, S.E.S. and sex | HAPP 1.1 | G' | +.39 | Gt' | 01 | Adults, New Hampshire, U.S.A.<br>Probability sample<br>N: 593, date: — | PHILL 67B<br>p. 288 |
| MENTAL ILLNESS | Twenty-two Item Screening Score (see above) | Unaffected by age<br>Index of Positive Affects: r = -.02 (ns)<br>Index of Negative Affects: r = +.57 (01) | AFF 2.3 | $r_{pm}$ | -.41 | $Chi^2$ | 01 | Adults, Houston, Texas, U.S.A.<br>Non-probability purposive quota sample stratified by age, sex, occupational skill level and ethnicity<br>N: 1441, date: autumn, 1969 | GAITZ 72<br>p. 65 |
| | | | COMP 1.1 | $r_{pm}$ | -.34 | $Chi^2$ | 01 | | |
| MENTAL HEALTH | 20-item checklist of psychoneurotic and psychophysiologic symptoms, indicative of mental health (Health Opinion Survey; see Leighton et al, 1963)<br>high stress vs low stress | | HAPP 1.1 | G' | +1.00 | Gt' | 01 | Student teachers, Chapel Hill, U.S.A.<br>Probability sample proportionally stratified by teaching level<br>N: 75, date: spring, 1967 | GUNZA 67<br>p. 126 |
| PSYCHIATRIC 'CASENESS' (probability that someone is suffering from a psychiatric disorder) | Rating by two psychiatrists on a 4-point scale, based on 6 years accumulated clinical information. | Index of Positive Affects: r = -.19 (05)<br>Index of Negative Affects: r = +.42 (01) | AFF 2.3 | $r_s$ | - | | s | Residents of Stirling County, Maritime, Canada<br>Probability sample stratified by sex, age, socio-environmental circumstances and mental health<br>N: 112, date: 1963 - 1968 | BEISE 74<br>p. 325 |
| PSYCHOLOGICAL RESOURCES (positive mental health) | 14 indicators of psychological resources including measures of mutuality (familial and extra-familial), resolution of losses, contextual and temporal perspective, growth, competence, insight, perceived and judged encroachment, hope, and satisfaction with intrapersonal and interpersonal competence in general. | In total significant correlations were found between two indicators of resources and psychological well-being. | HAPP 1.1 | r | + | | | People in transition, U.S.A.<br>Stratified random sample<br>N: 216, date: — | CHIRI 71<br>p. 603 |
| | | There were four significant or near significant correlations with positive affect, four with negative affect (including two inverse relationships), and eight with affect balance. | AFF 2.3 | r | + | | | | |
| PSYCHOLOGICAL DEFICITS (mental illness) | 10 indicators of psychological deficits including number of symptoms mentioned, plus a psychiatrist's ratings of the degree of psychopathology implicit in each symptom response, long- and short-term symptoms, and total symptom response set per respondent; Gottschalk anxiety scores, derived from TAT cards, global ratings by an interdisciplinary team of social scientists on perceived stress, stress impact, degree and direction of impairment. | Six of the deficit indicators correlated significantly (05) with both affect balance and with negative affect.<br>No relationships with positive affect were found | AFF 2.3 | r | - | | 05 | See above | CHIRI 71<br>p. 603 |
| EGO STRENGTH | 68-item index tapping a general factor of psychopathology, reflecting degree of maladjustment or ego-dysfunction, irrespective of differential diagnosis. (Ego Strength Scale; see Barron, 1956) | | AFF 2.1 | $r_{pm}$ | +.27 | | 01 | Female college seniors, U.S.A.<br>Non-probability chunk sample<br>N: 162, date: May - June, 1966 | PORTE 67<br>p. 93/95 |
| MALADJUSTMENT | Scale containing MMPI items, designed to identify maladjustment in a college population. (Mt scale; see Kleinmuntz, 1961) | Stronger among females: r = -.45 (05)<br>Lower among males : r = -.20 (ns) | COMP 1.1 | $r_{pm}$ | - | | | Undergraduate students, Ohio, U.S.A.<br>Non-probability accidental sample<br>N: 132, date: 1966/1967 | MILLE 68<br>p. 1082 |

## H 2.3.2 - SPECIFIC MENTAL HEALTH CHARACTERISTICS

| | | | | | | | | | |
|---|---|---|---|---|---|---|---|---|---|
| SEVERITY OF PATHOLOGY | Rating by a psychiatrist on the basis of a detailed symptom check-list<br>1-3 (minimal impairment) / 4-6 / 7-9 / 8-12 (marked impairment) | Index of Negative Affects: r = +.16 (ns)<br>U-shaped curve: Ss with pathology ratings of 7-9 having most negative feelings<br>Significant differences between those with ratings of 4-6 and those with ratings of 7-9 only.<br>Unrelated to the Index of Positive Affects | HAPP 1.1<br>AFF 2.3 | G'<br>r | -.27<br>- | Gt' | 01 | Non-hospitalized schizophrenic males, Monroe County, New York, U.S.A.<br>Probability sample drawn from the Monroe County psychiatric case register<br>N: 178, date: 1964 - 1965 | ALEXA 68<br>p. 29/67 |
| BEING DEFINITELY SCHIZOPHRENIC | Possibly schizophrenic vs definitely schizophrenic, as assessed by relative number of independant diagnoses, and having schizophrenic symptoms | | HAPP 1.1 | | | $Chi^2$ | ns | See above | ALEXA 68<br>p. 33 |
| NEUROTICISM | Adapted Super Neuroticism Scale, focussing on behavior and early childhood experiences, indicative of neuroticism (see Shaffer, 1968) | | AFF 2.1 | $r_{pm}$ | -.34 | | 01 | Married females, U.S.A.<br>Non-probability purposive sample by expert choice<br>N: 62, date: — | HARDE 69<br>p. 50 |
| EVER EXPECTED A NERVOUS BREAKDOWN | Direct questions<br>no vs yes | Index of Positive Affects:<br>males : G = +.04 (wave 3: G = -.05)<br>females: G = +.00 (wave 3: G = -.06)<br>Index of Negative Affects:<br>males : G = +.48 (wave 3: G = +.50)<br>females: G = +.47 (wave 3: G = +.35)<br>Unaffected by amount of worries | AFF 2.3 | G | - | | | Adults, urban areas, U.S.A.<br>Probability area samples<br>N: 2787, date: January, 1963 - January, 1964 | BRADB 69<br>p. 110 |
| EVER EXPECTED A NERVOUS BREAKDOWN | Direct question: no vs yes | males : $t_k$ = -.10 (05)<br>females: $t_k$ = -.11 (01) | HAPP 1.1 | $t_k$ | - | | 05 | Adult married population with children, U.S.A.<br>Probability area sample<br>N: 797, date: spring, 1957 | VEROF 62<br>p. 196 |
| EVER EXPECTED A NERVOUS BREAKDOWN | Direct question: no vs yes | Index of Positive Affects: G = +.08<br>Index of Negative Affects: G = +.19 | AFF 2.3 | G | - | | | Employed males, England<br>Non-probability purposive quota sample<br>N: 192, date: — | PAYNE 74<br>p. 17 |
| EXPECTED A NERVOUS BREAKDOWN MORE THAN ONCE | Direct question: no vs yes | Index of Positive Affects: G = +.44<br>Index of Negative Affects: G = +.41 | AFF 2.3 | G | | | | See above | PAYNE 74<br>p. 17 |
| NEED FOR HELP WITH EMOTIONAL PROBLEMS OR FAMILY TROUBLES | Closed question: 'During the past year did you ever feel that you could use some help in dealing with emotional problems or family troubles?'<br>never / not very often / sometimes / often | Computed for 1973 data only:<br>Index of Positive Affects: r = +.01 (ns)<br>Index of Negative Affects: r = +.40 (001) | AFF 2.3 | r | -.25 | | 001 | Adults, Los Angeles County, U.S.A.<br>Multi-stage probability samples of households<br>N: 1078 in 1972 and 1008 in 1973<br>date: spring, 1972 and spring, 1973 | CHERL 75<br>p. 197 |

## H 2.3.3 - BEING TREATED FOR MENTAL ILLNESS

| | | | | | | | | | |
|---|---|---|---|---|---|---|---|---|---|
| MENTAL DISTURBANCES | normals vs out-patients of psychiatric hospital, diagnosed as suffering from anxiety and depression<br>(Puerto Ricans vs validation sample; see sample construction in excerpt, Part II) | Index of Positive Affects: G' = +.03 (ns)<br>Index of Negative Affects: G' = +.65 (01) | HAPP 1.1<br>AFF 2.3 | G'<br>G' | -.35<br>-.57 | Gt'<br>Gt' | 01<br>01 | National adult population, Puerto Rico<br>Probability simple random sample<br>N: 1417, date: November, 1963 - January, 1964 and August - October, 1964 | MATLI 66<br>p. 44 |
| MENTAL ILLNESS | community subjects vs hospital subjects<br>(see sample construction in excerpt, Part II) | | HAPP 1.1<br>AFF 1.1<br>HAPP 2.1 | G'<br>G'<br>G' | -.50<br>-.57<br>-.47 | Gt'<br>Gt'<br>Gt' | 01<br>01<br>01 | Aged persons, San Francisco, U.S.A.<br>Probability sample of community subjects and non-probability chunk sample of hospital subjects<br>N: 435, date: — | PIERC 73<br>p. 88 |

| | | | | | | | | | |
|---|---|---|---|---|---|---|---|---|---|
| MENTAL HEALTH | normals vs psychiatric out-patients (see sample construction in excerpt, Part II) | Normal subjects also scored significantly higher than the psychiatric out-patients on the Index of Positive Affects (005) and lower on the Index of Negative Affects (001). | AFF 2.3 | DM | - | t | 001 | Aged persons, Los Angeles County, U.S.A.<br>Non-probability purposive samples by expert choice of psychiatric out-patients and normal community subjects<br>N: 27, date: 1971 | MORIW 74<br>p. 76 |
| MENTAL ILLNESS | expatients vs inpatients (see sample construction in excerpt, Part II) | Significant differences for the Index of Negative Affects only. | AFF 2.3 | | - | t | 05 | Aged mental patients, U.S.A.<br>Non-probability accidental sample<br>N: 36, date: 1966 | HACKE 69<br>p. 125 |
| HAVING RECEIVED PSYCHIATRIC TREATMENT PRIOR TO COLLEGE YEARS | controls vs patients (see sample construction in excerpt, Part II) | | AFF 1.1 | G' | -.68 | Gt' | 01 | Full-time university students, Berkeley Campus, California, U.S.A.<br>Probability samples<br>N: 280, date: 1971 - 1972 | ESTES 73<br>p. 471 |

## H 2.4 - LONGEVITY

| | | | | | | | | | |
|---|---|---|---|---|---|---|---|---|---|
| LONGEVITY | Longevity Index:<br>number of years lived after initial testing (1955 - 1959) | For those who are still living (about half the panel), an estimate was made of how many years they will have lived since initial testing by adding the present number of years since initial testing (about 15) to the expected number of years now remaining according to actuarial life expectancy tables, based on age, sex and race. | COMP 4.4 | r | +.01 | | | Aged non-institutionalized persons, North Carolina, U.S.A.<br>Non-probability accidental sample, using volunteers | PALMO 69<br>p. 248 |
| LONGEVITY | Longevity Quotient:<br>number of years lived after initial testing divided by the expected number of years remaining after examination for persons of a given age, sex and race | See above<br>Unaffected by sex and race | COMP 4.4 | r | +.26 | | | See above | PALMO 69<br>p. 249 |

## H 2.5 - VARIOUS FACTORS CONCERNING HEALTH

| | | | | | | | | | |
|---|---|---|---|---|---|---|---|---|---|
| REPORT OF HOPES CONCERNING HEALTH OF SELF OR FAMILY | Open-ended question on personal wishes and hopes for the future<br>Responses rated as concerning one's own health and health of family | | HAPP 3.1 | G' | +.29 | Gt' | 01 | Adult population of 5 westernized nations, 3 underdeveloped giants, 2 countries in the Middle East, 3 Caribbean nations and the Philippines<br>Representative sample<br>N: 18653, date: ± 1960 | CANTR 65/1<br>p. 263 |
| REPORT OF FEARS CONCERNING HEALTH OF SELF OR FAMILY | Open-ended question on personal worries and fears for the future<br>Responses rated as concerning ill health, accident, death; for self or for members of the family | | HAPP 3.1 | G' | +.22 | Gt' | 01 | See above | CANTR 65/1<br>p. 263 |
| MOST IMPORTANT WORRY: HEALTH (PERSONAL AND FAMILY) | Open-ended question on most important worry other worries vs health | Computed for those having worries only (N = 2040). | HAPP 1.1 | G' | +.15 | Gt' | 01 | National adult population, U.S.A.<br>Non-probability quota sample<br>N: 2377, date: February, 1946 | WESSM 56<br>p. 213 |
| DESIRED PERSONAL CHANGES: HEALTH | Open-ended question on desired personal changes other changes vs change mentioned | Computed for those who desire to change only. (N = 1591) | HAPP 1.1 | G' | -.12 | Gt' | 05 | See above | WESSM 56<br>p. 211 |

| | | | | | | | | | |
|---|---|---|---|---|---|---|---|---|---|
| THINKING OFTEN ABOUT HEALTH | Closed question: not at all / sometimes / often, during last week | Gammas computed on the basis of the proportion 'often' answers<br>Lower among those of high S.E.S. : G' = -.31 (01)<br>Stronger among those of low S.E.S.: G' = -.37 (01) | HAPP 1.1 | G' | - | Gt' | | Inhabitants of 4 small communities, Illinois, U.S.A.<br>Probability multi-stage samples<br>N: 2006, date: March, 1962 | BRADB 65/1<br>p. 54 |
| WORRYING ABOUT HEALTH OF SELF AND FAMILY | Direct question rated on an open graphic scale ranging from 'not worried' to 'very worried' | | HAPP 1.1 | G | +.24 | | | National adult population, The Netherlands<br>Probability area sample<br>N: 1552, date: June, 1968 | BAKKE 74<br>p. 27 |
| BEING INTERESTED IN HEALTH | Closed question | College students only<br>L-shaped curve: significant negative among unhappier students only | COMP 4.1 | | - | | | Students, U.S.A.<br>Non-probability chunk sample<br>N: 1651, date: — | SYMON 37<br>p.292 |
| HAVING PROBLEMS WITH HEALTH | Closed question | | COMP 4.1 | | | | ns | See above | SYMON 37<br>p. 292 |
| BEING INTERESTED IN MENTAL HYGIENE | Closed question | | COMP 4.1 | | | | ns | See above | SYMON 37<br>p. 292 |
| HAVING PROBLEMS WITH MENTAL HYGIENE | Closed question | high school students: significant positive relationship<br>college students: significant negative relationship<br>L-shaped curve: stronger among happier students<br>graduate students: negative relationship<br>L-shaped curve: significant negative among happier students only | COMP 4.1 | | | | | See above | SYMON 37<br>p. 292 |
| ALTERATIONS IN HEALTH STATUS | Major change in health during past 2 years | Unaffected by life change in general | AFF 1.3 | r | -.12 | | 05 | Adults, Renton, Washington, U.S.A.<br>Probability systematic random sample of households<br>N: 536, date: — | PESZN 75<br>p. 445 |

## H 2.6 - HEALTHCARE

## READINESS TO SEEK HELP:

| | | | | | | | | | |
|---|---|---|---|---|---|---|---|---|---|
| READINESS FOR SELF-REFERRAL (a person's psychological preparedness to turn to professional help with an emotional problem) | 3-item index, containing attitude to professional help, use of professional help, and perceived competence to handle one's problems oneself<br>strong self help / self help / might need help / could have used help / has used help | When elaborated for educational level:<br>grade school: G' = -.09 (05)<br>high school : G' = -.15 (01)<br>college : G' = -.24 (01) | HAPP 1.1 | G' | - | Gt' | | Non-institutionalized adults, U.S.A.<br>Probability multi-stage area sample<br>N: 2460, date: spring, 1957 | GURIN 60<br>p. 262 |
| READINESS FOR SELF-REFERRAL | 3 item index<br>(see above) | | HAPP 1.1 | G' | -.34 | Gt' | 05 | Students teachers, Chapel Hill, U.S.A.<br>Probability sample proportionally stratified by teaching level<br>N: 75, date: spring, 1967 | GONZA 67<br>p. 130 |
| READINESS TO SEEK CARE | Likelihood of seeking medical care in eight hypothetical situations involving pain and symptomatology | | AFF 1.1 | $r_{pm}$ | +.01 | | ns | Families of hourly workers and salaried employees, U.S.A.<br>N: 712, date: summer, 1973 | TESSL 75<br>p. 103 |
| NEED FOR HELP WITH EMOTIONAL PROBLEMS OR FAMILY TROUBLES | Closed question: 'During the past year did you ever feel that you could use some help in dealing with emotional problems or family troubles?'<br>never / not very often / sometimes / often. | Computed for 1973 data only.<br>Index of Positive Affects: r = +.01 (ns)<br>Index of Negative Affects: r = +.40 (001) | AFF 2.3 | r | -.25 | | 001 | Adults, Los Angeles County, U.S.A.<br>Multi-stage probability samples of households<br>N: 1078 in 1972 and 1008 in 1973<br>date: spring, 1972 and spring, 1973 | CHERL 75<br>p. 197 |

## AVAILABILITY OF HELP:

| Concept | Question / Measure | Remarks | Measure | Stat | Value | Type | Sign. | Population / Sample | Source |
|---|---|---|---|---|---|---|---|---|---|
| AVAILABILITY OF HELP IN CASE OF ILLNESS | Question: 'If you were sick in bed at home for a short time, is there someone you could count on for help?' | | HAPP 2.1 | G' | +.35 | Gt' | 05 | Aged chronically-ill patients, U.S.A.<br>Probability sample<br>N: 167, date: 1959 | HENLE 67<br>p. 70 |

## EVALUATION OF HEALTHCARE:

| Concept | Question / Measure | Remarks | Measure | Stat | Value | Type | Sign. | Population / Sample | Source |
|---|---|---|---|---|---|---|---|---|---|
| FAITH IN DOCTORS | Choice between the following alternatives:<br>- I have a great faith in doctors<br>- In general I think doctors do a good job<br>- In general I think doctors are overrated<br>- I distrust doctors | | AFF 1.1 | $r_{pm}$ | +.03 | | ns | Families of hourly workers and salaried employees, U.S.A.<br>N: 712, date: summer, 1973 | TESSL 75<br>p. 103 |
| SCEPTICISM TOWARDS MEDICAL CARE | 6-item index (see Bice & Kalimos, 1971)<br>A typical item is: 'Do you often doubt some of the things doctors say they can do?' | | AFF 1.1 | $r_{pm}$ | -.07 | | 05 | See above | TESSL 75<br>p. 103 |
| SATISFACTION WITH MEDICAL CARE | 11-item satisfaction with medical care index containing satisfaction with doctor's concern about health, warmth and personal interest, friendliness, training and technical competence, willingness to listen, amount of time spent with you, amount of privacy in doctor's office, amount of health information given, quality of medical care, adequacy of office facilities and equipment, and friendliness of nurses, receptionists etc. | Investigated among those who received some medical services in the past year | AFF 1.1 | $r_{pm}$ | +.12 | | 001 | See above | TESSL 75<br>p. 102 |
| SATISFACTION WITH MEDICAL CARE OF CHILDREN | 11-item satisfaction with medical care index rephrased so as to be appropriate to measure satisfaction with care received by children | Computed for Ss with children under 12 years only (N = 386) | AFF 1.1 | $r_{pc}$ | | | ns | See above | TESSL 75<br>p. 105 |
| SATISFACTION WITH COMMUNITY'S MEDICAL FACILITIES | Closed question rated on a graphic rating scale very dissatisfied / somewhat dissatisfied / neither dissatisfied nor satisfied / somewhat satisfied / very satisfied | males : r = +.09 (ns)<br>females: r = +.05 (ns) | HAPP 3.1 | $r_{pm}$ | + | t | ns | Workers, Columbia, Canada<br>Non-probability purposive sample by expert choice<br>N: 470, date: — | HULIN 69<br>p. 285 |
| SATISFACTION WITH AVAILABILITY OF DOCTORS IN THE COMMUNITY | See above | males only | HAPP 3.1 | $r_{pm}$ | +.13 | t | 05 | See above | HULIN 69<br>p. 285 |
| SATISFACTION WITH AVAILABILITY OF DENTISTS IN THE COMMUNITY | See above | males only | HAPP 3.1 | $r_{pm}$ | +.13 | t | 05 | See above | HULIN 69<br>p. 285 |
| SATISFACTION WITH MEDICAL SERVICES | Closed question | | HAPP 1.1<br>AFF 1.1 | mc<br>mc | +.15<br>+.20 | | | Urban Jewish population, Israel<br>Probability area sample using dwelling units<br>N: 1830, date: summer, 1973 | LEVY 75/2<br>p. 373 |
| POSITIVE EVALUATION OF THE WAY THE HEALTH MIN. HANDLES HEALTH PROBLEMS | Closed question | | HAPP 1.1<br>AFF 1.1 | mc<br>mc | +.13<br>+.04 | | | See above | LEVY 75/2<br>p. 373 |

# H 3 HOPES, ASPIRATIONS AND GOALS

see also 'Concerns, Interests (C 2)
'Values' (V 1)



## H 3.1 – ASPIRED LIFE CHANGE

### H 3.1.1 – ASPIRED GENERAL LIFE CHANGE

| | | | | | | | | | |
|---|---|---|---|---|---|---|---|---|---|
| WISH TO CHANGE LIFE | Closed question: like to continue in much the same way / change some parts / change many parts | first questioning : r = –.44<br>second questioning: r = –.39 | HAPP 3.1 (1st instr.) | $r_{pm}$ | –.45 | | | National adult population, U.S.A.<br>Probability area sample (third sample)<br>N: 1072, date: November, 1972 | ANDRE 74<br>p. 15 |
| | | | HAPP 2.1 (2nd instr.) | $r_{pm}$ | –.44 | | | | |
| | | | COMP 1.1 (3rd instr.) | $r_{pm}$ | –.36 | | | | |
| | | | HAPP 1.1 (4th instr.) | $r_{pm}$ | –.37 | | | | |
| | | | HAPP 3.1 (5th instr.) | $r_{pm}$ | –.37 | | | | |
| | | Index of Positive Affects: r = –.13<br>Index of Negative Affects: r = +.36 | AFF 2.3 (6th instr.) | $r_{pm}$ | –.35 | | | | |
| WISH TO CHANGE LIFE | Closed question: like to continue in much the same way / change some parts / change many parts | Index of Positive Affects: G = –.16 (05)<br>Index of Negative Affects: G = +.34 (05) | AFF 2.3 | G | –.33 | | 05 | Adults, urban areas, U.S.A.<br>Probability area samples<br>N: 2787, date: January, 1963 – January, 1964 | BRADB 69<br>p. 51/63/68 |
| | | Lower among males : G = –.57<br>Stronger among females: G = –.69 | HAPP 1.1 | G | – | | | | |
| | | Unaffected by sex<br>males : G = –.72<br>females: G = –.70 | CON 1.1 | G | – | | | | |
| WISH TO CHANGE LIFE | Closed question: like to continue in much the same way / change some parts / change many parts | | HAPP 2.1 | $r_{pm}$ | –.17 | | | National population, Britain<br>Non-probability quota sample<br>N: 213, date: March, 1971 | ABRAM 73<br>p. 21 |
| WISH TO CHANGE LIFE | Closed question: like to continue in much the same way / change some parts / change many parts | Index of Positive Affects: G = –.07<br>Index of Negative Affects: G = +.06 | AFF 2.3 | G | – | | | Employed males, England<br>Non-probability purposive quota sample<br>N: 192, date: — | PAYNE 74<br>p. 17 |
| DESIRE TO CHANGE | Open-ended question on desired personal changes (see next page, H 3.1.2)<br>nothing vs other | | HAPP 1.1 | G' | –.17 | Gt' | 01 | National adult population, U.S.A.<br>Non-probability quota sample<br>N: 2377, date: February, 1946 | WESSM 56<br>p. 211 |

## H 3.1.2 - ASPIRED SPECIFIC CHANGES

| | | | | | | | | | |
|---|---|---|---|---|---|---|---|---|---|
| DESIRED PERSONAL CHANGES MENTIONED: | Open-ended direct question<br>other changes vs change mentioned | Computed for those who desire to change only<br>(N = 1591) | | | | | | National adult population, U.S.A.<br>Non-probability quota sample<br>N: 2377, date: February, 1946 | WESSM 56<br>p. 211 |
| - CHARACTER CHANGES (worry less) | | | HAPP 1.1 | G' | +.12 | Gt' | 05 | | |
| - PHYSICAL APPEARANCE, weight, size, looks | | | HAPP 1.1 | G' | +.05 | Gt' | ns | | |
| - HEALTH | | | HAPP 1.1 | G' | -.12 | Gt' | 05 | | |
| - AGE | | | HAPP 1.1 | G' | +.09 | Gt' | ns | | |
| - MORE EDUCATION | | | HAPP 1.1 | G' | -.14 | Gt' | ns | | |
| - BETTER SOCIAL RELATIONSHIPS | | | HAPP 1.1 | G' | -.01 | Gt' | ns | | |
| - BETTER WORK AND ATTITUDES TOWARDS IT | | | HAPP 1.1 | G' | -.39 | Gt' | 01 | | |

## H 3.2 - SPECIFIC HOPES, ASPIRATIONS AND GOALS

### H 3.2.1 - PERSONAL HOPES, ASPIRATIONS AND GOALS

| | | | | | | | | | |
|---|---|---|---|---|---|---|---|---|---|
| PERSONAL HOPES AND ASPIRATIONS: | Content-analysis on the basis of an open-ended question on personal wishes and hopes for the future | | | | | | | National adult population 5 Westernized nations, 3 under-developed giants, 2 countries in the Middle East, 3 Caribbean nations and the Philippines.<br>Representative samples<br>N: 18653, date: ± 1960 | CANTR 65/1<br>p. 263 |
| - VALUES AND CHARACTER | Responses rated as concerning emotional stability and maturity; be a normal, decent person; self-development or improvement; acceptance by others; achieve sense of own personal worth; resolution of own religious, spiritual or ethical problems; lead a disciplined life; etc. | | HAPP 3.1 | G' | +.21 | Gt' | 01 | | |
| - ECONOMIC CONDITIONS | Responses rated as concerning improved or decent standard of living for self or family; have own business, own land, own farm; have own house; have modern conveniences; have wealth; etc. | | HAPP 3.1 | G' | -.27 | Gt' | 01 | | |
| - JOB OR WORK SITUATION | Responses rated as concerning good job, congenial work, employment, success in one's work, etc., for self, spouse, or other family members | | HAPP 3.1 | G' | -.01 | Gt' | ns | | |

| | | | | | | | | | |
|---|---|---|---|---|---|---|---|---|---|
| - HEALTH OF SELF OR FAMILY | Responses rated as concerning one's own health and health of family | | HAPP 3.1 | G' | +.29 | Gt' | 01 | | |
| - FAMILY REFERENCES | Responses rated as concerning happy family life; concern and hopes for relatives, children; etc. | | HAPP 3.1 | G' | +.11 | Gt' | 01 | | |
| - POLITICAL REFERENCES | Responses rated as concerning freedom and other aspirations having to do with the political situation | | HAPP 3.1 | G' | +.07 | Gt' | ns | | |
| - SOCIAL REFERENCES | Responses rated as concerning social justice; future generations; social security; etc. | | HAPP 3.1 | G' | +.06 | Gt' | 05 | | |
| - INTERNATIONAL REFERENCES | Responses rated as concerning peace; a better world; etc. | | HAPP 3.1 | G' | +.44 | Gt' | 05 | | |
| - WANT STATUS QUO | Responses indicative of happiness with things as they are now | | HAPP 3.1 | G' | +.49 | Gt' | 05 | | |
| PERSONAL GOALS IN JUNIOR YEARS: | Closed question on subjective relevance of each of the goals mentioned, rated on 7-point scales ranging from 'not at all important' to 'extremely important goal'<br>(Perceived Instrumentality of College Test; see Constantinople 1965, 1970) | This analysis pertains to the relationship of personal goals in junior years and happiness in senior years (N = $\pm$ 60). It is partly based on data from Constantinople (see remarks in excerpt, Part II).<br>Constantinople has performed the same analysis with her samples of undergraduate Rochester students, but could not find any relationship between the subjective relevance of the goals and happiness.<br>See excerpts CONST 65 and CONST 70 (Part II).<br>See also under 'Attitudes towards School' (Part III, E 1.2.1). | | | | | | Female college seniors, University of Rochester, U.S.A.<br>Non-probability chunk sample<br>N: 162, date: May - June, 1966 | PORTE 67<br>p. 96 |
| - LEARNING HOW TO LEARN FROM BOOKS AND TEACHERS | | | AFF 2.1 | | | | ns | | |
| - ACQUIRING AN APPRECIATION OF IDEAS | | | AFF 2.1 | | | | ns | | |
| - ESTABLISHING OWN PERSONAL, SOCIAL AND ACADEMIC VALUES | | | AFF 2.1 | | | | ns | | |
| - DEVELOPING RELATIONSHIPS WITH THE OPPOSITE SEX | | | AFF 2.1 | | | | ns | | |
| - CONTRIBUTING IN A DISTINGUISHE AND MEANINGFUL MANNER TO SOME CAMPUS GROUP | | | AFF 2.1 | | | | ns | | |
| - DEVELOPING THE ABILITY TO GET ALONG WITH DIFFERENT KINDS OF PEOPLE | | | AFF 2.1 | | | | ns | | |
| - BECOMING SELF-CONFIDENT | | | AFF 2.1 | | | | ns | | |

| | | | | | | | | | |
|---|---|---|---|---|---|---|---|---|---|
| - PERSONAL INDEPENDENCE | | | AFF 2.1 | | | | ns | | |
| - FINDING A SPOUSE | | | AFF 2.1 | | | | ns | | |
| - ACHIEVING ACADEMIC DISTINCTION | | | AFF 2.1 | | | | ns | | |
| - HAVING MANY GOOD FRIENDS | | | AFF 2.1 | | | | ns | | |
| - DISCOVERING OWN STRONG POINTS AND LIMITATIONS | | | AFF 2.1 | | | | ns | | |
| - PREPARING FOR A CAREER WHICH BEGINS RIGHT AFTER GRADUATION | | | AFF 2.1 | | | | s | | |
| - PREPARING FOR A CAREER WHICH REQUIRES FURTHER STUDY BEYOND THE B.A. OR B.S. | | | AFF 2.1 | | | | ns | | |
| PERSONAL GOALS IN SENIOR YEARS: | Closed question on subjective relevance of each of the goals mentioned, rated on 7-point scales ranging from ' not at all important' to 'extremely important goal'. (see above) | This analysis pertains to the relation of personal goals and happiness at the same time (senior years) | | | | | | Female college seniors, University of Rochester, U.S.A. (See last page) | PORTE 67 p. 96 |
| - FINDING A SPOUSE | | | AFF 2.1 | | | | ns | | |
| - ACHIEVING ACADEMIC DISTINCTION | | | AFF 2.1 | | | | ns | | |
| - PREPARING FOR A CAREER WHICH BEGINS RIGHT AFTER GRADUATION | | | AFF 2.1 | | | | ns | | |
| - PREPARING FOR A CAREER WHICH REQUIRES FURTHER STUDY BEYOND THE B.A. OR B.S. | | | AFF 2.1 | | | | ns | | |
| HAVING PLANS TO GO TO COLLEGE | Open-ended question on future plans; other plans vs plan to enter post-high school education | | COMP 1.2 | $r_{pm}$ | +.07 | | 05 | Public highschool boys, U.S.A. Probability multi-stage sample N: 2213 in 1966, 1886 in 1968 and 1799 in 1969, date: fall, 1966, spring, 1968 and spring, 1969 | BACHM 67/70 p. 243 |

## H 3.2.2 - HOPES AND ASPIRATIONS CONCERNING ONE'S COUNTRY

| | | | | | | | | | |
|---|---|---|---|---|---|---|---|---|---|
| NATIONAL HOPES AND ASPIRATIONS: | Content analysis on the basis of an open-ended question on wishes and hopes for the future of one's country | | | | | | | National adult populations 5 Westernized nations, 3 underdeveloped giants, 2 countries in the Middle East, 3 Caribbean nations and the Philippines | CANTR 65/1 p. 263 |

(to be continued on next page)

| | | | | | | | | | |
|---|---|---|---|---|---|---|---|---|---|
| - POLITICAL | Responses rated as concerning honest, efficient, balanced, democratic or representative, socialistic government; freedom; law and order; national unity; political stability, internal peace and order; etc. | U-shaped curve: moderately happy people being least concerned with politics | HAPP 3.1 | G' | -.05 | Gt' | ns | | |
| - ECONOMIC | Responses rated as concerning improved or decent standard of living; technological advances, greater productivity; economic stability; employment; etc. | | HAPP 3.1 | G' | -.10 | Gt' | 05 | | |
| - SOCIAL | Responses rated as concerning social justice; eliminate discrimination, prejudice or exploitation; education; improved labor conditions; control of labor; social security; housing; agrarian reform; public health; limited population growth; sense of social and political responsibility and awareness; morality, ethical standards, religion; etc. | | HAPP 3.1 | G' | +.17 | Gt' | 01 | | |
| - INTERNATIONAL | Responses rated as concerning peace; disarmament, limitation of armaments, control or banning of nuclear weapons; lessening of cold war; better relations with Communist bloc; friendly relations with all countries; better world; maintain neutrality; help other nations; increased foreign trade or exports; etc. | | HAPP 3.1 | G' | +.47 | Gt' | 01 | | |
| - INDEPENDENT STATUS | Responses rated as concerning military strength; maintain or attain the position of a world power; enhancement of status and importance of the nation; exert ideological or moral leadership; national independence; etc. | | HAPP 3.1 | G' | +.26 | Gt' | 01 | | |
| - PRESERVE NATIONAL STATUS QUO | Responses indicative of contentment with things as they are | | HAPP 3.1 | G' | +.75 | Gt' | 01 | | |

## H 3.2.3 - VARIOUS WISHES

| | | | | | | | | | |
|---|---|---|---|---|---|---|---|---|---|
| DESIRE FOR HAVING MORE AMUSEMENT | Whether one would like to go out more often in the evenings for entertainment | 33% of the relatively dissatisfied and 26% of the satisfied would like to go out more often.<br>Stronger among males<br>Unaffected by going out with spouse or not | HAPP 2.1 | D% | - | | s | Middle-aged, middle class married couples, U.S.A.<br>Non-probability accidental sample of couples<br>N: 416, date: 1952 - 1953 | ROSE 55<br>p. 18 |
| WANT TO SPEND MORE TIME IN WORK AROUND THE HOUSE | | Unaffected by sex | HAPP 2.1 | D% | + | | s | See above | ROSE 55<br>p. 18 |
| WANT TO SPEND LESS TIME IN WORK AROUND THE HOUSE | | Among females 44% of the dissatisfied and 27% of the satisfied want to spend less time in work around the house.<br>No relationship among males | HAPP 2.1 | D% | - | | s | See above | ROSE 55<br>p. 18 |
| DESIRE FOR LONGER SCHOOLING | | 75% of the relatively dissatisfied and 58% of the very satisfied desire longer schooling.<br>Unaffected by sex | HAPP 2.1 | D% | - | | s | See above | ROSE 55<br>p. 17 |

| | | | | | | | | | |
|---|---|---|---|---|---|---|---|---|---|
| PREFER TO CHANGE JOB WHEN POSSIBLE | Closed question: no / perhaps / yes | unmarried males: r = -.08<br>married males: r = -.09<br>unmarried females: r = -.33<br>married females: r = -.03 | HAPP 2.1 | $r_{pm}$ | - | $Chi^2$ | | Adults, Amsterdam, The Netherlands<br>Probability systematic random sample stratified by sex and marital status<br>N: 600, date: September - December, 1965 | JONG 69<br>p. 22 |
| PREFER TO CHANGE JOB | Closed question: 'If you had the choice, would you change your present job in agriculture for another occupation?'<br>no vs yes | | HAPP 2.1 | $T^2$ | +.10 | $Chi^2$ | 001 | Individual farmowners and their families, Poland<br>Non-probability purposive quota sample<br>N: 1002, date: June - July, 1960 | MAKAR 62<br>p. 110 |
| WANT TO CONTINUE LIVING IN ONE'S TOWN | Closed question ranging from 'definitely no' to 'definitely yes' | | HAPP 1.1<br>AFF 1.1 | mc<br>mc | +.23<br>+.12 | | | Urban adult Jewish population, Israel<br>Probability area sample, using dwelling units<br>N: 1940, date: spring, 1973 | LEVY 75/1<br>p. 372 |
| WANT TO MOVE TO ANOTHER TOWN | Closed question ranging from 'definitely no' to 'definitely yes' | | HAPP 1.1<br>AFF 1.1 | mc<br>mc | -.14<br>-.05 | | | See above | LEVY 75/1<br>p. 372 |

## H 3.3 - PERCEIVED REALIZATION OF ASPIRATIONS AND GOALS

### H 3.3.1 - PERCEIVED OVERALL REALIZATION OF ASPIRATIONS (CONTENTMENT)

see 'Contentment' (H 1.3)

### H 3.3.2 - PERCEIVED SPECIFIC UNFULFILLED ASPIRATIONS

| | | | | | | | | | |
|---|---|---|---|---|---|---|---|---|---|
| UNFULFILLED ASPIRATIONS MENTIONED: | Open-ended direct question<br>Other aspirations vs aspirations mentioned | Computed for those who have unfulfilled aspirations only (N = 1646) | | | | | | National adult population, U.S.A.<br>Non-probability quota sample<br>N: 2377, date: February, 1946 | WESSM 56<br>p. 210 |
| - TRAVEL, VACATION | | | HAPP 1.1 | G' | +.07 | Gt' | ns | | |
| - NEW HOME, BUILD HOME, OWN HOME | | | HAPP 1.1 | G' | -.01 | Gt' | ns | | |
| - MATERIAL POSSESSIONS (cars, coats) | | | HAPP 1.1 | G' | +.11 | Gt' | ns | | |
| - EDUCATION, FOLLOW A TALENT | | | HAPP 1.1 | G' | +.06 | Gt' | ns | | |
| - MONEY | | | HAPP 1.1 | G' | -.07 | Gt' | ns | | |
| - NEW JOB, BUSINESS OF OWN | | | HAPP 1.1 | G' | +.01 | Gt' | ns | | |
| - MOVE TO COUNTRY, BECOME FARMER | | | HAPP 1.1 | G' | +.00 | Gt' | ns | | |
| - MARRIAGE, CHILDREN, HUSBAND | | | HAPP 1.1 | G' | -.27 | Gt' | 05 | | |
| HAVING UNFULFILLED ASPIRATIONS | | Open-ended question on unfulfilled aspirations (see above)<br>nothing vs other | HAPP 1.1 | G' | -.23 | Gt' | 01 | See above | WESSM 56<br>p. 210 |

## H 3.4 - VARIOUS FACTORS CONCERNING HOPES, ASPIRATIONS AND GOALS

| | | | | | | | | | |
|---|---|---|---|---|---|---|---|---|---|
| STATUS OF OCCUPATIONAL ASPIRATIONS | Open question on 'What sort of work do you think you might do for a living?', coded and converted to the Duncan socio-economic status index (see Reiss, 1961) | | COMP 1.2 | $r_{pm}$ | +.06 | | ns | Public highschool boys, U.S.A.<br>Probability multi-stage sample<br>N: 2213 in 1966 , 1886 in 1968 and 1799 in 1969, date: fall 1966, spring 1968 and spring 1969 | BACHM 67/70<br>p. 247 |
| SATISFACTION WITH NEXT YEAR'S PLANS IN TERMS OF ACHIEVEMENT NEEDS | Closed question on 'the extent to which S's present plans for further education, career, or job fulfill her need to achieve, to fully utilize her capacities', rated on a 7-point scale ranging from 'highly unsatisfactory' to 'highly satisfactory'. | | AFF 2.1 | $r_{pm}$ | +.17 | | 05 | Female college seniors, U.S.A.<br>Non-probability chunk sample<br>N: 162, date: May - June, 1966 | PORTE 67<br>p. 101 |
| DEGREE IN WHICH HE WORKS WITH DISTANT OBJECTS IN VIEW (as opposed to living from 'hand to mouth') | Trained peer rating on a 7-point scale on the basis of observation | | AFF 5.2 | $r_{pm}$ | -.08 | | | Male students, England<br>Non-probability chunk sample<br>N: 194, date: 1912 - 1913 | WEBB 15<br>p. 26 |
| ROLE RELATED PLANNING ABILITIES (ability to conceptualize goals and the instrumental tasks necessary to their accomplishment and ability to maintain a judicious balance among the various roles) | Rating by psychiatrists on the basis of observations during 6 years | Non-significant relationship with the Index of Negative Affects. | AFF 2.3 | $r_{pm}$ | +.29 | | 01 | Residents of Stirling County, Maritime, Canada<br>Probability sample stratified by sex, age, socio-environmental circumstances and mental health<br>N: 112, date: 1963 - 1968 | BEISE 74<br>p. 325 |
| CHANGE ORIENTATION | 2-item index of closed questions on optimism about the future, and yearning for change | | HAPP 1.1<br>HAPP 3.1 | r<br>r | -.12<br>$\pm$ 0 | | | Adults, Metro Manila, Philippines<br>Probability area sample<br>N: 941, date: January - April, 1972 | BULAT 73<br>p. 233 |

# H 4 HOUSEHOLD



## H 4.1 - HOUSEHOLD COMPOSITION

see also 'Family' (F 1), 'Marital Status' (M 1)

| | | | | | | | | | |
|---|---|---|---|---|---|---|---|---|---|
| NUMBER / PERCENTAGE OF CHILDREN LIVING AT HOME | | Reported for females only | HAPP 2.1 | D% | $\pm$ 0 | | ns | Middle-aged, middle class married couples, U.S.A.<br>Non-probability accidental sample of couples<br>N: 416, date: 1952 - 1953 | ROSE 55<br>p. 16 |
| POSTPARENTAL STAGE | Children still living with parents vs 'empty nest' | Stronger among those of age 40-49: G' = +.29 (01)<br>Reversed among those of age 50-59: G' = -.11 (ns) | HAPP 1.1 | G' | +.16 | Gt' | 05 | Non-institutionalized middle-aged females, U.S.A.<br>Pooling of 3 Gallup surveys<br>N: 902, date: 1963, 1966 | GLENN 75 A/1<br>p. 106 |
| POSTPARENTAL STAGE | See above | Lower among those of age 40-49 : G' = +.10 (ns)<br>Stronger among those of age 50-59: G' = +.27 (ns) | HAPP 1.1 | G' | +.12 | Gt' | ns | Non-institutionalized middle-aged females, U.S.A.<br>Pooling of NORC surveys<br>N: 425, date: 1972, 1973 | GLENN 75 A/2<br>p. 106 |
| POSTPARENTAL STAGE | See above | Lower among those of age 35-49 : G' = +.19 (ns)<br>Stronger among those of age 50-64: G' = +.32 (ns) | COMP 1.1 | G' | +.12 | Gt' | ns | Non-institutionalized middle-aged females, U.S.A.<br>Roper survey<br>N: 319, date: 1971 | GLENN 75 A/3<br>p. 107 |
| CHILDREN IN OWN HOUSE | Number of children | | HAPP 2.1 | G | +.06 | $Chi^2$ | 002 | Male employees of age 40+, The Netherlands<br>Non-probability chunk sample<br>N: 13000, date: — | SONDE 75 |
| LIVING ALONE | Living with parents vs living alone | Computed for singles only.<br>Males : r = -.21 (ns)<br>Females: r = -.03 (ns) | HAPP 2.1 | $r_{pm}$ | - | $Chi^2$ | ns | Adults, Amsterdam, The Netherlands<br>Probability systematic random sample stratified by sex and marital status<br>N: 600, date: September - December, 1965 | JONG 69<br>p. 203 |
| LIVING ARRANGEMENT | alone / with a spouse / with a child / some other arrangement | When controlled for level of health and level of income no relationships among those in poorer health or with lower incomes. Among those with better health and with incomes over $ 4,000.- per year Ss living alone reported the highest morale and those who are unmarried and living with a child reported the lowest morale. | AFF 1.1 | | | $Chi^2$ | ns | Aged persons, Metropolitan Boston, U.S.A.<br>Probability area sample<br>N: 1335, date: 1965 | FOWLE 69<br>p. 733 |
| HOUSEHOLD COMPOSITION : | | Analysis on the basis of a comparison between the happiness of the category mentioned and the happiness of the entire population | | | | | | Aged chronically-ill patients, U.S.A.<br>Probability sample<br>N: 167, date: 1959 | HENLE 67<br>p. 71 |
| - LIVING ALONE | | | HAPP 2.1 | G' | -.14 | Gt' | ns | | |
| - LIVING WITH SPOUSE | | | HAPP 2.1 | G' | +.09 | Gt' | ns | | |

| | | | | | | | | | |
|---|---|---|---|---|---|---|---|---|---|
| - LIVING WITH SPOUSE AND CHILDREN | | | HAPP 2.1 | G' | +.48 | Gt' | ns | | |
| - LIVING WITH CHILDREN | | | HAPP 2.1 | G' | -.27 | Gt' | ns | | |
| - LIVING WITH OTHER COMBINATION OF RELATIVES | | | HAPP 2.1 | G' | +.48 | Gt' | ns | | |
| LIVING ALONE | Living with others vs living alone | | HAPP 2.1 | G' | -.22 | Gt' | ns | Aged chronically-ill patients, U.S.A. (see last page) | HENLE 67 p. 71 |
| QUALITY OF CONTACTS WITH HOUSEHOLD MEMBERS | Closed question: generally troubled / sometimes one, sometimes the other / generally pleasant | Computed for those who are living with others only | HAPP 2.1 | G' | +.42 | Gt' | 01 | See above | HENLE 67 p. 71 |
| OBJECTION TO LIVING ALONE | Closed question: no vs yes | Computed for those who are living alone only | HAPP 2.1 | G' | -.56 | Gt' | 01 | See above | HENLE 67 p. 71 |

## H 4.2 - HOUSEHOLD WORK

| | | | | | | | | | |
|---|---|---|---|---|---|---|---|---|---|
| AMOUNT OF TIME SPENT ON HOUSEWORK | Number of hours usually spent on housework per week | Computed for females only<br>24% of the relatively dissatisfied and 9% of the satisfied women spend 60 hours or more a week on housework.<br>About an equal percentage of satisfied and dissatisfied women spend less than 20 hours a week on housework. | HAPP 2.1 | D% | - | | | Middle-aged, middle class married couples, U.S.A.<br>Non-probability accidental sample of couples<br>N: 416, date: 1952 - 1953 | ROSE 55 p. 16 |
| HAVING PAID HOUSEHOLD HELP | | Computed for females only | HAPP 2.1 | D% | + | | s | See above | ROSE 55 p. 16 |
| GETTING HOUSEHOLD ASSISTANCE FROM CHILDREN OR HUSBAND | | Computed for females only | HAPP 2.1 | D% | ± 0 | | ns | See above | ROSE 55 p. 16 |
| WANT TO SPEND MORE TIME ON WORK AROUND THE HOUSE | | Unaffected by sex | HAPP 2.1 | D% | + | | s | See above | ROSE 55 p. 18 |
| WANT TO SPEND LESS TIME ON WORK AROUND THE HOUSE | | Among females 44% of the dissatisfied and 27% of the satisfied want to spend less time on work around the house.<br>No relationship among males | HAPP 2.1 | D% | - | | s | See above | ROSE 55 p. 18 |
| SATISFACTION WITH HOUSEWORK | Closed question: very little / a fair amount / a lot of pleasure and satisfaction | Computed for unemployed women only | HAPP 1.1 | G' | +.38 | Gt' | 01 | National adult population, U.S.A.<br>Non-probability quota sample<br>N: 2377, date: February, 1946 | WESSM 56 p. 198 |
| SATISFACTION WITH HOUSEWORK, work around the house | Closed question: 'How do you feel about . . .' terrible / unhappy / mostly dissatisfied / mixed / mostly satisfied / pleased / delighted | Unaffected by sex | HAPP 3.1 (1st instr.) | $h^2$ | .26 | | | National adult population, U.S.A.<br>Probability area sample (first sample)<br>N: 1297, date: May, 1972 | ANDRE 74 p. 17 |
| ENJOYING DOMESTIC WORK | Closed question: a little / much / very much | | HAPP 1.1 | $r_{pm}$ | +.34 | | | Housewives, The Netherlands<br>Probability area sample<br>N: 450, date: autumn, 1964 | PHILI 66 p. 66 |

# I 1 INCOME

I 1.1 Level of income (money)

I 1.2 Perceived sufficiency of income

I 1.3 Debts

I 1.4 Satisfaction with income, standard of living . . see A 2.2.14 , S 1.8.3, S 1.9.2

I 1.5 Concerns about income, money

I 1.6 Various indicators of income, standard of living

I 1.7 Change in income

## I 1.1 - LEVEL OF INCOME (MONEY)

| | | | | | | | | | |
|---|---|---|---|---|---|---|---|---|---|
| INCOME | low / medium / high | | HAPP 3.1 | G' | +.38 | Gt' | 01 | Adult population of 5 Westernized nations, 3 underdeveloped giants, 2 countries in the Middle East, 3 Caribbean nations & The Philippines<br>Representative samples<br>N: 18653, date: ± 1960 | CANTR 65/1<br>p. 259 |
| ECONOMIC STATUS | Classification by the interviewer<br>lower / middle / upper | | HAPP 1.1 | G' | +.24 | Gt' | 01 | National adult population, U.S.A.<br>Non-probability quota sample<br>N: 2377, date: February, 1946 | WESSM 56<br>p. 184 |
| INCOME | less than average / average / greater than average | See remarks in excerpt (Part II).<br>In 1946: negroes: G' = +.15 (ns)<br>whites : G' = +.24 (01)<br>In 1966: negroes: G' = -.32 (05)<br>whites : G' = +.26 (01) | HAPP 1.1 | G' | + | Gt' | | National adult populations, U.S.A.<br>Non-probability quota samples and probability area samples<br>N: 25617, date: 1946, 1947, 1948, 1956, 1966 | MANNI 72<br>p. 50 |
| INCOME | | Unaffected by educational level | HAPP 1.1 | | + | | s | Non-institutionalized adults, U.S.A.<br>Probability multi-stage area sample<br>N: 2460, date: spring, 1957 | GURIN 60<br>p. 216 |
| SOCIO-ECONOMIC LEVEL | low / middle / high | Cantril's book did not offer enough information to decide whether 'income' or 'S.E.S' was measured here. | HAPP 3.1 | G' | +.25 | Gt' | 01 | National adult population, U.S.A.<br>Probability sample<br>N: 1549, date: 1959 | CANTR 65/1<br>p. 378-380 |
| ECONOMIC LEVEL | income<br>lower / middle / upper one-third | | HAPP 2.1<br>HAPP 3.1<br>CON 1.1 | r<br>r<br>r | +.15<br>+.19<br>+.16 | | | National adult population, U.S.A.<br>Cantril (1965) modified probability sample<br>N: 1406, date: 1959 | BORTN 70<br>p. 44 |
| INCOME | lower / lower middle / upper middle / upper | See remarks in excerpt (Part II).<br>lower : Mean = 5.93 (6.27)<br>lower middle: Mean = 6.48 (6.52)<br>upper middle: Mean = 6.76 (7.03)<br>upper : Mean = 7.49 (7.41) | HAPP 3.1 | DM | + | | | Non-institutionalized national adult population, U.S.A.<br>Multi-stage probability sample, stratified by size of locality<br>N: 1588, date: January, 1971 (+ 1964) | CANTR 71<br>p. 66 |
| INCOME | 4-point scale | Gammas based on proportions 'very happy' answers.<br>Stronger among whites: G' = +.19 (01)<br>Not among blacks : G' = -.01 (ns) | HAPP 1.1 | G' | +.21 | Gt' | 01 | Non-institutionalized adults, U.S.A.<br>Type of sample construction unclear<br>N: 1602, date: March, 1972 | ALSTO 74<br>p. 100 |

| | | | | | | | | | |
|---|---|---|---|---|---|---|---|---|---|
| INCOME | | | HAPP 3.1 (1st instr.) | $h^2$ | .18 | | | National adult population, U.S.A.<br>Probability area sample (first sample)<br>N: 1297, date: May, 1972 | ANDRE 74<br>p. 20 |
| FAMILY INCOME | 12-point scale | Unaffected by age (under 65 vs 65+)<br>Unaffected by S.E.S. | HAPP 1.1 | $r_{pm}$ | +.13 | | 01 | Non-institutionalized adults, U.S.A.<br>Probability sample<br>N: 1547, date: 1972, 1973 | SPREI 74<br>p. 455/457 |
| INCOME | 8-point scale<br><br>4-point scale | Stronger among those of lower educational level<br>Stronger among older Ss | HAPP 1.1<br><br>AFF 2.3 | G'<br><br>G' | +.29<br><br>+.26 | Gt'<br><br>Gt' | 01<br><br>01 | Inhabitants of 4 small communities, Illinois, U.S.A.<br>Probability multi-stage samples<br>N: 2006, date: March, 1962 | BRADB 65/1<br>p. 9/23 |
| INCOME | 10-point scale | Significant among those of lower educational levels (less than high school graduate) and among high school graduates under the age of 35 only (05).<br>Unaffected by number of children.<br>Index of Positive Affects: $\bar{DR}$ = +.25 (05)<br>Index of Negative Affects: $\bar{DR}$ = -.10 (05)<br>Computation of Gamma on the basis of a 3-point scale:<br>less than $ 5,000 / 5,000-7,999 / 8,000 and more | AFF 2.3<br><br>HAPP 1.1 | $\bar{DR}$<br><br>G' | +.25<br><br>+.33 | BCI | 05 | Adults, urban areas, U.S.A.<br>Probability area samples<br>N: 2787, date: January, 1963 - January, 1964 | BRADB 69<br>p. 45/91/<br>95/99 |
| INCOME | Closed question on total income during last year<br>16-point scale | L-shaped curve: Stronger among lower income levels. Slightly stronger among persons of age 46-59. | HAPP 3.1 | $r_{pm}$ | +.10 | | | People of 46 and older, Duke, U.S.A.<br>Probability systematic random sample, stratified by age and sex<br>N: 502, date: 1968 | PALMO 72<br>p. 70 |
| SOCIO-ECONOMIC LEVEL | low / middle / high | Cantril's book did not offer enough information to decide whether 'income' or 'S.E.S.' was measured. | HAPP 3.1 | G' | +.88 | Gt' | 01 | National adult population, Dominican Republic<br>Probability samples<br>N: 814, date: ± 1960 | CANTR 65/1<br>p. 378-380 |
| SOCIO-ECONOMIC LEVEL | low / middle / high | See above | HAPP 3.1 | G' | +.52 | Gt' | 01 | National adult population, Panama<br>Probability sample, proportionally poststratified by dwelling and mortality<br>N: 642, date: ± 1960 | CANTR 65/1<br>p. 378-380 |
| SOCIO-ECONOMIC LEVEL | low / middle / high | See above | HAPP 3.1 | G' | +.16 | Gt' | 01 | National adult population, Cuba<br>Probability area sample<br>N: 992, date: ± 1960 | CANTR 65/1<br>p. 378-380 |
| INCOME | 8-point scale | Unaffected by educational level<br>Stronger among those of age 50+<br>Lower in rural areas (Q = +.13) | HAPP 1.1<br>AFF 2.3 | G'<br>G' | +.20<br>+.19 | Gt'<br>Gt' | 01<br>01 | National adult population, Puerto Rico<br>Probability simple random sample<br>N: 1417, date: November, 1963 - January, 1964 and August, 1964 - October 1964 | MATLI 66<br>p. 22 |
| SOCIO-ECONOMIC LEVEL | low / middle / high | See above at Cantril's sample from the Dominican Republic. | HAPP 3.1 | G' | +.38 | Gt' | 01 | National adult population, Brazil<br>Probability samples<br>N: 2168, date: ± 1960 | CANTR 65/1<br>p. 378-380 |
| SOCIO-ECONOMIC LEVEL | lower vs upper | See above<br>Stronger among those who have no children (01)<br>Lower among those who have children (01) | HAPP 3.1 | DM | + | DMRT | 01 | Married adults in the Dominican Republic, Panama and Yugoslavia<br>Pooling of the Cantril (1965) samples of the Dominican Republic, Panama and Yugoslavia<br>N: 4113, date: ± 1960 | BOHN 72<br>p. 31 |
| FAMILY INCOME | low / average / high | | HAPP 2.1<br>HAPP 1.1 | G'<br>G' | +.24<br>+.21 | Gt'<br>Gt' | 01<br>01 | National populations of nine European countries<br>Type of sample construction not reported<br>N: 9605 (9543), date: May, 1975 | COMMI 75<br>p. 139/153 |
| INCOME | 2-point scale | low income : Mean = 5.25<br>high income: Mean = 6.70 | HAPP 2.1 | DM | + | | | National population, Britain<br>Non-probability quota sample<br>N: 213, date: March, 1971 | ABRAM 73<br>p. 4 |

| | | | | | | | | | |
|---|---|---|---|---|---|---|---|---|---|
| SOCIO-ECONOMIC LEVEL | low / middle / high | Cantril's book did not offer enough information to decide whether 'income' or 'S.E.S.' was measured. | HAPP 3.1 | G' | +.23 | Gt' | 01 | National population, W. Germany<br>Probability area sample<br>N: 480, date: ± 1960 | CANTR 65/1<br>p. 370-380 |
| INCOME | 4-point scale | | HAPP 1.1 | G' | +.19 | Gt' | 05 | National adult population, The Netherlands<br>N: at least 1000, date: 1948 | NIPO 49<br>p. 4 |
| SOCIO-ECONOMIC LEVEL | low / middle / high | See above | HAPP 3.1 | G' | +.22 | Gt' | 01 | National adult population, Yugoslavia<br>Probability sample<br>N: 1523, date: ± 1960 | CANTR 65/1<br>p. 378-380 |
| SOCIO-ECONOMIC LEVEL | low / middle / high | See above | HAPP 3.1 | G' | +.55 | Gt' | 01 | National population, Israel<br>Probability sample<br>N: 1170, date: ± 1960 | CANTR 65/1<br>p. 378-380 |
| INCOME | lower / middle / upper | Lower income group : Mean = 4.0<br>Middle income group: Mean = 5.5<br>Upper income group : Mean = 6.5 | HAPP 3.1 | DM | + | | | National population, Israel<br>Probability sample<br>N: 1170, date: ± 1960 | CANTR 65/1<br>p. 369 |
| SOCIO-ECONOMIC LEVEL | low / middle / high | See above at Cantril's sample from W. Germany | HAPP 3.1 | G' | +.52 | Gt' | 01 | National adult population, Nigeria<br>Probability sample, proportionally stratified by dwelling and region<br>N: 1200, date: ± 1960 | CANTR 65/1<br>p. 378-380 |
| SOCIO-ECONOMIC LEVEL | low / middle / high | See above | HAPP 3.1 | G' | +.42 | Gt' | 01 | National population, India<br>Probability sample, proportionally poststratified by dwelling<br>N: 2366, date: 1958 | CANTR 65/1<br>p. 378-380 |
| INCOME | 4-point scale | Lowest income group : Mean = 3.0<br>Second income group : Mean = 3.8<br>Third income group : Mean = 4.3<br>Highest income group: Mean = 4.9 | HAPP 3.1 | DM | + | | | National population, India<br>Probability sample, proportionally poststratified by dwelling<br>N: 2366, date: 1958 | CANTR 65/1<br>p. 368 |
| SOCIO-ECONOMIC LEVEL | lower; lower middle / middle / upper middle; upper | See above at Cantril's sample from W. Germany<br>Upper, upper middle: Mean = 5.8<br>Middle : Mean = 5.3<br>Lower middle, lower: Mean = 4.3 | HAPP 3.1 | DM | + | | | National adult population, Japan<br>Probability sample<br>N: 972, date: ± 1960 | CANTR 65/1<br>p. 370 |
| SOCIO-ECONOMIC LEVEL | low / middle / high | See above at Cantril's sample from W. Germany | HAPP 3.1 | G' | +.44 | Gt' | 01 | National adult population, The Philippines<br>Probability sample, proportionally poststratified by dwelling<br>N: 500, ate: ± 1960 | CANTR 65/1<br>p. 378-380 |
| HOUSEHOLD INCOME | | Lower among males : G = +.21<br>Stronger among females: G = +.38 | HAPP 1.1 | G | + | | | Adults, Metro Manila, Philippines<br>Probability area sample<br>N: 941, date: January - April, 1972 | BULAT 73<br>p. 234-235 |
| | | males : G = +.53<br>females: G = +.50 | HAPP 3.1 | G | + | | | | |
| | | Index of Positive Affects:<br>males : G = +.25<br>females: G = +.26<br>Index of Negative Affects:<br>males : G = +.14<br>females: G = +.06 | AFF 2.3 | G | + | | | | |

SPECIAL GROUPS:

| Variable | Measure | Remarks | Dependent | Stat. | Value | Test | Sign. | Sample | Source |
|---|---|---|---|---|---|---|---|---|---|
| INCOME | Husband's income rated on a 3-point scale | | HAPP 1.1 | $r_{pm}$ | +.21 | | | Housewives, The Netherlands<br>Probability area sample<br>N: 450, date: autumn, 1964 | PHILI 66<br>p. 66 |
| INCOME | 4-point scale | Stronger among the handicapped: G' = +.49 (01)<br>Lower among normals : G' = +.09 (ns) | HAPP 2.1 | G' | +.31 | Gt' | 01 | Physically defective and normal persons, Detroit, U.S.A.<br>Non-probability purposive samples<br>N: 295, date: — | CAMER 71<br>p. 641 |
| INCOME | 4-point scale | Stronger among the handicapped: r = +.34 (01)<br>Lower among normals : r = +.11 (ns) | HAPP 2.1 | r | + | | | CAMER 71 sample; See above | CAMER 73/1<br>p. 209 |
| INCOME | 4-point scale | | HAPP 2.1 | | | | ns | Physically handicapped and normal persons, U.S.A.<br>Non-probability purposive samples<br>N: 90, date: — | CAMER 73/2<br>p. 211 |
| TOTAL ANNUAL FAMILY INCOME | | L- shaped curve: Significant among lower income levels only (below $ 4,000). | AFF 1.1 | | + | $Chi^2$ | s | Aged persons, Metropolitan Boston, U.S.A.<br>Probability area sample<br>N: 1335, date: 1965 | FOWLE 69<br>p. 734 |
| INCOME | Clinic fee rating based on an evaluation of the patient's total financial situation<br>3-point scale | When among the lowest income category the welfare Ss were compared with those dependent on Social Security or relatives, welfare status appears to be negatively related to happiness: G' = -.79 (01). | HAPP 2.1 | G' | +.37 | Gt' | 01 | Aged chronically-ill patients, U.S.A.<br>Probability sample<br>N: 167, date: 1959 | HENLE 67<br>p. 70 |
| INCOME | 4-point scale: less than $ 3,999 / 4,000 - 4,999 / 5,000 - 7,999 / 8,000 or more | Those with incomes between $ 5,000 and $ 7,999 generally are less happy than those with incomes of $ 4,000 - 4,999. | HAPP 1.1 | $t_{k_c}$<br>G | +.15<br>+.26 | | 01 | Non-hospitalized schizophrenic males, Monroe County, New York, U.S.A.<br>Probability sample, drawn from the Monroe County psychiatric case register<br>N: 178, date: 1964 - 1965 | ALEXA 68<br>p. 97/108 |

## I 1.2 - PERCEIVED SUFFICIENCY OF INCOME

| Variable | Measure | Remarks | Dependent | Stat. | Value | Test | Sign. | Sample | Source |
|---|---|---|---|---|---|---|---|---|---|
| SUFFICIENT FAMILY INCOME | Closed question ranging from 'insufficient' to 'definitely sufficient' | | HAPP 1.1<br>AFF 1.1 | mc<br>mc | +.35<br>+.35 | | | Urban adult Jewish population, Israel<br>Probability area sample, using dwelling units<br>N: 1940, date: spring, 1973 | LEVY 75/1<br>p. 372 |
| SUFFICIENT FAMILY INCOME | Closed question | | HAPP 1.1<br>AFF 1.1 | mc<br>mc | +.29<br>+.34 | | | Urban adult Jewish population, Israel<br>Probability area sample, using dwelling units<br>N: 1830, date: summer, 1973 | LEVY 75/2<br>p. 373 |
| PERCEIVED FINANCIAL ADEQUACY | Closed question: not enough to manage on / just enough to get by / comfortable | | HAPP 2.1 | G' | +.92 | Gt' | 01 | Aged chronically-ill patients, U.S.A.<br>Probability sample<br>N: 167, date: 1959 | HENLE 67<br>p. 70 |

## I 1.3 - DEBTS

| | | | | | | | | | |
|---|---|---|---|---|---|---|---|---|---|
| HAVING DEBTS | no debts vs debts | Data from the third interview wave were used here.<br>When elaborated for income:<br>less than \$ 5,000: $D\bar{R}$ = +.05 (ns)<br>\$ 5,000 - \$ 6,999: $D\bar{R}$ = .00 (ns)<br>\$ 7,000 - \$ 9,999: $D\bar{R}$ = -.04 (ns)<br>\$ 10,000 or more : $D\bar{R}$ = .00 (ns)<br>When those having debts were divided into those who could pay off debts and those who could not pay off their debts without borrowing, in all income groups the differences with those who have no debts were still non-significant.<br>Also when debt-level was assessed by the actual dollar debt instead of the subjective report of debt no significant relationships with hedonic level appear. | AFF 2.3 | $D\bar{R}$ | +.01 | B | ns | Adults, urban areas, U.S.A.<br>Probability area samples<br>N: 2787, date: January, 1963 - January, 1964 | BRADB 69<br>p. 100 |
| INABILITY TO PAY DEBTS | Could pay off debts vs could not pay off debts without borrowing | See above<br>Ss having no debts were excluded here.<br>Significant (05) among those with incomes between \$ 5,000 and \$ 7,000 only | AFF 2.3 | $D\bar{R}$ | -.06 | BCI | ns | See above | BRADB 69<br>p. 100 |
| INCREASE IN DEBT LEVEL | decreased / stable / increased | Analysis on the basis of a comparison between data from January, 1963 (wave 1) and October, 1963 (wave 3). | AFF 2.3 | $D\bar{R}$ | - | BCI | ns | See above | BRADB 69<br>p. 102 |
| WORRY ABOUT DEBTS | Closed question on worries about debts during the past few weeks<br>no vs yes | Lower among those with incomes of \$ 10,000 or more : $D\bar{R}$ = -.04 (05). | AFF 2.3 | $D\bar{R}$ | -.11 | BCI | 05 | See above | BRADB 69<br>p. 102 |

## I 1.4 - SATISFACTION WITH INCOME, STANDARD OF LIVING

see 'Satisfaction with Income, Standard of Living' (S 1.8.3), 'Satisfaction with Work, Job + Specific Aspects' (S 1.9.2), 'Types of Affect - Present Work' (A 2.2.14)

## I 1.5 - CONCERNS ABOUT INCOME, MONEY

| | | | | | | | | | |
|---|---|---|---|---|---|---|---|---|---|
| REPORT OF HOPES CONCERNING ECONOMIC CONDITIONS | Open-ended question on personal wishes and hopes for the future<br>Responses rated as concerning improved or decent standard of living for oneself or family; having own business, own land, own farm, own house, modern conveniences, having wealth, etc. | | HAPP 3.1 | G' | -.27 | Gt' | 01 | Adult populations of 5 Westernized nations, 3 underdeveloped giants, 2 countries in the Middle East, 3 Caribbean nations and the Philippines<br>Representative samples<br>N: 18,653, date: ± 1960 | CANTR 65/1<br>p. 263 |
| REPORT OF FEARS CONCERNING ECONOMIC CONDITIONS | Open-ended question on personal worries and fears for the future<br>Responses rated as concerning deterioration in or inadequate standard of living for oneself or family, etc. | | HAPP 3.1 | G' | -.29 | Gt' | 01 | See above | CANTR 65/1<br>p. 263 |

| | | | | | | | | | |
|---|---|---|---|---|---|---|---|---|---|
| UNFULFILLED ASPIRATIONS: MONEY | Open-ended question on unfulfilled aspirations other aspirations vs aspirations mentioned | Computed for those having unfulfilled aspirations only ( N = 1646) | HAPP 1.1 | G' | -.07 | Gt' | ns | National adult population, U.S.A.<br>Non-probability quota sample<br>N: 2377, date: February, 1946 | WESSM 56<br>p. 210 |
| MOST IMPORTANT WORRY: FINANCIAL WORRIES, MONEY | Open-ended question on most important worry other worries vs worry mentioned | Computed for those having worries only (N = 2040) | HAPP 1.1 | G' | -.23 | Gt' | 01 | See above | WESSM 56<br>p. 213 |
| THINKING OFTEN ABOUT MONEY | Closed question: not at all / sometimes / often, during last week | Gamma's computed on the basis of proportion 'often' answers.<br>Unaffected by S.E.S. | HAPP 1.1 | G' | -.22 | Gt' | 01 | Inhabitants of 4 small communities, Illinois, U.S.A.<br>Probability multi-stage samples<br>N: 2006, date: March, 1962 | BRADB 65/1<br>p. 54 |
| HAVING PROBLEMS WITH MONEY | Closed question | High school students only<br>L - shaped curve: Stronger negative among unhappier students | COMP 4.1 | | - | | s | Students, U.S.A.<br>Non-probability chunk sample<br>N: 1651, date: — | SYMON 37<br>p. 292 |
| BEING INTERESTED IN MONEY | Closed question | | COMP 4.1 | | | | ns | See above | SYMON 37<br>p. 292 |

## I 1.6 - VARIOUS INDICATORS OF INCOME, STANDARD OF LIVING

| | | | | | | | | | |
|---|---|---|---|---|---|---|---|---|---|
| SELF-EVALUATED COMPARATIVE FINANCIAL STATUS | 3-item index of closed questions on present financial situation compared with former expectations, former situation, situation of most relatives and friends<br>worse (stressful) vs better (non-stressful) | Unaffected by S.E.S. | AFF 1.3 | $\overline{DR}$ | +.12 | | 05 | Adults, Alameda County, U.S.A.<br>Probability sample<br>N: 6928, date: 1965 | BERKM 71<br>p. 41 |
| MATERIAL STYLE OF LIFE | Measures based on amount of material possessions and material wealth | Index of Negative Affects: r = -.16 (05)<br>No relationship with Index of Positive Affects | AFF 2.3 | $r_{pm}$ | + | | | Residents of Stirling County, Maritime, Canada.<br>Probability sample, stratified by sex, age, socio-environmental circumstances and mental health<br>N: 112, date: 1963 - 1968 | BEISE 74<br>p. 325 |
| LEVEL OF INCOME COMPARED WITH OTHER JOBS | Closed question: very small / small / average / large / very large | | HAPP 2.1 | $T^2$ | +.18 | $Chi^2$ | 001 | Individual farm owners and their families, Poland<br>Non-probability purposive quota sample<br>N: 1002, date: June - July, 1960 | MAKAR 62<br>p. 112 |
| LEVEL OF INCOME COMPARED WITH OTHER JOBS | Closed question: very small / small / average / large / very large | | HAPP 2.1 | $T^2$ | +.13 | $Chi^2$ | 001 | Persons gainfully employed outside agriculture, Poland<br>Non-probability purposive quota sample<br>N: 982, date: June - July, 1960 | MAKAR 62<br>p. 113 |
| BEING ABLE TO SAVE | Closed question | | HAPP 1.1<br>AFF 1.1 | mc<br>mc | +.23<br>+.25 | | | Urban adult Jewish population, Israel<br>Probability area sample, using dwelling units<br>N: 1830, date: summer, 1973 | LEVY 75/2<br>p. 373 |
| INCOME | Being vs not being a member of the sick-fund | Significant among lower educational levels only (025). | HAPP 1.1 | | + | $Chi^2$ | | Adults, Utrecht, The Netherlands<br>Probability sample, stratified by age<br>N: 300, date: autumn, 1967 | MOSER 69<br>p. 21 |
| WELFARE STATUS | formerly-welfare vs welfare | Significant (05) among husband-present females only. | HAPP 1.1 | DM | - | | | Low-income women with children, New York State, U.S.A.<br>Probability systematic random sample, stratified by employed status and presence or absence of a husband in the house (marital status)<br>N: 1325, date: — | BENDO 74<br>p. 77 |

| | | | | | | | | | |
|---|---|---|---|---|---|---|---|---|---|
| ECONOMIC DEPRIVATION | not deprived vs economically deprived | See remarks in excerpt (Part II).<br>Stronger among the gainfully employed: G'= -.54(01)<br>Stronger among those retirees who had a positive orientation to retirement when they were retired : G'= -.53(01)<br>Lower among those retirees who had a negative orientation to retirement : G'= -.40(ns) | COMP 1.2 | G' | -.55 | Gt' | 01 | Aged males (those satisfied in 1952), U.S.A.<br>Non-probability accidental sample<br>N: 787, date: 1952 - 1956 | THOMP 60<br>p. 168 |

## 1.1.7 - CHANGE IN INCOME

| | | | | | | | | | |
|---|---|---|---|---|---|---|---|---|---|
| REPORTED PAY-CUT DURING PAST YEAR | Closed question on pay-cut of chief wage earner during past year: no vs yes | | AFF 2.3 | $\bar{DR}$ | -.04 | BCI | ns | Adults, urban areas, U.S.A.<br>Probability area samples<br>N: 2787, date: January, 1963 - January, 1964 | BRADB 69<br>p. 104 |
| REPORTED PAY-RAISE DURING PAST YEAR | Closed question on pay-raise of chief wage earner during past year: no vs yes | | AFF 2.3 | $\bar{DR}$ | +.05 | BCI | 05 | See above | BRADB 69<br>p. 104 |
| INCREASE IN INCOME DURING ONE YEAR | Total family income of 1962 compared with total income in 1963<br>less / same / greater | In January, 1963 (wave 1) Ss were enquired after their total family income in 1962.<br>In October, 1963 (wave 3) Ss were enquired after their expected total income in 1963<br>Unaffected by level of income. | AFF 2.3 | $\bar{DR}$ | +.01 | BCI | ns | See above | BRADB 69<br>p. 104 |
| EXPECTING WAGE INCREASE DURING NEXT 5 YEARS | Closed question: decreasing / no change / increasing | | HAPP 2.1 | $T^2$ | +.17 | $Chi^2$ | 001 | Persons gainfully employed outside agriculture, Poland<br>Non-probability purposive quota sample<br>N: 982, date: June - July, 1960 | MAKAR 62<br>p. 112 |
| EXPECTING INCOME INCREASE DURING NEXT 5 YEARS | Closed question: decreasing / no change / increasing | | HAPP 2.1 | $T^2$ | +.16 | $Chi^2$ | 001 | Individual farm-owners and their families, Poland<br>Non-probability purposive quota sample<br>N: 1002, date: June - July, 1960 | MAKAR 62<br>p. 112 |

# I 2 INSTITUTIONAL LIVING

see also 'Being treated for mental illness' (H 2.3.3).

| | | | | | | | | | |
|---|---|---|---|---|---|---|---|---|---|
| RESTRICTIVENESS OF SETTING | open ward (ward A) vs closed ward (ward B) | See also sample construction in excerpt (Part II)<br>open ward : mean = 4.68<br>closed ward: mean = 5.39 | AFF 5.1 | DM | + | | 001 | Institutionalized mentally retarded males, U.S.A.<br>Non-probability chunk sample<br>N: 149, date: — | PÀNDE 71<br>p. 328 |
| LENGTH OF INSTITUTIONALIZATION | Number of years | open ward : r = +.14 (ns)<br>closed ward: r = -.06 (ns) | AFF 5.1 | $r_{pm}$ | | | ns | See above | PANDE 71<br>p. 329 |
| COOPERATIVENESS | Ratings by two experienced staff members who were familiar with all the patients on a 7-point 'rebellious - cooperative' scale | open ward : r = +.56 (001)<br>closed ward: r = +.60 (001) | AFF 5.1 | $r_{pm}$ | + | | 001 | See above | PANDE 71<br>p. 329 |
| AGGRESSIVENESS | Ratings by two experienced staff members who were familiar with all the patients on a 7-point 'passive - aggressive' scale | open ward : r = -.24 (05)<br>closed ward: r = -.34 (01) | AFF 5.1 | $r_{pm}$ | - | | 05 | See above | PANDE 71<br>p. 329 |
| POPULARITY | Ratings by two experienced staff members who were familiar with all the patients on a 7-point 'isolated - popular' scale | open ward : r = +.52 (001)<br>closed ward: r = +.47 (001) | AFF 5.1 | $r_{pm}$ | + | | 001 | See above | PANDE 71<br>p. 329 |
| SOCIABILITY | Score based on number of choices made in answering three open-ended questions:<br>- who do you like?<br>- who are your friends?<br>- who do you play with? | open ward : r = +.30 (01)<br>closed ward: r = +.04 (ns) | AFF 5.1 | $r_{pm}$ | + | | | See above | PANDE 71<br>p. 329 |
| REJECTION OF PEERS | Score based on number of choices made in answering three open-ended questions:<br>- who don't you like?<br>- who do you dislike?<br>- who don't you like to play with? | open ward : r = -.03 (ns)<br>closed ward: r = -.12 (ns) | AFF 5.1 | $r_{pm}$ | - | | ns | See above | PANDE 71<br>p. 329 |
| PEER POPULARITY | Score based on the number of times one is selected by his peers in answering three open-ended questions:<br>- who do you like?<br>- who are your friends?<br>- who do you play with? | open ward : r = +.04 (ns)<br>closed ward: r = +.30 (05) | AFF 5.1 | $r_{pm}$ | + | | | See above | PANDE 71<br>p. 329 |
| REJECTION BY PEERS | Score based on the number of times one is selected by his peers in answering three open-ended questions:<br>- who don't you like?<br>- who do you dislike?<br>- who don't you like to play with? | open ward : r = -.23 (05)<br>closed ward: r = -.32 (01) | AFF 5.1 | $r_{pm}$ | - | | 05 | See above | PANDE 71<br>p. 329 |

| | | | | | | | | | |
|---|---|---|---|---|---|---|---|---|---|
| ADJUSTMENT | Overall staff-ratings based on the staff's own conceptualization of adjustment | For 8 out of the 12 staff members a significant (05) relationship between their rankings on adjustment and satisfaction (= happiness measure) was found (range of r = +.27 to +.51).<br>Analysis of results suggest that in evaluating the residents the staff equated adjustment with external criteria, such as cooperation and conduct, more than with internal criteria, such as the feelings of the residents. | COMP 5 | $t_k$ | +.35 | | 02 | Male residents of a chronic care Veterans Administration nursing home, age 46 - 89, U.S.A.<br>N: 20, date: — | SCHNE 71 p. 63 |
| COOPERATION WITH STAFF | Overall staff-ratings on cooperation with the staff, conformity to rules, and conduct. | For 12 out of the 16 staff members a significant (05) relationship between their rankings on cooperation and satisfaction (= happiness measure) was found (range of r = +.32 to +.63). | COMP 5 | $t_k$ | +.46 | | 01 | See above | SCHNE 71 p. 63 |
| DEGREE OF MISPERCEPTION OF THE NEEDS OF THE RESIDENTS BY THE STAFF | 10-item inventory of statements which were intended to represent general needs of particular importance to residents of an institution for the aged (e.g. 'being able to do things for yourself', being with people who like you')<br>On the basis of paired comparisons the relative importance of each of the needs was assessed for each of the residents.<br>In the same way each staff member's perception of the relative importance of the needs for each of the residents was assessed.<br>A difference score was computed for the discrepancy between each resident's ordering and the overall staff's ordering of the needs. | Also the 20 difference scores of each individual staff member were ranked and then correlated with his rankings of the residents on satisfaction (= happiness measure). For only 2 of the 16 staff members a significant correlation was found. | COMP 5 | $t_k$ | -.14 | | ns | See above | SCHNE 71 p. 63 |

# L 1 LIFE HISTORY



## L 1.1 - CHILDHOOD SITUATION

This category contains indicators of the childhood situation in general only. Relationships of happiness with specific indicators of the childhood are reported in 'Family' (F 1), 'Education and School' (E 1), Confrontation with War' (W 1.1), etc.

| | | | | | | | | | |
|---|---|---|---|---|---|---|---|---|---|
| <u>LIFE HISTORY</u>: | 212-item inventory of past life experiences | 18 scores were derived, indicating good or bad past experiences in various life areas. Only a few scores were related to hedonic level. Other scores were not presented. | | | | | | Male college students, U.S.A.<br>Non-probability chunk sample<br>N: 17, date: ± 1960 | WESSM 66/2<br>p. 122 |
| - POOR LIFE EXPERIENCES | Over-all total score | | AFF 3.1 | $r_{pm}$ | -.41 | t | 05 | | |
| - LOW SCHOLARSHIP | Score consisting of items indicating past feelings of intellectual inferiority, feelings of academic failure and discouragement | | AFF 3.1 | $r_{pm}$ | -.50 | t | 05 | | |
| - DEPRESSION AND INSECURITY | | | AFF 3.1 | $r_{pm}$ | -.46 | t | 10 | | |
| - POOR PEER RELATIONS | | | AFF 3.1 | $r_{pm}$ | -.45 | t | 10 | | |
| - SIBLING CONFLICT | | | AFF 3.1 | $r_{pm}$ | -.39 | t | 10 | | |
| - PARENTAL TREATMENT AND RELATIONSHIPS | | A number of scores on parental treatment or relationships were derived. None of them appeared to show much relationship to mood level. | AFF 3.1 | | | t | ns | | |
| HAPPY LIFE HISTORY | Clinical rank on 'happy - unhappy life story', stressing auto-biographic reports and information for three years, concerning past life experiences up to the time of entering college | | AFF 3.1 | $r_{pm}$ | +.48 | t | 05 | See above | WESSM 66/2<br>p. 104 |
| <u>CHILDHOOD STRESS</u>: | 4-factor score (see below) | | AFF 1.3 | $D\bar{R}$ | -.09 | | 05 | Adults, Alameda County, U.S.A.<br>Probability sample<br>N: 6928, date: 1965 | BERKM 71<br>p. 42-43 |
| - BROKEN HOMES IN CHILDHOOD | S lived with real father / mother during the first 15 years of his life<br>yes vs no | | AFF 1.3 | $D\bar{R}$ | - | | 05 | | |
| - POSITIVE EVALUATION OF FATHER AND MOTHER AS A PARENT | Closed questions for mother and father separately<br>worse / about the same / better than most fathers/mothers | | AFF 1.3 | $D\bar{R}$ | +.08 | | 05 | | |

(to be continued on next page)

| | | | | | | | | | |
|---|---|---|---|---|---|---|---|---|---|
| - HAPPINESS OF PARENTS' MARRIAGE IN CHILDHOOD | Closed question: very unhappy / unhappy / somewhat unhappy / somewhat happy / happy / very happy | | AFF 1.3 | $\bar{DR}$ | +.08 | | 05 | | |
| - LONG OR SERIOUS ILLNESS IN FAMILY DURING CHILDHOOD | Closed question: no vs yes | | AFF 1.3 | $\bar{DR}$ | -.02 | | 05 | | |

## L 1.2 - LIFE CHANGE IN ADULTHOOD

This category contains indicators of general life change only.
Relationships of happiness with specific changes are reported in 'Change in Income' (I 1.7), 'Marital Status' (M 1), 'Retirement' (R 2), 'Social Mobility' (S 5.3), 'Change of Work' (W 2.3), etc.

| | | | | | | | | | |
|---|---|---|---|---|---|---|---|---|---|
| LIFE CHANGE | Number of life change units during the past two years as assessed by a modified form of the Schedule of Recent Events (see Holmes & Rahe,1967) | | AFF 1.3 | r | -.08 | | ns | Adults, Renton, Washington, U.S.A.<br>Probability systematic random sample of households<br>N: 536, date: — | PESZN 75<br>p. 445 |
| ALTERATIONS IN HEALTH STATUS | Major change in health during the past two years (item from the Schedule of Recent Events; see above) | Unaffected by life change | AFF 1.3 | r | -.12 | | 05 | See above | PESZN 75<br>p. 445 |
| EXPERIENCE OF RECENT LIFE CHANGES | Adapted Schedule of Recent Experiences (see Holmes & Rahe, 1967), scored for the past year | Index of Positive Affects: G = +.06<br>Index of Negative Affects: G = +.19 | AFF 2.3 | G | - | | | Employed males, age 30 - 60, England<br>Non-probability purposive sample by expert choice<br>N: 192, date: — | PAYNE 75<br>p. 101 |
| LIFE CHANGE | Number of life changes experienced after age 20, as assessed by a 15-item inventory | | HAPP 1.1 | G | +.15 | | | National adult population, The Netherlands<br>Probability area sample<br>N: 1552, date: June, 1968 | BAKKE 74<br>p. 28 |
| MAJOR LIFE CHANGES | Experience of a major life change (either positive or negative) in the past year | | AFF 1.1 | $r_{pm}$ | +.07 | | ns | Families of hourly workers and salaried employees, U.S.A.<br>N: 712, date: summer, 1973 | TESSL 75<br>p. 103 |
| GAINS IN SOCIAL STATUS OVER 4 YEARS | Comparison of data from 1967 and 1971<br>A significant move to a fully independent household, marriage, and taking paying employment were defined as status gains.<br>Institutionalization, the death of supportive family members and friends, and recent geographic dispersion of supportive children were defined as losses<br>losses / no change / gains | | AFF 2.3 | $t_k$ | +.13 | | ns | Aged female public housing residents, U.S.A.<br>Probability systematic random sample<br>N: 44, date: 1967 - 1971 | GRANE 73A<br>p. 7 |
| ROLE LOSS | number of lost roles | | AFF 2.3 | r | +.05 | | ns | Aged retired persons, Los Angeles County, U.S.A.<br>Non-probability purposive quota sample, proportionally stratified by marital status<br>N: 71, date: 1971 | MORIW 73<br>p. 229 |

# L 2 LIFE QUALITY



## L 2.1 - SUBJECTIVE LIFE QUALITY

This category contains among others invalid indicators of Happiness

## L 2.1.1- OVERALL JUDGMENTS OF LIFE

see also 'Happiness' (H 1)

| | | | | | | | | | |
|---|---|---|---|---|---|---|---|---|---|
| PROJECTIVE HAPPINESS | Over-all score on a scheme of 15 positive and 15 negative variables indicative of happy - unhappy themes, using stories that were told to the Standard Thematic Apperception Test cards (see Murray, 1943) | | AFF 3.1 | $r_{pm}$ | +.27 | t | ns | Male college students, U.S.A.<br>Non-probability chunk sample<br>N: 17, date: ± 1960 | WESSM 66/2<br>p. 120 |
| HAVING A GOOD LIFE | Closed question: bad / fair / good | | HAPP 1.1 | G' | +.54 | Gt' | 01 | National adult population, The Netherlands<br>N: at least 1000, date: 1948 | NIPO 49<br>p. 3 |
| HAVING A GOOD LIFE | Closed question: other answers (less than good) / good / very good | | HAPP 1.1 | $r_{pm}$ | +.29 | | | Housewives, The Netherlands<br>Probability area sample<br>N: 450, date: autumn, 1964 | PHILI 66<br>p. 66 |
| HEDONIC LEVEL OF FEELINGS ABOUT THE GOOD AND PLEASANT PARTS OF LIFE | Closed question: terrible / unhappy / mostly dissatisfied / mixed / mostly satisfied / pleased / delighted | | HAPP 3.1 (1st instr.) | $r_{pm}$ | +.37 | | | National adult population, U.S.A.<br>Probability area sample (second sample)<br>N: 1118, date: November, 1972 | ANDRE 74<br>p. 15 |
| | | | HAPP 2.1 | $r_{pm}$ | +.25 | | | | |
| | | | COMP 1.1 | $r_{pm}$ | +.34 | | | | |
| HEDONIC LEVEL OF FEELINGS ABOUT THE POOR ASPECTS OF LIFE (annoying, worrying things) | Closed question: terrible / unhappy / mostly dissatisfied / mixed / mostly satisfied / pleased / delighted | | HAPP 3.1 (1st instr.) | $r_{pm}$ | +.25 | | | See above | ANDRE 74<br>p. 15 |
| | | | HAPP 2.1 | $r_{pm}$ | +.27 | | | | |
| | | | COMP 1.1 | $r_{pm}$ | +.23 | | | | |
| ENJOYING LIFE | Closed question on enjoying life compared with other people of the same age: less / about the same / more | Index of Positive Affects: G' = +.15 (01)<br>Index of Negative Affects: G' = -.83 (01) | AFF 2.3 | G' | +.38 | Gt' | 01 | National adult population, Puerto Rico<br>Probability simple random sample<br>N: 1417, date: November, 1963 - January, 1964 and August - October, 1964 | MATLI 66<br>p. 13 |
| ENJOYMENT OF PREVIOUS DAY | Direct question rated on an 11-point self-anchoring scale | | HAPP 3.1 | $r_{pm}$ | +.25 | | | National adult population, U.S.A.<br>Probability sample<br>N: 1549, date: 1959 | CANTR 65/2<br>p. 268/415 |

| | | | | | | | | | |
|---|---|---|---|---|---|---|---|---|---|
| ENJOYMENT OF PREVIOUS DAY | Direct question rated on an 11-point self-anchoring scale | | HAPP 2.1<br>CON 1.1<br>HAPP 2.1<br>HAPP 3.1<br>CON 1.1 | $r_{pm}$<br>$r_{pm}$<br>r<br>r<br>r | +.38<br>+.28<br>+.33<br>+.27<br>+.31 | | | National adult population, U.S.A.<br>Cantril (1965) modified probability sample<br>N: 1406, date: 1959 | BORTN 70<br>p. 44 |
| SATISFACTION WITH OWN SATISFACTION LEVEL | Difference between level of satisfaction with life and level of satisfaction one thinks people like oneself are entitled to | Both questions were rated on an 11-point self-anchoring scale.<br>See also instrument in excerpt (Part II). | HAPP 2.1 | $r_{pm}$ | +.59 | | | National population, Britain<br>Non-probability quota sample<br>N: 213, date: March, 1971 | ABRAM 73<br>p. 21 |

## L 2.1.2 - ASPECT JUDGMENTS OF LIFE

see also 'Satisfaction with ...' (S 1), 'Types of Affect' (A 2.2), 'Problems, Worries and Fears' (P 5)

### MULTIPLE ASPECT JUDGMENTS

| | | | | | | | | | |
|---|---|---|---|---|---|---|---|---|---|
| LONG-TERM SATISFACTION | 3-item index of closed questions on like to continue one's life in much the same sort of way or like to change parts of it, success at planning one's life, and accomplished most of the things one would have liked to | Index of Positive Affects: r = +.21 (05)<br>Index of Negative Affects: r = -.33 (01)<br><br>When controlled for positive and negative affect: $r_{pc}$ = +.30 (001) | AFF 2.3<br><br>HAPP 1.1 | $r_{pm}$<br><br>$r_{pm}$ | +<br><br>+.45 | | s<br><br>001 | Residents of Stirling County, Maritime, Canada<br>Probability sample stratified by sex, age, socio-environmental circumstances and mental health<br>N: 112, date: 1963 - 1968 | BEISE 74<br>p. 323/325 |
| SATISFACTION WITH LIFE | 20-item index of agree / disagree statements; e.g.'I've gotten pretty much what I expected out of life'<br>(adapted Neugarten Life Satisfaction Index A; see Neugarten et al., 1961) | | COMP 5 | $t_k$ | + | | ns | Male residents of a chronic care Veterans Administration nursing home, age 46-89, U.S.A.<br>N: 20, date: — | SCHNE 71<br>p. 63 |
| SATISFACTION WITH LIFE | 12-item index including 6 open-ended questions and 6 checklist items; e.g. 'How happy would you say you are right now compared with earlier periods of your life ?'<br>(adapted Neugarten Life Satisfaction Index B; see above) | | COMP 5 | $t_k$ | +.28 | | 05 | See above | SCHNE 71<br>p. 63 |
| SATISFACTION WITH LIFE | Combined Neugarten Life Satisfaction Indices A and B<br>(see above) | | COMP 5 | $t_k$ | +.23 | | 10 | See above | SCHNE 71<br>p. 63 |
| POSITIVE INNER WELL-BEING | 17-item index of closed questions on pleasure, feeling happy, having life-goals, laughing, energy level, self-consciousness, trust in others, activity level, satisfaction with social participation, positive outlook on life, self-confidence, trust in own feelings, health, satisfaction with hobbies, love for children, sense of freedom, and interest in environment<br>(selected items from the Inner Well-Being questionnaire) | | COMP 1.1 (1st instr.)<br><br>COMP 1.1 (2nd instr.) | $r_{pm}$<br><br>$r_{pm}$ | +.55<br><br>+.40 | | | Secondary school pupils, The Netherlands<br>Non-probability chunk sample<br>N: 291, date:— | HERMA 73<br>p. 738/740 |

| Concept | Measure | Remarks | Code | Stat. | Value | Test | Sign. | Population / Sample | Source |
|---|---|---|---|---|---|---|---|---|---|
| NEGATIVE INNER WELL-BEING | 19-item index of closed questions on feelings of worthlessness, inferiority, powerlessness, anxiety, inner emptiness, loneliness, guilt, boredom and jealousy, degree of depressiveness, unhappiness, self-alienation, worries, self-dislike and lack of confidence, and perceived distance between oneself and others (selected items from the Inner Well-Being questionnaire) | | COMP 1.1 (1st instr.) | $r_{pm}$ | -.36 | | | Secondary school pupils, The Netherlands (see last page) | HERMA 73 p. 738/740 |
| | | | COMP 1.1 (2nd instr.) | $r_{pm}$ | -.60 | | | | |
| HAPPINESS | Ss with many negative feelings and few positive feelings (N = 58) vs Ss with few negative feelings and many positive feelings (N = 28) as assessed by the Inner Well-Being questionnaire (see above) | | AFF 3.1 | | + | | | Secondary school pupils, The Netherlands<br>Non-probability accidental sample<br>N: 89, date: after 1970 | RAMZY 73 p. 77 |
| NEGATIVE AFFECT STATES | 40-item index of closed questions on irritability (7 items), general anxiety (7 items), anxiety and tension (5 items), depression (6 items), anomy (8 items) and resentment (7 items) | | COMP 1.2 | $r_{pm}$ | -.51 | | 001 | Public high school boys, U.S.A.<br>Probability multi-stage sample<br>N: 2213 in 1966, 1886 in 1968 and 1799 in 1969<br>date: fall, 1966; spring, 1968 and spring 1969 | BACHM 67/70 p. 122 |
| OPTIMISM | Factor Optimism - Pessimism, based on indirect agree/disagree questionnaire items, e.g. chances of success in life, most endeavors are worthwhile, life consists of a procession of disillusionments, the future looks black as pitch | This questionnaire was filled up 2 years before hedonic level was assessed | AFF 3.1 | $r_{pm}$ | +.58 | t | 05 | Male college students, U.S.A.<br>Non-probability chunk sample<br>N: 17, date: ± 1960 | WESSM 66/2 p. 116 |
| **SINGLE ASPECT JUDGMENTS** | | | | | | | | | |
| HAVING FUN IN LIFE | Agree / disagree statement: 'I get a lot of fun out of life' | Stronger among females: G = +.88<br>Lower among males : G = +.83<br>When standardized on:<br>- usual mood and frequency of low mood: $G_s$ = +.65<br>- usual mood : $G_s$ = +.76<br>- frequency of low mood : $G_s$ = +.80<br>- tending to be a discouraged person : $G_s$ = +.80<br>- tending to be a lonely person : $G_s$ = +.73<br>- anxiety symptoms : $G_s$ = +.83<br>- participation in extracurricular activities : $G_s$ = +.85<br>- social class : $G_s$ = +.85 | HAPP 1.1 | G<br>V | +.85<br>.46 | $Chi^2$ | 01 | Juniors and seniors attending public high schools in New York State, U.S.A.<br>Probability cluster sample of 10 public high schools<br>N: sample A: 1682, sample B: 1664<br>date: 1960 | BRENN 70 p. 64/71/75/ 87/88/262/263 |
| | | Unaffected by sex | AFF 1.1 | G<br>V | +.68<br>.36 | $Chi^2$ | 01 | | |
| LIFE FRUSTRATION | Closed question: 'Do you find life frustrating?' never / infrequently / sometimes / frequently / constantly | Stronger among normals : r = -.44 (01)<br>Lower among the handicapped: r = -.29 (01) | HAPP 2.1 | r | - | | 01 | Physically defective and normal persons, Detroit, U.S.A.<br>Non-probability purposive samples<br>N: 295, date: — | CAMER 73/1 p. 209 |
| APPRAISED EASE OF LIFE | Closed question: 'How has your life been so far?' very difficult / difficult / average / easy / very easy | Stronger among normals : r = +.38 (01)<br>Lower among the handicapped: r = +.17 (05) | HAPP 2.1 | r | + | | | See above | CAMER 73/1 p. 209 |
| TIME SPENT IN DISLIKED ACTIVITIES | 2 direct questions on disliked activities and on amount of time spent doing these things | | HAPP 1.1 | G' | -.18 | Gt' | 01 | National adult population, U.S.A.<br>Non-probability quota sample<br>N: 2377, date: February, 1946 | WESSM 56 p. 212 |

| | | | | | | | | | |
|---|---|---|---|---|---|---|---|---|---|
| DOING THINGS ONE LIKES | Total number of activities engaged in during the past day, as assessed by a personal 160-item activity schedule for each S, administered for 30 days (160 most pleasant events from the Pleasant Events Schedule Form II; see Mac-Phillamy & Lewinsohn, 1971)<br>Two scores were deducted: a raw activity score (= number of activities) and a weighted activity score (= number of activities with each activity weighted for its pleasantness rating). | See instrument and remarks in excerpt (Part II).<br>Stronger for Depression score 1, than for score 2 (001) or score 3 (001)<br>Slightly stronger correlations with the weighted activity score than with the raw score (05)<br>Non-significant differences between the depressed, the psychiatric controls and the normal controls, and between males and females<br>Depression is more strongly related to pleasant activities engaged in during the same day than to activities during the previous or during the next day(s) (001).<br>Depression is not more strongly related to pleasant activities during previous day(s) than to activities during the next day(s) and vice versa | AFF 3.3 | $r_{pm}$ | + | t | 001 | College undergraduates, Oregon, U.S.A.<br>Non-probability purposive sample by expert choice stratified by psychic status and sex<br>N: 30, date: February - March, 1971 | LEWIN 72<br>p. 293 |
| DOING THINGS ONE LIKES | Raw activity score (see above under LEWIN 72)<br>The Pleasant Events Schedule Form III was used here (see MacPhillamy & Lewinsohn, 1971) | See remarks in excerpt (Part II)<br>The mean correlation between the activity score and the depression score of the same day for a period of 30 days was used.<br>Stronger among the depressed and psychiatric controls than among the normal controls (05):<br>depressed : r = +.36<br>psychiatric controls: r = +.43<br>normal controls : r = +.25<br>Stronger among females than among males (05):<br>females : r = +.39<br>males : r = +.29<br>Unaffected by age:<br>age 18-29 : r = +.30<br>age 30-49 : r = +.40<br>age 50+ : r = +.32 | AFF 3.3 | $r_{pm}$ | + | | | Adults, Oregon, U.S.A.<br>Non-probability purposive sample by expert choice stratified by psychic status and sex<br>N: 90, date: — | LEWIN 73<br>p. 264 |
| LONELINESS | 6-item index of statements on feeling lonely, nobody cares for you, difficulty making lasting contacts, coping with things alone, hard to find real friends, and alone in the world. | Unaffected by sex<br>Lower among married persons: G' = -.36 (01)<br>Stronger among singles : G' = -.50 (01) | HAPP 2.1 | G' | -.48 | Gt' | 01 | Adults, Amsterdam, The Netherlands<br>Probability systematic random sample stratified by sex and marital status<br>N: 600, date: September - December, 1965 | JONG 69<br>p. 197 |
| TENDING TO BE A LONELY PERSON | Closed question: not lonely / fairly lonely / very lonely | Unaffected by sex<br>When standardized on:<br>- usual mood : $G_s$ = -.56<br>- having fun in life : $G_s$ = -.50<br>- frequency of low mood : $G_s$ = -.62<br>- tending to be a discouraged person: $G_s$ = -.60<br>- anxiety symptoms : $G_s$ = -.66 | HAPP 1.1 | G<br>V | -.68<br>.32 | $Chi^2$ | 01 | Juniors and seniors attending public high schools in New York State, U.S.A.<br>Probability cluster sample of 10 public high schools<br>N: sample A: 1682, sample B: 1664, date: 1960 | BRENN 70<br>p. 71/75/87/88/268 |
| | | Stronger among males: G = -.55<br>Lower among females : G = -.49 | AFF 1.1 | G<br>V | -.31<br>.23 | $Chi^2$ | 01 | | |
| TENDING TO BE A DISCOURAGED PERSON | Direct agree/disagree statement | Unaffected by sex<br>When standardized on:<br>- usual mood : $G_s$ = -.59<br>- having fun in life : $G_s$ = -.47<br>- frequency of low mood : $G_s$ = -.57<br>- tending to be a lonely person : $G_s$ = -.53<br>- anxiety symptoms : $G_s$ = -.63 | HAPP 1.1 | G<br>V | -.67<br>.35 | $Chi^2$ | 01 | See above | BRENN 70<br>p. 71/75/265 |
| | | Unaffected by sex | AFF 1.1 | G<br>V | -.56<br>.29 | $Chi^2$ | 01 | | |

| | | | | | | | | | |
|---|---|---|---|---|---|---|---|---|---|
| DOUBT ABOUT MEANINGFULNESS OF OWN EXISTENCE | Direct question rated on a graphic scale ranging from 'never' to 'very often' | Stronger among those of age 25–40<br>Stronger among those of lower education<br>Unaffected by S.E.S.<br>Unaffected by sex | HAPP 1.1 | G | -.56 | | 05 | National adult population, The Netherlands<br>Probability area sample<br>N: 1552, date: June, 1968 | BAKKE 74<br>p. 29 |
| **ASPECT JUDGMENTS CONCERNING THE FUTURE** | | | | | | | | | |
| PERSONAL HOPES: WANT STATUS QUO | Open-ended question on personal wishes and hopes for the future<br>Responses indicative of happiness with things as they are now | | HAPP 3.1 | G' | +.49 | Gt' | 05 | Adult population of 14 countries<br>Representative samples<br>N: 18,653, date: ± 1960 | CANTR 65/1<br>p. 263 |
| EXPECTED EASE OF LIFE IN FUTURE | Closed question: very difficult / difficult / average / easy / very easy | Unaffected by physical status:<br>normals : r = +.44 (01)<br>handicapped: r = +.46 (01) | HAPP 2.1 | r | + | | 01 | Physically defective and normal persons, Detroit, U.S.A.<br>Non-probability purposive samples<br>N: 295, date: — | CAMER 73/1<br>p. 209 |
| CHANGE ORIENTATION | 2-item index of closed questions on optimism about the future, and yearning for change | | HAPP 1.1<br>HAPP 3.1 | r<br>r | -.12<br>± 0 | | | Adults, Metro Manila, Philippines<br>Probability area sample<br>N: 941, date: January – April, 1972 | BULAT 73<br>p. 233 |
| **L 2.2 - OBJECTIVE LIFE QUALITY** | | | | | | | | | |
| **L 2.2.1 - PERSONAL INDICATORS** | see also 'Health and Health Care' (H 2), 'Personality' (P 1), 'Self-Image' (S 2) | | | | | | | | |
| WELL-BEING | Ratings by two psychologists on a 5-point scale. The raters were instructed to rate on a dimension of well-being that ranged from spent, played out, almost senile in manner, to alive, zestful, vital even enthousiastic | | HAPP 2.1 | | + | | ns | Aged residents of an appartment building for the elderly, U.S.A.<br>Non-probability accidental sample<br>N: 122, date: — | STORA 75<br>p. 99 |
| HAVING EVER CONTEMPLATED SUICIDE | Closed question: no vs yes | Stronger among normals : r = -.28 (01)<br>Lower among the handicapped: r = -.11 (ns) | HAPP 2.1 | r | - | | | Physically defective and normal persons, Detroit, U.S.A.<br>Non-probability purposive samples<br>N: 295, date: — | CAMER 73/1<br>p. 209 |
| HAVING CONTEMPLATED SUICIDE DURING PAST MONTH | Closed question: no vs yes | Stronger among normals : r = -.34 (01)<br>Lower among the handicapped: r = -.21 (05) | HAPP 2.1 | r | - | | 05 | See above | CAMER 73/1<br>p. 209 |

## L 2.2.2 - SOCIAL INDICATORS

see also 'Level of Education' (E 1.1.1), 'Income' (I 1), 'Socio-Economic Status' (S 5), 'Work' (W 2); and 'Family' (F 1), 'Marital Status' (M 1), 'Social Participation' (S 4)

| Indicator | Description | Remarks | Variable | Measure | Value | Test | Sign. | Population / Sample | Source |
|---|---|---|---|---|---|---|---|---|---|
| DEPRIVATION | 3-item index on compulsory retirement, widowhood and physical disability | See remarks in excerpt (Part II)<br>Stronger among withdrawn Ss (those reporting reduction in family participation, in extra-family participation and/or in organizational activity during past year) : G' = -.90 (01)<br>Lower among not-withdrawn Ss : G' = -.51 (05) | HAPP 1.1 | G' | -.70 | Gt' | 01 | Non-institutionalized aged persons, San Fransisco, U.S.A.<br>Probability sample stratified by sex, age and social living arrangement<br>N: 269, date: 1960 - 1964 | LOWEN 65 p. 367 |
| | | Unaffected by social withdrawal:<br>withdrawn Ss : G' = -.70 (01)<br>not-withdrawn Ss: G' = -.65 (01) | HAPP 2.1 | G' | -.70 | Gt' | 01 | | |
| | | Stronger among withdrawn Ss : G' = -.64 (01)<br>Lower among not-withdrawn Ss: G' = -.40 (ns) | AFF 1.1 | G' | -.55 | Gt' | 01 | | |
| CHILDHOOD STRESS | 4-factor score containing broken homes in childhood, evaluation of mother and father as parents, happiness of parents' marriage during childhood, illness of family members during childhood. | | AFF 1.3 | $D\bar{R}$ | -.09 | | s | Adults, Alameda County, U.S.A.<br>Probability sample<br>N: 6928, date: 1965 | BERKM 71 p. 43 |
| ADULT STRESS | 5-factor score containing poor physical health, poor interpersonal relations, self-evaluated comparative financial status, marital satisfaction, parental worries | | AFF 1.3 | $D\bar{R}$ | -.22 | | s | See above | BERKM 71 p. 43 |
| STRESS | 9-factor score containing stress both in adult- and in childhood (see above) | | AFF 1.3 | $D\bar{R}$ | -.22 | | s | See above | BERKM 71 p. 43 |
| SOCIAL HEALTH | Index containing<br>- employability (including educational level, occupational level, and job stability)<br>- marital satisfaction<br>- sociability (including number of close relatives and friends, and frequency of contacts)<br>- community involvement (including church attendance, political activity, and organizational memberships) | | AFF 1.3 | $D\bar{R}$ | +.26 | BCI | 05 | See above (BERKM 71 sample) | RENNE 74 p. 42 |
| OVER-ALL ROLE ADJUSTMENT | Combined 13-item marital tension index and 3-item job satisfaction index | For indices of marital tension and job satisfaction see resp. 'Marriage: Characteristics of the Relationship' and 'Satisfaction with Work, Job in general' (Part III; M 2.4 and S 1.9.1) | HAPP 1.1 | G' | +.43 | Gt' | 01 | Males in the age of 25 - 49, 4 small communities, Illinois, U.S.A.<br>Probability multi-stage samples<br>N: 393, date: March, 1962 | BRADB 65/1 p. 38 |

## L 2.3 - VARIOUS FACTORS CONCERNING LIFE QUALITY

see also 'Aspired Life Change' (H 3.1)

| | | | | | | | | |
|---|---|---|---|---|---|---|---|---|
| PERCEIVED HAPPY IMAGE | Estimate of how friends would rate one's happiness: most miserable of all / about three-fourths of the population happier than you are / the average person of your own sex and age / happier on the whole than three-fourths of the population of similar age and sex / happiest of all | Stronger among females: r = +.35<br>Lower among males : r = +.22 | COMP 4.1 | $r_{pm}$ | + | | Graduate students of education, U.S.A.<br>Non-probability chunk sample<br>N: 388, date: — | WATSO 30<br>p. 88 |
| | | Stronger among females: r = +.49<br>Lower among males : r = +.26 | COMP 4.3 | $r_{pm}$ | + | | | |
| | | Unaffected by sex:<br>males : r = +.39<br>females: r = +.39 | AFF 1.3 | $r_{pm}$ | + | | | |
| WISH TO HAVE LIVED IN AN OTHER WAY IN THE PAST | Closed question on number of things one wants to change if one could relive one's life<br>not change any of it / change some parts / change many parts | | HAPP 2.1 | $r_{pm}$ | +.06 | | National population, Britain<br>Non-probability quota sample<br>N: 213, date: March, 1971 | ABRAM 73<br>p. 21 |
| SATISFACTION | Two closed questions on whether and how much one is closer in general satisfaction to the person one would most or to the person one would least like to be | | HAPP 2.1 | $r_{pm}$ | +.09 | | See above | ABRAM 73<br>p. 21 |
| TYPE OF SUBJECTIVE AGE RELATED DEPRIVATION | Ss were classified on the basis of present-self, past-self and future-self ratings using the Cantril (1965) question on 'best possible life' (see sample construction in excerpt, Part II). | In the second column, the types of deprivation are ordered from lowest to highest mean scores on the contentment measure resp. the life satisfaction measure. | | | | | National adult population, U.S.A.<br>Cantril (1965) national probability sample<br>N: 1294, date: 1959 | BORTN 74A<br>p. 539 |
| | (temporary deprivation (TD) / continuous deprivation (CD) / great expectations deprivation (GED)/ stereotyped non-deprivation (SND) / anticipatory deprivation (AD) | Non-significant differences between TD and CD, between CD and GED and between SND and AD. Other differences are significant (05). | CON 1.1 | DM | + | DMRT | | |
| | temporary deprivation (TD) / continuous deprivation (CD) / great expectations deprivation (GED)/ stereotyped non-deprivation (SND) / anticipatory deprivation (AD) | Non-significant differences between TD and CD, and between GED, SND and AD. Other differences are significant (05). | HAPP 2.1 | DM | + | DMRT | | |

# L 3 LIFE STYLE



## L 3.1 - CONSUMPTION PATTERN

### L 3.1.1 - CONSUMPTION OF FOOD

| | | | | | | | | | |
|---|---|---|---|---|---|---|---|---|---|
| CONSUMPTION OF MILK, YOGHURT, ETC. | Closed question on amount of consumption per day | | HAPP 1.1 | G | +.14 | | | National adult population, The Netherlands<br>Probability area sample<br>N: 1552, date: June, 1968 | BAKKE 74<br>p. 28 |
| CONSUMPTION OF MEAT, FISH AND EGGS | See above | | HAPP 1.1 | G | +.21 | | | See above | BAKKE 74<br>p. 28 |
| CONSUMPTION OF SUGAR | Closed question on number of cups of coffee, tea and chocolate; and number of spoons of sugar used in each cup | | HAPP 1.1 | G | +.05 | | ns | See above | BAKKE 74<br>p. 28 |
| CONSUMPTION OF FAT | Closed question on usual amount of consumption of bacon and drippings | | HAPP 1.1 | G | -.01 | | ns | See above | BAKKE 74<br>p. 28 |
| CONSUMPTION OF FRUIT | Closed question on amount of consumption of fresh fruit per week | | HAPP 1.1 | G | +.04 | | ns | See above | BAKKE 74<br>p. 28 |

### L 3.1.2 - CONSUMPTION OF ALCOHOL, TOBACCO, AND DRUGS

| | | | | | | | | | |
|---|---|---|---|---|---|---|---|---|---|
| USING ALCOHOL | Closed question on consumption of alcohol. total abstainers (always abstained and ex-drinkers) vs alcohol users | Reversed among those reporting not doing too well in getting things they want : G' = -.08 (ns)<br>Among those doing pretty well : G' = +.06 (ns) | HAPP 1.1 | G' | +.06 | Gt' | ns | Non-institutionalized adult population, U.S.A.<br>Probability multi-stage sample<br>N: 1453, date: summer, 1963 | BRENN 67<br>p. 671 |
| | | Stronger among those who are very happy : G' = +.42 (05)<br>Among the pretty happy : G' = +.12 (ns)<br>Not among the not too happy : G' = +.03 (ns) | CON 1.1 | G' | +.16 | Gt' | 05 | | |
| AMOUNT OF ALCOHOL CONSUMPTION | Closed question on using alcohol and amount of alcohol ordinarily consumed at one sitting. total abstainer / small amounts / medium or large amounts | Our Gamma (G') was computed by us on the basis of data available. The other Gammas (G) were sent to us by the author and not presented in the publication<br>(to be continued on next page) | | | | | | See above | BRENN 67<br>p. 671 |

| | | | | | | | | | |
|---|---|---|---|---|---|---|---|---|---|
| | | U - shaped curve: those drinking small amounts being most happy<br>Among those doing pretty well in getting the things they want : G = +.01 (ns)<br>- with no problems due to drinking: G = +.04 (ns)<br>Among those not doing too well : G = -.03 (ns)<br>- with no problems due to drinking: G = +.08 (ns) | HAPP 1.1 | G'<br>G | +.01<br>+.02 | Gt' | ns<br>ns | | |
| | | Stronger among those who are very happy: G' = +.24 (ns)<br>Among the pretty happy : G' = +.06 (ns)<br>Not among the not too happy : G' = -.01 (ns) | CON 1.1 | G' | +.09 | Gt' | ns | | |
| | small amounts vs medium or large amounts | Total abstainers were excluded here.<br>Among those with no problems due to drinking: G' = +.04 (ns)<br>Among those with problems due to drinking: G' = -.44 (01)<br>Among those doing pretty well in getting the things they want : G = -.09 (ns)<br>- with no problems : G = -.04 (ns)<br>- with problems : G = -.28 (ns)<br>Among those not doing too well : G = +.12 (ns)<br>- with no problems : G = +.52 (01)<br>- with problems : G = -.48 (05) | HAPP 1.1 | G | -.06 | | ns | | |
| | | Among those with no problems due to drinking: G' = +.11 (ns)<br>Among those with problems due to drinking: G' = -.25 (ns) | CON 1.1 | G' | +.08 | Gt' | ns | | |
| BEING AN EX-DRINKER | alcohol users vs ex-drinkers | Those who have always abstained were excluded here.<br>Reversed among those reporting not doing too well in getting the things they want: G' = +.17 (ns)<br>Among those doing pretty well : G' = -.10 (ns) | HAPP 1.1 | G' | -.12 | Gt' | ns | Non-institutionalized adult population, U.S.A. (See last page) | BRENN 67 p. 671 |
| | | Stronger among those who are very happy: G' = -.51 (05)<br>Among the pretty happy : G' = -.43 (01)<br>Not among the not too happy : G' = +.00 (ns) | CON 1.1 | G' | -.35 | Gt' | 01 | | |
| BEING AN EX-DRINKER | always abstained vs ex-drinkers | Alcohol users were excluded here.<br>Reversed among those reporting not doing too well in getting the things they want : G' = -.13<br>Among those doing pretty well : G' = +.05 | HAPP 1.1 | G' | -.08 | | | See above | BRENN 67 p. 671 |
| | | Stronger among those who are pretty happy: G' = -.46<br>Negative among the very happy : G' = -.17<br>Not among the not too happy : G' = +.02 | CON 1.1 | G' | -.28 | | | | |
| HAVING PROBLEMS DUE TO DRINKING | 5-item index of closed questions on specific problems due to drinking with health, employer, spouse or other familymembers, police.<br>no problems vs problems | Computed for alcohol users only.<br>Stronger among those who use medium or large amounts : G' = -.53 (01)<br>Lower among those who use small amounts: G' = -.09 (ns)<br>(to be continued on next page) | HAPP 1.1 | G' | -.31 | Gt' | 01 | See above | BRENN 67 p. 671 |

| | | | | | | | | | |
|---|---|---|---|---|---|---|---|---|---|
| | | Stronger among those reporting not doing too well in getting the things they want : G = -.31 (05)<br>Lower among those doing pretty well: G = -.14 (ns)<br><br>Stronger among those who use medium or large amounts : G' = -.64 (01)<br>Lower among those using small amounts: G' = -.38 (05)<br><br>Stronger among those who are not too happy: G' = -.59 (01)<br>Lower among the pretty happy : G' = -.39 (01)<br>Not among the very happy : G' = -.06 (ns) | CON 1.1 | G' | -.51 | Gt' | 01 | | |
| CONSUMPTION OF ALCOHOL | Closed question on amount of consumption, rated on a 6-point scale | | HAPP 1.1 | G | +.05 | | ns | National adult population, The Netherlands<br>Probability area sample<br>N: 1552, date: June, 1968 | BAKKE 74<br>p. 28 |
| ALCOHOL USAGE | Repeated yes / no question on usage during the past day; during one month | | AFF 3.1<br>HAPP 3.1 | $r_{pm}$<br>$r_{pm}$ | -.03<br>+.02 | | ns<br>ns | Undergraduate students, U.S.A.<br>Non-probability chunk sample<br>N: 67, date: summer, 1970 | GORMA 71<br>p. 216/222 |
| CIGARETTE SMOKING | Direct question on number of cigarettes | | HAPP 2.1 | G | -.06 | $Chi^2$ | 001 | Male employees of age 40+, The Netherlands<br>Non-probability chunk sample<br>N: 13000, date: — | SONDE 75 |
| CONSUMPTION OF TOBACCO | Direct question on number of cigars, cigarettes and pipes smoked per day | | HAPP 1.1 | G | +.04 | | ns | National adult population, The Netherlands<br>Probability area sample<br>N: 1552, date: June, 1968 | BAKKE 74<br>p. 28 |
| MARIJUANA USAGE | Repeated yes / no question on usage during the past day; during one month | | AFF 3.1<br>HAPP 3.1 | $r_{pm}$<br>$r_{pm}$ | -.03<br>-.35 | | ns<br>01 | Undergraduate students, U.S.A.<br>Non-probability chunk sample<br>N: 67, date: summer, 1970 | GORMA 71<br>p. 216/222 |
| AMPHETAMINE USAGE | See above | | AFF 3.1<br>HAPP 3.1 | $r_{pm}$<br>$r_{pm}$ | -.05<br>+.11 | | ns<br>ns | See above | GORMA 71<br>p. 216/222 |
| BARBITURATE USAGE | See above | | AFF 3.1<br>HAPP 3.1 | $r_{pm}$<br>$r_{pm}$ | -.02<br>-.38 | | ns<br>01 | See above | GORMA 71<br>p. 216/222 |

## L 3.2 - SLEEP RHYTHM

| | | | | | | | | | |
|---|---|---|---|---|---|---|---|---|---|
| AMOUNT OF SLEEP | Difference between the time one usually goes to sleep and the time one usually awakes | | HAPP 1.1 | G | $\pm$ 0 | | ns | National adult population, The Netherlands<br>Probability area sample<br>N: 1552, date: June, 1968 | BAKKE 74<br>p. 28 |

(to be continued on next page)

| | | | | | | | | | |
|---|---|---|---|---|---|---|---|---|---|
| AMOUNT OF SLEEP | Repeated direct question on number of hours sleep last night; during 6 weeks | | AFF 3.1 | $r_{pm}$ | +.25 | t | ns | Male college students, U.S.A.<br>Non-probability chunk sample<br>N: 17, date: ± 1960 | WESSM 66/2<br>p. 283 |
| AMOUNT OF SLEEP | Repeated closed question on amount of sleep last night; during one month<br>much less than average / less than average / average amount / more than average / much more than average | | AFF 3.1<br>HAPP 3.1 | $r_{pm}$<br>$r_{pm}$ | +.16<br>-.06 | | ns<br>ns | Undergraduate students, U.S.A.<br>Non-probability chunk sample<br>N: 67, date: summer, 1970 | GORMA 71<br>p. 216/222 |
| SATISFACTION WITH AMOUNT OF SLEEP | Closed question: 'How do you feel about the amount of sleep you get?'<br>terrible / unhappy / mostly dissatisfied /mixed / mostly satisfied / pleased / delighted | | HAPP 3.1<br>(1st instr.) | $h^2$ | .31 | | | National adult population, U.S.A.<br>Probability area sample (third sample)<br>N: 1072, date: November, 1972 | ANDRE 74<br>p. 19 |

## L 3.3 - USE OF LEISURE TIME

see also 'Social Participation' (S 4) and 'Sports' (S 6)

## L 3.3.1 - LEVEL OF ACTIVITY IN LEISURE TIME

| | | | | | | | | | |
|---|---|---|---|---|---|---|---|---|---|
| SOCIAL ACTIVITY | Number of hours spent during the last typical week attending a sport event; attending church, lectures, concerts ect.; doing volunteer work for church, other organizations, or relatives; visiting, telephoning, or writing friends or relatives; parties, eating out, or entertaining | Stronger among males: r = +.17 | HAPP 3.1 | r | +.09 | | | People of 46 and older, Duke, U.S.A.<br>Probability systematic random sample, stratified by age and sex<br>N: 502, date: 1968 | PALMO 72<br>p. 70 |
| ACTIVE LEISURE TIME | Closed question: no vs yes | | HAPP 2.1 | G | +.58 | $Chi^2$ | 000 | Male employees of age 40-65, The Netherlands<br>Non-probability chunk sample<br>N: 13,000, date: — | SONDE 75 |
| AMOUNT OF NON-ASSOCIATIONAL LEISURE ACTIVITY | Average number of hours per week | The relationship disappears when controlled for self-perceived health. | COMP 1.1 | $r_{pm}$ | +.28 | | 05 | White males who had experienced a first heart attack, Durham, North Carolina, U.S.A.<br>Non-probability quota sample<br>N: 56, date: 1970 | GARRI 73<br>p. 201 |
| ENGAGING IN HOBBIES | | Unaffected by sex | HAPP 2.1 | | + | | s | Middle-aged, middle class married couples, U.S.A.<br>Non-probability accidental sample of couples<br>N: 416, date: 1952 - 1953 | ROSE 55<br>p. 17 |
| HAVING HOBBIES | Direct question on number of hobbies<br>Weighted score based on number of hobbies and amount of skill involved | Index of Positive Affects: r = +.16 (05)<br>Index of Negative Affects: r = +.30 (01) | AFF 2.3 | $r_{pm}$ | | | | Residents of Stirling County, Maritime, Canada<br>Probability sample, stratified by sex, age, socio-environmental circumstances and mental health<br>N: 112, date: 1963 - 1968 | BEISE 74<br>p. 325 |
| CAMPUS ACTIVITY LEVEL | Non-required campus activities of any sort<br>no activities vs activities | | COMP 2.2 | | ± 0 | | ns | Female college students, New York, U.S.A.<br>Type of sample construction unclear<br>N: 238, date: — | WASHB 41<br>p. 283 |
| NUMBER OF EXTRACURRICULAR ACTIVITIES TAKEN PART IN | Open-ended direct question: 0 / 1-2 / 3+ | | HAPP 1.1<br><br>AFF 1.1 | G<br>V<br>G<br>V | +.14<br>.10<br>+.16<br>.10 | <br>$Chi^2$<br><br>$Chi^2$ | <br>01<br><br>01 | Juniors and seniors attending public high schools in New York State, U.S.A.<br>Probability cluster sample of 10 public high schools<br>N: sample A: 1682, date: 1960 | BRENN 70<br>p. 108/318 |

| | | | | | | | | | |
|---|---|---|---|---|---|---|---|---|---|
| TIME SPENT ON EXTRACURRICULAR ACTIVITIES | Open-ended direct question: 0 / 1-4 / 5 hours or more in an average week | | HAPP 1.1 | G<br>V | +.14<br>.09 | $Chi^2$ | 01 | Juniors and seniors attending public high schools in New York State, U.S.A.<br>(see last page) | BRENN 70<br>p. 108/314 |
| | | | AFF 1.1 | G<br>V | +.21<br>.12 | $Chi^2$ | 01 | | |
| PARTICIPATION IN EXTRACURRICULAR ACTIVITIES | 2-item index of open-ended questions on number of extracurricular activities taken part in, and number of hours spent on these activities in an average week | When standardized on:<br>- having fun in life : $G_s$ = +.07<br>- tending to be a lonely person : $G_s$ = +.10<br>- having faith in people : $G_s$ = +.10<br>- sensitivity to failure : $G_s$ = +.14<br>- educational level of mother : $G_s$ = +.12<br>- school social class : $G_s$ = +.12<br>- self-esteem : $G_s$ = +.12<br>- tending to be a lonely person, and having fun in life : $G_s$ = +.07<br>- having faith in people, and having fun in life : $G_s$ = +.04<br>- having faith in people, and tending to be a lonely person : $G_s$ = +.06<br>- educational level of mother, and having fun in life : $G_s$ = +.07<br>- educational level of mother, and tending to be a lonely person : $G_s$ = +.08<br>- educational level of mother, and having faith in people : $G_s$ = +.09<br>- school social class, and having fun in life : $G_s$ = +.06<br>- school social class, and tending to be a lonely person : $G_s$ = +.08<br>- school social class, and having faith in people : $G_s$ = +.08<br>- school social class, and educational level of mother : $G_s$ = +.11<br><br>Unaffected by stability of self-image<br>Unaffected by hours spent on work for pay<br>Positive in middle and upper class : G = +.14<br>When standardized on self-esteem : $G_s$ = +.10<br>Negative in lower class : $G_s$ = -.29<br>When standardized on self-esteem : $G_s$ = -.24<br>Unaffected by school social class | HAPP 1.1 | G<br>V | +.14<br>.07 | $Chi^2$ | 02 | See above | BRENN 70<br>p. 108/124 - 158/310 |
| | | When standardized on:<br>- having fun in life : $G_s$ = +.19<br>- tending to be a lonely person : $G_s$ = +.21<br>- having faith in people : $G_s$ = +.21<br>- sensitivity to failure : $G_s$ = +.24<br>- educational level of mother : $G_s$ = +.22<br>- school social class : $G_s$ = +.23<br>- tending to be a lonely person, and having fun in life : $G_s$ = +.19<br>- having faith in people, and having fun in life : $G_s$ = +.17<br>- having faith in people, and tending to be a lonely person : $G_s$ = +.18<br>- educational level of mother, and having fun in life : $G_s$ = +.19<br>- educational level of mother, and tending to be a lonely person : $G_s$ = +.19<br>- educational level of mother, and having faith in people : $G_s$ = + 18<br><br>(to be continued on next page) | AFF 1.1 | G<br>V | +.24<br>.11 | $Chi^2$ | 01 | | |

| | | | | | | | | | |
|---|---|---|---|---|---|---|---|---|---|
| | | - school social class, and having fun in life : $G_s = +.19$<br>- school social class, and tending to be a lonely person : $G_s = +.20$<br>- school social class, and having faith in people : $G_s = +.21$<br>- school social class, and educational level of mother : $G_s = +.21$<br>Stronger among those with medium and high stability of self-image : G = +.27<br>Lower among those with low stability of self-image : G = +.21<br>Stronger among those who did not spend time on working for pay : G = +.27<br>Lower among those who spent some hours on work for pay : G = +.22<br>Negative in lower class : G = -.13<br>Positive in middle and upper class : G = +.21<br>Unaffected by school social class | | | | | | | |
| EXTENT OF MENTAL WORK BESTOWED UPON PLEASURES (games etc.) | Class-master rating on a 7-point scale on the basis of observation | | AFF 5.3 | $r_{pm}$ | +.43 | | | Schoolboys, England<br>Non-probability chunk sample<br>N: 140, date: 1912 - 1913 | WEBB 15<br>p. 27 |
| DEGREE OF BODILY ACTIVITY IN PURSUIT OF PLEASURES | See above | | AFF 5.3 | $r_{pm}$ | +.47 | | | See above | WEBB 15<br>p. 27 |
| EXTENT OF MENTAL WORK BESTOWED UPON PLEASURES | Trained peer rating on a 7-point scale on the basis of observation | | AFF 5.2 | $r_{pm}$ | +.27 | | | Male students, England<br>Non-probability chunk sample<br>N: 194, date: 1912 - 1913 | WEBB 15<br>p. 26 |
| DEGREE OF BODILY ACTIVITY IN PURSUIT OF PLEASURES | See above | | AFF 5.2 | $r_{pm}$ | +.36 | | | See above | WEBB 15<br>p. 26 |

## L 3.3.2 - SPECIFIC LEISURE ACTIVITIES

## TIME SPENT ON TV, RADIO, NEWSPAPER

| | | | | | | | | | |
|---|---|---|---|---|---|---|---|---|---|
| AVERAGE TELEVISION VIEWING | Closed question on number of hours a day on the average one watched television last week, rated on a 7-point scale<br>1 hour or less / 2 hours / 3 hours or more | Index of Positive Affects only : G' = -.13 (ns)<br>Negative among those of high S.E.S.: G' = -.14 (ns)<br>Not among those of low S.E.S. : G' = +.02 (ns)<br>Among those of low S.E.S. U-shaped curve: Those watching television for about 2 hours a day having most positive feelings. | AFF 2.3 | G' | - | Gt' | ns | Males in the age of 25 - 49, 4 small communities, Illinois, U.S.A.<br>Probability multi-stage samples<br>N: 393, date: March, 1962 | BRADB 65/1<br>p. 44 |
| WATCHING TELEVISION | Direct question: 2 hours or less / more than 2 - 5 hours / more than 5 hours daily | | AFF 2.3 | $t_k$ | +.09 | | ns | Aged female public housing residents, U.S.A.<br>Probability systematic random sample<br>N: 44, date: 1967 - 1971 | GRANE 75<br>p. 703 |
| LISTENING TO RADIO | Direct question: less than 1 hour / 1 - 2 hours / more than 2 hours daily | Lower among those of age 66-75 : $t_k$ = +.03 (ns)<br>Stronger among those of age 82-92 : $t_k$ = +.45 (01) | AFF 2.3 | $t_k$ | +.19 | | 03 | See above | GRANE 75<br>p. 703 |
| READING NEWSPAPERS | Direct question on frequency in the past week not at all / once / more than once | Lower among males : G = +.21<br>Stronger among females: G = +.46 | HAPP 1.1 | G | + | | | Adults, Metro Manila, Philippines<br>Probability area sample<br>N: 941, date: January - April, 1972 | BULAT 73<br>p. 234 |
| | | Lower among males : G = +.42<br>Stronger among females: G = +.60 | HAPP 3.1 | G | + | | | | |

## GOING OUT

| | | | | | | | | | |
|---|---|---|---|---|---|---|---|---|---|
| FREQUENCY OF GOING OUT EVENINGS WITH SPOUSE | 2 or fewer evenings a month vs more | 33% of the very satisfied and satisfied, and 40% of the relatively dissatisfied women go out 2 or fewer evenings a month with their husband.<br>Among the men 29% of the very satisfied, 37% of the satisfied and 39% of the relatively dissatisfied report going out 2 or fewer evenings a month with their wives. | HAPP 2.1. | D% | + | | s | Middle-aged, middle class married couples, U.S.A.<br>Non-probability accidental sample of couples<br>N: 416, date: 1952 - 1953 | ROSE 55<br>p. 17 |
| GOING TO THE MOVIES | Direct question on frequency in the past week<br>not at all / once / more than once | Lower among males : G = +.02<br>Stronger among females: G = +.52 | HAPP 1.1 | G | + | | | Adults, Metro Manila, Philippines<br>Probability area sample<br>N: 941, date: January - April, 1972 | BULAT 73<br>p. 234 |
| | | Lower among males : G = +.24<br>Stronger among females: G = +.36 | HAPP 3.1 | G | + | | | | |
| EATING IN RESTAURANTS | See above | Lower among males : G = +.12<br>Stronger among females: G = +.46 | HAPP 1.1 | G | + | | | See above | BULAT 73<br>p. 234 |
| | | Lower among males : G = +.42<br>Stronger among females: G = +.53 | HAPP 3.1 | G | + | | | | |
| EATING IN RESTAURANTS | Closed question: not at all / once / several times or more during last week | Index of Positive Affects only : G' = +.23 (01)<br>Unaffected by S.E.S.<br>Stronger among males : G' = +.30 (01)<br>Lower among females : G' = +.23 (01) | AFF 2.3 | G' | + | Gt' | | Inhabitants of 4 small communities, Illinois, U.S.A.<br>Probability multi-stage samples<br>N: 2006, date: March, 1962 | BRADB 65/1<br>p. 48 |
| GOING FOR A TRIP IN A CAR | See above | Index of Positive Affects only : G' = +.23 (01)<br>Unaffected by sex<br>Unaffected by S.E.S. | AFF 2.3 | G' | + | Gt' | | See above | BRADB 65/1<br>p. 48 |
| DISTANCE TRAVELED FROM HOME DURING LAST WEEK | Closed question on furthest distance other than going to work, rated on a 10-point scale<br>less than 1 mile / 2-25 miles / 25 miles or more | Index of Positive Affects only : G' = +.08 (ns)<br>Among those of high S.E.S. : G' = -.07 (ns)<br>Among those of low S.E.S. : G' = +.15 (ns)<br>Among those of low S.E.S. U-shaped curve:<br>Those males who traveled 2 - 25 miles having the least positive feelings. | AFF 2.3 | G' | +.08 | Gt' | ns | Males in the age of 25 - 49, 4 small communities, Illinois, U.S.A.<br>Probability multi-stage samples<br>N: 393, date: March, 1962 | BRADB 65/1<br>p. 43 |
| DISTANCE TRAVELED FROM HOME DURING THE PAST FEW WEEKS | Closed question on furthest distance other than going to work, rated on a 7-point scale | Index of Positive Affects: G' = +.29<br>Index of Negative Affects: G' = -.04 | AFF 2.3 | G | + | | | Adults, urban areas, U.S.A.<br>Probability area samples<br>N: 2787, date: January, 1963 - January, 1964 | BRADB 69<br>p. 127 |

## OTHER LEISURE ACTIVITIES

| | | | | | | | | | |
|---|---|---|---|---|---|---|---|---|---|
| BETTING OR GAMBLING | Direct question on frequency in the past week<br>not at all / once / more than once | Negative among males : G = -.05<br>Positive among females: G = +.15 | HAPP 1.1 | G | + | | | Adults, Metro Manila, Philippines<br>Probability area sample<br>N: 941, date: January - April, 1972 | BULAT 73<br>p. 234 |
| | | Negative among males : G = -.03<br>Positive among females: G = +.28 | HAPP 3.1 | G | + | | | | |
| READING | Number of hours devoted to reading books, newspapers and magazines<br>less than 1 / 1 to 3 / more than 3 hours daily | | AFF 2.3 | $t_k$ | +.04 | | ns | Aged female public housing residents, U.S.A.<br>Probability systematic random sample<br>N: 44, date: 1967 - 1971 | GRANE 75<br>p. 703 |
| NUMBER OF LEADING ROLES PLAYED IN A PLAY | 2 questions on having played a leading role and number of roles | | AFF 6 | $r_{pm}$ | +.28 | | 05 | Female undergraduates, U.S.A.<br>Random sample<br>N: 72, date: — | LUDWI 71/75<br>p. 64 |

## L 3.3.3 - CHANGES IN LEISURE ACTIVITIES

| | | | | | | | | | |
|---|---|---|---|---|---|---|---|---|---|
| NEW ACTIVITIES ENGAGED IN | Closed question: no vs yes; during the past few weeks | Index of Positive Affects: G = +.36<br>Index of Negative Affects: G = +.08 | AFF 2.3 | G | + | | | Adults, urban areas, U.S.A.<br>Probability area samples<br>N: 2787, date: January, 1963 - January, 1964 | BRADB 69<br>p. 130 |
| NEW EGO-ORIENTED ACTIVITIES ENGAGED IN | 2 direct questions on new activities engaged in during the past few weeks, and type of activities; coded for those activities one engaged in alone | Index of Positive Affects: G = +.37<br>Index of Negative Affects: G = +.07 | AFF 2.3 | G | + | | | See above | BRADB 69<br>p. 130 |
| NEW OTHER-ORIENTED ACTIVITIES ENGAGED IN | 2 direct questions on new activities engaged in during the past few weeks, and type of activities; coded for those activities one engaged in with other people | Index of Positive Affects: G = +.36<br>Index of Negative Affects: G = +.08 | AFF 2.3 | G | + | | | See above | BRADB 69<br>p. 130 |
| GONE TO NEW PLACES | Closed question: no vs yes; during the past few weeks | Index of Positive Affects: G = +.25<br>Index of Negative Affects: G = +.04 | AFF 2.3 | G | + | | | See above | BRADB 69<br>p. 130 |
| NOVELTY | 3-item index of closed questions on new people met, new places gone to, and new activities engaged in during the past few weeks | Computed for Index of Positive Affects only: G = +.34<br>When controlled for S.E.S.: G = +.30<br>Unaffected by sociability<br>Stronger among those who are not satisfied with their social life: G = +.40<br>For question on new people met see 'Changes in Social Participation' (Part III, S 4.4). | AFF 2.3 | G | + | | | See above | BRADB 69<br>p. 132 |
| NEW ACTIVITIES OR HOBBIES ENGAGED IN | Closed question; during the last few weeks | Index of Positive Affects: G = +.30<br>Index of Negative Affects: G = +.22 | AFF 2.3 | G | | | | Employed males, England<br>Non-probability purposive quota sample<br>N: 192, date: — | PAYNE 74<br>p. 17 |
| WATCHING MORE TELEVISION | Repeated direct question on number of hours daily<br>Difference between scores in 1967 and 1971 | | AFF 2.3 | $t_k$ | +.10 | | ns | Aged female public housing residents, U.S.A.<br>Probability systematic random sample<br>N: 44, date: 1967 - 1971 | GRANE 75<br>p. 703 |
| LISTENING MORE TO THE RADIO | See above | Not among those of age 66 - 75: : $t_k$ = +.00(ns)<br>Stronger among those of age 82 - 92: $t_k$ = +.53(01) | AFF 2.3 | $t_k$ | +.23 | | 02 | See above | GRANE 75<br>p. 703 |
| READING MORE | See above | | AFF 2.3 | $t_k$ | -.07 | | ns | See above | GRANE 75<br>p. 703 |

## L 3.3.4 - ATTITUDES TOWARDS USE OF LEISURE TIME

see also 'Satisfaction with Leisure' (S 1.1)

| | | | | | | | | | |
|---|---|---|---|---|---|---|---|---|---|
| DESIRE FOR HAVING MORE AMUSEMENT | Whether one would like to go out more often in the evenings for entertainment | 33% of the relatively dissatisfied and 26% of the satisfied would like to go out more often.<br>Stronger among males<br>Unaffected by going out with spouse or not | HAPP 2.1 | D% | - | | s | Middle-aged, middle class married couples, U.S.A.<br>Non-probability accidental sample of couples<br>N: 416, date: 1952 - 1953 | ROSE 55<br>p. 18 |
| ATTITUDE TOWARDS AMOUNT OF TIME SPENT ON ENTERTAINMENT | Closed question: none / far too little / rather too little / sufficient | | HAPP 2.1 | $T^2$ | +.18 | $Chi^2$ | 001 | Non-agricultural population, Poland<br>Non-probability purposive quota sample<br>N: 1385, date: June/July, 1960 | MAKAR 62<br>p. 114 |
| ATTITUDE TOWARDS AMOUNT OF TIME SPENT ON ENTERTAINMENT | See above | | HAPP 2.1 | $T^2$ | +.13 | $Chi^2$ | 001 | Individual farmowners and their families, Poland<br>Non-probability purposive quota sample<br>N: 1002, date: June/July, 1960 | MAKAR 62<br>p. 114 |

| | | | | | | | | | |
|---|---|---|---|---|---|---|---|---|---|
| BEING INTERESTED IN RECREATION | Closed question | | COMP 4.1 | | | | ns | Students, U.S.A.<br>Non-probability chunk sample<br>N: 1651, date: — | SYMON 37<br>p. 292 |
| HAVING PROBLEMS WITH RECREATION | Closed question | | COMP 4.1 | | | | ns | See above | SYMON 37<br>p. 292 |

## L 3.4 - VARIOUS LIFE STYLE CHARACTERISTICS

| | | | | | | | | | |
|---|---|---|---|---|---|---|---|---|---|
| FREQUENCY OF BATHING | Closed question rated on a 6-point scale | | HAPP 1.1 | G | +.05 | | ns | National adult population, The Netherlands<br>Probability area sample<br>N: 1552, date: June, 1968 | BAKKE 74<br>p. 28 |
| FREQUENCY OF SHOPPING | Direct question on frequency in the past week<br>not at all / once / more than once | Lower among males : G = +.18<br>Stronger among females: G = +.45 | HAPP 1.1 | G | + | | | Adults, Metro Manila, Philippines<br>Probability area sample<br>N: 941, date: January - April, 1972 | BULAT 73<br>p. 234 |
| | | Stronger among males: G = +.45<br>Lower among females: G = +.40 | HAPP 3.1 | G | + | | | | |
| BEING INTERESTED IN MANNERS | Closed question | | COMP 4.1 | | | | ns | Students, U.S.A.<br>Non-probability chunk sample<br>N: 1651, date: — | SYMON 37<br>p. 292 |
| HAVING PROBLEMS WITH MANNERS | Closed question | high school students only<br>L-shaped curve: significantly positive among happier students only | COMP 4.1 | | + | | | See above | SYMON 37<br>p. 292 |

# L 4 LIVING ENVIRONMENT



## L 4.1 - COMMUNITY SIZE

| | | | | | | | | | |
|---|---|---|---|---|---|---|---|---|---|
| COMMUNITY SIZE | farm / rural nonfarm and under 2500 / 2500 - 9999 / 10,000 - 99,999 / 100,000 - 499,999 / 500,000 and over | See remarks in excerpt (Part II).<br>in 1946: negroes: G' = -.07 (ns)<br>whites : G' = -.02 (ns)<br>in 1956: negroes: G' = -.13 (05)<br>whites : G' = +.02 (ns)<br>in 1966: negroes: G' = -.30 (01)<br>whites : G' = +.01 (ns) | HAPP 1.1 | G' | | Gt' | | National adult populations, U.S.A.<br>Non-probability quota samples and probability area samples<br>N: 25617, date: 1946, 1947, 1948, 1956, 1966 | MANNI 72<br>p. 56 |
| COMMUNITY SIZE | country / under 25,000 / 25,000 - 500,000 / over 500,000 | Strongest among the well-to-do.<br>reversed among blacks and low-income whites. | HAPP 1.1 | $t_{k_b}$ | -.03 | | 01 | National population, U.S.A.<br>National probability sample<br>N: 2970, date: 1952 | FISCH 73/1<br>p. 226 |
| COMMUNITY SIZE | rural, small town, small city / suburb / metropole | U-shaped curve: Those living in suburbs being most happy.<br>No difference between those living in a rural dwelling, a small town, or a small city was found. | HAPP 1.1 | G' | -.06 | Gt' | ns | Adults, U.S.A.<br>Probability multi-stage area sample<br>N: 2460, date: spring, 1957 | GURIN 60<br>p. 229 |
| COMMUNITY SIZE | Country / under 25,000 / 25,000 - 500,000 / over 500,000 | Strongest among the well-to-do.<br>Reversed among blacks and low-income whites. | HAPP 1.1 | $t_{k_b}$ | -.01 | | 05 | National population, U.S.A.<br>National probability sample<br>N: 1605, date: 1957 | FISCH 73/2<br>p. 226 |
| COMMUNITY SIZE | country / under 25,000 / 25,000 - 500,000 / over 500,000 | Strongest among the well-to-do.<br>Reversed among blacks and low-income whites. | HAPP 1.1 | $t_{k_b}$ | -.01 | | ns | National population, U.S.A.<br>National probability sample<br>N: 1555, date: 1963 | FISCH 73/3<br>p. 226 |
| COMMUNITY SIZE | out of Standard Metropolitan Statistical Areas / in SMSA / in large SMSA | Stronger among migrants and among the well-to-do.<br>U-shaped curve among those who lived in communities of the same size as they were raised in: Those living in a SMSA being least happy.<br>When those living in a SMSA were compared with those living in a large SMSA: $t_k$ = -.06 (ns).<br>Those living in the center of towns and cities were less happy than those living in the outskirts: $t_k$ = -.07 (001) | HAPP 2.1 | $t_{k_b}$ | -.07 | | 01 | National population, U.S.A.<br>Probability sample with double-sampling of blacks<br>N: 1440, date: 1968 | FISCH 73/4<br>p. 226 |
| COMMUNITY SIZE | under 2500 / 2500 - 49,999 / 50,000 - 499,999 / over 500,000 | See remarks in excerpt (Part II).<br>under 2500 : Mean = 5.61 (6.11)<br>2500 - 49,999 : Mean = 5.82 (6.30)<br>50,000 - 499,999: Mean = 5.96 (5.83)<br>500,000+ : Mean = 5.72 (5.76) | HAPP 3.1 | DM | | | | Non-institutionalized national adult population, U.S.A.<br>Multi-stage probability sample stratified by size of locality<br>N: 1588, date: January, 1971 (+ 1964) | CANTR 71<br>p. 66 |

| | | | | | | | | | |
|---|---|---|---|---|---|---|---|---|---|
| SIZE OF HOME TOWN | less than 1000 / 1000 – 5000 / 5000 – 10,000 / 10,000 – 50,000 / 50,000 – 100,000 / over 100,000 | | HAPP 1.1 | $r_{pm}$ | | t | ns | Male undergraduates, U.S.A.<br>Non-probability chunk sample<br>N: 103, date: ± 1967 | [illegible] 69<br>p. 28 |
| COMMUNITY SIZE | less than 2500 (rural) / 2500 – 250,000 / 250,000+ (large city) | | HAPP 1.1 | G | -.25 | $Chi^2$ | 05 | Aged persons, U.S.A.<br>National probability sample<br>N: 319, date: 1973 | HYNSO 75<br>p. 65 |
| COMMUNITY SIZE | – 5000 / 5000 – 10,000 / 10,000 – 20,000 / 20,000 – 50,000 / 50,000+ / Havana | – 5000 : Mean = 5.3<br>5000 – 10,000 : Mean = 6.3<br>10,000 – 20,000: Mean = 6.0<br>20,000 – 50,000: Mean = 7.6<br>50,000+ : Mean = 6.3<br>Havana : Mean = 6.0 | HAPP 3.1 | DM | | | | National adult population, Cuba<br>Probability area sample<br>N: 992, date: ± 1960 | CANTR 65/1<br>p. 366 |
| COMMUNITY SIZE | rural / 2000 – 50,000 / 50,000 – 500,000 / 500,000+ | rural : Mean = 4.3<br>2000 – 50,000 : Mean = 4.9<br>50,000–500,000 : Mean = 5.6<br>500,000+ : Mean = 5.2 | HAPP 3.1 | DM | + | | | National adult population, Brazil<br>Probability samples<br>N: 2168, date: ± 1960 | CANTR 65/1<br>p. 365 |
| SIZE OF LOCALITY | village / small town / big town | | HAPP 2.1<br>HAPP 1.1 | G'<br>G' | -.04<br>-.02 | Gt'<br>Gt' | 05<br>ns | National population of nine European countries<br>Type of sample construction not reported<br>N: 9605 (or 9543; see remarks in excerpt, Part II)<br>date: May, 1975 | COMMI 75<br>p. 139/153 |
| COMMUNITY SIZE | rural / under 20,000 / 20,000 – 100,000 / over 100,000 / metro. Paris | Negative relationship among the well-to-do (05) | COMP 1.1 | DM | ± 0 | | | National population, France<br>N: 2175, date: 1967 | FISCH 73/5<br>p. 227 |
| COMMUNITY SIZE | – 2000 / 2000 – 10,000 / 10,000 – 100,000 / 100,000+ | – 2000 : Mean = 5.2<br>2000 – 10,000 : Mean = 5.3<br>10,000 – 100,000: Mean = 5.4<br>100,000+ : Mean = 5.3 | HAPP 3.1 | DM | + | | | National population, W. Germany<br>Probability area sample<br>N: 480, date: ± 1960 | CANTR 65/1<br>p. 376 |
| COMMUNITY SIZE | less than 5000 / 5000 – 20,000 / 20,000 – 50,000/ 50,000 – 100,000 / more than 100,000 | | HAPP 1.1 | G | +.06 | | ns | National adult population, The Netherlands<br>Probability area sample<br>N: 1552, date: June, 1968 | BAKKE 74<br>p. 27 |
| COMMUNITY SIZE | less vs more than 500,000 inhabitants | | HAPP 1.1 | $r_{pm}$ | -.11 | | | Housewives, The Netherlands<br>Probability area sample<br>N: 450, date: autumn, 1964 | PHILI 66<br>p. 66 |
| COMMUNITY SIZE | village (rural) / up to 10,000 / 10,000 – 20,000/ 20,000 – 100,000 / 100,000+ | village : Mean = 4.3<br>up to 10,000 : Mean = 4.3<br>10,000 – 20,000 : Mean = 4.5<br>20,000 – 100,000: Mean = 4.7<br>100,000+ : Mean = 4.6 | HAPP 3.1 | DM | + | | | National adult population, Poland<br>Probability samples<br>N: 1464, date: ± 1960 | CANTR 65/1<br>p. 374 |
| COMMUNITY SIZE | rural / 5000 – 20,000 / 20,000 – 100,000 / 100,000+ | rural : Mean = 4.7<br>5000 – 20,000 : Mean = 4.7<br>20,000 – 100,000: Mean = 4.6<br>100,000+ : Mean = 4.7 | HAPP 3.1 | DM | ± 0 | | | National adult population, Nigeria<br>Probability sample proportionally stratified by dwelling and region<br>N: 1200, date: ± 1960 | CANTR 65/1<br>p. 371 |
| COMMUNITY SIZE | rural / 5000 – 99,999 / 100,000+ | rural : Mean = 3.6<br>5000 – 99,999 : Mean = 4.1<br>100,000+ : Mean = 4.2 | HAPP 3.1 | DM | + | | | National population, India<br>Probability sample proportionally poststratified by dwelling<br>N: 2366, date: 1958 | CANTR 65/1<br>p. 368 |

## L 4.2 – RURAL VS URBAN DWELLING

| | | | | | | | | | |
|---|---|---|---|---|---|---|---|---|---|
| URBAN DWELLING | rural vs urban dwelling | | HAPP 3.1 | G' | +.14 | Gt' | 01 | Adult populations of 14 countries<br>Representative samples<br>N: 18653, date: ± 1960 | CANTR 65/1<br>p. 259 |

| | | | | | | | | | |
|---|---|---|---|---|---|---|---|---|---|
| URBAN DWELLING | rural vs urban dwelling | | HAPP 3.1 | G' | -.01 | Gt' | ns | National adult population, U.S.A.<br>Probability sample<br>N: 1549, date: ± 1960 | CANTR 65/1<br>p. 378-380 |
| LIVING IN AN URBAN AREA | rural / suburban / urban | | HAPP 1.1 | $r_{pm}$ | | t | ns | Male undergraduates, U.S.A.<br>Non-probability chunk sample<br>N: 103, date: ± 1967 | HEERE 69<br>p. 28 |
| LIVING IN A CITY OR A TOWN | village or country vs city or town | L-shaped curve: Negative relationship among unhappier females only. | COMP 2.2 | | - | | ns | Female college students, New York, U.S.A.<br>N: 238, date: — | WASHB 41<br>p. 283 |
| URBAN DWELLING | rural vs urban dwelling | | HAPP 3.1 | G' | +.56 | Gt' | 01 | National adult population, Dominican Republic<br>Probability samples<br>N: 814, date: ± 1960 | CANTR 65/1<br>p. 378-380 |
| URBAN DWELLING | rural vs urban dwelling | | HAPP 3.1 | G' | +.29 | Gt' | 01 | National adult population, Panama<br>Probability sample proportionally poststratified by dwelling and mortality<br>N: 642, date: ± 1960 | CANTR 65/1<br>p. 378-380 |
| URBAN DWELLING | rural vs urban dwelling | | HAPP 3.1 | G' | -.20 | Gt' | 01 | National adult population, Cuba<br>Probability area sample<br>N: 992, date: ± 1960 | CANTR 65/1<br>p. 378-380 |
| URBAN DWELLING | rural vs urban dwelling | | HAPP 3.1 | G' | +.30 | Gt' | 01 | National adult population, Brazil<br>Probability samples<br>N: 2168, date: ± 1960 | CANTR 65/1<br>p. 378-380 |
| URBAN RESIDENCE | rural vs urban dwelling | In Dominican Republic:<br>- Lower among those who have children (01)<br>- Stronger among those who have no children (01)<br>In Panama:<br>- Stronger among those who have children (01)<br>- Lower among those who have no children (ns)<br>In Yugoslavia:<br>- Stronger among those who have children (01)<br>- Lower among those who have no children (ns) | HAPP 3.1 | DM | + | DMRT | 01 | Adults in the Dominican Republic, Panama and Yugoslavia (married people only)<br>Pooling of the Cantril (1965) samples of the Dominican Republic, Panama and Yugoslavia<br>N: 4113, date: ± 1960 | BOHN 72<br>p. 31 |
| LIVING IN AN URBAN SETTING | inhabitants of rural communes vs Helsinki | Lower among males : G' = +.12 (ns)<br>Stronger among females: G' = +.25 (01) | HAPP 2.1 | G' | +.18 | Gt' | 01 | National population, Finland<br>Probability samples<br>N: 948, date: spring - summer, 1966 | HAAVI 71<br>p. 587 |
| URBAN DWELLING | rural vs urban dwelling | | HAPP 3.1 | G' | -.03 | Gt' | ns | National population, W.Germany<br>Probability area sample<br>N: 480, date: ± 1960 | CANTR 65/1<br>p. 378-380 |
| URBAN DWELLING | rural vs urban dwelling | | HAPP 3.1 | G' | +.26 | Gt' | 01 | National adult population, Yugoslavia<br>Probability sample<br>N: 1523, date: ± 1960 | CANTR 65/1<br>p. 378-380 |
| URBAN DWELLING | rural vs urban dwelling | | HAPP 3.1 | G' | +.22 | Gt' | 01 | National population, Egypt<br>Non-probability accidental sample proportionally post-stratified by dwelling<br>N: 499, date: ± 1960 | CANTR 65/1<br>p. 378-380 |
| URBAN DWELLING | rural vs urban dwelling | | HAPP 3.1 | G' | -.01 | Gt' | ns | National adult population, Nigeria<br>Probability sample proportionally stratified by dwelling and region<br>N: 1200, date: ± 1960 | CANTR 65/1<br>p. 378-380 |

| | | | | | | | | | |
|---|---|---|---|---|---|---|---|---|---|
| URBAN DWELLING | rural vs urban dwelling | | HAPP 3.1 | G' | +.28 | Gt' | 01 | National population, India<br>Probability sample proportionally poststratified by dwelling<br>N: 2366, date: 1958 | CANTR 65/1<br>p. 378-380 |
| URBAN DWELLING | rural vs urban dwelling | Rural : Mean = 4.8<br>Semi-urban: Mean = 5.3<br>Urban : Mean = 5.2 | HAPP 3.1 | G' | +.20 | Gt' | 01 | National adult population, The Philippines<br>Probability sample proportionally poststratified by dwelling<br>N: 500, date: + 1960 | CANTR 65/1<br>p. 373/378-380 |
| **L 4.3 - GEOGRAPHIC REGION** | | | | | | | | | |
| REGION: LIVING IN THE SOUTH | non-south vs south | See remarks in excerpt (Part II).<br>in 1946: negroes: G' = -.01 (ns)<br>whites : G' = +.00 (ns)<br>in 1956: negroes: G' = +.14 (ns)<br>whites : G' = -.02 (ns)<br>in 1966: negroes: G' = +.13 (ns)<br>whites : G' = -.06 (05) | HAPP 1.1 | G' | | Gt' | | National adult populations, U.S.A.<br>Non-probability quota samples and probability area samples<br>N: 25,617, date: 1946, 1947, 1948, 1956, 1966 | MANNI 72<br>p. 53 |
| REGION | South, Northeast, Midwest, or Far West | | HAPP 1.1 | | | | ns | Non-institutionalized adults, U.S.A.<br>Probability multi-stage sample<br>N: 2460, date: spring, 1957 | GURIN 60<br>p. 207/230 |
| REGION | East, Midwest, South or West | See remarks in excerpt (Part II).<br>East : Mean = 5.77 (5.87)<br>Midwest: Mean = 5.83 (6.07)<br>South : Mean = 5.58 (6.00)<br>West : Mean = 5.95 (5.65) | HAPP 3.1 | DM | | | | Non-institutionalized national adult population, U.S.A.<br>Multi-stage probability sample stratified by size of locality<br>N: 1588, date: January, 1971 (+ 1964) | CANTR 71<br>p. 66 |
| REGION | West, East, North | West : Mean = 4.1<br>East : Mean = 3.6<br>North : Mean = 5.5 | HAPP 3.1 | DM | | | | National adult population, Nigeria<br>Probability sample proportionally stratified by dwelling and region<br>N: 1200, date: + 1960 | CANTR 65/1<br>p. 371 |
| **L 4.4 - VARIOUS CHARACTERISTICS OF LIVING ENVIRONMENT** | | | | | | | | | |
| REGION | coop. settlement / new urban / long settled urban / Tel Aviv, Haifa / Jerusalem | coop. settlement : Mean = 5.3<br>new urban : Mean = 4.5<br>long settled urban: Mean = 5.5<br>Tel-Aviv, Haifa : Mean = 5.5<br>Jerusalem : Mean = 5.5 | HAPP 3.1 | DM | | | | National population, Israel<br>Probability sample<br>N: 1170, date: + 1960 | CANTR. 65/1<br>p. 369 |
| ECONOMIC DEPRESSION OF LOCAL ENVIRONMENT | Comparison of inhabitants of 4 communities varying in degree of economic depression<br>(see also sample construction in excerpt, Part II) | Negative among those of lower S.E.S. only.<br>Strongest among those of age 50+ and low S.E.S.<br>Slightly reversed among those of age 50+ and high S.E.S. | HAPP 1.1 | G' | -.17 | Gt' | 01 | Inhabitants of 4 small communities, Illinois, U.S.A.<br>Probability multi-stage samples<br>N: 2006, date: March, 1962 | BRADB 65/1<br>p. 62-65 |
| | | Index of Positive Affects: G' = -.12 (01)<br>Stronger among those under the age of 50<br>Positive among those of low S.E.S.<br>Not among those of high S.E.S.<br>Index of Negative Affects: G' = +.02 (ns)<br>Negative among those of age 50+ and lower S.E.S. only. (To be continued on next page) | AFF 2.3 | G' | - | Gt' | | | |

| | | | | | | | | | |
|---|---|---|---|---|---|---|---|---|---|
| | | Reversed among those under the age of 50 and higher S.E.S.<br>Not among those of age 50+ and higher S.E.S. and among those under the age of 50 and lower S.E.S. | | | | | | | |
| IMPROVING ECONOMIC CLIMATE OF LOCAL ENVIRONMENT | living in a prosperous vs an improving economic climate | This analysis is based on a comparison of the answers of the inhabitants of two communities (N = 1005)<br>Positive among those of lower S.E.S. only. | HAPP 1.1 | G' | +.10 | Gt' | ns | Inhabitants of 4 small communities, Illinois, U.S.A.<br>(see last page) | BRADB 65/1<br>p. 62 |
| PERCEIVED SAFETY | Direct question on whether it is safe to walk at night | | HAPP 1.1<br>AFF 1.1 | mc<br>mc | +.21<br>+.23 | | | Urban adult Jewish population, Israel<br>Probability area sample using dwelling units<br>N: 1830, date: summer, 1973 | LEVY 75/2<br>p. 373 |
| ESTIMATE OF CHANCES OF BEING ROBBED | Respondent's own evaluation | males : G = +.05<br>females : G = +.07 | HAPP 1.1 | G | + | | | Adults, Metro Manila, The Philippines<br>Probability area sample<br>N: 941, date: January - April, 1972 | BULAT 73<br>p. 234-235 |
| | | males : G = -.02<br>females : G = -.10 | HAPP 3.1 | G | - | | | | |
| | | Index of Positive Affects:<br>males : G = +.04<br>females: G = +.06<br>Index of Negative Affects:<br>males : G = +.01<br>females: G = +.06 | AFF 2.3 | G | | | | | |
| GETTING ON WELL WITH THE LOCAL AUTHORITIES | Closed question:<br>very badly / rather badly / average / fairly well / very well | | HAPP 2.1 | $T^2$ | +.16 | $Chi^2$ | 001 | Individual farmers and their families, Poland<br>Non-probability purposive quota sample<br>N: 1002, date: June - July, 1960 | MAKAR 62<br>p. 109 |

## L 4.5 - ATTITUDES TOWARDS LIVING ENVIRONMENT

see also 'Satisfaction with Living Environment' (S 1.2)

| | | | | | | | | | |
|---|---|---|---|---|---|---|---|---|---|
| LIVING CONDITIONS IN THE NEIGHBORHOOD | Respondent's own evaluation | males : G = +.15<br>females : G = +.19 | HAPP 1.1 | G | + | | | Adults, Metro Manila, The Philippines<br>Probability area sample<br>N: 941, date: January - April, 1972 | BULAT 73<br>p. 234-235 |
| | | Lower among males : G = +.17<br>Stronger among females: G = +.34 | HAPP 3.1 | G | + | | | | |
| | | Index of Positive Affects:<br>males : G = +.18<br>females: G = +.05<br>Index of Negative Affects:<br>males : G = -.12<br>females: G = -.07 | AFF 2.3 | G | + | | | | |
| POSITIVE EVALUATION OF NEIGHBORHOOD | Closed question ranging from 'not at all good' to 'very good' | | HAPP 1.1<br>AFF 1.1 | mc<br>mc | +.28<br>+.26 | | | Urban adult Jewish population, Israel<br>Probability area sample using dwelling units<br>N: 1940, date: spring, 1973 | LEVY 75/1<br>p. 372 |
| WANT TO CONTINUE LIVING IN ONE'S TOWN | Closed question ranging from 'definitely no' to 'definitely yes' | | HAPP 1.1<br>AFF 1.1 | mc<br>mc | +.23<br>+.12 | | | See above | LEVY 75/1<br>p. 372 |

| | | | | | | | | | |
|---|---|---|---|---|---|---|---|---|---|
| WANT TO MOVE TO AN OTHER TOWN | Closed question ranging from 'definitely no' to 'definitely yes' | | HAPP 1.1<br>AFF 1.1 | mc<br>mc | -.14<br>-.05 | | | Urban adult Jewish population, Israel<br>(see last page) | LEVY 75/1<br>p. 372 |
| GEOGRAPHIC MOBILITY | Number of times one moved his residence in the past 10 years | | HAPP 3.1 | r | -.05 | | | People of 46 and over, Duke, U.S.A.<br>Probability systematic random sample stratified by age and sex<br>N: 502, date: 1968 | PALMO 72<br>p. 70 |

# M 1 MARITAL STATUS



## M 1.1 - MARRIED

### M 1.1.1 - NEVER MARRIED VS MARRIED

| | | | | | | | | | |
|---|---|---|---|---|---|---|---|---|---|
| MARRIED | Never married vs married | | HAPP 1.1 | G' | +.28 | | | National adult population, U.S.A.<br>Non-probability quota sample<br>N: 2377, date: February, 1946 | WESSM 56<br>p. 190 |
| MARRIED | Never married vs married | Stronger among males: G' = +.50 (01)<br>Lower among females : G' = +.31 (01) | HAPP 1.1 | G' | +.41 | Gt' | 01 | Non-institutionalized adults, U.S.A.<br>Probability multi-stage sample<br>N: 2460, date: spring 1957 | GURIN 60<br>p. 232 |
| MARRIED | Never married vs married | See remarks in excerpt (Part II).<br>Among males : G' = +.38 (01)<br>age 18-39: G' = +.40 (01)<br>age 40-59: G' = +.22 (ns)<br>age 60+ : G' = +.42 (05)<br>Among females: G' = +.44 (01)<br>age 18-39: G' = +.57 (01)<br>age 40-59: G' = +.12 (ns)<br>age 60+ : G' = +.14 (ns) | HAPP 1.1 | G' | +.42 | Gt' | 01 | National adult population, U.S.A.<br>Combined data from 3 general surveys conducted by NORC<br>N: 3853, date: 1972, 1973, 1974 | GLENN 75B<br>p. 596 |
| MARRIED | Never married vs married | Lower among males : G' = +.39 (01)<br>Stronger among females: G' = +.56 (01) | HAPP 1.1 | G' | +.39 | Gt' | 01 | Non-institutionalized adults, U.S.A.<br>National probability sample<br>N: 1500, date: spring 1973 | SPREI 75<br>p. 242 |
| MARRIED | Never married vs married | Gammas based on proportions 'not too happy'answers<br>Stronger among males: G' = +.47 (01)<br>Lower among females : G' = +.18 (ns) | HAPP 1.1 | G' | +.38 | Gt' | 01 | Inhabitants of 4 small communities, Illinois, U.S.A.<br>Probability multi-stage samples<br>N: 2006, date: March, 1962 | BRADB 65/1<br>p. 13 |
| MARRIED | Never married vs married | Sign. among young males only: $\bar{DR}$ = +.17 (05)<br>No other sex or age differences<br>(to be continued on next page) | AFF 2.3 | $\bar{DR}$ | +.05 | BCI | ns | Adults, urban areas, U.S.A.<br>Probability area samples<br>N: 2787, date: January, 1963 - January, 1964 | BRADB 69<br>p. 149-154 |

| | | | | | | | | | |
|---|---|---|---|---|---|---|---|---|---|
| | | Index of Positive Affects: $D\bar{R}$ = +.01 (ns)<br>Stronger among those of age under 25: $D\bar{R}$ = +.07<br>Unaffected by sex (ns)<br>Index of Negative Affects: $D\bar{R}$ = -.05 (ns)<br>Stronger among males : $D\bar{R}$ = -.09 (05)<br>Lower among females : $D\bar{R}$ = -.01 (ns)<br>Strongest among males of<br>age under 25 : $D\bar{R}$ = -.15 (05) | | | | | | | |
| | | Unaffected by sex<br>males : G' = +.38<br>females: G' = +.42 | HAPP 1.1 | G' | + | | | | |
| | | Stronger among males under the age of 25<br>No other sex or age differences | | | | | | | |
| MARRIED | Never married vs married | Positive among males : G' = +.38 (ns)<br>Negative among females: G' = -.39 (ns) | COMP 1.1 | G' | | Gt' | ns | Adults, San Francisco, U.S.A.<br>Probability area sample, poststratified by drinking habits<br>N: 979, date: 1964 | KNUPF 66<br>p. 844 |
| MARRIED | Never married vs married | Never married persons reporting that they are often alone are the least likely to report that they are not satisfied with their present way of life.<br>Unaffected by age | HAPP 2.1 | G' | -.10 | Gt' | ns | Aged persons, Detroit, U.S.A.<br>Probability systematic random sample stratified by type of housing<br>N: 210, date: — | CUBRI 74<br>p. 110-111 |
| | | Unaffected by age | HAPP 1.1 | G' | +.04 | Gt' | ns | | |
| MARRIED | Never married vs married | | HAPP 2.1 | G' | +.21 | Gt' | ns | Aged chronically-ill patients, U.S.A.<br>Probability sample<br>N: 167, date: 1959 | HENLE 67<br>p. 69 |
| MARRIED | Never married vs married | | HAPP 1.1<br>AFF 2.3 | G'<br>G' | +.02<br>-.00 | Gt'<br>Gt' | ns<br>ns | National adult population, Puerto Rico<br>Probability simple random sample<br>N: 1417, date: November, 1963 - January, 1964 and August - October, 1964 | MATLI 66<br>p. 24 |
| MARRIED | Never married vs married | | HAPP 3.1 | DM | - | DMRT | 01 | Adults in the Dominican Republic, Panama and Yugoslavia<br>Pooling of the Cantril (1965) samples of the Dominican Republic, Panama and Yugoslavia<br>N: 5228, date: — | BOHN 72<br>p. 23 |
| MARRIED | Never married vs married | | HAPP 2.1<br>HAPP 1.1 | G'<br>G' | +.18<br>+.14 | Gt'<br>Gt' | 01<br>01 | National populations of nine European countries<br>Type of sample construction not reported<br>N: 9605 (or 9543; see remarks in excerpt, Part II), date: May, 1975 | COMMI 75<br>p. 140/153 |
| MARRIED | Never married vs married | | HAPP 1.1 | G' | +.06 | Gt' | ns | National population, Belgium<br>N: 1555 (1507), date: May, 1975 | COMMI 75<br>p. 155 |
| MARRIED | Never married vs married | | HAPP 1.1 | G' | +.05 | Gt' | ns | National population, United Kingdom (including Northern Ireland)<br>N: 1317 (1325), date: May, 1975 | COMMI 75<br>p. 155 |
| MARRIED | Never married vs married | | HAPP 1.1 | G' | +.22 | Gt' | 05 | National population, Denmark<br>N: 1039 (1073), date: May, 1975 | COMMI 75<br>p. 155 |
| MARRIED | Never married vs married | | HAPP 1.1 | G' | +.08 | Gt' | ns | National population, France<br>N: 1196 (1156), date: May, 1975 | COMMI 75<br>p. 155 |
| MARRIED | Never married vs married | | HAPP 1.1 | G' | +.15 | Gt' | ns | National population, W.Germany<br>N: 1039 (1039), date: May, 1975 | COMMI 75<br>p. 155 |

| | | | | | | | | | |
|---|---|---|---|---|---|---|---|---|---|
| MARRIED | Never married vs married | | HAPP 1.1 | G' | -.04 | Gt' | ns | National population, Ireland<br>N: 999 (996), date: May, 1975 | COMMI 75<br>p. 155 |
| MARRIED | Never married vs married | | HAPP 1.1 | G' | -.01 | Gt' | ns | National population, Italy<br>N: 1043 (1043), date: May, 1975 | COMMI 75<br>p. 155 |
| MARRIED | Never married vs married | | HAPP 1.1 | G' | +.12 | Gt' | ns | National population, Luxembourg<br>N: 324 (311), date: May, 1975 | COMMI 75<br>p. 155 |
| MARRIED | Never married vs married | | HAPP 1.1 | G' | +.29 | Gt' | 05 | National population, The Netherlands<br>N: 1093 (1093), date: May, 1975 | COMMI 75<br>p. 155 |
| MARRIED | Never married vs married | Unaffected by age<br>Stronger among males: G' = +.41 (01)<br>Lower among females : G' = +.27 (01) | HAPP 2.1 | G' | +.34 | Gt' | 01 | Adults, Amsterdam, The Netherlands<br>Probability systematic random sample, stratified by sex and marital status<br>N: 600, date: September - December, 1965 | JONG 69<br>p. 188 |
| MARRIED | Never married vs married | Unaffected by sex | HAPP 1.1 | G' | +.28 | Gt' | 05 | Adults, Utrecht, The Netherlands<br>Probability sample stratified by age<br>N: 300, date: autumn, 1967 | MOSER 69<br>p. 15 |

## M 1.1.2 - WIDOWED VS MARRIED

| | | | | | | | | | |
|---|---|---|---|---|---|---|---|---|---|
| MARRIED | Widowed vs married | | HAPP 1.1 | G' | +.45 | | | National adult population, U.S.A.<br>Non-probability quota sample<br>N: 2377, date: February, 1946 | WESSM 56<br>p. 190 |
| MARRIED | Widowed vs married | Stronger among males: G' = +.64 (01)<br>Lower among females : G' = +.53 (01) | HAPP 1.1 | G' | +.51 | Gt' | 01 | Non-institutionalized adults, U.S.A.<br>Probability multi-stage area sample<br>N: 2460, date: spring, 1957 | GURIN 60<br>p. 232 |
| MARRIED | Widowed vs married | Lower among those under age 65: r = +.05<br>Stronger among those of age 65+: r = +.18<br>Unaffected by S.E.S. | HAPP 1.1 | $r_{pm}$ | +.09 | | 01 | Non-institutionalized adults, U.S.A.<br>Probability sample<br>N: 1547, date: 1972, 1973 | SPREI 74<br>p. 457 |
| MARRIED | Widowed vs married | Stronger among males: G' = +.66 (01)<br>Lower among females : G' = +.43 (01) | HAPP 1.1 | G' | +.46 | Gt' | 01 | Non-institutionalized adults, U.S.A.<br>National probability sample<br>N: 1500, date: spring, 1973 | SPREI 75<br>p. 242 |
| MARRIED | Widowed vs married | See remarks in excerpt (Part II).<br>Among males: G' = +.39 (01)<br>age 60+ : G' = +.52 (01)<br>Among females: G' = +.42 (01)<br>age 40-59 : G' = +.60 (01)<br>age 60+ : G' = +.34 (01) | HAPP 1.1 | G' | +.35 | Gt' | 01 | National adult population, U.S.A.<br>Combined data from 3 U.S. general surveys conducted by NORC<br>N: 3853, date: 1972, 1973, 1974 | GLENN 75B<br>p. 596 |
| MARRIED | Widowed vs married | Gamma based on proportions 'not too happy' answers<br>Unaffected by sex | HAPP 1.1 | G' | +.66 | Gt' | 01 | Inhabitants of 4 small communities, Illinois, U.S.A.<br>Probability multi-stage samples<br>N: 2006, date: March, 1962 | BRADB 65/1<br>p. 13 |
| MARRIED | Widowed vs married | Index of Positive Affects: $\bar{DR}$ = +.13 (05)<br>Index of Negative Affects: $\bar{DR}$ = -.06 (ns)<br>Unaffected by sex | AFF 2.3 | $\bar{DR}$ | +.13 | BCI | 05 | Adults, urban area, U.S.A.<br>Probability area samples<br>N: 2787, date: January, 1963 - January 1964 | BRADB 69<br>p. 149-150 |
| | | Stronger among males: G' = +.69<br>Lower among females: G' = +.61 | HAPP 1.1 | G' | + | | | | |

| | | | | | | | | |
|---|---|---|---|---|---|---|---|---|
| MARRIED | Widowed vs married | Unaffected by age<br>Unaffected by age | HAPP 2.1<br>HAPP 1.1 | G'<br>G' | +.06<br>+.25 | Gt'<br>Gt' | ns<br>ns | Aged persons, Detroit, U.S.A.<br>Probability systematic random sample, stratified by type of housing<br>N: 210, date: — | GUBRI 74<br>p. 110-111 |
| MARRIED | Widowed vs married | | HAPP 2.1 | G' | +.23 | Gt' | ns | Aged chronically-ill patients, U.S.A.<br>Probability sample<br>N: 167, date: 1959 | HENLE 67<br>p. 69 |
| MARRIED | Widowed vs married | | HAPP 1.1<br>AFF 2.3 | G'<br>G' | +.35<br>+.20 | Gt'<br>Gt' | 01<br>ns | National adult population, Puerto Rico<br>Probability simple random sample<br>N: 1417, date: November, 1963 - January, 1964 and August - October, 1964 | MATLI 66<br>p. 24 |
| MARRIED | Widowed vs married | | HAPP 2.1<br>HAPP 1.1 | G'<br>G' | +.27<br>+.30 | Gt'<br>Gt' | 01<br>01 | National populations of nine European Countries<br>Type of sample construction not reported<br>N: 9605 (or 9543; see remarks in excerpt, Part II), date: May, 1975 | COMMI 75<br>p. 140/153 |

## M 1.1.3 - DIVORCED VS MARRIED

| | | | | | | | | | |
|---|---|---|---|---|---|---|---|---|---|
| MARRIED | Divorced vs married | | HAPP 1.1 | G' | +.49 | | | National adult population, U.S.A.<br>Non-probability quota sample<br>N: 2377, date: Febraury, 1946 | WESSM 56<br>p. 190 |
| MARRIED | Divorced vs married | Lower among males : G' = +.40 (01)<br>Stronger among females: G' = +.75 (01) | HAPP 1.1 | G' | +.62 | Gt' | 01 | Non-institutionalized adults, U.S.A.<br>National probability sample<br>N: 1500, date: spring, 1973 | SPREI 75<br>p. 242 |
| MARRIED | Divorced vs married | Index of Positive Affects: $\bar{DR}$ = +.05 (ns)<br>Index of Negative Affects: $\bar{DR}$ = -.05 (ns)<br>Unaffected by sex | AFF 2.3 | $\bar{DR}$ | +.07 | BCI | 05 | Adults, urban areas, U.S.A.<br>Probability area samples<br>N: 2787, date: January, 1963 - January, 1964 | BRADB 69<br>p. 149-150 |
| | | Unaffected by sex<br>males : G' = +.56<br>females: G' = +.61 | HAPP 1.1 | G' | + | | | | |
| MARRIED | Divorced vs married | Unaffected by age<br>Unaffected by age | HAPP 2.1<br>HAPP 1.1 | G'<br>G' | +.23<br>+.15 | Gt'<br>Gt' | ns<br>ns | Aged persons, Detroit, U.S.A.<br>Probability systematic random sample stratified by type of housing<br>N: 210, date: — | GUBRI 74<br>p. 110-111 |
| MARRIED | Divorced vs married | | HAPP 2.1 | Gt' | +.41 | Gt' | ns | Aged chronically-ill patients, U.S.A.<br>Probability sample<br>N: 167, date: 1959 | HENLE 67<br>p. 69 |
| MARRIED | Divorced vs married | | HAPP 1.1<br>AFF 2.3 | G'<br>G' | +.25<br>+.17 | Gt'<br>Gt' | 05<br>ns | National adult population, Puerto Rico<br>Probability simple random sample<br>N: 1417, date: November, 1963 - January, 1964 and August - October, 1964 | MATLI 66<br>p. 24 |
| MARRIED | Divorced vs married | | HAPP 2.1<br>HAPP 1.1 | G'<br>G' | +.47<br>+.39 | Gt'<br>Gt' | 01<br>01 | National population of nine European countries<br>Type of sample construction not reported<br>N: 9605 (or 9543; see remarks in excerpt, Part II), date: May, 1975 | COMMI 75<br>p. 140/153 |

## M 1.1.4 - SEPARATED VS MARRIED

| | | | | | | | | | |
|---|---|---|---|---|---|---|---|---|---|
| MARRIED | Separated vs married | Unaffected by sex<br>Index of Positive Affects: $\overline{DR}$ = +.11 (05)<br>Lower among males : $\overline{DR}$ = +.06 (ns)<br>Stronger among females : $\overline{DR}$ = +.14 (05)<br>Index of Negative Affects: $\overline{DR}$ = -.12 (05)<br>Stronger among males : $\overline{DR}$ = -.15 (05)<br>Lower among females : $\overline{DR}$ = -.08 (ns) | AFF 2.3 | $\overline{DR}$ | +.16 | BCI | 05 | Adults, urban areas, U.S.A.<br>Probability area samples<br>N: 2787, date: January, 1963 - January, 1964 | BRADB 69<br>p. 149-150 |
| | | Unaffected by sex<br>males : G' = +.70<br>females: G' = +.68 | HAPP 1.1 | G' | + | | | | |
| MARRIED | Separated vs married | | HAPP 1.1<br>AFF 2.3 | G'<br>G' | -.04<br>-.08 | Gt'<br>Gt' | ns<br>ns | National adult population, Puerto Rico<br>Probability simple random sample<br>N: 1417, date: November, 1963 - January, 1964 and August - October, 1964 | MATLI 56<br>p. 24 |
| MARRIED | Separated vs married | | HAPP 2.1<br>HAPP 1.1 | G'<br>G' | +.55<br>+.62 | Gt'<br>Gt' | 01<br>01 | National populations of nine European countries<br>Type of sample construction not reported<br>N: 9605 (or 9543; see remarks in excerpt, Part II), date: May, 1975 | COMMI 75<br>p. 140/153 |

## M 1.1.5 - NEVER MARRIED, WIDOWED, DIVORCED, OR SEPARATED VS MARRIED

### NOT PRESENTLY MARRIED VS MARRIED

| | | | | | | | | | |
|---|---|---|---|---|---|---|---|---|---|
| MARRIED | Not currently married vs married | | AFF 1.1 | $r_{pm}$ | -.06 | | ns | Families of hourly workers and salaried employees, U.S.A.<br>N: 712, date: summer, 1973 | TESSL 75<br>p. 103 |
| MARRIED | Having a husband in the home<br>husband-absent vs husband present | Stronger among unemployed females<br>Stronger among formerly welfare status females | HAPP 1.1<br>HAPP 2.1 | DM<br>DM | +<br>+ | | 001<br>001 | Low-income women with children, New York State, U.S.A.<br>Probability systematic random sample stratified by employed status ans marital status<br>N: 1325, date: — | BENDO 74<br>p. 74/78 |
| MARRIED | All others vs married persons living with their spouse | | HAPP 3.1 | r | +.05 | | | People of 46 and over, Duke, U.S.A.<br>Probability systematic random sample stratified by age and sex<br>N: 502, date: 1968 | PALMO 72<br>p. 70 |
| MARRIED | Never married, widowed or divorced vs married | Gammas based on proportions 'very satisfied' answers<br>Helsinki : G' = -.05 (ns)<br>rural communes: G' = +.05 (ns) | HAPP 2.1 | G' | +.02 | Gt' | ns | National population, Finland<br>Probability samples<br>N: 948, date: spring - summer, 1966 | HAAVI 71<br>p. 588 |
| MARRIED | Unmarried vs married | | HAPP 1.1 | | | | ns | National adult population, The Netherlands<br>N: at least 1000, date: 1948 | NIPO 49<br>p. 4 |

## WIDOWED, DIVORCED, SEPARATED VS MARRIED

| | | | | | | | | |
|---|---|---|---|---|---|---|---|---|
| MARRIED | Widowed, divorced or separated vs married | | HAPP 3.1 | DM | - | DMRT | 01 | Adults in the Dominican Republic, Panama and Yugoslavia<br>Pooling of the Cantril (1965) samples of Dominican Republic, Panama and Yugoslavia<br>N: 5228, date: — | BOHN 72<br>p. 23 |
| MARRIED | Widowed, divorced or separated vs married | | HAPP 1.1 | G' | +.51 | Gt' | 01 | National population, Belgium<br>N: 1555 (1507), date: May, 1975 | COMMI 75<br>p. 155 |
| MARRIED | Widowed, divorced or separated vs married | | HAPP 1.1 | G' | +.15 | Gt' | ns | National population, United Kingdom (including Northern Ireland)<br>N: 1317 (1325), date: May, 1975 | COMMI 75<br>p. 155 |
| MARRIED | Widowed, divorced or separated vs married | | HAPP 1.1 | G' | +.54 | Gt' | 01 | National population, Denmark<br>N: 1039 (1073), date: May, 1975 | COMMI 75<br>p. 155 |
| MARRIED | Widowed, divorced or separated vs married | | HAPP 1.1 | G' | +.39 | Gt' | 05 | National population, France<br>N: 1196 (1156), date: May, 1975 | COMMI 75<br>p. 155 |
| MARRIED | Widowed, divorced or separated vs married | | HAPP 1.1 | G' | +.52 | Gt' | 01 | National population, W. Germany<br>N: 1039 (1039), date: May, 1975 | COMMI 75<br>p. 155 |
| MARRIED | Widowed, divorced or separated vs married | | HAPP 1.1 | G' | +.09 | Gt' | ns | National population, Ireland<br>N: 999 (996), date: May, 1975 | COMMI 75<br>p. 155 |
| MARRIED | Widowed, divorced or separated vs married | | HAPP 1.1 | G' | +.32 | Gt' | 05 | National population, Italy<br>N: 1043 (1043), date: May, 1975 | COMMI 75<br>p. 155 |
| MARRIED | Widowed, divorced or separated vs married | | HAPP 1.1 | G' | +.45 | Gt' | 01 | National population, Luxembourg<br>N: 324 (311), date: May, 1975 | COMMI 75<br>p. 155 |
| MARRIED | Widowed, divorced or separated vs married | | HAPP 1.1 | G' | +.67 | Gt' | 01 | National population, The Netherlands<br>N: 1093 (1093), date: May, 1975 | COMMI 75<br>p. 155 |
| MARRIED | Widowed or divorced vs married | Unaffected by sex | HAPP 1.1 | G' | +.64 | Gt' | 01 | Adults, Utrecht, The Netherlands<br>Probability sample stratified by age<br>N: 300, date: autumn, 1967 | MOSER 69<br>p. 15 |

## DIVORCED, SEPARATED VS MARRIED

| | | | | | | | | | |
|---|---|---|---|---|---|---|---|---|---|
| MARRIED | Divorced or separated vs married | Lower among males : G' = +.35 (05)<br>Stronger among females: G' = +.55 (01) | HAPP 1.1 | G' | +.48 | Gt' | 01 | Non-institutionalized adults, U.S.A.<br>Probability multi-stage area sample<br>N: 2460, date: spring, 1957 | GURIN 60<br>p. 232 |
| MARRIED | Divorced or separated vs married | See remarks in excerpt (Part II).<br><br>Among males : G' = +.42 (01)<br>age 18 – 39: G' = +.72 (01)<br>age 40 – 59: G' = +.20 (ns)<br>age 60+ : G' = +.55 (05)<br><br>Among females: G' = +.61 (01)<br>age 18 – 39: G' = +.62 (01)<br>age 40 – 59: G' = +.75 (01)<br>age 60+ : G' = +.27 (ns) | HAPP 1.1 | G' | +.52 | Gt' | 01 | National adult population, U.S.A.<br>Combined data from 3 U.S. general surveys conducted by NORC<br>N: 3853, date: 1972, 1973, 1974 | GLENN 75B<br>p. 596 |
| MARRIED | Divorced or separated vs married | Gammas are based on proportions 'not too happy' answers.<br><br>Stronger among males: G' = +.59 (01)<br>Lower among females: G' = +.47 (01) | HAPP 1.1 | G' | +.51 | Gt' | 01 | Inhabitants of 4 small communities, Illinois, U.S.A.<br>Probability multi-stage samples<br>N: 2006, date: March, 1962 | BRADB 65/1<br>p. 13 |

## M 1.1.6 - LIVING AS MARRIED

| | | | | | | | | |
|---|---|---|---|---|---|---|---|---|
| CONSENSUAL UNION | Married vs consensual union | HAPP 1.1 | G' | -.17 | Gt' | 05 | National adult population, Puerto Rico<br>Probability simple random sample<br>N: 1417, date: November, 1963 - January, 1964 and August - October, 1964 | MATLI 66<br>p. 24 |
| | | AFF 2.3 | G' | -.17 | Gt' | 01 | | |
| CONSENSUAL UNION | Never married vs consensual union | HAPP 1.1 | G' | -.16 | | | See above | MATLI 66<br>p. 24 |
| | | AFF 2.3 | G' | -.17 | | | | |
| CONSENSUAL UNION | Widowed vs consensual union | HAPP 1.1 | G' | +.18 | | | See above | MATLI 66<br>p. 24 |
| | | AFF 2.3 | G' | +.04 | | | | |
| CONSENSUAL UNION | Divorced vs consensual union | HAPP 1.1 | G' | +.08 | | | See above | MATLI 66<br>p. 24 |
| | | AFF 2.3 | G' | -.11 | | | | |
| CONSENSUAL UNION | Separated vs consensual union | HAPP 1.1 | G' | -.11 | | | See above | MATLI 66<br>p. 24 |
| | | AFF 2.3 | G' | -.10 | | | | |
| LIVING AS MARRIED | Married vs living as married | HAPP 2.1 | G' | +.10 | Gt' | ns | National population of nine European countries<br>Type of sample construction not reported<br>N: 9605 (or 9543; see remarks in excerpt, Part II), date: May, 1975 | COMMI 75<br>p. 140/153 |
| | | HAPP 1.1 | G' | +.04 | Gt' | ns | | |
| LIVING AS MARRIED | Never married vs living as married | HAPP 2.1 | G' | +.27 | Gt' | 01 | See above | COMMI 75<br>p. 140/153 |
| | | HAPP 1.1 | G' | +.16 | Gt' | ns | | |
| LIVING AS MARRIED | Widowed vs living as married | HAPP 2.1 | G' | +.35 | Gt' | 01 | See above | COMMI 75<br>p. 140/153 |
| | | HAPP 1.1 | G' | +.30 | Gt' | 01 | | |
| LIVING AS MARRIED | Divorced vs living as married | HAPP 2.1 | G' | +.52 | Gt' | 01 | See above | COMMI 75<br>p. 140/153 |
| | | HAPP 1.1 | G' | +.38 | Gt' | 01 | | |
| LIVING AS MARRIED | Separated vs living as married | HAPP 2.1 | G' | +.56 | Gt' | 01 | See above | COMMI 75<br>p. 140/153 |
| | | HAPP 1.1 | G' | +.60 | Gt' | 01 | | |

## M 1.2 - NEVER MARRIED

### M 1.2.1 - MARRIED VS NEVER MARRIED

see above (M 1.1.1)

### M 1.2.2 - WIDOWED VS NEVER MARRIED

| | | | | | | | | |
|---|---|---|---|---|---|---|---|---|
| NEVER MARRIED | Widowed vs never married | HAPP 1.1 | G' | +.24 | | | National adult population, U.S.A.<br>Non-probability quota sample<br>N: 2377, date: February, 1946 | WESSM 56<br>p. 190 |

| | | | | | | | | | |
|---|---|---|---|---|---|---|---|---|---|
| NEVER MARRIED | Widowed vs never married | Stronger among males: G' = +.39 (05)<br>Lower among females : G' = +.30 (01) | HAPP 1.1 | G' | +.21 | Gt' | 05 | Non-institutionalized adults, U.S.A.<br>Probability multi-stage sample<br>N: 2460, date: spring, 1957 | GURIN 60<br>p. 232 |
| NEVER MARRIED | Widowed vs never married | See remarks in excerpt (Part II)<br>Among males : G' = +.01 (ns)<br>age 60+ : G' = +.12 (ns)<br>Among females: G' = -.03 (ns)<br>age 40 - 59: G' = +.51 (05)<br>age 60+ : G' = +.21 (ns) | HAPP 1.1 | G' | -.08 | Gt' | ns | National adult population, U.S.A.<br>Combined data from 3 general surveys conducted by NORC<br>N: 3853, date: 1972, 1973, 1974 | GLENN 75B<br>p. 596 |
| NEVER MARRIED | Widowed vs never married | Stronger among males: G' = +.46 (05)<br>Lower among females: G' = +.14 (ns) | HAPP 1.1 | G' | +.16 | Gt' | ns | Non-institutionalized adults, U.S.A.<br>National probability sample<br>N: 1500, date: spring, 1973 | SPREI 75<br>p. 242 |
| NEVER MARRIED | Widowed vs never married | Gammas based on proportions 'not too happy' answers.<br>Stronger among females: G' = +.57 (01)<br>Lower among males : G' = +.26 (ns) | HAPP 1.1 | G' | +.35 | Gt' | 01 | Inhabitants of 4 small communities, Illinois, U.S.A.<br>Probability multi-stage samples<br>N: 2006, date: March, 1962 | BRADB 65/1<br>p. 13 |
| NEVER MARRIED | Widowed vs never married | Stronger among females: $\overline{DR}$ = +.10 (ns)<br>Lower among males : $\overline{DR}$ = +.03 (ns)<br>Index of Positive Affects: $\overline{DR}$ = +.12 (05)<br>Unaffected by sex<br>Index of Negative Affects: $\overline{DR}$ = -.01 (ns)<br>Stronger among females : $\overline{DR}$ = -.03 (ns)<br>Reversed among males : $\overline{DR}$ = +.07 (ns) | AFF 2.3 | $\overline{DR}$ | +.08 | BCI | ns | Adults, urban areas, U.S.A.<br>Probability area samples<br>N: 2787, date: January, 1963 - January, 1964 | BRADB 69<br>p. 149-150 |
| | | Stronger among males : G' = +.42<br>Lower among females : G' = +.34 | HAPP 1.1 | G' | + | | | | |
| NEVER MARRIED | Widowed vs never married | Unaffected by age<br>Unaffected by age | HAPP 2.1<br>HAPP 1.1 | G'<br>G' | +.17<br>+.23 | Gt'<br>Gt' | ns<br>ns | Aged persons, Detroit, U.S.A.<br>Probability systematic random sample stratified by type of housing<br>N: 210, date: — | GUBRI 74<br>p. 110-111 |
| NEVER MARRIED | Widowed vs never married | | HAPP 2.1 | G' | +.02 | Gt' | ns | Aged chronically ill patients, U.S.A.<br>Probability sample<br>N: 167, date: 1959 | HENLE 67<br>p. 69 |
| NEVER MARRIED | Widowed vs never married | | HAPP 1.1<br>AFF 2.3 | G'<br>G' | +.36<br>+.20 | | | National adult population, Puerto Rico<br>Probability simple random sample<br>N: 1419, date: November, 1963 - January, 1964 and August - October, 1964 | MATLI 66<br>p. 24 |
| NEVER MARRIED | Widowed vs never married | | HAPP 2.1<br>HAPP 1.1 | G'<br>G' | +.11<br>+.17 | Gt'<br>Gt' | 01<br>01 | National population of nine European countries<br>Type of sample construction not reported<br>N: 9605 (or 9543; see remarks in excerpt, Part II), date: May, 1975 | COMMI 75<br>p. 140/153 |

## M 1.2.3 - DIVORCED VS NEVER MARRIED

| | | | | | | | | | |
|---|---|---|---|---|---|---|---|---|---|
| NEVER MARRIED | Divorced vs never married | | HAPP 1.1 | G' | +.29 | | | National adult population, U.S.A.<br>Non-probability quota sample<br>N: 2377, date: February, 1946 | WESSM 56<br>p. 190 |

| | | | | | | | | | |
|---|---|---|---|---|---|---|---|---|---|
| NEVER MARRIED | Divorced vs never married | Lower among males : G' = +.13 (ns)<br>Stronger among females: G' = +.57 (01) | HAPP 1.1 | G' | +.40 | Gt' | 01 | Non-institutionalized adults, U.S.A.<br>National probability sample<br>N: 1500, date: spring, 1973 | SPREI 75<br>p. 242 |
| NEVER MARRIED | Divorced vs never married | Unaffected by sex<br>Index of Positive Affects: $\bar{DR}$ = +.04 (ns)<br>Unaffected by sex<br>Index of Negative Affects: $\bar{DR}$ = .00 (ns)<br>Positive among males : $\bar{DR}$ = +.04 (ns)<br>Negative among females : $\bar{DR}$ = -.02 (ns) | AFF 2.3 | $\bar{DR}$ | +.02 | BCI | ns | Adults, urban areas, U.S.A.<br>Probability area samples<br>N: 2787, date: January, 1963 - January, 1964 | BRADB 69<br>p. 149-150 |
| | | Unaffected by sex<br>males : G' = +.27<br>females: G' = +.27 | HAPP 1.1 | G' | + | | | | |
| NEVER MARRIED | Divorced vs never married | Unaffected by age | HAPP 2.1 | G' | +.36 | Gt' | ns | Aged persons, Detroit, U.S.A.<br>Probability systematic random sample stratified by type of housing<br>N: 210, date: — | GUBRI 74<br>p. 110-111 |
| | | Unaffected by age | HAPP 1.1 | G' | +.12 | Gt' | ns | | |
| NEVER MARRIED | Divorced vs never married | | HAPP 2.1 | G' | +.22 | Gt' | ns | Aged chronically-ill patients, U.S.A.<br>Probability sample<br>N: 167, date: 1959 | HENLE 67<br>p. 69 |
| NEVER MARRIED | Divorced vs never married | | HAPP 1.1 | G' | +.25 | | | National adult population, Puerto Rico<br>Probability simple random sample<br>N: 1419, date: November, 1963 - January, 1964 and August - October, 1964 | MATLI 66<br>p. 24 |
| | | | AFF 2.3 | G' | +.17 | | | | |
| NEVER MARRIED | Divorced vs never married | | HAPP 2.1 | G' | +.34 | Gt' | 01 | National population of nine European countries<br>Type of sample construction not reported<br>N: 9605 (or 9543; see remarks in excerpt, Part II), date: May, 1975 | COMMI 75<br>p. 140/153 |
| | | | HAPP 1.1 | G' | +.27 | Gt' | 01 | | |

## M 1.2.4 - SEPARATED VS NEVER MARRIED

| | | | | | | | | | |
|---|---|---|---|---|---|---|---|---|---|
| NEVER MARRIED | Separated vs never married | Unaffected by sex<br>Index of Positive Affects: $\bar{DR}$ = +.11 (05)<br>Stronger among females : $\bar{DR}$ = +.13 (05)<br>Lower among males : $\bar{DR}$ = +.06 (ns)<br>Index of Negative Affects: $\bar{DR}$ = -.07 (ns)<br>Unaffected by sex | AFF 2.3 | $\bar{DR}$ | +.10 | BCI | 05 | Adults, urban areas, U.S.A.<br>Probability area samples<br>N: 2787, date: January, 1963 - January, 1964 | BRADB 69<br>p. 149-150 |
| | | Unaffected by sex<br>males : G' = +.44<br>females: G' = +.47 | HAPP 1.1 | G' | + | | | | |
| NEVER MARRIED | Separated vs never married | | HAPP 1.1 | G' | +.03 | | | National adult population, Puerto Rico<br>Probability simple random sample<br>N: 1419, date: November, 1963 - January, 1964 and August - October, 1964 | MATLI 66<br>p. 24 |
| | | | AFF 2.3 | G' | +.08 | | | | |
| NEVER MARRIED | Separated vs never married | | HAPP 2.1 | G' | +.44 | Gt' | 01 | National populations of nine European countries<br>Type of sample construction not reported<br>N: 9605 (or 9543; see remarks in excerpt, Part II), date: May, 1975 | COMMI 75<br>p. 140/153 |
| | | | HAPP 1.1 | G' | +.52 | Gt' | 01 | | |

## M 1.2.5 - WIDOWED, DIVORCED OR SEPARATED VS NEVER MARRIED

### WIDOWED, DIVORCED, SEPARATED VS NEVER MARRIED

| | | | | | | | | | |
|---|---|---|---|---|---|---|---|---|---|
| NEVER MARRIED | Widowed, divorced or separated vs never married | | HAPP 3.1 | DM | + | DMRT | 05 | Adults in the Dominican Republic, Panama and Yugoslavia<br>Pooling of the Cantril (1965) samples of the Dominican Republic, Panama and Yugoslavia<br>N: 5228, date: — | BOHN 72<br>p. 23 |
| NEVER MARRIED | Widowed, divorced or separated vs never married | | HAPP 1.1 | G' | +.46 | Gt' | 01 | National population, Belgium<br>N: 1555 (1507), date: May, 1975 | COMMI 75<br>p. 155 |
| NEVER MARRIED | Widowed, divorced or separated vs never married | | HAPP 1.1 | G' | +.11 | Gt' | ns | National population, United Kingdom (including N.Ireland)<br>N: 1317 (1325), date: May, 1975 | COMMI 75<br>p. 155 |
| NEVER MARRIED | Widowed, divorced or separated vs never married | | HAPP 1.1 | G' | +.32 | Gt' | 05 | National population, Denmark<br>N: 1039 (1073), date: May, 1975 | COMMI 75<br>p. 155 |
| NEVER MARRIED | Widowed, divorced or separated vs never married | | HAPP 1.1 | G' | +.30 | Gt' | 05 | National population, France<br>N: 1196 (1156), date: May, 1975 | COMMI 75<br>p. 155 |
| NEVER MARRIED | Widowed, divorced or separated vs never married | | HAPP 1.1 | G' | +.41 | Gt' | 05 | National population, W.Germany<br>N: 1039 (1039), date: May, 1975 | COMMI 75<br>p. 155 |
| NEVER MARRIED | Widowed, divorced or separated vs never married | | HAPP 1.1 | G' | +.13 | Gt' | ns | National population, Ireland<br>N: 999 (996), date: May, 1975 | COMMI 75<br>p. 155 |
| NEVER MARRIED | Widowed, divorced or separated vs never married | | HAPP 1.1 | G' | +.32 | Gt' | 05 | National population, Italy<br>N: 1043 (1043), date: May, 1975 | COMMI 75<br>p. 155 |
| NEVER MARRIED | Widowed, divorced or separated vs never married | | HAPP 1.1 | G' | +.38 | Gt' | ns | National population, Luxembourg<br>N: 324 (311), date: May, 1975 | COMMI 75<br>p. 155 |
| NEVER MARRIED | Widowed, divorced or separated vs never married | | HAPP 1.1 | G' | +.53 | Gt' | 05 | National population, The Netherlands<br>N: 1093 (1093), date: May, 1975 | COMMI 75<br>p. 155 |
| NEVER MARRIED | Widowed or divorced vs never married | | HAPP 1.1 | G' | +.40 | Gt' | ns | Adults, Utrecht, The Netherlands<br>Probability sample stratified by age<br>N: 300, date: autumn, 1967 | MOSER 69<br>p. 15 |

### DIVORCED, SEPARATED VS NEVER MARRIED

| | | | | | | | | | |
|---|---|---|---|---|---|---|---|---|---|
| NEVER MARRIED | Divorced or separated vs never married | Stronger among females: G' = +.34 (01)<br>Reversed among males : G' = -.08 (ns) | HAPP 1.1 | G' | +.18 | Gt' | ns | Non-institutionalized adults, U.S.A.<br>Probability multi-stage area sample<br>N: 2460, date: spring, 1957 | GURIN 60<br>p. 232 |
| NEVER MARRIED | Divorced or separated vs never married | See remarks in excerpt (Part II).<br>Among males : G' = +.04 (ns)<br>age 18 - 39: G' = +.45 (ns)<br>age 40 - 59: G' = -.01 (ns)<br>age 60+ : G' = +.18 (ns)<br>Among females: G' = +.23 (ns)<br>age 18 - 39: G' = +.07 (ns)<br>age 40 - 59: G' = +.70 (01)<br>age 60+ : G' = +.14 (ns) | HAPP 1.1 | G' | +.13 | Gt' | ns | National adult population, U.S.A.<br>Combined data from 3 U.S. general surveys conducted by NORC<br>N: 3853, date: 1972,1973, 1974 | GLENN 75B<br>p. 596 |

| | | | | | | | | |
|---|---|---|---|---|---|---|---|---|
| NEVER MARRIED | Divorced or separated vs never married | Gammas based on proportions 'not too happy' answers<br>Stronger among females: G' = +.32 (ns)<br>Lower among males : G' = +.16 (ns) | HAPP 1.1 | G' | +.17 | Gt' | ns | Inhabitants of 4 small communities, Illinois, U.S.A.<br>Probability multi-stage samples<br>N: 2006, date: March, 1962 | BRADB 65/1<br>p. 13 |

## M 1.3 - WIDOWED

### M 1.3.1 - MARRIED VS WIDOWED

see above (M 1.1.2)

### M 1.3.2 - NEVER MARRIED VS WIDOWED

see above (M 1.2.2)

### M 1.3.3 - DIVORCED VS WIDOWED

| | | | | | | | | | |
|---|---|---|---|---|---|---|---|---|---|
| WIDOWED | Divorced vs widowed | | HAPP 1.1 | G' | +.05 | | | National adult population, U.S.A.<br>Non-probability quota sample<br>N: 2377, date: February, 1946 | WESSM 56<br>p. 190 |
| WIDOWED | Divorced vs widowed | Stronger among females: G' = +.39 (01)<br>Reversed among males : G' = -.22 (ns) | HAPP 1.1 | G' | +.21 | Gt' | 05 | Non-institutionalized adults, U.S.A.<br>National probability sample<br>N: 1500, date: spring, 1973 | SPREI 75<br>p. 242 |
| WIDOWED | Divorced vs widowed | Slightly stronger among females: $\bar{DR}$ = -.07 (ns)<br>Not among males : $\bar{DR}$ = -.01 (ns)<br>Index of Positive Affects: $\bar{DR}$ = -.09 (ns)<br>Index of Negative Affects: $\bar{DR}$ = +.01 (ns)<br>Unaffected by sex | AFF 2.3 | $\bar{DR}$ | -.06 | BCI | ns | Adults, urban areas, U.S.A.<br>Probability area samples<br>N: 2787, date: January, 1963 - January, 1964 | BRADB 69<br>p. 149-150 |
| | | Stronger among males: G' = -.24<br>Lower among females : G' = -.11 | HAPP 1.1 | G' | - | | | | |
| WIDOWED | Divorced vs widowed | Unaffected by age | HAPP 2.1<br>HAPP 1.1 | G'<br>G' | +.18<br>-.12 | Gt'<br>Gt' | ns<br>ns | Aged persons, Detroit, U.S.A.<br>Probability systematic random sample stratified by type of housing<br>N: 210, date: — | GUBRI 74<br>p. 110-111 |
| WIDOWED | Divorced vs widowed | | HAPP 2.1 | G' | +.20 | Gt' | ns | Aged chronically-ill patients, U.S.A.<br>Probability sample<br>N: 167, date: 1959 | HENLE 67<br>p. 69 |
| WIDOWED | Divorced vs widowed | | HAPP 1.1<br>AFF 2.3 | G'<br>G' | -.11<br>-.05 | | | National adult population, Puerto Rico<br>Probability simple random sample<br>N: 1419, date: November, 1963 - January, 1964 and August - October, 1964 | MATLI 66<br>p. 24 |
| WIDOWED | Divorced vs widowed | | HAPP 2.1<br>HAPP 1.1 | G'<br>G' | +.23<br>+.10 | Gt'<br>Gt' | 01<br>ns | National populations of nine European countries<br>Type of sample construction not reported<br>N: 9605 (or 9543; see remarks in excerpt, Part II), date: May, 1975 | COMMI 75<br>p. 140/153 |

## M 1.3.4 - SEPARATED VS WIDOWED

| | | | | | | | | | |
|---|---|---|---|---|---|---|---|---|---|
| WIDOWED | Separated vs widowed | Unaffected by sex<br>Index of Positive Affects: $\bar{DR}$ = -.02 (ns)<br>Unaffected by sex<br>Index of Negative Affects: $\bar{DR}$ = -.06 (ns)<br>Stronger among males : $\bar{DR}$ = -.13 (ns)<br>Lower among females : $\bar{DR}$ = -.04 (ns) | AFF 2.3 | $\bar{DR}$ | +.03 | BCI | ns | Adults, urban areas, U.S.A.<br>Probability area samples<br>N: 2787, date: January, 1963 - January, 1964 | BRADB 69<br>p. 149-150 |
| | | Females only : G' = +.17<br>Not among males: G' = +.02 | HAPP 1.1 | G' | + | | | | |
| WIDOWED | Separated vs widowed | | HAPP 1.1<br>AFF 2.3 | G'<br>G' | -.28<br>-.14 | | | National adult population, Puerto Rico<br>Probability simple random sample<br>N: 1419, date: November, 1963 - January, 1964 and August - October, 1964 | MATLI 66<br>p. 24 |
| WIDOWED | Separated vs widowed | | HAPP 2.1<br>HAPP 1.1 | G'<br>G' | +.32<br>+.37 | Gt'<br>Gt' | 01<br>01 | National population of nine European countries<br>Type of sample construction not reported<br>N: 9605 (or 9543; see remarks in excerpt, Part II),<br>date: May, 1975 | COMMI 75<br>p. 140-153 |

## M 1.3.5 - DIVORCED OR SEPARATED VS WIDOWED

| | | | | | | | | | |
|---|---|---|---|---|---|---|---|---|---|
| WIDOWED | Divorced or separated vs widowed | Stronger among males : G' = -.38 (05)<br>Reversed among females: G' = +.05 (ns) | HAPP 1.1 | G' | -.04 | Gt' | ns | Non-institutionalized adults, U.S.A.<br>Probability multi-stage area sample<br>N: 2460, date: spring, 1957 | GURIN 60<br>p. 232 |
| WIDOWED | Divorced or separated vs widowed | See remarks in excerpt (Part II).<br>Among males : G' = +.03 (ns)<br>age 60+ : G' = +.04 (ns)<br>Among females: G' = +.25 (05)<br>age 40 - 59: G' = +.29 (ns)<br>age 60+ : G' = -.07 (ns) | HAPP 1.1 | G' | +.21 | Gt' | 05 | National adult population, U.S.A.<br>Combined data from 3 U.S. general surveys conducted by NORC<br>N: 3853, date: 1972, 1973, 1974 | GLENN 75B<br>p. 596 |
| WIDOWED | Divorced or separated vs widowed | Gammas based on proportions 'not too happy' answers<br>Stronger among females: G' = -.30 (ns)<br>Lower among males : G' = -.10 (ns) | HAPP 1.1 | G' | -.19 | Gt' | ns | Inhabitants of 4 small communities, Illinois, U.S.A.<br>Probability multi-stage samples<br>N: 2006, date: March, 1962 | BRADB 65/1<br>p. 13 |

## M 1.4 - DIVORCED

## M 1.4.1 - MARRIED VS DIVORCED

see above (M 1.1.3)

## M 1.4.2 - NEVER MARRIED VS DIVORCED

see above (M 1.2.3)

## M 1.4.3 - WIDOWED VS DIVORCED

see above (M 1.3.3)

## M 1.4.4 - SEPARATED VS DIVORCED

| | | | | | | | | |
|---|---|---|---|---|---|---|---|---|
| DIVORCED | Separated vs divorced | Index of Positive Affects: $\bar{DR}$ = +.07 (ns)<br>Index of Negative Affects: $\bar{DR}$ = -.07 (ns)<br>Unaffected by sex | AFF 2.3 | $\bar{DR}$ | +.09 | BCI | ns | Adults, urban areas, U.S.A.<br>Probability area sample<br>N: 2787, date: January, 1963 - January, 1964 | BRADB 69<br>p. 149-150 |
| | | Stronger among females: G' = +.28<br>Lower among males : G' = +.10 | HAPP 1.1 | G' | + | | | | |
| DIVORCED | Separated vs divorced | | HAPP 1.1<br>AFF 2.3 | G'<br>G' | -.18<br>-.11 | | | National adult population, Puerto Rico<br>Probability simple random sample<br>N: 1419, date: November, 1963 - January, 1964 and August - October, 1964 | MATLI 66<br>p. 24 |
| DIVORCED | Separated vs divorced | | HAPP 2.1<br>HAPP 1.1 | G'<br>G' | +.12<br>+.28 | Gt'<br>Gt' | ns<br>05 | National populations of nine European countries<br>Type of sample construction not reported<br>N: 9605 (or 9543; see remarks in excerpt, Part II)<br>date: May, 1975 | COMMI 75<br>p. 140/153 |

## M 1.5 - SEPARATED

## M 1.5.1 - MARRIED VS SEPARATED

see above (M 1.1.4)

## M 1.5.2 - NEVER MARRIED VS SEPARATED

see above (M 1.2.4)

## M 1.5.3 - WIDOWED VS SEPARATED

see above (M 1.3.4)

## M 1.5.4 - DIVORCED VS SEPARATED

see above (M 1.4.4)

## M 1.6 - VARIOUS COMPARISONS

| | | | | | | | | | |
|---|---|---|---|---|---|---|---|---|---|
| MARITAL STATUS | Widowed / divorced / never married / married | | HAPP 2.1<br>HAPP 3.1<br>CON 1.1 | r<br>r<br>r | +.06<br>+.04<br>+.01 | | | National adult population, U.S.A.<br>Cantril (1965) modified probability sample<br>N: 1406, date: 1959 | BORTN 70<br>p. 44 |

| | | | | | | | | | |
|---|---|---|---|---|---|---|---|---|---|
| CONTINUITY IN MARITAL STATUS | Incontinuity (widowed / divorced) vs continuity (never married / married) | Unaffected by age | HAPP 2.1 | G' | +.11 | Gt' | ns | Aged persons, Detroit, U.S.A.<br>Probability systematic random sample stratified by type of housing<br>N: 210, date: — | GUBRI 74<br>p. 110-111 |
| | | Unaffected by age | HAPP 1.1 | G' | +.24 | Gt' | ns | | |
| MARITAL STATUS | Widowed / married / unmarried | The unmarried are most happy (mean rating 6.00), followed by resp. the married (5.66) and the widowed (4.08) | HAPP 2.1 | DM | + | | | National population, Britain<br>Non-probability quota sample<br>N: 213, date: March, 1971 | ABRAM 73<br>p. 4 |
| MARITAL STATUS | Widowed / never married / married | Positive among males : G = +.18<br>Negative among females: G = -.06 | HAPP 1.1 | G | | | | Adults, Metro Manila, the Philippines<br>Probability area sample<br>N: 941, date: January - April, 1972 | BULAT 73<br>p. 232 |
| | | Lower among males : G = -.04<br>Stronger among females: G = -.16 | HAPP 3.1 | G | - | | | | |
| | | Index of Positive Affects:<br>males : G = +.12<br>females : G = +.16<br>Index of Negative Affects:<br>Stronger among males: G = -.20<br>Not among females : G = -.01 | AFF 2.3 | G | + | | | | |
| LEVEL OF ATTACHMENT OF MALE PARTNER | Closed question: recently terminated relationship / apparently not dating / won't marry present beau / will possibly marry present beau / will fairly certain marry present beau / engaged/ married | Females who are certain of getting married, who are engaged, or who are married are generally happier than those who are not (05) | AFF 2.1 | DM | + | $F^+$ | ns | Female college seniors, U.S.A.<br>Non-probability chunk sample<br>N: 162, date: May - June, 1966 | PORTE 67<br>p. 58 |

## M 1.7 - ATTITUDES TOWARDS MARITAL STATUS

| | | | | | | | | | |
|---|---|---|---|---|---|---|---|---|---|
| POSITIVE SELF-IMAGE | Extent of agreement with 3 positive statements about singles: singles having an easy carefree life, a better financial position, a lot of leisure time | Computed for singles only<br>Negative among males : r = -.08<br>Positive among females: r = +.10 | HAPP 2.1 | $r_{pm}$ | | | | Adults, Amsterdam, The Netherlands<br>Probability systematic random sample stratified by sex and marital status<br>N: 600, date: September - December, 1965 | JONG 69 |
| NEGATIVE SELF-IMAGE | Extent of agreement with 11 negative statements about singles: singles like being alone, live a frivolous life, are often jealous, shy, unattractive, reserved, etc. | Computed for singles only<br>Stronger among males: r = -.22 (005)<br>Lower among females : r = -.10 (ns) | HAPP 2.1 | $r_{pm}$ | - | $Chi^2$ | | See above | JONG 69<br>p. 200 |
| PERCEIVED POSITIVE IMAGE | Expected agreement of married persons with 3 positive statements about singles: singles have an easy carefree life, a better financial position, a lot of leisure time | Computed for singles only<br>males : r = -.04<br>females: r = +.06 | HAPP 2.1 | $r_{pm}$ | | | | See above | JONG 69 |
| PERCEIVED NEGATIVE IMAGE | Expected agreement of married persons with 11 negative statements about singles: singles like being on their own, live a frivolous life, are often jealous, shy, unattractive, reserved, etc. | Computed for singles only<br>Stronger among males: r = -.19<br>Not among females : r = -.03 | HAPP 2.1 | $r_{pm}$ | - | | | See above | JONG 69 |

# M 2 MARRIAGE



## M 2.1 - BEING MARRIED

see 'Marital Status - Married' (M 1.1)

## M 2.2 - ATTITUDES TOWARDS MARRIAGE

see also 'Satisfaction with Marriage' (S 1.7.2)

| | | | | | | | | | |
|---|---|---|---|---|---|---|---|---|---|
| POSITIVE ATTITUDE TOWARDS MARRIAGE | Closed question: 'In general, which do you think is happier - married people or single people?' single / no difference / married | | HAPP 1.1 | G' | +.32 | Gt' | 01 | National population, U.S.A.<br>Non-probability quota sample<br>N: 2377, date: February, 1946 | WESSM 56<br>p. 191 |
| THINKING OFTEN ABOUT MARRIAGE | Closed question: not at all / sometimes / often, during last week | Gammas computed on the basis of proportion 'often' answers<br>Unaffected by S.E.S.<br>high S.E.S.: G' = -.07 (ns)<br>low S.E.S. : G' = -.03 (ns) | HAPP 1.1 | G' | - | Gt' | | Inhabitants of 4 small communities, Illinois, U.S.A.<br>Probability multi-stage samples<br>N: 2006, date: March, 1962 | BRADB 65/1<br>p. 54 |
| EXPECTED SATISFACTION IF MARRIED | Closed question rated on a 5-point scale | Computed for singles only<br>males : r = +.06 (ns)<br>females: r = -.08 (ns) | HAPP 2.1 | $r_{pm}$ | | $Chi^2$ | | Adults, Amsterdam, The Netherlands<br>Probability systematic random sample stratified by sex and marital status<br>N: 600, date: September - December, 1965 | JONG 69<br>p. 193 |

## M 2.3 - CHARACTERISTICS OF THE SPOUSE

| | | | | | | | | | |
|---|---|---|---|---|---|---|---|---|---|
| BEING A WIFE OF A SKILLED WORKER | Being a wife of an unskilled / a semi-skilled / a skilled worker | Computed for presently married females only | HAPP 1.1 | G' | +.26 | Gt' | 01 | Non-institutionalized adults, U.S.A.<br>Probability multi-stage area sample<br>N: 2460, date: spring, 1957 | GURIN 60<br>p. 223 |
| EMLOYED STATUS OF SPOUSE | Ss with unemployed vs employed spouse | Computed for married respondents only<br>Lower among males : $\bar{DR}$ = +.04 (ns)<br>Stronger among females : $\bar{DR}$ = +.10 (05)<br>Index of Positive Affects : $\bar{DR}$ = +.06 (05)<br>Stronger among females : $\bar{DR}$ = +.19 (05)<br>Lower among males : $\bar{DR}$ = +.04 (ns)<br>Index of Negative Affects : $\bar{DR}$ = +.06 (05)<br>Unaffected by sex: males : $\bar{DR}$ = .00 (ns)<br>females: $\bar{DR}$ = +.02 (ns)<br>For further elaborations see 'Having Work' (W 2.1, Part III). | AFF 2.3 | $\bar{DR}$ | +.01 | BCI | ns | Adults, urban areas, U.S.A.<br>Probability area samples<br>N: 2787, date: January, 1963 - January, 1964 | BRADB 69<br>p. 187 |

| | | | | | | | | | |
|---|---|---|---|---|---|---|---|---|---|
| WIFE OF UNEMPLOYED CHIEF WAGE EARNER | Wife of employed vs unemployed chief wage earner | This analysis concerns only women who are not chief wage earners.<br>Index of Positive Affects: $\overline{DR}$ = -.19 (05)<br>Index of Negative Affects: $\overline{DR}$ = -.02 (ns) | AFF 2.3 | $\overline{DR}$ | -.10 | BCI | 05 | Adults, urban areas, U.S.A.<br>(See last page) | BRADB 69<br>p. 184/186 |
| | | | HAPP 1.1 | G | -.32 | | | | |
| SOCIAL STRATUM OF HUSBAND | Lower vs upper strata | Computed for married females only<br>Gammas based on proportion 'very satisfied' answers<br>Stronger among employed females: G' = -.31 (ns)<br>Lower among unemployed females: G' = -.20 (ns) | HAPP 2.1 | G' | - | Gt' | ns | Inhabitants of Helsinki, Finland<br>Probability sample<br>N: 442, date: spring - summer, 1966 | HAAVI 71<br>p. 595 |
| INCOME | Husband's income rated on a 3-point scale | | HAPP 1.1 | $r_{pm}$ | +.21 | | | Housewives, The Netherlands<br>Probability area sample<br>N: 450, date: autumn, 1964 | PHILI 66<br>p. 66 |
| BEING YOUNGER THAN SPOUSE | Same age or older vs younger | 35% of the relatively dissatisfied, 27% of the satisfied and 17% of the very satisfied were the same age as their husband or older (sign.).<br>No relationship among men | HAPP 2.1 | D% | + | | s | Middle-aged, middle class married couples, U.S.A.<br>Non-probability accidental sample of couples<br>N: 416, date: 1952 - 1953 | ROSE 55<br>p. 16 |
| LIFE SATISFACTION OF SPOUSE | Closed question rated on a 5-point scale (see instrument in excerpt, Part II). | 65% of the men, whose wives said they were very satisfied with their lives, also said they were satisfied, whereas this was only true for 15% of the men whose wives were relatively dissatisfied. | HAPP 2.1 | D% | + | | s | See above | ROSE 55<br>p. 16 |

## M 2.4 - CHARACTERISTICS OF THE RELATIONSHIP

see also 'Satisfaction with Marriage' (S 1.7.2)

| | | | | | | | | | |
|---|---|---|---|---|---|---|---|---|---|
| FEELINGS OF MARITAL INADEQUACY | Closed question of frequency of feeling not as good a husband/wife as one would like to be<br>never / once in a while / a lot of times | Stronger among males: $t_k$ = -.15 (01)<br>Not among females: $t_k$ = +.01 (ns) | HAPP 1.1 | $t_k$ | - | | | Adult married population with children, U.S.A.<br>Probability area sample<br>N: 797, date: — | VEROF 62<br>p. 196 |
| PROBLEMS IN MARRIAGE (in the past) | Open-ended question on problems getting along with each other<br>S never had problems vs mentions problems | Stronger among females: $t_k$ = -.24 (01)<br>Lower among males: $t_k$ = -.14 (01) | HAPP 1.1 | $t_k$ | - | | 01 | See above | VEROF 62<br>p. 196 |
| MARITAL TENSION | 13-item index of closed questions on marital problems concerning time spent with friends, how the house looks, household expenses, being tired, being away from home too much, disciplining children, in-laws, not showing love, work, how to spend leisure time, work around the house, religion, irritating personal habits, other | | HAPP 1.1 | G' | -.22 | Gt' | 01 | Males in the age of 25-49, 4 small communities, Illinois, U.S.A.<br>Probability multi-stage samples<br>N: 393, date: March, 1962 | BRADB 65/1<br>p. 37 |
| | | Index of Positive Affects: G' = +.04 (ns)<br>Index of Negative Affects: G' = +.43 (01) | AFF 2.3 | G' | - | Gt' | | | |
| MARITAL TENSION | 11-item index of yes/no questions on differences in opinion or problems concerning time spent with friends, household expenses, being tired, being away from home too much, disciplining children, in-laws, not showing love, your (husband's) job, how to spend leisure time, religion, irritating personal habits | Stronger among females: G = -.32<br>Lower among males: G = -.16<br>Index of Positive Affects:<br>Stronger among males: G = +.10<br>Not among females: G = +.00<br>Index of Negative Affects:<br>Slightly stronger among females: G = +.43<br>Lower among males: G = +.37<br>Unaffected by S.E.S.<br>(to be continued on next page) | AFF 2.3 | G | - | | | Adults, urban areas, U.S.A.<br>Probability area samples<br>N: 2787, date: January, 1963 - January, 1964 | BRADB 69<br>p. 164 |

| | | | | | | | | | |
|---|---|---|---|---|---|---|---|---|---|
| | | Stronger among females : G = -.37<br>Lower among males : G = -.25 | HAPP 1.1 | G | - | | | | |
| MARRIAGE COMPANIONSHIP | 5-item index of yes/no questions, on shared activities in the past few weeks: spent an evening just chatting with each other, had a good laugh together or shared a joke, been affectionate toward each other, taken a drive or gone for a walk just for pleasure, did something that the other one particularly appreciated | Lower among males : G = +.17<br>Stronger among females : G = +.29<br>Index of Positive Affects: $\overline{DR}$ = +.13 (05)<br>Stronger among females: G = +.33<br>Lower among males: G = +.22<br>Lower among males of high S.E.S. only: $\overline{DR}$ = +.04 (ns)<br>Index of Negative Affects:<br>Stronger among females: G = -.12<br>Lower among males: G = -.03 | AFF 2.3 | G | + | | | Adults, urban areas, U.S.A.<br>(See last page) | BRADB 69<br>p. 166 |
| | | Lower among males: G = +.20<br>Stronger among females: G = +.28 | HAPP 1.1 | G | + | | | | |
| MARRIAGE SOCIABILITY | 4-item index of yes/no questions on shared activities in the past few weeks: visited friends together; gone out together to a movie, bowling, sporting event or some other entertainment; entertained friends in your home; ate out in a restaurant together | Unaffected by sex<br>males: G = +.12<br>females: G = +.16<br>Index of Positive Affects: $\overline{DR}$ = +.11 (05)<br>Stronger among females: G = +.25<br>Lower among males: G = +.16<br>Stronger among females of high S.E.S. only: $\overline{DR}$ = +.20 (05)<br>Index of Negative Affects<br>males: G = -.02<br>females: G = +.00 | AFF 2.3 | G | + | | | See above | BRADB 69<br>p. 168 |
| | | Unaffected by sex<br>males: G = +.14<br>females: G = +.18 | HAPP 1.1 | G | + | | | | |
| FREQUENCY OF GOING OUT EVENINGS WITH SPOUSE | 2 or fewer evenings a month vs more | 33% of the very satisfied and satisfied and 40% of the relatively dissatisfied women go out 2 or fewer evenings a month with their husband.<br>Among the men 29% of the very satisfied, 37% of the satisfied and 39% of the relatively dissatisfied report going out 2 or fewer evenings a month with their wives. | HAPP 2.1 | D% | + | | s | Middle-aged, middle class married couples, U.S.A.<br>Non-probability accidental sample of couples<br>N: 416, date: 1952 - 1953 | ROSE 55<br>p. 17 |
| DESIRED INTERACTION WITH HUSBAND | 3-item index of closed questions on would enjoy seeing him every day, would spend most of my free time with him if possible, would like to see him more often | Computed for married females only | HAPP 1.1 | r | +.29 | | 004 | Females from the Seattle- Washington area, U.S.A.<br>Non-probability chunk sample<br>N: 153, date: — | BRIM 74<br>p. 437 |
| PERCEIVED ASSISTANCE FROM HUSBAND | 3-item index of closed questions on would ask him for the loan of a sizable amount of money if I were in serious need, would ask him to risk personal danger to help me out of a tight spot, would ask him to pick me up at the airport late at night if there were no other means of transportation available | See above | HAPP 1.1 | r | +.14 | | ns | See above | BRIM 74<br>p. 437 |
| CONCERN FOR HUSBAND | Closed question: Try to always remember his birthday | See above | HAPP 1.1 | r | +.07 | | ns | See above | BRIM 74<br>p. 437 |
| VALUE SIMILARITY WITH HUSBAND | 3-item index of closed questions on generally share the same philosophy of life with him, his ideals most nearly approach my ideals of 'the right way', have a great many interests in common with him | See above | HAPP 1.1 | r | +.42 | | 002 | See above | BRIM 74<br>p. 437 |

| | | | | | | | | | |
|---|---|---|---|---|---|---|---|---|---|
| SATISFACTION WITH LOVE LIFE | Closed question rated on an open graphic scale ranging from 'very dissatisfied' to 'very satisfied' | Lower for those of age 41-50 and 61-65<br>Stronger among those of low S.E.S.<br>No relation among those of high educational level<br>Unaffected by sex | HAPP 1.1 | G | +.70 | | 05 | National adult population, The Netherlands<br>Probability area sample<br>N: 1552, date: June, 1968 | BAKKE 74<br>p. 28 |
| SATISFACTION WITH SEX LIFE | Closed question: 'How do you feel about . . .' terrible / unhappy / mostly dissatisfied / mixed / mostly satisfied / pleased / delighted | | HAPP 3.1<br>(1st instr.) | $h^2$ | .40 | | | National adult population, U.S.A.<br>Probability area sample (third sample)<br>N: 1072, date: November, 1972 | ANDRE 74<br>p. 19 |

## M 2.5 - VARIOUS FACTORS CONCERNING MARRIAGE

| | | | | | | | | | |
|---|---|---|---|---|---|---|---|---|---|
| LEVEL OF ATTACHMENT TO MALE PARTNER | Closed question: recently terminated relationships / apparently not dating / won't marry present beau / will possibly marry present beau / will fairly certain marry present beau / engaged / married | Females who are certain of getting married, who are engaged, or who are married are generally happier than the females who are not (05). | AFF 2.1 | DM | + | $F^+$ | ns | Female college seniors, U.S.A.<br>Non-probability chunk sample<br>N: 162, date: May - June, 1966 | PORTE 67<br>p. 58 |
| AGE OF MARRIAGE | Under the age of 20 vs later | 20% of the relatively dissatisfied women and 6% of the satisfied women married under the age of 20 (sign.).<br>No relationship among men | HAPP 2.1 | D% | + | | | Middle-aged, middle class married couples, U.S.A.<br>Non-probability accidental sample of couples<br>N: 416, date: 1952 - 1953 | ROSE 55<br>p. 16 |
| AGE OF MARRIAGE | Under the age of 30 vs later | 12% of the dissatisfied and 7% of the satisfied women married at 30 years of age or later (ns)<br>No relationship among men | HAPP 2.1 | D% | - | | | See above | ROSE 55<br>p. 16 |
| DISSATISFACTION WITH AGE OF MARRIAGE | Wish to have been a little older / younger wher got married | 48% of the dissatisfied women and only 14% of the satisfied women wish to have got married when younger or older (sign.).<br>Among males 15% of the dissatisfied and 9% of the satisfied wish they had been a little older when chey got married (sign.). No difference in the proportion of males saying they wish they had married at a younger age. | HAPP 2.1 | D% | - | | | See above | ROSE 55<br>p. 16 |

# N 1 NATION



## N 1.1 - ATTITUDES TOWARDS THE NATION

see also 'Satisfaction with Nation' (S 1.3), and 'Politics' (P 3)

### N 1.1.1 - ATTITUDES TOWARDS THE NATION IN GENERAL

| | | | | | | | | | |
|---|---|---|---|---|---|---|---|---|---|
| POSITIVE EVALUATION OF PRESENT NATIONAL SITUATION | Closed question rated on an 11-point self-anchoring scale:<br>'Suppose your greatest hopes for (name of country) are at the top, your worst fears at the bottom. Where would you put (name of country) on the ladder at the present time?' | For self-anchoring scale see instrument in excerpt (Part II).<br>Stronger in countries were political changes took place recently (p. 223). | HAPP 3.1 | $r_s$ | +.55 | | 05 | Adult population 5 Westernized nations, 3 underdeveloped giants, 2 countries of the Middle East, 3 Caribbean nations and the Philippines<br>Representative samples<br>N: 18,653, date ± 1960. | CANTR 65/1<br>p. 184 |
| POSITIVE EVALUATION OF PRESENT NATIONAL SITUATION | See above | | HAPP 3.1 | $r_s$ | +.08 | | | National adult population, U.S.A.<br>Probability sample<br>N: 1549, date: ± 1960 | CANTR 65/1<br>p. 233 |
| POSITIVE EVALUATION OF PRESENT NATIONAL SITUATION | See above | | HAPP 3.1 | $r_s$ | +.28 | | | National adult population, Dominican Republic<br>Probability samples<br>N: 814, date: ± 1960 | CANTR 65/1<br>p. 233 |
| POSITIVE EVALUATION OF PRESENT NATIONAL SITUATION | See above | | HAPP 3.1 | $r_s$ | +.18 | | | National adult population, Panama<br>Probability sample, proportionally poststratified by dwelling and mortality<br>N: 642, date: ± 1960 | CANTR 65/1<br>p. 233 |
| POSITIVE EVALUATION OF PRESENT NATIONAL SITUATION | See above | | HAPP 3.1 | $r_s$ | +.38 | | | National adult population, Cuba<br>Probability area sample<br>N: 992, date: ± 1960 | CANTR 65/1<br>p. 233 |
| POSITIVE EVALUATION OF PRESENT NATIONAL SITUATION | See above | | HAPP 3.1 | $r_s$ | +.15 | | | National adult population, Brazil<br>Probability samples<br>N: 2168, date: ± 1960 | CANTR 65/1<br>p. 233 |
| POSITIVE EVALUATION OF PRESENT NATIONAL SITUATION | See above | | HAPP 3.1 | $r_s$ | +.30 | | | National population, W.Germany<br>Probability area sample<br>N: 480, date: ± 1960 | CANTR 65/1<br>p. 233 |

| | | | | | | | | | |
|---|---|---|---|---|---|---|---|---|---|
| POSITIVE EVALUATION OF PRESENT NATIONAL SITUATION | See last page | | HAPP 3.1 | $r_s$ | +.21 | | | National adult population, Yugoslavia<br>Probability sample<br>N: 1523, date: ± 1960 | CANTR 65/1<br>p. 233 |
| POSITIVE EVALUATION OF PRESENT NATIONAL SITUATION | See above | | HAPP 3.1 | $r_s$ | +.14 | | | National population, Egypt<br>Non-probability accidental sample, proportionally poststratified by dwelling<br>N: 499, date: ± 1960 | CANTR 65/1<br>p. 233 |
| POSITIVE EVALUATION OF PRESENT NATIONAL SITUATION | See above | | HAPP 3.1 | $r_s$ | +.12 | | | National population, Israel<br>Probability sample<br>N: 1170, date: ± 1960 | CANTR 65/1<br>p. 233 |
| POSITIVE EVALUATION OF PRESENT NATIONAL SITUATION | See above | | HAPP 3.1 | $r_s$ | +.16 | | | Members of kibbutzim, Israel<br>Non-probability purposive quota sample<br>N: 300, date: ± 1960 | CANTR 65/1<br>p. 233 |
| POSITIVE EVALUATION OF PRESENT NATIONAL SITUATION | See above | | HAPP 3.1 | $r_s$ | +.40 | | | National adult population, Nigeria<br>Probability sample, proportionally stratified by dwelling and region<br>N: 1200, date: ± 1960 | CANTR 65/1<br>p. 233 |
| POSITIVE EVALUATION OF PRESENT NATIONAL SITUATION | See above | | HAPP 3.1 | $r_s$ | +.30 | | | National population, India<br>Probability sample, proportionally poststratified by dwelling<br>N: 2366, date: 1958 | CANTR 65/1<br>p. 233 |
| POSITIVE EVALUATION OF PRESENT NATIONAL SITUATION | See above | | HAPP 3.1 | $r_s$ | +.31 | | | National adult population, Japan<br>Probability sample<br>N: 972, date: ± 1960 | CANTR 65/1<br>p. 233 |
| POSITIVE EVALUATION OF PRESENT NATIONAL SITUATION | See above | | HAPP 3.1 | $r_s$ | +.13 | | | National adult population, The Philippines<br>Probability sample, proportionally poststratified by dwelling<br>N: 500, date: ± 1960 | CANTR 65/1<br>p. 233 |
| POSITIVE EVALUATION OF PRESENT NATIONAL SITUATION | Closed question rated on an 11-point self-anchoring scale, based on Cantril (see above under CANTR 65/1) | | HAPP 2.1<br>HAPP 3.1<br>CON 1.1 | r<br>r<br>r | +.18<br>+.12<br>+.16 | | | National adult population, U.S.A.<br>Cantril (1965) modified probability sample<br>N: 1406, date: 1959 | BORTN 70<br>p. 44 |
| POSITIVE EVALUATION OF NATIONAL SITUATION 5 YEARS AGO | Closed question on 'where did the United States stand 5 years ago', rated on an 11-point self-anchoring scale | | HAPP 2.1<br>HAPP 3.1<br>CON 1.1 | r<br>r<br>r | +.13<br>+.09<br>+.12 | | | See above | BORTN 70<br>p. 44 |
| POSITIVE EXPECTATIONS OF NATIONAL SITUATION 5 YEARS FROM NOW | Closed question on 'where do you think the United States will be on the ladder 5 years from now?', rated on an 11-point self-anchoring scale | | HAPP 2.1<br>HAPP 3.1<br>CON 1.1 | r<br>r<br>r | +.15<br>+.10<br>+.10 | | | See above | BORTN 70<br>p. 44 |
| PERCEIVED IMPROVEMENT IN NATIONAL SITUATION DURING PAST 5 YEARS | Difference in ladder ratings:<br>Evaluation of present national situation minus evaluation of national situation 5 years ago (see above) | | HAPP 2.1<br>HAPP 3.1<br>CON 1.1 | r<br>r<br>r | +.05<br>+.02<br>+.04 | | | See above | BORTN 70<br>p. 44 |
| EXPECTED IMPROVEMENT IN NATIONAL SITUATION DURING NEXT 5 YEARS | Difference in ladder ratings:<br>Expectation of national situation 5 years from now minus evaluation of present national situation | | HAPP 2.1<br>HAPP 3.1<br>CON 1.1 | r<br>r<br>r | +.03<br>+.00<br>+.00 | | | See above | BORTN 70<br>p. 44 |

| | | | | | | | | |
|---|---|---|---|---|---|---|---|---|
| POSITIVE EVALUATION OF GENERAL SITUATION OF ISRAEL | Closed question | HAPP 1.1<br>AFF 1.1 | mc<br>mc | +.36<br>+.39 | | | Urban adult Jewish population, Israel<br>Probability area sample, using dwelling units<br>N: 1830, date: summer, 1973 | LEVY 75/2<br>p. 373 |

## N 1.1.2 - ATTITUDES TOWARDS THE GOVERNMENT

| | | | | | | | | |
|---|---|---|---|---|---|---|---|---|
| TRUST IN GOVERNMENT | 3-item index of closed questions on waste of tax money by government, trust in government, and smartness of government (see Robinson et al., 1969) | COMP 1.2 | $r_{pm}$ | +.23 | | 001 | Public highschool boys, U.S.A.<br>Probability multi-stage sample<br>N: 2213 in 1966, 1886 in 1968 and 1799 in 1969, date: fall, 1966, spring, 1968 and spring, 1969 | BACHM 67/70<br>p. 243 |
| POSITIVE EVALUATION OF THE WAY THE GOVERNMENT HANDLES ECONOMIC PROBLEMS | Closed question ranging from 'not at all good' to 'very good' | HAPP 1.1<br>AFF 1.1 | mc<br>mc | +.11<br>+.11 | | | Urban adult Jewish population, Israel<br>Probability area sample, using dwelling units<br>N: 1940, date: spring, 1973 | LEVY 75/1<br>p. 372 |
| POSITIVE EVALUATION OF THE WAY THE GOVERNMENT HANDLES ECONOMIC PROBLEMS | Closed question | HAPP 1.1<br>AFF 1.1 | mc<br>mc | +.12<br>+.07 | | | Urban adult Jewish population, Israel<br>Probability area sample, using dwelling units<br>N: 1830, date: summer, 1973 | LEVY 75/2<br>p. 373 |
| POSITIVE EVALUATION OF THE WAY THE GOVERNMENT HANDLES IMMIGRATION PROBLEMS | Closed question ranging from 'not at all successfully' to 'very successfully' | HAPP 1.1<br>AFF 1.1 | mc<br>mc | +.07<br>-.04 | | | Urban adult Jewish population, Israel<br>Probability area sample, using dwelling units<br>N: 1940, date: spring, 1973 | LEVY 75/1<br>p. 372 |
| POSITIVE EVALUATION OF WHAT THE GOVERNMENT IS DOING FOR THE ECONOMICALLY DEPRIVED TO IMPROVE THEIR CONDITION | Closed question ranging from 'much less than necessary' to 'much more than is necessary' | HAPP 1.1<br>AFF 1.1 | mc<br>mc | +.09<br>+.05 | | | See above | LEVY 75/1<br>p. 372 |
| POSITIVE EVALUATION OF WHAT THE GOVERNMENT IS DOING TO EXPLAIN ITS DECISIONS | Closed question ranging from 'government is doing almost nothing' to 'very much' | HAPP 1.1<br>AFF 1.1 | mc<br>mc | -.00<br>-.07 | | | See above | LEVY 75/1<br>p. 372 |
| POSITIVE EVALUATION OF THE WAY THE GOVERNMENT HANDLES CURRENT PROBLEMS | Closed question | HAPP 1.1<br>AFF 1.1 | mc<br>mc | +.20<br>+.12 | | | Urban adult Jewish population, Israel<br>Probability area sample, using dwelling units<br>N: 1830, date: summer, 1973 | LEVY 75/2<br>p. 373 |
| POSITIVE EVALUATION OF THE WAY THE GOVERNMENT HANDLES SECURITY PROBLEMS | Closed question | HAPP 1.1<br>AFF 1.1 | mc<br>mc | +.09<br>+.10 | | | See above | LEVY 75/2<br>p. 373 |
| POSITIVE EVALUATION OF THE WAY THE HEALTH MIN. HANDLES HEALTH PROBLEMS | Closed question | HAPP 1.1<br>AFF 1.1 | mc<br>mc | +.13<br>+.04 | | | See above | LEVY 75/2<br>p. 373 |

## N 1.1.3 - OTHER SPECIFIC ATTITUDES

| | | | | | | | | |
|---|---|---|---|---|---|---|---|---|
| POSITIVE EVALUATION OF CURRENT LABOR RELATIONS BETWEEN EMPLOYERS AND EMPLOYEES IN THE COUNTRY | Closed question ranging from 'not at all good' to 'very good' | HAPP 1.1<br>AFF 1.1 | mc<br>mc | +.06<br>+.03 | | | Urban adult Jewish population, Israel<br>Probability area sample, using dwelling units<br>N: 1940, date: spring, 1973 | LEVY 75/1<br>p. 372 |

| | | | | | | | | | |
|---|---|---|---|---|---|---|---|---|---|
| POSITIVE EVALUATION OF THE CONDITION OF NEW IMMIGRANTS IN THE PAST 12 MONTHS | Closed question ranging from 'not at all good' to 'very good' | | HAPP 1.1<br>AFF 1.1 | mc<br>mc | +.07<br>-.07 | | | Urban adult Jewish population, Israel<br>(See last page) | LEVY 75/1<br>p. 372 |
| POSITIVE EVALUATION OF RELATIONS BETWEEN NEW IM-MIGRANTS AND VETERANS AT THE MOMENT | Closed question ranging from 'not at all good' to 'very good' | | HAPP 1.1<br>AFF 1.1 | mc<br>mc | +.06<br>+.03 | | | See above | LEVY 75/1<br>p. 372 |
| POSITIVE EVALUATION OF SECURITY SITUATION OF ISRAEL | Closed question | | HAPP 1.1<br>AFF 1.1 | mc<br>mc | +.20<br>+.25 | | | Urban adult Jewish population, Israel<br>Probability area sample, using dwelling units<br>N: 1830, date: summer, 1973 | LEVY 75/2<br>p. 373 |
| POSITIVE EVALUATION OF EMPLOYER-WORKER RELATIONS | Closed question | | HAPP 1.1<br>AFF 1.1 | mc<br>mc | +.14<br>+.10 | | | See above | LEVY 75/2<br>p. 373 |
| POSITIVE EVALUATION OF ETHNIC RELATIONS | Closed question | | HAPP 1.1<br>AFF 1.1 | mc<br>mc | +.22<br>+.12 | | | See above | LEVY 75/2<br>p. 373 |
| POSITIVE EVALUATION OF ETHNIC INTEGRATION IN THE COUNTRY | Closed question | | HAPP 1.1<br>AFF 1.1 | mc<br>mc | +.06<br>-.07 | | | See above | LEVY 75/2<br>p. 373 |

## N I.2 - CONDITION OF THE NATION

| | | | | | | | | | |
|---|---|---|---|---|---|---|---|---|---|
| SOCIO-ECONOMIC DEVELOPMENT | Index containing:<br>- general welfare: GNP per capita, and number of doctors per 10,000 persons<br>- communications: number of vehicles, telephones, radios, and newspaper circulation, per 1000 persons<br>- industrialization: energy consumption per capita, and percentage of the economically active population in the non-agricultural sectors<br>- urbanization: percentage of the population in cities over 100,000<br>- education: percentage of the population literate, and primary school enrollment ratio | The mean happiness rating for each of the countries was correlated with the index of development.<br>L-shaped curve: stronger among unhappy Ss | HAPP 3.1 | $r_s$ | +.67 | | 01 | Adult populations 5 Westernized nations, 3 underdeveloped giants, 2 countries in the Middle East, 3 Caribbean nations and the Philippines.<br>Representative samples<br>N: 18.653, date: ± 1960 | CANTR 65/1<br>p. 194 |
| ECONOMIC PROSPERITY OF THE COUNTRY | Inhabitants of Puerto Rico vs inhabitants of highest income areas in the U.S.A. | Analysis on the basis of a comparison with data from Bradburn & Caplovitz (BRADB 65 - data) | HAPP 1.1 | G' | +.44 | Gt' | 01 | National adult population, Puerto Rico<br>Probability simple random sample<br>N: 1417, date: November, 1963 - January, 1964 + August - October, 1964 | MATLI 66<br>p. 5 |
| LIVING IN A PERIOD OF NATIONAL CRISIS | Comparison of data from March, 1962 with the data from October, 1962, during the Cuban crisis (Resp. BRADB 65/1 and BRADB 65/2 - data; see excerpts, Part II) | Unaffected by worrying about the crisis<br>Computed for the Index of Positive Affects only: G'= -.23 (01)<br>Stronger among Ss who were worrying about the crisis.<br>No relationship with the Index of Negative Affects | HAPP 1.1<br>AFF 2.3 | G'<br>G' | +.13<br>- | Gt'<br>Gt' | 05 | Inhabitants of 4 small communities, Illinois, U.S.A.<br>Probability multi-stage samples<br>N: 547, date: October, 1962 | BRADB 65/2<br>p. 82-85 |

# P 1 PERSONALITY

see also 'Self-image' (S 2)
'Mental health' (H 2.3)
'Affect' (A 2)

P 1.1 Locus of control

P 1.2 Coping capacity (Effectiveness) . . . . . . . . . see also P 1.8.1, H 2.3, S 2, T 1.1, C 1, P 5

P 1.3 Defensiveness

P 1.4 Stages of personality development
- 1.4.1 – Erikson's stages of psycho-social development
- 1.4.2 – Other indicators of personality development

P 1.5 Needs . . . . . . . . . . . . . . . . . . . . . . see also C 2, H 3, V 1
- 1.5.1 – Achievement motivation . . . . . . . . . . . . see also S 1.8, S 2.2, G 1.2, W 2.9
- 1.5.2 – Need for social approval
- 1.5.3 – Desire for excitement
- 1.5.4 – Desire for social participation . . . . . . . . see S 4, esp. S 4.5
- 1.5.5 – Various needs

P 1.6 Tendency to react positively

P 1.7 Morality . . . . . . . . . . . . . . . . . . . . see also A 2.2.8, A 2.2.13, V 1

P 1.8 Personality traits concerning interpersonal functioning . . . . . . . . . . . . . . . . . . see also S 4, P 4, S 2.2, T 2
- 1.8.1 – Interpersonal capability
- 1.8.2 – Trust in people
- 1.8.3 – Influence
- 1.8.4 – Various traits concerning interpersonal functioning

P 1.9 Various personality traits

## P 1.1 - LOCUS OF CONTROL

| | | | | | | | | | |
|---|---|---|---|---|---|---|---|---|---|
| INTERNAL CONTROL | Index containing four pairs of statements, e.g. 'some of the good and some of the bad things in my life have happened by chance' (external control). 'What's happened to me has been my own doing' (internal control).<br>Each S was asked which one of each pair is more true for him.<br>(from the Internal-External Control of Reinforcement Scale; see Jessor et al. (1968) | Unaffected by sex and age | HAPP 3.1 | r | +.16 | | | People of 46 and older, Duke, U.S.A.<br>Probability systematic random sample, stratified by age and sex<br>N: 502, date: 1968 | PALMO 72<br>p. 70 |
| INTERNAL CONTROL EXPECTATION | 4-item index of forced choice questions measuring the respondent's expectations concerning personal control over the events of one's life (items from the Rotter Internal vs External Locus of Control Scale; see Rotter, 1966) | In 1972: Affect balance: r = +.29 (001)<br>Positive affect: r = +.21 (001)<br>Negative affect: r = -.21 (001)<br>In 1973: Affect Balance: r = +.28 (001)<br>Positive affect: r = +.27 (001)<br>Negative affect: r = -.15 (001) | AFF 2.3 | $r_{pm}$ | + | | 001 | Adults, Los Angeles County, U.S.A.<br>Multi-stage probability samples of households<br>N: 1078 in 1972 and 1008 in 1973<br>date: spring, 1972 and spring, 1973 | CHERL 75<br>p. 197 |
| EXTERNAL LOCUS OF CONTROL | 23-item index<br>(Internal vs External Locus of Control Scale; see Rotter, 1966) | | AFF 3.1<br>HAPP 3.1 | $r_{pm}$<br>$r_{pm}$ | -.31<br>-.13 | | 05<br>ns | Undergraduate students, U.S.A.<br>Non-probability chunk sample<br>N: 67, date: summer, 1970 | GORMA 71<br>p. 215-218 |
| EXTERNAL LOCUS OF CONTROL | Items from the Rotter I-E Scale, measuring a belief concerning felt mastery over the course of one's life (see Mirels, 1970) | | AFF 3.1<br>HAPP 3.1 | $r_{pm}$<br>$r_{pm}$ | -.23<br>-.08 | | ns<br>ns | See above | GORMA 71<br>p. 215-218 |
| INTERNAL CONTROL | 12-item index<br>(items from Rotter's I-E Scale; see Rotter, 1966) | | COMP 1.2 | $r_{pm}$ | +.17 | | 001 | Public high school boys, U.S.A.<br>Probability multi-stage sample<br>N: 2213 in 1966, 1886 in 1968 and 1799 in 1969<br>date: fall, 1966; spring, 1968 and spring, 1969 | BACHM 67/70<br>p. 243 |
| OTHER DIRECTEDNESS | 36-item index<br>(I-O Social Preference Scale; see Karrarjian, 1962) | | HAPP 1.1 | $r_{pm}$ | -.16 | t | 05 | Male undergraduates, U.S.A.<br>Non-probability chunk sample<br>N: 103, date: ± 1967 | HEERE 69<br>p. 22 |
| INDEPENDENCE OF JUDGEMENT | 9-item index<br>(Independence of Judgement Scale; see Barron, 1965) | | HAPP 1.1 | $r_{pm}$ | | t | ns | See above | HEERE 69<br>p. 22 |

| Concept | Measure | Remarks | Indicator | Statistic | Value | Test | Sig. | Population / sample | Source |
|---|---|---|---|---|---|---|---|---|---|
| **ABILITY TO DO THINGS ONESELF TO INCREASE SATISFACTION** | Closed question rated on an 11-point self-anchoring scale: 'To what extent do you feel there is a good deal you can do yourself to make your life happier and more satisfying than it is, as contrasted to the feeling that there isn't very much you can do about it yourself?' | | HAPP 3.1<br>HAPP 2.1<br>CON 1.1 | $r_{pm}$<br>$r_{pm}$<br>$r_{pm}$ | +.29<br>+.35<br>+.25 | | | National adult population, U.S.A.<br>Probability sample<br>N: 1549, date: 1959 | CANTR 65/2<br>p. 268/415 |
| EFFICACY | Closed question rated on an 11-point self-anchoring scale (see above) | | HAPP 2.1<br>HAPP 3.1<br>CON 1.1 | r<br>r<br>r | +.35<br>+.28<br>+.27 | | | National adult population, U.S.A.<br>Cantril (1965) modified probability sample<br>N: 1406, date: 1959 | BORTN 70<br>p. 44 |
| INNER DIRECTEDNESS (tendency to be guided mainly by personal rather than external considerations) | 127-item Inner Directedness Scale (from Shostrom's Personal Orientation Inventory; see Shostrom, 1964) | | AFF 2.1 | $r_{pm}$ | +.19 | | ns | Married females, U.S.A.<br>Non-probability purposive sample by expert choice<br>N: 62, date: — | HARDE 69<br>p. 50 |

## P 1.2 - COPING CAPACITY (EFFECTIVENESS)

see also 'Interpersonal Capability' (P 1.8.1), 'Mental Health' (H 2.3), 'Self-Image' (S 2), 'Time Competence' (T 1.1), 'Cognition' (C 1), 'Problems, Worries and Fears' (P 5)

| Concept | Measure | Remarks | Indicator | Statistic | Value | Test | Sig. | Population / sample | Source |
|---|---|---|---|---|---|---|---|---|---|
| IDENTITY INTEGRITY | Composite clinical rank order on identity diffusion vs identity integrity, measuring continuity vs discontinuity of past, present and future; integration vs lack of integration in interpersonal and work relationships; integration vs lack of integration of the total personality; and effectiveness vs ineffectiveness in self-definition and achievement of ends | The criteria were largely based on Erikson's discussion of identity.<br>(See also under 'Erikson's Stages of Psychosocial Development'; Part III, P 1.4.1) | AFF 3.1 | $r_{pm}$ | +.66 | t | 05 | Male college students, U.S.A.<br>Non-probability chunk sample<br>N: 17, date: ± 1960 | WESSM 66/2<br>p. 124 |
| PSYCHOLOGICAL RESOURCES (positive mental health) | 14 indicators of psychological resources including measures of mutuality (familial and extra-familial), resolution of losses, contextual and temporal perspective, growth, competence, insight, perceived and judged encroachments, hope, and satisfaction with intrapersonal and interpersonal competence in general. | Indicators of both psychological resources and psychological deficits were developed and correlated with well-being and affect. The correlations concerning psychological deficits, and deficits and resources combined, were presented under 'Mental Health' (Part III, H 2.3.1) . | | | | | | People in transition, U.S.A.<br>Stratified random sample<br>N: 216, date: — | CHIRI 71<br>p. 603 |
| | | In total, significant correlations were found between two indicators of resources and psychological well-being. | HAPP 1.1 | r | + | | | | |
| | | There were four significant or near-significant correlations with positive affect, four with negative affect (including two inverse relationships), and eight with affect balance. | AFF 2.3 | r | + | | | | |
| RESOLUTION AND FORTITUDE | Content analysis of interview records by 2 independent judges (component of the Life Satisfaction Rating).<br>5-point scale:<br>5. Try and try again attitude. Active personal responsibility, takes the bad and the good and makes the most of it.<br>4. Can take life as it comes. Has no complaint of the way life has treated him. Assumes responsibility readily.<br>3. Has ups and downs. Shows a trace of extrapunitiveness or intropunitiveness concerning his difficulties in life.<br>2. Feels he hasn't done better because he has not gotten the breaks. Has worked hard but feels he never got anywhere. | See remarks in excerpt (Part II). | CON 1.4<br>COMP 1.4 | r<br>r | +.70<br>+.48 | | | White adult population of age 50+, Kansas City, U.S.A.<br>Stratified probability sample and non-probability quota sample<br>N: 177, date: — | NEUGA 61<br>p. 139 |

(to be continued on next page)

| | | | | | | | | | |
|---|---|---|---|---|---|---|---|---|---|
| | 1. Talks of hard knocks which he has not mastered (extrapunitive). Blames self a great deal (intropunitive). Feels helpless; overwhelmed by life. | | | | | | | | |
| ROLE RELATED PLANNING ABILITIES (ability to conceptualize goals and the instrumental tasks necessary to their accomplishment and ability to maintain a judicious balance among the various roles). | Rating by psychiatrists on the basis of observations during 6 years | Index of Positive Affects: r = +.29 (01)<br>Non-significant relationship with the Index of Negative Affects. | AFF 2.3 | $r_{pm}$ | + | | | Residents of Stirling County, Maritime, Canada<br>Probability sample stratified by sex, age, socio-environmental circumstances and mental health<br>N: 112, date: 1963-1968 | BEISE 74<br>p. 325 |

## SUBJECTIVE INDICATORS

| | | | | | | | | | |
|---|---|---|---|---|---|---|---|---|---|
| PROJECTIVE HELPLESSNESS | Score from told stories to the Standard Thematic Apperception Test cards (see Murray, 1943), indicative of feeling or being helpless, feeling weak or ineffectual, being dominated, dependent | | AFF 3.1 | $r_{pm}$ | -.56 | t | 05 | Male college students, U.S.A.<br>Non-probability chunk sample<br>N: 17, date: ± 1960 | WESSM 66/2<br>p. 120 |
| TENDING TO BE A DISCOURAGED PERSON | Direct agree / disagree statement | Unaffected by sex<br>When standardized on:<br>- usual mood : $G_s$ = -.59<br>- having fun in life : $G_s$ = -.47<br>- frequency of low mood : $G_s$ = -.57<br>- tending to be a lonely person: $G_s$ = -.53<br>- anxiety symptoms : $G_s$ = -.63 | HAPP 1.1 | G<br>V | -.67<br>.35 | $Chi^2$ | 01 | Juniors and seniors attending public high schools, New York State, U.S.A.<br>Probability cluster sample of 10 public high schools<br>N: sample A: 1682, sample B: 1664, date: 1960 | BRENN 70<br>p. 71/75/265 |
| | | Unaffected by sex | AFF 1.1 | G<br>V | -.56<br>.29 | $Chi^2$ | 01 | | |
| SUBJECTIVE ADAPTATION TO CHANGE | Question on coping with death of one of both parents, or separation of parents during childhood<br>very bad / rather bad / so-so / rather well / very well | Computed for those who reported death or separation of parents before the age of 20. | HAPP 1.1 | G | +.36 | | ns | National adult population, The Netherlands<br>Probability area sample<br>N: 1552, date: June, 1968 | BAKKE 74<br>p. 28 |

## P 1.3 - DEFENSIVENESS

| | | | | | | | | | |
|---|---|---|---|---|---|---|---|---|---|
| **DEFENSE MECHANISMS:** | Inventory containing 10 stories, dealing with the following conflict areas: authority, independence, masculinity (male form), femininity (female form), competition and situational.<br>After reading each story each S was asked to respond to four questions corresponding to four types of behavior evoked by the situation described in the story:<br>- proposed actual behavior<br>- impulsive behavior (in fantasy)<br>- thoughts<br>- feelings<br>Five responses are provided for each question, each response representing one of five defense mechanisms (see next page) | Correlations were presented for males only. These are reported in the next columns. Among females no relationships were found. | | | | | | Undergraduates, U.S.A.<br>Non-probability chunk sample<br>N: 55, date: — | CLUM 73<br>p. 509 |

| | | | | | | | | | |
|---|---|---|---|---|---|---|---|---|---|
| | Each S marked a plus for the response most representative for his reaction and a minus for the one least representative. (Defense Mechanism Inventory; see Gleser & Ihilevich, 1969) | | | | | | | | |
| TURNING AGAINST OTHERS: | Defenses that deal with conflict through attacking a real or presumed external frustrating object (Turning against Object cluster). | | | | | | | Undergraduates, U.S.A. (See last page) | CLUM 73 p. 509 |
| - ACTION BEHAVIOR | | | AFF 3.1 | r | -.33 | | ns | | |
| - FANTASY BEHAVIOR | | | AFF 3.1 | r | -.40 | | ns | | |
| - THOUGHT BEHAVIOR | | | AFF 3.1 | r | -.44 | | 05 | | |
| - AFFECT | | | AFF 3.1 | r | -.29 | | ns | | |
| - SUMSCORE | | Among females there was a tendency for the defence turning against others to be negatively related to hedonic level. | AFF 3.1 | r | -.57 | | 01 | | |
| PROJECTION: | Defenses which justify the expression of aggression towards an external object through first attributing negative intent or characteristics to it (Projection cluster) | | | | | | | See above | CLUM 73 p. 509 |
| - ACTION BEHAVIOR | | | AFF 3.1 | r | +.01 | | ns | | |
| - FANTASY BEHAVIOR | | | AFF 3.1 | r | +.05 | | ns | | |
| - THOUGHT BEHAVIOR | | | AFF 3.1 | r | -.40 | | ns | | |
| - AFFECT | | | AFF 3.1 | r | -.10 | | ns | | |
| - SUMSCORE | | | AFF 3.1 | r | -.21 | | ns | | |
| INTELLECTUALIZATION: | Defenses that deal with conflict through invoking a general principle that 'splits off' affect from content and represses the former; e.g. intellectualization, isolation, rationalization (Principalization cluster) | | | | | | | See above | CLUM 73 p. 509 |
| - ACTION BEHAVIOR | | | AFF 3.1 | r | +.33 | | ns | | |
| - FANTASY BEHAVIOR | | | AFF 3.1 | r | +.20 | | ns | | |
| - THOUGHT BEHAVIOR | | | AFF 3.1 | r | +.47 | | 05 | | |
| - AFFECT | | | AFF 3.1 | r | +.04 | | ns | | |
| - SUMSCORE | | | AFF 3.1 | | +.43 | | 05 | | |
| TURNING AGAINST SELF: | Defenses that deal with conflict through directing aggressive behavior towards S himself; e.g. masochism and autosadism (Turning against Self cluster) | | | | | | | See above | CLUM 73 p. 509 |
| - ACTION BEHAVIOR | | | AFF 3.1 | r | -.21 | | ns | | |
| - FANTASY BEHAVIOR | | | AFF 3.1 | r | -.22 | | ns | | |
| - THOUGHT BEHAVIOR | | | AFF 3.1 | r | -.13 | | ns | | |
| - AFFECT | | | AFF 3.1 | r | -.24 | | ns | | |
| - SUMSCORE | | | AFF 3.1 | r | -.28 | | ns | | |

| | | | | | | | | | |
|---|---|---|---|---|---|---|---|---|---|
| REVERSAL | Defenses that deal with conflict by responding in a positive or neutral fashion to a frustrating object which might be expected to evoke a negative reaction, e.g. negation, denial, reaction formation, and repression (Reversal cluster) | | | | | | | Undergraduates, U.S.A. (See last page) | CLUM 73 p. 509 |
| - ACTION BEHAVIOR | | | AFF 3.1 | r | -.10 | | ns | | |
| - FANTASY BEHAVIOR | | | AFF 3.1 | r | +.37 | | ns | | |
| - THOUGHT BEHAVIOR | | | AFF 3.1 | r | +.59 | | 01 | | |
| - AFFECT | | | AFF 3.1 | r | +.43 | | 05 | | |
| - SUMSCORE | | | AFF 3.1 | r | +.55 | | 01 | | |
| REPRESSION | 20-item index referring to denial of hostility towards significant others, avoidance of tension-producing activities, avoidance of recall of past events, etc. (DPI Repression Scale; see Jackson & Messick, 1964) | | AFF 3.1<br>HAPP 3.1 | $r_{pm}$<br>$r_{pm}$ | -.05<br>-.08 | | ns<br>ns | Undergraduate students, U.S.A. Non-probability chunk sample N: 67, date: summer 1970 | GORMA 71 p. 215/219 |
| GENERAL REPRESSION AND DENIAL OF UNPLEASANT AND DISTURBING AFFECTS | Clinical rank order on the basis of general clinical experience with the subjects and observation of their behavior and reactions to experimental situations | This rank was made one year before hedonic level was assessed | AFF 3.1 | $r_{pm}$ | -.01 | t | ns | Male college students, U.S.A. Non-probability chunk sample N: 17, date: ± 1960 | WESSM 66/2 p. 104 |
| SUPPRESSIVITY AND CONCEALMENT OF EMOTIONS | See above | See above | AFF 3.1 | $r_{pm}$ | +.42 | t | ns | See above | WESSM 66/2 p. 105 |

## P 1.4 - STAGES OF PERSONALITY DEVELOPMENT

### P 1.4.1 - ERIKSON'S STAGES OF PSYCHO-SOCIAL DEVELOPMENT

| | | | | | | | | | |
|---|---|---|---|---|---|---|---|---|---|
| PSYCHO-SOCIAL STAGES OF DEVELOPMENT: | 60-item Q sort, describing characteristics indicative of successful and unsuccessful resolutions of the first six developmental crises of Erikson's stages of psycho-social development (see Erikson, 1959)<br>The Q sort was filled out both in very elated and in very depressed moods for self-concept ('an accurate picture of yourself as you honestly feel and believe you are') | There were 5 items indicative of successful and 5 items indicative of unsuccessful resolution for each of the six stages. The subject was instructed to fit the set of items into a forced, seminormal distribution on a 7-point scale ranging from 'least characteristic' to 'most characteristic'.<br>In the next columns the upper correlations concern psycho-social development as assessed in elation, and the lower as assessed in depression. | | | | | | Male college students, U.S.A. Non-probability chunk sample N: 17, date: ± 1960 | WESSM 66/2 p. 107-109 |
| - SUCCESSFUL ORAL SENSORY: BASIC TRUST | Placid and untroubled / accessible to new ideas / imperturbable optimist / able to take things as they come / deep, unshakable faith in himself | | AFF 3.1 | $r_{pm}$<br>$r_{pm}$ | +.21<br>+.44 | t<br>t | ns<br>ns | | |

| | | | | | | | | | |
|---|---|---|---|---|---|---|---|---|---|
| - UNSUCCESSFUL ORAL SENSORY: BASIC MISTRUST | Incapable of absorbing frustration and everything frustrates him / can't share things with anybody / pessimistic, little hope / dim nostalgia for lost paradise / never gets what he really wants | | AFF 3.1 | $r_{pm}$<br>$r_{pm}$ | -.56<br>-.86 | t<br>t | 05<br>05 | | |
| - SUCCESSFUL MUSCULAR ANAL: AUTONOMY | Values independence above security / free and spontaneous / stands on his own two feet / quietly goes his own way / good judge of when to comply and when to assert himself | | AFF 3.1 | $r_{pm}$<br>$r_{pm}$ | +.03<br>+.50 | t<br>t | ns<br>05 | | |
| - UNSUCCESSFUL MUSCULAR ANAL: SHAME AND DOUBT | An automatic response to all situations / meticulous and over-organized / cautious, hesitant, doubting / feels as if he were being followed / always in the wrong, apologetic | | AFF 3.1 | $r_{pm}$<br>$r_{pm}$ | -.45<br>-.74 | t<br>t | ns<br>05 | | |
| - SUCCESSFUL LOCOMOTOR GENITAL: INITIATIVE | Adventuresome / dynamic / ambitious / inventive, delights in finding new solutions to new problems / sexually aware | | AFF 3.1 | $r_{pm}$<br>$r_{pm}$ | +.63<br>+.66 | t<br>t | 05<br>05 | | |
| - UNSUCCESSFUL LOCOMOTOR GENITAL: GUILT | Sexually blunted / afraid of impotence / thinks too much about the wrong things / big smoke but no fire / inhibited and self-restricted | | AFF 3.1 | $r_{pm}$<br>$r_{pm}$ | -.28<br>-.39 | t<br>t | ns<br>ns | | |
| - SUCCESSFUL LATENCY: INDUSTRY | Conscientious and hard working / interested in learning and likes to study / serious, has high standards / accomplishes much, truly productive/ excels in his work | | AFF 3.1 | $r_{pm}$<br>$r_{pm}$ | +.62<br>+.48 | t<br>t | 05<br>05 | | |
| - UNSUCCESSFUL LATENCY: INFERIORITY | Can't fulfill his ambitions / doesn't apply himself fully / fritters away his time / ineffective, doesn't amount to much / a playboy, always 'hacking' around | | AFF 3.1 | $r_{pm}$<br>$r_{pm}$ | -.56<br>-.62 | t<br>t | 05<br>05 | | |
| - SUCCESSFUL PUBERTY AND ADOLESCENCE: IDENTITY | Confidence is brimming over / natural and genuine / poised / knows who he is and what he wants out of life / pride in his own character and values | | AFF 3.1 | $r_{pm}$<br>$r_{pm}$ | +.42<br>+.54 | t<br>t | ns<br>05 | | |
| - UNSUCCESSFUL PUBERTY AND ADOLESCENCE: ROLE DIFFUSION | A poseur, all facade and pretence / spreads himself thin / attempts to appear at ease / never knows how he feels / afraid of commitment | | AFF 3.1 | $r_{pm}$<br>$r_{pm}$ | -.26<br>-.23 | t<br>t | ns<br>ns | | |
| - SUCCESSFUL YOUNG ADULTHOOD: INTIMACY | Candid, not afraid to expose himself / warm and friendly / has sympathetic concern for others / tactful in interpersonal relations / comfortable in intimate relationships | | AFF 3.1 | $r_{pm}$<br>$r_{pm}$ | +.67<br>+.69 | t<br>t | 05<br>05 | | |
| - UNSUCCESSFUL YOUNG ADULTHOOD: ISOLATION | Little regard for the rest of the world / preoccupied with himself / very lonely / cold and remote / secretly oblivious of the opinions of others | | AFF 3.1 | $r_{pm}$<br>$r_{pm}$ | -.71<br>-.66 | t<br>t | 05<br>05 | | |
| PSYCHO-SOCIAL DEVELOPMENT | Analysis of individual items from a 60-item Q sort, filled out both in very elated and in very depressed moods for both self-concept ('an accurate picture of yourself as you honestly feel and believe you are') and ideal-concept ('the picture of the sort of person you have hoped to become or fancied yourself to be') (see above) | The unhappy men were more concerned, in both their real-self and ideal-self, with Erikson's fourth developmental crisis Industry vs Inferiority, while the happy men were more concerned with the sixth stage Intimacy vs Isolation. (See also 'Congruency between Real and Ideal Self-Image', and 'Content of Self-Image'; Part III, S 2.1.1 and S 2.2) | AFF 3.1 | $r_{pm}$ | + | t | 05 | Male college students, U.S.A. (see last page) | WESSM 66/2 p. 112-113 |

| | | | | | | | | | |
|---|---|---|---|---|---|---|---|---|---|
| PSYCHO-SOCIAL DEVELOPMENT: | 60-item inventory describing characteristics indicative of successful and unsuccessful resolutions of the first six developmental crises of Erikson's stages of psycho-social development (adapted from Wessman & Ricks; see last pages) | Analysis on the basis of the 16 most happy and 16 least happy Ss in each of the 8 sex/class groups (N = 256)<br>The same items as in the Wessman & Ricks study were used. In this study each item was rated on a 7-point scale ranging from 'definitely most uncharacteristic of you' to 'definitely most characteristic of you'<br>Significance and elaboration were based on Analysis of Variance | | | | | | Undergraduate college students, U.S.A.<br>Non-probability chunk sample<br>N: 952, date: March, 1965 | CONST 65<br>p. 52-57 |
| - SUCCESSFUL FIRST STAGE: BASIC TRUST | | Unaffected by sex and stage of study | AFF 2.1 | DM | + | | 01 | | |
| - UNSUCCESSFUL FIRST STAGE: BASIC MISTRUST | | Lower in junior years, esp. among males<br>In senior years stronger among females | AFF 2.1 | DM | - | | 01 | | |
| - SUCCESSFUL SECOND STAGE: AUTONOMY | | Slightly negative among males<br>Slightly positive among females | AFF 2.1 | DM | | | ns | | |
| - UNSUCCESSFUL SECOND STAGE: SHAME AND DOUBT | | Stronger among females than among males<br>Unaffected by stage of study | AFF 2.1 | DM | - | | 01 | | |
| - SUCCESSFUL THIRD STAGE: INITIATIVE | | Unaffected by sex and stage of study | AFF 2.1 | DM | + | | 01 | | |
| - UNSUCCESSFUL THIRD STAGE: GUILT | | Among males stronger in freshman years<br>Among females strongest in senior years and lowest in junior years | AFF 2.1 | DM | - | | 01 | | |
| - SUCCESSFUL FOURTH STAGE: INDUSTRY | | Unaffected by sex and stage of study | AFF 2.1 | DM | + | | 01 | | |
| - UNSUCCESSFUL FOURTH STAGE: INFERIORITY | | Unaffected by sex and stage of study | AFF 2.1 | DM | - | | 01 | | |
| - SUCCESSFUL FIFTH STAGE: IDENTITY | | Among males strongest in sophomore years and lowest in senior years<br>Among females stronger in senior years | AFF 2.1 | DM | + | | 01 | | |
| - UNSUCCESSFUL FIFTH STAGE: IDENTITY DIFFUSION | | Unaffected by sex and stage of study | AFF 2.1 | DM | - | | 01 | | |
| - SUCCESSFUL SIXTH STAGE: INTIMACY | | Unaffected by sex and stage of study | AFF 2.1 | DM | + | | 01 | | |
| - UNSUCCESSFUL SIXTH STAGE: ISOLATION | | Unaffected by sex and stage of study | AFF 2.1 | DM | - | | 01 | | |
| PSYCHO-SOCIAL DEVELOPMENT: | 60-item Inventory of Psycho-Social Development (see above) | These data concern students from the Constantinople (1965) sample (see above).<br>In this analysis N = 581. | | | | | | Undergraduate college students, U.S.A.<br>Non-probability chunk sample<br>N: 581, date: March, 1965 | CONST 70<br>p. 10 |
| - SUCCESSFUL FIRST STAGE: BASIC TRUST | | Freshman males : r = +.34 (01)<br>Senior males : r = +.48 (01)<br>Freshman females: r = +.33 (01)<br>Senior females : r = +.43 (01) | AFF 2.1 | r | + | | | | |

| | | | | | | | | |
|---|---|---|---|---|---|---|---|---|
| - UNSUCCESSFUL FIRST STAGE: BASIC MISTRUST | | Freshman males : r = -.37 (01)<br>Senior males : r = -.58 (01)<br>Freshman females: r = -.21 (01)<br>Senior females : r = -.42 (01) | AFF 2.1 | r | - | | | |
| - SUCCESSFUL SECOND STAGE: AUTONOMY | | Freshman males : r = +.12 (ns)<br>Senior males : r = +.18 (05)<br>Freshman females: r = +.10 (ns)<br>Senior females : r = +.12 (ns) | AFF 2.1 | r | + | | | |
| - UNSUCCESSFUL SECOND STAGE: SHAME AND DOUBT | | Freshman males : r = -.10 (ns)<br>Senior males : r = -.21 (05)<br>Freshman females: r = -.07 (ns)<br>Senior females : r = -.25 (01) | AFF 2.1 | r | - | | | |
| - SUCCESSFUL THIRD STAGE: INITIATIVE | | Freshman males : r = +.19 (05)<br>Senior males : r = +.38 (01)<br>Freshman females: r = +.36 (01)<br>Senior females : r = +.24 (01) | AFF 2.1 | r | + | | | |
| - UNSUCCESSFUL THIRD STAGE: GUILT | | Freshman males : r = -.32 (01)<br>Senior males : r = -.46 (01)<br>Freshman females: r = -.18 (05)<br>Senior females : r = -.24 (01) | AFF 2.1 | r | - | | | |
| - SUCCESSFUL FOURTH STAGE: INDUSTRY | | Freshman males : r = +.14 (ns)<br>Senior males : r = +.25 (01)<br>Freshman females: r = +.09 (ns)<br>Senior females : r = +.16 (ns) | AFF 2.1 | r | + | | | |
| - UNSUCCESSFUL FOURTH STAGE: INFERIORITY | | Freshman males : r = -.13 (ns)<br>Senior males : r = -.21 (05)<br>Freshman females: r = -.15 (ns)<br>Senior females : r = -.23 (01) | AFF 2.1 | r | - | | | |
| - SUCCESSFUL FIFTH STAGE: IDENTITY | | Freshman males : r = +.18 (05)<br>Senior males : r = +.48 (01)<br>Freshman females: r = +.35 (01)<br>Senior females : r = +.42 (01) | AFF 2.1 | r | + | | | |
| - UNSUCCESSFUL FIFTH STAGE: IDENTITY DIFFUSION | | Freshman males : r = -.12 (ns)<br>Senior males : r = -.10 (ns)<br>Freshman females: r = -.01 (ns)<br>Senior females : r = -.21 (05) | AFF 2.1 | r | - | | | |
| - SUCCESSFUL SIXTH STAGE: INTIMACY | | Freshman males : r = +.14 (ns)<br>Senior males : r = +.39 (01)<br>Freshman females: r = +.19 (05)<br>Senior females : r = +.20 (05) | AFF 2.1 | r | + | | | |
| - UNSUCCESSFUL SIXTH STAGE: ISOLATION | | Freshman males : r = -.22 (01)<br>Senior males : r = -.36 (01)<br>Freshman females; r = -.27 (01)<br>Senior females : r = -.36 (01) | AFF 2.1 | r | - | | | |

## P 1.4.2 - OTHER INDICATORS OF PERSONALITY DEVELOPMENT

| Indicator | Measure | Comments | Code | Stat. | Value | Test | Sig. | Sample | Source |
|---|---|---|---|---|---|---|---|---|---|
| PSYCHO-SEXUAL STAGES OF DEVELOPMENT: | Composite clinical rank order on symptomatic characteristics indicative of degree of fixation at or regression to the various psycho-sexual stages | | | | | | | Male college students, U.S.A.<br>Non-probability chunk sample<br>N: 17, date: $\pm$1960 | WESSM 66/2<br>p. 124 |
| - ORAL RECEPTIVE | | | AFF 3.1 | $r_{pm}$ | | t | ns | | |
| - ORAL AGGRESSIVE | | | AFF 3.1 | $r_{pm}$ | | t | ns | | |
| - ANAL EXPULSIVE | | | AFF 3.1 | $r_{pm}$ | | t | ns | | |
| - ANAL RETENTIVE | | | AFF 3.1 | $r_{pm}$ | -.44 | t | 10 | | |
| - URETHRAL ICARIAN | | | AFF 3.1 | $r_{pm}$ | | t | ns | | |
| PERSONAL MATURITY AND INTEGRATION | Composite clinical rank order ranging from 'most neurotic, regressed, disintegrated' to 'most secure, mature, integrated' | | AFF 3.1 | $r_{pm}$ | +.59 | t | 05 | See above | WESSM 66/2<br>p. 124 |
| SELF-ACTUALIZATION | Rating by judges, using a form listing 15 qualities drawn from Maslow's (1954) description of the characteristics of the self-actualizing person | | AFF 2.1 | $r_{pm}$ | +.28 | | 05 | Married females, U.S.A.<br>Non-probability purposive sample by expert choice<br>N: 62, date: — | HARDE 69<br>p. 50 |
| SELF-PERCEIVED CREATIVITY AND MATURITY | 2-item index of direct questions on creativity and personality maturity compared with others | The subjects answered these questions at the end of an experimental situation in which their self-esteem was experimentally altered. This was done by means of a false personality report dealing with the subject's creativity, maturity and other things.<br>These questions formed a check on the acceptance of the personality report.<br>Correlation with self-perceived creativity : $r_{pm}$ = +.05 (ns)<br>Correlation with self-perceived maturity : $r_{pm}$ = +.17 (ns)<br>Unaffected by self-esteem<br>For happy Ss self-perceived creativity and maturity is unaffected by bolstered self-esteem and decreased by reduced self-esteem.<br>For unhappy Ss it is increased by bolstered self-esteem and unaffected by reduced self-esteem. | AFF 6 | F | + | | ns | Female undergraduates, U.S.A.<br>Random sample<br>N: 72, date: — | LUDWI 71/75<br>p. 64/207 |

## P 1.5 - NEEDS

see also 'Concerns, Interests' (C 2), 'Hopes, Aspirations & Goals' (H 3), 'Values' (V 1)

## P 1.5.1 - ACHIEVEMENT MOTIVATION

see also 'Satisfaction with Socio-Economic Level' (S 1.8) and 'Content of Self-Image' (S 2.2) for indicators of Achievement motivation among women see also 'Gender-role attitudes' (G 1.2) and 'Reasons for having a job' (W 2.9).

| | | | | | | | | |
|---|---|---|---|---|---|---|---|---|
| DESIRE TO EXCEL AT PERFORMANCES IN WHICH THE PERSON HAS HIS CHIEF INTEREST (whether of work, play or otherwise) | Class-master rating on a 7-point scale on the basis of observation | | AFF 5.3 | $r_{pm}$ | +.53 | | | Schoolboys, England<br>Non-probability chunk sample<br>N: 140, date: 1912 - 1913 | WEBB 15<br>p. 27 |
| DESIRE TO EXCEL AT PERFORMANCES IN WHICH THE PERSON HAS HIS CHIEF INTEREST (whether of work, play or otherwise) | Trained peer rating on a 7-point scale on the basis of observation | | AFF 5.2 | $r_{pm}$ | +.20 | | | Male students, England<br>Non-probability chunk sample<br>N: 194, date: 1912 - 1913 | WEBB 15<br>p. 26 |
| STATUS OF OCCUPATIONAL ASPIRATIONS | Open question on 'What sort of work do you think you might do for a living?', coded and converted to the Duncan socio-economic status index (see Reiss, 1961) | | COMP 1.2 | $r_{pm}$ | +.06 | | ns | Public high school boys, U.S.A.<br>Probability multi-stage sample<br>N: 2213 in 1966, 1886 in 1968, and 1799 in 1969<br>date: fall 1966, spring 1968, and spring 1969 | BACHM 67/70<br>p. 247 |
| AMBITIOUS JOB ATTITUDE | 13-item index of closed questions indicating preferences for 'a job that doesn't bug me' (no one to boss me, don't have to work too hard, not much responsibility, high prestige, etc.) and preference for 'a job that pays off' (learning new things, good chances for getting ahead, good pay, using one's skills, etc.) | Preference for 'a job that pays off' was related to happiness : r = +.21 (001)<br>Preference for 'a job that doesn't bug me' was unrelated to happiness: r = -.05 (ns) | COMP 1.2 | $r_{pm}$ | +.16 | | 001 | See above | BACHM 67/70<br>p. 243 |
| DESIRE FOR LONGER SCHOOLING | | Among women 76% of the relatively dissatisfied believe that further schooling would be desirable, whereas this is true of only 61% of the very satisfied.<br>Among men the comparable figures are 73% and 55% respectively | HAPP 2.1 | D% | - | | s | Middle-aged, middle class married couples, U.S.A.<br>Non-probability accidental sample of couples<br>N: 416, date: 1952 - 1953 | ROSE 55<br>p. 17 |
| THINKING OFTEN ABOUT GETTING AHEAD | Closed question: not at all / sometimes / often; during last week | Gammas computed on the basis of proportions 'often' answers<br>Among those of high S.E.S.: G' = -.06 (ns)<br>Among those of low S.E.S. : G' = +.01 (ns) | HAPP 1.1 | G' | - | Gt' | ns | Inhabitants of 4 small communities, Illinois, U.S.A.<br>Probability multi-stage samples<br>N: 2006, date: March, 1962 | BRADB 65/1<br>p. 54 |
| SATISFACTION WITH NEXT YEAR'S PLANS IN TERMS OF ACHIEVEMENT NEEDS | Closed question on 'the extent to which one's present plans for further education, career, or job fulfill her need to achieve, to fully utilize her capacities', rated on a 7-point scale ranging from 'highly unsatisfactory' to 'highly satisfactory' | | AFF 2.1 | $r_{pm}$ | +.17 | | 05 | Female college seniors, U.S.A.<br>Non-probability chunk sample<br>N: 162, date: May - June, 1966 | PORTE 67<br>p. 101 |

## P 1.5.2 - NEED FOR SOCIAL APPROVAL

| | | | | | | | | |
|---|---|---|---|---|---|---|---|---|
| NEED FOR SOCIAL APPROVAL | 10-item index of the true / false statements, such as: 'I never hesitate to go out of my way to help someone in trouble' and 'There have been times when I feel like rebelling against people in authority'<br>(shortened Social Desirability scale; see Crowne & Marlowe, 1964) | | HAPP 1.1 | G' | +.24 | Gt' | 01 | Adults in the New England and Mid-Atlantic States, U.S.A.<br>Probability cluster sample<br>N: 404, date: — | PHILL 72<br>p. 929 |

| | | | | | | | | | |
|---|---|---|---|---|---|---|---|---|---|
| NEED FOR SOCIAL APPROVAL | Marlowe - Crowne Social Desirability Scale (see Crowne & Marlowe, 1964) | | AFF 2.1 | $r_{pm}$ | +.24 | | ns | Married females, U.S.A.<br>Non-probability purposive sample by expert choice<br>N: 62, date: — | HARDE 69<br>p. 50 |
| SOCIAL DESIRABILITY | 33-item index (Marlowe - Crowne Social Desirability Scale; see Crowne & Marlowe, 1964) | | AFF 3.1<br>HAPP 3.1 | $r_{pm}$<br>$r_{pm}$ | +.14<br>-.07 | | ns<br>ns | Undergraduate college students, U.S.A.<br>Non-probability chunk sample<br>N: 67, date: summer, 1970 | GORMA 71<br>p. 215/218 |
| NEED FOR SOCIAL APPROVAL | 33-item index of true / false statements (Social Desirability Scale; see Crowne & Marlowe, 1964) | | HAPP 1.1 | $r_{pm}$ | +.28 | t | 005 | Male undergraduates, U.S.A.<br>Non-probability chunk sample<br>N: 103, date: ± 1967 | HEERE 69<br>p. 27 |
| NEED FOR SOCIAL APPROVAL | 31-item index of true / false statements (Social Desirability Scale; see Crowne & Marlowe, 1964) | | COMP 1.2 | $r_{pm}$ | +.28 | | 001 | Public high school boys, U.S.A.<br>Probability multi-stage sample<br>N: 2213 in 1966, 1886 in 1968 and 1799 in 1969<br>date: fall, 1966, spring, 1968 and spring, 1969 | BACHM 67/70<br>p. 242 |
| CARING ABOUT WHAT OTHER PEOPLE THINK ABOUT YOU OR WHAT YOU DO | Closed question: no vs yes | | HAPP 1.1 | G' | -.15 | Gt' | 01 | National adult population, U.S.A.<br>Non-probability quota sample<br>N: 2377, date: February, 1946 | WESSM 56<br>p. 203 |
| SENSITIVITY TO CRITICISM | 3-item index of closed questions on sensitivity to criticism, being hurt by criticism, feeling disturbed when laughed at or blamed | When standardized on social class: $G_s = -.22$ | HAPP 1.1<br><br>AFF 1.1 | G<br>V<br>G<br>V | -.23<br>.12<br>-.19<br>.11 | <br>$Chi^2$<br><br>$Chi^2$ | <br>01<br><br>01 | Juniors and seniors attending public high schools in New York State, U.S.A.<br>Probability cluster sample of 10 public high schools<br>N: sample A: 1682, sample B: 1664, date: 1960 | BRENN 70<br>p. 94/179/302 |
| DESIRE TO BE LIKED BY HIS ASSOCIATES | Class-master rating on a 7-point scale on the basis of observation | | AFF 5.3 | $r_{pm}$ | +.45 | | | Schoolboys, England<br>Non-probability chunk sample<br>N: 140, date: 1912 - 1913 | WEBB 15<br>p. 27 |
| DESIRE TO BE LIKED BY HIS ASSOCIATES | Trained peer rating on a 7-point scale on the basis of observation | | AFF 5.2 | $r_{pm}$ | +.38 | | | Male students, England<br>Non-probability chunk sample<br>N: 194, date: 1912 - 1913 | WEBB 15<br>p. 26 |
| EAGERNESS FOR ADMIRATION | Class-master rating on a 7-point scale on the basis of observation | | AFF 5.3 | $r_{pm}$ | +.46 | | | Schoolboys, England<br>Non-probability chunk sample<br>N: 140, date: 1912 - 1913 | WEBB 15<br>p. 27 |
| EAGERNESS FOR ADMIRATION | Trained peer rating on a 7-point scale on the basis of observation | | AFF 5.2 | $r_{pm}$ | +.12 | | | Male students, England<br>Non-probability chunk sample<br>N: 194, date: 1912 - 1913 | WEBB 15<br>p. 26 |

## P 1.5.3 - DESIRE FOR EXCITEMENT

| | | | | | | | | | |
|---|---|---|---|---|---|---|---|---|---|
| DESIRE FOR EXCITEMENT | Score, calculated by multiplying ratings of desire to engage in each of 75 activities by ratings of the extent of excitement associated with the relevant activities. (DX-test; see Jackson & Lyons, 1969) | | AFF 3.1 | r | +.07 | | ns | University students, U.S.A.<br>Probability sample<br>N: 45, date: — | LUDWI 70<br>p. 173 |
| EXCITEMENT | Repeated closed question on to what extent one felt like doing exciting things during the day, rated each night on a 4-point scale for at least 20 days | Analysis on the basis of the mean rating | AFF 3.1 | r | -.16 | | ns | See above | LUDWI 70<br>p. 173 |

| | | | | | | | | | |
|---|---|---|---|---|---|---|---|---|---|
| TRANQUILLITY | Repeated closed question on to what extent one feels like doing calm and tranquil things during the day, rated each night on a 4-point scale for at least 20 days | Analysis on the basis of the mean rating | AFF 3.1 | r | +.16 | | ns | University students, U.S.A. (see last page) | LUDWI 70 p. 173 |
| DESIRE FOR EXCITEMENT | Behavioral choice of which of three roles Ss would play in a scene to be videotaped for possible use in campus lectures on expressive behavior. One of these roles was a lead part, an other was a supportive role, and the third was a minor part. | The subjects answered this question (and the next questions; see below) in an experimental situation right after their self-esteem was experimentally altered. The relationship appeared to be unaffected by manipulated self-esteem. For both happy and unhappy Ss desire for excitement is unaffected by both bolstered and reduced self-esteem. Unaffected by manipulated perceived acting ability. | AFF 6 | $r_{pm}$ | +.32 | | 01 | Female undergraduates, U.S.A. Random sample N: 72, date: — | LUDWI 71/75 p. 32-33/64 |
| DESIRE FOR EXCITEMENT | Closed question on how much at this moment one feels like playing a lead role in a campus theatrical production | See above. Unaffected by manipulated self-esteem. For happy Ss desire for excitement is unaffected by both bolstered and reduced self-esteem. For unhappy Ss desire for excitement is increased by bolstered self-esteem, and unaffected by reduced self-esteem. Unaffected by manipulated perceived acting ability. | AFF 6 | $r_{pm}$ | +.35 | | 01 | See above | LUDWI 71/75 p. 33/64 |
| EXPECTED SUCCESS IN ACTING | Direct question on expected success in playing a lead role in a campus theatrical production | See above | AFF 6 | $r_{pm}$ | +.22 | | 10 | See above | LUDWI 71/75 p. 33/64 |
| EXCITEMENT IN ACTING | Direct question on the extent to which playing a lead role was perceived as exciting | See above | AFF 6 | $r_{pm}$ | +.37 | | 01 | See above | LUDWI 71/75 p. 64 |
| PERCEIVED ENJOYMENT IN ACTING | Direct question on the extent to which playing a lead role was perceived as enjoyable | See above | AFF 6 | $r_{pm}$ | +.46 | | 01 | See above | LUDWI 71/75 p. 33/64 |
| FEAR OF ACTING | Direct question on the extent to which playing a lead role was perceived as scary | See above | AFF 6 | $r_{pm}$ | -.16 | | ns | See above | LUDWI 71/75 p. 33/64 |
| DESIRE TO PARTICIPATE IN EXCITING ACTIVITIES | 6-item index of closed questions on whether at this moment one feels like engaging in activities which are characterized as exciting (+), relaxing (-), tranquil (-), or restful (-) (items from a 36-item Excitement Adjective Check-list). | See above. Unaffected by manipulated self-esteem. For happy Ss desire to participate is unaffected by bolstered self-esteem and increased by reduced self-esteem. For unhappy Ss desire to participate is unaffected by both reduced and bolstered self-esteem. Similar scores measuring desire for participation in risky activities, scary activities and challenging activities were composed. These scores were not related to hedonic level either. | AFF 6 | $r_{pm}$ | +.06 | | ns | See above | LUDWI 71/75 p. 34/64 |
| DESIRE FOR PARTICIPATION IN EXCITING ACTIVITIES | 4-item index of closed questions on whether at this moment one feels like being a lead actress in a play, dating with an attractive guy, driving a sports car, walking through a forest late at night ( see next page). (from the Activity Reaction Scale; see Jackson & Lyons, 1969) | See above. Unaffected by manipulated self-esteem. For both happy and unhappy Ss desire for participation is unaffected by both bolstered and reduced self-esteem. | AFF 6 | $r_{pm}$ | +.24 | | 05 | See above | LUDWI 71/75 p. 33/64 |

| | | | | | | | | | |
|---|---|---|---|---|---|---|---|---|---|
| DESIRE FOR PARTICIPATION IN SOCIAL EXCITING ACTIVITIES | 2-item index of closed questions on whether at this moment one feels like being a lead actress in a play and meeting an attractive guy for the first time and being asked out for a date (see last page). | See last page.<br>Affected by manipulated self-esteem (.10)<br>For happy Ss desire for participation is unaffected by both bolstered and reduced self-esteem.<br>For unhappy Ss desire for participation is unaffected by reduced self-esteem, and increased by bolstered self-esteem. | AFF 6 | $r_{pm}$ | +.30 | | 05 | Female undergraduates, U.S.A. (see last page) | LUDWI 71/75 p. 33/64 |
| DESIRE FOR PARTICIPATION IN NON-SOCIAL EXCITING ACTIVITIES | 2-item index of closed questions on whether at this moment one feels like driving a sports car as fast as it will go, and walking through a forest late at night by oneself. (see last page) | See above<br>Unaffected by manipulated self-esteem.<br>For both happy and unhappy Ss desire for participation is unaffected by both bolstered and reduced self-esteem. | AFF 6 | $r_{pm}$ | +.09 | | ns | See above | LUDWI 71/75 p. 34/66 |
| PERCEIVED EXCITEMENT IN EXCITING ACTIVITIES | 4-item index of exciting activities (see above), scored for 'how exciting does this activity seem to you right now?' | See above | AFF 6 | $r_{pm}$ | +.27 | | 05 | See above | LUDWI 71/75 p. 64 |
| PERCEIVED ENJOYMENT IN EXCITING ACTIVITIES | 4-item index of exciting activities (see above), scored for 'how enjoyable does this activity seem to you right now?' | See above | AFF 6 | $r_{pm}$ | +.33 | | 01 | See above | LUDWI 71/75 p. 64 |
| DESIRE FOR PARTICIPATION IN BORING ACTIVITIES | 4-item index of closed questions on whether at this moment one feels like sitting in the Rathskeller by oneself, being at a dull party, being in a slow moving academic discussion, and resting in bed (see below) (from the Activity Reaction Scale; see above) | See above<br>Unaffected by manipulated self-esteem.<br>For both happy and unhappy Ss desire for participation is unaffected by both bolstered and reduced self-esteem. | AFF 6 | $r_{pm}$ | | | ns | See above | LUDWI 71/75 p. 34 |
| DESIRE FOR PARTICIPATION IN SOCIAL BORING ACTIVITIES | 2-item index of closed questions on whether at this moment one feels like being at a dull party, and being at a slow moving academic discussion (see above) | See above<br>Unaffected by manipulated self-esteem | AFF 6 | $r_{pm}$ | | | ns | See above | LUDWI 71/75 p. 34 |
| DESIRE FOR PARTICIPATION IN NON-SOCIAL BORING ACTIVITIES | 2-item index of closed questions on whether at this moment one feels like sitting in the Rathskeller by oneself, and resting in bed (see above) | See above<br>Unaffected by manipulated self-esteem | AFF 6 | $r_{pm}$ | | | ns | See above | LUDWI 71/75 p. 34 |
| PERCEIVED BOREDOM IN BORING ACTIVITIES | 4-item index of boring activities (see above), scored for 'how boring does this activity seem to you right now?' | See above | AFF 6 | $r_{pm}$ | +.20 | | ns | See above | LUDWI 71/75 p. 64 |
| SENSATION SEEKING | Index containing forced-choice questions in which one choice in each item pair mentions a more prosaic, subdued activity, while the other choice mentions a novel, sensual, or active behavior.<br>The scale was scored for the number of active choices.<br>(Sensation-Seeking Scale; see Zuckerman et al., 1964) | | AFF 3.1<br>HAPP 3.1 | $r_{pm}$<br>$r_{pm}$ | +.28<br>+.18 | | 05<br>ns | Undergraduate students, U.S.A.<br>Non-probability chunk sample<br>N: 67, date: summer, 1970 | GORMA 71 p. 215/218 |
| EXTERNAL SENSATION SEEKING | Index containing exteroceptive activities, such as sports and exploration activities, scored for the number of activities S might prefer.<br>(External Sensation-Seeking Scale; see Pearson, 1970) | | AFF 3.1<br>HAPP 3.1 | $r_{pm}$<br>$r_{pm}$ | +.35<br>+.29 | | 01<br>05 | See above | GORMA 71 p. 215/216 |

| | | | | | | | | | |
|---|---|---|---|---|---|---|---|---|---|
| **INTERNAL SENSATION SEEKING** | Index containing interoceptive activities, such as fantasy and observation of bodily processes, scored for the number of activities S might prefer. (Internal Sensation-Seeking Scale; see Pearson, (1970). | | AFF 3.1<br>HAPP 3.1 | $r_{pm}$<br>$r_{pm}$ | +.33<br>+.13 | | 01<br>ns | Undergraduate students, U.S.A. (see last page) | GORMA 71 p. 215/216 |

## P 1.5.4 - DESIRE FOR SOCIAL PARTICIPATION

see 'Social Participation' (S 4), esp. 'Preferences with respect to Social Participation' (S 4.5)

## P 1.5.5 - VARIOUS NEEDS

| | | | | | | | | | |
|---|---|---|---|---|---|---|---|---|---|
| NEED FOR SELF-UTILIZATION | 9-item index containing closed questions on desiring to use one's skills (see Long, 1967) | | COMP 1.2 | $r_{pm}$ | +.29 | | 001 | Public high school boys, U.S.A.<br>Probability multi-stage sample<br>N: 2213 in 1966, 1886 in 1968 and 1799 in 1969<br>date: fall, 1966; spring, 1968 and spring, 1969 | BACHM 67/70 p. 242 |
| NEED FOR SELF-DEVELOPMENT | 15-item index containing closed questions on desiring to develop one's skills (see Long, 1967) | | COMP 1.2 | $r_{pm}$ | +.33 | | 001 | See above | BACHM 67/70 p. 242 |
| DESIRE TO IMPOSE HIS OWN WILL ON OTHERS (as opposed to tolerance) | Class-master rating on a 7-point scale on the basis of observation | | AFF 5.3 | $r_{pm}$ | +.36 | | | Schoolboys, England<br>Non-probability chunk sample<br>N: 140, date: 1912 - 1913 | WEBB 15 p. 27 |
| DESIRE TO IMPOSE HIS OWN WILL ON OTHER PEOPLE (as opposed to tolerance) | Trained peer rating on a 7-point scale on the basis of observation | | AFF 5.2 | $r_{pm}$ | +.17 | | | Male students, England<br>Non-probability chunk sample<br>N: 194, date: 1912 - 1913 | WEBB 15 p. 26 |

## P 1.6 - TENDENCY TO REACT POSITIVELY

| | | | | | | | | | |
|---|---|---|---|---|---|---|---|---|---|
| RECALLING PLEASANT ASSOCIATIONS IN CONNECTION WITH VERBAL STIMULI | Score based on the difference between the number of pleasant associations reported by each S, and the average number of pleasant associations reported by the whole sample on each of 5 lists of 50 stimulus words, using one series on each of 5 consecutive days.<br>Ss were asked: 'When I pronounce a word to you, observe what idea that word first calls to your mind, and report whether it is a pleasant or unpleasant idea. If it seems neither pleasant nor unpleasant, but indifferent, continue thinking until either a pleasant or unpleasant idea is suggested and report which it is'. | Analysis of the results strongly suggests the existence of a real positive correlation between exceeding or falling below the average number of pleasant associations and cheerfulness. | AFF 5.2 | | + | | | Female college students, U.S.A.<br>Non-probability chunk sample<br>N: 97, date: — | MORGA 19 p. 303-304 |
| RECALLING PLEASANT ASSOCIATIONS IN CONNECTION WITH VERBAL STIMULI | Total number of pleasant associations reported on 3 series of 50 stimulus words each, using one series on each of 3 consecutive days. (for question used, see above with MORGA 19) | | AFF 1.1<br>AFF 6 | G'<br>G' | +.57<br>+.52 | Gt'<br>Gt' | 05<br>05 | Female psychology students, U.S.A.<br>Non-probability chunk sample, poststratified by temperament<br>N: 67, date: — | WASHB 25 P. 455 |

| | | | | | | | | | |
|---|---|---|---|---|---|---|---|---|---|
| RECALLING PLEASANT ASSOCIATIONS IN CONNECTION WITH VERBAL STIMULI | Total number of pleasant associations reported on 3 series of 30 stimulus words each, using one series on each of 3 consecutive days (for question used, see last page with MORGA 19) | | AFF 6 | G' | +.55 | Gt' | 05 | Female psychology students, U.S.A.<br>Non-probability chunk sample, poststratified by temperament<br>N: 123, date: — | WASHB 26<br>p. 279 |
| PROMPTNESS OF PLEASANT ASSOCIATIONS IN CONNECTION WITH VERBAL STIMULI | Each S was given 5 stimulus words in succession with the instruction to recall an unpleasant associated personal experience; then 5 words with the instruction to recall a pleasant idea. When a word had suggested an (un)pleasant idea the S rapped on the table. The intervals between giving the word and the S's rap were measured by a stopwatch.<br>Sixty stimulus words were used, thirty each for the pleasant and unpleasant recalls. The average reaction time for the pleasant experiences was divided by the average reaction time for the unpleasant experiences. | The results offer some confirmation of the idea that there is a positive correlation between a cheerful temperament and especially slow recall of unpleasant ideas. | AFF 5.2 | | + | | | Female college students, U.S.A.<br>Non-probability chunk sample<br>N: 69, date: — | BAXTE 17<br>p. 156-157 |
| PROMPTNESS OF PLEASANT ASSOCIATIONS IN CONNECTION WITH VERBAL STIMULI | Average reaction time for unpleasant associations divided by the average reaction time for pleasant associations<br>3 series of stimulus words, each containing 6 groups of 5 words each were used, one series on each of 3 consecutive days<br>(for method used, see above) | | AFF 6 | G' | +.70 | Gt' | 05 | Female psychology students, U.S.A.<br>Non-probability chunk sample, poststratified by temperament<br>N: 123, date: — | WASHB 26<br>p. 279 |
| INCLINATION TO RECALL PLEASING WORDS | Ratio of pleasant and unpleasant words mentioned. Ss were required to write down pleasing and displeasing words. Conditions were arranged in such a way that it was equally possible to write down either pleasing or displeasing words | Correlation coëfficient was assessed by means of a scattergram using daily mood ratings and the percentage of recalled pleasant words on the same day (261 pairs of data were available) | AFF 3.1 | $r_{pm}$ | +.29 | | 04 | College students, U.S.A.<br>Non-probability chunk sample<br>N: 34, date: 1934 - 1935 | YOUNG 37B<br>p. 317 |
| BEING READILY PLEASED BY ODORS | Affective reaction test, employing a standard series of 14 odors, given for 9 consecutive days. Ss immediately reported for each odor 'I like it' or 'I dislike it' | The data also are presented in YOUNG 37A, p.331<br>When a scattergram was prepared, using daily mood ratings and affective reactions to odors on the same day (306 pairs of data): $r_{pm}$ = -.29 (03) | AFF 3.1 | $r_s$ | -.02 | | ns | See above | YOUNG 37B<br>p. 315 |

## P 1.7 - MORALITY

see also 'Types of Affect : Guilt' (A 2.2.8) and 'Personal Moral Judgment' (A 2.2.13); and 'Values' (V 1)

| | | | | | | | | | |
|---|---|---|---|---|---|---|---|---|---|
| ESTIMATE OF GENERAL EXCELLENCE OF CHARACTER | Class-master rating on a 7-point scale on the basis of observation | | AFF 5.3 | $r_{pm}$ | +.36 | | | Schoolboys, England<br>Non-probability chunk sample<br>N: 140, date: 1912 - 1913 | WEBB 15<br>p. 27 |
| 'FIRST IMPRESSION' ESTIMATES OF GENERAL EXCELLENCE OF CHARACTER | Estimate at a single short personal interview on a 7-point scale by two 3rd year students (school 1), the author and another member of the college staff (school 2 and 4), the author and a lady (school 3) | | AFF 5.3 | $r_{pm}$ | +.31 | | | See above | WEBB 15<br>p. 27 |
| ESTIMATE OF GENERAL EXCELLENCE OF CHARACTER | Trained peer rating on a 7-point scale on the basis of observation | | AFF 5.2 | $r_{pm}$ | +.19 | | | Male students, England<br>Non-probability chunk sample<br>N: 194, date: 1912 - 1913 | WEBB 15<br>p. 26 |
| ESTIMATE OF GENERAL EXCELLENCE OF CHARACTER BY LECTURERS | Rating on a 7-point scale on the basis of observation, by two staff-members | | AFF 5.2 | $r_{pm}$ | -.01 | | | See above | WEBB 15<br>p. 26 |

| | | | | | | | | | |
|---|---|---|---|---|---|---|---|---|---|
| TRUSTWORTHINESS (keeping his word or engagement, performing his believed duty) | Class-master rating on a 7-point scale on the basis of observation | | AFF 5.3 | $r_{pm}$ | +.18 | | | Schoolboys, England<br>Non-probability chunk sample<br>N: 140, date: 1912 - 1913 | WEBB 15<br>p. 27 |
| TRUSTWORTHINESS (keeping his word or engagement, performing his believed duty) | Trained peer rating on a 7-point scale on the basis of observation | | AFF 5.2 | $r_{pm}$ | +.07 | | | Male students, England<br>Non-probability chunk sample<br>N: 194, date: 1912 - 1913 | WEBB 15<br>p. 26 |
| CONSCIENTIOUSNESS (keenness of interest in the goodness and wickedness of actions) | Class-master rating on a 7-point scale on the basis of observation | | AFF 5.3 | $r_{pm}$ | +.19 | | | Schoolboys, England<br>Non-probability chunk sample<br>N: 140, date: 1912 - 1913 | WEBB 15<br>p. 27 |
| CONSCIENTIOUSNESS (keenness of interest in goodness and wickedness of actions) | Trained peer rating on a 7-point scale on the basis of observation | | AFF 5.2 | $r_{pm}$ | -.08 | | | Male students, England<br>Non-probability chunk sample<br>N: 194, date: 1912 - 1913 | WEBB 15<br>p. 26 |
| TENDENCY NOT TO ABANDON TASKS FROM MERE CHANGEABILITY | Class-master rating on a 7-point scale on the basis of observation | | AFF 5.3 | $r_{pm}$ | -.03 | | | Schoolboys, England<br>Non-probability chunk sample<br>N: 140, date: 1912 - 1913 | WEBB 15<br>p. 27 |
| TENDENCY NOT TO ABANDON TASKS FROM MERE CHANGEABILITY | Trained peer rating on a 7-point scale on the basis of observation | | AFF 5.2 | $r_{pm}$ | +.06 | | | Male students, England<br>Non-probability chunk sample<br>N: 194, date: 1912 - 1913 | WEBB 15<br>p. 26 |
| TENDENCY NOT TO ABANDON TASKS IN THE FACE OF OBSTACLES | Class-master rating on a 7-point scale on the basis of observation | | AFF 5.3 | $r_{pm}$ | +.40 | | | Schoolboys, England<br>Non-probability chunk sample<br>N: 140, date: 1912 - 1913 | WEBB 15<br>p. 27 |
| TENDENCY NOT TO ABANDON TASKS IN THE FACE OF OBSTACLES | Trained peer rating on a 7-point scale on the basis of observation | | AFF 5.2 | $r_{pm}$ | +.23 | | | Male students, England<br>Non-probability chunk sample<br>N: 194, date: 1912 - 1913 | WEBB 15<br>p. 26 |
| PURE-MINDEDNESS (extent to which he shuns telling or hearing stories of immoral meaning) | Trained peer rating on a 7-point scale on the basis of observation | | AFF 5.2 | $r_{pm}$ | -.19 | | | See above | WEBB 15<br>p. 26 |

## P 1.8 - PERSONALITY TRAITS CONCERNING INTERPERSONAL FUNCTIONING

see also 'Social Participation' (S 4), 'Popularity' (P 4), 'Content of Self-Image' (S 2.2), 'Institutional Living' (I 2)

### P 1.8.1 - INTERPERSONAL CAPABILITY

| | | | | | | | | | |
|---|---|---|---|---|---|---|---|---|---|
| EASE OF MAKING FRIENDS | Closed question: not very easy vs make friends easily | | HAPP 1.1 | G' | +.37 | Gt' | 01 | National adult population, U.S.A.<br>Non-probability quota sample<br>N: 2377, date: February, 1946 | WESSM 56<br>p. 202 |
| SUCCESS IN ACQUIRING FRIENDS | Closed question | | HAPP 1.1<br>AFF 1.1 | mc<br>mc | +.36<br>+.40 | | | Urban adult Jewish population, Israel<br>Probability area sample using dwelling units<br>N: 1830, date: summer, 1973 | LEVY 75/2<br>p. 373 |
| GETTING ON WELL WITH OTHER PEOPLE | Direct question rated on a graphic scale ranging from 'very bad' to 'very good' | Slightly lower among those of age 41 - 45<br>Lower among those of low S.E.S.<br>Stronger among those of lower education<br>Stronger among males than among females<br>Stronger among the unmarried | HAPP 1.1 | G | +.42 | | 05 | National adult population, The Netherlands<br>Probability area sample<br>N: 1552, date: June, 1968 | BAKKE 74<br>p. 27 |

| Variable | Measure | Remarks | Category | Stat. | Value | Test | Sig. | Population / sample | Source |
|---|---|---|---|---|---|---|---|---|---|
| SATISFACTION WITH HOW ONE GETS ON WITH PEOPLE | Closed question: 'How do you feel about. . ?' terrible / unhappy / mostly dissatisfied / mixed / mostly satisfied / pleased / delighted | Unaffected by sex | HAPP 3.1 (1st instr.) | $h^2$ | .31 | | | National adult population, U.S.A.<br>Probability area sample (first sample)<br>N: 1297, date: May, 1972 | ANDRE 74<br>p. 17 |
| NORMAL INTROVERSION (social participation) | Fusion factor indicative of social withdrawal or disturbed introversion (with shy, seclusive, submissive, guilty, depressed, masochistic personalities) vs social participation or normal extraversion (with poised, sociable, dominant, confident and spontaneous personalities)<br>(Fusion Factor A from the MMPI Scales; see Kassebaum et al., 1959) | Average hedonic level correlated significantly with a number of the MMPI scales. There were large negative correlations with most of the scales indicative of psychopathology.<br>Additional data were not presented. | AFF 3.1 | $r_{pm}$ | + | t | s | Male college students, U.S.A.<br>Non-probability chunk sample<br>N: 17, date: ± 1960 | WESSM 66/2<br>p. 116 |
| INTERPERSONAL REACTIVITY | Rating by psychiatrists on the basis of observation during 6 years.<br>High scores indicate emotional openness to others and ability to secure emotional support from them. | Index of Positive Affects: r = +.25 (01)<br>Index of Negative Affects: r = -.26 (01) | AFF 2.3 | $r_{pm}$ | + | | 01 | Residents of Stirling County, Maritime, Canada<br>Probability sample stratified by sex, age, socio-environmental circumstances and mental health<br>N: 112, date: 1963 - 1968 | BEISE 74<br>p. 325 |
| GIVING ONESELF EASILY | Direct question rated on a graphic scale, ranging from 'very difficult' to 'very easily' | | HAPP 1.1 | G | +.07 | | ns | National adult population, The Netherlands<br>Probability area sample<br>N: 1552, date: June, 1968 | BAKKE 74<br>p. 27 |
| DEGREE OF 'TACT' IN GETTING ON WITH PEOPLE | Trained peer rating on a 7 -point scale on the basis of observation | | AFF 5.2 | $r_{pm}$ | +.21 | | | Male students, England<br>Non-probability chunk sample<br>N: 194, date: 1912 - 1913 | WEBB 15<br>p. 26 |
| HAVING PROBLEMS WITH GETTING ALONG WITH OTHERS | Closed question | College students only<br>L - shaped curve : significant among happier students only | COMP 4.1 | | - | | | Students, U.S.A.<br>Non-probability quota sample<br>N: 1651, date: — | SYMON 37<br>p. 292 |
| TENDING TO BE A LONELY PERSON | Closed question: not lonely / fairly lonely / very lonely | Unaffected by sex<br>When standardized on:<br>- usual mood : $G_s$ = -.56<br>- having fun in life : $G_s$ = -.50<br>- frequency of low mood : $G_s$ = -.62<br>- tending to be a discouraged person: $G_s$ = -.60<br>- anxiety symptoms : $G_s$ = -.66 | HAPP 1.1 | G<br>V | -.68<br>.32 | $Chi^2$ | 01 | Juniors and seniors attending public high schools in New York State, U.S.A.<br>Probability cluster sample of 10 public high schools<br>N: sample A: 1682, sample B: 1664, date: 1960 | BRENN 70<br>p. 71/75/268 |
| | | Stronger among males: G = -.55<br>Lower among females : G = -.49 | AFF 1.1 | G<br>V | -.31<br>.23 | $Chi^2$ | 01 | | |
| LONELINESS | 6-item index of statements on feeling lonely, nobody cares for you, difficulty in making lasting contacts, coping with things alone, hard to find real friends, alone in the world | Unaffected by sex<br>Lower among the married: G' = -.36 (01)<br>Stronger among singles : G' = -.50 (01) | HAPP 2.1 | G' | -.48 | Gt' | 01 | Adults, Amsterdam, The Netherlands<br>Probability systematic random sample stratified by sex and marital status<br>N: 600, date: September - December, 1965 | JONG 69<br>p. 197 |
| THERAPIST'S FUNCTIONING IN THERAPEUTIC CONDITIONS: | Ratings of individual therapy sessions (recorded on audiotapes) by 3 advanced graduate students in counseling psychology.<br>Two 4-minute segments from each of 24 tapes were rated independently by the raters for each variable.<br>The average of these ratings per scale per therapist was used | | | | | | | Therapists, Columbia University, U.S.A.<br>Non-probability chunk sample<br>N: 12, date: 1970 | GURMA 72<br>p. 170 |
| - WARMTH | Expanded Truax Warmth Scale (see Truax & Carkhuff, 1967) | | AFF 3.1 | $r_s$ | +.55 | | 05 | | |
| - EMPATHY | Adapted Truax Empathy Scale (see Bergin & Solomon, 1970) | | AFF 3.1 | $r_s$ | +.40 | | 10 | | |

| Variable | Operationalization | Remarks | Code | Measure | Value | Test | Sig. | Sample | Source |
|---|---|---|---|---|---|---|---|---|---|
| - GENUINENESS | Expanded Truax Genuineness Scale (see Truax & Carkhuff, 1967) | | AFF 3.1 | $r_s$ | +.43 | | 10 | | |
| - SELF-DISCLOSURE | Self-Disclosure Scale (see Carkhuff & Berenson, 1967) | | AFF 3.1 | $r_s$ | +.44 | | 10 | | |
| - FACILITATIVE INTERPERSONAL FUNCTIONING | Gross Facilitative Interpersonal Functioning Scale (see Carkhuff et al., 1968) | | AFF 3.1 | $r_s$ | +.59 | | 02 | | |

## P 1.8.2 - TRUST IN PEOPLE

| Variable | Operationalization | Remarks | Code | Measure | Value | Test | Sig. | Sample | Source |
|---|---|---|---|---|---|---|---|---|---|
| ESTEEM FOR OTHERS | 3-item index of true / false statements containing 'most people are selfish and inconsiderate', 'it doesn't pay to put yourself out for other people', and 'most people can be trusted' | Computed for the Index of Positive Affects only: $\bar{DR}$ = +.08 (05)<br>Unaffected by S.E.S.<br>Stronger among those who are higher in sociability: $\bar{DR}$ = +.13 (05) | AFF 2.3 | $\bar{DR}$ | + | BCI | | Adults, urban areas, U.S.A.<br>Probability area samples<br>N: 2787, date: January, 1963 - January, 1964 | BRADB 69<br>p. 145 |
| TRUST IN OTHER PEOPLE | Direct question rated on a graphic scale ranging from 'none' to 'very much' | | HAPP 1.1 | G | +.22 | | ns | National adult population, The Netherlands<br>Probability area sample<br>N: 1552, date: June, 1968 | BAKKE 74<br>p. 27 |
| SOCIAL ISOLATION | 5-item index indicating a strong mistrust in other people (see Berting, 1968) | | HAPP 1.1 | G' | -.16 | Gt' | ns | Adults, Utrecht, The Netherlands<br>Probability sample stratified by age<br>N: 300, date: autumn, 1967 | MOSER 69<br>p. 42 |
| TRUST IN SOCIAL NETWORK MEMBERS | 3-item index of closed questions on whether one would trust him/her with important information, discuss with him/her psychological problems, tell him/her about a 'put down' someone had given her | These questions were answered for each social network member.<br>Those adults one sees at least once a month and who are 'important persons' in one's life were considered as social network members.<br>Unaffected by marital status | HAPP 1.1 | r | +.10 | | ns | Females from the Seattle-Washington area, U.S.A.<br>Non-probablity chunk sample<br>N: 153, date: — | BRIM 74<br>p. 437 |
| HAVING FAITH IN PEOPLE | 5-item index of agree/disagree statements on 'no one cares for you','human nature is cooperative', 'trust in people', 'people take advantage of you', 'most people tend to help others' | When standardized on participation in extra-curricular activities: $G_s$ = +.31 | HAPP 1.1 | G<br>V | +.34<br>.18 | $Chi^2$ | 01 | Juniors and seniors attending public high schools in New York State, U.S.A.<br>Probability cluster sample of 10 public high schools<br>N: sample A: 1682, sample B: 1664, date: 1960 | BRENN 70<br>p. 94/140/290 |
| | | | AFF 1.1 | G<br>V | +.27<br>.14 | $Chi^2$ | 01 | | |
| TRUST IN PEOPLE | 6-item index of closed questions on trust in people (see Robinson et al., 1969) | | COMP 1.2 | $r_{pm}$ | +.13 | | 001 | Public high school boys, U.S.A.<br>Probability multi-stage sample<br>N: 2213 in 1966, 1886 in 1968 and 1799 in 1969<br>date: fall, 1966, spring, 1968 and spring, 1969 | BACHM 67/70<br>p. 243 |

## P 1.8.3 - INFLUENCE

### ACTUAL INFLUENCE:

| Variable | Operationalization | Remarks | Code | Measure | Value | Test | Sig. | Sample | Source |
|---|---|---|---|---|---|---|---|---|---|
| DEGREE IN WHICH HE MAKES HIS INFLUENCE FELT AMONG THE FELLOWS | Class-master rating on a 7-point scale on the basis of observation | | AFF 5.3 | $r_{pm}$ | +.57 | | | Schoolboys, England<br>Non-probability chunk sample<br>N: 140, date: 1912 - 1913 | WEBB 15<br>p. 27 |

| | | | | | | | | |
|---|---|---|---|---|---|---|---|---|
| WIDENESS OF HIS INFLUENCE (i.e. the extent to which he makes his influence felt among any of his fellows whenever he speaks or acts) | Trained peer rating on a 7-point scale on the basis of observation | | AFF 5.2 | $r_{pm}$ | +.30 | | | Male students, England<br>Non-probability chunk sample<br>N: 194, date: 1912 - 1913 | WEBB 15<br>p. 26 |
| INTENSITY OF HIS INFLUENCE ON HIS SPECIAL INTIMATES | See above | | AFF 5.2 | $r_{pm}$ | +.40 | | | See above | WEBB 15<br>p. 26 |

## ATTEMPTED INFLUENCE:

| | | | | | | | | | |
|---|---|---|---|---|---|---|---|---|---|
| DESIRE TO IMPOSE HIS OWN WILL ON OTHERS (as opposed to tolerance) | Class-master rating on a 7-point scale on the basis of observation | | AFF 5.3 | $r_{pm}$ | +.36 | | | Schoolboys, England<br>Non-probability chunk sample<br>N: 140, date: 1912 - 1913 | WEBB 15<br>p. 27 |
| DESIRE TO IMPOSE HIS OWN WILL ON OTHERS (as opposed to tolerance) | Trained peer rating on a 7-point scale on the basis of observation | | AFF 5.2 | $r_{pm}$ | +.17 | | | Male students, England<br>Non-probability chunk sample<br>N: 194, date: 1912 - 1913 | WEBB 15<br>p. 26 |

## P 1.8.4 - VARIOUS PERSONALITY TRAITS CONCERNING INTERPERSONAL FUNCTIONING

see also 'Various Personality Traits during Childhood' (P 1.9)

| | | | | | | | | | |
|---|---|---|---|---|---|---|---|---|---|
| DISLIKE OTHERS | Direct question on number of people one dislikes, rated on a graphic scale ranging from 'none' to 'very much' | | HAPP 1.1 | G | -.24 | | ns | National adult population, The Netherlands<br>Probability area sample<br>N: 1552, date: June, 1968 | BAKKE 74<br>p. 27 |
| LIKING OTHERS | Closed question on how much one likes people in general<br>not at all / very little / somewhat / considerably / very much | Stronger among normals : r = +.54 (01)<br>Lower among handicapped: r = +.22 (01) | HAPP 2.1 | r | + | | 01 | Physically defective and normal persons, Detroit, U.S.A.<br>Non-probability purposive samples<br>N: 295, date: — | CAMER 73/1<br>p. 209 |
| PRESENTING A FALSE SELF | 2-item index of closed questions on putting up a front to people, putting on an act to impress people | | HAPP 1.1 | G<br>V | -.23<br>.11 | $Chi^2$ | 01 | Juniors and seniors attending public high schools in New York State, U.S.A.<br>Probability cluster sample of 10 public high schools<br>N: sample A: 1682, sample B: 1664, date: 1960 | BRENN 70<br>p. 94/294 |
| | | | AFF 1.1 | G<br>V | -.29<br>.10 | $Chi^2$ | 01 | | |
| HIDING TRUE FEELINGS | 2-item index of closed questions on not showing real feelings to others, not showing anger | | HAPP 1.1 | G<br>V | -.08<br>.05 | $Chi^2$ | 01 | See above | BRENN 70<br>p. 94/298 |
| | | | AFF 1.1 | G<br>V | -.04<br>.04 | $Chi^2$ | ns | | |
| TENDENCY TO SHOW KINDNESS | Class-master rating on a 7-point scale on the basis of observation | | AFF 5.3 | $r_{pm}$ | +.13 | | | Schoolboys, England<br>Non-probability chunk sample<br>N: 140, date: 1912 - 1913 | WEBB 15<br>p. 27 |
| IMPULSIVE KINDNESS | Trained peer rating on a 7-point scale on the basis of observation | | AFF 5.2 | $r_{pm}$ | +.20 | | | Male students, England<br>Non-probability chunk sample<br>N: 194, date: 1912 - 1913 | WEBB 15<br>p. 26 |
| TENDENCY TO DO KINDNESSES ON PRINCIPLE | See above | | AFF 5.2 | $r_{pm}$ | +.19 | | | See above | WEBB 15<br>p. 26 |

| Variable | Measure | Remarks | Happiness measure | Statistic | Value | Test | Significance | Sample | Source |
|---|---|---|---|---|---|---|---|---|---|
| READINESS TO ACCEPT THE SENTIMENTS OF HIS ASSOCIATES | Trained peer rating on a 7-point scale on the basis of observation | | AFF 5.2 | $r_{pm}$ | -.01 | | | Male students, England (see last page) | WEBB 15 p. 26 |
| DEGREE OF CORPORATE SPIRIT (in whatever body interest is taken, e.g. college, school, country, native place, etc.) | See above | | AFF 5.2 | $r_{pm}$ | +.42 | | | See above | WEBB 15 p. 26 |
| OFFENSIVE MANIFESTATION OF HIS SELF-ESTEEM (SUPERCILIOUSNESS) | See above | | AFF 5.2 | $r_{pm}$ | -.02 | | | See above | WEBB 15 p. 26 |

## P 1.9 - VARIOUS PERSONALITY TRAITS

| Variable | Measure | Remarks | Happiness measure | Statistic | Value | Test | Significance | Sample | Source |
|---|---|---|---|---|---|---|---|---|---|
| TEST-ANXIETY | 16-item index of questions on anxiety about exams and other tests (adapted Test Anxiety Questionnaire; see Mandler & Sarason, 1952) | | COMP 1.2 | $r_{pm}$ | -.16 | | 001 | Public high school boys, U.S.A.<br>Probability multi-stage sample<br>N: 2213 in 1966, 1886 in 1968, and 1799 in 1969<br>date: fall 1966, spring 1968 and spring 1969 | BACHM 67/70 p. 242 |
| IMPULSE CONTROL | Score based on test data, self-reports, staff ratings and interviewer's ratings for motor control, delay of gratification and reflectiveness | The correlations between life satisfaction and the separate measures of each of the three dimensions of impulse control were all non-significant. | HAPP 2.1 | $R^2$ | +.40 | | ns | Institutionalized white females, age 55-97, U.S.A.<br>Non-probability purposive sample<br>N: 91, date: — | KAHAN 75 p. 682-685 |
| RIGIDITY | 22-item index referring to preferences for routinized activities, adherence to social conventions, compulsions and obsessions (Gough-Sanford Rigidity Scale; see Rokeach, 1960) | For other measures of rigidity see also under 'Rigidity' (Part III, C 1.4) | AFF 3.1<br>HAPP 3.1 | $r_{pm}$<br>$r_{pm}$ | -.04<br>+.07 | | ns<br>ns | Undergraduate students, U.S.A.<br>Non-probability chunk sample<br>N: 67, date: summer, 1970 | GORMA 71 p. 215/218 |
| SENSITIVITY TO FAILURE | 3-item index of closed questions on 'feeling disturbed when done something badly', 'bothered by finding that someone has a poor opinion of you', 'disturbed when becoming aware of some fault or inadequacy in oneself' | | HAPP 1.1<br><br>AFF 1.1 | G<br>V<br>G<br>V | -.06<br>.07<br>-.06<br>.05 | <br>$Chi^2$<br><br>$Chi^2$ | <br>01<br><br>05 | Juniors and seniors attending public high schools in New York State, U.S.A.<br>Probability cluster sample of 10 public high schools<br>N: sample A: 1682, sample B: 1664, date: 1960 | BRENN 70 p. 94/306 |
| PERSONALITY TRAITS: | 16 Personality Factor Test (16 PF test; see Cattell, 1950) | Total factor scores for the two forms (one taken in elation, the other in depression) were correlated with the mean daily average score on the Elation-Depression Scale).<br>Only significant associations with the 16 factors were reported. | | | | | | Male college students, U.S.A.<br>Non-probability chunk sample<br>N: 17, date: ± 1960 | WESSM 66/2 p. 113-115 |
| - PARMIA (Parasympathetic Immunity) vs THRECTIA (Threat Reactivity) | | | AFF 3.1 | $r_{pm}$ | +.61 | t | 05 | | |
| - DOMINANCE vs SUBMISSIVENESS | | | AFF 3.1 | $r_{pm}$ | +.52 | t | 05 | | |
| - GUILT PRONENESS vs CONFIDENCE | | | AFF 3.1 | $r_{pm}$ | -.49 | t | 05 | | |
| LAW AND ORDER ATTITUDE | 4-item index ( items from a shortened Adorno F-Scale; see Weima, 1963) | | HAPP 1.1 | G' | +.21 | Gt' | 05 | Adults, Utrecht, The Netherlands<br>Probability sample stratified by age<br>N: 300, date: autumn, 1967 | MOSER 69 p. 39 |
| ADJUSTMENT | Bi-polar factor, having strong positive correlations with time competence (+.78), and inner directedness (+.74), and strong negative correlations with neuroticism (-.64) and anxiety (-.77). | | AFF 2.1<br>AFF 3.1 | $r_{pm}$<br>$r_{pm}$ | +.11<br>+.46 | | ns<br>01 | Married females, U.S.A.<br>Non-probability purposive sample by expert choice<br>N: 62, date: — | HARDE 69 p. 52/61 |

| | | | | | | | | | |
|---|---|---|---|---|---|---|---|---|---|
| OPENNESS | Bi-polar factor, having positive correlations with inner directedness (+.40), neuroticism (+.37), and anxiety (+.30), and strong negative correlations with need for social approval (-.82) and satisfaction with role (-.69) | | AFF 2.1<br>AFF 3.1 | $r_{pm}$<br>$r_{pm}$ | -.29<br>-.10 | | 05<br>ns | Married females, U.S.A.<br>(see last page) | HARDE 69<br>p. 52/63 |
| DEGREE OF SENSE OF HUMOR | Trained peer rating on a 7-point scale on the basis of observation | | AFF 5.2 | $r_{pm}$ | +.68 | | | Male students, England<br>Non-probability chunk sample<br>N: 194, date: 1912 - 1913 | WEBB 15<br>p. 26 |
| DEGREE OF AESTHETIC FEELING (love of the beautiful for its own sake) | See above | | AFF 5.2 | $r_{pm}$ | -.07 | | | See above | WEBB 15<br>p. 26 |
| <u>RESPONSE SETS:</u> | | Two other clinical rank orders, concerning repression and denial of unpleasant affects, were presented under 'Defensiveness' (Part III, P 1.3) | | | | | | Male college students, U.S.A.<br>Non-probability chunk sample<br>N: 17, date: ± 1960 | WESSM 66/2<br>p. 104-106 |
| - HYPOBOLIC - HYPERBOLIC VERBAL EXPRESSION | Clinical rank order on the basis of general clinical experience with the subjects and observation of their behavior and reactions to experimental situations, for the relative degree to which S understates and overstates and habitually uses strong words to express himself. | This rank was made a year before hedonic level was assessed. | AFF 3.1 | $r_{pm}$ | -.02 | t | ns | | |
| - TEST DISHONESTY | MMPI Lie Scale (See Gough, 1953), scored on a series of 'false' answers to questions that usually are answered 'true' | | AFF 3.1 | $r_{pm}$ | -.25 | t | ns | | |
| - ECCENTRIC TEST-ATTITUDE | MMPI Invalidity Scale (see Gough, 1953), supposedly indicative of gross eccentricity, carelessness in responding, or lack of personal restraint | Inspection of the individual items suggests that low scores would be indicative of well-adjusted conventionality and high scores of eccentric deviance with bizarre and unpleasant admissions. | AFF 3.1 | $r_{pm}$ | -.64 | t | 05 | | |
| - EVASIVE TEST-ATTITUDE (social-desirability) | MMPI Suppression Scale (see Gough, 1953), measuring the degree to which S has been guarded or evasive, or overly frank and self-critical in responding | | AFF 3.1 | $r_{pm}$ | -.01 | t | ns | | |
| - CONSISTENT (DIS)AGREEING RESPONSE TENDENCIES | Over-all agreement score (see Couch & Keniston, 1960), indicative of 'yea saying' or 'nay saying' | | AFF 3.1 | $r_{pm}$ | -.31 | t | ns | | |

## VARIOUS PERSONALITY TRAITS DURING CHILDHOOD

The happiness ratings at hand here are clinical ratings of hedonic level in infants, made between 8 and 36 months of age. These ratings are correlated with ratings of various personality traits made at different points in time: from characteristics observed just after birth to characteristics in childhood and adolescence.

| | | | | | | | | | |
|---|---|---|---|---|---|---|---|---|---|
| <u>NEWBORN ACTIVITY:</u> | Observation of movements of hands and feet by method of Kessen et al. (1961) using motion pictures of four observations on two consecutive days | Newborn activity was correlated with hedonic level at eight months | | | | | | 8 months old infants, U.S.A.<br>Non-probability quota sample<br>N: 24, date: — | MCGRA 68<br>p. 1249 |
| - NEWBORN ACTIVITY | Observation of movements of hands and feet | | AFF 5.1 | $r_{pm}$ | +.06 | | ns | | |
| - NEWBORN REACTIVITY<br>(to be continued on next page) | Difference between unstimulated activity and activity after S's forehead was rubbed | | AFF 5.1 | $r_{pm}$ | -.09 | | ns | | |

| Variable | Measurement | Remarks | Code | Statistic | Value | | | Population | Source |
|---|---|---|---|---|---|---|---|---|---|
| - NEWBORN REACTIVITY | Difference between unstimulated activity and activity after removal of a nipple | | AFF 5.1 | $r_{pm}$ | -.51 | | 01 | | |
| ACTIVITY | Examination by psychologist using a 9-point scale (Activity: 'inactive - vigorous' rating scale, from Bayley Infant Behaviour Profile) | Both hedonic level and the variable mentioned were assessed at eight months. | AFF 5.1 | $r_{pm}$ | +.59 | | 01 | 8 months old infants, U.S.A. (see last page) | MCGRA 68 p. 1249 |
| TENSION | Examination by psychologist using an 8-point scale (Tension rating scale, from Bayley Infant Behaviour Profile) | See above | AFF 5.1 | $r_{pm}$ | -.79 | | 01 | See above | MCGRA 68 p. 1249 |
| FEARFULNESS | Examination by psychologist using a 7-point scale (Fearfulness: 'reaction to the new or strange' rating scale, from Bayley Infant Behaviour Profile) | See above | AFF 5.1 | $r_{pm}$ | -.55 | | 01 | See above | MCGRA 68 p. 1249 |
| <u>CHILD CHARACTERISTICS BETWEEN THE AGES OF 10 AND 36 MONTHS:</u> | Repeated expert rating on the basis of observation of expressive behaviour in test situation on bi-polar 7-point scales | Each child was rated 12 times during this period on both hedonic level and the variable mentioned. Ratings at the ages of 10, 11 and 12; 13, 14 and 15; 18, 21 and 24; and 27, 30 and 36 months were combined.<br>See also instrument and remarks in excerpt (Part II).<br><br>columns: 10-12 / 13-15 / 18-24 / 27-36 | | | | | | Children, Berkeley, California, U.S.A.<br>Non-probability chunk sample<br>N: 54, date: 1928 - 1943 | SCHAE 63 p. 29 |
| - RESPONSIVENESS TO PERSONS | Slight - marked | boys:<br>10-12: -.20 -.32 -.17 -.21<br>13-15: -.17 -.12 -.03 -.12<br>18-24: $-.42^{x}$ $-.41^{x}$ -.26 -.21<br>27-36: +.16 -.02 -.10 -.08<br>girls:<br>10-12: +.19 +.08 +.04 +.03<br>13-15: -.15 +.03 +.04 +.10<br>18-24: -.14 -.23 -.20 -.12<br>27-36: +.10 +.00 -.03 +.20 | AFF 5.1 | $r_{pm}$ | | | | | |
| - ACTIVITY | Inactive - vigorous | boys:<br>10-12: -.08 -.18 -.06 -.27<br>13-15: -.02 +.03 -.01 -.17<br>18-24: +.19 +.24 $+.65^{x}$ +.29<br>27-36: +.25 +.07 +.21 +.14<br>girls:<br>10-12: +.03 +.11 +.07 -.07<br>13-15: +.01 +.09 +.29 +.10<br>18-24: +.07 +.12 +.34 +.01<br>27-36: +.06 +.02 +.20 +.23 | AFF 5.1 | $r_{pm}$ | | | | | |
| - SPEED OF MOVEMENTS | Slow - rapid | boys:<br>10-12: -.18 -.31 -.26 $-.39^{x}$<br>13-15: -.05 -.13 -.07 -.29<br>18-24: +.06 -.06 +.35 -.02<br>27-36: +.10 +.05 +.13 +.02<br>girls:<br>10-12: -.02 +.10 +.11 -.07<br>13-15: -.05 +.10 +.28 -.01<br>18-24: +.01 -.04 +.06 -.27<br>27-36: +.02 -.03 -.04 -.27 | AFF 5.1 | $r_{pm}$ | | | | | |
| - DEGREE OF STRANGENESS | Shy - unreserved | boys:<br>10-12: $+.49^{x}$ $+.43^{x}$ +.35 +.18<br>13-15: +.36 $+.66^{x}$ $+.43^{x}$ +.31<br>18-24: +.23 +.33 $+.61^{x}$ +.22<br>27-36: +.16 $+.38^{x}$ +.21 +.33<br><br>(to be continued on next page) | AFF 5.1 | $r_{pm}$ | | | | | |

| Variable | Measure | Group | Age | 10-12 | 13-15 | 18-24 | 27-36 | | | Population | Source |
|---|---|---|---|---|---|---|---|---|---|---|---|
| | | girls: | 10-12 | +.72$^x$ | +.50$^x$ | +.41$^x$ | +.48$^x$ | | | | |
| | | | 13-15 | +.61$^x$ | +.69$^x$ | +.60$^x$ | +.48$^x$ | | | | |
| | | | 18-24 | +.36 | +.60$^x$ | +.70$^x$ | +.60$^x$ | | | | |
| | | | 27-36 | +.29 | +.35 | +.58$^x$ | +.76$^x$ | | | | |
| - AMOUNT OF POSITIVE BEHAVIOUR | Negative - positive | boys: | 10-12 | +.59$^x$ | +.64$^x$ | +.44$^x$ | +.45$^x$ | AFF 5.1 | $r_{pm}$ | | |
| | | | 13-15 | +.53$^x$ | +.86$^x$ | +.61$^x$ | +.70$^x$ | | | | |
| | | | 18-24 | +.62$^x$ | +.60$^x$ | +.72$^x$ | +.49$^x$ | | | | |
| | | | 27-36 | +.40$^x$ | +.55$^x$ | +.42$^x$ | +.85$^x$ | | | | |
| | | girls: | 10-12 | +.76$^x$ | +.64$^x$ | +.40$^x$ | +.34 | | | | |
| | | | 13-15 | +.54$^x$ | +.74$^x$ | +.62$^x$ | +.48$^x$ | | | | |
| | | | 18-24 | +.48$^x$ | +.60$^x$ | +.73$^x$ | +.57$^x$ | | | | |
| | | | 27-36 | +.47$^x$ | +.54$^x$ | +.64$^x$ | +.78$^x$ | | | | |
| - IRRITABILITY (tendency to be sensitive to and react to stimulation) | Calm - excitable | boys: | 10-12 | +.67$^x$ | +.69$^x$ | +.42$^x$ | +.41$^x$ | AFF 5.1 | $r_{pm}$ | | |
| | | | 13-15 | +.63$^x$ | +.80$^x$ | +.52$^x$ | +.58$^x$ | | | | |
| | | | 18-24 | +.37 | +.68$^x$ | +.61$^x$ | +.55$^x$ | | | | |
| | | | 27-36 | +.37 | +.56$^x$ | +.51$^x$ | +.88$^x$ | | | | |
| | | girls: | 10-12 | +.74$^x$ | +.59$^x$ | +.40$^x$ | +.35$^x$ | | | | |
| | | | 13-15 | +.73$^x$ | +.84$^x$ | +.58$^x$ | +.44$^x$ | | | | |
| | | | 18-24 | +.52$^x$ | +.68$^x$ | +.82$^x$ | +.67$^x$ | | | | |
| | | | 27-36 | +.47$^x$ | +.49$^x$ | +.66$^x$ | +.75$^x$ | | | | |
| **CHILD CHARACTERISTICS BETWEEN THE AGES OF 27 AND 96 MONTHS:** | Repeated expert ratings on the basis of observation of expressive behaviour in test-situation on bi-polar 7-point scales | Each variable was correlated with the child's hedonic level at the ages of 10-36 months. See also instrument and remarks in excerpt (Part II). Each child was rated 14 times on the variables mentioned. Ratings at the ages of 27 and 30, 33 and 36, 42 and 48, 54 and 60, 66 and 72, 78 and 84, and 90 and 96 months were combined. For both boys and girls N=24 here. | | | | | | | | Children, Berkeley, California, U.S.A. Non-probability chunk sample N: 54, date: 1928-1943 | SCHAE 63 p. 98/103 |
| | | | | 10-12 | 13-15 | 18-24 | 27-36 | | | | |
| - FRIENDLINESS | 3-item index: - initial response to situation (negative - friendly) - secondary response to situation ( negative - friendly) - attitude towards task (unwilling - eager) | boys: | 27-30 | +.48$^x$ | +.35 | +.27 | +.48$^x$ | AFF 5.1 | $r_{pm}$ | | |
| | | | 33-36 | +.33 | +.26 | +.40 | +.40 | | | | |
| | | | 42-48 | +.06 | +.21 | -.02 | +.23 | | | | |
| | | | 54-60 | +.23 | +.32 | +.08 | +.23 | | | | |
| | | | 66-72 | +.26 | +.23 | +.34 | +.26 | | | | |
| | | | 78-84 | +.02 | +.07 | +.14 | +.15 | | | | |
| | | | 90-96 | -.12 | -.07 | +.05 | -.15 | | | | |
| | | girls: | 27-30 | +.16 | +.52$^x$ | +.75$^x$ | +.72$^x$ | | | | |
| | | | 33-36 | +.05 | +.33 | +.53$^x$ | +.66$^x$ | | | | |
| | | | 42-48 | -.10 | +.15 | +.19 | +.18 | | | | |
| | | | 54-60 | -.17 | +.04 | +.22 | +.29 | | | | |
| | | | 66-72 | -.50$^x$ | -.16 | +.15 | +.08 | | | | |
| | | | 78-84 | -.47$^x$ | -.27 | -.10 | -.20 | | | | |
| | | | 90-96 | -.39 | -.19 | -.22 | -.13 | | | | |
| - COOPERATIVENESS | 2-item index: - variability in cooperation (variable - consistent) - attention to instructions (inattentive - alert) | boys: | 27-30 | +.20 | +.00 | +.13 | +.23 | AFF 5.1 | $r_{pm}$ | | |
| | | | 33-36 | +.22 | +.04 | +.27 | +.25 | | | | |
| | | | 42-48 | +.06 | +.05 | -.02 | -.04 | | | | |
| | | | 54-60 | +.08 | +.18 | +.08 | +.22 | | | | |
| | | | 66-72 | -.01 | +.18 | +.20 | +.17 | | | | |
| | | | 78-84 | +.15 | +.19 | +.18 | +.23 | | | | |
| | | | 90-96 | -.11 | +.09 | +.00 | -.08 | | | | |

(to be continued on next page)

| Variable | Measure | Group | Age (months) | 10-12 | 13-15 | 18-24 | 27-36 | Code | Statistic | Population | Source |
|---|---|---|---|---|---|---|---|---|---|---|---|
| | | girls: | 27-30 | -.02 | +.21 | +.35 | +.16 | | | | |
| | | | 33-36 | -.22 | +.09 | +.34 | +.28 | | | | |
| | | | 42-48 | -.14 | +.12 | +.22 | +.08 | | | | |
| | | | 54-60 | -.25 | -.11 | +.08 | +.01 | | | | |
| | | | 66-72 | -.32 | -.18 | +.12 | +.06 | | | | |
| | | | 78-84 | -.52$^x$ | -.29 | -.08 | -.16 | | | | |
| | | | 90-96 | -.20 | -.15 | -.18 | +.06 | | | | |
| - ATTENTIVENESS | 3-item index: - external distraction (distractible - single-minded) - association (flighty - controlled) - maintenance of effort ( easily discouraged - persistent) | boys: | 27-30 | +.10 | -.12 | +.20 | +.26 | AFF 5.1 | $r_{pm}$ | | |
| | | | 33-36 | +.28 | -.05 | +.29 | +.16 | | | | |
| | | | 42-48 | +.14 | -.01 | +.14 | +.12 | | | | |
| | | | 54-60 | +.18 | +.18 | +.25 | +.34 | | | | |
| | | | 66-72 | +.05 | +.20 | +.32 | +.36 | | | | |
| | | | 78-84 | +.01 | +.10 | +.20 | +.29 | | | | |
| | | | 90-96 | -.02 | +.13 | +.15 | +.23 | | | | |
| | | girls: | 27-30 | -.56$^x$ | -.34 | -.10 | -.15 | | | | |
| | | | 33-36 | -.23 | -.03 | +.19 | +.28 | | | | |
| | | | 42-48 | -.05 | +.13 | +.21 | +.15 | | | | |
| | | | 54-60 | -.01 | +.00 | +.10 | +.04 | | | | |
| | | | 66-72 | -.27 | -.16 | +.07 | +.10 | | | | |
| | | | 78-84 | -.34 | -.14 | +.02 | -.10 | | | | |
| | | | 90-96 | -.24 | -.14 | -.14 | -.01 | | | | |
| - FACILITY | 3-item index: - comprehension of task (slow - swift) - verbal responses (vague - definite) - method of performance (random - systematic) | boys: | 27-30 | +.10 | +.12 | +.24 | +.45$^x$ | AFF 5.1 | $r_{pm}$ | | |
| | | | 33-36 | +.12 | +.15 | +.36 | +.53$^x$ | | | | |
| | | | 42-48 | -.07 | -.04 | +.18 | +.46$^x$ | | | | |
| | | | 54-60 | +.23 | +.23 | +.50$^x$ | +.62$^x$ | | | | |
| | | | 66-72 | +.19 | +.27 | +.50$^x$ | +.62$^x$ | | | | |
| | | | 78-84 | +.05 | +.13 | +.35 | +.55$^x$ | | | | |
| | | | 90-96 | +.08 | +.19 | +.39 | +.57$^x$ | | | | |
| | | girls: | 27-30 | -.22 | +.04 | +.19 | +.18 | | | | |
| | | | 33-36 | -.18 | +.03 | +.22 | +.25 | | | | |
| | | | 42-48 | -.11 | +.20 | +.33 | +.45$^x$ | | | | |
| | | | 54-60 | -.12 | +.02 | +.14 | +.24 | | | | |
| | | | 66-72 | -.18 | -.05 | +.12 | +.30 | | | | |
| | | | 78-84 | -.22 | -.14 | -.05 | -.01 | | | | |
| | | | 90-96 | -.12 | -.07 | -.16 | -.01 | | | | |

| Variable | Measure | Remarks | | | | | | Code | Statistic | Population | Source |
|---|---|---|---|---|---|---|---|---|---|---|---|
| <u>CHILD CHARACTERISTICS BETWEEN THE AGES OF 9 AND 12 YEARS:</u> | Repeated expert rating on the basis of observation of expressive behaviour in test situation on bi-polar 7-point scales | Each variable was correlated with the child's hedonic level at the ages of 10-36 months. See also instrument and remarks in excerpt (Part II). For boys N = 22 or 23, for girls N = 21 here. Each child was rated 6 times on the variables mentioned. Ratings at the ages of 9, 9½ and 10 years, and of 10½, 11 and 12 years were combined | | | | | | | | Children, Berkeley, California, U.S.A. Non-probability chunk sample N: 54, date: 1928 - 1943 | SCHAE 63 p. 99-104 |

| Variable | Measure | Group | Age (years) | 10-12 | 13-15 | 18-24 | 27-39 | Code | Statistic |
|---|---|---|---|---|---|---|---|---|---|
| - NOT SHY | Shy - at ease | boys: | 9-10 | -.00 | -.06 | +.08 | +.04 | AFF 5.1 | $r_{pm}$ |
| | | | 10½-12 | -.15 | -.02 | +.06 | +.05 | | |
| | | girls: | 9-10 | -.04 | -.22 | -.18 | +.03 | | |
| | | | 10½-12 | +.03 | +.09 | +.26 | +.22 | | |

| | | | | 10–12 | 13–15 | 18–24 | 27–36 | | |
|---|---|---|---|---|---|---|---|---|---|
| - FRIENDLY ATTITUDE TOWARDS EXAMINER | Unfriendly - friendly | boys: | 9–10 | +.03 | -.02 | +.04 | -.11 | AFF 5.1 | $r_{pm}$ |
| | | | 10½–12 | +.06 | +.26 | +.22 | +.07 | | |
| | | girls: | 9–10 | -.22 | -.33 | -.34 | -.16 | | |
| | | | 10½–12 | +.11 | +.16 | +.14 | +.08 | | |
| - COOPERATION | Unwilling - willing | boys: | 9–10 | +.05 | +.04 | +.07 | +.00 | AFF 5.1 | $r_{pm}$ |
| | | | 10½–12 | +.12 | +.29 | +.20 | +.06 | | |
| | | girls: | 9–10 | -.24 | -.12 | -.14 | +.05 | | |
| | | | 10½–12 | +.43 | +.40 | +.13 | +.34 | | |
| - ATTITUDE TOWARDS TASK (INTERESTED) | Bored - interested | boys: | 9–10 | +.15 | +.09 | +.06 | +.05 | AFF 5.1 | $r_{pm}$ |
| | | | 10½–12 | +.13 | +.29 | $+.43^{x}$ | +.26 | | |
| | | girls: | 9–10 | -.26 | -.16 | -.09 | +.08 | | |
| | | | 10½–12 | +.39 | $+.56^{x}$ | +.31 | $+.46^{x}$ | | |
| - EXERTS EFFORTS | Poor - excellent | boys: | 9–10 | +.08 | +.09 | +.06 | +.05 | AFF 5.1 | $r_{pm}$ |
| | | | 10½–12 | +.05 | +.24 | +.29 | +.17 | | |
| | | girls: | 9–10 | -.32 | -.05 | +.04 | +.14 | | |
| | | | 10½–12 | +.18 | +.33 | +.09 | +.20 | | |
| - ATTENTION TO INSTRUCTIONS | Inattentive - attentive | boys: | 9–10 | +.06 | +.11 | -.01 | +.13 | AFF 5.1 | $r_{pm}$ |
| | | | 10½–12 | -.01 | +.11 | +.16 | +.33 | | |
| | | girls: | 9–10 | -.09 | +.01 | -.10 | -.04 | | |
| | | | 10½–12 | +.24 | +.42 | +.16 | +.36 | | |
| - NOT DISTRACTIBLE | Distractible - intent on task | boys: | 9–10 | +.12 | +.12 | +.09 | +.20 | AFF 5.1 | $r_{pm}$ |
| | | | 10½–12 | +.12 | +.16 | +.22 | +.30 | | |
| | | girls: | 9–10 | -.15 | +.01 | -.02 | +.07 | | |
| | | | 10½–12 | +.22 | +.39 | +.12 | +.32 | | |
| - SYSTEMATIC METHOD OF PERFORMANCE | Random - systematic | boys: | 9–10 | +.04 | +.08 | +.22 | +.30 | AFF 5.1 | $r_{pm}$ |
| | | | 10½–12 | +.15 | +.27 | +.37 | +.41 | | |
| | | girls: | 9–10 | -.11 | -.01 | -.01 | +.19 | | |
| | | | 10½–12 | +.10 | +.33 | +.21 | +.24 | | |
| - RAPID EXECUTION OF TASKS | Slow - rapid | boys: | 9–10 | -.12 | +.03 | +.00 | +.14 | AFF 5.1 | $r_{pm}$ |
| | | | 10½–12 | +.08 | +.12 | +.19 | +.35 | | |
| | | girls: | 9–10 | -.12 | $-.44^{x}$ | -.43 | -.29 | | |
| | | | 10½–12 | +.04 | +.10 | +.08 | +.05 | | |
| - SWIFT COMPREHENSION OF TASKS | Slow - swift | boys: | 9–10 | +.12 | +.07 | +.26 | $+.46^{x}$ | AFF 5.1 | $r_{pm}$ |
| | | | 10½–12 | +.14 | +.19 | +.38 | +.42 | | |
| | | girls: | 9–10 | -.22 | -.31 | -.29 | -.02 | | |
| | | | 10½–12 | +.21 | +.31 | +.25 | +.26 | | |
| - ESTIMATED VALIDITY OF TEST | Low - high | boys: | 9–10 | +.27 | +.17 | +.13 | +.09 | AFF 5.1 | $r_{pm}$ |
| | | | 10½–12 | +.10 | +.26 | +.33 | +.14 | | |
| | | girls: | 9–10 | +.11 | +.12 | +.19 | $+.44^{x}$ | | |
| | | | 10½–12 | +.36 | +.27 | +.14 | +.30 | | |
| - ACTIVITY CONTROL | Overactive - underactive | boys: | 9–10 | +.36 | +.38 | +.41 | +.26 | AFF 5.1 | $r_{pm}$ |
| | | girls: | 9–10 | -.10 | -.25 | $-.46^{x}$ | -.27 | | |

| Characteristic | Measure | Results | | | | | Code | Statistic | | | | Population | Source |
|---|---|---|---|---|---|---|---|---|---|---|---|---|---|
| **CHILD CHARACTERISTICS BETWEEN THE AGES OF 12 AND 18 YEARS:** (boys only) | Adjective ratings on 7-point scales by two judges on the basis of notes from observations in test periods at different ages | Computed for boys only (N=21). Each variable was correlated with the child's hedonic level at the ages of 10 - 36 months. See also instrument and remarks in excerpt (Part II). | | | | | | | | | | Children, Berkeley, California, U.S.A. Non-probability chunk sample N: 54, date: 1928 - 1943 | SCHAE 63 p. 100 |
| | | | 10-12 | 13-15 | 18-24 | 27-36 | | | | | | | |
| - TIMID, COMPLIANT, INHIBITED, LACKS CONFIDENCE | Cluster of four adjective ratings | | -.15 | -.16 | -.30 | -.24 | AFF 5.1 | $r_{pm}$ | | | | | |
| - COURTEOUS, CONSCIENTIOUS, DEPENDABLE, RESPECTFUL, CONSERVATIVE | Cluster of five adjective ratings | | +.12 | -.11 | +.04 | -.02 | AFF 5.1 | $r_{pm}$ | | | | | |
| - TACTFUL, CALM, CONTENTED, APPRECIATIVE, CONSIDERATE, PATIENT, REFINED IN TASTE | Cluster of seven adjective ratings | | +.14 | -.08 | +.12 | +.02 | AFF 5.1 | $r_{pm}$ | | | | | |
| - FRIENDLY, CHEERFUL | Cluster of two adjective ratings | | +.16 | +.10 | +.27 | +.06 | AFF 5.1 | $r_{pm}$ | | | | | |
| - SOCIAL IN SITUATION, NATURAL | Cluster of two adjective ratings | | +.16 | +.11 | +.34 | +.05 | AFF 5.1 | $r_{pm}$ | | | | | |
| - INDEPENDENT, TALKATIVE, ASSERTIVE, TAKES INITIATIVE, OUTGOING | Cluster of five adjective ratings | | +.27 | +.26 | +.36 | +.22 | AFF 5.1 | $r_{pm}$ | | | | | |
| - BOLD, BOASTFUL, EXCITABLE, IMPULSIVE, PLEASURE-LOVING, DISTRACTIBLE, UNINHIBITED, SHOW-OFF | Cluster of eight adjective ratings | | +.00 | +.13 | +.17 | +.09 | AFF 5.1 | $r_{pm}$ | | | | | |
| - IRRITABLE, DOMINEERING, PUGNACIOUS, NOISY, DEMANDING, NOT DEPENDABLE | Cluster of six adjective ratings | | -.11 | +.02 | +.05 | +.01 | AFF 5.1 | $r_{pm}$ | | | | | |
| - RUDE, CRITICAL, OPINIONATED, COMPLAINS, DEFIANT | Cluster of five adjective ratings | | +.03 | +.08 | +.16 | +.26 | AFF 5.1 | $r_{pm}$ | | | | | |
| - HOSTILE, DESTRUCTIVE | Cluster of two adjective ratings | | -.12 | +.07 | -.07 | +.09 | AFF 5.1 | $r_{pm}$ | | | | | |
| - COLD, SUSPICIOUS, UNFRIENDLY | Cluster of three adjective ratings | | -.18 | +.05 | -.18 | +.17 | AFF 5.1 | $r_{pm}$ | | | | | |
| - RESERVED, UNCOMMUNICATIVE | Cluster of two adjective ratings | | -.14 | +.02 | -.18 | +.02 | AFF 5.1 | $r_{pm}$ | | | | | |
| **CHILD CHARACTERISTICS BETWEEN THE AGES OF 12 AND 18 YEARS:** (girls only) | Adjective ratings on 7-point scales by two judges on the basis of notes from observations in test periods at different ages | Computed for girls only (N=19). Each variable was correlated with the child's hedonic level at the ages of 10 - 36 months. See also instrument and remarks in excerpt (Part II). | | | | | | | | | | See above | SCHAE 63 p. 105 |
| | | | 10-12 | 13-15 | 18-24 | 27-36 | | | | | | | |
| - TIMID, SELF-CONSCIOUS, SENSITIVE, LACKS CONFICENCE, SHY, EASILY HURT, INHIBITED, SERIOUS, HUMORLESS, RIGID, PRECISE | Cluster of eleven adjective ratings | | +.24 | +.29 | -.05 | -.18 | AFF 5.1 | $r_{pm}$ | | | | | |

| | | 10-12 | 13-15 | 18-24 | 27-36 | | |
|---|---|---|---|---|---|---|---|
| - COURTEOUS, RESPECTFUL, CONSERVATIVE, COMPLIANT, TACTFUL, COOPERATIVE, PATIENT, CONSIDERATE | Cluster of eight adjective ratings | +.23 | +.12 | -.15 | -.06 | AFF 5.1 | $r_{pm}$ |
| - CONSCIENTIOUS, DEPENDABLE, PERSEVERING | Cluster of three adjective ratings | +.34 | +.22 | +.02 | +.04 | AFF 5.1 | $r_{pm}$ |
| - FRIENDLY, TALKATIVE, NOT UNFRIENDLY | Cluster of three adjective ratings | -.10 | -.07 | +.04 | -.02 | AFF 5.1 | $r_{pm}$ |
| - SOCIAL IN SITUATION, INTERESTED IN PEOPLE, NATURAL, STRAIGHT-FORWARD | Cluster of four adjective ratings | -.24 | -.18 | -.04 | -.01 | AFF 5.1 | $r_{pm}$ |
| - INDEPENDENT, ASSERTIVE, OUT-GOING, LEADER, RESOURCEFUL, TAKES INTITIATIVE, INDEPENDENT AT HOME | Cluster of seven adjective ratings | -.29 | -.17 | +.22 | +.20 | AFF 5.1 | $r_{pm}$ |
| - BOLD, BOASTFUL, IMPLUSIVE, UN-INHIBITED, SHOW-OFF, PLEASURE-LOVING, OPINIONATED | Cluster of seven adjective ratings | -.34 | -.24 | +.03 | -.06 | AFF 5.1 | $r_{pm}$ |
| - IRRITABLE, DISRESPECTFUL, DOMINEERING, PUGNACIOUS, NOISY, DEMANDING, TACTLESS, NOT DEPENDABLE, EXCITABLE, DIS-TRACTIBLE | Cluster of ten adjective ratings | -.14 | -.10 | +.08 | -.02 | AFF 5.1 | $r_{pm}$ |
| - DEFIANT, RUDE, SARCASTIC, CRITICAL | Cluster of four adjective ratings | -.02 | +.06 | +.24 | +.06 | AFF 5.1 | $r_{pm}$ |
| - HOSTILE, RESENTFUL | Cluster of two adjective ratings | +.03 | -.02 | +.04 | -.06 | AFF 5.1 | $r_{pm}$ |
| - SULKY, BITTER | Cluster of two adjective ratings | -.01 | +.00 | +.18 | +.09 | AFF 5.1 | $r_{pm}$ |
| - DISCONTENTED, UNHAPPY, DISSATISFIED, COMPLAINS | Cluster of four adjective ratings | +.09 | +.07 | +.02 | -.07 | AFF 5.1 | $r_{pm}$ |
| - GLOOMY, NOT CHEERFUL | Cluster of two adjective ratints | +.14 | +.21 | +.19 | -.09 | AFF 5.1 | $r_{pm}$ |
| - RESERVED, COLD, ALOOF, UNCOMMUNICATIVE | Cluster of four adjective ratings | +.15 | +.16 | +.12 | +.12 | AFF 5.1 | $r_{pm}$ |
| - POPULAR, BELONGS TO GROUPS | Cluster of two adjective ratings | -.06 | -.11 | +.09 | +.32 | AFF 5.1 | $r_{pm}$ |
| - CALM, NOT NERVOUS | Cluster of two adjective ratings | -.10 | -.22 | -.24 | +.10 | AFF 5.1 | $r_{pm}$ |

# P2 PHYSICAL CHARACTERISTICS



## P 2.1 - PHYSICAL APPEARANCE

see also 'Ethnicity' (E 2)

| | | | | | | | | | |
|---|---|---|---|---|---|---|---|---|---|
| LENGTH | 4-point scale | Unaffected by sex:<br>males : G' = +.11 (05)<br>females: G' = +.08 (05) | HAPP 1.1 | G' | + | Gt' | 05 | National adult population, U.S.A.<br>Non-probability quota sample<br>N: 2377, date: February, 1946 | WESSM 56<br>p. 180-181 |
| HEIGHT | Data obtained from hospital records | Open ward : r = -.23 (05)<br>Closed ward: r = +.01 (ns) | AFF 5.1 | $r_{pm}$ | - | | | Institutionalized mentally retarded males, U.S.A.<br>Non-probability chunk sample<br>N: 149, date: — | PANDE 71<br>p. 329 |
| WEIGHT | underweight / average / overweight; using standards relative to length | | HAPP 1.1 | G' | +.02 | Gt' | ns | National adult population, U.S.A.<br>Non-probability quota sample<br>N: 2377, date: February, 1946 | WESSM 56<br>p. 183 |
| RELATIVE WEIGHT | Broca-index | | HAPP 2.1 | G | +.10 | $Chi^2$ | 000 | Male employees of age 40+, The Netherlands<br>Non-probability chunk sample<br>N: 13000, date: — | SONDE 75 |
| WEIGHT | Data obtained from hospital records | Open ward : r = -.09 (ns)<br>Closed ward: r = -.13 (ns) | AFF 5.1 | $r_{pm}$ | - | | ns | Institutionalized mentally retarded males, U.S.A.<br>Non-probability chunk sample<br>N: 149, date:— | PANDE 71<br>p. 329 |
| APPEARANCE | Rating by staffmembers on a 7-point scale ranging from 'very unattractive' to 'very good-looking' | Open ward : r = +.16 (ns)<br>Closed ward: r = +.34 (01) | AFF 5.1 | $r_{pm}$ | + | | | See above | PANDE 71<br>p. 329 |
| DESIRED PERSONAL CHANGES: PHYSICAL APPEARANCE, WEIGHT, SIZE, LOOKS | Open-ended question on desired personal changes other changes vs change mentioned | Computed for those who desire to change only (N = 1591) | HAPP 1.1 | G' | +.05 | Gt' | ns | National adult population, U.S.A.<br>Non-probability quota sample<br>N: 2377, date: February, 1946 | WESSM 56<br>p. 211 |

## P 2.2 - PHYSICAL HEALTH

see 'Physical Health' (H 2.1)

## P 2.3 - VARIOUS PHYSIOLOGICAL CHARACTERISTICS

| | | | | | | | | | |
|---|---|---|---|---|---|---|---|---|---|
| MENSTRUATION | Comparison of mean daily ratings on hedonic level with daily ratings prior to and during menstruation | Of the 19 women reporting menstrual periods, 14 had an 'average' hedonic level lower than their general mean during the two days prior to menstruation (05) and 8 of the 19 reached their most depressed periods of the entire 6-week study on these two days. (to be continued on next page) | AFF 3.1 | | - | t | 05 | Female college students, U.S.A.<br>Non-probability chunk sample<br>N: 21, date: ± 1960 | WESSM 66/1<br>p. 63-64 |

| | | | | | | | | | |
|---|---|---|---|---|---|---|---|---|---|
| BEING PREGNANT | non-pregnant vs pregnant females | Eleven women also showed a lower 'average' hedonic level on the day the menstrual period commenced<br>Computed for females only<br>Twenty-two females were pregnant | HAPP 1.1 | G | -.28 | | 05 | National adult population, The Netherlands<br>Probability area sample<br>N: 1376, date: June, 1968 | VEENH 74<br>p. 500<br>BAKKE 74<br>p. 27 |
| BLOOD PRESSURE | 2-item index containing systolic and diastolic measurement | | HAPP 2.1 | G | -.02 | $Chi^2$ | ns | Male employees of age 40-65, The Netherlands<br>Non-probability chunk sample<br>N: 13,000, date: — | SONDE 75 |
| SERUM CHOLESTEROL LEVEL | Determination in laboratory, utilizing the Clark et al. (1968) method | During the two months of extensive training $r_{pm}$ ranged from -.70 (01) at the first measurement before the training started, to +.01 (ns).<br>15 out of the 16 measurements demonstrated negative correlations (mean $r_{pm}$ = -.28 (ns)). | AFF 3.3 | $r_{pm}$ | -.28 | | ns | Trainees on the U.S. Underwater Demolition Team, U.S.A.<br>Probability sample<br>N: 16-20, date: — | RAHE 71<br>p. 403 |
| GALVANIC SKIN RESPONSE | Average deviation on a galvanometer in an experimental situation<br>Ss were instructed to recall pleasant or unpleasant associations in connection with verbal stimuli. For each set of stimulus words the average deflection was used.<br>less than 5º / 5º - 10º / more than 10º deflection | About half the sample was used here.<br>For the cheerful Ss 93 averages were obtained, and for the depressed Ss 72 averages. | AFF 6 | G' | +.51 | Gt' | 05 | Female psychology students, U.S.A.<br>Non-probability chunk sample, poststratified by temperament<br>N: 67, date: — | WASHB 25<br>p. 455 |

# P 3 POLITICS

P 3.1 Political concern

P 3.2 Attitudes towards political situation . . . . . . . see also N 1.1, S 1.3

P 3.3 Political preference

## P 3.1 - POLITICAL CONCERN

| | | | | | | | | | |
|---|---|---|---|---|---|---|---|---|---|
| REPORT OF PERSONAL HOPES CONCERNING POLITICAL SITUATION | Open-ended question on personal wishes and hopes for the future<br>Responses rated as concerning freedom and other aspirations having to do with the political situation | | HAPP 3.1 | G' | +.07 | Gt' | ns | National adult population of 5 Westernized nations, 3 underdeveloped giants, 2 countries in the Middle East, 3 Caribbean nations and the Philippines<br>Representative samples<br>N: 18653, date: ± 1960 | CANTR 65/1 p. 263 |
| REPORT OF PERSONAL FEARS CONCERNING POLITICAL SITUATION | Open-ended question on personal worries and fears for the future<br>Responses rated as concerning lack of freedom; political instability; no improvement in present government; etc. | | HAPP 3.1 | G' | +.22 | Gt' | 01 | See above | CANTR 65/1 p. 263 |
| REPORT OF NATIONAL HOPES CONCERNING POLITICAL SITUATION | Open-ended question on wishes and hopes for the future of one's country<br>Responses rated as concerning honest, efficient, balanced, democratic or representative, socialistic government; freedom; law and order; national unity; political stability, internal peace and order; etc. | U-shaped curve: moderately happy people being least concerned with politics | HAPP 3.1 | G' | -.05 | Gt' | ns | See above | CANTR 65/1 p. 263 |
| REPORT OF NATIONAL FEARS CONCERNING POLITICAL SITUATION | Open-ended question on fears and worries for the future of one's country<br>Responses rated as concerning dishonest government; inefficient government; communism; no democracy or representative government; fear country will become socialistic; lack or loss of freedom; lack of law and order; disunity among people of the nation; political instability, chaos, civil war; high or increased taxes; etc. | U-shaped curve: moderately happy people being least concerned with politics | HAPP 3.1 | G' | -.04 | Gt' | 01 | See above | CANTR 65/1 p. 263 |
| REPORT OF PERSONAL HOPES CONCERNING SOCIAL SITUATION | Open-ended question on personal wishes and hopes for the future<br>Responses rated as concerning social justice; future generations; social security; etc. | | HAPP 3.1 | G' | +.06 | Gt' | 05 | See above | CANTR 65/1 p. 263 |
| REPORT OF PERSONAL FEARS CONCERNING SOCIAL SITUATION | Open-ended question on personal worries and fears for the future<br>Responses rated as concerning social injustice; future generations; no social security; etc. | | HAPP 3.1 | G' | +.27 | Gt' | 01 | See above | CANTR 65/1 p. 263 |

| | | | | | | | | |
|---|---|---|---|---|---|---|---|---|
| REPORT OF NATIONAL HOPES CONCERNING SOCIAL SITUATION | Open-ended question on wishes and hopes for the future of one's country<br>Responses rated as concerning social justice; eliminate discrimination, prejudice or exploitation; education; improved labor conditions; control of labor; social security; housing; agrarian reform; public health; limited population growth; sense of social and political responsibility and awareness; morality, ethical standards, religion; etc. | HAPP 3.1 | G' | +.17 | Gt' | 01 | National adult populations of 14 countries (see last page) | CANTR 65/1 p. 263 |
| REPORT OF NATIONAL FEARS CONCERNING SOCIAL SITUATION | Open-ended question on fears and worries for the future of one's country<br>Responses rated as concerning social injustice; continued discrimination, prejudice or exploitation; inadequate educational facilities and schooling; poor and unfair working conditions; abuses by labor; unlimited population growth; no sense of social and political responsibility or awareness; lack of morality, ethical standards, religion; too much mechanization and standardization, materialism, conformity; etc. | HAPP 3.1 | G' | +.11 | Gt' | 01 | See above | CANTR 65/1 p. 263 |
| REPORT OF PERSONAL HOPES CONCERNING INTERNATIONAL SITUATION | Open-ended question on personal wishes and hopes for the future<br>Responses rated as concerning peace; a better world; etc. | HAPP 3.1 | G' | +.44 | Gt' | 05 | See above | CANTR 65/1 p. 263 |
| REPORT OF PERSONAL FEARS CONCERNING INTERNATIONAL SITUATION | Open-ended question on personal worries and fears for the future<br>Responses rated as concerning war; militarism and armaments; misuse of nuclear energy; threat, aggression, domination by a communist power; etc. | HAPP 3.1 | G' | +.47 | Gt' | 01 | See above | CANTR 65/1 p. 263 |
| REPORT OF NATIONAL HOPES CONCERNING INTERNATIONAL SITUATION | Open-ended question on wishes and hopes for the future of one's country<br>Responses rated as concerning peace; disarmament, limitation of armaments, control or banning of nuclear weapons; lessening of cold war; better relations with communistic bloc; friendly relations with all countries; better world; maintain neutrality; help other nations; increased foreign trade or exports; etc. | HAPP 3.1 | G' | +.47 | Gt' | 01 | See above | CANTR 65/1 p. 263 |
| REPORT OF NATIONAL FEARS CONCERNING INTERNATIONAL SITUATION | Open-ended question on fears and worries for the future of one's countrv<br>Responses rated as concerning war; continued armament, no control or banning of nuclear weapons; no lessening of cold war; isolation from other nations; inability to maintain neutrality; etc. | HAPP 3.1 | G' | +.29 | Gt' | 01 | See above | CANTR 65/1 p. 263 |
| REPORT OF NATIONAL HOPES CONCERNING ECONOMIC SITUATION | Open-ended question on wishes and hopes for the future of one's country<br>Responses rated as concerning improved or decent standard of living; technological advances, greater productivity; economic stability; employment; etc. | HAPP 3.1 | G' | -.10 | Gt' | 05 | See above | CANTR 65/1 p. 263 |

| | | | | | | | | | |
|---|---|---|---|---|---|---|---|---|---|
| REPORT OF NATIONAL FEARS CONCERNING ECONOMIC SITUATION | Open-ended question on fears and worries for the future of one's country<br>Responses rated as concerning no improvement in or inadequate standard of living; no technological advances, economic backwardness, low productivity; failure to preserve present standard of living, economic instability; unemployment; etc. | | HAPP 3.1 | G' | -.08 | Gt' | 01 | National adult populations of 14 countries (see last page) | CANTR 65/1 p. 263 |
| REPORT OF NATIONAL HOPES CONCERNING INDEPENDENT STATUS | Open-ended question on wishes and hopes for the future of one's country<br>Responses rated as concerning military strength; maintain or attain the position of a world power; enhancement of status and importance of the nation; exert ideological or moral leadership; national independence; etc. | | HAPP 3.1 | G' | +.26 | Gt' | 01 | See above | CANTR 65/1 p. 263 |
| REPORT OF NATIONAL FEARS CONCERNING INDEPENDENT STATUS | Open-ended question on fears and worries for the future of one's country<br>Responses rated as concerning not to maintain or attain the position of a world power; lose or have no status or importance; failure to exert ideological or moral leadership; lack or loss of national independence; threat, aggression, domination by a communistic power of any foreign power, etc. | | HAPP 3.1 | G' | +.11 | Gt' | 01 | See above | CANTR 65/1 p. 263 |
| POLITICAL KNOWLEDGE | 4-item index of open-ended questions on names of politicians | | HAPP 6 | $r_{pm}$ | +.06 | | ns | Public high school boys, U.S.A.<br>Probability multi-stage sample<br>N: 2213 in 1966, 1886 in 1968 and 1799 in 1969<br>date: fall, 1966; spring, 1968 and spring, 1969 | BACHM 67/70 p. 243 |
| BEING INTERESTED IN CIVIC INTERESTS | Closed question | College students only<br>L-shaped curve: stronger among unhappier students | COMP 4.1 | | + | | s | Students, U.S.A.<br>Non-probability chunk sample<br>N: 1651, date: — | SYMON 37 p. 292 |

## P 3.2 - ATTITUDES TOWARDS POLITICAL SITUATION

see also 'Attitudes towards Nation' (N 1.1), and 'Satisfaction with Nation' (S 1.3)

| | | | | | | | | | |
|---|---|---|---|---|---|---|---|---|---|
| WISH TO PRESERVE NATIONAL STATUS QUO | Open-ended question on wishes and hopes for the future of one's country<br>Responses indicative of contentment with things as they are | | HAPP 3.1 | G' | +.75 | Gt' | 01 | National adult populations of 14 countries<br>Representative samples<br>N: 18653, date: ± 1960 | CANTR 65/1 p. 263 |
| HAVE NO FEARS FOR THE NATION | Open-ended question on fears and worries for the future of one's country<br>Responses indicating no fears or worries for the country | | HAPP 3.1 | G' | -.02 | Gt' | ns | See above | CANTR 65/1 p. 263 |
| MOST IMPORTANT WORRY: POLITICS, WORLD AND NATIONAL CONDITIONS | Open-ended question on most important worry other worries vs worry mentioned | Computed for those who have worries only (N = 2040) | HAPP 1.1 | G' | +.31 | Gt' | 01 | National adult population, U.S.A.<br>Non-probability quota sample<br>N: 2377, date: February, 1946 | WESSM 56 p. 213 |
| HAVING PROBLEMS WITH CIVIC INTERESTS | Closed question | Graduate students only<br>L-shaped curve: significant positive relationship among happier students only | COMP 4.1 | | + | | | Students, U.S.A.<br>Non-probability chunk sample<br>N: 1651, date: — | SYMON 37 p. 292 |

## P 3.3 - POLITICAL PREFERENCE

| | | | | | | | | | |
|---|---|---|---|---|---|---|---|---|---|
| POLITICAL AFFILIATION | Independent / Democrat / Republican | See remarks in excerpt (Part II)<br>Independent: Mean = 6.43 (6.88)<br>Democrat : Mean = 6.47 (6.67)<br>Republican : Mean = 6.77 (7.20) | HAPP 3.1 | DM | + | | | Non-institutionalized national adult population, U.S.A.<br>Multi-stage probability sample stratified by size of locality<br>N: 1588, date: January, 1971 (+ 1964) | CANTR 71<br>p. 66 |
| POLITICAL AFFILIATION | Communists / Social-Democratics / Religious centre parties (Catholics and Protestants) / Conservatives | Communists : 13% happy, 52% pretty happy, 22% unhappy<br>Social Democratics: 37% happy, 51% pretty happy, 4% unhappy<br>Catholics : 43% happy, 43% pretty happy, 6% unhappy<br>Protestants : 50% happy, 40% pretty happy, 3% unhappy<br>Conservatives : 52% happy, 41% pretty happy, 5% unhappy | HAPP 1.1 | D% | + | | | National adult population, The Netherlands<br>N: at least 1000, date: 1948 | NIPO 49<br>p. 4 |

# P 4 POPULARITY



## P 4.1 - ACTUAL POPULARITY

| Variable | Measurement | Results | Code | Stat. | Sign | | Sig. | Population | Source |
|---|---|---|---|---|---|---|---|---|---|
| POPULARITY | Rating by 2 experienced staff members who were familiar with all the patients, on a 7-point 'isolated-popular' scale | Open ward : r = +.52 (001)<br>Closed ward: r = +.47 (001) | AFF 5.1 | $r_{pm}$ | + | | 001 | Institutionalized mentally retarded males, U.S.A.<br>Non-probability chunk sample<br>N: 149, date: — | PANDE 71<br>p. 329 |
| PEER POPULARITY | Score based on the number of times one is selected by his peers in answering three open-ended questions:<br>- Who do you like?<br>- Who are your friends?<br>- Who do you play with? | Open ward : r = +.04 (ns)<br>Closed ward: r = +.30 (05) | AFF 5.1 | $r_{pm}$ | + | | | See above | PANDE 71<br>p. 329 |
| REJECTION BY PEERS | Score based on the number of times one is selected by his peers in answering three open-ended questions<br>- Who don't you like?<br>- Who do you dislike?<br>- Who don't you like to play with? | Open ward : r = -.23 (05)<br>Closed ward: r = -.32 (01) | AFF 5.1 | $r_{pm}$ | - | | 05 | See above | PANDE 71<br>p. 329 |

## P 4.2 - PERCEIVED POPULARITY

see also 'Types of Affect: Social Respect' (A 2.2.18)

| Variable | Measurement | Results | Code | Stat. | Sign | | Sig. | Population | Source |
|---|---|---|---|---|---|---|---|---|---|
| SELF-PERCEIVED POPULARITY WITH SAME SEX (in high school) | Direct question | Lower among males : r = +.03<br>Stronger among females: r = +.12 | COMP 4.1 | $r_{pm}$ | + | | | Graduate students of education, U.S.A.<br>Non-probability chunk sample<br>N: 388, date: — | WATSO 30<br>p. 104 |
| | | Stronger among males : r = +.22<br>Lower among females : r = +.10 | COMP 4.3 | $r_{pm}$ | + | | | | |
| | | Stronger among males : r = +.24<br>Lower among females : r = +.14 | AFF 1.3 | $r_{pm}$ | + | | | | |
| SELF-PERCEIVED POPULARITY WITH OPPOSITE SEX (in high school) | Direct question | Stronger among males : r = +.13<br>Lower among females : r = +.03 | COMP 4.1 | $r_{pm}$ | + | | | See above | WATSO 30<br>p. 104 |
| | | Positive among males : r = +.39<br>Negative among females: r = -.09 | COMP 4.3 | $r_{pm}$ | | | | | |

(to be continued on next page)

| | | | | | | | | | |
|---|---|---|---|---|---|---|---|---|---|
| | | Positive among males : r = +.15<br>Negative among females: r = -.02 | AFF 1.3 | $r_{pm}$ | | | | | |
| APPRAISED LIKING BY OTHERS | Closed question: 'How much do you think that people in general like you?'<br>not at all / very little / somewhat / considerably / very much | Stronger among normals : r = +.54 (01)<br>Lower among handicapped: r = +.33 (01) | HAPP 2.1 | r | + | | 01 | Physically defective and normal persons, Detroit, U.S.A.<br>Non-probability purposive samples<br>N: 295, date: — | CAMER 73/1<br>p. 209 |
| PERCEIVED APPRECIATION BY PEOPLE ONE IS WORKING WITH ON THE JOB | Closed question rated on a 3-point scale | unmarried males : r = +.16 (ns)<br>married males : r = +.08 (ns)<br>unmarried females: r = +.10 (025)<br>married females : r = +.16 (ns) | HAPP 2.1 | $r_{pm}$ | + | $Chi^2$ | | Adults, Amsterdam, The Netherlands<br>Probability systematic random sample stratified by sex and marital status<br>N: 600, date: September - December, 1965 | JONG 69<br>p. 191 |

## P 4.3 - VARIOUS FACTORS CONCERNING POPULARITY

| | | | | | | | | | |
|---|---|---|---|---|---|---|---|---|---|
| EASE OF MAKING FRIENDS | Closed question<br>not very easy vs make friends easily | | HAPP 1.1 | G' | +.37 | Gt' | 01 | National adult population, U.S.A.<br>Non-probability quota sample<br>N: 2377, date: February, 1946 | WESSM 56<br>p. 202 |
| SUCCESS IN ACQUIRING FRIENDS | Closed question | | HAPP 1.1<br>AFF 1.1 | mc<br>mc | +.36<br>+.40 | | | Urban adult Jewish population, Israel<br>Probability area sample using dwelling units<br>N: 1830, date: summer, 1973 | LEVY 75/2<br>p. 373 |
| SATISFACTION WITH ADMIRATION OR RESPECT BY OTHERS | Closed question: 'How do you feel about . . .?'<br>terrible / unhappy / mostly dissatisfied / mixed / mostly satisfied / pleased / delighted | | HAPP 3.1<br>(1st instr.) | $h^2$ | .34 | | | National adult population, U.S.A.<br>Probability area sample (third sample)<br>N: 1072, date: November, 1972 | ANDRE 74<br>p. 19 |
| BEING INTERESTED IN PERSONAL ATTRACTIVENESS | Closed question | High school students only<br>U-shaped curve: Those reporting 'average' happiness being most interested in personal attractiveness | COMP 4.1 | | + | | | Students, U.S.A.<br>Non-probability chunk sample<br>N: 1651, date: — | SYMON 37<br>p. 292 |
| HAVING PROBLEMS WITH PERSONAL ATTRACTIVENESS | Closed question | High school students only<br>L-shaped curve: Significant positive relationship among unhappier students only | COMP 4.1 | | + | | | See above | SYMON 37<br>p. 292 |

# P 5 PROBLEMS, WORRIES AND FEARS

see also 'Concerns, Interests' (C 2)
'Life quality' (L 2)



## P 5.1 - PROBLEMS

### P 5.1.1 - AMOUNT OF PROBLEMS

| | | | | | | | | |
|---|---|---|---|---|---|---|---|---|
| FEELING THAT LIFE IS FULL OF TROUBLES AND OBSTACLES | Closed question rated on an 11-point self-anchoring scale | | HAPP 3.1 | $r_{pm}$ | -.25 | | National adult population, U.S.A.<br>Probability sample<br>N: 1549, date: 1960 | CANTR 65/2<br>p. 268/415 |
| | | | HAPP 2.1 | $r_{pm}$ | -.35 | | | |
| | | | CON 1.1 | $r_{pm}$ | -.26 | | | |
| EXTENT OF PERCEIVED TROUBLES AND OBSTACLES IN LIFE | Closed question rated on an 11-point self-anchoring scale<br>(see above) | | HAPP 2.1 | r | -.35 | | National adult population, U.S.A.<br>Cantril (1965) modified probability sample<br>N: 1406, date: 1959 | BORTN 70<br>p. 44 |
| | | | HAPP 3.1 | r | -.29 | | | |
| | | | CON 1.1 | r | -.23 | | | |

### P 5.1.2 - SPECIFIC PROBLEMS

For problems with health see 'Health and Health Care' (H 2)

| | | | | | | | | |
|---|---|---|---|---|---|---|---|---|
| PROBLEMS WITH: | 15-item inventory of closed questions | | | | | | Students, U.S.A.<br>Non-probability chunk sample<br>N: 1651, date: — | SYMON 37<br>p. 292 |
| - HEALTH | | | COMP 4.1 | | | ns | | |
| - SEX | | High school students only<br>L-shaped curve: significant negative relationship among happier students only | COMP 4.1 | | - | | | |
| - SAFETY | | | COMP 4.1 | | | ns | | |
| - MONEY | | High school students only<br>L-shaped curve: stronger negative relationship among happier students | COMP 4.1 | | - | s | | |
| - MENTAL HYGIENE | | High school students: significant positive relationship<br>College students: significant negative relationship<br>L-shaped curve: stronger negative relationship among happier students<br>Graduate students: negative relationship<br>L-shaped curve: significant negative relationship among happier students only | COMP 4.1 | | | | | |

| | | | | | | | | | |
|---|---|---|---|---|---|---|---|---|---|
| - STUDY HABITS | | High school students only<br>L - shaped curve: significant positive relationship among happier students only | COMP 4.1 | | + | | | Students U.S.A.<br>(See last page) | SYMON 37<br>p. 292 |
| - RECREATION | | | COMP 4.1 | | | | ns | | |
| - PERSONAL AND MORAL QUALITIES | | College students only<br>L - shaped curve: significant positive relationship among happier students only | COMP 4.1 | | + | | | | |
| - FAMILY RELATIONSHIPS | | High school students only<br>L- shaped curve: significant negative relationship among happier students only | COMP 4.1 | | - | | | | |
| - MANNERS | | High school students only<br>L - shaped curve: significant positive relationship among happier students only | COMP 4.1 | | + | | | | |
| - PERSONAL ATTRACTIVINESS | | High school students only<br>L - shaped curve; significant positive relationship among happier students only | COMP 4.1 | | + | | | | |
| - DAILY SCHEDULE | | High school students only<br>U - shaped curve: students of average happiness having least problems with their daily schedule | COMP 4.1 | | - | | s | | |
| - CIVIC INTERESTS | | Graduate students only<br>L - shaped curve: significant positive relationship among happier students only | COMP 4.1 | | + | | | | |
| - GETTING ALONG WITH OTHERS | | College students only<br>L - shaped curve: significant negative relationship among happier students only | COMP 4.1 | | - | | | | |
| - PHILOSOPHY OF LIFE | | | COMP 4.1 | | | | ns | | |
| FAMILY PROBLEMS | Closed question: no vs yes | | HAPP 2.1 | G | -.55 | $Chi^2$ | 000 | Male employees of age 40+, The Netherlands<br>Non-probability chunk sample<br>N: 13,000, date: — | SONDE 75 |
| PROBLEMS IN MARRIAGE (in the past) | Open-ended question on problems getting along with each other.<br>S never had problems vs mentions problems | Stronger among females: $t_k$ = -.24 (01)<br>Lower among males : $t_k$ = -.14 (01) | HAPP 1.1 | $t_k$ | - | | 01 | Adult married population with children, U.S.A.<br>Probability area sample<br>N: 797, date: spring 1957 | VEROF 62<br>p. 196 |
| MARITAL TENSION | 14-item index of closed questions on marital problems concerning time spent with friends, how the house looks, household expenses, being tired, being away from home too much, disciplining children, in-laws, not showing love, work, how to spend leisure time, work around the house, religion, irritating personal habits, other | | HAPP 1.1 | G' | -.22 | Gt' | 01 | Males in the age of 25 - 49, 4 small communities, Illinois, U.S.A.<br>Probability multi-stage samples<br>N: 393, date: March, 1962 | BRADB 65/1<br>p. 37 |
| | | Index of Positive Affects: G' = +.04 (ns)<br>Index of Negative Affects: G' = +.43 (01) | AFF 2.3 | G' | - | Gt' | | | |
| MARITAL TENSION | 11-item index of yes/no questions on differences in opinion or problems concerning time spent with friends, household expenses, being tired, being away from home too much, disciplining children, in-laws, not showing love, your (husband's) job, how to spend leisure time, religion, irritating personal habits | Stronger among females : G = -.32<br>Lower among males : G = -.16<br>Index of Positive Affects:<br>Stronger among males : G = +.10<br>Not among females : G = +.00<br>Index of Negative Affects:<br>Slightly stronger among females: G = +.43<br>Lower among males : G = +.37<br>Unaffected by S.E.S. | AFF 2.3 | G | - | | | Adults, urban areas, U.S.A.<br>Probability area samples<br>N: 2787, date: January, 1963 - January, 1964 | BRADB 69<br>p. 164 |

(to be continued on next page)

| | | | | | | | | | |
|---|---|---|---|---|---|---|---|---|---|
| | | Stronger among females : G = -.37<br>Lower among males : G = -.25 | HAPP 1.1 | G | - | | | | |
| PARENTAL WORRIES | Score derived from an agree/disagree statement on children giving their parents more trouble than pleasure, and a 13-item inventory of parental problems | | AFF 1.3 | $\bar{DR}$ | - | | 05 | Adults, Alameda County, U.S.A.<br>Probability sample<br>N: 6928, date: betwee 1965 and 1971 | BERKM 71<br>p. 42 |
| HAVING PROBLEMS IN RAISING CHILDREN | Open-ended question on main problems<br>never had problems vs mentions problems | Stronger among males: $t_k$ = -.20 (01)<br>Lower among females: $t_k$ = -.05 (ns) | HAPP 1.1 | $t_k$ | - | | | Adult married population with children, U.S.A.<br>Probability area sample<br>N: 797, date: spring 1957 | VEROF 62<br>p. 196 |
| PROBLEMS WITH JOB (in the past) | Open-ended direct question<br>S never had problems vs mentions problems | Computed for males only | HAPP 1.1 | $t_k$ | -.03 | | ns | See above | VEROF 62<br>p. 196 |
| HAVING DIFFICULTIES IN KEEPING OCCUPIED | Closed question: no vs yes | See remarks in excerpt (Part II).<br>Lower among the gainfully employed: G' = -.43 (01)<br>Lower among retirees who had a positive orientation to retirement before they were retired : G' = -.38 (05)<br>Stronger among retirees who had a negative orientation to retirement: G' = -.64 (01) | COMP 1.2 | G' | -.49 | Gt' | 01 | Aged males, U.S.A.(Those satisfied in 1952)<br>Non-probability accidental sample<br>N: 787, date: 1952 - 1954 | THOMP 60<br>p. 168 |
| HAVING PROBLEMS DUE TO DRINKING | 5-item index of closed questions on specific problems due to drinking : with health, employer, spouse or other family members, police<br>no problems vs problems | Computed for alcohol users only<br>Stronger among those who use medium or large amounts : G' = -.53 (01)<br>Lower among those who use small amounts : G' = -.09 (ns)<br>Stronger among those not doing too well in getting the things they want : G' = -.31 (05)<br>Lower among those doing pretty well: G' = -.14 (ns) | HAPP 1.1 | G' | -.31 | Gt' | 01 | Non-institutionalized adult population, U.S.A.<br>Probability multi-stage sample<br>N: 1453, date: summer, 1963 | BRENN 67<br>p. 671 |
| | | Stronger among those who use medium or large amounts : G' = -.64 (01)<br>Lower among those using small amounts : G' = -.38 (05)<br>Stronger among not too happy Ss : G' = -.59 (01)<br>Lower among pretty happy Ss : G' = -.39 (01)<br>Not among very happy Ss | CON 1.1 | G' | -.51 | Gt' | 01 | | |

## P 5.2 - WORRIES AND FEARS

### P 5.2.1 - AMOUNT OF WORRIES AND FEARS

| | | | | | | | | | |
|---|---|---|---|---|---|---|---|---|---|
| AMOUNT OF WORRYING | Closed question: a little / a fair amount / a lot | | HAPP 1.1 | G' | -.32 | Gt' | 01 | National adult population, U.S.A.<br>Non-probability quota sample<br>N: 2377, date: February, 1946 | WESSM 56<br>p. 213 |
| EXTENT OF WORRIES | Closed question: never / not very much / sometimes / a lot / all the time | | HAPP 1.1 | G' | -.28 | Gt' | 01 | Non-institutionalized adults, U.S.A.<br>Probability multi-stage area sample<br>N: 2460, date: spring, 1957 | GURIN 60<br>p. 29 |

| | | | | | | | | | |
|---|---|---|---|---|---|---|---|---|---|
| EXTENT OF WORRIES AND FEARS THAT THINGS MIGHT GET WORSE FOR ONE-SELF AND FAMILY | Closed question rated on an 11-point self-anchoring scale | | HAPP 3.1 | $r_{pm}$ | -.27 | | | National adult population, U.S.A.<br>Probability sample<br>N: 1549, date: 1960 | CANTR 65/2<br>p. 268/415 |
| | | | HAPP 2.1 | $r_{pm}$ | -.24 | | | | |
| | | | CON 1.1 | $r_{pm}$ | -.23 | | | | |
| EXTENT OF WORRIES AND FEARS THAT THINGS MIGHT GET WORSE FOR ONESELF AND FAMILY | Closed question rated on an 11-point self-anchoring scale (see above) | | HAPP 2.1 | r | -.28 | | | National adult population, U.S.A.<br>Cantril (1965) modified probability sample<br>N: 1406, date: 1959 | BORTN 70<br>p. 44 |
| | | | HAPP 3.1 | r | -.30 | | | | |
| | | | CON 1.1 | r | -.23 | | | | |
| AMOUNT OF WORRYING | Closed question: never / a little / sometimes / a lot / all the time | | HAPP 3.1 (1st instr.) | $r_{pm}$ | -.21 | | | National adult population, U.S.A.<br>Probability area sample (second sample)<br>N: 1118, date: November, 1972 | ANDRE 74<br>p. 15 |
| | | | HAPP 2.1 | $r_{pm}$ | -.24 | | | | |
| | | | COMP 1.1 | $r_{pm}$ | -.13 | | | | |
| AMOUNT OF WORRYING | Closed question: never / a little / sometimes / a lot / all the time | first questioning : r = -.24<br>second questioning: r = -.27 | HAPP 3.1 (1st instr.) | $r_{pm}$ | -.28 | | | National adult population, U.S.A.<br>Probability area sample (third sample)<br>N: 1072, date: November, 1972 | ANDRE 74<br>p. 15 |
| | | | HAPP 2.1 | $r_{pm}$ | -.27 | | | | |
| | | | COMP 1.1 | $r_{pm}$ | -.16 | | | | |
| | | | HAPP 1.1 | $r_{pm}$ | -.24 | | | | |
| | | | HAPP 3.1 (5th instr.) | $r_{pm}$ | -.30 | | | | |
| | | Index of Positive Affects: r = -.12<br>Index of Negative Affects: r = +.32 | AFF 2.3 | $r_{pm}$ | -.31 | | | | |
| WORRYING | Closed question: not very much vs a lot | | HAPP 1.1 | G' | -.58 | Gt' | 01 | Males in the age of 25-49 of 4 small communities, Illinois, U.S.A.<br>Probability multi-stage samples<br>N: 393, date: March, 1962 | BRADB 65/1<br>p. 51 |
| | | Index of Negative affects: G' = -.49 (01)<br>No relation to the Index of Positive Affects | AFF 2.3 | G' | - | Gt' | | | |
| INTENSITY OF WORRYING | Closed question: never / not very much / a lot | Index of Positive Affects:<br>first interview: males: G = +.05<br>females: G = -.08<br>second interview: males: G = -.07<br>females: G = -.13<br>Index of Negative Affects:<br>first interview: males: G = +.43<br>females: G = +.42<br>second interview: males: G = +.53<br>females: G = +.52 | AFF 2.3 | G | - | | | Adults, urban areas, U.S.A.<br>Probability area samples<br>N: 2787, date: January, 1963 - January, 1964 | BRADB 69<br>p. 110 |
| AMOUNT OF WORRIES | 12-item index of yes/no questions on worries during the past few weeks about not having enough money, financial debts, work, getting along with wife/husband/girlfriend/boyfriend, moving ahead in the world, one's children, sexual problems, people one has troubles with, health, things that happen in one's neighborhood, world situation, growing old<br>(adapted from Srole et al., 1962) | Index of Positive Affects:<br>males: G = +.00<br>females: G = -.03<br>Index of Negative Affects:<br>males: G = +.40<br>females: G = +.41<br>Unaffected by expecting a nervous breakdown | AFF 2.3 | G | - | | | See above | BRADB 69<br>p. 110 |
| INCREASING AMOUNT OF WORRIES | Stable vs increasing worries, as measured by a 12-item worry index (see above)<br>The index was filled out twice with an interval of 10 months. | Computed for the Index of Negative Affects only: $\overline{DR}$ = +.06 | AFF 2.3 | $\overline{DR}$ | - | | | See above | BRADB 69<br>p. 111 |

| | | | | | | | | | |
|---|---|---|---|---|---|---|---|---|---|
| DECREASING AMOUNT OF WORRIES | Stable vs decreasing worries, as measured by a 12-item worry index (see last page)<br>The index was filled out twice with an interval of ten months. | Computed for the Index of Negative Affects only: $\overline{DR}$ = -.08 | AFF 2.3 | $\overline{DR}$ | + | | | Adults, urban areas, U.S.A.<br>(See last page) | BRADB 69<br>p. 111 |
| WORRYING | Closed question: never / sometimes / all the time | Unaffected by sex:<br>males: $t_k$ = -.19 (01)<br>females: $t_k$ = -.18 (01) | HAPP 1.1 | $t_k$ | - | | 01 | Adult married population with children, U.S.A.<br>Probability area sample<br>N: 797, date: spring 1957 | VEROF 62<br>p. 196 |
| EXTENT OF WORRIES | Closed question: never / not very much / a lot / all the time | | HAPP 1.1 | G' | +.00 | Gt' | ns | Student teachers, Chapel Hill, U.S.A.<br>Probability sample proportionally stratified by teaching level<br>N: 75, date: spring, 1967 | GONZA 67<br>p. 73 |
| HAVING NO WORRIES AND FEARS | Open-ended question on personal worries and fears for the future<br>Responses indicating that the respondent cannot think of any fears or worries. | See also 'Personal Worries and Fears' (Part III, P 5.2.2.1) | HAPP 3.1 | G' | +.29 | Gt' | 01 | Adult populations of 5 Westernized nations, 3 underdeveloped giants, 2 countries in the Middle East, 3 Caribbean nations and the Phippines<br>Representative samples<br>N: 18653, date: $\pm$ 1960 | CANTR 65/1<br>p. 263 |

## P 5.2.2 - SPECIFIC WORRIES AND FEARS

For worries and fears concerning health see 'Health and Healthcare' (H 2)

### P 5.2.2.1 - PERSONAL WORRIES AND FEARS

| | | | | | | | | | |
|---|---|---|---|---|---|---|---|---|---|
| PERSONAL WORRIES AND FEARS: | Content analysis on the basis of an open-ended question on personal worries and fears for the future | | | | | | | Adult populations of 5 Westernized nations, 3 underdeveloped giants, 2 countries in the Middle East, 3 Caribbean nations and the Philippines.<br>Representative samples<br>N: 18653, date: $\pm$ 1960 | CANTR 65/1<br>p. 263 |
| - VALUES AND CHARACTER | Responses rated as concerning emotional instability and immaturity; become anti-social; no self-development or improvement; not be accepted by others; no sense of personal worth; be a person without character; etc. | | HAPP 3.1 | G' | +.17 | Gt' | 01 | | |
| - ECONOMIC CONDITIONS | Responses rated as concerning deterioration in or inadequate standard of living for self or family; etc. | | HAPP 3.1 | G' | -.29 | Gt' | 01 | | |
| - JOB OR WORK SITUATION | Responses rated as concerning poor job, uncongenial work, unemployment, failure in one's work, etc., for self, spouse, or other family members | | HAPP 3.1 | G' | -.05 | Gt' | ns | | |
| - HEALTH OF SELF OR FAMILY | Responses rated as concerning ill health, accident, death for self or for members of the family | | HAPP 3.1 | G' | +.22 | Gt' | 01 | | |
| - FAMILY REFERENCES | Responses rated as concerning no or unhappy family life; worries and fears regarding relatives, children; etc. | | HAPP 3.1 | G' | +.08 | Gt' | 01 | | |

| | | | | | | | | | |
|---|---|---|---|---|---|---|---|---|---|
| - POLITICAL REFERENCES | Responses rated as concerning lack of freedom; political instability; no improvement in present government; etc. | | HAPP 3.1 | G' | +.22 | Gt' | 01 | Adult population of 14 countries<br>(See last page) | CANTR 65/1<br>p. 263 |
| - SOCIAL REFERENCES | Responses rated as concerning social injustice; future generations; no social security; etc. | | HAPP 3.1 | G' | +.27 | Gt' | 01 | | |
| - INTERNATIONAL REFERENCES | Responses rated as concerning war; militarism and armaments; misuse of nuclear energy; threat, aggression, domination by a Communist power; etc. | | HAPP 3.1 | G' | +.47 | Gt' | 01 | | |
| - HAVE NO FEARS | Responses indicating that the respondent cannot think of any fears or worries | | HAPP 3.1 | G' | +.29 | Gt' | 01 | | |
| WORRIES ABOUT FUTURE OF FAMILY MEMBERS | Direct question rated on an open graphic scale ranging from 'not worried' to 'very worried' | | HAPP 1.1 | G | +.30 | | ns | National adult population, The Netherlands<br>Probability area sample<br>N: 1552, date: June, 1968 | BAKKE 74<br>p. 28 |
| WORRIES ABOUT RELATIONSHIP WITH FAMILY MEMBERS | See above | Lower among those of age 40 - 50<br>Stronger among those of low S.E.S.<br>Not among those of higher education<br>Unaffected by sex | HAPP 1.1 | G | +.45 | | 05 | See above | BAKKE 74<br>p. 28 |
| PARENTAL WORRIES | Score derived from an agree/disagree statement on children giving their parents more trouble than pleasure, and a 13-item inventory of parental problems | | AFF 1.3 | $\overline{DR}$ | - | | 05 | Adults, Alameda County, U.S.A.<br>Probability sample<br>N: 6928, date: | BERKM 71<br>p. 42 |
| ANXIETY ABOUT FUTURE OF FARM | Closed question: not anxious at all / rather not anxious / little anxious / very anxious | | HAPP 2.1 | $T^2$ | -.16 | $Chi^2$ | 001 | Individual farm owners and their families, Poland<br>Non-probability purposive quota sample<br>N: 1002, date: June - July, 1960 | MAKAR 62<br>p. 113 |
| WORRY ABOUT DEBTS | Closed question: no vs yes | Lower among those with incomes of $ 10.000 or more | AFF 2.3 | $\overline{DR}$ | -.11 | BCI | 05 | Adults, urban areas, U.S.A.<br>Probability area samples<br>N: 2787, date: January, 1963 - January, 1964 | BRADB 69<br>p. 102 |

## P 5.2.2.2 - MOST IMPORTANT WORRY

| | | | | | | | | | |
|---|---|---|---|---|---|---|---|---|---|
| MOST IMPORTANT WORRY: | Open-ended direct question<br>Other worries vs worry mentioned | Computed for those who have worries only<br>(N = 2040) | | | | | | National adult population, U.S.A.<br>Non-probability quota sample<br>N: 2377, date: February, 1946 | WESSM 56<br>p. 213 |
| - FAMILY AND CHILDREN | | | HAPP 1.1 | G' | +.10 | Gt' | 05 | | |
| - HEALTH (personal and family) | | | HAPP 1.1 | G' | +.15 | Gt' | 01 | | |
| - FINANCIAL WORRIES, MONEY | | | HAPP 1.1 | G' | -.23 | Gt' | 01 | | |
| - SECURITY, JOB, FUTURE | | | HAPP 1.1 | G' | -.09 | Gt' | ns | | |
| - POLITICS, WORLD AND NATIONAL CONDITIONS | | | HAPP 1.1 | G' | +.31 | Gt' | 01 | | |
| - WORK CONDITIONS | | | HAPP 1.1 | G' | +.05 | Gt' | ns | | |
| - PERSONAL TRAITS | | | HAPP 1.1 | G' | -.05 | Gt' | ns | | |
| - HOUSING, PLACE TO LIVE | | | HAPP 1.1 | G' | -.25 | Gt' | ns | | |
| - VAGUE ANSWERS (anything, everything) | | | HAPP 1.1 | G' | -.03 | Gt' | ns | | |

## P 5.2.2.3 - WORRIES AND FEARS CONCERNING ONE'S COUNTRY

| | | | | | | | | | |
|---|---|---|---|---|---|---|---|---|---|
| NATIONAL WORRIES AND FEARS: | Content analysis on the basis of an open-ended question on fears and worries for the future of one's country | | | | | | | Adult population of 5 Westernized nations, 3 underdeveloped giants, 2 countries in the Middle East, 3 Caribbean nations and the Philippines<br>Representative samples<br>N: 18653, date: ± 1960 | CANTR 65/1<br>p. 263 |
| - POLITICAL | Responses rated as concerning dishonest government; inefficient government; communism; no democracy or representative government; fear country will become socialistic; lack or loss of freedom; lack of law and order; disunity among people of the nation; political instability, chaos, civil war; high or increased taxes; etc. | U-shaped curve: moderately happy people being least concerned with politics | HAPP 3.1 | G' | -.04 | Gt' | 01 | | |
| - ECONOMIC | Responses rated as concerning no improvement in or inadequate standard of living; no technological advances, economic backwardness, low productivity; failure to preserve present standard of living, economic instability; unemployment; etc. | | HAPP 3.1 | G' | -.08 | Gt' | 01 | | |
| - SOCIAL | Responses rated as concerning social injustice; continued discrimination, prejudice or exploitation; inadequate educational facilities and schoolings; poor and unfair working conditions; abuses by labor; unlimited population growth; no sense of social and political responsibility or awareness; lack of morality, ethical standards, religion; too much mechanization and standardization, materialism, conformity; etc. | | HAPP 3.1 | G' | +.11 | Gt' | 01 | | |
| - INTERNATIONAL | Responses rated as concerning war; continued armament, no control or banning of nuclear weapons; no lessening of cold war; isolation from other nations; inability to maintain neutrality; etc. | | HAPP 3.1 | G' | +.29 | Gt' | 01 | | |
| - INDEPENDENT STATUS | Responses rated as concerning not to maintain or attain the position of a world power; lose or have no status or importance; failure to exert ideological or moral leadership; lack or loss of national independence; threat, agression, domination by a communist power or any foreign power; etc. | | HAPP 3.1 | G' | +.11 | Gt' | 01 | | |
| - HAVE NO FEARS FOR NATION | Responses indicating no fears or worries for the country | | HAPP 3.1 | G' | -.02 | Gt' | ns | | |
| FEAR OF WAR | Item mentioned in open-ended question on fears and worries for one's personal future and/or for the future of one's country | The mean happiness rating for those who express fear of war is 5.1 and for those who do not express fear of war 4.8 (ns)<br>In each of the separate countries the differences were non-significant | HAPP 3.1 | DM | + | | ns | See above | CANTR 65/1<br>p. 264 |

# R 1 RELIGION

see also 'Values' (V 1)



## R 1.1 - RELIGIOUSNESS

| | | | | | | | | | |
|---|---|---|---|---|---|---|---|---|---|
| NON-RELIGIOUS | Church member vs non-member | | HAPP 1.1 | G' | -.27 | Gt' | 01 | National adult population, U.S.A.<br>Non-probability quota sample<br>N: 2377, date: February, 1946 | WESSM 56<br>p. 208 |
| NON-RELIGIOUS | Church member vs non-member | See also under 'Religious Denomination' (Part III, R 1.2) | HAPP 1.1 | G' | -.11 | | | National adult population, The Netherlands<br>N: at least 1000, date: 1948 | NIPO 49<br>p. 4 |
| NON-RELIGIOUS | Church member vs non-member | Unaffected by sex and marital status | HAPP 2.1 | | | $Chi^2$ | ns | Adults, Amsterdam, The Netherlands<br>Probability systematic random sample stratified by sex and marital status<br>N: 600, date: September - December, 1965 | JONG 69<br>p. 190 |
| NON-RELIGIOUS | Not being a member of a church | Gamma is based on a comparison of the happiness ratings of the non-religious and the happiness of the entire population. | HAPP 1.1 | G' | +.04 | Gt' | ns | Adults, Utrecht, The Netherlands<br>Probability sample stratified by age<br>N: 300, date: autumn, 1967 | MOSER 69<br>p. 23 |
| RELIGIOUSNESS | 5-item index:<br>1. I adhere strongly to the religion of my parents<br>2. I have adopted the religion of my parents, but do not take it very seriously<br>3. I have adopted a new religion to which I adhere strongly<br>4. I have adopted a new religion, but I do not take it very seriously<br>5. I do not adhere to any religion; I am essentially 'this worldly' in my outlook | The index was regarded as a 5-point scale; item 1 indicating most religious and item 5 least religious. | COMP 1.1 | $r_{pm}$ | +.33 | | s | Undergraduate college students, Hawaii<br>Non-probability accidental sample<br>N: 101, date: — | WILSO 65<br>p. 375 |
| RELIGIOUSNESS | 5-item index (see above) | For correlational purposes the items were scored in three ways:<br>- 5-point scale: item 1 indicating the most religious (as above):<br>males : r = +.01 (ns)<br>females: r = +.17 (ns)<br>- 3-point scale: item 1 or 3 (top category), 2 or 4 (middle), or 5 (lowest category):<br>males : r = -.00 (ns)<br>females: r = +.12 (ns)<br>- 5-point scale: item 3 (most religious), 4,1,2,5 (least religious):<br>males : r = +.00 (ns)<br>females: r = +.16 (ns) | COMP 1.1 | $r_{pm}$ | + | | ns | Undergraduate students, Ohio, U.S.A.<br>Non-probability accidental sample<br>N: 132, date: 1966/1967 | MILLE 68<br>p. 1082 |

| | | | | | | | | | |
|---|---|---|---|---|---|---|---|---|---|
| IMPORTANCE OF RELIGION IN ONE'S LIFE | Direct question rated on an 11-point self-anchoring scale, ranging from 'not at all important' to 'extremely important' | | HAPP 3.1 | $r_{pm}$ | +.11 | | | National adult population, U.S.A.<br>Probability sample<br>N: 1549, date: 1960 | CANTR 65/2<br>p. 268/415 |
| | | | HAPP 2.1 | $r_{pm}$ | +.18 | | | | |
| | | | CON 1.1 | $r_{pm}$ | +.15 | | | | |
| IMPORTANCE OF RELIGION IN ONE'S LIFE | Direct question rated on an 11-point self-anchoring scale (see above) | | HAPP 2.1 | r | +.17 | | | National adult population, U.S.A.<br>Cantril (1965) modified probability sample<br>N: 1406, date: 1959 | BORTN 70<br>p. 44 |
| | | | HAPP 3.1 | r | +.08 | | | | |
| | | | CON 1.1 | r | +.14 | | | | |
| RELIGIOUSNESS | Closed question on importance of religion<br>very unimportant / unimportant / of small importance / important / very important | Computed for normals only. | HAPP 2.1 | r | +.23 | | 01 | Physically defective and normal persons, Detroit, U.S.A.<br>Non-probability purposive samples<br>N: 295, date: — | CAMER 73/1<br>p. 209 |
| RELIGIOUSNESS | Direct question: 'Do you get much consolation and help from your religion?'<br>no vs yes | | HAPP 1.1 | G' | +.27 | Gt' | 01 | National adult population, U.S.A.<br>Non-probability quota sample<br>N: 2377, date: February, 1946 | WESSM 56<br>p. 207 |
| PRACTICING ONE'S RELIGION | Direct question<br>non-practicing vs practicing | Catholics : G' = +.46 (01)<br>Protestants: G' = -.05 (ns)<br>Jews : G' = +.17 (ns) | HAPP 2.1 | G' | + | Gt' | | Aged chronically-ill patients, U.S.A.<br>Probability sample<br>N: 167, date: 1959 | HENLE 67<br>p. 69 |
| INTEREST IN RELIGIOUS BELIEFS AND CEREMONIES (regardless of denomination) | Trained peer rating on a 7-point scale on the basis of observation | | AFF 5.2 | $r_{pm}$ | -.18 | | | Male students, England<br>Non-probability chunk sample<br>N: 194, date: 1912 - 1913 | WEBB 15<br>p. 26 |

## R 1.2 - RELIGIOUS DENOMINATION

| | | | | | | | | | |
|---|---|---|---|---|---|---|---|---|---|
| RELIGIOUS AFFILIATION | Protestant, Catholic, Jewish vs none, agnostics | No significant differences among those reporting Protestant, Catholic or Jewish religion | HAPP 1.1 | G' | +.27 | Gt' | 01 | National adult population, U.S.A.<br>Non-probability quota sample<br>N: 2377, date: February, 1946 | WESSM 56<br>p. 208 |
| RELIGION | Protestant / Catholic / Jewish | Protestant: Mean score = 6.5<br>Catholic : Mean score = 6.7<br>Jewish : Mean score = 7.1 | HAPP 3.1 | DM | + | | | National adult population, U.S.A.<br>Probability sample<br>N: 1549, date: ± 1960 | CANTR 65/1<br>p. 375 |
| CATHOLIC RELIGION | Protestant vs Catholic | | HAPP 1.1 | G' | -.02 | Gt' | ns | Non-institutionalized adults, U.S.A.<br>Probability multi-stage area sample<br>N: 2460, date: spring, 1957 | GURIN 60<br>p. 241 |
| CATHOLIC RELIGION | Protestant vs Catholic | Gammas are based on proportions 'very happy', 'high positive feelings', and 'high negative feelings' | | | | | | Adults, New Hampshire, U.S.A.<br>Probability sample<br>N: 600, date: — | PHILL 67A<br>p. 486 |
| | | | HAPP 1.1 | G' | -.05 | | | | |
| | | Index of Positive Affects: G' = -.15<br>Index of Negative Affects: G' = +.16 | AFF 2.3 | G' | - | | | | |
| CATHOLIC RELIGION | Protestant vs Catholic | Catholic : Mean score = 5.4<br>Protestant: Mean score = 5.3 | HAPP 3.1 | DM | + | | | National population, W. Germany<br>Probability area sample<br>N: 480, date: ± 1960 | CANTR 65/1<br>P. 376 |

| Variable | Operationalization | Remarks | Happiness measure | Statistic | Result | Test | Sig. | Population / sample | Source |
|---|---|---|---|---|---|---|---|---|---|
| RELIGIOUS AFFILIATION: | | The Gammas are based on a comparison of the happiness ratings of the category mentioned and the happiness of the entire population | | | | | | Adults, Utrecht, The Netherlands<br>Probability sample stratified by age<br>N: 300, date: autumn, 1967 | MOSER 69<br>p. 23 |
| - ROMAN CATHOLIC | | | HAPP 1.1 | G' | +.30 | Gt' | ns | | |
| - 'GEREFORMEERD' (FUNDAMENTALISTIC PROTESTANT) | | | HAPP 1.1 | G' | +.18 | Gt' | ns | | |
| - 'NEDERLANDS HERVORMD' OR OTHER (MODERATE PROTESTANT) | | | HAPP 1.1 | G' | -.15 | Gt' | ns | | |
| - NON-RELIGIOUS | | | HAPP 1.1 | G' | +.04 | Gt' | ns | | |
| RELIGIOUS DENOMINATION | Gereformeerd (Fundamentalistic Protestant / Ned. Hervormd (Moderate Protestant) / Roman Catholic / non-religious | Gereformeerd : 55% happy, 41% pretty happy<br>Ned.Hervormd : 45% happy, 45% pretty happy<br>Roman-Catholic : 39% happy, 46% pretty happy<br>Non-religious : 39% happy, 43% pretty happy | HAPP 1.1 | | | | | National adult population, The Netherlands<br>N: at least 1000, date: 1948 | NIPO 49<br>p. 4 |
| RELIGIOUS AFFILIATION | 'Collectivistic' type of church (e.g. Roman-Catholic) vs 'individualistic' type of church and non-religious | Unaffected by sex and marital status | HAPP 2.1 | | | $Chi^2$ | ns | Adults, Amsterdam, The Netherlands<br>Probability systematic random sample stratified by sex and marital status<br>N: 600, date: September - December, 1965 | JONG 69<br>p. 190 |
| RELIGION | Muslem / Christian / pagan | Muslem : Mean score = 5.3<br>Christian: Mean score = 4.3<br>pagan : Mean score = 3.8 | HAPP 3.1 | DM | + | | | National adult population, Nigeria<br>Probability sample proportionally stratified by dwelling and region<br>N: 1200, date: ± 1960 | CANTR 65/1<br>p. 371 |

## R 1.3 - RELIGIOUS PARTICIPATION

### CHURCH ATTENDANCE

| Variable | Operationalization | Remarks | Happiness measure | Statistic | Result | Test | Sig. | Population / sample | Source |
|---|---|---|---|---|---|---|---|---|---|
| CHURCH ATTENDANCE | Direct question: 'Do you attend church regularly?' no vs yes | | HAPP 1.1 | G' | +.31 | Gt' | 01 | National adult population, U.S.A.<br>Non-probability quota sample<br>N: 2377, date: February, 1946 | WESSM 56<br>p. 207 |
| CHURCH ATTENDANCE | Direct question: never / a few times a year / a few times a month / once a week / more than once a week | Analysis on the basis of the answers of Catholics and Protestants only.<br>Stronger among Catholics: G' = +.20 (01)<br>U-shaped curve: Those who attend church once a week are most happy<br>Lower among Protestants : G' = +.11 (01) | HAPP 1.1 | G' | +.14 | Gt' | 01 | Non-institutionalized adults, U.S.A.<br>Probability multi-stage area sample<br>N: 2460, date: spring, 1957 | GURIN 60<br>p. 240 |
| CHURCH ATTENDANCE | 10-point scale | Stronger among those under the age of 65: r = +.10<br>Not among those of age 65+ : r = -.01<br>The difference between the correlations is not significant<br>Unaffected by S.E.S. | HAPP 1.1 | $r_{pm}$ | +.08 | | 01 | Non-institutionalized adults, U.S.A.<br>Probability samples<br>N: 1547, date: 1972, 1973 | SPREI 74<br>p. 457 |
| CHURCH ATTENDANCE | Closed question: never / sometimes / once a week | Non-religious Ss were excluded<br>Stronger among Protestants (025)<br>Not among Catholics (ns)<br>(to be continued on the next page ) | HAPP 1.1 | G' | +.27 | Gt' | 01 | Adults, Utrecht, The Netherlands<br>Probability sample stratified by age<br>N: 300, date: autumn, 1967 | MOSER 69<br>p. 24 |

| | | | | | | | | | |
|---|---|---|---|---|---|---|---|---|---|
| | | When the non-religious were compared with the religious it appeared that those attending church once a week are about as happy as the non-religious. Those attending church sometimes, and especially religious Ss who never attend church are less happy. | | | | | | | |
| GOING TO CHURCH | Closed question on frequency in the past week: not at all / once / more than once | Lower among males : G = +.10<br>Stronger among females: G = +.28 | HAPP 1.1 | G | + | | | Adults, Metro Manila, Philippines<br>Probability area sample<br>N: 941, date: January - April, 1972 | BULAT 73<br>p. 232 |
| | | Lower among males : G = +.16<br>Stronger among females: G = +.32 | HAPP 3.1 | G | + | | | | |

## PARTICIPATION IN VARIOUS RELIGIOUS ACTIVITIES

| | | | | | | | | | |
|---|---|---|---|---|---|---|---|---|---|
| RELIGIOUS PARTICIPATION | 3-item index containing amount of time spent on religious activities, playing an active role, and holding a function | unmarried males : r = +.05 (ns)<br>married males : r = +.02 (ns)<br>unmarried females: r = +.15 (ns)<br>married females : r = +.14 (ns) | HAPP 2.1 | $r_{pm}$ | + | $Chi^2$ | ns | Adults, Amsterdam, The Netherlands<br>Probability systematic random sample stratified by sex and marital status<br>N: 600, date: September - December, 1965 | JONG 69<br>p. 203 |
| PARTICIPATION IN RELIGIOUS EVENTS | Open-ended question on how often one attended church services or other church sponsored events during the last month<br>none / 1-4 times / 5 or more times | Computed for those with current religious preferences only<br>Index of Positive Affects only: G' = -.04 (ns)<br>Positive among those of high S.E.S. : G' = +.10 (ns)<br>Negative among those of low S.E.S. : G' = -.35 (05) | AFF 2.3 | G' | -.04 | Gt' | ns | Males in the age of 25-49, 4 small communities, Illinois, U.S.A.<br>Probability multi-stage samples<br>N: 393, date: March, 1962 | BRADB 65/1<br>p. 44 |
| PARTICIPATING IN CHURCH ACTIVITIES | no church activities vs church activities | L-shaped curve: Positive among unhappier students only | COMP 2.2 | | + | | ns | Female college students, New York, U.S.A.<br>Type of construction unclear<br>N: 238, date: — | WASHB 41<br>p. 283 |
| ATTENDING RELIGIOUS SERVICES | Direct question: never / sometimes / weekly or more | Stronger among those of age 66-75: $t_k$ = +.67 (01)<br>Lower among those of age 82-92 : $t_k$ = -.10 (ns) | AFF 2.3 | $t_k$ | +.33 | | 01 | Aged female public housing residents, U.S.A.<br>Probability systematic random sample<br>N: 44, date: 1967 - 1971 | GRANE 75<br>p. 703 |
| ATTENDING RELIGIOUS SERVICES MORE OFTEN | Repeated direct question (see above)<br>Difference between scores in 1967 and 1971 | Lower among those of age 66-75 : $t_k$ = -.04 (ns)<br>Stronger among those of age 82-92: $t_k$ = -.17 (ns) | AFF 2.3 | $t_k$ | -.15 | | 07 | See above | GRANE 75<br>p. 703 |

## R 1.4 - VARIOUS FACTORS CONCERNING RELIGION

| | | | | | | | | | |
|---|---|---|---|---|---|---|---|---|---|
| SATISFACTION WITH RELIGIOUS FAITH | Closed question: 'How do you feel about . . .?' terrible / unhappy / mostly dissatisfied / mixed / mostly satisfied / pleased / delighted | Unaffected by sex | HAPP 3.1 (1st instr.) | $h^2$ | .24 | | | National adult population, U.S.A.<br>Probability area sample (first sample)<br>N: 1297, date: May, 1972 | ANDRE 74<br>p. 17 |
| SATISFACTION WITH COMFORT FROM RELIGION | Closed question rated on a 7-point self-anchoring scale, based on Cantril (1965) | | HAPP 2.1 | r | +.05 | | | Adult population of 8 major British conurbations<br>Non-probability quota sample<br>N: 593, date: October - November, 1971 | HALL 73<br>p. 100 |

# R 2 RETIREMENT

R 2.1 Being retired

R 2.2 Compulsory vs voluntary retirement

R 2.3 Various factors concerning retirement

## R 2.1 - BEING RETIRED

| | | | | | | | | |
|---|---|---|---|---|---|---|---|---|
| BEING RETIRED, INDEPENDENT | | Gamma based on difference in happiness between the retired and the entire population | HAPP 2.1 | G | -.04 | | National adult population, U.S.A.<br>Probability sample proportionally stratified by sex, age, occupation, S.E.S. and education<br>N: 1015, date: 1948 - 1949 | BUCHA 53<br>p. 213 |
| BEING RETIRED | | The Gammas are based on a comparison of those reporting 'not too happy' among those who are retired, and those reporting 'not too happy' in the entire population<br><br>males : G' = -.29 (01)<br>females: G' = -.27 (05) | HAPP 1.1 | G' | - | Gt' | Inhabitants of 4 small communities, Illinois, U.S.A.<br>Probability multi-stage samples<br>N: 2006, date: March, 1962 | BRADB 65/1<br>p. 14 |
| BEING RETIRED, INDEPENDENT | | See above at BUCHA 53 (U.S.A. sample). | HAPP 2.1 | G' | +.05 | | National adult population, Mexico<br>Probability sample proportionally stratified by sex, age, occupation, S.E.S. and education<br>N: 1752, date: 1948 - 1949 | BUCHA 53<br>p. 189 |
| BEING RETIRED, INDEPENDENT | | See above | HAPP 2.1 | G' | -.08 | | National adult population, Britain<br>Probability sample proportionally stratified by sex, age, occupation, S.E.S. and education<br>N: 1195, date: 1948 - 1949 | BUCHA 53<br>p. 138 |
| BEING AN OLD AGE PENSIONER | | The mean happiness score of the old age pensioners was compared with the mean happiness score of the entire population.<br><br>total population : Mean = 6.84<br>old age pensioners : Mean = 4.74 | HAPP 2.1 | DM | - | | National population, Britain<br>Non-probability quota sample<br>N: 213, date: March, 1971 | ABRAM 73<br>p. 4 |
| BEING RETIRED, INDEPENDENT | | See above at BUCHA 53 (U.S.A. sample). | HAPP 2.1 | G' | -.56 | | National adult population, France<br>Probability sample proportionally stratified by sex, age, occupation, S.E.S. and education<br>N: 1000, date: 1948 - 1949 | BUCHA 53<br>p. 148 |
| BEING RETIRED, INDEPENDENT | | See above | HAPP 2.1 | G' | -.28 | | National adult population, W. Germany<br>Probability sample proportionally stratified by sex, age, occupation, S.E.S. and education<br>N: 3371, date: 1948 - 1949 | BUCHA 53<br>p. 157 |

| | | | | | | | | | |
|---|---|---|---|---|---|---|---|---|---|
| BEING RETIRED, INDEPENDENT | | See last page at BUCHA 53 (U.S.A. sample) | HAPP 2.1 | G' | +.05 | | | National adult population, Italy<br>Probability sample proportionally stratified by sex, age, occupation, S.E.S. and education<br>N: 1078, date: 1948 - 1949 | BUCHA 53<br>p. 176 |
| BEING RETIRED, INDEPENDENT | | See above | HAPP 2.1 | G' | -.14 | | | National adult population, The Netherlands<br>Probability sample proportionally stratified by sex, age, occupation, S.E.S. and education<br>N: 942, date: 1948 - 1949 | BUCHA 53<br>p. 197 |
| BEING RETIRED, INDEPENDENT | | See above | HAPP 2.1 | G' | -.02 | | | National adult population, Norway<br>Probability sample proportionally stratified by sex, age, occupation, S.E.S. and education<br>N: 1030, date: 1948 - 1949 | BUCHA 53<br>p. 205 |
| BEING RETIRED, INDEPENDENT | | See above | HAPP 2.1 | G' | -.20 | | | National adult population, Australia<br>Probability sample proportionally stratified by sex, age, occupation, S.E.S. and education<br>N: 945, date: 1948 - 1949 | BUCHA 53<br>p. 131 |

AGED PERSONS ONLY:

| | | | | | | | | | |
|---|---|---|---|---|---|---|---|---|---|
| RETIREMENT | gainfully employed vs retired between 1952 and 1954 | See sample construction and remarks in excerpt (Part II).<br>Among those who were satisfied in 1952: G' = -.21<br>Among those who were dissatisfied in 1952: G' = +.11<br>When the gainfully employed were compared with retirees who had a positive orientation to retirement before they were retired : G' = +.13<br>When compared with retirees who had a negative orientation to retirement : G' = -.27<br>Unaffected by voluntary vs compulsory retirement<br>Among those who were satisfied in 1952:<br>Unaffected by economic deprivation<br>Among those in good health : G' = -.28<br>Among those in poor health : G' = +.12<br>Among those who have no difficulties in keeping occupied : G' = -.09<br>Among those who have difficulties in keeping occupied : G' = -.21 | COMP 1.2 | G' | -.07 | Gt' | ns | Aged males, U.S.A.<br>Non-probability accidental sample<br>N: 1559, date: 1952 - 1954 | THOMP 60<br>p. 167-168 |
| RETIREMENT | working full-time vs retired | Computed for males of age 65 - 70 only.<br>55% of those still working full-time, and 45% of the retired males report a high degree of life satisfaction. | HAPP 1.1 | D% | - | | | Non-institutionalized adults, U.S.A.<br>Probability samples<br>N: 1547, date: 1972, 1973 | SPREI 74<br>p. 456 |
| STILL WORKING | not working vs working | Computed for those of age 60+ only.<br>Among those who are still working 83% have life satisfaction, while among those who do not work 65% have life satisfaction. | HAPP 3.1 | D% | + | | | Adults, Japan<br>Probability sample<br>N: 2000 or more, date: September, 1973 | PALMO 75<br>p. 124 |
| YEARS OF RETIREMENT | 1-7 years | U-shaped curve: Those who retired in 1961, 1966 and 1967 were happier than those who retired during the years in-between. Especially those who had been retired for 4 years were relatively unhappy. | HAPP 1.1 | D% | | | | Retired university faculty members, U.S.A.<br>Probability systematic random sample<br>N: 547, date: 1968 | SKRAB 69<br>p. 68 |

## R 2.2 - COMPULSORY VS VOLUNTARY RETIREMENT

| | | | | | | | | | |
|---|---|---|---|---|---|---|---|---|---|
| COMPULSORY RETIREMENT | voluntary vs administrative retirement | See remarks in excerpt (Part II).<br>Computed for those who were retired only.<br>Unaffected by orientation to retirement before retirement. | COMP 1.2 | G' | -.08 | | | Aged males, U.S.A.<br>Non-probability accidental sample<br>N: 1559, date: 1952 - 1954 | THOMP 60<br>p. 168 |
| VOLUNTARY RETIREMENT | involuntary vs voluntary retirement | | COMP 4.2 | C | +.32 | $Chi^2$ | 001 | Retired aged males residing in a retirement hotel for the aged<br>Non-probability purposive quota sample matched on years of retirement, age, nature of retirement, occupational level, and length of stay at the establishment<br>N: 140, date: — | PERET 75<br>p. 134 |
| COMPULSORY RETIREMENT | not compulsory vs compulsory retirement | Only 83% of those retired under a policy of compulsory retirement considered themselves happy as compared with 90% of those who retired because they personally desired to do so. | HAPP 1.1 | D% | - | | | Retired university faculty members, U.S.A.<br>Probability systematic random sample<br>N: 547, date: 1968 | SKRAB 69<br>p. 68 |

## R 2.3 - VARIOUS FACTORS CONCERNING RETIREMENT

| | | | | | | | | | |
|---|---|---|---|---|---|---|---|---|---|
| POSITIVE PRE-RETIREMENT ATTITUDE TOWARD RETIREMENT | 3-item index of closed questions indicating a negative vs a positive orientation to retirement | See remarks in excerpt (Part II).<br>Computed for those who were retired between 1952 and 1954 only.<br>Among those who were satisfied in 1952:<br>Among the economically deprived : G' = +.27<br>Among those who are not deprived : G' = +.41<br>Among those in good health : G' = +.52<br>Among those in poor health : G' = +.30<br>Among those who have no difficulties in keeping occupied : G' = +.32<br>Among those who have difficulties in keeping occupied : G' = +.60 | COMP 1.2 | G' | +.40 | Gt' | 01 | Aged males, U.S.A.<br>Non-probability accidental sample<br>N: 1559, date: 1952 - 1954 | THOMP 60<br>p. 168 |
| ADVANCED PLANNING OF RETIREMENT | no plans / some plans / planned a great deal | ± 91% of those who had planned a great deal are happy in retirement as compared with 84% of those who had planned some, but comparatively little, and only 79% of those who had made no plans. | HAPP 1.1 | D% | + | | | Retired university faculty members, U.S.A.<br>Probability systematic random sample<br>N: 547, date: 1968 | SKRAB 69<br>p. 68 |
| POSITION AT THE TIME OF RETIREMENT | non-administrative vs administrative positions | Happy in retirement were:<br>- 100% of the former presidents<br>- 87% of the former deans or those who held administrative positions higher that that of head of department<br>- 93% of those who were heads of departments<br>- 81% of the full professors<br>- 83% of the assistant professors | HAPP 1.1 | D% | + | | | See above | SKRAB 69<br>p. 68 |
| FIELD OF ACTIVITY BEFORE RETIREMENT | professional and liberal arts colleges / other / college of agriculture and engineering | Computed for those who were actively engaged in teaching and /or research only. Those who held administrative positions were eliminated from consideration .<br>(to be continued on next page) | HAPP 1.1 | D% | + | | | See above | SKRAB 69<br>p. 68 |

| | | | | | | | | | |
|---|---|---|---|---|---|---|---|---|---|
| | | Retirees whose major activities were in the college of agriculture and engineering are relatively most happy in retirement.<br>Persons who were in the professional and liberal arts colleges are relatively least happy in retirement. | | | | | | | |
| SELF-PERCEIVED INCREASE IN OCCUPATIONAL PRESTIGE, AFTER MILITARY RETIREMENT | 3-item index of closed questions on present job in comparison with former military job with respect to: it's general importance, level of skill and knowledge required, authority over other people | Index of Positive Affects: G = +.30<br>Index of Negative Affects: G = -.01 | AFF 2.3 | G | +.22 | | | Middle-aged, presently employed army retirees, California, U.S.A.<br>Probability simple random sample<br>N: 362, date: August, 1970 | GARBE 71 p. 181 |
| SELF-PERCEIVED AMOUNT OF CHANGE IN OCCUPATIONAL ROLE CLUSTER | 5-item index of closed questions on amount of change in present occupation compared with former military occupation, rated on 4-point scales ranging from 'the same' to 'very different'<br>Items used: actual work performed, knowledge and skill used, amount of time spent working, type of organization, kind of people one works with | Index of Positive Affects: G = -.17<br>Index of Negative Affects: G = +.12<br>Among those with increased occupational prestige:<br>affect balance : G = -.29<br>positive affect: G = -.25<br>negative affect: G = +.20<br>Among those with the same occupational prestige:<br>affect balance : G = +.17<br>positive affect: G = +.05<br>negative affect: G = -.12<br>Among those with decreased occupational prestige:<br>affect balance : G = -.19<br>positive affect: G = -.17<br>negative affect: G = +.19 | AFF 2.3 | G | -.16 | | | See above | GARBE 71 p. 181 |
| CIVILIAN REFERENCE GROUP SALIENCE AFTER MILITARY RETIREMENT | 8-item index of statements indicating orientation towards and identification with civilian life and current civilian career | Presented for Index of Positive Affects only:<br>G = +.28 | AFF 2.3 | G | + | | | See above | GARBE 71 p. 196 |
| MILITARY REFERENCE GROUP SALIENCE AFTER MILITARY RETIREMENT | 8-item index of statements indicating orientation towards and identification with the army and former military career | Presented for Index of Positive Affects only:<br>G = +.10 | AFF 2.3 | G | + | | | See above | GARBE 71 p. 208 |
| ROLE LOSS | Number of lost roles | | AFF 2.3 | r | +.05 | | ns | Aged retired persons, Los Angeles County, U.S.A.<br>Non-probability purposive quota sample proportionally stratified by marital status<br>N: 71, date: 1971 | MORIW 73 p. 229 |

# S 1 SATISFACTION WITH . .

S 1.1 Satisfaction with leisure
- 1.1.1 – Leisure activities
- 1.1.2 – Leisure time

S 1.2 Satisfaction with living environment
- 1.2.1 – Housing
- 1.2.2 – Neighborhood
- 1.2.3 – Specific facilities
- 1.2.4 – Various aspects of the living environment

S 1.3 Satisfaction with nation
- 1.3.1 – Nation in general
- 1.3.2 – Government
- 1.3.3 – Various aspects of the nation

S 1.4 Satisfaction with oneself . . . . . . . . . . . see S 2.1

S 1.5 Satisfaction with one's own life . . . . . . . . see H 1, L 2

S 1.6 Satisfaction with physical health

S 1.7 Satisfaction with social life
- 1.7.1 – Family, relatives
- 1.7.2 – Marriage
- 1.7.3 – Friends, social contacts
- 1.7.4 – Various aspects of social life

S 1.8 Satisfaction with socio-economic level
- 1.8.1 – S.E.S. in general
- 1.8.2 – Level of education
- 1.8.3 – Income, standard of living . . . . . . . . . . . see also S 1.9.2

S 1.9 Satisfaction with work, job. . . . . . . . . . . . see also A 2.2.14
- 1.9.1 – Work in general
- 1.9.2 – Specific aspects of the job

S 1.10 Various domainsatisfactions

S 1.11 Satisfaction sumscores

## S 1.1 - SATISFACTION WITH LEISURE

### S 1.1.1 - LEISURE ACTIVITIES

| | | | | | | | | | |
|---|---|---|---|---|---|---|---|---|---|
| SATISFACTION WITH SPARE TIME ACTIVITIES | Closed question: 'How do you feel about . . .?' terrible / unhappy / mostly dissatisfied / mixed / mostly satisfied / pleased / delighted | Unaffected by sex | HAPP 3.1 (1st instr.) | $h^2$ | .41 | | | National adult population, U.S.A.<br>Probability area sample (first sample)<br>N: 1297, date: May, 1972 | ANDRE 74 p. 17 |
| SATISFACTION WITH SPARE TIME ACTIVITIES | See above | | HAPP 3.1 (1st instr.) | $h^2$ | .47 | | | National adult population, U.S.A.<br>Probability area sample (third sample)<br>N: 1072, date: November, 1972 | ANDRE 74 p. 19 |
| HAPPINESS WITH LEISURE TIME ACTIVITIES | Closed question rated on an 11-point self-anchoring scale, based on Cantril (1965) | | HAPP 1.1 | $r_{pm}$ | +.55 | | | Workers of a Utility Union, Greater Kansas City area, U.S.A.<br>Probability cluster sample<br>N: 213, date: — | GILLO 73 p. 124 |
| SATISFACTION WITH THINGS YOU CAN DO IN LEISURE TIME | Closed question rated on an 11-point self-anchoring scale, based on Cantril (1965) | | HAPP 2.1 | $r_{pm}$ | +.24 | | | National population, Britain<br>Non-probability quota sample<br>N: 213, date: March, 1971 | ABRAM 73 p. 21 |
| SATISFACTION WITH LEISURE TIME ACTIVITIES | Closed question ranging from 'not at all satisfied' to 'very satisfied' | | HAPP 1.1<br>AFF 1.1 | mc<br>mc | +.55<br>+.51 | | | Urban adult Jewish population, Israel<br>Probability area sample, using dwelling units<br>N: 1940, date: spring, 1973 | LEVY 75/1 p. 372 |
| SATISFACTION WITH POSSIBILITIES TO PURSUE ONE'S HOBBIES | Closed question rated on an open graphic scale ranging from 'very dissatisfied' to 'very satisfied' | Lower among those of age 41 – 50<br>Unaffected by S.E.S.<br>Stronger among those of medium educational level<br>Stronger among females | HAPP 1.1 | G | +.53 | | 05 | National adult population, The Netherlands<br>Probability area sample<br>N: 1552, date: June, 1968 | BAKKE 74 p. 27 |
| LITTLE SATISFACTION RECEIVED FROM SPORTS | Closed question: disagree / not sure / agree | Unaffected by sex<br><br>males: G = –.33 (01)<br>females: G = –.25 (ns) | HAPP 1.1<br>HAPP 2.1 | G<br>G | –.25<br>– | $Chi^2$<br>$Chi^2$ | ns | Adults, Toledo, Ohio, U.S.A.<br>Systematic random sample<br>N: 510, date: 1973 | SNYDE 74 p. 35 |

## S I.1.2 - LEISURE TIME

| | | | | | | | | | |
|---|---|---|---|---|---|---|---|---|---|
| SATISFACTION WITH AMOUNT OF TIME FOR DOING THE THINGS ONE LIKES | Closed question: 'How do you feel about . . .' terrible / unhappy / mostly dissatisfied / mixed / mostly satisfied / pleased / delighted | Unaffected by sex | HAPP 3.1 (1st instr.) | $h^2$ | .28 | | | National adult population, U.S.A.<br>Probability area sample (first sample)<br>N: 1297, date: May, 1972 | ANDRE 74 p. 17 |
| SATISFACTION WITH AMOUNT OF TIME FOR DOING THE THINGS ONE LIKES | See above | | HAPP 3.1 (1st instr.) | $h^2$ | .31 | | | National adult population, U.S.A.<br>Probability area sample (third sample)<br>N: 1072, date: November, 1972 | ANDRE 74 p. 19 |
| SATISFACTION WITH CHANCES FOR RELAXATION | See above | | HAPP 3.1 (1st instr.) | $h^2$ | .39 | | | See above | ANDRE 74 p. 19 |
| SATISFACTION WITH SPARE TIME | Closed question rated on a 7-point self-anchoring scale, based on Cantril (1965) | | HAPP 2.1 | r | +.40 | | | Adult population of 8 major British conurbations<br>Non-probability quota sample<br>N: 593, date: October - November, 1971 | HALL 73 p. 100 |
| SATISFACTION WITH POSSIBILITIES FOR LEISURE TIME ACTIVITIES | Closed question rated on a 4-point scale ranging from 'very unsatisfied' to 'very satisfied' | unmarried employed males: r = +.53 (05)<br>unmarried employed females: r = +.19 (05)<br>married employed males: r = +.28 (05)<br>married employed females: r = +.29 (05)<br>married non-employed females: r = +.54 (05) | HAPP 2.1 | $r_{pm}$ | + | | 05 | Inhabitants of Helsinki, Finland<br>Probability sample<br>N: 442, date: spring - summer, 1966 | HAAVI 71 p. 590 |

## S 1.2 - SATISFACTION WITH LIVING ENVIRONMENT

### S I.2.1 - HOUSING

| | | | | | | | | | |
|---|---|---|---|---|---|---|---|---|---|
| SATISFACTION WITH HOUSE, APARTMENT | Closed question: 'How do you feel about . . .' terrible / unhappy / mostly dissatisfied / mixed / mostly satisfied / pleased / delighted | Unaffected by sex | HAPP 3.1 (1st instr.) | $h^2$ | .36 | | | National adult population, U.S.A.<br>Probability area sample (first sample)<br>N: 1297, date: May, 1972 | ANDRE 74 p. 17 |
| SATISFACTION WITH HOUSE, APARTMENT | See above | | HAPP 3.1 (1st instr.) | $h^2$ | .44 | | | National adult population, U.S.A.<br>Probability area sample (third sample)<br>N: 1072, date: November, 1972 | ANDRE 74 p. 19 |
| SATISFACTION WITH HOUSING | Closed question rated on an 11-point self-anchoring scale, based on Cantril (1965) | | HAPP 2.1 | $r_{pm}$ | +.13 | | | National population, Britain<br>Non-probability quota sample<br>N: 213, date: March, 1971 | ABRAM 73 p. 21 |
| SATISFACTION WITH HOUSE | Closed question rated on a 7-point self-anchoring scale, based on Cantril (1965) | | HAPP 2.1 | r | +.19 | | | Adult population of 8 major British conurbations<br>Non-probability quota sample<br>N: 593, date: October - November, 1971 | HALL 73 p. 100 |
| SATISFACTION WITH HOUSING | Closed question rated on an open graphic scale ranging from 'very dissatisfied' to 'very satisfied' | Lower among those of medium S.E.S.<br>Stronger among those of high or low S.E.S.<br>Lower among those of medium and high educational level<br>Unaffected by age and sex | HAPP 1.1 | G | +.41 | | 05 | National adult population, The Netherlands<br>Probability area sample<br>N: 1552, date: June, 1968 | BAKKE 74 p. 27 |

| | | | | | | | | | |
|---|---|---|---|---|---|---|---|---|---|
| SATISFACTION WITH HOUSING | Direct yes / no question | unmarried males: r = +.30 (01)<br>married males: r = +.01 (ns)<br>unmarried females: r = +.29 (025)<br>married females: r = +.04 (ns) | HAPP 2.1 | $r_{pm}$ | + | $Chi^2$ | | Adults, Amsterdam, The Netherlands<br>Probability systematic random sample, stratified by sex and marital status<br>N: 600, date: September - December, 1965 | JONG 69<br>p. 192 |
| SATISFACTION WITH HOUSING | Direct yes / no question | | HAPP 2.1 | G | +.26 | $Chi^2$ | 000 | Male employees of age 40+, The Netherlands<br>Non-probability chunk sample<br>N: 13000, date: — | SONDE 75 |
| SATISFACTION WITH APARTMENT | Closed question ranging from 'very unsatisfied' to 'very satisfied' | | HAPP 1.1<br>AFF 1.1 | mc<br>mc | +.30<br>+.26 | | | Urban adult Jewish population, Israel<br>Probability area sample using dwelling units<br>N: 1940, date: spring, 1973 | LEVY 75/1<br>p. 372 |

## S I.2.2 - NEIGHBORHOOD

| | | | | | | | | | |
|---|---|---|---|---|---|---|---|---|---|
| SATISFACTION WITH COMMUNITY | Closed question: would rather live somewhere else vs like living in this community | | HAPP 1.1 | G' | +.34 | Gt' | 01 | National adult population, U.S.A.<br>Non-probability quota sample<br>N: 2377, date: February, 1946 | WESSM 56<br>p. 200 |
| SATISFACTION WITH NEIGHBORHOOD | 6-item index containing satisfaction with neighbors, community members, outdoor space, location and safety<br>Closed questions: 'How do you feel about . . .' terrible / unhappy / mostly dissatisfied / mixed / mostly satisfied / pleased / delighted | Unaffected by sex | HAPP 3.1<br>(1st instr.) | $h^2$ | .31 | | | National adult population, U.S.A.<br>Probability area sample (first sample)<br>N: 1297, date: May, 1972 | ANDRE 74<br>p. 17 |
| SATISFACTION WITH DISTRICT | Closed question rated on an 11-point self-anchoring scale, based on Cantril (1965) | | HAPP 2.1 | $r_{pm}$ | +.03 | | | National population Britain<br>Non-probability quota sample<br>N: 213, date: March, 1971 | ABRAM 73<br>p. 21 |
| SATISFACTION WITH DISTRICT | Closed question rated on a 7-point self-anchoring scale, based on Cantril (1965) | | HAPP 2.1 | r | +.24 | | | Adult population of 8 major British conurbations<br>Non-probability quota sample<br>N: 593, date: October - November, 1971 | HALL 73<br>p. 100 |
| SATISFACTION WITH NEIGHBORHOOD | Single direct question rated on an open graphic scale ranging from 'very dissatisfied' to 'very satisfied' | Unaffected by age and sex<br>No relation among those of highest or lowest S.E.S.<br>No relation among those of high educational level | HAPP 1.1 | G | +.42 | | 05 | National adult population, The Netherlands<br>Probability area sample<br>N: 1552, date: June, 1968 | BAKKE 74<br>p. 27 |
| SATISFACTION WITH LIFE IN ONE'S TOWN | Closed question ranging from 'not at all satisfied' to 'very satisfied' | | HAPP 1.1<br>AFF 1.1 | mc<br>mc | +.45<br>+.36 | | | Urban adult Jewish population, Israel<br>Probability area sample using dwelling units<br>N: 1940, date: spring, 1973 | LEVY 75/1<br>p. 372 |

## S I.2.3 - SPECIFIC FACILITIES

| | | | | | | | | | |
|---|---|---|---|---|---|---|---|---|---|
| SATISFACTION WITH SCHOOL FACILITIES IN THE AREA | Closed question: 'How do you feel about . . .' terrible / unhappy / mostly dissatisfied / mixed / mostly satisfied / pleased / delighted | Unaffected by sex | HAPP 3.1<br>(1st instr.) | $h^2$ | +.17 | | | National adult population, U.S.A.<br>Probability area sample (first sample)<br>N: 1297, date: May, 1972 | ANDRE 74<br>p. 17 |

| | | | | | | | | | |
|---|---|---|---|---|---|---|---|---|---|
| SATISFACTION WITH COMMUNITY'S SCHOOL FACILITIES | Closed question rated on a graphic rating scale very dissatisfied / somewhat disssatisfied / neither satisfied nor dissatisfied / somewhat satisfied / very satisfied | males: r = +.12 (05)<br>females: r = +.08 (ns) | HAPP 3.1 | $r_{pm}$ | + | t | | Workers, Columbia, Canada<br>Non-probability purposive sample by expert choice<br>N: 470, date: — | HULIN 69<br>p. 285 |
| SATISFACTION WITH SCHOOL TEACHERS IN THE COMMUNITY | See above | males: r = +.15 (01)<br>females: r = +.07 (ns) | HAPP 3.1 | $r_{pm}$ | + | t | | See above | HULIN 69<br>p. 285 |
| SATISFACTION WITH MEDICAL CARE | 11-item satisfaction with medical care index containing satisfaction with doctor's concern about health, warmth and personal interest, friendliness, training and technical competence, willingness to listen, amount of time spent with you, amount of privacy in doctor's office, amount of health information given, quality of medical care, adequacy of office facilities and equipment, and friendliness of nurses, receptionists, etc. | Investigated among those who received some medical services in the past year. | AFF 1.1 | $r_{pm}$ | +.12 | | 001 | Families of hourly workers and salaried employees, U.S.A.<br>N: 712, date: summer, 1973 | TESSL 75<br>p. 102 |
| SATISFACTION WITH MEDICAL CARE FOR CHILDREN | 11-item satisfaction with medical care index rephrased so as to be appropriate to measure satisfaction with care received by children | Computed for Ss with children under 12 only (N= 386) | AFF 1.1 | $r_{pc}$ | | | ns | See above | TESSL 75<br>p. 105 |
| SATISFACTION WITH COMMUNITY'S MEDICAL FACILITIES | Closed question rated on a graphic rating scale very dissatisfied / somewhat dissatisfied / neither dissatisfied nor satisfied / somewhat satisfied / very satisfied | males: r = +.09 (ns)<br>females: r = +.05 (ns) | HAPP 3.1 | $r_{pm}$ | + | t | ns | Workers, Columbia, Canada<br>Non-probability purposive sample by expert choice<br>N: 470, date: — | HULIN 69<br>p. 285 |
| SATISFACTION WITH AVAILABILITY OF DOCTORS IN THE COMMUNITY | See above | males only | HAPP 3.1 | $r_{pm}$ | +.13 | t | 05 | See above | HULIN 69<br>p. 285 |
| SATISFACTION WITH AVAILABILITY OF DENTISTS IN THE COMMUNITY | See above | males only | HAPP 3.1 | $r_{pm}$ | +.13 | t | 05 | See above | HULIN 69<br>p. 285 |
| SATISFACTION WITH MEDICAL SERVICES | Closed question | | HAPP 1.1<br>AFF 1.1 | mc<br>mc | +.15<br>+.20 | | | Urban adult Jewish population, Israel<br>Probability area sample using dwelling units<br>N: 1830, date: summer, 1973 | LEVY 75/2<br>p. 373 |
| SATISFACTION WITH CONSUMER FACILITIES | 3-item index containing satisfaction with the way you can get around to work, school, shopping, etc; doctors, clinics and hospitals; and the goods and services one can buy in the area<br>Closed questions: 'How do you feel about . . .' terrible / unhappy / mostly dissatisfied / mixed / mostly satisfied / pleased / delighted | Unaffected by sex | HAPP 3.1<br>(1st instr.) | $h^2$ | .31 | | | National adult population, U.S.A.<br>Probability area sample (first sample)<br>N: 1297, date: May, 1972 | ANDRE 74<br>p. 17 |
| SATISFACTION WITH GOODS AND SERVICES AVAILABLE IN THE AREA | Closed question: 'How do you feel about . . . .' terrible / unhappy / mostly dissatisfied / mixed / mostly satisfied / pleased / delighted | | HAPP 3.1<br>(1st instr.) | $h^2$ | .25 | | | National adult population, U.S.A.<br>Probability area sample (third sample)<br>N: 1072, date: November, 1972 | ANDRE 74<br>p. 19 |
| SATISFACTION WITH SHOPPING FACILITIES IN THE COMMUNITY | Closed question rated on a graphic rating scale very dissatisfied / somewhat dissatisfied / neither satisfied nor dissatisfied / somewhat satisfied / very satisfied | Stronger among males: r = +.22 (01)<br>Lower among females: r = +.10 (ns | HAPP 3.1 | $r_{pm}$ | + | t | | Workers, Columbia, Canada<br>Non-probability purposive sample by expert choice<br>N: 470, date: — | HULIN 69<br>p. 285 |
| SATISFACTION WITH RECREATION FACILITIES | 2-item index containing satisfaction with outdoor places and sports and recreation facilities<br>Closed questions: 'How do you feel about . . .' terrible / unhappy / mostly dissatisfied / mixed / mostly satisfied / pleased / delighted | Unaffected by sex | HAPP 3.1<br>(1st instr.) | $h^2$ | .22 | | | National adult population, U.S.A.<br>Probability area sample (first sample)<br>N: 1297, date: May, 1972 | ANDRE 74<br>p. 17 |

| | | | | | | | | |
|---|---|---|---|---|---|---|---|---|
| SATISFACTION WITH NEARBY PLACES OF RECREATION AND SPORTS | Closed question: 'How do you feel about . . .' terrible / unhappy / mostly dissatisfied / mixed / mostly satisfied / pleased / delighted | | HAPP 3.1 (1st instr.) | $h^2$ | .27 | | | National adult population, U.S.A. Probability area sample (third sample) N: 1072, date: November, 1972 | ANDRE 74 p. 19 |
| SATISFACTION WITH ADULT RECREATIONAL FACILITIES IN THE COMMUNITY | Closed question rated on a graphic rating scale very dissatisfied / somewhat dissatisfied / neither satisfied nor dissatisfied / somewhat satisfied / very satisfied | males: r = +.22 (01)<br>females: r = +.20 (ns) | HAPP 3.1 | $r_{pm}$ | + | t | | Workers, Columbia, Canada Non-probability purposive sample by expert choice N: 470, date: — | HULIN 69 p. 285 |
| SATISFACTION WITH RECREATIONAL FACILITIES FOR CHILDREN IN THE COMMUNITY | See above | Stronger among females: r = +.27 (05)<br>Lower among males: r = +.12 (05) | HAPP 3.1 | $r_{pm}$ | + | t | 05 | See above | HULIN 69 p. 285 |
| SATISFACTION WITH MUNICIPAL SERVICES, like garbage collection, fire and police protection | Closed question: 'How do you feel about . . .' terrible / unhappy / mostly dissatisfied / mixed / mostly satisfied / pleased / delighted | Unaffected by sex | HAPP 3.1 (1st instr.) | $h^2$ | .20 | | | National adult population, U.S.A. Probability area sample (first sample) N: 1297, date: May, 1972 | ANDRE 74 p. 17 |
| SATISFACTION WITH THE WAY THE POLICE AND THE COURTS DO THEIR JOB | Closed question rated on an 11-point self-anchoring scale, based on Cantril (1965) | | HAPP 2.1 | $r_{pm}$ | -.04 | | | National population, Britain Non-probability quota sample N: 213, date: March, 1971 | ABRAM 73 p. 21 |
| SATISFACTION WITH AVAILABILITY OF LIVING ACCOMMODATIONS IN THE COMMUNITY | Closed question rated on a graphic rating scale very dissatisfied / somewhat dissatisfied / neither satisfied nor dissatisfied / somewhat satisfied / very satisfied | Stronger among males: r = +.23 (01)<br>Lower among females: r = +.08 (ns) | HAPP 3.1 | $r_{pm}$ | + | t | | Workers, Columbia, Canada Non-probability purposive sample by expert choice N: 470, date: — | HULIN 69 p. 285 |

## S 1.2.4 - VARIOUS ASPECTS OF THE LIVING ENVIRONMENT

| | | | | | | | | | |
|---|---|---|---|---|---|---|---|---|---|
| SATISFACTION WITH LOCAL GOVERNMENT | 2-item index containing satisfaction with police and courts, and local government<br>Closed questions: 'How do you feel about . . .' terrible / unhappy / mostly dissatisfied / mixed / mostly satisfied / pleased / delighted | Stronger among males: $h^2$ = .31<br>Lower among females : $h^2$ = .18 | HAPP 3.1 (1st instr.) | $h^2$ | .23 | | | National adult population, U.S.A. Probability area sample (first sample) N: 1297, date: May, 1972 | ANDRE 74 p. 17 |
| SATISFACTION WITH COST OF LIVING IN THE COMMUNITY | Closed question rated on a graphic rating scale very dissatisfied / somewhat dissatisfied / neither satisfied nor dissatisfied / somewhat satisfied / very satisfied | Stronger among males: r = +.23 (01)<br>Lower among females: r = +.08 (ns) | HAPP 3.1 | $r_{pm}$ | + | t | | Workers, Columbia, Canada Non-probability purposive sample by expert choice N: 470, date: — | HULIN 69 p. 285 |
| SATISFACTION WITH COSTS OF HOUSING IN THE COMMUNITY | See above | males: r = +.09 (ns)<br>females: r = +.15 (ns) | HAPP 3.1 | $r_{pm}$ | + | t | ns | See above | HULIN 69 p. 285 |
| SATISFACTION WITH ATTRACTIVENESS OF TOWN | See above | Stronger among males: r = +.24 (01)<br>Lower among females: r = +.09 (ns) | HAPP 3.1 | $r_{pm}$ | + | t | | See above | HULIN 69 p. 285 |
| SATISFACTION WITH LOCATION OF THE COMMUNITY IN TERMS OF ISOLATION AND REMOTE LOCATION | See above | males: r = +.30 (01)<br>females: r = +.29 (01) | HAPP 3.1 | $r_{pm}$ | + | t | 01 | See above | HULIN 69 p. 285 |
| SATISFACTION WITH CONDITION OF NATURAL ENVIRONMENT IN THE AREA | Closed question: 'How do you feel about . . .' terrible / unhappy / mostly dissatisfied / mixed / mostly satisfied / pleased / delighted | Unaffected by sex | HAPP 3.1 (1st instr.) | $h^2$ | .13 | | | National adult population, U.S.A. Probability area sample (first sample) N: 1297, date: May, 1972 | ANDRE 74 p. 17 |
| SATISFACTION WITH SECURITY FROM THEFT | See above | | HAPP 3.1 (1st instr.) | $h^2$ | .27 | | | National adult population, U.S.A. Probability area sample (third sample) N: 1072, date: November, 1972 | ANDRE 74 p. 19 |

| | | | | | | | | | |
|---|---|---|---|---|---|---|---|---|---|
| **SATISFACTION WITH THE WEATHER** | See last page | Unaffected by sex | HAPP 3.1 (1st instr.) | $h^2$ | .12 | | | National adult population, U.S.A.<br>Probability area sample (first sample)<br>N: 1297, date: May, 1972 | ANDRE 74<br>p. 17 |
| **SATISFACTION WITH THE WEATHER** | Closed question rated on a graphic rating scale very dissatisfied / somewhat dissatisfied / neither satisfied nor dissatisfied / somewhat satisfied / very satisfied | males: r = +.25 (01)<br>females: r = +.23 (05) | HAPP 3.1 | $r_{pm}$ | + | t | 05 | Workers, Columbia, Canada<br>Non-probability purposive sample by expert choice<br>N: 470, date: — | HULIN 69<br>p. 285 |

## S 1.3 - SATISFACTION WITH NATION

### S 1.3.1 - NATION IN GENERAL

| | | | | | | | | | |
|---|---|---|---|---|---|---|---|---|---|
| SATISFACTION WITH THE WAY THINGS ARE GOING IN THE U.S.A | Closed question rated on an 11 point self-anchoring scale (see Cantril, 1965) | | HAPP 2.1<br>HAPP 3.1<br>CON 1.1 | r<br>r<br>r | -.11<br>-.09<br>-.11 | | | National adult population, U.S.A.<br>Cantril (1965) modified probability sample<br>N: 1406, date: 1959 | BORTN 70<br>p. 44 |
| DISSATISFACTION WITH PRESENT SOCIO-POLITICAL ORDER | 5-item index indicating anomia and powerlessness (from a shortened Adorna F-scale; see Weima, 1963) | | HAPP 1.1 | G' | +.13 | Gt' | ns | Adults, Utrecht, The Netherlands<br>Probability sample stratified by age<br>N: 300, date: autumn, 1967 | MOSER 69<br>p. 40 |

### S 1.3.2 - GOVERNMENT

| | | | | | | | | | |
|---|---|---|---|---|---|---|---|---|---|
| SATISFACTION WITH NATIONAL GOVERNMENT | 4-item index containing satisfaction with the way the government is operating, what the government is doing about the economy, national military activities, the way political leaders think and act<br>Closed questions: 'How do you feel about . . .' terrible / unhappy / mostly dissatisfied / neither satisfied nor dissatisfied / somewhat satisfied / very satisfied | Unaffected by sex | HAPP 3.1 (1st instr.) | $h^2$ | .26 | | | National adult population, U.S.A.<br>Probability area sample (first sample)<br>N: 1297, date: May, 1972 | ANDRE 74<br>p. 17 |
| SATISFACTION WITH NATIONAL GOVERNMENT | 3-item index containing satisfaction with what government is doing, and the way political leaders think and act<br>Closed questions (See above) | | HAPP 3.1 (1st instr.) | $h^2$ | .25 | | | National adult population, U.S.A.<br>Probability area sample (third sample)<br>N: 1072, date: November, 1972 | ANDRE 74<br>p. 19 |
| SATISFACTION WITH THE WAY THE GOVERNMENT HANDLES STRIKES | Closed question ranging from 'not at all satisfied' to 'very satisfied' | | HAPP 1.1<br>AFF 1.1 | mc<br>mc | +.01<br>-.04 | | | Urban adult Jewish population, Israel<br>Probability area sample using dwelling units<br>N: 1940, date: spring, 1973 | LEVY 75/1<br>p. 372 |
| SATISFACTION WITH THE WAY THE GOVERNMENT HANDLES STRIKES | Closed question | | HAPP 1.1<br>AFF 1.1 | mc<br>mc | +.08<br>+.08 | | | Urban adult Jewish population, Israel<br>Probability area sample using dwelling units<br>N: 1830, date: summer, 1973 | LEVY 75/2<br>p. 373 |

| | | | | | | | |
|---|---|---|---|---|---|---|---|
| SATISFACTION WITH THE WAY THE GOVERNMENT HANDLES PROBLEMS RELATED TO TERRORIST ACTIVITIES AGAINST ISRAELIS ABROAD | Closed question ranging from 'not at all satisfied' to 'very satisfied' | | HAPP 1.1<br>AFF 1.1 | mc<br>mc | +.09<br>+.04 | Urban adult Jewish population, Israel<br>Probability area sample using dwelling units<br>N: 1940, date: spring, 1973 | LEVY 75/1<br>p. 372 |

## S 1.3.3 - VARIOUS ASPECTS OF THE NATION

| | | | | | | | |
|---|---|---|---|---|---|---|---|
| SATISFACTION WITH STANDARDS AND VALUES OF TODAY'S SOCIETY | Closed question: 'How do you feel about . . .' terrible / unhappy / mostly dissatisfied / mixed / mostly satisfied / pleased / delighted | | HAPP 3.1 (1st instr.) | $h^2$ | .26 | National adult population, U.S.A.<br>Probability area sample (third sample)<br>N: 1072, date: November, 1972 | ANDRE 74<br>p. 19 |
| SATISFACTION WITH THE WAY YOUNG PEOPLE THINK AND ACT | See above | Stronger among females: $h^2 = .23$<br>Lower among males: $h^2 = .11$ | HAPP 3.1 (1st instr.) | $h^2$ | .15 | National adult population, U.S.A.<br>Probability area sample (first sample)<br>N: 1297, date: May, 1972 | ANDRE 74<br>p. 17 |
| SATISFACTION WITH THE WAY PEOPLE OVER FORTY THINK AND ACT | See above | Unaffected by sex | HAPP 3.1 (1st instr.) | $h^2$ | .22 | See above | ANDRE 74<br>p. 17 |
| SATISFACTION WITH LEVEL OF DEMOCRACY | Closed question rated on a 7-point self-anchoring scale, based on Cantril (1965) | | HAPP 2.1 | r | +.25 | Adult population of 8 major British conurbations<br>Non-probability quota sample<br>N: 593, date: October - November, 1971 | HALL 73<br>p. 100 |
| SATISFACTION WITH WELFARE SERVICES such as health, pensions, social workers, social security, etc. | Closed question rated on an 11-point self-anchoring scale, based on Cantril (1965) | | HAPP 2.1 | $r_{pm}$ | +.37 | National population, Britain<br>Non-probability quota sample<br>N: 213, date: March, 1971 | ABRAM 73<br>p. 21 |
| SATISFACTION WITH COST OF LIVING | Closed questions: 'How do you feel about . . .' terrible / unhappy / mostly dissatisfied / mixed / mostly satisfied / pleased / delighted | | HAPP 3.1 (1st instr.) | $h^2$ | .26 | National adult population, U.S.A.<br>Probability area sample (first sample)<br>N: 1297, date: May, 1972 | ANDRE 74<br>p. 17 |
| SATISFACTION WITH ECONOMIC SITUATION | Closed question | | HAPP 1.1<br>AFF 1.1 | mc<br>mc | +.19<br>+.15 | Urban adult Jewish population, Israel<br>Probability area sample using dwelling units<br>N: 1830, date: summer, 1973 | LEVY 75/2<br>p. 373 |
| SATISFACTION WITH THE WAY THE HISTADRUT HANDLES STRIKES | Closed question ranging from 'not at all satisfied' to 'very satisfied' | | HAPP 1.1<br>AFF 1.1 | mc<br>mc | -.03<br>-.07 | Urban adult Jewish population, Israel<br>Probability area sample using dwelling units<br>N: 1940, date: spring, 1973 | LEVY 75/1<br>p. 372 |
| SATISFACTION WITH MEDIA | 2-item index containing satisfaction with entertainment and information from TV, radio, newspapers, etc.<br>Closed questions: 'How do you feel about . . .' terrible / unhappy / mostly dissatisfied / mixed / mostly satisfied / pleased / delighted | Stronger among males: $h^2 = .22$<br>Lower among females: $h^2 = .12$ | HAPP 3.1 (1st instr.) | $h^2$ | .15 | National adult population, U.S.A.<br>Probability area sample (first sample)<br>N: 1297, date: May, 1972 | ANDRE 74<br>p. 17 |
| SATISFACTION WITH ISRAELI TV PROGRAMS | Closed question ranging from 'very unsatisfied' to 'very satisfied' | | HAPP 1.1<br>AFF 1.1 | mc<br>mc | +.02<br>-.08 | Urban adult Jewish population, Israel<br>Probability area sample using dwelling units<br>N: 1940, date: spring, 1973 | LEVY 75/1<br>p. 372 |

## S 1.4 - SATISFACTION WITH ONESELF

See 'Formal Aspects of Self Image' (S 2.1)

## S 1.5 - SATISFACTION WITH ONE'S OWN LIFE

See 'Happiness' (H 1) and 'Life Quality' (L 2)

## S 1.6 - SATISFACTION WITH PHYSICAL HEALTH

| | | | | | | | | | |
|---|---|---|---|---|---|---|---|---|---|
| SATISFACTION WITH HEALTH, PHYSICAL CONDITION | Closed question: 'How do you feel about . . .' terrible / unhappy / mostly dissatisfied / mixed / mostly satisfied / pleased / delighted | Unaffected by sex | HAPP 3.1 (1st instr.) | $h^2$ | .29 | | | National adult population, U.S.A.<br>Probability area sample (first sample)<br>N: 1297, date: May, 1972 | ANDRE 74 p. 17 |
| SATISFACTION WITH HEALTH, PHYSICAL CONDITION | See above | | HAPP 3.1 (1st instr.) | $h^2$ | .38 | | | National adult population, U.S.A.<br>Probability area sample (third sample)<br>N: 1072, date: November, 1972 | ANDRE 74 p. 19 |
| SATISFACTION WITH HEALTH | Closed question | Stronger among whites: G = +.33 (05)<br>Lower among blacks: G = +.04 (ns) | HAPP 1.1 | G | + | | | Non-institutionalized adults, U.S.A.<br>Type of sample construction unclear<br>N: 1602, date: March, 1972 | ALSTO 74 p. 101 |
| SATISFACTION WITH HEALTH | Closed question rated on an 11-point self-anchoring scale, based on Cantril (1965) | | HAPP 2.1 | $r_{pm}$ | +.10 | | | National population, Britain<br>Non-probability quota sample<br>N: 213, date: March, 1971 | ABRAM 73 p. 21 |
| SATISFACTION WITH HEALTH | Closed question rated on a 7-point self-anchoring scale, based on Cantril (1965) | | HAPP 2.1 | r | +.24 | | | Adult population of 8 major British conurbations<br>Non-probability quota sample<br>N: 593, October - November, 1971 | HALL 73 p. 100 |
| SATISFACTION WITH HEALTH | Closed question rated on an open graphic scale ranging from 'very dissatisfied' to 'very satisfied' | Unaffected by age and sex<br>Stronger among those of low S.E.S.<br>Lower among those of low educational level | HAPP 1.1 | G | +.60 | | 05 | National adult population, The Netherlands<br>Probability area sample<br>N: 1552, date: June, 1968 | BAKKE 74 p. 28 |
| SATISFACTION WITH HEALTH | Closed question rated on a 5-point scale ranging from 'dissatisfied' to 'very satisfied' | Stronger among males: In the different age groups r ranges from +.24 to +.42 (s)<br>Lower among females: r ranging from +.07 to +.22 (ns)<br>Stronger among those of age 50-65:<br>males: r = +.42 (s)<br>females: r = +.22 (ns) | HAPP 1.1 | $r_{pm}$ | +.29 | $Chi^2$ | s | Adults, Utrecht, The Netherlands<br>Probability sample stratified by age<br>N: 300, date: autumn, 1967 | MOSER 69 p. 32 |
| SATISFACTION WITH HEALTH IN RELATION WITH IMPORTANCE ATTACHED TO HEALTH | Satisfaction weighted for importance attached to good health | | HAPP 1.1 | G' | +.29 | Gt' | 01 | See above | MOSER 69 p. 33 |

## S 1.7 - SATISFACTION WITH SOCIAL LIFE

### S 1.7.1 - FAMILY, RELATIVES

| | | | | | | | | | |
|---|---|---|---|---|---|---|---|---|---|
| SATISFACTION WITH FAMILY | 3-item index containing satisfaction with children, wife/husband, and marriage<br>Closed questions: 'How do you feel about . . . terrible / unhappy / mostly dissatisfied / mixed / mostly satisfied / pleased / delighted | Unaffected by sex | HAPP 3.1 (1st instr.) | $h^2$ | .38 | | | National adult population, U.S.A.<br>Probability area sample (first sample)<br>N: 1297, date: May, 1972 | ANDRE 74 p. 17 |
| SATISFACTION WITH OWN FAMILY LIFE, wife/husband, marriage, children | Closed question: 'How do you feel about . . . .' terrible / unhappy / mostly dissatisfied / mixed / mostly satisfied / pleased / delighted | | HAPP 3.1 (1st instr.) | $h^2$ | .52 | | | National adult population, U.S.A.<br>Probability area sample (third sample)<br>N: 1072, date: November, 1972 | ANDRE 74 p. 19 |

| | | | | | | | | | |
|---|---|---|---|---|---|---|---|---|---|
| SATISFACTION WITH ONE'S FAMILY LIFE | Closed question rated on an 11-point self-anchoring scale, based on Cantril (1965) | | HAPP 2.1 | $r_{pm}$ | +.17 | | | National population, Britain<br>Non-probability quota sample<br>N: 213, date: March, 1971 | ABRAM 73<br>p. 21 |
| SATISFACTION WITH FAMILY LIFE | Closed question rated on a 7-point self-anchoring scale, based on Cantril (1965) | | HAPP 2.1 | r | +.38 | | | Adult population of 8 major British conurbations<br>Non-probability quota sample<br>N: 593, date: October - November, 1971 | HALL 73<br>p. 100 |
| SATISFACTION WITH FAMILY | Closed question rated on an open graphic scale ranging from 'very dissatisfied' to 'very satisfied' | Unaffected by age, S.E.S. and sex<br>No relation among those of high educational level | HAPP 1.1 | G | +.51 | | 05 | National adult population, The Netherlands<br>Probability area sample<br>N: 1552, date: June, 1968 | BAKKE 74<br>p. 27 |
| SATISFACTION WITH FAMILY LIFE | Closed question rated on a 4-point scale ranging from 'very unsatisfied' to 'very satisfied' | unmarried employed males: r = +.54 (05)<br>unmarried employed females: r = +.38 (05)<br>married employed males: r = +.30 (05)<br>married employed females: r = +.38 (05)<br>married non-employed females: r = +.54 (05) | HAPP 2.1 | $r_{pm}$ | + | | 05 | Inhabitants of Helsinki, Finland<br>Probability sample<br>N: 442, date: spring - summer, 1966 | HAAVI 71<br>p. 590 |
| SATISFACTION WITH ACTIVITIES WITH FAMILY | Closed question: 'How do you feel about . . .' terrible / unhappy / mostly dissatisfied / mixed / mostly satisfied / pleased / delighted | Unaffected by sex | HAPP 3.1<br>(1st instr.) | $h^2$ | .38 | | | National adult population, U.S.A.<br>Probability area sample (first sample)<br>N: 1297, date: May, 1972 | ANDRE 74<br>p. 17 |
| SATISFACTION WITH ACTIVITIES WITH FAMILY | See above | | HAPP 3.1<br>(1st instr.) | $h^2$ | .51 | | | National adult population, U.S.A.<br>Probability area sample (third sample)<br>N: 1072, date: November, 1972 | ANDRE 74<br>p. 19 |
| SATISFACTION WITH INTRA-FAMILY AGREEMENT ON HOW FAMILY INCOME SHOULD BE SPENT | See above | | HAPP 3.1<br>(1st instr.) | $h^2$ | .42 | | | See above | ANDRE 74<br>p. 19 |
| SATISFACTION WITH CLOSE ADULT RELATIVES | See above | Unaffected by sex | HAPP 3.1<br>(1st instr.) | $h^2$ | .22 | | | National adult population, U.S.A.<br>Probability area sample (first sample)<br>N: 1297, date: May, 1972 | ANDRE 74<br>p. 17 |

## S 1.7.2 - MARRIAGE

| | | | | | | | | | |
|---|---|---|---|---|---|---|---|---|---|
| SATISFACTION WITH MARRIAGE | Question whether one was happier when single yes vs no | Computed for married singles only | HAPP 1.1 | G' | +.39 | Gt' | 01 | National adult population, U.S.A.<br>Non-probability quota sample<br>N: 2377, date: February, 1946 | WESSM 56<br>p. 192 |
| MARITAL HAPPINESS | Closed question: not too happy / just about average / a little happier than average / very happy | married persons only<br>Computed by us on the basis of the original data | HAPP 1.1 | G' | +.68 | Gt' | 01 | Non-institutionalized adults, U.S.A.<br>Probability multi-stage area sample<br>N: 2460, date: spring 1957 | GURIN 60 |
| MARITAL HAPPINESS | See above | males : t = +.38 (01)<br>females: t = +.44 (01) | HAPP 1.1 | $t_k$ | + | | 01 | Adult married population with children, U.S.A.<br>Probability area sample<br>N: 797, date: spring 1957 | VEROF 62<br>p. 196 |
| MARITAL HAPPINESS | Closed question: not too happy / pretty happy / very happy | See remarks in excerpt (Part II).<br>Computed for married persons only (on the basis of 1973 and 1974 data)<br>Stronger among females: G' = +.85 (01)<br>Unaffected by age<br>Lower among males : G' = +.78 (01)<br>Stronger among males of age 18-39 (G' = +.86) and lower among those of age 60+ (G' = +.70) | HAPP 1.1 | G' | +.81 | Gt' | 01 | National adult population, U.S.A.<br>Combined data from 3 U.S. General Surveys conducted by NORC<br>N: 3853, date: 1972, 1973, 1974 | GLENN 75/B<br>p. 597 |

| | | | | | | | | | |
|---|---|---|---|---|---|---|---|---|---|
| MARITAL HAPPINESS | Closed question: not too happy / pretty happy / very happy | Stronger among those of high S.E.S.<br>Unaffected by sex<br>Third wave: Lower among males : G = +.68<br>Stronger among females: G = +.86 | HAPP 1.1 | G | +.72 | | | Adults, urban areas, U.S.A.<br>Probability area samples<br>N: 2787, date: January, 1963 - January, 1964 | BRADB 69<br>p. 158 |
| MARITAL SATISFACTION | 6-item index of closed questions on happiness in marriage, regrets about marriage, frequency of problems, seriously considered a divorce, understanding and affection | Strongest among white females<br>Lowest among white males<br>Among blacks unaffected by sex | HAPP 1.1 | | + | | | Married adults, Alameda County, California, U.S.A.<br>Probability area sample of households<br>N: 5163, date: 1965 | RENNE 70<br>p. 63 |
| MARITAL SATISFACTION | See above | | AFF 1.3 | $\bar{DR}$ | + | | 05 | Adults, Alameda County, U.S.A.<br>Probability sample<br>N: 6928, date: 1965 | BERKM 71<br>p. 42 |
| MARITAL HAPPINESS | Closed question | Married respondents only<br>Lower among males : G = +.41<br>Stronger among females: G = +.47 | HAPP 1.1 | G | + | | | Adults, Metro Manila, Philippines<br>Probability area sample<br>N: 941, date: January - April, 1972 | BULAT 73<br>p. 232 |
| | | Lower among males : G = +.21<br>Stronger among females: G = +.27 | HAPP 2.1 | G | + | | | | |
| | | Index of Positive Affects:<br>males : G = +.33<br>females : G = +.32<br>Index of Negative Affects:<br>Stronger among females: G = -.27<br>Lower among males : G = -.09 | AF 2.3 | G | + | | | | |
| SATISFACTION WITH MARRIAGE | Closed question rated on a 7-point self-anchoring scale, based on Cantril (1965) | | HAPP 2.1 | r | +.23 | | | Adult population of 8 major British conurbations<br>Non-probability quota sample<br>N: 593, date: October - November, 1971 | HALL 73<br>p. 100 |
| MARITAL HAPPINESS | Closed question | | HAPP 1.1 | G' | +.39 | Gt' | 01 | National adult population, The Netherlands<br>N: at least 1000, date: 1948 | NIPO 49<br>p. 3 |
| SATISFACTION WITH MARRIAGE | Closed question rated on an open graphic scale ranging from 'very dissatisfied' to 'very satisfied' | Computed for married persons only<br>Stronger among those of age 25-35<br>Lower among those of high S.E.S.<br>Stronger among those of medium educational level<br>Unaffected by sex | HAPP 1.1 | G | +.73 | | 05 | National adult population, The Netherlands<br>Probability area sample<br>N: 1552, date: June, 1968 | BAKKE 74<br>p. 27 |
| MARITAL SATISFACTION | Closed question on expectations re marriage: not up to / in accordance with / surpassed | Computed for married persons only<br>males : r = +.21 (ns)<br>females: r = +.49 (005) | HAPP 2.1 | $r_{pm}$ | + | $Chi^2$ | | Adults, Amsterdam, The Netherlands<br>Probability systematic random sample, stratified by sex and marital status<br>N: 600, date: September - December, 1965 | JONG 69<br>p. 193 |
| SATISFACTION WITH MARRIAGE | Closed question rated on a 5-point scale ranging from 'dissatisfied' to 'very satisfied' | Computed for married Ss only<br>Unaffected by sex | HAPP 1.1 | $r_{pm}$ | +.47 | $Chi^2$ | s | Adults, Utrecht, The Netherlands<br>Probability sample stratified by age<br>N: 300, date: autumn, 1967 | MOSER 69<br>p. 18 |
| SATISFACTION WITH MARRIAGE | Closed question | | HAPP 1.1 | $r_{pm}$ | +.44 | | | Housewives, The Netherlands<br>Probability area sample<br>N: 450, date: autumn, 1964 | PHILI 66<br>p. 66 |
| MARITAL HAPPINESS | Closed question: very unhappy / unhappy / average / happy / very happy | | HAPP 2.1 | $T^2$ | +.22 | $Chi^2$ | 001 | Married persons, Poland<br>Non-probability, purposive quota sample<br>N: 1746, date: June - July, 1960 | MAKAR 62<br>p. 108 |
| SATISFACTION WITH RELATIONSHIP TO SPOUSE | Closed question rated on a 4-point scale ranging from 'very unsatisfied' to 'very satisfied' | Computed for married Ss only<br>married employed males : r = +.27 (05)<br>married employed females : r = +.29 (05)<br>married non-employed females: r = +.50 (05) | HAPP 2.1 | $r_{pm}$ | + | | 05 | Inhabitants of Helsinki, Finland<br>Probability sample<br>N: 442, date: spring - summer, 1966 | HAAVI 71<br>p. 590 |

## S I.7.3 - FRIENDS, SOCIAL CONTACTS

| | | | | | | | | | |
|---|---|---|---|---|---|---|---|---|---|
| SATISFACTION WITH FRIENDS | Closed question: wish to move to a 'different circle' vs satisfied | Stronger among those who are not getting along well with their family and/or are dissatisfied with their job<br>Unaffected by sex, education, age, income, S.E.S., marital status, and race | HAPP 1.1 | G' | +.43 | Gt' | 01 | National adult population, U.S.A.<br>Non-probability quota sample<br>N: 2377, date: February, 1946 | WESSM 56<br>p. 201 |
| SATISFACTION WITH SOCIAL CONTACTS, FRIENDS | **2-item index containing** satisfaction with social contacts and the time spent with friends<br>Closed questions: 'How do you feel about . . .' terrible / unhappy / mostly dissatisfied / mixed / mostly satisfied / pleased / delighted | Unaffected by sex | HAPP 3.1<br>(1st instr.) | $h^2$ | .34 | | | National adult population, U.S.A.<br>Probability area sample (first sample)<br>N: 1297, date: May, 1972 | ANDRE 74<br>p. 17 |
| SATISFACTION WITH FRIENDS | Closed question: 'How do you feel about . . .' terrible / unhappy / mostly dissatisfied / mixed / mostly satisfied / pleased / delighted | | HAPP 3.1<br>(1st instr.) | $h^2$ | .36 | | | National adult population, U.S.A.<br>Probability area sample (third sample)<br>N: 1072, date: November, 1972 | ANDRE 74<br>p. 19 |
| SATISFACTION WITH SOCIAL LIFE | Closed question: not too satisfied / pretty satisfied / very satisfied | Computed for Index of Positive Affects only:<br>G = +. 18 (ns)<br>Stronger among those with very low sociability (.05)<br>Unrelated to Index of Negative Affects | AFF 2.3 | G | + | | | Urban areas, U.S.A.<br>Probability area sample<br>N: 2787, date: January, 1963 - January, 1964 | BRADB 69<br>p. 140 |
| SATISFACTION WITH ONE'S FRIENDSHIPS | Closed question rated on an 11-point self-anchoring scale, based on Cantril (1965) | | HAPP 2.1 | $r_{pm}$ | +.08 | | | National population, Britain<br>Non-probability quota sample<br>N: 213, date: March, 1971 | ABRAM 73<br>p. 21 |
| SATISFACTION WITH FRIENDS | Closed question rated on an open graphic scale ranging from 'very dissatisfied' to 'very satisfied' | Unaffected by age and sex<br>Lower among those of medium S.E.S.<br>Stronger among those of low educational level | HAPP 1.1 | G | +.59 | | 05 | National adult population, The Netherlands<br>Probability area sample<br>N: 1552, date: June, 1968 | BAKKE 74<br>p. 27 |
| SATISFACTION WITH FRIENDS AND ACQUAINTANCES | Closed question rated on a 5-point scale ranging from 'dissatisfied' to 'very satisfied' | | HAPP 1.1 | $r_{pm}$ | +.15 | $Chi^2$ | s | Adults, Utrecht, The Netherlands<br>Probability sample stratified by age<br>N: 300, date: autumn, 1967 | MOSER 69<br>p. 29 |
| SATISFACTION WITH SOCIAL GROUP | Closed question | | HAPP 1.1<br>AFF 1.1 | mc<br>mc | +.43<br>+.34 | | | Urban adult Jewish population, Israel<br>Probability area sample using dwelling units<br>N: 1830, date: summer, 1973 | LEVY 75/2<br>p. 373 |

## S 1.7.4 - VARIOUS ASPECTS OF SOCIAL LIFE

| | | | | | | | | | |
|---|---|---|---|---|---|---|---|---|---|
| SATISFACTION WITH HOW ONE GETS ON WITH PEOPLE | Closed question: 'How do you feel about . . .' terrible / unhappy / mostly dissatisfied / mixed / mostly satisfied / pleased / delighted | Unaffected by sex | HAPP 3.1<br>(1st instr.) | $h^2$ | .31 | | | National adult population, U.S.A.<br>Probability area sample (first sample)<br>N: 1297, date: May, 1972 | ANDRE 74<br>p. 17 |
| SATISFACTION WITH CHANCE TO KNOW PEOPLE ONE FEELS COMFORTABLE WITH | See above | Unaffected by sex | HAPP 3.1<br>(1st instr.) | $h^2$ | .31 | | | See above | ANDRE 74<br>p. 17 |
| SATISFACTION WITH ORGANIZATIONAL MEMBERSHIPS | See above | Unaffected by sex | HAPP 3.1<br>(1st instr.) | $h^2$ | .21 | | | See above | ANDRE 74<br>p. 17 |

| | | | | | | | | | |
|---|---|---|---|---|---|---|---|---|---|
| SATISFACTION WITH SEX LIFE | Closed question: 'How do you feel about . . .' terrible / unhappy / mostly dissatisfied / mixed / mostly satisfied / pleased / delighted | | HAPP 3.1 (1st instr.) | $h^2$ | .40 | | | National adult population, U.S.A.<br>Probability area sample (third sample)<br>N: 1072, date: November, 1972 | ANDRE 74<br>p. 19 |
| SATISFACTION WITH ADMIRATION OR RESPECT BY OTHERS | See above | | HAPP 3.1 (1st instr.) | $h^2$ | .34 | | | See above | ANDRE 74<br>p. 19 |
| SATISFACTION WITH RESPECT FOR YOUR RIGHTS BY OTHERS | See above | | HAPP 3.1 (1st instr.) | $h^2$ | .28 | | | See above | ANDRE 74<br>p. 19 |
| SATISFACTION WITH RELIABILITY OF PEOPLE YOU DEPEND ON | See above | | HAPP 3.1 (1st instr.) | $h^2$ | .38 | | | See above | ANDRE 74<br>p. 19 |
| SATISFACTION WITH PRIVACY | See above | | HAPP 3.1 (1st instr.) | $h^2$ | .37 | | | See above | ANDRE 74<br>p. 19 |
| SATISFACTION WITH LOVE LIFE | Closed question rated on an open graphic scale ranging from 'very dissatisfied' to 'very satisfied' | Lower among those of age 41-50 and 61-65<br>Stronger among those of low S.E.S.<br>No relation among those of high educational level<br>Unaffected by sex | HAPP 1.1 | G | +.70 | | 05 | National adult population, The Netherlands<br>Probability area sample<br>N: 1552, date: June, 1968 | BAKKE 74<br>p. 28 |

## S 1.8 - SATISFACTION WITH SOCIO-ECONOMIC LEVEL

### S 1.8.1 - S.E.S. IN GENERAL

| | | | | | | | | | |
|---|---|---|---|---|---|---|---|---|---|
| PERCEIVED SATISFACTION OF S.E.S.-GROUP ONE BELONGS TO | Closed question on perceived satisfaction of various S.E.S.-groups on an 11-point self-anchoring scale, based on Cantril (1965); and closed question on the S.E.S.-group S belongs to | | HAPP 2.1 | $r_{pm}$ | +.47 | | | National population, Britain<br>Non-probability quota sample<br>N: 213, date: March, 1971 | ABRAM 73<br>p. 21 |
| SATISFACTION WITH S.E.S. | Closed question rated on an open graphic scale ranging from 'very dissatisfied' to 'very satisfied' | Unaffected by age, S.E.S., and sex<br>Lower among those of high educational level | HAPP 1.1 | G | +.58 | | 05 | National adult population, The Netherlands<br>Probability area sample<br>N: 1552, date: June, 1968 | BAKKE 74<br>p. 27 |

### S 1.8.2 - LEVEL OF EDUCATION

| | | | | | | | | | |
|---|---|---|---|---|---|---|---|---|---|
| SATISFACTION WITH EDUCATION | Closed question rated on a 7-point self-anchoring scale, based on Cantril (1965) | | HAPP 2.1 | r | +.27 | | | Adult population of 8 major British conurbations<br>Non-probability quota sample<br>N: 593, date: October - November, 1971 | HALL 73<br>p. 100 |
| SATISFACTION WITH EDUCATIONAL LEVEL | Closed question ranging from 'very unsatisfied' to 'very satisfied' | | HAPP 1.1<br>AFF 1.1 | mc<br>mc | +.26<br>+.31 | | | Urban adult Jewish population, Israel<br>Probability area sample using dwelling units<br>N: 1940, date: spring, 1973 | LEVY 75/1<br>p. 372 |

## S 1.8.3 - INCOME, STANDARD OF LIVING

see also 'Satisfaction with Work, Job - Specific Aspects' (S 1.9.2)

| | | | | | | | | | |
|---|---|---|---|---|---|---|---|---|---|
| SATISFACTION WITH MATERIAL STANDARD OF LIVING | 2-item index containing satisfaction with income and standard of living<br>Closed questions: 'How do you feel about . . .' terrible / unhappy / mostly dissatisfied / mixed / mostly satisfied / pleased / delighted | Unaffected by sex | HAPP 3.1 (1st instr.) | $h^2$ | .47 | | | National adult pop U.S.A.<br>Probability area samp (first sample)<br>N: 1297, date: May, 1972 | ANDRE 74 p. 17 |
| SATISFACTION WITH MATERIAL STANDARD OF LIVING | See above | | HAPP 3.1 (1st instr.) | $h^2$ | .57 | | | National adult population, U.S.A.<br>Probability area sample (third sample)<br>N: 1072, date: November, 1972 | ANDRE 74 p. 19 |
| SATISFACTION WITH FINANCIAL SITUATION | Closed question | Stronger among blacks: G = +.65 (05)<br>Lower among whites: G = +.42 (05) | HAPP 1.1 | G | + | | | Non-institutionalized adults, U.S.A.<br>Type of sample construction unclear<br>N: 1602, date: March, 1972 | ALSTO 74 p. 101 |
| FINANCIAL SITUATION | Closed question: not satisfied at all / more or less satisfied / pretty well satisfied | Stronger among the aged: r = +.41<br>Lower among those under the age of 65: r = +.21<br>This difference is significant (05)<br>Unaffected by sex | HAPP 1.1 | $r_{pm}$ | +.24 | | 01 | Non-institutionalized adults, U.S.A.<br>Probability samples<br>N: 1547, date: 1972, 1973 | SPREI 74 p. 457 |
| SATISFACTION WITH FINANCIAL SITUATION | Closed question rated on an 11-point self-anchoring scale, based on Cantril (1965) | | HAPP 2.1 | $r_{pm}$ | +.52 | | | National population, Britain<br>Non-probability quota sample<br>N: 213, date: March, 1971 | ABRAM 73 p. 21 |
| SATISFACTION WITH STANDARD OF LIVING | Closed question rated on a 7-point self-anchoring scale, based on Cantril (1965) | | HAPP 2.1 | r | +.36 | | | Adult population of 8 major British conurbations<br>Non-probability quota sample<br>N: 593, date: October - November, 1971 | HALL 73 p. 100 |
| SATISFACTION WITH INCOME | Closed question rated on an open graphic scale ranging from 'very dissatisfied' to 'very satisfied' | Stronger among younger persons<br>Lower among those of high or low S.E.S.<br>Stronger among those of low educational level | HAPP 1.1 | G | +.44 | | 05 | National adult population, The Netherlands<br>Probability area sample<br>N: 1552, date: June, 1968 | BAKKE 74 p. 27 |

## S 1.9 - SATISFACTION WITH WORK, JOB

see also 'Types of Affect - Present Work' (A 2.2.14)

### S 1.9.1 - WORK IN GENERAL

| | | | | | | | | | |
|---|---|---|---|---|---|---|---|---|---|
| JOB SATISFACTION | Closed question: very little / fair amount / a lot of pleasure and satisfaction | Stronger among those who are not getting along well with their family and/or are not satisfied with their friends | HAPP 1.1 | G' | +.44 | Gt' | 01 | National adult population, U.S.A.<br>Non-probability quota sample<br>N: 2377, date: February, 1946 | WESSM 56 p. 194 |
| SATISFACTION WITH WORK | Closed question | Computed for employed Ss only<br>Stronger among whites: G = +.46 (05)<br>Lower among blacks: G = +.39 (05) | HAPP 1.1 | G | + | | | Non-institutionalized adults, U.S.A.<br>Type of sample construction unclear<br>N: 1602, date: March, 1972 | ALSTO 74 p. 101 |
| SATISFACTION WITH JOB | 5-item index containing satisfaction with job, co-workers, work, work situation, and availabilities for doing the job<br>Closed questions 'How do you feel about . . .' terrible / unhappy / mostly dissatisfied / mixed / mostly satisfied / pleased / delighted | Stronger among males: $h^2$ = .36<br>Lower among females: $h^2$ = .15 | HAPP 3.1 (1st instr.) | $h^2$ | .23 | | | National adult population, U.S.A.<br>Probability area sample (first sample)<br>N: 1297, date: May, 1972 | ANDRE 74 p. 17 |

| | | | | | | | | | |
|---|---|---|---|---|---|---|---|---|---|
| SATISFACTION WITH JOB | Closed question: 'How do you feel about. . .' terrible / unhappy / mostly dissatisfied / mixed / mostly satisfied / pleased / delighted | | HAPP 3.1 (1st instr.) | $h^2$ | .37 | | | National adult population, U.S.A.<br>Probability area sample (third sample)<br>N: 1072, date: November, 1972 | ANDRE 74<br>p. 19 |
| WORK SATISFACTION | 3-item index of closed questions on satisfaction with earnings, kind of work and the work as a whole: low / medium / high / very high | Computed for male chief wage earners only.<br>Positive relationship with Index of Positive Affects.<br>Stronger among higher occupational prestige levels in both white- and blue-collar jobs (05)<br>Not among lower prestige levels (ns)<br>Negative relation with Index of Negative Affects.<br>Significant among low prestige, blue-collar workers only (05) | AFF 2.3 | $\overline{DR}$ | + | BCI | | Adults, urban areas, U.S.A.<br>Probability area samples<br>N: 2787, date: January, 1963 – January, 1964 | BRADB 69<br>p. 203–205 |
| | | Computed for chief wage earners only. Female chief wage earners were almost without exception single women.<br>Stronger among males: G = +.43<br>Lower among females : G = +.28<br>In wave 3: males : G = +.41<br>females : G = +.44<br>Slightly stronger among people with low job statuses, particularly for women. | HAPP 1.1 | G | + | | | | |
| JOB SATISFACTION | Question on whether current job is the best one ever had<br>Have had better one vs is the best one | Computed for chief wage earners only (see above)<br>Index of Positive Affects: $\overline{DR}$ = +.08 (05)<br>Stronger among males : $\overline{DR}$ = +.09 (05)<br>Not among females : $\overline{DR}$ = +.02 (ns)<br>Index of Negative Affects: $\overline{DR}$ = –.05 (ns)<br>Unaffected by sex | AFF 2.3 | $\overline{DR}$ | + | BCI | | See above | BRADB 69<br>p. 197 |
| JOB SATISFACTION | Closed question: dissatisfied / ambivalent / satisfied / very satisfied | Computed for males only. | HAPP 1.1 | $t_k$ | +.13 | | 01 | Adult married population with children, U.S.A.<br>Probability area sample<br>N: 797, date: — | VEROF 62<br>p. 196 |
| JOB SATISFACTION | Believe that one is in the 'right' job | Stronger among females. | HAPP 2.1 | D% | + | | s | Middle-aged, middle class married couples, U.S.A.<br>Non-probability accidental sample of couples<br>N: 416, date: 1952 – 1953 | ROSE 55<br>p. 17 |
| JOB SATISFACTION | 3-item index of closed questions on satisfaction with over-all job, kind of work and wages | | HAPP 1.1 | G' | +.56 | Gt' | 01 | Males in the age of 25–49, 4 small communities, Illinois, U.S.A.<br>Probability multi stage samples<br>N: 393, date: March, 1962 | BRADB 65/1<br>p. 37 |
| | | Index of Positive Affects: G' = +.10 (ns)<br>Index of Negative Affects: G' = –.28 (01) | AFF 2.3 | G' | + | Gt' | | | |
| HAPPINESS WITH JOB | Closed question rated on an 11-point self-anchoring scale, based on Cantril (1965) | | HAPP 1.1 | $r_{pm}$ | +.37 | | | Workers of a utility union, Greater Kansas City area, U.S.A.<br>Probability cluster sample<br>N: 213, date: — | GILLO 73<br>p. 124 |
| JOB SATISFACTION | Closed question: somewhat or very unsatisfied / somewhat satisfied / very satisfied | Computed for employed Ss only<br>Index of Positive Affects: t = +.14 (01)<br>high S.E.S. group : t = +.33 (01)<br>medium S.E.S. group : t = +.16 (05)<br>low S.E.S. group : t = +.01 (ns)<br>Index of Negative Affects: t = –.26 (001)<br>high S.E.S. group : t = –.07 (ns)<br>medium S.E.S. group : t = –.35 (001)<br>low S.E.S. group : t = –.30 (001)<br>Affect Balance:<br>high S.E.S. group : t = +.27 (01)<br>medium S.E.S. group : t = +.32 (001)<br>low S.E.S. group : t = +.31 (01) | AFF 2.3 | t | + | | s | Non-hospitalized schizophrenic males, New York, U.S.A.<br>Probability sample, drawn from the Monroe County Psychiatric Case Register<br>N: 178, date: 1964 –1965 | ALEXA 68<br>p. 177/190 |

| | | | | | | | | | |
|---|---|---|---|---|---|---|---|---|---|
| | | No differences when happiness is used as dependent or independent variable: $d_{xy}$ and $d_{yx}$ are approximately equal. | HAPP 1.1 | t | +.23 | | 001 | | |
| SATISFACTION WITH JOB of oneself or husband | Closed question rated on an 11-point self-anchoring scale, based on Cantril (1965) | | HAPP 2.1 | $r_{pm}$ | +.24 | | | National population, Britain<br>Non-probability quota sample<br>N: 213, date: March, 1971 | ABRAM 73<br>p. 21 |
| SATISFACTION WITH JOB | Closed question rated on a 7-point self-anchoring scale, based on Cantril (1965) | | HAPP 2.1 | r | +.33 | | | Adult population of 8 major British conurbations<br>Non-probability quota sample<br>N: 593, date: October - November, 1971 | HALL 73<br>p. 100 |
| JOB SATISFACTION | Closed question on enjoying work:<br>do not enjoy / reasonably / enjoy | | HAPP 1.1 | G' | +.74 | Gt' | 01 | National adult population, The Netherlands<br>N: at least 1000, date: 1948 | NIPO 49<br>p. 3 |
| JOB SATISFACTION | Closed question: no / partly yes / partly no / yes | unmarried males : r = +.26 (025)<br>married males : r = +.13 (ns)<br>unmarried females: r = +.41 (005)<br>married females : r = +.29 (005) | HAPP 2.1 | $r_{pm}$ | + | $Chi^2$ | | Adults, Amsterdam, The Netherlands<br>Probability systematic random sample, stratified by sex and marital status<br>N: 600, date: September - December, 1965 | JONG 69<br>p. 195 |
| SATISFACTION WITH WORK | Direct yes / no question | | HAPP 2.1 | G | +.80 | $Chi^2$ | 000 | Male employees at the age of 40+, The Netherlands<br>Non-probability chunk sample<br>N: 13000, date: — | SONDE 75 |
| SATISFACTION WITH WORK | Closed question | | HAPP 1.1<br>AFF 1.1 | mc<br>mc | +.49<br>+.48 | | | Urban adult Jewish population, Israel<br>Probability area sample, using dwelling units<br>N: 1830, date: summer, 1973 | LEVY 75/2<br>p. 373 |
| SATISFACTION WITH WORK IN GENERAL | Closed question rated on a 4-point scale ranging from 'very unsatisfied' to 'very satisfied' | unmarried employed males : r = +.30 (05)<br>unmarried employed females: r = +.14 (ns)<br>married employed males : r = +.29 (05)<br>married employed females : r = +.21 (ns) | HAPP 2.1 | $r_{pm}$ | + | | | Inhabitants of Helsinki, Finland<br>Probability sample<br>N: 442, date: spring - summer, 1966 | HAAVI 71<br>p. 590 |
| JOB SATISFACTION | Closed question: 'Do you like your job?'<br>no / indifferent / yes / yes, very much | | HAPP 2.1 | $T^2$ | +.17 | $Chi^2$ | 001 | Housewives and persons gainfully employed outside agriculture, Poland<br>Non-probability purposive quota sample<br>N: 1251, date: June - July, 1960 | MAKAR 62<br>p. 110 |
| JOB SATISFACTION | Closed question: 'Do you like working in agriculture?'<br>no / indifferent / yes / yes, very much | | HAPP 2.1 | $T^2$ | +.11 | $Chi^2$ | 001 | Individual farmowners and their families, Poland<br>Non-probability purposive quota sample<br>N: 1002, date: June - July, 1960 | MAKAR 62<br>p. 110 |
| SATISFACTION WITH HOUSEWORK | Closed question: very little / a fair amount / a lot of pleasure and satisfaction | Computed for unemployed housewives only | HAPP 1.1 | G' | +.38 | Gt' | 01 | National adult population, U.S.A.<br>Non-probability quota sample<br>N: 2377, date: Febrauary, 1946 | WESSM 56<br>p. 198 |
| SATISFACTION WITH HOUSEWORK, work around the home | Closed question: 'How do you feel about. . . .'<br>terrible / unhappy / mostly dissatisfied / mixed / mostly satisfied / pleased / delighted | Unaffected by sex | HAPP 3.1<br>(1st instr.) | $h^2$ | .26 | | | National adult population, U.S.A.<br>Probability area sample (first sample)<br>N: 1297, date: May, 1972 | ANDRE 74<br>p. 17 |
| SATISFACTION WITH ROLE (i.e. career combined with homemaking or full-time housewives | Closed question : very dissatisfied / mildly dissatisfied / satisfied / very satisfied | | AFF 2.1 | $r_{pm}$ | +.24 | | ns | Married females, U.S.A.<br>Non-probability purposive sample by expert choice<br>N: 62, date: — | HARDE 69<br>p. 50 |

## S 1.9.2 - SPECIFIC ASPECTS OF THE JOB

| | | | | | | | | | |
|---|---|---|---|---|---|---|---|---|---|
| SATISFACTION WITH: | Cumulative point adjective check-list<br>(Job Descriptive Index; see Quinn & Kahn, 1967) | | | | | | | Workers, Columbia, Canada<br>Non-probability purposive sample by expert choice<br>N: 470, date: — | HULIN 69<br>p. 285 |

| | | | | | | | | |
|---|---|---|---|---|---|---|---|---|
| - ACTUAL WORK DONE | | Stronger among males: r = +.27 (01)<br>Lower among females : r = +.14 (ns) | HAPP 3.1 | $r_{pm}$ | + | t | | | |
| - PAY | | males only | HAPP 3.1 | $r_{pm}$ | +.20 | t | 01 | | |
| - PROMOTIONAL OPPORTUNITIES | | males only | HAPP 3.1 | $r_{pm}$ | +.15 | t | 01 | | |
| - SUPERVISION | | males only | HAPP 3.1 | $r_{pm}$ | +.13 | t | 05 | | |
| - CO-WORKERS | | males : r = +.20 (01)<br>females: r = +.23 (05) | HAPP 3.1 | $r_{pm}$ | + | t | 05 | | |
| SATISFACTION WITH: | Job Descriptive Index (See Smith et al., 1969)<br>(see also last page under HULIN 69) | See 'sample construction' in excerpt (Part II) | | | | | | Male supervisors of a chemical plant, U.S.A.<br>Probability samples<br>N: 69, date: — | IRIS 72<br>p. 302 |
| - WORK | | sample A: r = +.01 (ns)<br>sample B: r = +.31 (ns) | HAPP 2.1 | $r_{pm}$ | + | | | | |
| - PAY | | sample A: r = +.46 (01)<br>sample B: r = +.07 (ns) | HAPP 2.1 | $r_{pm}$ | + | | | | |
| - PROMOTIONS | | sample A: r = +.23 (ns)<br>sample B: r = +.36 (05) | HAPP 2.1 | $r_{pm}$ | + | | | | |
| - SUPERVISION | | sample A: r = +.40 (05)<br>sample B: r = +.30 (ns) | HAPP 2.1 | $r_{pm}$ | + | | | | |
| - CO-WORKERS | | sample A: r = +.04 (ns)<br>sample B: r = +.26 (ns) | HAPP 2.1 | $r_{pm}$ | + | | | | |
| SATISFACTION WITH MANAGEMENT'S RESPONSE TO COMPLAINTS | Closed question rated on a graphic rating scale very dissatisfied / somewhat dissatisfied / neither satisfied nor dissatisfied / somewhat satisfied / very satisfied | Stronger among males: r = +.22 (01)<br>Lower among females : r = +.06 (ns) | HAPP 3.1 | $r_{pm}$ | + | t | | Workers, Columbia, Canada<br>Non-probability purposive sample by expert choice<br>N: 470, date: — | HULIN 69<br>p. 285 |
| SATISFACTION WITH TRAINING OPPORTUNITIES | See above | Stronger among females: r = +.21 (ns)<br>Lower among males: : r = +.09 (ns) | HAPP 3.1 | $r_{pm}$ | + | t | ns | See above | HULIN 69<br>p. 285 |
| SATISFACTION WITH WORKING CONDITIONS | See above | males : r = +.16 (01)<br>females: r = +.12 (ns) | HAPP 3.1 | $r_{pm}$ | + | t | | See above | HULIN 69<br>p. 285 |
| SATISFACTION WITH WORK ITSELF | Closed question rated on a 5-point scale ranging from 'I dislike the work very much and would dearly like to do something else' to 'I like it very much and wouldn't want to do any other work' | Index of Positive Affects: G = +.06<br>Index of Negative Affects: G = -.09 | AFF 2.3 | G | + | | | Employed males, England<br>Non-probability purposive quota sample<br>N: 192, date: — | PAYNE 74<br>p. 17 |
| SATISFACTION WITH BOSS | Closed question rated on a 5-point scale ranging from 'not satisfied' to 'completely satisfied' | Index of Positive Affects: G = +.01<br>Index of Negative Affects: G = -.08 | AFF 2.3 | G | + | | | See above | PAYNE 74<br>p. 17 |
| SATISFACTION WITH COLLEAGUES | Closed question rated on a 5-point scale ranging from 'not satisfied' to 'completely satisfied' | Index of Positive Affects: G = -.07<br>Index of Negative Affects: G = -.03 | AFF 2.3 | G | | | | See above | PAYNE 74<br>p. 17 |
| SATISFACTION WITH PAY | Closed question rated on a 4-point scale ranging from 'inadequate - struggle to buy just basics, and quite often have to go into debt to do that' to 'completely adequate - meet all bills, buy things I want, have holidays I want and can save if choose to' | Index of Positive Affects: G = -.03<br>Index of Negative Affects: G = -.12 | AFF 2.3 | G | | | | See above | PAYNE 74<br>p. 17 |

| | | | | | | | | | |
|---|---|---|---|---|---|---|---|---|---|
| SATISFACTION WITH STATUS AT WORK | Closed question rated on a 4-point scale ranging from 'very unsatisfied' to 'very satisfied' | unmarried employed males : r = +.26 (05)<br>unmarried employed females: r = +.30 (05)<br>married employed males : r = +.25 (05)<br>married employed females : r = +.28 (05) | HAPP 2.1 | $r_{pm}$ | + | | 05 | Inhabitants of Helsinki, Finland<br>Probability sample<br>N: 442, date: spring - summer, 1966 | HAAVI 71<br>p. 590 |
| SATISFACTION WITH DAILY TRAVELLING | Closed question: no vs yes | | HAPP 2.1 | G | +.34 | $Chi^2$ | 000 | Male employees of age 40+, The Netherlands<br>Non-probability chunk sample<br>N: 13000, date: — | SONDE 75 |

## S 1.10 - VARIOUS DOMAINSATISFACTIONS

| | | | | | | | | | |
|---|---|---|---|---|---|---|---|---|---|
| SATISFACTION WITH PRESENT AGE | Closed question: wish to be younger vs satisfied with present age | | HAPP 1.1 | G' | +.22 | Gt' | 01 | National adult population, U.S.A.<br>Non-probability quota sample<br>N: 2377, date: February, 1946 | WESSM 56<br>p. 178 |
| SATISFACTION WITH PRESENT AGE | Closed question: wish to be older vs satisfied with present age | | HAPP 1.1 | G' | +.18 | Gt' | ns | See above | WESSM 56<br>p. 178 |
| SATISFACTION WITH RELIGIOUS FAITH | Closed question: 'How do you feel about. . .' terrible / unhappy / mostly dissatisfied / mixed / mostly satisfied / pleased / delighted | Unaffected by sex | HAPP 3.1<br>(1st instr.) | $h^2$ | .24 | | | National adult population, U.S.A.<br>Probability area sample (first sample)<br>N: 1297, date: May, 1972 | ANDRE 74<br>p. 17 |
| SATISFACTION WITH AMOUNT OF FUN | See above | Unaffected by sex | HAPP 3.1<br>(1st instr.) | $h^2$ | .51 | | | See above | ANDRE 74<br>p. 17 |
| SATISFACTION WITH AMOUNT OF FUN | See above | | HAPP 3.1<br>(1st instr.) | $h^2$ | .61 | | | National adult population, U.S.A.<br>Probability area sample (third sample)<br>N: 1072, date: November, 1972 | ANDRE 74<br>p. 19 |
| SATISFACTION WITH CHANCES TO ENJOY PLEASANT OR BEAUTIFUL THINGS | See above | | HAPP 3.1<br>(1st instr.) | $h^2$ | .55 | | | See above | ANDRE 74<br>p. 19 |
| SATISFACTION WITH OPPORTUNITY TO CHANGE THINGS | See above | | HAPP 3.1<br>(1st instr.) | $h^2$ | .37 | | | See above | ANDRE 74<br>p. 19 |
| SATISFACTION WITH ONE'S CREATIVITY | See above | | HAPP 3.1<br>(1st instr.) | $h^2$ | .32 | | | See above | ANDRE 74<br>p. 19 |
| SATISFACTION WITH CHANCES OF GETTING A GOOD JOB | See above | | HAPP 3.1<br>(1st instr.) | $h^2$ | .37 | | | See above | ANDRE 74<br>p. 19 |
| SATISFACTION WITH AMOUNT OF SLEEP YOU GET | See above | | HAPP 3.1<br>(1st instr.) | $h^2$ | .31 | | | See above | ANDRE 74<br>p. 19 |
| SATISFACTION WITH OWN SATISFACTION LEVEL | Difference-score of actual satisfaction and degree of satisfaction one feels to be entitled to; both rated on 11-point self-anchoring scales, based on Cantril (1965) | See also instrument in excerpt (Part II). | HAPP 2.1 | $r_{pm}$ | +.59 | | | National population, Britain<br>Non-probability quota sample<br>N: 213, date: March, 1971 | ABRAM 73<br>p. 21 |
| SATISFACTION WITH CHILDREN'S EDUCATION | Closed question rated on an 11-point self-anchoring scale, based on Cantril (1965) | | HAPP 2.1 | $r_{pm}$ | +.14 | | | See above | ABRAM 73<br>p. 21 |
| SATISFACTION WITH COMFORT FROM RELIGION | Closed question rated on a 7-point self-anchoring scale, based on Cantril (1965) | | HAPP 2.1 | r | +.05 | | | Adult population of 8 major British conurbations<br>Non-probability quota sample<br>N: 593, date: October - November, 1971 | HALL 73<br>p. 100 |

| | | | | | | | | | |
|---|---|---|---|---|---|---|---|---|---|
| SATISFACTION WITH DAILY ACTIVITIES | Closed question rated on an open graphic scale ranging from 'very dissatisfied' to 'very satisfied' | Lower among those of age 41 - 50<br>Stronger among those of high or low S.E.S., among those of medium educational level, among females and among the married | HAPP 1.1 | G | +.56 | | 05 | National adult population, The Netherlands<br>Probability area sample<br>N: 1552, date: June, 1968 | BAKKE 74<br>p. 27 |
| SATISFACTION WITH UNIVERSITY | Closed question rated on a 7-point graphic scale on satisfaction with one's experience as a student at the University of Rochester: extremely dissatisfied / neither satisfied nor dissatisfied / extremely satisfied | | AFF 2.1 | DM | + | t | 01 | Undergraduate full-time college students, University of Rochester, U.S.A.<br>Non-probability chunk sample<br>N: 952, date: March, 1965 | CONST 65<br>p. 71 |
| SATISFACTION WITH UNIVERSITY | Direct yes / no question: 'Given the same alternatives, would you again choose to come to the University of Rochester?' | Analysis on the basis of the 16 most and 16 least happy Ss in each of the 8 sex/class group: (N = 256) | AFF 2.1 | D% | + | | | See above | CONST 65<br>p. 74 |
| SATISFACTION WITH NEXT YEAR'S PLANS IN TERMS OF ACHIEVEMENT NEEDS | Closed question on 'the extent to which S's present plans for further education, career, or job fulfill her need to achieve, to fully utilize her capacities' rated on a 7-point scale, ranging from 'highly unsatisfactory' to 'highly satisfactory' | | AFF 2.1 | $r_{pm}$ | +.17 | | 05 | Female college seniors, University of Rochester, U.S.A.<br>Non-probability chunk sample<br>N: 162, date: May - June, 1966 | PORTE 67<br>p. 101 |
| SATISFACTION WITH OCCUPATIONAL PREFERENCE | 5-item index reflecting satisfaction with the appropriateness of stated occupational preference | See remarks in excerpt (Part II).<br>For males: r = +.26 (05)<br>- Stronger among those reporting high priority of work and a career: r = +.39 (01)<br>Lower among those reporting low priority: r = +.13 (ns)<br>- Unaffected by general attitudes towards work: low: r = +.22 (ns)<br>high: r = +.30 (05)<br>- Stronger among those reporting high career advancement and planning: r = +.40 (01)<br>Lower among those reporting low career advancement: r = +.04 (ns)<br>For females: r = +.30 (01)<br>- Stronger among those reporting high priority of work and a career: r = +.31 (05)<br>Lower among those reporting low priority: r = +.18 (ns)<br>- Stronger among those reporting low attitudes towards work: r = +.36 (01)<br>Lower among those reporting high attitudes towards work: r = +.13 (ns)<br>- Stronger among those reporting high career advancement and planning: r = +.53 (01)<br>Lower among those reporting low career advancement and planning: r = +.17 (ns) | COMP 1.2 | r | + | Z | s | Undergraduate college students, U.S.A.<br>Non-probability chunk sample<br>N: 203, date: — | GREEN 74<br>p. 54 |

## S 1.11 - SATISFACTION SUMSCORES

| | | | | | | | | | |
|---|---|---|---|---|---|---|---|---|---|
| SATISFACTION WITH MAJOR LIFE AREAS | 6-item index of closed questions on satisfaction with housing, neighborhood, friends, occupation, marriage, and children, rated on 7-point scales. unhappy with one or more / not unhappy with any / satisfied with all 6 of these areas | Each satisfaction was significantly related (001) to enjoyment | COMP 1.1 | G | +.50 | | 001 | Adults, U.S.A.<br>Probability cluster sample using households and probability multi-stage sample<br>N: 2168, date: 1972 | BRENN 75B<br>p. 354 |

| | | | | | | | | | |
|---|---|---|---|---|---|---|---|---|---|
| SATISFACTION WITH MARRIAGE, JOB, AND HEALTH | Factor analysis on the basis of answers on direct closed questions | | HAPP 1.1 | V | +.68 | | | Housewives, The Netherlands<br>Probability area sample<br>N: 450, date: autumn, 1964 | PHILI 66<br>p. 67 |

# S 2 SELF - IMAGE

see also 'Personality' (P 1)



## S 2.1 - FORMAL ASPECTS OF SELF-IMAGE

### S 2.1.1 - CONGRUENCY BETWEEN REAL AND IDEAL SELF-IMAGE

| | | | | | | | | | |
|---|---|---|---|---|---|---|---|---|---|
| SELF-ESTEEM (real-ideal congruency) | Correlation between self and ideal descriptions, as assessed by a 45-item Q sort, filled out both in very elated and in very depressed moods, for both self-concept ('the most accurate picture of yourself as you really believe you are now') and ideal-concept ('the picture of yourself as the kind of person you have hoped to become or have fancied yourself to be'). | For congruency in elation : $r_s$ = -.36 (ns)<br>For congruency in depression: $r_s$ = -.50 (05)<br>Both the happier and unhappier girls experience discrepancies between real-self and ideal-self in depression.<br>In elation the unhappier girls feel no consistent divergence from their ideals (primarily concerning intellectual ambitions), while the happier girls continue to feel areas of discontent (primarily concerning social and emotional qualities).<br>(see also 'Content of self-image'; Part III, S 2.2) | AFF 3.1 | $r_s$ | - | | s | Female college students, U.S.A.<br>Non-probability chunk sample<br>N: 14, date: October - December, 1957 | WESSM 60<br>p. 122-123 |
| REAL - IDEAL SELF CONGRUENCY | Correlation between self and ideal descriptions, as assessed by a 60-item Q sort, describing characteristics indicative of successful and unsuccessful resolutions of the first six developmental crises of the Erikson's stages of psychosocial development (see Erikson, 1959).<br>The Q sort was filled out in both very elated and in very depressed moods for both self-concept ('an accurate picture of yourself as you honestly feel and believe you are') and ideal-concept ('the picture of the sort of person you have hoped to become or fancied yourself to be'). | For congruency in elation : r = +.79<br>For congruency in depression: r = +.76<br>Both the happier and unhappier men experience more discrepancies between real-self and ideal-self in depression than in elation.<br>For the happier men the differences between the real-selves and ideal-selves concerned social and emotional qualities as well as work, while for the unhappier men the most extreme and consistent differences all dealt with unrealized ambition and inability to work (see also 'Content of self-image'; Part III, S 2.2).<br>For the unhappy men most discrepancies concerned the fourth developmental crisis: 'Industry vs Inferiority', while for the happy men most discrepancies concerned the sixth developmental crisis: 'Intimacy vs Isolation' (see 'Personality development'; Part III, P 1.4). | AFF 3.1 | $r_{pm}$ | + | t | 05 | Male college students, U.S.A.<br>Non-probability chunk sample<br>N: 17, date: ± 1960 | WESSM 66/2<br>p. 107-113 |

## S 2.1.2 - STABILITY OF SELF-IMAGE

| Concept | Measure | Remarks | Variable | Stat. | Value | Test | Sign. | Population / Sample | Source |
|---|---|---|---|---|---|---|---|---|---|
| CONSISTENCY OF SELF-CONCEPT | Correlation between self descriptions provided in elation and in depression, as assessed by a Q sort of 45 items, filled out both in extremely high and extremely low moods for self-concept ('the most accurate picture of yourself as you really believe you are now') | | AFF 3.1 | $r_s$ | +.09 | | ns | Female college students, U.S.A.<br>Non-probability chunk sample<br>N: 14, date: October - December, 1957 | WESSM 60<br>p. 122 |
| STABILITY OF SELF-IMAGE | 5-item index (Guttman scale) of agree / disagree statements on continuing or changing opinions and ideas about oneself | | HAPP 1.1 | G<br>V | +.25<br>.13 | $Chi^2$ | 01 | Juniors and seniors attending public high schools in New York State, U.S.A.<br>Probability cluster sample of 10 public high schools<br>N: sample A: 1682, sample B: 1664, date: 1960 | BRENN 70<br>p. 94/286 |
| | | | AFF 1.1 | G<br>V | +.22<br>.11 | $Chi^2$ | 01 | | |

## S 2.1.3 - SELF-ESTEEM

| Concept | Measure | Remarks | Variable | Stat. | Value | Test | Sign. | Population / Sample | Source |
|---|---|---|---|---|---|---|---|---|---|
| RESPECT FOR ONESELF | Direct question rated on an 11-point self-anchoring scale on respect for oneself as a person; feelings of being a worthwhile and worthy person, as contrasted to a feeling that one is a failure and doesn't amount to much | | HAPP 3.1 | $r_{pm}$ | +.21 | | | National adult population, U.S.A<br>Probability sample<br>N: 1549, date: 1960 | CANTR 65/2<br>p. 268/415 |
| | | | HAPP 2.1 | $r_{pm}$ | +.39 | | | | |
| | | | CON 1.1 | $r_{pm}$ | +.41 | | | | |
| SELF-RESPECT | Closed question rated on an 11-point self-anchoring scale (see above) | | HAPP 2.1 | r | +.36 | | | National adult population, U.S.A.<br>Cantril (1965) modified probability sample<br>N: 1406, date: 1959 | BORTN 70<br>p. 44 |
| | | | HAPP 3.1 | r | +.21 | | | | |
| | | | CON 1.1 | r | +.41 | | | | |
| SELF-ESTEEM | 10-item index (Guttman scale) of agree / disagree statements on feeling to be a person of worth, having a number of good qualities, feeling to be a failure, being able to do things as well as most other people, not having much to be proud of, positive attitude towards oneself, satisfaction with oneself, lack of self-respect, feeling useless at times, being no good at all (Rosenberg Self-Esteem Scale; see Rosenberg, 1965). | When standardized on:<br>- participation in extracurricular activities : $G_s$ = +.41<br>- social class : $G_s$ = +.42<br>Stronger in lower class : G = +.48<br>When standardized on participation in extracurricular activities : $G_s$ = +.42<br>Lower in middle and upper class : G = +.42<br>When standardized on participation in extracurricular activities : $G_s$ = +.40 | HAPP 1.1 | G<br>V | +.42<br>.20 | $Chi^2$ | 01 | Juniors and seniors attending public high schools in New York State, U.S.A.<br>Probability cluster sample of 10 public high schools<br>N: sample A: 1682, sample B: 1664, sample C: 1678<br>date: 1960 | BRENN 70<br>p. 94/141/154/274 |
| | | | AFF 1.1 | G<br>V | +.36<br>.19 | $Chi^2$ | 01 | | |
| SELF-ESTEEM | 10-item index of closed questions on being worthwhile as a person, having good qualities, being as able as others, not proud of oneself, positive attitude towards oneself, feeling not good at all, a useful guy, can't do anything right, do a job well, not very useful life<br>(item from Self-Esteem Indices from Rosenberg, 1965; and Cobb et al., 1966) | | COMP 1.2 | $r_{pm}$ | +.54 | | 001 | Public high school boys, U.S.A.<br>Probability multi-stage sample<br>N: 2213 in 1966; 1886 in 1968; and 1799 in 1969<br>date: fall, 1966; spring, 1968; and spring, 1969 | BACHM 67/70<br>p. 122 |

| | | | | | | | | | |
|---|---|---|---|---|---|---|---|---|---|
| SELF-ESTEEM | Index of agree / disagree statements, indicative of a successful life, self-confidence, success in achieving goals, etc. | Self-esteem was measured two years before hedonic level was assessed. | AFF 3.1 | $r_{pm}$ | +.50 | t | 05 | Male college students, U.S.A.<br>Non-probability chunk sample<br>N: 17, date: ± 1960 | WESSM 66/2<br>p. 117 |
| SELF-ESTEEM | Adjective checklist scored for 'how do you feel at the moment?'<br>(Modified Leventhal Self Esteem Scale; see Dabbs & Leventhal, 1966) | The subjects filled in this questionnaire in an experimental situation, right after their self-esteem was experimentally altered.<br>The relationship appeared to be unaffected by manipulated self-esteem.<br>For happy Ss self-esteem is unaffected by bolstered self-esteem and decreased by reduced self-esteem.<br>For unhappy Ss self-esteem is higher by bolstered self-esteem than by reduced self-esteem. | AFF 6 | $r_{pm}$ | +.35 | | 01 | Female undergraduates, U.S.A.<br>Random sample<br>N: 72, date: — | LUDWI 71/75<br>p. 64 |
| SELF-ESTEEM | Each subject was asked to place herself and 5 other persons (such as a friend, a selfish person, a grandmother, a sad person, a doctor, a strong person, etc.) in a line of 6 circles.<br>This was done 6 times with different combinations of persons.<br>Each placement of the self in the circle farthest to the left was most indicative of high self-esteem (score 6), and placement in the circle farthest to the right of low self-esteem (score 1).<br>(Ziller Self-Esteem Scale; see Ziller et al., 1964). | See above | AFF 6 | $r_{pm}$ | +.08 | | ns | See above | LUDWI 71/75<br>p. 64 |
| ESTEEM OF HIMSELF AS A WHOLE | Trained peer rating on a 7-point scale on the basis of observation | | AFF 5.2 | $r_{pm}$ | +.12 | | | Male students, England<br>Non-probability chunk sample<br>N: 194, date: 1912 - 1913 | WEBB 15<br>p. 26 |
| SELF-ESTEEM | 11-item index of 9-point Likert scales containing being honest, confident, etc. | Index of Positive Affects: G = +.09<br>Index of Negative Affects: G = -.11 | AFF 2.3 | G | + | | | Employed males, England<br>Non-probability purposive quota sample<br>N: 192, date: — | PAYNE 74<br>p. 17 |
| POSITIVE SELF-CONCEPT | Content analysis of interview records by 2 independent judges (component of Life Satisfaction Rating)<br>5-point scale:<br>5. Feels at his best. Thinks of self as wise, mellow; physically able or attractive; feels important to others<br>4. Feels more fortunate than the average. Is sure he can meet the exigencies of life. Compensates well for any difficulty of health. Feels in control of self in relation to the situation.<br>3. Sees self as competent in at least one area, e.g., work; but has doubts about self in other areas. Acknowledges loss of youthful vigor, but accepts it. Reports health better than average.<br>2. Feels that other people look down on him. Is defensive about what the years are doing to him.<br>1. Feels old. Feels in the way, or worthless. Makes self-disparaging remarks. | See remarks in excerpt (Part II). | CON 1.4<br>COMP 1.4 | r<br>r | +.73<br>+.82 | | | White adult population of age 50+, Kansas City, U.S.A.<br>Stratified probability sample and non-probability quota sample<br>N: 177, date: — | NEUGA 61<br>p. 139 |

| | | | | | | | | | |
|---|---|---|---|---|---|---|---|---|---|
| POSITIVE SELF-CONCEPT | 21 bipolar adjective 7-point scales (semantic differential scales; see Monge, 1971). The scales were scored for 'Myself - as I really am most of the time'. | Four principal self-concept components were extracted: Achievement / Leadership, Congeniality / Sociability, Psychological adjustment and Physical adjustment. Only Psychological adjustment appeared to be related to the Affect Balance Score (see also 'Content of real self image'; Part III, S 2.2.1). | AFF 2.3 | DM | + | D | 01 | Catholic sisters, U.S.A.<br>Non-probability chunk sample<br>N: 183, date: — | LEWIS 72<br>p. 67-69 |

## S 2.1.4 - SELF-CONFIDENCE

see also 'Types of Affect: Self Confidence' (A 2.2.16)

| | | | | | | | | | |
|---|---|---|---|---|---|---|---|---|---|
| CONFIDENCE IN ONESELF | Direct question rated on an 11-point self-anchoring scale on confidence in oneself in general; how sure one feels of oneself | | HAPP 3.1 | $r_{pm}$ | +.28 | | | National adult population, U.S.A.<br>Probability sample<br>N: 1549, date: 1960 | CANTR 65/2<br>p. 268/415 |
| | | | HAPP 2.1 | $r_{pm}$ | +.31 | | | | |
| | | | CON 1.1 | $r_{pm}$ | +.41 | | | | |
| SELF-CONFIDENCE | Closed question rated on an 11-point self-anchoring scale (see above) | | HAPP 2.1 | r | +.34 | | | National adult population, U.S.A.<br>Cantril (1965) modified probability sample<br>N: 1406, date: 1959 | BORTN 70<br>p. 44 |
| | | | HAPP 3.1 | r | +.26 | | | | |
| | | | CON 1.1 | r | +.41 | | | | |
| FEELING AS ABLE AS OTHERS TO DO THINGS | Closed question: strongly disagree / disagree / agree / strongly agree (item from Self-Esteem Scale; see 'Self-Esteem'; Part III, S 2.1.3). | | HAPP 1.1 | G<br>V | +.19<br>.10 | $Chi^2$ | 01 | Juniors and seniors attending public high schools in New York State, U.S.A.<br>Probability cluster sample of 10 public high schools<br>N: sample A: 1682, sample B: 1664, sample C: 1678<br>date: 1960 | BRENN 70<br>p. 94/282 |
| | | | AFF 1.1 | G<br>V | +.22<br>.11 | $Chi^2$ | 01 | | |
| BELIEF IN HIS OWN POWERS | Trained peer rating on a 7-point scale on the basis of observation | | AFF 5.2 | $r_{pm}$ | +.11 | | | Male students, England<br>Non-probability chunk sample<br>N: 194, date: 1912 - 1913 | WEBB 15<br>p. 26 |
| PROJECTIVE HELPLESSNESS | Score from told stories to the standard Thematic Appreciation Test cards (see Murray, 1943), indicative of feeling or being helpless, feeling weak or ineffectual, being dominated, dependent | | AFF 3.1 | $r_{pm}$ | -.56 | t | 05 | Male college students, U.S.A.<br>Non-probability chunk sample<br>N: 17, date: ± 1960 | WESSM 66/2<br>p. 120 |
| SOCIAL UNCERTAINTY (lack of self-confidence) | 2-item index indicating fear for other's opinion (criticism), and lack of self-confidence | | HAPP 1.1 | G' | -.35 | Gt' | 01 | Adults, Utrecht, The Netherlands<br>Probability sample, stratified by age<br>N: 300, date: autumn, 1967 | MOSER 69<br>p. 44 |
| FEELING UNCERTAIN AND UNDECISIVE | Closed question: no vs yes | | HAPP 2.1 | G | -.74 | $Chi^2$ | 000 | Male employees of age 40+, The Netherlands<br>Non-probability chunk sample<br>N: 13000, date: — | SONDE 75 |

## S 2.1.5 - SATISFACTION WITH ONESELF

| | | | | | | | | | |
|---|---|---|---|---|---|---|---|---|---|
| SATISFACTION WITH PERSONAL EFFICACY | 3-item index containing satisfaction with way of handling problems, way of accomplishment, and oneself (to be continued on next page) | Unaffected by sex | HAPP 3.1<br>(1st instr.) | $h^2$ | .55 | | | National adult population, U.S.A.<br>Probability area sample (first sample)<br>N: 1297, date: May, 1972 | ANDRE 74<br>p. 17 |

| | | | | | | | | | |
|---|---|---|---|---|---|---|---|---|---|
| | Closed questions: 'How do you feel about...' terrible / unhappy / mostly dissatisfied / mixed/ mostly satisfied / pleased / delighted | | | | | | | | |
| SATISFACTION WITH ONESELF | Single closed question: 'How do you feel about yourself – what you are accomplishing and how do you handle problems?' terrible / unhappy / mostly dissatisfied / mixed/ mostly satisfied / pleased / delighted | | HAPP 3.1 (1st instr.) | $h^2$ | .54 | | | National adult population, U.S.A.<br>Probability area sample (third sample)<br>N: 1072, date: November, 1972 | ANDRE 74<br>p. 19 |
| SATISFACTION WITH ONESELF AS A PERSON | Closed question: 'How do you feel about yourself as a person?'<br>not so good / could be better / just O.K / pretty good | Index of Positive Affects: r = +.03 (ns)<br>Index of Negative Affects: r = –.22 (01) | AFF 2.3<br><br>COMP 1.1 | $r_{pm}$<br><br>$r_{pm}$ | +.18<br><br>+.24 | $Chi^2$<br><br>$Chi^2$ | 01<br><br>01 | Adults, Houston, Texas, U.S.A.<br>Non-probability purposive quota sample, stratified by age, sex, occupational skill level, and ethnicity<br>N: 1441, date: autumn, 1969 | GAITZ 72<br>p. 65 |
| SATISFACTION WITH ONESELF | Closed question: strongly disagree / disagree / agree / strongly agree<br>(item from Self-Esteem Scale; see 'Self Esteem'; Part III, S 2.1.6). | | HAPP 1.1<br><br>AFF 1.1 | G<br>V<br>G<br>V | +.43<br>.25<br>+.35<br>.19 | $Chi^2$<br><br>$Chi^2$ | 01<br><br>01 | Juniors and seniors attending public high schools, New York State, U.S.A.<br>Probability cluster sample of 10 public high schools<br>N: sample A: 1682, sample B: 1664 sample C: 1678<br>date: 1960 | BRENN 70<br>p. 94/278 |

## S 2.1.6 – VARIOUS INDICATORS OF A POSITIVE SELF-IMAGE

see also 'Types of Affect: Social Respect' (A 2.2.18)

| | | | | | | | | | |
|---|---|---|---|---|---|---|---|---|---|
| SELF-ACCEPTANCE | Degree to which S gives a positive evaluation of the self in describing differences from others, as assessed by an open-ended question on differences from most other people<br>negative / ambivalent / neutral / positive / very positive | Unaffected by sex:<br>males : $t_k$ = –.01 (ns)<br>females: $t_k$ = +.02 (ns) | HAPP 1.1 | $t_k$ | | | ns | Adult married population with children, U.S.A.<br>Probability area sample<br>N: 797, date: spring, 1957 | VEROF 62<br>p. 196 |
| PERCEIVED STRONG POINTS IN THE SELF | Open-ended direct question<br>S sees no strong points vs mentions strong points | Unaffected by sex | HAPP 1.1 | $t_k$ | +.04 | | ns | See above | VEROF 62<br>p. 196 |
| SHORTCOMINGS IN THE SELF | Open-ended question on how one would like his children to be different from oneself<br>doesn't want children to be different vs wants children to be different | males only: $t_k$ = –.10 (05) | HAPP 1.1 | $t_k$ | – | | | See above | VEROF 62<br>p. 196 |
| SENSITIVITY TO FAILURE | 3-item index of closed questions on feeling disturbed when done something badly, bothered by finding that someone has a poor opinion of you, disturbed when becoming aware of some fault or inadequacy in oneself | | HAPP 1.1<br><br>AFF 1.1 | G<br>V<br>G<br>V | –.06<br>.07<br>–.06<br>.05 | $Chi^2$<br><br>$Chi^2$ | 01<br><br>05 | Juniors and seniors attending public high schools in New York State, U.S.A.<br>Probability cluster sample of 10 public high schools<br>N: sample A: 1682, sample B: 1664, | BRENN 70<br>p. 94/306 |

## S 2.2 – CONTENT OF SELF-IMAGE

## S 2.2.1 - CONTENT OF REAL SELF-IMAGE

| | | | | | | | | |
|---|---|---|---|---|---|---|---|---|
| REAL SELF DESCRIPTIONS: | Content analysis of a 45-item Q sort, filled out both in extremely high and in extremely low moods for self-concept ('the most accurate picture of yourself as you really believe you are now') | The group of Ss was divided in two according to their mean 'daily average mood' (see instrument in excerpt, Part II).<br>The Q sort descriptions provided by the seven relatively happy girls were compared with those of the seven relatively unhappy girls.<br>Only significant discrepancies between the descriptions of both groups were presented. | | | | | Female college students, U.S.A.<br>Non-probability chunk sample<br>N: 14, date: October - November, 1957 | WESSM 60<br>p. 123 |
| - FRIENDLY, SOCIABLE, AND OPEN TOWARDS OTHERS | | In both high and low moods the happy girls describe themselves as more friendly, sociable, more willing to give of themselves to others, and more interested in what others have to offer.<br>The unhappy girls describe themselves as more independent, self-sufficient and introspective. | AFF 3.1 | | + | | 05 | | |
| - SOPHISTICATED, CRITICAL, INTERESTED IN ACADEMIC WORK | | In both high and low moods the unhappy girls describe themselves as more critical, sophisticated, interested in academic work and introspective.<br>The happy girls describe themselves as more unorganized, tolerant and nervous. They are able to enjoy work without being preoccupied with it, and do not consider themselves sophisticated or poised. | AFF 3.1 | | - | | 05 | | |
| REAL-SELF DESCRIPTIONS: | Content analysis of a 60-item Q sort, describing characteristics indicative of successful and unsuccessful resolutions of the first six developmental crises of the Erikson's stages of psychosocial development (see Erikson, 1959).<br>The Q sort was filled out both in very elated and in very depressed moods for self-concept ('an accurate picture of yourself as you honestly feel and believe you are'). | See also under 'Personality development'(Part III, P 1.4)<br>The group of Ss was divided in two according to their mean 'daily average mood'(see instrument in excerpt, Part II).<br>The Q sort descriptions provided by the nine relatively happy men were compared with those of the eight relatively unhappy men.<br>Only significant discrepancies between the descriptions of both groups were presented. | | | | | Male college students, U.S.A.<br>Non-probability chunk sample<br>N: 17, date: ± 1960 | WESSM 66/2<br>p. 110-111 |
| - WARM, FRIENDLY AND COMFORTABLE IN CLOSE RELATIONSHIPS | | In general the happy men describe themselves as more social, while the unhappy men are more isolated and preoccupied with themselves.<br>In depression also the happy men experience a decrease in social interests, but are still concerned with others, while the unhappy men, in depression, were unable to share with others. | AFF 3.1 | | + | t | 05 | | |
| - ABLE TO EXCEL IN WORK, CONSCIENTIOUS, PRODUCTIVE | | Especially in elation the happy men describe themselves as productive, while the unhappy men, even in elation, are more given to wasting time and failing to apply themselves. | AFF 3.1 | | + | t | 05 | | |
| - UNABLE TO FULFILL AMBITIONS | | The unhappy men are more ambitious, but are less able to fulfill their ambitions.<br>Especially in depression they feel ineffective, unable to get what they want, pessimistic and unable to absorb frustation. | AFF 3.1 | | - | t | 05 | | |
| - OPTIMISM IN BAD SPIRITS | | The happy men perceive depression as temporary states which would be resolved when the problems which occasioned them had been resolved.<br>(to be continued on next page) | AFF 3.1 | | + | t | 05 | | |

| | | | | | | | | | |
|---|---|---|---|---|---|---|---|---|---|
| | | The unhappy men are more pessimistic, feel depression as permanent states of frustration and impotent desire. | | | | | | | |
| - TENDENCY TO DISREGARD THE WORLD | | Especially in depression the unhappy men felt a tendency to disregard the world, but also felt they were in the wrong and apologetic. | AFF 3.1 | | - | t | 05 | | |
| SELF-IMAGE: | Factors derived from self-ratings on a semantic differential of 28 bipolar adjective 7-point scales | | | | | | | Married female graduates of liberal arts college, U.S.A.<br>Probability cluster sample<br>N: 229, date: 1971 | GORDO 74<br>p. 243 |
| - POTENCY: EMOTIONAL AND PHYSICAL STRENGTH | | | HAPP 1.1 | r | +.25 | | 01 | | |
| - SUPPORTIVENESS: NURTURANT, AGREEABLE BEHAVIOR IN INTERPERSONAL SETTINGS | | | HAPP 1.1 | r | +.20 | | 01 | | |
| - SPONTANEITY: WILLINGNESS TO TAKE IMMEDIATE ACTION | | | HAPP 1.1 | r | | | ns | | |
| - EMOTIONALITY: LEVEL OF EMOTION | | | HAPP 1.1 | r | +.25 | | 01 | | |
| SELF-CONCEPT COMPONENTS: | Principal components, extracted from 21 bipolar adjective 7-point scales (semantic differential scales; see Monge, 1971).<br>The adjective scales were scored for 'Myself - as I really am most of the time'. | | | | | | | Catholic sisters, U.S.A.<br>Non-probability chunk sample<br>N: 183, date: — | LEWIS 72<br>p. 67-69 |
| - ACHIEVEMENT / LEADERSHIP | 7 items: inferior - superior, dull - sharp, follower - leader, dumb - smart, failure - success, weak - strong, worthless - valuable | | AFF 2.3 | DM | + | D | ns | | |
| - CONGENIALITY / SOCIABILITY | 4 items: cruel - kind, awful - nice, unfriendly - friendly, bad - good | | AFF 2.3 | DM | - | D | ns | | |
| - PSYCHOLOGICAL ADJUSTMENT | 6 items: dissatisfied - satisfied, unstable - stable, shaky - steady, sad - happy, unsure - confident, soft - hard | | AFF 2.3 | DM | + | D | 01 | | |
| - PHYSICAL ADJUSTMENT | 4 items: delicate - rugged, sick - healthy, nervous - relaxed, tired - refreshed | | AFF 2.3 | DM | - | D | ns | | |

## S 2.2.2 - CONTENT OF IDEAL SELF-IMAGE

see also 'Value Dimensions' (V 1.1)

| | | | | | | | | | |
|---|---|---|---|---|---|---|---|---|---|
| IDEAL-SELF DESCRIPTIONS: | Content analysis of a 45-item Q sort, filled out both in extremely high and in extremely low moods for ideal-concept ('the picture of yourself as the kind of person you have hoped to become and have fancied yourself to be') | See also under 'Content of real self-image' (Part III, S 2.2.1).<br>The group of Ss was divided in two according to their mean 'daily average mood' (see instrument in excerpt, Part II).<br>The Q sort descriptions provided by the seven relatively more happy girls were compared with those of the seven relatively less happy girls.<br>Only significant discrepancies between the descriptions of both groups were presented. | | | | | | Female college students, U.S.A.<br>Non-probability chunk sample<br>N: 14, date: October - November, 1957 | WESSM 60<br>p. 123 |

| | | | | | | | | | |
|---|---|---|---|---|---|---|---|---|---|
| - PRIMARILY CONCERNED WITH WORK | | In elation the unhappy girls place a high value on work, while the happy girls tend to place a higher value on friendliness and consideration for others. In depression both the happy and unhappy girls value work more than in elation, but this is more extreme for the unhappy girls. For these girls concern with work in depression took the form of more exclusive concern with intellectual creativity and achievement, while the happy girls in depression place a higher value on the inherent satisfactions in learning, and are more concerned with discovering what they want out of life. | AFF 3.1 | | - | | 05 | | |
| IDEAL-SELF DESCRIPTIONS: | Content analysis of a 60-item Q sort, filled out both in very elated and in very depressed moods for ideal-concept ('the picture of the sort of person you have hoped to become or fancied yourself to be'). | See also under 'Content of real self-image' (Part III, S 2.2.1).<br>The group of Ss was divided in two according to their mean 'daily average mood' (see instrument in excerpt, Part II).<br>The Q sort descriptions provided by the nine relatively happy men were compared with those of the eight relatively unhappy men.<br>Only significant discrepancies between the descriptions of both groups were presented. | | | | | | Male college students, U.S.A.<br>Non-probability chunk sample<br>N: 17, date: $\pm$ 1960 | WESSM 66/2<br>p. 111-112 |
| - PRIMARILY CONCERNED WITH EFFICIENT WORK AND AMBITION | | In general the unhappy men value nothing but efficient work and ambition, especially in their depressed moods.<br>The happier men value warmth and friendliness as much as their academic goals, and reject pretense, selfishness and pessimism more than they reject ineffectiveness, wasting of time and failure to fulfill ambitions. | AFF 3.1 | | - | t | 05 | | |

## S 2.3 - VARIOUS FACTORS CONCERNING SELF-IMAGE

| | | | | | | | | | |
|---|---|---|---|---|---|---|---|---|---|
| PERCEIVED UNIQUENESS OF SELF | Open-ended question on differences from most other people<br>S sees no difference with others vs mentions differences | unaffected by sex: males : $t_k$ = +.07 (ns)<br>females: $t_k$ = +.02 (ns) | HAPP 1.1 | $t_k$ | + | | ns | Adult married population with children, U.S.A.<br>Probability area sample<br>N: 797, date: spring, 1957 | VEROF 62<br>p. 196 |
| DESIRED PERSONAL CHANGES: CHARACTER CHANGES (worry less) | Open-ended question on desired personal changes<br>other changes vs change mentioned | Computed for those who desire to change only (N = 1591). | HAPP 1.1 | G' | +.12 | Gt' | 05 | National adult population, U.S.A.<br>Non-probability quota sample<br>N: 2377, date: February, 1946 | WESSM 56<br>p. 211 |
| MOST IMPORTANT WORRY: PERSONALITY TRAITS | Open-ended question on most important worry<br>other worries vs worry mentioned | Computed for those who have worries only (N = 2040). | HAPP 1.1 | G' | -.05 | Gt' | ns | See above | WESSM 56<br>p. 213 |
| REPORT OF HOPES CONCERNING VALUES AND CHARACTER | Open-ended question on personal wishes and hopes for the future<br>Responses rated as concerning emotional stability and maturity; being a normal, decent person; self-development or improvement; acceptance by others; achieve sense of own personal worth; resolution of own religious, spiritual, or ethical problems; lead a disciplined life; etc. | | HAPP 3.1 | G' | +.21 | Gt' | 01 | Adult population of 5 Westernized nations, 3 underdeveloped giants, 2 countries in the Middle East, 3 Caribbean nations and the Philippines<br>Representative samples<br>N: 18653, date: $\pm$ 1960 | CANTR 65/1<br>p. 263 |

| | | | | | | | | | |
|---|---|---|---|---|---|---|---|---|---|
| REPORT OF FEARS CONCERNING VALUES AND CHARACTER | Open-ended question on personal worries and fears for the future<br><br>Responses rated as concerning emotional instability and immaturity; become anti-social; no self-development or improvement; not be accepted by others; no sense of personal worth; be a person without character; etc. | | HAPP 3.1 | G' | +.17 | Gt' | 01 | Adult population of 14 countries (see last page) | CANTR 65/1 p. 263 |

# S 3 SEXUALITY



## S 3.1 - ATTITUDES TOWARDS SEX

### S 3.1.1 - ONE'S OWN ATTITUDES

| | | | | | | | | | |
|---|---|---|---|---|---|---|---|---|---|
| LIBERAL SEXUAL ATTITUDE (PRAGMATIC) | 6-item questionnaire of various sexual behaviors varying in intimacy, scored for how one would probably behave when possible on a first date, after several dates, with a steady, and with a fiancé(e). | | COMP 1.1 | $r_{pm}$ | -.15 | | ns | Undergraduate college students, Hawaii<br>Non-probability accidental sample<br>N: 101, date: — | WILSO 65<br>p. 375 |
| LIBERAL SEXUAL ATTITUDE (IDEAL) | 6-item questionnaire of various sexual behaviors varying in intimacy, scored for those behaviors one endorses or approves of on a first date, after several dates, with a steady and with a fiancé(e). | | COMP 1.1 | $r_{pm}$ | -.10 | | ns | See above | WILSO 65<br>p. 375 |
| LIBERALITY OF SEXUAL BEHAVIORS ENGAGED IN | 6-item questionnaire of various sexual behaviors varying in intimacy, scored for number of behaviors engaged in on a first date, after several dates, with a steady, with a fiancé(e). | Scores were weighted to reflect liberality of attitudes rather than liberality of behavior.<br>males : r = -.07 (ns)<br>females: r = -.01 (ns) | COMP 1.1 | $r_{pm}$ | - | | ns | Undergraduate students, Ohio, U.S.A.<br>Non-probability accidental sample<br>N: 132, date: 1966 / 1967 | MILLE 68<br>p. 1082 |
| LIBERALITY OF SEXUAL BEHAVIORS ENGAGED IN AND REVEALED TO PEERS | 6-item questionnaire (see above), scored for number of sexual behaviors engaged in and later disclosed to a member of one's peer group. | See above<br>Stronger among males: r = =.25 (05)<br>Not among females : r = +.03 (ns) | COMP 1.1 | $r_{pm}$ | - | | ns | See above | MILLE 68<br>p. 1082 |
| LIBERALITY OF SEXUAL BEHAVIORS ENGAGED IN AND REVEALED TO PARENTS | 6-item questionnaire (see above), scored for number of sexual behaviors engaged in and later disclosed to one or both parents. | See above<br>Positive among females: r = +.22 (ns)<br>Negative among males : r = -.14 (ns) | COMP 1.1 | $r_{pm}$ | | | ns | See above | MILLE 68<br>p. 1082 |
| LIBERALITY OF SEXUAL BEHAVIORS ONE WOULD LIKE TO ENGAGE IN WITH A DATE | 6-item questionnaire (see above), scored for number of behaviors one would like to engage in at different stages of a dating relationship. | Positive among females: r = +.12 (ns)<br>Negative among males : r = -.11 (ns) | COMP 1.1 | $r_{pm}$ | | | ns | See above | MILLE 68<br>p. 1082 |
| LIBERALITY OF SEXUAL BEHAVIORS DEEMED ACCEPTABLE IF EXPERIENCED PREVIOUSLY BY A FIANCE(E) | 6-item questionnaire (see above), scored for number of behaviors one would not seriously disapprove of if one's fiancé(e) had engaged in them before with someone else. | males : r = -.13 (ns)<br>females: r = -.16 (ns) | COMP 1.1 | $r_{pm}$ | - | | ns | See above | MILLE 68<br>p. 1082 |

## S 3.1.2 - PERCEIVED ATTITUDES OF OTHERS

| Variable | Description | Questions | Design | Statistic | Value | | Sig. | Sample | Source |
|---|---|---|---|---|---|---|---|---|---|
| PERCEIVED LIBERALITY OF SEXUAL ATTITUDES OF PEER GROUP | 6-item questionnaire of various sexual behaviors varying in intimacy, scored for those behaviors which one's peer group would not seriously disapprove of on a first date, after several dates, with a steady and with a fiancé(e). | | COMP 1.1 | $r_{pm}$ | +.02 | | ns | Undergraduate college students, Hawaii<br>Non-probability accidental sample<br>N: 101, date: — | WILSO 65<br>p. 375 |
| PERCEIVED LIBERALITY OF SEXUAL ATTITUDES OF PARENTS | 6-item questionnaire (see above), scored for sexual behaviors which one's parents would not seriously disapprove of. | | COMP 1.1 | $r_{pm}$ | -.04 | | ns | See above | WILSO 65<br>p. 375 |

## S 3.1.3 - ATTITUDINAL CONFLICTS

| Variable | Description | Questions | Design | Statistic | Value | | Sig. | Sample | Source |
|---|---|---|---|---|---|---|---|---|---|
| SEXUAL CONFLICT: | Discrepancy between various scores indicative of sexual liberality: | For questions used see above under 'Liberality of Sexual Attitudes' (S 3.1) and 'Perceived Liberality of Sexual Attitudes of Others' (S 3.2). | COMP 1.1 | | | | | Undergraduate college students, Hawaii<br>Non-probability accidental sample<br>N: 101, date: — | WILSO 65<br>p. 375 |
| | - Discrepancy between liberality of one's ideal sexual attitude and liberality of one's pragmatic sexual attitude | | COMP 1.1 | $r_{pm}$ | -.18 | | ns | | |
| | - Discrepancy between liberality of one's pragmatic sexual attitude and perceived liberality of sexual attitude of one's peer group | | COMP 1.1 | $r_{pm}$ | -.22 | | s | | |
| | - Discrepancy between liberality of one's ideal sexual attitude and perceived liberality of sexual attitude of one's peer group | | COMP 1.1 | $r_{pm}$ | +.14 | | ns | | |
| | - Discrepancy between liberality of one's pragmatic sexual attitude and perceived liberality of sexual attitude of one's parents | | COMP 1.1 | $r_{pm}$ | -.17 | | ns | | |
| | - Discrepancy between liberality of one's ideal sexual attitude and perceived liberality of sexual attitude of one's parents | | COMP 1.1 | $r_{pm}$ | -.09 | | ns | | |
| | - Discrepancy between perceived liberality of sexual attitudes of one's peers and one's parents | | COMP 1.1 | $r_{pm}$ | +.06 | | ns | | |
| SEXUAL CONFLICT: | Discrepancy between various scores indicative of sexual liberality: | For questions used see above under 'Liberality of Sexual Attitudes' (S 3.1) | | | | | | Undergraduate students, Ohio, U.S.A.<br>Non-probability accidental sample<br>N: 132, date: 1966 / 1967 | MILLE 68<br>p. 1082 |
| | - Difference between liberality of sexual behaviors engaged in and liberality of sexual behaviors engaged in and revealed to peers | Positive among males : r = +.23 (ns)<br>Negative among females: r = -.07 (ns) | COMP 1.1 | $r_{pm}$ | + | | ns | | |
| | - Difference between liberality of sexual behaviors engaged in and liberality of sexual behaviors engaged in and revealed to parents | Negative among females: r = -.15 (ns)<br>Not among males : r = +.03 (ns) | COMP 1.1 | $r_{pm}$ | - | | ns | | |
| | ( to be continued on next page) | | | | | | | | |

| | | | | | | | | | |
|---|---|---|---|---|---|---|---|---|---|
| | - Difference between liberality of sexual behaviors engaged in and liberality of sexual behaviors one would like to engage in with a date | Negative among females: r = -.15 (ns)<br>Not among males : r = +.03 (ns) | COMP 1.1 | $r_{pm}$ | - | | ns | | |
| | - Difference between liberality of sexual behaviors engaged in and liberality of sexual behaviors deemed acceptable if experienced previously by a fiancé (e) | Stronger among females: r = +.17 (ns)<br>Not among males : r = +.03 (ns) | COMP 1.1 | $r_{pm}$ | + | | ns | | |
| | - Difference between liberality of sexual behaviors engaged in and revealed to peers and liberality of sexual behaviors engaged in and revealed to parents | Stronger among males: r = -.21 (ns)<br>Lower among females : r = -.11 (ns) | COMP 1.1 | $r_{pm}$ | - | | ns | | |
| | - Difference between liberality of sexual behaviors engaged in and revealed to peers and liberality of sexual behaviors one would like to engage in with a date | Stronger among males: r = -.17 (ns)<br>Lower among females : r = -.08 (ns) | COMP 1.1 | $r_{pm}$ | - | | ns | | |
| | - Difference between liberality of sexual behaviors engaged in and revealed to peers and liberality of sexual behaviors deemed acceptable if experienced previously by a fiancé(e) | Negative among males : r = -.18 (ns)<br>Positive among females: r = +.18 (ns) | COMP 1.1 | $r_{pm}$ | | | ns | | |
| | - Difference between liberality of sexual behaviors engaged in and revealed to parents and liberality of sexual behaviors one would like to engage in with a date | males : r = -.00 (ns)<br>females: r = -.04 (ns) | COMP 1.1 | $r_{pm}$ | - | | ns | | |
| | - Difference between liberality of sexual behaviors engaged in and revealed to parents and liberality of sexual behaviors deemed acceptable if experienced previously by a fiancé(e) | Stronger among females: r = -.26 (05)<br>Not among males : r = -.01 (ns) | COMP 1.1 | $r_{pm}$ | - | | ns | | |
| | - Difference between liberality of sexual behaviors one would like to engage in with a date and liberality of sexual behaviors deemed acceptable if experienced previously by a fiancé(e) | Stronger among females: r = -.30 (05)<br>Not among males : r = -.01 (ns) | COMP 1.1 | $r_{pm}$ | - | | ns | | |
| SEX GUILT | Subscale from the Mosher Incomplete Sentences Test (see Mosher, 1961) | | HAPP 1.1 | DM | - | $r_1$ | 05 | University students, U.S.A.<br>Non-probability chunk sample<br>N: 313, date: 1966 - 1967 | BRADB 67<br>p. 64 |

## S 3.2 - QUALITY OF SEX LIFE

see also 'Types of Affect - Love and Sex' (A 2.2.11)

| | | | | | | | | | |
|---|---|---|---|---|---|---|---|---|---|
| SATISFACTION WITH SEX LIFE | Closed question: 'How do you feel about your sex life?'<br>terrible / unhappy / mostly dissatisfied / mixed/ mostly satisfied / pleased / delighted | | HAPP 3.1<br>(1st instr.) | $h^2$ | .40 | | | National adult population, U.S.A.<br>Probability area sample (third sample)<br>N: 1072, date: November, 1972 | ANDRE 74<br>p. 19 |
| SATISFACTION WITH LOVE LIFE | Closed question rated on an open graphic scale ranging from 'very dissatisfied' to 'very satisfied' | Lower among those of age 41-50 and 61-65<br>Stronger among those of low S.E.S.<br>Not among those of high educational level<br>Unaffected by sex | HAPP 1.1 | G | +.70 | | 05 | National adult population, The Netherlands<br>Probability area sample<br>N: 1552, date: June, 1968 | BAKKE 74<br>p. 28 |

| | | | | | | | | | |
|---|---|---|---|---|---|---|---|---|---|
| SEXUAL ENJOYMENT | Closed question on amount of pleasure and enjoyment during sex relations at the present time<br>none / mild / moderate / very much pleasure and enjoyment | | HAPP 3.1 | r | +.14 | | | People of 46 and older, Duke, U.S.A.<br>Probability, systematic random sample, stratified by age and sex<br>N: 502, date: 1968 | PALMO 72<br>p. 70 |
| HAVING PROBLEMS WITH SEX | Closed question | High school students only<br>L - shaped curve: Significantly negative among happier students only | COMP 4.1 | | - | | | Students, U.S.A.<br>Non-probability chunk sample<br>N: 1651, date: — | SYMON 37<br>p. 292 |

## S 3.3 - VARIOUS FACTORS CONCERNING SEX

| | | | | | | | | | |
|---|---|---|---|---|---|---|---|---|---|
| BEING HOMOSEXUAL | Other vs homosexual | Computed for single males only. | HAPP 2.1 | G' | -.36 | Gt' | ns | Adults, Amsterdam, The Netherlands<br>Probability systematic random sample, stratified by sex and marital status<br>N: 600, date: September - December, 1965 | JONG 69<br>p. 252 |
| BEING INTERESTED IN SEX | Closed question | | COMP 4.1 | | | | ns | Students, U.S.A.<br>Non-probability chunk sample<br>N: 1651, date: — | SYMON 37<br>p. 292 |

# S 4 SOCIAL PARTICIPATION



## S 4.1 - SOCIAL PARTICIPATION IN INTERPERSONAL NETWORKS

### S 4.1.1 - NUMBER OF INTERPERSONAL RELATIONSHIPS

| | | | | | | | | | |
|---|---|---|---|---|---|---|---|---|---|
| NUMBER OF INTIMATES, FRIENDS AND AQUAINTANCES | 3-item index of closed questions on number of people one can talk with about personal things, number of people one cares about, and number of acquaintances | unmarried males : r = +.09 (ns)<br>married males : r = +.12 (ns)<br>unmarried females: r = +.21 (ns)<br>married females : r = +.17 (01) | HAPP 2.1 | $r_{pm}$ | + | $Chi^2$ | ns | Adults, Amsterdam, The Netherlands<br>Probability systematic random sample, stratified by sex and marital status<br>N: 600, date: September – December, 1965 | JONG 69<br>p. 203 |
| NUMBER OF SOCIAL NETWORK MEMBERS | Closed question on number of adults seen at least once a month and considered as important persons in life | Positive among married females : r = +.12 (ns)<br>Negative among unmarried females: r = -.06 (ns) | HAPP 1.1 | r | + | | ns | Females from the Seattle – Washington area, U.S.A.<br>Non-probability chunk sample<br>N: 153, date: — | BRIM 74<br>p. 437 |
| NUMBER OF SIGNIFICANT OTHERS | Closed question on number of people who one considers to be close and with whom one can feel free and talk about personal things | When controlled for role loss: $r_{pc}$ = +.47 (01)<br>When controlled for age : $r_{pc}$ = +.45 (01)<br>When controlled for supported self-disclosure : $r_{pc}$ = +.45 (01) | AFF 2.3 | r | +.45 | | 01 | Aged retired persons, Los Angeles County, U.S.A.<br>Non-probability purposive quota sample, proportionally stratified by marital status<br>N: 71, date: 1971 | MORIW 73<br>p. 229 |
| HAVING A CONFIDENT | Closed question: 'Is there one person in particular you confide in or talk to about yourself or your problems?' no vs yes | Positive among males : r = +.15<br>Negative among females: r = -.07 | HAPP 3.1 | r | +.04 | | ns | People of 46 and older, Duke, U.S.A.<br>Systematic random sample, stratified by age and sex<br>N: 502, date: 1968 | PALMO 72<br>p. 70 |
| AVAILABILITY OF PEOPLE ONE CAN COUNT ON | Closed question: 'Can you count on other people in a crisis?' no vs yes | | HAPP 2.1 | $T^2$ | +.18 | $Chi^2$ | 001 | National adult population, Poland<br>Non-probability purposive quota sample, stratified by sex, age, type of local community, employment and S.E.S.<br>N: 2387, date: June/July, 1960 | MAKAR 62<br>p. 108 |
| NUMBER OF FRIENDS | Closed question: I live more or less on my own / I stick to the family / I only have a small number of friends / I have a lot of friends | | HAPP 2.1 | $T^2$ | +.19 | $Chi^2$ | 001 | Non-agricultural population, Poland<br>Non-probability purposive quota sample<br>N: 1385, date: June/July, 1960 | MAKAR 62<br>p. 108 |
| NUMBER OF SOCIAL CONTACTS | Index on number of contacts | Unaffected by health and income | AFF 1.1 | | + | $Chi^2$ | s | Persons over 65, Metropolitan Boston, U.S.A.<br>Probability area sample<br>N: 1335, date: 1965 | FOWLE 69<br>p. 734 |
| NUMBER OF NEIGHBORS KNOWN | Direct question on number of neighbors known well enough to visit with<br>0 / 1-3 / 4 or more | See remarks in excerpt (Part II).<br>Stronger among mentally ill than among mentally well persons (see PHILL 67B, p. 289) | HAPP 1.1 | G | +.22 | | | Adults, New Hampshire, U.S.A.<br>Probability sample<br>N: 600, date: — | PHILL 67A<br>p. 483-484 |
| | | Index of Positive Affects: G = +.12<br>high S.E.S. : d = +.04<br>medium S.E.S. : d = +.04<br>low S.E.S. : d = +.10<br>(to be continued on next page) | AFF 2.3 | G | + | | | | |

| | | | | | | | | | |
|---|---|---|---|---|---|---|---|---|---|
| | | Index of Negative Affects: G = +.01<br>high S.E.S. : d = -.10<br>medium S.E.S. : d = +.02<br>low S.E.S. : d = +.09<br>(see PHILL 69, p. 8) | | | | | | | |
| SOCIABILITY | Number of choices made in answering 3 open-ended questions:<br>- who do you like?<br>- who are your friends?<br>- who do you play with? | Open ward : r = +.30 (01)<br>Closed ward: r = +.04 (ns) | AFF 5.1 | $r_{pm}$ | + | | | Institutionalized mentally retarded males, U.S.A.<br>Non-probability chunk sample<br>N: 149, date: — | PANDE 71<br>p. 329 |
| PEER POPULARITY | 3 open-ended questions (see above)<br>Score based on number of times the respondent was selected by his peers. | Open ward : r = +.04 (ns)<br>Closed ward: r = +.30 (05) | AFF 5.1 | $r_{pm}$ | + | | | See above | PANDE 71<br>p. 329 |
| REJECTION OF PEERS | Score based on number of choices made in answering three open-ended questions:<br>- who don't you like?<br>- who do you dislike?<br>- who don't you like to play with? | Open ward : r = -.03 (ns)<br>Closed ward: r = -.12 (ns) | AFF 5.1 | $r_{pm}$ | - | | ns | See above | PANDE 71<br>p. 329 |
| REJECTION BY PEERS | 3 open-ended questions (see above)<br>Score based on number of times the respondent was selected by his peers. | Open ward : r = -.23 (05)<br>Closed ward: r = -.32 (01) | AFF 5.1 | $r_{pm}$ | - | | 05 | See above | PANDE 71<br>p. 329 |
| POPULARITY | Rating by 2 experienced staff members who were familiar with all the patients on a 7-point 'isolated-popular' scale. | Open ward : r = +.52 (001)<br>Closed ward: r = +.47 (001) | AFF 5.1 | $r_{pm}$ | + | | 001 | See above | PANDE 71<br>p. 329 |

## S 4.1.2 - FREQUENCY OF INTERPERSONAL CONTACTS

| | | | | | | | | | |
|---|---|---|---|---|---|---|---|---|---|
| SOCIABILITY | 3-item index of closed questions on number of times one got together with friends, number of telephone calls with friends, and number of times one was in touch with relatives, during the past few weeks. (see below) | Index of Positive Affects only: G = +.24<br>Unaffected by S.E.S.<br>Unaffected by novelty<br>Unaffected by satisfaction with social life<br>Stronger among those with high esteem for others | AFF 2.3 | G | + | | | Adults, urban areas, U.S.A.<br>Probability area samples<br>N: 2787, date: January, 1963 - January, 1964 | BRADB 69<br>p. 132 |
| INFORMAL SOCIAL PARTICIPATION | Direct question on number of contacts with family, friends or acquaintances, during the past week<br>0-3 / 4-5 / 6 or more | U-shaped curve: Those who had 4 or 5 contacts being most happy | HAPP 1.1 | G' | +.00 | Gt' | ns | Adults, Utrecht, The Netherlands<br>Probability sample, stratified by age<br>N: 300, date: autumn, 1967 | MOSER 69<br>p. 27 |
| CONTACTS WITH SOCIAL NETWORK MEMBERS | Closed question on how often one sees each network member<br>about once a month / once every week or two / several times a week / almost every day | Those adults one sees at least once a month and who are 'important persons' in one's life were considered as social network members.<br>married females : r = +.04 (ns)<br>unmarried females: r = -.01 (ns) | HAPP 1.1 | r | | | ns | Females from the Seattle-Washington area, U.S.A.<br>Non-probability chunk sample<br>N: 153, date: — | BRIM 74<br>p. 437 |
| PARTICIPATION IN INFORMAL SOCIABILITY | Sociability with relatives and friends, measured in terms of the average hours per week involvement.<br>non-involvement vs involvement | | COMP 1.1 | $r_{pm}$ | +.04 | | ns | White males who had experienced a first heart attack, Durham, North Carolina, U.S.A.<br>Non-probability quota sample<br>N: 56, date: 1970 | GARRI 73<br>p. 201 |
| CONTACTS WITH FRIENDS AND RELATIVES | Direct question on frequency of face-to-face interaction<br>monthly or less / about once a week / more than weekly | Stronger among those of age 66-75: $t_k$ = +.52 (01)<br>Stronger among those of age 82-92: $t_k$ = +.50 (01)<br>Lower among those of age 76-81 | AFF 2.3 | $t_k$ | +.43 | | 01 | Aged female public housing residents, U.S.A.<br>Probability systematic random sample<br>N: 44, date: 1967 - 1971 | GRANE 75<br>p. 703 |

| | | | | | | | | | |
|---|---|---|---|---|---|---|---|---|---|
| FREQUENCY OF TELEPHONE USE | Direct question<br>2 or less / 3 to 4 / 5 or more calls daily | | AFF 2.3 | $t_b$ | +.18 | | ns | Aged female public housing residents, U.S.A.<br>(see last page) | GRANE 75<br>p. 703 |

## FREQUENCY OF CONTACTS WITH RELATIVES

| | | | | | | | | | |
|---|---|---|---|---|---|---|---|---|---|
| CONTACTS WITH RELATIVES | Open-ended question on number of families<br>no / 1 / 2 / 3 or more families during last week | Index of Positive Affects only: G' = +.22 (01)<br>Unaffected by S.E.S. | AFF 2.3 | G' | + | Gt' | | Males in the age of 25–49, 4 small communities, Illinois, U.S.A.<br>Probability multi-stage samples<br>N: 393, date: March, 1962 | BRADB 65/1<br>p. 43 |
| CONTACTS WITH RELATIVES | Open-ended question on number of relatives one was in touch with during the past two weeks (visits, telephone calls, letters) | Index of Positive Affects: G = +.10<br>Index of Negative Affects: G = +.03 | AFF 2.3 | G | + | | | Adults, urban areas, U.S.A.<br>Probability area samples<br>N: 2787, date: January, 1963 – January, 1964 | BRADB 69<br>p. 127 |
| EXTENT OF FAMILIAL CONTACT OUTSIDE THE HOME | Respondents were classified according to the number of their living relatives, multiplied by the frequency of contacts with these relatives<br>sparse / occasional / many | | HAPP 2.1 | G' | +.28 | Gt' | 05 | Aged chronically-ill patients, U.S.A.<br>Probability sample<br>N: 167, date: 1959 | HENLE 67<br>p. 71 |

## FREQUENCY OF CONTACTS WITH FRIENDS

| | | | | | | | | | |
|---|---|---|---|---|---|---|---|---|---|
| CONTACTS WITH FRIENDS OTHER THAN RELATIVES | Closed question on frequency of contact during last week, rated on a 5-point scale<br>not at all / once / twice | Index of Positive Affects only: G' = +.31 (01)<br>Unaffected by S.E.S. | AFF 2.3 | G' | + | Gt' | | Males in the age of 25–49, 4 small communities, Illinois, U.S.A.<br>Probability multi-stage samples<br>N: 393, date: March, 1962 | BRADB 65/1<br>p. 43 |
| CONTACTS WITH FRIENDS OTHER THAN RELATIVES | Closed question on how many times one got together with friends, during the past few weeks, rated on a 6-point scale | Index of Positive Affects: G = +.25<br>Index of Negative Affects: G = +.04 | AFF 2.3 | G | + | | | Adults, urban areas, U.S.A.<br>Probability area samples<br>N: 2787, date: January, 1963 – January, 1964 | BRADB 69<br>p. 127 |
| CONTACTS WITH FRIENDS | Direct question on how many times one got together with friends during the past few weeks<br>0 / 1–2 / 3 or more | See remarks in excerpt (Part II).<br>Unaffected by mental health (see PHILL 67B, p.288) | HAPP 1.1 | G | +.22 | | | Adults, New Hampshire, U.S.A.<br>Probability sample<br>N: 600, date: — | PHILL 67A<br>p. 483–484 |
| | | Index of Positive Affects: G = +.34<br>high S.E.S. : d = +.11<br>medium S.E.S. : d = +.22<br>low S.E.S. : d = +.35<br>Index of Negative Affects: G = +.03<br>high S.E.S. : d = –.09<br>medium S.E.S. : d = +.02<br>low S.E.S. : d = +.07<br>(see PHILL 69, p. 7) | AFF 2.3 | G | + | | | | |
| CONTACTS WITH FRIENDS | Direct question on number of contacts in the past 4 weeks rated on a 6-point scale ranging from 'not at all' to 'five or more' | Index of Positive Affects: G = +.13<br>Index of Negative Affects: G = +.11 | AFF 2.3 | G | | | | Employed males, England<br>Non-probability purposive quota sample<br>N: 192, date: — | PAYNE 74<br>p. 17 |
| CONTACTS WITH FRIENDS | Closed question: less than once a month / between once a month and once a week / at least once a week | Index of Positive Affects only: G = +.19 (05) | AFF 2.3 | G | + | | | Non-hospitalized schizophrenic males, Monroe County, New York, U.S.A.<br>Probability samples, drawn from the Monroe County psychiatric case register<br>N: 178, date: 1964 – 1965 | ALEXA 68<br>p. 153 |

| | | | | | | | | | |
|---|---|---|---|---|---|---|---|---|---|
| TELEPHONE CONTACTS WITH FRIENDS | Closed question rated on a 6-point scale<br>none / less than one a day / once a day or more | Index of Positive Affects only : G' = +.22 (01)<br>U-shaped curve: Those with less than 1 telephone contact a day having most positive feelings<br>Lower among those of high S.E.S. : G' = +.12 (ns)<br>Stronger among those of low S.E.S.: G' = +.26 (ns) | AFF 2.3 | G' | + | Gt' | | Males in the age of 25–49, 4 small communities, Illinois, U.S.A.<br>Probability multi-stage samples<br>N: 393, date: March, 1962 | BRADB 65/1<br>p. 43 |
| CHATTING WITH FRIENDS ON TELEPHONE | Closed question on how many times a day during the past few weeks, rated on a 6-point scale | Index of Positive Affects: G = +.20<br>Index of Negative Affects: G = +.08 | AFF 2.3 | G | + | | | Adults, urban areas, U.S.A.<br>Probability area samples<br>N: 2787, date: January, 1963 – January, 1964 | BRADB 69<br>p. 127 |
| TALKING WITH FRIENDS ON TELEPHONE | Direct question on number of times per day, rated on a 5-point scale ranging from 'none' to '4 or more' | Index of Positive Affects: G = –.08<br>Index of Negative Affects: G = –.21 | AFF 2.3 | G | | | | Employed males, England<br>Non-probability purposive sample<br>N: 192, date: — | PAYNE 74<br>p. 17 |

## FREQUENCY OF VARIOUS SOCIAL CONTACTS

| | | | | | | | | | |
|---|---|---|---|---|---|---|---|---|---|
| EXTENT OF DATING | Open-ended question on number of dates this year | | HAPP 1.1 | G<br>V | +.23<br>.10 | $Chi^2$ | 01 | Juniors and seniors attending public high schools in New York State, U.S.A.<br>Probability cluster sample of 10 public high schools<br>N: sample A: 1682, date: 1960 | BRENN 70<br>p. 108/322 |
| | | | AFF 1.1 | G<br>V | +.11<br>.07 | $Chi^2$ | 05 | | |
| ATTENDING PARTIES | Direct question: not at all / once / more than once in the past week | Lower among males G = +.19<br>Stronger among females: G = +.53 | HAPP 1.1 | G | + | | | Adults, Metro Manila, Philippines<br>Probability area sample<br>N: 941, date: January – April, 1972 | BULAT 73<br>p. 232 |
| | | Lower among males : G = +.42<br>Stronger among females: G = +.47 | HAPP 3.1 | G | + | | | | |
| ATTENDING PARTIES | Direct question: never / once a month or less / more than once a month | Index of Positive Affects only: G = +.28 (05) | AFF 2.3 | G | + | | | Non-hospitalized schizophrenic males, New York, U.S.A.<br>Probability sample, drawn from the Monroe County psychiatric case register<br>N: 178, date: 1964 – 1965 | ALEXA 68<br>p. 153 |
| CONTACTS WITH NEIGHBORS | Direct question on frequency of face-to-face interaction<br>less than daily / about once a day / more than once a day | Stronger among those of age 76 – 81<br>Lower among those of age 66 – 75: $t_k$ = +.14 (ns)<br>Lower among those of age 82 – 92: $t_k$ = +.23 (ns) | AFF 2.3 | $t_k$ | +.28 | | 01 | Aged female public housing residents, U.S.A.<br>Probability systematic random sample<br>N: 44, date: 1967/1971 | GRANE 75<br>p. 703 |

## S 4.1.3 – QUALITY OF INTERPERSONAL RELATIONSHIPS

for characteristics of parent – child relationships see 'Family' (F 1), and of marital relationships see 'Marriage' (M 2)
See also 'Personality Traits concerning Interpersonal Functioning' (P 1.8)

| | | | | | | | | | |
|---|---|---|---|---|---|---|---|---|---|
| QUALITY OF INTIMATE RELATIONSHIPS | Score based on number of people one can talk with about personal things and people one cares about, frequency of contacts with these persons, and appreciation of these contacts | unmarried males : r = +.15 (ns)<br>married males : r = +.08 (ns)<br>unmarried females: r = +.30 (025)<br>married females : r = +.04 (ns) | HAPP 2.1 | $r_{pm}$ | + | $Chi^2$ | ns | Adults, Amsterdam, The Netherlands<br>Probability systematic random sample stratified by sex and marital status<br>N: 600, date: September – December, 1965 | JONG 69<br>p. 203 |
| CONCERN FOR SOCIAL NETWORK MEMBERS | Closed question on whether the respondent always tries to remember his/her birthday; scored for each social network member | Those adults one sees at least once a month and who are 'important persons' in one's life were considered as social network members.<br>Negative among married females : r = –.10 (ns)<br>Positive among unmarried females: r = +.40 (02) | HAPP 1.1 | r | | | | Females from the Seattle-Washington area, U.S.A.<br>Non-probability chunk sample<br>N: 153, date: — | BRIM 74<br>p. 437 |

| Concept | Operationalization | Specification | Code | Stat. | Value | Test | Sig. | Population / Sample | Source |
|---|---|---|---|---|---|---|---|---|---|
| TRUST IN SOCIAL NETWORK MEMBERS | 3-item index of closed questions on whether the respondent would trust him/her with important information, discuss with him/her psychological problems, tell him/her about a 'put down' someone had given her. The questions were answered for each social network member. | Unaffected by marital status | HAPP 1.1 | r | +.10 | | ns | Females from the Seattle-Washington area, U.S.A. (See last page) | BRIM 74 p. 437 |
| PERCEIVED ASSISTANCE FROM SOCIAL NETWORK MEMBERS | 3-item index of closed questions on whether the respondent would ask him/her for the loan of a sizeable amount of money, to risk personal danger to help her, to pick her up at the airport late at night. The questions were answered for each social network member. | Stronger among unmarried females: r = +.43 (007)<br>Reversed among married females : r = -.05 (ns) | HAPP 1.1 | r | + | | | See above | BRIM 74 p. 437 |
| VALUE SIMILARITY WITH SOCIAL NETWORK MEMBERS | 3-item index of closed questions on whether the respondent feels that his/her ideals approximate most her ideals of the 'right way', feels she has a great many interests in common with him/her, generally shares the same philosophy of life with him/her. The questions were answered for each social network member. | Positive among married females : r = +.34 (002)<br>Negative among unmarried females: r = -.19 (ns) | HAPP 1.1 | r | + | | | See above | BRIM 74 p. 437 |
| SUPPORTED SELF-DISCLOSURE | Number of important life areas for which support for self-disclosure from significant others is perceived.<br>Measurement by means of Supported Self-Disclosure Index (see Jourard & Lasakow, 1958), modified to include 38 content areas of concern to the elderly, including changes in social relations with age, status and role changes, bodily changes, self-feelings, financial and material problems, and health problems. | Those persons one considers to be close and with whom one can feel free and talk about personal things were considered as significant others.<br>L-shaped curve: Stronger positive among those reporting lower self-disclosure<br>When controlled for age : $r_{pc}$ = +.08 (ns)<br>When controlled for role loss : $r_{pc}$ = +.17<br>Stronger among those reporting low role loss : r = +.36 (01)<br>Negative among those reporting very high role loss : r = -.23 (ns) | AFF 2.3 | r | +.17 | | ns | Aged retired persons, Los Angeles County, U.S.A.<br>Non-probability purposive quota sample, proportionally stratified by marital status<br>N: 71, date: 1971 | MORIW 73 p. 229 |

## QUALITY OF FAMILY RELATIONSHIPS

| Concept | Operationalization | Specification | Code | Stat. | Value | Test | Sig. | Population / Sample | Source |
|---|---|---|---|---|---|---|---|---|---|
| QUALITY OF CONTACTS WITH FAMILY MEMBERS | Score based on number of family members mentioned among 4 most important social contacts, frequency of contacts with these family members, and appreciation of these contacts. | Computed for married persons only.<br>Stronger among females: r = +.36<br>Not among males : r = +.00 | HAPP 2.1 | $r_{pm}$ | + | $Chi^2$ | | Adults, Amsterdam, The Netherlands<br>Probability systematic random sample stratified by sex and marital status<br>N: 600, date: September - December, 1965 | JONG 69 p. 26 |
| CLOSE FAMILY LIFE | College student offspring rating | Females only: among 48% of the very satisfied women the total family life was 'very close'. Among the satisfied women this was 28%, and among the relatively dissatisfied women it was only 20%. | HAPP 2.1 | D% | + | | s | Middle-aged, middle class married couples, U.S.A.<br>Non-probability accidental sample of couples<br>N: 416, date: 1952 - 1953 | ROSE 55 p. 16 |
| STATE OF FAMILY RELATIONSHIPS | Closed question: 'How do you and your family get along?'<br>only so-so / fairly well / very well | Stronger among those who are dissatisfied with their job and / or friends | HAPP 1.1 | G' | +.64 | Gt' | 01 | National adult population, U.S.A.<br>Non-probability quota sample<br>N: 2377, date: February, 1946 | WESSM 56 p. 194 |
| POSITIVE EVALUATION OF ONE'S FAMILY LIFE | Closed question ranging from 'very bad' to 'very good' | | HAPP 1.1<br>AFF 1.1 | mc<br>mc | +.66<br>+.51 | | | Urban adult Jewish population, Israel<br>Probability area sample using dwelling units<br>N: 1940, date: spring, 1973 | LEVY 75/1 p. 372 |

| Indicator | Measurement | Remarks | Code | Stat. | Value | Test | Sign. | Population / Sample | Source |
|---|---|---|---|---|---|---|---|---|---|
| GETTING ON WELL WITH ONE'S FAMILY | Closed question: very badly / rather badly / average / fairly well / very well | | HAPP 2.1 | $T^2$ | +.22 | $Chi^2$ | 001 | Non-agricultural population, Poland<br>Non-probability purposive quota sample<br>N: 1385, date: June - July, 1960 | MAKAR 62<br>p. 108 |
| GETTING ON WELL WITH ONE'S FAMILY | See above | | HAPP 2.1 | $T^2$ | +.14 | $Chi^2$ | 001 | Individual farmowners and their families, Poland<br>Non-probability purposive quota sample<br>N: 1002, date: June - July, 1960 | MAKAR 62<br>p. 109 |

## QUALITY OF OTHER SPECIFIC RELATIONSHIPS

| Indicator | Measurement | Remarks | Code | Stat. | Value | Test | Sign. | Population / Sample | Source |
|---|---|---|---|---|---|---|---|---|---|
| QUALITY OF CONTACTS WITH HOUSEHOLD MEMBERS | Closed question: generally troubled / sometimes one, sometimes the other / generally pleasant | | HAPP 2.1 | G' | +.42 | Gt' | 01 | Aged chronically-ill patients, U.S.A.<br>Probability sample<br>N: 167, date: 1959 | HENLE 67<br>p. 71 |

## S 4.1.4 - OTHER CHARACTERISTICS OF INTERPERSONAL RELATIONSHIPS

| Indicator | Measurement | Remarks | Code | Stat. | Value | Test | Sign. | Population / Sample | Source |
|---|---|---|---|---|---|---|---|---|---|
| NUMBER OF MARRIED PEOPLE AMONG 4 CLOSEST FRIENDS | Direct questions | Computed for singles only<br>males : r = +.05<br>females: r = +.09 | HAPP 2.1 | $r_{pm}$ | + | | | Adults, Amsterdam, The Netherlands<br>Probability systematic random sample stratified by sex and marital status<br>N: 600, date: September - December, 1955 | JONG 69<br>p. 203 |
| NUMBER OF UNPLEASANT SOCIAL CONTACTS | Direct questions on number of social contacts one does not appreciate | unmarried males : r = +.08<br>married males : r = -.10<br>unmarried females: r = -.05<br>married females : r = +.03 | HAPP 2.1 | $r_{pm}$ | | | | See above | JONG 69<br>p. 22 |
| RELATIVE CLOSEDNESS OF CIRCLE OF ACQUAINTANCES | Closed question: 'Do your friends and acqaintances also know each other?'<br>Response categories ranged from 'no, practically none' (1) to 'yes, practically all' (5) | | HAPP 1.1 | G' | +.24 | Gt' | 05 | Adults, Utrecht, the Netherlands<br>Probability sample stratified by age<br>N: 300, date: autumn, 1967 | MOSER 69<br>p. 29 |

## S 4.1.5 - VARIOUS INDICATORS OF PARTICIPATION IN INTERPERSONAL NETWORKS

see also 'Types of Affect': 'Companionship' (A 2.2.3), 'Love and Sex' (A 2.2.11), and 'Sociability'(A 2.2.17)

see also 'Personality Traits concerning Interpersonal Functioning' (P 1.8) and 'Content of Self-Image' (S 2.2)

| Indicator | Measurement | Remarks | Code | Stat. | Value | Test | Sign. | Population / Sample | Source |
|---|---|---|---|---|---|---|---|---|---|
| TENDING TO BE A LONELY PERSON | Closed question: not lonely / fairly lonely / very lonely | Unaffected by sex<br>When standardized on:<br>- usual mood : $G_s$ = -.56<br>- having fun in life : $G_s$ = -.50<br>- frequency of low mood : $G_s$ = -.62<br>- tending to be a discouraged person: $G_s$ = -.60<br>- anxiety symptoms : $G_s$ = -.66 | HAPP 1.1 | G<br>V | -.68<br>.32 | $Chi^2$ | 01 | Juniors and seniors attending public high schools in New York State, U.S.A.<br>Probably cluster sample of 10 public high schools<br>N: sample A: 1682, sample B: 1664<br>date: 1960 | BRENN 70<br>p. 71/75/87/88/268 |
| | | Stronger among males: G = -.55<br>Lower among females : G = -.49 | AFF 1.1 | G<br>V | -.31<br>.23 | $Chi^2$ | 01 | | |
| LONELINESS | 6-item index of statements on feeling lonely, nobody cares for you, difficulty in making lasting contacts, coping with things alone, hard to find real friends, and alone in the world | Unaffected by sex<br>Lower among married persons: G' = -.36 (01)<br>Stronger among singles : G' = -.50 (01) | HAPP 2.1 | G' | -.48 | Gt' | 01 | Adults, Amsterdam, The Netherlands<br>Probability systematic random sample stratified by sex and marital status<br>N: 600, date: September - December, 1965 | JONG 69<br>p. 197 |

| | | | | | | | | | |
|---|---|---|---|---|---|---|---|---|---|
| DESIRED PERSONAL CHANGES: BETTER SOCIAL RELATIONSHIPS | Open-ended question on desired personal changes<br>other changes vs change mentioned | Computed for those who desire to change only (N = 1591). | HAPP 1.1 | G' | -.01 | Gt' | ns | National adult population, U.S.A.<br>Non-probability quota sample<br>N: 2377, date: February, 1946 | WESSM 56<br>p. 211 |
| HAVING PROBLEMS WITH GETTING ALONG WITH OTHERS | Closed question | College students only<br>L-shaped curve: Significant negative among happier students only. | COMP 4.1 | | | | | Students, U.S.A.<br>Non-probability chunk sample<br>N: 1651, date: — | SYMON 37<br>p. 292 |

## S 4.2 - SOCIAL PARTICIPATION IN VOLUNTARY ORGANIZATIONS

### ORGANIZATIONAL MEMBERSHIPS

| | | | | | | | | | |
|---|---|---|---|---|---|---|---|---|---|
| ORGANIZATIONAL MEMBERSHIPS | Direct question on belonging to organizations, clubs, or community groups | Stronger among females<br>Stronger among those of lower S.E.S. | HAPP 1.1 | G' | +.33 | Gt' | 01 | Inhabitants of 4 small communities, Illinois, U.S.A.<br>Probability multi-stage samples<br>N: 2006, date: March, 1962 | BRADB 65/1<br>p. 47 |
| | | Index of Positive Affects: G' = +.25 (01)<br>Stronger among females<br>Unaffected by S.E.S.<br>Index of Negative Affects: G' = -.19 (01)<br>Stronger among males<br>Unaffected by S.E.S. | AFF 2.3 | G' | + | Gt' | | | |
| ASSOCIATION MEMBERSHIPS | Direct question on memberships in voluntary associations other than religious services<br>none / one / 2 or more | Stronger among those of age 66-75: $t_k$ = +.62 (01)<br>Stronger among those of age 82-92: $t_k$ = +.54 (01)<br>Lower among those of age 76-81 | AFF 2.3 | $t_k$ | +.50 | | 01 | Aged female public housing residents, U.S.A.<br>Probability systematic random sample<br>N: 44, date: 1967 - 1971 | GRANE 75<br>p. 703 |
| ORGANIZATIONAL MEMBERSHIPS | Direct question on number of organizational memberships<br>0 / 1 / 2 or more | Index of Positive Affects only: G = +.17 (05) | AFF 2.3 | G | + | | | Non-hospitalized schizophrenic males, New York, U.S.A.<br>Probability sample, drawn from the Monroe County psychiatric case register<br>N: 178, date: 1964 - 1965 | ALEXA 68<br>p. 153 |
| SORORITY MEMBERSHIP | non-member vs member | Freshmen: negative relationship<br>L-shaped curve: Significant relationship among unhappier students only.<br>Juniors: positive relationship<br>L-shaped curve: Significant relationship among unhappier students only. | COMP 2.2 | | | | | Female college students, New York, U.S.A.<br>N: 238, date: — | WASHB 41<br>p. 283 |

### ORGANIZATIONAL ACTIVITY

| | | | | | | | | | |
|---|---|---|---|---|---|---|---|---|---|
| ORGANIZATIONAL ACTIVITY | Direct question on number of organizations, such as church and school groups, labor unions, or social, civic, and fraternal clubs one takes an active part in<br>0 / 1 / 2 | See remarks in excerpt (Part II). | | | | | | Adults, New Hampshire, U.S.A.<br>Probability sample<br>N: 600, date: — | PHILL 67A<br>p. 483-484 |
| | | Unaffected by mental health status<br>(See PHILL 67B, p. 289) | HAPP 1.1 | G | +.29 | | | | |
| | | Index of Positive Affects: G = +.27<br>high S.E.S. : d = +.13<br>medium S.E.S. : d = +.05<br>low S.E.S. : d = +.25<br>Index of Negative Affects: G = -.05<br>high S.E.S. : d = -.08<br>medium S.E,S. : d = -.05<br>low S.E.S. : d = +.07<br>(See PHILL 69, p.9) | AFF 2.3 | G | + | | | | |

| | | | | | | | | | |
|---|---|---|---|---|---|---|---|---|---|
| ORGANIZATIONAL ACTIVITY | Closed question on number of organizations such as church, school groups, labor unions, or social, civic, and fraternal clubs one takes an active part in, rated on a 5-point scale | Index of Positive Affects: G = +.22<br>Index of Negative Affects: G = -.08 | AFF 2.3 | G | + | | | Adults, urban areas, U.S.A.<br>Probability area samples<br>N: 2787, date: January, 1963 - January, 1964 | BRADB 69<br>p. 127 |
| PARTICIPATION IN VOLUNTARY ASSOCIATIONS | | | HAPP 1.1<br>HAPP 2.1 | G<br>G | +.11<br>+.12 | | | Adults, Toledo, Ohio, U.S.A.<br>Systematic random sample<br>N: 510, date: 1973 | SNYDE 74<br>p. 32 |
| FORMAL SOCIAL PARTICIPATION | Being active in some voluntary organization or community activity | Stronger among males: 52% of the dissatisfied and 81% of the satisfied men are active in some organization or activity.<br>Among females 48% of the dissatisfied compared with 61% of the satisfied are active. | HAPP 2.1 | D% | + | | s | Middle-aged, middle class married couples, U.S.A.<br>Non-probability accidental sample of couples<br>N: 416, date: 1952 - 1953 | ROSE 55<br>p. 17 |
| ORGANIZATIONAL ACTIVITY | Sum of the number of religious services and meetings of other groups such as clubs, unions, or associations which the respondent reported usually attending each month | Stronger among those of age 46-59: r = +.26<br>Lower among those of age 60-71 : r = +.10<br>Unaffected by sex | HAPP 3.1 | r | +.18 | | | People of 46 and older, Duke, U.S.A.<br>Probability systematic random sample, stratified by age and sex<br>N: 502, date: 1968 | PALMO 72<br>p. 70 |
| SOCIALLY PARTICIPANT BEHAVIOR | 3-item index of closed questions on number of formal organizations one belonged to during the previous year, number of times one attended during a month, and whether one held office. | Index of Positive Affects only: r = +.35 (01) | AFF 2.3 | $r_{pm}$ | + | | | Residents of Stirling County, Maritime, Canada<br>Probability sample, stratified by sex, age, socio-environmental circumstances and mental health<br>N: 112, date: 1963 - 1968 | BEISE 74<br>p. 325 |
| ORGANIZATIONAL ACTIVITY | 3-item index of direct questions on number of organizational memberships, amount of time spent on these organizations per month, and holding a function. | unmarried males : r = +.23 (05)<br>married males : r = -.08 (ns)<br>unmarried females: r = +.03 (01)<br>married females : r = +.05 (ns) | HAPP 2.1 | $r_{pm}$ | + | $Chi^2$ | | Adults, Amsterdam, The Netherlands<br>Probability systematic random sample, stratified by sex and marital status<br>N: 600, date: September - December, 1965 | JONG 69<br>p. 203 |
| FORMAL SOCIAL PARTICIPATION | 3-item index of closed questions on number of organizational memberships, attending meetings, and holding office in them. | | HAPP 1.1 | | + | $Chi^2$ | ns | Adults, Utrecht, The Netherlands<br>Probability sample, stratified by age<br>N: 300, date: autumn, 1967 | MOSER 69<br>p. 27 |
| ASSOCIATION ATTENDANCE | Direct question on attendance activity in voluntary associations other than religious services<br>never / sometimes / regularly | Stronger among those of age 66-75: $t_k$ = +.52 (01)<br>Stronger among those of age 82-92: $t_k$ = +.60 (01)<br>Lower among those of age 76-81 | AFF 2.3 | $t_k$ | +.43 | | 01 | Aged female public housing residents, U.S.A.<br>Probability systematic random sample<br>N: 44, date: 1967 - 1971 | GRANE 75<br>p. 703 |
| PARTICIPATION IN COMMUNITY ORGANIZATIONS | Measurement in terms of the average hours per week involvement<br>non-involvement vs involvement | | COMP 1.1 | $r_{pm}$ | +.12 | | ns | White males who had experienced a first heart attack, Durham, North Carolina, U.S.A.<br>Non-probability quota sample<br>N: 56, date: 1970 | GARRI 73<br>p. 201 |

## RELIGIOUS PARTICIPATION

| | | | | | | | | | |
|---|---|---|---|---|---|---|---|---|---|
| PARTICIPATION IN RELIGIOUS EVENTS | Open-ended question on how often one attended church services or other church-sponsored events during the last month<br>none / 1-4 times / 5 or more times | Computed for those with current religious preferences only.<br>Index of Positive Affects only : G'= -.04 (ns)<br>Positive among those of high S.E.S.: G'= +.10 (ns)<br>Negative among those of low S.E.S. : G'= -.35 (05) | AFF 2.3 | G' | -.04 | Gt' | ns | Males in the age of 25 - 49, 4 small communities, Illinois U.S.A.<br>Probability multi-stage samples<br>N: 393, date: March, 1962 | BRADB 65/1<br>p. 44 |
| PARTICIPATING IN CHURCH ACTIVITIES | no church activities vs church activities | L-shaped curve: Positive among unhappier students only | COMP 2.2 | | + | | ns | Female college students, New York, U.S.A.<br>Type of construction unclear<br>N: 238, date: — | WASHB 41<br>p. 283 |
| ATTENDING RELIGIOUS SERVICES | Direct question: never / sometimes / weekly or more | Stronger among those of age 66-75: $t_k$ = +.67 (01)<br>Lower among those of age 82-92 : $t_k$ = -.10 (ns) | AFF 2.3 | $t_k$ | +.33 | | 01 | Aged female public housing residents, U.S.A.<br>Probability systematic random sample<br>N: 44, date: 1967 - 1971 | GRANE 75<br>p. 703 |

| | | | | | | | | | |
|---|---|---|---|---|---|---|---|---|---|
| RELIGIOUS PARTICIPATION | 3-item index containing amount of time spent on religious activities, playing an active role and holding a function | unmarried males : r = +.05 (ns)<br>married males : r = +.02 (ns)<br>unmarried females: r = +.15 (ns)<br>married females : r = +.14 (ns) | HAPP 2.1 | $r_{pm}$ | + | $Chi^2$ | ns | Adults, Amsterdam, The Netherlands<br>Probability systematic random sample, stratified by sex and marital status<br>N: 600, date: September - December, 1965 | JONG 69<br>p. 203 |

## S 4.3 - OVERALL INDICATORS OF SOCIAL PARTICIPATION

see also 'Use of Leisure Time' (L 3.3), and 'Sports' (S 6)

| | | | | | | | | | |
|---|---|---|---|---|---|---|---|---|---|
| SOCIAL PARTICIPATION | 7-item index of closed questions on number of organizational memberships, number of times one got together with friends, chatted with friends on the telephone, attended a meeting, ate in a restaurant, went for a ride in the car, and furthest distance went from home other than going to work; during the last week | Index of Positive Affects only: G' = +.28 (01)<br>Unaffected by S.E.S. | AFF 2.3 | G' | + | Gt' | | Males in the age of 25 - 49, 4 small communities, Illinois, U.S.A.<br>Probability multi-stage samples<br>N: 393, date: March, 1962 | BRADB 65/1<br>p. 44 |
| SOCIAL ACTIVITY | Number of hours spent during the last typical week attending a sports event, church or other meetings, lectures, or concerts; doing volunteer work for church, other organizations, or relatives; visiting, telephoning, or writing friends or relatives; parties, eating out, or entertaining | Stronger among males: r = +.17 | HAPP 3.1 | r | +.09 | | | People of 46 and older, Duke, U.S.A.<br>Probability systematic random sample, stratified by age and sex<br>N: 502, date: 1968 | PALMO 72<br>p. 70 |
| SOCIAL CONTACTS | Number of reported voluntary visits or telephone conversations with children, close relatives, close friends, neighbors; and number of religious services or other meetings; during one month | | HAPP 3.1 | r | +.01 | | ns | See above | PALMO 72<br>p. 70 |
| SOCIAL PARTICIPATION | 3-item index of closed questions on frequency of contacts with friends, number of neighbors known and organizational activity | See remarks in excerpt (Part II).<br>Stronger among males : G = +.73<br>Lower among females : G = +.22<br>Stronger among Catholics: G = +.40<br>Lower among Protestants : G = +.23<br>age 21 - 34 : G = +.17<br>age 35 - 49 : G = +.22<br>age 50+ : G = +.47<br>low education : G = +.40<br>medium education : G = +.33<br>high education : G = +.01<br>low S.E.S. : d = +.30<br>medium S.E.S. : d = +.14<br>high S.E.S. : d = +.03<br>When elaborated for S.E.S. and age:<br>- smallest relationship (d = +.06) among those of age 21-49 and high S.E.S.<br>- strongest relationship (d = +.39) among those of age 50+ and medium or low S.E.S.<br>In the different S.E.S.-groups unaffected by sex and religious affiliation<br>(see PHILL 69, p. 17).<br>(to be continued on next page) | HAPP 1.1 | G | +.32 | | | Adults, New Hampshire, U.S.A.<br>Probability sample<br>N: 600, date: — | PHILL 67A<br>p. 483-484 |

| | | | | | | | | | |
|---|---|---|---|---|---|---|---|---|---|
| | | Mentally well Ss: G' = +.28 (01)<br>Mentally ill Ss : G' = +.32 (05)<br>(see PHILL 67B, p. 289) | | | | | | | |
| | | Index of Positive Affects: G = +.32<br>Index of Negative Affects: G = -.08<br>males : positive affect: G = +.41<br>: negative affect: G = +.17<br>females : positive affect: G = +.27<br>: negative affect: G = +.00<br>Catholics : positive affect: G = +.39<br>: negative affect: G = -.01<br>Protestants : positive affect: G = +.27<br>: negative affect: G = -.07<br>age 21 - 34 : positive affect: G = +.15<br>: negative affect: G = -.01<br>age 35 - 49 : positive affect: G = +.27<br>: negative affect: G = -.53<br>age 50+ : positive affect: G = +.50<br>: negative affect: G = +.10<br>low education : positive affect: G = +.37<br>: negative affect: G = -.16<br>medium education : positive affect: G = +.09<br>: negative affect: G = +.08<br>high education : positive affect: G = +.40<br>: negative affect: G = -.03<br>low S.E.S. : positive affect: d = +.41<br>: negative affect: d = +.15<br>medium S.E.S. : positive affect: d = +.16<br>: negative affect: d = -.09<br>high S.E.S. : positive affect: d = +.08<br>: negative affect: d = -.11<br>When elaborated for S.E.S. and age:<br>- Smallest relationship with positive affect (d = +.04), and strongest negative relationship with negative affect (d = -.12) among those of age 21-49 and high S.E.S.<br>- Strongest relationship with positive affect (d = +.33) and strongest positive relationship with negative affect (d = +.08) among those of age 50+ and medium or low S.E.S.<br>In the different S.E.S.-groups unaffected by sex and religious affiliation<br>(see PHILL 69, p. 10) | AFF 2.3 | G | + | | | | |
| POOR INTERPERSONAL RELATIONS | 2-item index of direct questions on number of close friends, and organizational memberships. non-stressful vs stressful | | AFF 1.3 | $\bar{DR}$ | -.12 | | 05 | Adults, Alameda County, U.S.A.<br>Probability sample<br>N: 6928, date: 1965 | BERKM 71<br>p. 41 |
| SOCIAL PARTICIPATIONS | 3-item index of direct questions on number of organizational memberships, frequency of contacts with friends and attending parties | | HAPP 1.1 | G | +.17 | | 01 | Non-hospitalized schizophrenic males, New York, U.S.A.<br>Probability sample, drawn from the Monroe County psychiatric case register<br>N: 178, date: 1964 - 1965 | ALEXA 68<br>p. 153/157 |
| | | Index of Positive Affects only: G = +.20 (01)<br>Stronger in high pathology group (01)<br>Lower in low pathology group (ns)<br>Not among those living alone<br>Stronger among those living with someone else than parents or spouse (boarding house, friends, etc.)<br>Not among married males living with their spouse<br>(to be continud on next page) | AFF 2.3 | G | + | | | | |

| | | | | | | | | | |
|---|---|---|---|---|---|---|---|---|---|
| | | Unaffected by employed status<br>Only among employed individuals living with their family of orientation the Index of Negative Affects is related to social participation: $t_{k_c} = -.27$ (05) | | | | | | | |

## S 4.4 - CHANGES IN SOCIAL PARTICIPATION

see also 'Changes in Leisure Activities' (L 3.3.3)

| | | | | | | | | | |
|---|---|---|---|---|---|---|---|---|---|
| HAVING MET NEW PEOPLE | Closed question on new people met during last week<br>no vs yes | Index of Positive Affects only: G' = +.48 (01)<br>Unaffected by S.E.S. | AFF 2.3 | G' | + | Gt' | | Males in the age of 25–49, 4 small communities, Illinois, U.S.A.<br>Probability multi-stage samples<br>N: 393, date: March, 1962 | BRADB 65/1<br>p. 43 |
| HAVING MET NEW PEOPLE | Open-ended question on number of new people met during the past few weeks | Index of Positive Affects: G = +.33<br>Index of Negative Affects: G = +.06 | AFF 2.3 | G | + | | | Adults, urban areas, U.S.A.<br>Probability area samples<br>N: 2787, date: January, 1963 - January, 1964 | BRADB 69<br>p. 127 |
| HAVING MET NEW PEOPLE | Direct question on new people met during past few weeks | Index of Positive Affects: G = +.18<br>Index of Negative Affects: G = +.20 | AFF 2.3 | G | | | | Employed males, England<br>Non-probability purposive quota sample<br>N: 192, date: — | PAYNE 74<br>p. 17 |
| HAVING MADE NEW FRIENDS | Closed question on new friends made in recent months<br>no vs yes | Index of Positive Affects: G = +.37<br>Index of Negative Affects: G = -.04 | AFF 2.3 | G | + | | | Adults, urban areas, U.S.A.<br>Probability area samples<br>N: 2787, date: January, 1963 - January 1964 | BRADB 69<br>p. 127 |
| NEW OTHER-ORIENTED ACTIVITIES ENGAGED IN | 2 direct questions on new activities engaged in during the past few weeks, and on type of activities; coded for activities one did with others. | Index of Positive Affects: G = +.36<br>Index of Negative Affects: G = +.08 | AFF 2.3 | G | + | | | See above | BRADB 69<br>p. 130 |
| CHANGE IN SOCIAL PARTICIPATION | 5-item index of repeated closed questions on number of times one got together with friends, number of telephone calls with friends, number of times one was in touch with relatives, number of new people met, during the past few weeks; and organizational activity<br>decreasing / stable / increasing social participation | Analysis on the basis of a comparison between data from January, 1963 (wave 1) and October, 1963 (wave 3).<br>Computed for Index of Positive Affects only.<br>Those with increased social participation are more likely, and those with decreased social participation are less likely to increase in positive affect than the sample as a whole (ns). | AFF 2.3 | $D\bar{R}$ | + | | ns | See above | BRADB 69<br>p. 137 |
| SOCIAL WITHDRAWAL | 3-item index of closed questions on reduction in contacts with relatives, other people, and organizational memberships during the past year | See remarks in excerpt (Part II).<br>Stronger among deprived Ss (compulsory retired, widowed, or physically disabled): G' = -.34 (ns)<br>Reversed among not-deprived Ss : G' = +.51 (ns) | HAPP 1.1 | G' | -.21 | Gt' | ns | Non-institutionalized aged persons, San Francisco, U.S.A.<br>Probability sample, stratified by sex, age and social living arrangement<br>N: 269, date: 1960 - 1964 | LOWEN 65<br>p. 367 |
| | | deprived Ss : G' = -.43 (05)<br>not-deprived Ss: G' = -.35 (ns) | HAPP 2.1 | G' | -.45 | Gt' | 01 | | |
| | | Stronger among deprived Ss : G' = -.48 (05)<br>Lower among not-deprived Ss: G' = -.19 (ns | AFF 1.1 | G' | -.41 | Gt' | 01 | | |
| CHANGES IN SOCIAL ACTIVITIES OVER 4 YEARS:<br>- HAVING MORE CONTACTS WITH FRIENDS AND RELATIVES | Repeated direct questions<br>Differences between scores in 1967 and 1971 | Stronger among those of age 66-75: $t_k = -.17$ (ns)<br>Reversed among those of age 82-92: $t_k = +.19$ (ns) | AFF 2.3 | $t_k$ | -.06 | | ns | Aged female public housing residents, U.S.A.<br>Probability systematic random sample<br>N: 44, date: 1967 - 1971 | GRANE 75<br>p. 703 |

| | | | | | | | | | |
|---|---|---|---|---|---|---|---|---|---|
| - HAVING MORE CONTACTS WITH NEIGHBORS | | Stronger among those of age 66–75: $t_k$ = +.42 (02)<br>Stronger among those of age 82–92: $t_k$ = +.54 (01)<br>Lower among those of age 76–81 | AFF 2.3 | $t_k$ | +.24 | | 02 | | |
| - HAVING MORE MEMBERSHIPS IN VOLUNTARY ASSOCIATIONS | | Lower among those of age 66–75 : $t_k$ = +.30 (05)<br>Stronger among those of age 82–92: $t_k$ = +.56 (01) | AFF 2.3 | $t_k$ | +.34 | | 01 | | |
| - ATTENDING MEETINGS OF VOLUNTARY ASSOCIATIONS MORE OFTEN | | Lower among those of age 66–75 : $t_k$ = +.10 (ns)<br>Stronger among those of age 82–92: $t_k$ = +.58 (01) | AFF 2.3 | $t_k$ | +.28 | | 01 | | |
| - ATTENDING RELIGIOUS SERVICES MORE OFTEN | | Lower among those of age 66–75 : $t_k$ = -.04 (ns)<br>Stronger among those of age 82–92: $t_k$ = -.17 (ns) | AFF 2.3 | $t_k$ | -.15 | | 07 | | |
| - USING THE TELEPHONE MORE OFTEN | | | AFF 2.3 | $t_k$ | +.02 | | ns | | |

## S 4.5 - PREFERENCES WITH RESPECT TO SOCIAL PARTICIPATION

### DESIRE FOR SOCIAL PARTICIPATION

| | | | | | | | | | |
|---|---|---|---|---|---|---|---|---|---|
| LIKE TO HAVE OTHER PEOPLE AROUND | Direct question rated on a graphic scale ranging from 'certainly not' to 'very much'. | | HAPP 1.1 | G | +.26 | | | National adult population, The Netherlands<br>Probability area sample<br>N: 1552, date: June, 1968 | BAKKE 74<br>p. 27 |
| APPRECIATION OF BEING ALONE | 5-item index of agree / disagree statements on possibilities to relax when alone, like to be alone, obligations towards others and too close ties with others as a consequence of social participation. | unmarried males : r = +.05<br>married males : r = -.05<br>unmarried females: r = -.61<br>married females : r = -.28 | HAPP 2.1 | $r_{pm}$ | | $Chi^2$ | | Adults, Amsterdam, The Netherlands<br>Probability systematic random sample, stratified by sex and marital status<br>N: 600, date: September - December, 1965 | JONG 69 |
| SOCIAL AUTONOMY | 4-item index of closed questions indicating preference for individual activity | | HAPP 1.1 | $r_{pm}$ | -.15 | $Chi^2$ | ns | Adults, Utrecht, The Netherlands<br>Probability sample stratified by age<br>N: 300, date: autumn, 1967 | MOSER 69<br>p. 43 |
| FONDNESS FOR COMPANIONSHIP, AS OPPOSED TO SOLITARINESS | Class-master rating on a 7-point scale on the basis of observation | | AFF 5.3 | $r_{pm}$ | +.58 | | | Schoolboys, England<br>Non-probability chunk sample<br>N: 140, date: 1912 - 1913 | WEBB 15<br>p. 27 |
| BEING INTERESTED IN GETTING ALONG WITH OTHERS | Closed question | | COMP 4.1 | | | | ns | Students, U.S.A.<br>Non-probability chunk sample<br>N: 1651, date: — | SYMON 37<br>p. 292 |
| DESIRE FOR PARTICIPATION IN SOCIAL ACTIVITIES | 5-item index of closed questions on whether at this moment one feels like engaging in activities which are characterized as social (+), conversational (+), non-social (-), withdrawn (-), or isolated (-).<br>(item from a 36-item Excitement Adjective Checklist). | The subjects filled in this questionnaire in an experimental situation, right after their self-esteem was experimentally altered. | AFF 6 | $r_{pm}$ | +.11 | | ns | Female undergraduates, University of Wisconsin, U.S.A.<br>Random sample<br>N: 72, date: — | LUDWI 71/75<br>p. 64 |
| DESIRE FOR PARTICIPATION IN DIFFERENT ORGANIZATIONS AND COMMUNITY ACTIVITIES | | Unaffected by sex | HAPP 2.1 | | | | ns | Middle-aged, middle class married couples, U.S.A.<br>Non-probability accidental sample of couples<br>N: 416, date: 1952 - 1953 | ROSE 55<br>p. 18 |

## SPECIFIC PREFERENCES

| Concept | Measure | Remarks | Happiness | Statistic | Value | | Significance | Population | Source |
|---|---|---|---|---|---|---|---|---|---|
| DESIRED INTERACTION WITH SOCIAL NETWORK MEMBERS | 3-item index of closed questions on whether the respondent would enjoy seeing him/her every day, would spend most of her free time with him/her if possible, would like to see him/her more often<br>The questions were answered for each social network member | Those adults one sees at least once a month and who are 'important persons' in one's life were considered as social network members.<br>Unaffected by marital status | HAPP 1.1 | $r$ | +.17 | | ns | Females from the Seattle-Washington area, U.S.A.<br>Non-probability chunk sample<br>N: 153, date: — | BRIM 74<br>p. 437 |
| FONDNESS FOR LARGE SOCIAL GATHERINGS | Trained peer-rating on a 7-point scale on the basis of observation | | AFF 5.2 | $r_{pm}$ | +.51 | | | Male students, England<br>Non-probability chunk sample<br>N: 194, date: 1912 - 1913 | WEBB 15<br>p. 26 |
| FONDNESS FOR SMALL CIRCLE OF INTIMATE FRIENDS | See above | | AFF 5.2 | $r_{pm}$ | -.14 | | | See above | WEBB 15<br>p. 26 |
| DESIRE FOR PARTICIPATION IN SOCIAL EXCITING ACTIVITIES | 2-item index of closed questions on whether at this moment one feels like being a lead actress, and whether one feels like dating with an attractive guy<br>(from Activity Reaction Scale; see Jackson & Lyons, 1969) | The subjects filled in this questionnaire in an experimental situation, right after their self-esteem was experimentally altered.<br>The relationship appeared to be unaffected by manipulated self-esteem (.10).<br>For happy Ss desire for participation is unaffected by both bolstered and reduced self-esteem.<br>For unhappy Ss desire for participation is unaffected by reduced self-esteem and increased by bolstered self-esteem. | AFF 6 | $r_{pm}$ | +.30 | | 05 | Female undergraduates, University of Wisconsin, U.S.A.<br>Random sample<br>N: 72, date: — | LUDWI 71/75<br>p. 33/64 |
| DESIRE FOR PARTICIPATION IN SOCIAL BORING ACTIVITIES | 2-item index of closed questions on whether at this moment one feels like being at a dull party, and whether one feels like being at a slow moving academic discussion<br>(See above) | See above<br>Unaffected by manipulated self-esteem<br>For both happy and unhappy Ss desire for participation is unaffected by both bolstered and reduced self-esteem. | AFF 6 | | | | ns | See above | LUDWI 71/75<br>p. 34 |
| COSMOPOLITAN ORIENTATION TOWARDS SOCIAL PARTICIPATION | 5-item index on agree / disagree statements, containing belonging to local clubs is more rewarding than to large nation-wide organizations; national and international events are less interesting than things that happen in the local community; a person from a well-established family usually is a better choice for a responsible job than a capable newcomer to the community; big cities are all right, but the local community is the backbone of America, I have a greater respect for an established local man than for a famous outsider.<br>(adapted Dye Localism - Cosmopolitan Scale; see Dye, 1963)<br>normatively local / intermediate / cosmopolitan | U-shaped curve: Those having an intermediate personal orientation being least happy | AFF 2.3 , | $t_k$ | -.08 | | ns | Aged female public housing residents, U.S.A.<br>Probability systematic random sample<br>N: 44. date: 1967 - 1971 | GRANE 73A<br>p. 6 |

## S 4.6 - SATISFACTION WITH SOCIAL PARTICIPATION

see 'Satisfaction with Social Life' (S 1.7)

## S 4.7 - VARIOUS FACTORS CONCERNING SOCIAL PARTICIPATION

| | | | | | | | | |
|---|---|---|---|---|---|---|---|---|
| PERSONAL ADJUSTMENT | Degree of correspondence between personal orientation towards social participation and actual social participation.<br><br>Personal orientation was measured by the adapted Dye (1963) Localism - Cosmopolitan Scale (see last page at GRANE 73A, under 'Specific Preferences with respect to Social Participation', (S 4.5).<br><br>Actual social participation was measured by 9 social communications activities, which were arrayed according to their degree of 'cosmopolitanness', using knowledge of the local / cosmopolitan characteristics of the people who are (in)active in them:<br>- cosmopolitan characteristics include visiting neighbors, friends and relatives and reading<br>- intermediate categories include church attendance, television viewing, and number of memberships in voluntary associations<br>- local characteristics include radio-listening, telephone use, and participation in voluntary associations. | AFF 2.3 | $t_k$ | -.02 | | ns | Aged female public housing residents, U.S.A.<br>Probability systematic random sample (survivors of the GRANE 73A sample)<br>N: 44, date: 1971 | GRANE 73B<br>p. 357 |

# S 5 SOCIO-ECONOMIC STATUS



## S 5.1 - SOCIO-ECONOMIC STATUS

see also 'Level of Education' (E 1.1.1), 'Level of Income' (I 1.1), 'Work Prestige' (W 2.4)

| | | | | | | | | | |
|---|---|---|---|---|---|---|---|---|---|
| S.E.S. | Interviewer's estimate: very poor / working class / middle class / well-to-do | | HAPP 2.1 | G' | +.30 | Gt' | 01 | National adult population, U.S.A.<br>Probability sample, proportionally stratified by sex, age, occupation, S.E.S. and education<br>N: 1015, date: 1948 - 1949 | BUCHA 53<br>p. 213 |
| CLASS | working / lower / lower middle / middle / upper middle / upper | upper : Mean = 7.2<br>upper middle: Mean = 7.4<br>middle : Mean = 6.8<br>lower middle: Mean = 5.7<br>lower : Mean = 4.6<br>working : Mean = 6.3 | HAPP 3.1 | DM | + | | | National adult population, U.S.A.<br>Probability sample<br>N: 1549, date: ± 1960 | CANTR 65/1<br>p. 375 |
| S.E.S. | 3-item index containing educational level, family income and occupational prestige | | HAPP 1.1 | $r_{pm}$ | +.14 | | 01 | Non-institutionalized adults, U.S.A.<br>Probability samples<br>N: 1547, date: 1972, 1973 | SPREI 74<br>p. 455 |
| SUBJECTIVE SOCIAL CLASS | Closed question: lower class / working class / middle class / upper class | Unaffected by S.E.S. (see above)<br>Stronger among those under age 65: r = +.18<br>Lower among those of age 65+ : r = +.06<br>The difference is not significant | HAPP 1.1 | $r_{pm}$ | +.15 | | 01 | See above | SPREI 74<br>p. 455-457 |
| S.E.S. | 3-item index containing family income, educational level, and occupational level<br>low vs high | Stronger in economically depressed areas<br>Strongest among those of age 50+ living in a depressed area | HAPP 1.1 | G' | +.28 | Gt' | 01 | Inhabitants of 4 small communities, Illinois, U.S.A.<br>Probability multi-stage samples<br>N: 2006, date: March, 1962 | BRADB 65/1<br>p. 9 |
| S.E.S. | 3-item index containing educational level, family income and occupational prestige<br>low / medium / high | Computed for Index of Positive Affects only: G = +.29<br>When controlled for sociability and novelty: $G_s$ = +.18<br>Unaffected by esteem for others | AFF 2.3 | G | + | | | Adults, urban areas, U.S.A.<br>Probability area sample<br>N: 2787, date: January, 1963 - January, 1964 | BRADB 69<br>p. 132 |
| S.E.S. | 3-item index containing income, educational level and occupational prestige<br>low / middle / high | | AFF 1.3 | $\bar{DR}$ | + | | ns | Adults, Alameda County, U.S.A.<br>Probability sample<br>N: 6928, date: 1965 | BERKM 71<br>p. 40 |
| S.E.S. | 2-item index containing occupational level and educational level (Hollingshead Two-Factor Index of Social Position; see Hollingshead, 1957)<br>low / medium / high | Stronger among those reporting low social participation : G' = +.69 (01)<br>Lower among those reporting medium and high social participation: G' = +.18 (ns), resp. G' = +.21 (05) | HAPP 1.1 | G' | +.30 | Gt' | 01 | Adults, New Hampshire, U.S.A.<br>Probability sample<br>N: 600, date: — | PHILL 69<br>p. 7-10/17 |
| | | Index of Positive Affects: G' = +.40 (01)<br>Index of Negative Affects: G' = -.16 (ns)<br>(to be continued on next page) | AFF 2.3 | G' | + | Gt' | | | |

| | | | | | | | | |
|---|---|---|---|---|---|---|---|---|
| | | Among those reporting high contact with friends:<br>Index of Positive Affects: G' = +.25 (01)<br>Index of Negative Affects: G' = -.25 (ns)<br>Among those reporting medium contact with friends:<br>Index of Positive Affects: G' = +.56 (01)<br>Index of Negative Affects: G' = -.05 (ns)<br>Among those reporting low contact with friends:<br>Index of Positive Affects: G' = +.42 (01)<br>Index of Negative Affects: G' = -.16 (ns)<br>Among those knowing a high number of neighbours:<br>Index of Positive Affects: G' = +.39 (01)<br>Index of Negative Affects: G' = -.18 (ns)<br>Among those knowing a medium number of neighbours:<br>Index of Positive Affects: G' = +.32 (01)<br>Index of Negative Affects: G' = -.03 (ns)<br>Among those knowing a low number of neighbours:<br>Index of Positive Affects: G' = +.49 (01)<br>Index of Negative Affects: G' = -.00 (ns)<br>Among those reporting high organizational activity:<br>Index of Positive Affects: G' = +.28 (05)<br>Index of Negative Affects: G' = -.12 (ns)<br>Among those reporting medium organizational activity:<br>Index of Positive Affects: G' = +.33 (05)<br>Index of Negative Affects: G' = -.09 (ns)<br>Among those reporting low organizational activity:<br>Index of Positive Affects: G' = +.40 (01)<br>Index of Negative Affects: G' = -.07 (ns)<br>Among those reporting high social participation:<br>Index of Positive Affects: G' = +.29 (01)<br>Index of Negative Affects: G' = -.18 (ns)<br>Among those reporting medium social participation:<br>Index of Positive Affects: G' = +.38 (01)<br>Index of Negative Affects: G' = +.01 (ns)<br>Among those reporting low social participation:<br>Index of Positive Affects: G' = +.48 (01)<br>Index of Negative Affects: G' = +.20 (ns) | | | | | | | |
| S.E.S. | Interviewer's estimate: very poor / working class / middle class / well-to-do | | HAPP 2.1 | G' | +.21 | Gt' | 01 | National adult population, Mexico<br>Probability sample, proportionally stratified by sex, age, occupation, S.E.S. and education<br>N: 1752, date: 1948 - 1949 | BUCHA 53<br>p. 189 |
| S.E.S. | Interviewer's estimate: very poor / working class / middle class / well-to-do | | HAPP 2.1 | G' | +.23 | Gt' | 01 | National adult population, Britain<br>Probability sample, proportionally stratified by sex, age, occupation, S.E.S. and education<br>N: 1195, date: 1948 - 1949 | BUCHA 53<br>p. 138 |
| SOCIAL GRADE | 6-point scale: E / D / $C_2$ / $C_1$ / B / A | AB social grade: Mean = 6.64<br>$C_1$ social grade: Mean = 5.56<br>$C_2$ social grade: Mean = 5.37<br>DE social grade: Mean = 4.73 | HAPP 2.1 | DM | + | | | National population, Britain<br>Non-probability quota sample<br>N: 213, date: March, 1971 | ABRAM 73<br>p. 4 |
| S.E.S. | Interviewer's estimate: very poor / working class / middle class / well-to-do | | HAPP 2.1 | G' | +.24 | Gt' | 01 | National adult population, France<br>Probability sample, proportionally stratified by sex, age, occupation, S.E.S. and education<br>N: 1000, date: 1948 - 1949 | BUCHA 53<br>p. 148 |

| | | | | | | | | | |
|---|---|---|---|---|---|---|---|---|---|
| S.E.S. | Interviewer's estimate : very poor / working class / well-to-do | | HAPP 2.1 | G' | +.18 | Gt' | 01 | National adult population, W. Germany<br>Probability sample, proportionally stratified by sex, age, occupation, S.E.S. and education<br>N: 3371, date: 1948 - 1949 | BUCHA 53<br>p. 156 |
| S.E.S. | Interviewer's estimate: very poor / working class / middle class / well-to-do | | HAPP 2.1 | G' | +.42 | Gt' | 01 | National adult population, Italy<br>Probability sample, proportionally stratified by sex, age, occupation, S.E.S. and education<br>N: 1078, date: 1948 - 1949 | BUCHA 53<br>p. 176 |
| S.E.S. | Interviewer's etimate: very poor / working class / middle class / well-to-do | | HAPP 2.1 | G' | +.34 | Gt' | 01 | National adult population, The Netherlands<br>Probability sample, proportionally stratified by sex, age, occupation, S.E.S. and education<br>N: 942, date: 1948 - 1949 | BUCHA 53<br>p. 197 |
| S.E.S. | Classification on the basis of (earlier) occupational prestige of chief wage-earner | | HAPP 1.1 | G | -.08 | | ns | National adult population, The Netherlands<br>Probability area sample<br>N: 1552, date: June, 1968 | BAKKE 74<br>p. 27 |
| S.E.S. | Interviewer's estimate: very poor / working class / middle class / well-to-do | | HAPP 2.1 | G' | +.34 | Gt' | 01 | National adult population, Norway<br>Probability sample, proportionally stratified by sex, age, occupation, S.E.S. and education<br>N: 1030, date: 1948 - 1949 | BUCHA 53<br>p. 205 |
| CLASS | working / lower / middle / upper middle; upper | upper; upper middle: Mean = 6.8<br>middle : Mean = 5.7<br>lower : Mean = 3.2<br>working : Mean = 4.7 | HAPP 3.1 | DM | + | | | National population, Israel<br>Probability sample<br>N: 1170, date: ± 1960 | CANTR 65/1<br>p. 369 |
| S.E.S. | Interviewer's estimate: very poor / working class / middle class / well-to-do | | HAPP 2.1 | G' | +.16 | Gt' | 05 | National adult population, Australia<br>Probability sample, proportionally stratified by sex, age, occupation, S.E.S. and education<br>N: 945, date: 1948 - 1949 | BUCHA 53<br>p. 130 |
| **SPECIAL GROUPS** | | | | | | | | | |
| EDUCATIONAL LEVEL OF FATHER | some grade school or grade school graduate / some high school or high school graduate / some college or college graduate / post graduate college work | | HAPP 1.1<br>AFF 1.1 | G<br>V<br>G<br>V | +.04<br>.03<br>+.03<br>.02 | $Chi^2$<br>$Chi^2$ | ns<br>ns | Juniors and seniors attending public high schools in New York State, U.S.A.<br>Probability cluster sample of 10 public high schools<br>N: sample A = 1682; sample B = 1664; sample C = 1678<br>date: 1960 | BRENN 70<br>p. 113/338 |
| EDUCATIONAL LEVEL OF MOTHER | some grade school or grade school graduate / some high school or high school graduate / some college or college graduate / post graduate college work | When standardized on:<br>- participation in extracurricular activities : $G_s$ = +.09<br>- social class : $G_s$ = +.06 | HAPP 1.1<br>AFF 1.1 | G<br>V<br>G<br>V | +.09<br>.04<br>+.04<br>.03 | $Chi^2$<br>$Chi^2$ | 05<br>ns | See above | BRENN 70<br>p. 113/342 |
| INCOME LEVEL OF FATHER'S OCCUPATION | Under $ 3400 / $ 3400-5000 / over $ 5000 | | HAPP 1.1<br>AFF 1.1 | G<br>V<br>G<br>V | +.07<br>.04<br>+.01<br>.02 | $Chi^2$<br>$Chi^2$ | ns<br>ns | See above | BRENN 70<br>p. 113/334 |
| SOCIAL CLASS | weighted score based on the medium score of father's occupation, father's education and father's primary source of income<br>lower / middle / upper | When standardized on:<br>- having fun in life : $G_s$ = +.07<br>- frequency of low mood : $G_s$ = +.15<br>- tending to be a lonely person : $G_s$ = +.08<br>- self-esteem : $G_s$ = +.08<br>- having faith in people : $G_s$ = +.09<br>- sensitivity to criticism : $G_s$ = +.09<br>(to be continued on next page) | HAPP 1.1 | G<br>V | +.12<br>.05 | $Chi^2$ | ns | See above | BRENN 70<br>p. 113/330 |

| | | | | | | | | | |
|---|---|---|---|---|---|---|---|---|---|
| | | - presenting a false self : $G_s$ = +.13<br>- participation in extracurricular activities : $G_s$ = +.14<br>- extent of dating : $G_s$ = +.14<br>- hours spent on work for pay : $G_s$ = +.12<br>- disruption of family relationships: $G_s$ = +.12<br>- number of children in the family : $G_s$ = +.10<br>- school social class : $G_s$ = +.12<br>- having fun in life, and tending to be a lonely person : $G_s$ = +.07<br>- having fun in life, and self-esteem : $G_s$ = +.06<br>- tending to be a lonely person, and self-esteem : $G_s$ = +.06<br>- having faith in people, and self-esteem : $G_s$ = +.07<br>- sensivity to criticism, and self-esteem : $G_s$ = +.05<br>When Ss are regrouped, so that the upper third of middle class = upper class, and the lower third of middle class = lower class : G = +.06<br>When standardized on educational level of mother : $G_s$ = +.04 | | | | | | | |
| | | When standardized on:<br>- having fun in life : $G_s$ = +.03<br>- frequency of low mood : $G_s$ = +.08<br>- tending to be a lonely person : $G_s$ = +.04<br>- self-esteem : $G_s$ = +.03<br>- having faith in people : $G_s$ = +.02<br>- sensivity to criticism : $G_s$ = +.04<br>- presenting a false self : $G_s$ = +.06<br>- participation in extracurricular activities : $G_s$ = +.06<br>- extent of dating : $G_s$ = +.07<br>- hours spent on work for pay : $G_s$ = +.03<br>- disruption of family relationships: $G_s$ = +.05<br>- number of children in the family : $G_s$ = +.05<br>- school social class : $G_s$ = +.05<br>- tending to be a lonely person, and having fun in life : $G_s$ = +.04<br>- self-esteem,and having fun in life: $G_s$ = +.01<br>- self-esteem, and tending to be a lonely person : $G_s$ = +.02<br>- self-esteem, and having faith in people : $G_s$ = +.01<br>- self-esteem, and sensitivity to criticism : $G_s$ = +.02<br>When Ss are regrouped, so that the upper third of middle class = upper class and the lower third of middle class = lower class : G = +.01<br>When standardized on educational level of mother : $G_s$ = .00 | AFF 1.1 | G<br>V | +.05<br>.03 | $Chi^2$ | ns | | |
| SUBJECTIVE SOCIAL CLASS POSITION | Closed question: lower / working / lower middle / middle / upper middle / upper class | Stronger in lower class : G = +.33<br>Lower in middle and upper class : G = +.23 | HAPP 1.1 | G<br>V | +.25<br>.12 | $Chi^2$ | .01 | Juniors and seniors attending public high schools in New York State, U.S.A.<br>(see last page) | BRENN 70<br>p. 120/358 |
| | | Unaffected by social class | AFF 1.1 | G<br>V | +.21<br>.10 | $Chi^2$ | .01 | | |

| | | | | | | | | | |
|---|---|---|---|---|---|---|---|---|---|
| SCHOOL SOCIAL CLASS (S.E.S. of the pupils of one's school | Score on the basis of percentage of juniors and seniors of 'upper class' status | When standardized on participation in extracurricular activities : $G_s$ = +.12<br>Stronger in middle and upper class : $G$ = +.11<br>Lower in the lower class : $G$ = +.05 | HAPP 1.1 | G<br>V | +.14<br>.08 | $Chi^2$ | .01 | Juniors and seniors attending public high schools in New York State, U.S.A.<br>(See last page) | BRENN 70<br>p. 113/149/182/346 |
| | | When standardized on participation in extracurricular activities : $G_s$ = +.04<br>Unaffected by social class | AFF 1.1 | G<br>V | +.07<br>.04 | $Chi^2$ | .01 | | |
| S.E.S. | weighted score on the basis of father's occupational status, father's education, mother's education, possessions in the home, number of books in the home, number of rooms per person in the home | Happiness was measured in each of the three interview waves, while S.E.S. was measured only in the first interview.<br>See also instrument and remarks in excerpt (Part II).<br>Correlation with first measurement of happiness : r = -.00<br>with second measurement : r = +.00<br>with third measurement : r = -.01 | COMP 1.2 | $r_{pm}$ | ± 0 | | ns | Public high school boys, U.S.A.<br>Probability multi-stage sample<br>N: 2213 in 1966; 1886 in 1968 and 1799 in 1969<br>date: fall 1966, spring 1968 and spring 1969 | BACHM 67/70<br>p. 209 |
| HIGH EDUCATIONAL STATUS OF FATHER | Non-graduate vs college graduate | U-shaped curve: girls with a non-graduate father reporting significantly more 'average happiness' | COMP 2.2 | | ± 0 | | ns | Female college students, New York, U.S.A.<br>Type of sample construction unclear<br>N: 238, date: — | WASHB 41<br>p. 283 |
| S.E.S. | 2-item index containing occupational level and educational level (Hollingshead Two-Factor Index of Social Position; see Hollingshead, 1957) | | COMP 1.1 | $r_{pm}$ | +.08 | | ns | White males who had experienced a first heart attack, Durham, North Carolina, U.S.A.<br>Non-probability quota sample<br>N: 56, date: 1970 | GARRI 73<br>p. 201 |
| S.E.S. | Hollingshead Two-Factor Index of Social Position (see above) | Index of Positive Affects: $t_k$ = +.23 (001)<br>G = +.34<br>Index of Negative Affects: $t_k$ = +.03 (ns)<br>G = +.05 | HAPP 1.1<br>AFF 2.3 | $t_{kc}$<br>$t_{kc}$<br>$G^c$ | +.17<br>+<br>+ | | 001 | Non-hospitalized schizophrenic males, Monroe County, New York, U.S.A.<br>Probability sample, drawn from the Monroe County psychiatric case register<br>N: 178, date: 1964 - 1965 | ALEXA 68<br>p. 97/122-123 |

## S 5.2 - SATISFACTION WITH S.E.S

see 'Satisfaction with Socio-Economic Level' (S 1.8)

## S 5.3 - SOCIAL MOBILITY

### INTERGENERATIONAL MOBILITY

| | | | | | | | | | |
|---|---|---|---|---|---|---|---|---|---|
| SOCIAL MOBILITY | Discrepancy between the respondent's S.E.S. and his father's S.E.S. | Both upward and downward social mobility are unrelated to happiness | HAPP 1.1 | G | +.03 | | ns | National adult population, The Netherlands<br>Probability area sample<br>N: 1552, date: June, 1968 | BAKKE 74<br>p. 28<br>VEENH 75<br>p. 13 |

## JOB ADVANCEMENT

| | | | | | | | | | |
|---|---|---|---|---|---|---|---|---|---|
| JOB ADVANCEMENT | 4-item index of closed questions on whether current job is the best one ever had, raise in pay during past year, promotion during past year and chances for advancement<br>very low / low / medium / high / very high | Computed for male chief wage earners only<br>Index of Positive Affects:<br>- Among white-collar workers:<br>Positive relationship (05) among both workers of high occupational prestige and workers of medium or low prestige.<br>- Among blue collar-workers:<br>Positive relationship (05) among workers of high or medium occupational prestige only.<br>Not among workers of low prestige.<br>Index of Negative Affects:<br>- Slightly negative (ns) among blue-collar workers of low occupational prestige only.<br>- No relationships among the other occupational categories. | AFF 2.1 | $\bar{DR}$ | + | BCI | | Adults, urban areas, U.S.A.<br>Probability area sample<br>N: 2787, date: January, 1963 - January, 1964 | BRADB 69<br>p. 199 |
| ACHIEVING HIGHER JOB | Closed question: no vs yes | | HAPP 2.1 | G | +.05 | $Chi^2$ | ns | Male employees of age 40 - 65, The Netherlands<br>Non-probability chunk sample<br>N: 13.000, date: — | SONDE 75 |
| SELF-PERCEIVED INCREASE IN OCCUPATIONAL PRESTIGE, AFTER MILITARY RETIREMENT | 3-item index of closed questions on present job in comparison with former military job, with respect to: its general importance, level of skill and knowledge required, authority over other people | Index of Positive Affects: G = +.30<br>Index of Negative Affects: G = -.01 | AFF 2.3 | G | +.22 | | | Middle-aged, presently employed army retirees, California U.S.A.<br>Probability simple random sample<br>N: 362, date: August, 1970 | GARBE 71<br>p. 181 |

## STATUS INCONSISTENCY

| | | | | | | | | | |
|---|---|---|---|---|---|---|---|---|---|
| SOCIAL MOBILITY | Discrepancy between level of school education and actual occupational status | For over-achievement : G = +.02 (ns)<br>For under-achievement: G = +.07 (ns) | HAPP 1.1 | G | +.04 | | ns | National adult population, The Netherlands<br>Probability area sample<br>N: 1552, date: June, 1968 | BAKKE 74<br>p. 28<br>VEENH 75<br>p. 13 |
| ACHIEVEMENT | Difference between educational level and occupational level | Positive relationship with over-achievement (ns)<br>Negative relationship with under-achievement (ns)<br>Only among those of medium education the under-achievers are significantly less happy (05). | HAPP 1.1 | | | $Chi^2$ | ns | Adults, Utrecht, The Netherlands<br>Probability sample, stratified by age<br>N: 300, date: autumn 1967 | MOSER 69<br>p. 21 |

## S 5.4 - VARIOUS FACTORS CONCERNING S.E.S.

| | | | | | | | | | |
|---|---|---|---|---|---|---|---|---|---|
| UPWARD CAREER ANCHORAGE | 6-item index of forced choice statements measuring whether a person tends to evaluate success in terms of how far a person has come (downward anchorage) or in terms of how far a person has to go before he reaches the top of his career (upward anchorage).<br>(Career-Anchorage Scale; see Tausky & Dubin, 1965). | | HAPP 3.1 | r | +.03 | | ns | People of 46 and older, Duke, U.S.A.<br>Probability systematic random sample, stratified by age and sex<br>N: 502, date: 1968 | PALMO 72<br>p. 70 |
| THINKING OFTEN ABOUT GETTING AHEAD | Closed question: not at all / sometimes / often, during last week | Gamma computed on the basis of proportion 'often' answers.<br>(to be continued on next page). | HAPP 1.1 | G' | - | Gt' | ns | Inhabitants of 4 small communities, Illinois, U.S.A.<br>Probability multi-stage samples<br>N: 2006, date: March, 1962 | BRADB 65/1<br>p. 54 |

| | | | | | | | | | |
|---|---|---|---|---|---|---|---|---|---|
| | | high S.E.S.: G' = −.06 (ns)<br>low S.E.S. : G' = +.01 (ns) | | | | | | | |
| PERCEIVED SUBJECTIVE SOCIAL CLASS POSITION IN FUTURE | Closed question on the general standing of expected future business or profession: below average / average / good / excellent | Stronger in middle and upper class: G = +.22<br>Lower in lower class : G = +.09 | HAPP 1.1 | G<br>V | +.23<br>.10 | $Chi^2$ | 01 | Juniors and seniors attending public high schools in New York State, U.S.A.<br>Probability cluster sample of 10 public high schools<br>N: sample B= 1664, date: 1960 | BRENN 70<br>p. 120/182/362 |
| | | Unaffected by social class | AFF 1.1 | G<br>V | +.15<br>.08 | $Chi^2$ | 01 | | |
| PREFERENCE FOR 'A JOB THAT DOESN'T BUG ME' | 7-item index of closed questions indicating preference for: no one to boss me, don't have to work too hard, clean job, not a lot of responsibility, lot of free time, high prestige, and not learning a lot of new things | | COMP 1.2 | $r_{pm}$ | −.05 | | ns | Public high school boys, U.S.A.<br>Probability multi-stage sample<br>N: 2213 in 1966, 1886 in 1968 and 1799 in 1969<br>date: fall 1966, spring 1968, spring 1969 | BACHM 67/70<br>p. 243 |
| PREFERENCE FOR 'A JOB THAT PAYS OFF' | 6-item index of closed questions indicating preference for: steady job, learning new things, good chances for getting ahead, good pay, using one's skills, nice friendly people | | COMP 1.2 | $r_{pm}$ | +.21 | | 001 | See above | BACHM 67/70<br>p. 243 |
| AMBITIOUS JOB ATTITUDE | 13-item index of closed questions indicating preference or 'a job that doesn't bug me' and preference for 'a job that pays off' (see above) | | COMP 1.2 | $r_{pm}$ | +.16 | | 001 | See above | BACHM 67/70<br>p. 243 |
| KNOWLEDGE ABOUT OCCUPATIONS | 25-item test containing questions on income, status, working hours, requirements, etc. of different occupations (Job Information Test) | | COMP 1.2 | $r_{pm}$ | −.01 | | ns | See above | BACHM 67/70<br>p. 242 |

# S 6 SPORTS



## S 6.1 - SPORTS - PRACTICE AND ABILITY

| | | | | | | | | | |
|---|---|---|---|---|---|---|---|---|---|
| BEING AN ATHLETE | College women (sample 1) vs athletes (sample II) | See also sample construction in excerpt (Part II). | AFF 1.1 | G' | +.39 | Gt' | 01 | College women and woman athletes, U.S.A.<br>Non-probability chunk samples<br>N: 603, date: — | SNYDE 75<br>p. 195 |
| | | | COMP 1.1 | G' | +.32 | Gt' | 01 | | |
| | | | COMP 1.1 | G' | +.32 | Gt' | 01 | | |
| BEING A GYMNAST | Basketball players vs gymnasts | Computed for athletes only | AFF 1.1 | G' | +.17 | Gt' | ns | See above | SNYDE 75<br>p. 197 |
| | | | COMP 1.1 | G' | +.22 | Gt' | ns | | |
| | | | COMP 1.1 | G' | +.12 | Gt' | ns | | |
| ATHLETICS, skill in and devotion to - | Cl- -master rating on a 7-point scale on the basi. of observation | | AFF 5.3 | $r_{pm}$ | +.30 | | | Schoolboys, England<br>Non-probability chunk sample<br>N: 140, date: 1912 - 1913 | WEBB 15<br>p. 27 |
| ATHLETICS | Rating on 7-point scales by (student)captains of various athletic clubs and by a staff member | | AFF 5.2 | $r_{pm}$ | +.39 | | | Male students, England<br>Non-probability chunk sample<br>N: 194, date: 1912 - 1913 | WEBB 15<br>p. 26 |
| PLAYING SPORTS | No sports vs sports | L-shaped curve: significant relationship among the more unhappy students only. | COMP 2.2 | | + | | s | Female college students, New York, U.S.A.<br>Type of construction unclear<br>N: 238, date: — | WASHB 41<br>p. 283 |
| PARTICIPATING IN SPORTS | Closed question: not at all / once / more than once in the past week | Lower among males: G = +.06<br>Stronger among females: G = +.46 | HAPP 1.1 | G | + | | | Adults, Metro Manila, Philippines<br>Probability area sample<br>N: 941, date: January - April, 1972 | BULAT 73<br>p. 232 |
| | | Lower among males: G = +.19<br>Stronger among females: G = +.24 | HAPP 3.1 | G | + | | | | |
| PLAYING SPORTS | Closed question: infrequently or never / some / frequently | Lower among males: G = +.04 (ns)<br>Stronger among females: G = +.24 (01) | HAPP 1.1 | G | +.14 | $Chi^2$ | | Adults, Toledo, U.S.A.<br>Systematic random sample<br>N: 510, date: 1973 | SNYDE 74<br>p. 34 |
| | | Lower among males: G = +.07 (ns)<br>Stronger among females: G = +.16 (ns) | HAPP 2.1 | G | +.10 | $Chi^2$ | ns | | |
| PARTICIPATING IN GAMES OR SPORTS ACTIVITIES | Closed question: not at all / once / several times / every day / more than once a day during last week | Computed for Index of Positive Affects only: G' = +.15 (05)<br>Stronger among males: G' = +.20 (01)<br>Lower among females: G' = +.10 (01)<br>Unrelated to Index of Negative Affects | AFF 2.3 | G' | + | Gt' | | Inhabitants of 4 small communities, Illinois, U.S.A.<br>Probability multi stage samples<br>N: 2008, date: March, 1962 | BRADB 65/1<br>p. 49 |
| ACTUAL SPORTING | Closed question: no vs yes | | HAPP 2.1 | G | +.07 | Chi | ns | Male employees of age 40+, The Netherlands<br>Non-probability chunk sample<br>N: 13000, date: — | SONDE 75 |

## S 6.2 - INTEREST IN SPORTS

| | | | | | | | | | |
|---|---|---|---|---|---|---|---|---|---|
| WATCHING SPORTS | Closed question: infrequently or never / sometimes / frequently | Lower among males: G = +.08 (ns)<br>Stronger among females: G = +.33 (01) | HAPP 1.1 | G | +.19 | $Chi^2$ | | Adults, Toledo, Ohio, U.S.A.<br>Systematic random sample<br>N: 510, date: 1973 | SNYDE 74<br>p. 34 |
| | | Stronger among females: G = +.30 (05)<br>Lower among males: G = +.15 (ns) | HAPP 2.1 | G | +.20 | $Chi^2$ | | | |
| TALKING ABOUT SPORTS | Closed question: infrequently or never / sometimes / frequently | Lower among males: G = +.23 (ns)<br>Stronger among females: G = +.39 (01) | HAPP 1.1 | G | + | $Chi^2$ | | See above | SNYDE 74<br>p. 34 |
| | | Males: G = +.29 (ns)<br>Females: G = +.33 (01) | HAPP 2.1 | G | + | $Chi^2$ | | | |
| READING SPORTS PAGE | Closed question: not at all / sometimes / thoroughly | Lower among males: G = +.13 (ns)<br>Stronger among females: G = +.28 (05) | HAPP 1.1 | G | + | $Chi^2$ | | See above | SNYDE 74<br>p. 34 |
| | | Males: G = +.26 (ns)<br>Females: G = +.29 (05) | HAPP 2.1 | G | + | $Chi^2$ | | | |
| SUBSCRIBE/READ SPORTS MAGAZINES | Direct yes/no question | Lower among males: G = +.01 (ns)<br>Stronger among females: G = +.19 (ns) | HAPP 1.1 | G | + | $Chi^2$ | ns | See above | SNYDE 74<br>p. 34 |
| | | Lower among males: G = +.11 (ns)<br>Stronger among females: G = +.25 (ns) | HAPP 2.1 | G | + | $Chi^2$ | ns | | |
| BEHAVIORAL INVOLVEMENT IN SPORTS | 5-item index of closed questions on playing sports, watching sports, talking about sports, reading sports page, and subscribe/read sports-magazines<br>(see above) | Stronger among females<br>Lower among males | HAPP 1.1 | G | +.24 | | | See above | SNYDE 74<br>p. 32 |
| | | Stronger among females<br>Lower among males | HAPP 2.1 | G | +.23 | | | | |
| KNOWLEDGE ABOUT SPORTS | Measurement by having respondents match a 12-item list of famous sports personalities with their appropriate sports sphere | | HAPP 1.1 | G | +.07 | | | See above | SNYDE 74<br>p. 32 |
| | | | HAPP 2.1 | G | +.07 | | | | |
| ATTENDING GAMES OR SPORTS ACTIVITIES | Closed question: not at all / once / several times / every day / more than once a day during last week | Computed for Index of Positive Affects only: G' = +.19 (01)<br>Unaffected by sex<br>Stronger among those of high S.E.S.: G' = +.15 (05)<br>Lower among those of low S.E.S.: G' = +.07 (ns)<br>Unrelated to Index of Negative Affects | AFF 2.3 | G' | | Gt' | | Inhabitants of 4 small communitites, Illinois, U.S.A.<br>Probability multi stage samples<br>N: 2006, date: March, 1962 | BRADB 65/1<br>p. 48 |

## S 6.3 - ATTITUDES TOWARDS SPORTS

| | | | | | | | | | |
|---|---|---|---|---|---|---|---|---|---|
| SPORTS SEEN AS A WAY TO RELAX | Closed question: disagree / not sure / agree | Males: G = +.06 (ns)<br>Females: G = +.13 (ns) | HAPP 1.1 | G | + | $Chi^2$ | ns | Adults, Toledo, Ohio, U.S.A.<br>Systematic random sample<br>N: 510, date: 1973 | SNYDE 74<br>p. 35 |
| | | Males: G = +.15 (ns)<br>Females: G = +.08 (ns) | HAPP 2.1 | G | + | $Chi^2$ | ns | | |
| SPORTS SEEN AS A WASTE OF TIME | Closed question: disagree / not sure / agree | Stronger among males: G = -.26 (ns)<br>Lower among females: G = -.10 (ns) | HAPP 1.1 | G | - | $Chi^2$ | ns | See above | SNYDE 74<br>p. 35 |
| | | Stronger among males: G = -.36 (01)<br>Lower among females: G = -.08 (ns) | HAPP 2.1 | G | - | $Chi^2$ | | | |

| | | | | | | | | | |
|---|---|---|---|---|---|---|---|---|---|
| LITTLE SATISFACTION RECEIVED FROM SPORTS | Closed question: disagree / not sure / agree | Unaffected by sex | HAPP 1.1 | G | -.25 | $Chi^2$ | ns | Adults, Toledo, Ohio, U.S.A. (See last page) | SNYDE 74 p. 35 |
| | | Males: G = -.33 (01)<br>Females: G = -.25 (ns) | HAPP 2.1 | G | - | $Chi^2$ | | | |
| SPORTS SEEN AS HELP AGAINST WORRIES AND PRESSURES OF THE DAY | Closed question: disagree / not sure / agree | Males: G = +.02 (ns)<br>Females: G = +.03 (ns) | HAPP 1.1 | G | + | $Chi^2$ | ns | See above | SNYDE 74 p. 35 |
| | | Stronger among males: G = +.13 (ns)<br>Lower among females: G = +.03 (ns) | HAPP 2.1 | G | + | $Chi^2$ | ns | | |
| AFFECTIVE INVOLVEMENT IN SPORTS | 4-item index of agree/disagree statements on sports are a way to relax, sports are a waste of time, little satisfaction received from sports and sports are a help against worries and pressures (see above) | Unaffected by sex | HAPP 1.1 | G | +.16 | $Chi^2$ | | See above | SNYDE 74 p. 32 |
| | | Stronger among males<br>Lower among females | HAPP 2.1 | G | +.15 | | | | |

# T 1 TIME PERSPECTIVE



## T 1.1 - TIME COMPETENCE

| | | | | | | | | | |
|---|---|---|---|---|---|---|---|---|---|
| ORGANIZATION OF TIME: | Temporal Behavior Questionnaire, in which 201 ways of experiencing, arranging, and estimating time in work, daily activities, and fantasies were rated in terms of the degree to which the subject was characteristically disposed or not disposed to engage in them | The instrument was scored on a number of a priori and factorically derived scales. The group of subjects was divided into two, according to their mean 'daily average mood' (see instrument in excerpt, Part II). Only significant correlations with average mood level were presented. | | | | | | Male college students, U.S.A.<br>Non-probability chunk sample<br>N: 17, date: ± 1960 | WESSM 66/2<br>p. 117-119 |
| - UNFILLED VS FILLED TIME PERSPECTIVE | The happy men commit and hold themselves to responsibilities and they plan and schedule their time far in advance. The unhappy men shy away from long-term responsibilities and keep the future open and uncommitted. They are anxious about the unknown future. | | AFF 3.1 | $r_{pm}$ | + | t | 05 | | |
| - LIFE IS FELT AS DICRETE VS CONTINUOUS | The happy men are aware of enduring themes and patterns in their life, and have a strong sense of their own identity. The unhappy men experience events as discrete, and life as a series of abrupt transformations. For them time is broken, chopped up, and without direction. | | AFF 3.1 | $r_{pm}$ | + | t | 05 | | |
| - PROCRASTINATING AND INEFFICIENT VS PUNCTUAL AND EFFICIENT USE OF TIME | The happy men work efficiently without wasting time and energy. They can manage each day to do everything they want to do. The unhappy men never begin or finish a task on time. They procrastinate too long, and feel themselves working below capacity. | | AFF 3.1 | $r_{pm}$ | + | t | 05 | | |
| EXPERIENCE AND USE OF TIME: | 80-item questionnaire, representing the 10 most positively and 10 most negatively loaded items on each of 4 orthogonal bi-polar factors (Ricks - Epley - Wessman Temporal Experience Questionnaire) | The factors were extracted from the 201-item Temporal Behavior Questionnaire, using a sample of 110 Ss. (see above) | | | | | | Male college students, U.S.A.<br>Wessman & Ricks (1966) sample (see above) | WESSM 73<br>p. 109-111 |
| - IMMEDIATE TIME PRESSURE | 20-item index measuring relaxed mastery and adaptive flexibility vs harassed lack of control | | AFF 3.1<br>COMP 5 | | | | ns<br>ns | | |
| - LONG-TERM PERSONAL DIRECTION | 20-item index measuring discontinuity and lack of direction vs continuity and steady purpose | | AFF 3.1<br>COMP 5 | r<br>r | $>$ +.48<br>$>$ +.48 | | 05<br>05 | | |

| Variable | Measure | Remarks | Code | Stat. | Value | Test | Sig. | Population / Sample | Source |
|---|---|---|---|---|---|---|---|---|---|
| - EFFICIENT TIME UTILIZATION | 20-item index measuring procrastination and inefficiency vs efficient scheduling | | AFF 3.1<br>COMP 5 | | | | ns<br>ns | | |
| - PERSONAL INCONSISTENCY | 20-item index measuring consistency and dependability vs inconsistency and changeability | | AFF 3.1<br>COMP 5 | | | | ns<br>ns | | |
| HAVING PROBLEMS WITH DAILY SCHEDULE | Closed question | High school students only<br>U-shaped curve: students of 'average' happiness having least problems with their daily schedule | COMP 4.1 | | - | | s | Students, U.S.A.<br>Non-probability chunk sample<br>N: 1651, date: — | SYMON 37<br>p. 292 |
| TIME COMPETENCE | 23-item index measuring whether one 'lives fully in the here and now and is able to tie past and future to the present in meaningful continuity' (Time Competence scale, from Shostrom's Personal Orientation Inventory; see Shostrom, 1964) | | AFF 2.1 | $r_{pm}$ | +.10 | | ns | Married females, U.S.A.<br>Non-probability purposive sample by expert choice<br>N: 62, date: — | HARDE 69<br>p. 50 |

## T 1.2 - TIME SPAN

| Variable | Measure | Remarks | Code | Stat. | Value | Test | Sig. | Population / Sample | Source |
|---|---|---|---|---|---|---|---|---|---|
| LENGTH OF PROSPECTIVE TIME SPAN | Score obtained from a set of 30 stories, using Thematic Apperception Test cards (see Ricks & Epley, 1960) | | AFF 3.1 | $r_{pm}$ | +.54 | t | 05 | Male college students, U.S.A.<br>Non-probability chunk sample<br>N: 17, date: ± 1960 | WESSM 66/2<br>p. 120-121 |
| LENGTH OF RETROSPECTIVE TIME SPAN | See above | | AFF 3.1 | $r_{pm}$ | +.44 | t | 10 | See above | WESSM 66/2<br>p. 120-121 |
| DEGREE IN WHICH ONE WORKS WITH DISTANT OBJECTS IN VIEW (as opposed to living 'from hand to mouth') | Trained peer rating on a 7-point scale on the basis of observation | | AFF 5.2 | $r_{pm}$ | -.08 | | | Male students, England<br>Non-probability chunk sample<br>N: 194, date: 1912 - 1913 | WEBB 15<br>p. 26 |
| FUTURITY | Closed question on how much one looks forward to next month<br>not at all / very little / somewhat / considerably / very much | Stronger among normals : r = +.43 (01)<br>Lower among handicapped: r = +.28 (01) | HAPP 2.1 | r | + | | 01 | Physically defective and normal persons, Detroit, U.S.A.<br>Non-probability purposive samples<br>N: 295, date: — | CAMER 73/1<br>p. 209 |
| FUTURITY | Number of items mentioned on open-ended question on personal wishes and hopes for the future | Computed by us on the basis of data available in book<br>See also 'Personal Hopes, Aspirations and Goals' (Part III, H 3.2.1). | HAPP 3.1 | G' | +.07 | Gt' | 05 | Adult population of 5 Westernized nations, 3 underdeveloped giants, 2 countries in the Middle East, 3 Caribbean nations & The Philippines<br>Representative samples<br>N: 18,653, date: ± 1960 | CANTR 65/1<br>p. 263 |
| FUTURITY | Number of items mentioned on open-ended question on personal worries and fears for the future | Computed by us on the basis of data available in the book<br>See also 'Personal Worries and Fears' (Part III, P 5.2.2.1) | HAPP 3.1 | G' | +.07 | Gt' | 05 | See above | CANTR 65/1<br>p. 263 |

T 1.3 - ATTITUDES TOWARDS TIME

| | | | | | | | | |
|---|---|---|---|---|---|---|---|---|
| EXPERIENCE OF TIME: | Time Metaphor Test, in which 214 metaphors concerning time were rated in terms of their closeness or distance from the subject's experience of time | The instrument was scored on a number of a priori and factorially derived scales.<br>The group of subjects was divided into two according to their mean 'daily average mood' (see instrument in excerpt, Part II).<br>Only significant correlations with average mood level were presented. | | | | | Male college students, U.S.A.<br>Non-probability chunk sample<br>N: 17, date: ± 1960 | WESSM 66/2<br>p. 117-119 |
| - DESCENDING VS ASCENDING | The happy men experience time in terms of ascending, upwardly soaring images: 'a soaring bird', 'a mountain flame of hope'.<br>The unhappy men experience time in terms of descending, declining images: 'a flower falling to the mold', 'the grave of aspiration'. | | AFF 3.1 | $r_{pm}$ | + | t | 05 | | |
| - DECOMPOSITION VS COMPOSITION | The happy men experience time as organic composition, growth and fertility: 'a succession of new forms', 'pregnancy and birth'.<br>The unhappy men experience time as decomposition, deterioration, corruption, and decay: 'a rotting tree trunk', 'dust setting in an ancient house'. | | AFF 3.1 | $r_{pm}$ | + | t | 05 | | |
| - A BAD VS A GOOD PERSON | The happy men personify time as a good person, a beneficent friend and wise teacher: 'the voice of encouragement', 'the wisest of counselors'.<br>The unhappy men personify time as a bad person, a malevolent adversary and opponent: 'the old bad cheater', 'a chronic thief', 'a relentless antagonist'. | | AFF 3.1 | $r_{pm}$ | + | t | 05 | | |
| - A DARK VS BRIGHT FUTURE | For the happy men a bright future lies ahead, with favorable anticipation of gain and increase: 'a promising career', 'good prospects'.<br>For the unhappy men a dark future lies ahead, with unfavorable anticipation, and dreaded foreboding: 'future misfortune', 'increasing darkness'. | | AFF 3.1 | $r_{pm}$ | + | t | 05 | | |
| - MONOTONOUS, BARREN AND EMPTY VS HARMONY AND COMPLEXITY | The happy men experience a sense of harmony in time, with active order and rhythmic pace in its complexity: 'the order of nature', 'a harmony of wishes'.<br>The unhappy men experience a sense of monotony in time. It is slow, tedious, barren and empty: 'the marching of tired feet', 'a retarded clock', 'an empty room'. | | AFF 3.1 | $r_{pm}$ | + | t | 05 | | |
| - PASSIVE VS ACTIVE | The happy men experience time as the setting for active oriented effort: 'the thrust of forward purpose', 'continuity of aim'.<br>The unhappy men express a feeling of passive subjection to time; it is something they cannot master or control to their own purposes: 'boredom unrelieved', 'something you can never stop', 'something you are never ready for'. | | AFF 3.1 | $r_{pm}$ | + | t | 05 | | |

| | | | | | | | | | |
|---|---|---|---|---|---|---|---|---|---|
| **TEMPORAL ORIENTATION:** | | | | | | | | | |
| - TIME ANXIETY | 16-item index referring to anxiety about the flow of time, fear of the future, longing for the past<br>(Time Anxiety Scale; see Calabresi & Cohen, 1968) | | AFF 3.1<br>HAPP 3.1 | $r_{pm}$<br>$r_{pm}$ | -.31<br>-.31 | | 05<br>05 | Undergraduate students, U.S.A.<br>Non-probability chunk sample<br>N: 63, date: summer, 1970 | GORMA 71<br>p. 215-218 |
| - TIME SUBMISSIVENESS | 9-item index referring to a conforming, pedantic attitude towards punctuality<br>(Time Submissiveness Scale; see Calabresi & Cohen, 1968) | | AFF 3.1<br>HAPP 3.1 | $r_{pm}$<br>$r_{pm}$ | -.03<br>+.07 | | ns<br>ns | | |
| - TIME POSSESSIVENESS | 5-item index referring to a greedy and possessive attitude towards time<br>(Time Possessiveness Scale; see Calabresi & Cohen, 1968) | | AFF 3.1<br>HAPP 3.1 | $r_{pm}$<br>$r_{pm}$ | -.15<br>-.30 | | ns<br>05 | | |
| - TIME FLEXIBILITY | 8-item index referring to an accepting and flexible attitude towards time<br>(Time Flexibility Scale; see Calabresi & Cohen, 1968) | | AFF 3.1<br>HAPP 3.1 | $r_{pm}$<br>$r_{pm}$ | +.24<br>+.09 | | ns<br>ns | | |
| BEING INTERESTED IN DAILY SCHEDULE | Closed question | High school students only. | COMP 4.1 | | - | | s | Students, U.S.A.<br>Non-probability chunk sample<br>N: 1651, date: — | SYMON 37<br>p. 292 |

# V 1 VALUES

see also 'Religion' (R 1)



## V 1.1 - VALUE DIMENSIONS

see also 'Specific Hopes, Aspirations and Goals' (H 3.2), 'Content of Ideal Self-Image' (S 2.2.2)

| Value | Indicator | Results | Happiness measure | Statistic | Value | | Significance | Population | Source |
|---|---|---|---|---|---|---|---|---|---|
| INSTRUMENTAL VALUES: | 18-item inventory (Rokeach Instrumental Values Scale; see Rokeach, 1968)<br>The values mentioned were rated on a 7-point 'important - unimportant' scale (absolute measure).<br>They were also ranked in the order of 'importance as guiding principles' in one's life (relative measure). | Since not many differences appeared between the correlations with the first and with the second happiness measure, only correlations with the first instrument are presented here.<br>Correlations obtained from the absolute measure are presented first; those from the ranking procedure second.<br>See also remarks in excerpt (Part II).<br>males / females | | | | | | Undergraduate university students, California, U.S.A.<br>Non-probability chunk sample<br>N: 86, date: November - December, 1971 | FORDY 72<br>p. 160/167 |
| - AMBITIOUS | | abs.: r = -.14 (ns) +.00 (ns)<br>rel.: r = -.19 (ns) -.20 (ns) | AFF 3.1 | $r_{pm}$ | -.00<br>-.01 | | ns<br>ns | | |
| - BROADMINDED | | abs.: r = -.31 (10) +.10 (ns)<br>rel.: r = -.00 (ns) +.11 (ns) | AFF 3.1 | $r_{pm}$ | -.00<br>+.01 | | ns<br>ns | | |
| - CAPABLE | | abs.: r = +.00 (ns) -.13 (ns)<br>rel.: r = +.23 (ns) -.29 (05) | AFF 3.1 | $r_{pm}$ | -.01<br>-.01 | | ns<br>ns | | |
| - CHEERFUL | | abs.: r = +.22 (ns) +.28 (05)<br>rel.: r = +.50 (01) + 38 (01) | AFF 3.1 | $r_{pm}$ | +.23<br>+.39 | | 05<br>01 | | |
| - CLEAN | | abs.: r = +.12 (ns) +.12 (ns)<br>rel.: r = +.29 (10) + 12 (ns) | AFF 3.1 | $r_{pm}$ | +.11<br>+.15 | | ns<br>ns | | |
| - COURAGEOUS | | abs.: r = +.00 (ns) +.07 (ns)<br>rel.: r = +.00 (ns) +.11 (ns) | AFF 3.1 | $r_{pm}$ | +.01<br>+.01 | | ns<br>ns | | |
| - FORGIVING | | abs.: r = -.19 (ns) +.30 (10)<br>rel.: r = -.22 (ns) +.36 (05) | AFF 3.1 | $r_{pm}$ | +.12<br>+.15 | | ns<br>ns | | |
| - HELPFUL | | abs.: r = -.26 (ns) +.00 (ns)<br>rel.: r = -.10 (ns) -.13 (ns) | AFF 3.1 | $r_{pm}$ | -.01<br>-.01 | | ns<br>ns | | |
| - HONEST | | abs.: r = -.00 (ns) +.15 (ns)<br>rel.: r = +.23 (ns) +.17 (ns) | AFF 3.1 | $r_{pm}$ | +.07<br>+.19 | | ns<br>10 | | |
| - IMAGINATIVE | | abs.: r = -.18 (ns) -.18 (ns)<br>rel.: r = +.00 (ns) -.00 (ns) | AFF 3.1 | $r_{pm}$ | -.17<br>-.00 | | ns<br>ns | | |

| Item | Measure of value | Correlations | Happiness measure | Statistic | Value | | Significance | Population | Source |
|---|---|---|---|---|---|---|---|---|---|
| | | males / females | | | | | | | |
| - INDEPENDENT | | abs.: r = -.17 (ns) / -.00 (ns)<br>rel.: r = -.11 (ns) / +.01 (ns) | AFF 3.1 | $r_{pm}$ | -.01<br>+.00 | | ns<br>ns | | |
| - INTELLECTUAL | | abs.: r = -.48 (01) / -.01 (ns)<br>rel.: r = -.38 (05) / -.01 (ns) | AFF 3.1 | $r_{pm}$ | -.22<br>-.19 | | 05<br>10 | | |
| - LOGICAL | | abs.: r = -.00 (ns) / -.00 (ns)<br>rel.: r = -.13 (ns) / -.22 (ns) | AFF 3.1 | $r_{pm}$ | -.12<br>-.19 | | ns<br>10 | | |
| - LOVING | | abs.: r = -.23 (ns) / +.01 (ns)<br>rel.: r = -.21 (ns) / +.17 (ns) | AFF 3.1 | $r_{pm}$ | -.12<br>+.00 | | ns<br>ns | | |
| - OBEDIENT | | abs.: r = +.13 (ns) / +.00 (ns)<br>rel.: r = +.01 (ns) / -.18 (ns) | AFF 3.1 | $r_{pm}$ | +.08<br>-.01 | | ns<br>ns | | |
| - POLITE | | abs.: r = +.01 (ns) / +.10 (ns)<br>rel.: r = -.00 (ns) / -.01 (ns) | AFF 3.1 | $r_{pm}$ | +.01<br>-.01 | | ns<br>ns | | |
| - RESPONSIBLE | | abs.: r = +.00 (ns) / -.01 (ns)<br>rel.: r = +.01 (ns) / -.26 (10) | AFF 3.1 | $r_{pm}$ | -.00<br>-.12 | | ns<br>ns | | |
| - SELF-CONTROLLED | | abs.: r = -.45 (01) / -.01 (ns)<br>rel.: r = -.35 (05) / -.16 (ns) | AFF 3.1 | $r_{pm}$ | -.12<br>-.22 | | ns<br>05 | | |
| TERMINAL VALUES: | 18-item inventory (Terminal Values Scale; see Rokeach, 1968)<br>The values mentioned were rated on a 7-point 'important - unimportant' scale (absolute measure).<br>They were also ranked in the order of 'importance as guiding principles' in one's life (relative measure). | Since not many differences appeared between the correlations with the first and with the second happiness measure, only correlations with the first instrument are presented here.<br>Correlations obtained from the absolute measure are presented first; those from the ranking procedure second.<br>See also remarks in excerpt (Part II). | | | | | | Undergraduate university students, California, U.S.A,<br>Non-probability chunk sample<br>N: 86, date: November - December, 1971 | FORDY 72<br>p. 159/160 |
| | | males / females | | | | | | | |
| - A COMFORTABLE LIFE | | abs.: r = +.23 (ns) / -.01 (ns)<br>rel.: r = +.32 (10) / -.11 (ns) | AFF 3.1 | $r_{pm}$ | -.01<br>+.03 | | ns<br>ns | | |
| - AN EXCITING LIFE | | abs.: r = +.23 (ns) / -.01 (ns)<br>rel.: r = +.40 (05) / +.00 (ns) | AFF 3.1 | $r_{pm}$ | +.00<br>+.14 | | ns<br>ns | | |
| - A SENSE OF ACCOMPLISHMENT | | abs.: r = -.01 (ns) / -.01 (ns)<br>rel.: r = -.19 (ns) / -.28 (05) | AFF 3.1 | $r_{pm}$ | -.10<br>-.22 | | ns<br>05 | | |
| - A WORLD AT PEACE | | abs.: r = +.00 (ns) / +.21 (ns)<br>rel.: r = +.00 (ns) / +.00 (ns) | AFF 3.1 | $r_{pm}$ | +.16<br>+.00 | | ns<br>ns | | |
| - A WORLD OF BEAUTY | | abs.: r = +.14 (ns) / -.01 (ns)<br>rel.: r = -.01 (ns) / +.01 (ns) | AFF 3.1 | $r_{pm}$ | +.00<br>+.00 | | ns<br>ns | | |
| - EQUALITY | | abs.: r = -.23 (ns) / +.22 (ns)<br>rel.: r = -.00 (ns) / +.00 (ns) | AFF 3.1 | $r_{pm}$ | +.01<br>+.01 | | ns<br>ns | | |
| - FAMILY SECURITY | | abs.: r = +.17 (ns) / +.01 (ns)<br>rel.: r = +.35 (05) / -.01 (ns) | AFF 3.1 | $r_{pm}$ | +.10<br>+.01 | | ns<br>ns | | |
| - FREEDOM | | abs.: r = -.18 (ns) / +.00 (ns)<br>rel.: r = -.35 (05) / +.01 (ns) | AFF 3.1 | $r_{pm}$ | -.01<br>-.01 | | ns<br>ns | | |

| | | | | | | | | |
|---|---|---|---|---|---|---|---|---|
| | | males / females | | | | | | |
| - HAPPINESS | | abs.: r = +.01 (ns) +.19 (ns)<br>rel.: r = +.17 (ns) +.18 (ns) | AFF 3.1 | $r_{pm}$ | +.13<br>+.15 | | ns<br>ns | | |
| - INNER HARMONY | | abs.: r = -.20 (ns) -.00 (ns)<br>rel.: r = -.27 (ns) +.01 (ns) | AFF 3.1 | $r_{pm}$ | -.01<br>-.01 | | ns<br>ns | | |
| - MATURE LOVE | | abs.: r = -.23 (ns) -.01 (ns)<br>rel.: r = -.18 (ns) -.09 (ns) | AFF 3.1 | $r_{pm}$ | -.12<br>-.13 | | ns<br>ns | | |
| - NATIONAL SECURITY | | abs.: r = +.17 (ns) +.00 (ns)<br>rel.: r = +.01 (ns) -.19 (ns) | AFF 3.1 | $r_{pm}$ | +.12<br>-.13 | | ns<br>ns | | |
| - PLEASURE | | abs.: r = +.30 (05) +.01 (ns)<br>rel.: r = +.26 (ns) -.00 (ns) | AFF 3.1 | $r_{pm}$ | +.15<br>+.01 | | ns<br>ns | | |
| - SALVATION | | abs.: r = -.24 (ns) +.14 (ns)<br>rel.: r = -.37 (05) +.26 (05) | AFF 3.1 | $r_{pm}$ | -.02<br>+.01 | | ns<br>ns | | |
| - SELF-RESPECT | | positive among males<br>negative among females | AFF 3.1 | $r_{pm}$ | -.07<br>-.11 | | ns<br>ns | | |
| - SOCIAL RECOGNITION | | abs.: r = +.21 (ns) -.00 (ns)<br>rel.: r = +.01 (ns) -.00 (ns) | AFF 3.1 | $r_{pm}$ | -.00<br>+.00 | | ns<br>ns | | |
| - TRUE FRIENDSHIP | | abs.: r = +.01 (ns) +.32 (05)<br>rel.: r = +.22 (ns) +.13 (ns) | AFF 3.1 | $r_{pm}$ | +.16<br>+.19 | | ns<br>05 | | |
| - WISDOM | | abs.: r = -.30 (ns) +.00 (ns)<br>rel.: r = -.41 (05) +.17 (ns) | AFF 3.1 | $r_{pm}$ | -.01<br>-.00 | | ns<br>ns | | |
| PERSONAL VALUES: | Content analysis of each Ss written philosophy of life by 5 judges, using a list of 68 frequently mentioned values (selected out of the entire set of philosophies by the author). | Analaysis on the basis of a comparison of the most happy and the most unhappy subjects (top and bottom 27% on the basis of their happiness scores; see first instrument in excerpt, Part II). | | | | | | Undergraduate university students, U.S.A.<br>Non-probability chunk sample<br>N: 68, date: Novemeber - December, 1971 | FORDY 72<br>p. 193-198 |
| - HAPPINESS (pleasure, joy, satisfaction, contentment, etc.) | | Unaffected by sex | AFF 3.1 | | + | $Chi^2$ | 05 | | |
| - ENJOYMENT OF LIFE | | Unaffected by sex | AFF 3.1 | | | $Chi^2$ | ns | | |
| - INNER PEACE (calmness) | | Unaffected by sex | AFF 3.1 | | + | $Chi^2$ | 05 | | |
| - LIVING LIFE TO ITS FULLEST (living each moment fully) | | Unaffected by sex | AFF 3.1 | | | $Chi^2$ | ns | | |
| - FUN, EXCITEMENT, GOOD TIMES | | Unaffected by sex | AFF 3.1 | | + | $Chi^2$ | ns | | |
| - AN EDUCATION | | Unaffected by sex | AFF 3.1 | | | $Chi^2$ | ns | | |
| - LEARNING | | Unaffected by sex | AFF 3.1 | | | $Chi^2$ | ns | | |
| - MEANING AND PURPOSE FOR LIFE | | Unaffected by sex | AFF 3.1 | | + | $Chi^2$ | 05 | | |
| - LOVE OF LIFE | | Unaffected by sex | AFF 3.1 | | + | $Chi^2$ | 05 | | |
| - LIVE DAY-BY-DAY; LIVING IN THE PRESENT (in the here and now) | | Unaffected by sex | AFF 3.1 | | | $Chi^2$ | ns | | |
| - AN ACTIVE LIFE | | Unaffected by sex | AFF 3.1 | | | $Chi^2$ | ns | | |
| - A SLOWER PACE TO LIFE (a relaxed pace) | | Unaffected by sex | AFF 3.1 | | | $Chi^2$ | ns | | |
| - SIMPLICITY IN LIVING | | Unaffected by sex | AFF 3.1 | | | $Chi^2$ | ns | | |

| | | | | | | | |
|---|---|---|---|---|---|---|---|
| - FLOWING WITH THE TIDE OF LIFE | | Unaffected by sex | AFF 3.1 | | | Chi$^2$ | ns |
| - OPENNESS TO EXPERIENCE | | Unaffected by sex | AFF 3.1 | | | Chi$^2$ | ns |
| - VARIETY OF EXPERIENCE | | Unaffected by sex | AFF 3.1 | | | Chi$^2$ | ns |
| - INTERPERSONAL RELATIONSHIPS; FRIENDSHIP | | Unaffected by sex | AFF 3.1 | | | Chi$^2$ | ns |
| - MARRIAGE AND FAMILY LIFE | | Unaffected by sex | AFF 3.1 | | | Chi$^2$ | ns |
| - LOVE (in general) | | Unaffected by sex | AFF 3.1 | | | Chi$^2$ | ns |
| - LOVE FOR OTHERS | | Significant (01) among females only | AFF 3.1 | | + | Chi$^2$ | 05 |
| - BEING TOLERANT, ACCEPTING, AND NON-JUDGMENTAL TOWARDS OTHERS (letting them be) | | Significant (05) among females only | AFF 3.1 | | + | Chi$^2$ | ns |
| - SYMPATHY, EMPATHY, UNDERSTANDING | | Unaffected by sex | AFF 3.1 | | | Chi$^2$ | ns |
| - BEING KIND AND CARING TOWARDS OTHERS | | Significant (05) among females only | AFF 3.1 | | + | Chi$^2$ | ns |
| - BEING NEEDED BY OTHERS | | Unaffected by sex | AFF 3.1 | | | Chi$^2$ | ns |
| - PLACING OTHERS ABOVE SELF | | Unaffected by sex | AFF 3.1 | | | Chi$^2$ | ns |
| - PLACING SELF ABOVE OTHERS | | Unaffected by sex | AFF 3.1 | | | Chi$^2$ | ns |
| - RESPECT FOR OTHERS (valuing every human being) | | Unaffected by sex | AFF 3.1 | | | Chi$^2$ | ns |
| - HELPING OTHERS | | Unaffected by sex | AFF 3.1 | | | Chi$^2$ | ns |
| - MAKING A CONTRIBUTION TO MAN OR SOCIETY | | Unaffected by sex | AFF 3.1 | | | Chi$^2$ | ns |
| - REALIZING POTENTIALS (growth, utilizing talents, self-actualization, self-improvement) | | Unaffected by sex | AFF 3.1 | | | Chi$^2$ | ns |
| - BEING CAPABLE (mastery) | | Unaffected by sex | AFF 3.1 | | | Chi$^2$ | ns |
| - STRIVING FOR GOALS; ACCOMPLISHMENT (challenges) | | Unaffected by sex | AFF 3.1 | | | Chi$^2$ | ns |
| - PERFECTION | | Unaffected by sex | AFF 3.1 | | | Chi$^2$ | ns |
| - CREATIVITY | | Unaffected by sex | AFF 3.1 | | | Chi$^2$ | ns |
| - WORLD PEACE | | Unaffected by sex | AFF 3.1 | | | Chi$^2$ | ns |
| - MATERIAL COMFORT; PROSPERITY | | Unaffected by sex | AFF 3.1 | | | Chi$^2$ | ns |
| - ANTI-MATERIALISM; ANTI-CAPITALISM | | Unaffected by sex | AFF 3.1 | | | Chi$^2$ | ns |
| - SECURITY | | Unaffected by sex | AFF 3.1 | | | Chi$^2$ | ns |
| - ANTI VARIOUS ASPECTS OF AMERICAN SOCIETY | | Unaffected by sex | AFF 3.1 | | | Chi$^2$ | ns |
| - ANTI-TECHNOLOGY | | Unaffected by sex | AFF 3.1 | | | Chi$^2$ | ns |
| - ANTI-PREJUDICE | | Unaffected by sex | AFF 3.1 | | | Chi$^2$ | ns |
| - ANTI WORRIES AND PROBLEMS | | Unaffected by sex | AFF 3.1 | | | Chi$^2$ | ns |
| - SPORTS AND PHYSICAL ACTIVITY | | Unaffected by sex | AFF 3.1 | | | Chi$^2$ | ns |
| - APPRECIATE NATURE | | Unaffected by sex | AFF 3.1 | | | Chi$^2$ | ns |
| - BEAUTY, ART, MUSIC | | Unaffected by sex | AFF 3.1 | | | Chi$^2$ | ns |
| - SELF-CONTROL | | Unaffected by sex | AFF 3.1 | | | Chi$^2$ | ns |
| - OPTIMISM (looking on the bright, positive side of living | | Unaffected by sex | AFF 3.1 | | + | Chi$^2$ | 05 |

| | | | | | | | | |
|---|---|---|---|---|---|---|---|---|
| - PESSIMISM | | Unaffected by sex | AFF 3.1 | | | $Chi^2$ | ns | | |
| - BEING GENUINE (being natural; not fake) | | Unaffected by sex | AFF 3.1 | | | $Chi^2$ | ns | | |
| - TRUTHFULNESS, HONESTY | | Unaffected by sex | AFF 3.1 | | | $Chi^2$ | ns | | |
| - BEING INDIVIDUALISTIC | | Unaffected by sex | AFF 3.1 | | - | $Chi^2$ | ns | | |
| - INNER DIRECTED (doesn't let others influence decisions; think for own self; self-determined) | | Unaffected by sex | AFF 3.1 | | - | $Chi^2$ | 05 | | |
| - OTHER DIRECTED (considers others's opinions and reactions in making decisions; pleases others | | Unaffected by sex | AFF 3.1 | | | $Chi^2$ | ns | | |
| - CONFORMITY IN SOCIETY | | Unaffected by sex | AFF 3.1 | | | $Chi^2$ | ns | | |
| - SELF-CONFIDENCE, BELIEF IN SELF | | Unaffected by sex | AFF 3.1 | | | $Chi^2$ | ns | | |
| - SELF-LOVE, PRIDE, SELF-RESPECT | | Unaffected by sex | AFF 3.1 | | | $Chi^2$ | ns | | |
| - BEING CONSERVATIVE | | Unaffected by sex | AFF 3.1 | | | $Chi^2$ | ns | | |
| - BEING LIBERAL | | Unaffected by sex | AFF 3.1 | | | $Chi^2$ | ns | | |
| - RESPECTING AUTHORITY; OBEDIENCE (to God, law, authority) | | Unaffected by sex | AFF 3.1 | | | $Chi^2$ | ns | | |
| - REALISTIC | | Unaffected by sex | AFF 3.1 | | | $Chi^2$ | ns | | |
| - TRUST (in self and others) | | Unaffected by sex | AFF 3.1 | | | $Chi^2$ | ns | | |
| - FREEDOM (of choice and action) | | Unaffected by sex | AFF 3.1 | | - | $Chi^2$ | ns | | |
| - FAIRNESS, JUSTICE | | Unaffected by sex | AFF 3.1 | | - | $Chi^2$ | 05 | | |
| - FLEXIBILITY (openness to change) | | Unaffected by sex | AFF 3.1 | | | $Chi^2$ | ns | | |
| - THANKFULNESS, BEING GRATEFUL | | Unaffected by sex | AFF 3.1 | | | $Chi^2$ | ns | | |
| - SOLITUDE, WITHDRAWAL FROM OTHERS | | Unaffected by sex | AFF 3.1 | | - | $Chi^2$ | ns | | |
| - OPEN-MINDEDNESS | | Unaffected by sex | AFF 3.1 | | | $Chi^2$ | ns | | |
| - EQUALITY | | Unaffected by sex | AFF 3.1 | | | $Chi^2$ | ns | | |
| PERSONAL VALUES | Combination scores of frequently mentioned values on the basis of content analysis of each S's written philosophy of life (see two pages back) | See 2 pages back | | | | | | Undergraduate university students, California, U.S.A.<br>Non-probability chunk sample<br>N: 86, date: November - December, 1971 | FORDY 72<br>p. 196-198 |
| - HAPPINESS | Combination score of:<br>- happiness;<br>- enjoyment of life;<br>- inner peace;<br>- living life to its fullest;<br>- love of life;<br>- fun, excitement, good times | Unaffected by sex | AFF 3.1 | | + | $Chi^2$ | 01 | | |
| - SOCIAL VALUES | Combination score of all values relating to social interests (N = 12) | Significant (01) among females only | AFF 3.1 | | + | $Chi^2$ | 01 | | |
| - STRIVING VALUES | Combination score of all values relating to striving, accomplishment, goal seeking | Unaffected by sex | AFF 3.1 | | | $Chi^2$ | ns | | |

(to be continued on next page)

| | | | | | | | | | |
|---|---|---|---|---|---|---|---|---|---|
| - SELF VALUES | Combination score of all values of self-confidence, self-esteem, etc. | Unaffected by sex | AFF 3.1 | | | $Chi^2$ | ns | | |
| - LEARNING VALUES | Combination score of all educational and learning values | Unaffected by sex | AFF 3.1 | | | $Chi^2$ | ns | | |
| <u>VALUE DIMENSIONS:</u> | Study of Values Inventory (see Allport et al., 1951).<br>Six standardized scores were developed from Ss' responses to a number of value-related questions and choice procedures contained in the inventory. | Since not many differences appeared between the correlations with the first and with the second happiness measure, only correlations with the first instrument are presented here.<br>See also remarks in excerpt (Part II). | | | | | | Undergraduate university students, California, U.S.A.<br>Non-probability chunk sample<br>N: 86, date: November - December, 1971 | FORDY 72<br>p. 154/155 |
| - THEORETICAL (dominant interest in the discovery of truth, empirical, critical, rational, 'intellectual' approach) | | males : r = -.17 (ns)<br>females: r = -.21 (ns) | AFF 3.1 | $r_{pm}$ | -.22 | | 05 | | |
| - ECONOMIC (emphazising useful and practical values; 'average American businessman' | | males : r = -.01 (ns)<br>females: r = -.06 (ns) | AFF 3.1 | $r_{pm}$ | -.06 | | ns | | |
| - AESTHETIC (placing the highest values on form and harmony; judging and enjoying each unique experience by its grace, symmetry, or fitness) | | males : r = +.16 (ns)<br>females: r = -.02 (ns) | AFF 3.1 | $r_{pm}$ | +.07 | | ns | | |
| - SOCIAL (altruism, philantropy) | | males : r = +.08 (ns)<br>females: r = -.06 (ns) | AFF 3.1 | $r_{pm}$ | +.00 | | ns | | |
| - POLITICAL (primarily interested in personal power, influence, and renown) | | males : r = -.10 (ns)<br>females: r = -.12 (ns) | AFF 3.1 | $r_{pm}$ | -.14 | | ns | | |
| - RELIGIOUS (mystical, concerned with unity of all experience, and seeking to comprehend the cosmos as a whole) | | males : r = -.01 (ns)<br>females: r = +.36 (01) | AFF 3.1 | $r_{pm}$ | +.26 | | 01 | | |
| <u>WAYS TO LIVE:</u> | 13-item inventory (Morris Ways to Live Survey; see Morris, 1956)<br>Each way to live was rated on a 7-point important - unimportant scale (Likert Type) (absolute measure)<br>The 13 ways to live were also ranked in the order of preference by each Ss | Since not many differences appeared between the correlations with the first and with the second happiness measure, only correlations with the first instrument are presented here.<br>Correlations obtained from the absolute measure are presented first; those from the ranking procedure second.<br>See also remarks in excerpt (Part II).<br>males / females | | | | | | See above | FORDY 72<br>p. 184-187 |
| - PRESERVE THE BEST THAT MAN HAS ATTAINED | | abs.: r = +.06 (ns) -.08 (ns)<br>rel.: r = +.06 (ns) -.18 (ns) | AFF 3.1 | $r_{pm}$ | -.03<br>-.09 | | ns<br>ns | | |
| - CULTIVATE INDEPENDENCE OF PERSONS AND THINGS | | abs.: r = -.11 (ns) -.19 (ns)<br>rel.: r = +.03 (ns) -.21 (ns) | AFF 3.1 | $r_{pm}$ | -.25<br>-.12 | | 05<br>ns | | |
| - SHOW SYMPATHETIC CONCERN FOR OTHERS | | abs.: r = -.15 (ns) +.16 (ns)<br>rel.: r = -.07 (ns) +.31 (05) | AFF 3.1 | $r_{pm}$ | +.02<br>+.16 | | ns<br>ns | | |

| | | | | | | | | | |
|---|---|---|---|---|---|---|---|---|---|
| | | males / females | | | | | | | |
| - EXPERIENCE FESTIVITY AND SOLITUDE IN ALTERNATION | | abs.: r = -.00 (ns) / -.19 (ns)<br>rel.: r = +.00 (ns) / -.01 (ns) | AFF 3.1 | $r_{pm}$ | -.17<br>-.00 | | ns<br>ns | | |
| - ACT AND ENJOY LIFE THROUGH GROUP PARTICIPATION | | abs.: r = -.13 (ns) / +.22 (ns)<br>rel.: r = +.00 (ns) / +.20 (ns) | AFF 3.1 | $r_{pm}$ | +.10<br>+.11 | | ns<br>ns | | |
| - CONSTANTLY MASTER CHANGING CONDITIONS | | abs.: r = -.16 (ns) / -.20 (ns)<br>rel.: r = -.13 (ns) / -.18 (ns) | AFF 3.1 | $r_{pm}$ | -.14<br>+.16 | | 05<br>ns | | |
| - INTEGRATE ACTION, ENJOYMENT, AND CONTEMPLATION | | abs.: r = +.12 (ns) / -.24 (ns)<br>rel.: r = +.21 (ns) / +.00 (ns) | AFF 3.1 | $r_{p,}$ | -.01<br>+.12 | | ns<br>ns | | |
| - LIVE WITH WHOLESOME, CAREFREE ENJOYMENT | | abs.: r = +.01 (ns) / -.14 (ns)<br>rel.: r = +.00 (ns) / -.10 (ns) | AFF 3.1 | $r_{pm}$ | -.00<br>-.03 | | ns<br>ns | | |
| - WAIT IN QUIET RECEPTIVITY | | abs.: r = -.19 (ns) / +.00 (ns)<br>rel.: r = -.01 (ns) / +.15 (ns) | AFF 3.1 | $r_{pm}$ | -.01<br>+.01 | | ns<br>ns | | |
| - CONTROL IN SELF STOICALLY | | abs.: r = -.37 (05) / -.15 (ns)<br>rel.: r = -.35 (05) / +.01 (ns) | AFF 3.1 | $r_{pm}$ | -.29<br>-.12 | | 01<br>ns | | |
| - MEDITATE ON THE INNER LIFE | | abs.: r = -.01 (ns) / -.26 (10)<br>rel.: r = -.08 (ns) / -.25 (10) | AFF 3.1 | $r_{pm}$ | -.22<br>-.18 | | 05<br>10 | | |
| - CHANGE ADVENTURESOME DEEDS | | abs.: r = +.13 (ns) / -.01 (ns)<br>rel.: r = +.24 (ns) / +.01 (ns) | AFF 3.1 | $r_{pm}$ | +.00<br>+.15 | | ns<br>ns | | |
| - OBEY THE COSMIC PURPOSES | | abs.: r = +.12 (ns) / +.32 (05)<br>rel.: r = +.13 (ns) / +.32 (05) | AFF 3.1 | $r_{pm}$ | +.26<br>+.26 | | 05<br>05 | | |
| LAW AND ORDER ATTITUDE | 4-item index containing children need law and order; one should feel love and respect for one's parents; there are just strong and weak people (items from a shortened F-scale; see Weima, 1963) | | HAPP 1.1 | G' | +.21 | Gt' | 05 | Adults, Utrecht, The Netherlands<br>Probability sample stratified by age<br>N: 300, date: autumn, 1967 | MOSER 69<br>p. 39 |
| DISSATISFACTION WITH PRESENT SOCIO-POLITICAL ORDER | 5-item index indicating anomy and powerlessness: we need less laws and institutions and more courageous leaders; most politicians are in-capabale; people should talk less and live a more natural and active way of life (items from a shortened F-scale; see Weima, 1963) | | HAPP 1.1 | G' | +.13 | Gt' | ns | See above | MOSER 69<br>p. 40 |
| DISAGREEMENT WITH THE PROTESTANT ETHIC | 4-item index containing agree/disagree statements: when the workday is finished a person should forget his job and enjoy himself; the principal purpose of a man's job is to provide him with the means for enjoying his free time; whenever possible a person should relax and accept life as it is, rather than always striving for unreachable goals; people who 'do things the easy way' are the smart ones (non-Protestant Ethic score) | students : r = -.09 (ns)<br>low skill workers: r = -.06 (ns) | HAPP 2.1 | r | - | $Chi^2$ | ns | Airmen, U.S.A.F., U.S.A.<br>Non-probability chunk sample<br>N: 420, date: — | BLOOD 69<br>p. 457 |
| AGREEMENT WITH THE PROTESTANT ETHIC | 4-item index containing agree/disagree statements: hard work makes a man a better person; wasting time is as bad as wasting money; a good indication of a man's worth is how well he does his job; it is better to have a job with a lot of responsibility than one with little responsibility (pro-Protestant Ethic score) | students : r = +.08 (ns)<br>low skill workers: r = +.17 (01) | HAPP 2.1 | r | + | $Chi^2$ | | See above | BLOOD 69<br>p. 457 |

| | | | | | | | | | |
|---|---|---|---|---|---|---|---|---|---|
| ACCEPTANCE OF SOCIAL VALUES | 33-item index of closed questions on honesty (7 items), kindness (4 items), reciprocity (7 items), self-control (5 items), social responsibility (4 items), and social skills (6 items) | | COMP 1.2 | $r_{pm}$ | -.26 | | 001 | Public high school boys, U.S.A.<br>Probability multi-stage sample<br>N: 2213 in 1966, 1886 in 1968 and 1799 in 1969<br>date: fall 1966, spring 1968 and spring 1969 | BACHM 67/70<br>p. 243 |
| TENDENCY TO DO KINDNESSESS ON PRINCIPLE | Trained peer rating on a 7-point scale on the basis of observation | | AFF 5.2 | $r_{pm}$ | +.19 | | | Male students, England<br>Non-probability chunk sample<br>N: 194, date: 1912 - 1913 | WEBB 15<br>p. 26 |

## V 1.2 - VALUE SIMILARITY

| | | | | | | | | | |
|---|---|---|---|---|---|---|---|---|---|
| VALUE SIMILARITY WITH SOCIAL NETWORK MEMBERS | 3-item index of closed questions on whether the respondent feels that his/her ideals most nearly approach her ideals of 'the right way', feels she has a great many interests in common with him/her, generally shares the same philosophy of life with him/her<br>The questions were answered for each social network member | Those adults one sees at least once a month and who are 'important persons' in one's life were considered as social network members<br>Positive among married females : r = +.34 (002)<br>Negative among unmarried females: r = -.19 (ns) | HAPP 1.1 | r | + | | | Females from the Seattle-Washington area, U.S.A.<br>Non-probability chunk sample<br>N: 153, date: — | BRIM 74<br>p. 437 |
| VALUE SIMILARITY WITH HUSBAND | 3-item index (see above), scored for the husband | Computed for married females only. | HAPP 1.1 | r | +.42 | | 002 | See above | BRIM 74<br>p. 437 |

## V 1.3 - VARIOUS FACTORS CONCERNING VALUES

see also 'Morality' (P 1.7)

| | | | | | | | | | |
|---|---|---|---|---|---|---|---|---|---|
| BEING INTERESTED IN PHILOSOPHY OF LIFE | Closed question | college students only<br>L-shaped curve: stronger positive relationship among unhappier students | COMP 4.1 | | + | | | Students, U.S.A.<br>Non-probability chunk sample<br>N: 1651, date: — | SYMON 37<br>p. 292 |
| HAVING PROBLEMS WITH PHILOSOPHY OF LIFE | Closed question | | COMP 4.1 | | | | ns | See above | SYMON 37<br>p. 292 |
| BEING INTERESTED IN PERSONAL AND MORAL QUALITIES | Closed question | | COMP 4.1 | | | | ns | See above | SYMON 37<br>p. 292 |
| HAVING PROBLEMS WITH PERSONAL AND MORAL QUALITIES | Closed question | college students only<br>L-shaped curve: significant positive relationship among happier students only | COMP 4.1 | | + | | | See above | SYMON 37<br>p. 292 |

# W 1 WAR

W 1.1 Confrontation with war

W 1.2 Thinking about war

## W 1.1 - CONFRONTATION WITH WAR

| | | | | | | | | | |
|---|---|---|---|---|---|---|---|---|---|
| CONFRONTATION WITH WAR | 5-point scale: students from Switzerland (not confronted with war) / U.S.A. / England / W.Germany - Goettingen / W.Germany - W.Berlin (most directly confronted with war) | | HAPP 1.2 | G' | -.36 | Gt' | 01 | Female college students from England, Switzerland, W. Germany and the U.S.A.<br>Wall (1948) Non-probability chunk sample<br>N: 493, date: 1949 - 1951 | BARSC 51<br>p. 179 |
| HAVING CONCENTRATION CAMP EXPERIENCE | No concentration camp experience vs having been in a Nazi concentration camp during World War II | | HAPP 3.1 | G' | -.36 | Gt' | 01 | Females in the age of 45 - 54, Israel<br>Probability sample<br>N: 287, date: 1968 | ANTON 71<br>p. 188 |

## W 1.2 - THINKING ABOUT WAR

| | | | | | | | | | |
|---|---|---|---|---|---|---|---|---|---|
| FEAR OF WAR | Item mentioned in open-ended question on fears and worries for one's personal future and/or for the future of one's country | See also 'Specific Worries and Fears' (Part III, P 5.2.2)<br>The mean happiness rating for those who express fear of war is 5.1 and for those who do not express fear of war 4.8 (ns)<br>In each of the separate countries the differences were non-significant too. | HAPP 3.1 | DM | + | | ns | Adult population of 5 Westernized countries, 3 underdeveloped giants, 2 countries in the Middle East, 3 Caribbean nations and the Philippines<br>Representative samples<br>N: 18653, date: ± 1960 | CANTR 65/1<br>p. 264 |
| THINKING OFTEN ABOUT THE ATOM-BOMB OR FALLOUT | Closed question: not at all / sometimes / often; during last week | Lower among those of high S.E.S. : G' = -.04 (ns)<br>Stronger among those of low S.E.S.: G' = -.26 (05)<br>Gammas computed on the basis of proportions 'often' answers | HAPP 1.1 | G' | - | Gt' | | Inhabitants of 4 small communities, Illinois, U.S.A.<br>Probability multi-stage samples<br>N: 2006, date: March, 1962 | BRADB 65/1<br>p. 54 |

# W 2 WORK



## W 2.1 - HAVING WORK

see also 'Retirement' (R 2)

| | | | | | | | | | |
|---|---|---|---|---|---|---|---|---|---|
| NON-LABOR | | Gamma is based on the difference in happiness between the 'non-labor' category and the entire population (including 'non-labor'). Housewives were not considered as 'non-labor'. See also under 'Type of Work' (Part III, W 2.2). | HAPP 3.1 | G' | +.04 | Gt' | ns | Adult population of 5 Westernized nations, 3 underdeveloped giants, 2 countries in the Middle East, 3 Caribbean nations and the Philippines<br>Representative samples<br>N: 19653, date: ± 1960 | CANTR 65/1<br>p. 259 |
| NON-LABOR | | The mean happiness score of the 'non-labor' was compared with the mean score of the entire population (including the 'non-labor'). Housewives probably were considered as 'non-labor' here. See also under 'Type of Work' (Part III, W 2.2). | HAPP 3.1 | DM | -0.3 | | | National adult population, U.S.A.<br>Probability sample<br>N: 1549, date: ± 1960 | CANTR 65/1<br>p. 375 |
| NON-LABOR FORCE | | The mean score on perceived realization of aspirations of the 'non-labor' was compared with the mean score of the entire population. See also under 'Type of Work' (Part III, W 2.2). | HAPP 3.1 | DM | ± 0 | | | Non-institutionalized national adult population, U.S.A.<br>Multi-stage probability sample, stratified by size of locality<br>N: 1588, date: January, 1971 (+ 1964) | CANTR 71<br>p. 66 |
| EMPLOYMENT STATUS: | | The Gammas are based on a comparison of those reporting 'not too happy' in the occupational group mentioned and in the entire population. | | | | | | Inhabitants of 4 small communities, Illinois, U.S.A.<br>Probability multi-stage samples<br>N: 2006, date: March, 1962 | BRADB 65/1<br>p. 14 |
| - SELF-EMPLOYED | | Stronger among males: G' = +.33 (05)<br>Lower among females : G' = +.02 (ns) | HAPP 1.1 | G' | + | Gt' | | | |
| - EMPLOYED | | males : G' = +.20 (01)<br>females: G' = +.20 (ns) | HAPP 1.1 | G' | + | Gt' | | | |
| - PART-TIME EMPLOYED | | Computed for females only: G' = +.07 (ns) | HAPP 1.1 | G' | + | Gt' | ns | | |
| - UNEMPLOYED | | Stronger among males: G' = -.41 (01)<br>Lower among females : G' = -.28 (ns) | HAPP 1.1 | G' | - | Gt' | | | |
| - RETIRED | | males : G' = -.29 (01)<br>females: G' = -.27 (05) | HAPP 1.1 | G' | - | Gt' | | | |
| - NOT IN LABOR FORCE | Full-time housewives; disabled; etc. | Stronger among males: G' = -.28 (ns)<br>Not among females : G' = +.00 (ns) | HAPP 1.1 | G' | - | Gt' | ns | | |
| EMPLOYED STATUS AS CHIEF WAGE EARNER | Unemployed vs employed chief wage earner | Stronger among females : $\bar{DR}$ = +.21 (05) (primarily single women)<br>Lower among males : $\bar{DR}$ = +.13 (05)<br>(to be continued on next page) | AFF 2.3 | $\bar{DR}$ | +.15 | BCI | 05 | Adults, urban areas, U.S.A.<br>Probability area samples<br>N: 2787, date: January, 1963 - January, 1964 | BRADB 69<br>p. 184-186 |

| | | | | | | | | | |
|---|---|---|---|---|---|---|---|---|---|
| | | Index of Positive Affects: $D\bar{R}$ = +.13 (05)<br>Unaffected by sex<br>Index of Negative Affects: $D\bar{R}$ = -.12 (05)<br>Stronger among females : $D\bar{R}$ = -.19 (05)<br>Lower among males : $D\bar{R}$ = -.10 (ns)<br><br>Stronger among males: G' = +.66<br>Lower among females : G' = +.57 | HAPP 1.1 | G' | + | | | | |
| WIFE OF EMPLOYED CHIEF WAGE EARNER | Wife of unemployed vs employed wage earner | This analysis concerns only women who are not chief wage earner.<br>Index of Positive Affects: $D\bar{R}$ = +.19 (05)<br>Index of Negative Affects: $D\bar{R}$ = +.02 (ns) | AFF 2.3<br>HAPP 1.1 | $D\bar{R}$<br>G | +.10<br>+.32 | BCI | 05 | Adults, urban areas, U.S.A.<br>(See last page) | BRADB 69<br>p. 184-186 |
| EMPLOYED STATUS | Unemployed vs employed | Computed for married respondents only.<br>Stronger among males : $D\bar{R}$ = +.15 (05)<br>with employed wife : $D\bar{R}$ = +.11 (ns)<br>with unemployed wife : $D\bar{R}$ = +.16 (05)<br>Lower among females : $D\bar{R}$ = +.08 (05)<br>with employed husband : $D\bar{R}$ = +.08 (05)<br>with unemployed husband: $D\bar{R}$ = -.05 (ns)<br><br>Index of Positive Affects : $D\bar{R}$ = +.02 (ns)<br>males with employed wife : $D\bar{R}$ = +.15 (ns)<br>males with unemployed wife : $D\bar{R}$ = +.17 (05)<br>females with employed husband : $D\bar{R}$ = +.04 (ns)<br>females with unemployed husband: $D\bar{R}$ = +.03 (ns)<br>Index of Negative Affects : $D\bar{R}$ = -.10 (05)<br>males with employed wife : $D\bar{R}$ = -.09 (ns)<br>males with unemployed wife : $D\bar{R}$ = -.11 (ns)<br>females with employed husband : $D\bar{R}$ = -.09 (05)<br>females with unemployed husband: $D\bar{R}$ = +.11 (ns) | AFF 2.3 | $D\bar{R}$ | +.08 | BCI | 05 | See above | BRADB 69<br>p. 187 |
| EMPLOYED STATUS OF SPOUSE | Ss with unemployed vs employed spouse | Computed for married respondents only.<br>Lower among males : $D\bar{R}$ = +.04 (ns)<br>employed males : $D\bar{R}$ = +.03 (ns)<br>unemployed males : $D\bar{R}$ = +.08 (ns)<br>Stronger among females: $D\bar{R}$ = +.10 (05)<br>employed females : $D\bar{R}$ = +.18 (05)<br>unemployed females : $D\bar{R}$ = +.05 (ns)<br><br>Index of Positive Affects: $D\bar{R}$ = +.06 (05)<br>employed males : $D\bar{R}$ = +.04 (ns)<br>unemployed males : $D\bar{R}$ = +.06 (ns)<br>employed females : $D\bar{R}$ = +.19 (05)<br>unemployed females : $D\bar{R}$ = +.18 (05)<br>Index of Negative Affects: $D\bar{R}$ = +.06 (05)<br>employed males : $D\bar{R}$ = .00 (ns)<br>unemployed males : $D\bar{R}$ = -.02 (ns)<br>employed females : $D\bar{R}$ = -.11 (ns)<br>unemployed females : $D\bar{R}$ = +.09 (ns) | AFF 2.3 | $D\bar{R}$ | +.03 | BCI | ns | See above | BRADB 69<br>p. 187 |
| GETTING EMPLOYED | Staying unemployed vs changing from unemployment to employment | Computed for chief wage earners only.<br>Analysis on the basis of a comparison between data from January 1963 (wave 1) and October 1963(wave 3).<br><br>Index of Positive Affects: $D\bar{R}$ = -.01<br>Index of Negative Affects: $D\bar{R}$ = -.04 | AFF 2.3 | $D\bar{R}$ | +.05 | | | See above | BRADB 69<br>p. 189 |
| FALLING UNEMPLOYED | Staying employed vs changing from employment to unemployment | See above<br><br>Index of Positive Affects: $D\bar{R}$ = -.19<br>Index of Negative Affects: $D\bar{R}$ = -.03 | AFF 2.3 | $D\bar{R}$ | -.13 | | | See above | BRADB 69<br>p. 189 |

| | | | | | | | | | |
|---|---|---|---|---|---|---|---|---|---|
| EMPLOYED STATUS | Not working vs working full- or part-time | in 1972:<br>Affect Balance : r = +.11 (ns)<br>Index of Positive Affects: r = +.14 (001)<br>Index of Negative Affects: r = -.02 (ns)<br>in 1973:<br>Affect Balance : r = +.17 (001)<br>Index of Positive Affects: r = +.18 (001)<br>Index of Negative Affects: r = -.08 (01)<br>Unaffected by sex | AFF 2.3 | r | + | | | Adults, Los Angeles County, U.S.A.<br>Multi-stage probability samples of households<br>N: 1078 in 1972 and 1008 in 1973, date: 1972 and 1973 | CHERL 75<br>p. 197 |
| EMPLOYED STATUS | Not having a job or business vs having one | Unaffected by sex | HAPP 3.1 | r | +.06 | | | People of 46 and over, Duke, U.S.A.<br>Probability, systematic random sample, stratified by age,sex<br>N: 502, date: 1968 | PALMO 72<br>p. 70 |
| EMPLOYED STATUS | Not in labor force / unemployed / employed | males : G = +.18<br>females: G = +.15 | HAPP 1.1 | G | + | | | Adults, Metro Manila, Philippines<br>Probability area sample<br>N: 941, date: January - April, 1972 | BULAT 73<br>p. 234-235 |
| | | Lower among males : G = +.10<br>Stronger among females: G = +.22 | HAPP 3.1 | G | + | | | | |
| | | Index of Positive Affects:<br>males : G = +.03<br>females: G = +.03<br>Index of Negative Affects:<br>males : G = -.06<br>females: G = -.13 | AFF 2.3 | G | + | | | | |

FEMALES:

| | | | | | | | | | |
|---|---|---|---|---|---|---|---|---|---|
| BEING A HOUSEWIFE (if no head of house-hold) | | Gamma is based on the difference in happiness between the housewives and the entire population (including the housewives).<br>See also under 'Type of Work' (Part III, W 2.2). | HAPP 3.1 | G' | -.06 | Gt' | ns | Adult population of 5 westernized nations, 3 underdeveloped giants, 2 countries in the Middle East, 3 Caribbean nations & The Philippines<br>Representative sample<br>N: 18653, date: ± 1960 | CANTR 65/1<br>p. 259 |
| BEING A HOUSEWIFE | | Gamma is based on the difference in happiness between the housewives and the entire population (including the housewives)<br>See also under 'Type of Work' (Part III, W 2.2) | HAPP 2.1 | G' | -.03 | | | National adult population, U.S.A.<br>Probability sample proportionally stratified by sex, age, occupation, S.E.S. and education<br>N: 1015, date: 1948 - 1949 | BUCHA 53<br>p. 214 |
| BEING A HOUSEWIFE | | See above | HAPP 2.1 | G' | +.07 | | | National adult population, Mexico<br>Probability sample proportionally stratified by sex, age, occupation, S.E.S. and education<br>N: 1752, date: 1948 - 1949 | BUCHA 53<br>p. 189 |
| BEING A HOUSEWIFE | | See above | HAPP 2.1 | G' | -.12 | | | National adult population, Great Britain<br>Probability sample proportionally stratified by sex, age, occupation, S.E.S. and education<br>N: 1195, date: 1948 - 1949 | BUCHA 53<br>p. 138 |
| BEING A HOUSEWIFE | | See above | HAPP 2.1 | G' | -.06 | | | National adult population, France<br>Probability sample proportionally stratified by sex, age, occupation, S.E.S. and education<br>N: 1000, date: 1948 - 1949 | BUCHA 53<br>p. 148 |
| BEING A HOUSEWIFE | | See above | HAPP 2.1 | G' | -.07 | | | National adult population, W. Germany<br>Probability sample proportionally stratified by sex, age, occupation, S.E.S. and education<br>N: 3371, date: 1948 - 1949 | BUCHA 53<br>p. 157 |

| | | | | | | | | | |
|---|---|---|---|---|---|---|---|---|---|
| BEING A HOUSEWIFE | | Gamma is based on the difference in happiness between the housewives and the entire population (including the housewives)<br>See also under 'Type of Work' (Part III, W 2.2) | HAPP 2.1 | G' | +.08 | | | National adult population, Italy<br>Probability sample proportionally stratified by sex, age, occupation, S.E.S. and education<br>N: 1078, date: 1948 - 1949 | BUCHA 53<br>p. 176 |
| BEING A HOUSEWIFE | | See above | HAPP 2.1 | G' | +.06 | | | National adult population, Norway<br>Probability sample proportionally stratified by sex, age, occupation, S.E.S. and education<br>N: 1030, date: 1948 - 1949 | BUCHA 53<br>p. 206 |
| BEING A HOUSEWIFE | | See above | HAPP 2.1 | G' | -.09 | | | National adult population, Australia<br>Probability sample proportionally stratified by sex, age, occupation, S.E.S. and education<br>N: 945, date: 1948 - 1949 | BUCHA 53<br>p. 131 |
| BEING A HOUSEWIFE | | The mean happiness score of the housewives was compared with the mean happiness score of the entire population (including the housewives).<br>See also under 'Type of Work' (Part III, W 2.2). | HAPP 3.1 | DM | $\pm$ 0 | | | National adult population, Yugoslavia<br>Probability sample<br>N: 1523, date: $\pm$ 1960 | CANTR 65/1<br>p. 377 |
| EMPLOYED STATUS | Housewife / part-time work / full-time work | Computed for females only.<br>Unaffected by marital status<br>Among females with 12 or fewer years of education: C = +.13 (05)<br>Among females with 13 or more years of education: C = +.19 (ns)<br>The role of full-time housewife appears to be slightly associated with both low and high degrees of happiness. | HAPP 1.1 | C | +.11 | $Chi^2$ | ns | Non-institutionalized adults, U.S.A.<br>National probability sample<br>N: 1500, date: spring, 1973 | SPREI 75<br>p. 243 |
| BEING A HOUSEWIFE | Respondents (males and females) employed outside the house vs housewives | | AFF 1.1 | $r_{pm}$ | -.02 | | ns | Families of hourly workers and salaried employees, U.S.A.<br>Samples from two large industrial firms<br>N: 712, date: summer, 1973 | TESSL 75<br>p. 103 |
| EMPLOYED STATUS | non-employed vs employed | Not among husband-present females<br>Positive among husband-absent females | HAPP 1.1 | DM | + | | | Low-income women with children, New York State, U.S.A.<br>Probability systematic random sample, stratified by employed status and marital status<br>N: 1325, date: — | BENDO 74<br>p. 75 |
| BEING EMPLOYED OUTSIDE THE HOUSE AT PAID TASKS | | Reported for married females only.<br>64% of the dissatisfied and 76% of the satisfied women have paid work | HAPP 2.1 | D% | + | | s | Middle-age, middle class married couples, U.S.A.<br>Non-probability accidental sample of couples<br>N: 416, date: 1952 - 1953 | ROSE 55<br>p. 17 |
| EMPLOYED STATUS | non-employed vs employed | Computed for females only.<br>Gamma based on proportion 'very satisfied' answers<br>Stronger among females with husbands of high S.E.S.<br>Slightly reversed among females with husbands of low S.E.S. | HAPP 2.1 | G' | -.02 | Gt' | ns | Inhabitants of Helsinki, Finland<br>Probability sample<br>N: 442, date: spring - summer, 1966 | HAAVI 71<br>p. 595 |

## SPECIAL GROUPS:

| Variable | Measure | Remarks | Happiness | Stat. | Value | Test | Sig. | Population / sample | Source |
|---|---|---|---|---|---|---|---|---|---|
| HOURS SPENT ON WORK FOR PAY | Direct question on number of hours per week during the school year | Among those of lower social class : G = +.01<br>Among those of middle and upper class: G = -.05 | HAPP 1.1 | G<br>V | -.02<br>.03 | $Chi^2$ | ns | Juniors and seniors attending public high schools in New York State, U.S.A.<br>Probability cluster sample of 10 public high schools<br>N: sample A: 1682, sample B: 1664, sample C: 1678<br>date: 1960 | BRENN 70<br>p. 108/182/326 |
| | | Among those of lower social class : G = +.04<br>Among those of medium and upper class: G = -.05 | AFF 1.1 | G<br>V | -.03<br>.03 | $Chi^2$ | ns | | |
| HAVING OUTSIDE WORK (for board, room, pay) | Non-working vs working | L-shaped curve: positive relationship among happier females only. | COMP 2.2 | | + | | ns | Female college students, New York, U.S.A.<br>Type of construction unclear<br>N: 238, date: — | WASHB 41<br>p. 283 |
| HAVING GAINFUL EMPLOYMENT | Absence vs presence of gainful employment | The relationship disappears when controlled for self-perceived health. | COMP 1.1 | $r_{pm}$ | +.36 | | 01 | White males who experienced a first heart attack, Durham, North Carolina, U.S.A.<br>Non-probability quota sample<br>N: 56, date: 1970 | GARRI 73<br>p. 201 |
| EMPLOYED STATUS | Unemployed vs employed | | HAPP 1.1 | $t_{k_c}$ | +.25 | | 001 | Non-hospitalized schizophrenic males, Monroe County, New York, U.S.A.<br>Probability sample, drawn from the Monroe County psychiatric case register<br>N: 178, date: 1964 - 1965 | ALEXA 68<br>p. 175 |
| | | Index of Positive Affects: $t_k$ = +.19 (001)<br>Index of Negative Affects: $t_k$ = -.02 (ns) | AFF 2.3 | $t_{k_c}$ | + | | | | |
| EMPLOYMENT HISTORY | Percentage of time employed during last five years, corrected for time in hospital<br>0 - 49% / 50 - 89% / 90 - 100% | | HAPP 1.1 | $t_{k_c}$ | +.21<br>+.48 | | 001 | See above | ALEXA 68<br>p. 173-174 |
| | | Index of Positive Affects: $t_k$ = +.25 (001)<br>Index of Negative Affects: $t_k$ = -.07 (05) | AFF 2.3 | $t_{k_c}$ | + | | | | |
| EMPLOYED STATUS | Unemployed vs employed | | HAPP 2.1 | G' | +.46 | Gt' | 05 | Aged chronically-ill patients, U.S.A.<br>Probability sample<br>N: 167, date: 1959 | HENLE 67<br>p. 69 |

## W 2.2 - TYPE OF WORK

see also 'Household Work' (H 4.2)

| Variable | Measure | Remarks | Happiness | Stat. | Value | Test | Sig. | Population / sample | Source |
|---|---|---|---|---|---|---|---|---|---|
| OCCUPATION: | | Gammas are based on a comparison of the happiness ratings of the occupational group mentioned and the happiness of the entire population. | | | | | | Adult population of 5 westernized nations, 3 underdeveloped giants, 2 countries in the Middle East, 3 Caribbean nations and the Philippines,<br>Representative samples<br>N: 18653, date: ± 1960 | CANTR 65/1<br>p. 259 |
| - PROFESSIONALS, BUSINESSMEN, TECHNICIANS | | | HAPP 3.1 | G' | +.55 | Gt' | 01 | | |
| - MANAGERS, OFFICIALS | | | HAPP 3.1 | G' | +.50 | Gt' | 01 | | |
| - WHITE COLLAR WORKERS | | | HAPP 3.1 | G' | +.35 | Gt' | 01 | | |
| - SKILLED WORKERS | | | HAPP 3.1 | G' | +.09 | Gt' | ns | | |
| - UNSKILLED WORKERS | | | HAPP 3.1 | G' | -.10 | Gt' | 01 | | |
| - FARMERS | | | HAPP 3.1 | G' | -.12 | Gt' | 01 | | |
| - NON-LABOR | | | HAPP 3.1 | G' | +.04 | Gt' | ns | | |
| - HOUSEWIVES (if no head of the house - hold) | | | HAPP 3.1 | G' | -.06 | Gt' | ns | | |

| | | | | | | | |
|---|---|---|---|---|---|---|---|
| OCCUPATION: | Gammas are based on a comparison of the happiness ratings of the occupational group mentioned and the happiness of the entire population. | | | | | National adult population, U.S.A.<br>Probability sample proportionally stratified by sex, age, occupation, S.E.S. and education<br>N: 1015, date: 1948 - 1949 | BUCHA 53<br>p. 214 |
| - PROFESSIONAL WORKERS | | HAPP 2.1 | G' | +.09 | | | |
| - OWNERS OF BUSINESS AND LARGE, MEDIUM SHOPS | | HAPP 2.1 | G' | +.28 | | | |
| - WORKERS ON OWN ACCOUNT, OWNERS OF SMALL SHOPS | | HAPP 2.1 | G' | +.02 | | | |
| - SALARIED-MANAGERIAL AND TOP-GRADE CLERICAL WORKERS | | HAPP 2.1 | G' | +.11 | | | |
| - OTHER CLERICAL WORKERS, SHOP-ASSISTENTS, etc. | | HAPP 2.1 | G' | -.03 | | | |
| - MANUAL WORKERS | | HAPP 2.1 | G' | -.10 | | | |
| - FARM WORKERS, FISHERMEN, GARDENERS | | HAPP 2.1 | G' | -.15 | | | |
| - FARM OWNERS | | HAPP 2.1 | G' | +.32 | | | |
| - HOUSEWIVES | | HAPP 2.1 | G' | -.03 | | | |
| - RETIRED, INDEPENDENT | | HAPP 2.1 | G' | -.04 | | | |
| - STUDENTS | | HAPP 2.1 | G' | -.02 | | | |
| OCCUPATION: | Computed for presently married employed persons only.<br>Males were categorized according to their own occupation and females according to their husband's occupation.<br>Gammas are based on a comparison of the happiness ratings of the occupational group mentioned and the happiness of all the married males and females | | | | | Non-institutionalized adults, U.S.A.<br>Probability multi-stage area sample<br>N: 2460, date: spring, 1957 | GURIN 60<br>p. 223 |
| - PROFESSIONALS, TECHNICIANS | Lower among males : G' = +.12 (ns)<br>Stronger among females: G' = +.30 (01) | HAPP 1.1 | G' | + | Gt' | | |
| - MANAGERS, PROPRIETORS | Stronger among males: G' = +.21 (05)<br>Lower among females : G' = +.15 (ns) | HAPP 1.1 | G' | + | Gt' | | |
| - CLERICAL WORKERS | Negative among males : G' = -.11 (ns)<br>Positive among females: G' = +.09 (ns) | HAPP 1.1 | G' | | Gt' | | |
| - SALES WORKERS | males : G' = +.25 (05)<br>females: G' = +.28 (05) | HAPP 1.1 | G' | + | Gt' | | |
| - SKILLED WORKERS | Negative among males : G' = -.03 (ns)<br>Positive among females: G' = +.03 (ns) | HAPP 1.1 | G' | | Gt' | | |
| - SEMI-SKILLED WORKERS | females only: G' = -.16 (ns) | HAPP 1.1 | G' | - | Gt' | | |
| - UNSKILLED WORKERS | Lower among males : G' = -.24 (05)<br>Stronger among females : G' = -.36 (01) | HAPP 1.1 | G' | - | Gt' | | |
| - FARMERS | Stronger among males: G' = -.16 (ns)<br>Lower among females : G' = -.08 (ns) | HAPP 1.1 | G' | - | Gt' | | |

| Variable | Remarks | Measure | Statistic | Result | Population | Source |
|---|---|---|---|---|---|---|
| OCCUPATION: | The mean happiness score of the occupational group mentioned was compared with the mean happiness of the entire population (mean score: 6.6) | | | | National adult population, U.S.A.<br>Probability sample<br>N: 1549, date: ± 1960 | CANTR 65/1<br>p. 375 |
| - PROFESSIONALS, BUSINESSMEN | Mean happiness score: 7.1 | HAPP 3.1 | DM | + | | |
| - WHITE COLLAR WORKERS | Mean happiness score: 6.6 | HAPP 3.1 | DM | ± 0 | | |
| - SKILLED WORKERS | Mean happiness score: 6.6 | HAPP 3.1 | DM | ± 0 | | |
| - UNSKILLED WORKERS | Mean happiness score: 6.3 | HAPP 3.1 | DM | - | | |
| - FARMERS | Mean happiness score: 6.5 | HAPP 3.1 | DM | - | | |
| - NON-LABOR | Mean happiness score: 6.3 | HAPP 3.1 | DM | - | | |
| OCCUPATION: | See remarks in excerpt (Part II).<br>The mean happiness score of the occupational group mentioned was compared with the mean happiness of the entire population ( 1964: 6.85; 1971: 6.56). | | | | Non-institutionalized national adult population, U.S.A.<br>Multi-stage probability sample, stratified by size of locality<br>N: 1588, date: January, 1971 (+ 1964) | CANTR 71<br>p. 66 |
| - PROFESSIONALS; BUSINESSMEN | Mean: 7.26 (1964); 7.18 (1971) | HAPP 3.1 | DM | + | | |
| - WHITE COLLAR WORKERS | Mean: 7.03 (1964); 6.49 (1971 ) | HAPP 3.1 | DM | + | | |
| - FARMERS | Mean: 6.78 (1964); 6.12 (1971) | HAPP 3.1 | DM | - | | |
| - MANUAL WORKERS | Mean: 6.61 (1964); 6.33 (1971) | HAPP 3.1 | DM | - | | |
| - NON-LABOR FORCE | Mean: 6.88 (1964); 6.50 (1971) | HAPP 3.1 | DM | ± 0 | | |
| OCCUPATION: | Gammas are based on a comparison of the happiness ratings of the occupational group mentioned and the happiness of the entire population | | | | National adult population , Mexico<br>Probability sample proportionally stratified by sex, age, occupation, S.E.S. and education<br>N: 1752, date: 1948 - 1949 | BUCHA 53<br>p. 189 |
| - PROFESSIONAL WORKERS | | HAPP 2.1 | G' | +.17 | | |
| - OWNERS OF BUSINESS AND LARGE, MEDIUM SHOPS | | HAPP 2.1 | G' | -.00 | | |
| - WORKERS ON OWN ACCOUNT, OWNERS OF SMALL SHOPS | | HAPP 2.1 | G' | -.10 | | |
| - SALARIED-MANAGERIAL AND TOP-GRADE CLERICAL WORKERS | | HAPP 2.1 | G' | -.03 | | |
| - OTHER CLERICAL WORKERS, SHOP-ASSISTANTS, etc. | | HAPP 2.1 | G' | +.11 | | |
| - MANUAL WORKERS | | HAPP 2.1 | G' | -.10 | | |
| - FARM WORKERS, FISHERMEN, GARDENERS | | HAPP 2.1 | G' | -.18 | | |
| - FARM OWNERS | | HAPP 2.1 | G' | +.43 | | |
| - HOUSEWIVES | | HAPP 2.1 | G' | +.07 | | |
| - RETIRED, INDEPENDENT | | HAPP 2.1 | G' | +.05 | | |

| Occupation | | Remarks | Measure | Stat. | Value | | | Population / Sample | Source |
|---|---|---|---|---|---|---|---|---|---|
| **OCCUPATION:** | | Gammas are based on a comparison of the happiness ratings of the occupational group mentioned and the happiness of the entire population. | | | | | | National adult population, Britain<br>Probability sample proportionally stratified by sex, age, occupation, S.E.S. and education<br>N: 1195, date: 1948 - 1949 | BUCHA 53<br>p. 138 |
| - PROFESSIONAL WORKERS | | | HAPP 2.1 | G' | +.42 | | | | |
| - OWNERS OF BUSINESS AND LARGE, MEDIUM SHOPS | | | HAPP 2.1 | G' | -.00 | | | | |
| - WORKERS ON OWN ACCOUNT, OWNERS OF SMALL SHOPS | | | HAPP 2.1 | G' | -.11 | | | | |
| - SALARIED-MANAGERIAL AND TOP-GRADE CLERICAL WORKERS | | | HAPP 2.1 | G' | +.32 | | | | |
| - OTHER CLERICAL WORKERS, SHOP-ASSISTANTS | | | HAPP 2.1 | G' | -.05 | | | | |
| - MANUAL WORKERS | | | HAPP 2.1 | G' | -.10 | | | | |
| - FARM WORKERS, FISHERMEN, GARDENERS | | | HAPP 2.1 | G' | +.10 | | | | |
| - FARM OWNERS | | | HAPP 2.1 | G' | +.47 | | | | |
| - HOUSEWIVES | | | HAPP 2.1 | G' | -.12 | | | | |
| - RETIRED, INDEPENDENT | | | HAPP 2.1 | G' | -.08 | | | | |
| OCCUPATION: | | The mean happiness score of the occupational group mentioned was compared with the mean happiness of the entire population (mean score: 5.53) | | | | | | National population, Britain<br>Non-probability quota sample<br>N: 213, date: March, 1971 | ABRAM 73<br>p. 4 |
| - BUSINESS EXECUTIVES; COMPANY DIRECTORS | | Mean happiness score: 6.84 | HAPP 2.1 | DM | + | | | | |
| - PROFESSIONAL WORKERS ( doctors, teachers, investors, shareholders, etc.) | | Mean happiness score: 5.91 | HAPP 2.1 | DM | + | | | | |
| - OFFICE WORKERS | | Mean happiness score: 6.04 | HAPP 2.1 | DM | + | | | | |
| - SKILLED MANUAL WORKERS | | Mean happiness score: 5.64 | HAPP 2.1 | DM | + | | | | |
| - UNSKILLED MANUAL WORKERS | | Mean happiness score: 4.75 | HAPP 2.1 | DM | - | | | | |
| - SMALL BUSINESSMEN; SHOPKEEPERS | | Mean happiness score: 4.10 | HAPP 2.1 | DM | - | | | | |
| - OLD AGE PENSIONERS | | Mean happiness score: 4.74 | HAPP 2.1 | DM | - | | | | |
| OCCUPATION: | | Gammas are based on a comparison of the happiness ratings of the occupation group mentioned and the happiness of the entire population | | | | | | National adult population, France<br>Probability sample proportionally stratified by sex, age, occupation, S.E.S. and educattion<br>N: 1000, date: 1948 - 1949 | BUCHA 53<br>p. 148 |
| - PROFESSIONAL WORKERS | | | HAPP 2.1 | G' | +.10 | | | | |
| - OWNERS OF BUSINESS AND LARGE, MEDIUM SHOPS | | | HAPP 2.1 | G' | +.39 | | | | |
| - WORKERS ON OWN ACCOUNT, OWNERS OF SMALL SHOPS | | | HAPP 2.1 | G' | +.08 | | | | |

(to be continued on next page)

| | | | | | | | | |
|---|---|---|---|---|---|---|---|---|
| - SALARIED-MANAGERIAL AND TOP-GRADE CLERICAL WORKERS | | | HAPP 2.1 | G' | +.45 | | | | |
| - OTHER CLERICAL WORKERS , SHOP ASSISTENTS | | | HAPP 2.1 | G' | +.05 | | | | |
| - MANUAL WORKERS | | | HAPP 2.1 | G' | -.22 | | | | |
| - FARM WORKERS, FISHERMEN, GARDENERS | | | HAPP 2.1 | G' | -.11 | | | | |
| - FARM OWNERS | | | HAPP 2.1 | G' | +.29 | | | | |
| - HOUSEWIVES | | | HAPP 2.1 | G' | -.06 | | | | |
| - RETIRED, INDEPENDENT | | | HAPP 2.1 | G' | -.56 | | | | |
| OCCUPATION: | | Gammas are based on a comparison of the happiness ratings of the occupation group mentioned and the happiness of the entire population | | | | | | National adult population, W. Germany<br>Probability sample proportionally stratified by sex, age, occupation, S.E.S. and education<br>N: 3371, date: 1948 - 1949 | BUCHA 53<br>p. 157 |
| - PROFESSIONAL WORKERS | | | HAPP 2.1 | G' | -.09 | | | | |
| - OWNERS OF BUSINESS AND LARGE, MEDIUM SHOPS | | | HAPP 2.1 | G' | -.07 | | | | |
| - WORKERS ON OWN ACCOUNT, OWNERS OF SMALL SHOPS | | | HAPP 2.1 | G' | +.15 | | | | |
| - SALARIED-MANAGERIAL AND TOP-GRADE CLERICAL WORKERS | | | HAPP 2.1 | G' | +.12 | | | | |
| - OTHER CLERICAL WORKERS, SHOP ASSISTANTS | | | HAPP 2.1 | G' | +.19 | | | | |
| - MANUAL WORKERS | | | HAPP 2.1 | G' | -.08 | | | | |
| - FARM WORKERS, FISHERMEN, GARDENERS | | | HAPP 2.1 | G' | -.15 | | | | |
| - FARM OWNERS | | | HAPP 2.1 | G' | +.02 | | | | |
| - HOUSEWIVES | | | HAPP 2.1 | G' | -.07 | | | | |
| - RETIRED, INDEPENDENT | | | HAPP 2.1 | G' | -.28 | | | | |
| OCCUPATION: | | See above | | | | | | National adult population, Italy<br>Probability sample proportionally stratified by sex, age, occupation, S.E.S. and education<br>N: 1078, date: 1948 - 1949 | BUCHA 53<br>p. 176 |
| - PROFESSIONAL WORKERS | | | HAPP 2.1 | G' | +.00 | | | | |
| - OWNERS OF BUSINESS AND LARGE, MEDIUM SHOPS | | | HAPP 2.1 | G' | +.26 | | | | |
| - WORKERS ON OWN ACCOUNT, OWNERS OF SMALL SHOPS | | | HAPP 2.1 | G' | +.09 | | | | |
| - SALARIED-MANAGERIAL AND TOP-GRADE CLERICAL WORKERS | | | HAPP 2.1 | G' | +.14 | | | | |

(to be continued on next page)

| | | | | | | | | |
|---|---|---|---|---|---|---|---|---|
| - OTHER CLERICAL WORKERS, SHOP ASSISTANTS, etc. | | | HAPP 2.1 | G' | -.15 | | | |
| - MANUAL WORKERS | | | HAPP 2.1 | G' | -.33 | | | |
| - FARM WORKERS, FISHERMEN, GARDENERS | | | HAPP 2.1 | G' | -.36 | | | |
| - FARM OWNERS | | | HAPP 2.1 | G' | +.29 | | | |
| - HOUSEWIVES | | | HAPP 2.1 | G' | +.08 | | | |
| - RETIRED, INDEPENDENT | | | HAPP 2.1 | G' | +.05 | | | |
| OCCUPATION: | | Gammas are based on a comparison of the happiness ratings of the occupation group mentioned and the happiness of the entire population. | | | | | National adult population, The Netherlands<br>Probability sample proportionally stratified by sex, age, occupation, S.E.S. and education<br>N: 942, date: 1948 - 1949 | BUCHA 53<br>p. 197 |
| - PROFESSIONAL WORKERS | | | HAPP 2.1 | G' | +.39 | | | |
| - OWNERS OF BUSINESS AND LARGE, MEDIUM SHOPS | | | HAPP 2.1 | G' | +.35 | | | |
| - WORKERS ON OWN ACCOUNT, OWNERS OF SMALL SHOPS | | | HAPP 2.1 | G' | -.04 | | | |
| - SALARIED-MANAGERIAL AND TOP-GRADE CLERICAL WORKERS | | | HAPP 2.1 | G' | +.43 | | | |
| - OTHER CLERICAL WORKERS, SHOP ASSISTANTS, etc. | | | HAPP 2.1 | G' | +.20 | | | |
| - MANUAL WORKERS | | | HAPP 2.1 | G' | -.22 | | | |
| - FARM WORKERS, FISHERMEN, GARDENERS | | | HAPP 2.1 | G' | -.12 | | | |
| - FARM OWNERS | | | HAPP 2.1 | G' | -.00 | | | |
| - RETIRED, INDEPENDENT | | | HAPP 2.1 | G' | -.14 | | | |
| OCCUPATION: | | Gammas are based on a comparison of the happiness ratings of the occupation group mentioned and the happiness of the entire population. | | | | | National adult population, Norway<br>Probability sample proportionally stratified by sex, age, occupation, S.E.S. and education<br>N: 1030, date: 1948 - 1949 | BUCHA 53<br>p. 206 |
| - PROFESSIONAL WORKERS | | | HAPP 2.1 | G' | +.38 | | | |
| - OWNERS OF BUSINESS AND LARGE, MEDIUM SHOPS | | | HAPP 2.1 | G' | +.39 | | | |
| - WORKERS ON OWN ACCOUNT, OWNERS OF SMALL SHOPS | | | HAPP 2.1 | G' | +.19 | | | |
| - SALARIED-MANAGERIAL AND TOP-GRADE CLERICAL WORKERS | | | HAPP 2.1 | G' | +.41 | | | |
| - OTHER CLERICAL WORKERS, SHOP ASSISTANTS, etc. | | | HAPP 2.1 | G' | +.06 | | | |
| - MANUAL WORKERS | | | HAPP 2.1 | G' | -.03 | | | |
| - FARM WORKERS, FISHERMEN, GARDENERS | | | HAPP 2.1 | G' | -.52 | | | |

| | | | | | | | | |
|---|---|---|---|---|---|---|---|---|
| - FARM OWNERS | | | HAPP 2.1 | G' | -.24 | | | |
| - HOUSEWIVES | | | HAPP 2.1 | G' | +.06 | | | |
| - RETIRED, INDEPENDENT | | | HAPP 2.1 | G' | -.02 | | | |
| OCCUPATION: | | The mean happiness score of the occupational group mentioned was compared with the mean happiness of the entire population (mean score: 4.4). | | | | | National adult population, Poland<br>Probability samples<br>N: 1464, date: ± 1960 | CANTR 65/1<br>p. 374 |
| - FARMERS | | Mean happiness score: 4.1 | HAPP 3.1 | DM | - | | | |
| - UNSKILLED WORKERS | | Mean happiness score: 3.7 | HAPP 3.1 | DM | - | | | |
| - SKILLED WORKERS, CRAFTSMEN | | Mean happiness score: 4.5 | HAPP 3.1 | DM | + | | | |
| - WHITE COLLAR WORKERS | | Mean happiness score: 4.9 | HAPP 3.1 | DM | + | | | |
| - OTHERS; STUDENTS | | Mean happiness score: 4.8 | HAPP 3.1 | DM | + | | | |
| OCCUPATION: | | The mean happiness score of the occupational group mentioned was compared with the mean happiness of the entire population (mean score : 5.0) | | | | | National adult population, Yugoslavia<br>Probability sample<br>N: 1523, date: ± 1960 | CANTR 65/1<br>p. 377 |
| - STATE EMPLOYEES | | Mean happiness score: 5.9 | HAPP 3.1 | DM | + | | | |
| - WORKERS | | Mean happiness score: 4.9 | HAPP 3.1 | DM | - | | | |
| - FARMERS | | Mean happiness score: 4.6 | HAPP 3.1 | DM | - | | | |
| - HOUSEWIVES | | Mean happiness score: 4.9 | HAPP 3.1 | DM | - | | | |
| OCCUPATION: | | The mean happiness score of the occupational group mentioned was compared with the mean happiness score of the entire population (mean score : 3.7) | | | | | National population, India<br>Probability sample, proportionally poststratified by dwelling<br>N: 2366, date: 1958 | CANTR 65/1<br>p. 368 |
| - PROFESSIONALS; STUDENTS | | Mean happiness score: 4.5 | HAPP 3.1 | DM | + | | | |
| - CLERKS; TEACHERS | | Mean happiness score: 4.2 | HAPP 3.1 | DM | + | | | |
| - SKILLED WORKERS | | Mean happiness score: 3.7 | HAPP 3.1 | DM | ± 0 | | | |
| - UNSKILLED WORKERS | | Mean happiness score: 3.2 | HAPP 3.1 | DM | - | | | |
| - FARM OWNERS | | Mean happiness score: 3.7 | HAPP 3.1 | DM | ± 0 | | | |
| - FARM WORKERS | | Mean happiness score: 3.1 | HAPP 3.1 | DM | - | | | |
| - OTHERS | | Mean happiness score: 4.1 | HAPP 3.1 | DM | + | | | |
| OCCUPATION: | | Gammas are based on a comparison of the happiness ratings of the occupation group mentioned and the happiness of the entire population. | | | | | National adult population, Australia<br>Probability sample proportionally stratified by sex, age, S.E.S. and education<br>N: 945, date: 1948 - 1949 | BUCHA 53<br>p. 131 |
| - PROFESSIONAL WORKERS | | | HAPP 2.1 | G' | +.19 | | | |
| - OWNERS OF BUSINESS AND LARGE, MEDIUM SHOPS | | | HAPP 2.1 | G' | +.20 | | | |

| | | | | | | | | | |
|---|---|---|---|---|---|---|---|---|---|
| - WORKERS ON OWN ACCOUNT, OWNERS OF SMALL SHOPS | | | HAPP 2.1 | G' | -.05 | | | | |
| - SALARIED-MANAGERIAL AND TOP-GRADE CLERICAL WORKERS | | | HAPP 2.1 | G' | +.05 | | | | |
| - OTHER CLERICAL WORKERS, SHOP ASSISTANTS, etc. | | | HAPP 2.1 | G' | -.03 | | | | |
| - MANUAL WORKERS | | | HAPP 2.1 | G' | +.04 | | | | |
| - FARM WORKERS, FISHERMEN, GARDENERS | | | HAPP 2.1 | G' | +.19 | | | | |
| - FARM OWNERS | | | HAPP 2.1 | G' | +.10 | | | | |
| - HOUSEWIVES | | | HAPP 2.1 | G' | -.09 | | | | |
| - RETIRED, INDEPENDENT | | | HAPP 2.1 | G' | -.20 | | | | |
| OCCUPATIONAL LEVEL | Farmers, farm labourers / service workers / semi- and unskilled workers / skilled workers / white collar / business executives / (semi-) professionals | See remarks in excerpt (Part II).<br>in 1946: negroes: G' = +.09 (ns)<br>whites : G' = +.09 (01)<br>in 1956: negroes: G' = -.03 (ns)<br>whites : G' = +.13 (01)<br>in 1966: negroes: G' = -.17 (05)<br>whites : G' = +.13 (01) | HAPP 1.1 | G' | | Gt' | | National adult populations, U.S.A.<br>Non-probability quota samples and probability area samples<br>N: 25617, date: 1946, 1947, 1948, 1956, 1966 | MANNI 72<br>p. 43 |
| OCCUPATIONAL LEVEL | Retired / unskilled / semi-skilled / skilled / service / sales / clerical / business / farm / professional | | HAPP 2.1<br>HAPP 3.1<br>CON 1.1 | r<br>r<br>r | +.02<br>+.09<br>+.02 | | | National adult population, U.S.A.<br>Cantril (1965) modified probability sample<br>N: 1406, date: 1959 | BORTN 70<br>p. 44 |
| OCCUPATION | Unskilled / semi-skilled / skilled / clerical and sales / professional | Computed for employed Ss only.<br>Clerical and sales workers are less happy than skilled workers. | HAPP 1.1 | $t_{k_c}$<br>G | +.15<br>+.30 | | 01 | Non-hospitalized schizophrenic males, Monroe County, New York, U.S.A.<br>Probability sample, drawn from the Monroe County Psychiatric Case Register<br>N: 178, date: 1964 - 1965 | ALEXA 68<br>p. 97/108/ 121 |
| | | Presented for Index of Negative Affects only. | AFF 2.3 | | | | ns | | |

## OCCUPATIONAL SKILL LEVEL

| | | | | | | | | | |
|---|---|---|---|---|---|---|---|---|---|
| SKILLED WORKER | Unskilled / semi-skilled / skilled | Computed for presently married males only (N=908). | HAPP 1.1 | G' | +.09 | Gt' | ns | Non-institutionalized adults, U.S.A.<br>Probability multi-stage area sample<br>N: 2460, date: spring 1957 | GURIN 60<br>p. 223 |
| WIVE OF SKILLED WORKER | Wife of unskilled / semi-skilled / skilled worker | Computed for presently married females only (N=963) | HAPP 1.1 | G' | +.26 | Gt' | 01 | See above | GURIN 60<br>p. 223 |
| OCCUPATIONAL SKILL LEVEL | Low vs high | Mexican males : DM = +1.1<br>Mexican females: DM = +0.5<br>Black males : DM = +1.0<br>Black females : DM = +0.8<br>Anglo males : DM = +0.5<br>Anglo females : DM = +0.4 | AFF 2.3 | DM | + | | | Adults, Houston, Texas, U.S.A.<br>Non-probability purposive quota sample stratified by age, sex, occupational skill level and ethnicity<br>N: 1441, date: autumn, 1969 | GAITZ 72<br>p. 63-64 |
| | | Trend indicated, but non-significant | COMP 1.1 | | + | $Chi^2$ | ns | | |

## MANUAL VS NON-MANUAL

| | | | | | | | | | |
|---|---|---|---|---|---|---|---|---|---|
| OCCUPATIONAL LEVEL | Manual vs non-manual | See remarks in excerpt (Part II).<br>in 1946: negroes: G' = -.04 (ns)<br>whites : G' = +.17 (01)<br>in 1956: negroes: G' = -.07 (ns)<br>whites : G' = +.14 (01)<br>in 1966: negroes: G' = -.36 (01)<br>whites : G' = +.16 (01) | HAPP 1.1 | G' | | Gt' | | National adult populations, U.S.A.<br>Non-probability quota samples and probability area samples<br>N: 25617, date: 1946, 1947, 1948, 1956, 1966 | MANNI 72<br>p. 47 |
| OCCUPATIONAL LEVEL | Blue vs white collar | Gammas based on proportions 'very happy' answers. Farmers were excluded<br>Among whites : G' = +.22 (01)<br>Reversed among blacks: G' = -.34 (ns) | HAPP 1.1 | G' | +.22 | Gt' | 01 | Non-institutionalized adults, U.S.A.<br>Type of sample construction unclear<br>N: 1602, date: March, 1972 | ALSTO 74<br>p. 100 |
| WHITE-COLLAR JOB | Blue-collar vs white-collar workers | Computed for chief wage earners only.<br>Female chief wage earners were, almost without exception, single women.<br>Index of Positive Affects : $D\bar{R}$ = +.11 (05)<br>- males : $D\bar{R}$ = +.10 (05)<br>Not in high income group: $D\bar{R}$ = -.02 (ns)<br>Unaffected by occupational prestige<br>- females : $D\bar{R}$ = +.13 (05)<br>Stronger among higher occupational prestige levels<br>Index of Negative Affects : $D\bar{R}$ = +.02 (ns)<br>- males : $D\bar{R}$ = +.01 (ns)<br>Unaffected by occupational prestige<br>- females : $D\bar{R}$ = -.02 (ns)<br>Slightly positive among higher occupational prestige levels (ns) | AFF 2.3 | $D\bar{R}$ | + | BCI | | Adults, urban areas, U.S.A.<br>Probability area samples<br>N: 2787, date: January, 1963 - January, 1964 | BRADB 69<br>p. 191-205 |
| | | - males : G' = +.03<br>- females : G' = +.06<br>G' based on proportions 'very happy' answers<br>When among the males occupational prestige was controlled : $G_{pt}$ = -.04 | HAPP 1.1 | G' | + | | | | |

## W 2.3 - CHANGE OF WORK

| | | | | | | | | | |
|---|---|---|---|---|---|---|---|---|---|
| GETTING EMPLOYED | Staying unemployed vs changing from employment to employment | Analysis on the basis of a comparison between data from January, 1963 (wave 1) and October, 1963 (wave 3).<br>Computed for chief wage earners only.<br>Index of Positive Affects: $D\bar{R}$ = -.01<br>Index of Negative Affects: $D\bar{R}$ = -.04 | AFF 2.3 | $D\bar{R}$ | +.05 | | | Adults, urban areas, U.S.A.<br>Probability area samples<br>N: 2787, date: January, 1963 - January, 1964 | BRADB 69<br>p. 189 |
| FALLING UNEMPLOYED | Staying employed vs changing from employment to unemployment | See above<br>Index of Positive Affects: $D\bar{R}$ = -.19<br>Index of Negative Affects: $D\bar{R}$ = -.03 | AFF 2.3 | $D\bar{R}$ | -.13 | | | See above | BRADB 69<br>p. 189 |

| | | | | | | | | | |
|---|---|---|---|---|---|---|---|---|---|
| SELF-PERCEIVED INCREASE IN OCCUPATIONAL PRESTIGE AFTER MILITARY RETIREMENT | 3-item index od closed questions on present job in comparison with former military job, with respect to: its general importance, level of skill and knowledge required, authority over other people | Index of Positive Affects: G = +.30<br>Index of Negative Affects: G = -.01 | AFF 2.3 | G | +.22 | | | Middle-aged presently employed army retirees, California, U.S.A.<br>Probability simple random sample<br>N: 352, date: August, 1970 | GARBE 71<br>p. 181 |
| SELF-PERCEIVED AMOUNT OF CHANGE IN OCCUPATIONAL ROLE CLUSTER | 5-item index of closed questions on amount of change in present occupation, compared with former military occupation, rated on 4-point scales ranging from 'the same' to 'very different'.<br>Items used: actual work performed, knowledge and skill used, amount of time spent working, type of organization, kind of people one works with | Index of Positive Affects: G = -.17<br>Index of Negative Affects: G = +.12<br>Among those with increased occupational prestige:<br>affect balance : G = -.29<br>positive affect: G = -.25<br>negative affect: G = +.20<br>Among those with the same occupational prestige:<br>affect balance : G = +.17<br>positive affect: G = +.05<br>negative affect: G = -.12<br>Among those with decreased occupational prestige:<br>affect balance : G = -.19<br>positive affect: G = -.17<br>negative affect: G = +.19 | AFF 2.3 | G | -.15 | | | See above | GARBE 71<br>p. 81 |
| CIVILIAN REFERENCE GROUP SALIENCE AFTER MILITARY RETIREMENT | 8-item index of statements indicating orientation towards and identification with civilian life and current civilian career | Presented for Index of Positive Affects only:<br>G = +.28 | AFF 2.3 | G | + | | | See above | GARBE 71<br>p. 196 |
| MILITARY REFERENCE GROUP SALIENCE AFTER MILITARY RETIREMENT | 8-item index of statements indicating orientation towards and identification with the Army and former military career | Presented for Index of Positive Affects only:<br>G = +.10 | AFF 2.3 | G | + | | | See above | GARBE 71<br>p. 208 |

## W 2.4 - WORK PRESTIGE

see also 'Socio-Economic Status' (S 5), and 'Type of Work' (W 2.2)

| | | | | | | | | | |
|---|---|---|---|---|---|---|---|---|---|
| OCCUPATIONAL PRESTIGE | 10-point scale (Duncan prestige scale; see Duncan, 1961) | Lower among those under the age of 65: r = +.09<br>Stronger among those of age 65+ : r = +.26<br>This difference is significant (05).<br>When controlled for S.E.S.:<br>Lower among those under the age of 65: $r_{pc}$ = +.01<br>Stronger among those of age 65+ : $r_{pc}$ = +.19 | HAPP 1.1 | $r_{pm}$ | +.11 | | 01 | Non-institutionalized adults, U.S.A.<br>Probability samples<br>N: 1547, date: 1972, 1973 | SPREI 74<br>p. 455/457 |
| OCCUPATIONAL PRESTIGE | 10-point scale of occupations, ranked for occupational prestige (Duncan prestige scale; see Duncan, 1961)<br>Respondents in white-collar jobs were dichotomized into medium and low vs high prestige. Respondents in blue-collar jobs were dichotomized into low vs medium and high prestige. | Computed for chief wage earners only.<br>Female chief wage earners were, almost without exception, single women.<br>Index of Positive Affects:<br>- Among white-collar workers: $\bar{DR}$ = +.07 (05)<br>males : $\bar{DR}$ = +.08 (05)<br>medium income group only: $\bar{DR}$ = +.12 (ns)<br>females : $\bar{DR}$ = +.05 (ns)<br>- Among blue-collar workers : $\bar{DR}$ = +.08 (05)<br>males : $\bar{DR}$ = +.09 (05)<br>unaffected by income<br>females : $\bar{DR}$ = -.03 (ns)<br>Index of Negative Affects:<br>- Among white-collar workers: $\bar{DR}$ = .00 (ns)<br>males : $\bar{DR}$ = -.01 (ns)<br>females : $\bar{DR}$ = +.06 (ns)<br>(to be contined on next page) | AFF 2.3 | $\bar{DR}$ | + | BCI | | Adults, urban areas, U.S.A.<br>Probability area sample<br>N: 2787, date: January, 1963 - January, 1964 | BRADB 69<br>p. 191-205 |

| | | | | | | | | | |
|---|---|---|---|---|---|---|---|---|---|
| | | - Among blue-collar workers : $D\bar{R}$ = -.07 (05)<br>males : $D\bar{R}$ = -.05 (ns)<br>females : $D\bar{R}$ = -.05 (ns)<br><br>When among the males white/blue-collar job was controlled:<br>Index of Positive Affects : $G_{pt}$ = +.23<br>Index of Negative Affects : $G_{pt}$ = -.08<br>Stronger among the blue-collar workers : $G_{pt}$ = -.15<br>Not among white-collar workers<br><br>The reported differences in affect appeared to be largely determined by differences between the occupational categories in job advancement level and work satisfaction. | | | | | | | |
| | | Among white-collar males : G' = +.17<br>Among white-collar females : G' = +.11<br>Among blue-collar males : G' = +.14<br>Among blue-collar females : G' = -.25<br>Gammas based on proportions 'very happy' answers<br><br>When among the males white/blue-collar job was controlled : $G_{pt}$ = +.19 | HAPP 1.1 | G' | + | | | | |
| PERCEIVED JOB PRESTIGE | Question: 'Do the people you know think of you as having a good job, an average job, or not too good a job?'<br>not too good or average vs good | Computed for male chief wage earners only.<br><br>Index of Positive Affects:<br>- Among white-collar workers : $D\bar{R}$ = +.15 (05)<br>high occupational prestige : $D\bar{R}$ = +.19 (05)<br>medium and low prestige : $D\bar{R}$ = +.09 (ns)<br>- Among blue-collar workers : $D\bar{R}$ = +.10 (05)<br>high and medium prestige : $D\bar{R}$ = +.14 (05)<br>low prestige : $D\bar{R}$ = +.06 (ns)<br>Index of Negative Affects:<br>- Among white-collar workers : $D\bar{R}$ = -.03 (ns)<br>Unaffected by occupational prestige<br>- Among blue-collar workers : $D\bar{R}$ = -.04 (ns)<br>Unaffected by occupational prestige | AFF 2.3 | $D\bar{R}$ | + | BCI | | Adults, urban areas, U.S.A.<br>(see last page) | BRADB 69<br>p. 201 |
| OCCUPATIONAL PRESTIGE | | Housewives and retirees were excluded in order to rank occupations from low to high degrees of prestige. | HAPP 1.1<br>HAPP 2.1 | G<br>G | +.01<br>+.05 | | | Adults, Toledo, Ohio, U.S.A.<br>Systematic random sample<br>N: 510, date: 1973 | SNYDE 74<br>p. 32 |
| SOCIAL STRATUM | Working in prestigeous occupations, rated on a 9-point scale | Computed for employed Ss only.<br><br>Positive among males<br>Negative among females | HAPP 2.1 | | | | | Inhabitants of Helsinki, Finland<br>Probability sample<br>N: 442, date: spring - summer, 1966 | HAAVI 71<br>p. 594 |
| SOCIAL STRATUM | Social stratum of husband, rated on a 9-point scale (see above) | Computed for married females only.<br>Gammas based on proportions 'very satisfied' answers.<br><br>Stronger among employed females: G' = -.31 (ns)<br>Lower among unemployed females : G' = -.20 (ns) | HAPP 2.1 | G' | - | Gt' | ns | See above | HAAVI 71<br>p. 595 |
| OCCUPATIONAL PRESTIGE | 10-point scale | unmarried males : r = +.08 (ns)<br>married males : r - +.05 (ns)<br>unmarried females: r = +.03 (ns)<br>married females : r = +.07 (ns) | HAPP 2.1 | $r_{pm}$ | + | $Chi^2$ | ns | Adults, Amsterdam, The Netherlands<br>Probability systematic random sample, stratified by sex and marital status<br>N: 600, date: September - December, 1965 | JONG 69<br>p. 190 |

| | | | | | | | | | |
|---|---|---|---|---|---|---|---|---|---|
| OCCUPATIONAL LEVEL | Low / medium / high | Married females were coded for the occupational level of their husbands<br>U-shaped curve: those of medium occupational level being most happy.<br>Unaffected by sex and age. | HAPP 1.1 | G' | +.10 | Gt' | ns | Adults, Utrecht, The Netherlands<br>Probability sample stratified by age<br>N: 300, date: autumn, 1967 | MOSER 69<br>p. 20 |
| PERCEIVED OCCUPATIONAL PRESTIGE | Question: 'Is your job generally respected and looked up to by people?'<br>not at all / little / average / yes, rather / yes, very much | | HAPP 2.1 | $T^2$ | +.13 | $Chi^2$ | 001 | Housewives and persons gainfully employed outside agriculture, Poland<br>Non-probability purposive quota sample<br>N: 1251, date: June - July, 1960 | MAKAR 62<br>p. 112 |
| PERCEIVED OCCUPATIONAL PRESTIGE | Question: 'Is farming generally respected and looked up to by people?'<br>not at all / little / average / much / very much | | HAPP 2.1 | $T^2$ | +.11 | $Chi^2$ | 001 | Individual farmowners and their families, Poland<br>Non-probability purposive quota sample<br>N: 1002, date: June - July, 1960 | MAKAR 62<br>p. 113 |

## W 2.5 - CAREER ORIENTATION

| | | | | | | | | | |
|---|---|---|---|---|---|---|---|---|---|
| UPWARD CAREER ANCHORAGE | 6-item index of forced choice statements measuring whether a person tends to evaluate success in terms of how far a person has come (downward anchorage) or in terms of how far a person has to go before he reaches the top of his career (upward anchorage). (Career-Anchorage Scale; see Tausky & Dubin, 1965). | | HAPP 3.1 | r | +.03 | | ns | People of 46 and older, Duke, U.S.A.<br>Probability systematic random sample, stratified by age and sex<br>N: 502, date: 1968 | PALMO 72<br>p. 70 |
| PREFERENCE FOR 'A JOB THAT DOESN'T BUG ME' | 7-item index of closed questions indicating preference for: no one to boss me, don't have to work too hard, clean job, not a lot of responsibility, lot of free time, high prestige, and not learning a lot of new things. | | COMP 1.2 | $r_{pm}$ | -.05 | | ns | Public high school boys, U.S.A.<br>Probability multi-stage sample<br>N: 2213 in 1966, 1886 in 1968 and 1799 in 1969<br>date: fall 1966, spring 1968 and spring 1969 | BACHM 67/70<br>p. 243 |
| PREFERENCE FOR 'A JOB THAT PAYS OFF' | 6-item index of closed questions indicating preference for: steady job, learning new things, good chances for getting ahead, good pay, using one's skills, nice friendly people. | | COMP 1.2 | $r_{pm}$ | +.21 | | 001 | See above | BACHM 67/70<br>p. 243 |
| AMBITIOUS JOB ATTITUDE | 13-item index of closed questions indicating preference for: 'a job that doesn't bug me' and preference for 'a job that pays off' (see above). | | COMP 1.2 | $r_{pm}$ | +.16 | | 001 | See above | BACHM 67/70<br>p. 242 |
| KNOWLEDGE ABOUT OCCUPATIONS | 25-item test containing questions on income, status, working hours, requirements, etc. of different occupations (Job Information Test). | | COMP 1.2 | $r_{pm}$ | -.01 | | ns | See above | BACHM 67/70<br>p. 242 |

## W 2.6 - CHARACTERISTICS OF ONE'S JOB

see also 'Income' (I 1)

| | | | | | | | | | |
|---|---|---|---|---|---|---|---|---|---|
| FREEDOM ON THE JOB | Closed question: none / some / much freedom | | HAPP 2.1 | $r_{pm}$ | + | $Chi^2$ | ns | Adults, Amsterdam, The Netherlands<br>Probability systematic random sample stratified by sex and marital status<br>N: 600, date: September - December, 1965 | JONG 69<br>p. 191 |

| Variable | Measurement | Remarks | Happiness measure | Stat. | Result | Test | Sign. | Population / Sample | Source |
|---|---|---|---|---|---|---|---|---|---|
| ACCEPTABLE WORKLOAD | Closed question: no vs yes | | HAPP 2.1 | G | +.75 | $Chi^2$ | 000 | Male employees of age 40+, The Netherlands<br>Non-probability chunk sample<br>N: 13000, date: — | SONDE 75 |
| WORKING IN SHIFTS | Closed question: no vs yes | | HAPP 2.1 | G | +.18 | $Chi^2$ | 000 | See above | SONDE 75 |
| WORKING IN OWN HOUSE | Closed question: no vs yes | | HAPP 2.1 | G | +.20 | $Chi^2$ | 000 | See above | SONDE 75 |
| DISTANCE TO WORK | Amount of time spent travelling | | HAPP 2.1 | G | -.20 | $Chi^2$ | ns | See above | SONDE 75 |
| POSITIVE EVALUATION OF EXISTING WORK RELATIONS BETWEEN EMPLOYEES AND EMPLOYERS in one's of spouse's place of work | Closed question ranging from 'not at all good' to 'very good' | | HAPP 1.1<br>AFF 1.1 | mc<br>mc | +.23<br>+.26 | | | Urban adult Jewish population, Israel<br>Probability area sample, using dwelling units<br>N: 1940, date: spring, 1973 | LEVY 75/1<br>p. 372 |
| PERCEIVED OPPORTUNITY TO USE ONE'S SKILLS IN PRESENT JOB | Closed question: not at all / insufficiently / only partly / yes, completely | | HAPP 2.1 | $T^2$ | +.15 | $Chi^2$ | 001 | Persons gainfully employed outside agriculture, Poland<br>Non-probability purposive quota sample<br>N: 982, date: June - July, 1960 | MAKAR 62<br>p. 110 |
| PERCEIVED SECURITY IN OCCUPATION | Closed question: insecure / average / secure / very secure | | HAPP 2.1 | $T^2$ | +.11 | $Chi^2$ | 001 | See above | MAKAR 62<br>p. 113 |
| EXTENT OF THE NECESSARY INTER-ACTION IN THE JOB SETTING | 2-item index of closed questions on necessary talking to other employees, and to customers, clients or just the general public:<br>no / rarely or sometimes / often or all day | Computed for employed Ss only.<br>No relationships with happiness and with both positive and negative affect.<br>Also no relations with the two separate questions. | HAPP 1.1<br>AFF 2.3 | | ± 0<br>± 0 | | ns<br>ns | Non-hospitalized schizophrenic males, Monroe County, New York, U.S.A.<br>Probability sample, drawn from the Monroe County Psychiatric Case Register<br>N: 178, date: 1964 - 1965 | ALEXA 68<br>p. 195 |
| EXTENT OF POTENTIAL INTERACTION IN THE JOB SETTING | 2-item index measuring amount of time spent working around three or more fellow-workers:<br>very little or some / most / all the time | Presented for Index of Negative Affect only:<br>G' = -.42 (05) | AFF 2.3 | G' | + | Gt' | | See above | ALEXA 68<br>p. 199 |

## W 2.7 - ADJUSTMENT TO ONE'S JOB

see also 'Satisfaction with Work, Job' (S 1.9)
and 'Types of Affect - Present Work' (A 2.2.14)

| Variable | Measurement | Remarks | Happiness measure | Stat. | Result | Test | Sign. | Population / Sample | Source |
|---|---|---|---|---|---|---|---|---|---|
| JOB ADVANCEMENT | 4-item index of closed questions on whether current job is the best one ever had, raise in pay during past year, promotion during past year and changes for advancement<br>very low / low / medium / high / very high | Computed for male chief wage earners only.<br>Index of Positive Affects:<br>- Among white-collar workers:<br>Positive relationship (05) among both workers of high occupational prestige and workers of medium or low prestige.<br>- Among blue-collar workers:<br>Positive relationship (05) among workers of high or medium occupational prestige only.<br>Not among workers of low prestige.<br>Index of Negative Affects:<br>- Slightly negative (ns) among blue-collar workers of low occupational prestige only.<br>No relationships among the other occupational categories. | AFF 2.3 | $\bar{DR}$ | + | BCI | | Adults, urban areas, U.S.A.<br>Probability area samples<br>N: 2787, date: January, 1963 - January, 1964 | BRADB 69<br>p. 199 |
| FEELINGS OF INADEQUATE JOB PERFORMANCE | Two closed questions on feeling one is not doing as good a job as one would like to, and frequency of these feelings during the past few weeks<br>never / once or twice / often | Computed for chief wage earners only.<br>Female chief wage earners were almost without exception single women.<br>(to be continued on next page) | AFF 2.3 | $\bar{DR}$ | | | | See above | BRADB 69<br>p. 207 |

| | | | | | | | | | |
|---|---|---|---|---|---|---|---|---|---|
| | | Positive relationships with both the Index of Positive Affects and the Index of Negative Affects.<br>- Among males slight positive relationship with positive affect and stronger positive relationship with negative affect.<br>- Among females positive relationship with positive affect and lower positive relationship with negative affect. | | | | | | | |
| INCREASED FEELINGS OF INADEQUATE JOB PERFORMANCE | Changes in frequency of feelings of inadequacy over a period of 9 months<br>decreased / remained the same / increased | Computed for male chief wage earners only.<br>Analysis on the basis of a comparison between data from January, 1963 (wave 1) and October, 1963 (wave 3).<br>Computed for the Index of Negative Affects only:<br>DR = + (05)<br>- Among white-collar workers:<br>Lower among those of high occupational prestige (ns)<br>Stronger among those of medium or low prestige (ns)<br>- Among blue-collar workers:<br>Stronger among those of high or medium occupational prestige (05)<br>Lower among those of low prestige (ns) | AFF 2.3 | $\bar{DR}$ | - | BCI | | Adults, urban areas, U.S.A.<br>(see last page) | BRADB. 69<br>p. 208 |
| SUCCESS IN PERFORMING JOB | Closed question | | HAPP 1.1<br>AFF 1.1 | mc<br>mc | +.29<br>+.31 | | | Urban adult Jewish population, Israel<br>Probability area sample, using dwelling units<br>N: 1830, date: summer, 1973 | LEVY 75/2<br>p. 373 |
| PERCEIVED ADEQUACY IN PERFORMING JOB | Closed question: not very good / average / little better than average / very good | Computed for males only. | HAPP 1.1 | $t_k$ | -.09 | | 05 | Adult married population with children, U.S.A.<br>Probability area sample<br>N: 797, date: spring, 1957 | VEROF 62<br>p. 196 |
| PROBLEMS WITH JOB (in the past) | Direct question<br>S never had problems vs mentions problems | Computed for males only. | HAPP 1.1 | $t_k$ | -.03 | | ns | See above | VEROF 62<br>p. 196 |
| MOST IMPORTANT WORRY: WORK CONDITIONS | Open-ended question on most important worry:<br>Other worries vs worry mentioned | Computed for those having worries only (N=2040). | HAPP 1.1 | G' | +.05 | Gt' | ns | National adult population, U.S.A.<br>Non-probability quota sample<br>N: 2377, date: February, 1946 | WESSM 56<br>p. 213 |
| PERCEIVED APPRECIATION BY PEOPLE ONE IS WORKING WITH ON THE JOB | Closed question rated on a 3-point scale | unmarried males : r = +.16 (ns)<br>married males : r = +.08 (ns)<br>unmarried females: r = +.10 (025)<br>married females : r = +.16 (ns) | HAPP 2.1 | $r_{pm}$ | + | $Chi^2$ | | Adults, Amsterdam, The Netherlands<br>Probability systematic random sample stratified by sex and marital status<br>N: 600, date: September - December, 1965 | JONG 69<br>p. 191 |
| GETTING ON WELL WITH SUPERIORS AT WORK | Closed question: very badly / rather badly / average / fairly well / very well | | HAPP 2.1 | $T^2$ | +.18 | $Chi^2$ | 001 | Persons gainfully employed outside agriculture, Poland<br>Non-probability purposive quota sample<br>N: 982, date: June - July, 1960 | MAKAR 62<br>p. 109 |
| GETTING ON WELL WITH WORK-FELLOWS | Closed question: very badly / rather badly / average / fairly well / very well | | HAPP 2.1 | $T^2$ | +.11 | $Chi^2$ | 001 | See above | MAKAR 62<br>p. 109 |

## W 2.8 - PERCEIVED IMPORTANCE OF SPECIFIC ASPECTS OF ONE'S JOB

| | | | | | | | | |
|---|---|---|---|---|---|---|---|---|
| PERCEIVED IMPORTANCE OF SPECIFIC ASPECTS OF THE JOB: | Closed questions rated on 7-point scales ranging from 'unimportant' to 'important', using items from the Job Descriptive Index (see Smith et al., 1969). | See 'sample construction' in excerpt (Part II). | | | | | Male supervisors of a chemical plant, U.S.A.<br>Probability samples<br>N: 69, date: — | IRIS 72<br>p. 302 |
| - ACTUAL WORK DONE | | sample A: r = -.52 (01)<br>sample B: r = +.59 (01) | HAPP 2.1 | $r_{pm}$ | | | | |
| - PAY | | sample A: r = -.11 (ns)<br>sample B: r = +.17 (ns) | HAPP 2.1 | $r_{pm}$ | | | | |
| - PROMOTIONAL OPPORTUNITIES | | sample A: r = -.53 (01)<br>sample B: r = +.18 (ns) | HAPP 2.1 | $r_{pm}$ | | | | |
| - SUPERVISION | | sample A: r = -.39 (05)<br>sample B: r = +.22 (ns) | HAPP 2.1 | $r_{pm}$ | | | | |
| - CO-WORKERS | | sample A: r = -.24 (ns)<br>sample B: r = +.03 (ns) | HAPP 2.1 | $r_{pm}$ | | | | |

## W 2.9 - REASONS FOR HAVING A JOB

| | | | | | | | | |
|---|---|---|---|---|---|---|---|---|
| REASONS FOR EMPLOYMENT: | Open-ended direct question | | | | | | Employed married females, Helsinki, Finland<br>Probability sample<br>N: 72, date: spring - summer, 1966 | HAAVI 71<br>p. 599 |
| - UTILIZE THE EDUCATION ATTAINED | | | HAPP 2.1 | $r_{pm}$ | -.05 | ns | | |
| - SATISFACTION WITH WORK | | | HAPP 2.1 | $r_{pm}$ | +.11 | ns | | |
| - NOT ENOUGH TO DO AT HOME | | | HAPP 2.1 | $r_{pm}$ | +.08 | ns | | |
| - GETTING INDEPENDENCE | | | HAPP 2.1 | $r_{pm}$ | +.10 | ns | | |
| - LACKING INTEREST IN HOUSEWORK | | | HAPP 2.1 | $r_{pm}$ | +.14 | ns | | |
| - MEETING PEOPLE | | | HAPP 2.1 | $r_{pm}$ | +.07 | ns | | |
| - RETAINING CONNECTION WITH THE WORK LIFE | | | HAPP 2.1 | $r_{pm}$ | +.04 | ns | | |
| - RAISING THE STANDARD OF LIVING | | | HAPP 2.1 | $r_{pm}$ | -.11 | ns | | |
| - EARNING NECESSARY INCOME FOR FAMILY | | | HAPP 2.1 | $r_{pm}$ | -.01 | ns | | |
| ECONOMIC REASONS MOST IMPORTANT FOR EMPLOYMENT | See above | In the lower social stratum, wives worked for money. In the upper stratum also for other reasons, but especially to utilize the education attained. | HAPP 2.1 | $r_{pm}$ | -.28 | 05 | See above | HAAVI 71<br>p. 599 |

## W 2.10 - DESIRE FOR CHANGE OF JOB

| | | | | | | | | | |
|---|---|---|---|---|---|---|---|---|---|
| UNFULFILLED ASPIRATIONS: NEW JOB, OWN BUSINESS | Open-ended question on unfulfilled aspirations: other aspirations vs aspiration mentioned | Computed for those having unfulfilled aspirations only (N=1646) | HAPP 1.1 | G' | +.01 | Gt' | ns | National adult population, U.S.A.<br>Non-probability quota sample<br>N: 2377, date: February, 1946 | WESSM 56<br>p. 210 |
| UNFULFILLED ASPIRATIONS: MOVE TO COUNTRY, BECOME FARMER | See above | See above | HAPP 1.1 | G' | +.00 | Gt' | ns | See above | WESSM 56<br>p. 210 |
| DESIRED PERSONAL CHANGES: BETTER WORK AND ATTITUDES TOWARDS IT | Open-ended question on desired personal changes: other changes vs change mentioned | Computed for those who desire to change only (N = 1591). | HAPP 1.1 | G' | -.39 | Gt' | 01 | See above | WESSM 56<br>p. 211 |
| PREFER TO CHANGE JOB WHEN POSSIBLE | Closed question: no / perhaps / yes | unmarried males : r = -.08<br>married males : r = -.09<br>unmarried females: r = -.33<br>married females : r = -.03 | HAPP 2.1 | $r_{pm}$ | - | $Chi^2$ | | Adults, Amsterdam, The Netherlands<br>Probability systematic random sample, stratified by sex and marital status<br>N: 600, date: September - December, 1965 | JONG 69<br>p. 22 |
| DESIRE FOR CHANGE OF JOB | Question: 'If you had the choice, would you change your present job in agriculture for an other occupation?'<br>no vs yes | | HAPP 2.1 | $T^2$ | +.10 | $Chi^2$ | 001 | Individual farmowners and their families, Poland<br>Non-probability purposive quota sample<br>N: 1002, date: June - July, 1960 | MAKAR 62<br>p. 110 |

## W 2.11 - VARIOUS ATTITUDES TOWARDS WORK

| | | | | | | | | | |
|---|---|---|---|---|---|---|---|---|---|
| REPORT OF HOPES CONCERNING JOB OR WORK SITUATION | Open-ended question on personal wishes and hopes for the future<br>Resonses rated as concerning good job, congenial work, employment, success in one's work, etc.; for oneself, spouse, or other family members. | | HAPP 3.1 | G' | -.01 | Gt' | ns | Adult population of 5 Westernized nations, 3 underdeveloped giants, 2 countries in the Middle East, 3 Caribbean nations and the Philippines<br>Representative samples<br>N: 18653, date: ± 1960 | CANTR 65/1<br>p. 263 |
| REPORT OF FEARS CONCERNING JOB OR WORK SITUATION | Open-ended question on personal worries and fears for the future<br>Responses rated as concerning poor job, uncongenial work, unemployment, failure in one's work, etc.; for oneself, spouse, or other family members. | | HAPP 3.1 | G' | -.05 | Gt' | ns | See above | CANTR 65/1<br>p. 263 |
| THINKING OFTEN ABOUT WORK | Closed question: not at all / sometimes / often, during last week | Gammas computed on the basis of proportions 'often' answers.<br>Unaffected by S.E.S.<br>high S.E.S.: G' = -.08 (ns)<br>low S.E.S. : G' = -.11 (05) | HAPP 1.1 | G' | - | Gt' | | Inhabitants of 4 small communities, Illinois, U.S.A.<br>Probability multi-stage samples<br>N: 2006, date: March, 1962 | BRADB 65/1<br>p. 54 |
| ANXIETY ABOUT FUTURE OF FARM | Closed question: not anxious at all / rather not anxious / little anxious / very anxious | | HAPP 2.1 | $T^2$ | -.16 | $Chi^2$ | 001 | Individual farmowners and their families, Poland<br>Non-probability purposive quota sample<br>N: 1002, date: June - July, 1960 | MAKAR 62<br>p. 112 |

# X 1 MISCELLANEOUS

| | | | | | | | | | |
|---|---|---|---|---|---|---|---|---|---|
| LAUGHING AND SINGING OFTEN | Closed question: no vs yes | | HAPP 2.1 | G | +.52 | $Chi^2$ | 000 | Male employees of age 40+, The Netherlands<br>Non-probability chunk sample<br>N: 13000, date:— | SONDE 75 |
| FREQUENCY OF LAUGHING | Repeated open-ended question on number of occasions one laughed during the past 24 hours; scored twice with an interval of 16 days | | AFF 1.1 | $r_{pm}$ | +.28 | | | College students, U.S.A.<br>Non-probability chunk sample (test – retestgroup)<br>N: 180, date: 1934/1935 | YOUNG 37A<br>p. 330 |
| PERCEIVED ACTING ABILITY | Closed question on acting ability compared with other people, rated on a 7-point scale miserable in acting / about average / highly talented in acting | This question figured in a mailed questionnaire together with a letter requesting the subject's participation in an experimental study. | AFF 6 | $r_{pm}$ | +.31 | | 05 | Female undergraduates, U.S.A.<br>Random sample<br>N: 72, date: — | LUDWI 71/75<br>p. 64 |
| SELF-PERCEIVED ACTING ABILITY | Direct question on acting ability compared with others | The subjects answered these questions at the end of an experimental situation in which their self-esteem was experimentally altered. This was done by means of a false personality report dealing with the subject's creativity, maturity, acting ability, and other things. These questions formed a check on the acceptance of the personality report. | AFF 6 | $r_{pm}$ | +.11 | | ns | See above | LUDWI 71/75<br>p. 64 |
| WRITING FIRMNESS | S's signature | | AFF 6 | $r_{pm}$ | -.12 | | ns | See above | LUDWI 71/75<br>p. 64 |
| DAY OF WEEK (Monday, Tuesday, etc.) | Differences between the day's averages on the happiness score and the mean of the other days, during a period of 21 days; as assessed by an analysis of variance, using days of the week as units for the analysis. | No day of the week was significantly different from the other days.<br>Fridays and Saturdays averaged the highest and Mondays and Tuesdays the lowest (ns). | AFF 3.1 (1st instr.) | F | | | ns | Undergraduate college students, California, U.S.A.<br>Non-probability chunk sample<br>N: 86, date: November – December, 1971 | FORDY 72<br>p. 152 |
| 'SPECIAL' DAY | Differences between the day's averages on the happiness score and the mean of all days, during a period of 21 days; as assessed by an analysis of variance, using the 21 days as units for the analysis. | The period covered in the study included the Thanksgiving Holidays, several weekends, an important examination, and the last day of the school term.<br>None of the day's averages was significantly different from the mean of all days.<br>Thanksgiving day, weekend, and the last-school-day's-eve rating showed the highest averages (ns). | AFF 3.1 (1st instr.) | F | | | ns | See above | FORDY 72<br>p. 152 |

| | | | | | | | | | |
|---|---|---|---|---|---|---|---|---|---|
| THE WEATHER | Mean daily temperature for the days of the experiment; temperature at the time of the experiment; mean daily humidity | | AFF 3.1 | | | | ns | College students, U.S.A.<br>Non-probability chunk sample<br>N: 236, date: 1934 - 1935 | YOUNG 37A<br>p. 328 |
| LENGTH OF LABOR | short vs long | The children's length of labor was correlated with hedonic level at eight months | AFF 5.1 | $r_{pm}$ | +.23 | | ns | 8 months old infants, U.S.A.<br>Non-probability quota sample<br>N: 24, date: — | MCGRA 68<br>p. 1249 |
| CLUSTER OF VARIABLES ASSOCIATED WITH NEUROSIS | Factor containing:<br>female sex; many children; low education; low use of milk; high use of sugar, tobacco, and alcohol; high social mobility; desintegration of family of origin; many worries; dissatisfaction with place of residence, lovelife, S.E.S., and with filling in the questionnaire<br>(see Aakster, 1972) | Unaffected by age and sex<br>Lower among those of medium S.E.S.<br>Stronger among those of higher educational level, except for the highest category<br>Stronger among those who were formerly married | HAPP 1.1 | G | -.67 | | 05 | National adult population, The Netherlands<br>Probability area sample<br>N: 1552, date: June, 1968 | BAKKE 74<br>p. 29 |
| CLUSTER OF VARIABLES ASSOCIATED WITH DEPRESSION | Factor containing:<br>female sex; many children; low bathing-frequency; high tobacco use; high social mobility; desintegration of family of origin; many worries; dissatisfaction with place of residence, lovelife, and S.E.S.<br>(see Aakster, 1972) | Same elaborations as above. | HAPP 1.1 | G | -.55 | | 05 | See above | BAKKE 74<br>p. 29 |

# PART IV

# PUBLIC HAPPINESS

**Distributions of Responses to Questions about Happiness in 121 Surveys in 32 Countries between 1940 and 1975**

## INTRODUCTION.

This part contains distributions of happiness, hedonic level of affect and contentment in samples that can be considered as representative for the populations of specific countries or larger areas.

Data sources: The data were partly obtained from publications in Part II of this volume. Additionally, data from four other sources are presented. Although partly published after 1975, we decided to include them because they contain highly relevant data for the prior period. These sources are:

1. A publication by Tom W. Smith: 'Time trends, Seasonal Variations, Intersurvey Differences, and Other Mysteries', Social Psychology Quarterly, 1979, vol. 42, no. 1, p. 18-30;
2. A publication by Richard A. Easterlin: 'Does Economic growth Improve Human Lot? Some empirical evidence'. In 'Nations and Households in Economic Growth' by David, P.A. & Melvin, W.R. (eds), Stanford University Press, 1974, Palo Alto, California;
3. Data from the 'Human Needs and Satisfactions'-survey, performed by the Charles F. Kettering Foundation and Gallup International Research Institutes in 1975. These data were offered us by the Dutch participating research organization NIPO and are partly published in e.g. The Public Opinion Quarterly, winter 1976-1977, vol. 41, p. 459-467.
4. Partly unpublished data from an international inquiry performed by the Gallup Institutes in 1970, published by the Netherlands Institute for Public Opinion (NIPO report 1398).

We will refer to the data from the publications already presented in Part II by means of the usual codes (f.i. WESSM 56). Data from Smith will be referred to as SMITH 79, from Easterlin as EASTE 74, from the Gallup-Kettering survey as GALLU 76, and from the NIPO as NIPO 70. Some of the data are presented in more than one publication. In these cases we refer to the foremost publication(s) only.

Ordering the data: It was our aim to present all the data in such a way that both within-country and cross-national comparisons can be made. In order to facilitate comparison, we ordered the material according to type of happiness question. For this purpose we used the categorization of questions already presented in Part I (see exhibit 1, p. 14). Most data concern overall happiness (type HAPP). Hedonic level of affect (type AFF) and contentment (type CON) have been assessed in a few national samples only: mainly in US ones. Composite indicators of happiness did not figure in any national sample at all.

The happiness questions used in (cross) national studies are listed in the exhibit on the next page.

HAPPINESS INVESTIGATIONS IN NATIONAL POPULATIONS, BY TYPE OF QUESTION.

| Table | Questions used | Regions / countries covered |
|---|---|---|
| OVERALL HAPPINESS | | |
| Table a | Questions like: 'In general, how happy would you say you are - very happy, fairly happy, or not happy?' (type HAPP 1.1) | Anglo America; U.S.A., Canada<br>Western Europe; France, W. Germany, Great Britain, Italy, Benelux, Scandinavia, Netherlands, Norway<br>Latin America; Brazil, Mexico<br>Africa<br>Asia; India, Japan, Malaysia, Philippines, Thailand<br>Australia |
| Table b | Questions like: 'Taken all together, how would you say things are these days - would you say that you are very happy, pretty happy, or not too happy?' (type HAPP 1.1) | U.S.A., Belgium, Denmark, France, W. Germany, United Kingdom, Ireland, Italy, Luxembourg, Netherlands |
| Table c | 'How satisfied are you with the way you are getting on now - very, all right, dissatisfied, don't know?' (type HAPP 2.1) | U.S.A., France, W. Germany, Great Britain, Italy, Netherlands, Norway, Mexico, Australia |
| Table c | 'All things considered, how satisfied or dis-satisfied are you with your life as a whole these days - very satisfied, fairly satisfied, not satisfied at all, don't know?' (type HAPP 2.1) | Belgium, Denmark, France, W. Germany, United Kingdom, Northern Ireland, Ireland, Italy, Luxembourg, Netherlands |
| Table e | Questions on satisfaction with one's life as a whole, rated on 11-point scales (type HAPP 2.1) | Anglo America; U.S.A., Canada<br>Western Europe; France, W. Germany, United Kingdom, Ireland, Italy, Benelux, Belgium, Netherlands, Luxembourg, Scandinavia, Denmark<br>Latin America; Brazil, Mexico<br>Africa<br>Asia; India, Japan<br>Australia |
| Table f | Questions on present situation compared with best and worst possible life, rated on 11-point self-anchoring scales based on Cantril (1965) (type HAPP 3.1) | Anglo America; U.S.A., Canada<br>Western Europe; France, W. Germany, United kingdom, Italy, Benelux Scandinavia, Yugoslavia, Poland<br>Latin America; Brazil, Cuba, Dominican Republic, Mexico, Panama<br>Africa; Egypt, Nigeria<br>Asia; India, Israel, Japan, Philippines<br>Australia |
| Table g | Various questions on overall happiness | U.S.A., Netherlands, Poland, Puerto Rico |
| HEDONIC LEVEL OF AFFECT | | |
| Table h | Questions on perceived occurrance of specific affects, using Affect Balance Scales (type AFF 2.3) | U.S.A., Puerto Rico |
| CONTENTMENT | | |
| Table i | Various questions on contentment (type CON 1.1) | U.S.A. |

## DISTRIBUTIONS OF OVERALL HAPPINESS

Table a: RESPONSES TO QUESTIONS LIKE: 'IN GENERAL, HOW HAPPY WOULD YOU SAY YOU ARE – VERY HAPPY, FAIRLY HAPPY, OR NOT HAPPY?' (TYPE HAPP 1.1, AIPO VERSION)[1]

| Countries[2] | Date | Code[1] | Proportions[3] | | | | N | Source |
|---|---|---|---|---|---|---|---|---|
| | | | 'very happy' | 'fairly happy' | 'not very', 'not (too)', and/or 'not at all happy' | don't know/ no answer | | |
| ANGLO-AMERICA | 1975 | A8 | 40 | 51 | 8 | 1 | 2046 | GALLU 76 |
| – U.S.A. | 46/2 | A2 | 46 | 45 | 8 | 1 | 2377 | WESSM 56, p. 170 (POS-417) |
| | 46/4 | A2 | 39 | 50 | 9 | 2 | 3152 | WESSM 56, p. 170 (AIPO-369) |
| | 46/6 | A3 | 38 | 57 | 4 | 1 | 3089 | WESSM 56, p. 170 (AIPO-399) |
| | 47/9 – 48/1 | A1 | 43 | 47 | 10 | | 1416 | SMITH 79, p. 22 (AIPO-410T) |
| | 48/5 | A5 | 36 | 54 | 9 | 1 | 1627 | WESSM 56, p. 170 (AIPO-418) |
| | 48/9 | A6 | 43 | 44 | 12 | 1 | ±1500 | NIPO 49, p. 3 (AIPO-425K) |
| | 52/11 | A7 | 47 | 43 | 9 | 1 | 2862 | WESSM 56, p. 170 (AIPO-508) |
| | 56/8 | A5 | 50 | 44 | 6 | | 2240 | SMITH 79, p. 22 (AIPO-569) |
| | 56/9 | A6 | 54 | 41 | 5 | | 1969 | SMITH 79, p. 22 (AIPO-570) |
| | 56/9 | A6 | 53 | 42 | 5 | | 2184 | SMITH 79, p. 22 (AIPO-571) |
| | 57/3 | A4 | 54 | 43 | 3 | | 1606 | SMITH 79, p. 22 (AIPO-580) |
| | 63/7 | A6 | 47 | 49 | 4 | | 1555 | SMITH 79, p. 22 (AIPO-675) |
| | 66/9-10 | A6 | 52 | 45 | 3 | | 1569 | SMITH 79, p. 22 (AIPO-735) |
| | 66/10 | A6 | 46 | 47 | 7 | | 1588 | SMITH 79, p. 22 (AIPO-736) |
| | 77/12 | A6 | 43 | 48 | 6 | 3 | ±1500 | NIPO 70 |
| | 1975 | A8 | 40 | 50 | 9 | 1 | 1014 | GALLU 76 |
| – Canada | 46/10 | A2 | 32 | 55 | 13 | 0 | | WESSM 56, p. 166 |
| | 1975 | A8 | 36 | 59 | 4 | 1 | 1032 | GALLU 76 |
| WESTERN EUROPE | 1975 | A8 | 20 | 60 | 18 | 2 | 2241 | GALLU 76 |
| – France | 46/7 | A2 | 8 | 44 | 40 | 8 | | WESSM 56, p. 166 |
| | 48/fall | A? | 11 | 52 | 33 | 4 | | NIPO 49, p. 3 |
| | 1965 | A1/2 | 12 | 65 | 18 | 5 | 1228 | EASTE 74, p. 107 |
| | 1975 | A8 | 22 | 66 | 10 | 2 | 330 | GALLU 76 |
| – W. Germany | 1965 | A1/2 | 20 | 66 | 11 | 3 | 1255 | EASTE 74, p. 107 |
| | 1975 | A8 | 12 | 63 | 19 | 6 | 303 | GALLU 76 |
| – Great Britain | 46/12 | A2 | 38 | 56 | 6 | 0 | | WESSM 56, p. 166 |
| | 48/fall | A? | 39 | 53 | 5 | 3 | | NIPO 49, p. 3 |
| | 1965 | A1/2 | 53 | 42 | 4 | 1 | 1179 | EASTE 74, p. 107 |
| | 70/fall | A? | 47 | 47 | 6 | 0 | | NIPO 70 |
| | 1975 | A8 | 38 | 54 | 7 | 1 | 707 | GALLU 76 |
| – Italy | 1965 | A1/2 | 11 | 52 | 33 | 4 | 1166 | EASTE 74, p. 107 |
| | 1975 | A8 | 9 | 59 | 31 | 1 | 309 | GALLU 76 |
| – Benelux | 1975 | A8 | 34 | 58 | 8 | 0 | 300 | GALLU 76 |
| – Scandinavia | 1975 | A8 | 28 | 67 | 4 | 1 | 330 | GALLU 76 |
| – Netherlands | 48/fall | A? | 43 | 44 | 6 | 7 | | WESSM 56, p. 166; NIPO 49, p. 3 |
| | 70/fall | A? | 78 | 19 | 2 | 1 | | NIPO 70 |
| – Norway | 48/fall | A? | 26 | 54 | 10 | 10 | | NIPO 49, p. 3 |
| LATIN AMERICA | 1975 | A8 | 32 | 38 | 28 | 2 | 2059 | GALLU 76 |
| – Brazil | 1975 | A8 | 36 | 45 | 18 | 1 | 382 | GALLU 76 |
| – Mexico | 1975 | A8 | 26 | 34 | 37 | 3 | 350 | GALLU 76 |

(to be continued on next page)

Table a: CONTINUED

| Countries[2] | Date | Code[1] | Proportions[3] 'very happy' | 'fairly happy' | 'not very', 'not (too)', and/or 'not at all happy' | don't know/ no answer | N | Source |
|---|---|---|---|---|---|---|---|---|
| AFRICA | 1975 | A8 | 18 | 50 | 31 | 1 | 914 | GALLU 76 |
| ASIA | 1975 | A8 | 7 | 41 | 50 | 2 | 872 | GALLU 76 |
| - India | 1975 | A8 | 6 | 31 | 62 | 1 | 354 | GALLU 76 |
| - Japan | 1975 | A8 | 9 | 56 | 23 | 12 | 337 | GALLU 76 |
| - Malaysia | 1965 | A1/2 | 17 | 64 | 15 | 4 | 502 | EASTE 74, p. 107 |
| - Philippines | 1965 | A1/2 | 13.5 | 73 | 13.5 | 0 | 500 | EASTE 74, p. 107 |
| - Thailand | 1965 | A1/2 | 13 | 74 | 12 | 1 | 500 | EASTE 74, p. 107 |
| AUSTRALIA | 48/fall | A? | 53 | 39 | 3 | 5 | | NIPO 49, p. 3 |
| | 70/fall | A? | 53 | 42 | 2 | 3 | | NIPO 70 |
| | 1975 | A8 | 37 | 57 | 6 | 0 | 301 | GALLU 76 |

Remarks: 1. Questions: - Question wordings:

A1: "In general, how happy would you say you are - very happy, fairly happy, or not very happy?" ("Not at all" additional precoded response)
A2: "In general, how happy would you say that you are - very happy, fairly happy, or not very happy?" ("Not at all" additional precoded response)
A3: "In general, how happy would you say you are - very happy, fairly happy, or not at all happy?"
A4: "In general, how happy would you say you are - fairly happy, very happy or not very happy?"
A5: "In general, how happy would you say you are - very happy, fairly happy, not very happy, or not at all happy?"
A6: "In general, how happy would you say you are - very happy, fairly happy, or not happy ("Not at all" additional precoded response)
A7: "In general, how happy would you say you are - very happy, fairly happy, or not happy?"
A8: "Generally speaking, how happy would you say you are - very happy, fairly happy, or not too happy?"

- Smith demonstrated that in the U.S.A. happiness questions offering the 'fairly happy' answer category cause different answer patterns than questions offering the 'pretty happy' category. He concludes that ".. . the substitution of 'fairly' for 'pretty' leads more people to classify thenselves as 'very' happy. Apparently 'fairly' is perceived as a less positive ranking than 'pretty'. When forced to chose between 'fairly' vs 'very', rather than 'pretty' vs 'very', more people switch to the 'very' category, since the middle choice does not appear sufficiently positive. This effect is reasonably stable across time." (SMITH 79, p. 23). Following Smith, we distinguished both types of questions (compare table a and b). However, we do not know whether the subtle differences between 'fairly happy' and 'pretty happy' are translatable into other languages. Since most data of 'from outside the U.S.A.' are reported in English, and because not all investigators are aware of these differences, it is not possible to distinguish these data properly. We divided the data from outside the U.S.A. on the basis of the (English) information offered.

2. Countries: - The data presented by GALLU 76 contain six major regions:

- Anglo America : U.S.A., Canada;
- Latin America : Brazil, Colombia, Mexico, Puerto Rico, Argentina, Peru, Venezuela, Chile, Equador, Guatemala, Bolivia, Uruguay, El Salvador, Paraguay, Nigaragua;
- Western Europe : France, Italy, United Kingdom, Western Germany, the Netherlands, Spain, Denmark, Switzerland, Finland, Belgium, Sweden, Norway, Portugal, Greece, Austria, Ireland, Luxembourg;
- Africa (Sub-Sahara): Nigeria, Tanzania, Kenya, South Africa, Uganda, Upper Volta, Mali, Malawi, Ivory Coast, Senegal, Rhodesia;
- Asia : India, Japan, Indonesia, the Philippines, Thailand, South Korea, Rep. of China, Sri Lanka, Malaysia, Singapore;
- Australia

When reliable also data from seperate countries are offered.

- Great Britain: the NIPO publications refer to 'England', WESSM and EASTE to 'great Britain' and GALLU to 'United Kingdom'.

3. Proportions: - In all cases we rouded the proportions to obtain a total of 100%.

- U.S.A. data were most extensively reported by SMITH. Unfortunately he omitted the proportions 'don't know/no answer'. By reasons of comparability we presented the data including the non-response from other sources when available.

4. Source: - AIPO = American Institute of Public Opinion ( Gallup)
POS = Public Opinion Survey (Gallup)
The data for the European and Asian countries presented by EASTE are from World Survey III, 1965 (Gallup).

- A number of studies are presented in more than one publication. Sometimes, minor differences existed in the information offered. In these cases we included those data that seemed most reliable.

Table b: RESPONSES TO QUESTIONS LIKE: 'TAKEN ALL TOGETHER, HOW WOULD YOU SAY THINGS ARE THESE DAYS – WOULD YOU SAY THAT YOU ARE VERY HAPPY, PRETTY HAPPY, OR NOT TOO HAPPY?' (TYPE HAPP 1.1, SCR/NORC VERSION)[1].

| Countries[2] | Date | Code[1] | Proportions | | | | N | Source |
|---|---|---|---|---|---|---|---|---|
| | | | 'very happy' | 'pretty happy' | 'not too happy' | don't know/ no answer | | |
| U.S.A. | 57/3 | S1 | 35 | 54 | 11 | | 2451 | GURIN 60; SMITH 79, p.22 (SRC-422) |
| | 63/5 | S2 | 32 | 51 | 17 | | 1501 | SMITH 79, p. 22 (NORC-160) |
| | 64/5 | S2 | 38 | 48 | 14 | | 1489 | SMITH 79, p. 22 (NORC-630) |
| | 64/10 | S2 | 37 | 52 | 11 | | 1966 | SMITH 79, p. 22 (NORC-760) |
| | 65/6 | S2 | 30 | 53 | 17 | | 1468 | SMITH 79, p. 22 (NORC-857) |
| | 71/7-8 | S3 | 29 | 61 | 10 | | 2147 | SMITH 79, p. 22 (SRC-811) |
| | 72/2-3 | S2 | 30 | 53 | 17 | | 1599 | SMITH 79, p. 22 (GSS-72) |
| | 72/4-5 | S3 | 27 | 65 | 8 | | 1254 | SMITH 79, p. 22 (SRC-OMNI) |
| | 72/11-73/2 | S2 | 27 | 59 | 14 | | 1459 | SMITH 79, p. 22 (NORC-5046) |
| | 72/11-73/2 | S3 | 22 | 67 | 11 | | 1056 | SMITH 79, p. 22 (SCR-ELEC) |
| | 73/3 | S2 | 36 | 51 | 13 | | 1496 | SMITH 79, p. 22 (GSS-73) |
| | 73/4-5 | S2 | 33 | 54 | 13 | | 723 | SMITH 79, p. 22 (CNS-1) |
| | 73/5-6 | S2 | 33 | 55 | 12 | | 647 | SMITH 79, p. 22 (CNS-2) |
| | 73/6-7 | S2 | 33 | 50 | 17 | | 642 | SMITH 79, p. 22 (CNS-3) |
| | 73/7-8 | S2 | 29 | 53 | 18 | | 615 | SMITH 79, p. 22 (CNS-4) |
| | 73/8-9 | S2 | 31 | 50 | 19 | | 639 | SMITH 79, p. 22 (CNS-5) |
| | 73/9-10 | S2 | 29 | 55 | 16 | | 630 | SMITH 79, p. 22 (CNS-6) |
| | 73/10-11 | S2 | 32 | 54 | 14 | | 681 | SMITH 79, p. 22 (CNS-8) |
| | 73/11-12 | S2 | 29 | 55 | 16 | | 696 | SMITH 79, p. 22 (CNS-8) |
| | 74/1 | S2 | 27 | 55 | 18 | | 696 | SMITH 79, p. 22 (CNS-9) |
| | 74/2 | S2 | 23 | 57 | 20 | | 692 | SMITH 79, p. 22 (CNS-10) |
| | 74/3 | S2 | 38 | 49 | 13 | | 1496 | SMITH 79, p. 22 (GSS-74) |
| | 74/3-4 | S2 | 28 | 57 | 15 | | 610 | SMITH 79, p. 22 (CNS-11) |
| | 74/5 | S2 | 33 | 55 | 12 | | 656 | SMITH 79, p. 22 (CNS-12) |
| | 75/3 | S2 | 33 | 54 | 13 | | 1481 | SMITH 79, p. 22 (GSS-75) |
| | 75/7 | S2 | 32 | 50 | 18 | | 581 | SMITH 79, p. 22 (NORC-5059) |
| | 76/2-4 | S2 | 34 | 53 | 13 | | 1499 | SMITH 79, p. 22 (GSS-76) |
| | 76/4-5 | S3 | 29 | 60 | 11 | | 1520 | SMITH 79, p. 22 (SRC-OMNI) |
| | 76/6-8 | S3 | 31 | 58 | 11 | | 2207 | SMITH 79, p. 22 (SRC-MH) |
| | 76/9 | S2 | 36 | 52 | 12 | | 1317 | SMITH 79, p. 22 (NORC-4239) |
| | 77/2-3 | S2 | 35 | 53 | 12 | | 1524 | SMITH 79, p. 22 (GSS-77) |
| WESTERN EUROPE | 75/5 | S3 | 16 | 54 | 27 | 3 | 9651 | COMMI 75 |
| - Belgium | 75/5 | S3 | 36 | 51 | 10 | 3 | 1555 | COMMI 75 |
| - Denmark | 75/5 | S3 | 38 | 49 | 6 | 7 | 1073 | COMMI 75 |
| - France | 75/5 | S3 | 16 | 55 | 27 | 2 | 1196 | COMMI 75 |
| - W. Germany | 75/5 | S3 | 11 | 63 | 21 | 5 | 1039 | COMMI 75 |
| - United Kingdom | 75/5 | S3 | 22 | 50 | 27 | 1 | 1328 | COMMI 75 |
| - Ireland | 75/5 | S3 | 17 | 53 | 29 | 1 | 1000 | COMMI 75 |
| - Italy | 75/5 | S3 | 6 | 48 | 44 | 2 | 1043 | COMMI 75 |
| - Luxembourg | 75/5 | S3 | 24 | 50 | 21 | 5 | 324 | COMMI 75 |
| - Netherlands | 75/5 | S3 | 31 | 54 | 10 | 5 | 1093 | COMMI 75 |

Remarks: See next page.

Table b: CONTINUED

Remarks: 1. Questions: - Question wordings:

S1: "Taking things all together, how would you say things are these days - would you say you're very happy, pretty happy or not too happy these days?"

S2: "Taken all together (altogether), how would you say things are these days - would you say that you are very happy, pretty happy, or not too happy?"

S3: "Taking all things together, how would you say things are these days - would you say that you're very happy, pretty happy, or not too happy these days?"

- See remark 1, below table a (second part).

2. Countries: - the distribution for Western Europe is based on the proportions for the countries presented.

- United Kingdom including Northern Ireland.

3. Proportions: - In all cases we rounded the proportions to obtain a total of 100%.

- U.S.A.-data were most extensively reported by SMITH. Unfortunately he omitted the proportions 'don't know/no answer'. These data were not to be found in other publications either.
SMITH also offered happiness distributions after our cut-off date of 1975. However, we could not think of a good reason for not presenting them here.

- The distribution for Western Europe is based on the proportions for the countries presented.

4. Source: - SRC : Survey Research Center, University of Michigan
SRC-OMNI: SRC Omnibus Survey
SRC-ELEC: SRC Election Survey
SRC-MH : SRC Mental Health Survey
NORC : National Opinion Research Center
GSS : General Social Survey, NORC
CNS : Continuous National Survey, NORC

- The U.S.A.-data are partly presented in other publications as well (e.g. BRADB 69).

- The European data were not presented in the publication of the Commission of the European Communities, but were offered to us by the Belgian Archives for the Social Sciences (BASS).

Table c: RESPONSES TO THE QUESTION: 'HOW SATISFIED ARE YOU WITH THE WAY YOU ARE GETTING ON NOW - VERY SATISFIED, ALL RIGHT, DISSATISFIED, DON'T KNOW?' (TYPE HAPP 2.1)[1].

| Countries[2] | Date | Proportions | | | | N |
|---|---|---|---|---|---|---|
| | | 'very satisfied' | 'all right' | 'dis-satisfied' | 'don't know'/ no answer | |
| U.S.A. | 48/9-10 | 15 | 57 | 26 | 2 | 1015 |
| WESTERN EUROPE | 1948-49 | 7 | 50 | 39 | 4 | 8616 |
| - France | 48/6-7 | 2 | 27 | 56 | 15 | 1000 |
| - Western Germany | 48/8 | 2 | 51 | 44 | 3 | 3371 |
| - Great Britain | 48/7 | 12 | 52 | 33 | 3 | 1195 |
| - Italy | 48/7 | 5 | 45 | 46 | 4 | 1078 |
| - Netherlands | 1948 | 8 | 54 | 34 | 4 | 942 |
| - Norway | 48/4 | 21 | 67 | 10 | 2 | 1030 |
| Mexico | 48/12-49/1 | 20 | 18 | 61 | 1 | 1752 |
| AUSTRALIA | 1948 | 22 | 57 | 20 | 1 | 945 |

Remarks: 1. Source: BUCHA 53; Appendix D, p. 125-126.

2. Countries: The distribution for Western Europe is based on the proportions for the countries presented.

Table d: RESPONSES TO THE QUESTION: 'ALL THINGS CONSIDERED, HOW SATISFIED OR DISSATISFIED ARE YOU WITH YOUR LIFE AS A WHOLE THESE DAYS - VERY SATISFIED, FAIRLY SATISFIED, NOT VERY SATISFIED , NOT SATISFIED AT ALL, DON'T KNOW?' (TYPE HAPP 2.1)[1,2].

| Country | Date | Proportions[3] | | | | | N |
|---|---|---|---|---|---|---|---|
| | | 'very satisfied' | 'fairly satisfied' | 'not very satisfied' | 'not at all satisfied' | don't know/ no answer | |
| WESTERN EUROPE | 73/9 | 41 | 52 | 5 | 1 | 1 | 13484 |
| | 75/5 | 33 | 52 | 7 | 2 | 6 | 9605 |
| - Belgium | 73/9 | 43 | 49 | 6 | 2 | 0 | |
| | 75/5 | 39 | 52 | 5 | 2 | 2 | 1555 |
| - Denmark | 73/9 | 51 | 44 | 4 | 1 | 0 | |
| | 75/5 | 51 | 41 | 4 | 0 | 4 | 1039 |
| - France | 73/9 | 15 | 62 | 17 | 4 | 2 | |
| | 75/5 | 16 | 59 | 16 | 7 | 2 | 1196 |
| - Western Germany | 73/9 | 16 | 66 | 15 | 2 | 1 | |
| | 75/5 | 13 | 66 | 16 | 2 | 3 | 1039 |
| - United Kingdom (incl. N. Ireland) | 73/9 | 33 | 52 | 11 | 3 | 1 | |
| | 75/5 | 33 | 53 | 9 | 3 | 2 | 1317 |
| Northern Ireland | 75/5 | 37 | 49 | 8 | 3 | 3 | |
| - Ireland | 73/9 | 53 | 39 | 6 | 2 | 0 | |
| | 75/5 | 36 | 52 | 9 | 3 | 0 | 999 |
| - Italy | 73/9 | 8 | 57 | 27 | 7 | 1 | |
| | 75/5 | 7 | 52 | 28 | 10 | 3 | 1043 |
| - Luxembourg | 73/9 | 40 | 49 | 9 | 2 | 0 | |
| | 75/5 | 26 | 45 | 15 | 7 | 7 | 324 |
| - Netherlands | 73/9 | 41 | 52 | 5 | 1 | 1 | |
| | 75/5 | 33 | 52 | 7 | 2 | 6 | 1093 |

Remarks: 1. Source: COMMI 75, p. 139-141.

2. Questions: The same question was also answered by means of an 11-point scale (see table e).

3. Proportions: The distribution for western Europe is based on the proportions for the countries presented.

Table e: RESPONSES TO QUESTIONS ON SATISFACTION WITH ONE'S LIFE AS A WHOLE, RATED ON 11-POINT SCALES, RANGING FROM 0 TO 10 (TYPE HAPP 2.1)[1].

| Countries[2] | Date | Code[1] | Proportions[3] high (7-10) | medium (4-6) | low (0-3) | don't know / no answer | Mean | N | Source |
|---|---|---|---|---|---|---|---|---|---|
| ANGLO AMERICA | 1975 | M | 75 | 21 | 3 | 1 | 7.6 | 2046 | GALLU 76 |
| - U.S.A. | 59/8 | L1 | | | | | 7.6 | 1549 | CANTR 65/2 |
| | 1975 | M | 75 | 21 | 3 | 1 | 7.6 | 1014 | GALLU 76 |
| - Canada | 1975 | M | 79 | 18 | 2 | 0 | 7.6 | 1032 | GALLU 76 |
| WESTERN EUROPE | 1975 | M | 64 | 31 | 5 | 0 | 7.0 | 2242 | GALLU 76 |
| | 75/5 | C | | | | | 7.4 | 9605 | COMMI 75, p. 208 |
| - France | 1975 | M | 57 | 37 | 5 | 1 | 6.6 | 330 | GALLU 76 |
| | 75/5 | C | | | | | 6.7 | 1196 | COMMI 75, p. 208 |
| - W. Germany | 1975 | M | 71 | 27 | 2 | 0 | 7.3 | 303 | GALLU 76 |
| | 75/5 | C | | | | | 7.0 | 1039 | COMMI 75, p. 208 |
| - United Kingdom | 71/3 | L2 | 24 | 27 29 | 20 | | 5.5 | 213 | ABRAM 73, p. 3 |
| | 1975 | M | (58<br>74 | 29 13<br>26 | 0<br>0 | 0<br>0) | 7.5 | 307 | GALLU 76 |
| | 75/5 | C | | | | | 7.5 | 1317 | COMMI 75, p. 208 |
| - Ireland | 75/5 | C | | | | | 8.2 | 999 | COMMI 75, p. 208 |
| - Italy | 1975 | M | 48 | 43 | 9 | 0 | 6.3 | 309 | GALLU 76 |
| | 75/5 | C | | | | | 6.3 | 1043 | COMMI 75, p. 208 |
| - Benelux | 1975 | M | 63 | 31 | 6 | 0 | 6.9 | 300 | GALLU 76 |
| - Belgium | 75/5 | C | | | | | 7.8 | 1555 | COMMI 75, p. 208 |
| - Netherlands | 75/5 | C | | | | | 7.5 | 1093 | COMMI 75, p. 208 |
| - Luxembourg | 75/5 | C | | | | | 7.7 | 324 | COMMI 75, p. 208 |
| - Scandinavia | 1975 | M | 86 | 13 | 1 | 0 | 8.0 | 330 | GALLU 76 |
| - Denmark | 75/5 | C | | | | | 8.3 | 1039 | COMMI 75, p. 208 |
| LATIN AMERICA | 1975 | M | 58 | 32 | 9 | 1 | 6.8 | 2059 | GALLU 76 |
| - Brazil | 1975 | M | 63 | 29 | 7 | 1 | 7.0 | 382 | GALLU 76 |
| - Mexico | 1975 | M | 69 | 22 | 9 | 0 | 7.0 | 350 | GALLU 76 |
| AFRICA | 1975 | M | 25 | 46 | 29 | 0 | 4.9 | 914 | GALLU 76 |
| ASIA | 1975 | M | 16 | 45 | 37 | 1 | 4.3 | 872 | GALLU 76 |
| - India | 1975 | M | 8 | 36 | 54 | 2 | 3.5 | 354 | GALLU 76 |
| - Japan | 1975 | M | 41 | 52 | 7 | 0 | 6.0 | 337 | GALLU 76 |
| AUSTRALIA | 1975 | M | 83 | 15 | 1 | 1 | 7.9 | 301 | GALLU 76 |

Remarks: 1. Question wordings: C : 11-point scale. 0 = not satisfied at all, 10 = very satisfied:
"All things considered, how satisfied or dissatisfied are you with your life as a whole these days?" (This questions was also answered by means of fixed answer categories; see table d).

L1: 11-point Ladder Rating (Cantril Satisfaction with Life rating; see CANTR 65/2):
"Some people seem to be quite happy and satisfied with their lives, while others seem quite unhappy and dissatisfied. Now look at the ladder again. Suppose that a person who is entirely satisfied with his life would be at the top of the ladder (step 10) and a person who is extremely dissatisfied with his life would be at the bottom of the ladder (step 0). Where would you put yourself on the ladder at the present stage of your life in terms of how satisfied or dissatisfied you are with your own personal life?"

L2: 11-point Ladder Rating, based on CANTR 65:
"How satisfied would you say you are with things in general today? This is a scale with complete satisfaction at the top (10) and complete dissatisfaction at the bottom (0). Whereabouts on the ladder would you put yourself?"

M : 11-point Mountain Rating, based on CANTR 65 (a mountain with 11 ascending steps instead of a ladder was used):
"Now taking everything about your life into account, how satisfied or dissatisfied are you with your life today?"

Table e: CONTINUED

2. Countries: - for countries used in GALLU-study see remark no. 2 (first part) below table a.

- the distribution for western Europe from the COMMI-study is based on the proportions for the nine countries presented in the table, while in the GALLU-study it is based on the scores for 17 countries.

- United Kingdom: the COMMI-data include Northern Ireland. In the case of the GALLU-data this is uncertain. They refer to the 'United Kingdom'. The ABRAM-sample covers the 'British population as a whole'.

3. Proportions: - In all cases we rounded the proportions to obtain a total of 100%.

- For the United Kingdom ABRAM offers the following proportions: 24% score 8-10; 27% score 6-7; 29% score 4-5; 20% score 0-3. To facilitate comparison we also presented proportions based on the same division for the British sample from the GALLU-study.

Table f: RESPONSES TO QUESTIONS ON PRESENT SITUATION COMPARED WITH BEST AND WORST POSSIBLE LIFE, RATED ON 11-POINT SELF-ANCHORING SCALES, BASED ON CANTRIL (1965) (TYPE HAPP 3.1)[1].

| Countries[2] | Date | Code[1] | Proportions[3] high (7-10) | medium (4-6) | low (0-3) | don't know/ no answer | Mean | N | Source |
|---|---|---|---|---|---|---|---|---|---|
| ANGLO AMERICA | 1975 | M | 56 | 37 | 6 | 1 | 6.7 | 2046 | GALLU 76 |
| - U.S.A. | 59/8 | L | 51 | 41 | 7 | 1 | 6.6 | 1549 | CANTR 65, p. 258 |
| | 1964 | L | | | | | 6.9 | | CANTR 71, p. 66 |
| | 1971 | L | | | | | 6.6 | 1588 | CANTR 71, p. 66 |
| | 1975 | M | 56 | 37 | 6 | 1 | 6.7 | 1014 | GALLU 76 |
| - Canada | 1975 | M | 63 | 34 | 3 | 0 | 7.0 | 1032 | GALLU 76 |
| WESTERN EUROPE | 1975 | M | 45 | 46 | 8 | 1 | 6.3 | 2241 | GALLU 76 |
| - France | 1975 | M | 36 | 52 | 12 | 0 | 5.8 | 330 | GALLU 76 |
| - Western Germany | 57/9 | L | 24 | 59 | 14 | 3 | 5.3 | 480 | CANTR 65, p. 258 |
| | 1975 | M | 50 | 43 | 3 | 4 | 6.6 | 303 | GALLU 76 |
| - United Kingdom | 1975 | M | 53 | 45 | 2 | 0 | 6.8 | 307 | GALLU 76 |
| - Italy | 1975 | M | 32 | 52 | 16 | 0 | 5.6 | 309 | GALLU 76 |
| - Benelux | 1975 | M | 43 | 47 | 10 | 0 | 6.0 | 300 | GALLU 76 |
| - Scandinavia | 1975 | M | 78 | 19 | 3 | 0 | 7.6 | 330 | GALLU 76 |
| - Yugoslavia | 62/spring | L | 21 | 57 | 21 | 1 | 5.0 | 1523 | CANTR 65, p. 258 |
| - Poland | 62/spring | L | | | | | 4.4 | 1464 | CANTR 65, p. 258 |
| LATIN AMERICA | 1975 | M | 44 | 43 | 13 | 0 | 6.0 | 2059 | GALLU 76 |
| - Brazil | 60/late - 61/early | L | 18 | 35 | 28 | 19 | 4.6 | 2168 | CANTR 65, p. 258 |
| | 1975 | M | 42 | 48 | 10 | 0 | 6.2 | 382 | GALLU 76 |
| - Cuba | 60/4-5 | L | 45 | 43 | 9 | 3 | 6.4 | 992 | CANTR 65, p. 258 |
| - Dominican Republic | 62/4 | L | 1 | 13 | 84 | 2 | 1.6 | 814 | CANTR 65, p. 258 |
| - Mexico | 1975 | M | 42 | 51 | 7 | 0 | 6.2 | 350 | GALLU 76 |
| - Panama | 62/3-1 | L | 18 | 54 | 26 | 2 | 4.8 | 642 | CANTR 65, p. 258 |
| AFRICA | 1975 | M | 17 | 55 | 28 | 0 | 4.6 | 914 | GALLU 76 |
| - Egypt | 60/fall | L | 30 | 51 | 17 | 2 | 5.5 | 499 | CANTR 65, p. 258 |
| - Nigeria | 62/9 - 63/spring | L | 21 | 46 | 28 | 5 | 4.8 | 1200 | CANTR 65, p. 258 |
| ASIA | 1975 | M | 12 | 43 | 44 | 1 | 4.1 | 872 | GALLU 76 |
| - India | 62/summer | L | 4 | 42 | 39 | 15 | 3.7 | 2366 | CANTR 65, p. 258 |
| | 62/fall | L | | | | | 3.4 | 2014 | CANTR 65, p. 92 |
| | 1975 | M | 7 | 36 | 55 | 2 | 3.4 | 354 | GALLU 76 |
| - Israel | 61/11-62/6 | L | 29 | 50 | 19 | 2 | 5.3 | 1170 | CANTR 65, p. 258 |
| - Japan | 62/fall | L | | | | | 5.2 | 972 | CANTR 65, p. 258 |
| | 1975 | M | 32 | 58 | 10 | 0 | 5.8 | 337 | GALLU 76 |
| - Philippines | 59/spring | L | 21 | 54 | 24 | 1 | 4.9 | 500 | CANTR 65, p. 258 |
| AUSTRALIA | 1975 | M | 62 | 35 | 3 | 0 | 7.0 | 301 | GALLU 76 |

Remarks: see next page

Table f: CONTINUED

Remarks: 1. Question wordings: L: 11-point Ladder Rating (Cantril Present Personal Rating; see CANTR 65/1):
"Here is a picture of a ladder. Suppose we say that the top of the ladder (step 10) represents the best possible life for you and the bottom (step 0) represents the worst possible life for you. Where on the ladder do you feel you personally stand at the present time?"

M: 11-point Mountain Rating, based on CANTR 65 (A mountain with 11 ascending steps was used instead of a ladder):
"To indicate how you feel about your life at this time, would you use this card. Suppose the top of the mountain (step 10) represents the best possible life you can imagine, and the bottom step of the mountain (step 0) represents the worst possible life you can imagine. On which step of the mountain would you say you personally feel you stand at this time - assuming that the higher the step the better you feel about your life, and the lower the step the worse you feel about it? Just point to the step that comes closest to how you feel".

2. Countries: For countries used in the GALLU-study see remark no 2 (first part) below table a.

3. Proportions: In all cases we rounced the proportions to obtain a total of 100%.

Table g: VARIOUS QUESTIONS ON OVERALL HAPPINESS[1].

| Country | Date | Type of question[1] | Question / Distribution | N | Source |
|---|---|---|---|---|---|
| Netherlands | 68/6 | HAPP 1.1 | "Generally speaking, are you a happy person?"<br>very happy ––––– very unhappy<br>Each S could indicate his positions with an X (Later translated into a 7-point scale).<br>62% score 1 (high); 18% score 2 ; 10% score 3; 8% score 4; 2% score 5, 6 or 7 (low). | 1552 | BAKKE 74 |
| Puerto Rico | 63-64/winter and 64/fall | HAPP 1.1 | "All things considered, how would you describe yourself these days? Would you say you are..?"<br>17% 'very happy'; 50% 'fairly happy'; 33% 'not too happy'. | 1417 | MATLI 66, p. 5 |
| U.S.A. | 1968 | HAPP 2.1 | "In general, how satisfying do you find the way you're spending your life these days? Would you call it ...?"<br>23% 'completely satisfying'; 66% 'pretty satisfying', 11% 'not very satisfying'. | 1440 | FISCH 73/4, p. 226 |
| Poland | 60/6-7 | HAPP 2.1 | "On the whole, are you satisfied with life?"<br>16% 'definitely yes'; 53% 'rather yes'; 10% 'don't know'; 16% 'rather no'; 5% 'definitely no'; 1% no reply. | 2387 | MAKAR 62, p. 106 |

Remarks: 1. This table contains various questions that could not be placed in the former tables, because question and/or answer categories were not comparable with those presented there. In the case of MATLI 66 we could not decide whether the question used was comparable with the AIPO-version or with the SCR/NORC-version (See remark no 1, second part, below table a).

DISTRIBUTIONS OF HEDONIC LEVEL OF AFFECT

Table h: QUESTIONS ON PERCEIVED OCCURRENCE OF SPECIFIC AFFECTS, USING 'AFFECT BALANCE SCALES' (TYPE AFF 2.3)[1].

| Countries | Date | Mean Scores[2] | | | N | Source[3] |
|---|---|---|---|---|---|---|
| | | Positive affect | Negative affect | Affect balance | | |
| U.S.A. | 73/4-5 | 3.40 | 1.59 | 7.80 | 723 | SMITH 79, p. 26 (CNS-1) |
| | 73/5-6 | 3.23 | 1.58 | 7.66 | 647 | SMITH 79, p. 26 (CNS-2) |
| | 73/6-7 | 3.29 | 1.71 | 7.57 | 642 | SMITH 79, p. 26 (CNS-3) |
| | 73/7-8 | 3.05 | 1.65 | 7.40 | 615 | SMITH 79, p. 26 (CNS-4) |
| | 73/8-9 | 3.12 | 1.57 | 7.55 | 639 | SMITH 79, p. 26 (CNS-5) |
| | 73/9-10 | 3.15 | 1.50 | 7.64 | 630 | SMITH 79, p. 26 (CNS-6) |
| | 73/10-11 | 3.32 | 1.52 | 7.81 | 681 | SMITH 79, p. 26 (CNS-7) |
| | 73/11-12 | 3.18 | 1.48 | 7.70 | 696 | SMITH 79, p. 26 (CNS-8) |
| | 74/1 | 3.01 | 1.38 | 7.63 | 696 | SMITH 79, p. 26 (CNS-9) |
| | 74/2 | 3.02 | 1.39 | 7.65 | 692 | SMITH 79, p. 26 (CNS-10) |
| | 74/3-4 | 3.03 | 1.43 | 7.60 | 610 | SMITH 79, p. 26 (CNS-11) |
| | 74/5 | 3.26 | 1.46 | 7.79 | 656 | SMITH 79, p. 26 (CNS-12) |
| Puerto Rico | 63-64/winter and 64/fall | 1.02<br>Distribution for Affect Balance: 14% score 2 or 3; 23% score 1, 29% score 0; 19% score -1 or -2, 15% score -3 or less. | 1.32 | -0.3 | 1417 | MATLI 66, p. 10-13 |

Remarks: 1. Instruments used: U.S.A.-data: Bradburn Affect Balance Score (see BRADB 69):

"During the past few weeks, did you ever feel . . . ." yes/no

1. particularly excited or interested in something?
2. so restless that you couldn't sit long in a chair?
3. proud because someone complimented you on something you had done?
4. very lonely or remote from other people?
5. pleased about having accomplished something?
6. bored?
7. on top of the world?
8. depressed?
9. that things were going your way?
10. upset because someone criticized you?

Positive affects: items 1,3,5,7,9 / Negative affects: items 2,4,6,8,10 / Affect Balance: Positive affect score minus Negative affect score plus 6.

Puerto Rico-data: adapted Bradburn Affect Balance Score:

"During the past week, did you ever feel . . . ." yes/no

1. on top of the world?
2. pleased about having accomplished something?
3. proud because someone complimented you on something you had done?
4. very lonely or remote from other people?
5. depressed or very unhappy?
6. bored?
7. so restless you couldn't sit long in a chair?
8. vaguely uneasy about something without knowing why?
9. that you could not do anything simply because you could not start it?

Positive affects: items 1,2,3 / Negative affects: items 4,5,6,7,8,9 / Affect Balance: Positive affect score minus Negative affect score.

2. Mean scores: The U.S.A.-data and the Puerto Rico-data are not fully comparable. In the case of the U.S.A. 5 positive and 5 negative affect items were used, leading to a possible range from 0 to 5 for Positive and for Negative affect and from 1 to 11 for Affect Balance. In Puerto Rico 3 positive and 6 negative items were used, leading to a possible range from 0 to 3 for Positive affect, from 0 to 6 for Negative affect, and from -6 to 3 for Affect Balance.

3. Source: CNS = Continuous National Survey (NORC).

## DISTRIBUTIONS OF CONTENTMENT

Table i: RESPONSES TO VARIOUS QUESTIONS ON CONTENTMENT (TYPE CON 1.1).[1]

| Date | Question/Distribution | N | Source |
|---|---|---|---|
| 59/8 | 11-point Ladder-rating: "How would you rate yourself as to how successful or unsuccesful you have been in terms of achieving your own goals and aims in life? Think of the top of the ladder (step 10) as being completely successful, the bottom (step 0) as being entirely unsuccessful". Mean score: 6.7 | 1549 | CANTR 65/2 |
| 63/5 | "When you think of the things you want from life, would you say that you're doing pretty well or you're not doing too well now in getting the things you want?" 82% 'doing pretty well'; 18% 'doing not too well'. | 1453 | BRENN 67, p. 669 (NORC 160) |

Remarks: 1. Both data are not fully comparable. We presented both questions in one table, because, as far as we know, no other information regarding contentment is published.

# APPENDIX A

## Technical Terms Used in the Excerpts

Not all authors use the same technical terms in describing their investigations: what is called a 'pseudo-random sample' by one author is for instance labeled as an 'ordinal sample' by an other. Likewise some refer to a 'scale' as a series of questions on one subjectmatter, while others use the same term to denote an answer device for a multiple choice question. Similarly there are great differences in the meaning attached to common words, such as 'reliability' and 'validity'. This confusion of tongues once necessitated the compilation of current technical jargon into a book named 'Thesaurus of Social Research Terminology' (Van der Merwe, 1974). In order to allow comparison between the various investigations, their design must obviously be described in one same language. Therefore all technical terms used in this book are enumerated and explained below. They are ordered in sequence of their appearance on the notationsheet by means of which the reports were excerpted. This notationsheet was presented in exhibit 4 on page 24.

## type of study

**descriptive or explanatory**

A study is considered *descriptive* when its aim is to give a picture of the distribution of certain variables in a sample. For example, a poll to assess the percentage of unhappy citizens in a country. When the investigator wants to do more than describe how things are and he also wants to know 'why', the study is said to be *explanatory*.

**explorative or testing**

A study is considered *explorative* when the investigator has hardly any pre-assumptions about the field of investigation. When, however, he has developed specific expectations and wants to assess the tenability of these, we speak about 'hypothesis *testing* research'.

**special group or local or national population**

The subjects involved in the study can be selected in two ways: by considering people who share some special characteristics, such as age, income, occupation, etc., or by investigating all persons living in a region. In the first case we speak about a *special group*, in the latter about *local*, *regional* or *national population*, depending on the region involved.

**snapshot or longitudinal**

A study is considered *longitudinal* when its data are gathered at different points in time. If not, we speak about a *snapshot* study. This latter type of study is sometimes also denoted as *synchronic*.

**experimental or non-experimental**

A study is considered *experimental* when during the course of the investigation a change is induced by the investigator and when the effects of that change on the dependent variable are assessed; eventually by comparing with a control group. In all other cases studies are considered '*non-experimental*'.

## data gathering

**observation**

Information about the subject can be gathered in several ways. First of all by observation: observations of the subject's behavior in their normal daily routine and setting (*field observation* or *naturalistic observation*) or in a laboratory situation where he is confronted with controlled stimuli (*laboratory observation*). The investigator may make his observations hidden behind a one-way mirror (*disguised observation*) or he may decide for *open observation*, If observation involves the sharing of daily activities with the subject, we speak about *participant observation*. Observation may be *structured* (*systematic or controlled*), using detailed observation schedules or *unstructured* (*natural, simple or qualitative observation*).

**interrrogation**

A more common way of data gathering in happiness research is by posing questions. Questions may vary in their degree of structure.

- open-ended question
- closed question

Open-ended, free answer or unrestricted answer questions leave the subject free to formulate his answer. When closed questions are used (sometimes called: cafetaria questions, multiple choice questions or fixed answer questions), the respondent is asked to choose from a list of assorted words or statements one or more that best represents his view.

- direct question
- indirect question

When using direct questions the interviewer asks directly what he wants to know. If he chooses to pose his question in a more hidden way so that the respondent should not become aware of his interests, we use the term indirect questioning. Sometimes this latter method involves projective techniques (see below).

interrogation by questionnaires
- highly structured questionnaire
- lowly structured questionnaire

Questions may be presented in written questionnaires. Highly structured questionnaires use specific and often closed questions. This method is often used in mailed questionnaires and large scale survey research. Low structured questionnaires use less specific questions, for example, a request to write a story on a certain subject or to give one's opinion on a handful of topics.

interrogation by interview
- structured interview
- half-structured interview
- focused interview
- clinical interview
- depth interview

Questions can also be posed verbally in an interview-situation. In a structured interview the interviewer fills out a questionnaire on the basis of the subject's responses on standardized questions. This technique is often used in telephonic interviews. It is often referred to as 'standardized personal interview' The half-structured, open or qualitative interview does not use identical questions for all subjects. The interviewer is more sensitive to directions in the conversation opened by the subject himself. Other names for this kind of data gathering are non-directive, non-schedule, or exploratory interview. When the interviewer concentrates his questions on some limited number of points we speak about focused interview. If the term clinical interview is used we aim at an interview of this kind which is specially focused on assessing the psychological condition of the subject: usually in a therapeutic setting. The term depth interview denotes an even more specific interview of this kind which focuses upon unconscious motivations and ideas, using techniques of free association, indirect questions, projective devices, etc.

Interviews are usually conducted at the house of the subject, but also in a laboratory setting, in a clinical setting, at the place of work, or by telephone.

<u>content analysis</u>

Another way of data gathering is analyzing written documents, dairies, essays, correspondence, etc. In case this involves objective, systematic and qualitative description of the manifest content of the documents, the term content analysis is used. This requires the development of a scheme of analysis according to which information can be selected and categorized. The term does not concern loose attempts to 'feel one's way into the matter'.

<u>projective techniques</u>

Finally, information can be gathered by observing the subject's verbal and expressive behavior when being confronted with ambiguous stimuli and asked to react by, for instance, making free associations on the forms he discovers in an inkblot; writing a story about a series of pictures shown to him; enumerating pleasant and unpleasant words that come to his mind, etc. This technique requires a subsequent content analysis of the answers.

- pictorial techniques

Pictorial techniques use pictures as projective material, for instance the inkblot in the Rohrschach test or the series of pictures in the Thematic Apperception Test.

- verbal techniques

Verbal techniques are sentence completion tests, word association test and indirect open-ended questions.

- role-playing

Role-playing is sometimes used to evoke projections as well. As such it figures in techniques like psychodrama, sociodrama and doll-playing.

---

## sample construction

(see column 9 in Part III)

---

Sampling is the process by which inference is made to the whole by examining only a part. Usually a limited amount of the subjects is selected out of a wider population. When the process of sampling is spread over a longer period we speak of time sampling or multiphase sampling.

probability sampling

Two types of sampling methods can be distinguished; probability sampling and non-probability sampling. Probability sampling implies selection of subjects at random and allows generalizations over the population out of which this random selection took place. Non-probability methods on the other hand use implicit or explicit criteria for selection and therefore in principle provide no basis for generalization. Only when the sample thus constructed can be shown to equal the population in the distribution of some relevant characteristics some generality may be claimed. Non-probability methods are often used in exploratory research where the focus is on generating new ideas. Probability methods fit better with the objectives of describing and testing studies .
The following variants of probability sampling can be mentioned:

simple random sampling

Simple random sampling is selecting respondents without any system or criterion. For example haphazardly picking names out of parish registers. The only system allowed in this method is preventing that the same person is invited more than once to cooperate in the study.

systematic random sampling

Systematic probability sampling allows for some system in choosing the subjects, as long as this system does not interfere with the aim of the study. For example drawing every 10th name out of a register or inviting the head of the household of house nr 5 of every street in town. This procedure is also known as pseudo-random sampling and ordinal sampling. A variant of this method is random start sampling . Here some files of a register are choosen at simple random and thereafter used in a systematic way. The procedure is also known as the method of interpenetrating subsamples.

stratified sampling

More criteria are introduced with stratified sampling. Here the distribution of special characteristics in the sample is manipulated. This procedure is also known as controlled sampling, oversampling, optimal sampling and weighting. For example the age of the subjects may be controlled. If the investigator wants the distribution of his sample to be equal to the distribution of age in his population, he draws a sample proportionally stratified by age. If he wants to be sure that there will be enough 90 year old subjects in his sample he will be inclined to draw a disproportionate sample with relatively more old people. Stratification can take place at the moment of sampling itself. We then speak of stratified or balanced sampling. Another possibility is random discard of some subjects with characteristics judged to be sufficiently represented in the sample. We speak here of post-stratification.

cluster sampling

— area sampling

— multi stage sampling

Often the population is too great to take a simple random sample. The inhabitants of a nation are not all represented in one great file. So for convenience's sake samples are sometimes drawn from clusters, such as towns, companies, households, schools, etc. Usually they are selected by simple or stratified random sampling methods. When the cluster is geographically defined, we speak of area sampling. The method of first selecting a number of areas, next a number of households within these areas and finally the subjects within the households is called multi-stage sampling.

non-probability sampling

accidental sampling

The following non-probability methods of sampling can be distinguished: The most widely used method of non-probability sampling is accidental sampling. One simply reaches out and takes the cases that fall to hand, continuing the process untill the sample reaches a designed size, without paying attention to possible distortions in the distribution of essential variables due to the way of selection.

chunk sample

When the selection is not totally haphazard but a group is taken which allows some prediction of the distortion in the distribution of the variables aimed at, we use the term chunk sample. For example a class of students, members of a club, employees of a firm, etc.

purposive sampling

— expert choice

— quota sampling

Purposive sampling is selecting subjects on basis of some criteria which are relevant for the variables in the study. When these criteria are vague and complex, this selection often takes place by expert choice. For example in a study of drug addiction a police-officer can select high addiction districts in the town or he can bring the investigator into contact with some addicts who on their turn can supply more subjects (snowball sampling). Expert choice is also used when the composition of two contrasting samples is necessary: for example healthy and unhealthy employees by the factory-doctor.
An other form of non-probability purposive sampling is quota sampling, also called stratified non-random sampling and interviewer selected sampling. Here the interviewer chooses the subjects himself on the basis of some instructions. For example, he is instructed to find subjects of certain age, sex and educational level.

---

## non-response; N

---

N

The number of subjects actually participating in the investigation is symbolized by 'N'. Usually the number is lower than the numbers that were selected for the study. This may be due to several reasons, e.g.:
Unattainable: contact could not be established with the subject for reasons of illness, wrong address, change of address, etc.
Refusal: subject refuses to participate.
Incomplete: the subject participates, but due to misunderstanding or incomplete responses his data have to be omitted.

non-response

The subjects who failed to participate in the study for these or other reasons are known as the non-response category. Their number is usually expressed as a percentage of the original sample.

A high non-response can interfere with the representativeness of the sample. When there is a high non-response due to illness among elderly people, the sample is no longer representative for age and all conclusions may be severely distorted. To cope with this problem a mini-study of the non-response group is sometimes made in order to establish the degree of deviance on a limited amount of variables; usually some variables which are easily measured such as sex, age and income. The non-response group is said to be unaffected by sex if this study does not reveal significant differences in the distribution of sex. If this is not the case and it turns out for example that the percentage of females in the non-response group is significantly higher/lower than in the response group, females are said to be overrepresented/ underrepresented in the non-response group.

unaffected by ...

overrepresentation/ underrepresentation of ...

---

## author's happiness label

---

Under the heading of 'label' in the notation sheet we note the name the original investigator gave to what we call 'happiness'. As mentioned earlier, different labels are often used for similar phenomena. Most investigators use labels like 'morale', 'general satisfaction', 'elation', etc. Sometimes, however, different names are used, indicating quite an other interpretation of the observations: for example: 'psychological health' and 'adjustment'. Differences in labeling sometimes go together with differences in conceptualization, but not always.

dependent variable

The concept of happiness can be used in different ways in the inquiry process. First of all it can be used as a dependent variable. The investigator then looks upon happiness as a resultant of a process and tries to identify the factors which make people happy. When the investigation is exclusively devoted to this purpose happiness is the only dependent variable. If the investigator is at the same time interested in the determinants of other factors as well, we say that happiness is one of the dependent variables in the investigation.
A reversed position in the inquiry process is also possible. Happiness can be seen as a determinant of another phenomenon. For example the feeling of happiness could foster physical health, improve interpersonal contact or give rise to a tolerant attitude. In such-like cases happiness is used as an independent variable. Studies of this type are rare.

independent variable

indicator

More often observations which we consider a valid indicator for our concept of happiness are used as indicator for quite an other matter. For example: happiness of children can be used as an indicator of 'parental adequacy' in a study of child rearing patterns and social class. Similarly happiness questions have been used to assess 'mental health'.

---

## happiness-indicator

(column 4 in Part III)

---

instrument

With the term indicator we aim at the empirical measures or the instrument' used; the concrete and specific definition of the variables in terms of the operations by which observations are to be categorized. A classification of happiness indicators was presented in exhibit 1 on page 13.

scheme of analysis

When happiness is assessed in an indirect way by behavioral observation or by projective techniques, these operations are framed in the instructions for subsequent content analysis. We call this a *scheme of analysis*.

question
rating scale

When happiness is measured by direct questioning the term 'indicator' refers to the *question* used and their answer-categories. Responses to closed questions are usually recorded on a *rating scale*. For example:

'Do you feel:

very happy ______________________________ unhappy '
1 2 3 4 5 6

- .... point scale
- graphic scale

When such a rating scale has six answer categories it is said to be a *six-point scale*. These items can be points on a linear scale or seperate multiple choice statements, such as 'very happy', 'happy', 'not too happy', or 'unhappy'. When *graphic scales* are used the subject indicates his rating by simply placing a check at the appropriate point on a line that runs from one extreme of the attribute in question to the other.

index
- .... item index
- simple index
- weighted index

Often several questions are used to assess one variable and the scores for these questions are added up. In that case we speak of an *index*. For example, popularity can be measured by perceived esteem of one's, boss, one's friend and one's spouse. When the answers on three of these questions are summed up into one score we speak of a *three item index*. When the investigator assigns equal weight to the items, we speak of a *simple index*, if not, of a *weighted index*.

Sometimes series of questions are first tested for 'scalability'. A cross-check is made as to whether other people also consider the question to be indicators of the same variable. Moreover one often tries to select questions in such a way that the answers offer a more accurate picture of the continuum on which the variable may vary. This is commonly called a 'scale'. The word scale here has an other meaning than that of the 'rating scale' mentioned above. We therefore stick to the term 'index'.

Several types of indices can be contructed: among other ones: *cumulative* indices, in which the items are supposed to represent an increasing monotonic function of the variable. Variants of this type index are e.g. the so-called *Thurstone-scales*, *Likert-scales* and *Guttman-scales*.

## reliability

The term *reliability* refers to the consistency of data yielded by an indicator irrespective of what it may measure. This can be assessed in the following ways:

stability
- repeat reliability
- retest reliability

An indicator is *stable or constant* when its measures do not change over time. This can be assessed by repeating the same questions at different times in the course of the interview (*repeat reliability*), or by retesting some weeks or years later in a special interview and than assessing the association between the responses in both instances. We then speak of *across-time stability or retest-reliability*.

equivalence

When an indicator contains more than one item it can be tested for e q u i v a l e n c e, c o n s i s t e n c y or c o n g r u e n c e. This refers to the degree in which these items measure the same phenomenon. Equivalence is assessed by the association between items. High association is considered as an indication that they cover the same factor. Current measures of equivalence are a l p h a (Cronbach, 1951) and o m e g a (Heise & Bornstedt, 1970), both ranging from zero to one.

---

## validity

---

An indicator is considered v a l i d if it measures what it is supposed to measure: if it is free of bias, systematic or non-sampling errors. This is one of the greatest problems in social research and in happiness research in particular. Does a set of questions on happiness tap the evaluation of life of the subject or does it reflect a value-orientation, a defensive self-image, a social norm, etc.? The validity of an indicator can be assessed in two ways: by the logical consistency of its items and by its correspondence with other indicators of the same phenomenon or related phenomena.

internal validity

structural validity

In the first case we speak of i n t e r n a l v a l i d i t y. This kind of validity is assessed by checking whether the questions or other observational devices we want to pose all represent the same meaning: its s u b s t a n t i v e v a l i d i t y. This can be done by carefully inspecting the matter ( f a c e- v a l i d i t y t e s t i n g) or by an inter-subjective procedure of c o n t e n t- v a l i d i t y t e s t i n g, often using judges. A final check on this substantive testing is the intercorrelation of test items when used on a larger group of subjects. We call this a testing for s t r u c t u r a l v a l i d i t y, or i t e m - a n a l y s i s. Here the same procedure is followed as with testing for equivalence, only the view-point is slightly different.

external validity

congruent validity

concurrent validity

— predictive validity
— retrodictive validity

A second method of validity testing is assessing correspondence with other indicators. We speak here of e x t e r n a l v a l i d i t y, p r a c t i c a l or e m p i r i c a l v a l i d i t y. Two variants can be discerned:

Firstly, estimates of validity can be made by assessing the association with other indicators of the same variable. For example, a happiness question can be validated on other happiness questions, facial expression, expert ratings, peer report, etc. We speak here of c o n g r u e n t v a l i d i t y.

Sometimes happiness indicators are validated on essentially other phenomena known to be related to happiness, such as mental health, social adjustment or social participation. We then speak of c o n c u r r e n t v a l i d i t y. This method is not very easy to apply in happiness research because the relations of these factors are neither complete nor constant. When congruent or concurrent validity is assessed by the association with later events, we speak of p r e d i c t i v e v a l i d i t y. When phenomena of the past are taken as a point of reference, we speak of r e t r o d i c t i v e v a l i d i t y.

---

## (frequency) distribution

---

The frequency distribution of answers reflects the number of subjects scoring on the different answer categories. For example, the frequency distribution of a single happiness question in a national sample can be: 30% very happy, 50% moderately happy and 20% unhappy.

unimodal or bimodal

There are different types of frequency distributions: unimodal or multimodal. We use the term 'unimodal' when the distribution shows one peak: f.e. 10%, 20%, 40%, 30% and 'bimodal' when the distribution shows two peaks: f.e. 10%, 30%, 10%, 40%, 10%.
Unless specially mentioned all frequency distributions mentioned are unimodal.

symmetry

Unimodal frequency distributions may vary in symmetry, that is the division of cases on either side of the mode. See below.

- positively skewed
- negatively skewed

subjects in % negatively skewed positively skewed symmetric

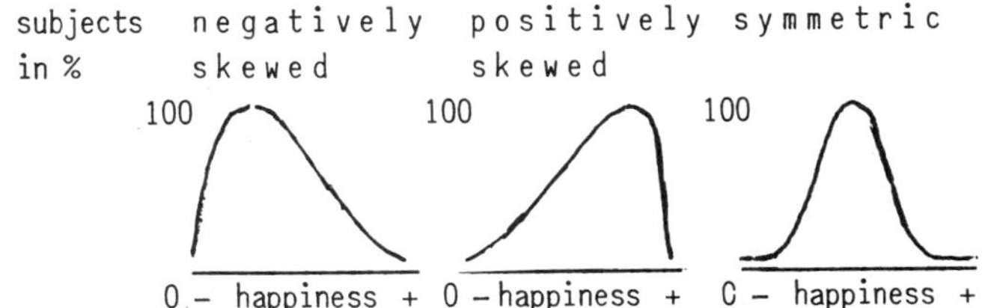


range

- possible range
- actual range

Frequency distributions may vary in range: the number of categories they cover. An investigator may distinguish ten different levels of happiness, but he may also do with splitting up between happy and unhappy subjects. The theoretical range does not necessarily coincide with the actual range; the subjects do not always use all answer categories the investigator offers them.

mean

modus

median

The center of a frequency distribution of happiness scores can be indicated in several ways. First by computing the mean or average which is the sum of happiness scores, divided by the number of subjects. A second indication is the modus: the category which yielded most scores. The third is the median: the point on the range which has as many observations on its left side as on its right side.

SD

Frequency distributions may differ in dispersion of scores. This dispersion is usually expressed in what is called the standard deviation (SD); the positive square root of the variance.

---

## association

(columns 5 and 6 in Part III)

---

Two variables are said to be associated or correlated when changes in one variable are systematically accompanied by changes in the other. For example happiness is said to be associated with health when people who say thay feel happy report more often that they feel healthy than unhappy people do.

direction of association

Association has aspects of direction and strength. Happiness and health are said to be positively associated when happiness goes hand in hand with good health and negatively when it is accompanied by bad health. This direction is indicated by + and - signs in the column 'value of association' in the excerpts (column 6 in Part III). Some practical problems may arise in indicating the direction of the relation. When we say there is an association of G = +.50 between happiness and education, the direction is clear; the more education, the more happiness and vice verse. Difficulties arise, however, when a variable is labeled so that the direction of the relation is less clear. For example, when an investigator reports an association of G = +.50 between happiness and marital status. Now it is not clear whether being married is positively associated with happiness or negatively. To interpret this information we must keep in mind that the association reported represents the following relation.

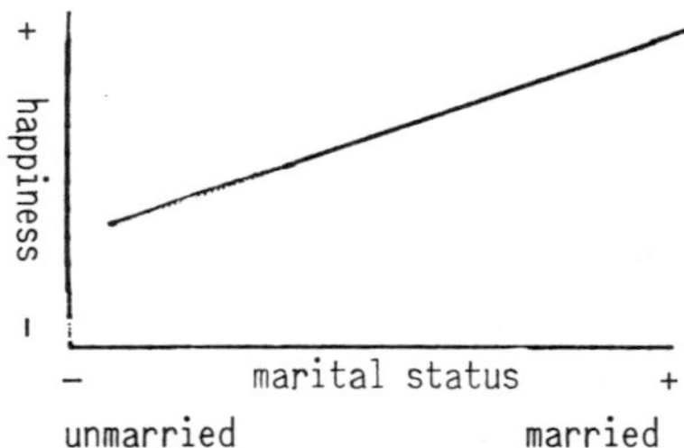


In the column of 'operationalisation' we write therefore 'unmarried vs married' which means that married status is associated with happiness.

value of association

Association reaches its highest possible value when all happy people are healthy and all unhappy people are unhealthy. Association is zero when as many people are healthy as unhappy people and negative when happy people turn out to be less healthy than unhappy people. Values of association are usually expressed by us in a number between one and zero.

measures of association

There are many ways of expressing the strength of associations. These measures of association use different assumptions and statistical techniques. It would lead us too far to discuss their pro's and contra's and their limitations. We may do with a review of basic assumptions, names, symbols and ranges in Appedix B.

---

## significance

(columns 7 and 8 in Part III)

---

The term significance refers to the likelihood that an observed empirical relationship results from sampling error. A relationship is said to be significant at the .05 level ($p < .05$) if the likelihood of its being only a function of sampling error is no greater than 5 percent. Assessing whether chances of sampling error are sufficiently small is called testing for significance. Such procedures make sense only when representativeness can be assumed.

p < .01

The character 'p' denotes usually the probability that in spite of the association found in the sample the actual association in the population is zero. For example when in a sample of the Dutch population we find a correlation of G = +.40 between health and happiness which is significant at the 99% level ($p < .01$) this means that there is a chance of less than 1% that in the Dutch population as a whole health and happiness are unrelated. Sometimes it is not the chance of a zero association which is computed but other points of reference are chosen. For example, when the association between health and happiness is +.30 for males and +.50 for females, it is possible to compute the likelihood that this difference is due to error. Unless stated otherwise significance calculations refer to the probability that there actually is no association at all in the population the sample was drawn from.

**s** **ns** Sometimes the investigator does not report 'p' values but merely claims to consider his results significant. In these cases we note 's'. If the investigator considers his results non-significant we note 'ns'. Usually p> 05 is considered non-significant.

## correlates of happiness

(column 1 and 2 in Part III)

Correlates of happiness are phenomena found to be associated with happiness. For example, when people claiming that they tend to be very happy are found to be healthier than people who tell te be rather unhappy on an average, health is said to be a correlate of happiness.

**conceptualization** Conceptualization is distinguishing an aspect of reality and attaching a name to it. Concepts are often highly theoretical and have no direct connection with the observable reality.

**operationalisaztion** Operationalization is translating them into observable terms. Devising a measure, instrument, or indicator. Such translation often requires a further specification of dimensions in the original concept. See for example the operationalization of the concepts of health and happiness below.

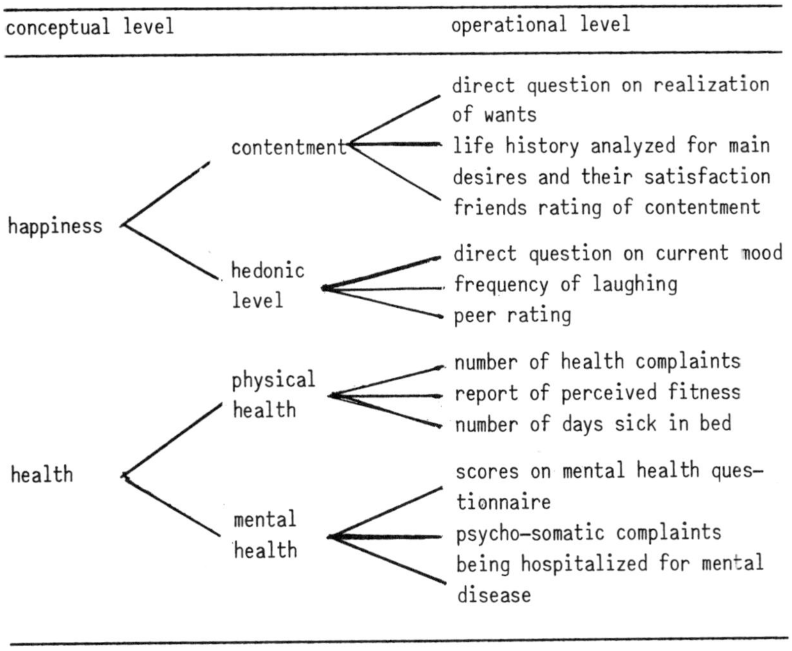

| conceptual level | | operational level |
|---|---|---|
| happiness | contentment | direct question on realization of wants |
| | | life history analyzed for main desires and their satisfaction |
| | | friends rating of contentment |
| | hedonic level | direct question on current mood |
| | | frequency of laughing |
| | | peer rating |
| health | physical health | number of health complaints |
| | | report of perceived fitness |
| | | number of days sick in bed |
| | mental health | scores on mental health questionnaire |
| | | psycho-somatic complaints |
| | | being hospitalized for mental disease |

This scheme does not cover all dimensions and operationalizations which could be devised for these two concepts. There are many more possibilities. This makes it clear that operationalization of the same concept can differ widely. So it is evident that when interpreting associations we should not rely too much upon the labels used, but focus on the operational definitions instead.

## elaboration

(column 3 in Part III)

specification

If in a certain population happiness is found statistically related to for example education, these phenomena are not always equally linked in all parts of that population. Happiness may be related to education among young adults but not among the elderly, or may be more strongly related to educational level among males than among females. Inspection for such differences is called *specification*.

stronger among ....
lower among ....
not among ....

If in the example at hand happiness is indeed more strongly related to education among males than among the population at large, the association is said to hold *stronger among* males and in the reverse to be lower in this category. If there is no correlation at all in this part of the population, we note *not among* males.

reversed among ....

Sometimes the direction of the association is different in a part of the population. For instance, it is observed that people who managed to earn a good income in spite of a low education, are particularly happy. We then write *reversed among* the highest income brackets.

explanation

A statistical relationship between happiness and education does not necessarily mean that education fosters happiness or that happiness adds to the chance that one does well at school. The variables may in fact be unrelated because one or more intervening variables are involved. Good health and high intelligence could for instance be responsible for a spurious correlation because they both add to educational success and to a positive appreciation of life. It is also possible that education as such does not add to happiness but that it favors indirectly a positive appreciation: for example because it opens doors to good paying jobs. One same factor can in fact be both a spurious factor and a link in a causal chain between education and happiness. Good health may inflate the correlation as far as it works spuriously, but at the same time it can also be responsible for a reality link: happiness fostering health and thereby happiness.

partial correlation

Such effect can be demonstrated by specification procedures as mentioned above. They can also be checked by computing *partial correlations*, that is assessing the correlation that remains when effects of one or two more further variables are checked. Partial correlation coefficients are symbolized with '$r_{pc}$', partial (or standardized) gammas with 'G' and partial taus with '$t_s$'. The results of such control procedures are noted as follows:

disappears when controlled for ....
lower when controlled for....

If the correlation between happiness and education appears to be mediated by income, we write that it *disappears when controlled for* income. If at least part of the common variance remains, we say that it appears *lower when controlled for that matter*.

reversed when controlled for...

Controls can also demonstrate an actually reversed relationship. Happiness could for instance be positively related to education, while education is in fact detrimental to it. That could be so, when negative effects were masked by the fact that highly educated people are typically born in the higher social ranks and for that reason enjoy greater self-respect and a better financiel start. In that case we note that the correlation is *reversed when controlled for* social milieu of origin. Likewise it is possible that a zero correlation masks a reality link. A positive effect of education on happiness could for instance be disguised by the fact that members of minority groups be diguised by the fact that members of minority groups are overrepresented in the higher educational levels, education being the only chance for mobility. These people may in fact take more enjoyment in life because of their educational achievement, but discrimination may still prevent their happiness to be above average. If such an effect is demonstrated by the existence of positive correlations in both the minority and and the majority or when a positive partial correlation appears we say that a correlation did appear when controlled for minority status.

... appears when controlled

Quite often such procedures reveal that suspicions about spuriousness of hypotheses about mediating variables are false. We then note that the correlation appeared unaffected by the control variable(s).

unaffected by ...

shape of the relation

Measures of association inform us about the strength of association. They do not provide information about the pattern of association, but more or less suggest a linear pattern. However, associations may follow non-linear patterns as well. For example a positive correlation between happiness and education may cover a great variety of patterns, some of which are shown below. Uncovering such patterns is called elaboration for shape. The following technical terms are used in that context:

linear

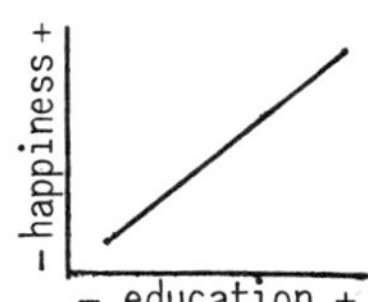


lineair relation: the more education, the more happiness

U-shaped

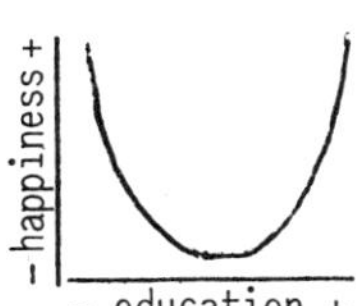


U-shaped curve: mediumly educated people being least happy

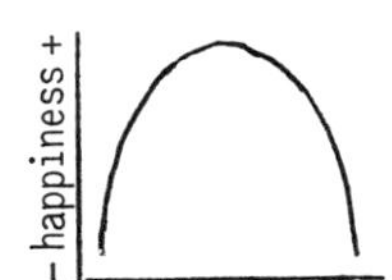


U-shaped curve: mediumly educated people being most happy

L-shaped

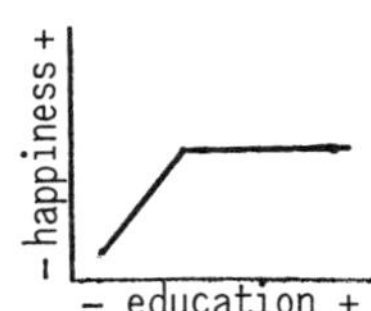


L-shaped curve: the relationship holds in the lower educational ranks only

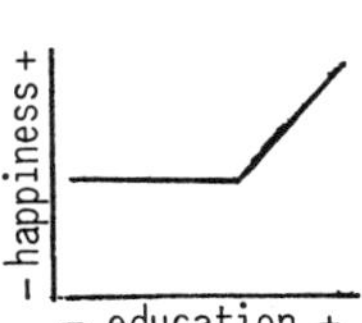


L-shaped curve: the relationship holds in the higher educational ranks only

Z-shaped curve

Z - s h a p e d c u r v e : the relationship does not hold in the middle educational ranks

Z - s h a p e d c u r v e : the relationship holds in the middle educational ranks

Usually relationships are supposed to be linear. Relatively few investigators assess whether this is in fact the case. We report about the shape of the relationship only when there is evidence that it is not linear.

noteworthy differences

These elaboration procedures involve often the comparison of association values: comparion of associations found in subpopulations (mutually and with the association found in the general population) or between controlled and uncontrolled associations. It is often not clear whether the differences that appear are really worthwhile. Tests of significance are seldom performed on such differences. A better criterion failing, we applied the rule that differences greater than .10 are worth mentioning whatever the measure of association, if only it ranges from one to zero. For studies involving 500 subjects or more, this threshold was lowered to .05. When differences smaller than that appeared, we noted 'unaffected by'. In the few cases that differences were checked for significance, the results of that check are mentioned.

---

## APPENDIX B

### Measures of Association Used in One or More of the Studies

The studies covered used quite different statistics to demonstrate co-variance with happiness. These measures of association are based on different assumptions of the mathematical quality of the data and are hence not fully comparable.

Though different in many respects, the bulk of the measures of association is at least equal with respect to the range in which they express the degree of co-variance. Most are standardized on a variation between one and zero. As such they allow at least a rough comparison.

Comparison is more difficult where unstandardized measures are involved, such as differences in means (DM), F, or the wellknown Chi-square ($X^2$). Therefore it was of little use to mention such values in the excerpts. It sufficed to note whether there was any relationship at all and if so, whether this was positive or negative (0, + or -). Neither was there use in enumerating differences in percentages (D%), the size of such differences depending too much on the number of categories involved and whether rows or columns are compared.

The various measures of association that figured in one or more of the investigations are listed below in alphabetical order. Assumptions about the level of measurement being quite crucial, differences on that matter are summarized in connection. More detail about formulas and strong and weak points can be found with the authors mentioned in the right column.

MEASURES OF ASSOCIATION USED IN ONE OR MORE OF THE STUDIES, IN ALPHABETICAL ORDER.

| symbol used here | name and other symbols used | range | assumptions about mathematical quality of the data | remarks | further information in |
|---|---|---|---|---|---|
| C | Pearson's contingency coëfficient | 0 to 1 | Assumes either ordinal level of measurement of both variables or one ordinally and the other dichotomous. | | McNemar, 1969: 227-231 |
| DM | Difference in means | 0 to $\infty$ | Assumes that both variables are measured at the interval level. | Differences not mentioned in the excerpts. It sufficed to note whether there was a difference and in what direction (0, + or -). | |
| $D\bar{R}$ | Difference in average ridits | 0 to 1 | Assumes that both variables are measured at the nominal level. | | Bross (1958) |
| D% | Difference in percentages. When both variables are dichotomized called Epsilon and symbolized with $\varepsilon$ | 0 to 100 | All levels of measurements. | Differences not mentioned in the excerpts. It sufficed to note whether there was a difference and in what direction (0, + or -). | |
| F | variance ratio | 0 to $\infty$ | Assumes that either both variables measured at the interval level or one at the nominal level and one at the interval level. Assumes also symmetry of distributions. | Values not mentioned because they are not standardized. It sufficed to note whether there was any association and in what direction (o, + or -). | McNemar, 1969: 282-287 |
| G | Goodman & Kruskal's Gamma $\gamma$ | -1 to +1 | Assumes ordinal level of measurement for both variables and symmetry of distribution. Works on the basis of grouped data. | The higher the number of knotted pairs (ties) the lower the significance of the association. | Mueller et al, 1970: 279-192 |
| G' | Gamma as mentioned above, computed by us on the basis of a frequency distribution in the original report. | | | | |

| symbol used here | name and other symbols used | range | assumptions about mathematical quality of the data | remarks | further information in |
|---|---|---|---|---|---|
| Gs | Standardized Gamma or partial Gamma ($G_{pt}$). Gamma as above from which the effect of one or more third variables is filtered away. | | | | |
| $h^2$ | correlation ratio, eta | 0 to 1 | Assumes nominal level of measurement for one variable and interval level for the other. Assumes a-symmetry. | Because of a-symmetry $h^2_{xy}$ not always identical with $h^2_{yx}$. | Mueller et al., 1970:326 |
| mc | Guttman's monotonicity coëfficient | 0 to 1 | Assumes interval level of measurement for both variables | | Guttman, 1977 |
| Q | Yule's Q | -1 to +1 | Assumes that both variables are dichotomized and symmetry of distributions | | Mueller et al., 1970: 290-292 |
| $r_{pc}$ | Partial correlation. The correlation in $r_{pm}$ (see below) that remains when the effect of one or more third variables is filtered away. | | | | |
| $r_{pm}$ | Product moment correlation. Pearson's correlation coëfficient, mostly simply referred to as 'r' | -1 to +1 | Assumes that both variables are measured at the interval level, that distributions are symmetric and the relationship linear. | | Mueller et al., 1970: 315-318 |
| $r_s$ | Spearman's correlation Rho $\rho$ | -1 to +1 | Assumes that both variables are measured at the ordinal level | | Mueller et al., 1970: 267-276 |
| tau | Goodman & Kruskal's tau $\tau$ | -1 to +1 | Assumes that variables are both measured at the nominal level or one nominally and the other dichotomous. Assumes symmetry of distributions. | | Mueller et al., 1970: 279-292 |

| symbol used here | name and other symbols used | range | assumptions about mathematical quality of the data | remarks | further information in |
|---|---|---|---|---|---|
| $t_k$ | Kendall's tau | -1 to +1 | Assumes that both variables are measured at the ordinal level. | Three variants:<br>$-t_{ka}$ equal number of categories in both variables, not corrected for knots<br>$-t_{kb}$ equal number of categories in both variables, corrected for knots<br>$-t_{kc}$ unequal number of categories in both variables, not corrected for knots | Mueller et al., 1970: 257-263 |
| $T^2$ | Tschuprow's T | 0 to 1 | Assumes that either both variables are measured at the nominal level or one nominally and the other dichotomous. | | Blalock, 1979: 304-315 |
| $V^2$ | Cramer's V | 0 to 1 | Assumes that either both variables are measured at the nominal level or one nominally and the other dichotomous. | | Hays, 1973: 745 |
| $X^2$ | Chi-square $\chi^2$ | 0 to $\infty$ | Assumes that both variables are measured either both nominally or both dichotomous or one nominally and the other dichotomous. | Values not mentioned in the excerpts. It sufficed to note whether there was any association and in what direction (0, + or -) | Mueller et al., 1970: 432-434 |

# APPENDIX C

## Test Statistics Used in One or More of the Studies

Tests of significance are methods for estimating the likelihood that observed patterns are due to sampling error. As such they make sense only when representativeness can be assumed. Most of the studies at hand here used such tests for assessing whether the associations they found in their sample are sufficiently sizable to be sure that there is also some association in the population this sample as drawn from. Next to tests of association some investigations involved procedures to ascertain that differences in association in sub-samples correspond with differences in the wider reality. Another few used tests for differences in center-measures (mean, modus, median) and methods to ascertain whether the frequency distribution meets specific demands: the so-called 'goodness of fit' tests.

All the methods that figured in one or more of the investigations covered in this book are enumerated on the next page.

TEST STATISTICS USED IN ONE OR MORE OF THE STUDIES COVERED IN ALPHABETICAL ORDER.

| symbol | name, description | used for | assumptions | further detail in: |
|---|---|---|---|---|
| B | Test for correlation using expected normal scores | association ($r_{pm}$)<br>- 1 sample | - simple random sample<br>- interval level of measurement | Fisher, 1958:201 |
| BCI | Bross' confidence interval for ridit values | goodness of fit<br>- 1 sample<br>- 2 independent samples | - simple random samples<br>- ordinal level of measurement | Bross, 1958 |
| D | Hotelling & Pabst's test for rank-correlation, also called 'Spearman's rank correlation test' (when used for trends called Daniels test). | association ($r_s$)<br>- 1 sample | - simple random sample<br>- ordinal level of measurement<br>- continual distribution of variables | Siegel, 1956:210. |
| DMRT | Duncan's Multiple Range Test | difference between pairs of means in analysis of variance | - simple random samples<br>- interval level of measurement | Kirk, 1968:93/94 |
| $F^+$ | Frazer's test for difference | center (median)<br>- 1 sample<br>- 2 dependent samples | - simple random sample<br>- ordinal level of measurement<br>- continual distribution of variables | |
| Gt | Goodman & Kruskal's test for Gamma | association (G)<br>- 1 sample | - simple random sample<br>- ordinal level of measurement | Goodman & Kruskal, 1979:76 |
| Gt' | Gamma test computed by us on the basis of frequency distributions in the original reports | | | |
| NK | Neuman-Keuls test | differences between pairs of means in analysis of variance | | Kirk, 1968:9–93 |
| $r_1$ | Fisher's exact test | goodness of fit (proportion)<br>- 2 independent samples | - simple random sample<br>- dichotomized variables<br>- nominal level of measurement | Blalock, 1979:292/7 |
| t | student t-test<br>included: confidence intervals for the mean | center (mean)<br>- 1 sample ($H_o : \mu = k$)<br>- 2 dependent samples ($H_o : \mu_1 - \mu_2 = k$)<br>- 2 independent samples ($H_o : \mu_1 - \mu_2 = k$)<br>- association ($r_{pm}$)<br>- 1 sample ($H_o : r_{pm} = 0$) | - simple random sample(s)<br>- at least interval level of measurement<br>- normal distribution of population<br>- when used for association: bivariate normal distribution of population | Hays, 1973:392-4 |
| W | Wilcoxon's signed rank test | center (median)<br>- 2 independent samples | - simple random sample(s)<br>- at least ordered metric level of measurement<br>- continual distribution of variables<br>- when used for 1 sample: population distribution is symmetric | Hays, 1973: 780-2 |
| $X^2$ | $X^2$, Chi-square | association<br>- 1 sample<br>goodness of fit<br>- 1 sample<br>- 2 independent samples | - simple random sample<br>- nominal level of measurement<br>- large sample(s) | Mueller et al., 1970:435-7 |
| Z | Z-test for association<br>Critical Ratio (CR) | association ($r_{pm}$)<br>- 1 sample ($H_o : r_{pm} = k$)<br>- 2 independent samples ($H_o : r_1 - r_2 = k$) | - simple random sample(s)<br>- at least interval level of measurement<br>- bivariate normal distribution of population | Mueller et al., 1970:407-9 |

# REFERENCES


AAKSTER, C.W., 1972. 'Sociocultural variables in the etiology of health-disturbances'. (Diss.) Groningen, The Netherlands.

ABRAMS, M & HALL, J., 1972. 'The conditions of the British people: report on a pilot survey using self-rating scales'. Unpubl. paper, Social Science Research Council, London. Partly reported in 'Measuring the quality of life using simple surveys', in Stöber et al.: 'Technology assessment on the quality of life', Elsevier 1973, Amsterdam, The Netherlands.

ACH, N., 1910. 'Ueber den Willensakt und das Temperament', Leipzig, Germany. ('Intentional behavior and temperament')

ADAMS, D.L., 1971. 'Correlates of satisfaction among the elderly'. In: 'Gerontologist', vol. 11, nr. 4, pt 2, p. 64-68.

ALDRICH, C.K., 1964. 'Personality factors and mortality in the relocation of the aged'. In: 'Gerontologist' vol. 4, p. 92-93.

ALEXANDER, W.E., 1968. 'Some sociological aspects of psychological well-being in a schizophrenic population: social class, participation and work'. Unpubl. doct. diss. Syracuse University, USA.

ALLPORT, G.W., VERNON, P.E. & LINDZEY, G., 1951. 'Study of values' (3rd ed). Boston USA, Houghton Mifflin.

ALSTON, J.P., LOWE, G.D. & WRIGLEY, A., 1974. 'Socioeconomic correlates for four dimensions of self-perceived satisfaction 1972'. In: 'Human Organization', vol. 33, nr. 1, p. 99-102.

AMONS, R.B. & AMONS, C.H., 1962. 'The quick test (QT): provisional manual. In: 'Psychological reports', vol. 11. Monograph suppl. 7-VII.

ANDREWS, F.M., 1974. 'Social indicators of perceived life quality'. In: 'Social Indicators Research I', p. 279-299.

ANDREWS, F.M. & WITHEY, S.B., 1973. 'Developing measures of perceived life quality. Result from several national surveys'. Paper presented at the Meeting of American Sociology Association, New York, U.S.A. In 1974 published in 'Social Indicators Research', vol. 1, p. 1-26

——. 1976. 'Social indicators of well-being'. Plenum Press. New York, USA.

ARKOFF, A, eds., 1975. 'Psychology and personal growth', Allyn & Bacon, Boston, USA.

ANTONOVSKY, A., MAOZ, B., DOWTY, N. & WIJSENBEEK, H., 1971. 'Twenty-five years later: A limited study of sequelae of the concentration camp experience'. In: 'Social Psychiatry', vol. 6, nr. 4, p. 186-193.

ARNOLD, M.B., 1960. 'Emotion and personality', University Press, Columbia, USA.

BACHMAN, J.G., KAHN, R.L., MEDNICK, M., DAVIDSON, T.N. & JOHNSON, L.D., 1967. 'Youth in transition I - Blueprint for a longitudinal study of adolescent boys'. Institute for Social Research, Ann Arbor, Mich.USA.

BACHMAN, J.G., 1970. 'Youth in transition II - The impact of family background on intelligence in the 10th grade boys'. Institute for Social Research, Ann Arbor, Mich. USA.

BAKKER, P. & BERG, N. van de, 1974. 'Determinanten en correlaties van geluk' (Determinants and correlates of happiness). Unpubl. essay, Erasmus University Rotterdam, The Netherlands.

BARRON, F., 1956. 'An egostrength scale which predicts response to psychotherapy'. In: G. Welsh & W. Dahlstrom (eds.) 'Basic reading on the MMPI in psychology and medicin', p. 226-234.

BARRON, F., 1965. 'The psychology of creativity'. In: 'New directions in psychology II'. Holt, Rinehart & Winston, New York City, USA.

BARRON, F. & WELSH, G.S., 1952. 'Artistic preference as a factor in personality style: Its measurement by a figure preference test'. In:'Journal of Psychology', vol. 33, p. 199-203.

BARSCHAK, E., 1951. 'A study of happiness and unhappiness in the childhood and adolescence of girls in different cultures'. In: 'Journal of psychology', vol. 32, p. 173-215.
Separatedly published by the Journal Press. Province Town (Mass.), USA.

BAXTER, M.F., YAMADA, K. & WASHBURN, M.F., 1917. 'Directed recall of pleasant and unpleasant experiences'. In: 'American Journal of Psychology', vol. 28, p. 155-157.

BAYLEY, N., 1933. 'Mental growth during the first three years: A developmental study of 61 children by repeated tests'. In: 'Genetical Psychological Monographs', vol. 14, p. 1-92.

BECK, A.T., WARD, C.H., MENDELSON, M., MOCK, J. & ERBAUGH, J., 1961. 'An inventory for measuring depression' In: 'Archives of General Psychiatry', vol. 4, p. 561-571.

BEISER, M., 1974. 'Components and correlates of mental well-being'. In: 'Journal of Health and Social Behavior', vol. 15, nr. 4, p. 320-327.

BELLOC, N.B., BRESLOW, L. & HOCHSTIM, J.R., 1971. 'Measurement of psychical health in a general population survey'. In: 'American Journal of Epidemology', vol. 93, p. 328-336.

BENDO, A.A. & FELDMAN, H., spring 1974. 'A comparison of the self-concept of low-income women with and without husbands present'. In: 'The Cornell Journal of Social Relations', vol. 9, nr. 1, p. 53-85.

BERGIN, A.E. & SOLOMON, B., 1970. 'Personality and performance correlates of empathic understanding in psychotherapy'. In: TOMLINSON, T. & HART, J. (eds) 'New directions in client-centered therapy'. Houghton Mifflin, Boston, USA.

BERKMAN, P.L., 1971. 'Lifestress and psychological well-being: A replication of Langner's analysis in the Midtown Manhattan Study' . In: 'Journal of Health & Social Behavior', vol. 12, p. 35-45.

BERNARD, J., 1972. 'The future of marriage'. Bantam Books, New York City, U.S.A.

BERTING, J., 1968. 'In het brede maatschappelijk midden'. (Diss.). Boom, Meppel, The Netherlands. (The middle strata)

BICE, T.W. & KALIMOS, E., 1971. 'Comparisons of health related attitudes. A cross-national factor analytic study'. In: 'Social Science and Medicin', vol. 5, p. 283-318

BIDERMAN, A.D. & SHARP, L.M., 1967. 'Out of uniform; the employment experience of retired military personel' . In: 'Monthly Labor Review', vol. 90, nr. 1, p. 15-21.

——. 1967. 'Out of uniform'(II). In: 'Monthly Labor Review', vol. 90, nr. 2, p. 39-47.

——. 1968. 'The convergence of military and civilian occupational structures: Evidence from studies of military retired employment. In: 'American Journal of Sociology', vol. 73, p. 381-399.

BLALOCK, H.M., 1979. 'Social Statistics' Revised second ed. McGraw Hill, New York City, USA.

BLOOD, M.R., 1969. 'Work values and job satisfaction'. In: 'Journal of Applied Psychology', vol. 53, nr. 6, p. 456-459.

BLOOD, M.R. & HULIN, C.L., 1967. 'Alienation, environmental characteristics and worker responses'. In: 'Journal of Applied Psychology', vol. 51, p. 284-290.

BLOOD, R.O. & WOLFE, D.M., 1960. 'Husbands and wives - the dynamics of married living'. Free Press, Glencoe (Ill.), USA.

BOHN, C.J., 1972. 'The effects of children upon life satisfaction. A thesis in child development and family relationships'. Unpubl. master thesis. Pennsylvania State University, USA.

BORTNER, R.W. & HULTSCH, D.F., 1970. 'A multivariate analysis of correlates of life satisfaction in adulthood' In: 'Journal of Gerontology', vol. 25, nr. 1, p. 41-47.

——. 1972. 'Personal time perspective in adulthood'. In: 'Developmental psychology', vol. 7, nr. 2, p. 98-103.

——. 1974. 'Patterns of subjective deprivation in adulthood'. In: ' Developmental Psychology', vol. 10, nr. 4, p. 534-545.

BORTNER, R.W., BOHN, C.J. & HULTSCH, D.F., 1974. 'A cross-cultural study of the effects of children on parental assessment of past, present and future'. In: 'Journal of Marriage and the family, p. 370-384.

BOTT, E., 1955. 'Urban families: Conjugal roles and social networks'. In: 'Human Relations', vol. 8, p. 345-384.

——. 1957. 'Family and Social Network'. Tavistock Publication, London, Gr. Britain.

BRADBURN, N.M., 1964. 'Measures of psychological well-being'. In: 'NORC working paper, survey 458'.

——. 1969. 'The structure of psychclogical well-being'. Aldine Publ. Co., Chicago, USA.

BRADBURN, N.M. & CAPLOVITZ, D., 1965. 'Reports on happiness: a pilot study of behavior related to mental health'. Aldine Publ. Co., Chicago, USA.

BRADBURY, B.R., 1967. 'A study of guilt and anxiety as related to certain psychological and sociological variables'. Unpubl. doct. diss. North Texas State University, USA.

BRAYLEY, L.S. & FREED, N.H., 1971. 'Modes of temporal orientation and psychopathology'. In: 'Journal of Consulting and Clinical Psychology', vol. 36, p. 33-39.

BRENNER, B., 1967. 'Patterns of alhccol use, happiness and the satisfaction of wants'. In: 'Quarterly Journal of Studies on Alcohol', vol. 28, nr. 4, p. 667-675.

——. 1970. 'Social factors in mental well-being at adolescence'. Unpubl. doct. diss. The American University, Washington D.C., USA.

——. 1975. 'Quality of affect and self-evaluated happiness'. In: 'Social Indicators research', vol. 2, nr.3 p. 315-331.

——. 1975. 'Enjoyment as a preventive of depressive affect'. In: Journal of Community Psychology', vol. 3, nr. 4, p. 346-357.

BRESKIN, S., 1968. 'Measurement of rigidity: A non-verbal test'. In: 'Perceptual and minor skills', vol. 27, p. 1203-1206.

BRICKMAN, P. & CAMPBELL, D.T., 1971. 'Hedonic relativism and planning the good society'. In: Appley (eds) 'Adaptation level theory - a synposium', Academic Press, London, Gr. Britain.

BRIM, J.A., 1974. 'Social network correlates of avowed happiness'. In: 'Journal of Nervous & Mental Disease', vol. 158, nr. 6, p. 432-439.

BRONFENBRENNER, U., 1967. 'The split-level American family'. In: 'Saturday Review', vol. L, nr. 40.

BROSS, I.O.J., 1958. 'How to use Ridit analysis'. In: 'Biometrics', vol. 14, March nr., p. 18-38.

BUCHANAN, W. & CANTRIL, H., 1953. 'How nations see each other. A study in public opinion'. University of Illinois Press, Urbans, USA.

BULATAO, R.A., 1973. 'Measures of happiness among Manila residents'. In: 'Philippine Sociological Review', vol. 21, nr. 3-4, p. 229-238.

CALABRESI, R. & COHEN, J., 1968. 'Personality and time attitudes'. In: 'Journal of Abnormal Psychology', vol. 73, p. 431-439.

CAMERON, P., van HOECK, D., WEISS, N. & KOSTIN, M., 1971. 'Happiness or life-satisfaction of the malformed' In: 'Proceedings of the 79th Annual Convention of the American Psychological Association', vol. 6, nr. 2, p. 641-642.

CAMERON, P., TITUS, D.G., KOSTIN, J. & KOSTIN, M., 1973. 'The life satisfaction of nonnormal persons'. In: 'Journal of Consulting & Clinical Psychology', vol. 41, nr. 2, p. 207-214.

CAMPBELL, A., 1976. 'Subjective measures of well-being'. In: 'American Psychologist', vol. 31, nr. 2, p. 117-124.

CAMPBELL, A. & CONVERSE, P., 1970. 'Monitoring the quality of American life', research proposal to the Russell Sage Foundation, S.R.C. Paper, New York City, USA.

CANTRIL, H., 1965. 'The pattern of human concern' 1/2. Rutgers University Press, New Brunswick (N.J.), USA.

CANTRIL, A.H. & ROLL, C.W. jr., 1971. 'Hopes and fears of the American people'. Universe Books, New York City, USA.

CARKHUFF, R.R. & BERENSON, B.G., 1967. 'Beyond counseling and therapy'. Holt, Rinehart & Winston, New York City, USA.

CARKHUFF, R.R., KRATOCHUIL, D. & FRIEL, T., 1968. 'The effect of professional training communication and discrimination of facilitative conditions'. In: 'Journal of Counseling Psych.', vol. 15, p. 68-74.

CASON, H., 1931. 'General curves and conditions of feeling'. In: 'Journal of Applied Psychology', vol. 15 p. 126-148.

CATHEY, C.W., REDMOND, R.F. & WOLF, S., 1957. 'Serum cholesterol, diet and stress in patients with coronary artery disease'. In: 'Journal of Clin. Invest.', vol. 36, p. 897.

CATTELL, R.B., 1950. 'The sixteen personality factor questionnaire'. Institute for Personality and Ability Testing, Champaign (Ill.), USA

CATTELL, R.B. & SCHREIER, I.H., 1963. 'Handbook for the IPAT Anxiety Scale Questionnaire'. Institute for Personality and Ability Testing, Champaign (Ill.), USA.

CAVAN, R.S., BURGESS, E.W., HAVIGHURST, R.J. & GOLDHAMMER, H., 1949. 'Personal adjustment in old age'. Science Research Associates, Chicago (Ill.), USA.

CHERLIN, A. & REEDER, L.G., 1975. 'The dimensions of psychological well-being; a critical review'. In: 'Sociological Methods and Research', vol. 4, p. 189-214.

CHIRIBOGA, D. & LOWENTHAL, M.F., 1971. 'Psychological correlates of perceived well-being'. In: 'Proceedings of the Annual Convention of the American Psychological Association', vol. 6, p. 603-604.

CLARK, B.R., RUBIN, R.T. & ARTHUR, R.J., 1968. 'A new micromethod for determination of cholesterol in serum', In: 'Anal. Biochem.', vol. 24, p. 27-33.

CLAYTON, M.B. & Jackson, D.N., 1961. 'Equivalence range, acquiescence, and overgeneralization'. In: 'Educational and Psychological Measurement', vol. 21, p. 371-381.

CLUM, G.A. & CLUM, J., 1973. 'Choice of defensemechanisms and their relationship to mood level'. In: Psychological reports', vol. 32, p. 507-510.

COBB, S., BROOKS, G.H., KASL, S.V. & CONELLY, W.E., 1966. 'The health of people changing jobs: A description of a longitudinal study. In: 'American Journal of Public Health', vol. 56, p. 1476-1481.

COFER, Ch. N. & APPLEY, M.H., 1964. 'Motivation: theory and research'. John Wiley & Sons Inc., New York,-USA - London, Gr. Britain.

COLEMAN, J.S., CAMPBELL, E.Q, HOBSON, C.J., McPARLAND, J. & MOOD, A.M., 1966. 'Equality of educational opportunity'. US Government Printing Office, Washington D.C., USA.

COMMISSION OF THE EUROPEAN COMMUNITIES, 1975. 'European men and women - A comparison of their attitudes to some of the problems facing society'. Commission of the European Communities, Brussels, Belgium.

CONSTANTINOPLE, A.D., 1965. 'Some correlates of happiness and unhappiness in college students'. Unpubl.diss. University of Rochester, USA.

CONSTANTINOPLE, A., 1967. 'Perceived instrumentality of the college as a measure of attitudes toward college'. In: Journal of Personality & Social Psychology', vol. 5, p. 196-201.

——. 1970. 'Some correlates of average level of happiness among college students'. In: 'Developmental Psychology', vol. 2, p. 447.

COUCH, A. & KENISTON, K., 1960. 'Yeasayers and naysayers: agreeing response set as a personality variable'. In: 'Journal of Abnormal & Social Psychology', vol. 60, p. 151-174.

COOK, S.W. & SELLTIZ, C., 1964. 'A multiple-indicator approach to attitude measurement'. In: 'Psychological Bulletin', vol. 62, p. 36-55.

COTTLE, T.J., 1971. 'Temporal correlates of dogmatism'. In: 'Journal of Consulting and Clinical Psychology', vol. 36, p. 70-81.

CRAWFORD, C.O., 1971. 'Health and the family: A medical-sociological analysis'. McMillan Co., New York, USA.

CRONBACH, L.J., 1951. 'Coefficient alpha and the internal structure of tests'. In: 'Psychometrica', vol. 16, p. 297-334.

CROWNE, D.P. & MARLOWE, D., 1964. 'The approval motive'. Wiley, New York, USA.

CUMMINGS, E., DEAN, L.R. & NEWELL, D.S., 1958. "What is 'morale'? A case history of a validity problem". In: 'Human Organizations', vol. 17, p. 3-8.

CUMMING, E. & HENRY, W.E., 1961. 'Growing old: the process of disengagement'. Basic Books, New York, USA.

DABBS, J.M. & LEVENTHAL, H., 1966. 'Effects of varying the recommendations in a fear-arousing communication'. In: 'Journ. Pers. & Soc. Psych.', vol. 4, p. 525-531.

DAVIS, H. et al., 1971. 'Incidence and type of psychiatric disturbance in dropouts from a state university'. In: 'Journal of the American college health association', vol. 19, p. 241-246.

DAVITZ, J.R., 1969. 'The language of emotion'. Academic Press, New York, USA.

——. 1970. 'A Dictionary and Grammar of Emotions'. In: ARNOLD, M. (ed.) 'Feelings and Emotions'. The Loyola Symposium, Academic Press, New York, USA - London, Gr. Britain, p. 251-258.

DEAN, D.G., 1961. 'Alienation - its meaning and measurement'. In: 'American Sociological Review', vol. 26.

DENTLER, R.A. & MACKLER, B., 1961. 'The socialization of retarded children in an institution'. In: 'Journal of Health & Human Behavior', p. 243-252.

DEUTSCH, H., 1945. 'The psychology of women'. Grune & Stratton, New York, USA, vol.2

DEUTSCHER, I., 1964. 'The quality of postparental life'. In: 'Journal of Marriage and the Family', vol. 26, p. 52-59.

DIRKEN, J.M., 1967. "Het meten van 'stress' in industriële situaties". Wolters, Groningen, The Netherlands. ('Measuring stress').

DOUVAN, E., 1960. 'Sex differences in adolescent character processes'. In: 'Merril-Palmer Quarterly', vol. 6, p. 203-211.

DUNCAN, O.D.A., 1961. 'A socioeconomic index for all occupations' (ch. 6) and 'Properties and characteristics of the socioeconomic index' (ch. 7). In: A.J. Reiss jr. 'Occupations and social status'. Free Press of Glencoe, New York, USA. p. 109-161.

DYE, T.R., 1963. 'The local-cosmopolitan dimension and the study of urban politics'. In: 'Social Forces', vol. 41, p. 239-246.

DYSINGER, D.W., 1937. 'A study of mood'. In: 'Psychological Records', vol. 1, p. 147-156.

——. 1938. 'The fluctuations of mood'. In: 'Psychological Records', vol. 2, p. 115-123.

EASTERLIN, R.A., 1974. 'Does economic growth improve human lot? Some empirical evidence'. In: DAVID, P.A. & MELVIN, W.R. (eds.) 'Nations and households in economic growth'. Stanford Univ. Press, Palo Alto (Cal.) USA.

ERIKSON, E.H., 1959. 'Identity and the life cycle: Selected papers'. In: 'Psychological Issues', vol. 1.

ESTES, R., 1973. 'Determinants of differntial stress levels among university students'. In: 'Journal of the American College Health Association', vol. 21, p. 470-476.

FALLDING, H., 1964. 'The source and burden of civilization illustrated in the use of alcohol'. In: 'Quart. 7 Stud. Alc.', vol. 25, p. 714-724.

FAND, A.B., 1955. 'Sexrole and self concept'. Unpubl. doct. diss., Cornell University, USA.

FELLOWS, E.W., 1966. 'Happiness: a survey of research'. In: 'Journal of Humanistic Psychology', vol. 6, p.17-30.

FERSTER, C.B., 1965. 'Classification of behavior pathology'. In: Krasner, L. & Ullman, L.P. (eds) 'Research in behavior modification', Harper & Row, New York, USA.

FISCHER, C.S., 1972. 'Urbanism as a way of life - a review and an agenda'. In: 'Sociological Methods and Research', vol. 1, p. 187-242.

——. 1973. 'Urban malaise'. In: 'Social Forces', vol. 52, p. 221-235.

FISHER, R.A., 1958. 'Statistical methods for Research workers'. Oliver & Boyd, London, Gr. Britain.

FISHER, S., 1973. 'The female orgasm'. New York, USA.

FLANAGAN, J.C., DAILEY, J.T., SHAYCROFT, M.F., GORHAM, W.A., ORR, D.B. & GOLDBERG, I., 1962. 'Designs for a study of American Youth'. Houghton Mifflin, Boston (Mass.), USA.

FLUEGEL, J.C., 1925. 'A quantative study of feeling and emotion in everyday life'. In: 'British Journal of Psychology', vol. 15, p. 318-355.

FORDYCE, M.W., 1972. 'Happiness, its daily variation and its relation to values', United States International Univ., order no. 72-23,491. USA.

FOWLER, F.J. jr. & McCalla, M.E., 1969. 'Correlates of morale among aged in Greater Boston'. In: 'Proceedings of the 77th Annual Convention of the American Psychological Association', vol. 4 (pt-2), p. 733-734.

FRENCH, J.W., EKSTROM, R.B. & PRICE, L.A., 1963. 'Manual for reference tests for cognitive factors'. Educational Testing Service, Princeton (N.J.), USA.

FRIEDSAM, H.J. & MARTIN, H.W., 1963. 'A comparison of self and physician's health ratings in an older population'. In: 'Journal of Health & Social Behavior', vol. 4, p. 179-183.

FROMM, E, 1955. 'The same society'. Rinehart, New York, USA.

GAITZ, C.M. & SCOTT, J., 1972. 'Age and the measurement of mental health'. In: 'Journal of Health and Social Behavior', vol. 13, p. 55-67.

GALLUP, G.H., winter 1976/1977. 'Human Needs and Satisfactions: A global survey'. In: Public Opinion Quarterly', vol. 4, p. 459-467.

GARBER, D.L., 1971. 'Retired soldiers in second careers: self assessed change, reference group salience, and psychological well-being'. Unpubl. diss. University of Southern California, USA. Order nr. 72-552.

GARDNER, R. & HOLZMAN, P.S., KLEIN, G.S., LINTON, H. & SPENCE, D.P., 1959. 'Cognitive controls: A study of individual consistencies in cognitive behavior'. In: 'Psychological Issues', vol. 1.

GARRITY, T.F., 1973. 'Social involvement and activeness as predictors of morale 6 months after myocardinal infarction'. In: 'Social Science and Medicine', vol. 7, p. 199-207.

GATES, A.T., 1958. 'Gates Reading Survey Form I'. Teachers College, Columbia University, New York, USA.

GEORGE, P.M., 1965. 'Occupational choices of college students: Centrality of occupation and evaluation-cognitive congruence'. Unpubl. doct. diss. University of North Carolina, Chapel Hill, USA.

GILLO, M.W., 1973. 'Studies on the nature of the relationships between job and life satisfactions: Towards a comprehensive model'. University of Kansas. Order no. 73-30.814. Unpubl. diss.

GLENN, N.D., 1975. 'Psychological well-being in the postparental stage: some evidence from national surveys'. In: 'Journal of Marriage and the Family', vol. 37, p. 105-110.

——. 1975. 'The contribution of marriage to the psychological well-being of males and females. In: 'Journal of Marriage and the Family', vol. 37, p. 594-601.

GLESER, G.C. & IHILEVICH, D., 1969. 'An objective instrument for measuring defense mechanisms'. In: 'Journal of Consulting and Clinical Psychiatry', vol. 33, p. 51-60.

GOFFMAN, E., 1959. 'The moral career of the mental patient'. In: 'Psychiatry', vol. 22, p. 123-142.

GOLD, M., 1966. 'Undetected delinquent behavior'. In: 'Journal of Research in Crime and Delinquency', vol. 3, p. 27-46.

GOLDSTEIN, K., 1952. 'Human nature in the light of psychopathology'. Harvard University Press, Cambridge (Mass.), USA.

GONZáLEZ, J.R., 1967. 'Study of student teacher's life adjustment'. Diss. The University of N. Carolina, Chapel Hill. USA.

GOODMAN, L.A. & KRUSKAL, W.A., 1979. 'Measures of association for cross-classification'. Springer, New York, USA, p. 76-310.

GORDON, F.E. & HALL, D.T., 1974. 'Self-image and stereotypes of femininity: Their relationship to women's role conflicts and coping'. In: 'Journal of Applied Psychology', vol. 59, p. 241-243.

GORMAN, B.S., 1971. 'A multivariate study of the relationship of cognitive control and cognitive style principles to reported daily mood experiences'. The City University of New York, USA. Order No. 72-5071.

GORMAN, B.S. & WESSMAN, A.E., 1974. 'The relationship of cognitive styles and moods'. In: 'Journal of clinical Psychology', vol. 30, p. 18-25.

GOUGH, H.C., 1953. 'Minnesota multiphasic personality inventory'. In: WEIDER, A, (ed.) 'Contributions toward medical psychology: theory and psychodiagnostic methods', vol. 2. Ronald, New York, USA, p. 545-567.

GRANEY, M.J., 1973. 'The affect balance scale and old age'. Paper presented at the Annual Meeting of the Mid-west Sociological Society, April 26, 1973, Milwaukee (Wisc.), USA.

—. 1973. 'Happiness and social participation in aging'. In: 'Gerontologist', vol. 13, p. 84. Same article published in 1975 in: 'Journal of Gerontology', vol. 30, p. 701-706.

GRANEY, M.J. & GRANEY, E.E., 1973. 'Scaling adjustment in older people'. In: 'International Journal of Aging & Human Development', vol. 4, p. 351-359.

GREENHAUS, J.H., 1973. 'A factorial investigation of career salience'. In: 'J. Voc. Behav.', vol. 3, p. 95-98.

—. 1974. 'Career Salience as a moderator of the relationship between satisfaction with occupational preference and satisfaction with life in general'. In: 'Journal of Psychology', vol. 86, p. 53-55.

GROOVER, M.E. jr., JERNIGAN, J.A. & MARTIN, C.D., 1960. 'Variations in serum lipid concentration and clinical coronary disease'. In: 'American Journal Medical Science', p. 133-139.

GRUHN, H. & KRAUSE, S., 1968. 'Zum Sozialverhalten Körperlich auffalliger Kinder & Jugendlicher'. In: Probleme und Ergebnisse der Psych.', p. 23, 73, 86.

GUBRIUM, J.F., 1974. 'Marital desolation and the evaluation of everyday life in old age'. In: 'Journal of Marriage and the Family', p. 107-113.

GURIN, G., VEROFF, J. & FELD, S., 1960. 'Americans view their mental health - A nationwide interview survey'. Basic Books Inc., New York, USA.

GURMAN, A.S., 1972. 'Therapists's mood patterns and therapeutic facilitativeness'. In: 'Journal of Counseling Psychology', vol. 19, p. 169-170.

GUTTMAN, L., 1944. 'A basis for scaling quantative data'. In: 'Am. Soc. Rev.', vol. 9, p. 139-150

—. 1977. 'What is not what in statistics?'. In: 'The Statistician', vol. 26, p. 81-107.

HAAVIO-MANNILA, E., 1971. 'Satisfaction with family, work, leisure and life among men and women'. In: 'Human Relations', vol. 24, p. 585-601.

HACKER, S.L. & GAITZ, C.M., 1969. 'The moral career of the elderly mental patient'. In: 'The Gerontologist', vol. 9, p. 120-127.

HALL, C.A. & LINDZEY, G., 1957. 'THeories of Personality'. Wiley, London, Gr. Britain.

HALL, D.T. & LAWLER, E.E., 1971. 'Job pressures and research performance'. In: 'American Scientist', vol. 59, p. 64-73.

HALL, J., 1973. 'Measuring the quality of life using simple surveys'. In: STOEBER, J. et al. 'Technology assessment and the quality of life'. Elsevier, Amsterdam, The Netherlands.

—. 1976. 'Subjective measures of quality of life in Britain: 1971 to 1975, some developments and trends', In: 'Social trends' # 7, HMSO 1976, vol. 7, p. 47-60.

HAMILTON, M.A., 1960. 'Rating scale for depression'. In: 'Journ. Neurol. Neurochir. Psychiatr.', vol. 23, p. 56-62.

HARDER, J.M., 1969. 'Self-actualization, mood, and personality adjustment in married women'. Diss. Columbia University (Teachers College), U.S.A.

HAVIGHURST, R.J. & ALBRECHT, R., 1953. 'Older people'. Longmans Green & Co., New York, USA.

HAYS, W.L., 1973. 'Statistics for the social sciences'. Holt, London, Gr. Britain.

HEATH, R.G., 1964. 'Pleasure Integration and Behavior'. Hoeber, New York, USA.

HEEREN, S.D., 1969. 'Entrepreneurial vs bureaucratic fathers, as related to family structure, happiness, and two measures on independence'. University of Kansas, USA, order no. 70-11,029.

HEISE, D.R. & BOHRNSTED, G.W., 1970. 'Validity, Invalidity and Reliability'. In: BORGATTA & BORNSTEDT (eds.) San Francisco, USA. Publ.: Jossey-Bay.

HENLEY, B. & DAVIS, M.S., 1967. 'Satisfaction and dissatisfaction: a study of the chronically-ill aged patients', In: 'Journal of Health & Social Behavior', vol. 8, p. 65-75.

HERMANS, H.J. & TAK-v.d.VEN, 1973. 'Are there arguments in favor of an original dimension "positive psychological well-being"?'. In: 'Nederlands tijdschrift voor de psychologie en haar grensgebieden', vol. 27, p. 731-754.

HEYMANS, G. & WIERSMA, E., 1906-1909. 'Beiträge zur speziellen Psychologie auf Grund einder Massenuntersuchung', In: 'Zeitschrift für Psychologie', p. 42-51. ('Contribution to special psychology based on surveys').

HOLLINGSHEAD, A.B., 1957. 'Two factor index of social position'. Mimeographed publ. Hollingsworth, A.B., Jale Station, New Haven, (Conn.), USA.

HOLMES, T.H. & RAHE, R.T., 1967. 'The social readjustment rating scale'. In: Journ. Psychom. Res', vol. 11, p. 213-218.

HOMANS, G.C., 1961. 'Social Behavior: Its elementary forms'. Harcourt, Brace & World, New York, USA.

HULIN, C.L., 1969. 'Source of variation in job and life satisfaction: the role of community and job-related variables'. In: 'Journal of Applied Psychology', vol. 53, p. 279-291.

HYNSON, L.M., 1975. 'Rural-urban differences in satisfaction among the elderly'. In: 'Rural Sociology', vol. 40, p. 64-66.

IRIS, B. & BARRETT, G.V., 1972. 'Some relations between job and life satisfaction and job importance'. In: 'Journal of Applied Psychology', vol. 56, p. 301-304.

ISAGER, H., 1948. 'Factors contributing to happiness among Danish college students'. In: 'Journal of Social Psychology', vol. 28, p. 237-246.

JACKSON, D. & LYONS, M., 1969. 'A factor analytic description of excitement'. Unpubl. paper, University of Wisconsin, USA.

JACKSON, D.N. & MESSICK, S., 1964. 'Differential Personality inventory' Form M. Unpubl.

JAHODA, M., 1958. 'Current Concepts of Positive Mental Health', Basic Books, New York, USA.

JARVIK, L.F. & FALEK, A., 1963. 'Intellectual ability and survival of the aged'. In 'Journal of Gerontology', vol. 18, p. 173-176.

JENCKS, C. , 1972. 'Inequality: a reassessment of the effect of family and schooling in America'. Basic Books, New York, USA.

JESSOR, R. et al., 1968. 'Society, personality, and deviant behavior'. Holt, Rinehart & Winston, New York, USA.

JOHNSON, W.B., 1937. 'Euphoric and depressed moods in normal subjects' I and II. In: 'Journal of Character and Personality', vol. 6, p. 79-98 & 188-202.

JONES, H.M., 1953. 'The pursuit of happiness'. Harvard University Press, Cambridge, (Mass.), USA.

de JONG- GIERVELD, J., 1969. 'De ongehuwden'. Samson, Alphen a/d Rijn, The Netherlands. ('The unmarried').

JOURARD, S.M., 1959. 'Healthy Personality and Self-Disclosure'. In: 'Mental Hygiene', p. 499-507.

JOURARD, S.M. & LASAKOW, P., 1958. 'Some factors of self-disclosure'. In: 'Journal of Abnormal and Social Psycology', vol. 56, p. 91-96.

KAHANA, B. & KAHANA, E., 1966. 'Age changes in impulsivity among chronic schizophrenics'. In: Proceedings of the 7th Congress of Gerontology, Vienna, Austria.

—— 1975. 'The relationship of impulse control to cognition and adjustment among institutionalized aged women'. In: 'Journal of Gerontology', vol. 30, p. 679-686.

KASSARJIAN, W.M., 1962. 'A study of Riesman's theory of social character'. In: 'Sociometry', vol. 25, p. 213-230.

KASSEBAUM, G.G., COUCH, A.S. & SLATER, P.E., 1959. 'The factorial dimensions of the MMPI'. In: 'Journ. Consult. Psychology', vol. 23, p. 226-236.

KATZ, M.M. & LYERLY, S.B., 1963. 'Methods for measuring adjustment and social behavior in the community'. In: 'Psychological Reports', vol. 13, p. 503-535.

KATZELL, R., BARRET , R. & PARKER, T., 1961. 'Job satisfaction, job performance and situational characteristics', In: 'Journal of Applied Psychology', vol. 45, p. 65-72.

KENYON, G.S., 1969. 'Sport Involvement: a conceptual go and some consequences thereof'. In: KENYON, G.S. (ed.) 'Aspects of contemporary sport sociology', The Athletic Institute, Chicago, USA.

KEPHART, W., 1966. 'The family, society and the individual'. Houghton Mifflin, New York, USA.

KESSEN, W., HENDRY, A.L.S. & LEUTZENDORF, A.M., 1961. 'The measurement of movement in the human newborn: a new technique'. In: 'Child development', vol. 32, p. 95-105.

KIRK, R.E., 1968. 'Experimental design: procedures for the behavioral sciences'. Wadsworth Publ. Comp. Inc., Belmont (Cal.), USA.

KLEINMUNTZ, B., 1961. 'The college maladjustment scale (Mt) norms and predictive validity'. In: 'Educational Psychologic Measurement', vol. 21, p. 1029-1033.

KNUPFER, G., CLARK, W. & ROOM, R., 1966. 'The mental health of the unmarried'. In: 'American Journal of Psychiatry', vol. 122, p. 841-851.

KORNHAUSER, A., 1965. 'The mental health of the industrial worker'. Wiley, New York, USA.

KREISBERG, L., 1970. 'Mothers in poverty'. Aldine Publ. Co., Chicago, USA.

KRYSTAL, H. (ed.), 1968. 'Massive psychic trauma'. International University Press, New York, USA.

KUHLEN, R.G., 1959. 'Aging and life adjustment'. In: BIRREN, J.F. (ed.) 'Handbook of aging and the individual', University of Chicago Press, Chicago, USA. , P. 852-897.

KUNIN, T., 1955. 'The development of a new type of attitude measure'. In: 'Personnel Psychology', vol. 8, p.65-78.

KUTNER, B., FANSHEL, D., TOGO, A.M. & LANGNER, T.S., 1956. 'Five hundred over sixty'. Russel Sage Foundation, New York, USA.

KWANT, R.C., 1962. 'Wijsgerige analyse van isolatie en communicatie'. In: v.d.BERG, G.J. 'Isolatie en communicatie in de samenleving'. Spectrum, Utrecht, The Netherlands. ('Analysis of isolation and communication').

LANDERS, D., 1970. 'Psychological feminity and the prospective female physical educator'. In: 'Research Quarterly', vol. 41, p. 164-170.

LANDIS, J., 1940. 'Attitudes and adjustments of aged rural people in Iowa'. Diss. Lousisiana State University, USA.

LANGNER, T.S., 1962. 'A twenty-two item screening score of psychiatric symptoms indicating impairment'. In: 'Journal of health and human behavior', vol. 3, p. 269-276.

LANGNER, T.S. & MICHAEL, S.T., 1963. 'Life stress and mental health'. The Free Press, New York, USA.

LARSON, R., 1978. 'Thirty years of research on the subjective well-being of older Americans'. In: 'Journal of Gerontology', vol. 33, p. 109-125.

LAWTON, M.P. & COHEN, J., 1974. 'The generality of housing impact on the well-being of older people'. In: Journal of Gerontology', vol. 29, p. 194-204.

LEIGHTON, D.C. et al., 1963. 'The Stirling County study of psychiatric disorder and sociocultural environment', Vol. 8: 'The Character of danger'. Basic Books, New York, USA.

LENSKI, G., 1961. 'The religious factor'. Doubleday, New York, USA.

LEVY, S. & GUTTMAN, L., 1975. 'On the multivariate structure of well-being'. In: 'Social Indicators Research', vol. 2, p. 361-388.

LEWINSOHN, P.M., 1973. 'Clinical and theoretical aspects of depression'. In: CALHOUN, K.S., ADAMS, H.E. & MITCHELL, K.M. (eds.) 'Innovative treatment methods in psychotherapy', Wiley, New York, USA.

LEWINSOHN, P.M. & ATWOOD, G.F., 1969. 'Depression: a clinical research approach'. In: 'Psychotherapy: Theory, Research and Practice', vol. 6, p. 166-171.

LEWINSOHN, P.M. & GRAF, M., 1973. 'Pleasant activities and depression'. In: 'Journal of Consulting & Clinical Psychology', vol. 41, p. 261-268.

LEWINSOHN, P.M. & LIBET, J., 1972. 'Pleasant events, activity schedules and depressions'. In: 'Journal of abnormal psychology', vol. 79, p. 291-295.

LEWIS, M.A., 1972. 'Actual and perceived age differences in self-concept and psychological well-being for Catholic sisters'. Syracuse University (N.Y.), USA. Order no. 73-7741.

LONG, J.M., 1967. 'Self-actualization in a sample of high-school boys'. Unpubl. doct. diss. University of Michigan, USA.

LOWENTHAL, M.F. & BOLER, D., 1965. 'Voluntary vs involuntary social withdrawal'. In: 'Journal of Gerontology', vol. 20, p. 363-371.

LOWENTHAL, M.F. & HAVEN, C., 1968. 'Interaction and adaptation: intimacy as a critical variable'. In: 'American sociological review', vol. 33, p. 20-30.

LUBIN, B., 1965. 'Adjective checklists for the measurement of depression'. In: 'Archives of general psychology', vol. 12, p. 57-62.

LUDWIG, L.D., 1970. 'Intra- and inter-individual relationships between elation-depression and desire for excitement'. In: 'Journal of personality', vol. 38, p. 167-176.

LUDWIG, L.D., 1971. 'Elation-depression and skill as determinants of desire for excitement'. Unpubl. doct.diss. University of Wisconsin, U.S.A. Partly published in the 'Journal of Personality' 1975, vol. 43, p. 1-22.

MADDOX, G.L., 1963. 'Activity and morale: a longitudinal study of selected elderly subjects'. In: 'Social Forces', vol. 42, p. 195-204.

——. 1968. 'Persistence of lifestyle among the elderly: A longitudinal study of patterns of social activity in relation to life satisfaction'. In: NEUGARTEN, B.L. (ed.)'Middle age and aging', University of Chicago Press, Chicago, USA.

MAKARCZYK, W., 1962. 'Factors affecting life satisfaction among people in Poland'. In: 'Polish sociol. Bulletin', vol: 1-2. p. 105-116. Poland.

MANDLER, G. & SARASON, S.B., 1952. 'A study of anxiety and learning'. In: 'Journal of abnormal and social psychology', vol. 47, p. 166-173.

MANNING GIBBS, R.A., 1972. 'Relative deprivation and self-reported happiness of blacks 1946-1966'. Unpubl. doct. diss. University of Texas, Austin, USA.

MARCUSE, H., 1963. 'Obsolence of psychoanalysis'. Talk delivered to the Annual Meeting of the American Political Science Association.

MARSDEN, D., 1969. 'Mothers alone'. The Penguin Press, London, Gr. Britain.

McGRADE, B.J., 1968. 'Newborn activity and emotional response at eight months'. In: 'Child development', vol. 39, p. 1247-1252.

McGRADE, KESSEN, W & LEUTZENDORF, A.M., 1965. 'Activity in the human newborn as related to delivery difficulty'. In: 'Child Development', vol. 36, p. 73-79.

McMILLAN, A.M., 1957. 'The health opinion survey. Technique for estimating prevalence of psychoneurotic and related types of disorder'. In: 'Psychological Reports', vol. 3, p. 325-329.

McNEMAR, Q., 1969. 'Psychological statistics'. John Wiley & Sons, Inc., New York, USA. (4th ed.)

McPHILLAMY, D. & LEWINSOHN, P.M., 1971. 'The pleasant event schedule'. Eugene, University of Oregon', Oregon, USA.

MASLOW, A.H., 1954. 'Motivation and personality'. Harper, New York, USA.

MATLIN, N., 1966. 'The demography of happiness'. University of Puerto Rico, School of Medicine, Department of Public Health, San Juan, Puerto Rico (Puerto Rico master sample, Survey of Health & Welfare, series 2, nr.3).

MECHANIC, D., 1968. 'Medical sociology'. Free Press, New York, USA.

——. 1972. 'Public expectations and health care'. John Wiley - Interscience, New York, USA.

MERTON, R.K. & ROSSI, A.S., 1968. 'Contributions to the theory of reference group behavior'. In: MERTON, R.K. 'Social theory and social structure' (p. 279-335). The Free Press, New York, USA.

MERWE, C. v.d., 1974. 'Thesaurus of social research terminology'. Universitaire Pers, Rotterdam, The Netherlands.

MESSICK, S. & KOGAN, N., 1965. 'Categorizing styles and cognitive structures'. ETS Research Bulletin, Princeton (N.J.): Educational Testing Service.

METHANY, E., 1965. 'Symbolic forms of movement: the feminine in sports'. In: 'Connotations of movement in sports and dance'. p. 43-56. Wm. C. Brown Co. Dubuque (Iowa), USA.

MILLER, H. & WILSON, W., 1968. 'Relation of several behaviors, values and conflict to avowed happiness and personal adjustment'. In: 'Psychological reports', vol. 23, p. 1075-1086.

MIRELS, H.L., 1970. 'Dimensions of internal vs external control'. In: Journal of Consulting & Clinical Psychology', vol. 34, p. 226-228.

MONGE, R.H., 1971. 'Patterns of self-concept in adolescence, maturity and old age'. Paper presented at the annual meeting of the Gerontological Society, Houston, USA.

MORGAN, C.M., 1937. 'The attitudes and adjustments of recipients of old age assistance in upstate and metropolitan New York'. In: 'Archives of Psychology'.

MORGAN, E., MULL, H.K. & WASHBURN, M.F., 1919. 'An attempt to test moods or temperaments of cheerfulness and depression by directed recall of emotionally toned experiences'. In: 'American Journal of Psychology', vol. 30, p. 302-304.

MORIWAKI, S.Y., 1973. 'Self-disclosure, significant others and psychological well-being in old age'. In: 'Journal of Health and Social Behavior', vol. 14, p. 226-232.

——. 1974. 'The Affect Balance Scale: a validity study with aged samples'. In: 'Journal of Gerontology', vol.29, p. 73-78.

MORRIS, C., 1956. 'Variety of human value'. University of Chicago Press, Chicago, USA.

MOSER-PETERS, C.M.J., 1969. 'Backgrounds of happiness feelings' (in Dutch). Ned. Inst. voor Preventieve Geneeskunde (TNO). Leiden, The Netherlands.

MOSHER, D.L., 1961. 'The development and validation of a sentence completion measure of guilt'. Unpubl. doct. diss. Department of Psychology, Ohio State University, Columbus (Ohio), USA.

MOWRER, O.H., 1961. 'The crisis in psychiatry and religion'. Van Nostrand, Princeton (N.J.), USA.

MUELLER, J.H., SCHNESSLER, K.F. & COSTNER, H.L., 1970. 'Statistical Reasoning in Sociology'. Houghton Miffin, Boston (Mass.), USA.

MURRAY, H.A., 1943. 'Thematic Apperception Test'. Harvard University Press, Cambridge (Mass.), USA.

NETTLER, G., 1976. 'Social concerns'. McGraw Hill, New York, USA.

NEUGARTEN, B.L., HAVIGHURST, R.J. & TOBIN, S.S., 1961. 'The measurement of life satisfaction'. In: 'Journal of Gerontology', vol. 16, p. 134-143

NICHOLI, J.N., 1967. 'Harvard dropouts: some psychiatric findings'. In: 'American Journal of Psychiatry', vol. 124, p. 105-112

NIPO (Netherlands Institute of Public Opinion), 1949. 'The things that make people happy' (in Dutch). In: 'De Publieke Opinie', vol. 3, p. 3-4., Amsterdam, The Netherlands.

——. 1970. NIPO report nr. 1398. Netherlands Institute of Public Opinion, Amsterdam, The Netherlands.

NOWLIS, V., 1965. 'Researsch with the Mood Adjective Checklist' in TOMKINS, S. & IZARD, C. (eds) 'Affect, Cognition and Personality'. Springer, New York, USA.

NOWLIS, V. & NOWLIS, H.H., 1956. 'The analysis of mood'. In: 'New York Academy of Science', vol. 65, p. 345-355.

OFFER, D. & SABSHIN, M., 1966. 'Normality'. Basis books, New York, USA.

OSGOOD, C.E., 1971. 'Exploration in semantic space: a personal diary'. In: 'Jour nal of Social Issues', vol. 27, p. 5-64.

PALMORE, E.B., 1969. 'Predicting longevity: a follow-up controlling for age'. In: 'Gerontologist', vol. 9, p. 247-250.

——. 1969. 'Physical, mental and social factors in predicting longevity'. In: 'Gerontologist', vol. 9, p.103-108.

——. 1975. 'The honorable elders. A cross-cultural analysis of aging in Japan'. Duke University Press, Durham, (N. Car.) USA.

PALMORE, E.B. & LUIKART, C., 1972. 'Health and social factors related to life satisfaction'. In: 'Journal of Health and Social Behavior', vol. 13, p. 68-80.

PANDEY, C., 1971. 'Popularity, rebelliousness and happiness among institutionalized retarded males'. In: 'American Journal of Mental Deficiency', vol. 76, p. 325-331.

PAYNE, R.L., 1974. 'N.M. Bradburn's measures of psychlogical well-being: an attempt at replication'. M.CR. Social and Applied Psychology Unit, Department of Psychology, Univ. of Sheffield, Gr. Britain. Memo no. 61.

——. 1975. 'Recent life changes and the reporting of psychological states'. In: 'Journal of Psychosomatic Research, vol. 19, p. 99-103.

PEAK, H., 1955. 'Attitude structure and motivation'. In: JONES, M. (ed.) 'Nebraska symposium on motivation', University of Nebraska Press, Lincoln, USA. p. 149-189.

PEARSON, P.H., 1970. 'Relationships between global and specific measures of novelty seeking'. In: 'Journal of Consulting and Clinical Psychology', vol. 34, p. 199-204.

PERETTI, P.O. & WILSON, C., 1975. 'Voluntary and involuntary retirement of aged males and their effect on emotional satisfaction, usefulness, self-image, emotional stability and interpersonal relationships'. In: 'International Journal of aging and human development', vol. 6, p. 131-138. and in: Giornale di Gerontologia, vol. 23, p. 38-51.

PESZNECKER, B.L. & McNEIL, J., 1975. 'Relationship among health habits, social assets, psychological well-being, life change, and alterations in health status'. In: 'Nursing Research', vol. 4, p. 442-447.

PETTIGREW, T.F., 1958. 'The measurement and correlates of category width as a cognitive variable. In: 'Journal of Personality', vol. 26, p. 532-544.

PHILIPS, Nederland, N.V., 1966. 'The Dutch housewife' (in Dutch). Philips Nederland N.V., Eindhoven, The Netherlands.

PHILLIPS. D.L., 1967. 'Social participation and happiness'. In: 'American Journal of Sociology', vol. 72 p. 479-488.

——. 1967. 'Mental health status, social participation and happiness'. In: 'Journal of Health & Social Behavior', vol. 8, p. 285-291.

——. 1969. "Social class, social participation, and happiness: A consideration of 'interaction-opportunities' and investment'". In: 'Sociological Quarterly', vol. 10, p. 3-21.

PHILLIPS, D.L. & CLANCY, K.J., 1972. "Some effects of 'social desirability' in survey studies". In: 'American Journal of Sociology', vol. 77, p. 921-940.

PIERCE, R.C. & CLARK, M.M., 1973. 'Measurement of morale in the elderly'. In: 'International Journal of Aging and Human Development', vol. 4, p. 83-11.

PLUTCHIK, R., 1980. 'A language for the emotions'. In: 'Psychology Today', p. 68-78.

POMMER, E.J. & VAN PRAAG, C.S., 1978. 'Satisfaction and lifesituation' (in Dutch), SCP cahier nr. 13, Sociaal Cultureel Planbureau, Den Haag, The Netherlands.

PORTER GUMP, J., 1972. 'Sex-role attitudes and psychological well-being'. In: 'Journal of social issues', vol. 28, p. 79-92

PORTER, J., 1967. 'Sex-role concepts, their relationship to psychological well-being and to future plans in female college seniors'. University of Rochester, USA. Order no. 67-13,639.

QUINN, R.P. & KAHN, R.L., 1967. 'Organizational psychology'. In: 'Annual Review of Psychology', vol. 18, p. 437-466.

RAHE, R.H., 1972. 'Subjects' recent life changes and their near future illness reports'. In: 'Ann. Clin. Res.', vol. 4, p. 250-265.

RAHE, R.H. & ARTHUR, R.J., 1967. 'Stressful underwater demolition training. Serum urate and cholesterol variability'. In: 'Jama', nr. 202, p. 1052-1054.

RAHE, R.H., RUBIN, R.T., GUNDERSON, E.K. & ARTHUR, R.J., 1971. 'Psychologic correlates of serum cholesterol in man: A longitudinal study'. In: "Psychosomatic Medicine', vol. 33, p. 399-410.

RAMZY-SALEH, GUIRGUIS, N. & HERMANS, H.J., 1973. 'Correlates of psychological well-being and emotionality'. In: 'Gedrag, Tijdschrift voor Psychologie', vol. 1, p. 64-91.

RASKIN, A., SCHULTERBRANDT, J, REATING, N. & McKEON, J.J., 1969. 'Replication of factors of psychopathology in interview, ward behavior and self-report ratings of hospitalized depressives'. In: 'Journal of Nervous and Mental Disease', vol. 148, p. 87-98.

REICHARD, S., 1962. 'Aging and personality', John Wiley and Sons, New York, USA.

REISS, A.J. jr., 1961. 'Occupations and social status'. The Free Press, New York, USA.

RENNE, K.S., 1970. 'Correlates of dissatisfaction in marriage'. In: 'Journal of Marriage and the Family', vol. 32, p. 54-69.

——. 1974. 'Measurement of social health in a general population survey'. In: 'Social Science Research', vol. 3, p. 25-44.

RICKS D.F. & EPLEY, D, 1960. 'Foresight and hindsight in the TAT'. Paper read at the Eastern Psychological Association New York, USA.

RIEGEL, K.F., RIEGEL, R.M. & MEYER, G.A., 1967. 'A study of the dropout rates in longitudinal research on aging and the prediction of death'. In: 'Journal of Personality & Social Psychology', vol. 5, p. 342-348.

ROBINSON, J.P., ALTHANASIOU, R. & HEAD, K.B., 1969. 'Measures of occupational attitudes and occupational characteristics'. The University of Michigan, Ann Arbor (Mich.), USA.

ROBINSON, J.P. & SHAVER, P.R., 1969. 'Measures of psychological attitudes. Appendix B to measures of political attitudes'. Institute for Social Research, Survey Research Center, University of Michigan, USA.

——. 1973. 'Measures of Social Psychological Attitudes' (revised ed.). Institute of Social Research, University of Michigan, USA.

ROKEACH, M. 1960. 'The open and closed mind'. Basic Books, New York, USA.

——. 1968. 'Beliefs, attitudes and values'. Bassey, New York, USA

ROLLINGS, B.C. & FELDMAN, H., 1970. 'Marital satisfaction over the family life cycle'. In: 'Journal of Marriage and the Family', vol. 32, p. 20-27.

ROSE, A, 1951. 'The adequacy of women's expectations for adult roles'. In: 'Social Forces', vol. 30, p. 69-77.

——. 1955. 'Factors associated with the life satisfaction of middle-class, middle aged persons'. In: 'Marriage and Family Living', vol. 17, p. 15-19.

ROSEN, J.L. & BIBRING, G.L., 1966. 'Psychological relations of male patients to a heart attack'. In: 'Psychosom. Med.', vol. 28, p. 808.

ROSENBERG, M., 1965. 'Society and the adolescent self-image'. Princeton University Press, Princeton, USA.

ROSOW, I., 1967. 'Social integration of the aged'. The Free Press, New York, USA.

ROTTER, J.B., 1966. 'Generalized expectancies of internal vs external control of reinforcement'. In: Psychological Monographs', vol. 80, nr. 1 (whole no. 609).

SCHAEFER, E.S., 1959. 'A circumplex model for maternal behavior'. In: 'Journal of Abnormal Social Psychology', p. 226-235.

SCHAEFER, E.S. & BAYLEY, N., 1963. 'Maternal behavior, child behavior and their intercorrelations from infancy, through adolescence. (Monography of the Society for Research). In: 'Child Development', serial no. 87, vol. no. 28, p. 3.

SCHLOSBERG, H., 1954. 'Three dimensions of emotion'. In: 'Psychological Review', vol. 61, p. 81-88.

SCHNEIDER, F.W. & COPPINGER, N.W., 1971. 'Staff-resident perceptions of the needs and adjustment of nursing home residents'. In: 'Aging & Human Development', vol. 2, p. 59-65.

SCHWAB, D.P. & CUMMINGS, L.L., 1970. 'Theories of performance and satisfaction: Re-review '. In: 'Industrial Relations', vol. 9, p. 408-430.

SCHWARZ, D. & STRAIN, F., 1972. 'Psychometric investigations on well-being in psychiatric and medical patients'. In: 'Archiv für Psychiatrie und Nervenkrankheiten', vol. 216, p. 70.

SCOTT, W.A., 1958. 'Research definitions of mental health'. In: 'Psychological Bulletin', vol. 55, p. 29-45.

——. 1962. 'Cognitive complexity and cognitive flexibility'. In: 'Sociometry', vol. 25, p. 405-414.

SHAFFER, W.F., 1968. 'Tests among hypotheses relating psychopathology and extreme upward mobility'. Unpubl. doct. diss. Teachers College, Columbia University, Columbia (Ohio), USA.

SHOSTROM, E.L., 1964. 'Personal Orientation Inventory' - An inventory for the measurement of self-actualization. Educational and Industrial Testing Service, Palo Alto, USA.

SIEGEL, S., 1956. 'Nonparametric Statistics', McGraw Hill, New York, USA.

SJöBERG, L., SVENSSON, E. & PERSSON, L.O., 1979. 'The measurement of mood'. In: 'The Scandinavian Journal of Psycology, vol. 20, p. 1-18.

SKRABANEK, R.L., 1969. 'Adjustment of former university faculty members to retirement'. In: 'Proceedings of the Southwestern Sociological Association', vol. 19, p. 65-69.

SMITH, M.B., 1959. 'Research strategies toward a conception of positive mental health'. In: 'American Psychologist', vol. 14, p. 673-681.

SMITH, P.C., KENDALL, L.M. & HULIN, C.L., 1969. 'The measurement of satisfaction in work and retirement'. Rand-McNally, Chicago (Ill.), USA.

SMITH, T.W., 1979. 'Happiness, Time Trends, Seasonal Variations, Intersurvey Differences, and Other Mysteries'. In: 'Social Psych. Quarterly', vol. 42, p. 18-30.

SNYDER, E.E. & KIVLIN, J.E., 1975. 'Women athletes and aspects of psychological well-being and body image'. In: 'Research Quarterly', vol. 46, p. 191-199.

SNYDER, E.E. & SPREITZER, 1974. 'Involvement in sports and psychological well-being'. In: 'International Journal of Sports Psychology', vol. 5, p. 28-39.

SONDERMEYER, B., 1975. 'Health correlates of happiness (in Dutch). Unpubl. report , Rotterdam, The Netherlands.

SPREITZER, E. & SNYDER, E.E., 1974. 'Correlates of life satisfaction among the aged'. In: 'Journal of Gerontology', vol. 29, p. 454-458.

——. 1975. 'Age marital-status and labor-force participation as related to life satisfaction '. In: 'Sexroles', vol. 1, p. 235-247.

SROLE, L. et al., 1962. 'Mental health in the Metropolis: The midtown Manhattan study'. McGraw Hill Book Co., New York, USA.

STANFIEL, J.D., TOMPKINS, W.G. & BROWN, H.L., 1971. 'A daily activities list and its relation to measures of adjustment and early environment'. In: 'Psychological Reports', vol. 28, p. 691-699.

STORANDT, M, WITTELS, I. & BOTWINIC, J., 1975. 'Predictors of a dimension of well-being in relocated healthy aged'. In: 'Journal of Gerontology', vol. 30, p. 97-102.

STOUFFER, S.A., GUTTMAN, L., SUCHMAN, E.A.. LAZARSFELD, P.F., STAR, S.A. & CLAUSEN, J.A., 1950. 'Studies in social psychology in World War II'. In: 'Measurement and Prediction', Vol. 4.

STOUFFER, S.A., SUCHMAN, A.E., de VINNEY, L.C., STAR, S.A. & WILLIAMS, R.M. jr., 1949. 'The American soldier: Adjustment during army life' vol.1. Princeton University Press, Princeton (N.J.), USA.

STREIB, G.F., 1956. 'Morale of the retired'. In: 'Social Problems', vol. 3, p . 270-276.

STREIB, G.F. & SCHNEIDER, C.J., 1971. 'Retirement in American society: Impact and process'. Cornell University Press, Ithaca, USA.

SUCHMAN, E.A., PHILLIPS, B.S. & STREIB, G.F., 1958. 'Analysis of the validity of health questionnaires'. In: 'Social Forces ', vol. 36, p. 223-232.

SULLIVAN, D.F., 1966. 'Conceptual problems in developing an index of health'. National Center for Health Statistic Series 2, no. 17, Washington D.C. , USA.

SULLIVAN, E.T., 1922. 'Mood in relation to performance'. In: 'Arch. Psychol.', vol. 8.

SUPER, D.E., 1957. 'The multi-factor tests: summing up'. In: 'Personal Guidance Journal', vol. 36, p. 17-20.

SWENSEN, C.H., 1963. 'Sexual behavior and psychopathology: a study of college men'. In: 'Journal of Clinical Psychology', vol. 19, p. 403-404.

SYMONDS, P.M., 1937. 'Happiness as related to problems and interests'. In: 'Journal of Educational Psychology' vol. 28, p. 290-294.

——. 1946. 'The dynamics of human adjustment'. D. Appleton - Century company, New York, 1946.

TAUSKY, C. & DUBIN, R., 1965. 'Career anchorages: manegerial moblity motivations'. In: 'American Sociological Review', vol. 30. p. 725-735.

TAYLOR. J.A., 1953. 'A personality scale of manifestanxiety'. In: 'Journal of Abnormal and Social Psych.' vol. 48, p. 285-290

TESSLER, R. & MECHANIC, D., 1975. 'Consumer satisfaction with prepaid group practice: A comparative study'. In: 'Journal of Health & Social Behavior', vol. 16, p. 95-113.

THOMPSON, W.E., STREIB, G.F. & KOSA, J., 1960. 'The effect of retirement on personal adjustment: a panel analysis'. In: 'Journal of Gerontology', vol. 15, p. 165-169.

TISSUE, T., 1972. 'Another look at self-rated health among the elderly'. In: 'Journal of Gerontology', vol. 27, p. 91-94.

TOBIN, S.S. & NEUGARTEN, B.L., 1961. 'Life satisfaction and social interaction in the aging'. In: 'Journal of Gerontology', vol. 16, p. 344-346.

TOWNSEND, P., 1957. 'Family life of older people'. Rontledge & Kegan Paul, London, Gr. Britain.

TRUAX, C.B. & CARKHUFF, R.R., 1967. 'Toward effective counseling and psychotherapy: Training and practice'. Aldine, Chicago, USA.

TUNSTALL, J., 1966. 'Old and alone; a sociological study of old people'. Rontledge & Kegan Paul, London, Gr. Britain.

VAUGHT, G.M., 1965. 'The relationship of role identification and ego strength to sex differences in'the rod-and-frame test. In: 'Journ. Pers.', p. 271-283.

VEENHOVEN, R., 1970. 'Het geluk als onderwerp van wetenschappelijk onderzoek'. In: 'Sociologische Gids', p. 115-122.('Happiness as subject of scientific inquiry')

—. 1974. 'Is there an innate need for children?'. In: 'Eurpoean Journal of Social Psychology', vol. 14, p. 495-501.

—. 1984. 'Conditions of Happiness'. Reidel, Dordrecht, The Netherlands.

VEENHOVEN, R. & BAKKER, P., 1975. 'Schooleducation and psychological well-being'. Unpubl. paper. Erasmus University, Rotterdam, The Netherlands.

VEROFF, J., FELD, S. & GURIN, G., 1962. 'Dimensions of subjective adjustment'. In: 'Journal of Abnormal and Social Psychology', vol. 64, p. 192-204.

WASHBURNE, J.N., 1941. 'Factors related to social adjustment of college girls'. In: 'Journal of Social Psychology', vol. 13, p. 281-289.

WASHBURN, M.F., BOOTH, M.E., STOCKER, S. & GLICKSMANN, E., 1926. 'A comparison of directed recall and free recalls of pleasant and unpleasant experiences'. In: 'American Journal of Psychology', vol. 37, p. 278-280.

WASHBURN, M.F., HARDING, L., SIMONS, H. & TOMLINSON, P., 1925. 'Further experiments on directed recall as a test of cheerful and depressed temperaments'. In: 'American Journal of Psychology', vol. 36, p. 454-456.

WATSON, G., 1930. 'Happiness among adult students of education'. In: 'Journal of Educational Psychology', vol.21, p. 79-109.

WEBB, E., 1915. 'Character and intelligence - an attempt at an exact study of character'. In: 'British Journal of Psychology'.

WEBER, M., 1958. 'The Protestant Ethic and the Spirit of Capitalism'. Scribner, New York, USA.

WECHSLER, D., 1955. 'Manual for the Wechsler Adult Intelligence Scale'. The Psychological Corp., New York, USA.

WEIMA, J., 1963. 'Psychologie van het anti-papisme' ('Psychology of the anti-papism'), Brandt, Hilversum, The Netherlands.

WEINERMAN, E.R., 1964. 'Patients's perceptions of group medical care'. In: 'American Journal of Public Health', vol. 54, p. 880-889.

WESSMAN, A.E., 1956. 'A psychological inquiry into satisfactions and happiness'. Unpubl. doct. diss. Princeton University, USA.

—. 1973. 'Personality and the subjective experience of time'. In: 'Journal of Personality assessment', vol. 37, p. 103-114.

WESSMAN, A.E., RICKS, D.F. & TYL, M. McI., 1960. 'Characteristics and concomitants of mood fluctuation in college women'. In: 'Journ. abnorm. soc. Psychol.'. p. 117-126.

WESSMAN, A.E. & RICKS, D.F., 1966. 'Mood and personality'. Holt, Rinehart & Winston, New York, USA.

WILSON, W.R., 1965. 'Relation of sexual behaviors, values, and conflicts to avowed happiness'. In: 'Psychological Reports', vol. 17, p. 371-378.

—. 1967. 'Correlates of avowed happiness'. In: 'Psychological Bulletin', vol. 67, p. 294-306.

WIRTH, L., 1938. 'Urbanism as a way of life', vol. 44, p. 3-24.

WITKIN, H.A., DYK, R.B., FATTERSON, H.F., GOODENOUGH, D.R. & KARP, S.A., 1962. 'Psychological differentiation', Wiley, New York, USA.

WITKIN, H.A., LEWIS, H.B., HARTZMAN, M., MACHOVA, K., MEISSER, P.B. & WAPNER, S., 1954. 'Personality through perception'. Harper, New York, USA.

WOHLFORD, P., 1966. 'Extension of personal time affective states, and expectation of personal dealth'. In: 'Journal of Personality and Social Psychology', vol. 3, p. 559-566.

YOUNG, P.T., 1937. 'Laughing and weeping, cheerfulness and depression: A study of moods among college students'. In: 'Journal of Social Psycholcgy', vol. 8, p. 311-334.

—. 1937. 'Is cheerfulness - depression a general temperamental trait?'. In: 'Psychological Review', vol.44, p. 313-319.

ZERSSEN, D.v., KOELLER, D.M. & REY, E.R., 1970. 'Die Befindlichkeitsskala (B-5), ein einfaches Instrument zur Objektivierung van Befindlichkeitsstörungen, insbesondere im Rahmen von Längsschnittuntersuchungen'. In: Arzneimittel-Forsch.', vol. 20, p. 915-918. ('The sensitivity scala - a longitudinal analysis').

ZILLER, R., MEAGS, J. & DECENCIO, D., 1964. 'Self-social constructs of normals and acute neuropsychiatric patients. In: 'J. Consulting Psychology', vol. 28, p. 59-63.

ZIMMERMAN, J., 1970. 'Die Messung und Differenzierung von paranoîden und depressiven Tendenzen mit einem item- und faktorenanalysierten Selbstbeurteilungs-fragebogen'. Med. Diss. München. W. Germany

ZUCKERMAN, M, KOLIN, E.A., PRICE, L. & ZOOB, I., 1964. 'Development of a sensation-seeking scale'. In: 'Journal of Consulting Psychology', vol. 28, p. 477-482.

# AUTHOR INDEX

# SUBJECT INDEX

(to be continued on next page)